Netherlanders in America

Dr. Albertus C. Van Raalte, 1811-1876
Founder of the colony of Holland in Ottawa County, Michigan

Netherlanders in America

A Study of Emigration and Settlement
in the Nineteenth and Twentieth Centuries
in the United States of America

Volumes 1 and 2

Jacob Van Hinte

Robert P. Swierenga, *General Editor*
Adriaan de Wit, *Chief Translator*

Heritage Hall Archives, Calvin College and Seminary, Sponsor

BAKER BOOK HOUSE
Grand Rapids, Michigan 49506

Translation of *Nederlanders in Amerika: Een Studie over Landverhuizers en Volkplanters in de 19ᵉ en 20ˢᵗᵉ Eeuw in de Vereenigde Staten van Amerika, Eerste en Tweede Deel*, published by P. Noordhoff, 1928, Groningen, The Netherlands.

Library of Congress Catalog Card Number: 84-72133

ISBN: 0-8010-9296-5

Author's Dedication

To the memory of the Dutch pioneers
in the United States of America, and
Albertus C. Van Raalte and so many
other men and women of action.

Editor's Dedication

To Jacob Van Namen, Robert Euser, and Neal Mast,
Dutch sons of the soil whose stories are the
equal of any immigrant saga portrayed here.

Contents

Volume 1

Part One **The Older Branch of the Dutch Trunk**

Seventeenth Century

The oldest voyage of Netherlanders to North America. The first ship with emigrants to the New Netherlands. The oldest "bacon letters": America the land of plenty. Patroonships and propaganda. Van der Donck as "booster." The colony of Niewer Amstel. Plockhoy uses America as a social laboratory and places poetry in the service of land advertising. America the land of liberty. William Penn as founder of utopia and land dealer. Earthly paradise moved to Pennsylvania. Labadists, tobacco, and slaves.

The restless mentality of seventeenth-century people. The Netherlands itself offered work for many. The flourishing

cheated by everybody. Final appreciation.

**9   The Rooting of the Young Dutch Branch
     in Iowa   265**

   A. Prairie Pioneers   265

       The Van Raalte and Scholte colonies compared. Social stand-
       ing determined the choice of many. The first settlement on the
       prairie: dugouts and sod houses. The town of Pella. Agricul-
       ture, cattle-raising, and gardening. Rapid development in busi-
       ness. Reverses. Money shortage and floods. New colonists and
       gold seekers restore prosperity.

   B. Transportation Problems   275

       Good and inexpensive transportation becomes the great prob-
       lem. Great expectations concerning the Des Moines River. A
       town, Amsterdam, accordingly laid out. The river disappoints,
       the town disappears. Railroad plans. Dreams and land specu-
       lation that result only in neighborhoods: no villages emerge.

   C. Political and Spiritual Life   280

       No union with the Reformed Church. An apostolic congrega-
       tion in which the pastor's office is not acknowledged. Grietje
       Noordtzij causes a revival. Intense quarrels over money mat-
       ters. Scholte suspended. Church disunity the result. Elemen-
       tary education. Striving for a university. Evening gatherings.
       Selection.

**10 The Rooting of the Young Dutch Branch
     in Wisconsin and Illinois   293**

   A. The Protestant Colonies in Wisconsin   293

       Reverend Zonne also advertises his settlement. It holds the
       middle between those in Michigan and Iowa. Van Raalte found
       much bitterness and division there.

   B. The Settlements in Illinois   296

       Rural life. Chicago's nearness. High Prairie already a railway
       station in 1852. Religious life.

   C. The Roman Catholic Settlements in Wisconsin   299

       A colony in the woods. Similar difficulties as in Michigan. No
       difficulty too much for the godly.

   D. Forgotten (Partially Run-down) Settlements   302

       The Ravenna, Michigan, colony fails, partially due to the insta-
       bility of Reverend Budding. A woodcutters' colony on Grand
       Island, New York, fails because of too much prosperity.

   E. Netherlanders in the Cities   307

       Sifting. Many believers also leave settlements, for example, B.
       Broere. Americanization develops more slowly in the cities

ments cause church quarrels. Also in Graafschap, Drenthe, Chicago, etc. Strong-willed leaders. Quarrels in Holland and Pella. Scholte more of a merchant than a shepherd.

B. The First Split   366

The less-educated insist on separation from the Reformed Church. "We have been sold out without our knowledge." Haan and his followers no genuine pioneers. Haan stirs up dissatisfaction. April 8, 1857, birthday of the Christian Reformed Church. A reaction to Americanization. Van Raalte resigns himself to it. Revivals. Clapper. Saloons stood empty, streets lay deserted, but God's house was filled. Growth of both denominations. The Reformed Church grows more rapidly. Statistics.

C. The Second Split   381

After 1880 rapid growth of the True [Ware] brothers. Anti-Free-Masonry movement. Secession under leadership of Reverend L. J. Hulst. Only a few pioneers among them. No room for a third Dutch church denomination. Change of views in the Netherlands.

13   Cultural Change: *Education and Missions*   389

A. Education   389

Broader interest. Sacrificial spirit. Neither in Holland nor in Pella are parochial schools wanted. However in Grand Rapids they are wanted. The East supports higher education. Van Vleck Hall. Dr. Phelps. Hope College in 1866. Desire for a university. A theological faculty. Suspended temporarily. Student life. The majority not interested in education. "In order to get through without working." In Pella also a desire for more education initiated by the leaders. A Baptist university. Later purchased by the Calvinists. A theological school in Grand Rapids. The first students accepted with "fear and trembling." A teacher who teaches twenty subjects. Preacher culture. Leads to clashes with old religious convictions. Some also study to become doctors and engineers. The seminary in Dubuque first Dutch, then Ost Frisian, then German. The Catholics have their parochial schools and use English because of their mixed character. Much later a college: They lack the activity of the Calvinists.

B. Missions   407

Mission work and mission spirit everywhere present. Strengthened by the Reformed Church and brought to the masses. A mission ship. E. J. Heeren the pioneer missionary. Otte, Oltmans, and Zwemer follow. Influences of missions. Little among the Christian Reformed: among the Roman Catholics, none.

14   Cultural Change: *Political Life*   415

A. Local Politics   415

Office seeking and mutual jealousy. Incorporation of Pella, Holland, Zeeland, and South Holland.

Volume 2

Part Four   **New Shoots on the Young Dutch Branch**

Part Five **Plants That Did Not Take Root**

Emigration and Colonization Since the Second Half
of the Nineteenth Century

The Parks. Railway interests and colonization. Oewel. The Colorado Land and Emigration Company. No success. Van Motz advertises Manitou and surroundings. Maxwell Land Grant Co. The Christian Reformed Church in Maxwell City. The Netherlands American Land and Emigration Company presents itself as a philanthropic institution based on Christianity. Believing Netherlanders are exploited and deceived. With initial success. Many embark. Disappointments. Underhand dealings at Ellis Island as in the Netherlands and elsewhere. Alamosa. The San Luis Valley turns out not to be volcanic but of sandstone; infertile. Land purchased for $26 per acre, not worth even $5. The brochure of the Christian Utrecht Company a string of lies. It did not even own land, only an option on 15,000 acres. A "Farmer-Committee" formed; buys other land. Crook and Rilland. Both fail. Reasons for the disaster. The Heersinks remain.

Interest rates. The Dutch mortgage business in America. Influence on emigration and colonization. A fjord-rich coast and a basalt-rich interior. De Smet. Spokane. Van Wijk gives pointers. The Spokane flour mills. Phoenix Lumber Co. Holland Bank and Holland Land Company. Insinger. A colony at Springdale. The Yakima Valley. The Puget Sound draws more Netherlanders. Whidbey Island. Fugitives from Canada. As in the days of Van Raalte. Countryside and towns. A coming and going. Church life.

Interior states. Immigration encouraged by the Carey Act and Desert Act. Dry farming. Mortgage business. Manhattan. Conrad and Choteau. Wormser City. Big Timber and Billings. Roman Catholics in Montana. "Little more than a living for his labor." Americans are uneasy about settling on irrigated land. A changeable climate. Montana for a great part uninhabitable. Acknowledgement of this by the government. Settlements that were total failures.

Shortage of laborers. The homesteader driven from the Northwest to the South by drought. Panegyrics of Charles Boissevain. The Boissevains and Norfolk. No success in Maryland.

Haagsma defends the South. Capital from the Netherlands and the Kansas City Southern Railroad. Port Arthur Land Company. Nederland, a rice and market gardening colony. Colonists of every stripe. A coronation feast as advertising. A cultural image. A failure. Port Arthur and its Dutch institutions. "Citizenship in Port Arthur means something." The settlement of Winnie. Bloemendaal takes a look and meets an enthusias-

Part Six The Contemporary Significance of Dutch Americans

groups. Socialism languishes. Orthodoxy does not tolerate it. Things are too good for the Hollanders and spirituality has "turned moldy." Judgments become milder and more broad-minded, even as "a protest against social evils." J. Groen a pioneer. Labor unions. The judgment of the Christian Reformed church postponed. Prohibition. Ku Klux Klan and imperialism.

Financially supported during the elections. The strict orthodox papers are politically independent. The best papers in factory centers. The losers. Newcomers. Survey of existing papers. Contents. The Mormons read the secular articles with the richest content. The more orthodox the paper, the better the Dutch. "English" papers. A newspaper war. *The American Daily Standard*.

Its development. Mulder and his work. Reflections of colonial life. Translations. "Zwaantje No Longer Speaks Dutch."

Results of individual emigration. Kuipers, Bok, De Kruif, Van Loon, and many others. Not all succeeded. By preference one does not associate with compatriots.

They made room and reduced unemployment. Influence on our agriculture was minor. Coopersburg. Remigration.

Apparently few Dutch characteristics remained. Neither in city layout, home design, nor in daily life. Desire for ostentation and prestigious churches. "Rank and Dignity reign supreme." Naive character of social life. Family days. Halloween. The elderly act boyish: the young act maturely. A coachman who studies to become a minister. "Self-made people."

Sunday rest. Neatness. Homelife. Tenacity of the Dutch language. Dialects. "*Mien Moudertoal*" ["My Mother tongue"]. Young people little inclined to study Dutch. Squeezed out. Language maintains itself longest in the churches. English six days a week, Dutch on Sunday in church. What is still read in Dutch. The A.N.V. not popular among the Dutch Americans. Does not belong there. Our language doomed to die out. Ellerbroek taught all his children Dutch. Dries Bosch tells much evil about the Netherlands but taught his ten children to read and write in Dutch. Dutch spirit strongest in the Midwest. The women's share in the language deterioration. With the language other values are lost. Psychological and physical changes. No Indian types. Even Bok is still viewed as a foreigner. Homesickness and race-consciousness. Group spirit. A devastating judgment. Concluding remarks.

List of Photos, Charts, and Maps

Editor's Preface

Since the 1960s American ethnic groups have sought as never before to honor their heritage and return to their roots. Dutch Americans are no exception. In 1982 they proudly and enthusiastically commemorated two hundred years of friendship and uninterrupted diplomatic ties between the United States and the Netherlands. Dutch citizens likewise looked across the ocean at their American offspring with fresh interest and even a sense of pride at their accomplishments in this, the "first new nation." Jacob Van Hinte would have reveled in the bicentennial activities and readily contributed to the scholarly conferences from his vast storehouse of historical knowledge of Dutch immigration and settlement. This publication in English of his monumental two-volume history *Nederlanders in Amerika* (Groningen: P. Noordhoff, 1928) is thus a fitting capstone of the bicentennial commemoration.

Nederlanders in Amerika has long been out of print and is therefore quite rare and almost unobtainable, even in the Netherlands. For Americans who face the language barrier, the book is entirely closed. Its inaccessibility has long been a source of frustration and an impediment to a full understanding of Dutch-American history and culture. *Nederlanders in Amerika* is the only comprehensive history of Dutch settlement in America written by a Netherlander, from the perspective of a Netherlander, and intended for a Netherlandic readership. Indeed, to this day Van Hinte is the only Dutch scholar to take a lifelong professional interest in the historical sweep of Dutch settlement in North America from the seventeenth to the twentieth century. This seminal work is the essential starting point for all who desire to learn about and understand the Dutch experience in America. Van Hinte's personal interviews with elderly immigrants in 1921 and his ready access to original sources, particularly letters, pamphlets, and newspapers, many of which are no longer available, makes this work all the more valuable.

This translation of *Nederlanders in Amerika* into English is a faithful reproduction of the entire original text. But in the interest of clarity and readability, sentence structure and paragraphing were sometimes altered. In the first two chapters Van Hinte quotes liberally from documents written in archaic Old Dutch; thus in the translation some of the original flavor is inevitably lost. Editorial clarifications have also been inserted and placed in brackets or added as footnotes.* The documentary end notes of Van Hinte were revised to conform to current scholarly practice and the list of references was rearranged and realphabetized, again according to current practice. The index of names in the original book has also been expanded to include subject and place references in the text and notes.

The American style of capitalization of Dutch surnames has been consistently used throughout the book. All Dutch surnames beginning with *van, de,* etc., are capitalized whether or not they appear with given names, initials for given names, or titles. Likewise, the indexing of these names is according to American practice. A name such as *De Jong* will appear in the index with names beginning with "D", not "J". Van Hinte himself probably would have adopted this approach, since he favored rapid assimiliation of the immigrant into the American scene. Yet we respect those individuals who continue to use the Dutch style, for the spelling of one's name is a highly personal matter.

The project to provide an English translation of *Nederlanders in Amerika* began in 1978, and only the unstinting efforts of numerous persons have brought the task to completion. As a third-generation Dutch American and a serious student of Dutch immigration and settlement in America, I had long felt a compelling desire to be able to utilize fully this rich storehouse of fact and interpretation, and to make it available for my children and grandchildren. From the outset, Professor Herbert J. Brinks, director of the Heritage Hall Archives at Calvin College, and his research archivist and secretary, Mrs. Zwanet C. Janssens, provided encouragement and assistance in recruiting translators, as also did Mr. Ralph Haan, genealogical specialist at the Herrick Public Library at Holland, Michigan. Eventually ten persons offered to translate various chapters. Only one was Dutch-born; one was an academic; several were retired. Mr. Dick Hoogeveen of Saskatchewan, an electrical engineer who emigrated in the 1950s and subsequently taught English to fellow immigrants, was the first to volunteer. He completed chapters 3 and 4 and part of chapter 11 in volume one. Professor John Yzenbaard of Western Michigan University, a specialist in Dutch immigrant history, did yeoman service in translating chapters 1 and 2 in volume one and chapters 3–5, 13–14, and part of 15 in volume two. He also served as a consultant and advisor. The other translators who helped complete the first draft were Mrs. Peter Slink nee Tien (I, 7–8; II, 1–2, 16), Mr. Hero Bratt (II, 10), and Reverend Gerrit Vander Ziel (II, 15 pt.), all from Holland, Michigan; Mrs. Julie M. Overton nee Van Ginkel of Yellow Springs, Ohio (I, 14–15); Mr. Peter H. Bouma of Grandville, Michigan. (I, 9–10, 12–13; II, 9, 11); Mr. John

*The few original footnotes by Van Hinte are identified as such.

Dahm, Jr. (I, 5, 11 pt.; II, 8), Mr. Egbert R. Post and Mr. David F. Van Vliet (I, 6; II, 6–7, 12, 15 pt.), all of Grand Rapids; and Mrs. Annette Boomker nee Doezema of South Holland, Illinois (Introduction, Table of Contents, and other front matter).

By the end of 1980 the combined effort had produced a complete initial draft. At this point, my colleague, Adriaan de Wit, professor of Romance Languages at Kent State University and a native-born Netherlander, agreed to join the project and to prepare a final draft of the basic translation that would be accurate and faithful to the original text, uniform in style, and lucid in contemporary phraseology. This tedious task he admirably accomplished during the next three years, and whatever merits this translation deserves are due to his conscientious efforts. Meticulous attention to detail, extensive knowledge of language structure and grammar, and the ability to translate German, French, and Latin words and phrases in the text are the hallmarks of his work.

A number of specialists assisted in explaining obscure terms, identifying persons mentioned, checking bibliographic references, and translating poetry in the text. Dr. Cornelis Smits of Haren (Netherlands), author of a multi-volume work on the Afscheiding of 1834, initially helped me contact Mr. Jan E. and Miss G. Van Hinte, the author's brother and sister who live in Delft, and his nephew, Professor Jan E. Van Hinte of the Free University of Amsterdam. Subsequently Dr. Smits compiled a bibliography of J. Van Hinte's publications and consulted for me a number of Dutch encyclopedias and dictionaries that were not readily available here. He also contacted the Drachten architect G. J. A. Bouma regarding the Frisian building called a *dwarshuizinge* noted in the text. Other consultants in the Netherlands were Dr. Pieter R. D. Stokvis, city historian of the Hague, Drs. Henry Van Stekelenburg of Vucht, and Drs. H. Van Zon of the Nederlands Agronomisch-Historisch Instituut in Groningen. Dr. Walter Lagerwey, Queen Juliana Professor Emeritus of Dutch Language, Literature, and Culture at Calvin College, provided considerable information on Dutch literary works and authors. Professor Elton J. Bruins of Hope College and director of the Netherlands Museum Archives at Holland, Michigan, located some obscure data, as did Hope College Archivist Andrew Vander Zee and Peter De Klerk, theological librarian at Calvin Theological Seminary. Other American scholars consulted were Vice-President Glenn Niemeyer of Grand Valley State College; Conrad Bult, Assistant Library Director for College-Related Matters at Calvin College and Seminary; Professor Richard L. Doyle of Mount Union College and a Pella expert; Dr. David G. Vanderstel, a specialist on the Grand Rapids Dutch settlements; Mr. Ross K. Ettema of South Holland, Illinois, a genealogist and historian of the Roseland and South Holland colonies; Dr. Hendrik Edelman of Rutgers University Library; Dr. Harry Boonstra of Hope College Library; and Emeritus Professor Bernard Fridsma of Calvin College. Professor Geart B. Droege of Ohio State University and editor of the Frisian Information Service bulletin, translated the Frisian poem in volume one, chapter 8, as well as other Frisian phrases and words. Mr. Marvin Baas of Holland, Michigan, translated the poem in the Groninger dialect in volume two, chapter 16.

Mr. Jan E. and Miss G. Van Hinte, whom I had the pleasure of visiting in their home in Delft in 1981, provided encouragement and financial assistance. Miss Van Hinte, the author's legal heir, also readily granted permission to publish this translation. Dr. Dennis Hoekstra of Palos Heights, Illinois, introduced me to Mr. Jacob Van Namen of Alsip, Illinois, a Dutch immigrant who is one of Chicago's largest wholesale florists. Van Namen and his business associates Robert Euser of Wheatfield, Colorado, and Neal Mast of Muskegon, Michigan, provided significant financial support for the project. The dedication of the book to these men reflects the crucial role they played in its preparation. Kent State University generously assumed some of the incidental costs and indirect expenses of the project, for which I am appreciative. Mr. Lester Ippel, Calvin College Treasurer, efficiently managed the account books of the Van Hinte Translation Project.

Mr. Herman Baker, President of Baker Book House, encouraged me by taking a personal interest in the project, and editor-in-chief Dan Van 't Kerkhoff and production manager Gordon De Young provided expert advice and warm support during all stages of production. My wife, Joan Swierenga nee Boomker, patiently typed the various drafts, despite often heavily marked copy. Melissa Ludvigsen, secretary in the Department of Romance Languages at Kent State University, typed the final draft with her usual accuracy and proficiency. Marjorie Evans, secretary in the History Department, and various student assistants at Kent State and also at Calvin College's Heritage Hall, typed some parts of the early drafts.

Finally, I cannot lay down my editorial pen without gratefully acknowledging my parents, grandparents, and wider family circle from whom I learned to appreciate and value my heritage. My maternal grandmother, Mrs. Peter A. (Alice) Hoekstra nee Clausing, who at this writing is ninety-nine years of age, provides a living link to the past. Her awareness of ethnic identity increased my own self-understanding and sharpened my sense of personhood. Only those who have shared the experience can understand the emotional impact of standing in the Old Country home of one's ancestor or in reestablishing contact with family members that had been broken for generations. For those who have not had this opportunity, reading Jacob Van Hinte's *Netherlanders in America* may provide vicariously some of the same feelings and emotions. If so, these efforts will have been richly rewarded.

Editor's Introduction

Embarking on his research trip to visit the Dutch "colonies" in America in 1921, Jacob Van Hinte, then a thirty-two-year-old recent university graduate, decided to keep a travel diary. As the S.S. *Rotterdam* set sail from Amsterdam to New York on July 11, he penned these telling words: "Emigrants! A word that already fascinated me when I was a boy and which I still feel carries such a deep connotation of the tragedy of life. Thus nothing has spellbound me more intensely than the pursuit of my investigation of the lives of these people who attempted to forge for themselves a new existence and livelihood far away from their native soil."[1] Since no one of Van Hinte's immediate family had emigrated, his sensitivity for the pathos involved and his wonderment at the outcome must have been the vicarious feelings of a bright, inquisitive youth. Whatever the cause, it is no wonder that with emotions as deep as these, Van Hinte would devote most of his scholarly career to the study of Dutch immigration to America.

Jacob Van Hinte was born in 1889 in the village of Muiden and grew up in Alkmaar.[2] History was his first love and major subject in college, where he studied with the famous Professor I. J. Brugmans. Later at the University of Amsterdam he studied social geography with the renowned scholar S. R. Steinmetz. Van Hinte taught geography and history at the high school level for the next six years in the cities of Leeuwarden (1912–1915), Den Helder (1915–1917), and Amsterdam (1917–1918). In 1919 he joined the geography faculty of the Public Commercial School (Openbare Handelsschool) in Amsterdam, which post he held for nearly thirty years until his untimely death in 1948. He was well beloved and respected by his students, who among themselves affectionately referred to him by the nickname "Jochem."[3]

While teaching in Amsterdam Van Hinte seized the opportunity to continue graduate studies at the Municipal University, completing a dissertation in 1920 on the subject of Dutch emigration to America. His mentor, Professor Steinmetz, was vitally interested in questions of the human response to geographical forces, of which migration was central. Also, in 1915 Professor H. Blink published the first scholarly study of Dutch emigration, and Van Hinte certainly must have been aware of this work. Van Hinte's older brother, Jan E. Van Hinte, worked for Royal Dutch Shell and had lived in the United States for a time. Jan's experiences perhaps stimulated Jacob's curiosity. In any case, Van Hinte's dissertation became the basis for the first volume of the 1928 publication, *Nederlanders in Amerika*. In the summer of 1921, Van Hinte began work on the companion volume by taking a six-week research trip to the USA. He visited all the major colonies and settlements from Paterson, New Jersey, to Sioux Center, Iowa, spoke at length with first- and second-generation colonists, read available primary documents and books, and took copious notes. Many of his sources and all the pioneers he interviewed are now gone. It was a prodigious effort to squeeze all this activity into such a short summer break, but the Amsterdam city fathers had refused to grant his request for a year's leave without pay. Nevertheless, Van Hinte made the most of the opportunity, and all through the 1920s he drew upon the capital stock accumulated in 1921 and continued writing. By 1928, on the eve of his fortieth birthday, he completed the task and was promoted *cum laude* upon the publication of his tome, which had grown to thirty-one chapters totaling 1,128 large pages, including eighty-five illustrations such as photographs, maps, and diagrams. To this day Van Hinte's work remains the most detailed account of this topic.

For most scholars such an effort is a life-long task and even Van Hinte admitted that one writes this type of book "only once in a life time." One reviewer called it a "*kerelswerk*" [he-man's work], doubtless because of the tremendous amount of material that Van Hinte processed, the balance he achieved between a scientific approach and a sense of humanity, and his amazing ability to capture the spirit of the times and the thinking of the immigrants, despite spending such a short time in the United States.[4]

During the 1930s Van Hinte broadened his inquiry to include Dutch immigrant settlements in the East Indies, South Africa, and Scandinavia. In 1933, in fact, he embarked on an extensive research trip to Asia and Africa, and in 1938 he returned to the East Indies once more. He published the fruits of his work and other research in more than forty articles in professional and popular journals.[5] He also served on numerous government geographical commissions and was a long-time director, beginning in 1933, of the Royal Netherlands Geographical Society (Koninklijk Nederlandsch Aardrijkskundig Genootschap). Later he served the Netherlands-South African Geographical Association as well. Only the rise of the Nazis and the Second World War interrupted his professional career. A Dutch nationalist to the core of his being, Van Hinte was *persona non grata* among government officials who collaborated with the Nazis. Several years before the War, he was nominated to be the first holder of the Steinmetz Chair in Geography at the University of Amsterdam, but the city fathers put a National Socialist Party member in the Chair. In September of 1941 Van Hinte even resigned from the Royal Netherlands Geographical Society because he believed it had come under Nazi influence and control. There was some criticism of his action from colleagues within the leadership of the Society, but in 1946, upon the death of the president of the editorial board of the Society's journal, *Tijdschrift van het Koninklijk Nederlandsch Aardrijkskundig Genootschap* (T.K.N.A.G.), Van Hinte was named to this prestigious post, a position he held until his death two years later.

In these depressed post-war years Van Hinte's long time scholarly interest in Dutch overseas emigration was stirred anew by the mass exodus of hundreds of thousands of his compatriots. Specifically, he believed the time had come to translate into English his 1928 work and perhaps to add a third volume covering the 1930s and 1940s, provided an American publisher would underwrite the project.

In late 1946 Van Hinte expressed his desires to his friend, Dr. Wybo Jan Goslinga, then head of the government department of education of Curaçao in the former Dutch West Indies, who occasionally visited the United States. Goslinga endorsed the project and in February of 1947 met with the publisher William B. Eerdmans, Sr., in Grand Rapids.[6] The timing was perfect. Eerdmans had only days earlier purchased the Van Raalte estate, including the original homestead and the dominie's library and personal papers, with the intent of establishing a Van Raalte Memorial Library. Eerdmans, who had hosted Van Hinte during his 1921 visit in Grand Rapids and frequently had sent research material and books to the Dutch scholar, was delighted to learn of his aspirations, especially since Van Raalte was the major hero of Van Hinte's book. Indeed, Van Hinte had dedicated his book to Van Raalte and included a full page picture of his hero immediately preceding the title page. Eerdmans wrote immediately to encourage the Dutch scholar in his plans and also to solicit from him manuscript material and books on immigration for the Van Raalte Library.

With Goslinga acting as the go-between, Van Hinte replied by directly asking Eerdmans to provide funds to enable him "to come to America to complete his third book and to render them in the English language."[7] The shrewd Eerdmans sidestepped this request by seeking to obtain a part-time position for Van Hinte either at Hope College or in a newly-proposed Dutch Chair at the University of Michigan, for which the Netherlands government was willing to pay half the salary. To make the offer irresistibly tempting, Eerdmans promised to provide Van Hinte with office space in the Van Raalte homestead if he would serve as curator of the library. "It seems to me," Eerdmans wrote, "you would be the logical man to develop the history and the historical significance and everything that goes with it of the early Dutch settlements in Michigan and other States."[8]

Eerdmans may have had ulterior motives as well, for he added, "Personally I am very anxious to have you come to America and if you do come you should take your library along and place it in the old homestead—part in the fireproof chamber and part in the library—and become Curator of the

Historical Foundation. However, all these things in the final analysis resort to that nasty little word 'money.' "[9] And at that time Eerdmans apparently was unwilling to part with any of his. But he did use his personal contacts to convince the University of Michigan to name Van Hinte as the first holder of the Dutch Chair. By July of 1947 Van Hinte had agreed to come. "One cannot ask for more," he wrote Eerdmans.[10] But this was not to be. Van Hinte died after a brief illness on March 1, 1948, only a few months before he was to take up residency in Ann Arbor.

In July of 1948 Eerdmans made one last attempt to purchase the immigration part of Van Hinte's library, but he was too late. Already in May, Jacob's brother and executor had disposed of the bulk of the collection of seven hundred books through a public auction house. Unsold books and all manuscript material were donated to the Royal Library (Koninklijke Bibliotheek) in The Hague. Eerdmans also indicated in a final letter to Jan E. Van Hinte that, "We have not made definite plans in regard to the translation of his two volumes on *Netherlanders in America*. This would be a huge work and it would be very difficult to procure a translator."[11] Eerdmans' practical business sense, unfortunately, overrode his interest in scholarship; he never did underwrite the venture.

This is a pity, because Van Hinte's work is an interesting period piece that remains a landmark in Dutch immigration history that can never be superseded by subsequent writings. It is narrative history at its best—imaginative, interpretive; and always stimulating and thought-provoking. The first of the six major parts describes the colonial Dutch, whom Van Hinte calls the "older branch"; next comes a detailed account of the transplanting of the "young branch" in the mid-nineteenth century. The third section traces the problems of adjustment in American social, economic, religious, and political life. In part four Van Hinte describes the successful shoots from the young branch: the planting of new colonies throughout the Midwest, such as Orange City, Iowa, and New Holland, South Dakota, which he calls a "daughter" and "granddaughter" of Pella. Part five takes the reader back to the agricultural crisis in the Old Country in the 1880s and the out-migration it spawned, to newer Dutch settlements in California, the Pacific Northwest, the Rocky Mountain region, and the South. Most of these later settlements, says Van Hinte, were plants "that did not take root" (p. 577). Many failed at the hands of swindlers, misguided promoters, and land companies, and others suffered from simple ignorance of farming in low rainfall areas or southern humid zones. The sixth and final part covers the first two decades of the twentieth century, when the second- and third-generation Dutch Americans moved speedily along the path of assimilation, due in large part to the hyper-Americanism during the First World War and its aftermath.

Americanization, indeed, is the central theme of Van Hinte's history of the Dutch settlers. It was, for the most part, a "slow and steady process" that was as desirable as it was inevitable, according to the author. It would be "tragic" for the Netherlanders to become American citizens and yet desire to remain Dutch, declared Van Hinte (p. 368). They could not contribute to American life, if such attitudes prevailed.

Having said this, there is also the hint, particularly in the concluding chapters, that the author viewed as no less a tragedy the gradual loss of the transplanted Dutch culture. If there could not truly be a "New Netherlands" in America, then, should the Fatherland ever be in ultimate jeopardy from totalitarian movements in Europe, there could be no haven abroad for the survival of Dutch culture.

Van Hinte's belief that the Dutch should jump into the American melting pot, which is surprising given his strong Dutch nationalism, can only be attributed to his political liberalism. He was willing to tolerate the loss of Dutch identity for a higher good—the success of the American democratic experiment of creating one nation out of many peoples. Of course, he also believed that Dutch culture contributed significantly to that final product, the American.

Van Hinte was above all a proud Netherlander. That he jeopardized his professional career to resist Nazism in the years 1935–1945 is quite consistent with the extreme nationalistic tone of his writings in the 1920s. From beginning to end, *Nederlanders in Amerika* is one long paean of praise to his Netherlandic readers, as they basked in the accomplishments of their departed kinfolk. Van Hinte repeatedly refers to the Dutch Americans with personal pronouns—"us," "our Hollanders," "our clan," "our Groningers," "our Frisians," or simply "our brethren in America."

Everything is written in terms of what "our Netherlanders" accomplished. This is understandable since, according to the author, the Dutch are racially "one of the best" races of mankind (p. 74). Although few in number, "their quality has been outstanding." "By sheer will power they [Van Raalte and his followers] confronted and conquered all their problems and difficulties." They succeeded because of their "character," "their enterprising adventurous Dutch spirit," whereas other groups failed, even fellow Calvinists like the Hungarian colony in Iowa. The Dutch throughout the frontier years proved to be "real Americans," abounding in restless energy and straining to get ahead like the "Transvaal trekkers." The Dutch frontiersmen in Kentucky were "veritable Daniel Boones." Patriotic Dutch young men readily volunteered in the Civil War, and during the heyday of slavery Dutch colonists in Pella and Chicago operated way stations on the Underground Railroad. Even Dutch Catholic immigrants are "*echte Hollanders*," although they displayed less of the Calvinist work ethic than did the Protestants, in the author's view.

Van Hinte chides American historians for downplaying the Dutch presence in Colonial America, especially in Pennsylvania, and he claims as his own every notable person of Dutch ancestry—the Presidents Martin Van Buren and Theodore Roosevelt (he would gladly have added Franklin D. Roosevelt to the list); the pioneer labor leader Samuel Gompers; Edward Bok, the originator and publisher of the *Ladies' Home Journal*; and countless others.

In contrast to the Dutch in America, the other nationalities pale by comparison. The English, Irish, and to a lesser extent, the Germans, fare poorly in Van Hinte's work. The "English cloud" hung as a pale over the New Netherlands in the seventeenth century, and the English throughout American history displayed a "haughty, opinionated," and "arrogant" spirit.

In modern scholarship, ethnic historians who excessively tout the accomplishments of their own nationality are called "filiopietists." Most scholars of Van Hinte's generation suffered from a similar myopia, and he is no exception. If readers can accept this boastful spirit as a cultural artifact of the time, they will be able to appreciate the bit of quaint humor it adds to the story.

Besides being a proud Dutchman, Van Hinte was a proud *Reformed* Dutchman, although of liberal leanings. "Faith is the tie that binds" in his account, but also the tie that breaks. In one emotional passage Van Hinte declared his American cousins to be a bunch of "believing, theologizing, psalmsinging, quarreling, snarling, mutually slandering pilgrims" (p. 362). While not belonging to the Seceder tradition, Van Hinte tried, not always successfully, as the above quote suggests, to understand that movement as an expression of Calvinism. He especially revered Albertus Christiaan Van Raalte and devoted himself to perpetuating the memory of his career. By the same token, the independent-minded Hendrik Pieter Scholte, who refused to affiliate with the Reformed Church in America and who in Van Hinte's opinion was ambiguous on the slavery issue, is given an extremely biased treatment. Van Hinte calls Scholte a "sphinx" and a "chameleon" (p. 426). Similarly, the 1857 Seceders and their successors, the Christian Reformed Church, are condemned for their self-righteousness and pettiness. Making a pun of their original denominational name, the True Dutch Reformed Church, Van Hinte almost always referred to them as the *"Ware" broeders* (True brethren). Once he called them "twice Seceders," which subsequent research has shown to be erroneous.[12]

On the other hand, Van Hinte is exceptionally perceptive in realizing that a salient issue in the conflict between the Reformed Church of America and the Christian Reformed Church was a difference of attitudes regarding Americanization. The Reformed Church of America favored and promoted assimilation, whereas the Christian Reformed Church tried to forestall it and preserve a Dutch identity and culture. This was the source of much of the denominational conflict over Freemasonry, American-style revivals, English-language worship services, and theological education. Van Hinte also concluded that the urban Dutch in Grand Rapids, Paterson, and Chicago were, theologically and culturally, more conservative than the rural colonists in Holland and Pella. Additionally, the settlers in the Michigan forests were more conservative than the prairie pioneers, because, as Van Hinte theorized, the forests were a harsh, confining environment, compared to the open, rolling prairies with their easily farmed soil.

Van Hinte was more than a proud Reformed Dutchman; he was a proud Reformed Dutch *scholar* with typical elitist attitudes. Learned people are portrayed as tolerant, open-minded, and liberal; uneducated persons are bigoted, close-minded, and reactionary. As one would expect of a European scholar, Van Hinte was fluent in four languages—Dutch, English, German, and French, and his book is sprinkled with quotations and citations in these languages.

Since this work is a greatly expanded version of the author's doctoral dissertation, the writing style is characteristically academic. Van Hinte wrote in a ponderous German-like style, with complex sentence syntax, some sentences stretching to twelve lines, with numerous dependent clauses. Rather than composing finely crafted sentences, however, Van Hinte used a free form, somewhat similar to the modern stream of consciousness writing, in which he expressed his thoughts in a string of incomplete sentences punctuated with numerous exclamation marks to convey emotion. He also employed negatives and double negatives to convey very strong positive thoughts. This personalized style makes for fascinating reading. At times Van Hinte was disarmingly simplistic, for example, when he condemned the use of alcohol or asserted that the colonists succeeded because of their faith in God.

As an academic, Van Hinte shared in the intellectual currents of his age. Causative forces in his history include: class consciousness; Teutonic racial superiority, which he derived from the neophyte eugenics movement; environmental determinism, for which he cited the German political geographer Frederich Ratzel and the American frontier historian Frederick Jackson Turner; melting pot ideals drawn from Turner and the American geographer Ellen Churchill Semple; and personality theories, which he took from the sociologist Edward A. Ross. But above all, Van Hinte was influenced by his mentor, S. R. Steinmetz, one of the most eminent geographers in Europe and the founding theorist of sociography. Unlike the environmental determinists, who believed that land makes a people, Steinmetz and his pupil insisted that "people and geography influence each other." In fact, since the environment is constantly changing, the character of a people is more important in successful colonization than are physical surroundings. The Dutch were a people forged in the perennial fight against the sea and the dominant power of Catholic Spain. It was this cultural and psychological heritage upon which the Dutch settlers drew in their attempts to alter their American environment by chopping down the forests, draining swamps, digging harbors, and damming and channeling rivers, often with the most primitive hand tools. In short, Van Hinte as a sociographer emphasized social and psychological factors more than physical and economic forces, and he concentrated his attention on particular local communities rather than using a large-scale, national approach. "By sheer will power," wrote Van Hinte the romanticist, the Dutch "tried to confront and conquer all their problems and difficulties" (p. 226).

The aspect of Van Hinte's scholarship that is most admirable was his speculative mind. He had a gift for drawing comparisons and posing perceptive and intriguing questions: How did the seventeenth-century emigration differ from that of the nineteenth century, and was there a direct link between the two, given the fact that Michigan was a "daughter state" of New York Dutch colonists? Were the Dutch Calvinists in America like the New England Puritans? Were the Dutch who emigrated more energetic and aggressive or more lackadaisical than those who remained at home? Did the developmental pattern differ in the various midwestern colonies, especially Holland, Pella, Sheboygan, and Sioux County? Why did Pella spawn numerous successful colonies and not Holland? Why did Van Raalte mistakenly choose Virginia for his only subsequent colonial venture? In what ways were the Dutch who settled in "elevator towns" affected differently than those in homogeneous "church villages"? How comparable was the clerical and business leadership in the different settlements? Did urban and rural dwellers differ? Did the Dutch farm like their American neighbors or retain Old Country cropping practices and animal husbandry? What impact did the coming of railroads such as the Pere Marquette have in western Michigan? How did the emigrants of the 1880s, with its agricultural crises, differ from those of the 1840s, with its religious and economic troubles? Did the difference between Calvinist energy and personal commitment and Roman Catholic leniency and universalism affect the survival of a Dutch identity? What impact did the disastrous Holland fire of 1871 have on the psychological and physical makeup of the city for the next generations? Why did the Dutch switch their political allegiance from the Democrats to the Republicans in the 1850s and 1860s? Did a generation gap develop between fathers and sons in the second generation? And the list goes on and on.

Perhaps most intriguing is the question that Van Hinte never clearly articulated but which seemed to be on his mind and heart in the late 1920s when the specter of fascism was on the rise in Europe. Could there truly be a "New Netherlands" in the United States, a place of refuge from totalitarianism? Could America be a place to preserve Dutch culture or even, if necessary, a place to begin anew on its virgin soil? Reluctantly, Van Hinte had to give up this hope as his research convinced him otherwise. The growing awareness of the inevitability of Americanization is thus also an underlying tragic theme in the book.

Truly, Van Hinte was a gifted historian whose insights and hypotheses have guided and challenged all future students of Dutch immigration and colonization. It is my hope that many will take the opportunity to read *Netherlanders in America*. Much can be learned from this Dutch scholar who understood the social and geographical forces in the transplanting and who had the gift of empathy for the emigrants as did few Netherlanders of his or any other generation. None need ask for more.

Notes

1. This quotation is taken from the first entry on page 1 of Jacob Van Hinte's handwritten diary, entitled "Naar Amerika" (1921), consisting of ninety-four pages, detailing the events of the trip, persons met, and even the cost of his travels in the United States from July 12 until August 31, 1921. Van Hinte visited numerous Dutch communities in various cities and towns: Hoboken, New York City, Paterson, Rochester, Grand Rapids, Holland, Chicago, Pella, and Orange City, plus Washington, D.C. A typed transcription of the diary by his grandniece Josephine Monique Van Hinte (1981) is located at Heritage Hall, Calvin College Library, Grand Rapids, Michigan. The original is in the possession of Van Hinte's brother J. E. Van Hinte and his sister G. Van Hinte, Oostsingel 22, Delft, Netherlands (hereafter cited as part of the Van Hinte Papers).

2. For sketchy biographical information on Van Hinte see "In Memoriam, Dr. J. Van Hinte," *Tijdschrift van het Koninklijk Nederlandsch Aardrijkskundig Genootschap*, 65, No. 3 (1948), 19–20; and P. J. Risseeuw, "In Memoriam van Dr. J. Van Hinte," *Missionary Monthly*, May, 1949, p. 155.

3. Quoted from a retirement address of a former student, J. G. Morrean, July 12, 1946, Van Hinte Papers.

4. "*Het Kompas*," May, 1947; and Dirk Nieland to J. Van Hinte, April 4, 1929, both in Van Hinte Papers.

5. For a complete bibliography of Van Hinte's publications, see Gretha Landman, "Jacob van Hinte; bio- en bibliografische gegevens," typescript, Nederlands Agronomisch-Historisch Instituut, Groningen, ca. 1979. A selected list of publications on American immigration follows these notes.

6. Van Hinte's postwar plans are described in the correspondence of W. J. Goslinga and William B. Eerdmans, Sr., with Van Hinte during the period 1946–1948, Van Hinte Papers. Interestingly, Goslinga was also a high school teacher of geography in Curaçao, and among his students was Adriaan de Wit, chief translator of this volume.

7. William B. Eerdmans, Sr., to W. J. Goslinga, May 27, 1947, Van Hinte Papers.

8. William B. Eerdmans, Sr., to J. Van Hinte, June 6, 1947, Van Hinte Papers.

9. Ibid.

10. William B. Eerdmans, Sr., to J. Van Hinte, June 17, 1947, and August 4, 1947, Van Hinte Papers.

11. William B. Eerdmans, Sr., to J. E. Van Hinte, July 14, 1948, Van Hinte Papers.

12. This view is expressed in volume one, chapter 15. For a reinterpretation of the 1857 secession based on new evidence, see Robert P. Swierenga, "Local-Cosmopolitan Theory and Immigrant Religion: The Social Bases of the Antebellum Dutch Reformed Schism," *Journal of Social History*, 14 (Fall 1980), 13–36, and Swierenga, "A Denominational Schism from a Behavioral Perspective: The 1857 Dutch Reformed Separation," *Reformed Review*, 34 (Spring 1981), 172–185.

Selected Bibliography of Jacob Van Hinte's
Published Works on the Subject of Immigration
(in chronological order of publication)

1. "De naam van Koning Willem I misbruikt," *Tijdschrift van Geschiedenis, Land- en Volkenkunde* 33 (1918), 183–188.

2. "Werkloosheid en Emigratie," *Tijdschrift voor Economische Geographie* 13 (Dec. 1922), 425–428.

3. "De industrieële ontwikkeling van Nederlandsch Oost-Indië (een overzicht)," *Tijdschrift van het Koninklijk Nederlandsch Aardrijkskundig Genootschap*, second series, XLII (1925), 349–385. (Hereafter T.K.N.A.G.)

4. "Europa in Amerika," *Onze Aarde* (1929), 493–552.

5. "Nederlandsche Nederzettingen in de Verenigde Staten van Amerika," in *Geschiedkundige Atlas van Nederland* (Martinus Nijhoff: 's -Gravenhage, 1934), 9–23.

6. "Een Nederlandsche nederzetting in Denemarken," T.K.N.A.G., LV (1938), 2–70.

7. "Nieuw Guinee als kolonisatiegebied voor Nederlanders," *Nieuw Guinee*, III (1939), 947–999.

8. "Europese invloeden op de ontwikkeling van de Verenigde Staten van Amerika," *Het Gemeenebest* (Maandblad voor het Nederlands Volksgeheel en tot bevordering van de Volksgemeenschap), 7 (Dec. 1946), 117–126.

9. "Nederlandse nederzettingen in de Verenigde Staten van Amerika," T.K.N.A.G., LXIV (1947), 411–422.

10. "De Frans-Canadezen," T.K.N.A.G., LXIV (1947), 715–733.

11. "Michigan; honderd jaren Nederlands leven in de V.S.," Amsterdam, Stichting I.V.I.O., 1947.

Author's Preface*

More than 230,000 Netherlanders have established themselves in the Republic of the United States since it achieved its independence in 1783 [the year in which the Treaty of Paris, the Anglo-American peace treaty, became final, with England recognizing American independence]. The "rooting" in the American soil, the adaptation to the American nation, in short, the whole process of adaptation and assimilation, Americanization in the fullest sense of the word, of a great proportion of these Netherlanders, will under close scrutiny prove to have been most influenced by the descendants of those clansmen of ours who, though in much smaller numbers, came to the New World in the seventeenth and eighteenth centuries.

It will also be seen that the material and spiritual ideals that motivated thousands of our countrymen in the nineteenth and twentieth centuries to migrate westward are essentially the same ones that attracted hundreds of these migrants to America a few centuries earlier.

These various factors aroused my interest and curiosity and led me to examine beforehand when and in what manner people in the Netherlands began to fashion a picture, a vision of America, the country of abundance and also of liberty. Subsequently, I wanted to find an explanation for the following phenomenon: in the enterprising seventeenth-century Netherlands so relatively few responded to the siren voice of the New World, while in the spiritless, spineless Netherlands of the nineteenth century so many responded. Almost all were drawn by "*le mirage américain*" [the American mirage], the delusion of an American earthly paradise.

Although this study and research gives mainly a deeper insight into the nature of the [nineteenth- and twentieth-century] immigrant, it is also of value in tracing in a cursory manner the process of transplantation of both the seventeenth- and eighteenth-century pioneers. This is done not only for the sake of the significance, already indicated, of the nineteenth- and twen-

*For the sake of clarity the sequence of paragraphs has been revised. The first six paragraphs which appear here are Van Hinte's final paragraphs.

xlv

tieth-century clansmen, but especially also because this process shows, in addition to all kinds of differences, so many resemblances and parallels with the adaptation process of the nineteenth- and twentieth-century immigrants. Thus we shall obtain a clearer view of the actual factors at work, *above all* the strength, the tenacity of the Netherlandic stock.

Up to now, no single, comprehensive study concerning the nineteenth- and twentieth-century emigration had been available. For that matter, there is also a lack of local studies; in fact, with one or two exceptions, there are far too few. Therefore, in many areas I had to do pioneer research myself and I spent years collecting and studying data often very difficult of access. I even found it necessary to research various archives and in so doing I found I was able to correct some wrong opinions.

In conclusion, respect for the great accomplishments of so many *kleine luyden* [little people or common folk] who are in actuality often "very great people," justifies the broad range of this study. Moreover, at the present time, emigration and colonization stand at the focus of interest. Perhaps the perusal of my work can contribute to a better insight into both matters, and it may be able to caution those who aspire to migrate and those who promote migration to use the greatest prudence and to help them realize even better the great responsibility of their decisions in this matter.

As I complete this study my thoughts go first to you, highly esteemed [S. R.] Steinmetz, who for so many years and with such warm interest has observed my labor. I am very grateful for your interest and help and for the many valuable observations you have shared with me, broadening my vision and deepening my understanding.

There are many others who in one way or another have been helpful. Many have kindly assisted me by word of mouth: Dutch Americans who temporarily sojourned in our land, such as consuls, mortgage bank representatives, preachers, merchants; remigrants of all kinds, a factory worker, a farmer, a businessman, or attorney in the United States; Netherlanders who had lived in America for longer or shorter periods, whether for their own pleasure or because of their professional responsibilities—they all shared with me their experiences. I have pleasant memories of all these conversations, for which I had to travel up and down our country. I went to Oosterbeek and Arnhem, then to Kampen, several times to the Hague, then to Nijmegen, occasionally to Middelburg, next to Leeuwarden, often to Amsterdam, once or twice to Dordrecht, then to Irnsum—everywhere people welcomed me and shared information. I conversed with people in many different types of environments—sometimes in the mansions of wealthy patricians, sometimes in humble homes, in the plush offices of foreign or domestic ministries, then again in a simple, second-story flat, sometimes in the private office of one of the "great men," also at times in the small, slow train between Amstelveen and Amsterdam, even amid the lively buzz of voices on a Monday afternoon at Kras [the Krasnapolsky restaurant in Amsterdam]. How varied and colorful were these glimpses of human life, how all these contacts carried me out of the sphere of daily existence! For example, what contrasts there were between a common laborer who went to America but did not succeed there and returned disappointed, and former ambassador Jonkheer De Graeff who, although he had been appointed to the high office of Governor-General of the Netherlands East Indies, found time and opportunity to share with me in a personal interview some of his impressions of the Dutch Americans.

Even greater is the number of those who furnished me with written data. They also were a colorful mixture: archivists and librarians, publishers of newspapers and books, consuls and bank directors, merchants and clergymen, farmers and factory workers. It often happened that a personal encounter led to an extensive correspondence. I am deeply indebted to the following individuals: Meester J. C. A. Everwijn and Meester F. E. H. Groenman, who sent me valuable reports from the commerce division of the former Department of Agriculture, Industry and Commerce; also to Jonkheer J. C. C. Sandberg of the Nederlandsche Vereeniging "Landverhuizing" [Dutch Association "Emigration"], and to C. Van Son of the Algemeen Nederlandsch Verbond [A. N. V. or American-Netherlands Association]. Further, I give thanks to Professor Meester N. W. Posthumus of the Economical-Historical Archives, to the firm of R. W. P. De Vries at Amsterdam, to the *Leeuwarder Courant*, to the Provincial Library at Leeuwarden, and the library of the Theological School at Kampen and to the following individuals: L. Emond, O.S.C., at St. Agatha; J. Kuiken at St. Anna Parochie; W. Van der Meulen at Leeuwarden; E.J. Everwijn Lange; Prof. Dr. J. P. Kleiweg De Zwaan and G. Trouw at Amsterdam; Meester H. A. van Coenen Torchiana at San Francisco; A.P. Van den Burch at Philadelphia; Paul D. Evans at Yale, New Haven, Connecticut; A. Van C.P. Huizinga at Thompson, Connecticut; G. Elferink at Rochester, New York; Rev. S. De Bruine, formerly at Oskaloosa, Iowa; D. Nieland at Grand Rapids, Michigan, to whom I am indebted for many photographs taken at my request; G.G. Gaass at Pella; and very many others.

Both the conversations and the letters roused ever more strongly in me the desire to go for a personal visit to America and the Dutch colonies there. How much I would have liked, therefore, to have been able to thank the Amsterdam city administration for its great generosity and broad pedagogical insight in granting my request for a year's leave of absence without any burden on the city's finances. It turned out otherwise. The administration decided it had to deny my request and consequently I was compelled to limit my stay in the United States to the summer vacation of 1921. Therefore I had to decline many an invitation to stay for a longer time with various Dutch-American families.

However, I was able to assemble a mass of information, priceless data were shared with me, rare documents were liberally donated. I am again unable to acknowledge every donor. However, I should mention a few. First, W. B. Eerdmans, publisher in Grand Rapids, Michigan, who for many years had been sending me from America, free of charge, countless documents and writings and whose house guest I was during my extended stay in the Furniture City. Next and above all, Dr. Henry Beets, also in Grand Rapids, who gave me the privileged access to his extensive library, and who did not hesitate when I ran out of time to compile all the data to mail the rare material to me overseas. I was also graciously received by secretaries of the A.N.V. in various areas as follows: Mr. Brons at Paterson and F. E. H. Gebhardt at New York; Prof. J. B. Nykerk at Holland, Michigan; J. H. Hoekstra at Chicago-Roseland; Prof. M. Hoffman at Pella, Iowa; Rev. J. Engelsman at Orange City in Sioux County, Iowa. I was also privileged to meet many leaders: the late Rev. T. Jongbloed and J. Van Twisk at Hoboken; Prof. Dr. A. J. Barnouw at New York; the late C. Spoelstra at Paterson; Rev. J. E. Struyck, A. J. F. Van Laer, and Quarles de Quarles at Albany. Also, Dr. H. Hulst, Dean Prof. [Albertus J.] Rooks, J. Steketee and D. Nieland, at Grand Rapids; Hope College President E. D. Dimnent and professors E. J. Blekkink and A. Raap, at Holland. Also, Mrs. Gilmore-Van Raalte; Honorable G. J. Diekema (former senator of the Congress at Washington, D.C.); W. O. Van Eyck, postmaster, and the late justice of the peace G. Van Schelven, Mr. H. Brink, all the latter of Holland, all of whom made scarce data available to me; the late judge, P. De Jong at South Holland, Illinois; the Cook and Gaass families and H. P. Scholte, Jr. at Pella, Iowa; P. J. Oggel, P. Mouw, and the then mayor G. Klay at Orange City, to whom I am indebted for a remarkable atlas of Sioux County, Iowa.

It is hardly necessary for me to say how significant all these personal contacts with the various colonial settlements and their leaders have been for me. The many conversations with gray-haired pioneers, such as Honorable [Cornelis] Van Loo at Zeeland, A. Van Stigt at Pella, and H. Van der Waa at Orange City, as well as the journey itself, have made an indelible impression on me.

Finally, I also thank my brother-in-law, Chr. Angel, and Miss H. Van der Laars for their assistance in preparing this book for publication, especially the latter for compiling the index.

Netherlanders in America

Volume 1

"Settlements are built—
but on the bones of the settlers."

Part One

The Older Branch
of the Dutch Trunk
Seventeenth Century

1

The First Emigrants and Settlers
How America Became a Land of Promise

The real interest of the Dutch in North America began in the second half of the sixteenth century. A desire for profit caused such businessmen as Gerrit Bicker and others, in 1597 and 1598, to outfit ships to sail to the North American coast where, besides fishing operations, trade with the Indians was already promising. Names such as Duincaep, Stormcaep, and others along the Canadian coast attest to this.[1]

Interest in trading and shipping circles grew after Hudson's famous voyage of 1609, in which he used both English and Dutch crew members on the *Halve Maan* [*Half Moon*], sailing under the Dutch flag. However, one should remember that Hudson had not been commissioned by his superiors to go to North America but rather to find the "northeast passage" around northern Asia in a search for the Indies. He had been expressly prohibited to search for the "northwest passage" while sailing along the American coasts. Altogether peremptorily and contrary to his given orders, Hudson, probably influenced by charts given him by a Captain Smith of Virginia,[2] soon sailed westward hoping to find a "western sea," a region that had been more or less forgotten after Verrazano's voyage of 1524 and the coastline of which, between Chesapeake Bay and Cape Malabar, was no longer known.[3] Everyone knows the consequence—the discovery of the Hudson River.

Although the English government did not permit Hudson to return to the Netherlands and deprived him of his charts, people in Holland soon learned of his discoveries either through Van Meteren—the well-known Dutch consul in London—or through a portion of Hudson's log or a resumé of it that he had probably sent to Amsterdam. In any case, interest in America grew. In 1610 some of our merchants sent a vessel to the newly discovered river and gave it the significant name of "Manhattes."[4]

This growth was also shown in the activity of a navigator, Jan Corneliszoon May, who in 1611 was instructed to accomplish what Hudson had neglected to do—to search for a northeast passage to India. If he were unsuccessful in this, according to supplementary oral instructions, he was to explore the coast of Nova Francia, that is, Canada.[5] Preparations for May's voyage were kept secret because others were interested in similar projects. May reached the American coast on October 24, 1611, when he sighted Terranoef (Newfoundland), a "high rugged land with many islands and cliffs . . . but no anchoring place that would suit us."[6] A few other ships—including one from Amsterdam and one from Sardam (Zaandam)—happened in to buy fish. May did not explore further south than 41°30'. There were no significant results from this voyage. May did not find the river discovered by Hudson, but interest in America grew. May's men had engaged in some trading with the Indians, having received special permission to do so. Back home they were full of talk about these Indians who smoked pipes fitted with large bowls and on whose land there were "vine stalks as thick as a man."[7]

More ships were dispatched to find the Hudson River. The first to do so was Adriaen Block in 1614. His ship, de Fortuyn [The Fortune] was skippered by Hendrick Christiaenszoon and it returned to the Netherlands laden with beaver skins. Block had lost his own ship through fire but continued his exploration in de Onrust [The Restless], a yacht he had constructed in America. The reports of the skippers increasingly spread the fame of America as a land of wealth. In that same year of 1614 thirteen merchants received permission from the States-General to send their ships—five of them—on four voyages to these newly named New Netherlands during the next three years.

At that same time the first, though temporary, colony—the trading post Fort Nassau—was founded in the New Netherlands. It was situated deep inland where the tide was still noticeable, allowing ships to go that far, near present-day Albany. "Further up, the river was dry; it is scarcely possible for rowboats to navigate there." Thus reports the writer De Laet, better known as a historian than as a geographer.[8] Within a few years the fort was no longer fit for use; it was situated on low ground and subject to flooding. In addition, the trading privileges of the directors of the New Netherlands had not been renewed.[9]

Others also wished to profit from the riches of America, and they obtained permission from the States-General after the expiration of the previously mentioned monopoly grant. Many merchants sent out their personnel; they did not confine themselves to the Hudson River area but ventured to the banks of the Susquehanna and those of the South River in Delaware where earlier explorations had been made.

However, in 1621 this "free" trade came to a temporary halt when the West India Company was founded and the New Netherlands area was included in its charter. All "free" traders were then required to leave the region by July 1, 1622; however, this edict did not meet with immediate compliance by all.[10] The earlier traders had established colonies of various sizes for temporary periods at the mouth of the Hudson or on Manhattan Island and Nut Island, and more northerly near Fort Nassau, that was now in ruins, and furthermore on the Delaware. Under the auspices of the West India Company, permanent settlements were made.

A new element was now introduced. America was not only suitable for trade, but also for agriculture and cattle raising. The Dutch area in America thus became a region for colonization. Various skippers, enthusiastic about the beaver trade, had also mentioned the agricultural possibilities. Among them was Cornelis Jacobszoon May of Hoorn who in 1620 not only spoke of the inhabitants but also called attention to the lumber riches. These accounts encouraged the Walloons in our country to ask the States of Holland for permission to go to the New Netherlands as colonists.

When the West India Company heard of this they agreed on November 3, 1623, to send a trading vessel "to Virginia"—also the generic name for the Hudson and Delaware areas—"for further trade, and to take along also for that purpose five or six families to found a colony there."[11] This was to have important consequences. A ship, the *Nieuw-Nederland* [*New Netherland*] was equipped and, under command of Cornelis Jacobszoon May, sailed for the New World on or after March 31, 1624, with thirty families on board, "most of them Walloons." This was the first Dutch emigrant ship, carrying also Dutch emigrants to North America. Many were to follow!

Thanks to the research of Professor A. Eekhof, we have recently learned from primary, rather than secondary, sources about the arrival of these first immigrants. Willem Van der Hulst, the second director of the colony, was evidently a passenger on the *Nieuw-Nederland* enroute "to Virginia and arriving at the Montagne River* went north for forty miles past a place called Maeykans, where we found a yacht called *Den Omvallende Nooteboom* [*The Falling Nut Tree*]. We took the ship and lodged the families in it until they could build adequate houses for the families."[12]

It is thus obvious that the first residence of these colonists, who in France and Belgium are still wrongly regarded as the founders of New Amsterdam, was actually at "Maeykans," which was really a settlement of Mohican Indians in the proximity of the former Fort Nassau. Not far away and slightly to the north, May erected Fort Orange—the site of present-day Albany. It was an ideal location for fur trading.

Economic and geographic factors dictated, as in so many other areas, that the oldest river trading posts should be as far inland as possible. This is still true today and explains why many great commercial centers have inland locations. Strategic considerations also dictated that, as may be seen elsewhere, a harbor capable of defense was needed; and so Fort Amsterdam was erected at the mouth of the Hudson River. Construction began in July, 1625, under the direction of Crijn Frederickszoon, an engineer, on what director Verhulst decided as the most appropriate island, Manhattan. The simultaneous birth of the town of New Amsterdam was thus not

---

*Another name for the river that was also called Manhattan River, North River, or Mauritius River. Since 1664 this "Great River" was called the Hudson River [Van Hinte].

due to Walloons but, as F. C. Wieder, proved conclusively, to Dutch colonists, among whom were several "landworkers" or farmers. They had left the Netherlands in April, 1625, aboard vessels named *de Macreel* |*the Mackerel*|, *Paert* |*Horse*|, *Koe* |*Cow*|, and *Schaep* |*Sheep*|.[13]

Some of the 1624 colonists had immediately begun farming in the Fort Orange region. Later some families were relocated at Nut Island, in the Hudson estuary, and a small fort was even constructed there. Still others were relocated on the South River or Delaware where the "Southern Colony" was being "actualized." Fort Wilhelmus was built somewhere else, but its site no longer can be found. A small settlement was even made on the Connecticut or "Fresh" River.[14]

It is necessary for us to consider how the "America fever" developed and how the concept of America filled the heads of increasingly more people. More than anything else the New Netherlands remained a land of beaver skins—a land for trade. Colonization was subordinate to it, and served to feed the traders and soldiers necessary to insure a peaceful trade, as was noted in the phrase "for that purpose" in the regulations for the 1623 colonists. It is expressed in an even stronger fashion in the development of agriculture and cattle raising on Manhattan Island where the Company itself took over agriculture and laid out five "boweries," each under the direction of a master farmer who, in turn, had other landworkers or tenant farmers under his jurisdiction; all were contract workers of the Company. Trading on one's own account was strictly forbidden, as were other vocations. These farmers were, in fact, "officials" appointed for a fixed number of years. Even the "free colonists" had to agree to serve for at least six years; in exchange for that they received free passage and a grant of land from the Company. Everything else provided by the Company was at their own charge and trade with anyone outside of the Company was strictly forbidden.[15]

This dominance of their instinct for trading is reflected in the management of the West India Company. The Company was the landlord. The "Directors" treated the colony as though it were a commercial sailing enterprise. "The Commander—or Director—with his council, to which the officiating skippers belong, and the Administrative Clerk and Secretary, along with the Comforter of the Sick, transfer as a unit from ship to land and continue their leading and administrative functions as soon as they land." Administrative Clerk Verhulst, second to May, was ordered to eat with his family at the same table as the Comforter of the Sick—a well-known figure aboard ships and substitute chaplain—and the members of the council. As Wieder mentions, "that was the custom in the cabin aboard ship."[16]

There was no mention of the rights of the colonists or their influence on government, which, although not a characteristic Dutch trait, was a general vogue of the times. In various English, French, and Spanish holdings the white element—not to mention the natives—had nothing to say either; even in the so-called "democratic" Pilgrim colonies there existed the greatest compulsion, although in another form. We seek in vain during the seventeenth century for the modern American concepts of freedom and equality for all, except for an occasional instance. In spite of the geographical "space," there was no democratic society. Geographical "space" by itself does not foster democracy, as is sometimes mistakenly believed. The New Netherlands colonists were divided into more than ten castes!

Although the government was that of a dominant monopoly and freedom was very limited—it was even necessary to get the consent of the West India Company to return to the Netherlands—North America was seen more and more as a land with a future for agriculture. Letters written by colonists and other unconscious and sometimes conscious propaganda contributed to this and ultimately resulted in what was to occur in the nineteenth century.

Letters to friends, laden with praise about the newly-adopted land, engendered the myth of seventeenth-century America by portraying it as "the legendary country of rice and porridge mountains," where with little or no work one could become wealthy within a few years. But dozens were disappointed (as thousands were in the nineteenth century), and the first chaplain of the New Netherlands, Jonas Michaëlius, complained in 1628—just as did his colleague of two centuries later, [Albertus Christiaan] Van Raalte—that "many of the common people preferred to be idle and wanted to make a living and become rich without working; saying that they had not come to work—they could have remained at home and done that."[17] Such was the repercussion of this illusion!

The author Baudertius was one of the first to publish such letters. In 1624 he published a letter from colonists who had gone that same year, holding forth about the beauty of the New World and its riches of fruit, game, birds, and fish. The colonists also praised the fertility of the soil and the friendliness of the inhabitants. They were only awaiting the arrival of some promised cattle. When they would come, the colonists would no longer desire to return to Holland "because everything we could wish for in the Paradise of Holland is here. You will not regret coming here with your family."[18] We shall see later that the difference between this letter and the nineteenth-century so-called "bacon letters," in which the great quantities of inexpensive meat are extolled, is not very great.

The scholar Nicholaas Janszoon Wassenaer regularly extolled the lot of the early colonists to the Dutch public, telling of grain sown shortly after arrival that had grown to the height of a man during the same year and of the Indians who were very good-natured if not molested. So immigration increased, although the second group of immigrants, totaling forty-six, which arrived in 1625, had fewer privileges. In November of 1626 Wassenaer wrote that the colony numbered two hundred souls and that thirty houses were to be found on Manhattan Island.[19]

De Laet, manager of the West India Company in the New Netherlands, was even more enthusiastic than Wassenaer in 1624 and subsequent years. In 1625 he wrote about the New Netherlands and its colonization. He concerned himself not only with the flourishing trade "in beaver skins, otter, fox and bear hides," etc., but also with the "beautiful and pleasant land, covered with beautiful forests and vineyards. All that was needed was work and industry of people to turn it into one of the most fruitful lands of that area." Hudson himself and those who arrived after him, so continues De Laet, "know how to say wonderful things of the trees that grow here." Hudson even declared that this "is the most beautiful land to cultivate that I ever trod upon in my life."[20] The same ideas were expressed by the nineteenth-century colonists and those associated with colonization. Thus the saying had already a very "modern" ring.

Because De Laet quotes Hudson, we may assume—although there is no proof for this—that De Laet must have had in hand some report of the explorer.[21] It is also possible, I think, that De Laet, using the psychology of a nineteenth-century land agent, knew what impression and what confidence is fostered by a first person account of land "seen by myself." He was, to be specific, a great promoter of colonization and soon a landowner himself in the New Netherlands. I am strengthened in this view also by De Laet's summation: "In sum it is a land well suited for our people because of the similarity of the air and of the weather."[22]

De Laet's portrayal is especially significant because it expresses a new current of thought among the Directors of the West India Company. They had previously seen the New Netherlands almost exclusively as a trade area in which only a few civil servants should be admitted to buy furs. Every real colonist was viewed as a clandestine fur dealer intent on breaking the Company's monopoly. Some Directors, however, came gradually to the conclusion that the colony would never attain the mercantile importance of the East Indies and so it would be better to send people to develop the land even though that would only make it a transshipment port for the West India trade—not a settlers' colony.[23] Even these ideas were still not in support of a settlement, but of trade. But through this line of thought the idea of a settlers' colony gained importance.

Still the colonization theme persisted. It had, no doubt, already been strengthened by the publication in 1625 of Robert Juet's journal. Juet had been Hudson's second mate. This account, published in English, must have attracted also the attention of the members of the West India Company— particularly De Laet and other promoters of colonization. Juet and his men greatly admired the forest resources: "The land is filled with huge and heavy oaks." They described the fields as "the most desirable they had ever seen, covered with grasses, flowers, and large trees, with a pleasant aroma wafting over it." On the return voyage, about ten miles south from the goal of the trip, which had extended to the later site of Fort Nassau, Juet and his men went ashore, "where they found excellent meadow land for cereals and other crops and many fine oak, walnut, and chestnut trees, elms and aromatic woods in abundance and in addition, much slate for houses and other useful kinds of stones."[24]

Of more immediate importance were two letters from men who had actually settled in the colony. Isaäck de Rasière, born in Middelburg, was named Clerk of the New Netherlands in 1626, while Pierre Minuit was Director-General. Rasière wrote—apparently after he had returned to the Netherlands in 1628 (the letter is undated)—a detailed account to Samuel Blommaert, a director closely involved in the New Netherlands. He pointed out how fit the land was for development, particularly on the higher areas along the river. "The high east side of the upper river is covered with tall trees and in some places good land can be found and this was once settled by many people but most of them have died or been driven out by force of arms."[25]

At about the same time, the first minister in the New Netherlands, Jonas Michaëlius, happened to describe this area in a letter written on August 8, 1628: "Not long ago I located some good spots where the soil is good. At the upper end of the River, near Fort Orange, there is available a large piece of land, wonderfully pleasant and fruitful."[26] In a second letter of August 11, 1628, Michaëlius commented on the shortage of colonists. "We still lack about 10 or 12 farmers with horses, cows, and sufficient laborers to supply us with bread, milk, and other necessities." He also mentioned how this land might be acquired, following a centuries-old pattern. "There are places situated nearby that are desirable and easy to defend, lands that could be purchased cheaply with a few trinkets from the Indians or we could just take the land without further ado because we could make better use of it than has been done in the past." Michaëlius specifically referred to lands near Fort Orange, from which the Indians had fled. "The Mohicans have fled and the land lies open, pleasant, and fruitful; it is a pity that we have no people or instructions from the Directors to occupy it."[27]

The Directors of the West India Company were much influenced by the contents of these latter letters; in particular those who were concerned with the affairs of the New Netherlands, men such as Blommaert, |Kiliaen| Van Rensselaer and, later De Laet.[28] Shortly thereafter Blommaert, Van Rensselaer and |Samuel| Godyn—the latter had received a previously unknown letter from Michaëlius and the first two letters were sent to a certain |Jan| Van Foreest (in Hoorn) and to the Reverend Smoutius |Adriaan Smout| in Amsterdam—sent out two men to explore the land and report on it. On January 13, 1629, these three "gentlemen" informed the West India Company that they would undertake what the Company had neglected to do— establish colonies. On July 7, 1629, the Company finally gave its consent by issuing the so-called "Freedoms and Exemptions." Anyone who desired to go to the New Netherlands could do so, take up a piece of land of his choice, and govern it as he wished. But there was one condition—at their own cost they would have to "plant" fifty adult colonists in the area of their choice, within four years.

Expressly included in the "Freedoms" was a provision that a single "patroon" might not have more than four miles on one river bank or two miles on each shore. But this regulation was not strictly observed. For example, Van Rensselaer gave his agent instructions to buy as much land as possible, both above and below Fort Orange—the land which Michaëlius had described as being so "pleasant." It was also decreed that the land was to be "bought" from the natives. Michaëlius had some advice about this. Earlier, the Company had made sure that Verhulst and his successor, Minuit, "bought" Manhattan Island from the Indians.[29]

Many wanted to purchase a "patroonship." In some cases two or more individuals pooled their resources and designated one of their number to function as landlord. In North America, as in the so-called "West,"* patroonships were formed in the area of the West India Company charter: the stately "Rensselaerswijck" of Kiliaen van Rensselaer and "associates" around Fort Orange, Michiel Pauw's "Pavonia" more southward on the right bank of the North River, and Samuel Godyn's and Samuel Blommaert's "Swanedael" on the right bank of the South River or Delaware River. In addition, Pauw declared himself the owner of a tract on the Thames River in Connecticut, Burgh claimed an area on the left bank of the Delaware, Samuel Blommaert claimed land on the Fresh River in Connecticut, etc., etc.[30]

It is not my intention to pursue the development of these "patroonships" in detail. I see them as factors that helped increase interest in North America to recruit colonists: the patroons acted as recruiters of colonists. Consequently, I will not deal with the difficulties that arose between the new "landlords" and the West India Company. The former considered themselves as vassals of the States-General and even as virtual sovereigns, despite the restrictions of the "Freedoms and Exemptions." The West India Company felt continually threatened in its privileges, especially in the fur trade. I mention this only because the constant opposition of the Company and its representatives in America seriously hampered the patroons in their plans for colonization. After a few years, they felt hopeless about the future and sold their rights to the Company, with one exception: Rensselaerswijck remained independent and developed into a flourishing colony. However, the Company itself no longer made any efforts at colonization. There were also troubles with the Indians who received us gladly as traders but not as farmers, since each farm meant a smaller hunting preserve.

The colony on the South River had an auspicious beginning. It had been "occupied" by twenty-eight hopeful colonists in 1631. In July of that year "their cows had calved" and "their lands has been planted and were covered with beautiful crops." But the year following they were massacred by the "Savages." One of the "planters," David Pieterszoon De Vries, calmly reports that "our little fort was destroyed by the savages and thirty-two men that were working their lands outside of the fort were killed."[31] From this instance we can get a picture of the dangers that threatened the immigrants. It is also interesting that about thirty men could have been found

---

*"West" refers to the former Dutch West Indies, as "Oost" does to the former Dutch East Indies.

for this single colony: an indication of some desire for emigration. This desire was dampened less by the danger of Indians than by the quarrels and machinations of the powerful leaders who claimed the best lands for themselves. De Vries informs us: "And so, because of all the quarrels the land was neither settled nor developed. Though there were enough people who wanted at that time to settle the land, because of the quarrels of the Directors, settlement lagged. The Directors themselves did not want to engage in the promotion of settlements; they preferred to see profits coming their way rather than to speak of settled colonies."[32]

The need for colonists became so acute that the States-General in 1640 more or less forced the West India Company to busy itself with emigration, and to open to all colonists the trade in the New Netherlands and along the North American coasts. The States-General ordered the Company to give up its fur monopoly and to facilitate the granting of patroonships so that anyone who came to the New Netherlands with five additional persons above age fifteen would receive two hundred morgens* of land and hunting and fishing rights. Indeed, the Company must even offer free passage to all compatriots who wished to leave with their families for the New Netherlands. These were to receive all the necessities, even a farm, complete with horses and cattle, which they could rent from the Company for a period of six years; meanwhile they could purchase their food and supplies on credit, if needed.[33] We can find similar conditions in the nineteenth and twentieth centuries.

In this manner the States-General indirectly promoted emigration, motivated by the realistic fear that other world powers would otherwise conquer the New Netherlands. For instance, the English had already built three cities on the Fresh River in Connecticut. One of these small towns was even close to the Dutch "Huys de Hoope" fort. David Pieterszoon De Vries, in the name of the Director-General of the New Netherlands, brought a protest in June, 1639. The English governor, John Haynes, who had hospitably invited De Vries to dine with him, answered that "the lands were vacant and we have been here for many years and so it really doesn't matter; it would be a shame to leave such good land undeveloped, land that would produce such fine grain."[34] This is a rationale that can still be heard today regarding the vast empty spaces of Australia.

The desire of our excellencies was fulfilled "to invite for emigration all good residents of the Netherlands." Their efforts were successful. Many people came from the Netherlands to settle as tenants in the New Netherlands under the prescribed conditions. Among them were several well-to-do families who arrived, bringing their servants with them. Some engaged in trade, which in turn gave rise to important coastal trade with the English colonies; others developed one of the trades that were no longer regulated. The relative tolerance attracted other nationalities such as the English, the French, the Germans, etc. With the French came particularly the Huguenots,

---

*A morgen (morning) is the area plowed in one morning, about two acres.

who suffered from increasing religious restrictions in France. There were even Swedes and Norwegians, usually classed together as "Northmen," who were chiefly interested in the riches of the woods and forest products. They had been invited to come by the patroons, as well as by the Company itself. It was assumed that these men were forestry specialists; they did not come, as Professor Colenbrander states, because there was a lack of Hollanders.[35]

Prosperity quickly came not only to the small trade and shipping center of New Amsterdam but also to the surrounding area. Within a short time "one could see thirty boweries built and provided with animals as beautiful as could be found in Europe, as well as a hundred plantations that would be bowery estates in two or three years. For as soon as the tobacco had been harvested, cereals were planted without replowing being necessary. During winter the settlers worked at preparing new land."[36]

The "plantations" were usually little patroonships and the best known was that of David Pieterszoon De Vries. He had first located on Staten Island and then on the right bank of the Hudson, about two miles above New Amsterdam, where he "planted" the Vriesendael colony. There was also the colony of Cornelis Melyn from Holland who, after De Vries' people "had been killed by the savages and the Raritans," tried in 1641 to colonize Staten Island, and the one of Meyndert Meyndertsen and that of a man from Utrecht, Van Nederhorst, who founded a "patroonship" southwest of Vriesendael, "only an hour away" in the Hackensack Valley. Also well known were the colonies of Cornelis Antonissen Van der Slijck from Breukelen and Adriaen Van der Donck from Breda, etc.[37] This also resulted in a more active propaganda for America in our country, as is obvious.

Emigration and colonization were short-lived, because of the covert—and later, more open—opposition of the West India Company, whose Directors were primarily interested in trade profits, which they felt were increasingly being threatened. Soon there was no more free passage or free transport of cattle. Land ownership was curtailed and the colonists were subject to arbitrary taxation. Even worse was the disgraceful attitude of Director-General Kieft, who stupidly caused some bloody wars with the Indians. Terrible cruelty was inflicted by both sides and farms and "plantations" were devastated. All desire for colonization ceased and many left. Peace was not restored until August, 1645. By then the number of Dutch colonists had dwindled from 3,000 to 1,000; the population of New Amsterdam and its environs, which in 1643 numbered about 2,500 souls, had declined to 500![38]

It is no wonder that there was considerable dissatisfaction. In 1645 the West India Company was forced to relinquish its monopoly of operating cargo ships between the colony and the fatherland as well as to Brazil and the West Indies. It had to open up the trade to everybody. As a consequence, New Amsterdam quickly revived. The discharge of Kieft was demanded and he was replaced by the able, though very despotic, |Peter| Stuyvesant, who refused the colonists' request to have an important voice in the government. This led the colonists, in 1649, to send to the Netherlands some confidential agents, headed by Adriaen Van der Donck. This visit was of importance for our goals, because it again strongly spurred emigration to the New Netherlands. In the "Memorial" and "Remonstrance" addressed to the States-General, the settlers asked for self-government as well as a reduction of many taxes, the abrogation of the West India Company's sovereignty over their holdings, strong promotion of emigration, etc.

Much interest was now shown in the colony and once again there was a desire for emigration. Van der Donck and his party had been in the Netherlands only a short time and already their propaganda efforts were so successful that hundreds of people wanted to go. Soon two hundred had left and Van der Donck urged two hundred more to go at Company expense. An even larger number awaited passage! A number of privileges were wrung from the Company. In 1652 New Amsterdam was given self-government. Trading privileges of the colonists were liberalized—for example, the slave trade, formerly a monopoly, was opened. Fares for passage were considerably reduced.[39]

Although the first Anglo-Dutch War (1652–1654) was a deterrant, still during those years both calculated and less purposeful preparations were made for emigration. In 1655 there appeared two very important publications that more than any previous ones must have impressed on Dutch minds the wonders of America. Both were of more significance than De Laet's *Nieuwe Wereldt* [*New World*], which had a second, enlarged Dutch edition in 1630, a Latin one in 1633, and a French version in 1640. The two new publications were also more important than Wassenaer's *Historisch Verhael* [*Historical Account*] of 1632. The works to which I refer were written by eye witnesses, whose firsthand accounts made a far deeper impression than some books that had appeared earlier, such as that printed in Alkmaar in 1644 and entitled *Een Kort Ontwerp van de Mahakvase Indiaenen* . . . door Johannem Megapolensem junioren [*A Short Account of the Mohawk Indians* . . . by Johannes Megapolensis, Jr.], pastor at Rensselaerswijck; also that which appeared in Amsterdam in 1651, *Beschrijvinghe van Virginia, Nieuw-Nederlandt, Nieuw-Engelandt* [Description of Virginia, New Netherlands, and New England], containing Megapolensis' "Short Account" and De Laet and Van der Donck's "Remonstrance."[40]

The first [of the two new items] concerned itself primarily with an Indian tribe; the second was a compilation. Appearing in 1655, they must have been of greater significance, since they were written by men who had themselves established patroonships and so were aware of what colonization meant.

Another work published in Alkmaar was *Korte Historiael, ende Journaels Aenteyckeninge, van verscheyden Voayagiens in de vier deelen des Wereldts-Ronde, als Europa, Africa, Asia ende Amerika gedaen* door D. David Pietersz. de Vries [*A Short History and Journal Notes Dealing with Various Voyages to the Four Continents of the World-Globe—Europe, Africa, Asia and America*, compiled by D. David Pieterszoon De Vries].

One can imagine how much those seventeenth-century people, such as Jan Huygen of Linschoten, loved reading of de Vries' experiences in America, just as our present-day generation "enjoy reading about strange lands and accounts of unusual happenings for which they had a particular liking and which amused them." What a paradise the New Netherlands must have seemed—such riches. David Pieterszoon found there "the most beautiful woods eyes could behold. . . . The open spaces of the old Maya land were so full of strawberries that one would lie down to eat them; there were also good blue grapes that are delicious." He had heard of "great herds of deer that had two fingers of fat on their ribs" and "of lots and lots of turkeys," etc.[41] It must have made a great impression on aspiring colonists that Brand Pijlen, one of the Rensselaerswijck farmers, had "twelve successive bountiful wheat crops, without suffering from summer diseases." Even more remarkable was the fertility of De Vries' own "plantation." It was "a neat place along the river bank at the foot of a hill, and an hour and a half further on, there was a valley where I could raise enough fodder for 200 cattle; I also had thirty morgens of grainland and raised wheat taller than any man in the land." De Vries also commented about the excellent rye, barley, oats, and peas that were sown and about the excellent beer that was brewed. He added: "We only lack people to work; it is a pleasant and attractive land that should be inhabited by our own people."[42] Thus we must assume that people were eager to emigrate and their fear of Indians faded into the background.

This fear had developed because colonists were killed in many areas. The fear grew because, when David Pieterszoon sought out the South River for the second time, "he found, here and there, skulls and skeletons of those of our people who had been killed and occasionally horse and cow heads of our animals that had also been killed." This fear decreased when it was realized time and again that the Dutch themselves, particularly the officials of the Company, had unleashed these cruelties. Governor-General Kieft was most guilty of all; "he wanted to blame the Indians for what his own people had done." De Vries had warned him in vain. "Stop this action. You want to crush the savages; but you will also cause our nation to be murdered." Kieft was later dismissed and, in what seemed to be a judgment of God, on his return to the fatherland with his gains of about *fl.* 400,000, he "lost his life in an accident,"* as the managers wrote to his successor, Stuyvesant.

De Vries himself got along well with the "savages": "They are very friendly to us and we do not fear them; we enter the forests with them and sometimes encounter them one or two hours from home and they behave the same as do any Christians we may encounter." Indeed, the Indians— one of them told De Vries himself—had been favorably inclined toward the first Dutch and after the ships had left they had taken care of those who had stayed behind. They "had protected them as the apple of their eye and

---

*Literally, "lost his life in the wrong channel, God forbid."

had urged their daughters to sleep with them and they had had children by them; there was many a savage running around with Dutch features but they were now rebelling and killing those of our own blood."[43] The "savages" were not so bad, provided one treated them well.

The second publication of great importance for emigration concerned itself directly with the question of colonization. Written by the capable Adriaen Van der Donck and also published in 1655, it was entitled *Beschrijvinge van Nieuw-Nederlant* [A *Description of the New Netherlands*]. A second edition came out in Amsterdam in 1656, which indicates its popularity and significance. Much of the content was not new, however, having previously appeared in the "Remonstrance" of 1649, the first section of which concerned itself with "the Situation, Fertility and the Sober State of Same" [of the New Netherlands]. It was published in The Hague in 1650. The "Remonstrance," of which Van der Donck is still considered to be the principal contributor,[44] and his *Description* made this "*jonkheer*" the chief propagandist for America in the seventeenth century. His title is still commemorated in the name of Yonkers, a suburb of New York City. The "Memorial" and the "Remonstrance" of 1649 had already inspired a general interest in the New Netherlands and it appeared to the Amsterdam office of the West India Company, as they wrote to Stuyvesant, as if all the heavens and earth were interested.[45] Even in Antwerp a pamphlet was published concerning the colony: "To the United Dutch Provinces."[46] The Company, assisted by one of its officials, Van Tienhoven, had managed to calm the storm; the Anglo-Dutch War was also a factor as previously noted.

The *Description* of 1655 again called attention to the New Netherlands. It was now generally assumed that in America there was plenty of work for all. This was an assumption promoted by all colonization agents and simultaneously strengthened by their stress on "over-population" in the old country and the "fallow" land to be worked in America. These propaganda motifs were used by Van der Donck in his vigorous propaganda campaign. The "Remonstrance" referred to the New Netherlands as "a noble province," which could be a refuge for all the "needy" in our land, "for high and middle class elements as well as for the lowest. Because for those who want to work here, it is much easier than in the Netherlands to earn their living." What groups were needed? "Farmers, farm hands and other needy persons . . . whom the fatherland could easily spare." In the *Description*, in which the advantages of colonization were summarized, we find reiterations such as, "Fifth, as is known, many people have commonly come to this land and there have never been too many; everyone can find employment and because there is peace it is obvious that there is work and so it could easily come to pass that our needy and superfluous people could easily establish another Netherlands outside the Netherlands to the benefit and support of the State."[47]

Emigration was promoted by Van der Donck not primarily for the benefit of the emigrants but for the state, as had been the case previously. This was easy to understand as long as the New Netherlands was one of our colonies. Once again free passage was given, this time to all artisans and farmers who could provide for themselves; many, who had not yet been able to make use of this offer, availed themselves of this opportunity. However, the Company still did not see the importance of colonization and was not at all inclined to promote it.

Meanwhile another propagandist arose, seemingly under the influence of Van der Donck's writings: the city of Amsterdam. The officials of the city had thoroughly studied the *Remonstrance*! They, too, had "plenty to spare." For example, the Amsterdam orphanage was filled to capacity! The New Netherlands could use the orphan boys and probably even more so, the orphan girls. In the nineteenth century ships filled with residents of all kinds of institutions were sent to America in order to reduce European public welfare costs. This was not a new idea—it was centuries-old. Indeed, overseas possessions were often overly endowed for this purpose! In this case, Amsterdam in 1652 offered the West India Company 150 boys and girls "from God's house [the almshouse] who were willing to be transported at a cost of *fl.*30 per head or to pay their keep at 8 stuivers [nickels] per day." The Company agreed, although the plan was somewhat delayed by the Anglo-Dutch War; nevertheless ten orphan girls and seven boys were shipped off.[48] The city of Amsterdam also managed, when the passage fare of *fl.*50 turned out to be too high, to arrange "that people of small means would be sent over by the skippers for the sum of *fl.*30." This arrangement considerably increased the number of emigrants.

Amsterdam's importance in the emigration increased when it decided to found an autonomous colony. In 1655, when the West India Company was in financial straits, the city purchased the patroonship on the South River that had just been recaptured by Stuyvesant from the Swedes who had founded a New Sweden there. A prospectus, containing some thirty-five "Conditions," was jointly drawn up by the city and the Company and printed and distributed separately, while they were also printed—which is typical for the relationship I have mentioned—on the back of the second edition of Van der Donck's *Description of the New Netherlands* that appeared in that same year of 1656.[49]

Amsterdam led a heavy propaganda campaign for colonization. It agreed to furnish the colony, called the "Nieuwer Amstel," "with a capable person who would serve as a school teacher and also function as a lay reader of the Holy Scriptures and lead in the singing of psalms." Already on December 21, 1656, the first colonists—a total of 113 souls—boarded the *Prins Maurits* "as colonizers, free artisans, soldiers—all with their families" under the leadership of Jacob Alrichs, the newly appointed vice-director of Nieuwer Amstel.

For some unaccountable reason, the voyage was entrusted to a captain and crew that had never been to the New Netherlands. In addition to this, a terrible storm caused the *Prins Maurits* to suffer shipwreck near Long Island.

However, Alrichs was able to reach land and, augmented by several New Amsterdamers, succeeded in reaching the South River with 125 persons on April 25, 1657. As behooved a good colonizer, his letters back home to Amsterdam were full of praise for the new area. On one of his expeditions he had found "beautiful land for development" where a couple of thousand "hardy" farmers "could raise a wonderful crop."

Despite the hazardous ocean voyage that was involved, three hundred colonists were prepared to leave for Nieuwer Amstel in March, 1657, and a minister was being sought to accompany them. Prospects for the new colony were so favorable that the Amsterdam classis reported "that sundry families are leaving to be transported thither." Shortly thereafter a second ship, *de Wagh*, left with about four hundred persons on board. In addition to the Hollanders there were many Waldensians—Protestants from the West Alpine area who had been persecuted by the Duke of Savoy and had fled to Amsterdam. Within two years there were six hundred settlers in Nieuwer Amstel.

As was true of many other new settlements, there were setbacks. Pietersen, the school teacher who had charge of twenty-five students, not only lacked paper, slates, and slate pencils but what was worse, there were insufficient provisions and so there were "murmurings" among the colonists. Letters of discontent were written, which gave "such a scare" that more than thirty families on Manhattan Island abandoned their plans to move to Nieuwer Amstel.[50]

Conditions worsened with the arrival of the second ship. Because of heavy rains the crops were destroyed and contagious disease resulted in the loss of many lives. The city of Amsterdam had to provide support for which it had little desire, and so it lost interest. The second edition of the "Conditions" was printed in 1659, and they were far less favorable than before; Asher was the first to call attention to this.[51] Because of this, and also because many of the colonists left for neighboring Virginia and Maryland, the promising undertaking died out.

The propaganda effects of the works of David Pieterszoon De Vries and Adriaen Van der Donck became apparent again in 1662 when *Kort Verhael van Nieuw-Nederlants Gelegentheit, Deughden, Natuerlyke Voorrechten, en byzondere bequaemheidt ter bevolkingh* [*A Short Account of the New Netherlands Location, Merits, and Natural Advantages and Its Peculiar Suitability for Colonization*] was published.[52] It included also various "Requests, Representation and Deductions," etc. that had been "presented" to the Amsterdam government "by various interested parties at various times, about the end of the year 1661." The first section of this work was altogether borrowed from the writings of De Vries and Van der Donck, and so we can safely conclude that the author of the *Short Account* drew from the Amsterdam propaganda and from the second edition of Van der Donck's *Description*, and that through reading of these works he hit upon the idea to realize, if possible, his communist ideals in America, promulgated already earlier in England—as Professor Quack has already pointed out.[53]

This assumption is true only if one can identify the author of the *Short Account* as that most remarkable inhabitant of Zeeland, Pieter Corneliszoon Plockhoy, of Zierikzee, a seventeenth-century precursor of both Robert Owen and Charles Fourier. Plockhoy had hopes of establishing a "Society" in America based on "Equality," in which no one "will ever strive to obtain the upper hand or commanding lead in this Society.... Since all matters shall be resolved or determined by a two-thirds vote of the entire Society and for the common good, they shall also be observed and kept, according to one's best ability as a truly peace-loving Christian person." Although Plockhoy had been brought up as a Mennonite [*Doopsgezind*] himself, people "of conflicting beliefs" could become members of the Society. Thus, there would be no preacher for the time being; "... it would be impractical for such a fledgling Society, as well as an inevitably ruinous plague to all peace and unity without which a well-ordered Society cannot be started or promoted, and much less made durable." Moreover, the colonists would be supplied "with the best of the best"—the Holy Scriptures. "All individual quarrels and sectarianism in matters of Religion" had to be eschewed.

The city of Amsterdam as well as the West India Company was concerned about the loss of the North American colonies after the accession of Charles II to the throne in 1660. Because the colonies could only be saved through an influx of settlers, they essentially approved Plockhoy's plans and drew up a contract with him. In one provision Plockhoy agreed that "as soon as possible he and twenty-four men would depart on one or more ships to go to the aforementioned colony, establish themselves, and support it with farming, fishing, industry and otherwise." They would "occupy" some land in common—Plockhoy's ideal—"while in addition each member of this society could from time to time choose for himself in particular, occupy and take up such other lands as they will be able and willing to cultivate and use as pastures."[54] Plockhoy, who had already demonstrated to be a practical idealist by allowing for individual holdings next to what for many was still a somewhat unusual "communal area," showed himself to be a businessman by the way he promoted the New Netherlands. His prospectus compared favorably with that of the most gifted land agent of the nineteenth and twentieth centuries. He even arranged to have poets of reputation spread the fame of the land waiting for colonization.

No less a person than Jacob Steendam, the famous first poet of the New Netherlands, who had already gained fame by his "*Klacht van Nieuw-Amsterdam in Nieuw-Nederland tot haar moeder*" ["Complaint of New Amsterdam in New Netherlands to her Mother"] (1659) and "'*t Lof van Nieuw-Nederland*" ["In Praise of New Netherlands"] (1661), wrote some "stimulating verses":[55]

> The New Netherlands are the best, the most noble of lands
> Rich in blessings, flowing with milk and honey,
> That the All-Highest has (with double bounteous hands)
> Endowed: indeed overfilled with all that grows there.

> The air, the earth and the sea are laden with his gifts:
> To sustain (those who are in need) even without effort.*

This and some other stanzas dealt with the New Netherlands in general, but knowing that Plockhoy's colony would be founded on the South River, the ninth stanza is dedicated to it:

> The New Netherlands South River: or the second Almosanas
> Provides for you (on her banks) with a pleasure grove as residence.
> You can choose Swanendal, where Oset's domain and throne were,
> Or some other place, for the benefit of your enterprise.
> You have the choice of all; you are free to choose
> Consider well this privilege; you will not lose it.†

In the "verses" of Steendam, according to a Holland-American of the twentieth century, we find for the first time "the real American spirit with the love and sympathy for the American country."[56] In addition to Steendam's verses, a sonnet of Karel Verloove was included. Both poets—this being mentioned to show their idealism as well as Plockhoy's—were in many respects kindred spirits to him and belonged to a group of "reformers" whose leader, Jan Zoet, according to Plockhoy's belief, dared to sing:

> The greatest evil I ever found
> Is the terrible lying committed in the churches.‡[57]

Thus we find expressed an attitude of anti-clericalism that was gaining ground at that time. Plockhoy and his followers showed, in addition, that they belonged, if not to the "deeper" stream, then to the wider stream of Free Thinkers or New Lights who, as children of their time, were more or less influenced by the mysticism of Boehme that expressed the spirit of the age. They organized themselves under such names as Pietists, Labadists, Quakers, etc. Plockhoy's real importance, which according to my knowledge has not been specifically mentioned before, is primarily that he was the first who tried to realize in America his social ideas that, like those of the other Free Thinkers, were closely related to their "religious" notions. This attempt

---

*   Nieuw-nederland is 't puyck, en 't eelste van de Landen
    Een Seegen-rijck gewest, daer Melck en Honigh vloeyd,
    dat d' allerhoogste heeft (met dubbeld milde handen)
    Begaeft: ja opgevult, in 't geen daer wast en groeyd.
    De Lugt, de Aerd en Zee, sijn swanger met haer gaven:
    Om (die behoeftigh is) oock sonder moeyt te laven.

†   Nieuw-neer-lands Zuyd-revier: of 't (t)weede Almosanas
    Schaft (op haer oevers) u een lusthof tot verblijf.
    Gy kiest of Swanendal (daer Osets rijck en troon was)
    Of wel een ander plaets, tot nut van u bedrijf.
    Gy hebt de keur van al: het staet u vry te kiesen
    Betracht dit voor-recht wel, gy sult het niet verliesen.

‡   Het allerkwaadste kwaad, dat ik ooit weet te vinden,
    Is 't schriklik liegen, dat men in de Kerkken doet.

in America was not due to the fact that America was known already at that time as the ideal land of freedom—people knew better—but because there was room enough not only for the Puritans and other primarily religious groups, but also for people with more social reformist feelings who wished to live there.

The Dutchman Plockhoy was the first one to make America into a laboratory for social experimentation. Quakers and Labadists, some of whom were Hollanders, would follow him in this. "America" as an ideal had gained a wider meaning. It is a credit to the city of Amsterdam that it gave Plockhoy an opportunity to prove the viability of his ideas in the New World, ideas which even today are considered with derision, not to say with animosity. His ideas were put forth at a time when the Puritans in New England were a most vicious, bigoted, and criminally intolerant group and when no Huguenots were tolerated in French Canada.

Plockhoy, the pioneer from Zeeland, again expounded his views in a pamphlet, "A Short and Clear Design for the Purpose of a Mutual Agreement to Ease the Toil, Dissatisfactions and Difficulties of all Sorts of Craftsmen, by Establishing a Mutual Company or Settlement." The colonists were to live as one large family—a united, peace-loving group that would work voluntarily six hours daily for the communal good. The profits would be divided equally among them. Terms like *servant* and *maid* would be unknown in the colony. If any colonist should still hire another to work for him, he too would be required to put in his six-hour stint. The school children of the community were not to be indoctrinated in any particular faith, but they were to be taught the Holy Scriptures and in particular also natural sciences and languages so that their minds would not be harmed by opinions inculcated before they were able to use their common sense. We already know about Plockhoy's concept of government: "a general council" would receive suggestions for improvement from any member, and these would be implemented by a two-thirds majority vote.[58]

In that same year of 1662, twenty-five Mennonite families—Mennonites have always indicated a prediliction for egalitarian ways—left for America with Plockhoy. They settled near the aforementioned patroonship of Swanendal on the South River. I am unaware as to whether others joined them, either attracted by Plockhoy's communism or by Steendam's utopian assurance that the riches of the New Netherlands could sustain people with its rice and porridge mountain "without effort"—a poetic reinforcement of the illusion of the legendary land of Cockaigne. Two years later Plockhoy's colony, just as Nieuwer Amstel, was destroyed by the English; the inhabitants of both were dispersed and several sold as slaves in Virginia.

In the meantime, the West India Company, repenting over its previous misconceptions, was strongly encouraging emigration to North America. It offered to the colonists a greater voice in the government and ordered more tolerance in religious matters. After that, the population quickly grew in numbers and prosperity. In addition to New Amsterdam and Rensselaerswijck, several other new villages came into being and those already in existence expanded. On Long Island there were settlements with names such as Middelburg, Heemstede, Vlissingen and 's Gravensande, largely inhabited by the English; also such villages as Breuckelen, Amersfoort, Midwoud, New Utrecht, and finally, Boswijck—in each of which there was a predominant Dutch element. New Haarlem arose on Manhattan Island. In the vicinity of Fort Orange, the hamlet of Beverwijck, which had only ten houses in 1646, had grown to such an extent that by 1657 it had its own minister.

Midway between New Amsterdam and Beverwijck a settlement had been founded, which in 1657, according to the accounts of Reverends J. Megapolensis and S. Drisius, constituted "an extremely pleasant area in which some Dutch households" had been established "and were doing exceedingly well." This hamlet, which was often called Esopus after the Indians, was re-named "Wiltwijck" by the "duytsche" [Dutch], that is, the Hollanders. To the south and on the other side of the North River—in present-day New Jersey—Bergen arose, where thirty families had settled, according to a report of Stuyvesant in 1660.[59]

Under Kieft the "English" villages had obtained a measure of self-government; the same thing happened in New Amsterdam in 1652 (more completely in 1653). In 1654 Stuyvesant was forced to give the Dutch hamlets a share in their government—they set up alderman seats. In 1663 and 1664, under the force of circumstances, a sort of colonial representative body was convened. In April of 1664, Jeremias van Rensselaer opened the first assembly [Landdag], in which, for the first time, all the Dutch areas were represented.

There was also increasing freedom in religious matters. Religious tolerance had earlier attracted people of various beliefs to the New Netherlands, although this tolerance should not be overestimated and must be considered in relation to the times and be compared in particular with the environment. As early as 1646 the freedom in New Amsterdam attracted the attention of the Jesuit [Isaac] Jogues. Calvinists were the most numerous element and only the Reformed Church was established; but there were also Catholics, "English Puritans," Lutherans, and Baptists.[60] Jews and Quakers were later arrivals. The colony also provided education. At first there was elementary education and after 1656 higher learning, with the founding of a Latin school in New Amsterdam. This education had a very colonial character in spite of its modern strivings. Some parents complained that the students fought with each other and tore the clothing from the backs of others, and the principal complained "that his hands were tied because some parents had forbidden him to punish their children."[61] Soon afterwards, this educational system functioned with fewer problems. Even though "freedom" of education played a very subordinate role among the "attractions" of America in those days, yet Plockhoy's "Short and Clear Plan" indicates that it was a factor.

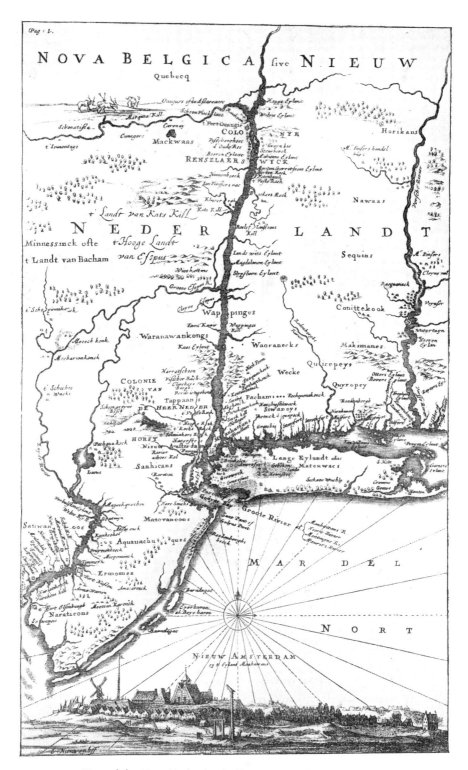

Map of the New Netherlands (from A. Van der Donck, 1656).

All these factors together explain why, around 1660, emigration to the New Netherlands was growing rapidly. When England in 1664 forced Stuyvesant to surrender the New Netherlands on the basis of very dubious claims, there were ten thousand residents there compared to two thousand in 1646 when Stuyvesant took charge. Among these, however, were about four thousand English, as well as Walloons, Huguenots, Waldensians, and other groups. These were people who had usually been persecuted in their homelands, and who had found hospitality in the Netherlands and the New Netherlands and who had built, especially in the latter place, a new existence for themselves.

The population of the New Netherlands had always been international in composition. The Director-General informed Jogues in 1646 that eighteen languages were spoken on Manhattan Island and in the surrounding area.[62] After all, that was nothing strange in such a typical trade and shipping center as New Amsterdam—then already the most important settlement on Manhattan Island. A petition from the mayors of New Amsterdam to Governor Stuyvesant, asking him to fortify the town indicates that the significance of these various languages and nationalities should not be overestimated. In this request it was noted that the residents "were mainly Dutch" and that the city in case of an English attack, would have to serve "as a refuge and succor for so many villages and hundreds of farms with houses, crops, lands, animals, and ten thousand souls—most of them Netherlanders—in addition to some French." Also at the same time some of the so-called "English" hamlets on Long Island had "been settled and inhabited by Netherlanders" for thirty to forty years.[63]

It has already been noted that the Dutch lost their North American holdings in 1664 just as it was becoming a very important agricultural colony; indeed, it looked like it would become "a granary for our fatherland." With the loss of the New Netherlands, emigration from our land to North America slackened, although it did not entirely cease. For more than a century the Hudson River area, rebaptized as New York and New Jersey, was supplied with preachers from the Netherlands. This resulted in an emigration of a number of intellectuals who not only exercised a far-reaching influence on church life, but their descendants were to dominate political life under the new English regime.

Although official propaganda for America ceased in the Netherlands, private means were employed to portray it as a wonderland. Even more so than previously, the common people were urged to seek an earthly paradise on the other side of the Atlantic Ocean. For example, now it was the well-known Englishman, William Penn, who advertised the former Dutch area, Pennsylvania, which was granted to him on the right bank of the South River, now exclusively called the Delaware. Following Plockhoy, it was the Quaker Penn who was to set up an ideal state in the New World. From London and Rotterdam, his project was advertised in English, German, French, and Dutch, and thus made known to western

Europe; the idealists—if from the continent—sailed from Rotterdam to the utopia.

Penn had visited the Netherlands and Germany in 1671 and 1677, and had found kindred souls in both areas. He had exchanged ideas in Friesland with the Labadists in Wieuwerd. Being the son of a Dutch mother—Margaretha Jasper of Rotterdam—he was eager to see "other foreign nationalities" in addition to Englishmen in his colony, in particular from the aforementioned countries. For that purpose he published in 1681 his *Short Account . . . of the Province called Penn-Sylvania, Located in America*. It is significant that in this pamphlet spiritual matters were in the primacy, although material matters were not overlooked. The prerogatives, freedoms, and privileges of the English nation would be granted there. Penn's goal was "to institute a free colony in which justice and diligence would prevail, . . . with freedom of conscience for each one in matters of religion, and public worship services." To this end he wished to sell blocks of five thousand acres of land to newcomers, if need be with "co-participants," for £100 plus an annual quitrent of one English shilling for each one hundred acres. Less well-to-do people would be able to rent up to two hundred acres for an annual quitrent of one English penny per acre.

Penn enumerated the groups he particularly desired. "Through the Providence of God the most desirable colonists were" (1) "industrious home owners and day laborers," (2) "industrious artisans," (3) "sharp minds" who because of inexpensive colonial living "would have plenty of time and opportunity to follow up on their good intentions to continue their scientific endeavors and be helpful in developing the nations," (4) "younger sons of families of but small fortune," and (5) "men with a Universal mind" to aid in government. Penn honestly warned that the first two or three years would not be easy: "the winter must be survived in order to enjoy the summer." They should carefully weigh "the present difficulties against the future comfort and abundance so that nobody will move motivated by presumptions and unsteady considerations, but by steady and solid ones. More than anything else, they must have an eye for God's Providence in making their decisions." They should only go with "the consent" of their nearest "Blood Friends" so that a "friendly and useful correspondence" could be maintained.

Information was distributed by "Jan Roelofszoon Van der Werf, who lived in the gilded Five Corners on the Amsterdam Heerestraat, and by Benjamin Furly, an English merchant living in the Shipbuilders harbor on the corner of Bierstraat in the house that was formerly called the Brewery of the Crown at Rotterdam." In addition and to stress the point, a letter of Penn was published concerning the importance of religious freedom, the suppression of which only created hypocrites.[64]

Two years later Penn changed the colonization terms so that for a hundred pounds one would not receive five thousand acres but "only" three thousand because Penn had to pay the Indians ten times as much for the land as previously. Now each purchaser also had to pledge "to settle a family" within three years on each thousand acres. Less well-to-do individuals would get fifty acres per household member, servants included, for a perpetual annual quitrent of one English penny per acre per year. Moreover, all would be "free residents." The spirit of brotherhood would be strengthened in the colony by the stipulation that although "sharp minds" were to be most desired, nevertheless those lawyers, attorneys, and solicitors who "would charge for their services" would be "banished to prevent anyone from profitting at the expense of another, and not to instigate parties to start lawsuits against each other."

It was frequently emphasized that no "established" church would be instituted and that everyone, regardless of religion, nationality, or rank, could be chosen to any office. However, one had to profess belief in "the one Almighty Eternal God, the Creator, Sustainer and Ruler of the World." "Wagers, Comedies, Gambling, Card Playing, Masquerades and all cursing, swearing, lying," etc., however, were forbidden. This pamphlet also contained favorable accounts of the land available for colonization and of the abundance of products and "the huge numbers of feathered creatures, the pleasant weather," etc. It seems to have been rapidly distributed because in 1684 the second edition of "A Letter from William Penn" appeared, in which a Hollander living in Pennsylvania highly praised the colony to which "many had come from Crevelt [Krefeld] and the surrounding areas in Meurslant."[65]

I have wanted to describe the basis of Penn's colony in some detail. First, it brings so clearly to the fore its close relationship with Plockhoy's endeavors and Plockhoy's significance as a "precursor—one among the most extraordinary of the memorials of American colonization"—comes out all the stronger.[66] In the second place, after the colonization of Pennsylvania and after the publication of pamphlets in so many languages, people began to view America even more than previously as the ideal land of freedom. William Penn was seen as the typical American. Later in France, according to [Gilbert] Chinard, Benjamin Franklin was considered above all as a Quaker, a follower of Penn. Franklin understood so well that his and America's popularity rested on an error that, as a good politician interested in the welfare of his country, he quietly let this *erreur populaire* run its course![67]

Although Penn's ideals were not unfamiliar to the Netherlanders and although his ideals were already alive previously in many a Dutch heart, the number of Hollanders that went to Pennsylvania was not of such importance that it led to the establishment of more or less self-sustaining colonies. It is true that, in cooperation with people from Krefeld and its vicinity, they helped to found Germantown in 1683. This town, now a part of Philadelphia, is considered the first permanent German settlement in the United States, but the role of the Hollanders, although incidentally mentioned, is usually forgotten.[68] In a "Deutschland ueber alles" frame of mind, many a Dutch name has been Germanized. Nor is it thought of at all that the area of Meurs, from which many of the founders of Germantown came, could certainly be considered a part of the Greater Netherlands at that time. In 1870 the Dutch language was still spoken there, and in this connection it should be remembered that many Krefelders originally were part of the Netherlands, or in the strict sense, of Holland.

Along the way it should be mentioned that not only the Germans, but also the French are responsible for detracting from the influence of the Dutch in the colonization of America. For example, there is the rather hilarious case of how [A. B.] Faust, the German-American scholar Germanized Pierre Minuit to Minnewit—considered until recently as the founder of New Amsterdam and consequently as a person of historical importance— and claimed him for Germany.[69] The French-American, Chinard, claims him as a Walloon for France and even adds the daring presumption that in the early days in New Amsterdam the French-Walloon element must have been predominant![70] In this instance also, it is completely overlooked that Minuit's birthplace—Wezel—was an entirely "Dutch" city in the cultural sense, not to mention Minuit's Dutch career. It is important to indicate this because as a result of the influence of such cases, one is inclined to underrate the Dutch role, small as it was, in the colonization of Pennsylvania. We should therefore also notice that on the first ship that sailed for Penn's colony there were next to the "Germans" (in this case the Low Dutch of the Lower Rhine region) also Dutch emigrants, mostly Mennonites—three brothers named Dirck, Abraham and Herman Op den Graeff and their families.[71]

The soul of the Germantown colony was a Dutch merchant named Jacob Telner, who had converted to the Mennonites in Amsterdam and had arranged for the purchase of about 18,000 morgens [9,000 acres] of land from Penn, of which 5,000 morgens [2,500 acres] were for himself. This assertion was made by the historian S. W. Pennypacker, who according to his own account, was of Dutch descent. The Pannebakkers were from Noord Brabant, but Faust, among others, considered them as Germans. According to Pennypacker, Telner "seems to have been the central figure of the whole emigration." He lived in Germantown for thirteen years and like his co-pioneers, the Dutch baker Cornelis Bom and [?] Van Bebber who owned 1,000 morgens [500 acres] of land, he wrote letters in Dutch to Holland. They were printed in Rotterdam and distributed for the promotion of emigration.[72]

Bom's very encouraging "Missive" was even reprinted. It must be said that Bom was extremely satisfied. He had a cow that gave plenty of milk, a riding horse and some pigs that multiplied so rapidly that, beginning with two, he soon had seventeen! In addition he had a garden and, before long, an orchard, etc., etc. According to A. C. Myers, this now very rare letter was an excellent example of propaganda.[73] Telner later went to London where he was a member of the Dutch colony and acted as an agent for emigration to Pennsylvania. As late as 1709, he facilitated the settling of eight or nine families on Penn's lands.[74]

Other Hollanders in Germantown and its surroundings were Jan Willemse Bockenogen from Haarlem, Gerhard Hendricks, the Schoenmakers, perhaps also the Kassels, as well as the Pannebakkers, Arent Klincker, and especially William Rittinghuysen, who came from Arnhem, where his family had been engaged in the typical Gelderlandic business of making paper. Willem and his two sons—Gerhard and Klaas—established the first paper mill in America in 1690, near Philadelphia. William Bradford, America's earliest printer, used their paper. Reasons enough for Faust and the like not to refer to Willem Rittinghuysen but to Wilhelm Ruttinghausen![75] Mention should be made that famous descendants of Willem, among others his scholarly great-grandson David—a friend of Franklin, are preferably referred to by our neighbors [the Germans], among others by R. Cronau, as Rittenhausen![76]

In addition to this I also call attention to another Dutch element in the person of a baker, Jan Duplouvys, married to Wijntje Van Sanen, and to a certain De Wees. There was also Dirck Keyser, a silk merchant from Amsterdam (as were so many Mennonites), Cornelis Siverts from Friesland, Dirck Van Kolk, Jan Doeden, Reinier Jansen from Alkmaar, etc. To conclude, there was another one, a well-known one. In 1694 an old, blind man led by his wife arrived in Germantown and won so much sympathy, not only from his countrymen Jan Doeden and Willem Rittinghuysen, but from all the other villagers, that they gave him citizenship free from all taxes, and after a collection by the two Hollanders they also gave him a house. The name of the blind wanderer—a bit of American tragedy—was none other than Pieter Corneliszoon Plockhoy, who had sought relief, as is so common in foreign lands, among his fellow countrymen and fellow believers.[77]

Even though the number of Hollanders in Germantown was not very large, their importance lay mostly in their cultural contributions. In this connection I have already mentioned Rittinghuysen. It is also interesting that among the first four proponents of the celebrated protest against slavery that originated in Germantown in 1688—"the first glimmering of the dawn of the contest"—there were three Netherlanders: Dirck and Abraham Op den Graeff and Gerhard Hendricks.[78] The famous German Pastorius was, as is known, the force behind this anti-slavery movement. We mention the protest in passing; thus, it did not originate with the "English" Quakers, but rather with the Dutch and Low Dutch Mennonites.

It is no wonder that all American writers such as Pennypacker, Gibbons, C. H. Smith, and others have strongly emphasized the role of the Hollanders in the development of Germantown.[79] There is an abundance of evidence concerning their importance in a communication written in Germantown on September 3, 1708, addressed to the Mennonites in Amsterdam, in which "catechism booklets" [vraeghboeckjes], "small Testaments for the young," psalm books, and Bibles were requested. A Dutch committee also arranged for a further emigration to Pennsylvania from the Netherlands and the bordering German and Swiss Rhinelands and concerned itself not only with the spiritual needs of the colonists, but also the secular needs of the aspiring emigrants.[80]

But the most astounding propaganda literature came from England and was even sponsored by the government. Distributed in the Rhineland, the legend of a wonderful America was trumpeted as much as possible. During the course of the eighteenth century there was, as a result, a veritable exodus from the Rhine area. In the seventeenth century, Amsterdam had been the port of embarkation for those bound for America, with Rotterdam playing only a minor role in this trade; now Rotterdam replaced it and played such a role that it became the great emigrant port.[81]

It is a striking fact that many of the pamphlets about America, not only in Dutch, but also in the German and French languages, were published in Rotterdam, The Hague, Amsterdam, Leyden, that is, in Dutch cities.[82] The English-American land sales, as far as the continent was concerned, were largely made via the Netherlands. Queen Anne and later George I, following the example of Penn, had their agents here who issued the most enticing descriptions to promote western Pennsylvania, now that the eastern part had become too expensive. They stated that there was to be the same freedom of worship and that the land was so productive—for ten to twenty years it would not have to be worked!—that the most humble person could enjoy a better life there than the greatest nobleman in Europe. The "*mirage américain*" was in full operation and caused a "Westward Ho" movement that can be viewed as a forerunner of the nineteenth- and twentieth-century exodus.

Due to all this propaganda, the attention of Dutch Labadists in Frisian Wieuwerd had already been directed earlier toward America. In 1679 they had sent out two representatives—Jasper Danckaerts and Peter Sluyter— and this led to a colonization in 1684. A New Netherlander named A. Herman, born in Prague, who was "annexed" by Faust for Germany, just as the two Labadists—here also the Dutch role is almost totally ignored— offered for that purpose part of his holdings in the present state of Delaware. Sluyter, formerly a resident of Haarlem, ruled here as a bishop and in this capacity he appeared not to have obtained a large following. He introduced tobacco growing and the slave trade, and consequently at the time of his death he was very well-to-do.[83] The entire operation, even if of but little importance, attests anew that all elements thought they could find a social laboratory in America. The coercion in certain areas was forgotten and more and more the name "America" was identified with "freedom."

In addition to the wonderful tales about American fertility that we have previously related, it was especially this freedom that attracted Germans *en masse* during the eighteenth century and also, following the revocation of the Edict of Nantes, dozens of Frenchmen who left for the New World, many via the Netherlands. At times their numbers were so large that the States-General had to take special steps so that the stream could be handled in an orderly way, particularly so that the poverty stricken would not remain in our land.

It speaks almost for itself that Hollanders also must have been affected by this America fever due to the propaganda literature and the sight of the departure of so many. Accounts concerning this are scarce, however, and so far as I am aware, no statistics are available. The number from our country could not have been large or even of somewhat noticeable size. Penny-packer mentions a few colonists from Gelderland. Because of circumstances as well as the sandy lands, it was the province for transit *par excellence* at the beginning of the eighteenth century.[84] C. Henry Smith, in his book, *The Mennonites of America*, mentions a number of settlers from Holland who after 1724 located in Lehigh County, Pennsylvania, near Coopersburg.[85] We also encounter Hollanders elsewhere. A. Gillon, from Rotterdam, achieved success in South Carolina. Pieter Le Poole from Leyden became a figure of importance in Charleston. Even today there are descendants there of these seventeenth- and eighteenth-century countrymen—some of whom arrived from the New Netherlands after the English took over, now well-known families like the Vedders in Charleston[86] and the Mazycks, who apparently had settled here earlier in company of French Calvinist fellow believers, just as the Huguenots had chosen to settle by preference in the New Netherlands, while the Germans were more attracted to Pennsylvania, although not exclusively. After 1772 the name of a distiller, G. Van Erkelens, is found in Connecticut. Dircks, originally from Overijsel, came from Surinam to America and for a time served as an officer during the Revolution.[87] Even more numerous are the unknown and the less prominent.

Ever since then, the illusion about America has not vanished from Dutch minds; indeed, it rather increased. Especially the American Revolution was a powerful force to that effect. In addition to the aspiring emigrants, traders became more and more interested in America, and in close relation with them, the politicians. Our poets described how people viewed America in the second half of the eighteenth and the first half of the nineteenth century. Not only John Paul Jones, but especially men such as Franklin and Washington, were admired as ideal Americans, in part as a consequence of the attitude of France, where no less a person than Voltaire praised America, and in particular because the "Quaker" had become an "in" figure. Especially Bellamy and his circle, which in addition to "artists" also included politicians and the passionate patriot Quint Ondaatje, idealized America and Americans. Besides |Jacobus| Bellamy himself and his friends |Johannes| Kinker and |Rhijnvis| Feith, |Jan Pieter| Kleyn and |Hieronymus| Van Alphen, there were the patriot |Johan Hendrik| Swildens and the philologist |Theodorus| Van Kooten, as well as F. Jeronimo De Bosch, who glorified America in general and men like Washington in particular and portrayed "Liberated America" to our whole nation as the land of liberty *par excellence*. Thus it is not by accident that the earliest Dutch emigrants who were going to the Republic of the United States were attracted by ideals, in particular by ideals of political freedom. I am referring to the group of "Patriotten."

2

Why the Number of America-Goers Remained Small in the Seventeenth and Eighteenth Centuries

It is a remarkable fact that the total number of Dutch emigrants who departed for North America during the seventeenth and very probably also the eighteenth centuries never exceeded 6,000, while in the nineteenth century, merely during the period 1845–1849 this figure was topped by 500; and after that more than 6,000 repeatedly came in a single year; in 1881 there were 8,597, and in 1882 even 9,517 Dutch emigrants![1]

This seems all the more remarkable when it is recalled that the seventeenth century in the Netherlands [the Golden Age] was a strongly entrepreneurial one, when the nation also reached a spiritual peak. But during the first half of the nineteenth century Dutch national endeavor had fallen to a minimum and did not improve again until the eighties. It may be recalled that men like Jan Huygen van Linschoten were typical of the seventeenth-century Dutch. From Goa in 1584 he wrote to his parents and expressed thoughts like these: "My heart is resolved day and night to only one thing and that is to see distant lands. Then there will be something to talk about when I am old. Time is wasted in no worse manner by a young man than to remain in his mother's kitchen, like an infant, not knowing what poverty nor riches are nor what is out there in the world. This is frequently the cause of its ruin."[2] Compare this to the ideals of a "young" man of about the 1840s, for example, Gerrit Witse, who wanted "a solid practice" and for this he needed—what a hero!—an appropriate and similarly solid wife.[3] We see the contrast between the sparkling, rough and tumble seventeenth-century life style portrayed by Bredero in his "Moortje" and "Spaansche Brabander"—not to mention Jan Steen and the like—and the drowsiness, the apathy, which characterized most of our languishing nation in the first half of the nineteenth century as shown in the literary portraits of everyday people by Nicolaas Beets, in particular in "De Leidsche Peuëraar" ["The Niggler of Leyden"].

I repeat, it seems all the more remarkable because in this psychological contrast we must look for one of the deeper causes for the relatively minor significance of Dutch colonies in the seventeenth century and the abundant blossoming of Dutch colonies—although under another flag—in the nineteenth century. The true settlements, especially of an agricultural nature, demanded permanent residence. The enterprising Hollander of the Golden Age set out voluntarily on exploration trips, like Jan Huygen, "desirous to see foreign and unknown lands or to seek adventure."[4] At the same time he tried to advance himself by trading in distant areas, but was too restless to settle down as a squatter and lead the rather monotonous life of a farmer.

Another example of this may be found in the case of the well-known seafarer and colony founder, David Pieterszoon De Vries, who first established a colony on the Delaware (or South) River in 1631. Later, in 1634, he founded one in Guyana, and following this he established one on Staten Island near the Hudson (or North) River in 1639. In February of 1640 he founded a colony a few miles north of New Amsterdam called "Vriesendael," as we already know.[5] However, all these colonies failed; the "planter" gave up too soon. Some circumstances, which we shall mention later, may have contributed to that. But, in particular, De Vries and so many of his contemporaries lacked the inner peace which, in addition to a spirit of determination, was essential to the successful founding of a colony. Both characteristics marked the nineteenth-century colonizers, although circumstances also contributed. The seventeenth century counted only one in that category, Kiliaen Van Rensselaer, and even he did not reside in his colony; he never visited it but administered it from his residence in Amsterdam![6] Colonies for trade and possessions, the so-called "colonies d'exploitation" that were content with a constant change of leadership, could be established anywhere in the world by our ancestors of the Golden Age and they flourished so much that they provoked the envy of our neighbors.

These ancestors were above all merchants who wanted fortified settlements to protect their businesses. The opening of trading posts obviously led to the exploitation of the surrounding area, but seldom to intensive cultivation of the land. Ratzel remarked that "trade does not require colonies,"* and he made particular reference to agricultural settlements.[7] From this it follows that commercial New Amsterdam was always far more important than the agricultural New Netherlands.

In the first three-quarters of the nineteenth century it was just the other way around. We were forced to abandon many important trading posts, while others led only a precarious existence. During that same period, as I have mentioned before, several flourishing Dutch settlements came into being on American soil. But they were Dutch colonies on alien soil. R. Gonnard refers to them as "colonies sans drapeau" [colonies without a flag], Dutch settlers living under a foreign flag.[8] They were the sorry result of the lassitude and apathy that caused the loss of so much good sap, in part unnecessarily, for the Dutch presence in the world.

---

*Der Handel braucht an und für sich keine Kolonien.

During these placid, unruffled forties, fifties, sixties, and even seventies of the nineteenth century, many left the fatherland, not necessarily voluntarily, and surely not in search of adventure. Pressing economic conditions, and often their more or less conscious rebellion against the lax spirit of the age, especially in religious matters, impelled them to go to the New World to improve their condition in more ways than one. It was not a spirit of adventure or of unrest that drove the nineteenth-century colonist to the ever-widening western areas, as was true of the seventeenth-century Dutch who did not lack leaders keen on adventure and profit for their own pockets. That these prosaic men [of the nineteenth century] had a greater chance of being successful was also due to the quiet determination and complete dedication to their task of leaders such as Van Raalte. The Gerrit Witses and not the Jan Huygens are the material that ideal colonists are made of!

Naturally, one can not say that those in the nineteenth century who moved to lands unknown to them were possessed of an inner peace, for that peace was disturbed by economic, religious, and political dissatisfaction, making way for an increasing restlessness from the moment that the idea "to America!" crossed their minds and stuck there permanently. Migration increases destabilization. Roscher has remarked that restlessness is a characteristic of "colonizing nations," and it is all the more noticeable if the nation is younger.[9] Proof of this can be found in the unabated emigration today to Canada, the United States, and elsewhere, of which the Dutch emigration is also a element.

Much larger—not in an absolute but in a relative sense, since their numbers were so much smaller—was this migration among the far more restless "colonist folk" in the seventeenth century. Many of them remained only a few years in the new settlements and then returned to the old country; sometimes they would remove to the New World again, though at the insistence or at the expense of others. Remigration was relatively much more common among the seventeenth-century colonizers than it was among those of the nineteenth century. As for many other Dutch aspects concerning emigration, exact statistics are not available. But there are some data. In the first place, the seventeenth-century emigrant could not envision himself as remaining permanently in the New World. So, at the end of his contract, after he had been in the employ of others (the West India Company or patroons) in the Hudson River area for a certain number of years—usually six, but sometimes three years, which supposedly would have facilitated the development of roots in the new soil—he returned with his family to the Netherlands even if he had been employed in agriculture. Many "free colonists" also returned after a few years.

Such restless persons cannot always be considered as real emigrants, since the latter intend to leave their fatherland permanently.[10] In many cases the contract settlers were like "officials" who left the homeland only for a few years. However, even among these officials there were some who became permanent settlers. The last Dutch Governor-General, Stuyvesant, is an example. If, in the modern sense, we cannot style all colonists as immigrants, neither can we refer to all of those who returned as remigrants. Nor can they be classified as seasonal workers. We can only speak of a floating population constantly on the move.

Unfortunately, there are no exact figures to determine how large this kind of remigration might have been—remigration never received much attention. However, we do have one example. A ship, *De Princesse* [The Princess], left New Amsterdam on August 16, 1647, for the Netherlands with more than a hundred persons on board.[11] Excluding the crew of about twenty-five men, there were several "officials" [civil servants] on board, including former Governor-General Kieft and a minister named Bogardus, plus a large number of remigrants. The vessel was shipwrecked in the Bristol Channel (as was mentioned earlier) and no less than eighty-one souls—men, women and children—were drowned. This accident, which cost both Kieft and Bogardus their lives, calls striking attention to the large number of people on board, this large number being all the more remarkable since between those two Amsterdams there was, for those times, a busy ship traffic. There must have been at least fifty remigrants on this one single ship, which is a very significant number when one considers that there were only about a thousand Hollanders living in the New Netherlands at the time. So far as I am aware, the remigration of the Dutch element in the nineteenth century was of very little significance, although this cannot be substantiated by official figures either. No particulars exist indicating any significant return.

Just as striking as the difference is between the scanty emigration of the seventeenth century and the considerable emigration of the nineteenth is the difference between the relatively large remigration of the seventeenth century and the relatively very low remigration of the nineteenth century. Here we also see expressed, in my view, the difference between the adventurous, restless Jan Huygen types of the Golden Age and the extremely steady, solid Gerrit Witse characters of the nineteenth century.

It is obvious that other factors also contributed to these differences. We should especially call attention to the different job opportunities and contrasts between the Netherlands and America, then and now. Proportionally, the pull that the Netherlands exerted in the Golden Age was no less than the one exerted today by the magnet commonly called "*Dollarica*," [i.e., "dollar-mania"]. The necessity for leaving, particularly for economic reasons, was much less pressing then, not only because the seventeenth-century Netherlands were relatively much more prosperous, but more importantly, because the density of population was much less. This was true in the first place in an absolute sense, but also in a relative sense, that is, when one keeps in mind the opportunities for employment at the time.

Yet we must not rate too highly the seventeenth-century situation, particularly in rural areas. There was considerable prosperity in the northern and western, so-called sea-oriented, provinces, but not in the eastern agricultural provinces. Agriculture, the principal source of income in the central and eastern sections was very backward; during the Eighty Years War it had even been sliding back. During the Golden Age we can consider conditions as downright bad.[12]

This explains why so many of the colonists in the New Netherlands were largely from Gelderland and Utrecht, generally peasants from the eastern sections of our country, even all the way to Drenthe, which was so isolated by peat bogs. The chance circumstance that someone like Van Rensselaer had holdings in the Veluwe region [of Gelderland] and that contacts with the farmers of the sandy soils may have encouraged their departure, seems to me to be greatly exaggerated.[13] Van Rensselaer mainly engaged former agricultural workers of the West India Company and, aside from a few foreigners, he also recruited his men from other provinces, even from Friesland and Zeeland.

That conditions in the Netherlands during their Golden Age may not have been rosy everywhere came to light in 1639 when a number of residents in the province of Utrecht, "noting that the taxes on their lands were greatly increasing so that a husbandman could hardly make his living," petitioned the West India Company to settle them as colonists in the New Netherlands.[14] This case also demonstrates that "impressment," as Professor Colenbrander erroneously assumed to exist, did not have to be used to get "colonists." They were so anxious to leave—and here is another significant point—that when they could not come to terms with the Company they turned to the government of Sweden and in 1860, under the leadership of Joost Van den Boogaerdt, located in the Swedish colony on the Delaware! This Swedish settlement included a definite Dutch element from the outset. In 1638 there were twenty-three persons at Fort Christina and twenty-two of these were Hollanders; only the commander was a Swede![15]

Although the emigration from our land to North America was not large, the urge for emigration in the seventeenth century should not be minimized. Not only were [Dutch] merchants and sailors found far outside the boundaries of our land; this was also true of "farmers and laborers." In addition to Dutch mercantile colonies in Nantes, Bordeaux, London, Götenborg, Smyrna, and everywhere else, and colonies such as Frederiksstad in Holstein, which was entirely founded by Netherlanders, there were also numerous farmers' settlements. Already in the sixteenth century there existed a gardening colony on the island of Amager in Denmark. Dutch farmers settled near Jönköping in Sweden and even to the present day good cattle are called "Hollandsk" and dairy production "Hollanderi." In Germany also, "Hollanderei" denotes dairy farming. The Dutch farmers who settled in Sweden were led by Johan Wijngaard, who had been a bailiff in Brandenburg.

Others were attracted to England. A Zeelander, Cornelis Vermuyden, diked in some land near Wash Bay in the Fens. Names such as Holland and

Dutch River remind us of our young poldermen ("*navvies*") and our farmers just as in the case of the "*digue des Hollandais*" |dyke of the Dutch| on the lower Seine River in France. There our countrymen drained the swamps called Marais Verniers. Agricultural settlements also arose near Arles, Gilles, and "*la petite Flandre*" |Little Flanders| near La Rochelle.[16] This all took place during the seventeenth century, which is proof once more that rest-lessness and entrepreneurship had also infected the farming population. It also proves that our trade, shipping, and industry were thriving, which was not the case for agriculture.

Why did not a larger number of our farmers venture to North America? For the very same reasons that very much hindered their settlement in South Africa. They wished to be free, not tenants as on the "boweries" of the West India Company, under whose aegis they could not even be masters in their own homes.[17] The awarding of privileges caused them to settle among the English, who were hardly well intentioned toward them. Privileges drew them to Germany, France, and elsewhere.

Nothing but compulsion and injustice awaited them in North America. This greatly conflicted with the ideas that were even beginning to percolate to the common people, namely that America was not only a land of pros-perity but above all a land of freedom and equality. As long as they could not fulfill these ideals, they refused to go there. Therefore we have, to use Colenbrander's own words, "the poor quality of the scraped-up human material" that lent itself to be used as colonists for the big companies and their managers![18] It was not only the prosperity of the Republic and its religious tolerance, which Colenbrander overemphasized, but it was espe-cially the inordinate greed for immediate wealth and the abject tunnel vision of the "high and mighty gentlemen" in charge of the Company—who, according to David Pieterszoon De Vries, "were nothing but rogues,"[19]—that accounted for the slight interest of our farmers to emigrate to Dutch North America.

There was plenty of interest, however! When the West India Company was forced by losses, and especially disgrace, to grant at least minimal freedoms and rights, the number of emigrants increased immediately. "More than a thousand farmers and laborers would soon have followed," if the Company had provided more passage and if the "high and mighty gentlemen" of the Company—now and forever primarily dealers in the highly prized beaver hides!—had not actively frustrated the stream of emi-gration for which they could not have cared less.[20]

But we can still wonder, or rather ask, why more Hollanders did not settle in William Penn's territory where, more than anywhere else in seventeenth-century America, people believed in the ideals of freedom that we still consider—though unjustly—as characteristic of the New World. For this the same answer can be given as that for the limited emigration from our country to the "former" New Netherlands, where, certainly at least after 1674, the greedy West India Company, eager for plunder, was no longer in control. The Englishmen who ruled then were just as unacceptable, due to the long-standing Dutch antipathy towards the haughty Englishmen bursting from their overwhelming conceit.

This antipathy was as strong among the New Netherlands colonists as among our sailors, and was expressed without disguise by David Pieterszoon De Vries and Adriaen Van der Donck. The feeling is still strongly alive in the memory of the descendants of the New Netherlanders, as in the case of the aristocratic Mrs. J. King Van Rensselaer, whose book, *The Social Ladder*, gives a vivid portrayal of it.[21] Politically, Pennsylvania was also an English colony, and William Penn was first of all an Englishman. In his prospectus prepared for the Hollanders, he referred to the English nation as "being considered the biggest and best in Europe."[22]

Such an attitude had a totally adverse effect even on those Hollanders who were hankering for America. It was this same attitude that caused many in the New Netherlands, even among the well-to-do, to return to the mother country after the English takeover, while others went deeper into the interior to minimize contact with the new subjugators so that, according to De Vries, they would not be beaten "with the tail" |cat-o'-nine-tails| or, as Van der Donck put it, to "be used as a doormat and be ridiculed afterwards."[23]

The American lode star, dimmed by the English cloud, would not shine in its full splendor until after the War for Independence in the second half of the eighteenth century, and then it was to draw large numbers of Netherlanders.

3

What Happened to the Old Dutch Branch

A. Under English Rule

In the previous chapters it was pointed out that the approximately six thousand Netherlanders who were in North America by 1644 experienced but few reinforcements since that date. Nevertheless, the study of their subsequent development and that of their descendants shows all the more strongly the strong national roots that characterized these Netherlanders all the way to the first half of the nineteenth century. This was evident in the fact that they retained for generations the language, manners, and customs of their fathers; and that they remained attached even to the present day, although it may be in a somewhat altered fashion, to the faith of their fathers—that very distinctive Dutch Calvinism. It should immediately be recognized that this Calvinism in turn contributed to the maintaining of the old language, manners, and customs; and one can speak of a mutual influence, since national origin and religion are so closely related in many ways.

To this day the Dutch language is maintained among the colonists of the nineteenth century, in part and until recently due to the unending stream of "new" immigrants from the motherland. The same could not be said for the second half of the seventeenth and the eighteenth centuries. Of this period one can speak at most—although this should not be underrated—of individual emigrations. The early "New Netherlanders" had to depend, therefore, largely on their own inner strength, without outside help. That they succeeded is largely due to the tremendous vitality which characterized these colonists in particular and the seventeenth-century Dutch in general. It was a more select group than our present emigrants.

The Dutch national spirit was so strong in those days that many of the foreign elements then taking up residence in the Netherlands—and there were many!—were absorbed by the population and soon had been almost completely "Netherlandized." Rudolf Häpke commented that many Sea-Germans, who settled in Bruges and Antwerp in the sixteenth century and after, continued to be Germans and helped to internationalize these cities, but that Amsterdam completely "Netherlandized" [hollandisierte] his fellow countrymen, just as was the case with many other foreign merchants.[1] The same happened in the New Netherlands, not only in New Amsterdam but also in all other areas where these "foreigners" were not an overwhelming majority. On the other hand, on Long Island, where the Dutch were greatly outnumbered by the English, the situation was not reversed and there was no "Anglicization" of the Dutch.

This "Dutchification" was first of all marked by the use of the Dutch language and then by religious services. The French and Walloons, often Calvinists too, in reverse fashion also learned Dutch rapidly because of their similarity in religion. Finally it was shown by the inter-marriages, in particular those between the French and the Dutch, who were already united by a common religion, which increased as time went by. On August 11, 1628, Jonas Michaëlius, New Amsterdam's first preacher, wrote to Smoutius in Amsterdam: "The only Sunday services among the Walloons and French are in the Dutch language, for there are few who do not understand the Dutch language."[2] However, we should not overlook the fact that many of these foreigners had been acquainted with our language and customs during their stay in the Netherlands.

An excellent example of this "Dutchification" may be seen in the case of Nieuw Haarlem, a village on Manhattan Island. It was "organized" in 1658 and by 1661 had thirty-two adult males—singles or heads of households. This group consisted of eleven Frenchmen, four Walloons, seven Hollanders, four Danes, three Swedes, and three Germans. If on the one hand this example illustrates the very cosmopolitan composition of this group, it is interesting to note on the other hand that among them a Reformed congregation was already organized in 1660, although it did not yet have a preacher. Services were conducted by a lay reader; to this post was nominated one of the well-known Montagnes. These settlers felt so "Dutch" that in 1664 they accepted with reluctance the rulership of the English, and on that occasion they stubbornly refused to give up the name of Nieuw Haarlem, which had been conferred by Stuyvesant, to replace it with that of Lancaster. Also, later efforts to change the name met with such resistance that the name "Haarlem" has been in use until the present day.[3]

It is significant that this "Dutchification" continued during the period of English control. Thus the news of the raid of Evertsen on the New Netherlands in 1673 was received with great rejoicing in Nieuw Haarlem, and even after this short-lived joy, the use of the Dutch language continued. For the next half-century municipal records were written in Dutch and calculations were made in guilders and stuivers [five-cent pieces]. Haarlem, which was not an isolated village but part of the present-day northern section of New York City, was so thoroughly Dutch that it still had Dutch characteristics in the early part of the nineteenth century, as shown in the architecture and furnishings of the homes as well as in the manners and customs and, more particularly, in the religious services.[4]

Although a few among the French had refused at times to contribute to the support of the lay reader, because there was a French resident preacher in New York, this was an exception. Haarlem was so Dutch, to a large part due to mixed marriages, that a minister straight from the Netherlands, [Johannes] Ritzema, served there from 1744 to 1765.[5] It is obvious that this development should be more evident in the interior settlements. An interesting example is that of the French settlement of Nouveau Palatinat [New Palatine], which was founded in 1660 by Walloons and Huguenots who had formerly enjoyed a few years of hospitality in the Palatinate in Germany. They settled in the fertile region of Esopus [Aesop] on the Hudson River where the Dutch had founded the village of Wiltwijck, now known as Kingston. Nouveau Palatinat was to become the most French settlement in North America at the time with a more or less autonomous government, which became known as "*Dusine*" [dozen: twelve men]. For fifty years the minutes of this "council" were published in French but in the early eighteenth century and, surprisingly, for the next seventy years they were mostly in Dutch!

For years these French had managed to stay independent, even in their religious services. In the end some began to go to church in Wiltwijck and then the assimilation began. In 1691 the first marriage took place there between a Frenchman and a young Dutch woman. It had happened earlier and more frequently in New Amsterdam;[6] this marked the beginning of the end of French autonomy. In 1733 a Hollander, Reverend J. Van Driessen, was called to be the preacher at the Reformed Church in Nouveau Palatinat and Dutch became the language of the church services; it did not change to English usage until 1800![7] This evidence of the strength of the Dutch spirit in absorbing various foreign elements was also shown in South Africa where, at about the same time, Frenchmen and Germans became characteristic "Dutch" boers.

Closely related to this phenomenon is the fact of the size of colonial families. Large families were common among both the upper and lower classes of society. As a case in point, ten children were born to Philip Pieterszoon Schuyler (from Amsterdam) and Margaretha Van Slichtenhorst, youngest daughter of Brant Van Slichtenhorst, the representative of the Rensselaers of Rensselaerswijck. Their wedding had been a great social event among the colonists. Brant was a man of some importance and under his jurisdiction Beverwijck, a modest "live-together place" of "only three small cottages" grew to become Albany, with "about a hundred residences." Therefore, Brant is sometimes considered to be the founder of Albany.[8] His grandchildren would later make their name in the history of the nation. The capacity to assimilate and the large families, which were also often characteristic of the French, especially in rural areas, explain why the Dutch dominance remained strong in the Hudson River area. This Dutch "stamp" remained unchanged, in spite of the revocation of the Edict of Nantes in 1685 that resulted in the settlement of many French Calvinists, and in spite of the increasing number of Englishmen who settled there after 1664.

Not only were the Netherlanders numerically the most important for a long time, but they were also of significance on the social level. In spite of the English takeover they set the tone in politics and contributed to the formation of a conservative nucleus, which the Hollanders in the United States of today still provide. In 1695 J. Miller, an English ecclesiastic, gave a report on the New York colony, and from this it appears that there were 3,525 church-going families at the time; 1,754 of these families were Dutch. If we calculate six persons per family—a very low estimate—it is evident that this colony totaled at least 21,000 whites, the larger part of which was Dutch. Also, one should not forget that there were individuals who did not have any church affiliations. In addition, some Hollanders were also found among the Lutherans, Jews, and other separately-listed denominations. On top of all that there were the Dutch in nearby New Jersey, whose numbers grew sharply after 1664, and whom we have not included.

Albany and the surrounding area were exclusively Dutch—from four to five hundred Dutch families were established there; the city itself had about two hundred houses. In Kingston and vicinity there were three hundred households, mostly Dutch, but "some English and French." Among the latter were those of Nouveau Palatinat. Kingston itself, formerly known as Wiltwijck, had one hundred houses. But even the city of New York, the center of the English administration, was still overwhelmingly Dutch. In and around the city, which counted eight hundred houses itself, there were at least five hundred Dutch families, two hundred French families, and more than a hundred "of English stock."[9]

It is also significant that Miller refers to the Hollanders as "well-to-do," the English as being in "moderate circumstances," while the French were portrayed as "poor." In this connection it should be noted that numerous Hollanders had worked themselves up. This is significant, now that there was no longer, to employ the terse language of David Pieterszoon De Vries, a "hostelry" with a West India Company "that wants the Fruit of the Merchants even before they are grown."[10]

Opinions concerning the social standing of the earliest Dutch colonists vary widely. It all depends whether one espouses the typical Dutch view of reduction and denigration or whether one assumes the just as typical American view of enlargement and exaggeration, which is all the more understandable—but not forgivable!—since these views may at times apply to one's own ancestors. Thus the Dutch scholar H. T. Colenbrander views the oldest people of New Amsterdam as a "loose and easy hodge-podge."[11] But Mrs. King Van Rensselaer referred to them as "men and women of education and refinement" who had established themselves in the city in the middle of the seventeenth century; they were "individuals who, in any other country than a Republic, would have been members of the aristocracy!"[12]

Exaggeration is plainly evident on both sides. It is a bit comical to hear this American lady speak not only of New York's but of America's oldest "society," among whose "leaders" she reckoned next to their "brilliant women" one such as Anneke Jans, the daughter of a New Netherlands' midwife.[13] On the other hand, we are saddened by the low esteem accorded to the "colonial" element by the Dutch viewpoint. Without doubt there have always been those among the immigrants who were persons of no account, good-for-nothings. Even today, when a person leaves his home country for good, people tend to be suspicious and ascribe evil motives, often because they themselves totally lack the courage to emigrate. The patroon Kiliaen Van Rensselaer once wrote: "The better elements seldom go so far overseas." He, as well as his eldest son—the so-called orphan-patroon, never saw their American holdings bacause these gentlemen did not care to make the voyage.

There are many examples of colonists of rather dubious character. If one reads the letters of the New Netherlands preachers, they form but one long complaint. In 1628 Jonas Michaëlius found the people "for the most part rather rough and dissolute,"[14] and one of his successors, Johannes Coneliszoon Baeker, described the New Amsterdam congregation in 1648 as "mostly ignorant in matters of religion and much inclined to drunkenness; the seventeen taverns established here contribute to that greatly."[15] It was not much better in the "rural areas" such as Rensselaerswijck. Their first preacher, Johannes Megapolensis, complained in 1643 of the drunkenness and laziness of the colonists and, what was worse, of their lack of respect for the clergy: they swore at him! In 1651 they even threatened his life![16]

Brant Van Slichtenhorst, previously described as the manager at Rensselaerswijck (1648–1652), later remarked "that the colonists (except for the devout who comprise but a few) are usually a wild and unruly bunch gathered from all over; one had been a privateer, another an exile, the third was a bankrupt, the fourth was a murderer, and so forth. You may well believe that we have had trouble because of so many discordant and queer "fish" being brought together."[17] Stuyvesant, the governor of New Amsterdam, complained in 1648 of the community in general. "The people are wild and without discipline."[18] He conceded that much of this was due to the misgovernment of his predecessor and the misconduct of the minister—both deceased.

In reading the above, one would be rather inclined to side with those who underestimated, such as Colenbrander, rather than with those, such as King Van Rensselaer, who exaggerated. One should, however, compare these descriptions with contemporary situations in our own and surrounding countries. There are tens of villages where even today the minister could complain about the drunkenness of perhaps some of his most pious brothers. Many tourists who, until rather recently, have visited such villages on a Sunday could testify to this! Nor should we be too appalled at the seventeen tap houses; New Amsterdam was primarily a port city. We should look only at the number of inns and beerhouses in similar port cities of today. Also, note the number of *"estaminets"* [taverns] among our neighboring Belgian villages that are hours distant from the thirst-producing sea. Would anyone dare to call the people of Staphorst, Bunschoten, Huizen (I speak from experiences collected while roaming through the dear fatherland!), or even of a Belgian village, a "loose and easy hodgepodge?" It should also be remembered that four or five troublemakers attract more attention than a hundred peaceful citizens. It is a well-known psychological phenomenon that the teacher remembers the names of the "troublemakers" in his class but forgets the names of the good students who may be ten times larger in number.

There were many, such as Brant Van Slichtenhorst himself, who were also influenced by the alluring accounts referred to earlier. An adventurous spirit led some to America, as was the case with the well-known Doctor Jan de la Montagne who had settled in the New World; others were originally farmers and officials and had come either at their own cost or at that of the patroons or in the service of the [West India] Company. Van Slichtenhorst himself had to admit that many well-intentioned people were found among them in addition to some less desirable elements. Besides the "little fellows" [kleine luyden], there were many young men from more well-to-do families. Often they were born into large families and came to the New World in hopes of achieving greater prosperity sooner than was possible in the mother country. Such an example is the Van Curlers family, which included Arend Van Curler, who founded Schenectady in 1661. Many of these families were shareholders, often minor, in the West India Company. As shareholders some became officials of the Company, such as the Van Twillers. The Company brought them and others to establish themselves in the New World, which after all was their property. It is because of this particular connection with the West India Company, as Beernink pointed out, that so many families from the Geldersche Vallei,* among whom were people of renown, settled on the Hudson River.[19] Kiliaen Van Rensselaer, one of the big stockholders, was responsible for convincing several of these to buy shares. Thus there is also much validity to the observations of Mrs. King Van Rensselaer, herself the descendant of an old lineage. In sum, we find diverse elements in the New Netherlands, ranging from the most lowly to those of patrician families. The Van Rensselaers belonged to the latter group; Jan Baptist Van Rensselaer was the first of the name to actually settle, doing so in 1651, after the death of Kiliaen's first heir.

Only after the influence of the West India Company had ended and the New Netherlands had become a "free land," free in the economic sense, was there a full unfurling of activity and trade and opportunities for settlers to release the energy pent up in them. Thus it was not a coincidence that

---

*This is a large valley running northeast-southwest from the Rhine to the Ysselmeer between the Veluwe and the Utrechtse Heuveling (Hill Range). It has been a traditional line of defense against invasions from the East due to its many swamps.

only after the English had taken control did important Dutchmen of the New Netherlands colony come to the fore. This should not be ascribed exclusively to the freedom that came with English rule, but also to the fact that the early difficulties, which go hand in hand with any new settlement, had been overcome. So people had finally adapted fully and only then could they expand. It is understandable that these types of men were found first of all among the merchant class, because New Amsterdam was primarily a trade and shipping center. Even among American geographers it became the accepted notion that these Dutch inhabitants were "the most active agents in the early coastal trade," as Ellen Semple confirms.[20]

Cornelis Steenwijck, already an influential person during the Dutch period, and Pieter Jacob Marius are examples of two merchant princes of former New Amsterdam who are still being pilloried today in the international literature devoted to "anti-capitalism," accused of the "crime" of using their own "talents" and energy to accumulate sums in America considered huge for their time.[21] Steenwijck, significantly enough, was a liquor dealer. He was reckoned the richest man in the province of New York, who at his death in 1686 left a cash fortune of around 53,000 gulden—plus a long list of debtors! Marius, an office holder in the Reformed Church, was honored during his lifetime as a big merchant and also influential because nearly all Manhattan Island was in debt to him. He became famous at his death in 1703 and was mourned by many. His funeral also attracted many, and as an indication of one of the Old World customs that was still observed, at this "solemnity" there were consumed twenty-nine gallons of wine, a half barrel of beer, and eight hundred cakes. Marius was thus buried "as a gentleman." The De Peysters were also well known in commercial circles.

At times, closely allied to this aristocracy of trade and at times originating from them, was an aristocracy of land owners, who were no less influential than the first group. The Van Rensselaers have been mentioned several times in connection with the patroonships. During the English regime other families rose to prominence. The English authorities not only confirmed the patroons in their holdings and associated privileges but went even further than the West India Company in granting lands on a large scale. Although Rensselaerswijck, with its 700,000 acres, constituted an enormous holding, there were during the second half of the eighteenth century three properties of more than a million acres each, plus many others of 200,000 or more acres.[22] Not only did the proprietors enjoy all kinds of feudal rights, just as the old patroons; they also enjoyed hereditary tenure and managed, through their influence on the administration, of which they often were members themselves, to evade all taxation on their domains. The Schuylers, Van Dams, Beekmans, Van Brughs, |Van| Cortlandts, and many others, along with the Van Rensselaers, formed the landed aristocracy with very un-American rights. It reminds one more of the medieval rights like hunting privileges, mill rights, bakery rights, etc., than of the rights that existed at that time in the Netherlands themselves.

Even the American Revolution effected little change in these arrangements because the new government was of the opinion that private property should not be touched. Although the Van Rensselaers voluntarily gave up their manorial rights, the hereditary rents continued without interruption—fourteen bushels of corn per hundred acres, four fat hens and a day's service (or a quantity of wood in lieu of this) for each 1,600-acre farm. A bitter anti-rent war had to be waged in the first half of the nineteenth century by the American farmers before this anachronism—as they considered it—came to an end.

In Europe, however, America was more or less identified with Pennsylvania. The freedom prevalent there, as well as in the West, was considered as typical of the entire New World. Quite the contrary was true. In the same year (1846) that thousands of Hollanders were on their way to the land of freedom, many of them under the leadership of Reverend Van Raalte, countless numbers of the New Netherlanders' farm wagons laden with grain, chickens, and wood blocked the roads leading to the manor house at Rensselaerswijck, the home of the landlord.[23] This state of affairs |patroonships| was typical not only for the former New Netherlands but also for a considerable part of "colonial" America—in Virginia, and in some of the other reaches. It lasted even longer in the former Spanish-Mexican territories with their "*Estados*" and in the St. Lawrence area of Canada with its "*Seignuries*." All these are proofs to show how dangerous it is to place in a causal relationship such concepts as "space," "freedom," and "broadness," as some geographers do. The development of wholesale trade, coupled with the growth of vast land ownership—for just as in the mother country the traders sought to increase their standing by land purchases, created a "rich" class, which, like a true society of regents, kept itself increasingly aloof from the common people. A class division ensued that was much more pronounced than in the Old Country, which is reflected in the fact that in certain American provinces the populace were forbidden to wear silks, jewelry, etc.!

Thus, in the third quarter of the seventeenth century, there was already a sharp cleavage among the mere four thousand residents of New York, a distinction between the ruling aristocracy and the proletariat. The latter group succeeded in getting temporary control of the government when the government of England passed from the pro-Catholic James to the Calvinistic William. This led to confusion in colonies such as New York. Leisler emerged as a born demagogue and became the leader of the common people. He was a completely "Dutchified," New York "German" merchant, born of Huguenot parents and of increasing influence, allied to the Bayards and Van Cortlandts, but yet not fully accepted in their circles. Despotically, he assumed temporary charge of the government, all in the name of William. The Dutch aristocrats, if not Jacobites, were nevertheless bound to the civil servants who exercised James' authority and were also, in part, bound to them through the land grants. They refused to recognize Leisler, who thereupon imprisoned some of them. However, the aristocrats were so powerful that, when William's rule was finally established in England, they brought about the death sentence of Leisler—a revolutionary after all!

The attitude of the Reformed Church was characteristic. Although Leisler was one of its most devoted members, the Reverends Selyns, Varick, and Dellius (the latter of whom was soon to be a big landholder himself!) insisted on passing sentence after this verdict. But Daillé, the more strongly anti-Jacobite (i.e., anti-papist) French minister and champion of the poor people, opposed this in vain.[24] This was an extremely conservative attitude on the part of the Dutch Reformed Church and revealed its deep aristocratic bent. It is still conservative today; later I shall return to this phenomenon.

The great influence of the Dutch "aristocracy" on the government of New York was shown in 1683 when James finally granted— it is said on the advice of William Penn—the oft-expressed wish of the colonists to have a voice in the government. When the legislative body met for the first time in that year, more than 60 percent of the eighteen members were Netherlanders. This influence grew during the reign of King William. Under his aegis the aristocratic Assembly, overthrown by Leisler, was restored and placed under immediate jurisdiction of the crown in 1691. Thus New York was changed from a "proprietor colony" to a "crown colony." All the members were opposed to Leisler and called for his execution.

As the Dutch influence became more pronounced in New York, Dutch characteristics were strengthened, especially under the influence of the church. The English influence also became more evident in the English areas to the north and south. According to Turner, there were places in Massachusetts where the residents could not change their place of residence without leave of the governor and his council.[25]

It can be said that the Dutch Reformed Church* made its entrance in the New Netherlands when in 1624 a caffa worker (caffa is a kind of silk fabric or serge), Bastiaen Janszoon Krol, was appointed as a comforter of the sick.[26] The actual founding of the Reformed Church in America dates from 1628 when Jonas Michaëlius, who apparently was a cultured individual, became the minister on Manhattan Island.[27] The influence of this church increased in America, and in 1664, when we lost the New Netherlands, there were eleven congregations and two "stations." Even after that year the influence of the Church continued to grow because the conditions under which the English took over were very mild and peaceful.[28] Not only were the residents allowed to nominate their own officials, but they also retained great freedom in religious affairs. They could organize their church governance and worship as they wished. Thus the change in government affected the

---

*Eekhof mentions the "Hervormde Kerk," which only dates from 1816. Among the colonists it was the "Gereformeerde Kerk" and this is what I am referring to [Van Hinte].

church but little; in spite of the takeover, even church relations were maintained with the Netherlands.

The West India Company, whose Amsterdam chamber had been entrusted with the management of the New Netherlands, at first left church governance to the church council of Amsterdam. After 1636 the council's activities were under the jurisdiction of the Classis of Amsterdam,* which appointed a committee of four brothers to have jurisdiction over the church affairs of the New Netherlands—even after 1664. The church in New York even submitted a disciplinary matter to the Classis in 1669, but the Classis refused to consider it because it realized that, in fact, it had no jurisdiction over English subjects. However, new ministers destined for America were ordained by the Classis of Amsterdam, as in the case of Willem Van Nieuwenhuysen in 1671, while, on the contrary, a request of the "American" teacher A. Luyck to be ordained in America was denied (1667). The Classis insisted upon keeping this right for itself.

The recapture of New York in 1673, which was renamed New Orange (Albany became Willemstad), strengthened the power of the Reformed Church, which the English were secretly undermining in favor of the Episcopalian Church. The States General inaugurated a monthly day of thanks that still survives in the American Thanksgiving holiday in November.

At the 1674 Treaty of Westminster the Dutch permanently ceded their North American possession. But the Dutch character of the colony continued. It showed itself first in the physical appearance of the cities; Albany and New York were laid out on Dutch models and provided with those remarkable city canals, just as was the case in the tropics, i.e., Batavia [now Djakarta, Indonesia]. The street system in New York, so carefully laid out in advance, had such names as Heerenstraat, Hoogstraat, Singel, Brouwersstraat, Heerengracht, etc., and the well-known stepgable architecture of Albany during the first half of the nineteenth century also reminds us of the mother land.[29] The dwellings of the Indians did not offer much to inspire the Hollanders. Even building materials, especially bricks, were usually brought over as ballast from the Netherlands. Everywhere Dutch cattle grazed in the fields, thanks to the resourcefulness of Pieter Evertsen Hulft's method of transportation across the ocean.[30] Later on, Adriaen Van der Donck remarked that English cattle fared better in America, and this was also experienced by the Dutch colonists of the nineteenth century.[31]

The Dutch way of life was even more evident in daily life, in customs and manners. I have already cited examples of this. It was most obvious in religious life, which was entirely brought in harmony with Dutch practice by Michaëlius, both in matters of religious services and of basic worship. The adherence was so great that when the renowned Reverend Nicolaas Van Rensselaer, a friend of King Charles II and the son of the powerful patroon

*The Protestant churches are often organized on a provincial basis and these are sub-divided into "classes," and then in turn into "circles," and all hold their respective meetings [Van Hinte].

Kiliaen, lord of Rensselaerswijck, was to be appointed with the cooperation of the English governor as pastor of the Reformed Church in Albany, he was stubbornly refused there because he had been ordained by the Anglican bishop of Salisbury and thus was an Episcopalian and not Reformed![32]

In the meantime the Reformed Church was constantly under threat, secretly if not openly, from the English national church, and so it wished to establish itself on a firmer footing. In 1696 the Reformed congregation of New York was the first to obtain a charter that gave more legal rights, and this example was later followed by numerous Reformed churches and also by the Episcopalians. Thus the Dutch Reformed Church was able to hold its own, in contrast to the French who were progressively Anglicized and who with few exceptions became affiliated with the Episcopalian Church, in part also because then they could draw on its financial support. The Reformed Church grew in spite of the strong opposition of several English governors, such as Cornbury. By 1708 there were thirty-four congregations and, after a religious revival (the Great Awakening), this number increased to sixty-five during the first half of that century.

The supply of ministers to serve these churches came largely from the Netherlands and, as was related earlier, the immigration of these intellectuals should not be underrated. They must have contributed to the adherence to the old ways, particularly to usage of the old language, yet the importance of these scholars should not be overvalued. There were not enough of them to be really important. Several, such as Reverends [Henry] Boel, Theodore J. Frielinghuysen, J. Ritzema, and many others, were among these immigrant preachers who, although they were English subjects, still sent their children, as Frielinghuysen did, to Holland for study and "ordination."

The increasing prosperity of the colonists in America's coastal region automatically caused a struggle for greater independence. Some of the settlers, less endowed by the blessings of destiny than others and thus ineligible to participate in government, migrated westward and left the tidewater area where people had lived up to this time. A pioneer spirit developed in the area between the "fall line"—where the navigability of tidal rivers ends—and the Allegheny Mountains, a region that became known as the "Old West."

If up to this time all eyes had been kept exclusively on Europe, now there were those who considered themselves fully as children of their country, as Americans. Also, as a result of the class struggle between the old "aristocratic" or well-to-do elements on the east coast and the poor independent backwoodsmen who had only themselves to rely on at the frontier of the "civilized" world, a new feeling—the American spirit—was born.[33] This new spirit was not only directed against England; it came from a deeper source and opposed the Old World in general. It emerged among the Dutch also, particularly in church life, since this was most reminiscent of the Netherlands. They wanted to break away from narrow, characteristic Dutch customs. The first organ in a Reformed Church was heard in 1727 in New York.

On the other hand, there were complaints about sermons being too long. There were also families that did not wish to be separated by sex but preferred to sit together as a group. The young people, of New York in particular, wished to introduce the English language in church life.

Furthermore, some wished to dissociate themselves from the supervision of the Classis of Amsterdam and wanted to prepare their own body, "Coetus" by name. But this was so contrary to the Dutch sense of hegemony and national spirit that a long and bitter struggle ensued between the progressives (the Coetus faction) and the conservatives, who later were to form the Conferentie group. At the insistence of the first group, the liturgy, psalms, and hymns were translated into English in 1745 but, due to the influence of the Conferentie group, these were infrequently used and often not even permitted. It is of some interest that the leader of the progressives lived in the largely Dutch town of Albany—on the frontier—while Ritzema, the leader of the conservative faction, lived in New York.

Apart from that, we should be careful here because it was also in New York—where the most well-to-do "Dutch" lived and also those who dealt mostly with the English officials—that in 1763 a bilingual preacher, a certain Scotsman, the Reverend Archibald Laidlie, was called to serve in tandem with a Dutch minister. He came from the "English" Reformed Church of Vlissingen in the Netherlands. He introduced services in both languages in the Reformed Church in America and many who were at the point of leaving the church chose to remain.

The struggle between the Coetus and Conferentie factions came to an end when, after a period of decadence, a new resurgence was anticipated. The conflict ended under the influence of John Henry Livingston, who was of Scottish descent and whose forebears had settled in Rotterdam and had been "Dutchified" there. He emigrated to the Dutch settlements on the Hudson like so many other Dutch folks. Livingston was the last of the contemporary "American" young men who in 1766 had gone to the Netherlands, to Utrecht, to pursue theological studies. After being ordained in the Netherlands, he became the second English-speaking preacher of the Reformed Church in New York, assisting in lightening Laidlie's work. Through his energetic efforts the differences were finally resolved in 1772, when the "Dutch Reformed Church of America" came into being as an independent organization. It is typical of the Dutch spirit that our overseas kinsfolk and fellow believers did not accept the proposal put forth by—of all institutions!—the city of Amsterdam, that they join with the Presbyterians and send their theological students to Presbyterian Princeton. The Dutch-Americans wanted their own educational system, Calvinistic and according to Dutch concepts, and so they established their own college at New Brunswick in New Jersey. The school, chartered in 1770, was called Queens College. It was primarily a church institution, and expanded in 1810 into a seminary.[34]

The Americanization of the young church organization proceeded very slowly. It was not until 1764 that a second organ was installed in the progressive New York area while other places had still to do without for years. Most of the churches retained their typical Dutch-Calvinist starkness. In addition to the preacher, who often preached up to two hours, there was, in the tradition of the fatherland, a psalm leader—a position not often found any longer in America today. He was a person of importance who opened the services with a Bible reading and who announced the psalms to be sung. Hymns were scarcely heard.

The American Revolution, an expression of the same spirit of restlessness that gave the Reformed Church its independence, of course also hastened the development of the church.

B. During and After the War of Independence

To a considerable extent the Hollanders were on the side of the revolutionaries and even provided some leadership. The first battle for freedom took place at Golden Hill on Manhattan Island in January, 1770. The Dutch element in New York was strongly opposed to the Stamp Act and among them were Livingston, the Scotsman who turned completely Dutch, the Roosevelts, Rutgers, and others. It was also the Dutch who captured the traitor André at Tarrytown. These are events "English" Americans choose to "forget."

According to A. Todd, ministers such as |C. F.| Foering, |J. R.| Hardenbergh, |Dirck| Romeyn, |E.| Westerlo, and others, proved themselves to be real heroes. The Dutch churchmen opted so strongly for the rebels that the embittered English especially chose to plunder and burn Dutch churches![35] Because of this outspoken English animosity against Dutch churches, everywhere the old, deep-rooted hatred against the arrogant English burst into flames even more strongly. Nowhere was this more clearly evident than in Albany and the surrounding area. In 1748 the Swedish traveler Kalm had noticed this hatred of the English for the Albany residents, but he also added, "The people of Albany hate the English even more than the English hate them."[36]

Frontier life had developed military traits in the Albany area more than elsewhere, especially as a result of the wars against the French and the Indians. So it is not surprising the frontier area saw the emergence of no less than three Revolutionary War generals—Philip Schuyler, Pieter Gansevoort, and Abraham Ten Broeck—all of them the pride of Albany, the former Beverwijck, and Willemstad. Of the Van Rensselaers in this same region, twelve of the eighteen males fought against the English; two were too old and four too young. Others joined in and served well—|Th. J.| Frielinghuysen, |Philip (1794–1831), son of Pierre| Van Cortlandt, |Henry| Rutgers, |Abraham| Van Vechten, etc. It is known that Washington considered the Dutch as some of his best troops, and while he was in New Jersey he frequently stayed with Dutch families. He often referred to his "loyal Dutch Belt."

The Hollanders never considered themselves to be "English"; in Pennsylvania the well-known Pastorius complained that even his Dutch maids did not get along with his English maids! But they were proud to be "Americans," not in the least because they themselves had fought so valiantly for the independence of the republic. We all know that war creates a feeling of nationalism or causes it to become stronger.

Just as in the case of the later Civil War, the Revolutionary War drove the whites further into the interior. The settlement of the "Old West," which had already started earlier, was vigorously pursued, spurred by the war. F. J. Turner, known for his studies about the frontier, neglected—one would almost think deliberately—to mention the Dutch element, and he even refers to "the absence of expansive power" in the New York area.[37] Yet the Dutch had the hardest task: to defend the land against both the powerful Iroquois and against the French. That explains their slow progress westward. This slow westward trek was also caused by the fact that in the Hudson area enormous estates were the rule, and the people of ordinary means were not attracted to settle there. This was particularly true in the case of the poor Palatines.[38] How contemptuously the Dutch landowners looked down upon them! What a class gap even on the frontier!

Turner neglects to mention that as early as 1661 the Hollanders at Albany were already moving westward and had established an outpost in the Mohawk Valley at Schenectady. Was the name taken from the Dutch *Schoon Echtenbeek* [Beautiful Echtenbeek]? Thus Hollanders belonged to the first pioneers of the "Old West." As early as 1680 Schenectady had a Reformed Church and in 1682 it obtained its own minister, [Peter] Tesschenmaker, who had studied at Utrecht. Turner also passes over the fact that in 1691 Schenectady was plundered and its inhabitants massacred by the French and Indians, who had planned a joint attack on Albany and New York.[39] Sixty individuals, including the minister Tesschenmaker, were slaughtered during that single Saturday night. Nor does Turner mention the youthful Johannes Schuyler who, as a twenty-two-year-old captain, had led an expedition to Canada in 1690 and had reached the western prairies. Finally, Turner forgets that the task of the Dutch was truly the most difficult one. It was to defend the most important traffic route in all of North America: the Mohawk and Hudson valleys. That route was even then already of overwhelming significance both commercially and strategically. In the French and English colonial wars, these two valleys, the Hudson valley even more so than the Mohawk valley, were the major battlefields. They were the "Gateway to the West." For a long time they had been a buffer zone where first the Indians, then the Dutch, and finally also the Palatines, were the victims. Such was the case of Kingston also, which had often been attacked previously and was burned by the English during the Revolutionary War in 1777.

Such was "Dutch" frontier life! Yet they continued to spread westward, so that at the beginning of the eighteenth century they had settled in the Schoharie River valley area. Among them were the Vroomans, who had large holdings and who were known for a conflict with their German neighbors.[40] The towns of Vroomans and Middelburg recall the efforts of the Dutch and the name of Schuyler, closely identified with the defense of the region, occurs not once but several times in topographic nomenclature. The Holland Land Company, which will be considered in more detail later, was to promote settlements here toward the end of the eighteenth century when, after the end of the Revolutionary War, a great speculative period began in the settlement of the Old West.

Even more than the Mohawk Dutch, the Jersey Dutch would become significant. Their pioneer spirit manifested itself in still another direction, although it was denied to them by "English scholars" such as Turner. A few individuals had settled earlier in New Jersey under the auspices of the West India Company, but most of these settlements were temporary. Permanent Dutch settlements occurred about 1660 and, as was mentioned earlier, after 1664, when many wanted to escape direct English rule, the less severe government of New Jersey proved attractive. Others—"three shiploads," in fact—went to South Carolina.

The first Reformed congregation of Bergen (present-day Jersey City) was founded in 1660. From Bergen further treks went westward. A Pole from the Netherlands—Albert Zaborowski, who was married to a Dutch "*juffrouw*" [miss] named Van der Linde—settled in Hackensack, one of the trading posts, and obtained a large grant, the so-called Paramus-patent. One of his five sons, Jacob, was the first white resident of Paramus. Johannes Van Emburgh purchased a large area adjacent to the Paramus-patent and became the first resident of present-day Ridgewood. A number of Hollanders—the Ackermans, Bantas, Bogerts, Hoppers, Van Houtens, and others—settled there and their descendants still live there.[41] The number of Hollanders in New Jersey increased when New York's Governor [Lord] Cornbury (1702–1708), contrary to the regulations of 1664, made life difficult for the Reformed Church people in his territory. Many crossed the Hudson and settled in the Raritan and Millstone Valleys of New Jersey. So many congregations flourished there that later it became known as "the garden of the Dutch Church."

It was also in this area, as we already know, that the preparatory school for theologians—Queens College—was founded in New Brunswick. Many Hollanders from Albany had settled there earlier, and one of the streets was even named Albany Street. Several other Dutch communities arose in New Jersey—Hoppertown (later known as Ho-ho-kus), after the Hopper family; Wortendyke, after Cornelius Wortendyke; and others. These are all towns that today are in the forefront of America's industrial areas. In the nineteenth century thousands of additional Hollanders were to settle there in order to work, mostly in the factories. Foremost among them was Paterson, founded somewhat later.

The increased westward movement following the War of Independence—Turner to the contrary notwithstanding—also affected our Hollanders.

When the cosmopolitan Cazenove (about whom more later) worked for the Holland Land Company in 1794, he made a long journey through New Jersey and Pennsylvania and stayed with a very well-to-do Hollander, Lucas Van Beeverhoud in Troy. Van Beeverhoud held no less than 1,650 acres of land. From there he journeyed through Boonton village, where a Reformed church had been organized and every two weeks services were held in Dutch. Such bi-weekly services do not attest to a densely settled Dutch area. This is understandable, because Van Beeverhoud himself complained about the low fertility of the land, which was much too stony, and on which winter wheat would not grow.[42]

Continuing on his trip through Pennsylvania, Cazenove apparently did not encounter any more Hollanders because he does not refer to them. Still there were numerous Dutchmen there, chiefly the younger generation from New Jersey who settled in York and Adams counties. They were independent of the much older Dutch settlements on the Delaware at "Nieuw Kasteel" [Newcastle] and at the more recent Germantown in the same state. Before the Revolution, in 1765, they had settled in the area west of the Susquehanna River, and two Reformed congregations, Conowago and Hanover, were organized. Conowago, near the later famous battlefield of Gettysburg, had 150 households, a total of seven hundred souls. The Bantas and Westervelts from the previously mentioned Bergen County were here, as well as the Montfoorts (from Harlingen) in the Millstone Valley. In addition there were the Van Nuys, Schomps, Van Arsdales, and others. In 1768 the Van Arsdales were the first landowners in this area.

The restlessness and wanderlust were now so strong in these people—a psychological phenomenon to which I shall return later—that in 1781 and in the following years nearly all had left.[43] As a consequence, only five Dutch families were left in 1817. Kentucky exercised a great drawing power then and many of the Dutch backwoodsmen also went there. Settlers from Conowago, York County, and Hanover, Adams County in Pennsylvania, and also from Bergen and Somerset Counties in New Jersey turned up in Kentucky and settled originally near the Salt River in Mercer County. No less than four families of the Frisian Bantas were among them. They purchased more than 1,200 acres of land, known as "The Low Dutch Tract."

In the nineties more journeyed to "the cane lands of Kaintuckee." They were underway for weeks, the cattle driven ahead of their big, heavy wagons that were filled with household goods and sometimes also with the women and children. They would camp in the wilderness at night, and only Sundays were permitted as days of rest and for holding church services. They crossed the mountains to the headwaters of the Ohio River and traveled along the river through unfriendly areas to settle finally in Mercer County, Kentucky.

Among them were Bantas, Terhunes, Demarests, Voorheeses, Verbryckes, Huffs, and Van Nuyses. Between 1789 and 1802 the Kentucky Hollanders bought large tracts of land. Some of them went on to the Salt River, where a church congregation was organized in 1800, during a Saturday evening gathering. At a later date a simple church structure was built on the Salt River, and for a time, from 1802 to 1816, they had their own preacher in the person of Thomas Kyle. When the church celebrated its centennial in 1900, the little church building was still standing, known and loved by the colonists as "the Old Mud Meeting House."[44]

Thus Hollanders also contributed to the founding and growth of one of the most remarkable states in the union—Kentucky—a state of outspoken individualists "where men die standing."[45] The Hollanders were veritable Daniel Boones, who was as we know the most typical of backwoodsmen, but not all could stick it out there. The numerous land companies, organized by the rich speculators in the "ruling," rich Eastern cities—the famous Washington is a good example—offered land under the most favorable of terms, and this totally disturbed the inner rest of the pioneer—as far as one could speak of inner rest. And so, some left Mercer County for Henry County while still others sought lands north of the Ohio.

Another group of these Pennsylvania colonists went northward in 1793 to New York State, where the Genesee tract in the northwestern part of the state offered large speculative prospects. The Holland Land Company was to operate here also. A Revolutionary War "colonel," J. L. Hardenbergh, had bought land here, having become acquainted with it during the wars against the Indians and the English. He became the first inhabitant of what later was known as Auburn. About ten Dutch families from Conowago, Pennsylvania, settled near Owasco Lake, probably as a result of his influence. Among them were the Brinckerhoffs, Jansens, Van Tines, Lysters, and others. A church congregation was also organized here.[46]

We can see that the Dutch also showed expansive power. We should not forget, though, that the English—and later the Germans—settled in much greater numbers in America and so had a greater impact on the Old West than did the Netherlanders. Starting out from this Old West, in the last half of the eighteenth century and the beginning of the nineteenth, we find our countrymen helping to people the New West. Since then, we find them in many states. They were found in Van Brugh County, Indiana, as well as in other places. They came here patently as Southerners—from Kentucky. The Voorhees family, in particular, including a few members of the New Jersey branch of that family, gained some importance through their eloquence and oratory skills, which were perhaps hereditary in the family. One of them, Daniel W. Voorhees, served in Washington as a member of the United States House of Representatives from the "Hoosier State," as Indiana is known. So did Schuyler Colfax who was probably Dutch also. Both of them served during the Civil War. The former is still remembered among the Hoosiers as "Dan Voorhees, the tall sycamore of the Wabash . . . prominent in Indiana politics," thanks to his "oratorical gifts, his sympathetic nature, and reputation for generosity," according to Meredith Nicholson, himself a Hoosier.[47]

Dutch Americans also settled elsewhere in the West. "Nobody could live along the Erie Canal in those days without feeling the suck of the forests, and catching a breath now and then of the prairie winds," a saying of J. T. Vandemark as reported by the writer [Herbert] Quick, who chose no "Englishman" as informant and who obviously was better acquainted with our countrymen than Turner. Vandemark, who "began to feel the West calling to [him] with a thousand voices which echoed back and forth along the Erie Canal, and swelled to a chorus at the western gateway, Buffalo," became for Quick the typical Iowa pioneer.[48]

Others of our countrymen journeyed to Illinois and still many, many more to Michigan. This state, whose capital is named for the well-known Dutch Lansing family of Albany, attracted so many colonists from New York State (Turner asserts that "the vast majority of the settlers were New Yorkers") that people used to call the southern peninsula of Michigan the daughter of the Empire State, New York State. Naturally Turner, who thinks only of the English, neglects to mention that there were numerous influential Old Dutch families among these "New Yorkers," and that they were highly esteemed by the New Englanders.[49] Later on we shall see how significant this Old Dutch nucleus would be for those who left their homeland in the nineteenth century. For the moment this important fact should be stressed: most of the nineteenth century immigrants settled in this daughter state as a consequence of the stream of Old Dutch that had gone there previously. Turner totally ignores this. Still later some were to forge on to the Far West, and one of them, [Clarence D.] Van Duzer, served as a Senator from Nevada.

This dispersion of the Old Dutch element, particularly in the Middle West, led to meetings with the "young Hollanders." Although these were not always the most pleasant, nevertheless these encounters were sometimes of a hallmark nature, for they marked the level of Americanization to which the Old Hollanders had advanced. In 1835, K. Jz. [Klaas Janszoon] Beukma, an enterprising farmer from Groningen (more about him later) traveled westward through the Hudson and Mohawk valleys to Schenectady and elsewhere. On his way he met "people who could still speak a slightly antiquated Dutch" and he wrote further: "Often I found them less than charming and with very little knowledge or interest about the land of their ancestors."[50]

Further west, on a farm near Cincinnati, Beukma was moved when he met a very old woman who "spoke better Dutch than anyone I had encountered on this side of New York." She had been brought up in New York but had moved this far with her husband and children. "It did her real good that she could still make herself understood in her beloved Dutch. . . . She wanted me to read to her from her *Nederduitsche* [Dutch] Bible." At the same time Beukma became acquainted with a bit of family tragedy that must have been so common among transplanted families of any age, but not to such an extent as this. She related that the children, having obviously associated much more with English-speaking people, had Americanized much more than their mother, and that they no longer understood Dutch. Indeed, when they heard their mother speak Dutch they said that she was mentally deranged.[51]

Various large stretches of land along the Illinois River (in the region bearing the same name) apparently belonged to a Van Rensselaer, granted by the United States for war and other services. Beukma wrote this in a letter of later date.[52] The Holland-Americans evidently dealt in land speculation following the example set by their English fellow citizens, such as Washington.

This expansion of Dutch people obviously also meant the growth of the Reformed Church, since the Old Dutch element was extremely church minded if not always so very religious. In 1792, when the church was organized, there were 116 congregations. In 1821 there were 187 and in 1845— before the huge new arrivals from the Netherlands—there were 274. Although most of these were in New York State and in New Jersey, there were others scattered throughout Pennsylvania, Illinois, Michigan, and other states. Indeed they had been formed into Classes and into two particular synods—New York and Albany—both organized in 1800. At the organizational top stood the general synod that had served since 1794 as the highest ecclesiastical body.

Closely related to the expansion was the formation of new classes, largely as the result of regrouping of some older congregations: Classis Philadelphia in Pennsylvania (1814), Classis Schenectady in western New York State (1826), Classis Schoharie, in western New York State (1826), Classis Illinois (1841), and Classis Michigan (1841). In addition, Canada, Virginia, and Kentucky were asking for ministers to serve the colonists in those areas.[53]

That church life was influenced more strongly all the time by Americanization speaks for itself. It is important to pursue this point, for it is precisely in this area of life that the Americanization process developed very slowly. There are good reasons for this because, as everywhere else, religion shows itself to be conservative in relation to language, customs, and manners. Hence, there is no better yardstick to measure the attachment to the old national base than this religious life, considering the fact that Calvinism is so tightly bound to our people.

It is clear that social and geographical circumstances also play a role in the Americanization process, since a more or less isolated location and existence can be of much influence. So it is not accidental that English appeared next to Dutch as the language of the pulpit for the first time in 1764 in the commercial and longtime government city of New York. In Albany, where in 1744 the people were still described as "entirely Dutch," the change came about only in 1782. This was very likely a result of the Revolutionary War and of "frontier life," both of which stimulated the developing patriotism. A visit of Washington to the city in that same year may also have contributed its share.[54] On the other hand, in the more rural

Kingston, located halfway between the two cities, the old language lasted until 1808, although English intruded into the Reformed Church "amid the murmurings of those who held in strong affection the Holland tongue and litany of their sires."[55]

From this it appears that English had not taken over entirely yet. The use of two languages was first a compromise to satisfy the desires of the young and those who thought that English had more "class" and that speaking Dutch was no longer respectable. This was especially true because, since the days of the West India Company, American Hollanders had kept Negro slaves and the Dutch language had become the language of the Negroes—the so-called Negro-Dutch. To curtail "walk-outs" from the church and switches to the English-speaking Presbyterians and—even worse—to the Episcopalians, two languages were used. This decision was supported even by older people who were very attached to their Dutch language but who were even more concerned about keeping the strength of their church. One of these supporters of English once said to Laidlie, "Oh, Pastor, we have offered up many earnest prayers in Dutch for your arrival amongst us and surely the Lord heard us in English and sent you to us." No more striking example could be given.

Still the Dutch language held its own, so much so that at the beginning of the nineteenth century, Dutch was the language for "preaching the Gospel" for approximately 250,000 Americans.[56] As late as 1789, Reverend Gehrhardus A. Kuypers accepted a charge in New York because he could "purely and readily" speak Dutch. His father had come from the Netherlands. With the passing of the older generation the number of his parishioners dwindled and the last Dutch sermon was given in New York in 1803.[57] Other towns dropped the use of Dutch later, in part because of the American chauvinism engendered by the War of 1812 with England, and perhaps even more so because of the influence of the westward movement, which more strongly than ever before generated an American spirit.

By about 1820, the English language was the common language of the Reformed churches.[58] However, Dutch could still be heard occasionally. For example, there was the Reverend [John] Gosman in Kingston who would waken those who, in good Dutch fashion, would take a nap in church. On one such occasion he received the testy retort from an awakened dreamer: "*Wat begeert U van mij, Dominee Gosman?*" ["What do you wish from me, Reverend Gosman?"][59] In some places Dutch psalms continued to be sung for a long time and at Communion services aged ministers gave speeches in Dutch. Dr. Thomas De Witt in 1844 pronounced the last Dutch benediction in the Middle Church on New York's Nassau Street.[60] The church was then permanently closed.

However, the language did not yet vanish. Quite to the contrary, it continued to exist among the decreasing number of older Dutch Americans. In 1886 General [G. H.] Sharpe of Kingston, writing of his youth, recounts this charmingly after having referred to the Anglicization of the church. "For a long period, however, and even within my own recollection, the close of the service and the pronunciation of the benediction was followed by an immediate resumption of the Dutch language by the congregation passing down the aisles and issuing from the doors."[61]

When the Dutch patriot Van der Kemp settled in New York State in the last half of the eighteenth century, he was agreeably surprised that Dutch was still spoken, even by the well-to-do element there, and this was particularly agreeable to his wife, who spoke no English. This eased her lot as the spouse of an "exile." In the autobiography that Van der Kemp wrote for his children, he mentioned: "Mrs. Clinton, Mrs. Tappan and Mrs. Hamilton"—ladies from America's highest circles and of Old Dutch ancestry—"conversed with your mother in Dutch. This was unexpected."[62]

Even more suprised were the Dutch immigrants who arrived in America in the middle of the nineteenth century when they were addressed in a somewhat old-fashioned Dutch. H. Van Eijk, whose son lent me his father's unpublished journal when I visited Holland, Michigan, had written in New York, under the date of July 25, 1847, that many Old Hollanders had visited him and his fellow travelers daily. They could still speak "old Low Dutch." "We received much friendship and help from some of them." For a while Van Eijk lived in Schraalenburgh, New Jersey, and under the date of September 9, 1847, his diary mentions the people there: "In their daily comings and goings nearly all use the old Dutch language." Although it was no longer used in school or church, Van Eijk and his companions spent many an evening with the Old Dutch preacher, [Isaac] Blauvelt. These "memorable" evenings closed with the singing of a Dutch psalm and prayer. For a time Van Eijk lived on Long Island and here also the Dutch language and customs reminded him of the Fatherland.[63]

Others had similar experiences. During the forties the Reverend [Nicholas J.] Marselus of New York addressed the Albany settlers in their own language, although he himself had been born in the Mohawk Valley and "had not read any Dutch for five years."[64] A group of immigrants from Drenthe, while enroute westward, had spent the larger part of the 1846–47 winter in Albany and were treated in a most friendly fashion. One of the Drenthe immigrants, [Jan Hendrikus] Stegink, stated that "many of the old residents of Dutch descent could still speak and understand Dutch."[65]

Even in the most American groups among the backwoodsmen, our language was still used. In 1855 it was said of a group of such backwoodsmen, real pioneers near Grand Rapids, "that they can still understand the Dutch language rather well although they speak it brokenly."[66] Decades later young Dutch ministers were still surprised at the tenacity of the Old Dutch language. In 1871 [B.] De Beij and [A.] Zwemer asserted: "In New Jersey and eastern New York we still find old fathers and mothers who like to speak in their antiquated Dutch to their newly arrived Holland brethren."[67] And H. E. Dosker wrote in 1888: "Even today and not without pride, many an eastern member of our church opens his State Bible to read a few passages and prove to you that, even after three hundred years the mother language has not been forgotten entirely."[68]

From this we can ascertain the role that religion and particularly the State Bible played in maintaining the Dutch language, although the book of "Father" |Jacob(us)| Cats* should also be considered. In the rural areas particularly, the work of Cats was held to be second only to the old Bible. In addition, some American clergymen about 1850 read Dutch periodicals and books—the magazine *De Vereeniging* |The Association| and Groen Van Prinsterer's *Handboek der Nederlandsche Geschiedenis* |Handbook of Dutch History|.[69]

The flow of thousands of immigrants in the nineteenth century quickened an interest in Dutch. Therefore, the General Synod of the Dutch Reformed Church in America strongly encouraged its theological students "to become so familiar with the Dutch tongue that they would be able to preach in the language."[70] As a result of numerous nineteenth-century Dutch immigrants settling in New Jersey, a close contact arose between the old and the new Dutch in America.

Considering the experiences of Van Eijk and others, it is entirely wrong to assume that there was little association between the two groups, as was asserted by Prof. J. Van Ginneken, S.J., in his *Handboek der Nederlandsche Taal* |Handbook of the Netherlands Language|.[71] He maintained that the Old Dutch element in Paterson and the surrounding area wanted little to do with the new arrivals. He quoted various statements such as, "Our Language is Low Dutch and theirs is Dutch and there is quite a difference. I can understand some of it quite well, but some of it I cannot."† From this it cannot be deduced that the "oldsters" viewed the newcomers as speaking a strange tongue. In fact, many of them took delight in proving that they could still speak Dutch! With considerable pride an Old-Dutch American approached Dr. M. Cohen Stuart when the latter was visiting in the Cats-kills, the land of Rip Van Winkle. "*Main heer, ik kan spiek Duitsch.*" |"Sir, I can speak Dutch."| Cohen Stuart was pleased to find that one of his hosts, the American Thomas De Witt, "still read a lot of Dutch," as D. Buddingh had mentioned earlier.[72] Mrs. K. Van Rensselaer reports that in the highest circles people still used many Dutch expressions for years and that the children learned Dutch songs and rhymes. No less a personage than Theodore Roosevelt, a contemporary from the same town as Mrs. Van Rensselaer, accurately recalled these children's songs during his visit to our land.

To what extent did the new Dutch contribute to the maintenance and

---

*Jacob(us) Cats (1577–1660) was a writer and statesman of little distinction and made his money at one time by farming. He was a verse writer rather than a poet, very didactic and uninspired. His lines drone on with the imperturbability of a metronome and have a soporific effect that is matched by no other poet. Yet his contemporaries were ardent fans and in many households the only two books present were the Bible and a volume by good old "Father" Cats.

†The phonetic transcript reveals that this Low Dutch was heavily tainted by English words and pronunciation: "Onze taal ez leech duits en hulliez ez Hollenz, kwait different. En pertie ken ek kwait choet verstane, mer en pertie ken ek niet."

change of the old language? Van Ginneken assumes, but does not prove, that the mutual influence could "obviously not be great." This could well be the subject of a productive study which, as far as I know, has not been undertaken as yet. From the previously mentioned Old-Dutch citations, it appears that there have been quite some changes in this Dutch during the passage of centuries. How strange it may have sounded in the ears of the nineteenth-century immigrants, particularly when they heard it from the mouths of very cultured Americans. J. Van't Lindenhout found it hilarious.[73] In 1886 he sojourned in Albany and was visited by an old, very cultured American lady who wanted to "put new life in her Dutch heart." She referred to her grandmother as *"een sterke frommes,"* but she meant in pure, peasant Frisian "a strong woman"! So it is easy to understand than when Teunis C. Bergen, an Old-Dutch American of high standing, talked with our consul-general [John Rutger] Planten in New York, they were unable to communicate because he used "Colonial Dutch" and the consul used Dutch. This was mentioned by Bergen in 1896.[74]

All this goes to show that many Dutch Americans would think twice before making use of their quaint and often dialectical Dutch in the presence of Netherlanders, although they often understood pure Dutch being spoken. In my numerous discussions with cultured descendants of the mid-nineteenth-century immigrants, I have had similar experiences. But it should also be mentioned that when the immigrant leader, Reverend H. P. Scholte, was in the city of Albany in 1848, he preached in his native language. He wrote that "there were many in the city who understood Dutch."[75] In the same year his countryman, Reverend H. J. Budding, preached in New York to Hollanders "and Americans who still speak and understand Dutch."[76] A third man of the cloth, A. C. Van Raalte, who was also in the area in 1846 could testify, however, that the Old Dutch families, most of whom were rich landowners, "had nearly all forgotten the Dutch speech."[77] But this was a consequence of false pride.

Forty years ago [about 1880] the Old-Dutch tongue was still very common in New York and New Jersey, particularly in the rural areas where it was also spoken by French, German, and English colonists, which was a result of the vigorous seventeenth-century Dutch ability to absorb. This absorption ability has decreased since then. Under the auspices of the Holland Society, which was then one of the most aristocratic groups in New York, "a sentimental journey," as they called it themselves, was made by members to the fatherland in 1888, and among them there were still some who spoke the Dutch of the Hudson and Mohawk River valleys. Due to their fluency in Old Dutch they were, more than the others, particularly impressed by the traditional visit to the island of Marken: "We seemed to have been suddenly taken back some two hundred years or more to the primitive days. . . . Those of our party who spoke the Dutch of the Mohawk and the Hudson found a tongue like their own."[78]

Although I myself do not dare to judge the value of these remarks, still it is of significance that the singsong, lilting mode of speech, especially typical for Noord Holland, is still found today among some Old-Holland Americans, even among those where the old language has been completely lost. Yet the language still exists and occasionally is "rediscovered" here and there. For example, around 1910 J. Dyneley Prince visited Bergen County in New Jersey and found two hundred elder residents who could still speak our language.[79] Should a Hollander call this a "discovery"? In New York's Mohawk Valley and in the valley of New Jersey the Old Dutch is still found today and it is labeled by our ancestral stock as Mohawk Dutch or New Jersey Dutch to distinguish it from the German Pennsylvania Dutch that contains more German elements. In 1920 I spent a short time in Midland Park, a heavily wooded area in New Jersey, and had the privilege to become acquainted with an Old Hollander, a certain Mr. Hopper, already advanced in years, whose New Jersey Dutch I found very difficult to understand. His portrait and residence are reproduced herewith.

Kindly forgive me for elaborating so much on the death of the Old Dutch language. It is obvious that with its disappearance the characteristic Dutch way of life also vanished. J. H. Halbertsma once noted, "The greater the faithfulness with which words are pronounced in the old ways, the greater is the faithfulness with which people continue to observe the old modes of life."[80] Therefore, the decadence of language is also important to sociographers.

With the decline of the language came a weakening of everything that was considered Dutch. This showed itself also in church life. When, toward the end of the eighteenth century the eight-four Articles, which had been drawn up by the famous Synod of Dordt as the basis for the Reformed Church, were translated into English, seventy-three supplementary articles were added in agreement with the changed concepts of the Americans. Since then, this church has become "thoroughly American," but it has preserved a healthy conservatism that is so typical of the Dutch element. Americanization resulted in, among other things, promotion for the training of their own ministers. This was already taking place at Queens College—later known as Rutgers College, after one of its greatest benefactors. In 1795 Schenectady Union College was founded for the same purpose. Both colleges are still active today in preparing students for the theological seminary at New Brunswick.

After 1810 all correspondence with the Classis of Amsterdam seems to have ceased. This should not be seen only as an expression of the American spirit of independence, because it may also be due to laxness on the part of the Netherlanders who often answered slowly or not at all. Prayer sessions became typical for the Reformed element in America, and young people attended them in increasing numbers. Sunday schools were instituted, and in addition to the psalms, people began more and more to sing also the hymns. A strong missionary spirit developed, about which more will be written later.

Old Dutch memories in New York and New Jersey. Top: The little Dutch church of Sleepy Hollow to the north of Terrytown in 1875 (from Dr. M. Cohen Stuart, *Zes Maanden in Amerika*). Middle: The eighty-year-old Dutch American Hopper in front of his home at Midland Park near Paterson in 1921 (original photo, J. Van Hinte). Bottom: Albany in 1805 (H. L. Pruyn Rice, H. *Bleecker*).

The slow Americanization of the church had caused many to join the Presbyterians or the Episcopalians. But others thought that Americanization was too rapid, especially in more outlying areas. In 1822 this even led to a break and separation by the more conservative elements who protested against the neglect of church discipline and the backsliding—as they termed it—from a true spiritual life. They saw as dead an orthodoxy that became more and more watered down, threatening a fall into Hopkinsianism and Arminianism—in short, into too much tolerance. Dr. S. Froeligh, minister at Hackensack and Schraalenburgh, with four other ministers and five consistory members representing eight congregations in all, seceded from the Dutch Reformed Church and organized the "True Reformed Dutch Church in the United States of America." Within three years the new denomination consisted of twenty-one congregations, grouped into two classes which met in an annual general synod. The new denomination did not really flourish, but on the contrary showed signs of floundering because of a lack of facilities for higher education, a too strong emphasis on the doctrine of predestination, with its sterile spirituality, and particularly because of the increasing Americanization of its members—a process that left no one untouched.[81] Later we shall note how this church group contributed, though in many instances unwittingly, to a breaking down of the unity of the nineteenth-century Dutch colonists. In part it was due to the fact that among these American seceders many could still read Dutch well and speak Jersey Dutch.[82]

The observations of D. Buddingh, who visited America in 1851, and became well acquainted with the Hervormde Hollandsche Kerk [Reformed Dutch Church], attest to the liberalization of American Calvinism during the nineteenth century. He noted that there was in the church a very wide freedom concerning baptism; "a quite higher viewpoint was observed" and a more "Christlike spirit" prevailed than ever before. The American Synod had remained free from the "blackmailing" of people into a confession of creed, which was "such an execrable, papal procedure.[83] The position of lay readers and "*voorzangers*" [psalm leaders] had also ceased among the Americans. Buddingh attended a funeral at Bethlehem, near Albany, where the Reverend Isaac N. Wyckoff officiated. If a funeral service in a Reformed Church seemed strange in the first place, our very liberal-minded countryman was even more astonished to find twenty-four Freemason brothers, all clad in the regalia and insignia of their order, in attendance and to see them take a very active part in that service.[84] Freemasonry had intruded on American Calvinism. This was of some significance because it was this same Wyckoff—to whom hundreds of Netherlands immigrants were grateful for the great help he had extended them—who was responsible for the affiliation of these nineteenth-century immigrants with the Reformed Church. However, for many of them the greatest objection was Freemasonry, and they blamed the church—often unjustly, as others claimed—for this!

An example of how far Americanization had progressed was evidenced in 1873 when Cohen Stuart preached in the Reformed Church in Peekskill on the Hudson. The most widely circulated newspaper advertised that "a true Dutchman" could be seen there that Sunday morning at the eleven o'clock service! When Cohen Stuart conducted services in the really old-fashioned Dutch village church of neighboring Cortlandttown, the Peekskill brass band was on hand. "The band sat in the narrow, small gallery and these young Levites broke into such full sound—lacking neither verve nor breath—that the old walls shook, and it must have awakened in alarm the Peeks, Van Cortlandts, and Hazebroeks, sleeping in the adjacent peaceful church yard."[85] This "Sacred Band" did not confine its efforts to this special occasion only; it had the duty of making all worship services "attractive," in order to be able to compete better with other denominations. It was something new, "quite a novelty in America."

Ten years later the Reformed Church was still considered as "perhaps the most rigid and unbending . . . of all churches in America that had originated in the times of the Reformation."[86] It is quite understandable that there are Dutch immigrants who, precisely because of their Calvinistic rearing and convictions, still shiver at the thought of joining this rigid(!) church, although the spirit of the times has also influenced Dutch Calvinism to no small extent. Modernism has a secure place also in the Netherlands. We are reminded of [Hendrikus] Colijn's* lectures on capital investment, given by this Calvinist in Reformed Church auditoriums! The process of increasing Americanization finally also affected the name of the church itself. In 1867, shortly after the Civil War, the word *Dutch* was dropped. Since then it has officially been known as "The Reformed Church in America."

The changes in language and religious worship are closely related to the mentality of the people. One can also see an interaction here. Speaking of character traits of the Dutch colonists, these also were Americanized, though extremely slowly. A typical example is the Dutch propensity for thrift, which is in sharp contrast to the American generosity and laxness in financial matters of the "real" Americans. The Swedish traveler Kalm, who was in Albany in 1749, was annoyed by the custom among the residents of sitting in the evening in good weather on the benches in front of their homes. If a pedestrian did not want to give offense, he would have to doff his hat to each one. But Kalm was even more aggravated by the "insatiable avarice and stinginess" of the "Albanians." "I had to pay much more for all items here than in any other place in the country and in addition the service was poor. One had to motivate them by paying for even the smallest thing."[87] The Hollanders in New York were much more reasonable, and this observation brings once more into focus the contrast between the urban and the rural areas. In 1848 the Reverend H. J. Buddingh noted that the

*Hendrikus Colijn (1869–1944) was a Dutch military officer and statesman, leader of the Antirevolutionary party, prime minister under Queen Wilhelmina.

offerings taken up in open plates in the New York Dutch churches produced very little. "Most people gave only one American penny; seldom were there any silver coins."[88]

This thriftiness was as characteristic of the well-to-do as it was of those not so well-off. This appears in the letters of Harmanus Bleecker, an Albany attorney and statesman who served as Minister to The Hague. In 1842 he wrote to Albany asking that American newspapers be sent to him only "if they can be sent without too much expense." Some months later, looking forward to his return to Albany with his young Dutch wife, he instructed that one of his houses be made ready but "with as little expense as possible."[89] There must have been a connection between being Dutch and thrifty, for these observations are gathered from a period when Dutch was still being spoken rather widely in America, and in this particular case no American spoke the language more fluently than did this very Mr. Bleecker.

At this time interest in the Netherlands increased, helped in part by the works of Washington Irving, although few were pleased by his depiction of the "Knickerbockers." The organization of St. Nicholas societies in the 1820s in Albany and in New York in 1835 are evidence of the Dutchness and historical sense of our brethren in America. The feast of St. Nicholas, a celebration that is as Dutch as can be, was promoted by these otherwise very aristocratic organizations, which observed it with a banquet on the fifth or sixth of December. Although the New York group was interested in its historical value "as the rallying point for historic New York,"[90] the Albany group was also more concerned with philanthropy and was therefore known as "The Saint Nicholas Benevolent Society." It was "founded with the object not only of keeping the feast of St. Nicholas, but also of affording relief to those of Dutch descent who were poor and in need of help."[91] Here we have another example of how Dutch usage of thrift and philanthropy can go very well together. The Dutchness of such traditions was again marked by Harmanus Bleecker, the thrifty ambassador who was the moving spirit in the Albany association, which reached its peak under his leadership.

Interest in "the good Vaderland" was also shown by the relatively large number of well-to-do Americans who visited the land in spite of primitive travel accommodations—the steamship was barely on its way to replace the sailing vessel. Bleecker, who had long wished to do so, made the trip when he was in his sixties, after a busy career. Other patricians such as Beekman, Duyckink, and the Van Rensselaers also visited our land around 1840. Some of them became so enamored with things Dutch that they began the study of the Dutch language and literature. I already referred to Bleecker in this connection. Appointed as American ambassador to the Netherlands by President [Martin] Van Buren, a fellow Dutch descendant, he spoke Dutch so well that when he presented his credentials in 1839, King Willem I asserted: "You speak better Dutch than we are accustomed to do in Holland."[92] Was the king secretly poking fun at the old-fashioned or "biblical" tone of Bleecker's language and pronunciation?

There is also the pleasing image given us by the young patrician, James W. Beekman, who traveled to Europe with Bleecker in 1839. He bought many Dutch books—among them those by Wagenaar*—and, having traveled through Europe, he did not return to America, but went to Holland because, as he wrote, he was "desirous of seriously undertaking the study of the Dutch language." For a time he served as secretary to Ambassador Bleecker.[93] The most famous example is that of J. Romeyn Brodhead, who, related to the Bleeckers, Van Cortlandts, and Van Schaicks, sailed to the Netherlands and went to work at the American embassy and found time to do the research for his famous *Colonial History of the State of New York.*

Many Americans sent inquiries to Bleecker, asking for information about the Old Country. It is extremely interesting to read these letters, which often concerned themselves with materialistic matters such as asking about claims on legacies of relatives in the Netherlands, etc. This is enough to prove that when, about 1845, so many Netherlanders left for America, there was already a good deal of interest among Dutch-Americans about the Netherlands. I am not aware if this interest had any direct influence on the increasing emigration from our land. I am not referring here to the help which was given in America, particularly by the churches.

More importantly, I was unable to find any influence exerted on the emigration movement by the "Dutch-packed" American embassy in The Hague or by all those Americans traveling in our land, although the emigrant literature sporadically mentions journeys by Americans. Their names or possible Dutch descent, however, are never mentioned. There could not have been much contact mainly because the travelers were usually of the "upper crust," whereas most of the emigrants belonged to the poorer classes of society—a social fact that, especially in those days, even concerned Americans.

We are aware that especially after the middle of the nineteenth century the Dutch influence in America was waning fast. The Civil War once more greatly strengthened "the American spirit." We know this from things like the altered name and practices of the |Dutch Reformed| Church. The rapid growth, especially of New York but also of Albany and other towns, contributed to the decline of a Dutch "presence" in outside life and of Dutch-American life itself and in many respects it even disappeared altogether. Even the characteristic Dutch houses gradually disappeared, although isolated examples could still be found.

The growth of the cities also resulted in the emergence of many "new rich" among the Dutch Americans. A tremendous surge in real estate speculation jacked up the prices of land so much, especially near the big cities, that many of our countrymen also piled up wealth. The Schermerhorns, the Rutgers, and the Roosevelts are interesting examples.[94] The enormous de-

---

*Lutzen Wagenaar (1855–1910) was a Frisian writer who became a Reformed preacher and followed the "Doleantie" movement. He wrote lyric poetry, drama, and fairy tales.

velopment of America's potential also offered our gifted brothers opportunities to exercise their talents. The Van der Bilts were among the first American millionaires. In his book dealing with the great American fortunes, Myers relates how in a thoroughly American way the young Cornelius Van der Bilt, "the Commodore," began with a ferryboat and later owned an entire commercial fleet! He had been born on Staten Island in 1794, the son of an ordinary ferryman, but became the richest man in America, the founder of "a dynasty of riches." During the Civil War a fortune of fifteen million dollars was considered as out of the ordinary, as almost unthinkable, yet this Dutch American left a personal fortune of 105 million dollars at his death in 1877. The entire "dynasty" of the "Vanderbilts" now controls an estimated 700 million dollars![95]

A thorough Americanization of an important segment of the Old Dutch element was not only reflected in the lives of the business people, among whom among others of importance, such as the "Vanderlips." New names kept popping up, like the Cleveland, Ohio, railroad magnates, the Van Sweringens, and Van Lear Black of Baltimore.[96] Many were also in politics and the scholarly professions.

It is a peculiar American practice to measure the accomplishments of an ethnic group by their number that enter the field of politics, since it dominates American life. The Old Dutch can point with pride to two presidents—Martin Van Buren (1837–1841) and Theodore Roosevelt (1901–1909). All of the other presidents were Anglo-Americans; no French or German Americans, much larger in numbers, have attained this high office. We can also enumerate some Dutch-American vice-presidents and numerous members of Congress; by 1910 New York State alone had contributed about sixty.[97] Many others have represented New Jersey, Pennsylvania, Michigan, and even—as we have noted—Indiana and Nevada.

Others have become governors. Prior to and during the Revolutionary War, A. De Peyster, P. Schuyler, and Rip Van Dam were in charge of the administration of New York. DeWitt Clinton became the first governor of New York State and is remembered because the Erie Canal was planned during his administration. A Frielinghuysen served as governor of New Jersey and much later, a Pennypacker in Pennsylvania, etc. The present governor of Michigan is A. J. Groesbeck; he too is a descendant of Old Dutch ancestry. An even greater number have served as legislators in the various state governments. The first mayor of Greater New York was a Van Wyk. Finally, some have served in the diplomatic corps abroad. We have already mentioned H. Bleecker who, like Henry Van Dyke later, were ministers to what they themselves referred to as "the dear old fatherland"—the Netherlands.

Many of these officials had distinguished themselves first in legal affairs. Some practiced law either as lawyers or as judges. Among those we find in the second half of the nineteenth century were a Van Vorst, a Depew—counsel for the Vanderbilts, and a Van Voorhees, all of great fame. At the present time, J. H. Van Winkle is Attorney-General for Oregon. Generals of note in this century were a De Peyster and a Verplanck; a Van Rensselaer served as such during the Civil War.

In the areas of science the name of Rittinghuysen—since changed to Rittenhouse—has already been mentioned. Simon De Witt was an important geographer who placed his services at the disposal of liberty, serving as a staff officer under Washington and later chosen as Surveyor-General of New York State. In the first half of the nineteenth century, G. Crommelin Verplanck was a noted literary figure.[98] Old Dutch blood also flowed through the veins of his contemporaries and colleagues—Paulding, who popularized the name "Brother Jonathan," just as his friend Irving did for the Knickerbockers, and Hoffman.[99] Henry Van Dyke was a gifted writer of the late nineteenth century. Notable examples in the field of history were R. Schuyler—whose work is often cited, Mrs. Schuyler Van Rysselaer, and the previously mentioned J. Romeyn Brodhead.

More than in anything else, the Old Dutch distinguished themselves in theology. Many became professors at New Brunswick Seminary, having been preceded by Livingston, the son of the Scottish preacher at Rotterdam and completely "Dutchified." Others, such as C. V. A. Van Dijck, became very gifted individuals on the mission field, gaining for themselves world reputations.

In conclusion, it should be noted that until fifty years ago, the Dutch gave leadership to the social life of New York and thus to the entire United States. Following are just a few examples. Miss E. Van Rensselaer was the forerunner of American "high life." Shortly after the Civil War, she decided to take up a more rewarding life and became a nurse, which occasioned quite some consternation both in aristocratic and church circles. "Ministers preached against this new departure in work for women as though it had been a transgression against the Decalogue. Newspapers deplored the step that Miss Van Rensselaer had taken, or else poked fun at her."

In the forties, George Schuyler organized New York's first yacht club, starting out with a simple boathouse, "the humble origin from which the palatial clubhouses and the hundreds of craft owned by the members have sprung." Later, at the time of the "gold rush," when the expansion with all its potential made itself felt also in New York's society, Mrs. Schermerhorn dared to give the first costume ball, "a forerunner of the epidemic of fancy balls that attacked fashionable New York at this period" (around 1870). "The ball was meant to be the greatest affaire-de-luxe New Yorkers had ever seen."[100] Later, when the Western invasion of "steel barons, coal lords, dukes of wheat and beef, of mines and railways" threatened New York society, the Old Dutch set the tone.

A former senator and presidential aspirant, ninety-three-year-old Chauncey M. Depew, above all an able attorney and a faithful member of the Holland Society in New York, is today considered America's best toastmaster, "the prince of after dinner speakers."[101] Mrs. Stuyvesant Fish, a descendant of famous "wooden Pete," shortly before the |First| World War instituted the "fifty-minute dinner" among the "four hundred" and introduced jazz at parties.[102] She was the last of "the Old |Dutch| Guard" to give such social leadership. The war profiteers were so numerous in society that they took over and nothing could be done to keep them out, as was the case, for instance, with Commodore Van der Bilt who himself in spite of his millions was not invited to join. He did not trouble himself about it, but his children and especially his grandchildren, "the third generation," gained a place.

The "climbers," due to their money, became too numerous and too powerful, since next to birth and profession money became all powerful. And although the 1910 New York telephone directory had no less than nineteen columns beginning with "Van," and the one of Brooklyn, twelve, and the Social Register and Blue Book show nine columns of "Van," little notice is paid to the Old Dutch aristocracy.[103] This is not because they have become less important in an absolute sense; in fact the Vanderbilt dynasty, for instance, has widened, but in a relative sense they have diminished due to the successive invasions of ambitious empire builders especially those from the West—no less than four waves—and perhaps because of a generalized rise of an ambitious class since the |First| World War. Mrs. J. K. Van Rensselaer, a descendant of one of the oldest patroon families and a member of the present American aristocracy, related the following sad news in 1925 when she wrote her *Memoirs*:

> Very recently one of the descendants of one of New York's oldest Dutch families gave a banquet for some fifty acquaintances, all of whom were able to trace their American ancestry prior to the English take-over in 1664. It was a dinner for New York's oldest aristocracy. Not a single New York City paper mentioned it—and for those who know American newspapers, this tells a lot! This was "first |and this shows the old pride, still a Dutch trait|,* because the old régime did not and still does not believe that publicity is necessary to social success, and second |and this shows the tragedy|,* because the city at large has forgotten the families who built it."[104]

The latter statement is confirmed by others, among whom are Ernest Gruening and Charles E. Wood in their book *These United States*. In the chapter, "No New Yorkers Know New York," the former comments that the city has become too vast and too heterogeneous "for either intimate acquaintance or deep affection." The latter comments that "the story of the Dutch settlers is foreign history as far as the school children of New York are concerned."[105] What is worse, there are Americans who do not wish to be reminded of their Dutch ancestry but who, when there are memorial festivities to celebrate New York's "founding," prefer to "leave" this honor to the French and Belgians, and more particularly to the Huguenots.

This brings me to the last question. How do these Old-Dutch Americans

---

*Van Hinte's interjection.

feel toward the Netherlands today? The answer, with some exceptions, is that they are less than indifferent! That is why especially New England, as portrayed in Turner's frontier studies, has been able to lay its hands on American history, in spite of the fact that there are an estimated two million of Young Dutch descent![106] Many of these are still farmers in New York and New Jersey, but they have also spread over the Western prairies and, on the whole, this rural population is usually still devoted to the Reformed Church. It was this church, as will appear later, that accepted so many of the nineteenth-century Dutch immigrants. Through this church they hear about the Netherlands and come in touch with residents from the Old Country, but there is little talk of sympathy [for the Netherlands] among them; they are Americans and farmers first of all.

It is somewhat different with the city dwellers in the mideastern states, who are more isolated from the inhabitants of the rural areas than one is wont to notice in America. That is, the urban areas in the East are more Americanized that the rural areas, yet one would think that people there would be more interested in the Old Country due to their greater education. Indeed, we saw evidences of this in the organization of St. Nicholas societies, the founding of the New York Historical Society, and of the literary *Knickerbocker Magazine*. But thereafter this interest flagged in the cities, simultaneously with the rejuvenation cure that went along with America's westward expansion. There was no longer time available for memories. A revival came in the eighties. The Holland Society was founded in New York in 1885. There were stirring speeches at the annual banquets of this group, proof of a certain amount of worship for the old fatherland, which resulted, as mentioned earlier, in a pilgrim journey in 1888. The "Vans," as they liked to call themselves, were welcomed in a most friendly way. This was "the home sentiment greeting the members of the family after an absence of 250 years."[107] The sense of ethnic unity was still so strong that, during the Dutch-English difficulties in South Africa, the guests at a June, 1889, dinner meeting of the Society in New York, sent greetings to the Afrikaaners, since both groups were descendants of the seventeenth-century Dutch.[108] After Jameson's famous raid, one of the foremost Hollanders in Pennsylvania, I. R. Pennypacker, a member of the Netherlands Society of Philadelphia, recited the patriotic poem "Krugersdorp."[109]

One should not misjudge the true character of these societies that were really not Dutch in the first place but were above all, and of course justly so, American. They were similar to the Huguenot Society of America (founded around the same time as the Holland Society), the Huguenot Society of South Carolina, and similar New England organizations. They all reflect a growing sense of history and all wanted to study their history, particularly their genealogy. They were more than historical societies, for they set up a class organization whose membership was drawn from those in the higher ranks. This society, as was mentioned above, which fell under the threat of being overwhelmed by the new rich, tried to withdraw and more than ever to close its ranks by basing membership largely, although not exclusively, on genealogy. So most of these organizations can be viewed as a sort of order of the nobility, a positive proof that also in America there existed a class society, as is the case in all societies, after all, even among animals. Our ethnic brothers of this "aristocracy" recognized this openly; it was spelled out in the bylaws. One could be a member of the Holland Society only if one were "the descendant in the direct male line of a Dutchman who was a native or resident of New York or of the American colonies prior to the year 1675," provided one were also "of respectable standing in society."

Henry Van Dyke put it even more clearly when he described membership in the Holland Society as being equivalent to proof of nobility. "We hold our Americanism by a title older than many an English duke holds his dukedom and with a greater pride."[110] Van Dyke openly acknowledged that present-day Holland should not expect much from this present "nobility," despite expressions of sympathy and friendship, despite "a supreme admiration."[111] And he continues: "We rejoice that our blood is drawn from the United Netherlands in the days of their brightest glory and of their highest power." The "young" Holland, although an "admirable nation" (Van Dyke was both a literary figure and a diplomat) was viewed as "only a cousin land about eight or nine generations removed." In connection with this we need only note the attitude of President [Theodore] Roosevelt during the last Boer War! Pollard commented that Roosevelt "would hardly be cited as evidence of an un-English strain in American politics."[112]

More and more self-glorification seems to have become the rut of the Holland Society, in spite of the unveiling of various historical plaques in the Netherlands, which can be condoned as promoting ancestor worship, but which served mainly to confirm the membership's nobility. It is this attitude which, though not excusable, makes understandable the scant interest among many of the Old Dutch Americans with respect to the Young Dutch element, with the exception once more of a few such as the sympathetic Mrs. H. L. Pruyn Rice in Albany and others, particularly, Americans of the Reformed Church. It is this attitude that explains the affront to the Dutch people, in spite of Dutch-American millionaires such as the Vanderbilts and the Vanderlips, when at the time of the Hudson-Fulton celebration in 1909, the Dutch gave a beautiful replica of the vessel "Halve Maan" [Half Moon] to commemorate the greatest period in Dutch history but left the vessel to rot in a neglected creek near Cohoes, north of Albany, after it had first been used in a disgraceful manner to advertise some land speculations.

It is also a demonstration of an attitude, if not of indifference at least of half-heartedness, on the part of the Holland Society that it took no action when the city of New York refused its gift, a replica of the statue of William the Silent in The Hague. The gift was tucked away for a while in an obscure corner of Van Cortlandt Park and finally given to Rutgers College in New

Jersey.[113] Was this not a justified occasion for a protest by at least a part of the two million Americans of Old Dutch descent? Shouldn't they have protested even if they would have had to give in anyway to the superior members of the Irish Catholics?

The experience of our former ambassador to Washington, Jonkheer [*Meester*]* A. C. D. De Graeff—now the Governor-General of the Dutch East Indies—was also sad. His Excellency confirmed to me personally the laxity of the Dutch Americans and also related that when, in that year of 1926, the 300th anniversary of New York's founding was to be celebrated, the members of the Holland Society were primarily interested in using the festivities to give a little shine to their increasing loss of brilliance. "They will not be interested in honoring the Netherlands but only themselves," was the substance of the comment of Jonkheer De Graeff.[114] It is true that much of the interest in the Netherlands in the days of Harmanus Bleecker was of a similar nature. One of the Gansevoorts asked ambassador Bleecker to find out if he was descended from the famous Wessel Gansfoort, of Lux Mundi, "the Light of the World!"[115]

If most of these episodes pain us—a few are comical—they prevent us from overrating the love these Americans profess for the Netherlands. They are valuable historical proofs, though, and give abundant evidence of the fact that the awareness of ethnic Dutch unity was losing out and that this was happening in close connection with the loss of the Dutch language. The Reformed faith of many Dutch-Americans and cases of Dutch character traits—people noticed the un-American sense of thrift even in millionaire Vanderbilt—are tokens which remind us of Dutch descent. We find them more widely in the rural areas of the East. There one is also struck by Dutch facial traits due not in the least to inter-marriages which, if we think of Mendel's laws of heredity, preserve the "Dutch look." All one has to do is study the portraits of these Americans. Even the facial traits of members of the Holland Society, related more than others to non-Netherlanders, cannot deny their Dutch origin. This is understandable according to Mendel's laws. In July, 1920, I visited Mr. A. J. F. Van Laer, Albany's well-known state archivist; he said that he was repeatedly struck by the Dutch facial features of many people in his area. This is corroborated by others. The Reverend A. Van Arendonk, who had a charge for a while at Gansevoort and Northumberland near Schuylerville in New York State, referred to his parishioners who were descendants of the seventeenth-century Dutch folk: "Some of them look so much like typical Dutchmen that I must control myself from speaking to them in Dutch!"[116] It may be cause for sadness that this Young Dutch American, Reverend Van Arendonk, like so many of his fellow countrymen in our times—now that the World War has again strengthened the "American spirit"—could only make himself understood to the Old

---

*"*Meester*" is the Dutch title given to people who have studied law, although they have not completed their doctorate, since Dutch students often dispense with writing the taxing dissertation.

Dutch Americans in English. It goes to prove once more the superior power of nationality over that of national descent. In this case the language of their shared nationality proved to be stronger than the language of their shared ethnic descent. American national consciousness is so strong that the more than 200,000 Netherlanders who settled in the United States in the nineteenth and twentieth centuries have not been able to save their language. But little can be said for rejuvenation of the Old Dutch language, no matter how vigorous the Young Dutch element has been, which indeed has proven to be racially one of the best.

More about this now.

Part Two

Transplanting of the Young Dutch Branch
Nineteenth Century

4

The Causes of Emigration in the First Half of the Nineteenth Century

A. Social Conditions

For us people of 1928, who live in the chaos that originated after the World War, it will not be difficult to imagine the social conditions that developed in Western Europe after the Napoleonic Wars. After the flush of victory in the wars of liberation was over, an enormous depression set in, a depression both in the material as well as the spiritual spheres. All strata of society, laborers as well as intellectuals, city people as well as rural residents, the higher classes as well as the lower ones, were at one time or another more or less affected by these events. Especially deplorable were conditions in the area of agriculture, trade, and industry.

In England, with its large land holdings, agricultural land was constantly being converted into grassland and then into hunting preserves. The sheep were displaced by deer. Also in Germany as it then existed, agriculture was very backward. The Continental System had severely harmed trade, particularly in Western Europe. The Americans, as the only "neutrals," had taken over shipping from the Europeans to a large extent. England, which at that time was already very industrialized, was hampered in the export of its industrial products for many years. This created overproduction and many factories had to be closed. The numerous wars had especially devastated the continent. The purchasing power of the population had shrunk and many people were reduced to poverty. Indifference and sometimes bitter despair overwhelmed many.

Faith, which for many was such a strong support during their struggle for life, was undermined by the influence of Enlightenment ideas and often was replaced by unbelief. Increasingly, discontent and embitterment accompanied it, especially because disappointment was encountered in the pursuit of political ideals, as well as in the illusions of freedom. Everywhere, instead of the promised government by the people, there was a return to the pre-1789 conditions and the enlightened despot emerged again. Had people fought so many years to come to that point? How much different were conditions in young America!

The Republic of the United States started to develop strongly after the initial difficult years. During the Napoleonic Wars especially, American foreign trade developed strongly. American shipping experienced an unprecedented increase, only to be interrupted because of the war with England in 1812. But then industry started to develop, and above all, agriculture. When peace was reestablished in Europe in 1815, the predominance of American shipping declined and more attention was paid to the home country. A new period, the one of National Expansion, began (1815–1860).[1]

Until then, America, situated between the Appalachian Mountains and the Atlantic Ocean, had closely followed events in Europe, but now it turned its sights westward. The great movement of colonization of the West began. First, the forests in the lake districts were cleared, and later the prairies to the south were developed and transformed into beautiful agricultural lands. Good roads were required. Country roads were constructed and canals dug; among the latter was the Erie Canal, built from 1817 to 1825. Steamships appeared on the rivers and quickly became indispensable. In 1818 about twenty steamboats were in use in the West, and this number rose to about 1,200 in 1848!

In the meantime competition appeared. In 1830 a start was made with the Baltimore and Ohio Railroad. Numerous opportunities were created and everywhere there were plenty of jobs. A wonderful sense of optimism prevailed among Americans. The future belonged to them! This was quite a contrast to tired Europe where the development of America did not remain unknown. The flood of emigrants from England actually never subsided. During the eighteenth century, Germans had established themselves in Pennsylvania as well as elsewhere. Moreover, many English and German mercenaries, brought over to the New World during the War of American Independence, had established themselves permanently there. Neither were the French strangers in America.

The letters of these colonists were avidly read in the old countries and created an urge to go West, because in the light of American optimism the European conditions looked even more bleak. In addition, many publications about America appeared in Europe. Many were travel accounts and these were eagerly read by the more educated, and once more their attention was directed to the United States. As an example we can cite *Voyage en Amérique* of |François R. A.| Chateaubriand.[2] In the spring of 1791 he had embarked from St. Malo like so many other Frenchmen, who in those days tried to find a refuge in the land of freedom by escaping from the "freedom" of their own country. When peace was restored in Europe after the Napoleonic Wars and travel became less dangerous, many followed this example. Already in 1815 a mass movement of emigrants to the port cities took place: The French to Le Havre; the English, Scotch, and Irish to Liverpool; the Swiss and Southern Germans to Rotterdam and Amsterdam; and somewhat later, the North Germans to Hamburg and Bremen. From these cities they tried to reach the promised land.

During the years 1817 and 1818 more than 30,000 Germans left their birthplace.[3] After this the number of emigrants declined, but after 1820 it increased again. American statistics of immigration published that year indicate that in the year 1820 the number of immigrants totalled 8,385.[4] These immigrants came mainly from the countries mentioned above, because, due to the geographic location of their lands, these nationals were dependent on America for their traffic. They were also more familiar with American conditions than any other peoples, due to their history and civilization. Having arrived in the United States and established themselves there, these colonists wrote stimulating letters to those who had stayed behind. They told about the great wealth in the New World. This again stimulated many others to make the trip across the ocean. Often they were incited to emigrate by recruiting agents of shipping companies who were already operating their usually loathsome trade in Switzerland and in the Rhine area.[5]

The number of immigrants in America reached a first apex in 1837, with 79,340. Because of the economic crisis that year, the number declined in 1838 to 38,914, but increased rapidly again after that. The interruption of the American boom period proved to be of short duration and recovery took place quickly, starting the "Golden Age." With this recovery, the number of immigrants also increased: in 1839, 68,069; in 1847, 234,968; reaching its second apex in 1854, 427,833!

It is no wonder that the great prosperity in the United States also attracted Netherlanders. The conditions in our country in the first half of the nineteenth century were not such that in the long run this appeal could be resisted. Initially, conditions in the rural areas, where half of the population then lived, were not bad. The decline of trade in the latter part of the eighteenth century had compelled many impoverished merchants to sell their lands. The glut had lowered the price of land to such an extent that many a tenant could become an owner. Obstacles to overseas trade during the French era* had caused an increase in grain prices and other food products. These included also the potato, which only recently was being cultivated as an indigenous plant. Farmers were thus able to obtain high prices for their products.[6] In 1816 our agriculture still belonged to the richest agricultural enterprises in Europe. There were many well-to-do farmers. The return to more normal conditions abroad, abundant harvests after 1817, the closing of British, French, and other foreign markets to foreign grains, and the flooding of our country with Prussian and Russian grains around 1820 dramatically changed all that and caused a rapid decline in grain prices. In 1816–1817, a "last"† of wheat would sell for fl.390

*France ruled the Netherlands during the Napoleonic era from 1796 to 1815.
†One "last" equals 2,000 kg.

and a "last" of rye for *fl.*225, while in 1823 these prices had declined to *fl.*100 and *fl.*84 respectively.

Especially the provinces that exported agricultural products, such as Groningen and Zeeland, were most severely affected. The clay farmers were the hardest hit because large scale farming had seen its greatest development among them, and hence they were most dependent on world markets. The life of the sand farmer was simpler and not so much subject to the swing between years of prosperity and poverty. He had to work harder than the clay farmer and therefore was accustomed to a more frugal existence. The situation among the cattle and dairy farmers was also different. During the years of low grain prices they still made a decent profit. Nevertheless they suffered difficult years. Cattle disease in 1826 caused great losses. Agriculture and stock breeding were both heavily hit by the great floods of 1825. The entire rural area suffered further from the bad harvests of 1828–1830. On top of all that, the Belgian rebellion in 1830 severely affected them. Heavy taxes were also levied. Taxes on milling and on brandy kept the grain prices low as well. We can therefore see that grain farmers especially encountered difficult times. It probably is no coincidence that the first emigration that came to public attention in 1835 and 1836 involved farmers from grain areas such as the sea-clay provinces of Groningen and Zeeland.

Only when the farmers convinced the government to restrict the import of foreign grain in 1835 by means of levying the so-called "scale duties" was their situation improved. Also, because of the rapid industrial development that took place in England, an increasing demand for our agricultural products was created there. In 1845, potato blight and bad grain harvests again struck, although farmers received some compensation in the higher prices they obtained for their products. The situation of their laborers was closely connected with the economic situation of the large and small farmers. Here again, differences occurred depending on whether laborers worked on clay or on sand soils, in agriculture or in stock raising, in a large enterprise or small one, or whether they worked for owners or tenants. In Friesland especially, the situation of the laborers was anything but an enviable one. A day's pay of the permanent laborers, the best situated group, was so small that it was a wonder that a laborer, who often had a large family, could even survive. Farmers hired less and less laborers on their permanent workforce because they had to pay high rents, heavy costs, and taxes. Because of this, many laborers were unemployed during the winter and spring when the soil was too wet, and they would go to the public assistance committee for welfare aid.[7] In 1850 in Ferwerderadeel, one could find twelve to fourteen permanent laborers against one hundred casual workers. This ratio was about the same in West Dongeradeel. In Friesland the least unfavorable situation could be found in the southwest, the "*Greidhoek*," where laborers specialized more in mowing. This type of work was traditionally left to foreigners, because the Dutch usually considered it too heavy. The worst conditions prevailed on the heath fields where the laborers lived in nearly subterranean huts, as for example, in Rottevalle and Surhuisterveen. Such conditions also prevailed in Drenthe, where the dwellings differed little from pigsties. The economic picture was a bit more favorable for the population on sandy soils. In the rural area of Salland [in Zeeland Province], a little prosperity prevailed, created by the higher prices for grain, cattle, and butter. This in turn accounted for the slightly higher wages being paid there. Extra earnings were also made by knitting and weaving. In Staphorst, for example, the knitting of stockings and mittens was so profitable that the members of the town council, dressed in their wooden shoes, attended council meetings and knitted during the discussion of community issues.[8] The prosperity of the remainder of the rural population is obviously closely connected to the well-being of the farmers and their laborers.

In cities conditions in general were equally bad. Trade, after a short revival in 1816, had stagnated again because of the lack of purchasing power of the population. Moreover, the character of trade had changed because of the transition from a protected trading system to a free one. Because of this the years in the middle of the nineteenth century were among the most difficult encountered by Dutch traders.[9] As trade played such a very important role, next to agriculture and stock raising, the aforementioned transition influenced conditions over the whole country. Many communities hardly advanced and in some the population even declined. Amsterdam, for instance, had 221,000 inhabitants in 1795. In 1815 this figure was reduced to 180,179, after which it slowly increased again to 211,349 in 1840.[10] However, trade continued to decline. The many and important commission houses, especially in Amsterdam, that traded with America, lost almost all of their importance after 1846. The American Republic introduced a more moderate [tariff] system in 1846 and the Dutch commission houses were replaced as go-betweens, since the Americans realized more and more the advantages of direct sales. Also the German States, which were strengthened through the Zollverein [a German customs union], encouraged imports through German ports, especially Bremen. The merchants of Amsterdam did not keep up with the times and adapt. This is the reason that their commission houses disappeared in the long run.

King Willem I, the "merchant king," tried to encourage trade and industry through the construction of a better transport network of highways, canals, and railroads. Cooperation, however, was minimal. Inertia and lack of development characterized also the higher social classes in those days. The founding of the "Netherlands Trading Company" was only possible after the King had pledged his own fortune to guarantee an interest rate of 4½ percent. This company not only tried to encourage trade and shipping but also industry, such as the weaving industry in Twente after 1830. Its beneficial influence only gradually became apparent. It appeared as if all energy and drive had disappeared from the Netherlands in those days. "In this little, forgotten corner of Europe, listlessness and an aversion for the new festered for a long time, as well as a superstitious fear of fate."[11] There was no sense of enterprise, there was no leadership, and there was no initiative. King Willem I was one of the few favorable exceptions, but he could not do everything; he could not set an example everywhere.

In 1860 [J. H.] De Bosch Kemper stated in the second printing of his well-known *Geschiedkundig Onderzoek naar de Armoede in ons Vaderland* [Historical Research on Poverty in our Country]: "There are many fortunes in our fatherland which are lying idle. Only when expertise is applied and guarantees for financially profitable returns are given, will they create work for thousands."[12] Also, the enthusiastic B. P. G. Van Diggelen mentioned repeatedly the enormous amount of work that still had to be done in our country. Already in 1849 he published a work about the Zuiderzee, the Frisian mudflats, and the Lauwerzee, in which he recommended that they should be recreated into fertile farms [by polderization]: "Our soil is a product of which no overproduction is to be feared."[13] However, his voice was not listened to either, and everything remained as it was.

Only unemployment increased, and with this poverty also increased, which was a threat to the cities as well as the rural areas. It was threatening because a large part of the population suffered from the potato harvest failure when potato blight ravaged all of Western Europe in 1845. Grains had been too costly for a long time, and hence potatoes had become a staple diet. The potato rebellions that occurred in many cities in our country showed the extremes to which people could be driven. Many minds were set thinking and the creation of relief work was encouraged everywhere. Hence the remark in a pamphlet of the Governor of Gelderland in March, 1848: "Peace and stability in the State cannot be bought at too high a price."[14] It is not that there was a lack of concern before that time. On the contrary, General [Johannes] Van den Bosch* and others founded the Society of Charity in 1818, during a time when our country had more than 700,000 needy out of a total population of more than 2,000,000. This proves that, even in those days, as people like Van Diggelen later realized "that the poor could only maintain their self-respect as independents if they could earn their living by their own effort."[15] The Society of Charity with a subsidy from the state, purchased thousands of hectares† of land and founded a few agricultural colonies: Wilhelminaoord in Friesland, Willemsoord in Overijsel, and Frederiksoord in Drenthe. Many an unemployed worker found a new existence there.

The charity of the Dutch is renowned. In the middle of the nineteenth century, our country boasted no less than 3,744 institutions of charity. In 1848, 8.5 million guilders was spent on public assistance institutions, not counting special assistance.[16] [A.] Brummelkamp and [A. C.] Van Raalte

---

*Johannes Van den Bosch (1780–1844) was a Dutch statesman and philanthropist, made Graaf [count] in 1839.

†A hectare equals 2.4 acres.

wrote in 1846 that the expenditures for maintenance of the poor was 20 million guilders per annum![17] One wished that the right initiatives had been stronger and that funds for them had been diverted from charity! Already it was realized that a country cannot become prosperous by means of collections, and that charity which was very great here, was "conducted too much by the heart and too little by the brain"; because of that, it had deteriorated to a cancerweed.[18]

It also happened, as is the case today, that many showed no inclination to work. Many considered all types of work too heavy and left it to foreigners, specifically Germans, who were more robust. Germans came to our country in great numbers to earn a living and they either established themselves permanently, or they were like the migratory birds who came to feed themselves but disappeared in the fall. They could be recognized, and even today some of them are still there as grassmowers, peat diggers, peat cutters, seed cutters, meatcutters of animals and horses, and others. They were found not only in the lower ranks of our society. While huge numbers of Dutch young men were enrolled at the theological faculties of the universities, many young offspring of the German middle class came "to be grafted on the branches of our trade."[19]

Among the Dutch the number of people to whom charity was distributed did not decrease but rather increased.[20] In 1841 there were 331,627 welfare recipients versus 2,599,516 not receiving welfare, or a 13:100 ratio; in 1845 there were 460,023 welfare recipients versus 2,593,691 not receiving welfare, an 18:100 ratio; and in 1850 there were 646,605 welfare recipients versus 2,426,791 not receiving welfare, a ratio of 27:100. Because of this, the costs of welfare reached enormous levels. In those days this was an important reason for many well-to-do to leave the country. In 1845 the very well educated Frisian farmer, W. Van Peyma, complained in one of his letters to his friend Eeckhoff in Leeuwarden about the "heavy and inequitable taxes for the maintenance and assistance of the poor, who have increased at an amazing rate and are still increasing."[21]

In Friesland the system of welfare was the most unfavorable. Because of silly welfare laws, which allocated welfare even to capable men, some of the farmers were forced to pay from fl.500 to fl.600 per year for support of the poor, in addition to all other taxes.[22] In West Dongeradeel, a preacher with an income of fl.600 paid fl.53 to welfare! This was in spite of the fact that, because of the war with Belgium and the expensive armistice that followed, the tax burden was already very heavy. Somebody who owned fl.50,000 would be assessed fl.2,200.[23]

The less-well-to-do were particularly burdened by excise duties. Although De Bosch Kemper asserted that "in general the amount of our taxes cannot be the general reason of poverty," yet taxes were for many day laborers the reason for their departure to the almost tax-free America of those days.[24] Especially the excise on milling, butchering, and peat was a thorn in the side of many. In the rural areas the tax official was a most hated man who always seemed to know the exact time when a day laborer, in deep secret, was butchering his pig. Although the rural inhabitants could eat a bit of pork, meat and wheat bread were unknown luxuries to the laborers in the cities. Excise taxes, at about *fl.*20 per year, as well as other taxes, were oppressive for the laborers. The license system especially imposed constraints and forced many to go elsewhere to make a living. A rural carpenter, for instance, went to America because in the Netherlands he was compelled to pay not only his license fee as a carpenter, but also as a wagon maker, wheelwright, chairmaker, foot stove maker, cabinet maker, etc. Many carpenters, therefore, left our country.[25]

The economic situation that was described earlier was anything but encouraging. Time and again there were setbacks in agriculture, and only very slow growth or even stagnation or decline in trade and industry. This all was disproportionate to the rapidly increasing population, and the consequences were unemployment, poverty, and welfare allocations. All this, of course, had to leave its mark on the moral life of the population. There were thousands of people in our country who, through lack of moral principles, were kept from working, lamented De Bosch Kemper.[26] A great portion of the wages was spent on alcohol and life was lived without a worry because of the anticipation of welfare funds. In 1850 a most dismal picture is painted for us about the spirit of the Frisian laborers.[27] They related to other members of our society like slaves in body and soul. They concerned themselves little with society; they were dead to society, but they had a slavish fear of the ones on whom they depended. To the other social classes, these helots were a subject of pressing worry and concern. Their energy was used like that of machines. They formed a kind of caste "which slowly has become like a stagnant pool in which vices and immorality have become prominent to a great degree." This picture was given to us by a person of that place and time!

The spirit was not much better in the cities of our country. Already the ill-fated consequences of increasing child labor in the factories were becoming evident. Industry "parasitized" more and more on child labor, which would ultimately become a disaster for our country. In 1841 the Provincial Government of Zuid Holland warned against child labor, and depicted a situation that equaled the misery found in rural Friesland: "Also in our factory cities the population, degenerated in body and soul, is testimony to the perverse influence of premature or overexerting labor in childhood."[28] Also, the middle class of those days was far from perfect. There was a desire for frills and insipid entertainment "through which money and mind were wasted." The entrepreneurial spirit was entirely lacking. When, in 1839, the government of the energetic Willem I proposed to build the Rhine railway from Amsterdam to Arnhem, our Parliament rejected this proposal with forty-six against two votes. Undoubtedly our representatives reflected the spirit of the greater portion of the people. They had no nerve. People with capital were satisfied with a moderate but assured interest. The young people, mirror images of Pieter Stastok,* rather stayed home than go to the colonies or other countries to create trade connections. "They live on their capital and they consume, but they do not produce."

Religious life for the greater portion of the population was in accordance with this spirit. Real devotion and Christian living were hard to find.[29] Churchgoing was very mechanical and there was much talk about dogmas, but little was applied in practice. The doctrine of election in connection with that of predestination gave many a great sense of powerlessness. The influence of one's own will and power was denied, which alleviated the sense of responsibility of many. Mysticism and fatalism had penetrated very deeply, especially among the lower classes.[30] In such an atmosphere, it is hardly possible to find an interest in politics or government affairs.

B. Opposition to the Spirit of the Age

Gradually, however, a change occurred in this slumbering mental attitude of the Dutch people. Willem De Clercq, the well-known first secretary of the Nederlandsche Handelmaatschappij [Netherlands Trading Company] was right when he wrote in his Dagboek [Diary] in 1829 that the Dutch nation was apathetic and there was "everywhere sullenness and insipidity."[31] Less acceptable is his assertion that in 1834, the year of the church Secession, "one can hear a leaf drop in the northern Netherlands, because everything is as dead as can be." This is true, of course, only if he referred to trade and shipping, because in the spiritual area there were clearly signs that a change was afoot. The resignation and apathy were changing into dissatisfaction, which became even more evident after the shock of the Belgian rebellion, and sometimes it led to resistance. There are those who did not understand this change and even in 1850 still attributed it to preachers and teachers of the youth who were too little concerned with the actual upbringing of children. They were supposed to instill in children "a satisfaction with the class into which it had behooved God to place them."[32]

Much earlier already, traces of dissatisfaction had appeared, but being at first at the local level, they were not noticed initially. It must not have been a coincidence that the objections against the spirit of the century were first and most sharply evident among the lower classes of the population, who were the ones most threatened economically. Neither could it have been coincidental that change was manifested by a renewed interest in religion through the church and through a tendency toward mysticism, to which a great portion of our people were inclined. Bad eco-

*Stastok is a Dutch character from Nicolaas Beets' Camera Obscura, denoting a very stiff, rigid, middle class, "stick-in-the-mud" type of person. Nicolaas Beets (1814–1903), man of letters and Protestant minister, wrote as a theological student under the pen name of Hildebrand. His Camera Obscura was a series of critical and ironic portraits of his contemporaries, like the Stastok family, Gerrit Witse, and others. He was active in the Reveil movement and gave a more serious direction to the Hervormde Kerk.

nomic conditions are fertile soil for the forming of new thoughts or reawakening of old ones in the religious sphere as well as in the economic sphere. In addition, depending on one's ability and education, feelings and intellect vie for priority.

This connection of religious and social grievances against the prevailing opinions is quite evident in the Zwijndrechtsche Nieuwlichters [Zwijndrecht Newlights] of Stoffel Muller.[33] Muller, a simple barge man, who was born in 1771 at Puttershoek, proposed his ideas for the first time in 1816. He declared himself against the decadent Christianity of his day, and preached instead about the ideal first Christian communities of Jerusalem. His ideas were communal property, no civil marriage, no birth registration, no military service, but instead love and charity and non-resistance. Even his opponents admitted the peace-loving nature of his followers by stating that "one could walk over their bodies or cut them up." Muller and his adherents, among whom the bailiff Dirk Valk of Waddingsveen, Maria Leer, and the chocolate manufacturer Mets of Vlissingen were of some importance, preached the equality of all human beings. They testified that "love wants to level all mountains of wealth, dominion, and power among people and raise all valleys of poverty, scorn and ignorance, that equality will come to all." These communistic ideas, according to [H. P. G.] Quack, originated from religious ideas in our country, and expressed a socialistic current which in the second quarter of the nineteenth century became a torrent through the whole of Europe.[34] They were not the result of the thinking of some intellectually well-educated, scholarly person, but came from the minds of people of the lower classes such as peat bargemen, day laborers, and sulphur-match peddlers. In everything and in everybody, God's name had to be venerated and praised.

Initially the group used a Rhine barge at Puttershoek, but later the sect divided into two groups, one at Zwijndrecht under Muller and the other at Mijdrecht under Valk. Many adherents lost their jobs because of their convictions. Valk was fired from his bailiff position. Also some were sentenced for vagrancy and contempt of court. On the whole, however, they were left alone. Because they were conscientious objectors, the government was lenient enough to let them serve their time as cooks in the military barracks. After Muller's death the group declined. Some emigrated to America, while others joined the group of Valk at Mijdrecht. This group also finally ceased to exist in 1848 after having been deserted by the younger ones. After that they could mainly be found scattered in the villages of Zuid Holland province until 1863. That was the year that the news spread among them in these villages that the Spirit had called them to join the Mormons in North America.

Of even more local character was the movement about 1824 of Jan Mazereeuw at Opperdoes in West Friesland.[35] This prophet, initially a wealthy farmer who later went downhill, foretold the end of the world. His followers sold their farms for ridiculous prices, cut down their orchards for firewood, and each day expected the end of everything. They dissociated themselves from the |Netherlands| Hervormde Kerk |Reformed Church|, and they did not send their children to school. The parents themselves instructed their children in religion. They were frugal and modest, and shunned all jewelry and color. Later they joined the Gereformeede Kerk and a few returned to the Hervormde Kerk. However, the memory lives on very strongly and today there are still people who call themselves "Mazereeuwers."[36]

The mystically-tainted religious revival was also evident in more well-to-do circles, namely the "Réveil."*[37] As the name indicates, this revival was undoubtedly influenced by foreign ideas. |Nicolaas| Schotsman, a preacher, had created interest in our country for the church revival in Geneva, Switzerland, where many had already seceded from the State Church in 1817. Swiss seceders such as César Malan and others attended the "soirées religieuses" |religious evenings| of their upper class co-religionists in Amsterdam on a regular basis. Merle d'Aubigné, who was deposed from his ministry by the State Church of Geneva, became the Court Preacher at the court of Willem I at Brussels where Groen Van Prinsterer met him regularly. Nevertheless, the Dutch Réveil acquired a national character, not only because of |Willem| Bilderdijk† who is sometimes called the father of the Réveil, but also because of his followers: Groen, |Isaac| Da Costa, |Abraham| Capadose‡ and others. Willem De Clercq§ especially influenced it as one of "the most gifted, and surely the most likeable son of the Réveil." They were orthodox in the acceptance of the old-church dogmatics, but for many, feelings took precedence over thinking.

Because of their orthodoxy they were in touch, more so than other circles of the well-to-do middle class, with the "kleine luyden" |common folk|. Already Bilderdijk was attracted to the "Bijltjes van Kattenburg"|| , those behind the cloister in Rotterdam, and the weavers and printers in Leiden. Among them he rediscovered, "when the cold breath of Rationalism passed over our country," "the delicate green shoots of the Reformed Confession, although yellowed and molded, saved from extinction."[38] Also, others were impressed by their orthodoxy of belief and visited the religious gatherings of these plain people, for example in Leiden, where even academic intellectuals attended the "oefeningen" |literally, exercises, prayer meetings| or con-

*The Réveil was a Protestant religious revival that began in Geneva, Switzerland, around 1810, as a reaction against Enlightenment rationalism. It was influenced by English Methodism and German pietism. Aristocratic circles in the Netherlands strongly supported the Réveil, and the movement had a great influence on Dutch society, church, and state.

†Willem Bilderdijk (1756–1831) was a noted Dutch poet, scholar, lawyer.

‡Abraham Capadose (1795–1894) of Portuguese-Jewish descent, was converted to the Hervormde Kerk and was a leader in the Réveil.

§Willem De Clercq (1795–1844) was a merchant and writer, and made the first comparative literature study in Europe. He played a leadership role in the Réveil.

||Bijltjes |little hatchets| was the popular name given to the ship carpenters in Kattenburg, the Amsterdam shipyard section.

venticles. In this manner, the religious revival of the well-to-do was initiated while, at the same time, giving them new food and new forces drawn from what was alive among the common folk. Their feelings also brought the men of the Réveil closer to the people. They, more than anybody else perhaps, were moved by the misery of the lower classes.[39]

The emigration of many underprivileged to America was witnessed with great indifference by a great portion of the middle class, but it caught the real attention of the men of the Réveil. Emigration, as well as welfare, therefore has been influenced by them, although in opposite ways. Encouraging charity was in accordance with their character; but prompting emigration required more fortitude and was initially considered a "sad plan" not in accordance with Scriptures.[40] With anxiety they witnessed the departure of hundreds from the country. Groen Van Prinsterer wrote in 1847 to his "Very Esteemed Friend and Brother," J. A. Wormser: "The responsibility of the ones who so much encourage emigration is a heavy one. In many aspects the disadvantage to Country and Church is evident." Hesitantly he added: "However, much of this may turn to an advantage if a true Dutch Christian Colony is founded that maintains close ties with the Christians in this country."[41] But within the circles of the Réveil there was no real opposition. They met one another in intimate reunions in the Amsterdam "*zaaltjes*" [rooms] or at no less private dinner gatherings at the homes of friends. It was not until 1845 that they felt the need for certain meetings of Christian friends which, under the leadership of Groen, would turn the spirit of the Réveil into action. Since that time they have had great influence in the area of church and state, school and society.

More sympathy than for those in the Réveil is undoubtedly due to the men and women who seceded from the Netherlands Hervormde Kerk in the 1830s because of their deep religious beliefs. They were subject to almost unbelieveable persecution, but they showed that, because of their belief and convictions, they were willing to suffer just like the martyrs of times past. The Réveil, as a movement, expressed great disapproval of the spirit of the century, but in line with this spirit, they shrank from action and initially they even more or less disavowed the men of action.[42] The Réveil and Secessionists went together in Switzerland. In this country they diverged. The aristocrats of the Réveil, with only a few exceptions, shrank from following the democrats of the Secession, an attitude which no doubt must have disappointed many.

Shortly after Willem I in 1813 had accepted the position of sovereign ruler, church matters required his attention. Immediately he took care of the payment of clerical salaries, since clergymen had suffered great poverty under the French regime. In 1816 he instituted new regulations for the management of the Hervormde Kerk, which were meant to replace the Church Order of Dordt of 1618. Although this was an arbitrary action of the King, these regulations were considered a great improvement in church organization and many accepted them as a great blessing. Not everyone viewed the regulations as an improvement, however. The action itself was a consequence of the paternalistic opinion that the King held about authority, an opinion that could be found elsewhere in Europe in those days. Two months after its declaration the Classis of Amsterdam presented its objections to the King, and expressed the fear that a domineering pope or bishop-like rule might result, and stated that it expected division and separation.[43] The government took little notice of this warning because the original classes were being disbanded anyway by the new regulations and replaced by new ones.

The actions of the consistory members at Axel in Zeeland were more direct. All but one refused to accept the new regulations and the protesters were consequently removed from office. However, this did not stop the opposition. Part of the population, which was devoted to the old Calvinistic religion and especially wanted to retain the old church order, rallied around the lay-preacher [oefenaar] [Johan Willem] Vijgeboom.[44] Vijgeboom, originally a farmer, resisted "the blind spirit of dreadful tolerance" and the evangelical hymns that he branded as "Remonstrant." He objected to the new church organization and especially to the far-reaching heterodoxical dogmas that were being preached from the Hervormde pulpits. On the advice of the new consistory the government hindered the meetings led by Vijgeboom. On January 22, [1823] Vijgeboom and the members of his group seceded from the Hervormde Kerk and took the name "*De Herstelde Kerk van Christus*" [The Restored Church of Christ]. They wished to return to the Three Formularies of Unity and the Church Order of Dordt; in other words, they wished to return to the creed of the old Gereformeerde Kerk. Vijgeboom took the pulpit in many towns in our country and was persecuted wherever he led groups of twenty or more persons, on the basis of articles 291 to 294 of the Napoleonic penal code. His secession did not succeed, perhaps because he was only a lay preacher and not an ordained minister, but more importantly because the spirit of the people was still dormant. Here as elsewhere, only after 1830 was there a turning of the tide of this spirit among a great part of the population.

Although the population was not ready for secession in 1823, it was ready in 1834. Poverty in the country had increased, and the Belgian rebellion had awakened many. An even more dangerous enemy appeared. It was the cholera epidemic that claimed thousands of victims in 1832 and 1833. Then it disappeared, but returned with such severity in 1848 that during 1848 and 1849 more than 22,000 people died of this illness in our country alone.[45] Many became indifferent or disheartened; but people with a different mental outlook searched for help in God. For instance, A. C. Van Raalte, who later was a leader of the emigration and who was still a student at Leiden in 1832, wrote how after the first cholera epidemic, the preaching of the Gospel became his sole purpose and prayer.[46] C. Van der Meulen, another leader of the emigration who was originally a well-to-do contractor at Middelharnis [Zuid Holland Province], was converted because of the loss of two children to cholera, and became a minister.[47] Also |Hendrik| De Cock, the man who gave the signal for Secession in the church, was converted in a similar manner. When he was installed as the preacher at Ulrum, Groningen, in 1829 he was not yet converted. Under the influence of a few of the simple members of his congregation and several articles written by Count Van Zuylen Van Nijevelt, his eyes were opened to the great decline in religious teachings. The pressing circumstances of the times, the Belgian revolution, and the cholera epidemic also contributed "to add a somber and melancholy tint to his feelings that were running very high at the time." From that time onward, people came from far and wide, even from Friesland and Drenthe, to listen to De Cock's preaching.

His changed ideas induced De Cock to baptize children of other congregations, which brought him in conflict with his classical board. This board was also annoyed by the fact that he disliked the evangelical hymns, which he considered as merely the work of man. He antagonized the entire clergy, however, with his bitter articles against two preachers: "Two wolves in the sheep-fold who can preach much better about eating and drinking, nice weather and long days, about gardening and farming, about newspapers and war, than about the Kingdom of Heaven, as they lead the way for their congregations to the markets and horse races, drinking and singing until early dawn, or attending meetings for the so-called |society for the| common good."[48] De Cock was suspended for libel on December 19, 1833, by the Classical Board of Middelstum but his salary was not withheld. The Provincial Board of Groningen unfrocked him on May 29, 1834, but the General Synod reinstated him on July 16, 1834, giving him six months from that date to show that he was repentant and to make amends.

During that same period, the orthodox clergyman H. P. Scholte, preached in the district of Heusden |Utrecht Province| for the same type of population which, as in Groningen and elsewhere, had remained attached to the old religion and the old church order. Scholte, who was an Amsterdamer by birth, had only started his studies at a relatively late date. He first studied at the Athanaeum in Amsterdam, during which time he met Da Costa, among many others. Afterwards he studied at Leyden where he was one of the faithful visitors of the group of |Joannes| Le Feburé. When the Belgian insurrection broke out he volunteered in the Chasseurs and participated in the campaign, after which he again returned to Leyden. There he became the center of a club of Secessionist students, called the Scholte Club, that spawned many Secessionist preachers such as |Antonie| Brummelkamp, Van Raalte, |Simon| Van Velzen, and others.[49] In March, 1833, Scholte was installed as clergyman at Doveren, Gansoyen, and Genderen in Noord Brabant. Soon thereafter the rumor spread of his keen and strict Reformed preaching, which made people from the whole district of Heusden gather to listen to this young minister who was extolled as a miracle of God.

Scholte also resisted the modern preachers and did not want anything to do with the evangelical hymns. It is no wonder that he followed the events in Ulrum with great interest. He entered into correspondence with De Cock, and after De Cock's visit to the manse at Doveren, he traveled to Ulrum and preached there, although Reverend |N.| Smith, the "*consulent*" |adviser| of the village of Leens, had refused him this opportunity. The suspension of Scholte was answered by him and his church council with the momentous decision made on November 1, 1834, to secede from the Hervormde Kerk. This followed the example of De Cock and his church council, who had already on October 13, 1834, signed the Instrument of Secession or Restoration. Many clergymen and their followers joined the Secession. A. Brummelkamp at Hattem, G. F. Gezelle Meerburg at Almkerk, S. Van Velzen at Drogeham in Friesland, and others, were unfrocked by the Hervormde Kerk. The postulant for the ministry, A. C. Van Raalte, was rejected, and he severed all connections with the church hierarchy and also joined the Seceders. Although originally of a local character, the Secession movement spread and became provincial, and quickly acquired a national character. The movement even crossed political boundaries and spread into Bentheim and Oost-Friesland.

Everywhere, in the cities as well as in the rural areas, the preaching of De Cock and his followers struck a responsive chord in the hearts of the simple people, who cultivated the religious inner life, and also among the pietists who adhered less to dead orthodoxy and stressed personal rebirth and conversion. But everywhere they met with reactionary forces. The government was irritated by the revolution in Belgium and considered that it had to act against these religious opponents in the same manner as it had in Belgium; and some even compared De Cock with |Louis| De Potter from Ulrum.*[50] The government cooperated everywhere and, therefore, the General Christian Synod of the Hervormde Kerk asked to interfere with and hinder the meetings of the Seceders. The Napoleonic Code, Articles 291 to 294, which was the accepted Penal Code, gave the legal ground for such action. According to these articles, no associations or groups of more than twenty persons could be formed without the permission of the government, and conditions could be imposed on such an association as the government deemed necessary. The Seceders appealed in vain on the basis of Article 190 of the Constitution, which stated that "the complete freedom of religion is guaranteed to everyone," and also Article 191 which stated: "All existing religious beliefs in the Kingdom will receive equal protection." Their opponents argued, however, that the term *existing* referred to the year 1815, in which year this new denomination did not yet exist.[51] Not only did the government support the Hervormde ministers, but also the better-situated citizens who threatened Seceders in their employ with dismissal. Support also came from the community at large, "which was always irritated by non-conformists, and which always reacted massively against secretive meetings." They resorted to arson, breaking of windows, assault, and

*Louis De Potter was a Belgian revolutionary journalist.

all sorts of other aggravating actions, to make life more difficult for the Seceders.[52]

The number of Seceders increased in spite of jail terms and high fines, and in spite of the billeting in their homes of some of the roughest elements of our army—the notorious dragoons. Just because of this persecution many others decided to join, because they were impressed with the Seceders' steadfastness. They also were embittered by the unchristian attitude of many of the Hervormde ministers with respect to the Seceders. After the Secession at Ulrum, 150 infantry soldiers were billeted in this village, mainly at the homes of the Seceders. De Cock was even required to take twelve. In an uncalled-for manner, the soldiers acted extremely roughly, probably under orders of the lesser elements among the officers of those days. Shortly thereafter De Cock was sentenced by the Court in Appingedam to three weeks in jail and a fine of *fl.*150 for "disturbing the peace." The same treatment was received by many other ministers, not once but many times. Reverend H. J. Budding, who preached three times each Sunday, and often during the week four times while moving from town to town, was required to pay *fl.*40,000 in fines!

Neither fines nor prison terms nor even persecution by the rabble could hold back these courageous ministers. On a November day in 1836, after Van Raalte had conducted a Communion service in Ommen [Overijsel Province], twenty-five houses in which Seceders lived were later attacked violently by a mob, and in a bombardment of heavy stones and bricks many windows and roof tiles were broken. A few days later Van Raalte was taken prisoner and guarded by the riffraff, who made it amply clear to him through threats and curses that he would be killed if he ever entered Ommen again. During the same month of November he was given a three-month jail sentence, because he spoke up and upbraided a burgomaster who interrupted a religious service and thereby showed himself to be an enemy of God and God's people.

Sometimes, when soldiers and the rabble made it impossible for Seceders to meet on land, they would meet on water. This happened at Oud-Loosdrecht on June 9, 1837, where H. P. Scholte planned to preach and baptize. The military prevented any service from being held, and therefore it was decided to gather on the lake in the ship of brother N. Pos, who made it available. At 8 A.M. the church ship sailed with the parents on board, as well as their children who were to be baptized. They were gaped after by the soldiers who had been called to arms! From all sides the members of the congregation converged on the ship in small boats. Scholte also went on board and preached twice that Sunday, entirely without interference. A week later he preached and served Communion on board a ship on the Zuider Zee for the brothers and sister of Bunschoten. Finally, even these gatherings on water were prevented.[53] Not everybody agreed with this persecution. The members of the Réveil defended the Seceders, and there were also Liberals such as Rinse Posthumus who considered the persecution foolish.[54] The protest of these men was passive and their opposition made very little difference. Groen, for example, who was a religious sympathizer of the Seceders, remained undismayed in the service of the King, who was ultimately responsible.

Having grown tired of the persecution, the Seceder congregation at Utrecht, led by Scholte, decided to request the King's recognition on the basis of the conditions laid down by the Government in 1836. They submitted this request in December 1838 and received recognition in February 1839. After this, many congregations under De Cock, Brummelkamp, Van Velzen, and others requested legal recognition. These requests were not always granted. Only after 1840, during the reign of Willem II, did recognition become easier. This King also forbade the use of the army against the Seceders. Fines, however, were still imposed until the end of 1848. Thus, peace returned slowly.

For a long time division remained among the Seceders themselves, not only about the requests for "freedom," which many did not wish to make, but also about baptism, church order, lay preachers, clerical dress, and other problems. These problems were often closely connected with the character of the people and the ensuing way of thinking, which among the Seceders led to a northern, more "precise" way of thinking and a southern, more "stretchable" way of thinking.[55] The internal struggle became so fierce, that in 1838 a schism took place among the brothers. The result of this was that a new church group was formed, namely "*De Gereformeerde Kerken onder het Kruis*" [The Reformed Churches under the Cross]. Even the fathers of the Secession, De Cock and Scholte, became mutual opponents. How deep this division had become was evident at the Synod at Amsterdam, the famous Pirate Synod of 1843, where the adherents split into three factions and had to leave without achieving their goals.[56] No wonder that, with all this haggling, with such a spirit of separation, sympathy for the Seceders diminished, although it can be glossed over as the adolescent crisis of the Seceder movement. No wonder also that the continuous quarreling made easier the people's decision to start all over again in America. This was undoubtedly the case for Scholte, one of the leaders of the migration movement.[57]

Not only the Hervormde people were dissatisfied. The church policy of the government, which aimed at government supremacy over the church, displeased others also. Lutherans and Jews were compelled to accept an organization that many did not want. Willem I even considered a union of Protestants and Roman Catholics. Then he would not only be the spiritual head of his Protestant subjects, but also of his Roman Catholic subjects, and in this way he could achieve the ideal of religious peace.

Because of this aspiration, government educational policy was also influenced. The 1806 law on elementary education of Van den Ende, which was maintained under Willem I, was meant to bring together the different denominations. However, the stronger this aspiration became, the more the schools of 1806 lost their positive Christian character and the reading of the Bible was neglected.[58] Schools became progressively more neutral, which pleased many but displeased a great many others. The result was that among the orthodox segment of the different churches, Roman Catholics as well as Protestants, there was an increasing desire to found their own private schools. The Jews already had their own schools. The thought of being able to found schools in the United States completely in accordance with one's own religious conviction, as well as education free from government interference, made many think about migration.

Emigration also became a necessity for economic reasons—to obtain a better livelihood. Especially after 1830, a change in the state of mind of the population became evident, not only in the religious sphere but also in other areas. Already with the Newlights of Zwijndrecht, besides their religious grievances, economic complaints were so strong that one is inclined to consider them as religious socialists. Among them, too, there was a strong desire for more equality among the people, a desire that, since the French Revolution, had been loudly proclaimed elsewhere, but only seldom realized. Equal rights again became a slogan in the nineteenth century, first among the young people, and after that in more and more strata of society. This movement also took place in our country. The middle class, initially satisfied with the patriarchal rule of Willem I, in the long run began to resist the King's paternalistic authority. Willem's policy after the Belgium uprising, which cost a fortune and led to heavier taxes, and the taxes needed to fight the increasing poverty, were undoubtedly major causes for dissatisfaction. This dissatisfaction, however, had deeper causes. The new spirit that demanded more self-governing in religious matters also expressed itself in the political arena. The old desire for independence, which had long been dormant, again came alive. An increasing segment of the population demanded participation and a voice in government. They no longer were satisfied with elections in which they only had an indirect vote through the electoral college, and they wanted nothing more to do with unresponsible governmental departments.

In Friesland this spirit not only prevailed in the cities, as in other parts of the country, but also in the country as well. Especially in areas with clay soil, such as Dongeradeel "... Here the fertility of the soil, combined with the common sense of the people, led, sooner than anywhere else, to the introduction of any tested novelty. To this should be added their sober lifestyle. All this had created among the farmer class a prosperity that gave new life and resilience to the old spirit of independence."[59] It was in this area that the gifted and progressive-thinking farmers' minister, Rinse Posthumus, from his hospitable manse at Waaxens again tried to awaken "silent Friesland." In this region there also lived the remarkable Frisian Worp Van Peyma, a plain but very well educated farmer who was a trusted adviser of the government in matters pertaining to the maintenance of sea dikes. In his spare time Van Peyma read Jean-Jacques Rousseau, and thus was very familiar with the French and American freedom ideals. The desire for freedom, as well as economic pressure, made him decide to sell his considerable properties. Although he was already in his fifties, he moved to the United States with his children and grandchildren to seek a better-governed homeland.[60] This example was not only followed by more than one levelheaded and well-to-do farmer in the north and northwest of Friesland, but also by inhabitants of Het Bilt, the West Frisians, who were no less spirited than the true Frisians, the "oudlanders."

Elsewhere this urge for freedom was also the reason why many farmers and other citizens decided to leave the country. A farmer by the name of |Klaas Janszoon| Beukma, who had left Groningen in 1835, explained in 1838 that his departure from the Netherlands was to provide for his children "in a country where the life of the inhabitants is more secure and the rights of people are supported and practiced as something of importance."[61] Political problems were the center of discussion, remarked an anonymous Roman Catholic person in 1846, after he had asserted that people had left the country for political reasons.[62] These reasons were not only the heavy tax burden but also a lack of improvement in political rights and an extension of civil rights. The greater part of the people, the so-called masses, worried little about politics and only asked for work and bread. However, the urge for freedom also took hold of them. This desire did not express itself in specific demands but rather in a more general but vague feeling of dissatisfaction. As this self-respect emerged, and because of this awareness, the pride of the citizens was hurt more deeply. Injustice was felt more acutely. Resistance arose against the middle class, which used to look down with contempt on "the laborers who are a despicable class of enemies that has only crime and rebellion on its mind."

There was also Stoffel Muller and his supporters, true mirrors of what was alive among the lowest classes of our nation, who held the opposite view of this opinion of the lower classes.[63] They wanted nothing to do with this feeling of grandeur and they turned against those "church meetings where pride and splendor sit up front and the poor are put in the rear." They cried out: "Watch out, you rich, powerful, proud show-offs, possessors of fortunes, gathered over many years. You possess only to satisfy your own desires. You suppress your lessers . . . and let the poor go hungry and naked."

Among the Seceders, who had already shown this democratic spirit in their religious struggle, there were many who did not primarily reject the political situation but the social situation of that epoch. They did not want to have anything to do with the slavish respect that was required, and they held a strong grievance about this. Even their fellow believers, the men of the Réveil, in spite of their similarity of belief, looked down on their "lesser" brothers. They were concerned about the salvation of these "lesser" souls, but without forgetting that God had created both poor and rich.[64] When speaking about the "lesser" brothers, Groen spoke not about the beloved brothers, but only of the brothers . . . in Christ![65]

The ones who moved to America were, in most instances, impressed with the prevailing equality. The letters of the Seceders and others who had emigrated mention this equality frequently. "The lesser are equal here to the rich and one need not lift one's hat for anybody. The rich people are considerate of the poor who work for them," wrote one of them, and then continued, "Religion is good here and God's people are many, and in this we acquiesce."[66] Characteristic of this spirit is a letter of one of the most respected leaders of the believing emigrants, the preacher Seine Bolks, written from the town of Overisel, which was founded by him in Michigan.[67] Bitterly he wrote in this letter: "Nobody longs for the land of our birth. We all feel liberated from all the torturing shackles on our souls and bodies." "It is not a country here where the workingman has to bring his sweat to the country's offices, while being cursed. Also a lesser citizen or poor man is not put back or despised; indeed, the opposite is true, he is respected and liked." Only after having relieved his feelings in this way did he continue: "What is more important, one is not hindered here in serving and preaching our dear God and Savior Jesus Christ." And further on: "The poorest here are better off than the richest in Holland. One works here for oneself and is no slave of anyone."

C. The Quandary—Go or Stay

The realization that one is human, and therefore feels an increasing urge for freedom, is the true reason why many leave the fatherland to build a new future in an area where one thinks he can pursue personal growth in a better way than is possible in the country of origin.[68] In general, this urge for freedom is expressed on the material level. To carve out an existence that is wider in scope and more independent is no doubt the most frequently stated reason for emigration. The fact that many came to the decision, not just because of themselves but to assure a better future for their children, gives to the economic reason an even higher moral value. There were (and are) people who not only because of economic considerations but also for religious and political reasons decided to migrate. Sometimes any one of these reasons may be the sole factor that motivates the emigration. There is no doubt that the social conditions in our country, described earlier, were the main reason for creating the urge for freedom. In broad outlines these conditions did not differ from those in surrounding countries. Sometimes they were almost the same, but at other times somewhat different than elsewhere in Western Europe. These conditions caused "grievances," be they social, religious, or political, to grow to such an extent that many finally decided to emigrate.

A decision to emigrate is so important, so far-reaching in its consequences, and its execution requires such will power, that it should be viewed with the greatest respect. This respect should not be diminished because of the fact that besides the hundreds of thousands who leave their home country for idealistic reasons, there are hundreds who do so with a less noble motivation, in which case the urge for freedom has often turned to lawlessness. For instance, there was a considerable number of Dutchmen who, to avoid the law, found a haven in the perennial lawless areas of the United States of America, or even worse, they found a new field of endeavor for their devious practices. Such people were found in ports such as New York and Baltimore, where they offered their services to their newly arrived compatriots. They used the trust created by a common language to relieve them of as many of their possessions as possible. The letters from emigrants are full of complaints about these "scoundrels," "shanghaiers" and "deceivers" of their own countrymen, who often appeared to be familiar with their relationships, their plans, and everything else. Even today there are still enough of this sort of "helping" countrymen who, together with the memory of former encounters with them, cause established colonists to be suspicious of any visiting countryman, and even distant relatives, as this writer personally experienced. The extradition treaty between the United States and the Netherlands, signed in 1872, has modified that category of immigrant, if not in quantity at least in quality.

Freedom is also highly desired by those who, even though they may not be conscientious objectors, hope to evade military service by emigrating. During the days of the replacement system, which is the system by which one could buy a replacement for military service, and which, obviously, worked in favor of the well-to-do, it can be easily understood that this system led to great dissatisfaction. Many young Dutchmen eligible for the draft moved to America where conscription in peacetime did not exist. Even today there are people who are against "serving," which is a deciding factor for their departure abroad. Our society has a far more lenient attitude toward this sort of emigrant. People knew how rough and mind-deadening a soldier's life usually was. A member of Parliament from Overijsel remarked in 1851 that if lessons in reading, writing, etc., were given in the service, this could have been a blessing for many.[69] Not only were men withdrawn from more useful work, but also from marriage, exactly "at an age that such a liaison is most ardently desired," according to a writer in De Economist in 1869.[70]

More or less compulsory is also the emigration of those who leave the fatherland on the insistence and with the support of the family. Many a good-for-nothing or black sheep in the family, and also those who wished to evade the law in the Netherlands, surprised everyone by becoming energetic workers in a country such as America, with its entirely new environment without prejudice. Their names were originally only whispered, but now they are mentioned openly and with pride, and even the hope of a rich uncle (and inheritance) in America is secretly fostered. Of course, there are also those who cannot get used to the American freedom and they go under, irretrievably. Various circumstances, some of which had nothing to do with those in the Fatherland, have made the decision to emigrate easier.

Americans exaggerate if they say, like Warne, that the enormous migrations from England, Germany, and the Netherlands were not governed by the economic situation in these countries but rather by conditions in America.[71] According to Warne, the latter formed the "basal cause"—the single powerful force drawing immigration to our shores," with western European conditions only as a "secondary cause." There undoubtedly is some truth in this opinion. However, it applies better to each of the mass movements that took place in the second half of the nineteenth century and the beginning of the twentieth century, rather than to the ones of the first half of the nineteenth century. Undoubtedly, in addition to the thrust away from the European states, the attraction of other nations, especially of America, should be taken into account as well. In the first half of the nineteenth century and again after the World War, people were primarily tired of the Continent and therefore sought a new place to live in Africa, as well as in Australia, in South America, and in Central and North America. Experience quickly indicated that of all these places to live, the United States offered the best chances for western Europeans.

The Netherlanders came to this conclusion after having learned their lesson in Algeria, as well as in southeast Australia, even though they had in the tent city of Ballarat their Kalverstraat and Noordeinde!*[72] They were also disappointed in Argentina, Brazil (where some literally died from hunger), Venezuela, and Guatemala, and also in their own colony of Surinam. The stream of Dutch emigrants was therefore also mainly directed to North America, to the country of Franklin and Washington. In our country people were just as well informed about North America as people of the countries mentioned at the beginning of this chapter. The American War of Independence had been followed in Holland with great interest. Great interest existed for the young Republic at the political level and even more at the trading level. The merchants had supported the Republic financially and were trading extensively with it. When the borrowed sums were paid off by the Americans, these monies were used to acquire vast stretches of territory in New York and Pennsylvania.

The literature about America was extensive and varied, both as original works in Dutch or as translated works. During the first half of the nineteenth century our country was flooded with this kind of material. The first volume of the magazine De Gids [The Guide] was almost entirely devoted to discussing new publications about America in order to acquaint Netherlanders with this land. It has continued with this task ever since, and in this matter acted as intended by the founder-editor [Everhardus J.] Potgieter,† who

---

*Well-known Dutch streets in Amsterdam, similar to Fifth Avenue or Sunset Boulevard for Americans.

†Everhardus Iohannes Potgieter (1808–1875) founded the important literary magazine De Gids (The Guide), for which he wrote most of the articles. His critical story, Jan, Jannetje en hun jongste kind, [John, Joannie and Their Youngest Child] (1842), is an attack on the prevailing negative spirit in all of Dutch life of the time. Since the Dutch language has various types denoted by Jan, Potgieter introduces in his story all the sons of Jan (Janmaat the sailor, Jan Contant and Jan Crediet who represent Dutch trade, Jan Compagnie the adventurer who made good in the colonies, and many others). All of those made the country great through their energy and enterprise, but their achievements are jeopardized by the youngest son Jan Salie (a creation of Potgieter), a good-for-nothing who represents everything in Dutch life that is dull and apathetic. One New Year's Eve father Jan and his energetic sons put Jan Salie in an old men's home to get rid of him. Jan Salie is still the contemporary epithet for a person without drive and energy.

showed a lifelong interest in the development of the young Republic and the hardy souls who emigrated to it. The above-mentioned volume of 1837 contained the well-known ode of Boxman, "Farewell to Europe from an Emigrant." This ode expressed what many young intellectuals felt:

> "Farewell, greying Europe! Close to your last breath,
> You see your states staggering while their foundations and
>   supports decay......
> We rush to the hemisphere where, young and full of strength,
> The states rise up;
> Where freedom sits on a throne in solemn splendor,
> And where suppression and rebellion are unknown."*

It expressed what was repulsive in "dying Europe," but also what was the drawing power of youthful America.

America also received the attention of the lesser-educated people. Our countrymen were deeply impressed by the streams of emigrants from Switzerland and Germany, who since 1815, via our rivers and roads, tried to reach the port cities of Amsterdam and Rotterdam, from where they started their journey across the ocean. A few decades later, an anonymous person reminisced: "We saw whole crowds of emigrants from Wurtemburg lying in the worst kind of misery on the sides of the roads. They were exhausted and starved and could not carry on, and as such created quite a problem for the local authorities."[73] All these strangers had only one destination: America, which they considered as their salvation. In the harbors it was the sailors of the many American ships and of the ships that regularly sailed to America who generated quite a bit of interest for the New World.

No wonder that many Dutchmen from rural areas as well as from the cities made the decision and moved to that wonderland. From there they soon wrote back, sometimes within a year, giving their favorable experiences. The farmers wrote about the "exceptionally fertile" soil, which consisted often of black clay, on which one has "plenty of grass and honey." Cattle could stay outdoors the year round, and in a short time, with only a little money, one could become a large landowner. The laborers told about the plentiful opportunities, where the earnings of one day equaled those of a week in the Netherlands. Even the laborers on public works were given three meals a day with meat and whiskey, and the food was so plentiful that leftovers were not kept, but fed to the dogs. The women hardly had a thing to do, and bachelors became rich. Most of them spoke about the easy way in which one could become a citizen, how one was permitted to vote, and

---

* *Vaarwel, grijzend Europa! dat uw' doodsnik nabij,*
Uw staten ziet wagglen bij 't molmen van grondvest en
*   schoren.....*
Wij ijlen naar 't halfrond, waar jong en vol kracht,
De staten opwaarts stijgen;
Waar vrijheid ten troon zit in staätlijke pracht,
En dwang en oproer zwijgen.

how religion could be freely exercised. A school teacher emigrant summed it all up by saying that he had come to the conclusion that his adopted fatherland was "a land blessed by God, in natural, social, and spiritual matters."[74] These letters were not only being read by relatives who had stayed behind, but they were passed from hand to hand in the village. Often they were printed, and in this manner they were read in an entire province, or even the whole country. These letters helped to make up the minds of those who still hesitated.

Besides letters there also appeared many "guides" and "information sheets" for the emigrants. In these America was usually praised sky-high and even referred to as having such fertile soils that, with only cursory cultivation, a harvest with a sixty-fold return could be obtained.[75] These instructions and informations were, of course, not of the most reliable kind, and much more influence was exerted by previous countrymen who, after they had become well-off, returned to pay a visit to the village of their birth. Van Peyma and other Frisians had already thought about emigration since 1830, being impressed by conversations with an American who traveled in Friesland at that time. It really made an impression when, a few years after emigrating to the promised land, a plain farmer's son returned, neatly dressed and wearing good shoes. Like a "gentleman," he was free and easy in his manner without any servility! Even the most suspicious person in the village was set thinking. When the old comrade then told about his adopted fatherland, where one could eat as much meat as one liked, where beer was cheap and plentiful, where land only cost one rijksdaalder (fl.2.50) per acre, where a day's wage was fl.2.50, where nobody had to be addressed with "Sir," where no royal court needed to be maintained, no large standing army, no costly bureaucracy; where there were no polder and dike charges, where no poor taxes had to be paid, then all reservations disappeared and many decided to go with this missionary to his second fatherland. The representatives of shipping companies, and later the agents of American land companies, also added their encouragement to emigration.[76]

There were also people who, even though they seriously thought about emigration, did not take that great step. All sorts of objections served as so many brakes that neutralized both the negative conditions in our country and the attractions of America. In the first place, there is the attachment to one's own country and surroundings. However, it is difficult to determine if this attachment is a real love for the country "which, for a truly moral and religious person assumes a more sacred, and really patriotic character,"[77] or if it is inertia, the fear of breaking with old habits and ideas.

Emigration in earlier centuries was sometimes considered a crime and hence punishable, and even in the early part of the nineteenth century many considered emigration as unpatriotic and hence morally reprehensible. This feeling was even more prevalent in religious circles, especially among the men and women of the Réveil. In their magazine *Christelijke Stemmen* [*Christian Voices*], departure from the Fatherland for economic and religious reasons was considered as "fleeing in the face of God, because God gave you a place as sentries, expecting that His servants would not walk off."[78] This opinion was held by many of the Seceders. Even the leaders who came later, such as the preachers Scholte[79] and Van der Meulen,[80] initially did not even want to consider emigration. The minister Lammert J. Hulst, who for years was one of the leaders in the Christian Reformed Church of America, said in his memoirs quite honestly that in his youth he was against emigration because of the stigma attached to it.[81] Many Roman Catholics shared the same view.[82] Emigration was condemned, especially if it was not directed to one's own colonies, but went by preference to the United States. Mercantilism |with its connotations of protected trade| was a prime consideration in this opinion. The departure of so many to a non-Dutch territory was seen as a great loss to the country, and emigration was considered as a social plague, an "illness," that had to be eradicated as soon as possible.[83] Also, because of this reason, emigration was not very patriotic.

Not everybody was successful in setting aside and overlooking these deep-rooted social prejudices against emigration. In addition, it was very difficult for many who considered leaving the country, because in the process they would withdraw from the circle of their acquaintances and especially from their parents' home. The attachment to these is an important element in our patriotism. Love for their parents was a factor for many young men who decided against emigration. For example, Tjibbe Geerts Van der Meulen, a well-known Frisian folkpoet and writer who considered emigration in 1848, was held back by the ties to his parental home.[84] For him this was not a passing fancy; all his life he remained interested in America—"That country of dreams and wishes"—where he later visited his brother. He also encouraged many a Frisian to emigrate there.[85] Not only did this attachment to the soil, the people, and the surroundings in which one had grown up restrain many from going, but it also caused many to return to their country of birth after they started their journey, or even after they had established themselves in America. Homesickness, which would increase as a result of troubles during the journey and the problems of settlement, was such a strong force drawing them back to the old country, that even the disdain and ridicule awaiting them there was disregarded. The attraction of the United States, which was sometimes a consequence of too high expectations of that country, was also mitigated.

Apart from the overly enthusiastic letters and guides about the promised land, some also appeared in which judgment about America and its future was described entirely differently. Those who had been disappointed in their expectations expressed themselves bitterly at times and advised their friends not to come: "Don't be tempted by those dollars"; keep in mind that "a dollar also has only one hundred cents."[86] Another remark: "Before coming to America, one should wait until one is really starving. For people who feel at home with pigs, it may be good, but not for city folks who know of some conveniences."[87] These disappointed people especially warned others not to believe the exuberant writers: "The reason why they write in this exuberant manner is self-interest, in order to entice rich relatives or acquaintances to come over in order to benefit from them. You can rest assured that almost all those letters do not even come close to the truth."[88] Such remarks, which undoubtedly were written in a mood of resentment and as such are only acceptable with reservations, nevertheless reduced many a candidate's emigration fever.

Some freely admitted that they wrote this "praise" to convince friends to go to America. "Derk and Louise Arnoud and children," a Seceder family, for example, admitted having written extensively in this fashion " . . . to entice you to come to us. Dear People, please do come soon!"[89] Writers of pamphlets issued many a warning against deciding too hastily, and they gave a pessimistic view of America: It is the country of freedom for all robbers, scoundrels, rogues, and scum of all types. They described America as a country where honesty had been made a farce and where the Indians roamed around plundering. "And you would like to live amongst these wild, uncivilized, rapacious, and plundering hordes?"[90] Even the writer M. P. Lindo, who like Potgieter also showed great interest in emigration, viewed it with apprehension. While the writer of Jan and Jannetje* looked at emigration from the courageous viewpoint, Lindo sensed the tragic side of it and hence wrote his *Wenken voor Landverhuizers* [*Suggestions for Emigrants*] to safeguard them against disappointment.[91] He pointed out that the apparently cheap property had first to be prepared for agriculture by means of very heavy labor especially when it was forested land. On the prairies, wood and water were lacking. Also, "A single raid by marauding Indians could destroy years of labor." The chances of those who did not want to become farmers were also considered unfavorable by Lindo. Very often laborers would look for work for weeks because of competition, especially from the many Irishmen. One of those spitting images of Nurks,† whom we have quoted above, had had a dire personal experience of that sort in Chicago and complained that since the Irish have come to America, "it is spoiled here for the working man." Many, therefore, wanted to return to the Netherlands.

More forceful was the warning of the gifted political scientist S. V. [S. Vissering] in *De Gids* of 1847. In discussing a pamphlet about emigration, he holds the writer responsible "if he had induced but one single wretched soul to take an irresponsible step. . . . " Immigrants in America, Vissering asserted, were forced to go to the wilderness of the West to make that habitable. They arrived in regions where "the development of the mind and soul are stifled by the deadening loneliness," where the distant home-

---

*Jan and Jannetje refers to Potgieter's poem, "Jan, Jannetje en hun jongste kind." See footnote on page 98.

†Nurks is a character from Nicolaas Beets' *Camera Obscura*, the epitome of a crabby, negative person; used as a generic name, the same way as a Scrooge denotes a miserly person in the English language.

steader was deprived of all help and at last "succumbs from misery and grief." The editor of *De Gids* was not the only one to make this somber prediction. Others also remarked that usually the first generation was sacrificed to prepare the way to prosperity for the next generation. The virgin earth takes revenge on everyone who violates her for the first time.[92]

Seeing returnees and hearing personal stories made an even greater impression in this regard. Many returned in great misery to the Netherlands, either via Rotterdam or Amsterdam, en route to their original place of residence. When these America-goers returned poor and fed up with that country to which they originally had departed with some funds and plenty of hope, and told to their fellow townspeople, now that they were poor and destitute and bitterly disappointed, what their experiences had been with American "freedom," this must also have yanked off "the veil of deceit with which the new world is still clothed for so many."[93]

If judgment about America varied, the sea voyage was almost always judged the same. Even now when one reads about the extortions and deceit to which the emigrants were subjected by the shipbrokers and shipowners, as well as the captain and crew, the question arises how all this was possible.[94] The emigrants were treated like cattle, and lived in extremely confined quarters for weeks, even lacking proper sleeping accommodations. They suffered because of the delays in the journey due to adverse winds, and they also suffered outbreaks of illnesses. Many of them succumbed. If, in addition, one looks at the cost, which was about *fl*.100 for a steerage passage in the forties, it is also understandable why many decided against such a journey.[95] The sea voyage from Rotterdam to New York, the route that was followed by most of the less well-to-do Dutch emigrants, lasted usually six or seven weeks, and with adverse winds, as much as ten or twelve weeks. Sometimes the ships had to be pulled through the Voorn canal by ten or twelve horses and for weeks await a favorable sailing wind at Hellevoetsluis. This could mean that Holland was not left until after a delay of up to one month. The passengers were required to maintain themselves, and also to cook for themselves and use their own bed linen, etc. They were entitled only to fire, drinking water, and a place to sleep, and only in case of mechanical trouble were they granted compensation, but not if the delay was caused by officials or unseasonable weather. By paying the ship company in advance, it was possible to insure against shortages of food.

An impression of such a journey can be obtained from letters of a number of inhabitants of the districts of Het Bilt and Barradeel in Friesland who left in 1847 for America.[96] These emigrants were "in their circles very respectable members of society" and have done well in their second Fatherland. At 4 A.M. on Friday, March 26, 1847, these emigrants left St. Anna Parochie by coach. Among them was the S. Osinga family, who, while staying at their friend's V. De V. "spent this last night on Frisian soil, sleepless and suffering from contradictory emotions, being in high spirits one minute and down again the next." Some friends accompanied them to Harlingen. In St. Jacobi Parochie, as at St. Anna Parochie before, many people were up and about, and in passing greeted them "with a good morning." At seven o'clock they arrived in Harlingen, where, in the office of the steamboat *Friso*, a few powerful speeches were delivered by T. W. and A. N., but Osinga could not find words to reply. At eight o'clock, the *Friso* left for Amsterdam, from where they traveled that same night to Gouda by nightboat and from there by steamboat to Rotterdam. The Frisians had booked space on the Prussian brig *Emil*. When Osinga protested that the space was insufficient and the sleeping accommodations too primitive, the captain refused to take them aboard. The ship left Rotterdam on the second of April with seventy-two passengers, but without the Osinga family; it was not until the eleventh that the ship sailed from Hellevoetsluis. It reached New York after a journey of eighty-two days.

During all these days the passengers had spent their time between decks, where even during the day it was so dark that people could barely see one another. Perhaps this was a blessing in disguise, because there were only a few cooking spots and battles took place sometimes to determine who should do their cooking first. The drinking water was bad and the food ran out and further purchases had to be made from the captain. In the meantime, the Osinga family had had to wait for another opportunity for passage. Only on the twelfth of April could they embark on the *Prinses Sophia*, which was also boarded by a number of people from Zeeland under the leadership of their preacher Van der Meulen. At Nieuwesluis they had to wait for high tide so that the passage through the canal could take place. Then there proved to be more than two hundred persons on board, which according to American laws, was one hundred too many! If she were to arrive with that many on board in an American port, the ship would be confiscated and the captain imprisoned. Because of a measles epidemic that raged on board ship, many children died, among them a daughter of Osinga. He decided to leave the ship because the number of passengers had to be reduced by one hundred anyway. "It was impossible for us to remain between the contaminated decks, where the sordid death stench prevailed."

Because of disagreement between the shipowners and shipbrokers, the ship remained in Hellevoetsluis, where Osinga asked assistance from the navy to fumigate the ship! When the ship finally departed, a number of emigrants remained, waiting for yet another ship, the *Louisa*. Some already started to suffer because they did not receive any compensation. Osinga, however, wrote to the American Consul, and because of this he was awarded *fl.*30 in damages. When finally, after a long wait, the *Louisa* was ready, the crew mutinied. Because of all these reasons, she finally sailed on June 22. During the voyage a collision with another ship, a brig, was narrowly averted, and also constant adverse winds meant that the port of New York was not reached until the 4th of August. Osinga looked in vain for work for a month, after which he left for Albany, where he found a spot in a bookbinding shop, earning $3.00 per week.

Such experiences during journeys were no exception; quite the opposite was true. If one went via foreign ports the experiences were not much better. The sailing ships that left from Bremerhaven were even less recommended, because of the vermin and the lack of hygiene, while the accommodation on board French ships was "distressingly dirty, nasty, loathsome, and raffish."[97] The conditions on board ships that sailed from Liverpool were just as deplorable. It often happened that, from a family of ten to twelve members, only one would reach the other side; the others—parents and children—would be buried at sea. The death rate on board British ships was the highest. In the first week of June, 1847, when eighty-four British emigrant ships reached the Gulf of St. Lawrence, they all had cases of typhoid on board! On some ships this amounted to one-quarter, while on others one-third, and sometimes even half, of the crowded passengers were affected. One to two hundred passengers died daily![98]

The crew on board ships was as crude as the workhands ashore. This was experienced by a number of Frisians who in 1853 traveled to North America via Liverpool with the *William and Mary*.[99] The captain and mates continually held back on the provisions that were agreed upon. This caused many a fight in which even knives were drawn. When the ship ran aground near the Bahama Islands because the mates were "dead drunk" and had steered too far south, the captain was the first to flee the ship in spite of the efforts of the emigrants to prevent him from doing so. Before the captain and the greater part of the crew left, the anchor was dropped, "so that we would be sacrificed to the sea and unable to witness to their shameful act." It was terrible to see how a young man who tried to climb in the boat "had his fingers cut off by the ax wielded by the savage crew members, and subsequently how he drowned." After a few days of great anguish the shipwrecked were picked up by an English wrecking schooner. The Frisian and German emigrants were put ashore on Grand Bahama. Their luggage and other possessions, however, were the booty of the schooner captain. With the help of the friendly natives of these islands the shipwrecked were provided with new clothing and transported to New Orleans.

But even after arriving in American ports, a traveler was not out of danger. The ship journey along the Mississippi for those who arrived in New Orleans and whose destination was the West, as well as the journey across the Great Lakes for those who traveled to the West via New York—the preferred route—was often miserable, partly because of the tempestuousness of the lakes, but mostly because of the roughness and carelessness of the crews, who were often drunk. For that reason, the German emigrant J. F. Diederichs called this last part of the journey "the hardest and most dangerous part of our journey from Europe."[100] This experience was especially applicable to a great number of Dutch emigrants from Winterswijk, Varseveld, Oosterbeek, Apeldoorn, and Holten, who embarked at Buffalo on the *Phoenix* en route to

Wisconsin. Within view of the eagerly awaited shores, the ship caught fire, mostly as a result of the negligence of the crew, of whom a number were drunk. About 250 people, including 127 of our countrymen, died a terrible death. Only 46 people, including 25 Netherlanders, were saved. It goes without saying that the news of this tragedy made a deep impression on people in the respective home communities. No wonder that their urge to emigrate subsided drastically, at least temporarily.[101]

In those days it took real courage to undertake the journey to America. Brummelkamp remarked, and justly so, that "the journey to America required a farewell, which made one think of a deathbed." Especially married men had to think twice before they subjected their wives and daughters to the dangers among such coarse sailors. Special measures for the protection of the female passengers proved to be necessary more than once, and sometimes even government measures were taken.[102]

Considering these difficult emigration circumstances, we cannot help but let our thoughts dwell upon the thousands of women who have sacrificed so much to follow their men abroad. The women must have said farewell with much greater difficulty; by nature they were more attached to their surroundings and family circle. Also they would probably have been more resigned under the pressure of the times and taken it in a more submissive way. Theirs was not the urge for freedom that drove the men to America. Being fully dedicated to their homelife, they thought less about emigration, and for them the name America meant something entirely different; if often meant nothing to them. The journey to America was more trouble for the women, and many a child was born on board an emigrant ship. Many more children died in misery on board the ships and were buried at sea.[103] For women, and especially for mothers, emigration was often something dreadful. They moved because they followed their men, not because they shared their men's ideals or spirit. Rather, they resigned themselves to the fact and went along. The British painter Erskine portrays this on a small but colorful canvas in the Tate Gallery in London. It is titled "Emigrants" and shows the emigrant confident and self-assured, anticipating the future, while in contrast his wife sits on the meager baggage with sorrow in her eyes, but resigned and deep in thought.

However, it is incorrect and contradictory to the facts to consider the attitude of all women to be passive toward emigration. Their characters are too diverse to assume this. The name *America* lost its deterrent sound for many after the letters of the first emigrants indicated that life for women was much better in the New World, and that it was even called the "Paradise for Women." Women also intoned the cry, "It's God's wish," after a few preachers, concerned with emigration, tried to give the movement a religious character. The spirit that moved the Seceders' wives is evident from a letter of Mrs. Arnoud in which she tells about a fearful stormy night when everybody thought that the ship would go down. For her, however, it was "a blissful night. I was in Heaven." "I sang continuously in my heart: Just as happened after Moses' prayer, even though thy path goes through the sea, no wave will overwhelm thee. . . . "[104] Also the thought of the future of their children made many women active and sometimes they even were leaders.

The recollections of the Honorable Cornelis Van Loo at the commemoration of the sixtieth anniversary of the Zeeland colony in Michigan are of particular interest.[105] His father, even though he was a Seceder, did not feel like emigrating and refused assistance in 1847 from the well-to-do farmer |Jannes| Van de Luyster, who was going to America himself and who offered to pay the journey to America for the entire family. One reason was that he again had plenty of work as a carpenter. Two years later the wealthy farmer Jan Smallegange wanted to take him along. "Father hesitated, but mother, who was a bright woman and considered the future of her children, convinced father. This is the way we arrived in this good land, like many others, kindly assisted by Smallegange." There were also women, who by will power, prevented men from emigrating. Among the leading colonists of the forties was Pieter De Jong, teacher at Kerkebuurt in the community of Haringcarspel, who founded the ever-prosperous settlement of Roseland, now part of Chicago. His brother Dirk intended to go with him and had already sold his belongings, packed his baggage, and paid for his journey. However, Dirk's wife changed her mind and did not want to go along. For that reason Dirk remained in Holland, where he served as an elder in the Seceders' Church at Krabbendam until his death.[106] How much it would also have pleased Johannes De Jonge, a baker from Goes, to have gone to America with his preacher, H. J. Budding. His wife, who knew that he would leave everything behind out of love for his preacher, threw a monkey wrench in the works and Johannes did not go to America. "My husband knew quite well that (my) yes is yes and no is no," said the forthright woman later.[107]

5

The Emigration

A. Forerunners of the Great Trek, 1790–1840

Already before the Napoleonic Wars many English, Scottish, Irish, German, and French people, as well as a number of Netherlanders, had established themselves in the United States. The Revolutionary War was of great interest and was followed closely by Dutch merchants as well as by democratic politicians. Both groups in those days supported the American rebels via St. Eustatius [an island in the former Dutch West Indies], which many called the Golden Rock. Through that island they supported the rebels commercially by supplying them with the necessary materials, financially by enabling them to consummate loans, and morally by recognizing them as independent people after having become involved in the war themselves.

All these involvements more or less influenced the immediate Dutch emigration to the young Republic. After the restoration of the House of Orange in 1787, many Patriots* saw the necessity of leaving the Northern Netherlands. Many established themselves in the Southern Netherlands and the northern part of France, whereas others chose North America as their new home.[1] Therefore, the first emigration of some importance from the Netherlands to the United States bore political overtones and was not without idealistic significance.

Among the political exiles who left in the years 1788–1790 and settled in America with their families were Francis Adrian Van der Kemp, Adam Gerard Mappa, and Henry De Clercq; all were men of some note.[2] The most interesting among them is Van der Kemp, the Baptist preacher who during the so-called Time of the Patriots, after having conducted the morning

*"Patriots" was the name of proponents in the last half of the eighteenth century in Holland who favored a reorganization of government and society in the United Netherlands. They strove for defeat of the regents' oligarchy, influence of the common people on the composition of representative bodies of government, control of these bodies, freedom of thinking in the widest sense, and a positive economic policy of the government. The American and French Revolutions contributed to many of their ideas, even of abandoning the House of Orange, if need be.

service, would don his citizen soldiers' uniform to train in the use of arms.[3] He even left his Leiden parish to head a corps of volunteers! Mappa also had been commander of a small and quickly organized army.

Those early influences still had other consequences. In the Amsterdam business world, after an initial hesitation to participate in loans for America, there was an increasing interest in the finances of America. Especially the Amsterdam financier, Pieter Stadnitski, succeeded in calling attention to American bonds. After that time big profits were made by speculation in these bonds. This led Stadnitski to draw attention to the vast land areas that were offered for sale by the Union and the several states due to their shortage of money, and which offered the opportunity of "even much bigger profits."[4]

Since the War of Independence, the United States had become *"colonies de l'Europe entière"* [colonies of all of Europe]. Due to increasing emigration, much land could be resold "for as many guilders as it was bought for nickels." After a few companies had already bought big areas of land, Stadnitski's promotional activities led to forming a land speculation consortium in September, 1792. Participants were some business firms that traded with America, such as W. and J. Willink, the Van Staphorsts, the Van Eeghens, Ten Cate and Vollenhoven, the financier P. Stadnitski, and the lawyer Rutger Jan Schimmelpenninck,[5] the future ambassador and grand pensionary, who by his great knowledge of the French and English languages had become the legal advisor of many business firms.[6] Shortly thereafter, other enormous pieces of land were purchased by the firm of Stadnitski and Son, and by Messrs. W. Willink, N. Van Staphorst, C. Van Eeghen, H. Vollenhoven, and R. J. Schimmelpenninck. Both purchases, in addition to some other private domains of the members of the "Six Houses," are still known by the public at large as those of the "Holland Land Company."

The cosmopolitan Cazenove, born in Amsterdam, who arrived in America already in March, 1790, to conduct financial business on behalf of some Netherlands bankers, officiated as general agent for the Holland Land Company. On his return to Europe in 1799 he was succeeded in the same capacity by the Italian Paul Busti.[7] [Paul] Evans told me that the Company bought up three and a half million acres in western New York State—the Genessee lands, which were mainly in the Mohawk region and the area east of Lake Erie and south of Lake Ontario. In addition, they bought half a million acres in western Pennsylvania near Meadville and a million acres in the northern part of the state.[8] Due to all these purchases, which were a safe investment considering the uncertain European situation, the Holland Land Company was regarded as the main landowner of the United States.[9]

Yet its influence on emigration from the Netherlands was not as big as could be expected. During the Napoleonic years our farmers were not too badly off. Why then move? No matter how Stadnitski pointed to the riches and variety of timber and the "many natural pastures full of clover especially in the valleys" and to the woods that "with many herbs offer an abundance of food for horses and cattle," all by themselves his words seem to have made a greater impression on the moneymen than on the Dutch farmers.[10] Aside from that, it seems that on the lands of the Holland Land Company the Dutch immigrants had to struggle with too many difficulties, even those who were at home with farming. Therefore, in 1810 the general agent advised his bosses in Amsterdam to discontinue sending Dutch colonists.[11]

This attempt that failed seemingly escaped Evans. He wrote me, "I am not sure that they actually sent any colonists to America," except for "officials" of the Company. Van Eeghen and others tried to sell part of their land to some Germans and Swiss people who were passing through the Netherlands on their way to America. "Since no success resulted from any such ventures, they soon gave them up."[12] Mainly Yankees and Welsh people colonized the possessions of the Holland Land Company.[13]

Among those who settled on the holdings of the Holland Land Company were also a few of the Dutch political exiles. A number of them even acted as agents of the Company and in this capacity they helped to found many a village. Thus they played an important role in developing American life, materially as well as in the spiritual sense. For example, Van der Kemp belonged to the pioneers of western New York State. Already for years he had wanted to settle in America, as he wrote to John Adams, American ambassador in London: It is "the object of my most ardent desires."[14] But Van der Kemp's wife disliked the idea. After he had been taken captive at Wijk by Duurstede, which made staying in the Netherlands impossible, his wife also agreed. The Van der Kemps settled among the Old Dutch families in the Hudson region at Esopus, where he bought a "country place" and applied himself to farming. At one time he made a trip from Esopus through the Mohawk region to Oneida Lake. It was then a lonely place far from civilization, but he was struck by the beauty of the lake. According to Governor De Witt Clinton, who later received the description of Van der Kemp's trip, he had the honor of making "the original invention of the Erie route."

Many Indians were still living in the Oneida region in 1788–1791 when the Van der Kemp family settled in this "howling wilderness." They did so after they had become impoverished during their apprenticeship years of farming and because for financial reason they could no longer stay in Esopus. The only settlement there was the village of Rotterdam, which consisted of a single good wooden house and twelve poorly constructed log cabins. Van der Kemp built a home four to five miles east of this settlement with a Dutch-style barn and with a wing for living quarters for the black servants, and named it Kempwijk. The Van der Kemp family settled in this lonely spot, where the nearest neighbors were miles away, and for years they lived the life of pioneers with all its privation and hardship.

Van der Kemp made the best of his situation in a remarkable way. He made himself available as assistant justice of the peace and even founded an agricultural society for western New York State. Mrs. Van der Kemp for years also adapted herself remarkably well to her new frontier life. No matter how difficult it was, "she bore it with honour to her race."[15] Nevertheless, in the long run loneliness overtook her and she became very sick. Therefore Van der Kemp made the great sacrifice in 1797. He left Kempwijk and moved a day's travel northeastward to Oldenbarneveld in Oneida County, where the Boon, Mappa, and other families lived.

Oldenbarneveld, which later became Trenton, but was then called Barneveld, was founded by [Gerrit] Boon, a former resident of Rotterdam. Boon was a member of the Beeftingh & Boon Company and came in 1791 to America to build, if possible, a maple sugar enterprise.[16] To accomplish this he bought an extensive area of land. However, the sugar undertaking proved to be a failure. From then on Boon, as well as his company, was involved only with land speculations and merged with the "Six Houses." Therefore we see him act as an "agent" of the Holland Land Company. Boon was the first settler in Oneida County in 1793. By building a blacksmith shop and sawmill, he made his creation of Oldenbarneveld of more importance. In 1798 he returned to the Netherlands. Boonville, his second creation, is still a reminder of his labors in Oneida County.[17]

The former Netherlands officer, Mappa, succeeded Boon as an agent and as such has contributed his share to America's development. Mappa also had a few difficult years behind him already before he came to Boon's settlement. He arrived in New York in December, 1789, and brought with him a typefoundry for western languages and even for eastern languages—a first for America. Due to the lack of qualified workers, he offered his type foundry for sale and moved to Oldenbarneveld a year later. It was among these families that Van der Kemp settled, and he received much support from Boon.

Van der Kemp's life thereafter has been of great importance for America but also for the Netherlands, due to his scholarly work. New York's governor DeWitt Clinton gave him an assignment to translate some forty volumes containing documents of the West India Company and this kept him occupied for years. Later these volumes were shipped to Albany. Van der Kemp also translated "*Korte beschrijving van de ontdekking en der verdere lotgevallen van Nieuw-Nederland*" ("*Brief Description About the Discovery and Further Adventures of New Netherland*") by Lambrechtsen Van Rithem. The role of the Netherlands in the formation of America was plainly brought to light through this work of Van der Kemp. Governor DeWitt Clinton was also of Dutch descent, and it was in Oldenbarneveld where for the first time he met Van der Kemp, whose knowledge he greatly respected. He wrote after that first meeting: "I have discovered the most learned man in America."[18] The governor also revived the old Dutch custom of celebrating a thanksgiving day. For the rest, Van der Kemp wrote about a great many subjects. This drew the attention of the famous Harvard University, which granted him the honorary L.L.D. degree. Van der Kemp was also a member of a number of scholarly societies in Boston, New York, and Philadelphia. Adams called him "a star of the first magnitude under a deep cloud."

However much Van der Kemp felt at home in America and considered himself to be an American, yet his thoughts constantly went to his birthplace. Nevertheless, he became a naturalized citizen in 1789 and in 1814 his son fought on the American side against the English. "Much of his thought is of Holland. . . . He seems to hear again the old music of his youth, though on muted strings, and wonders if his friends think of him in the Western woods of America." But Van der Kemp's friends did not forget him. |Cornelis| De Gijselaar and |Jean| Luzac, and especially Vreede, continually sent him letters and books. In return, the last letter of Van der Kemp was addressed to his bosom friend Pieter Vreede in Holland. It was the same with the other colonists; also Mappa. He too associated with educated Americans, but his thoughts stayed with the Netherlands. He still received the *Gazette de Leyden* |*Leyden Gazette*| and this gave many an occasion for conversation about the Old Country and the Old World in general. Indeed, not only the exiles of the Netherlands but even their neighbor, the well-known |Friedrich Wilhelm Baron| Von Steuben, former aide-de-camp of Frederik the Great, took part in these meetings of minds. The liberation of the Netherlands in 1813 was also commemorated in Oldenbarneveld. Mappa and Van der Kemp received this news with tears of joy and thankfulness.[19] In Utica—the former Fort Schuyler—Van der Kemp's oration on the liberation was even published.

In 1828 Mappa and Mrs. Van der Kemp died, and Van der Kemp followed them in death one year later. His daughter living in Oldenbarneveld remained there with her youngest brother. The oldest son who succeeded Busti as general agent for the Holland Land Company lived in Philadelphia and so did the daughter of Mappa. Miss Van der Kemp outlived both her brothers and died in 1868 at the age of 83. She was highly regarded and loved by the people of the village as "the last of the exiles, who came from Holland so long before."

The Holland Land Company had still other capable Netherlanders in its employ. In 1790 Colonel John Lincklaen came to America in the company of Gerrit Boon and became the Company's agent for the lands south of Lake Oneida. He settled in Cazenovia near Lake Cazenovia, both named after the first general agent. The village of Lincklaen lying south of Cazenovia still reminds us of his labors for the Land Company. But the family of Lincklaen also played a prominent part in American cultural life. Mrs. Helen Lincklaen Fairchild, who still lives in Cazenovia, drew attention to the labors of these notable immigrants by her publication both in New York and London of the *Journals* of John Lincklaen and her book on Francis Adrian Van der Kemp (1903). Thus she made a permanent record for future Americans.

The most peculiar character was Harmen Jan Huidekoper, agent of the Holland Land Company in western Pennsylvania. In the circles of the Unitarian Church he was honored for founding in his hometown of Meadville the Meadville School for Unitarians. As "the eager enlightened student of advanced Biblical criticism," Huidekoper obtained such influence that, so they dared to say, if he had been the only immigrant from the Netherlands to date, "it could not be said that she [the emigration] was wholly without influence on the psychology of America."[20] So influential was this typical Dutch patrician that when someone asked about the fundamentals of Unitarian beliefs, the answer for a long time was: "Nobody knows but Huidekoper and he won't tell."[21] Huidekoper died in 1854. His descendants are still living in Meadville, where they belong to "the most prominent people," and contribute, however modestly, to the cultural rapprochement between America and the Netherlands.[22]

In the beginning of the nineteenth century the number of emigrants from the Netherlands had been small but the quality, no doubt, was outstanding. Their number had also been strengthened by the immigration of persons who were banished by [Herman Willem] Daendels from the Island of Java.[23] This immigration at an end of the eighteenth and beginning of the nineteenth century has more or less visibly strengthened the Dutch tradition in the states of New York and Pennsylvania. It even perpetuated the use of the Dutch language and contributed to the promotion of American culture.

However, one must not overestimate the significance of the Holland Land Company for immigration and its appeal for America itself. Many town names and other names in western New York State, to be sure, remind one of its activities. Today there is still a Rotterdam in the Mohawk Valley (not to be confused with the village of the same name on Lake Oneida that goes today by the name of Constantia) and the important industrial town of Amsterdam. North of the Mohawk in Oneida County are town names like Holland Patent, Barneveld, and Boonville. More to the north in Lewis County one finds Port Leyden and West Leyden. South of Lake Oneida lie Cazenovia and De Ruyter in Madison County, and Lincklaen in Chenango County. To the northwest of Chenango County one is struck by the name of Zealand, located on Otiosco Lake in Onondaga County.

A second group of Dutch names are found in the more westerly section. In 1792 the intermediate lands containing 1,200,000 acres near the Lower Genessee and Lake Ontario, were bought by an English association, Pulteney and Co., for £75,000. Especially in this region many Netherlanders settled, mostly from Zeeland. To the west of these "English" areas, we again find many Dutch names. In Genessee County there are Bergen and Batavia. In Batavia the office of the agent of New York State is today converted into a museum. In Wyoming County we find Orangeville and Java village; and in Erie County the names of Holland and Willinck, both lying on the Cazenovia River. We also find in the southwesterly county of New York State, Chautauqua, a town that is a reminder of Busti, the second general agent of the Holland Land Company.[24] A Pennsylvania county also has the name of Holland. Even more important is perhaps Huidekoper's description of this area.

The residents of all these towns and areas are seldom of Dutch descent.

It was only in the 1850s that the Dutch settled there, and then sparingly. An example is Buffalo, which in 1801 was laid out by the Holland Land Company as the city of New Amsterdam, and whose typically Dutch inner city canal reminded us for years of its true origin.[25] Even before the Holland Land Company had bought this land, there were already white people in the vicinity of Buffalo, including Dutch people—[Frederick Jackson] Turner notwithstanding. they were Cornelius Winne and others who came from the Hudson area but seemingly pulled out again. Evans told me that in the first thirty years of its existence no fellow Netherlander of any account dwelled in the city. Not so today, as we shall see later; our Frisians took care of that!

At that time the Holland Land Company no longer existed. Due to troubles with revolting colonists, the Company in 1836 and the following years had been forced to sell all of its possessions. A certain [?] Van Hall looked after the interests of the Company in New York State, and in 1846 it no longer possessed a single acre. So around 1855, after all current business matters were completed, the Company ceased to exist. Thus the Holland Land Company had been of only very relative importance for the emigration of our Netherlanders. Ruth Putnam stated that it "left a history of much effort and little result," and more particularly that "little Dutch trace is left on the scene of this enterprise."[26] The interesting study of Paul Evans endorses these remarks. Still he pointed out to me that the Company "did leave a record of honest and, on the whole, broad-minded administration in a peculiarly vexing and complicated business."[27]

However interesting it may have been, the emigration from the Netherlands to America had not been extensive during the latter part of the eighteenth century and the beginning of the nineteenth century. Stadnitski, who in 1792 spoke of the "considerable number of emigrants from Europe to America," added that "from our country itself there have gone [only] a few."[28] It has also been shown that the number of emigrants had not greatly increased since the founding of the Holland Land Company. The total number of immigrants in the United States for the period 1776–1820 is estimated at 250,000. The first counting of numbers really started in 1820, the birth year of American immigration statistics. In that year the Netherlands were already listed separately, but since emigrants were not recorded individually, it is impossible to trace how many emigrants came from the northern part [Holland] or the southern part of the Netherlands [Belgium]. The concept of "immigrant" has also constantly been viewed differently, and in addition many evaded the control [the requirement to register with the government]. So these numbers are an approximation and thus far from accurate. However, they are of great importance for comparative purposes, also for Dutch emigration, because they illustrate the interesting fact that the highpoints of emigration to America usually conincide for all western European nations.

The economic character of this emigration is strongly evident when one notes that the largest numbers occurred during and immediately after American boom periods, while the smallest number—"the ebb of immigration"—coincided with the crisis periods or "panic years." The great appeal of the land of the dollar comes strongly to the fore, although in varying degrees. It was all the stronger as conditions in one's own country became poorer. In a reverse manner the repulsion by one's own country was felt more strongly in proportion to the increased attraction by America.

These things come to light in these first years of statistics. From 1820 to 1834 the numbers of Dutch emigrants to America were as follows:

Year	No.	Year	No.	Year	No.
1820	49	1825	37	1830	22
1821	56	1826	176	1831	175
1822	51	1827	245	1832	205
1823	19	1828	263	1833	39
1824	40	1829	169	1834	87

The flood of 1825 and other disasters may explain the sudden increase in 1826 and following years. The Belgian uprising explains the decrease in 1830.

In America's first boom period in 1835, 1836, and 1837, the numbers strongly increased. Dutch emigration stood then at 124, 301, and 312 respectively—the first peak! It is characteristic for this emigration that the migrations to America from other West European nations reached their peaks simultaneously. The small size of Dutch emigration stands out, nevertheless, when compared to figures from other nations:

Year	Netherlands	France	Germany	Ireland and Great Britain
1837	312	5,074	23,740	79,340
1838	27	3,675	11,683	38,914

However, in 1837 a panic broke out in America and then one sees the number of immigrants quickly decline.

The cited figures of the Dutch emigration in the 1830s show an increase, though very modest. The slowly awakening urge for more freedom in economic, political, and religious areas, as described in chapter four, brought many to the thought of emigrating to America, and it became a reality for many. That it was specifically Groningen and Zeeland farmers whose emigration was the first to attract attention was closely connected with the critical farmers' situation already described. It was also due to the interesting letters from the seemingly bright and very energetic Groninger K. Jz. [Klaas Janszoon] Beukma, a "former farmer on the Castor farm in the parish of Zuurdijk in the municipality of Leens, who moved to the United States of North America in the year 1835." These Groningers and Zeelanders were followed, if not immediately, then later, by many of their landsmen. They established important Dutch settlements where hundreds of others settled subsequently and where the Dutch language is often still used in the churches.

Among the Groningers, Beukma was the most interesting character. He belonged to that set of well-prepared, liberal, and freedom-loving farmers who were plentiful in the province of Groningen and especially also in the province of Friesland. Time and again we shall meet them among the immigrants, which is not altogether by chance! No wonder that during the bad agricultural years experienced in West Europe, Beukma's thoughts went to the rapidly rising America. His wife's death and his concern over the future of his four children also contributed to these emigration thoughts. The departure to Missouri of the well-known Ost Frisian geographer [Fridrich] Arends, the describer, among other things, of the North Sea Coasts, must also have put weight on the balance.

Beukma prepared for his trip by studying the much-read work of the Duke of Saxon-Weimar, *Reise durch Nord-Amerika in 1825 und 1826* [*Trip Through North America in 1825 and 1826*], which was translated into Dutch, and also the German booklet of Gerke, *Amerikanischen Rathgeber* [*American Advisor*].[29] Moreover, he obtained recommendations for fellow countrymen in New York. However, Beukma had no knowledge of the Holland Land Company.[30] Seemingly the Company was still following the advice given by Busti in 1810.

The Beukmas left Rotterdam on an American ship on May 20, 1835, and they arrived on July 13 in New York, where, thanks to the letters of introduction, they received a hearty welcome and much support from the previously settled Netherlanders. It seems that many enterprising Dutch had settled in New York City, trusting the growing pace of this city. Beukma observed that the rate of construction was unusually fast and they even demolished substantial buildings to make room for shops. Our Groninger already saw and felt it then and wrote in one of his letters: "Everything looks as if the center of the world's commerce shall be established here."[31]

However, being a true son of the soil, he did not want to stay in the big city, but was driven to the West, as were so many others. This was in spite of the advice against it by the Dutch Consul, since great sacrifices were required in the West. However, Beukma did not know in which part of the West he would make his new home. Many recommended Michigan; others, Illinois. In Buffalo he would make up his mind. The Holland Land Company had expanded its possessions by purchasing Grand Island's 17,800 acres near Niagara Falls, but Beukma concluded that the Company asked too much for their land. Therefore, he left Buffalo to go to Cincinnati by way of Cleveland. He then intended to move to the farthest part of the West, but by necessity gave it up. "This step would possibly be too strange and thus too hard to make us a homestead in the wilderness in an area with no roads and therefore thinly populated."

In Cincinnati Beukma came at last to a decision and after various investigations, discussions, study of maps, etc., he decided to try to buy some land near Lafayette in the state of Indiana in the area of the Wabash River, a tributary of the larger Ohio River that had great potential for future shipping traffic. At Cincinnati Beukma bought a couple of covered wagons with four horses and the courageous fellow set out with his family on the dangerous trip through the thinly populated areas and almost trackless country, guided only by the mere knowledge of his maps. It is touching to read the sober description of this trip and the difficulties that he encountered. One of the horses refused to obey, at which one wagon was destroyed; rivers had to be forded when bridges were lacking; after that they had to negotiate hills. He tackled it all calmly. One then understands why a man like Beukma who had so much pioneer spirit no longer felt at home in the Netherlands of his time.

At last the Beukmas came near Lafayette, moved into a loghouse and from there went in search of suitable land. Beukma bought a piece of land six miles "above" Lafayette on the Wabash River, near the future diggings of the Wabash Canal, after having enquired about cost, soil, and future opportunities for shipping traffic. He paid $955 for 181 acres, partly woods and partly wet prairie, both so-called bottom or low-lying land and upland lying on the bluffs. Beukma built his home and barns on the higher-lying land, which was sandy and thus very suitable for raising corn, wheat, and buckwheat. The low land, likewise of choice sand and clay that reminded Beukma of the Oldambster polder soil, was usable both as forest and farm land, but only after the heavy work of clearing. "Yet what sacrifice can be or may be too heavy," he wrote, "for one to provide an honest and independent living for himself and his own?"

Beukma did not live there for long. After a few years, together with his fellow emigrant Van K(ingma?) he bought land closer to town, two and a half miles north of Lafayette—seventeen acres of choice prairie land at $30 per acre—in order to start a nursery and market garden. He did all this for the benefit of his children, so that they could become better acquainted with Americans. Beukma's wish for them was "to ,initiate them through closer companionship and contact to this worthy nation."[32] For the time being, the farm was rented out and later Beukma's oldest son came to live there, while the youngest son worked in the market garden business with his father. The second son became a carpenter in Lafayette.[33]

With wishes fulfilled concerning his children, Beukma's pioneer spirit was not yet satisfied. His thoughts as a man from the flat Groningerland were constantly on the "grand prairy" [sic], the great treeless open spaces, in other words, the real prairie, which in his day most Americans considered unfit for living or farming. "Only with difficulty can they conceive of it as a basis for life," observed Beukma.[34] A few times he traveled to these areas more to the north and to the west of Lafayette that were the possessions of a Dutch American named Rensselaer. The prairie landscape made a deep impression on Beukma. He had visions of establishing a Netherlands' colony there. This stayed with him "as a favorite idea, however much I know that this likely will never materialize, to buy a piece of choice land on the nearby grand-prairy [sic], and settle it with a few of you or even with a few other vigorous Groninger families. We would settle there first as a community, and then divide it amongst ourselves after it has been brought under cultivation."

In the province of Groningen conditions had somewhat improved, at least for the farmers, since the levying of import duties on foreign wheat. Therefore, only a few families followed Beukma, including a certain Van der Kraak with his family, the three Muller brothers, two of whom settled in northern Indiana at the little St. Joseph River, but the third one wanted to return. The last family named [T. J.] Aapkens, who came from Landschapspolder, originally settled in northwestern Ohio near Defiance on the Maumee River, also on the Wabash Canal route. They seemed to have moved partly to Lafayette later on. Here one of the sons started a brick works and married Beukma's only daughter.[35]

Beukma's wish to settle a Holland colony on the prairie has not been fulfilled. However, his homesteading near Lafayette later caused many a Netherlander to go to this city. The previously mentioned families who had come to America in 1847 from the "*grietenijen*"* [municipalities] of Het Bilt and Barradeel in Friesland, had a letter of recommendation with them for the Beukmas. A few of them, K. J. De Vree, Oolberg, and J. Jonk got a job enroute in Albany; others such as G. R. Wassenaar, A. T. Halma, and W. S. Osinga got jobs enroute at Toledo. The rest traveled to Lafayette where Beukma's carpenter son provided living quarters for them. Three of them, J. Bolman, J. De Jong, and Jelle De Bildt went to work for the brickmaker Aapkens for $12 per month. H. G. Holwerda became a drayman [brewer's hand]. W. J. Jonk earned as much as $20 per month and boarded at J. W. De Jong and his wife S. S. De Bildt, his travel companions, while S. T. Krap rented eight acres of land next to that of Beukma. For the rest, the soil near Lafayette was a disappointment. This place was better fit for craftsmen than for farmers.

The Netherlands element was thus reinforced here with these Frisian families, eighteen persons in all. Later on because of their letters, many more were brought to this city. One of them wrote: "Because of the language barrier we would be pleased to have a Holland preacher and medical doctor here."[36] Their wishes materialized. At the time of the arrival of the Beukmas, Lafayette counted only two thousand inhabitants. At the present time, through the expansion of industry and business, it has more than twenty thousand souls and also a Christian Reformed and a Reformed congregation. The first was organized in 1865 and permanently founded in 1869, and the second in 1888. In 1927 the Christian Reformed Church counted 147 families (648 souls), and the Reformed Church had 53 families.[37]

Many immigrants, however, already had found work enroute to Lafayette,

*A *grietenij* prior to 1851 was the district in Friesland of a *grietman*, a civil servant with judicial and administrative power.

which led to permanent settlements. This especially explains the presence of a number of Netherlanders in Indianapolis. Here also a Reformed congregation was organized that today counts twenty-five families. Sizable Dutch settlements in the factory cities of Cleveland and Cincinnati owe their existence to the fact that many who were enroute to the states around Lake Michigan and to Iowa passed through these big cities and found work.

In the 1830s Zeelanders, next to the Groningers, comprised most of the emigrants. Beukma informs us in one of his letters, dated September 14, 1836, that some twelve Zeeland farm families boarded a vessel in New York to travel to the vicinity of Buffalo.[38] A certain Zeelander, |Jan| Cappon, from the island of Walcheren, settled that same year in Pultneyville, Wayne County, east of Rochester in the state of New York in the territory of the aforementioned Pulteney and Co. association.[39] In 1840 a Zeeland family, De Kruif, lived in this same town. Since then numerous Zeelanders settled in Pultneyville or vicinity. For example, in 1842 the Daan family came from Westkapelle; they later moved to Sheboygan County in Wisconsin where the village of Oostburg was founded.[40] In 1843 the three Eernisse brothers from Kadzand, Zeeuws-Vlaanderen, tried to find a living west of Pultneyville in the more important town of Rochester. Their parents and youngest brother also came to this city in the following year.[41]

Since then many important settlements came into being there. Moreover, the Erie Route, the main road leading to the West, led through these regions. This was followed in those days by an increasing stream of immigrants. The industry in the cities and the orchards in the country made many Netherlanders, especially Zeelanders, but later also Frisians, decide to settle among their fellow countrymen and preferably home province precursors.

B. The Great Trek

1. The Psychological Moment

With these Zeelanders we have now come to the 1840s, which was a period when the western European situation deteriorated and the growth of the United States increased. These developments strongly spurred migration in general and particularly to America.

Year	Netherlands	Germany	France	Great Britain and Ireland
1840	57	29,704	7,419	42,726
1841	214	15,291	5,006	53,960
1842	330	20,370	4,504	73,347
1843	330	14,441	3,346	28,100
1844	184	20,731	3,155	47,843
1845	791	34,355	7,663	64,031
1846	979	57,561	10,583	73,932
1847	2,631	74,281	20,040	128,838

The little people such as farmhands, artisans, and small farmers were, as everywhere else, suffering the most. Scarcity of work, low wages, and increasing food prices gave very little hope for the future. They found themselves faced with the poorhouse, welfare, handouts from the deaconate of the church, and scornful epithets like *"gasthuisbiggen"* |charity pigs|!

Already then some realized that charity alone could not produce lasting solutions. Here, as in so many other areas of life of those days, preachers tried to give leadership. Their profession brought them closer to the needs of the people than anyone else. Perhaps they saw and understood better the change occurring in the thoughts of these people, and perceived sooner the increasing dissatisfaction. Already plans were made in 1839 by such ministers of the Gospel as |Johannes H.| Betting at Beets |Beesd|, |Arend| Van den Brandhof at Elst near Amerongen, and |Dirk| Copijn at Wilnis, who detected the slumbering energy among their people and hoped to provide a broader field of activity for it through emigration.[42]

That these preachers' thoughts went out to our colonies is understandable. They even succeeded in obtaining cooperation from the government. On January 25, 1843, there appeared a Royal Decree by which the Reverend Betting with two farmers was appointed to prepare the colonization, by Dutch farmers, of Surinam, which overseas territory of the empire was still highly valued. Betting became disappointed when he learned about the surroundings in Surinam, and was recalled, but colonization on the lower Saramacca River continued. Four ships carried the emigrants to their new homes. They were so badly furnished, lacked so much in everything, and the heat was so unbearable that the whole emigration attempt failed. Of the 384 emigrants, 189 succumbed and only eleven remained in good health. Some of the survivors went back to the Netherlands but the rest stayed, strengthened by the words of the courageous Reverend Copijn who shared in their sufferings. He crawled in their hovels to comfort the sick and close the eyes of the dying. This man was full of self-sacrifice and had the patience of Job.[43] In 1853 the "remainders" moved to the vicinity of Paramaribo, where their descendants the other day commemorated the seventy-fifth anniversary of this dreadful colonization. In that same year of the Saramacca colonization, the year 1845, a very hard winter set in, and conditions in the Netherlands and western Europe became generally more desperate than ever before.

Perhaps there has never been experienced a greater misery than in 1845, the year the potato disease broke out. This resulted in famine in many places, because the potato had become more and more the staple diet for many people. It is the Frisian |Worp| Van Peyma who described the potato disease in one of his letters: "The disease is present here on many farms. It is as bad here as anywhere else on various soils and in different varieties of potatoes. At first the leaves wilt, or rather get small dark spots on them, after which they more or less shrivel together, lose their juice, and before long dry up altogether. I suspect up to now that this disease is transmitted by the seed of a variety of mold that is dusted far and wide over the leaves. This parasitic growth draws an amazing amount of moisture, hence the infected leaves soon wither. The many rainy days have favored the growth of the fungus so much that they develop seed to spread to the neighboring soil and fields and thus contaminate and rot the foliage of the plants."[44]

The food shortage caused by the disease was so great that even the middle class had to feed itself with food usually only fed to animals, broad beans and old peas. "Help us or we starve!" was the cry of distress, and the pleading appeal for public charity made in many municipalities.[45] Facing this prospect, many came to the conclusion to leave a country where deeper-lying causes had already been present for years. So the potato disease—it may sound somewhat matter of fact—was the reason that no longer dozens, but hundreds, and elsewhere thousands, left their fatherland. Especially in 1846 and 1847, when the distress became sharper because the existing supplies further dwindled, many moved to America. The earlier emigrants wrote letters telling how wonderful America was, the land of promise, where "the most flavorful dishes and the most delicious white bread" smiled upon the starving Europeans! Thus, in these years, emigration grew to the proportions of an exodus! Great Britain, Ireland, and also Germany experienced an enormous departure. Misery, on the one hand, and the hopeful letters from America on the other, created unrest and excitement which gripped numberless people and caused whole villages to move.

Many had an overwhelmingly mystical feeling; they felt like they *had* to leave. Europe had reached a turning point; it was near sinking, as at one time Africa and Asia had submerged into the night, and America was to become the last ruler of the world. Hence came this uncontrollable drive to the West. As Arends said: "It is an impulse flowing from the innermost recess of the heart. Providence itself seems to summon us to that. It engenders in us an obscure feeling that drives us to leave the homes of our fathers."[46]

It was perhaps from Germany that this exodus movement, containing economic but also mystical elements, crossed our borders.[47] At least this movement was first observed in the outlying part of the province of Gelderland, the Achterhoek, in the vicinity of Eibergen, Neede, Winterswijk, and Dinxperloo, the areas nearest the German border. In 1836 Beukma met in Buffalo a Gelderland merchant family that had already lived in America for one year.[48] Around 1842 several families from the neighborhood of Eibergen had emigrated to the United States.[49] In 1844, 45 families emigrated not only from Gelderland but also from the provinces of Zeeland and Noord-Brabant, while a year later 181 families, numbering 680 souls, crossed the ocean from Gelderland alone.[50]

The trek continually grew stronger. In an incidental way the attention of the Reverends A. Brummelkamp and A. C. Van Raalte had been drawn to this phenomenon. They remarked: "From village to village and from city to city it begins to penetrate the land of our fathers." It happened as follows:

On a certain day the dissenting preacher Brummelkamp was visited in Arnhem by A. Hartgerink. He was a simple brother from the province, "not a farmer but every inch a Geldersman, who introduced himself as the schoolmaster of Neede, a small village behind Zutphen."[51] The conversation went as follows:

"Whereabouts are you going for the trip?"

"To North America."

"To America?" and with a tone of amazement he added with absolute sincerity: "And what are you going to do there?"

Thereupon the teacher let Brummelkamp read letters received from former emigrants. "I read, was amazed, and, full of emotion; I sent for Van Raalte. We both knew that the writers of these letters had been poor as church mice; but these lines spoke of an abundance such as was no longer imaginable in the Fatherland. We were speechless. A light dawned on us in the darkness of the diaconate's welfare program. God opened our eyes and we saw that a great deal of the inconvenience in which we found ourselves was caused by the builders of the Babel tower. Just as these tower builders, we were crowding each other out here. . . . When a farmyard was for rent or came up for sale, there were twenty or forty people speculating on it. If a house had to be built, twenty carpenters wanted the work; otherwise they would be without work. Now we saw that on God's earth there was plenty of room; one only had to move over a bit!"

In this way the leaders of the Dissenters "discovered" America. A light descended upon them. By emigrating to America their fellow believers too could avert poverty and increasing unemployment. There was a threatening danger, however. Most of these very simple immigrants might become lonely and scattered among the Americans whose language they did not understand, and they and their children might fall prey to degeneration of religion and morals. To prevent this the clerics resolved to support the endeavor and to offer themselves as counselors for those who would want advice and through this means to give leadership. In consultation with others, among whom was [Johan Adam] Wormser, a friend of Brummelkamp, they developed various plans to regulate the emigration and amply discussed them. However, the distress was so extreme that action had to be taken immediately.

At Arnhem the small congregation held meeting upon meeting to discuss the all-important question: To America or not? And both preachers, Van Raalte and Brummelkamp, immediately made haste to attend these meetings to be of service for advice and leadership. After discussion here, new foundations were laid. In short, "an agreement was designed and drawn up that, although it did not state it specifically, really had only one aim, to aid the impoverished brothers and sisters in the Lord to earn a living in America."[52] This document, entitled "*Grondslagen der Vereeniging van Christenen voor de Hollandsche Volksverhuizing naar de Vereenigde Staten in N.-America*" [*Foundations of the Society of Christians for the Emigration of Hollanders to the United States of*

North America], became historically significant for the colonization of the states of Michigan and Wisconsin. To this day, it determines its social-geographical and primarily its religious character. Of the total of sixteen articles, it is especially Article 7 that reflects the character of this settlement and the resultant progress of the colonization: "The first mission is to create a Colony that is Christian. Therefore, it is recommended to the Committee taking care of the acceptance, help, and sending of emigrants, to find such 'salting' elements for the colony as are necessary to insure a Christian majority. Therefore, it will not accept any persons for colonization other than those who will be expected to submit to the Lord's Word, so that in that way not only a Christian consistory but also a Christian government will be present in order to uphold the law of God which is the foundation of every state."

As Article 7 points to the religious character, so Article 8 stipulates that the Christians who were threatened the most by social circumstances would be considered first for transportation. "People who are members of or are included in the Colony, and who cannot contribute anything to their passage or first settling costs, etc., will remain altogether free citizens, and will not be discriminated against in comparison to the other inhabitants. In order to cover the disbursement made in their favor, one-fifth of all income or profits of their lands, no matter what they will be called, will be set aside until all advanced money with its interest (5 percent) shall have been paid off. Only after this will they have full ownership privileges of any real estate." Later we shall see how this article made possible the passage of the poorest immigrants and at the same time how it limited the choice of land to be purchased.

The Dutch character of the colony-to-be appeared from Article 9: "In order that not every immigrant may be burdened by the difficulties and the dangers and expense of land buying, and that the dispersion of colonists and the anticipated intrusion of strangers may be prevented, the buying of land shall take place by and in the name of the Association. The citizens of the colony will have an opportunity to buy these lands via contract of transfer signed by the double Committee in the name of the Association and for the same amount, plus expenses as paid by the Committee." This was declared at the home of Reverend Brummelkamp on April 15, 1846, at a meeting of Dissenters. The following month of May, the Association helped two very needy families go to America—the families of Derk Arnoud, cabinetmaker, and Willem Kwinkelenberg, painter, who were joined by a third family, also named Arnoud.

Eight days later, in the first part of June, 1846, R. Sleyster, deacon of the Velp congregation and the Brusse brothers from Varseveld, departed as representatives to find a good opportunity to buy land in the interior of America. Numerous parishioners with wives and children sailed the ocean with them. In the meantime Brummelkamp and Van Raalte had also asked advice from other friends among the Dissenters and the Hervormde Kerk.

The Reverend H. P. Scholte considered the emigration to America not yet to be inevitable, although in general according to the Lord's Word it was not prohibited—since a Christian too might, due to temporal circumstances, leave the country of his birth.[53] But he admitted at the same time "that if in many respects there is no change, then the present situation will grow so much worse that for a Christian it will be impossible to find employment in any social position without harming his conscience." However, our Hervormde [Reformed] friends who were men of the Réveil would have very little to do with the emigration to America. At the meetings held in Amsterdam, they propagated the idea of colonization in the Netherlands' colonies. For example, the well-known preacher [Otto G.] Heldring, who originally wanted to promote emigration to Port Natal in South Africa, was influenced by [J. P.] Freyss, a businessman. Subsequently Heldring became a warm advocate of colonization of the highlands in Java or one of the sparsely populated islands.[54] Although Scholte had already been thinking of moving to America, Heldring persuaded him to go to the minister of colonies for an audience to ask for permission to settle at Ceram or at Ubi, "especially at Ceram, which had on its west side a high and beautiful plateau that in every respect fulfilled Scholte's requirements." However, when Scholte demanded freedom and independence in religion and education the request was refused.[55]

Brummelkamp and Van Raalte also reflected on all these ideas. In an interesting pamphlet, "*Landverhuizing, of waarom bevorderen wij de volksverhuizing naar Noord-Amerika en niet naar Java?*" ["Emigration, or Why We Promote the Migration to North America and Not to Java?"], they gave public account of the decision to lead the emigration stream to America. "It is not necessary at this time to speak about the West," considering the past failure of the Saramacca colonization. The East was closed for Christians and in general also for Netherlanders. Moreover, the Governor-General could prohibit both preaching and religious education. Therefore, the Dissenters did not go to the colonies, no matter how glorious it might have been to labor in Java, also among the heathen, and to found there a central point from which to spread the Gospel. In that case "they would have forgotten all about America!" After all, and this also pertained to South Africa, who would pay for the expensive passage, point out the farmland, and provide work?[56]

In addition, the question remained to what extent both preachers could have succeeded in redirecting the stream of emigrants somewhere else, now that it was headed more and more exclusively to North America. Expectations ran high because numerous letters had already been received about this fairyland. There were even Netherlanders who imagined no longer having to work there![57] The distributed pamphlet, which in 1846 ran through four editions, made a deep impression, at least in the circles of the Dissenters and the Réveil. These booklets were of great influence in the resulting emigration out of the Netherlands and even out of neighboring border areas.

In addition to political and mystical motives, these emigrants had an overwhelming economic motive. This was also true of the Dissenters. H. P. Scholte acknowledged this when he said: "The messages from North America of former acquaintances who are settled there and according to the standards of the world are enjoying some prosperity, are to be considered mostly as the first cause that generated the desire also of Christians.[58]

This economic factor, generally speaking, remained decisive. Brummelkamp and Van Raalte in the above-named pamphlet made it clear that they would support emigration: "In the fullness of the most vivid conviction that this is the way, the only way, to alleviate their dire needs and the needs of many thousands who shall follow and whose needs increase daily as long as they stay here. They are faced every winter by a more fearful future and their hearts are tormented by the somber thought of having to rely in the last resort on the altogether sober and humiliating support of parochial welfare!" Later they even publicly accused the writer of having put the material aspect in the foreground. On this Brummelkamp observed: "We have indicated the material aspect as the cause why many *must* move, but we have also pressed the point that this is to be achieved in a religious and God-glorifying manner."[59]

But the emigration resulting from this pamphlet carried still another characteristic, a religious one. Although people were already permitted to practice their religion provided they made a request for "freedom," those who refused to make this request were still fined. Even though this seldom happened, it occurred the last time in 1846, which is why it was mentioned in the pamphlet: "Also even today citizens are dragged to court and fined because they lent their home without the government's permission for religious purposes or preaching to more than twenty persons." The accompanying note again expressed the flare-up of dissatisfaction and sense of independence. These symptoms were found throughout the whole of western Europe and expressed a spirit: "We shall continue to preach in barns and houses and in unrecognized congregations."

It may be correct that a great many Dissenters, especially the more "precise," conservative elements among them, had little inclination for Christian education and were satisfied with the non-religious public school.[60] "The parents must provide knowledge of religion by sending their children to catechism." Others, the followers of Brummelkamp and Van Raalte, as reflected in the pamphlet, strongly felt the grievance that the local government bodies dodged in any way possible the issue of giving permission to establish Christian schools, a position "to which the law compels them." "In this dodging they were supported by the higher authorities." It is in the light of these circumstances that both writers gave emigration a higher place. People were striving not only for material gain but also for spiritual deliverance. For many the ideal became that of freedom of religion and of education. Thus, the grievances were many.

Meanwhile among the wealthy there prevailed "pride and luxury that spares neither extravagance nor knows any bounds." The rich were greedy while the misery of the poor increased daily. The consequences were bound to come. "The Netherlands face their bleakest future. Its remaining survivors, sons and daughters, shall be banished, thus says the Lord. . . . Mindful of these words we are ripe to leave the House of Orange and the Netherlands. . . . Ruler and Nation, great and small, we sincerely are calling upon all of you to awaken out of the sleep of carelessness and indifference. Also many people of the Dissenters, who had no intention of leaving you, are waking up! They shall not request any longer the freedom of preaching the gospel and of establishing Christian schools. We pray that you may return to the God of your fathers and serve Him, . . . so that the heat of the wrath of God be turned away." This impressive writing struck a responsive chord especially among the religious followers. Many who had been wavering were now convinced that there was only one way out: To America!

This was understandable, because the distress was high among the Dissenters. They already belonged to a materially disadvantaged part of the population, and their burdens were made still heavier by the payment of many fines in the days of persecution. In the province of Friesland alone, *fl.* 16,860 |$6,672| was collected in fines up to February 1837, and in Zuid Holland and Lower Gelderland fines already totaled *fl.*11,323 |$4,530|![61]

Legal persecutions and fines slowly abated, but the worse social persecutions remained. For a long time, even in the 1850s, the Dissenters were shunned by the village folk and townspeople and even before that they were called abusive names such as *Cocksianen, Knikkers, en Fijnen** and employers took away all available employment and ruined them in business, as happened to the shoemaker |Jakob| Noordewier and many others.[62] Not everybody knew, as did the father of the Honorable |Cornelis| Van Loo, how to regain the public's sympathy and thereby the customers.[63] After that, crowds of emigrants converged upon harbor cities, especially Rotterdam. Lindo, the writer, reported: "We saw in their ranks grey-headed men, youths, delicate children and robust men, old and young women, and whole households."[64]

They were warned, and their fellow church member Van der Meulen, the apostle of the province of Zeeland, urged them in a stimulating writing: "We pray that the Lord may spare His children not to leave the land of their birth because of worldly-mindedness and go to foreign lands to find a roomier existence."[65] In the periodical of the men of the Réveil, they were accused of going to America not under the pressure of God and not as they claimed to serve God in private, but actually "to work and to make money, as much money as possible." They were accused of being weak, ignorant people who "let themselves be carried away by the glitter of gold."[66]

But all these warnings and reproofs were of no avail. On the contrary, the

---

*The word *Cocksianen* refers to followers of Hendrik De Cock. The word *Knikkers* refers to *kale knikker*, meaning bald pate; it has the same meaning as *Geuzen* or Beggars, the nickname for Dutch Protestants who rebelled against the Spanish in the 16th century. The word *Fijnen* means pious-ones or ultra-orthodox.

stream became continually stronger. Even if there were among the Dissenters those who were aggravated by the prophesy described in the pamphlet, that God would and in fact already had abandoned the Netherlands, in the simple mind of the common people, already so prone to all that had a semblance of mysticism, the conviction grew that Church and State were in the process of collapsing and that the Providence of God opened a way of escape.[67]

Many up to now might have been driven by the conscious striving for improvement of their lot, but others were more mystically minded and acted in "a fever of obscure excitement" driven by "a restless seeking for something new." This had already been observed earlier in Germany.[68] But now emigration for the Dissenters had acquired a new significance, a religious significance: It is God's will! Van Raalte himself, who had recovered from a massive typhoid attack, had so far not thought of leaving the Netherlands any more than did Brummelkamp.[69] But now they came to the conclusion that the emigrants, whom they themselves also had spurred on, should not be left to their fate in that big and foreign country. Van Raalte also thought about the future of his own boys. "Look at the children," he said to his spouse, "we must go to America!" And with that he convinced his wife. On September 24, 1846, he left Arnhem and the following October 2, with a company of emigrants, he boarded *The Southerner* bound for New York.

His departure caused many others to take the weighty step, among whom were some preachers. Scholte who had already made up his mind before, departed in 1847, as did Van der Meulen, who was originally against emigration and called it "too worldly."[70] He became convinced "that God's judgments were hanging over the head of this country." He followed a great many Zeelanders, at their request, to serve as their pastor in the New World. In Friesland under the leadership of Reverend |Marten| Ypma and in the province of Overijsel under Reverend |Seine| Bolks, people also made ready to leave the fatherland.

Not only the less fortunate but also many prosperous believers listened to the urgings of their hearts and sold their possessions to raise money for the trip to America. Among the Gelderland and Overijsel immigrants on the ill-fated ship that sank in Lake Michigan were many who belonged to the better class in the Netherlands; some were definitely well-to-do. The rescued Geerling family from Apeldoorn and a few others lost all their money, which was appraised at approximately $50,000.[71] More than seventy well-to-do families, mainly from the province of Zuid Holland, joined the ranks of Reverend Scholte and also agreed to finance the passage of many less fortunate families.[72] Among the Zeeland emigrants there also were moneyed families such as |Jan| Wabeke, |Jan| Smallegange, and especially Jannes Van de Luyster. The latter sold his farmstead in the vicinity of Borsele for *fl.* 60,000 |$24,000| and on his own account took seventy-seven persons overseas to America; most were the less fortunate and some had nothing to their name.[73]

What went on in the mind of these rich men is evident from the diary left behind by Van de Luyster.[74]

> In the affairs of America, the Lord gave me an insight into His judgments that already pressed and still threatened, and were well defined by Paul's words to the Jews: "Whereas you have rejected the Gospel, we turned to the heathen, which was affirmed immediately, so that the Lord withheld His blessings and Spirit from the Jews. The heathen accepted the Word and thus the downfall of the Jews was the salvation of the heathen." (Acts 13:46–48). This also is the case of the Netherlands. In Europe where the Gospel shone for so many centuries but has been rejected by the masses, which resulted in a careless and godless life, there is still a small remnant, the elect, who remain true to the word of God. Thus was my heart turned the other way and also the heart of my wife who also found favor in the eyes of the Lord for all eternity and also the hearts of our four children who are still at home. My heart was freed from everything to accept deliverance and to take the way of the Lord who has opened it for us to leave everything and proceed to North America."

Hundreds felt and thought the same way as Van de Luyster and left. The latest example was [Aart] Kool, father of the American politician and historical writer, who even gave up his father's inheritance. In vain was he promised his uncle's rich inheritance if he remained in Holland. In vain his mother up to the last moment appealed to him to stay.[75] Not by accident did the poet Da Costa reflect in the same year of 1847 in his poem "*Wachter, wat is er van den Nacht?*" ["Watchman, What of the Night?"] what happened in the adventurous minds of part of his fellow believers:

> For eighty years, our century has been seeing at the western beaches
> with an eye, desirous of salvation and outstretched hands,
> another glitter of glory, another star of hope
> for old and drudging and overflowing Europe! . . .
>
> Thither! from where for the first time that fresh sound of "Free"
> thundered throughout Europe: Thither! for those in need of air and life
> for those who want to rove beyond substance and society,
>   . . . who want labor
> whether for a bite of bread which only stills hunger,
> or for abundance and treasure.*

Van Raalte recalled twenty-five years later at the silver anniversary of the Holland colony in Michigan that the idea of emigration in those days moved as a breath of God throughout the whole country.[76]

*On zeeeuw, sints tachtig jaar, ziet aan die Westerstranden
met heilverlangend oog, met uitgebreide handen,
een andren glans van roem, een andre ster van hoop
voor 't oude en afgetobde en overvolle Euroop! . . .*

*Daarheen! van waar het eerst die versche klank van "Vrij"
Euroop doordaverde. Daarheen! wie lucht en leven
behoeft, wie boven stof en maatschappij wil zweven, . . .
wie arbeid wil,
't zij voor een bete broods die slechts den honger still',
hetzij om overvloed en schat.*

It is necessary to recognize this religious spirit. Although material considerations may have led most people to emigrate, and religious factors played
a role only later on, yet religion certainly gave a definite and peculiar
character to this emigration. It is because of religious considerations that
many left their fatherland in groups rather than individually. This was also
because preachers especially took the lead and also priests, as we shall see
later. These same ideas ensured that emigration did not lead to dispersal of
the Netherlanders once they had reached the New World. Rather, it led to
colonization, to the birth of the later flourishing Dutch settlements in the
United States. And religion also explains the great will power with which
many colonists knew how to combat the many and appalling difficulties. It
surely is not by accident that precisely those Dutch colonies in the United
States came to great prosperity where, next to material motives, the prime
mover had been religious motives. Still today these settlements are characterized by their religious quality. Finally, their cultural value for the United
States still lies primarily in their godly devotion.

2. Whither?

Already we have seen how the involvement of preachers gave some
leadership to the emigration movement. To America! was the slogan for all,
but still the question remained, to what part of the United States? For an
answer to this question they decided not only to send the above-named
representatives, |Roelof| Sleyster and |Jan| Brusse, for investigation, but
they tried also to get in touch with American fellow believers. Therefore
Brummelkamp and Van Raalte wrote a letter, dated May 25, 1846, "To the
Believers in the United States of North America," in which they sketched
who they were and how their congregations came into being under persecutions at home and how they now labored under a heavy yoke. They described the tragic economic situation and explained that these material
circumstances, plus the will of God that everyone should work, had made
them look for another area. "Our wish is that there is a place for our people
in the interior of America so that they may find temporal sustenance by
farming and to rescue their generation from the distress of a sinking society." At the same time the writers expressed the wish that their people
should come to live in villages so that their children could take advantage
of Christian education. They would also like to spread the word of God
among the pagans. This remarkable letter ended with an elaborate appeal
for assistance.[77]

Sleyster took this letter along and handed it to |Hendrik| Hengerveld,
one of his travel companions, who finally handed the letter to Reverend
I. N. Wyckoff, preacher in Albany, the state capital of New York. The letter
could probably not have fallen in better hands. Wyckoff, as his name indicates, was an American of Old-Netherlandic descent and besides he be-

longed to the already well-known Dutch Reformed Church of America, as did so many of his fellow countrymen.

Now it is true that the Dutch language was no longer in use in this denomination, but in a remarkable way, as one will remember, it was just at this time that there was an increasing interest in the history of the denomination and the general history of New York State.[78] No wonder that this letter was immediately translated into English by Wyckoff and published in the *Christian Intelligencer*, the denominational weekly, dated October 15, 1846. This letter made a deep impression on many Americans, the more so because it not only concerned fellow Dutch citizens but especially persecuted fellow Protestants.[79]

In a cordial reply to Van Raalte, Wyckoff suggested sending two or three competent men in order to select, with the assistance of some American brothers, a suitable colonization area in one of the western states, and in addition he promised all the necessary help to the oppressed brothers. For this purpose Wyckoff in Albany formed "The Protestant Evangelical Holland Immigration Society,"and soon a similar organization was also formed in New York City. Thus relationships began that were of immediate, temporary usefulness, due to the great amount of aid they brought to the immigrants, aid that "indeed put to shame, that is to say, put Holland to shame."[80] They also became of permanent value, since they resulted in a great cooperation, even association in church matters. These established American-Dutch ties have certainly favored the process of assimilation, the adaptation of the Dutch elements to American society. These relationships also gave an easier solution to the question in the minds of many immigrants: "Where to settle in the United States?" This was certainly the case for Van Raalte in his search for a colonization spot.

In the previous twenty years suitable areas for colonization had greatly increased due to new improvements in transportation. Initially, western New York State and western Pennsylvania were the immigration areas where, under the influence of land companies, many Europeans settled among Americans. Soon after, the Ohio Valley, long known to the Americans, also became important to the immigrants. The growing steam navigation on the Ohio and Mississippi Rivers brought increasing numbers of immigrants to Ohio, Indiana, and Illinois. The opening of the Erie Canal in 1825, and the resulting increase in navigation on the Great Lakes, made not only the entrance to Illinois easier, but brought additional "new" territories, such as Michigan and Wisconsin, to the attention of immigrants.

In these territories the number of white settlers increased rapidly. Around 1800 barely 1,000 whites lived in the lake areas of Michigan, Indiana, Illinois, Wisconsin, and Minnesota. This number had not yet reached 5,000 in 1810. After immigration became stronger in the thirties, the inhabitants of Michigan alone amounted already to 212,000 in 1840 and the more westerly situated Wisconsin population increased to 30,945. While many Americans settled in Michigan, in Wisconsin their numbers shrank in comparison to

European immigrants. Already in 1837 Michigan was elevated to statehood while Wisconsin came into the Union in 1848. These facts, as we shall see later, influenced Van Raalte's choice.

However, the European migration was generally more inclined toward Wisconsin.[81] In contrast to Michigan, which was largely covered with dense woods and where Americans felt more at home than Europeans, Wisconsin offered more variation between forest and prairie, and in general its soil was more fertile. Of even greater significance was the fact that most immigrants followed the waterways since they were much cheaper. Wisconsin was easier to reach this way than lower Michigan, which had dangerous coasts due to shallows and surf breakers, so that large ships, the "liners," stayed away from there. Many harbors were built along the west shore of Lake Michigan in Wisconsin and Illinois. In some instances, those increased in prosperity with phenomenal speed. In 1834 Milwaukee was a mere fur trading post of the Frenchman Salomon Juneau and in 1840 it barely counted 1,000 inhabitants, but in 1846 it already had 9,000 inhabitants, which in 1850 grew to 20,000. In 1830 Chicago was a trading post counting 70 souls, in 1841 it was a town of 5,700, and in 1851 it grew to a city of 34,000 inhabitants.

In contrast, along the east shore, sand dunes formed by westerly winds sometimes reached sixty meters [197 feet].[82] In those days there was hardly a town of importance found along that east shore and these regions could only be served from the Wisconsin side by transferring to smaller vessels. In addition to this, Wisconsin, in contrast to other states, had no state debt and therefore did not demand taxes. Moreover, the immigrants after a short period of residence were able to obtain the right to vote.

In Wisconsin, therefore, the population increased faster than in Michigan. In 1850 Michigan counted 398,000 inhabitants, or 186,000 more than in 1840. In the same period Wisconsin saw an increase of 275,000 people and had in 1850 upwards of 305,000. Thus Wisconsin was booming. The flood of Netherlands immigrants, who after 1840 freed themselves from areas near the German border, even as the Germans themselves had done, turned to Wisconsin and to a lesser extent to Illinois. That is why Milwaukee became a gathering place and the starting point from which to settle a colony.

3. *Enroute with Van Raalte*

With this idea of Wisconsin in mind, Van Raalte landed with his party at New York City on November 17, 1846. Because of the Hudson River and Erie Canal, New York became the most important port of entry for the immigrants, who could also use the railroads running through the Hudson and Mohawk valleys. After a brief stop in which Van Raalte exchanged opinions about his plans with a variety of people, the party traveled by steamboat to Albany. There Rev. Wyckoff and the members of his congregation received the immigrants hospitably and gave them all kinds of help. After making a brief stop, the immigrants traveled on via "steamwagon" [railroad] to Buffalo, where they were held up because of stormy weather. Not until November 27 did they depart for Detroit, in hopes of possibly being able to reach Milwaukee before winter.

But upon arriving in Detroit they learned that the steamboat traffic had come to a halt because of ice on the lakes. Since travel overland would be too expensive, they decided to spend the winter in Detroit. A friendly Scotsman loaned the immigrants a warehouse and a dwelling for a temporary place to stay. Van Raalte himself rented an upstairs town apartment for his family. Here also the immigrants found all kinds of cooperation, especially from the clergy, since the Secession was placed on a par with that in Scotland "so that here in God-fearing circles it is rather a crown than a defamation." In these same circles, as so many in Europe, they were indeed convinced on the basis of Biblical prophecy that "a terrible storm of God's judgments would burst forth over Europe." They believed that now the saying was applicable: "Get out, my people, lest thou shalt have a share in their plagues."[83]

For the rest, much love, piety, and will power was necessary to lead these people. They were mostly plain people of the land, people without the barest of education and of whom many had never been outside the area of their village of birth. Now they were driven through hunger and mystical religious conviction to a foreign country. One can thus visualize the demands that were placed on Van Raalte, as leader of these emigrants, and the difficulties with which he had to contend. Already upon arrival in New York there were swindlers galore who saw in these unsuspecting immigrants an easy prey. Later in Holland, Michigan, Reverend Jacob Van der Meulen expressed it tersely: "Like flies on meat in the dog days, they bore down on the immigrants, like mosquitoes on the first settlers in these woods."[84] There was indeed much need for leadership.

Van Raalte had to pay attention to everything and take care of everyone. There was only one capable man among his company who was willing and able to help. "The rest were good for nothing on the trip," so Van Raalte wrote in one of his letters. One thing and another also made it difficult to get employment. "The unappealing appearance, the surliness of our people, and above all not knowing the English language made it very difficult for our people to obtain work. They depend on me for everything and still most of them are ungrateful."

Luckily Van Raalte succeeded in obtaining employment for the group, because in St. Clair, fifty miles north of Detroit, a steamboat was under construction. But for Van Raalte himself, the winter stayover was not a period of hibernation. On the contrary, more than ever he felt the responsibility to look for a suitable colonization area. The preacher became a geographer. For weeks he was occupied with what is known in America as prospective geography. Like a geographical engineer Van Raalte had to study the potential for further growth of various regions that were considered good colonization spots—and that not only in his study chamber.

Van Raalte's thoughts were all in favor of Wisconsin and also in a lesser degree in favor of Illinois and Iowa, but already in New York he was advised by a much-traveled Zeelander to settle in Michigan. Detroit at that time was the capital of Michigan. During his stay, the state legislature had just met and our preacher thus was able to meet several lawmakers who centered his thoughts on Michigan. Being under the persuasion of Michigan's notables, Van Raalte gave up his intentions to explore Chicago, Milwaukee, and St. Louis and thus abandoned the possible colonization plans in Illinois, Wisconsin, and Iowa.

Numerous handicaps were cited by the Michigan authorities against settlement in these other states, some of which later on proved to be untrue. They must not settle, at any rate, south of Milwaukee because of unhealthful climatic conditions. Therefore, Iowa, Illinois, and southern Wisconsin did not come into consideration because they were (supposedly) too hot for Netherlanders. Still more important were the objections in connection with the flow of traffic that partly resulted from the climate. If they settled in western Wisconsin or in Iowa, they would have to depend on the Mississippi River and New Orleans would be the nearest marketplace. In summertime this would be a severe disadvantage because of the southern heat, while in winter the river would be frozen above St. Louis. The Great Lakes too would be of little use in winter. The lack of railroad facilities was also severely felt in the northwestern states. Southern Michigan, on the other hand, already had some railroads and there they were now busy connecting them through Canada with New York. New York City, the market to which they would have to look in the future, was reachable year round. In addition, Michigan was known to have a "certified healthful climate."

The clincher, however, resulted from other circumstances, since Van Raalte was dissuaded from settling in regions where there were no roads, no matter how cheaply the land was offered. He should settle in a region "where the rough edges have been taken off" and where already a few families were living. There were no whites living in western Wisconsin and northern Iowa. In eastern Wisconsin, due to the influence of the steamboat associations, there were quite large numbers of white settlers. But here lived a mixed number of Europeans who were indifferent to Holland immigrants. Because of that, the region had "little to recommend itself" to Van Raalte. It was different in Michigan, which had come more exclusively into the hands of older Americans. There dwelled a more scholarly, religious, and enterprising nucleus among whom the families of Old-Dutch origin found great respect and influence. Van Raalte and his followers also benefited from this situation.

Once Michigan was chosen, the question still remained about what part of the state in which to locate, since this state was nearly six times the size of the Netherlands. The solution of this question was facilitated, among other things, by the advice given by an Old-Dutch lawyer [Theodore] Romeyn and the preachers [George] Duffield and [?] West of Detroit, [Ova P.]

Hoyt of Kalamazoo, |Andrew B.| Taylor of Grand Rapids, and especially by
Judge |John R.| Kellogg of Allegan. Various parts of Michigan were con-
sidered, as for example the Saginaw Valley on the east side of the state
where many Dutch Roman Catholic farmers subsequently settled.[85] Van
Raalte's attention was drawn to western Michigan and more particularly to
the part lying between the Kalamazoo and Grand rivers, both of which had
an outlet to Lake Michigan. G. Van Schelven, the well-known justice of the
peace in Holland, Michigan, and also an historian, explained in his series of
articles in *De Grondwet*: "It always has been our presumption, and still is
today, that next to God we owe it mostly to the influence of Judge Kellogg
that this region was given preference."[86]

It was in this area, favorable for traffic by land or water and surrounded
by many smaller and larger market places, that Van Raalte decided to make
a personal investigation. He received this opportunity through the mediation and continual help of Judge Kellogg. Sometimes on horseback but
many times on foot, Van Raalte for weeks roamed through the heavy snow,
which made it all the more difficult to go through the forests. "Along the
banks of the rivers one finds many toppled trees and dense undergrowth,
and one had to leave the horses because they could not cross the river by
walking over tree trunks as we did." Often Van Raalte sank exhausted in the
snow. On one occasion, overtaken by darkness, he got lost, although he
carried a compass. In this manner Van Raalte finally completed his difficult
and responsible mission.

His choice fell on an area where the small Black River flows into Black
Lake, which in turn has an open connection with Lake Michigan. The
chosen area lies between larger rivers, eighteen miles from the Grand River
and twelve miles from the Kalamazoo River. Numerous geographic factors
were considered by Van Raalte. In the first place was the location. This was
not only favorable because of the climate that he considered to be excellent
both with regard to health and the growing of products such as wheat and
maize, but especially with regard to the future market places. It was within
reach of Allegan, Kalamazoo, Grand Rapids, etc., which were the nearest
towns. Milwaukee, Racine, and Chicago, etc., on the opposite side of Lake
Michigan were also readily available. Even New Orleans and New York, far
away as they were, could be reached by canal, lake, and river.

The condition of the soil also attracted Van Raalte's attention, even
though later there were differences of opinion about this. The elevated
wood area where numerous rivulets flowed, provided necessary water
sources and he saw that the overabundant water safely ran off without
danger of flooding. This was looked upon as a very healthy and fertile land
by virtue of the numerous varieties of trees growing there. However, Van
Raalte initially saw only one objection—the chosen area was almost totally
covered with heavy and dense woods; prairies, except for a few cornfields,
were lacking. "At first," he wrote, "this caused me great frustration. Often I
could not answer the question of what is more important: 'prairies or a

favorable location for market places and trade?' Still, it is my judgment that wooded areas can become prairies, whereas any unfavorable position for trade cannot be changed."

Still other circumstances were added to the prairie versus woods question, and Van Raalte had to consider those also. For example, sod-busting made the prairies very unhealthful in the first few years. Moreover, only since the thirties was this open endless plain with its icy north wind and lack of wood considered habitable. The real old-time Americans still shunned it, as one remembers from Beukma's observation in 1837. Especially the lack of wood for building and fuel material made living on the prairie too expensive; it required too much wealth. "The rich farmer may feel at home on the prairies, but in no other occupation or trade is this the case," asserted Van Raalte and rightly so at that time. Among his party there were no rich farmers. On the contrary, had he not taken to heart the misfortune of the poorest who were supported by this Colonization Society? And they were not all farmers or farmhands; there were craftsmen among them.

These circumstances of Van Raalte's decision must be taken into serious consideration when evaluating his choice of a location. The clearing of woods for sufficient cropland and pasture may have been pictured as too simple by Van Raalte. No doubt his conviction was quite correct that one could build a new home in the chosen area in the cheapest way possible and that various crafts could soon be started there. He not only had in mind farmers and cattle-raisers, but also coopers, basketmakers, tanners, carpenters, and cabinetmakers. He contemplated the possibility of establishing sawmills and shipyards, and constructing a harbor in order to export timber products to the treeless parts of Illinois and southern Wisconsin. He even had an eye already on the possibility of developing a fishing industry.

With everybody in mind, he established the basis for the broad development of a colony. Even today the people are grateful to Van Raalte for that. "A deep feeling of admiration and appreciation should even now be stirring our soul for the insight, the courage, the dedication, and the spirit of enterprise of this principal director of the Netherlands emigration." Thus spoke Van Schelven, justice of the peace.[87] Van Raalte felt the heaviness of his responsibility. As he said in one of his letters, "I feel that I am living at a tremendous point in time." Therefore, after he had made his research trip, he invited a few of his American friends to Detroit to discuss his chosen area. They not only ratified his choice but in addition appointed committees in Detroit, Marshall, Kalamazoo, Allegan, Grand Rapids, Grand Haven, and Saugatuck to assist the Netherlanders in cooperation with the already-established Netherlands Society in Albany.

After again having re-examined the desired area with some members of the committees, Van Raalte bought a considerable section of it in his name, with the assistance of some prominent men. Sellers were the Federal government and some speculators holding land near the Black River. From the government alone, they bought nearly one thousand acres.[88] With this land near Black Lake, they got the key to a much greater upland region. The Detroit committee, which was financially better off, even decided to purchase the adjacent lands and sell them later to the Dutch colonists when they could afford to buy. The settling and potential expansion of a considerable settlement was now possible. If they had settled in the more densely populated Grand River and Kalamazoo River valleys, they would have paid more for the land but also would have had less chance of expansion because there they would have been more enclosed by established owners.

It was the Netherlander |Bernardus| Grootenhuis, accompanied by his wife and assisted by four American laborers dispatched by the Detroit committee, who took the very first preparatory step—that of chopping a road through the dense woods. After that, the first small crowd of immigrants under the leadership of Van Raalte arrived on the evening of February 9, 1847, near the mouth of the Black River. The following day after a fervent prayer, they began building the first log cabin and after it was finished the men called for their wives and children who had been left behind in Allegan. The working families who were left behind in St. Clair also joined them and even immigrant families who had arrived in New York and New Orleans. Thus were the foundations laid for the later prosperous Holland colony in Ottawa and Allegan counties on Michigan's western shore.[89]

4. *Enroute with Scholte*

Van Raalte's wish that the preacher H. P. Scholte and his followers would also settle in Michigan did not materialize. Scholte preferred the prairies of Iowa, and thus disappointed many who had hoped to see the development of one big Christian Dutch colony in the United States. At first one may regret this split from the viewpoint of religion, for it revealed a lack of unity. Nevertheless, it is fully understandable if one takes into account the purely material considerations. In Scholte's choice, economic factors were also decisive.

Originally both leaders cooperated in the emigration. In Scholte's periodical *De Reformatie* |The Reformation| of May 1846 those who wished to move to North America were advised to seek information either from the editor, Scholte, or from |Antonie| Brummelkamp, brother-in-law of Van Raalte. In this manner they hoped to come "to a reasonable cooperation in order to settle a Free Holland Colony in one of the fertile regions of North America." Many people applied, among whom were a great many paupers. In July 1846 *De Reformatie* reported that "the registration of persons who want free transportation to North America has increased very much."

Although one does not read anywhere that a definite agreement was made between Van Raalte and Scholte, they nevertheless came to a division of labor that made the different choices in America very understandable. We already saw how Van Raalte had worked in the sandy, woody, and relatively poor eastern part of the Netherlands and had been concerned for the poor people, especially those of Gelderland and Overijsel. The poverty of his followers also made him decide to settle in the very forested state of Michigan. Scholte, on the contrary, had lived mostly in clay- and bog-like level country in the comparatively prosperous western part of the Netherlands and thus cast his lot with people of means, primarily those from the provinces of Zuid Holland and Utrecht.

Thus, in addition to the society established in Arnhem by Brummelkamp and Van Raalte for resettling poor immigrants, there was founded in Utrecht a second society, "The Society for Emigration to North America," whose board only accepted those "who can pay their own way and establish themselves." At a meeting held before the founding in August, 1846, they had already gathered nearly seventy moneyed families, mainly from the province of Zuid Holland. When they met again on September 4, 1846, orders were given jointly to buy twelve sections of land |one section contains 640 acres|. In December of the same year the purchase was expanded to eighteen sections. On December 25, 1846, the following members were voted unanimously to administrative positions: H. P. Scholte at Utrecht, president; A. J. Betten at Noordeloos, vice-president; I. Overkamp at Utrecht, secretary; and advisors J. F. De Cocq at Amsterdam, A. Wigneij at Dordrecht, G. H. Overkamp at Leerdam, and J. Rietveld at Noordeloos. All of them were from the flat western countryside.[90]

The group was somewhat acquainted with the various regions recommended for colonization, partly because of Scholte's cooperation on a translation from the High German of Moritz Beyer, *Het Boek der Landverhuizers, of Gids en Raadsman bij de Verhuizing naar Noord-Amerika* |*The Book of Emigrants, or Guide and Advisor for Moving to North America*|. Principally, attention was centered on the prairie sections of southern Wisconsin, northern Illinois, and Iowa. However, Scholte was mostly impressed by Professor J. G. Buttner's "*Briefe aus und über Nord-Amerika*" |"Letters From and About North America"|, and he greatly favored Iowa, despite the fact that at that time he still expected Van Raalte to settle in Wisconsin. Iowa, in Beyer's words, was a "state called into being as if by magic." Buttner praised it on account of its healthful climate, the extensive open areas for farming, the abundance of wood and water, and a place without wet low-lying areas and swamps.[91]

Just as a few brethren had declared themselves ready to undertake a tentative land investigation with the Van Raalte society, so some others also made themselves available to the Scholte organization. The latter would travel on their own expense and try to work together with Van Raalte and his advisors. But nothing came of this planned cooperation.

Thus the vanguard of the Holland Society left from Rotterdam on October 2, 1846. It consisted of the families H. Barendregt, C. Van Nieuwenhuizen, J. H. Schijf, A. Den Hartog, D. Van Ham, P. Stavast, |G.| Rouwert, J. Mergels, and the bachelors K. De Hoog, T. Keppel, J. Schaap, H. Boomgaars, and J. Baay. After a very stormy trip, they arrived in New Orleans on November 19. "The Lord had assisted us perceptibly."[92]

New Orleans was a city in the making. "Everything seems to be in its beginning, hundreds of houses are under construction, and everything here is in turbulence, in unusual turbulence from the movement of wagons and carts. Six hundred sea-going vessels lie docked three abreast at the wharves in addition to numerous steamships, mostly of a very large kind, though of a different design than those in Holland. They tell me that 1,300 boats sail the Mississippi and I believe this when I see all the commotion. One sees no sailing vessels on the river; they cannot be used because of the sharp bends in the river. Therefore, the boats running upstream cannot catch the wind. The water always runs downstream and the banks are covered with woods so that no horse or man can be used for towing." So wrote Barendregt, who was accustomed to the tow-path and the tranquil Netherlands villages and cities, in a very interesting letter from the city of St. Louis to the "Very Esteemed Teacher and Brother in the Lord," H. P. Scholte.[93]

After a nine-day trip on the Mississippi River, the party arrived in St. Louis, having stayed only a short time in New Orleans. Because of the arrival of winter, the vanguard gave up plans to continue the trip to Iowa or Wisconsin. In St. Louis they met, among others, many brethren from Winterswijk and also from Germany, some of whom were acquainted with the situation in Iowa so that they could help complete the questionnaire that Scholte had given along.

Barendregt's letter was received and read with great interest and taken to heart. And, indeed, his advice not to arrive in New Orleans in the boiling heat of summer was followed by Scholte and the Society. Scholte with wife and children made the trip from Rotterdam to Liverpool via London, and from there the steamship *Sarah Sand** took them across the ocean in thirteen days to Boston, where they arrived the first part of May, 1847.

The Society chartered four sailboats: *Nagasaki, Pieter Floris, Catharina Jackson,* and *Maasstroom.* These ships could transport a total of 160 families and a number of bachelors, since Barendregt had advised the farmers to take farmhands along with them. A grand total of eight hundred to nine hundred persons set out on the journey under the leadership of the board members of the society. In early April the ships sailed from Rotterdam, with the exception of the *Pieter Floris,* which sailed from Amsterdam. They arrived in Baltimore in the later part of May and the first part of June, after a generally uneventful trip. Two old persons and eighteen children died at sea, but a number of babies were also born.

No one wanted to remain for long in the sinful city of Baltimore because, although it was an important seaport, it was anything but a charming city. They had "in many places [to] plow through the mud above the ankles, and everywhere chickens, pigs, and cows were roaming freely through the streets of the city."[94] In Baltimore they made arrangements for further transporta-

*According to the U.S. ship passenger manifests, Scholte actually sailed with his family on the Steamer *Caledonia* from Liverpool to Boston, arriving on May 6, 1847, manifest No. 589. See National Archives Microfilm Series M-237, Reel No. 23.

tion, both for the people and also the baggage. Here again they had heeded Barendregt's advice and had taken along crates full of household furnishings and food supplies and various tools, even large farm wagons! However, the greatest care was bestowed on the heavy money chest containing the wealth of the immigrants, in particular their golden "*Willempjes*" [named after King Willem I whose effigy adorned the Dutch gold coins]. The strongest among the men had to guard the chest and they were not without success. As a matter of pride, this chest is still today on display in Pella's National Bank as a memorial of "the old country," and I had the honor of seeing it there. Scholte had also made the necessary arrangements for inland travel, and he left immediately for Baltimore after the arrival of the first ship. Luckily he was able to keep his fellow Christians out of the hands of the many shanghaiers who had heard about the anticipated arrival of so many rich Hollanders.The swindlers rushed the ships and tried to force their aid on these people.[95]

The group boarded the train to Columbia, Pennsylvania. There, with bag and baggage, they were packed in a few canalboats like sardines in a can enroute to Hollidaysburg, Pennsylvania. There they boarded another train, this time on the Portage Railway and were "portaged" over the Allegheny Mountains to Johnstown, and from there they were packed once more into canalboats to Pittsburgh. From there they took the steamboat on the Ohio River "the gateway to the West," past the city of Cincinnati, and then on to the Mississippi River to reach St. Louis, their temporary goal.

In spite of the fact that this three-week inland trip was marked by a variety of stimulating experiences, the concerns of the travelers were too great to enjoy the usually beautiful landscape. They had not only to take in stride cramped quarters, "but on top of the aggravation of crying children who had need of a warm meal that was impossible to get. If in desperation somebody finally dared to leave the boat to cook some food on shore, hoping to be ready before the boat would leave again, but would fail and be left behind with porridge, pot and all, that surely was enough to douse the last poetic spark (if present at all) in the human breast. And what is even more of a burden when traveling like this is to lose a dear one whose body is hastily brought on shore and buried so that the trip can be resumed with as little delay as possible. Such circumstances require more than human strength in order not to be consumed by sorrow."[96]

A number of houses were rented in St. Louis for these immigrants, and for those who could not find a house a few wooden sheds were built on a donated space. Although nobody spoke Dutch in this city, the immigrants were received with the same affection as was Van Raalte in Albany and elsewhere. One of the Presbyterian churches in the city even gave permission to the Hollanders "regularly to make use of a large assembly hall on the day of rest without cost, and including heat in winter; and they helped with our needy and sick."[97]

While waiting for a permanent place to settle, most immigrants tried to get some work in St. Louis. "Some active ones happily succeeded while others who had imagined, like children, that America was a wonderland, were less fortunate in finding what they were not looking for very seriously."[98]

In the meantime a committee of investigation, consisting of H. P. Scholte, I. Overkamp, J. Rietveld, T. Keppel, and G. Van der Pol went out to find a suitable place for colonization. For that matter Scholte had already immediately upon his arrival in Boston gathered all possible information concerning colonization. He had traveled for that purpose to Washington as well as to New York City and Albany where he obtained admission to several circles through the recommendations of the American representative in the Netherlands. Here he was fortified in his conviction that he should settle in one of the western States, but not in Michigan. Although during his stay in New York and Albany, the Hollanders in Michigan were given all aid possible, yet they advised Scholte not to join with Van Raalte.

It also made a big impression on Scholte that deacon Sleyster, who had preceded Van Raalte as a land searcher in Wisconsin, did not care for Michigan at all after he had investigated the colony there. It was also a fact that numerous Hollanders who had already lived in St. Louis for months and who had been invited by Van Raalte to Michigan refused after investigation to settle there. This refusal also gave Scholte second thoughts.[99] Apparently referring to Van Raalte's optimistic letter from Detroit, dated January 30, 1847, Scholte observed: "I am of the opinion that a good place recommends itself, not by what one might do there but by what has been done and is being done there, etc."[100]

Scholte abandoned Michigan altogether as a colonization area for Netherlanders. Slightly mocking Van Raalte's remarks about the wealth of the woods and the beautiful location of Michigan's west side, Scholte formulated his objections to Michigan as follows:

1st. The position of the area was too far north; 2nd. The total lack of suitable roads to reach the area; 3rd. The lack of sufficient prairie suitable for farming, since nearly everything is covered with dense woods of heavy trees; 4th. The nearness of Indians and the distance from white inhabitants and organized villages. Taking this altogether, I resolved that for the kind of Netherlanders with whom I was to colonize, this territory could not be considered as suitable. A Dutch farmer who has already lived half of his life on the level land of meadows and fields could not be pleased by the unaccustomed combat with trees and a long continuous scene of leftover tree stumps amid pasture and farmland. Although not underestimating Michigan for its fertility or the worth of its many varieties of timber nor the pleasantness of its many feathered denizens chirping away in the cool shade of the virgin woods, I had, however, learned and lived long enough to realize that for the farmers tree stumps are unpleasant obstacles and the value of timber decreases markedly when everything is woods and woods. Besides, I was absolutely convinced that the newly-arrived Hollanders in North America were more prosaic rather than

poetic and consequently that their first thought would be not to gratify the
eye and ear but to find soil suitable to cultivate and the easier the better. I
knew that the Dutch country folk of which our society mainly consisted were
very much set to have pastures with milk cows without delay, and to drive
their plows and harrows through the fields and that they were altogether
disinclined to choose an axe instead of a spade and become lumber
traders."[101]

That Michigan's guaranteed healthful climate was far from perfect, like
the climate of any other place in the world, had become apparent to
Scholte from an advertisement by the Dutch colony that appeared in a New
York paper, and which requested a certain kind of pills! So it is understandable that the committee in the first place turned to the excellent prairie
land of Iowa, which in the last years so many immigrants with some capital
had already settled. Indeed, so many had done so that, although land had
been purchased from the Indians only recently, the state was incorporated
in 1846.

At first Scholte had in mind the so-called "half breed tract" in southeastern Iowa, which was formerly occupied by half-blood Indians who sold it to
a syndicate of New York gentlemen. This sale caught Scholte's interest in
this tract. Fertile though it was, however, it was already too populated to be
considered for a Holland colony.

The committee therefore turned further to the West to the city of Fairfield
in Jefferson County where General [Verplank] Van Antwerp, the Receiver at
the government land office and an American of Old Dutch descent, received
Scholte with the greatest kindness and cooperation. In Fairfield Scholte
accidently met Moses J. Post, a Baptist minister, who was well acquainted
with the surrounding territory in which he had traveled as a missionary for a
period of six years. When Post learned of the Hollanders' plans, he recommended a few areas for colonization.

Scholte, "having recognized God's hand," was able to persuade Post to
visit the intended area. Then, when in agreement with the committee, they
decided to buy the land, Post helped to buy out the claims of the various
established American colonists. This land still belonged to the government,
although the American settlers had the first option to buy it. In general
American farmers are easily inclined to move and change dwellings. Already
in 1792 Pieter Stadnitski pointed out in a pamphlet their strong urge to
move, and also Beukma and Van Raalte pointed out this phenomenon.
Scholte even persuaded them to leave their farms within one month. In order
to achieve this objective he included the unharvested crops in the purchase
price, also the cattle and other inventories. Scholte had no authority to do
this; moreover the money on deposit was woefully inadequate for this type of
deal. "But feeling the leading of the Lord, seeing the good opportunity, and
the excellent fertility of the soil and the easiness with which it could be
worked, I did not hesitate to purchase it on my own responsibility."

Scholte could not, at that time, foresee the difficulties that would result from this "premature" deal. But in this way the Hollanders came into possession in one week's time, from Thursday to the following Monday, of a number of farms and of very fertile, sprawling, rolling government lands. This area lay in Marion County between the Des Moines and Skunk* rivers, including also Lake Prairie and Jefferson townships. All kinds of grains could be grown and the land was also excellent for raising cattle. Here and there were found larger and smaller clumps of trees, with the heaviest trees standing along the rivers that were to be prepared for navigation.

After the committee reported its findings in St. Louis, the greater part of the tarrying immigrants decided to leave immediately for Marion County in Iowa. They proceeded to Keokuk, "the Gate City of Iowa," on a chartered steamboat in the first half of the same month, August 1847, in which the deal was concluded. From there the trek west was by wagon, horse, or on foot. During that last part of the trip, three persons died struggling through the heavy rainstroms. People and freight reached their destination with only a short interval between. A big disappointment awaited the colonists. Scholte had instructed a few Americans to construct some fifty log cabins during his absence. However, on arrival they found nothing but a great number of boards that had been ordered. From these boards shelters were hastily constructed. In the meantime the vacating of farms began and these were immediately occupied by a few families.[102]

At the same time plans for the city were laid out in the middle of the prairies at one of the highest parts of the area between the rivers. Scholte called it "Pella," a name altogether inapplicable geographically, since it means "basin," but psychologically it was easily explained: Did not the disciples of Jesus flee to Pella when Jerusalem was to be taken and ravaged by the Romans? Many have since "fled" to this new Pella, and firstly those who still remained behind in St. Louis in the same year of 1847. Some came after wintering in St. Louis the next spring and numerous others came in 1849 and also in years following.

5. To Van Raalte or to Scholte?

Many were disappointed that Van Raalte and Scholte had not settled in the same area. Reverend Cornelius Van der Meulen, who had joined Van Raalte in America, but who had studied theology with Scholte, explained that, had that been the case, two years after having been established "we in union could have done great things with the blessing of the Lord."[103] Also for those with less foresight than Van der Meulen, at the outset anyway, the separation of both leaders was unpleasant. The numerous Dissenters who had stayed behind in the Netherlands and who felt strongly inclined

---

*Actually the *South* Skunk River, as indicated on today's maps. In the area it is popularly referred to as the Skunk River. Van Hinte uses the popular designation here and in subsequent references.

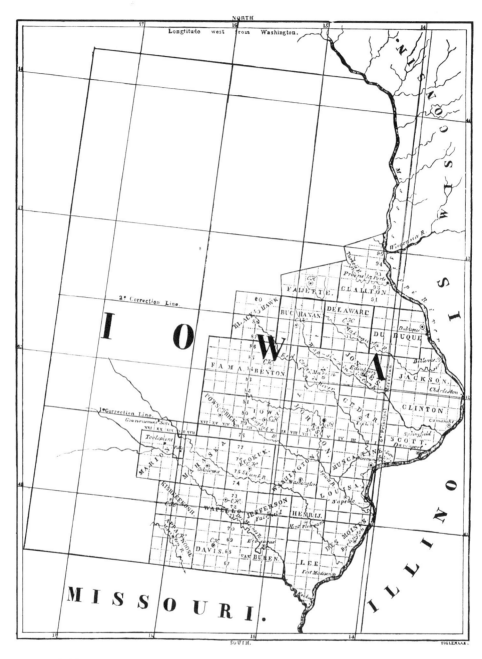

Map of the state of Iowa at the arrival of the Netherlanders. The small square blocks indicate the surveyed townships (rural municipalities).

towards emigration and those who were already decided now had to come to the difficult decision whom to join.

The question of going to Van Raalte or Scholte became the subject of many conversations and even meetings. The situation became more complicated when both Scholte and Van Raalte tried to draw emigrants. Both understood that the success of their colonization depended on increasing immigration. Therefore, both were trying to paint the best possible picture of living in their respective communities. For example, Scholte made less of an issue of the lack of wood on the prairies, but Van Raalte in turn overrated the woods. His observation was: "It is very much easier to get accustomed to the presence of woods than to the lack of them."[104] Seemingly this was not applicable to everyone, because there were many who fled the forests. Yet, not only were the leaders trying to recommend their own territory, which often led to overblown expectations by the immigrants, but indirectly or directly they found fault with each other's choice. Van der Meulen expressed his disappointment: "Everything bears the mark of envy, carnality, and working without faith."[105] A certain jealousy, even a certain rivalry, developed in recruiting. This was very strongly manifested in 1847 when a great number of Zeelanders came to the United States.

Earlier we saw how already in the thirties a great number of Zeelanders came to the United States and settled in the general area of western New York and how the emigration fever originated among the Zeeland Dissenters. In the spring of 1846, Anthonie De Bree with his family left his village of Oudelande and settled in Oakland County, Michigan. After having lived there a few years, he moved to Greenville in Montcalm County in the same state, where his family has since stayed amid Americans.[106] Zeelanders, however, were more impressed when the wealthy farmer, Jannes Van de Luyster, departed for America with his family. Many wished to go with him.

In the spring of 1847 at the city of Goes, three meetings were held among those who were "moving-disposed," in which they not only decided to emigrate jointly but even like the Pilgrim fathers of 1620 to organize themselves on a church basis and to set out on the ocean trip as a Christian congregation. Jannes Van de Luyster and Johannes Hoogesteger were chosen as elders, Jan Steketee and Adriaan Glerum as deacons, while Reverend Cornelius Van der Meulen—a longtime "provincial" evangelist and later minister of a church in Goes—was called to serve the immigrant congregation.

Van der Meulen, who was originally an opponent of emigration, was more and more struck by the prevailing frivolous and indifferent attitude in the Netherlands concerning the truth. "His thoughts were led to observe the course of the Gospel, which throughout time had traveled from East to West like the sun; thus his attention was likewise drawn to this western hemisphere."[107] For fear that "the Dutch sun of prosperity was setting, especially in relation to religion, and that the judgments of God were hanging above their heads," he decided in the interest of his posterity to transplant them to America. He took the call of the congregation that now paid his traveling expenses.

We saw already that Van De Luyster had paid the passage for 77 persons. The total number departing came to 450, some leaving from Antwerp and some from Rotterdam. However, they could not come to an agreement where to settle or whom to join. Therefore they made an arrangement that the leader of the first ship to arrive in New York would have to choose and leave a message behind with Dr. Thomas De Witt in New York.

Jannes Van de Luyster took the leadership of three hundred emigrants, not only from Goes and vicinity but also from Kadzand, Axel, etc. On April 10, 1847, they hoped to leave from Antwerp. However, in Antwerp it turned out that the ship in question did not have sufficient room so that only part of the company could sail at the given date. That party was under the leadership of |Jan| Steketee. Van de Luyster with the remainder had to wait ten days, but still they arrived in New York first. His ship took only forty-five days to make the trip while the ship of Steketee required sixty-three days to cross the ocean.

Another part of the congregation, totaling 157 people, departed under the leadership of Jan Kaboord and Reverend Van der Meulen. The latter preached his farewell sermon to his congregation in Goes "with reference to Acts 20:25–27 under much emotion and heart-rending tears."[108] On April 8, 1847, they went from Goes to Rotterdam, where they had booked passage on the *Prinses Sophia*, on which was also booked a Frisian by name of S. Osinga. Osinga, himself not a Seceder, sketched in his diary the spirit of the Zeelanders as follows: "There sits one singing out of an old worn psalm-book and here is one orally reading a prayer out of an old prayerbook."[109]

When it developed that the ship had too many passengers on board, it occasioned a delay of several weeks at Hellevoetsluis. Many of the immigrants, among them Osinga, were finally transferred to a ship called *Louisa*. During all that time, Van der Meulen preached a series of farewell sermons to the surrounding congregations, which enabled him to gather more funds via the collections to support his very poor Zeelanders. He succeeded in keeping his party on the *Prinses Sophia*.[110] This ship did not leave Hellevoet-sluis until May 27, but after a very successful voyage docked on July 2 in New York City, which was after Van de Luyster's and Steketee's arrival.

Scholte, who had waited for the Zeelanders in New York, persuaded Van de Luyster, who had arrived first and according to the agreement was to choose a place of settlement, to go with him to St. Louis until he, Scholte, could find a suitable colonization area. However, in Buffalo, because of a misunderstanding, there arose much dissatisfaction in spite of the fact that Van de Luyster had already bought and paid for the tickets to St. Louis, that they changed plans and went instead to Van Raalte in Michigan.[111] Arriving in Michigan, Van de Luyster bought 1,680 acres of land from the govern-

The receipt of ownership (deed) of Jannes Van de Luyster.

ment about six miles east of Van Raalte's Holland settlement, sections 17 and 19, and an additional 400 acres in section 9. He designated part of this for the establishment of a village called Zeeland.[112]

The rest of the Zeeland leaders also opted for Michigan. Upon his arrival in New York, Van der Meulen received letters from Van Raalte and Scholte "who had made arrangements for us all the way to our place of settlement, although we have during our trip over there met nothing but difficulty and deceit."[113] Van der Meulen and his party had gone on board the steamboat in New York bound for Albany, but instead they landed in Troy. When the Zeelanders rented two canalboats, they already turned out to be half-filled with strangers. And they were cheated left and right when their baggage was weighed. When Van der Meulen pointed out the injustice of the overweight, they would not allow him to board the canalboat and even tried to push him into the water! So Van der Meulen traveled to Albany and returned to New York "to assert his rights, and the immigrants thought it better not to object to this."

At Buffalo he again rejoined his party. "When we went to the steamboat that would take us to Black Lake, we had no idea what awaited us there. The trip lasted five days and the further we went, the more unbroken woods we saw along the shores. Now and then the boat landed at a log cabin.

During the trip a woman died. Her body was left in the hands of strangers for burial. However, we always were under the impression that we would come to a city—the city of Holland. At Grand Haven we met Hollanders and we woke up from our dream when we heard the dreadful rumors of sickness and starvation in Holland.... When we arrived at Black Lake we saw nothing at our feet but sand dunes and trees. There was a heavy surf and the little rowboat of the steamship was narrow, so it could not land us on shore. First a few men, among them also my father, waded ashore. The men had to walk through the surf and carried us on shore. When no one else dared to follow our example, the boat left with the rest of the immigrants, plus the baggage, back to Grand Haven."[114]

When it turned out that there was no lodging at the outlet of Black Lake, Van der Meulen decided to send his family back to Grand Haven. This was possible since just then a family with a flat-bottomed boat planned to set out on the dangerous trip. However, they got no farther than Port Sheldon Creek where they were overtaken by stormy weather and for safety's sake decided to sail the boat up the creek. A heavy thunder storm compelled them to abandon the flatboat and to seek shelter in a deserted wooden shed at Port Sheldon.

In the meantime Reverend Van der Meulen in the company of a few men left for Holland and from there went to Grand Haven where he heard about the residence of his family. At Grand Haven a few flatboats were rented, which picked up those who were stranded there and also those at Port Sheldon. They were ferried to Black Lake. "On a beautiful moonlight night we sailed along the silent banks to Black Lake where we arrived in the morning. From there we continued our journey with the flatboats and in the afternoon we saw the 'city of Holland' before our eyes. When we came on shore we saw everywhere shelters made of branches."

Five wooden sheds were constructed for the arrival of the Zeelanders, but the parties of Van de Luyster and Steketee had already occupied them. Before the trip started, Zeelanders "had imagined something like a foretaste of heaven," but now they began to "grumble and became dejected." However, Reverend Van der Meulen gave as his opinion: "Without a clear conscience we may not choose another way, because the Lord had brought so many of His children here."[115] Finally they found temporary shelter in a dilapidated log cabin. No matter how many difficulties they had to face, still Van der Meulen had no regrets about his choice. Among the Zeelanders there were only a few well-to-do who had paid their fare, "but surely many more had to be helped by still others."[116] Thus there was not enough money to buy the necessary wood for cabins, barns, and fuel on the prairies, so they were relegated to the forests.

Just one-third of the original number who had left the province of Zeeland with three ships settled in the colony of Zeeland.[117] Of the remainder, some had died at sea and on land, and others had found work in Albany. Many stayed in Rochester, New York, where already numerous compatriots resided, and others went to Milwaukee, Wisconsin. Also many stayed in Van Raalte's colony in Holland.

A number of the Frisian Seceders in Holland also decided to travel to Michigan. To organize the trip, they came together at Leeuwarden on November 19, 1846. This group unanimously called the Reverend Marten A. Ypma at Hollum "to go with them as their shepherd and instructor and to live with them where the Lord would lead." Accepting the call, Ypma left from Rotterdam on April 7, 1847, with his congregation of forty-nine adults and a number of children; they sailed on the English ship *Vesta*. In the latter part of June they arrived in Ottawa County, Michigan, where the majority found a temporary home with the Van Raalte colony in Holland. After a few weeks of preparation and searching for suitable land, they found a fertile clay region twelve miles east of Holland. Here they set up the village of Vriesland on sections 16, 21, 22, and 23.

Shortly after the founding of Vriesland, a number of people from Drenthe came to America, among whom there were a few very well-to-do. A few came from the picturesque village of Staphorst. They settled one mile southeast of Vriesland and formed the village of Drenthe. Four miles east of Holland the bustling village of Groningen sprang up, established by the enterprising Jan Rabbers from the province of Drenthe and populated by a number of Groningers.

Also a number of inhabitants from Graafschap [County] Bentheim [some five miles across the German border at Overijsel] decided to settle with Van Raalte. They were not only closely allied to the Netherlands by religion but also by speech dialect. Therefore, about five miles southwest of Holland they founded the village of Graafschap in 1847. Because of the good clay soil and favorable position, more Graafschappers, and also Drenthers, Gelderlanders, and Zeelanders from the old country emigrated and joined the new village.[118]

Also of significance was the emigration of a number of Overijselers, especially from the village of Hellendoorn, under the guidance of the energetic Reverend S. Bolks. On August 18, 1847, they departed from Hellendoorn, traveled over Zwolle, and arrived on August 21 in Rotterdam. From there the company left for London by steamship and started the ocean voyage with a sailboat on September 3. They arrived in New York City in the first half of October. However, they stayed in the city of Syracuse for the winter and from there looked for a suitable place to settle. "Because there were bad rumors afoot about Michigan, their intentions were not to go there, but to go to Wisconsin or choose any other region for settlement."[119] The thought even arose to settle on an island above Buffalo, but this place was judged unfit.

While the immigrants in Syracuse got work "and made good wages," Reverend Bolks and brother G. H. Veldhuis made various trips and spoke with many people, especially Americans of Old Dutch descent. Finally, for the sake of getting off cheaply and taking into account the poverty of their emigrants, they decided to move to the woods of Michigan. Moreover, Reverend Bolks had received a call to the recently established village of Graafschap. They departed May 1, 1848, from Syracuse and arrived in early June via Grand Haven at the mouth of Black Lake. From here they went to Holland where the party was quartered for the time being.

To settle in the village of Graafschap seemed difficult, so they sought a suitable place elsewhere. After a search they settled nine miles southeast of Holland in Allegan County in an area consisting of clay alternating here and there with sandy soil. This area was partly owned by the government and partly by speculators from whom the necessary land was bought jointly [by the colonists]. Bolks was very favorably impressed: "Everything was heavy clay and could be obtained for a modest price." We live on "the most exquisite grounds," so he wrote to the fatherland. A Dutch clay farmer would perhaps have been less satisfied than his colleagues from the Overijsel sandy soils.

Numerous log cabins were built and a new village, Hellendoorn, soon came into being. But since many other immigrants arrived from Den Ham and other villages of the old Oversticht, the town was renamed Overijssel [Overisel]. Subsequently other settlements were founded, such as Beaverdam, North Holland, and South Holland—so named according to their location in relation to "*de stad*" Holland, Noordeloos, and Filmore.[120] Continuously the stream to Michigan grew, stimulated by letters of Van Raalte.

Iowa was the goal of many immigrants.[121] In the spring and summer of 1849 the dangerous journey of numerous Netherlanders began. They came partly from the Society founded in 1846 by Scholte and others, namely J. Hospers, A. C. Kuyper, and J. Maasdam, who were the leaders. Among them were found those of very good social position and well educated, but "what stood them in good stead" was that many "were well supplied with golden *Willempjes*." Some of them settled in Pella, others concentrated on farming in the vicinity, and bought out a few American farmers there. For example, Maarten A. Witsenburg bought four hundred acres of land from Daniel Earl who lived four to five miles west of the city. The Witsenburgs were Frisians.

Not only Hollanders followed Scholte but also emigrants of the other provinces. The "Frisian Neighborhood" west of Pella, the hamlet of Kockengen north of Pella named after the well-known village in the province of Utrecht, and the Herwijnen neighborhood named for the well-known village in the province of Gelderland, for a long time were reminders of that.[122] The pick of the Dutch emigrants of those years settled in Pella. Old Mister Van Schelven recalled from his younger years how the immigrants in "the name of Scholte" were told that he could not place those entirely without means in the open prairie. Van Raalte let it be known that those without means were just the folks who were welcome by him. "And both were right in this."[123]

6. The Trek to Wisconsin and Illinois

Not all emigrants, even among the Seceders, followed Van Raalte or Scholte. The spontaneous emigration movement, which originated in the forties in the Achterhoek of Gelderland and spread out all over the Netherlands, as we have seen before, settled first of all in Wisconsin. They went to Milwaukee, the main port of this state, where many vessels overflowing with immigrants landed. Many Dutch pioneers also settled in and around the city. There woods and pastures alternated, which seemed to be the ideal country for small farmers with some capital.

One of the first letter writers, [A.] Hollerdijk, bought sixty acres mostly of pasture but including some woodland near Milwaukee.[124] In May of 1845 various families from the Achterhoek settled in this vicinity. Sleyster and Brusse, Van Raalte's advisors, also turned to Wisconsin, and they found ten Holland families in Milwaukee, but Sleyster himself moved farther inland. After first having become an American citizen, he "claimed" 160 acres of land near Waupun in Fond du Lac County, eighty-six miles northwest of Milwaukee.[125] Other Achterhoek families also resided there: [B.] Te Beest, [Gerrit] Boland, [John W.] Rensinck, and others from Dinxperloo and Winterswijk. Letters of these colonists later drew numerous family members and acquaintances, despite the colonies in Michigan and Iowa.

The arrival at Milwaukee of Reverend P. Zonne was of importance to the Wisconsin colonists. This Seceder preacher, the last one to be fined, rejected Michigan. "It seems quite true that Michigan is very unhealthy, espe-

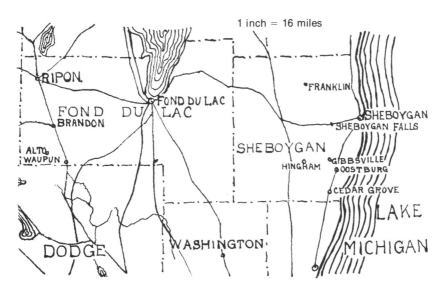

Protestant settlements in Wisconsin.

cially the place chosen by Van Raalte for colonization. I don't know of any place more unfit than the one of the concocted plan, and the advantages so liberally depicted by Van Raalte are nine-tenths, if not entirely, exaggerated."[126]

Although the number of Netherlanders in Milwaukee continually increased, so that in 1848 it reached 500 among a largely German population of 14,000, still Reverend Zonne lived here only shortly. Already in 1847 he moved with a number of Netherlanders northward to Sheboygan County. Its southeastern part consisted of heavy clay alternating with sandy hills and, as in Michigan, it was covered with woods. Different farmers bought eighty acres and formed a Holland colony, later known as Cedar Grove. In the latter part of 1852 the colony counted more than two hundred cleared farms with four thousand to six thousand acres of cultivated land.[127]

In the same Sheboygan County there arose still other Netherlands settlements. Zeelanders founded the village of Oostburg where the Daan family, originally residents of Pultneyville, New York, settled as one of the first families and contributed much to the prosperity of Oostburg. Already in 1844 the [Jan] Zuvelt [Zeevelt] family lived in this vicinity.[128] Some distance to the north the village of Gibbsville was established, where, as in Cedar Grove and Milwaukee, settlers included some of the Hollanders who were rescued from the ill-fated steamer *Phoenix*. Numerous Hollanders chose as their residence Sheboygan, the port city in this county.

The settlement of Reverend Baay in Wisconsin in 1848 also became important.[129] In February of that year, he traveled with a great company from Apeldoorn to Rotterdam and on March 7 departed from Hellevoetsluis on the Bremen ship *Wichelhausen*, arriving in the first part of May in New York City, after a stormy voyage of sixty-four days. During the trip the heavy weather had broken the bowsprit, the beam of the foremast, and the top of the main mast. From New York on, Baay had the same experiences as so many before and after him. In the first place he had to warn his party about their countrymen who were out to cheat and lead them astray. However, in Albany he found much friendliness from Americans of Old Dutch parentage. Baay paid too much for the boat trip to Buffalo and also had to battle constantly against the high prices of food. Deceit was everywhere!

The settlers' intentions to go to Wisconsin were largely blocked by a letter received in Buffalo, written by Van Raalte, in which he warned against Baay's choice, because in Wisconsin there were living too many Germans and Catholics. But in Baay's view this was incorrect.[130] The final result was that when the immigrants landed in Milwaukee, the greater part of them crossed the Big Lake from there to Michigan. Only two families followed Baay to the interior of Wisconsin to a region in the vicinity of Waupun, where different families already lived, especially those from the province of Gelderland. This was near Alto, south of Lake Winnebago, Baay's goal of the trip. Van Raalte, for a long time, also had had his eye on this territory.

On June 5 the much smaller party started from Milwaukee in two wagons. The first day they traveled exclusively through the forest, the following day along "cultivated fields of various grains, alternating with pastures that provided abundant food for the cattle." In his letter to his Dutch friends, Baay continues about his experiences: "Nowhere did I see such beautiful cattle and never did I drink such rich milk."

Waupun and Alto together had upwards of thirty families, most of them possessing eighty acres of land and some even three or four times eighty acres! And it had a healthy climate! "For twenty-eight years my wife was in poor health and here she is healthy and strong." No wonder that, in spite of the letters of Van Raalte and Scholte, many an immigrant of means went to Wisconsin. Sleyster, on August 25, 1846, had written from Waupun that "those who brought 1,500 guilders to the interior of the country could be prosperous farmers in a short time." But "those who have no money, I know not what advice to give."

Wisconsin thus remained a competitor and not without success. In 1849, some 150 families from the province of Zeeland under the guidance of Reverend H. G. Klijn and the elders J. Kotvis, J. De Pree, and P. Lankester traveled to Michigan, where Reverend Klijn received a call to the congregation of Graafschap.[131] A few of these families stayed behind in Rochester, New York, including the subsequently famous Zwemer family from Oostkappelle, but many more went on to Wisconsin.[132] The elders Kotvis and Lankester, with twenty-five families, founded the village of Franklin, fifteen miles southwest of Milwaukee. In this way the number of Netherlanders in Wisconsin grew and increased. Some of them came directly from Europe; some others had already lived a few years on American soil, either in New York State, Michigan, or elsewhere, where they had waged the battle for existence.

Illinios was still a fourth area drawing a number of believing emigrants. From this state J. A. Buekenhorst in Decatur already had written on June 16, 1845: "Those who can should come here." Thirty persons went there in the fall of 1845. This prairie state had also been mentioned by the leaders of the emigration movement in the Netherlands. Later Van Raalte declared it unfit; it was located too far south and the land in this state was too expensive for his emigrants without means, while Scholte gave preference to the western and cheaper Iowa.

Still there were farmers whose thoughts remained centered on Illinois. Four families of the province of Zuid Holland—those of P. Killewinger, C. Arentse, C. Schaai, and A. De Ruiter—landed in the spring of 1847 in the booming city of Chicago, port city of Illinois, to seek suitable prairie land in the vicinity of this city.[133] In May, 1847, this led to a settlement near the Little Calumet River, about twenty miles south of Chicago, in a fertile gently rolling territory. In 1846 the American government "paid out" this area, which was valued at $1.25 per acre, as a way of paying the soldiers who had fought in the Mexican War. They, in turn, sold it to a certain |John Mason|

Peck, a land speculator, at seventy-five cents per acre.* The farmers negotiated with Peck and set up their tents near the Little Calumet. Their numbers were reinforced by the newly arrived families of H. De Jong, R. Van
Vuren, W. Gouwens, A. Zwijnenberg, and a few Benschop families. They
bought the riverside lands along the Little Calumet for $1.75 and $2.75 an
acre. The farmers after that concentrated on cattle raising and also on
farming. That is how the first Dutch settlement originated in Illinois and
was called "*Lage Prairie*" [Low Prairie].

The village increased from the immigration of relatives and acquaintances to such an extent that Reverend W. C. Wust on September 3, 1848,
already could organize the Holland people into a church congregation.[134]
Mostly a colony of people from the province of Zuid Holland, it was at the
suggestion of Peter De Jong, Zwarte Piet [Black Pete], who had emigrated in
1859 with his parents, that in 1869 it was renamed South Holland, a name it
still bears today.

A number of people from the province of Noord Holland learned about the
settlement on the prairies of Illinois. In the spring of 1849 they considered
the plan to improve their lot in America. Some of them belonged to the
Seceder Church, followers of which held meetings since 1842 in Krabbendam
and there were led to organize a Seceder congregation in 1845. Another
Seceder was Pieter De Jong, a school teacher in Kerkebuurt in the district of
Haringcarspel, who acted as leader of the emigrants. Among others who went
with Pieter was his brother Jacob (brother Dirk stayed behind in the Netherlands because of his wife), J. Ton, H. and G. Eenigenburg, K. Akkerman, K. and
P. Dalenberg, Cornelis Kuyper, and Jan Vermeulen.[135] The last person, J. Vermeulen, was a Roman Catholic shopkeeper in Eenigenburg who had sided
with the Seceder congregation in Krabbendam. His dissent caused his former
fellow Catholics to turn so hostile that it not only bankrupted his business
but even his life was threatened. There were fifteen families in the party, all
from the province of Noord Holland, except the [Leendert] Van der Syde
family, who hailed from the province of Zuid Holland. Only two of the emigrants were not married; one of them, J. Ton, was a farmhand.

On April 16, 1849, they boarded a Frisian barge in Schoorl that took them
to Rotterdam, from where they departed via steamboat to Hâvre and finally
boarded the American sailboat *Boston*. At Hâvre the party tarried four days
and shopped for necessary provisions. Among these was a barrel of wine.
However, once on board the vessel, the barrel was emptied by sailors in a
few days, "leaving nothing but air for the tired travelers." The sea voyage,
shared by many Zeelanders, lasted forty-two days and they landed virtually
famished in New York City.

From here began the land trip that lasted sixteen days; first via steamboat to Troy, and from there via Erie canalboat to Buffalo. For once there

---

*The reference is to military bounty land warrants that Congress gave to soldiers who served in the
Mexican War.

were no complaints about the canalboat. They were treated with bread and brown sugar! At Buffalo the party boarded the Great Lakes ship *Key Stone State* to Chicago. On July 4, 1849, they arrived in this expanding city, which already had 25,000 inhabitants. They were fortunate and succeeded in finding an unfurnished house for a temporary stay. They had to wade through the muddy streets; the main ones were covered with heavy boards so that one would not sink away in the quagmire!

A few members of the party left and investigated Low Prairie. A certain Klaas Pool, whom they met by chance, took them to the settlement. On the way back, the delegates passed a ten- to twenty-foot high prairie ridge near the Calumet River. The ridge was covered with two-foot tall grass and wild flowers, which pleased them so much that they decided to settle there. Through the mediation of |Levi| Osterhoudt, who lived near Riverdale and spoke Low German, 200 acres were purchased at $5 per acre.[136] This land was distributed as follows: K. Dalenberg, 40 acres; P. De Jong, 35; Jb. De Jong, 40; C. Kuyper, 15; P. Dalenberg, 10; L. Van der Syde, 18; and G. Eenigenburg, 10 acres. The purchase spread out between the present 99th Street and 115th Street and between State Street and Lake Calumet. Later they bought still more land westward to the present Halsted Street. They found temporary shelter in a few homes in the vicinity of Messrs. Lob |Hamilton Lopp| and Bruell |Charles H. Buhl|. The wood necessary for building homes was hauled by oxcart from Chicago, and soon the first house was built with the aid of carpenter Abram De Koker from Green Bay, Wisconsin.

Thus the foundation was laid for the second Dutch settlement in Illinois, called after its higher elevation, "*Hooge Prairie*" |High Prairie|. This area was not only suitable for farming and raising cattle but also for trade because of its favorable position on the former "Indian Trail" to Michigan and Canada, which today is the busy Michigan Avenue to Detroit. This colony also was soon reinforced by many people from the mother country, such as the families of C. Ton, Jacob Schoon, P. and M. Madderom, P. and B. Prins, T. Maat, I. Snip, B. Van Mijnen, M. Van der Star, C. Roggeveen, H. Van der Bilt, and others. The farmers continued to call it High Prairie. The businessmen gave it the name *Calumet*; later both names were replaced by *Roseland*; probably after the beautiful rose garden in front of the home of Van de Winde |William Van Winden(?)|.[137]

The spiritual atmosphere in these settlements is shown by the fact that for the first Sundays they went to church in Low Prairie, a distance of fourteen miles, on overloaded oxcarts "while singing long metric psalms." On September 23, 1849, they already organized their own church congregation, starting with eighteen members and meeting in the barn of K. Dalenberg. The services were led by Jb. De Jong, chosen as elder.

The city of Chicago worked its way up to Queen of the Lakes due to its location at the most southern end of Lake Michigan, which dips deep into the area there. It is therefore understandable that many Netherlanders were drawn to this most important business center. Especially those who did not feel at home in "*de Kolonie*"—in Michigan—and could not get enough work, came to Chicago. There were people such as K. Koelewijn, who left for Chicago, where men were constantly hired to work in the lumber harbor and for building of roads and houses. Finally the supply of labor outpaced the demand "because there is a flood of people; since the Irish and the *nooretlui* [Norsemen] have come to America, things have been spoiled for the workmen here."[138]

But many Netherlanders went directly to Chicago, especially those from the provinces of Zuid Holland and Noord Holland, and from the Groningen villages of Uskwerd [Usquert], Uithuizen, Uithuizermeeden, etc. Among them were the Van Dellens who are well known today among the Christian Reformed people.[139] Already in 1859 there was a "Groninger quarter" in Chicago and even before that, in 1853, the first Reformed congregation was organized among the Netherlanders.

While the craftsmen stayed in the city, the farmers, either independently or as hired hands, soon tried to take up dairy farming and make butter and cheese, since the low and marshy land gave excellent pasture but little farming land.

In spite of these settlements, Illinois has never had the importance for the Netherlands Seceders that Michigan, Iowa, and Wisconsin have obtained. It is also striking that the emigration to Illinois had never been under the leadership of a preacher. Hence it lacked the eloquent preacher's pen to spread the word about the Illinois settlements, no matter how "deeply religious" their people were.[140] In the other settlements, Van Raalte, Scholte, Van der Meulen, Bolks, Baay, and Zonne all publicized their settlements. Scholte's *Eene Stem uit Pella* [A Voice from Pella] was even translated into German in abbreviated form.[141] In spite of this lack of clerical publicists, the tempting "*spekbrieven*" ["baconletters"] of Illinois have not remained without results, as we noted previously.

6

The Emigration
(*Continued*)

A. Frisians and Roman Catholics

There are people who think that it was "almost exclusively" the Seceders who took part in the migration of the years 1845–1850, the "Great
Trek," as the Holland-Americans, who feel kinship with the |South Afri-
can| Boers, like to call it. From the Reformed side in the Netherlands,
some have tried to emphasize this perception, although acknowledging
that there were also those who went along who belonged to a mixed
group. In this regard they relied upon an anonymous writer about whom
they had nothing to relate but bad things. In an "extremely scanty little"
sermon about the emigration, this anonymous writer, for example, made
one remark that people eagerly accepted: "As everywhere else, so it is
also here (in the area of Heusden and Altena) that Seceders almost
exclusively are the people who exhibit a definite inclination toward
emigration."[1]

The facts, however, speak a different language. Nowhere is it reported
that the emigrants who left for America in the spring of 1845 or in the
previous years belonged to the Seceders. Only in the fall of 1845 is there a
mention of them, specifically in a letter that Brummelkamp and Van Raalte
sent to the believers in America. In this letter, dated May 25, 1846, they
speak of a "group of thirty souls from our congregations and other respectable citizens" who departed for Illinois in the fall of the previous year. In
the same letter it is reported that a total of fifty souls hoped to leave the
following month, including "some members of our congregations, and
some other Christian fellow citizens."

The incorrectness of the point of view of the anonymous writer, which
was so strongly stressed by the Reformed spokesmen, appears also from a
report of Scholte in *De Reformatie* of June, 1846, in which he relates regarding
emigration that a few contributions had come in and very many inquiries,
the latter mostly from those in need. "The majority of the wholly needy

ones, however, were not among the Seceders. If possible, all would be helped, but the Seceders would have preference."[2]

Let it be said to the credit of Van Raalte, Scholte, and other leaders that they fulfilled this promise. In Article 8 of the Constitution of the Arnhem Emigration Society, no mention was ever made of Seceders, but of Christians, of an effort to make the colony a Christian one, and of making provision for a Christian majority. Recently in Christian Reformed circles in America, E. J. Tuuk, with a certain satisfaction, pointed out this liberal attitude of the leaders: "Bear in mind they were men of the Secession of '34 but there was nothing petty or small about them in this enterprise."[3]

We may safely assume that there were among the colonists very many "non-Seceders," as [Jannes] Van de Luyster called a part of his Zeelanders. Van Raalte's "*stad*" Holland, for example, numbered not only Seceders but also many other Christians and even a few worldly citizens.[4] Scholte declared in *Eene Stem uit Pella* [A Voice from Pella]: "Although those who were called Christians in the Netherlands were divided among different denominations, here they still form only one congregation."[5] Of the families who emigrated between 1835 and 1848, only one-fourth reported that they belonged to the Seceders. So it may even be assumed that members of the Hervormde Kerk made up the large majority.

With regard to the ecclesiastical controversies that later broke out in the different settlements and the subsequent splitting of churches, non-Seceders have not been without influence. How large their number was, in the end, is difficult to determine, especially since the need had become so great in our fatherland that Brummelkamp and Van Raalte declared: "Catholics and Protestants volunteer to leave their faith or to renounce it, as they say, if only we will help them in external matters!"[6]

If there were then a number of non-Seceders who considered themselves more or less related and took part in the colonization of the Seceders, many others emigrated entirely independently from them, either as individuals or in smaller or larger groups. Only among the Roman Catholics did emigration lead to colonization, just as among the Seceders. Among the other emigrants, as far as I know, colonization has not occurred or occurred permanently because many lacked the will or the stamina, sometimes both, especially since such a binding and strengthening element as the Faith was not present in most cases. Regarding the individual emigration of Hollanders, one finds evidence of it in almost every American city of some importance, and here and there also in rural areas. One can open almost any [telephone] directory in America and find a few Van's and other Dutch names, although it is not always possible to make out from the spelling which names date back to the seventeenth century and which date to the nineteenth and twentieth centuries.

Regardless of the less desirable elements of Dutch blood with whom immigrants came into contact everywhere, the Groninger [Klaas Janszoon] Beukma was surprised by the great number of former Hollanders whom he became acquainted with in 1835 in New York, "from whom I received a great deal of advice and friendship."[7] It also struck Van Raalte that he found and met a large number of Hollanders on his trip to the West. In Rochester, New York, according to him, there were a couple hundred Hollanders in residence, among whom Visscher [Johannes De Visser] from Zeeland preached. "There are also many worldly Hollanders," he declared. Even in Detroit, Van Raalte came across two worldly Dutch families who had lived there for four months already. The many Groningers in Chicago were by no means all Seceders. To the contrary, they were indeed known "to have sunken so deeply that they prefer to spend the Sabbath in idleness rather than in worship and going to church." The Synagogue of Satan was first recreated by Cornelius Van der Meulen (1859–1861) into a paradise of God.[8]

1. *Worp Van Peyma and His Followers.*

Among the group immigration, only that of the Frisians, as far as I know, attracted any degree of attention, whether in the letters regarding their travels that appeared in print or concerning the place that the emigrants occupied in social life. In another connection references have already been made to the departure of a number of emigrants from the *"grietenijen"* [municipalities or districts] of Het Bilt and Barradeel, at least the majority of whom had undertaken the ocean trip to New York in April, 1847. Yet most of them, after a longer or shorter period of time, depending on whether they had earned some money on the way in Albany, New York, or Cleveland, Ohio, reached their goal of Lafayette, Indiana, the residence of Beukma. Mention of this has already been made. Two years later a company of mostly wealthy Frisians and a few Groningers left. Some of the Frisians were from clay soils in the northwest and some from the eastern sandy soils in the vicinity of Bergum.

Although improvement of their lot was their primary reason for leaving, there were also those among them just as many Seceders who were driven by more idealistic motives, who regarded America not only as a place where pork was eaten three times a day, but primarily as a land of freedom. Dissatisfaction with the government, its tax system, its officialdom, the shortsighted dragoon policy, and its fines against the Seceders, in short, its vexation with the "German" methods of governing, primarily those of Willem I, had, next to economic worries, led to the ripening of the plan to escape to America. *"Tous, tant que nous sommes, l'Amérique est notre asile commun."*[9] [For all of us, as many as we are, America is our common refuge.]

The most interesting among these Frisians, indeed one of the most important figures among the Dutch emigrants of that time, was the farmer Worp Van Peyma at Ternaard, an aristocrat-farmer and descendant of an old patrician family from Westdongeradeel, whose estate at one time stood at the Paesens, not far from Hantumhuizen. At the age of nineteen, Van Peyma was an independent farmer. In addition to engaging directly in farming, he made himself available for service in the Frisian dike defenses against the sea. From 1820 until he left for America in 1849, Van Peyma was "a member of the working board for dike maintenance and the works in Oostdongera-deel and Westdongeradeel, that had its own dike lock, Ezumazijl, and was completely separated from the dike maintenance department of the province." He wrote this information from America to a friend at the age of eighty-one.[10] He was one of the consultants for the government in connection with the management of sea dikes. After the dike breaks of 1825 he wrote a study about the construction of sea dikes and was able to have his plans accepted and executed in spite of the opposition of the dike boards, all with the cooperation of the governor [C.] Van Zuylen Van Nijevelt.

Van Peyma liked to tackle scientific problems, often preferring the study chamber to farming. But in the already very difficult times, Van Peyma had a hard struggle to make a living and found it necessary, as did so many farmers in those days, to participate in ordinary work in the field in order to save himself the wages of one farmhand.

Feeling attracted by the French and American spirit, and thus being even more strongly aggravated by the enlightened despotism of Willem I, Van Peyma was influenced by all kinds of factors working together to make him regard America as the land of the future for himself and his children. Already in 1830, when at the home of [Roelof Hessels] Hommema, one of his friends, he met an American who highly praised his fatherland, and this turned Van Peyma's thoughts in that direction. Still it was not until 1849 that he made the weighty decision to liquidate most of his substantial property. With his children and grandchildren and a number of good friends he left for America by way of Hamburg in May, 1849. Only a few were concerned about this departure, but among those few was Van Peyma's brother-in-law and spiritual friend, the many-sided, talented minister Rinse Posthumus, who in a gripping "*Farwol!*" [farewell] reported what went on in the hearts of Friesland's best sons.[11]

How hard it is, thus to take leave of one another,
Consoled that you went to the land of Washington,
And Franklin, through whose counsel and deeds
Freedom won out over servitude.

We people can only thrive in freedom;
That's how God wants it, He makes us so free:
That's what America tells us in the gladdening
Of those who come to freedom's school and shelter.
There we are human beings and citizens; before the law
No one has an advantage, except by their virtue.
No citizens are crushed by a heavy burden:
There a new world is growing in happy youth.

Oh Frisians! Netherlands! across the sea, to the west,
Lies the land where there is room for you to work.

To forget the land, where Mom cradled me and fed me
With mother's milk, where my parents' remains lie,
No one can: Nay! The human heart must bleed
When it, for the last time, bids that land farewell!*

Arriving in New York, the Van Peyma group spent the first weeks becoming acquainted. They received a great deal of help from Leendert Kingma, formerly of Makkum, who owned a brickyard and a lime kiln between Albany and New York at Wawarsing and who had traveled through a large part of the United States.

The Groningers, namely the Beukmas, Borgmans, and Van Houtens, finally settled in Plainfield, New Jersey, where the stony soil truly caused difficulties for agriculture and was better suited for orchards, but where the proximity of the rapidly growing city of New York furnished an important market for agricultural and garden crops as well as for dairy products. In addition, it was an inhabited region where one lived among the most cultured Americans, partly also of Old Dutch descent.

When a year later C. Borgman from Kloosterburen visited his family at Plainfield and with them went to the Presbyterian church, he was quite surprised "about the dresses, especially of the women who attended this church. They had provided themselves with parasols and fans for protection against the sun and heat and very generally dressed according to Parisian fashion."

The picturesqueness and liveliness of this area also struck him. Six times a day the train provided good connections, but what especially drew his attention were the numerous riders "among whom were even ladies in their riding habits galloping about unafraid." A single family, S., also from Groningen, settled on the equally stony Staten Island and there bought fifty acres of land. They applied themselves to cattle raising and gardening, which provided "very substantial advantages because of the proximity of New York."[12]

The Frisians, namely the Van Peymas, Koopmans, Zuidemas, Dijkstras, and others, seemingly were not attracted by the social life to the degree of our Groningers. They also found the land here to be too expensive and too poor; thus they traveled farther to the North, where they bought land near the town called Lancaster, ten miles east of Buffalo, and there they indeed established a Frisian colony covering an area of about three [square] miles. The land there, especially on both sides of Buffalo Creek, consists of excellent clay, which according to the aforementioned Borgman, who also visited

Ho swier it falt, sa fen elkor te schieden,
It treast, dat jou nei 't lân fen Washington
In Franklin gonch, jae, troch wans ried in dieden,
De frijheit der de tjienstberheit oerwon,

Wij minsken kinne alline yn frijheit tierje;
Sa wol it God, hij makket uus sa frij:
Sa seit Amerika uus yn 't opblierjen
Fen dij 't der komme yn frijheits schoelle in lij.
Der is men minske in borger; for de wetten

Het nimmen eat foruut, as troch syn deuchd.
Nin borgers wurd' troch swiere laest forplette:
Der groeit in nije wrâd yn bliere jeuchd.

O Friesen! Nederlân! oer see, yn 't westen,
Leit 't lân, wer 't roemtme for jimme arbeid is.

Forjitte it lân, wer 't mem uus widze in fiede
Mei tate, wer 't uus âders stof yn leit,
Kin nimmen: Nee! it minske-hart' mat bliede,
As it dat lân for 't laeste: farwol! seit.

the Frisians, is certainly much better than the soil of New Jersey and is not inferior to the best clay lands of Holland.[13]

Worp Van Peyma settled nearest to Lancaster and bought eighteen acres of land on which there were three residences.[14] The main house, which he himself occupied, was very near the highway to the village. It was "a beautiful country seat . . . surrounded by a beautiful garden." One of the other two much smaller homes was occupied by a workman and his wife whom Van Peyma had taken with him. The third he rented out.

Twenty minutes further, J. D. and R. Van Peyma each bought ninety acres of land and applied themselves as true Frisians to the raising of cattle. In 1850 they each owned thirty head of cattle, produced butter and cheese that was just as good as in Friesland, and also sold a great deal of the milk in Buffalo. R. Van Peyma also owned a "beautiful and fine, well-situated white residence, two stories high, in front of which was a lawn sloping to the highway, shaded by luxurious trees." Ten minutes beyond, D. |Dijkstra|, K. |Koopman| had purchased 125 acres of mostly very fertile and low clay soil for $60 per acre and beyond that another 110 acres of woods. He also devoted himself principally to cattle raising. The widow D. |Sarah Dijkstra, widow of Gerrit Jans| had 150 acres farther on, mostly heavy clay soil, including 50 acres of woods. In addition this enterprising woman operated a brick factory in which German laborers worked for one-third of the profits.

On the other side of the railroad that ran through the colony, J. Z. |Jan H. Zuidema| had sixty acres of land purchased at $50 per acre and, just as the widow D., busied himself principally with farming. Because of that, both of these farms appealed the most to |C.| Borgman, the Groninger, upon his visit. He himself acknowledged this, "because cultivation was the principal activity and not cattle raising."[15] Finally, Dr. |Jacob| Van Peyma, apparently the son of Worp and Z's |Zuidema's| nearest neighbor, who lived the farthest from Lancaster, had paid $40 per acre for thirty acres of land, mostly still wooded and only partially cleared. He served as a doctor and already in 1850 had a "satisfactory practice," especially also among the Americans and Germans who disliked quackery and whose confidence he had won.

One cannot escape the impression that this colony must certainly have been the richest and that it was founded with the least amount of effort of all those established in those days by our fellow countrymen. However, this obviously required a considerable amount of capital. Settlement there was thus possible only for the affluent. According to Borgman, the colonists seemed "on the whole to feel at home" already in 1850, all the more so since they did not have to pay high taxes "nor the notorious poor tax." And they foresaw a good future open for their children.

As far as the Van Peymas were concerned, this prosperity is confirmed in the interesting unpublished letters of Worp Van Peyma, who after a few years sold the greater part of his holdings at a very large (one-third) profit, and opened a steam tannery and owned a discount bank. How typically American! No matter how great the changes in his material life, his love for science continued and at that time he had a study room added. He read a great deal of French and German and applied himself energetically to the study of the English language. To do this, he not only allowed his correspondence to lapse "for a while," but even found it necessary "to push behind the bench his otherwise most beloved Dutch reading materials. . . . Now I delight myself concerning the latter, since I now read and understand English almost as easily as my mother tongue. The latter, however, still has preference, especially when I must elaborate on something and have to write it down. . . . Since the Hollanders here in Lancaster are with few exceptions all Frisians, I have in the fifteen to sixteen years since we have been here heard or spoken very little Dutch. It is Frisian or English in my home, and outside either English or a variety of "low" or "high" German. But the Dutch language still is uppermost in my mind, although I no longer pay much attention to grammar or orthography. It remains in my eyes a beautiful language, although English in some respects is shorter in expression and may be more easily acquired."[16]

From the letters written to his *Frisian* friends in the *Dutch* language, one notices that Van Peyma had not yet forgotten this language. Indeed, he had taken with him across the ocean almost all of the works published by his friend [W.] Eekhoff of Leeuwarden, and had later publications sent to him. In 1877 he admitted: "While reading quite a bit of French, High German and especially a great deal of English, the mother tongue has certainly been the loser, although I continue to cling to it above all others."[17] Included in his Dutch readings were those concerning dike maintenance. These were his favorites, "in which I still always continue to have the same interest as when I was among you."[18] While living in America, Van Peyma had written an essay about the silt deposits of the Wadden that was published through the efforts of his brother-in-law [Rinse] Posthumus and of his notary Klaasensz in Holland.

It is moving to notice with what truly deep interest the "American" Van Peyma continued to follow events in the Old Country and how he sympathized, for example, with the high water levels of January 30, 1877, and their consequences. He even allowed his thoughts to be directed to the plans for the draining the Zuiderzee and studied and compared the opinions about this of Beyerink and [J. A.] Van Diggelen. It is also moving to read in one of his last letters concerning his Zuiderzee studies: "Whether I will ever be in a position to collect these particular comments into a systematic whole is very uncertain, since I have already celebrated my eighty-first birthday last month."[19] And a few months later this energetic eighty-one-year-old wrote: "Should I still write about defense against the sea and the acquiring of land from the sea, then I will possibly also get to the topic of the Zuiderzee and give reasons why the Zuiderzee was not silted up still more during so many centuries. I greatly differ with many people on this point and certainly also cannot agree with all of Van Diggelen's views."[20] Assuredly there is truth in the observation made from the Frisian side: "It is an indictment that there is no longer a place between the Flie and the Lauwers* for a man with such a wide horizon and such talents."[21]

For the rest, Van Peyma felt happy in America: "We are living by ourselves in abundant ease up to this time." He busied himself a great deal with the education of his children. Three of his sons became doctors, one a lawyer, and one an educator. Two of his children moved with their families to Iowa and Kansas to take up farming. Van Peyma's family finally numbered only three members, himself, his second wife, and one daughter.

Van Peyma refused to accept any kind of job. However, he had many experiences, which prompted him to make such a notable remark in his last letter to his friend W. Eekhoff in Leeuwarden: "Meanwhile I had to look upon myself many a time as an already too old, transplanted tree, transferred and brought over to a far country, which for a long time would not flourish so well as in the soil of the fatherland."[22] This energetic man died in June, 1881, at Lancaster.

The settlement of the Groningers in Plainfield, New Jersey, and the Frisians in nearby Lancaster, New York, caused more colonists to come to these places since that time. For example, the Dutch family De B. K. had settled in Plainfield already in 1850 and had purchased a farm of 110 acres for $6,000. It seems that same year an Utrecht family had settled nine miles from Lancaster on a rented farm, while five miles east of the "village" a Hollander, Forell, tried to farm. In Lancaster, a former student at Leyden, K., who had participated in the Greek war for independence and later had wandered in Mexico, had "a prospering well-patronized store."[23]

In 1855 the total number of colonists was estimated to be a couple of hundred around the two towns. Neither of the two settlements, however, became large. Either the unfertile soil or the expensive land was a continuing deterrent to settlement. Then, too, a few of the most educated among the Van Houtens and also a few of the Van Peymas in the long run did not feel at home in America.[24] Van Houten, who after the death of his first wife, whose maiden name was Borgman, remarried a daughter of Worp Van Peyma, and later moved to Pella, Iowa, where we will meet him in 1869 as host of the Dutch businessman, "Mr."† A. E. Croockewit.

2. O. H. *Bonnema and His Followers.*

Although not occurring within the years of the real Great Migration, two more Frisian "migrations," both of which took place in 1853, merit our interest. In Friesland especially, there was an increase in the number of

---

*The Flie (Vlie or Vliestroom) is the sea passage between the Wadden Islands of Vlieland and Terschelling on the northwest coast of Friesland. The Lauwerszee (today Lauwersmeer) is a bay of the Waddenzee on Friesland's eastern border with Groningen. Hence, the Flie and the Lauwers are on the western and eastern borders of Friesland Province.

†The abbreviation of *Meester*, a Dutch title for lawyers; see footnote on page 73.

those who considered emigration as "the only way to escape from the bonds of poverty and need, and to open a source of prosperity." This conviction brought a number of Frisians from different parts of the province to unite themselves under the leadership of O. H. Bonnema, a grain dealer at Kimswerd. The group left the country from Harlingen on February 26, 1853, in order to "free themselves from that general recession that is so clearly in evidence in our fatherland."[25] The farewell was heart-rending. "We shall never forget, as we parted from Frisian soil, the tense moments that were spent among the hundreds of relatives and friends when people shouted "farewell" once more to each other. Never did I waver more between hope and fear than I did during those moments. Driven forward by a brisk Northeaster, the crowd soon disappeared from our sight and nothing remained but the coast of Friesland which, covered with snow, looked like a bank of chalk."

After the arrival of the steamship *City of Norwich* at Lowestoft, on which the group totaling ninety-two persons made the trip, they traveled by rail to Liverpool, attracting attention everywhere because of the wooden shoes and the silver ear decorations of the women. The Frisian women especially aroused pity because of their bonnets, which prompted the English to cry out: "Oh God! These women have no hair!" On the other hand, the edifying manner in which the English observed the Sabbath in Liverpool made a big impression on them: "In that great business center a deathlike quiet reigned on that day, which affords the citizen an opportunity to honor the Almighty in a proper manner." The company consisted mostly of "worldly" Frisians. "The Bible came into the hands of only a few." B. B. Haagsma, Bonnema's bookkeeper, who described this trip, was offended in this regard by his associates because on June 5, the Lord's day, "our people lay upon the deck almost the entire day like cattle in the pasture. . . . In the matter of observing the Sabbath in a pious manner we were far inferior to the English, indeed to many colored people."

On March 21, eighty-six of the Frisians sailed—a total of six had returned to Friesland because of the impression the journey had made thus far—on the beautiful three-masted *William and Mary*, a ship of five-hundred English tons famous for its great speed. The events of this sea voyage have already been described in chapter 4. There was the repeated warning given before leaving Friesland: "Almost all ships are wrecked," which prophecy had even prevented a few from undertaking the trip. In this instance, it became a fact. In spite of the cowardly conduct of the English captain, when the ship was wrecked near the Bahama Islands, the migrants were rescued by a beachcomber's schooner and brought to shore on the islands. However, three Frisians who were picked up by an American ship landed in Liverpool! The generally poor island folk cared for the migrants lovingly and provided them with necessary clothing: "Everyone here (in the small town of Nassau) seems to make it a point of honor to do good." Finally, the trip so rudely interrupted was continued to New Orleans. On June 10, 1853, they landed in this city, where our Frisians were dumbfounded to learn that not only the ship *William and Mary* had been wrecked, but [supposedly] that two hundred passengers, including the Frisians, had perished in the waves!

Ministered to by the agent of a German society for assistance to emigrants, the shipwreck victims were provided by the city treasury with provisions for the trip upriver and each was given $5.50, as a result of which the Frisians had at their disposal a total of $440. Already by June 11 they boarded a riverboat to sail up the Mississippi: "Alternately, we saw beautiful plantations with majestic oak woods behind, then again densely covered woodlands down to the shoreline, indeed even up to twenty to thirty feet into the river. Thousands of turns provided various surprising views constantly!" For five days they remained in St. Louis where they bought tools; then they continued the river trip, passing by a number of towns. One of them was Davenport, a new town of two thousand inhabitants, "where someone standing on the river bank asked us: 'Where are you from?' in Frisian. So we knew from what province he was and answered his unexpected question. 'I am from Wolvegae' he finally said. This was the first Frisian we met in America although we had already met Hollanders in various cities."

On June 29 the immigrants arrived at Galena in northern Illinois. The men left the women and children behind in this city while they traveled farther the following day to seek a suitable colony site. In the vicinity of the city of Prairie La Crosse in Wisconsin, a city which had existed for only seven years, they began a more detailed investigation. They even inspected the land on the opposite side of the river in Minnesota. Fertile as it was, however, it was judged to be unsuitable because it had insufficient transportation facilities. But Bonnema "bought" a house with eighty acres of land from a German there, three miles distant from the river, upon which two families settled. They were probably the first Dutch colonists in Minnesota.

The rest of the Frisians, however, settled north of the city of La Crosse in the Black River area near a little town called Onalaska where 640 acres of land were "purchased," or rather "claimed," by Bonnema with the help of a Dutch gentleman, Van Rensselaar. This Hollander, a native of Amsterdam, had moved to America with his parents when only six years old and now occupied important posts in this state. Fortunately, he still could understand the Dutch *"in lyts bytsje"* ["a little bit"] as he said in Dutch heavily tainted with English. At Onalaska they purchased the necessary lumber for the building of homes and transported it eight miles to the claimed area, where they speedily erected two serviceable "tents." In this way, the foundation was laid for the colony of "Frisia." Sixty Frisians finally settled in this colony. Fourteen had died during the trip by sea, and one family had remained in St. Louis; so two-thirds of the original number had reached their goal.

During the next three months, six homes were constructed, in addition to a carpenter shop and a blacksmith shop. All were "built more or less in the Frisian style" near the shore of a stream flowing into the Black River.

This farming colony, however, did not prosper. Soon a few left, among them the carpenter. The young settlement's population in 1855 had dwindled to fifty. Haagsma called urgently to the affluent, as well as the less wealthy and poor compatriots, to settle in Frisia: "Not a soul needs to harbor the opinion that good fortune and satisfaction are solely connected with the land of one's birth." It is nowhere apparent to me that there were many who gave heed to this call. A brother of Bonnema did go to take a peek at the colony once and then remained in America.

Frisia, however, died entirely. The laborers who had been brought over at the expense of their leader to establish a large farming project with him did not wish to remain in the service of Oepke Haitzes [Bonnema] but rented or bought land elsewhere. The two Bonnemas found themselves forced to resume their former business of grain dealing, but they had a hard time, as a second cousin, E. Bonnema of Jelsum, informed me. One of them later occupied the position of city treasurer. One of their brothers who had remained in the Netherlands, E. Bonnema's grandfather, said frequently: "If they had only remained in the Netherlands, then they would certainly have become rich, especially in the years 1860–1880, since the price of grain increased so much locally while it decreased in America."[26] Now, just as so many wealthy Hollanders who left for America, they died there in comparative poverty around 1892. Bonnema's bookkeeper, Haagsma, later settled in St. Louis where he served his compatriots as Netherland's consul.

The name Frisia no longer appears in the vicinity of La Crosse. There are a few other colonies—New Amsterdam and Mindorp to the north and Brinkman to the south of this city—which are reminders of Hollanders, because already earlier a Reformed mission station had been established in New Amsterdam in 1877.

3. *Balk Mennonites*

The second Frisian emigration in the year 1853 calling for our attention was of an entirely different character. It involved a number of Mennonites from Balk who, like many Seceders—and probably more strongly than most—left the fatherland because of their religious convictions. The trend of greater involvement in religious life, emphasized in chapter 4, also came to expression among the Mennonites. But in contrast to what was noticed among the Dutch Hervormden [Reformed], it led them to greater tolerance. As a result, it became possible to amalgamate the various groups among which the Mennonites were divided.[27]

In a few places people would have nothing to do with this, as for example, the congregation of the "*Nieuwe Vermaning*" [New Admonition] (that is, the church) at Aalsmeer and the congregation of the Old Frisians at Balk.[28] People said of this last named Old Mennonite congregation, numbering thirty-five members and eighty-nine souls in 1838, that with regard to cooperation, "these people of Balk still seem to remain the most obstinate."[29] We learn about these "*Fijnen*" [hairsplitting orthodox ones], as they were called in contrast to the "*Groven*" [coarse ones], from the interesting "*Mededeelingen*" [information] concerning them that were printed as an appendix of S. Blaupot ten Cate's *Geschiedenis der Doopsgezinden in Friesland* [History of the Mennonites in Friesland].[30] The rigidity of their religious opinions is indicated there. After the service of Baptism, for example, which like Communion was held only once a year, one of the Teachers one of the Eldest—there were four Teachers: two Eldest and two Assistants—"lifts up those baptized, greets them with a Christian love kiss and admonishes them to remain true to the profession made."

The church service was still "in its infancy" among them and consisted of a not too well sounding singing, "the silent prayer, during which the Members knelt with their backs turned to the Teacher and of a Sermon very simple in language and style that consists largely of Bible texts." The footwashing, practiced earlier here and there, was "no longer practiced in Balk as a Church ceremony, but as a service of love, so that when one or more Brethren from another Congregation would be sent to them to render some spiritual service, they greet them with a holy kiss of love and as a symbol of humility and eagerness to oblige upon their arrival, wash the feet of same at the place where they have taken up abode. . . . 'Outmarriage,' that is to say a marriage of a Brother or Sister with someone not belonging to the congregation, resulted in an Ecclesiastical ban, to the extent that the person involved was excommunicated from the Fellowship." Except for that, in contrast to the religiously equally very conservative Seceders, the Mennonites were "friendly and helpful toward everyone" in their workaday life.

Concerning their social life, they distinguished themselves particularly "by a simple, not very comfortable clothing, and a very sober lifestyle. No gold or silver is worn on the person nor tolerated for domestic use. The majority do not smoke tobacco nor use strong drink. What is not absolutely necessary for bodily sustenance is labeled by them as waste. Their homes are austere and can be recognized by the special and uniform architecture and color. Their furniture is very inexpensive and meager; but their material circumstances, amassed through industry and frugality, are on the whole favorable." It seems clear to me from an interesting writing by a brother from Aalsmeer to the minister R. J. Smit of Balk, that there were already evidences among those who emigrated in 1853, especially among the youth, of departure from the strict rules of living and related convictions described above that were encountered among the Balkers in the year 1839.[31] From this writing it appeared to me that not only the use of strong drink but also smoking was opposed most strongly by Smit and others. It must thus have been a disappointment for the Balkers, once they had established themselves in America, to find fellow believers who did not seem to be opposed to smoking. This is one of the reasons apparently why the Balkers were not inclined to a complete affiliation. More about this later.

It is also understandable that Mennonites, with this spiritual attitude, would have nothing to do with the bearing of arms, and that our Balkers in this respect were in complete contrast with "fellow believers" like the formerly-discussed emigrant Van der Kemp, the Mennonite minister and army commander! The prevailing opinion in our Mennonite circles "that military service by government order is a duty for every citizen" was not shared by the Balkers.[32]

In regard to the Frisian Mennnonites in 1839, Blaupot ten Cate remarked, ". . . that they now live as faithful and obedient inhabitants of the State, that they gave strong evidence of this not least of all by their contribution in 1830 and subsequently, that the reputation which was then enjoyed by the Frisians is also due to them. They do not find from their position any reason for complaint about the Government of the country, but honor and respect the King, given to us by God; they love him as Father of the Fatherland."[33] The Balkers would not have taken responsibility for this remark! At first they only developed an inner resistance, but under the influence of the previously-described "shift" in the national consciousness, they submitted petitions to the government for "dispensation from bearing arms." When this did not help, some of them decided to leave the country for America, where Congress had particularly warranted freedom from military service to the Mennonites.[34]

They did not have to leave the country for economic reasons. What was stated regarding their "temporal" situation in 1839 was also true for the year 1853, when they left for America. Their contemporary and friend, D. S. Gorter, in contrast to Bonnema's bookkeeper, Haagsma, considered that "our earthly well-being and our life's fortunes [are] most closely bound to fatherland and home." He addressed those leaving as follows: "You had rented good farms here with land and acreage developed by your industry, manured and made fertile by your sweat, which nourished you abundantly and promised you an unencumbered living to the time of your death; and all of this you are giving up in order to seek an uncertain existence abroad."[35] In addition, a Mennonite from Balk, who was closely associated with the Mennonite emigrants, declared after further investigation: "They were not all what one would call rich, but well-to-do. Their greatest motive was freedom from bearing arms."[36] Gorter also wrote that they were leaving for religious reasons ". . . and in this way you are giving to this spineless and argumentative century an example of a mighty sacrificial faith, . . . a silent rebuke to those who remain."[37]

On April 15, 1853, the small group left from Rotterdam—the ministers R. J. Smit and R. J. Symensma with two other families, Visser and Huitema, for a total of seventeen souls, all Mennonites. A few others joined them. By way of Goole and Liverpool, where they wandered about for a few days "to everyone's amazement" with wooden shoes, and even "slippers and socks," the "*Mennisten*" |Mennonites| traveled to Philadelphia.[38] The steamer *Glasgow* brought them over the Atlantic Ocean. While enroute, the thus-far childless marriage of R. and J. was blessed with a newborn baby who was given the name of the boat. She gained an advantage from this because, at the age of twenty, she was permitted to travel to Europe at the expense of the steam-ship company.[39] The trip by sea was so pleasant that Symensma's wife declared, "If we could earn our bread on the sea, I would risk it to spend my life there." This was then an exception to what we have previously noted about the ocean trips.

For our Mennonites the troubles first began after arrival in the United States. In part, let it be admitted, it was their own fault and due to outright ineptness. There had certainly been very little preparations. The Balkers would not hear of making contact with the descendants of the Dutch "*Mennisten*" who had already settled in America in the seventeenth century, as for example Van Raalte and Scholte had done in relation to the Reformed folk. "For certain reasons they did not follow the advice of friend G., to look up the brethren in Lancaster, Pennsylvania, first; but they went directly to Pittsburgh by rail, thinking that they would be able to make inquiries everywhere."[40]

Smit and his people just wished to sojourn in America "as strangers and aliens." Well, they experienced what this means! They were so completely surrounded by crooks from the moment that they sojourned on American soil, that—so Smit wrote—"Had I had but worldly experiences, probably despair would have taken possession of me in the first port, although I knew on the other hand that it would have to happen that way."

The Balkers experienced more severe tests. Just as so many others, they learned "that the poor emigrants in wagons and ships are frequently treated as herds of cattle or as baggage." Probably it is for that reason too that Smit and his people preferably traveled on foot, seeking for like-minded Mennonite brethren whom they hoped to find first in Ohio and later in Indiana. Certainly the Amish brethren, the "Bearded Men," were supposed to live there. Among the numerous groups of Mennonites of the most scattered variety who had settled in America since the seventeenth, but especially in the eighteenth century, these Amish brethren belonged to the most conservative. They are named after the Swiss Mennonite minister, Jacob Amman from the Bern Canton, who had introduced among other things footwashing among his followers and the use of hooks and eyes on coats and other clothing.* Banished from Switzerland in 1711, they escaped by way of Amsterdam to America, where they still preserve these customs to the present day.

These Amish brethren, just as many of their fellow believers, had settled in and around Lancaster, Pennsylvania. Because of a shortage of land and the wish to live more separated from the other inhabitants in order better

---

*The use of buttons on clothing was considered militaristic. The wearing of mustaches, too!

to maintain the old customs, many of them and other Mennonites in the beginning of the nineteenth century moved farther to the west through the Ohio valley. A few groups settled in Ohio; others traveled farther westward after 1840, where they were impressed by the fertility of Indiana. They applied themselves to farming and cattle-raising on the prairies in this state and in the forests east of the city of Goshen in Elkhart County, and later in the neighboring counties.[41]

From what we have previously related about the religious notions of the Balkers, it is understandable for us that they must have felt quite at home among the Amish brethren and followed literally in their footsteps, as indeed the Amish brethren had done previously [sic]. After suffering all kinds of hardships, they reached the town of Zoar, in Ohio, where they looked in vain for the bearded men, who seemed to have settled five and a half hours farther on in Waynesburg. The land, however, seemed to be too expensive here, so they traveled still farther west to Indiana, except for a few laborers who had found work in the vicinity of the city of Dover.

Finally, again after the most unusual travel experiences, three of the families arrived in Goshen on June 1. This was more than seven weeks after leaving Friesland; twenty-two days were spent in roaming around in the United States. "We have missed a bed for more than three weeks and without doubt have not been undressed for fourteen days. We have spent many nights wobbling on benches because there was no room for us to stretch out upon the floor."

Finally, however, there came an end to all trouble. After two innkeepers in Goshen had refused to take in the exhausted emigrants, they found lodging at the third. And once they had become acquainted with the ministers and Mennonites in and around Goshen, they were cared for by them in a most hospitable manner. Also, with the help of the Mennonites in the area, the Balkers looked over four "eighties" (parcels of land of eighty acres), "next to each other," ten miles south of Goshen, near the village of New Paris. Included was a "beautiful log cabin, garden, and courtyard." The owner had already cleared fifty acres of land. "First each of us took a drink of water from his well, [then we] asked about the price and conditions. While discussing this and inspecting the land, we came near to a stump and sitting on it we bought this property for *fl.*7,900 [$3,160]."[42]

The purchased land was divided among the three families of Smit, his brother-in-law Symensma, and that of a certain B. W., in such a way that each received seventeen acres of "cleared" land and ninety acres of woodland. Our Frisians began chopping the trees already a day after the purchase. "It was on the ninth of June that the first of our axe-bites echoed in the American forest. In less than a half hour the sweat ran from our faces, but less than an hour and half had gone by before twelve trees lay felled and soon there were fires burning as big as I've ever seen."

Meanwhile others also came from Ohio, among them the lucky parents R. and J.; but three men remained in Ohio. In August, 1853, the small colony numbered twenty individuals. With the help of the neighbors they built log cabins for all the families. These neighbors also helped our believers in every other possible way to make pioneer life easier. The Mennonites were very numerous here "and treated us with the greatest of love," even though there was some difference in church customs.

Although "union was sought by them earnestly," the Balkers temporarily remained independent in church matters. The Mennonite neighbors belonged to various groups: real Mennonites, as well as Amish brethren, and in the matter of morals the most genuine *"Thunkers"* [Dunkers] were found among them. That the members of all these groups smoked "small pipes little larger than a thimble" surprised our people, still more because many of the women also used these little pipes, to which they ascribed a wholesome influence upon health.

The Balkers, temporarily at least, postponed the founding of their own "admonition" [church] on the land purchased by them, where they also thought of laying out a cemetery. One of the ministers urged this by calling to their attention "that this would be a hindrance to our fraternization [assimilation]." They were permitted to use a church building that was used once in four weeks and was situated one hour away; on other Sundays they could use it "without hindrance." "The key was at our disposal."[43] For many years, nevertheless, at least according to C. H. Smith, the Balkers formed a more or less independent congregation where they held services according to their own admonition and in their own language.[44]

Now, however, they are no longer a separate congregation, but have gone over to the "Amish." However, a division existed among these "Amish." One faction was getting too worldly, and the conservatives, or the "Old Order," would have nothing to do with the buggy, bicycle, telephone, curtains, and musical instruments. They still wore long beards, the trimming of which, just as the use of buttons instead of hooks and eyes, resulted in banishment from the congregation. So there was also a schism among the Balkers and their descendants. Most of them, including Smit and Symensma, joined the very conservative "Old Mennonites," the bearded men, and were a part of the Salem congregation. Others, such as a few Huitemas, now belong to the "Mennonite Brethren of Christ," the most Methodistic group among the Mennonites.[45] Two Huitemas are now even ministers in this latter group: D. Hygema, an Americanization of Huitema, at Nappanee, Indiana, the original settlement of the Mennonites near Elkhart, and J. Hygema at Milford, Nebraska.

In material matters, things have gone well with the Mennonites, since most of them are industrious and thrifty. Among their descendants there are, besides farmers, also businessmen and even bankers. The Vissers have become prominent. Klaas, who was born in Balk in 1840, had come over with his parents, and later married a daughter of Symensma, joined "the Mennonite Church" in 1891, and died in 1924. He had five children, of which two daughters, Mrs. Duker and Mrs. Vandervier, married countrymen, as is indicated by their names.[46] It is, however, two of his cousins who have made the most progress, Martin Fisher, a businessman, and his brother, the bank director.

Whether the colony was reinforced by new arrivals is not known to me. Reverend Leendertz, whom I asked, never heard about this. One of the Huitemas later went to Friesland to convert his former fellow believers, but without any results.[47] J. M. Leendertz, a Mennonite minister, recently visited them and met there two old men born in Friesland. They could still speak Frisian and could understand the Dutch of Reverend Leendertz. Otherwise not much of the Dutch has remained. Surprisingly, while in other respects they are such conservative people in contrast with other more modern Holland-Americans, as we have seen previously, yet they have Americanized their names: Smit became Smith and Visser became Fisher.

Although the Balker emigration in its results has not been of great importance compared to that of the Seceders and that of the Catholics, as we shall see later, it still deserves this elaborate discussion. In no single group of Dutch emigrants in the nineteenth century did the idealistic motive for emigration come to the fore so genuinely and so exclusively as with these truly sober but courageous Frisians.

4. Roman Catholic Emigration

Now we must still deal with one very important emigration, namely that of the Roman Catholics. Although on the whole very little interest has been shown in the pioneers of the nineteenth century in the United States—and what is known about them is known almost exclusively in ecclesiastical circles—this is true to an even greater extent regarding the Catholics among them. As a result, unjust opinions have been formed regarding the emigration of Catholics. For example, the Seceders were warned by some quarters in 1846 not to leave the country because Protestantism would be victimized since Catholics, "who never showed much zeal for emigration," would then expand there and Ultramontanism would gain influence as a result.[48] It was unjustly considered by these quarters that the writing of Brummelkamp and Van Raalte had no influence upon them. We have already pointed out how the facts indicated something quite different!

In our day, H. Blink has repeatedly indicated the existing phenomenon as he saw it, that emigration from Catholic areas was very limited and that primarily Protestants moved.[49] Professor Blink associates this with the already-mentioned subdivided land ownership and with the small-scale farming operations that resulted, but he thinks also that the Roman Catholic Church tied a person closer to the parish of his birthplace than was the case for Protestants.[50] Others associate this supposedly limited zeal for emigration with "race." "The attachment to their birthplace and still more the aversion to travel by sea is a typical racial characteristic of the majority of the population of Noord Brabant," the government's archivist at 's Hertogenbosch wrote to me.[51] This view has also been expressed frequently regarding other nations, even though they finally provided the largest numbers of emigrants.

Whether the more than 40,000 Dutch Roman Catholic emigrants from Noord Brabant and Limburg who have settled in the United States—to say nothing about those living in other countries—would confirm the above remarks is very doubtful! Think also of the more than four million Roman Catholic Italians and millions of Roman Catholic Irish in the Republic! Or think of the more than two million Lutheran Norwegians, Swedes, and Danes who were considered in the first half of the nineteenth century to be afflicted with this same "racial peculiarity." The authoritative Potgieter expressed the opinion that the Norwegian farmers were too much attached to the soil. "From such wood, so firmly grown into the soil, from such wood no emigrants are hewn."[52] And now?

Conditions among the Catholics were no better than those among other groups of the population. They also had to wage a severe struggle to make a living. Also among them the ecclesiastical and school policies of the government aroused great dissatisfaction, all the more so since they were more often the victims, like the Seceders. Was not a Roman Catholic priest exiled for six years because he had opened a Christian school?[53] It happened at a time when Catholics also expressed their "complaints" in several of their own papers and magazines, some of which were already founded at the time of Willem I.[54] Even a pro-government person declared: "Being a Catholic myself I feel very much grieved about what the Catholics must endure in our country. Frequently my freedom-breathing soul is deeply shocked, and a blush of indignation spreads over my face."[55] Honest people resigned themselves to the circumstances, in language like we heard from the men of the Réveil: "My exalted religion, though, teaches me to be submissive to lawful authority and teaches me especially the sweet hope and unwavering trust that rests upon the infallible promises of our Divine Creator." He did not wish to "flee from" his Fatherland any more than they.

But also among the Catholics there were those who thought and *acted* differently, whose protest was not limited to a blushing face. Among the educated, the "shift" came to expression in gatherings, in books and papers either in poetry or in prose. The more simple in spirit exhibited their "opposition" in another manner. Their growing activism drove them to America. Already in 1845 the departure of Roman Catholics attracted attention second only to that of the Seceders. They also considered emigration to be "a mainstay of hope and deliverance."

De Catholijke Nederlandsche Stemmen [The Catholic Netherlands Voices][56] of 1846 (established in 1843!) contained the following announcement:

> Since the Dutch Catholics for more than thirty years have been bereft of the enjoyment of the most precious liberties, and because of more and more pressing taxes and the increasing cost of food, their material as well as

religious and moral welfare has for some time been noticeably reduced; Catholics in various parts of the fatherland, as well as non-Catholics, have therefore made the decision to move to the United States of *North America*, to purchase land, and to settle there. This aim can never be realized more easily and better than by the cooperation of everyone who has made the same decision. At *Nijmegen*, Province of *Gelderland*, various wealthy Catholic families who have made a decision to leave next February, 1847, for *North America*, and to buy land along the Missouri, have appointed a committee for the purpose of making all the provisions and arrangements necessary for their departure. A meeting place has been decided upon now where everyone who has the same plan and possesses the necessary means can join, to the end of helping carry out the plan jointly and to prevent parties arriving in *America* independently from being separated by great distances from one another and settling in various places in isolation. By intelligent cooperation an entire area could be purchased in order to establish a Dutch Catholic Colony.

The secretary of this committee "for the promotion of regular emigration of Dutch Catholics to North America" was Meester C. Verwayen of Nijmegen to whom those interested could refer "preferably in person or with postpaid letters," at the latest by the end of November, 1846.

The main idea was the same as that of the Seceders: colonization preferably by fellow believers. Clerical leadership was lacking, however, in these Nijmegen plans. Presumably as a result, nothing came of the famous colony near the Missouri where the Catholic Church had much influence.

Not that people did not emigrate. To the contrary; but they went in small groups. This emigration had at least in the early years an individual character. Many left, especially from the southern portion of our country situated "above" the Waal, but also—let it be said with emphasis—from other areas. For example, four Roman Catholic families moved from the Noord Holland village of Warmenhuizen in 1846, two of them to Evansville. A. C. Robbers joined the latter "in order to be with her parents and her husband, who had moved there previously and were settled there." From Alkmaar four Roman Catholic families left in 1847, a total of sixteen individuals; the heads were respectively a watchmaker, cabinetmaker, surgeon, and shopkeeper. From Nibbikswoud in the same year three Roman Catholic families and three singles undertook the dangerous journey. They were indigent folk, with "little education and training," and were driven in part by a "desire for the improvement of their status," the turnabout! ["*kentering*"]. However, they did not know "the place of their destination."[57]

Most Catholics followed the general stream of European immigration: through the valleys of the Hudson and Mohawk to the West. Thus Van Raalte already wrote in his frequently mentioned letter from Buffalo of November 27, 1846, about the "Catholic Hollanders" who lived there. He made a less complimentary remark two weeks later from Detroit: "The Catholics who have dropped down here are mostly bad people." The Seceders were just no friends of the Catholics!

This, however, did not deter the Catholics from following with great interest, and even with sympathy, the emigration movement among the Seceders. For example, *De Catholijke Nederlandsche Stemmen*, agreeing with Scholte's articles about migration in *De Reformatie*, welcomed and very elaborately reprinted them.[58] This Catholic paper made mention of "a remarkable article" in which Scholte made "strong, but concise reproofs" to the *Handelsblad*. "*De Reformatie* tells this Amsterdam stockmarket paper hard truths and contends that that paper is incompetent or displays bad faith. The *Staatscourant* [the official government paper] also received its share of well-earned blame that *De Reformatie* casts upon all opponents of emigration, who without knowledge of the facts write in a partisan or misleading manner about emigration to *North America*."

However, those in Catholic circles became acquainted with America and with the areas suited for colonization in other ways. Among the numerous Jesuits, who since the beginning of the seventeenth century attempted to bring faith and culture into Canada as well as in "America," and as "elite troops" of the Catholic Church established numerous mission posts among Indians and whites, there were also priests from the southern and northern Netherlanders. These clergymen did not neglect to report to family members and acquaintances about the long journey and the frequently wonderful experiences they had. These were sometimes so interesting that the letters were circulated in print and thus were widely spread. Very detailed, for example, is the *Rijsverhaal* [*Travel Narrative*] of B. G. Krijnen, S. J. that appeared in 1837 in 's Hertogenbosch.[59] On September 23, 1835, he left from Antwerp with two other priests, Th. De Leeuw and A. Eysvogels, and four other individuals, among them a baker and a cabinetworker, all assigned to North American missions. On December 22 they arrived in St. Louis and were received "with thousands and thousands of benedictions." The priests were originally from Breda and Oss.

5. With *Van den Broek* to *Wisconsin*

Of overriding importance for the emigration of Catholic Hollanders have become the life and activities of Father [Theodorus] Van den Broek, O. P. This priest, born in 1783 in Amsterdam and originally admitted to the Franciscan Order, later changed to the Dominican Order following a dispensation by the Pope in 1817. From 1819 to 1830 he was a parish priest at Alkmaar and likewise from 1830 to 1832 at Tiel. Later he received permission to go to North America as a missionary to proclaim the gospel among Indians in the area between the Mississippi River, Lake Michigan, and Lake Superior. In a very elaborate description sent from "Grand Cocalin above Green Bay, Wisconsin T[erritory], N[orth] America," reprinted in the *Godsdienstvriend* [Friend of Religion] of 1843, this pioneer priest reported on his work among the Indians and among the German and Irish immigrants.[60]

On July 15, 1832, he sailed with six other missionaries from Antwerp to

Baltimore, from where they traveled further to Cincinnati. The vicar of this city sent Van den Broek to the cloister at St. Rosa in Kentucky to study there for some time. Already in October he went to Somerset "in the Ohio" to the cloister of St. Joseph, charged by his provincial, [P.] De Young (De Jong?) to administer the holy sacraments among more than ten thousand Germans settled in the surrounding large cities "which are situated one hundred to two hundred miles from each other." In 1833, however, Van den Broek received permission to go to Detroit, in the vicinity of which he narrowly escaped death: "My horse sank with me into a morass, so that all rescue seemed impossible; however, I was fortunate enough to get off the horse backwards and to reach solid ground. I offered a prayer of faith and began to cry out loud with all my might. Beyond all expectations, I heard a voice from the other side of the lake and soon help came to me from there. . . . Two men succeeded with the help of poles to rescue my horse."

The bishop of Michigan sent Van den Broek to Wisconsin, to Green Bay, "a bay which is situated 42°43' North latitude and is called Green Bay because of the green territories which are found at this bay's entrance." In this area, a flourishing Dutch colony would later arise. Upon his arrival on July 4, 1834, the missionary found only nine or ten houses, "but very many Indians." There he erected the church and the parsonage and witnessed the number of inhabitants increase to one thousand, the number of settlements increase by three, among them the village of Rapides des Pères, later on usually called De Pere. The Americans gave the village this name "because there is a rapid waterfall there, and 150 years before there was a Jesuit station with two fathers, of which one was killed by the wild Indians and whose remains were thrown into the rapids. They hacked the missionary to pieces, and in order that he would not resurrect, as they said, they burned the remains and threw the ashes in the river."

More than two years later, on December 6, 1836, Van den Broek was ordered by his bishop to leave his station and to settle "twenty-four miles further away in the forest with the wild Indians, in a place called La Petite Chûte, a small waterfall near Grand Cocalin." With the help of converted Indians, a church and a parsonage were built here also. For years Van den Broek performed his sacrificial task here among the Menomonee Indians, and among the Winnebago Indians who lived more to the south. He labored in poverty "without receiving support from Europe except what was sent to me by my mother and a few friends." His task was made much more difficult by the many Germans, French-Canadians, and Irish who settled in these areas: "My activities are unbelievably great. On Sundays I preach in the forenoon nowadays in the French, English, and High-German languages, and in the afternoon in the Indian language. In addition, I conduct school every day and often make missionary journeys. I am, however, in spite of all these tiresome duties very healthy, and I find everything easy due to the Divine support at my age of sixty." This, to state it properly, was "not the work of a giant but that of a saint."

Spiritual leaders of the immigrants. Top: Reverend C. Van der Meulen, a leader of the Zeelanders. Middle: Father T. J. Van den Broek, O.P., the founder of the Roman Catholic colony in Wisconsin. Bottom: Reverend H. P. Scholte, the founder of Pella in Marion County, Iowa.

In 1847 our missionary received permission to return for some time to the Netherlands to take care of his own affairs. Having arrived there he discovered that the Amsterdam notary who had taken care of his interests had disappeared, taking with him a large sum of money, including *fl.*10,000 [$4,000] that had remained of Van den Broek's inheritance following the death of his parents! In addition to this sad history, other matters kept the Dominican busy. Already in America he had thought about a possible colonization by his fellow believers and compatriots and now he attempted to work out this idea further. In the writing mentioned above, he already pointed to the many Germans who had settled in his locale and remarked further: "The land where I live lies along the Fox River; La Petite Chûte is a very pleasant place, where at the time of my arrival there was only forest; but where I can now already sow one hundred bushels of grain. It is a very healthful and fertile land there. In the Wisconsins, as our area is called, are grown very good winter-wheat, corn, oats, peas, beans, potatoes, etc.; all kinds of trees are found there. There are many copper, lead, iron, and coal mines."

In Holland Van den Broek now wrote a small book about his stay at Fox River, in which he pictured the beauty of the country, the fertility of the soil, and the healthfulness of the climate in such glowing colors that many of his fellow countrymen wished to respond to his call to emigrate to the land of freedom.[61]

In addition, he also addressed an open letter to his "Fellow Countrymen in Jesus Christ!" to support his mission but also to follow him: "Now still one more word to you, Roman Catholics in Holland, who because of accidents or adversity wish to attempt your luck in my missions in the New World. Say with the apostle Paul: 'Oh, the depths of the riches both of the wisdom and the knowledge of God! How unsearchable are His judgments, and His ways past finding out!' [Rom. 11:33]. In the hands of Divine Providence your crosses and trials will become the instrument for the spreading of the faith and by the example of your faith and fiery zeal, you will bring converts to a more spiritual life. Prepare yourself carefully and well. I am always ready—as I have said in the book which I published—to furnish you all kinds of information."[62]

From all sides emigrants streamed in, from Holland and Zeeland as well as from Noord Brabant and Gelderland. Their number was so great that Van den Broek negotiated with the firm of Hugo and Blokhuizen of Rotterdam for the lease of three ships. Various matters were simplified for him, in that the Brabander Cornelis Van de Hey from the village of Zeeland [Noord Brabant], who had long considered emigration and now after reading Van den Broek's pamphlet had reached a definite decision, was able to accumulate a sum of *fl.*9,000 among his fellow emigrants. As a result of this cooperation, the passage, except for provisions, would cost only *fl.*56.

On March 19, 1848, the *Maria Magdalena* left from Rotterdam with Father Van den Broek and a few Amsterdamers also on board. One of the latter,

J. C. Van Niel, described how a man and a woman with their two-year-old child wept so bitterly about the step taken "that the captain considered it to be his duty to send the unfortunate couple back to Holland in a life boat, although we had been at sea two days." He also told about religious life aboard ship. On the stern of the ship a desk served as an altar upon which the Father read the holy mass daily, assisted by Jan Wigman, who later would become "one of the greatest and most famous lawyers in the northern states." "Every evening Father Van den Broek came with us to pray the Rosary and after that the singers sang the 'Salve Regina'."

Wigman, also an Amsterdamer, tells us about a severe storm that the emigrants experienced: "Tuesday afternoon it had reached its worst. Everything was swept from the deck by the high waves that dashed over the ship. The captain and the crew had even tied themselves to the ship. When by evening there did not seem to be a possibility of a let up, the captain asked for an axe to chop down the main mast in order yet to save the ship in this way."

Where was Father Van den Broek during this storm? "His cabin was across from mine. I lay in bed because it was impossible to remain standing, for the ship rocked terribly and was rolled up and down by the stormy waves. From all sides one heard cries of distress. It was more than pathetic. As I thought I had reached my final hour, I stood up and looked for Father Van den Broek. I found him in his cabin, kneeling before his crucifix, praying to God with warm tears for deliverance. When he heard that the captain was at the point of chopping down the mast, he jumped up, left his cabin and, although the waves were rolling over the deck, rushed to the captain and kept him from carrying out his plan. The captain stood dismayed, but followed the advice of our brave priest-leader, and see, soon the storm abated."

After having arrived at New York, they followed the well-known way over Albany to Buffalo. Here Van den Broek had an argument with the captain of the canal boat, who demanded a second payment for the trip that had already been paid for. After the Father had returned to New York to settle this "misunderstanding," the emigrants left for Mackinac, where Lake Huron joins with Lake Michigan, and from there they sailed in small ships to Green Bay and further along the Fox River to Little Chute. The Hollanders arrived June 10, 1848, after having been on their way for eighty-three days.

Meanwhile two other ships had left Holland with emigrants, the *Amerika* enroute to Philadelphia and the *Libra* bound for Boston.[63] The emigrants aboard the latter ship totaled eighty individuals. They were under the leadership of the Franciscan Father Gothard and were largely from the environs of Uden in Noord Brabant. From this community their trunks and travel requisites were transported by cart to Vechel. "From Vechel we traveled by two boats to 's [Hertogen] Bosch, where the same barge was towed by a steamer to Rotterdam, where we embarked on March 10 on the small three-masted ship *Libra*." After a sea journey of fifty-two days they arrived safely on May 5, 1848, in Boston, where three families remained behind. The others left by way of Buffalo and Mackinac to Green Bay, where just as at

Buffalo a family remained behind. The others soon left the green bay: "From there we left for Kaukana with a flat-bottomed barge that was pro- pelled by six men with poles, which took two full days. From there we continued on to Little Chute, where we arrived at the end of May and remained for a few days to rest and make further plans for the future."

In the beginning of June, very likely at the suggestion of Father Gothard, he and the families Verkuilen, Van den Berg, Ebben, Verboort, and Driek Van der Hey laid out the village of Franciscus Bosch [Francis' Woods] a few miles east of Little Chute in the middle of the forest. After the departure of Father Gothard two years later, the village with good reason was renamed Holland, because it was the first settlement in the vicinity established exclusively by Hollanders, in contrast to the somewhat older villages of Little Chute, Freedom, and Bay Settlement, where Germans, Frenchmen, and Irish had preceded the otherwise very numerous Hollanders.

The Dutch pioneers were followed by many others. In the spring of 1849 numerous emigrants left for America from the communities of Zeeland, Uden, Vechel, etc.[64] They were, however, without any spiritual leadership. In 1850 this prompted the Honorable. G. J. B. Van den Heuvel, who was "driven solely by zeal for the salvation of souls, voluntarily to leave kith and kin, and also the community of Boekel whose highly esteemed chaplain he was, to undertake the care of the souls of the numerous families of Noord Brabanters in the far country."[65] Two hundred additional Noord Brabanters went with him![66] In proportion to the increase in the number of emigrants, there occurred a corresponding lack of spiritual help, and people in the young colony longed for priests. "If the Crozier Fathers [Kruisheeren] from Uden and St. Agatha knew to what danger our souls are exposed, they

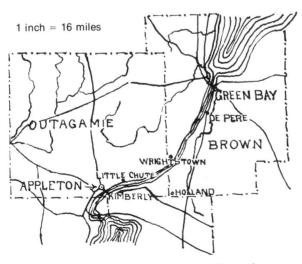

Roman Catholic settlements in Wisconsin.

would certainly come to help us." Indeed, "this appeal to the ancient Order's willingness to sacrifice found an enthusiastic response in its cloisters." In September, 1850, the friar-missionaries Wilhelm De Jonge and Hubert Nuyts, priests from the cloister at Uden, left for Wisconsin. They were the first of a long list from this order who to the present day fulfill sacrificial mission tasks in the Midwest.

For many Catholics who still delayed seeking their fortune in America, the final hindrance disappeared with the arrival of these friars. They now joined those who had settled previously in the Fox River Valley and with them laid the foundation for the later very prosperous Dutch colony. "Some may have felt disappointed when they landed, because while still in the Netherlands they could not have imagined the virgin forests in the western hemisphere. Some may also have regretted taking the step and when seated on stumps in the dense woods, they yearned for their motherland and despaired of a future in the New World. But this certainly did not last long." Indeed the pioneers were strengthened by a steady reinforcement of their numbers from the motherland.

Apparently the emigration by Catholic Hollanders has been more important than is usually recognized. Even in the year 1853, two Catholics emigrated compared to three Reformed folk, and one must keep in mind also that at that time scarcely more than a third of the population of Holland was Catholic.[67]

The Catholic Church as such, however, has not taken a part in emigration, neither promoting nor encouraging it. Whenever priests went along with emigrants or followed them, this was on their personal initiative.[68] Their number was small, however, because most of the Dutch priests would have nothing to do with this "trek." For example, the pastor at the time in the Brabant village of Zeeland, from the vicinity of which so many left the country, believed that America was a strange and bad country. "And although he knew very little about the priests who lived there, yet he considered them not to be of the best kind."[69]

All the more striking is the great number of Catholic emigrants, since Catholics in the first half of the nineteenth century were hardly welcome. Americans belonging to the Reformed Church of America wished very much to help Dutch emigrants, provided they were not part of the Roman Catholic Church![70]

This spirit was evident also among a number of other denominations. Due to the arrival of so many predominantly Irish and German Catholics, essentially Protestant America feared the increasing influence of the Roman Catholic Church and the resulting weakening of democratic institutions.[71] Therefore, immigration of Catholics was considered to be "of the devil," so says [Frank Julien] Warne. According to somber predictions in the newspapers, this would indeed lead "to the submerging of our institutions and the inevitable downfall of the Republic through Catholicism."[72]

Serious disturbances even occurred in New York, Boston, and Philadelphia against the Irish and in Cincinnati against the Germans. Undoubtedly, economic causes had contributed. Mayo Smith sees a "no popery excitement" in this;[73] others view it as a product of economic jealousy [*broodnijd*].[74] Still, these disturbances bore primarily an anti-Catholic character. They were, as Lauck and Jenks confirmed, "largely based on opposition to the immigration of Catholics rather than to that of persons undesirable for other reasons."[75] People were especially aggravated, as Mayo Smith also points out, because they thought that Catholics voted according to the orders of their priests.[76]

B. Postscript

In summary, it appears to us that not only Seceders left the country, although their emigration undoubtedly was the most noticeable, but also a number of more or less orthodox Hervormde Kerk members, many Roman Catholics, numberless "worldly" Netherlanders, a few Mennonites, and some Zwijndrecht Newlights. To what extent the number of Seceders has been exaggerated and Catholics underestimated is evident from the fact that of the 2,331 emigrant heads of families who left from 1835 to 1848, only 653 declared themselves to be Seceders and 449 Roman Catholic!

Socially, the large majority of emigrants belonged to the "*kleine luyden*" [common folk]. However, there were also many affluent among them. Think of the Pella colonists and of those who left with Van Peyma. Most of the emigrants came from rural areas, but a smaller number came from cities. Of those who emigrated in the period from 1845 to 1847, seven-eighths came from the countryside.[77] America must have exerted a greater attraction upon those from the country than from the cities. Religious zeal must also have been of great influence in these years. On the whole, however, it can be stated that people of different religions, social status, and occupations left for the New World, although differing in their relative numbers. Understandably, as we have seen, they were moved in this matter by different motives of an economic, religious, or even a political nature.

I would gladly have confirmed these various matters on the basis of exact statistics. But most unfortunately, in the realm of statistics there is probably no material less trustworthy than that associated with emigration. Even the concept "emigrant" is, to the present day, subject to continuous revision and despite a few efforts put forth to that end, its definition is still not internationally established. I have already indicated elsewhere the comparative worthlessness of emigration statistics.[78]

How carefully American statistics must be used may be shown by the fact that Americans regarded travelers who traveled first and second class as immigrants only after January 1, 1903. As a result of this genuine administrative revision in the concept of *immigrant*, the total of immigrants suddenly increased by 12 percent! Other revisions, however, caused the total to decrease again, with the result that the statistical totals again were more nearly accurate, although they remained doubtful. For example, before January 1, 1906, whenever a foreigner came to the United States, he was regarded as an immigrant. But anyone returning from a foreign visit after that date was no longer looked on as such; as a result the statistics of total immigration were reduced by more than 10 percent![79]

When one is reminded that numerous Hollanders did not migrate as mere steerage passengers, it is understandable that for that reason alone the American figures must be lower than those of Holland for the period covered. This is even more the case since the number of visits to the Old Country was still very small then, and only later when people had achieved greater prosperity did it become more important.

But also, the migration statistics of the Netherlands are today so incomplete that recently two authorities relying upon these statistics—the incident is not without humor—attempted to point out the exact opposite![80] In "appreciation" of these Netherlands figures, let it be stated here that they were acquired in three different ways.[81] The "*Commissies van toezicht over den doortocht en het vervoer van landverhuizers*" ["The Commissions of Supervision over the Passage and Transportation of Emigrants"] furnished annual reports, which however apply only to overseas emigration and only to steerage passengers. The more affluent and in general those who left via foreign ports, therefore, are not included. The statistical yearbook *Bijdragen tot de statistiek van Nederland* [*Contributions to the Statistics of Holland*] contains the figures obtained from the mayors' reports, but these were not bound by a definite interpretation of the concept of "emigrant" and usually regarded only those of less wealth as such. A third set of figures is derived from the population registers [*bevolkingsregisters*] of the communities in which the names of those leaving are removed "because of departure to foreign countries." This record thus includes also the more prosperous emigrants. However, all these reports are very inaccurate, especially the last two data sets, regarding the country to which the person who left has emigrated. For these reasons the Dutch statistics on emigration to America during the period I have covered may be assumed to be somewhat too low.* It should also not be forgotten that many an America-bound person more or less intentionally did not think he had to give information about his leaving.

How different the American and the Netherlands statistics are may become evident from a few examples. From the years of Beukma's emigration in 1835 to and including the year 1843, according to the Dutch reports 124 Hollanders settled in the United States; but according to the American report, there were 1,780 Hollanders! I have previously given the total of Dutch immigrants up to the year 1848, based on American statistics. During the years 1845 to 1847 the number would then have been 791 + 979 + 2,631 = 4,401. But according to the Dutch reports, there would have been in 1846 from Winterswijk alone, 538 families totaling 1,755 persons leaving for America, and in the year 1847 alone from all of Holland, 1,520 families totaling 5,322 persons![82]

*Van Hinte actually uses the phrase "too high," but the context indicates clearly that Dutch statistics underreport emigration.

A committee appointed by the Society for the Benefit of the Public in 1847 to estimate the total emigrants for the three years 1845 to 1847, which relied also on information furnished by the Dutch government, gave as a figure almost 7,000, that is 1,100 to 1,200 families. Although these numbers do not agree with the "official" ones mentioned, we may regard them as more trustworthy, considering the very special investigations.

That one cannot speak of a decreasing emigration after 1847 is apparent from the following American statistics regarding Dutch immigration: 1848, 918; 1849, 1,190; 1850, 684; 1851, 352; 1852, 1,719; 1853, 600; 1854, 1,534; and 1855, 2,588. These figures must also be viewed as a minimum!

After 1855 the attraction of America decreased, at least for a short time, because of an economic crisis that occurred there. European conditions in agriculture and industry meanwhile had improved since 1850, so that the urge to leave ["*afstooting*"] had decreased. Gradually, these changes also were of importance in Holland. Already by 1850 emigration was less a matter of religion and politics and more one of an economic or "worldly" character. This is very clear from an official Netherlands report for the year 1853, according to the *Netherlandsche Staatscourant*, when 1,654 individuals emigrated.[83] Of these, 21 left because of poverty, 543 because of a desire for improvement in status (the turnabout!), 18 because of the example of others, and 11 because of religious principles. It would be interesting to know the exact numbers for different religions. The Committee cited above, however, mentioned only a "coincidence of various circumstances." The reports regarding the province of Groningen say something about the year 1853.[84] From that area 107 heads of families and independent individuals, a total of 246 persons, left for "overseas." Included in the 107 were 76 *Hervormden* [Reformed], 2 Mennonites, 17 Seceders, and 12 Roman Catholics.

From which areas the Dutch emigrants originated appears from the Netherlands reports for the years 1845 to 1854, during which period 20,417 Hollanders emigrated to overseas countries: Gelderland, 5,192; Zeeland, 4,745; Zuid Holland, 2,897; Noord Brabant, 1,585; Overijsel, 1,418; Groningen, 1,376; Friesland, 1,175; Noord Holland, 989; Drenthe, 594; Utrecht, 367; and Limburg, 69. Although these totals are "subject to revision," they are useful to show the incorrectness of Professor Blink's contention that the provinces with the least agricultural enterprises (Gelderland, Overijsel, Noord Brabant, and Limburg) produced the smallest number of emigrants.[85] This may be true at certain times because of definite circumstances, but this opinion certainly does not apply for the period of 1845 to 1854, and therefore not in general.

Although Brummelkamp's prediction that emigration to North America "must have the most dire consequences for Holland," did not become a reality, the sudden departure of so many did not remain without effect. In the centers of emigration, in the provinces of Gelderland and Zeeland, where the "epidemic" raged the strongest and several proceeded to the immediate sale of farms and dwellings, of furniture and crops standing in the field, the value of property decreased very severely. The rental of homes and leases decreased by 15 to 20 percent, while the value of real estate, especially of land, decreased by even 25 to 35 percent. No wonder that those involved thought about the future "with dread"![86]

Less noticeable at first, but of greater long-run importance, was the fact that it was precisely the energetic, the most active element that left our country. Large as the sums of money might have been that the emigrants took with them and therefore withdrew from our natural resources, far greater for our Fatherland was the loss of spiritual capital. Men of action like Van Raalte, Bolks, and so many others, we could hardly do without. People who dared to express themselves openly regarding religious issues as well as other problems were not too numerous in Holland around 1850!

The comments of [Wilhelm Georg Friedrich] Roscher about emigration in general also applied to the Netherlands: usually the ranks of the lower middle class were especially reduced and the gulf between poor and rich became considerably greater because of it.[87] As a result, the need for welfare support was not diminished in our country, regardless of the increasing emigration, but became greater not only comparatively but also in the absolute sense as we noted in the fourth chapter.

Emigration in our country has thus not remained unnoticed. This already became clear to us from the different quoted pamphlets and magazine articles relating to emigration, especially of the Seceders, that appeared for the purpose of encouragement or opposition. What a warm, if only tempo-rary, interest people showed, for example, in the circles of the Réveil! But also elsewhere! Unjustly and knowing better, people here in *Christelijk Gere-formeerde* [Christian Reformed] circles attempted to create the opinion that folks looked down upon the emigrants only "with proud disdain or with sympathetic shrugging of the shoulders," "upon these ostracized pariahs," who were actually "cast out" by the fatherland as "exiles."[88]

This is exemplified in an episode related by Jacob Van der Meulen in his "Reminiscences" in memory of his father, Cornelius, the apostle of Zee-land.[89] When the *Prinses Sophia*, the ship on which our Zeeland emigrants were aboard, was hailed by another Dutch ship, the captain or one of the crew seems to have answered the question regarding what he had on board by stating: "Counterfeit money no longer current in Holland." This was an answer, says one of our present-day church historians, "that only echoed the general feeling of ruling Liberalism."[90]

Certainly there were those for whom the concept "emigrant" denoted some wrongdoing or something pitiful and who therefore looked down upon them in disdain or pity, and not only upon the Seceders among them. In 1847 there even appeared a carnival poster by C. Campagne from Tiel on which the sad story of the miseries of Scholte and Van Raalte with their believers are pictured enroute to the *Nieuw-Luilekkerland* [New Wonderland]. From this, it is clear how little some people valued the activism of the emigrants.[91] It is evidence of a non-scientific approach, not to mention a lack of the Christian love of truth, to ascribe similar feelings to all of Liberalism. What a bitter injustice would be done by this to Potgieter and his adherents!

How were the Seceder emigrants pictured in the liberal journal *De Gids*? As men and women belonging to the nucleus of the farming and middle class, with muscular arms and fine heads, full of enthusiasm and energy, whose departure one regarded with sorrow. "No matter how little sympathy the exaggerations of the Separatists may inspire in us, they were compatriots, twigs from the same trunk."[92] That people among the more simple folk regarded this departure with sorrow may be clear from a somewhat saccharine outpouring appearing in the year 1847:[93]

> They are brothers, though, whom we miss,
> On the soil of the Fatherland,
> Where love at one time bound us together,
> Who wander off to foreign shores
> Where apparently liberty dwells,
> But where nevertheless no perfection rules.*

And this was preceded by the declaration:

> Indeed, it is the pronouncement of our heart;
> We, we see them go with sorrow.†

People not only sympathized with the Seceders alone, but with emigrants in general. Listen, for example, to the unusually bitter "The Emigrants' Farewell to Europe" by A. Winkler Prins, appearing about that time (1852):

> My asking for enlightenment and warmth,
>   That gave spirit and life to the old soil, was in vain;
> A spectator threatens . . . gradual growth of poverty!
>   It wanders everywhere—it wanders in an ominous manner;
> Thou killest industry through thy burdens,
>   Thou demandest thy part of the beggar's bread and salt,
> And the flunkies of the treasury thou entertainest as
>   Frolicsome guests with gold obtained through torture.‡

The way in which others could also very strikingly depict how the wanderers of that time cast a glance upon the New World is proven to me by the fact that even recently one of the oldest colonists in Michigan declared

---

* 't Zijn toch broeders, die wij derven,
  Op den Vaderlandschen grond,
  Waar de liefde ons eens verbond,
  Die naar vreemde kusten zwerven
  Waar de vrijheid schijnbaar woont,
  Maar toch geen volmaaktheid troont.

† Ja! 't is de uitspraak van ons hart;
  Wij, wij zien hen gaan met smart.

‡ 'k Vroeg vruchtloos naar verlichting en verwarming
    Die geest en leven gaf aan d'ouden grond;
  Een spooksel dreigt. . . . gestadige verarming!
    't Waart overal,—'t waart onheilspellend rond;
  De nijverheid vermoordt ge door uw lasten,
    Gij vergt uw deel van 's beedlaars brood en zout,
  En schatkistknechten onthaalt ge als dartle gasten
    Met afgepijnigd goud.

with typical American pathos: "And with dying lips I will sing along with the Dutch poet Ter Haar":[94]

> America! which poet's song
> Will not rise to a higher tune?
> Where thou ringest the sound of thy name?
> Who can sketch us what thou wilst become?
> What beautiful future shines for thee
> When already Europe is sinking in its grave;
> Although the old world is perishing,
> O, young and beautiful America.*

However, it was not only the finer-tuned soul of the author and poet who, sympathetic to the immigrant, was either struck by the courage or else by the tragedy of his undertaking. The interest soon spread out in broader circles. The Maatschappij tot Nut van het Algemeen [Society for the Benefit of the Public] appointed a commission in 1847 to study the emigration question and it collected a great deal of information. The commission finally produced a report in which emigration to North America was discouraged. The question also was discussed elsewhere: in the local chapters of the Society where lectures were given;[95] in the departments of the Maatschappij ter bevordering van Nijverheid [Society for the Advancement of Industry]; even from the pulpits it was considered to be proper to discourage emigration![96] Still others desired to promote emigration, and a few liberals in Amsterdam even intended to publish a weekly *De Landverhuizing* [The Emigration].[97]

Nor did the government remain neutral regarding the loss of so many subjects. What seems to have remained unknown to Potgieter and others became clear to me in the examination of the archives regarding emigration, namely that already before the Society began to work on this, the Minister of Home Affairs requested a report from the governors of the provinces noting "what emigration had taken place."[98] For this purpose questionnaires were prepared, shown in the accompanying photo of a facsimile, which had to be sent in by the "City or Community Boards" on or before January 10, 1848, with information about those who in 1847 or earlier "have moved to America or other overseas places." Details would even have to be secured "from information furnished by their remaining relatives or friends." Similar reports would be expected annually on or before January 10. These reports are still being used, as we have seen previously, to compile Netherlands statistics.

Amerika! welk dicht'renlied,
Verheft tot hooger galm zich niet?
Waar gij 't geklank uws naams laat hooren.

Wie schetst ons wat gij worden zult?
Wat schoone toekomst u gaat blinken
Als reeds Euroop' in 't graf gaat zinken;
Schoon d'oude wereld onderga,
O, jong en schoon Amerika.

Nº 12881 RZ A° 1847   Haarlem, den 10. December 1847.

Nº 219/9700.

Overeenkomstig de bestaande voorschriften moeten door UEA, na den afloop van elk jaar, opgaven worden ingezonden van de Geboorten, Sterfte en Verhuizingen, welke er gedurende hetzelve binnen Uwe Gemeente hebben plaats gehad.

Bij de nu en dan voorkomende landverhuizingen naar Noord-Amerika of andere Overzeesche Gewesten, is het mij niet onbelangrijk voorgekomen, eenige inlichtingen te ontvangen aangaande de Personen, die met voormeld doel, deze Provincie mogten hebben verlaten, en werkelijk, hetzij afzonderlijk of met hunne gezinnen, naar de voorzeide Gewesten ter inwoning zijn vertrokken.

Het is om die reden dat ik de eer heb UEA, door deze uittenoodigen, om, gelijktijdig met de inzending der Staten van Geboorten Sterfte enz, die gedurende den Jare 1847, ten Uwent zijn aangegeven, alhier overteleggen eene opgave van de Ingezetenen Uwer Gemeente, welke, gedurende dat Jaar, naar Noord-Amerika of andere Overzeesche Gewesten zijn vertrokken, ten einde zich aldaar te vestigen.

Die opgave zal dienen in te houden:

De namen en voornamen der betrokken lieden, hun beroep, ouderdom en godsdienstige gezindheid; de vermoedelijke redenen van vertrek; de plaats waarheen zij zich begeven hebben en eindelijk alle zoodanige bijzonderheden ten hunnen opzigte, wier mededeeling door UEA niet ondienstig mogt worden geacht.

Mogten er zoodanige landverhuizingen ten uwent niet zijn voorgekomen, dan zal het voldoende zijn dat zulks blootelijk aan mij worde kenbaar gemaakt.

Overigens verzoek ik UEA om, voor zoo verre ten deze geene nadere voorschriften mogten worden gegeven, jaarlijks met het doen van dergelijke opgave voorttegaan.

De Staatsraad, Gouverneur
der Provincie Noord-Holland,
van Ewijck.

Aan de Stedelijke en Gemeente-Besturen
in de Provincie Noord-Holland.

A document that denies supposed indifference of our government (Municipal Archives, Amsterdam). [This letter from the governor of Noord Holland Province to the Municipal councils of the province required compilation and forwarding of annual lists of overseas emigrants, in addition to the usual statistics of births, deaths, and changes of residence. If there were no overseas emigration, this fact was to be reported as well.]

GEMEENTE ARCHIEF VAN AMSTERDAM

Yet another document which proves the concern of the government for the emigration (Municipal Archives, Amsterdam). [This is a copy of one of the emigration reports from Amsterdam, listing the heads of families and single adults; it includes information concerning profession, age, religion, social class, tax category, number of women, children, and servants, reasons for departure, destination, with space for remarks.]

It was the data received from this government investigation that was processed largely by the above-mentioned Benefit Society Commission. This commission, "consisting of men living in the different provinces of the Fatherland," addressed, among others, the governor of Noord Holland in a letter dated January 14, 1848, signed by the chairman of the Commission, Brüno Tideman, from which the following is quoted:

> The undersigned Chairman of the Commission was prepared to come to ask Your Excellency's influential help for the collection of the statistical reports from Noord Holland, when he received the Provincial Paper, dated December 30, number 82, and noticed therein that Your Excellency requested almost identical reports from the Community Boards before January 10, which the Commission had intended to collect. He, therefore, now approaches Your Excellency with the humble request that it may please Him to order the aforesaid Commission and also the Benefit Society to furnish a copy or excerpts of the general table that will presumably be made up for the various reports, while it will please the Society to cooperate with the latter on the same basis as the national government, in order to give to the desire for emigration at least such regulation as will best promote the real interest of the individuals involved, as well as that of the Fatherland.[99]

Compared with foreign countries such as Germany and England, where the government scarcely took note of emigration and regarded it with great indifference, even though thousands emigrated compared to dozens in our country, one can still be amazed at the interest displayed, especially considering the spirit of the times. But let us be on our guard against overestimating the interest! Because exactly that same unfortunate spirit of the times was the cause for the bulk of Dutch folk, alarmed for a time, to slip again into apathy. People also became accustomed to emigration! As a result, even the departure of a Van Peyma in 1849 no longer made an impression outside of the circle of his friends and acquaintances. The people as well as the government viewed his leaving with indifference, as if he were the most common German emigrant.[100]

It is true that the Benefit Society appointed still another commission in 1849, this one consisting of three members in Amsterdam, and it offered its golden medal in December 1850 for the best essay on the question of "The Increasing Desire for Emigration." Yet nothing was subsequently heard from the commission or about this prize contest—no more than about the paper that was to be started at Amsterdam, De Landverhuizing, or of the afore-mentioned Roman Catholic Emigration Committee at Nijmegen.

The Dutch people were once again so soundly asleep that even the Crimean War was not able to awaken them. Only the Franco-Prussian War of 1870 seemed able to shake them awake!

7

The New Environment
Soil, Climate, and People

Between 1845 and 1855 approximately 23,000 Netherlanders migrated to the United States. Many settled among the Americans, either in the cities or in the rural areas. Their difficult struggle for existence, especially during those first years, was often aggravated by a burning homesickness for the Old Country and by bitter disappointments in their efforts to cope with the process of Americanization. However, in this chapter it is not these "Argonauts" who are our primary concern. Those with whom we shall be most concerned are the men and women who followed Van Raalte, Scholte, and others to more remote and isolated areas of North America that at that time were inhabited by white people. We have already seen how these immigrants were more or less bound together by a common religious faith and sought a region where they could lead an existence both materially and spiritually independent, according to their convictions, and as much as possible free from alien influences. This drive was so strong among the two leaders that the colonies they established in Michigan and Iowa still bear in our day distinctive qualities that set them apart from their environment.

This distinctiveness is less discernible in other Dutch settlements, such as those in Illinois and Wisconsin, where they settled beside and among other European immigrants or vice versa. In the Fox River valley the Hollanders live like brothers with their German, Irish, and French-Canadian fellow Roman Catholics, while more southward in Wisconsin the Dutch Calvinists and Germans are the best of neighbors.

The desire on the part of the immigrants to colonize, to settle in groups based on preference for religious beliefs or national origin, was made somewhat easier by their usually limited financial means. If they wished to be landowners they naturally gravitated to thinly populated "marginal" or "borderline" areas where land was obviously cheaper. Their sense of solidarity was thereby strengthened in no small way and has even survived to the present time. Around 1845 the "boundaries" of settlement in America extended as far as Michigan's Grand River Area[1] and on the Iowa prairies to

193

the area between the Des Moines and Skunk Rivers.[2] Therefore, it was by no means accidental that Van Raalte and Scholte, once they had narrowed their choices to these states, settled in these areas.

Their colonies, as well as those in Illinois and Wisconsin, joined with the existing settlements of Americans and Europeans and thus became a very modest part of the vast frontier line that had been reached by the settlement movement due to the then general push to the West—Westward Ho! Therefore, Netherlanders also became outposts on the brink of civilization, pioneers in the true sense of the word. By so doing they took their more or less destined place and became instrumental in bringing about a world-event—making habitable a new continent. This was a majestic task that they accomplished with courage, albeit at the cost of many lives, for it can be said of them, as of millions of others, that they built flourishing settlements, "but on the bones of the settlers."

However, we should not consider their contribution as being merely one of passive endurance, as some German historians have described the numerous "*Pfarrer und Schulmeister*" [Pastor and Schoolmaster] and other colonies in non-German districts. For example, Lamprecht and Hassert have asserted with some bitterness that these early colonies provided only cultural manure—"*Kulturdünger*"!—for the future development of the designated states.[3] That was not the case at all, because in my view these colonists demonstrated a great deal of will power, initiative, and idealism that belied such a viewpoint, and they also maintained their identity. They were not merely instruments to be used—they became leaders. Precisely for that reason these men and women, coming mostly from the lowest levels, if not the scum of society in the Netherlands, deserve our full attention.

As we review once again the reasons why the Dutch pioneers settled where they did, it becomes evident that in their search they were not influenced solely by historic cultural boundaries that limited their way westward and northwestward, but also that within these boundaries other factors, mainly geographical, made their influence felt. The composition of the soil, the climate, and the nature of the inhabitants limited their options southward and made them decide to settle north of the Ohio and Missouri rivers. The social condition of the immigrants finally determined whether they would settle more northward in the forests or more southward on the prairies. Thus the many Dutch colonies came into existence, and most of these, it should be noted, were located on or "near" Lake Michigan, that is, near by American standards.

However, from this location one should not draw the conclusion, so often heard but not demonstrated by the facts, that the Netherlanders preferred to settle near water, in the Old Country tradition. Indeed, the facts indicate otherwise! Only under very favorable conditions are we willing, when abroad, to do battle against the watery element. There is no doubt that the proximity of Black Lake did influence Van Raalte's choice of location. He envisioned turning it into a "splendid harbor" and in his imagination he saw it visited by many merchant and fishing vessels and surrounded by a thriving shipbuilding industry.[4] As it turned out, it was not the water, but the forests and their cheap price that became the deciding factor for settlement. The development of the woods became the chief concern of Van Raalte's followers while the lake remained of minor significance and expectations in this direction never materialized. After having visited the colony in Michigan, Cohen Stuart commented that it is only near shorelines and coasts that Netherlanders feel really at home, and that water and wind are natural elements for us. However, this is totally out of place here.[5] For that matter, nowhere does it appear that the Dutch colonists of the nineteenth century felt drawn to waterways. On the contrary, since most of them were landlubbers, they purposely shunned water and chose higher ground on which to settle. With the single exception of the lake harbor at Holland, Michigan, all attempts, as we shall see later, to build harbors in Wisconsin and Iowa failed. The fact that the Roman Catholic Netherlanders settled in the watery Fox River valley was due to the chance circumstance that their leader, Van den Broek, had been active there for years previously. They also, having mostly come from the countryside, seem to have had little concern about water. It was no special preference, but rather the general considerations we have outlined that brought our countrymen to the states surrounding Lake Michigan. Since many of them arrived in the cities surrounding this lake, they settled in these cities and their surrounding areas, and especially in Wisconsin this led to many a settlement.

A. Soil Composition

It is important to note the nature of the soil into which the "young branch" from the Dutch stock was transplanted. In this connection we may observe that the growth of this offshoot was eased to no small degree by the great similarities between the soil type of their new base and that of the Fatherland, in spite of many differences. How important this was is demonstrated by subsequent Dutch colonization attempts in Colorado and California, where the soil was so completely different from that of the Netherlands that the immigrants did not know how to use it to best advantage, and the colonies failed.

The area they occupied is geologically very old. It is built up of rocks of the "primary" or Paleozoic era. Various geological periods of this era are represented here. The core in Wisconsin and Illinois consists of the so-called Cambrian and Ordovician layers, merging into the Silurian eastward to Lake Michigan's western shore and westward to near the Mississippi; to the Devonian in northern Iowa and southern Michigan and also to the Carboniferous in these same states. Below these rocks are found various valuable limestones and sandstones. The upper Carboniferous is found in the Des Moines River and Skunk River area in Iowa and the Saginaw region in Michigan, consisting largely of very valuable layers of coal. During this early time period various mineral lodes were formed.[6]

The Netherlands colonists found various other minerals of value. Already in his publication, *Eene Stem uit Pella* |A *Voice from Pella*|,[7] Scholte referred to the wealth of limestone and sandstone: "The burned lime is of the first quality." He noted other metallic ores, and added that "at many locations coal of excellent quality is found." Many a farmer later found that he had a coal mine on his farm, which he worked especially during winter.[8] In Michigan Van Raalte considered setting up an iron foundry.[9] Although the importance of the coal veins in the Saginaw area decrease in a southern direction, those in the Grand River area were exploited and developed during Van Raalte's time.[10]

During the passage of thousands of years, various factors altered the land surface. The variations between summer heat and winter cold, between daytime and nighttime temperatures, the precipitation, the wind, etc., eroded the rocks, and the water carried away the debris, thereby contributing strongly to further erosion. Thus, river valleys were constantly broadened and leveled, high areas worn down, and the land surface from the middle of Texas to southern Wisconsin and Michigan became an endless tertiary peneplain.[11] This monotonous plain, interrupted only by river valleys, the breadth and depth of which were determined by previous local "raisings" in the soil, by precipitation, the hardness of the subsoil, etc., and also by the divides between the river valleys, became the prairie plains of today that formed the basis of this peneplain where many a Dutch colonist tried to wrest for himself a new existence. We recall the testimony of Bonnema and his associates in the driftless area in southwestern Wisconsin and of others in Indiana, etc.

However, the northern section of the plains underwent great changes due to alterations in the climate in the beginning of the quaternary period. An average decline of about five degrees centigrade brought about the formation of tremendous ice masses in both Europe and North America, glaciers that moved southward and covered great land areas. One of these glaciers, the Keewatin, had great significance for this area. It spread out into the Mississippi basin as far as the valleys of the Ohio and Missouri rivers. These rivers owe their origin to the glacier. "They may be pictured as two great drainage arms, embracing the border of the ancient ice sheet and carrying away its waters."[12]

During the ice age in which periods of lesser cold alternated, the so-called interglacial periods, it appears that the Keewatin glacier moved southward six times, for varying distances, plowing through the sedimentary top layers, breaking down the hard subsoil, crumbling and re-arranging the eroded debris, leaving many terminal moraine hills. These altered the courses of the rivers and often impeded the flow of the water, thus forming moraine lakes. The glacier ice also gouged out areas of the basic rocks, forming many lakes. Indeed, the Great Lakes owe their origin mainly to this gouging and damming, in addition to tectonic changes.[13]

The moraine landscape, originating in the oldest part of the ice age in the Sub-Aftonian, Kansan, Illinoian, and Iowan periods, has but few distinguishable characteristics today. Chamberlin and Salisbury ascribe this to the fact that the last three of the above-mentioned time periods did not bring about much hill formation.[14] On the other hand, Bowman affirms that these ice ages are many thousands of years further into the past and therefore erosion has reduced the differences in height much more drastically. However that may be, much more obvious are the distinguishing features of the more recent era of the ice age, the so-called Earlier and Later Wisconsin Invasions, between a "mere" 20,000 and 150,000 years ago.[15] This "younger" glacial landscape still displays all the evidence of its youth, especially in Wisconsin and Michigan. Here one finds extensive ranges of terminal moraine hills. In addition, especially in eastern Wisconsin where they are numerous, are the drumlins formed by ground moraines formed under the ice: "rather definite elongate shapes, with their longer axes in the direction of ice-movement and two to ten times the shorter." There are also the kames, which are "primarily phenomena of the margin of the ice developed by running water, the active agent, in association with ice, the passive partner." Next are the eskers, some very high and very long but mostly short, and finally the sanders, outwash "fans" [plains] in front of glacial hills, composed of washed-out sand. The drumlines and the kames were preferred by the colonists as home sites because they felt safer on high ground and the locations were healthier than the lower lying and therefore often swampy areas.[16]

The "youth" of the landscape is evident also in the water. Drainage was often impeded, resulting in unhealthy marshes and swamps as well as the countless numbers of lakes. It was these marshes and swamps that first gave Michigan such a "sinister reputation—not without cause—although it was their mosquitoes and not their 'miasmatic exhalations' that were responsible for the bone-racking ague of the early settlers," of which the Dutch immigrants could also testify![17] The rivers carved out new routes for themselves, cutting through the newly-formed ridges of glacial deposit, resulting in rapids and waterfalls. These still limit the navigation value of the rivers in Michigan and elsewhere. However, they proved to be useful for the development of industry, also among the Dutch colonists.

More than any other state, Michigan was affected by the ice age. The average thickness of the layers of glacial debris in the northern part of the Southern Peninsula is 90 meters [295 feet], even reaching a depth of 210 to 240 meters [689–787 feet] in places! Various hills and kames reach a height of 300 to 360 meters [984 to 1,181 feet], some as high as 450 meters [1,476 feet].[18] These features of the landscape in Michigan and Wisconsin (and in other areas as well)—the many hills and elevations in what would otherwise have been level land—are primarily due to the ice age. In these states there are areas inhabited by Dutch colonists, especially those not more than 300 meters [984 feet] above sea level, in which are found striking similarities with the eastern part of our own European Netherlands that likewise originated in the diluvial period. These similarities also struck Cohen Stuart while visiting the colonial settlements in Michigan, where in some places he was under the impression of being in Gelderland and in others, Drenthe.[19] Some years later, R. P. J. Tutein Nolthenius said that the rail line from Chicago to Grand Rapids passed through landscape "that more than any other part of America brought before his mind's eye his own fatherland."[20]

Even more strongly are we reminded of our own country by the changes that originated in the alluvial period—the clay and peat deposits, and especially the formation of sand dunes out of glacial material, due to the predominating strong westerly winds that built up sand dunes on the west coast of the Peninsular State. South of Muskegon they reach an impressive height in the "Creeping Joe" dunes that are comparable with our sand dunes in the Netherlands. Thanks to them, beaches and seaside resorts became important resources for the colonies, but at the same time the dunes restricted and impeded the development of harbor facilities, as at the city of Holland.

Although the diluvial and alluvial deposits characterize the landscape features and the morphology of the areas occupied by our former fellow citizens from the Netherlands, they are also very important in determining the composition of the upper layers of the earth, the actual farmland. Various factors, primarily the climate with its variations, and secondly the plant life dependent on both weather and soil, continually modified the characteristics and weathering of the rock base and eventually resulted in the presently existing soil types. It was first of all these surface soils, "the skin of the earth," that drew the attention and interest of the colonists and made prosperous citizens of many of them.

In this connection we should first mention the layers of loess that cover the southern part of the glacial area—Illinois, Iowa, Nebraska, and the neighboring states to the south. Although originally a "rock," it was reduced to "soil" by plant life.[21] The northern portion of this area (this loess can be found up to thirty-five miles south of St. Paul in Minnesota) was covered by more recent glaciers and therefore came into existence during or before the Iowan ice age. Although originating in part from the Great Plains east of the Rocky Mountains, American loess, like the European sort, consists mostly of very fine glacial debris: "angular undercomposed particles of calcite, dolomite, feldspar, mica, and a certain number of rarer minerals"; it is strikingly porous, "owing in part to vertical tubes usually found in it and supposedly due to root action." Mainly transported by wind action, loess is an aeolian formation with traces here and there of fluvial influence. It has an average thickness of six decimeters [2 feet]; however, in many places one finds layers of three meters |almost 10 feet| and in others as deep as 30 meters |almost 100 feet|![22]

The meager forest growth on the prairies and the relative treeless condition of the western plains is chiefly ascribed to this layer of loess, but so is their wealth and variety of all kinds of grasses and general fertility.[23] The actual loess, light brown in color, buffish brown sometimes, with a bluish cast, is a variety of silt intermediate in size of grain between the finest sand and clay and was seldom mentioned or referred to in the writings of the Holland colonists who simply called it clay.[24] As a soil type it was found only in the higher parts of the basin; the bluffs were covered with it and it was first called "bluff deposits," and described as "an unusual soil type, yellow in color, composed of fine particles, mixed with clay and limestone, very fertile, producing a wealth of grain and garden products."[25]

As a result of luxuriant vegetation closely related to generally inadequate drainage, the upper layers of loess, especially in the broad valleys, became mixed in such a way with organic materials of plant origin, called humus, that "new" soil types arose.[26] These soils, which are sometimes peaty, very rich in humus, and therefore dark and very often black in color, are similar to the chernozem, the black soil of Russia and Siberia. They became the foundation of the most flourishing and prosperous of the Dutch settlements in America.

Over the years the immigrants in their letters and memoirs repeatedly referred to and described these soil types. According to Scholte, the prairie on which Pella was built was easy to cultivate, once it had been plowed up. In general the soil resembles "rich, mellow, black garden soil."[27] One of the colonists from Gelderland, whom I quoted earlier, called it "black marl clay."[28] The presence of loess constituents in the soil, especially in Iowa's soil, is more clearly expressed in the writings of another Gelderlander, Bloemendaal, who described the soil as "very fine grained, consisting of continually decomposing grass and leaves. When it is wet it is as fine and slippery as soft soap, but exceptionally fertile. The color of the prairie soil is black or grayish, while that of the forest soil is yellowish." In northwestern Iowa, where numerous flourishing villages later came into existence, Bloemendaal described these soils as of "unprecedented fertility." He said, "It is neither clay nor sand. Here they call it muck. It is not heavy and can always be worked with two horses."[29]

Further north, in Wisconsin and Michigan, in areas of more recent glacial deposits, are many soil types that differ greatly from one another. Within relatively very short distances, especially by American norms, one may find many varying grades of soil. The terminal moraines contain many stones; the eskers, gravel; while the kames are generally very sandy. In various places the ground also contains heavy loam of glacial origin; elsewhere it is gravelly.[30] After the glacial period peat bogs formed in places where there was no sufficient drainage, but once they are drained they become valuable. In other places the increasing decomposition of plant residue in these bogs produced "muck," called "*mok*" by the Dutch settlers, which like the "peats" is excellent for various types of horticulture. In many areas clay sediment settled on the lake bottoms as well as in the broadened river beds. For example, the coastal regions between the Great Lakes, the moraine hills in the interior, and the "Lake Plains" near Chicago, Green Bay, and Saginaw Bay became important because of their clay base. In these areas glacial ice tongues (lobes) gouged out shallow valleys and flooded them, after which the clay settled.

Everywhere in Michigan and Wisconsin those who work the soil are reminded of the effects of the ice age. The remnants of glacial debris were important to the Dutch immigrants, as shown by Bloemendaal's description of the land around Alto, Wisconsin: "The lay of the land is hilly. One can hardly find forty continuous acres of level land. There were also large stones in the soil that a farmer frequently struck with his plow." Some places, especially hills, are so full of stones they cannot be plowed at all and have to be left as they are.[31] A farmer often followed the plowman with an iron crowbar to dig out and remove the stones. Some stones were so large and heavy they could not be moved. Then one either worked around them or dug underneath to bury them. This was perhaps not an unfamiliar task for many of our Dutch sand farmers who were accustomed to digging out boulders, which activity is called "*roden*" in Dutch. However, these stones are not worthless. They are burned to obtain lime for mortar or they are used as foundations under houses and barns. Bloemendaal saw an entire church building constructed of these stones. Often they are used to make storm shelters for cattle underneath barns. Besides, the limestone in the soil served as a natural lime fertilizer, saving enormous sums of money. Huntington and Cushing have asserted in their *Principles of Human Geography* that the various glacial components have been worth an estimated $50,000,000 annually to the state of Wisconsin alone.

The many divergent soil types recurring in Wisconsin and Michigan account for the equally divergent opinions expressed by writers and historians, especially concerning Van Raalte's colony, such as [K.] Koelewijn's statement, referring to Holland, Michigan, that "there is nothing there and nothing can grow there yet, because it is nothing but sand and trees," and Bolk's description, previously quoted, of the soil at Overijsel as being heavy clay and very valuable.[32]

B. The Climate

Also, in respect to the climate, there are similarities between the colonies and the Old Country, although the latter lies about 10 degrees further north. The colonies lie between 41 and 45 degrees north latitude, the Old Country between 50 and 54 degrees. Both the Netherlands and the colonies lie in the temperate zone. When the average annual temperatures are compared we find that both lie in an area with yearly isotherms of 4 to 12 degrees C. [39 to 54 degrees F.][33] The average annual temperature at De Bilt is 10 degrees C. [50 degrees F.]; Milwaukee, 7 degrees C. [45 degrees F.]; Chicago, 9.1 degrees C. [48 degrees F.]; and Des Moines, 9.2 degrees C. [49 degrees F.]. The atmospheric pressure in both countries, in summer and winter, is in the relatively high range of 760 millimeters [29.92 inches] and above. Also the average precipitation coincides, amounting to 50 to 100 centimeters [20 to 40 inches] spread over the seasons, although most of the rainfall occurs during the warmer half of the year. However, in the American settlements the heaviest rainfalls occur in early summer while in the Netherlands the heavy rains come in the latter part of the summer and early fall. The average annual rainfall is as follows: De Bilt, 827 millimeters [32.6 inches]; Detroit, 805 millimeters [31.7 inches]; Chicago, 833 millimeters [32.8 inches]; and Des Moines, 810 millimeters [31.9 inches]. These figures on annual temperatures and rainfall are of interest to us chiefly as bases for comparison, and they indicate a measure of similarity in our two countries. However, to the farmer and dairyman the monthly averages are more important.

It goes without saying that the similarity of climate with that of the Old Country was important to the colonists in adapting to the new environment. Later attempts at colonization, such as Van Raalte's venture in Virginia, settlements in Florida and Texas, and also in the Far West, did not succeed, largely because of the great differences in climate. One should not conclude that in the Midwest the colonists found that the climate was very much like that of the Netherlands. Quite the contrary! The contrasts were so great that it often required much will power of our countrymen to see it through. Not everyone succeeded. Many were financially ruined; some even lost lives in the struggle.

The summer and winter temperatures in the Netherlands are moderated by the sea, and there are generally no great contrasts in the day-to-day weather. On the other hand, midwestern America has an inland climate—high summer and low winter temperatures—with surprisingly great variations. This is indicated by the charts of average January and July temperatures:

	Netherlands	**Middle West**
January isotherms	0–4° C. [32–39 F.]	0-minus 4° C. [32–25 F.]
July isotherms	20–16° C. [68–61 F.]	20–24° C. [68–75 F.]

The contrasts are even more evident when one compares specific localities:

	January	**July**
DeBilt	2° C. [36 F.]	18° C. [64 F.]
Groningen	1° C. [34 F.]	18° C. [64 F.]
Chicago	−4.6° C. [22 F.]	22.4° C. [72 F.]
Des Moines	−4.6° C. [22 F.]	24.4° C. [76 F.]

In Chicago in winter the thermometer may register far below zero C. |32 degrees F.|, while in summer it may go up to and above 32 degrees C. |90 degrees F.| for eight to ten successive days. But more dangerous than these extremes is the suddenness of the changes. In a few hours the thermometer may drop 20 or 30 degrees C. |36 or 54 degrees F.|!

Indeed, sudden changes in the weather are common to the entire American continent. There is no east-west range of mountains to obstruct the air currents. As a result, the warm winds from the southeast penetrate the extreme northern areas, and conversely, the cold northern and northwestern storms cross over into southern areas. These sudden changes, especially the killing frosts at night, may be very damaging to crops. Also, the periods of drought, sometimes continuing for months, can be disastrous. Many a settlement, also among the Netherlanders, has been completely ruined by droughts. Forest fires, caused by drought, devasted the greater part of the city of Holland in the fire year of 1871, the exact same time as the great Chicago fire.

The rapid and extreme changes in temperature and in precipitation, or the lack of it, are generally accompanied by storms. Midwest America is notorious for its northwestern storms, the "Northers," whose "cold waves" invade the south and suddenly drop the temperatures to below zero C. |32 degrees F.|, and for the hailstorms that destroy the crops. Even more dangerous are the blizzards in midwinter, which, like the purgas in northern Russia and the burans in Siberia, drive fine dry snow across the endless plains at times for days without end, making travel difficult and even impossible.[34] These storms occur chiefly in the northern part of the Mississippi basin. One of the farmers of this prairie area, a Mr. |G.| Draayom, originally from the province of Overijsel in the Netherlands, relates how he was overtaken by a blizzard on his way home with a load of hay:

> By this time the wind was howling out of the northwest, soon followed by snow flurries that made it impossible to see any further ahead than the length of my wagon. The oxen repeatedly stood still and although I used the whip on them they would not move. I got down and tried to find out what the trouble was. No wonder! The animals had their eyes so full of snow they could not see the road and stood still. As soon as we cleared the snow from their eyes, they went on. . . . We had to do it again and again: Clear their eyes, climb back on my load and leave it entirely to the oxen to find their way home.[35]

In summer it was often the dust storms, accompanied by heat waves, that damaged the crops. This was especially true in the Great Lakes area and the Mississippi valley, both characterized by stormy weather. The city of Chicago, around which Dutch settlements were clustered, rightly came to be called the "Windy City." This is the friction area between the cold north and the warm south, which accounts for the frequency and the violence of the Northers and the blizzards and gives rise also to the tornadoes,[36] the scourge of the area.

Our colonists also repeatedly experienced the violence of tornadoes. Already in 1848 residents of Pella reported that "buildings under construction were leveled to the ground in an instant."[37] Perhaps even worse was the storm of June 18, 1871, whose description by K. Van Stigt, unwittingly reveals that the colonies lay in an area of climatological disturbances: "Sunday evening, about 6:00 P.M., dark clouds gathered from the southwest and northwest, rising higher and denser and darker, almost black. Between them in the west, the sky was just as dark. We all watched with alarm those black clouds from both corners for more than two hours and then, suddenly, the dark clouds began to move against one another from the northwest to the southwest and for forty to fifty minutes we had such a terrible storm as we had never experienced since the founding of the colony. Many houses, both in the city and in the country, lost their roofs; others were completely demolished. Fruit trees and shade trees were destroyed or snapped like pipestems and many were completely uprooted. Fortunately, no one was killed."[38]

Some years later, in 1902, a tornado struck a new colony at Sioux Center, in northwest Iowa, settled mostly by immigrants from Gelderland, in which four Hollanders were killed on the spot and many others were injured, some of whom died later. An entire house was picked up by the wind and the occupants thrown into a nearby group of trees.[39] It is not surprising that in building a house people kept the tornadoes in mind and provided a deep storm cellar underneath in which to take refuge.

Because of their location east of Lake Michigan, under the influence of the prevailing westerly winds, the climatic contrasts and atmospheric disturbances in Michigan are less severe than those elsewhere in the Midwest, and in their area one could almost speak of a "sea climate" like that of the Netherlands.[40] The winters are milder and the summers cooler, while precipitation is more equally distributed, maintaining a moderate water level in the rivers. The rainy, drizzly day is known in Michigan as well as in the Netherlands. Destructive storms, although not entirely unknown, occur less frequently in Michigan, especially near the lakes. Likewise, the hot, dry winds that destroy crops are not so frequent here as in neighboring states. However, also in Michigan the weather can be highly changeable, as appears from a news item from Muskegon, printed in De Grondwet |The Constitution| in Holland, Michigan, on February 22, 1921: "Yesterday the temperature reached 60 degrees F. and above, and the sand dunes along Lake Michigan were full of men and women without coats or jackets. But today the beaches are deserted and a howling northwester accompanied by driving snow and a 40-degree drop of the mercury forcefully reminded everyone that winter is not yet over."[41]

C. Flora and Fauna

Since there are so many overall similarities in soil composition and climate between the Netherlands and the colonies, it is not surprising that one should observe the same similarities in the plant and animal world. Both the Netherlands and the colonial settlements lie in the temperate zone and their tree growth belongs in the general classification of the northern hemisphere, where trees with needle-type foliage are found in the more northern areas and broad-leafed types thrive in the south.[42] No doubt the settlement of colonists was facilitated by the presence of the same types of trees they were familiar with in the homeland, such as firs and spruces in the north, and oaks, elms, beeches, and other well known species in the areas further south.

Nevertheless, there were also differences that made adaptation more difficult. To begin with, in America the immigrants found many varieties of trees they had never seen. Not only were there differences within the same general classifications—for example, Europe lists twenty types of oak trees, the United States, fifty; Europe has ten types of pine trees, North America, thirty or forty—but there are tree species there that are totally unknown in our part of the world. The Hollanders in Michigan encountered nine varieties of hickory, the wood of which resembles our ash.[43] Also in America are found tree types going back to the tertiary period, which have died out in Europe, such as certain varieties of pines, the tulip tree, and the sassafras in Michigan, and in other areas, the swamp cypress, sequoia, and other species. In short, in northern Europe there are approximately forty varieties of trees native to the region, while in America there are about four hundred!

This relative unfamiliarity with the differing tree types had a direct bearing on the colonists' problems in selecting suitable land for cultivation, especially during winter |when there was no foliage on the trees by which to identify them.| It is generally possible to evaluate the soil by the type of tree growing on it, although it must be remembered that trees, indeed all plants, possess to a great degree the ability to adjust, having "a certain physiologic plasticity or power of self-regulation."[44] In addition to the soil, the climate is also a factor: "The home of the tree is the soil and the air."[45] As a consequence, in the Midwest the softwoods, such as fir and spruce, are generally found growing on sandy soils, and the hardwoods, such as ash, maple, beech, and others, are found on clay soils; but the reverse is sometimes encountered and in Michigan white pine can be found on heavy clay and hardwoods in sand six feet deep.[46] These contrasts occur most frequently in the colonial settlements in Wisconsin and Michigan since several of these colonies lie in the line of transition between the needle- and broad-leaf type foliage trees and both kinds are found growing side by side. For example, Van Raalte spoke not only of "our hemlock, pine, and cedar tracts" but also of nearby "sugar maple woods."[47]

The colonists' efforts to evaluate the soil by the trees growing on it was especially difficult in the Great Lakes area because in this climatological transition zone is found a very great diversity of vegetation and the number of "unknown" varieties growing side by side is therefore that much larger. Fairly recently the botanist, J. P. Lotsy, was amazed to find in the Calumet district, east of Chicago in an area where many Hollanders live, a cactus native to the south, the "Opuntia Raffinesquii," growing beside the "Pinus Banksiana," a post-glacial relic still frequently found in the far north of Labrador![48] It is not surprising that the immigrants in search of good farming soil dared not make their decisions on the basis of the trees growing in the area but called in the assistance of others. Committees of investigation were helpful. Later, the selection of good farmland for the settlers became a lucrative business for certain highly competent persons experienced in this matter, who were specifically appointed for this task.[49]

Experience demonstrated to the colonists the close connection between vegetation and soil composition, in particular in relation to ground moisture. A writer from the colonial period, "Een Gelderschman," classified the soil in Iowa in three grades according to the trees, as follows: "Large elms, linden or lime trees, chestnuts, walnuts and maples indicate the richest soil. Smaller elms, black and red oak trees identify the second grade. The poorest soil is covered with white oaks, with a few black oaks mixed in."[50]

Other variations in plant growth, perhaps of even greater importance to the colonists, are the contrasts that occur here just as they do in the American climate. The almost impenetrable forests in Michigan and northern Wisconsin are very unlike the sparse tree growth in parts of Illinois, Iowa, and other western states. In the latter areas, forests are found chiefly along the rivers, but further west the diminishing rainfall and increasing winds cause the forests to thin out and to disappear entirely.[51] No doubt there were other contributing factors, "secondary causes," such as the kind of soil in these western states—the fine loess less suitable for tree growth—and perhaps the poisonous excretions from the roots of certain kinds of prairie plants.[52]

In periods of prolonged drought, forest and grass fires, ignited by lightning or by Indians, did considerable damage. According to the writer Koelewijn, the forests at Holland, Michigan, were "so dense one could hardly get through them and the trees were as tall and large as the largest trees in all of the Netherlands."[53] Forest giants as we know them in California and Oregon are also found in other places in America. The Netherlanders in Wisconsin and Michigan became all too familiar with them and at first stood powerless "before the tall, heavy pines and maples and the wildly majestic oaks, tossing their crowns through the branches of other trees!"[54] The Bible-reading Hollanders called them "children of Anak!" [Canaanite giants, Josh. 15:13]. There was such overwhelming abundance of wood that finally, at their wits' end, they simply burned it off to get rid of it.

By contrast, those colonists from Noord Holland and Zuid Holland who settled on the "Grand Prairie" southwest of Chicago saw the flat lands adorned with the most beautiful flowers and grass up to two feet high, but the trees were lacking. The lumber needed for building and the wood needed for fuel had to be brought from the "Windy City" by ox cart.[55] The same was true of other areas. As one goes further west even the "gallery woods," narrow stretches of wooded areas along river banks, give way to small groups of trees, "*bouquets de bois*" [groves of trees], and then to solitary specimens and even these eventually are succeeded by treeless steppes.[56] The total lack of building material brought many colonists to the point of digging homes out of the ground "like real earthworms," the "dug-outs" and "sod-houses" of the Pella and Sioux County settlers.

Next to the trees, other forms of vegetation came to have value for the immigrants. The impenetrability of the northern forests was increased due to many types of scrub brush and undergrowth: the underwoods. Some of this undergrowth had economic value, producing edibles, like berries. Various kinds of grasses, like the "buffalo grasses," were used by dairy farmers to feed cattle. Reed grasses were used to make roofs for their sod houses and fuel for their cooking fires. From among the very limited number of native agricultural plants, corn became most valuable for the immigrants.

The animals they encountered in this new environment contributed in a lesser degree to the "rooting" of the immigrants. In the animal kingdom they also found many similarities between the American types and those of northern and central Europe, especially in the case of the larger kinds such as bears, wolves, deer, foxes, etc.[57] From the beginning they called the animals they were not familiar with by their American names, such as minks, raccoons, skunks, woodchucks, etc. Sometimes the American names were translated very literally into Dutch, e.g., *catfish* became "*katvisch*." On the whole the Netherlanders suffered little damage from dangerous wild animals. There were no fatalities, only fright after such encounters. The Michigan and Wisconsin forests were rich in game—deer, wolves, bears, foxes, wildcats, beavers, skunks, porcupines, wild geese, turkeys, ducks, and wood pigeons—and were a hunter's paradise, richly rewarding the chase.[58]

The prairies were also rich in game. Sjoerd Aukes Sipma wrote from Pella to his former village neighbors in the Netherlands: "There are many ducks, geese and swans, partridges, turkeys and peacocks, forest and prairie wolves, but no large ferocious animals."[59] One of the writers among the colonists, "*Een Gelderschman*," described the wildlife in Iowa in considerable detail.[60] He reassured his readers that "while the jaguar, forest wolf, and bison are no longer found here, pigs and sheep are occasionally attacked by the smaller prairie wolf. Wildcats, foxes, lynxes, weasels, and the smaller preying animals are still fairly numerous. The badger, raccoon, the opposum are found almost everywhere. Also elk, deer, fallow deer and roebucks, beavers, otters and muskrats.... There are many different kinds of squirrels in large numbers and west of the Mississippi is found the prairie dog, a rodent belonging to the marmot and squirrel and which has nothing in common with our domestic dog except its bark. Also moles, mice, rats, and unbelievable numbers of hares and rabbits." Also the bird world is well represented, although we miss the magpie and the house sparrow we are so familiar with in Holland. The rivers and lakes are full of fish—pike, perch, bass, carp, trout, salmon, sturgeon, bream and salmon trout, but the catfish "is the most numerous" in both northern and southern waters.

Although in general none of the animals were dangerous to the colonists they could certainly be troublesome and annoying. Those that devoured the field crops were more of a problem than the flesh-eating ones. Deer repeatedly ate the "greening corn" and pastured in the growing crop fields. Deer hunting was therefore a constant necessity. After a mild winter the smaller animals, especially the squirrels, were so numerous that they devoured all growing crops and caused a virtual disaster. In those first years rats and mice were a terrible problem. "It was so bad that at night while we were asleep they gnawed the buttons off our clothes and if there was any food in the house we had to eat it promptly or the mice would get to it first." The devout colonists, who often prayed long prayers before their meals, had to reckon with these invaders who did not hesitate to help themselves from the tables during the quiet moments![61]

There were other problems, such as the disastrous grasshopper plagues. The colonists had to wear heavy boots to protect themselves from the fangs of the many, many snakes. However, the greatest threat was from the mosquitoes. The "anopheles" mosquito, the carrier of malaria germs, has struck fear in the most northernmost regions of America, as far as Alaska. Many of the Netherlands immigrants in those early years, especially in the swampy areas of Michigan, lost their lives by the "agency" of these insects.

Many domestic animals were imported over the years. The first to be brought in were cows, pigs, and a few oxen; later, chickens, dogs, and cats came. In the beginning a horse was such a rare sight that when one passed by on a woodland path, women and children came running out to look.[62]

D. The People

The immigrants not only had to adjust to different types of soil, to differences in climate and day-to-day weather, and to learn how to deal with unfamiliar plants and animals; they were also to some degree dependent on the people among whom, or next to whom, they came to live. In this respect, the immigrants of the nineteenth and twentieth centuries found that the Americans with whom they had their first contacts were of their own level of thinking, civilization, and culture. They had far less contacts with the Negroes of the south or with Indians, and then usually with semi-civilized ones. Therefore, the Americanization of our countrymen was of a totally different sort than that of their seventeenth-century predecessors who established themselves not only in an untouched wilderness but also among "untouched"—and therefore "wild"—primitive peoples. On their trek to the Middle West our immigrants had already met the most varied types of Americans in the most varied ways, and as we saw, not always with pleasure! Once they had reached their destination they had to deal with them again for the purchase of the necessary land. More than once they were disappointed in the trustworthiness of the Yankees, despite all their carefulness, which is an experience present land buyers still encounter![63]

To whom did the land available for colonizing belong? When England acknowledged the independence of the thirteen states in 1783 it also gave up all claims to the territory east of the Mississippi. Various Appalachian states had already laid claim to portions of this area and were using the proceeds of land sales to pay their state debts. However, at the insistence of the state of Maryland, these claims were renounced and title to the land was given over to the Union and declared as far as still possible to be public property under the jurisdiction of Congress.[64] These public lands were greatly enlarged by the Louisiana Purchase. This territory west of the Mississippi for many years belonged to France and temporarily to Spain, but it was formally signed over to the American representative by Napoleon in Paris in 1803.

The greater part of this public land was temporarily "administered" by federal officials as "districts" or as "territories." Later, after many immigrants had occupied a district, it became a territory, and then in time a self-governing state. Out of the Northwest Territory that lay between the Ohio and upper Mississippi rivers, there came into existence successively the state of Ohio in 1802, Indiana in 1816, Illinois in 1818, and as we already noticed, Michigan in 1837, and Wisconsin in 1848.[65] Louisiana [Territory] was first divided into the Louisiana District and the more southerly Orleans Territory. Later, after all kinds of changes, Louisiana officially became a state in 1812, Missouri in 1821, Arkansas in 1836, and Iowa in 1846.[66] The more northern and western parts of the original Louisiana Purchase were organized later, after they had become more settled.

All this colonial expansion was preceded by important governmental regulations. Although the Union officially owned these immense areas, in reality the administration usually exercised only sovereignty rights and the actual owners were the various Indian tribes native to the region. As the white colonists moved in, the Indians were in effect dispossessed and compelled to give way. Gradually the Indians migrated further west to regions not yet earmarked for colonization. Many treaties were made with the Indians in which they were compensated by pensions or annuities and by absolving them from their debts that were at times considerable. Among these treaties were some of special interest to the Netherlanders. For example, in 1821 the Ottawas, Potawatomis, and others relinquished their land in southwestern Michigan south of the Grand River, where Van Raalte and his followers later settled.[67] In 1842 the Chippewas gave up a good share of Wisconsin, and the Winnebagos were compelled to do the same. A large part of the present state of Iowa was taken from the Indians in 1831 following the Black Hawk War, "a series of massacres," and the capture of their chief, Black Hawk. The Sacs and Foxes, who had earlier displaced other

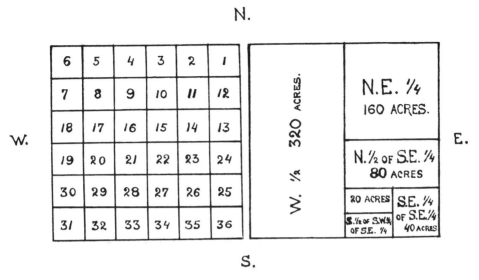

A section and its further division.

Indian tribes in Iowa, were also forced to leave their lands after the "Black Hawk Purchase" was made in 1832 and the "New Purchase" ten years later. Only the Sioux Indians in the northwest retained, at least for the time being, their hunting grounds, but eventually whites, such as Scholte and his people, took over.[68]

After the Union had come into "legal" possession of the land by these usually "peaceful" means of "purchase," they were measured by United States surveyors and recorded on maps. Following a resolution passed by the Continental Congress in 1785, a new method of surveying and mapping was adopted, the "Rectangular System," which greatly simplified the old inaccurate and cumbersome system of designating property by "metes and bounds."[69] According to the "Old Congressional Plan" of 1785, first used in Ohio and afterwards applied to all the "new" areas, the land was surveyed in sections six miles long and six miles wide, the so-called "townships." By this method two lines were established as accurately as possible by astronomical measurement, an east-west "baseline" and a north-south line, called the "principal meridian," drawn at right angles to each other. Parallel to the baseline, at equal six-mile intervals, the "township lines" were indicated and parallel to the principal meridian the same six-mile distances were called the "range lines." The townships were then numbered by their locations north or south of the baseline and by their line "range" west or east of the principal meridian.

Each township is as nearly as possible thirty-six square miles in size and comprises 23,040 acres. However, lakes and rivers, state boundary lines, converging meridians, and inaccurate measurements made these figures sometimes more imaginary than real. Each township is divided into thirty-six "sections," each if possible one mile long and one mile wide, encompassing 640 acres, providing there are no "fractional sections." The sections are all numbered in the same order, beginning with No. 1 in the northeastern corner, continuing left or westward through No. 6. South of No. 6 lies No. 7 and the numbering continues again, eastward to the right, and so on, repeating the order. Each section is in turn divided into four parts of 160 acres each, designated as NE, NW, SE, and SW "quarters." Each "quarter-section" is again divided into "quarter of the quarters" covering forty acres, the smallest legal description shown on the surveyor's charts of the Union. These "forties" and "eighties" became an important part of the American farmer's way of life and daily discussions—much as hogs were in the Netherlands!

The townships and sections were all marked out by the surveyors and "corner posts" were placed at all the corners with numbers and letters to identify the tract. In the forests these were marked with "blazes" on the trees. [These *"blessen,"* as the Dutch called them, were ax marks on the trunk to show the white wood underneath.] In addition, the quarters were all identified with "quarter posts." A land buyer was thus able, with the help of a good map and a compass, to find the property he had bought which would otherwise have been most difficult in the thick forests or the prairies with their man-high tall grasses. Later the roads and highways were laid out along the borders of the sections and sometimes also alongside the quarters—the sectionlines and quarterlines, which account for the typical chessboard effect of the countryside, similar to the pattern of our drainage canals, reminding us of the Beemster and other polders.

The townships became the smallest units of local government, the "civil townships." As many localities grew into cities they incorporated into separate units, for example, in Michigan the city of Zeeland adjacent to Zeeland township. Thus the boundaries of the "civil townships" and the "congressional" or government townships no longer always coincided. The townships were combined into counties.

After land was mapped by surveyors it was registered in the General Land Office at Washington, the agency responsible for the administration of the public lands. Parties interested in purchasing these lands can still make application to this bureau today, as Scholte did, or to one of the branch land offices in the various states. Hollanders in Michigan and Iowa dealt with branch land offices in Ionia, Michigan, and in Fairfield, Iowa, both of which have now been closed.

Only the surveyed lands were available for purchase, and in 1807 Congress forbade any settlement on unsurveyed land. Public auctions were held and the land sold to the highest bidder. It could also be bought by "private entry." The demand for land in the mid-nineteenth century was so great, however, and the general situation was of such a kind that many immi-

grants ignored completely the Congressional prohibition of 1807 and became "squatters." They were of the opinion that the land belonged to
anyone who used it and could keep possession of it. In an arbitrary manner
they marked out their own claim with corner posts or tree blazes and
demanded recognition of their "claims" by the officials. In Iowa the viola-
tors of the law ("trespassers") formed powerful organizations, "claim associations." At public auctions they competed with land speculators, defend-
ing their "claims" at times with violence, and succeeded in having these
"claims" acknowledged and recorded in the official records. At auctions the
claim owners received the right to buy first. They paid the minimum price of
$1.25 per acre, plus costs, and thus many laid hands on as much as 160
acres of excellent quality farmland at very low prices. It is not surprising
that a brisk business developed, not only in land, but in "claims."[70] Two
important laws evolved out of this unwritten "claims" right, the Pre-
emption Act [of 1841] and the Homestead Act of 1862. Under the latter, any
American citizen, or prospective citizen could come into possession of 160
acres of land, paying only the expense of registration, providing that he
signed a pledge that, among other things, he would live on the land for five
years. These early "claims" caused our Netherlands colonists great difficulties, involving them in complex lawsuits and very strained relationships
with the Americans.

The Union had at its disposal much land but not much money, so it
fulfilled many of its obligations by grants of land, in the manner of the
European feudal lords of earlier days. After the wars with England (1812)
and Mexico (1846), and after the Civil War in 1865, the soldiers received
their premiums and pensions in land "warrants." Often the veterans, not
wishing to farm the land themselves, or lacking the means to do so, sold
their land warrants for half price or more to land speculators. One of these,
for example, was a certain [John Mason] Peck in Illinois, who in turn sold
the land at a good profit to the Zuid Hollanders,[71] or directly to the colonists, such as Dominie Ypma in Vriesland, Michigan.[72]

Congress gave thousands of acres of public land away to the various
states, especially for the benefit of education. The famous Ordinance of
1787 [Northwest Ordinance] specified that Section 16 of each township be
given to the state to provide, from the proceeds [from the sale] of the
school land, for the establishment and maintenance of elementary schools
("public schools"). For high schools and colleges, and especially for setting
up courses in agriculture, the states also received payment in land. All this
"State land," as distinguished from "Congress land," could be obtained by
colonists by going to the land bureau located in the state capital of the
specified state. Especially after 1850, large areas of swampland were
granted to various states so that better drainage could be provided. As a
result this, state-owned land took on great importance.

Major companies such as canal and railroad companies were supported
by both federal and state land grants. Since 1856 Congress passed a series

of resolutions by which federal lands were ceded to the states for such support. Very often pieces of sections, as far as they were not yet sold, lying on both sides of a railroad or canal, were given as "land grants" to the construction companies, who were able to sell these properties at higher prices, since they lay closer to the canal or railroad.

Many land speculators bought large areas of Congress land and State land, at times also the railway and canal lands. They organized into corporations and endeavored to sell these acres at great profit to the immigrants streaming in. These "land sharks" were among the most dangerous enemies of the Dutch colonists.

However, concerning these real estate transactions, there were wide differences in the experiences of the colonists. Some found the acquisition of their property rights to be involved and intricate processes, all too often based on dubious and questionable dealings with "real estate men." On the other hand, certain American traits worked to their advantage, continuing even to the present time to promote the grouping together of Dutch settlers. I am thinking about the restlessness of the Americans, a trait that had also been noticed by many other "colonizing" nations. According to Arends,[73] they were proud of their country, but apparently not at all attached to their homes. According to Beukma, "almost every American has his property for sale."[74] Van Raalte remarked that "Americans move hundreds of miles for a trifle."[75] Because of this American trait, many a Netherlander with some capital was able to buy rather easily a piece of farmland already under cultivation, an "improved farm." This saved him the effort of first development. We saw that Scholte in Iowa bought a number of farms, including the livestock and growing crops. Thus it was possible to move into areas already inhabited and block out contiguous settlements by "buying out" not just some American farmers but many of them.

To the extent that Americans remained living among the Netherlanders, or as newcomers to the area chose to settle among the Dutch, they gave our countrymen much assistance from their experience in felling great trees in the forests or in the building, and the "raising" of their houses. A readiness to help, an urge to share a neighbor's problems, is certainly one of the most sympathetic characteristics also of the American pioneer. The official agencies of both the federal and state governments also assisted the Hollanders in many ways and by so doing helped along the Americanization process of colonists they were happy to acquire as citizens.

The native Americans were of much less influence on our countrymen, who while still in Europe had heard many scary "Indian tales." Potgieter wrote one of them, and Rinse Posthumus had translated into the Dutch language a story about the Indian warrior Black Hawk. The Dutch feared the Indians. Van Raalte rejected the proposal to settle in Wisconsin and Scholte likewise refused to go to Michigan because of these tales. But in America they learned to know them as a peaceful people. The women were occupied with raising corn and beans while the men spent their time hunting and fishing or "lying full length on the ground in front of their huts." They knew how to get sugar from the sugar maples. They were prone to be beggars, which was annoying but never dangerous, except when they had drunk too much "fire water" (whiskey). They roamed in tribal groups through the territory they had themselves previously sold to the white settlers. In the fall of 1847 about fifty Indians, men, women and children, came on foot through Pella. Sipma wrote: "We met them as we came from church one Sunday morning. They all appeared to be thick and fat. In no way could we tell that they harbored any hatred against the whites."[76] How different was the reality from their earlier fears!

The Dutch saw less of the Negroes. The only immigrants who en-countered them—and then only sporadically—were those who came by way of New Orleans and St. Louis, and in a lesser degree those who came via Baltimore. By and large, the influence of the Negroes upon the Dutch immigrant movement was minimal or negative. Their presence in the south-ern states was one of the reasons, along with the climate, why the Nether-landers did not establish colonies in those areas. They would have nothing to do with Negro slavery, with the possible exception of Scholte.[77] Indeed, they took an active part in the freeing of many a Negro slave.

Having learned something of the environment into which the "young branch" from the Netherlands was transplanted, let us now follow the process of its "rooting."

8

The Rooting of the Young Dutch Branch in Michigan

A. Forest Pioneers

The colonists had to cope with many difficulties almost impossible to overcome in those first years, in the forests as well as on the prairies, despite the noted similarities. On the evening of February 9, 1847, six men and one woman—A. C. Van Raalte, E. Frederiks, J. Laarman, J. Lankeet, E. Sagers, and Mr. and Mrs. W. Notting, led by the American G. Harrington—arrived in the woods on the south side of Black Lake to begin a struggle for a new life against the giants of the forest in Michigan.[1] Unimpressive as they appeared, they were heroes. The valiant [Bernardus] Grootenhuis who so courageously assisted Van Raalte for many years, had begun that struggle already a few days before. How strange for these Netherlanders, unaccustomed to the forest, to have come to this heavily wooded area, where the trees stood so thick there were hardly any open spaces to build the planned houses! The forest stretched for miles in every direction, interspersed with streams and rivers, swamps and ponds, without any paths or bridges. The trees were of many unfamiliar varieties, depending on the terrain, which alternated from hilly to flat, from sandy and dry to clay and wet, and even swampy sometimes. There were oaks, beeches, pines, hemlocks, sycamores, walnut trees, cedars, sugar maples, elms and basswoods, ashes, willows and alders, many measuring six feet and more in circumference. "Only roving half-civilized Indians and wild forest animals could live here, and they challenged each other for control of this unbroken wilderness."[2]

Most of these trees would have to be cut down to obtain land for farming and space, and building materials for homes and roads. But this kind of work was totally unfamiliar to most of the Hollanders. However, they were fortunate to have the assistance and instruction of a few Americans, who were more familiar with this type of work and who helped them fell the first forest giants and build the first primitive log cabin.

Thus did the gallant little band, working for days with inadequate tools

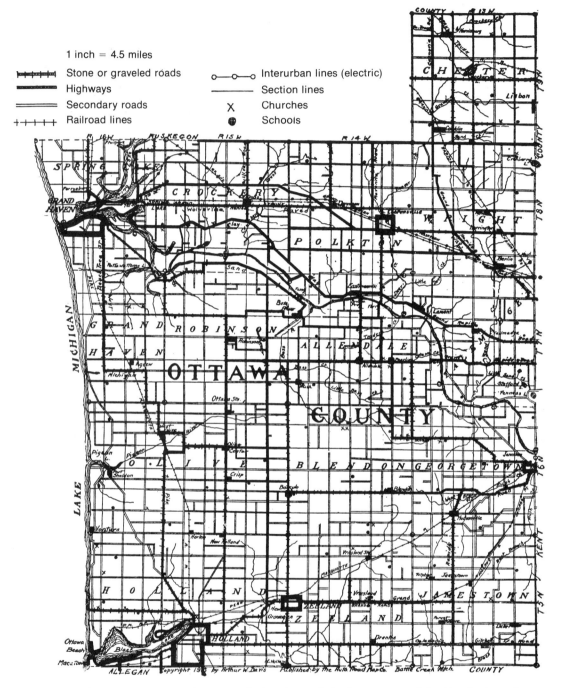

Map of Ottawa County, Michigan, in which is located the largest part of the Van Raalte colony.

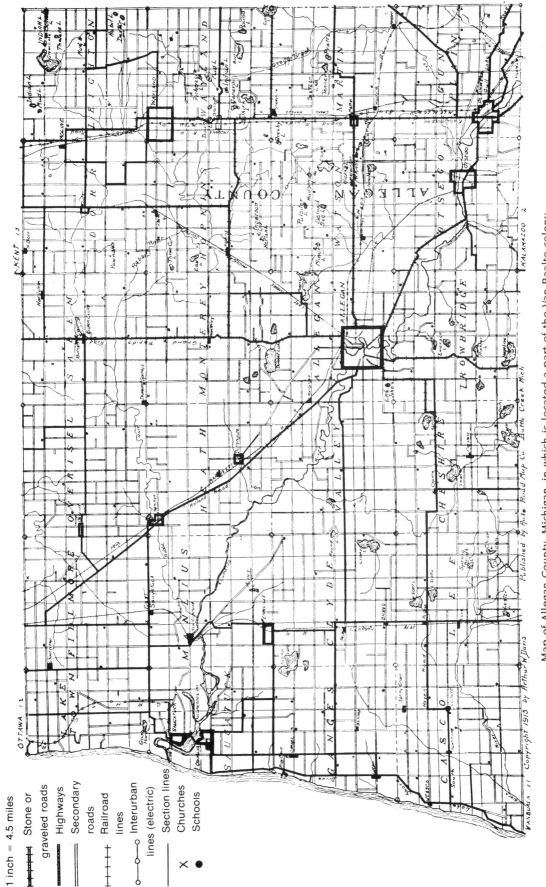

1 inch = 4.5 miles

Stone or
graveled roads

Highways

Secondary
roads

Railroad
lines

Interurban
lines (electric)

Section lines

Churches

Schools

Map of Allegan County, Michigan, in which is located a part of the Van Raalte colony.

Published by Auto Road Map Co. Battle Creek Mich

Copyright 1913 by Arthur H. Davis

and equipment in snow more than two feet deep, succeed in providing for themselves a shelter into which they moved. Until this time they had enjoyed the liberal hospitality of the Reverend G. N. Smith, an American missionary to the Indians, and a shelter under the roof of Isaac Fairbanks, a government agricultural advisor to the Potawatomi Indians. Although Smith and Fairbanks both lived several miles south of Black Lake, they were the colonists' nearest neighbors, and gave them invaluable help and encouragement. Some distance beyond lived two American farmers, |Gilbert| Cranmer and |Anton| Schorno, who played a far lesser role for the immigrants.[3] The settlers soon built a second log cabin, next to the first, and then sent for the wives and children who had been left behind in Allegan. The cabins were situated on a hill, the location of which was for many years afterwards known as the "Van der Haar farm," one mile east of the present city of Holland. The cabins could be reached by a road Grootenhuis and his men had cleared from Fairbank's farm onwards, but the road was not continued further because of a cedar swamp.

In the meantime, in the spring of 1847, immigrants were streaming into the colony from every direction. Most of them came by boat across Lake Michigan from Chicago or Milwaukee, landing at Grand Haven. From there they came to Black Lake in smaller boats or on foot. Many others, alarmed by the many shipwrecks on the big lakes, came by train by way of Buffalo and Detroit to Kalamazoo, proceeding from there by ox-drawn wagon to Allegan and then by sleds or, after the thaw, on foot to their destination. Some walked all the way from Buffalo![4]

The colony was not prepared for this influx and the two log cabins were inadequate. Thus, despite the abundance of raw building materials available in the felled trees, shelter was the colonists' most immediate and desperate need and they had to make do in the strictest way imaginable. Many found a temporary solution in a few buildings at Port Sheldon, a lengthy eight miles north of Black Lake, which had been abandoned by a bankrupt land company that in the years from 1830 to 1840 had speculated on developing a port city. Others found shelter in the abandoned huts of migrating Indians who went north in the spring in search of game and absented themselves for long periods of time. They even appropriated a structure the Indians and their missionary had used as a church.

However, most of the colonists improvised shelters by setting up posts and covering them with bed sheets or lengths of cotton cloth, or by cutting a few young trees, pruning them so they would have a fork on top, after which they were put in the ground with a pole in two forks. Leafy branches were put against this framework. Others stuck branches in the ground, the tops converging like a tepee; the sides would be covered with bark mats or reed mats. Boxes, cloths, or bedsheets were used for doors; there were plenty of openings left for the smoke to escape![5]

Especially in stormy and rainy weather they found out how utterly inadequate these make-shift shelters were. Often they were rudely awakened in

How an American chops down a tree (R., *Amerikaansche Levenservaring*).

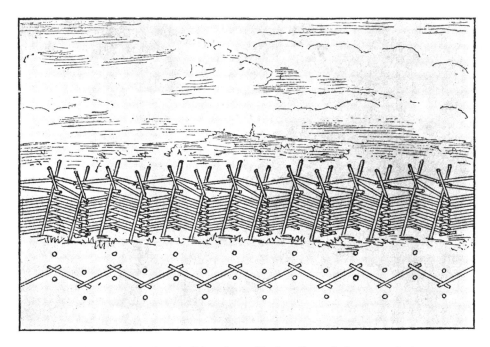

How an American builds a fence (R., *Amerikaansche Levenservaring*).

the night and were compelled to take cover under a table or an umbrella—a valuable item if they had one—against the pouring rain.[6] Since most of the cooking, baking, and washing of clothes had to be done out in the open, and since the first year of their arrival was unusually rainy, many went around for days in wet clothing, much to the detriment of their health.

The construction of more houses proceeded only slowly, partly because the colonists were so inexperienced in cutting the necessary wood and partly because there were as yet no sawmills. Only the wealthy could afford the luxury of a house built of planks. Planks were available in areas not too far distant, but since there were few means of transporting them they were scarce and expensive.

The felling of trees was not only time-consuming but also dangerous. At first it took the colonists a whole day to cut down one single tree but after becoming more accustomed to the work they cut down as many as twenty or thirty per day. At first the Hollanders with their unwieldy square axes girdled the trees close to the ground, and the forest giants finally would fall but no one could predict in which direction. Many an immigrant chopped off a toe or a foot and some were wounded or killed by a falling tree. Also, crashing trees often damaged a log cabin or destroyed the fragile leaf-shelters.[7] "Almost every one of the first settlers could later show the scars of the injuries he received in this battle with the children of Anak."[8]

Both the Indians and Americans who had settled here earlier or who would pass through gave the inexperienced colonists instructions in the proper techniques of the genuine backwoodsman: "Small notches, and large chips; strike the axe each time in the place from which it came; make the cut as far from the ground as half the length of a man's body." Rows of trees were thus prepared, ready to fall. Then when the last tree was cut it fell against the next one and all of them fell together, domino-fashion, with a tremendous crash. At first they also dug out the stumps but later they decided it cost more than it was worth, so they were left standing. Part of the tree trunks were used to build the log cabins, but most of the logs of the cleared land were stacked in piles and left to dry for several years and eventually burned as being worthless. Scholte had previously warned that in time they would have a shortage of timber and his predictions proved to be true! Thus also the Netherlanders, as so many others, including the Americans themselves in the first place, were responsible for the wholesale destruction of timber worth millions of dollars, which resulted later in a lumber shortage.

The building of the log cabins was equally awkward and wasteful, largely because the colonists did not have the proper equipment. Saws and hammers, drills, and axes were their only tools, while wooden pegs usually served as nails. When after strenuous exertion the necessary tree trunks were obtained and the branches trimmed off, a few logs were laid in a square to serve as a foundation. The ends were notched so that they would fit together at the corners and to keep them from coming apart. The bottom logs were also notched at intervals so that the floor crossbeams could be fitted into place. Then a second square of logs was placed upon the first, and a third upon the second, etc., until a height of five or six feet was obtained. Then the spaces for the doors and windows were sawed out and framed with planks. Then more logs were laid in place, and across the top-most ones beams were laid to form a ceiling. At the corners long nails or wooden pegs were inserted to keep all the logs in place. Finally, rafters were added to form a peaked roof.

After they had reached that point they would move into the "building" and finish the interior. The doors were hung, the windows covered (first with cloth, later with glass) and the roof covered, first with bark or small boards called "shakes," later to be replaced with shingles that were much more watertight. The walls were not always wind and watertight—Van der Veen's log cabin looked like a big bird-cage. To remedy this, the open spaces were stuffed with branches and leaves and then smeared on both sides with wet clay. This kept out the cold and water.[9] A fireplace was made of large, flat stones, cemented together with clay; a chimney was made of boards or woven twigs. To guard against the danger of setting fire to the house, the inside of the chimney and the wall against which the fireplace was built were covered with a thick layer of clay.

The furnishings in these log cabins were in harmony with the structure. A tree stump that had been left in the ground within the enclosed space—or a piece of a sawed-off tree trunk—served as a table. Before they had laid the floor boards, they would sit on the floor cross-beams. After the floor boards had been laid they would sit on blocks of wood or in hollow tree trunks cut to length. Wooden boxes brought from the Old Country also served as tables and seats, but usually as wardrobes. They slept on the floor or on a few planks laid across the ceiling beams, which was very dangerous. Mattresses consisted of leafy twigs and later of animal skins or the bedsize sacks they had brought along stuffed with leaves or moss. Flour or meal barrels, easily made into cradles, became particularly valuable, especially to those colonists more richly blessed with children than with money. For lighting, some used lamps they had brought with them from the Old Country, but now fueled with animal fat and with a piece of cotton for a wick. Others had bought candles in neighboring communities. Later they made their own candles or simply filled a cup or saucer with fat and inserted a small piece of cloth as a wick.

Most of the women had no adequate cooking utensils. These were improvised from most unlikely sources. Again the flour barrel proved to be a precious possession. A whole barrel became a butter churn. Sawed through in the middle it became a washtub in which the weekly laundry could be done with lye substituting for soap. Brooms and scrubbing brushes were made from twigs. Spoons and forks were carved out of wood. Chips were used as table knives and wooden trays served as plates and bowls.

One absolute essential was an iron cooking pot. In it the colonists baked their bread. The pot was filled with dough and then buried and covered with glowing charcoal. The same pot was used to make coffee, to boil potatoes, to soak corn [maize], to roast meat, and to fry bacon. A few families would jointly own a coffee grinder, which was also used to grind corn. Corn was also ground by crushing it with a heavy iron bar on a stone placed in a hollow tree stump.[10] Gradually the housing shortage was overcome. The colonists became more experienced, especially in construction, and soon a log cabin could be erected in a few days instead of a week or longer. They acquired a few oxen to help move the heavy tree trunks, and that eased the work considerably.

In April, 1847, at the urging of Van Raalte, some twenty-five men went to the mouth of Black Lake where it opens into Lake Michigan. There, with great effort, without a carpenter, without good tools, even without sufficient food, using boards and beams washed up on the shore, these men built a shed on the beach for the benefit of the immigrants. J. Vinke was appointed the first caretaker, shortly succeeded by C. Van der Veere. They were to meet the colonists arriving by boat, advise them, and direct them to the city of Holland and also act as beachcombers for the colony. Later in this same year, so many newcomers arrived that the temporary shelter, called Castle Garden, became overcrowded not only with healthy guests but mostly with sick ones, so that many were forced to spend nights in the open, under the trees or on the cold beach sand. Many were so exhausted by the difficult and dangerous journey and the inadequate food that, undermined by illness, they succumbed to these final hardships. Like Moses, they had reached the border of the promised land and had beheld it from a distance but did not enter it. Their bodies were hastily buried in shallow trenches in the shifting dunes. Later, the winds uncovered their bones and reminded subsequent immigrants of the courageous pioneers who had preceded them.[11]

A message was received that three companies of Zeelanders were on their way to the colony and in preparation five sheds were built for their use. However, a group of Frisians and Graafschappers preceded the Zeelanders and they occupied the sheds for a very brief period before vacating them in favor of the Zeelanders under the leadership of Van de Luyster and Steketee. After the Zeelanders had left, these sheds in turn continued to serve as temporary living quarters for other groups. Several colonists first stayed in these sheds for a while, scouted around in the forests and selected a location, built their log cabin, and then brought their families from the city of Holland.[12]

Incidentally, Holland looked little like a city yet. People sarcastically wrote about it as a "city of trees."[13] So far as I know, Cornelia M. Van Malsen was the only woman among the early correspondents of the colony, and she reported in July, 1847: "Many already live in log cabins, but many still live in shelters made from leafy tree branches. There are forty of us, young and old, living together in one house."[14] In December of the same year the now

Cornelia M. Van de Luyster wrote: "There are now already 120 houses in our city, not including the later arrivals from Zeeland, Friesland, and Drenthe," [who were still in temporary camps].

A year later, in August of 1848, H. Van Eijk arrived in Holland and recorded his first diary impressions as follows: "At first sight the 'city' is most unattractive. Here and there one sees a house, or a house under construction, in small openings in the impenetrable virgin forest, surrounded by stumps two or three feet high. There is a street, called 8th Street, along which are some thirty houses. Several others are lined up along the lake front, and there are some twenty spread at random. But there is much building going on and much cutting of trees. Everywhere there are woods and felled tree trunks are lying everywhere so that one can hardly see five rods in any direction."[15]

Regardless of what the actual house count was—whether it was Cornelia's too high estimate of 120 or Van Eijk's too low estimate of 50 more than six months later—in either case the expectations of the newly arrived immigrants were greatly disappointed by the reality. Being partly misled by the inducements set forth by certain "gentlemen" in New York, the newcomers had expected to find in Van Raalte's colony a populous large city with regular streets, good hotels, and well-stocked stores. One such person had imagined it to be an earthly paradise, a place of luxury. Another person had thought she could rent an attractive home and "to have everything as pleasant as she had in Amsterdam."[16] How bitter the disillusionment was we have already observed concerning the arrival of the Zeelanders.

Equally as difficult as the matter of housing was the problem of provisions, and it came quite soon at that. Some of the immigrants still had food left over from the journey when they arrived at the mouth of Black Lake. Others, like the Van der Meulen family, had bought flour in Grand Haven, in Chicago, or other stopping places. But there were others who had landed without any reserves of food at all and were glad that the Indians were willing to sell them some corn. In the surrounding communities plentiful supplies of all kinds were available, but because of the forests and swamps and the absence of any roads or trails these supplies were not readily accessible. So long as the colonists had any money, enterprising American dealers took advantage of that situation and raised their prices tenfold and more. This was all the more despicable since the quality of these supplies left much to be desired; for example, after one bought a barrel of flour the top layers would be okay, but, at home, the bottom layers of the flour would be found to be moldy and inedible.[17]

In the spring after the heavy snows melted and the showers came, the forest trails became impassable, while the swollen and fast flowing rivers and streams were too dangerous for navigation. The delivery of flour, potatoes, etc., was then no longer possible and people went for days and even weeks with only some corn, bean soup, and salted meat to eat. Only the strongest and most courageous among the colonists ventured out on the dangerous trails through the forests and swamps, across rivers and streams, to Allegan, Grand Rapids, Grand Haven, or Singapore to get some provisions. Although these cities were "only" 24, 30, 32 and 14 miles from Holland respectively, the trip took days and sometimes weeks, providing they did not get lost, or worse! A few tried to get food by hunting deer or other game, and others increasingly followed their example. Food shortages were at times greatly complicated when large new groups of immigrants arrived at the same time.

The first few months were bad enough, but worse was still to come. They ran out of money. After their golden "Willempjes," their guilders and even their "stuivers" were gone, and little or no American money had come in, the American merchants and peddlers were no longer so accommodating and stayed away. This was all the more serious because the transition from forest to farmland proceeded very slowly and there was no prospect of their becoming self-supporting in the immediate future. All open spaces within ten or fifteen miles, even the clearings left by the migrating Indians, were appropriated by the colonists for the planting of potatoes, corn, and buckwheat to have at least some stores for the coming winter.[18]

Meals were very simple, even monotonous. Three times a day they ate nothing but Indian maize boiled in water, occasionally replaced by potatoes, peas, or beans. No desserts. Those who had flour sometimes also had bread, but it was not very tasty since the balls of dough were baked in hot ashes. Sometimes the flour was used for pancakes, porridge, or pudding, according to the skill of the housewife. Only after they had acquired cows, pigs, and chickens and American-type cookstoves did the food become more appetizing and of better quality. "Juffrouw" [Mrs.] Van Raalte showed many of the women a better method of making bread. Coffee and tea were so expensive, they had to make do with extracts from roasted peas, beans, and corn to which they sometimes added milk and sugar as a special luxury. Some brewed a kind of beer from sassafras and herbs from the forest.

Their clothes also showed their initially increasing poverty. The children wore garments they had outgrown, while many an older person also had to go around in his wornout togs, unable to show in his dress any difference between weekdays and Sundays. Fathers went to the Sunday services wearing worn-out overalls, everyday blue shirts and patched trousers, wooden shoes, or "klompstevels" (wooden shoes on which. are nailed the shafts of boots or animal skins). The skills of those women who could sew and mend were severely tested. Fortunately some had friends "out East" who donated clothing that was rationed out to even the very poorest.[19]

When a population moves from one soil and climate region to a totally different one, illnesses are likely to result. This was especially true in this case because the colonists were already exhausted from the journey and then they also had to cope with uncleared land and inadequate food, clothing, and protection from the weather. Poor drainage resulted in very damp ground—swamps, pools, and puddles—in which malaria-bearing mosquitoes multiplied, a condition aggravated by the continual digging out of tree stumps. Moisture evaporating from the open ground added to the dampness. Moreover, the climate in Michigan is much more subject to sudden changes than in the Netherlands. Especially the quick variations in temperature were difficult to get adjusted to.

The sharpest contrasts in this regard were found in the small clearings in the forest. In the summer air temperatures reached 180 |sic| degrees F. and more. The air in these small clearings was practically motionless. On the other hand, in these small clearings the nighttime temperatures were the first to reach the freezing point and remained there longest. The Finnish immigrants fared better in this respect than the Netherlanders. Since they had forests in their homeland too, they had learned from experience to link their clearings together, which promoted air circulation and thus equalized the temperature.[20] The cold, damp fogs lying along the lakes in Michigan were also very unhealthy.

As a result there was much illness—malaria, typhus, smallpox, scarlet fever, etc.—especially among those who, because they had come from higher and dryer regions in the Netherlands, were most susceptible.[21] Others, who had come from low-lying swampy provinces, seemed better able to withstand these extremes (as the Beukma family had previously experienced in Indiana.)[22] Naturally, their psychological reactions had a bearing on their physical conditions. Precisely this last aspect of their situation, the undernourishment and the hardships, made many so discouraged that they succumbed and died, not necessarily because the illness was so severe or uncurable but because they lost the will to live.

During the summer of 1847 the situation deteriorated so greatly that the whole colony became one great hospital. In nearly every log cabin, in every hut and tent, was serious illness, even death. Almost every family mourned the loss of one or more members, indeed whole families died out. From a company of Frisians that had come to Holland eleven had died by April of 1848.[23] The population of the village of Groningen was reduced by half before the end of the first year.

So great was the number of the dead that finally there were no longer boards with which to make caskets, and many of the survivors were themselves too ill to bury the dead. A proper funeral could not even be considered. A certain |Josias| De Regt, for example, whose wife had died, simply wrapped the body in a bedsheet and buried it in a grave he dug behind the cabin.[24] For lack of assistance others buried their wives and children in like manner. There was no designated burial area, no "cemetery," the corpses were simply committed to the earth near their homes. Only after the first church had been built was an area set aside for a cemetery around the church, as was the Old Dutch custom.

The only doctor in the colony, Dr. |J. S. M. C.| Van Nus, was practically powerless to do anything without the needed medicine and without experience in these illnesses and this kind of situation. Many "doctors" from the surrounding communities came, but it soon became evident that they were quacks who came "to make money and then go away when their pockets were filled and their ignorance of medical art and medicine came to light."[25] Many a colonist was thus tricked out of his last money (one of them even traded his old silver watch) for what was merely quinine or a potion that turned out to be only brandy!

The best doctor proved to be their leader, Van Raalte, "the active brain of the whole enterprise." He worked tirelessly, supported and encouraged by his wife. He functioned as preacher, justice of the peace, police officer, real estate dealer, woodcutter, and carpenter! During this period of illness he also proved himself a good physician, even an obstetrician, saving lives by patiently comforting and encouraging those who were suffering. Every morning there gathered at his house those who came to consult him about their ailing families. He tried always to give some measure of help, whether with quinine or medicinal rhubarb, or with advice and recommendations. He spent his afternoons calling with words of comfort and encouragement on the sick in their homes, widely scattered in the forest.

Sorrow and grief were present everywhere, here turned to despair, there to hopeless resignation. It seemed as if everyone expected to die. But there was bitterness too. There were those who, knowing their Bible, accused Van Raalte, as the people of Israel had accused Moses: "Why did you bring us up out of Egypt, to die in this wilderness, and to bring us to this evil place?"[26] Many left the colony and moved to Illinois or Wisconsin to try their luck there, and they warned newcomers not to go to Holland: "The people there are dying like mice from illness and want." Even Van Raalte feared, in a moment of faint-heartedness, that the colony would fail and come to nothing. At least once it was too much for him to bear. One Sunday evening during that first disastrous summer, standing in the open air on the trunk of a tree, he preached on the Scripture verse, "See, the Judge standeth before the door." His audience was small, most of his congregation was ill, many had died, and others had left and gone to other areas. During the prayer he was overcome and in a voice choked with tears he cried out, "O Lord, must we now all die?"[27]

With the approach of winter the total number of those who were ill was somewhat reduced, housing was improved, and supplies more plentiful. Nevertheless, in 1848 conditions were still anything but rosy. H. Van Eijk, who arrived in the colony in August of that year, reported that there were many persons ill, as many as five to seven in one home. There were fewer deaths, though fever reigned everywhere and he wrote, "The colonists looked as if they had returned from the land of the dead back to the world."[28]

By sheer will power they tried to confront and conquer all their problems and difficulties. The dangers shared by the whole community, composed of such heterogeneous elements, brought about in the colony a spirit of solidarity that, thanks to the leadership qualities of Van Raalte, resulted in a communal cooperation such as they would never know again and which many an aged pioneer afterward recalled with nostalgia. It was at the urging of Van Raalte that the colonists erected the temporary shelters at the mouth of Black River for the accommodation of arriving immigrants. For Van Raalte himself a house was built of cedar logs. It was on his recommendation that a few doctors were asked to come from Kalamazoo, to be paid out of a common fund.[29]

As time went on, steady progress was made with the erection of houses. In 1849 the Reverend I. N. Wyckoff visited the villages and recorded the number of dwellings as follows: Holland and surrounding area, 225; Zeeland, 175; Groningen, 30; Drenthe, 45; Vriesland, 69; Overisel, 35; and Graafschap, 50; for a total of 629, inhabited by approximately three thousand persons.* In addition there were about three thousand acres of cleared land available for settling. Gradually, in one way or another conditions improved.

An interesting plan was devised to solve the problem of purchasing food. Already in August of 1847 the Zeelanders had appointed some of their men to go to Grand Rapids and buy supplies for the whole group.[30] In the late summer of the same year a general meeting of all the various groups was held, at which it was decided to set up a common fund for the purpose of buying supplies in wholesale lots in New York and to make these available to the colonists at cost, plus pro-rated expenses. Everyone who still had some funds loaned them at low interest and so "a sort of apostolic stock company" was organized.[31] One of the colonists, B. Grootenhuis, and an Old Dutch resident of Grand Rapids, E. De Young, traveled together to New York and there purchased large quantities of goods, not only food but all kinds of household goods, tools, even children's toys, and "Yankee notions." They paid for half of it and charged the remainder to the account of "Van Raalte and Company." In the meantime a trading post was set up east of Black Lake, with personnel appointed and Grootenhuis put in charge.

At the insistence of Jannes Van de Luyster, a member of the Zeeland group, and largely with his money, the colonists purchased a ship for $800, a 100-ton, two-masted schooner, the A. E. *Knickerbocker*, manned by Hollanders with [Ale] Steginga as mate. The intention and purpose was to ship not only supplies into the colony and products out, but in addition to transport incoming immigrants from Buffalo, Milwaukee, and Chicago and by so doing to promote the growth of the Michigan colony.

Neither the store nor the ship proved to be a profitable venture. The projects lacked both sufficient capital and competent management, in spite of the good will of the promoters, among whom was J. Van de Luyster, Jr.[32] Some of the merchandise arrived in spoiled condition. Articles needed for winter did not arrive until spring. The ship was run inefficiently. Because of

---

*The erroneous figures for Holland (235), Graafschaap (20), and the total (639) have been corrected.

the sand banks at the entrance of Black Lake, loading and unloading of merchandise and farm and forest products was difficult and not without danger and damage. Also, many immigrants arriving on the ship declined to pay the passage. Was not the ship the common property of the colony?[33]

With one thing and another the venture sustained so many losses that it soon became apparent it could not be continued. There was too much competition from newly developed private enterprise. The "cooperative" fell apart in 1847. The ship was sold for $400 and the left-over merchandise divided among the "stock-holders" as equitably as possible. The one suffering the greatest loss was Jannes Van de Luyster, Sr. In fact, he was reduced to poverty and later his family, after renewed reverses, had to be given financial assistance.[34] The unpaid debts were charged against "Van Raalte and Company" and since the company no longer existed, Van Raalte himself was held responsible. He was rescued from imminent bankruptcy by Christian brothers in New York State and New Jersey.[35]

Other communal projects undertaken to provide food for the group were likewise dismal failures. At one of the first general meetings it was decided to try to rent with common funds some farms near Saugatuck, southwest of Holland.[36] [Arend] Kampers and two other farmers were appointed to manage the undertaking and bring the produce to Holland. There is no record of results. A colonial fishery was also considered. R. Schilleman made some inquiries in St. Joseph and Chicago about American methods of fresh-water fishing. A fishing vessel was actually built and outfitted but, due to lack of cooperation from the colonists who were established deeper inland, it had to be sold for $5.[37]

It has been asserted, unfairly, that these various endeavors failed only because they were communal or cooperative in nature.[38] We shall see that private and individual ventures also failed. They lacked adequate financial resources, skilled craftsmen, and more than anything else, good roads, etc. Other colonies of pioneers had the same histories of failures and successes.

Our colonists soon realized that the isolation in which they found themselves greatly complicated the problems of providing the basic housing, food, and other necessities. In addition to these, they needed good roads, which would benefit farmers and all kinds of industry and commerce. In no other area did the common goal hold the community together so long and so strongly as this common need for trade routes. Also, this problem did not lend itself to individual enterprise. It could only be accomplished by people working together.

When the immigrants first arrived, the only "road" through the dense woods was formed by an Indian trail from Allegan past the Fairbanks farm to the Indian village on Black Lake. This trail was widened up to the farm, but the tree stumps were not removed, so that only with great caution would it accommodate wagons and sleighs. As more colonists were scattered throughout the forests and more settlements were established, paths connecting them with the "city" of Holland were laid out by marking the trees with blazes. But these blazes were often so small and inconspicuous that many a traveler got lost and wandered around in the forest for hours, even for days and nights, to the great concern of their families, as also once happened to the senior Van de Luyster.[39] Often one could hear, especially toward evening, the cries of distress of the lost wanderers echoing through the forest. Not every lost traveler would succeed, guided by a light in a window or by the solemn sound of the singing of psalms, in finding a place to spend the night.

A good part of that first winter and much time thereafter was invested in cutting down trees to make roads. At a general meeting it was agreed that the colonists would work in shifts without pay to do this unaccustomed labor. Since Grootenhuis and his coworkers had previously laid out a road from the Fairbanks home to the first dwellings, this road was extended through the cedar swamp to the city of Holland. In the meantime the village of Zeeland had been settled, and it likewise was connected to Holland by a similar road. The connection from Van Raalte's home to the first log church and the adjoining cemetery across a swamp became a very significant one. No other road in the colony had quite the same importance. Alike in birth, marriage, and death, everyone at one time or another followed that same road.[40] The greatest obstacle was caused by swamps that had to be crossed; especially when the surplus water could not be drained. That is why it took two years to lay a road between the villages of Vriesland and Zeeland, which were separated by a swamp. The first attempt was abandoned, and a new attempt was made in another location. The road from the village of Overisel to Zeeland also ran through a swamp, first drained by the digging of drainage canals. Forest roads were built by cutting and hauling away as many trees as needed to allow for wagon and cart traffic. But swamp roads required more work. The logs were laid out across the road closely packed next to each other. After heavy rains or after spring thaws set in, such a "cross road" or "corduroy road" looked more like a wooden raft than a traffic road and it was dangerous for both vehicles and pedestrians. Later it was learned that some of these early trails or "roads" did not comply with American regulations and had to be relocated!

All this work was not done entirely without financial aid. At their own expense the merchants of Grand Rapids laid out a road to the colony to facilitate trade, while the state of Michigan took responsibility for the construction of a road from Kalamazoo to Grand Haven by way of Allegan and Holland. Besides, the state of Michigan assisted with subsidies, paid out in land grants, as was often done in those times when the state had more land than money. So, in the spring of 1848, four hundred acres of state land were designated for the cost of a bridge over the Black River, and in 1849 a total of three thousand acres of state land had already been given to encourage more road building. Most of the "bridges" consisted simply of a few logs laid across a small stream. However, the Black River close to the lake was much too wide for that and many a town gathering was held to plan and prepare for the Grand Haven bridge. No builder or contractor could be found to undertake this project and finally, in November 1848, again at the urging of Van Raalte, the colonists together began the big job.[41] However, progress was very slow and the committee charged with the supervision was compelled to use gentle coercion. Absentees were required to get an able substitute or pay a fine of $1.50 per day. All participants would share in the profits from the sale of the land grants. They hoped to complete the job in May 1849.

In the beginning a traveler through the forest made no more than two or three miles per day. Travel by water was no faster or less dangerous. How dangerous the landing was at Black Lake was demonstrated by the experience of the Zeelanders who had to contend with many sandbanks and one of the frequent storms causing heavy surf. Because of this, transfer of goods and persons to smaller boats was often impossible. Navigation and commerce suffered. Once on Black Lake, one was still not safe, and had to face many heavy tree trunks floating around in the water and the danger of running aground on the shallows. Many an already "unseaworthy" flatboat or scow incurred a leak in its hull, and passengers and goods arrived in Holland thoroughly soaked.

Groups of colonists who wished to establish themselves further inland proceeded up the Black River, as far as they could, an undertaking which proved to be no less arduous. They purchased lumber from which they built a raft, and on the raft they loaded their wives, children, and household goods while the men pulled the raft upstream. "It was continually sticking fast, here on a tree trunk, there on a stone, or pushed by the water currents against the bank. Many a time the men had to wade into the water and with a united effort lift the raft free. When night fell, the raft got stuck so solidly that the travelers decided to take a well-deserved rest." They built a fire on the bank, hung their wet upper clothes around it to dry and spent the night sleeping on the ground around the fire. The next morning it was for the men to jump "back into the water up to the waist, lift the raft free, load aboard the thirteen wives and children and continue on up the stream." So traveled the founders of the village of Drenthe![42]

Van Raalte realized that these and similar transportation problems made the growth of shipping and trade practically impossible and that they seriously threatened the development of his creation—Holland. A good harbor was an absolute necessity for which no effort should be too great. Various attempts to open "the mouth" and maintain a channel into Black Lake failed from lack of money and equipment. It is true, the state of Michigan made available for the project four thousand acres of state land and the government in Washington, $5,000, but these amounts proved to be far from sufficient and offical cooperation left much to be desired. An adequate harbor landing was not achieved, according to Van Raalte, "either because it is difficult to work with land [to raise money] or because the commissioner in charge of such government works does not care about our prosperity."[43] A request was made to the government for $45,000 to complete the project. Van Raalte asked that an estimate of the cost be made. One of the officials of the Bureau of Topographical Engineers, J. B. Bowes, entrusted by the government to make such an estimate, gave a figure of at least $100,000. A second estimate, made by him in June 1850, induced Congress to allot $8,000 for the time being, after which the work was immediately begun. Unfortunately, President [Franklin] Pierce withdrew the grant because (it was said) the state of the treasury would not permit the use of government funds for the advancement of regional projects. Economy measures were in full swing after the Mexican War. Secretly it was whispered by his Republican opponents that the real reason was that this Democratic "southern" president was prejudiced against a "northern" project.[44]

The colonists, deeply disappointed but not discouraged, called a general meeting and after discussion decided to tackle the job themselves. Scores of workers gathered at the mouth of Black Lake with shovels and other simple implements and began to dig a channel. A shopkeeper by the name of [Alderd] Plugger, one of the most interested parties in the project, offered to pay for their daily food out of his own pocket. That was their only pay.[45] They kept at it until they had dug a channel through which flatboats from Black Lake could reach Lake Michigan. Goods could now be transferred directly from the schooners to the scows. Previously it had usually been necessary to carry freight by hand over the sandbanks. However, the strong west winds soon filled the channel with sand again and it turned out the labor had been fruitless. For more than ten years the colonists wrestled with this problem, which greatly hindered the growth of both Holland and the surrounding inland territory. Business and the slowly developing agriculture and industry were all greatly hampered by the lack of water transportation.

B. Sources of Income

Van Raalte's followers were largely landlubbers who wished to establish themselves as farmers. For them the forests had to be transformed, re-created into farmland. This "cleaning" of the land was a very slow and laborious process. It involved not only the felling of trees but also the digging out of the stumps, which for the time being was impossible. The normal procedures of plowing and harrowing the soil was thus also impossible. Since they had to work with hand tools between the stumps, they were limited to the types of crops they were able to plant, such as potatoes, corn, beans, and peas. Later, after the stumps had been removed and the land could be plowed, they raised wheat, rye, and oats. Some attempted to raise buckwheat and chicory as they had been accustomed to do in the Old Country, but they found the soil less suitable.[46] They also tried raising tobacco, but only briefly, because they found that trade brought in better and cheaper kinds of tobacco.

All types of farming were handicapped by the primitive implements they had, for they had to improvise as best they could from the materials available in the forests. Pitchforks were made of hickory, grain was threshed—"scourged" ["*geeselen*"]—by beating it with long sticks. Wagons, sleds, and harrows were made entirely from wood. Even the harnesses for the oxen were primitive: towing thongs for oxen were made of the tough strips of bark from young linden trees!

Their American neighbor [George S., Sr.] Harrington, brought in the first yoke of oxen and rented them out to the Hollanders at $2 per day.[47] Later the more affluent farmers bought their own oxen and some others bought them in joint ownership. Most either did without or hired them once in a while as they were able. "Ox farmers" soon found, following Harrington's example, that the animal rental business was a good source of income. These farmers also came to serve a valuable purpose in the colony as freight carriers.

Next in importance to the production of food crops was the raising of cattle and other livestock. Because they had as yet no barns or stables or fodder for the animals for the winter, they were reluctant to invest in livestock. However, their American neighbors allowed their cattle to roam at will in the forests where there was plenty of forage. The first winters were not extremely severe, so the colonists followed the example of those "neighbors" and bought a few cows to range in the woods. Even some of those who owned no land at all bought one or two cows and turned them loose to "pasture" in the woods and they began producing milk, butter, and cheese on a very limited scale.

This activity brought about new problems. The cows invaded the clearings, so the colonists built fences to keep them out, as well as the deer and the bears, etc. A second and more serious problem was that the cattle continuously wandered away and were lost in the woods so that the owners sustained substantial losses.[48] They tied a bell around the neck of each cow but a better way was to keep the young calves at home, since the mothers always returned. The winter of 1848–1849 was very severe and this "American" system of keeping livestock showed its weaknesses: a shortage of feed and no shelter. Not everyone was willing to share his log cabin with his cow! The Zeelanders lost a third of their investment in livestock! Pigs and chickens were also shipped in and found plenty of food in the woods. Thus, gradually the colonists were able to provide for their own needs and had some left over to export.

So it appeared that all the difficulties associated with the settlement had been conquered—until the disastrous year 1851. That year, continuous rains considerably reduced the grain harvest, and what the colonists were able to salvage was almost entirely devoured by invaders—mice, porcupines, raccoons, woodchucks, and especially squirrels. Squirrels became a veritable plague. "They climbed up the cornstalks and ate the kernels right off the ears. They invaded barns and houses, penetrated into the attics and under the beds—wherever grain was stored these robbers seemed to be able to find it."[49]

Many who had persevered to this point became discouraged and left the colony. They moved to Grand Rapids, Kalamazoo, Allegan, Grand Haven, or other places. Some gave up farming and switched to commerce and industry. More than had been the case heretofore, attention was given to the resources of the forest, and people tried to make a living exploiting them. As early as January, 1847, Van Raalte had called attention to the wealth of cranberries growing wild in two peat bog areas between the Black and Grand rivers. They could be sold in surrounding areas for a very fair price.[50] Before the disastrous year of 1851 not much attention had been paid to this source of income. They also found they could make and sell maple sugar, since the maple trees were plentiful. They learned from the Indians how to tap the trees in the spring and boil the sap down into sugar which they then used for themselves or sold to wholesalers for an average price of seven cents per pound. Another of the forest products that could be sold, although less profitably, was lye made from the ashes of burned maples. Especially after 1851, many eeked out a wretched existence in this way. According to Van Raalte, an acre of maple trees yielded five or six dollar's worth of lye.[51] As they became more familiar with the demands of the American market, they learned that the trees of the forest, which had to be cut down anyway for farmland and pasture, yielded other saleable products. For example, they found that the bark of the hemlock was used to make tannic acid, which was much in demand in the tanneries in Chicago. Many a colonist spent his days peeling bark.

Others cut the trees into firewood and sold it in surrounding areas. Still others made barrel staves and bottoms, churns, axe handles, and shingles. The latter were so profitable that Dominie Van der Meulen said he made more money from seven pine trees cut into "schinkels" than he had paid for his twenty acres of land.[52] Also chairmakers and wooden shoemakers made a living from the woods. The wooden shoes found a ready market also among the American farmers and even city dwellers paid well for them. In various ways the trees of the forest became increasingly important. Many a farmer profited in two ways; selling his wood brought income and it also cleared his land.

This exploitation of the forest naturally led to the manufacture of various products. Also in this area communal projects were initially attempted. A community sawmill was built in part with some assistance from those same Christian brethren in the East.[53] A factory for the making of wood shingles was also started, but neither of these succeeded.[54] A lack of adequate capital and experienced workmen caused them to fail just as various other colonial private industries.

The lack of a good sawmill was especially irksome. It was ironical that in the very midst of dense forests they had to bring in rafts of lumber for building from other areas, and it often arrived in damaged condition. A few

enterprising pioneers in the settlements of Groningen and Vriesland and in
"*de stad*" Holland concentrated their efforts on constructing a sawmill. Especially the village of Groningen seemed destined to become the industrial
center of the colony because of its favorable location, equidistant from all
the other settlements, while at that point the Black River became navigable.
Jan Rabbers, the founder of Groningen, had observed the advantages of this
location and in cooperation with others he had already begun in the mild
winter of 1847–48 to build a sawmill that was put into operation in April of
1848.[55] The undertaking was plagued with many adversities. While it was still
under construction it was crushed by a falling tree. After it had gone into
operation and all colonists had their wood sawed there, the dam was
washed out several times. Rabbers was compelled to borrow money to
rebuild. He consistently asked every newly-arrived colonist, "Didya bring
also som' money?"[56] In the end the expenses became too high and after the
strong water current had destroyed the mill dam several times, the enterprise had to be discontinued. But, undiscouraged and undismayed, Rabbers, the *Matthijs de Sterke* [Paul Bunyan] of the colony, now built a gristmill
for the grinding of grain. One of his neighbors, J. Kolvoort, built a similar
gristmill in a newer settlement further north, also named Groningen.

In the city of Holland in 1848, O. Van der Sluis, with the help of American
workmen, built a steam sawmill.[57] This project also failed, and the promoter
was financially ruined like so many a pioneer. However, later on the enterprise prospered. A windmill, built by J. Schrader near the Grand Haven
bridge, was not successful either. The dense forest surrounding the "*meulen*"
[mill] on three sides obstructed the windcurrents too much. In the village of
Vriesland two brothers, L. and G. Bosch, also pioneered in the mill business
but their "mill" was extremely primitive. Later, a water-powered gristmill
was built and an oil mill.[58]

Van Raalte tried to encourage the development of these various industries in every way possible. He announced: "The village of Holland will
make suitable land available for all such projects for free." Van Raalte
himself, in cooperation with an American, H. D. Post, set up a processing
plant in which the "black salt" obtained by burning trees was reworked into
potash that could be sold. Many a poverty-stricken immigrant was helped
to make a living by working here.[59] However, it too lasted only a short time.

Attempts were made in both Holland and Zeeland to establish a leather-
tanning business, but without success. Greater success was obtained with a
shipyard set up by [Jan] Slag, one of the colonists. His first ship, *The Wooden
Shoe Dutchman*, outsailed even the government vessels on Lake Michigan. On
the other hand, a pottery begun by one of the Frisians in Holland soon ran
out of funds and came to an end. The one project that thrived from the
beginning was the brickyard begun by B. J. Veneklaasen. But he was his own
craftsman! He had previously been a brickmaker by trade in the Netherlands. In 1848 he started a brickyard three miles southeast of Holland. A
year later Van Raalte reported. "The brick business has been exceptionally

successful."[60] A few years later the brickyard was moved to the village of Groningen, where it fared equally well. It should be said that Veneklaasen had four sons who worked with him! Still later, the brickyard was moved again, this time near Zeeland, where it still is today one of the most important and modern industries in the area, giving good employment to many laborers.

On the whole, of all the various kinds of projects initiated in the colony, manufacturing encountered the most obstacles and was the least successful. Merchandising did better, but it also developed slowly and it too was far surpassed by the growth of farming and livestock endeavors. This was due in part to the extremely primitive means of transportation at first, and consequently the postal service was also very poor. The nearest post office at that time was at Manlius, near the present New Richmond in Allegan County. The first Dutch postman in the area was Willem Notting, who lived in a settlement then called South Holland on the county line between Ottawa and Allegan counties. Once a week Notting went on the trail to Manlius, a distance of twelve miles through dense forest, carrying the mail back and forth. Vrouw Notting carried the mail the remaining three miles from their home to Holland. In Holland it was sorted in the store of the American merchant Post, and then K. Van den Hoek was, among others, responsible for its delivery to Zeeland, Drenthe, and Vriesland.

Only after the trails to Allegan, Grand Haven, and Grand Rapids had become roads did stage drivers take over Notting's difficult task. They not only carried the mail but as "the only medium of intercourse with the outer world," they also did errands and assignments for the colonists. Thus they became the middlemen, the commission agents, even for the retail trade, "the general purchasing agent, purveyor and commission man, broker and confidential man of all his fellow-colonists," whose importance went far beyond, for instance, that of the freight carriers of our day. Van Schelven himself, in his paper on the early postal service of Holland, went so far as to declare: "The stage driver of old was one of the indispensable factors in the general make-up of our primitive commercial life." For some time he was the only one who had cash and who transacted "cash business."

In the beginning these "mail carriers" transported the mail only once a week; later it was twice a week. So it went until 1870 when the first railway to Holland was opened, greatly improving business communications. After that the glory of the postilions was a thing of the past. The retail trade was no longer so dependent on them and the storekeeper now became the economic power.

In the beginning, the overriding necessity for basic foodstuffs brought about a cooperative for buying and selling supplies. But before long, those colonists who possessed some capital funds of their own began personal retail businesses.[61] J. Binnenkant and |Willem| Houtkamp opened a grocery store in Holland. A. Plugger followed suit. |J.| Van der Veen, a coppersmith, became a dealer in hardware, while A. Visser opened the first bakery shop.

At first Visser had few customers because "everyone does his own baking."[62] However, the Van der Veen family became his first good patrons.[63] K. Smit and J. Busquet opened a retail store in Zeeland and our miller Jan Rabbers did the same at Groningen.

The failure of the cooperatives turned out for the better because it resulted in more individual ventures. In August of 1848 Van Eijk recorded in his diary that there were a sufficient number of stores and no shortage of foodstuffs anymore, and even good housing could be had. The opening of a "hotel" by Binnenkant contributed to the latter. In Holland alone in 1852 there were seven stores, two hotels, a bakery, a brass and copper smithy, a tailor shop and even a goldsmith's shop.[64] There also were some wagon-makers and blacksmiths.

Among the small businessmen, storekeepers especially became men of importance. They are comparable to our grocers who sell the greatest variety of goods. As everywhere else in the West, and also earlier in New England, they had a great influence on the development of the colonies.[65] The pioneer grocers, the "grocerymen," have generally been pictured as "tyrants, uncrowned kings, who ruled the entire community from behind their counters with iron scepters,"[66] against whom revolt is of no use, whose power is unlimited and against whom even the freedom-loving Americans had no recourse. However, this description was not altogether valid in the Dutch settlements, thanks to the usually strong religious character of the community. Here it was the preacher and the consistory [kerkeraad] who formed a counterweight in case economic dictatorial tendencies should develop.[67]

The power exercised by the storekeeper, also in the Dutch settlements, was due to the extreme poverty of those early years when the colonists had constant expenses and when there was hardly any income. True, during the food shortage the young people, the teenagers, at Van Raalte's urging went into the American community to work and they earned some money which they brought or sent home for the benefit of their parents, while also newly-arrived immigrants brought in some capital, but it was hardly enough to buy even the first necessities for living. So acute was the cash shortage that the preacher himself was paid in corn or "personal labor." A year's work for a carpenter netted him only twenty-five cents in cash, and the barber's charge of three cents for a shave was likewise paid for in field products or work.[68] It was with the storekeepers that the colonists had the highest outstanding accounts, especially when they could not pay off their debts in groceries with products from their land. There were immigrants who worked in the forests for months to pay off the "grocerymen."

Through their dealings with the American business community, the merchants in Holland were able to find buyers for the goods produced by the Hollanders, and so they became the foremost providers of employment in the colony. A. Plugger in Holland and H. Keppel in Zeeland exported great quantities of barrel staves and other products from the forests, and the latter even outfitted a ship for this trade.[69] These businessmen bought from the colonists (at low prices) all types of goods—butter and eggs from one, hand-made stools and chairs from another—paying for them in food supplies. Almost everybody had an open account with a storekeeper. For a long time people paid one another not in money but in "store notes," a type of private draft or check that could be used as payment at the grocery. The "store" became the colonial bankinghouse! For many years this system of barter and exchange and "store pay" was part of colonial life.[70] This continued until the sixties, until after roads had been laid out and improved, and especially after harbor facilities were completed and traffic greatly increased and commerce jumped fourfold. Then finally the lack of cash ceased. Both farming and manufacturing also increased. Everyone was making money!

C. Administration of the Colony

It is understandable that all the previously recorded struggles, difficulties, and stresses associated with the establishment of a new community in totally unfamiliar terrain would dominate the social life of the colonists and promote the pioneer spirit in all walks of life. But on the other hand, it is equally understandable that the thirst for freedom and a great religious zeal, present in a small nucleus, would influence that struggle for existence and put their stamp on the young colony. It was precisely these characteristics, present from the very beginning, that caused the settlement of Netherlanders to differ economically from many American and other settlements, and caused them even more so to differ in their spiritual life.

Especially in Van Raalte's creation this became evident. There, as in so many other communities in the hard struggle for existence, the storekeepers wielded the economic clout, but they were influential also in other areas. To quote Clive Day: "The country-store was the focus of the village, not only in economic, but in political and social life as well."[71] Day had written this concerning eighteenth-century America but it applied just as well to the mid-nineteenth-century Far West and also, up to a point, to the pioneers from the Netherlands. For example, in *"de stad"* Holland important decisions were made in a community gathering held in the home of storekeeper Binnenkant.[72] Midweek religious evening gatherings were held in his hotel. He owned a newspaper, *De Hollander*, and also published a religious periodical, *De Verzamelaar* [The Compiler].[73] Another storekeeper, H. D. Post, one of the first Americans who settled among the Hollanders, thanks to that combination was named postmaster in 1848 and a year later chosen supervisor (township mayor). Beyond that I was not able to ascertain any "domineering" by the storekeeper in daily public affairs. In conformity with the "fundamental agreement" drawn up in the Netherlands before the migration, all colonists having reached their majority were to have equal rights and were to take part in the governance of the colony, at least as long as it was still left to its own resources.

By the time the Netherlanders arrived in western Michigan there were already established communities in the valley of the Kalamazoo River, such as Kalamazoo, Otsego, and Allegan. Further north, in the valley of the Grand River (where in 1821 the first white man, Rix Robinson, a fur-trader, settled)[74] were towns like Grand Haven, founded in 1834, and Grand Rapids and Grandville of later dates. These areas had been organized into counties.

The Black River valley, Van Raalte's choice, lying between these two larger rivers, belonged for the most part to Ottawa County; but the smaller part, the southern section, was in Allegan County. In the words of Michigan's governor in 1847, this area was still such "a stretch of unbroken wilderness," inhabited by Indians and only a single white man, that there was hardly any governmental supervision.[75] The Hollanders, like so many other "frontier men," had to fend for themselves. As early as February 8, 1847, they held their first general meeting in the forest, at which Van Raalte's colonization plan was approved.[76] Later, many similar "popular meetings" were held, first under the trees, then in front of Van Raalte's home, after that (take note!) in the church. Matters of common interest were discussed and a work plan was set up. In these meetings the previously mentioned decisions to solve the food shortage and other problems were taken, usually after being proposed by the leader.

In the beginning these gatherings involved the entire colony, but in time various groups separated and formed more or less independent villages whose inhabitants, mostly farmers, seldomly met. As far as they were organized into a church they would also leave the administration of the community affairs to the care of the minister and the consistory, as soon happened in Zeeland and Vriesland. Therefore, in February, 1849, Van Raalte remarked in his writings all too discreetly, that he was "entirely ignorant concerning the home affairs of the *Dorpskommen* |village communities| that were slowly arising all around him."[77]

The city of Holland was the first settlement officially laid out by E. B. Bassett, the Allegan county surveyor, in the fall of 1847.[78] With the help of a compass the north-south, east-west directions of the "streets" were officially determined. The intervening areas were divided into blocks or parceled into lots, marked by "blazes" on the trees. When the surveyor became ill, his work was completed by J. Dumont, assisted by B. Grootenhuis, after which "the village of Holland" was officially inscribed in the county records by a county official. The first street, now "Eighth Street," was "opened" after the trees were felled. In a similar manner the surrounding villages were established and officially recorded. In Zeeland the preacher Van der Meulen, a former builder, served as surveyor; in Overijsel a baker did the same.[79]

The public meetings were henceforth mainly concerned with Holland. They were generally held once a week, from seven to nine in the evening, in the home of one of the members. The chairman of the evening was chosen anew at each meeting but the secretary remained in office for two months.

The meeting was begun with prayer and then opened for general discussion of any topic whatsoever concerning the village that anyone in the meeting was free to bring up. Then, sometimes after very lengthy exchanges, certain decisions were made.[80] The matter of bridge building was often on the agenda, the decisions concerning which have been mentioned earlier; then the construction of roads, the building of a school, etc. The cost of these projects was mostly met by voluntary subscription, the remainder by levies or taxes imposed by the governing body. There were also other matters to be settled, such as the increasing number of pigs running unrestrained through the community, raiding vegetable gardens and damaging crops. It was decided that not until the first of November were pigs to be released.

The religious convictions of many of the colonists also came to expression in the decisions of these public meetings. The Christian Indians who respected the Sabbath were offended when they saw the Dutch colonists navigating on Black Lake on Sunday.[81] Worse was the fact that these Dutch colonists, sometimes forced by circumstances, would use that day to transship store goods. At a general meeting it was decided, therefore, that this was henceforth to be strictly forbidden. Actually, these decisions, as many realized, were not based on any governmental or religious jurisdiction, and this became clear in the case of the liquor problem. The prohibition rules were totally disregarded and the governing body attempted to restrict the sale of gin by imposing import duties. There is no record in the minutes, however, that these duties were collected. Although Van Raalte strongly expressed his opposition, several taverns or saloons were opened, which caused endless discussions at the general meetings on how to deal with the matter.[82] It required all of Van Raalte's oratorical charisma to bring about the closing of these establishments. Finally in 1855 he obtained legal enforcement power when the state of Michigan enacted a law prohibiting the sale of liquor.

The impact of these "frontier laws," based on the will of the majority, should not be underestimated. For example, in Iowa, when it was still only a territory, the American colonists did not hesitate to impose the death penalty. [Andrew] Jackson, president of the United States at the time, did not attempt to reverse the verdict on the grounds "that the laws of congress had not been extended over the territory."[83]

From the foregoing it would appear that these public assemblies appropriated for themselves not only legislative powers but also executive and even to some degree judicial powers. However, an important part of the executive power was apparently moving into the hands of a commission, the Board of Trustees, while the consistory of the church exercised most of the judicial power. But both bodies invaded the areas of the lawmaking body, which gave rise to many difficulties, arguments, and great bitterness, all the more so because the powers of the general assembly were not delineated nor circumscribed by either the Board of Trustees or the consistory.

Title to the land designated for the founding of Holland was made out in

Van Raalte's name, although four others, the aforementioned merchants, J. Binnenkant, J. Rabbers, Kolvoort, and one [Jan] Stegeman had each paid for eighty acres. These four were planning to engage in real estate promotion and speculation "to make money" but were strongly resisted by Van Raalte who considered this contrary to the basic communal plan of the colony. He induced them to abandon their plan and submit to the authority of the general assembly.[84] This body appointed a commission, the previously mentioned Board of Trustees, of which Van Raalte was chairman and J. Van der Veen, J. A. Verhorst, J. Schrader, and J. Slag were members. They were entrusted with the sale of the colony's real estate and the financial management of the village. The first building lots were sold for $15 each, but the price was soon raised to $48 for corner lots and $38 for middle lots. After the debts were paid, the profits were divided into various funds such as those for the support of the preacher, the treasury of the church, the development of a harbor, etc.

The Board of Trustees did not limit itself to sales and finances but rather became more and more like "B. and W." [Burgemeester and Wethouders, i.e., Mayor and Commissioners], the executive power of the colony. But according to the public assembly they encroached too much on legislative territory. They forbade the butchering of cattle inside the village limits, the erection of fences made of rotted wood or branches, and the sale of liquor in Holland. They decreed that anyone could cut down any tree inside the village limits, provided the entire tree and stump were removed, etc. Also it was this Board that conceived the idea of a communal shingle factory. At the general meetings of the whole colony, more than once questions were raised about the Board of Trustees, about their competence, the length of time they were to hold office, and the extent to which they were answerable to the people, etc. This led to some "heated discussions," especially after the colony store started to become a failure and ran deeply into debt.[85] In the spring of 1850 it was decided to abandon the trustee system and turn over the management of all community property—including the debts!— exclusively to Van Raalte.

Even greater than the authority of the Board was that of the consistory, not only in religious matters but also in secular matters. In the surrounding villages the consistory ran the whole show, but in Holland they handled, as far as the secular sector was concerned, chiefly the meting out of justice. A wide variety of matters came under consideration—the selling of land and other real estate, cattle, wages, the management of the school, etc. A woman convicted of slander was compelled to confess her sin in public. A man whose son had taken a tree from a neighbor was declared guilty and sent home; his penalty was to read in the Old Testament the story of Eli, the indulgent father who failed to discipline his sons. A brother butchered a pig, mistakenly believing it was his, and was ordered to pay $4 to make good. However, he was able to pay only $2 and so Van Raalte and the consistory paid the remaining $2. Domestic affairs were also dealt with—

complaints against a troublesome mama-in-law and a young girl who had run away from the home of her stepfather, etc. Even the punishment of the school children was committed to Van Raalte.

For many, the worst punishment was to be denied the privilege of taking Holy Communion at the church, or still more severe, to be cut off from church membership.[86] The elders and deacons were especially active as guardians of the public morals and they were second to none, including our present church fathers. Already in those days too, an elder expressed alarm because a woman wore a dress with a collar that had not been properly closed. And when in the fifties a circus owner put up his tent in Holland, two elders posted themselves at the entrance with the result that the promoter soon left "this d— hole."[87]

The most important morality problem was undoubtedly that of marriage. During this early period many colonists died, both men and women. Many large households mourned the loss of father or mother, sometimes both. The difficult living conditions induced many a widow or widower to marry again and much sooner than was considered proper in normal times in order to provide for the care of the children. The consistory recommended that a widow wait at least nine months after the death of her husband before marrying again, a recommendation by no means always followed.

This problem of remarrying and the matter of establishing a school were the only two subjects not directly involving religious matters, and they continued to be discussed even after dismissal of the meeting. They were discussed at the first meeting of the "classis," a gathering of the pastors and consistories of all the churches of all the villages in the Dutch settlement, held for the first time in 1848. Five years later, in 1853, they came to a united decision: although the Bible does not mention the matter, it was advisable that a widow should wait nine months, and widower three months, before marrying again.[88]

Since Van Raalte and the consistory also exercised great influence in the general public meetings and since Van Raalte was also the chairman of the Board of Trustees, the administration of the entire colony came to have a very theocratic character, reminiscent of Calvin in Geneva and the Pilgrims in the New England states.

Not everyone was in favor of this theocracy and many saw in the "democracy" of Van Raalte actually his "autocracy"—democracy and autocracy are often closer to each other than we are aware. This displeasure was expressed in many letters to the editor printed in the colonial newspaper, De Hollander. Articles with titles like "Playing Boss" and "The Pope and His Cardinals," obviously aimed at Van Raalte personally and at the "irrevocability" of the consistory, could only be interpreted as opposition to the theocratic regime. One of the most impartial writers of personal memoirs among the pioneers, the highly regarded Engbertus Van der Veen, wrote: "Pope and Cardinals is often repeated by worldly people and others with malcontented spirits."[89]

In an earlier paragraph I related that in many midwestern settlements the merchants came into complete control of the community, but this was definitely not the case in Holland. To what extent and to what degree the "business interests" were involved in the opposition to the theocracy cannot be ascertained. For that matter, several of the merchants were members of the church; a few were even in the consistory. But Van Raalte and the consistory were able to hold their ground. Convinced that the tenor of the newspaper would "lead to destruction of the church and state," a general meeting of several of the colonial churches was held on May 8, 1852. Besides Holland, the churches of Graafschap, Drenthe, and Overijsel were represented. Zeeland decided to abstain. The writings of "some would-be politician" in the paper were strongly condemned and the editor, H. Doesburg, was denied the right to partake of Holy Communion.[90] The situation was so tense that Van Raalte considered leaving Holland and going to the colony at the Cape of Good Hope. However, the editor publicly acknowledged and repudiated his errors and confidence was gradually restored.

In the meantime there had been new developments on a higher governmental level and the Dutch colonists found themselves no longer entirely undisputed lords in their own castle. In the spring of 1849 the township of Holland was officially organized, which included all that part of the area lying in Ottawa County. Most of the Dutch were thereby united in a single rural municipality, somewhat comparable to the extensive municipalities in our Friesland Province and elsewhere. However, they had not lived in America long enough to be citizens and therefore had no voting rights to elect officials. At the first election, on April 2, 1849, held at the home of Van Raalte, the only qualified voters were Americans. There were only some ten present and so each one was elected to an office. H. D. Post became supervisor; J. Bronson, township clerk; and H. G. Post, treasurer, etc.[91]

According to the laws of that time, immigrants could not apply for their citizenship "first papers" until after they had been residents for two and one-half years. When that time arrived, so many in the colony indicated they wished to apply that Van Raalte requested the county clerk, H. Griffin, to come to Grand Haven to make out the papers for this "wholesale naturalization." There were three hundred applicants from Holland, one hundred from Zeeland and forty from Vriesland. Because of the large number, the papers were processed at one half the usual fee.[92] Following this, they were able to vote in the election of 1851, at which time they could, if they wished, replace the American township officials with men of Dutch ancestry.

Because Zeeland was located in the center of the township, the first election in which Dutch voters took part was held in the log church there. It was typically American, caucus-style! Reverend Van der Meulen as chairman kept order only with difficulty. There was vehement language and loud outcries. Repeatedly the chairman had to remind people of the sacred precinct in which they were gathered, crying out "Brothers! O, Brothers!" thereby preventing people from coming to blows![93] As the opposing candidates were vying with one another, it became evident that there was sharp competition between Holland and Zeeland. In the meantime others tried to start a scuffle outside in front of the church!

All kinds of grievances and opposing views came to expression in these elections. In the first place there was resentment over the autocracy of Van Raalte and his theocracy; furthermore, there was competition between the "city people" and the villagers. People kept referring to "*de stad*" of Holland in a venomous tone. This attitude, like a "prickly little thorn," was still noticeable in the nineties.[94] Historian Van der Veen records: "The Zeeland and Stateland men (from the village of Drenthe and surrounding area) were full of anger on [against] the Holland city men." The "country people" seemed to have gained the advantage. Van der Veen tells it as follows: "After the caucus we went home in a body. My, but some of the office-seekers were angry and jealous and made remarks as to why the Zeeland men captured all the best offices. Pieter Van der Berg said, 'Holland is ignored.' Others said, 'Well, well! The old Hulst from Stateland justice of the peace? That man with such a rebellious character? He is more for war than for peace!'"

Apparently this underlying jealousy between "*de stad*" of Holland and the "village" of Zeeland, which was actually a small-scale continuation of the age-old animosity between the Hollanders and the Zeelanders in early days in the Old Country, led to the organization of Zeeland as a separate township in 1851.

It seems that the last general citizens' meeting was held on February 21, 1849; that at least is the date of the final minutes. However, the authority of the church in secular matters continued much longer. It was not until January 18, 1859, ten years later, that the consistory of Van Raalte's church declared that they would no longer make decisions in matters that properly belonged to the civil authorities.[95] But in the villages surrounding Holland it appears that the church continued to exercise much influence in the civil realm, in spite of the "American" government. For example, in Zeeland, the elders A. Van Bree and J. G. Van Hees, were elected justices of the peace, but when some civil case came before them they handled it in the manner of church elders and tried to reach a settlement.[96]

But the Hollanders could be stern judges, as appears from one case in which for the first time a jury trial was held. Two young men, instead of attending church one Sunday, went into the forest, and had wantonly broken the windows of the orphanage. Both boys were tried before a jury and found guilty. One, considered too young to be jailed, was fined. The other was sentenced to thirty days in jail at Grand Haven. The sheriff in Grand Haven apparently felt that the sentence was too severe, for he kept the boy in his own home for thirty days and treated him as a member of his family.[97]

D. Religious Life

The influence of the church on the civil administration of the colony was one of the many expressions of the religious spirit that permeated the lives of a great many of these colonists. It was the spirit that had sustained and strengthened them through the severest persecutions in the Netherlands and had brought them finally to the decision to leave the Fatherland with the accompaniment of prayer and psalm singing.

It was this same spirit that gave them strength to endure in the difficult struggle in the Michigan forests. It was their faith in God, "the staff upon which they leaned," that helped them bear the heaviest blows. Since God had led them here, He would continue to care for them. It was to God they turned in frightening moments and after being encouraged, they would go back to work. One of the old settlers gave this testimony: "A pilgrim walked with joy a bumpy trail in the evening. He could hear in the distance the singing of psalms that filled the forest during quiet weather. Now he passed log cabins: here he heard hymns, there prayers. In another cabin he saw the occupants all kneeling in thankful prayer. Elsewhere there was mutual testimony of the great deeds of the Lord. Over there a man wrestled with his God for his dear ones."[98]

Two years later the American, [Isaac] Wyckoff, visited the colony and reported as follows on the spiritual attitudes of the colonists: "Their religious customs are very strict and devout. They do everything with prayer and thanksgiving. They sing and pray in the morning, after dinner, and after supper. They pray before they transact any business. When they meet to do common work together they pray. The city council opens its meetings with prayer. The standing and tenor of their worship is purer and higher than any I ever heard before and seems like those of the first Christians and very beautiful."[99] The Reverend Van der Meulen wrote: "It would be difficult to find a home where someone or other did not fear God. Indeed, one hears prayers ascending to heaven from every hut."[100] This religious spirit came to its fullest expression on Sunday when the colonists, regardless of how hard they had worked during the week, were early on their way to the church service to listen to the sermons of the preachers—words of comfort and encouragement by Van Raalte, Van der Meulen, or Ypma, originally the only pastors in the colony.

The first worship services were held in the open air, in the great temple of God's creation, in the forests of Michigan, as Van Raalte expressed it.[101] They had cleared some open places in the forest for that purpose. Tree trunks laid in rows served as pews for the women and children and the elderly, while the able men stood throughout the service. A tree stump was the pulpit.[102] In bad weather the service was held in the preacher's home or the largest dwelling available. Later in the season when poor weather put an end to their hedge sermons and the home of the preachers proved to be too small, the Zeelanders gathered for worship in the log cabin of J. Wabeke, "which was the largest in the village."[103] The Vrieslanders met in the cabin of S. Kaslander, an elder, while the Hollanders met for evening services in Binnenkant's hotel.[104] During that first summer they also celebrated the communion service in the open air, and since they had no table they received the sacraments of bread and wine standing, as the Jews do at the Passover meal in memory of the exodus from Egypt. Even the first marriage vows were said in the forest under the open sky. Van Raalte recorded in the marriage register: "Lambert Floris, aged twenty-seven years, and Jantjen Meijering, aged twenty-eight years, both of Holland, Ottawa, Michigan, in a church meeting in the woods in Section 2S. T5N. R15W. near the house of A. C. Van Raalte, in the presence of G. Van Rhee and C. J. Van Raalte of Holland, on 25th of July, 1847."[105]

As early as the summer of 1847 they started building a church made of logs in an area that had been selected as a burying place (now known as Pilgrim Home Cemetery) so that during the first winter they could use part of the building. The following summer the church, complete with pulpit and old style pews, was finished under the leadership of G. J. Kroon, architect.[106] After a while it became apparent that the church was too small, and not ideally situated, being too far away from Holland. In the very beginning all the people in the surrounding villages "churched" at Van Raalte's. But in time these villages—Overijsel, Drenthe, and Groningen—formed their own congregations, called their own pastors and built their own churches.[107] At the same time Holland itself was expanding more and more to the West, to the lake front. This left the log church in an isolated position in the East. In 1853 it was decided to build a new church more centrally located.

The new church, now built of planks, was expected to cost $2,500. The amount was raised with great difficulty by private subscriptions and loans. To their dismay they found that it would cost at least $1,000 more, so the building activities begun in 1854 were temporarily halted due to lack of funds. Van Raalte strongly insisted that the building be completed and declared that "he would not continue to preach in the unfinished church, without ceiling or plaster, as this was affecting his health," whereupon it was completed and dedicated in June, 1856. The church was designed by architect Jacobus Schrader more or less in the neo-classic style. At that time that style, although lacking in originality, was very popular in Europe and especially in America it had made heavy inroads. This accounts for the unusual combination of an extremely orthodox Calvinistic congregation worshiping in a church in the style of a "heathen" temple.

In the tower they hung the great bell bought in 1850 with funds raised by individual offerings. Following the Old Country custom, the bell was rung for church services, at funerals, and as a fire alarm. On weekdays it also chimed the work hours at 7 A.M. and noon, and 1 P.M. and 6 P.M., a custom still followed in many Dutch villages to this day. Until 1856 the bell had hung in the center of Holland in a heavy wooden frame, three meters |ten feet] high. H. Doesburg, one of the first teachers in Holland, was also the first bell-ringer, as goes without saying.[108]

This plank church, called the Pillar Church because of the columns across the front—the people's church *par excellence*—was spared during the fierce and destructive forest fire of 1871 and thus remains one of the historical buildings in Holland. So intimately were the lives of the old colonists intertwined with the "good old church" that they cannot speak without emotion of "this blessed old house of the Lord, blessed place of holy consecration and communion with the Lord's people—holy place you were ever dear to me and many others."[109]

Likewise in the village of Zeeland, very early, almost before the colonists themselves had roofs over their heads, they built a log church. When Cornelia Van Malsen, the writer referred to earlier, visited Zeeland in the beginning of November of 1847 the church was already half finished.[110] Also this church, in which the song leader [*voorzanger*] sat on the pulpit platform beside the preacher, was soon too small and was replaced by a larger log church measuring forty by sixty feet. Wyckoff, who liked to exaggerate, described it as "quite an ornamental building."[111] In the tower of this church they hung a bell that not only sounded the call to worship, but which was also rung when someone was thought to be lost in the forest. Then everyone left his work and joined the search teams until the missing son or daughter was found. It was not until 1849 that the village of Vriesland built a log church, which served until 1852, when they built a "plank" church. The other smaller villages had to make do for a longer time. Worship services in Overisel were held in the home of Wolterink, one of the colonists, where part of the congregation, due to lack of space, sat in the unfinished attic.[112] Over the years each settlement did the same—first they built a "log" church, later a "plank" church. Worship services were faithfully attended. If anyone was absent there was only one conclusion: he must be ill.

In 1849 a couple of American civil engineers came to Holland to study the problems involved in constructing harbor facilities at Black Lake and happened to arrive on a Sunday morning. The entire town appeared dead. They saw no living soul. At last it dawned on them that the people were all at church, so they went to the church building. Suddenly they stood still, astonished. They were met by the sound of solemn, stately psalm singing. "It was like the sound of rushing waters," testified one of the Americans later.[113]

The majority of the colonists were thoroughly acquainted with the Bible, no matter how uneducated and parochial they might be otherwise. Like real theologians they listened critically to the preacher's sermons and if they judged any statement of his to be "un-Biblical" they did not hesitate to ask him to explain more fully afterwards. The congregation thought Van Raalte was a wealthy man. His annual salary, which was only $600, was not even paid in full, and of that, part was not in cash but in work service. Every male in the congregation over the age of eighteen was required to work for Van

In pioneer days. Top: A characteristic log cabin. Middle: The first School building in "de Kolonie." Bottom: The first church building. (*Historical Souvenir*.)

Raalte one day out of every six weeks. No wonder then, that with a large family he constantly found himself in financial difficulty, yet the congregation thought they were justified in criticizing his work. In 1852 the consistory thought that the congregation was spiritless.[114] A year later, they rebuked him for spending too much time preaching in the outlying churches and doing paper work. (From the beginning in 1847 until August 5, 1958, he was not only the president of the consistory but also the secretary.) They said that due to this "for a few years already his preaching had lost its power." Van Raalte, a Calvinist to the backbone [*hart en nieren*, literally heart and kidneys], must have been aware of this himself, for he acknowledged it in these simple words: "I am busy from morning till evening and often far into the night, almost beyond my strength. I totally lack the time for even the most elementary study."[115]

There were two sides to the coin. On the reverse side, Van Raalte demanded the full attention of his hearers. Now and then, a brother or sister of the congregation, worn out by the arduous and unaccustomed labor of the week and wearied by the long walk to the church early in the morning around stumps and over logs, would fall asleep during the service. Then the vigilant preacher (as we saw it being done by the Old Dutch preacher Gosman in the East) would waken him or her by calling out the name loud and clear.[116]

In other ways the worship service proceeded more amiably and informally. Just inside the door of the old block church in Holland stood a pail of water and a dipper and anyone who felt thirsty could go and take a drink.[117] If the children became restless during the long service, which began at 9:30 and lasted two to three hours, they were soothed with peppermint candy. The women refreshed themselves from time to time with eau de cologne, passing the small bottle inconspicuously from hand to hand along the pews.[118] During winter a roaring fire had to be kept going. In the church in Holland there were two old-fashioned kitchen stoves and the earliest arrivals appropriated seats as near the stoves as possible. They would even put their feet up on it and in typical colonial manner so remain throughout the service as if this were the most common thing in the world.[119] In some churches there was no chimney and if the well-chosen words of the teacher did not bring forth tears, the "bitter" smoke did![120]

The early churches were by no means weather-tight; in Zeeland it actually happened that when the congregation gathered for a Sunday morning service, they found the floor, the pews, and the pulpit snowed under. But the preacher stood on a pew, the listeners stood gathered around the stove "and the service went on as if nothing out of the ordinary had occurred."[121]

Some aspects of these primitive conditions in the churches had their humorous side and this was not entirely lost on the colonists in spite of their stern Calvinism. One of the residents in the village of Groningen, [H.] Van Eijk, relates the following: "Everything was simple and primitive. Most of us wore our "*klompenstevels*" [wooden shoes with leather tops] to church, including the preacher. On the way to church, wet snow, which lay around all winter long on paths and in the woods, adhered to the wooden soles and made it very difficult to remain standing on the slippery floor. The preacher could hardly stay on his feet himself and was slipping and sliding on the platform and the young people, watching this, almost burst out laughing."[122]

If the Sunday sermon was the only spiritual refreshment for the colonists in those early years, their church-going was likewise the only recreation. The desperate struggle for bare existence left them no time or energy to desire more, so they looked forward to Sunday as the only break. Then the young fellows looked at the girls and talked with them. The adults enjoyed seeing their friends again, especially those who originally came from the same villages in the Netherlands.[123] They felt the need for this fellowship so greatly that many came to church earlier than necessary, just to have the opportunity to visit together before the service began. After the service almost no one went home. They had brought bread from home and ate their meager lunch together. They talked about the events of the week and reminisced about the Old Country. They encouraged each other; they sang together; they prayed together. But for the children Sunday was a dull day. They were not allowed to play. They were not even allowed to be noisy. Mrs. G., the daughter of Van Raalte, told me herself that she remembered how people complained because there was too much laughter from the young people coming from the preacher's house on Sunday!

As an example of how the colonists relaxed during the week, T. Ulberg from Vriesland tells this: "In the evening, if the weather was nice, we sat on the foundation logs of the unfinished portion of our log cabin. In the Old Country I had learned to play the German flute and I had promised the Lord that I would never play anything but psalms. So we sat on the cross pieces of the foundation. I played. My wife and children all joyfully sang psalms. How beautiful it sounded in the forest!"[124]

There were very few musical instruments in the colony. The first piano we know of belonged to one of the American families in Holland in 1851. Many colonists had scruples even against the use of organs in the church. They were introduced very gradually and not without opposition. In time, with greater prosperity and more liberal concepts, pianos and organs became more numerous and many families owned one or the other. However, in the church the "voorzanger" still remained for a long time a dominant figure. The first concert in the colony was given in Holland in 1858. Despite the fact that it consisted entirely of sacred music and was performed in the chapel of the Van Vleck Hall, it aroused considerable criticism, especially since de Juffrouw—the Dominie's wife—and her daughter attended.[125] In view of the foregoing, it is not surprising to see that the longer the colonists lived in the colony and founded additional villages, the more they went their own way, while exactly the opposite was true in everything concerning the church. The desire for cooperation in religious matters even grew stronger. There were many ecclesiastical questions on which individual consistories dared not pass judgment and for which they felt the need of joint deliberation and discussion. This led to the first meeting of Classis on April 23, 1848. According to the minutes of [D.] Versteeg, it was held at the home of H. Broek, located between Holland and Groningen.[126] The trio of preachers, Van Raalte, Van der Meulen, and Ypma, were present with their consistories, plus the consistory of "Allegan County," apparently referring to Graafschap.[127] They actually constituted themselves a "Classis," later officially designated as the Classis of Holland.[128] They agreed to meet twice annually on the last Wednesdays of April and October. After 1850 these meetings were held in Zeeland because it was the most centrally located, because it was the largest church in the colony, and because overnight lodging was widely available here. The members of the churches took these meetings so seriously that the day of the Classis meeting in Zeeland was considered a holiday and many attended and listened with great interest to the public discussions. This interest was heightened because not only church but also civil matters were discussed.

At the first meeting it was expressly stated that they would adhere to the teaching and doctrines of the Gereformeerde Kerk. They made some decisions regarding religious feast days and the length of the term of elders and deacons. Among the problems that surfaced were also those of marriage and remarriage, as was noted before, while during subsequent meetings the church leaders dealt with purely secular matters, such as the building of roads and bridges, etc. After June 29, 1859, Classis met in Holland so that the seminary students could also attend "and thus gain some insight into the mysteries of church government and civil administration."

As "de Kolonie" expanded so did the importance of the Classis. In 1849 there were already seven congregations represented, of which four had their own preacher and five had their own church building: Holland (Van Raalte), 225 families, 250 members; Zeeland (Van der Meulen), 175 families, 225 members; Vriesland (Ypma), 69 families, 125 members; Overisel (Bolks), 35 families, 80 members; Graafschap,* 50 families, 100 members; Drenthe, 45 families, 79 members; and Groningen, 30 families, 63 members. If we compare these statistics, compiled by Wyckoff, with an earlier account of the number of houses, and assuming that each house was occupied by a family, we would have to conclude that all the families in "de Kolonie" belonged to a church and that consequently the Classis represented the whole colony. The very reliable historian, Van der Veen, called the "majority" of the colonists Christians. Perhaps both Wyckoff and Van der Veen are correct. In that case, using Van der Meulen's expression, we would have to say that some of the settlers were "mouth confessors" and "Sunday Christians."

---

*The erroneous figure of 150 for Graafschap has been corrected.

E. Union with the Reformed Church

One of the most compelling questions faced by the Classis was to determine what the colony's relationship should be to the organization at that
time called the "Reformed Protestant Dutch Church." The question and its
solution have had far-reaching consequences. It has continued to excite
interest to the present time and still moves many a pen.[129]

In previous statements I related with what sympathy the brothers of the
Reformed Church in America followed the religious persecution in our land
and with what dedication they obeyed the call of Brummelkamp and Van
Raalte to help the immigrants as much as possible. In particular one should
remember the countless services the Reverend Dr. I. N. Wyckoff of Albany
rendered in behalf of the Protestants among the Dutch immigrants, partly
because of their common heritage and partly because of their common
faith.

It goes without saying that the Reformed Church went beyond the initial
contact. Driven by the same bonds of faith and blood, they desired closer
fellowship with the immigrants that they considered as "a new company of
Pilgrims from the land of our forefathers."[130] And so these "Pilgrims of the
West," at the time of the second classical meeting on September 27, 1848,
received an invitation to attend the meeting of the Reformed Church Synod.
The invitation was not immediately accepted. The Classis stated that "although we acknowledge that we should strive for closer fellowship and that
love demands that fellowship be practiced, yet because of the many internal difficulties and problems associated with getting settled it is still difficult at the present time."[131]

The Board of Domestic Missions of the Reformed Church then requested
Reverend I. N. Wyckoff to make a trip west and personally acquaint himself
with the situation among the immigrants. This visit eventually led to the
affiliation of the Hollanders with the Reformed Church, and to the important report that we have mentioned several times earlier.[132] Wyckoff was
received in the colony almost "literally with shouts of joy" and paid visits to
the various settlements. He arrived on Thursday, May 31, 1849.[133] The following day, Friday, he visited "*de stad* Holland" and on Saturday the surrounding area, "following Indian trails from one clearing and settlement to the
next." The following Tuesday Wyckoff, accompanied by Van Raalte and a few
others, visited the various outlying churches. Wyckoff rode the doctor's
horse (the only one in the colony), Van Raalte and the others went along on
foot. "After wading through Black River we went to Groningen, the next
stop, and then along a foot path to Zeeland. We spent the evening there
with Dominie Van der Meulen and his congregation. We started out again
early Wednesday morning and went to Drenthe. We ate our noon lunch
there—bread, butter, and coffee—and then started out for Vriesland but
lost our way. A kind woman offered to be our guide. At last we located
Dominie Ypma and after having seen the area of his labors and received his

hospitality, we spent the night there. We returned to the city the following day, in spite of rain."[134]

That the colonists greatly appreciated this visit also appears in Wyckoff's written report: "The thought that we at last were concerned for them, cared for them, and although belatedly were willing to help them, touched their hearts. Many prayers of thanksgiving were sent up to God for this charitable work and many blessings were prayed down upon the head of your representative."

The most important day of the visit was undoubtedly Monday, June 4. On that day Wyckoff met with the preachers and some of the elders of the colony in Holland and discussed the possibility of affiliation with the Reformed Church. Although this was not a meeting of Classis according to church regulations, they came together at what Wyckoff called a "classical meeting." Wyckoff reports: "The brethren were a little fearful to enter upon an ecclesiastical union with us, although they believe in the unity of the brethren and long for Christian sympathy and fellowship. They have experienced the harsh and painful shackles of ecclesiastical domination so strongly and have seen with such sorrow how a tightly structured organization, set up according to human rules, can lead on the one hand to religious formalism and on the other hand to repression of conscience, that they hardly know what to say. Naturally I assured them," so continued Wyckoff, "that it was farthest from our intention to bring them into subjection to human authority or to exercise ecclesiastical tyranny over them. I suggested to them that, if at any time in the future they found the association with the Reformed Church 'opposed to their religious prosperity or enjoyment,' they had the greatest possible freedom to bid us a brotherly farewell and go their own way again."

How strongly the colonists wished to conclude the union appears in the written report Van Raalte made of the consultation held with Wyckoff. Later, in an evil hour, the Reverend H. E. Dosker dubbed this report "The Union Document." In the report they state as follows: "We feel very strongly the need for the communion of the saints. We abhor the sectarian spirit. . . . Therefore we seek the closest possible union with God's church, wherever it manifests itself anywhere on earth, if it knows and practices the way of salvation. All the more we feel this unity with those churches that have the same confession of faith, the same liturgy and the same organizational structure that we have. . . . We have never considered ourselves as being anything other than a part of the Hollandsche Gereformeerde Kerk. We long, therefore, to live in fellowship with those churches and wish to send our representatives to its official meetings."[135]

Although one could have reservations about the legality within church policy of this semi-official meeting called together in haste and where these preliminary discussions took place, to which Henry Beets and others of like mind later called attention,[136] yet there is less doubt about the legitimacy of the classical meeting the following April, 1850. It was at that meeting,

whose minutes were more in accordance with the regular proceedings [Acta]
of a legal and well-prepared church meeting, that the decision was made
definitely to join.[137] For this purpose Van Raalte was appointed to attend
the meeting of the Particular Synod of the Reformed Church at Schenectady
in May 1850 as their delegate, ". . . instructing him to give in our name all
necessary information, and to ask what would promote the desired
union."[138] Since neither Van Raalte nor his congregation had the funds for
the expenses of the trip to "the East," Wyckoff and some American friends
provided these to enable Van Raalte to carry out his charge.

The result was that after the Synod had heard Van Raalte, an official
declaration was adopted as follows: "Since by due process a request has
been received from the Classis of Holland, Michigan, to be permitted to
join this Synod, therefore be it resolved that, taking into consideration the
unusual circumstances surrounding the matter, this body concurs in the
actions taken by the above-mentioned Classis of Holland, concerning the
way it is organized, and will bring the request for its affiliation to the
attention of the General Synod and ask that the Holland Classis be advised
to which particular Synod it will be assigned."[139] The General Synod meeting
was held June, 5, 1850, and following days at Poughkeepsie, New York. They
appointed a committee consisting of the Reverends John Knox, I. N. Wyckoff, J. A. Liddel, and the elders A. Van Nest and A. Van Bergen. Their
mandate was to report on the possible admission of Classis Holland. The
interesting report of that committee is as follows:

> This Classis consists of nine organized churches with an average membership
> of 100 each and it enjoys the services of six pastors. The people making up
> these congregations are immigrants from Holland who, driven by the joint
> pressures of temporary economic necessity caused by heavy taxes and a large
> over-population, and by a grievous interference with the rights of their con-
> science, found a refuge in this land of freedom. Here in their new home they
> have already earned great respect by their orderly and industrious behavior
> and especially by their steadfast and exemplary observance of Christian be-
> havior. It can be foreseen that they can take their place among the best and
> most solid sectors of our society. It was naturally to be expected that we
> would extend help to these exiles from the fatherland, coming from that same
> time-honored church [in the Netherlands] from which in its heyday the Re-
> formed Church of North America had derived its respected religious stan-
> dards and privileges. Accordingly they have been welcomed with cordial and
> liberal sympathy in New York, Albany, Buffalo, and Detroit and other towns
> where they arrived. Foreigners in a foreign land, beloved for their own sake
> and for the sake of their fathers, they deserve a hearty welcome in our church
> fellowship, which they desire, and all appropriate help in establishing them-
> selves in the place of their choice.
>
> The committee recommends the adoption of the following resolutions:
> 1. Resolved, That the Classis of Holland be received under the care of the
> General Synod and be assigned to the Particular Synod of Albany. 2. Re-

solved, That the religious condition and necessities of the Holland immigrants, wherever they are dispersed throughout our country, be commended
to the particular attention of the Board of Domestic Missions.[140]

The report was immediately accepted by the General Synod without any
deliberation and therewith the union became an accomplished fact. "Thus,
for the exiles from the fatherland the period of separation from the guidance and oversight of the church in the Netherlands had ended in the
union with the church in America."[141] According to the proponents it was
the unity in the Spirit that led to the organizational union, which was a
blessing for the hundreds who were thus kept for the Reformed Church and
its confessions.[142]

However, opponents saw in this union an ecclesiastical marriage between two parties who had known each other for only a very short time,
who did not understand each other's language, and who had not had the
opportunity to develop esteem for each other. In short, it was a union that
lacked the essential basis for a true and durable marital love relationship.[143]
More than that, they considered it an unlawful marriage, because neither in
the mandate of the Classis Holland meeting of April 1850, nor in the
minutes of the two Synods, was there any reference to Wyckoff's promise of
June 4, 1849, that if at any time in the future the colonists found that this
union was contrary to "their religious prosperity or enjoyment" they were
free to separate again. In the omission of this "stipulation," of this "condition," they saw a serious shortcoming.[144] On the other hand, those who
supported the union thought it folly to give official sanction to Wyckoff's
informal remarks, asserting that it was only incidental, a purely personal
comment made in passing.[145]

How difficult it is to form a right judgment in this matter appears from
the subsequent developments: the Gereformeerde Kerk in the Netherlands,
which was most closely related to the immigrants, at first accepted the
conclusions of the supporters of the union, but later changed its mind and
shared the opinion of the opponents, while now it again tends to incline
toward its original position.[146] Professor H. Bouwman wavered between the
two positions for several years, expressing himself as follows: "Although it
goes a bit too far to say that the union was unlawful, it is certainly true that
the transaction was not carried out according to proper ecclesiastical procedure."[147] The well-known preacher, G. Keizer, has entirely revised his opinion and has come to believe at the present time that the reservation or
stipulation expressed by Wyckoff was never formally made a part of the
transaction and that too much importance has been attached to the word
condition.[148] Very firmly he states: "I conclude therefore that the immigrants
can not properly say that the union was carried out 'contrary to ecclesiastical regulations,' neither can the Dutch Reformed Church properly say that
the admission of the immigrants to their fellowship was 'unlawful'."[149]

The "Union" itself and the manner in which it came about and the varying opinions that were expressed concerning it, both in America and in the Netherlands, have reached a level of importance that goes far beyond the immediate church concerns. The whole course of events demonstrates once more the great value of the presence of an Old Dutch element in American society for the rooting of the colonists, which was very strongly promoted by the common religious bond and by the high regard and esteem in which Van Raalte and his followers were held.

In many cases religion and its closely related church organization have hindered the assimilation of immigrants abroad, not in the least due to the rigid adherence to their native language. But the colonists here |in Holland, Michigan| were greatly aided by their union with the Reformed Church in America. Thanks also to their stout Calvinism, they did not lose their own convictions, which are so often lost when people assimilate into a new environment.

This "Union" has been greatly conducive to the assimilation into American society not only of Van Raalte and "his people" but also of many of the thousands of Netherlanders who followed them, continuing up to the present time, in the United States and even in Canada, especially for those who became members of the Reformed Church. In particular this matter of church membership was often decided upon before they had even left the Netherlands, in consulation if possible with the preacher of the congregation to which they belonged there. This explains the importance that must be attached to the opinions in the Netherlands concerning the church union.[150]

It should be pointed out that the influence of the "Union" upon the Americanization of Van Raalte's colonists had been somewhat limited from the very onset, due to the Holland congregation's urgent request that they not be made a part of the English-speaking Classis of Michigan, in existence since 1841, but that they be organized as a separate classis of Holland. Because of this the immigrants automatically had less contact with their American brothers-in-faith than would otherwise have been the case. Secondly, the influence of the union was diminished when after some years a group of the colonists apparently still felt so little at home in the Reformed Church that they separated from this church and at least for the time being went their own way. The influence of the Reformed Church was to come to expression in two other areas, namely in the work of "Domestic Missions" and especially in the realm of education, more in particular in a college and seminary.

F. Education

At the very first classical meeting Van Raalte brought up the matter of education. Very soon after the coming of the first colonists a few Dutch teachers settled among them. However, they had very little material and equipment at their disposal. Desks, slates, blackboards, and textbooks were an unknown luxury in those first years, and buildings for the purpose were unthinkable. "Here, classes were held in a kitchen, there in a loft, somewhere else in a church." At first there were very few pupils, partly because many parents saw little value in education and kept the children at home to work in the fields, partly because parents were afraid their children would get lost in the woods.[151]

In the matter of education, Zeeland was the most progressive. In his journal Van Eijk writes that "a school teacher (H. De Bruin) and a suitable school building are matters that raise this village even beyond the level of a city." Van Eijk also writes that in the village of Groningen the first school house was destroyed by fire. The village of Overisel had the first female teacher in the colony, who later became the wife of Reverend [Gerrit J.] Nijkerk. She taught in an attic. Drenthe and Holland obtained teachers from the Netherlands too.

At first most of the colonists showed little interest in this matter of education. Their children had more important things to do than to spend time learning, and it could be proved by "at least a hundred verses from the Bible" how unnecessary it was! But their leaders, particularly Van Raalte, continued to stress it. Therefore, at the second meeting of Classis, held on September 7, 1848, it was decided: "Schools should be promoted and supported by the congregation since they are an important part of the Christian calling of God's people on earth. All indifference and lukewarmness in this matter must be condemned and punished." During a subsequent meeting the leaders showed that they understood quite well the importance of a good education: "The character, the destiny and the prosperity of a nation depend on education." So state the minutes of October 30, 1850.

Van Raalte and some of the others also saw clearly that instruction should be given in the English language, lest they should become, as others wanted, "transplanted Netherlanders" instead of a real part of the American nation. The matter of language was thus an issue from the very beginning. In Holland they hired an American, I. Hoyt from Kalamazoo, who during the winter of 1847–1848 instructed children by day and parents in the evening in the English language.[152] To make it possible not only for those living in "*de stad*" but also those further removed to take the lessons, the first classes were held in a small structure in the center of the first cluster of houses, afterwards in the church by the cemetery and finally, after the surrounding villages began to go their own way, in the center of Holland in a room in the home of storekeeper [Willem] Houtkamp. Hoyt, who was a Methodist, began all lesson sessions with prayer, with everyone kneeling except the orthodox ones. They considered Hoyt a barbarian because he prayed in a foreign language and—poor man— probably did not know what he was praying anyway, since he could not pray in Dutch! Bibles with parallel columns, one in Dutch and one in English, served as textbooks.

On June 29, 1848, the first school district was formed according to the American pattern and the first school board elected as follows: A. C. Van Raalte as moderator, the American H. D. Post, director, and W. J. Mulder, assessor. The following year a woman teacher, Miss Elvira Langdon from Allegan, was hired. Zeeland and the other villages now also formed their own school districts and their boards were charged with the appointment of teachers. English was used in teaching, although it was inadequately done in some places.

Already during the first years Van Raalte's thoughts and plans went in the direction of higher education. He realized that the colonists could not carry the costs of higher education and, in those early years, they had no appetite for it either, so he turned again to "the East" for help.[153] The Particular Synod of Albany, to whose jurisdiction classic Holland had been assigned at the time of the union, was willing to help and voted their approval in the autumn of 1850 at Schenectady. Leaders in the Reformed Church had been urging higher education in the West as early as 1836 and 1843.[154] Especially J. Romeyn was a spokesman for these views; his motto was "Train Western men, for Western work, on Western soil."[155]

In that same year of 1850 Reverend John Garretson, secretary of the Board of Domestic Missions, who had come to Michigan, instigated an inquiry and promised Van Raalte support in this matter. Once the colonists were assured of this, they decided at a meeting of the Classis on April 30, 1851, to establish an institute where young people could be prepared for higher learning. In consultation with Reverend Garretson this institute was set up that fall on a very limited scale for the time being as "a high school to prepare sons of the colonists from Holland for Rutgers College, and also to educate daughters of said colonists." Walter Taylor, who was an elder in the Reformed Church at Geneva, New York, was appointed the teacher of this Pioneer School.[156] His son and two daughters assisted him and all instruction was in the English language. The Americanizing influence of the union was thus strongly in evidence right away.

However, all this did not pass without a reaction, and problems arose over the language issue. In 1852 Dominie Ypma recommended that a teacher be hired "who would be qualified to instruct students of this school with good knowledge but also to teach the basic use of the Dutch language, the pure use of which is sadly being lost. And this is occurring in spite of everyone's conviction that in the interest of religion it is absolutely necessary that the language, which is yet indispensable for many years, must be upheld so that the preaching will not become ridiculous due to the mixing of the languages. People should also, when needed, be able to wield the pen well in their native tongue."[157] Dominie Ypma even suggested that the Classis invite Dominie Brummelkamp [in the Netherlands] to take charge of this education. Taylor himself encouraged this suggestion by assuring them that "the East" would continue to support the young institution. Brummel-kamp, who had encouraged the migration movement, admitted that his conscience smote him with the accusation—"You urge others to take the risks of going, but you yourself stay at home."[158] Diligently he and his family began, therefore, to study English in preparation. However, he could not bring himself to accept the challenge, even though it was his own people who were calling for his help. When he declined, the people in Holland gave up the attempt "to Hollandize the Academy."[159]

Interest in the youthful institution continued to grow, largely through the endeavors of Van Raalte and Van der Meulen, who both constantly reminded the colonists of the value of such a school not only for Holland but for the whole colony. Both continued to urge the churches strongly to support the school: "We must not let the years fly by without training our children to take over the positions and responsibilities in church, school, and society. As supervisors, fathers, and leaders of the people, we can not die with a clear conscience if we do not, while it is still day, work to leave behind us successors and shepherds and if we do not see to it in time that the people grow and mature to assume, in the right way, the responsibilities God has entrusted us with in this place."

Everyone's help was welcome. Reverend Van der Meulen said at a Classis meeting: "Should not a man be able to set aside [as an offering] a thousand barrel staves, or a few cords of [hemlock] bark, or a farmer ten bushels of corn, or some potatoes, or pork or butter? Should not a day laborer be able to set aside a few days of his wages for this purpose?"[160]

At the same classical meeting of September 1, 1852, when Van der Meulen spoke those words, it was decided that "children from other villages would be placed in one, two, or more boarding houses in order to supervise their behavior and activities, also outside of school hours." At the same time a committee consisting of all the preachers and one elder from each of the churches represented at Classis was charged with the supervision and administration of the "Institute." More strongly than before, this gave the school a "colonial" rather than a merely local character and thereby also a greater chance of success. When the teacher, Taylor, turned in his first report, Van Raalte wrote under it: "This is my anchor of hope for this people and for their future."[161] Rightly so!

This zeal for education in "*de Kolonie*" has very greatly increased the social significance of the Dutch element not only in Michigan but, indeed, throughout the United States. Therefore, its growth and development deserve our careful observation, but also for other reasons. It demonstrates anew what a driving force Van Raalte was! He and his coleaders were farsighted men with high ideals and in no area was this more clearly shown than in this broadminded striving for education, a broadmindedness that was sharply contrasted by the parochialism of their followers. In later years the colonists were highly praised for their idealism, all the more strongly so as their Americanization progressed and not only at jubilees. This praise was unjustified because these ideals lived, consciously at least, only in their leaders.

No doubt one's sympathies are aroused to hear a prominent Dutch American, the former Congressman G. J. Diekema, exclaim in an address: "Think of these poor, half-starved, half-naked immigrants, building a college before they had provided for actual personal wants, before they had felled the forests or drained the swamps!"[162] This shows the gratitude of the descendant who reaped the fruits of the labors of the pioneers. From this statement we see also to what extent Diekema had been Americanized culturally. For us it is an expression of the typical American ancestor worship that sometimes exaggerates the position and overlooks the reality.

We see this also when we consider that Taylor's salary was not paid to him for a long time because some colonists failed to cooperate; indeed, they resisted it. Van Raalte was again compelled to appeal urgently to the East for help. Finally he complained: "If the next nine years are spent in the same way, they will prove that these Dutch people have as a whole demonstrated that they do not yet understand or appreciate their position, their calling, or their own best interests. They know, indeed, how to acquire good farms, earn money, etc., but they are not motivated, either by love for the Fatherland, nor by religious commitments, to dedicate themselves to more noble pursuits, such as the establishment and development of a Christian community."[163]

G. The Pilgrims of the West

The Honorable Diekema asserted in 1907 and repeated in 1917: "Great men they were, who had high ideals, thought great thoughts, did great deeds, followed great leaders and worked out a great destiny."[164] However, in 1849 Van Raalte wrote: "Worldliness and worry, ignorance, unbelief, pride are rumbling here too. Some do not care to work or think the pay is not high enough. Others cannot get accustomed to bartering or they isolate themselves by the attitude: 'I can't do that, I never did it before.' Not everyone has the right tongue to savor the freedom we have here."[165]

How difficult it is to believe in these "great thoughts"; how small we see these immigrants, these "great men" appear in the report of the greatly respected (but not ultra-orthodox) Reverend Van Eijk who wrote on June 8, 1851: "Reviling, uncharitable and unrighteous judgments are my portion. People here have Jehu's passion for the strictest orthodoxy. They try to brand me an erring spirit. Painful as this is, I try not to hate these slanderers. They are like those who in their mad zeal burned heretics at the stake in the Middle Ages. Yet I wish to pray for them."[166] Nevertheless this true Christian, "to escape the slander and lies," had to leave the village of Groningen. "For slander and lies had reached a shocking height in Groningen, so small and insignificant in other ways." It was an outrageous case of intolerance, a mockery of all love for one's fellow man!

Others have thought of these colonists as saints, comparing them with the Pilgrims of 1620. In a report to the General Synod of the Reformed Church the following statement appears: "A new company of Pilgrims has reached our shores,"[167] while in the newspaper of this church, the *Christian Intelligencer*, a similar sentiment had already been expressed. That evaluation has since come to be generally accepted. Diekema goes so far as to assert that this Dutch colonization is "the only immigration that in spirit and purpose, can truly be said to resemble the settlement of New England by the Pilgrim Fathers. It was thus that the city of Holland became to American Hollanders what Plymouth Rock is to the New Englanders."[168]

The similarity is perhaps even more striking than appears up to this point, when one takes into account that the English Pilgrims, as well as the Dutch, were in the first place human beings—in many respects even very, very small human beings—and only after that they were Christians who came from similar social and spiritual backgrounds and likewise were transplanted into similar environments. Even though acknowledging this, I do not wish to judge them unfairly thereby. On the contrary, when one also considers their faults—how narrow-minded, selfish and unkind, albeit unconsciously, these Pilgrims often showed themselves to be—then one remains faithful to the truth, which is the first duty of a Christian, and by so doing the value and importance of their influence becomes all the more evident. Such a stand causes one also to become all the more impressed by the greatness of character of men like Van Raalte and Van der Meulen, and others, who must have possessed unusual gifts indeed, to be able to bring out whatever was good and noble and great in these "*kleine luyden*" and to get them to work together constructively, in spite of all kinds of controversy and disagreement, to produce such final good results.

To their credit it can be said that many of the immigrants or their children openly acknowledged their shortcomings, some more and some less. The honest Van der Veen declared: "The majority of the first settlers were Christians, but yet so imperfect which showed itself in so many ways."[169] [A. J.] Pieters admits, more casually, that the colonists, although "a God-fearing group, were intensely human."[170]

Indeed, how often we have observed that! We know what kind of religious atmosphere was prevalent in the colony. But this atmosphere did not prevent many so-called Christians from going out and getting drunk. Van Raalte tried to stop the sale of liquor and to prevent the opening of a saloon but many had whiskey in their homes and would invite friends in for a "so-called drink and the effect might make them high-spirited and full of merriment." Van der Veen writes: "There was also too many of this class of people."[171] Clandestine liquor sales were numerous. Many instances of public drunkenness are recorded in the minutes of Holland's first consistory. As noted previously, also the first general community gatherings dealt with this problem, but to no avail. Saloons were opened. A part of Visser's bakery was remodeled so that on Sunday, church-goers could gather to discuss the sermon and the Bible as they smoked and drank! This saloon, "always full of the good Christians(?)," came to have a certain renown as the "church saloon."

It also seemed difficult for some to distinguish between "mine and thine." Even the Indians experienced this at the hands of the Hollanders. In this respect, too, there are noteworthy similarities with the Pilgrims of 1620. Like them, the Dutch owed much to the Indians. The Indians provided them with food; from them the Dutch learned how to grow corn and make maple sugar. Just as among the New England Pilgrims there were thieves (read the account of Friederici) who "with the help of the Lord" stole the corn supplies from the natives, considering them to be "the good gifts of God,"[172] so there were also among the Netherlanders those who (so says Versteeg) "seemed to feel no pangs of conscience when they stole or destroyed the pot and kettles of the Indians during their absence."[173]

One Sunday, as the morning worship service had ended, four Indians, accompanied by J. Pickard, a French half-breed, the only one among the Indians who could speak some Dutch, came to Van Raalte and told him that his people had stolen some utensils out of their tents. While the translator was still speaking, Van Raalte became so indignant that he shouted "*Jan Rap en zijn maat* [Jan Rap and his comrade, meaning Ragtag and Bobtail] are here among us! Now we are being shamed before the Indians!" During the afternoon service, he directed his whole sermon at the thieves and said that this incident had disgraced the name of the Hollanders and ordered those who were guilty of such base acts to leave "*de Kolonie*" and the sooner the better! Miss Pieters called this "an amusing incident!"[174] On another occasion game was stolen from the Indians.

In spite of the strictest prohibition, the Hollanders sold liquor to the Indians as the Puritans had done before them.[175] What was still worse, the Puritans desecrated the graves of the Indians, although respect for the dead is one of the most commendable and moving traits of the Indians.[176] It must be said: similar violations occurred also in "*de Kolonie*."[177] As more and more colonists came, the Indians lost their hunting grounds and no longer felt themselves at home in the area around Black Lake. Most of them, under the leadership of Chief Waukazoo, who was described as being "in every respect a noble man with a big heart [and] great abilities," migrated in 1848 to the northern part of the lower peninsula, to Traverse Bay. There, through his contacts with "civilization," Chief Waukazoo, as so many others of his race, became an alcoholic and went to his grave as a drunkard. The Indians returned several times to visit the graveyard which was fenced in and in which many tombs were also surrounded with a fence and decorated with flowers and crosses. One day they discovered that the graves had been vandalized. They were so outraged that many of the colonists "feared that the Indians would wreak bloody vengeance, which they probably would have done if the savages had not been outnumbered."

Aside from these regrettable incidents, on the whole there was a good and cordial relationship between the Hollanders and the Indians, chiefly

due to the tact and diplomacy of their leaders. There was none of the
barbarity toward the Indians such as was committed by the 1620 Pilgrims.
In that respect conditions were far different from those of the seventeenth
century!

Especially in their relationships among themselves, there were similarities between the Puritans and Pilgrims of the West. Although both groups
had migrated primarily to improve their economic condition, in both groups
were found those who insisted they had come for religious reasons only
and they looked down with contempt on those who openly admitted "they
had come to America for the purpose of making a better living."[178] Van Eijk
and others found out that "all those who did not, just like them, read a
chapter from the Bible three times a day, sing a few verses from the psalms,
and talk about their spiritual experiences" were not Christians!

In both groups a theocratic oligarchy developed—the members of the
consistory in Holland considered themselves to be irremovable—and in
both groups this clerical authority extended itself to the smallest details.
This led to spiritual presumptuousness—they both thought themselves to
be Chosen People, the elect.

Among the Pilgrims of the East, as well as among those of the West, were
many who put a higher value on faith than on love. In regard to the New
England Pilgrims, Friederici wrote: "There was no evidence of nobleness of
spirit. The ingratitude they manifested, even against the benefactors from
their own group, seems not to have troubled their conscience."*[179] As concerns the Calvinistic immigrants in Michigan, the same attitudes repeatedly
revealed themselves. How often their great leader, Van Raalte, experienced
this! Van der Meulen wrote in 1847: "We all—immigrants from Holland,
Drenthe, Friesland, Gelderland, and Zeeland—live together in love and talk
about the spiritual life."[180]

In 1849 Van Raalte wrote of the dissatisfaction and criticism expressed by
some of his people, but later wrote that on the whole "the majority were
happy and contented and felt themselves fortunate."[181] However, below the
surface there was a great deal of rivalry between the "*stad*" and the villages,
especially between Holland and Zeeland, and also in the city itself, often
coming to expression in the general public meetings and in the consistory.

In all the disagreements the most heated arguments occurred in the area
of church affairs. They were all the more violent when less time and attention
was needed to be paid to the struggle for material existence, that is, when the
communities became more strongly rooted. How little "love" or contentment
actually existed was sometimes shown in the church gatherings. At one of
these meetings an eyewitness reported: "I saw, to my astonishment, such
antagonism and disorderly behavior that it looked more like a saloon than

---

*Von Edelmut hatten sie keine Spur, und Undankbarkeit selbst gegen Wohltäter aus ihrer eigenen Mitte scheint nie ihr
Gewissen beschwert zu haben."

like a classical meeting."[182] At another meeting, where four preachers were present, among others, the crowd "became so excited and unruly that some people threatened to do violence to Dr. Van Raalte personally."

In spite of these quarrels, jealousy, suspicion, and ingratitude, etc., the colony managed to survive and prosper. In fact, the Michigan colony under the leadership of Van Raalte had a great influence on the other settlements of Calvinistic Netherlanders in America, especially in the realm of church and school, an influence that is still discernible today. For these seemingly insignificant people possessed a power that was almost superhuman, a determination induced by their faith. Especially in this respect, the Pilgrims of the West and those of the East were similar.

In conclusion: In regard to the settlement of the Dutch Puritans there exists yet another misunderstanding. One should not overestimate the assistance they received from the Americans. Too often the impression is given that Van Raalte and his people were received with open arms in this freedom loving and hospitable America. True, the Reformed Church gave them a most cordial welcome and considerable help, especially that part of the church that was of Old Dutch descent. But one should keep in mind that this church, although one of the oldest in the United States, occupied a subordinate place in the mass of Americans. Only a very small number belonged to that church and most people knew nothing of it. The great majority of Americans were totally indifferent to the immigrants. Indeed, there were some who disdained the Netherlanders, and there were perhaps even more who tried to defraud them, as we have seen before. How far these fraud attempts would go was shown when some of the colonists, now firmly established on their own land, bought more state land, which dishonest land speculators tried to repossess, with the help and cooperation of state officials, of all people! Van Raalte, at considerable expense, appealed to judicial authorities, but in vain. At his wits' end, he finally went directly to Governor |Lewis| Cass in Detroit, which was then the capital.[183] Only after having threatened the governor that he and all his people would leave Michigan and settle in Illinois instead, did he manage to obtain justice. Michigan was thinly populated and the governor was reluctant to lose the Dutch settlers and so "the land under dispute came back to the settlement."

There were Americans in Michigan who would have liked to see the Hollanders leave. Although |John R.| Kellogg at Allegan deserves everlasting credit for his support of the Netherlanders, his colleague, |F. J.| Littlejohn, also a "leading resident" and other citizens, would have none of them. They "talked loud against the Dutch settlers" and wished "that they would move away," because if they did not, they would have "such a lot of paupers" to support that it would raise the taxes.[184]

In 1922 the oldest church in Holland celebrated its 75th anniversary. One of the speakers was the American church historian, Dr. Henry Beets. In his address he referred to the less-than-hospitable way the Dutch immigrants were received: "They were very disappointed when, after a long and arduous journey, they arrived here and were looked upon as unpatriotic subjects, like our present-day tramps and vagabonds."[185]

The tremendous effort exerted by the colonists in establishing themselves on American soil, the great determination, the perseverance, and above all the faith in God they demonstrated, have gradually changed the contempt with which they were at first regarded into respect, even admiration. One of their American neighbors, A. D. Botsford of Otsego in Allegan County, acknowledged this openly some years later in a public address: "When I look at your fields and cultivated farmlands, your substantial houses and barns, filled with cattle and grain, your churches and scientific institutions, open to everyone, then I must say, 'Well done, good and faithful servants. Let us all benefit from your example!'"[186]

9

The Rooting of the Young Dutch Branch in Iowa

A. Prairie Pioneers

In addition to the Van Raalte colony in the forests of Michigan, the Scholte colony on the prairies of Iowa drew the most attention. However, its direct influence on Dutch immigration was not as important. Thousands went "to Van Raalte" and only hundreds followed Scholte. Yet the Iowa colony deserves our full attention, even though its influence in the United States of America is less than that of the Michigan colony. We are again dealing with a group of fellow countrymen at the time that the national spirit of the mother country was at its lowest ebb. They were also firmly determined to try to build themselves a new life abroad, and were motivated by material and spiritual concerns.

The Pella colony's interest also lies in the fact that it differed in many respects from the one in Michigan. Already in the Netherlands differences were evident. Van Raalte, as we have seen, led the totally destitute immigrants, while most of the well-to-do followed Scholte. This social contrast greatly influenced the choice of a place to settle; for the poor, the forest seemed the most suited, while the more well-to-do preferred the prairies. Settling on the prairies entailed entirely different problems, but it also offered totally different "opportunities" than did colonizing in the forests. Thus the differences in location, type of soil, and climate, explain the variation in ways of making a living. The decisive factor in such choices was usually social standing.

The human factor in both colonies differed in still another sense. In the Pella colony there were relatively many well-to-do people, including a number of very educated people, a few preachers, a medical doctor, a former notary public, a former mayor, even a former high school teacher, and businessmen. They not only influenced the growth of the economy, but also helped to develop the spiritual nature of Pella.

Scholte had an entirely different personality than Van Raalte, and this also influenced the rooting and development of Pella compared with the Holland colony. This personality difference of the leaders has even influenced the development of the settlements to the present day!

The relative wealth of the Pella colonists undoubtedly facilitated their establishment there. In spite of all the hardships one usually encounters on such long trips, the voyage to the promised land had been less unpleasant for the Pella people, because they had always traveled in close-knit groups. Thus, they did not have to go through the aggravations, for instance, that of drunk Irishmen. One penniless Pellian wrote the following about the overland trip: "Never have I been better pleased than with my trip through North America."[1] None of the Michigan settlers ever dared to claim such satisfaction!

A committee was chosen with Scholte as chairman and they decided where to settle. Nonetheless, quite a large number of immigrants remained in St. Louis and spent the winter there, in a spirit of "Easy does it." Some of them decided to take possession of the land they had purchased and arrived in groups between August 19 and 22, 1847.[2] Several Netherlanders were housed on the farms that had been bought from the Americans, and if Iowans had followed up on Scholte's order to build some fifty log cabins, the housing problem would have been no problem. Unfortunately, as we have mentioned earlier, the newly arrived Dutchmen found no buildings at all but only some planks that were moreover far from sufficient to fill their needs. This was a bitter blow that was felt all the more sharply because among these first colonists there were a number of city people, of the lower middle class, who were not at all acquainted with farm life, let alone pioneer life. "Imagine a number of bread and pastry bakers, tailors, shoemakers, painters, clerks, business representatives, and people of the same ilk, who had spent all their lives as city dwellers in European towns." Some of them hardly knew what a cow or pig looked like or knew anything about farm equipment. They had left neat and comfortable homes and had never known or seen anything else. Just imagine such people suddenly transferred to the open prairie with only a grove here and there, seeing nothing but grass, trees, and the open sky, and having no protection from the elements of nature. When the day was ended and the lengthening shadows announced the coming of night, they could find no proper resting place for their worn-out bodies and tired heads, but they had to wrap themselves in a blanket of some sort and lay down their tired limbs on mother earth. However, even during this makeshift night rest, they were disturbed by howling wolves. "Imagine all this and then you get some idea about the real living conditions of the early settlers in Pella, Iowa and surrounding areas," so relates K. Van Stigt, who was one of them.[3]

Very soon the pile of planks was used to build a sizeable shelterhouse where many found cover. Others used boards and crates in an attempt to make shelters and tents which they covered with oil cloth, bushes, and the long prairie grass. Soon they realized that in the open fields, these shelters and tents furnished poor protection against the weather. Because of the lack of appropriate building material, many followed the way indicated by soil and climate and began to dig homes in the slopes of the "rolling" prairie, as other pioneers had done before them and as others would do after them. As they dug, the soil was used for walls and these were raised even higher with sod. Then small fir-tree rafters, chopped from the woods north of the "town," were placed over the structures. The roofs were covered with reeds or straw. Only a few sod houses and dugouts had a wooden floor; most merely had bare, hardpacked soil. Some had a wooden front door while others used a cloth drape, since planks were scarce. Many of these homes were dug on the northwest side of town, where the Oakwood Cemetery is now located. Thus the notorious "Straw Town" came into existence.[4]

Two years after the first settlement, these "homes" were still used as protection against cold and wind. At times snakes would crawl through the "walls" and one time an ox walked over a verdant roof and fell in. Yet, people took it in stride and "there reigned more solidarity and satisfaction in these dwellings that today we would call unfit even for cattle than in the present-day homes that are provided with all the comforts and frills," remarked a pioneer in 1897.[5]

While many dug temporary homes this way, Scholte as soon as possible contacted the District Surveyor to plat the center of town so that solid homes could be built there. As early as September 2, 1847, the County Surveyor could write this description on his plat of the new "town": "Pella is beautifully located on an elevation from which one scans the surrounding territory; the streets are a hundred feet wide; the "blocks and square" are four hundred feet square. The blocks are divided into eight lots as can be seen on the map. The town is located near the center of the section line dividing sections 3 and 10, running east and west. The town is laid out in a rectangular shape. A stone is placed on each corner of the town square from which further surveying must begin."[6] And he added, "I, Claiborne Hall, Surveyor of Marion County, declare to have surveyed accurately sixty-four lots in the above named 'town'." Thus we see that Pella as well as Holland (Michigan) were platted by an American, and this determined to a great extent the American appearance of the town.

The names given to the "streets" then and in '48 reflect the spirit of many of the colonists: Avenues were called Entrance, Inquiring, Perseverance, Reformation, Gratitude, Experience, Patience, Confidence, Expectation, and Accomplishment; and the streets were named Columbus, Washington, Franklin, Liberty, Union, Independence, and Peace.

The 640 acres used for the town included two cornfields purchased at a high price. On one of the cornfields stood a log cabin where the colonists had had their first noonday meal and after November 1847, served as the abode of M. J. Post, a Baptist missionary. On the other field there was only a crib which the Hollanders rebuilt into a log cabin.[7] Since Scholte was one of the first "city" dwellers, this house on Garden Square became the home for him and his family, who arrived from St. Louis in November, 1847. Soon, however, construction of a larger dwelling was started.

Others also bought lots and had homes built, so that hopefully they would have adequate shelter before winter. Among them were G. H. Over-kamp, [John H.] Wolters and [Jacob] Smeenk, J. H. Schijf, [Jacob] Van de Roovaart, [Adrianus] Veenman, [J. J.] Hasselman, etc., some of them businessmen. Lumber was scarce and had to be obtained some miles south of town from the American [W.] Nossaman, the sawmill owner. Due to the high cost of this building material, homes were slow in coming. In spite of the mild winter, Pella had only forty homes in September, 1848, while at that time Holland and Zeeland in the wooded areas of Michigan already had several hundred.[8] A great number of the colonists—and not only farmers—settled permanently in the vicinity of the town and adjoining countryside.

For this development, Scholte also had taken the preparatory steps. With the aid of John A. Graham, "one of the most distinguished citizens of Keokuk," Scholte became the owner of 18,000 acres of land in Prairie Lake Township. With the help of Graham, he had bought many land warrants for $60 to $80 each.[9] Each warrant covered 160 acres. With as many of these warrants as were available, they "entered" Congress land. Land bought without "warrants" had to be paid for in cash. We already know that in buying this land, "claims," etc. had also to be taken into account.

How did the immigrants become individual land owners? Scholte himself tells us how this took place and, as we shall see later, this led to much dissention and hard feelings. He wrote:

> As soon as the farms were vacated, the Netherlanders willing to buy took possession. Since the Association had not acquired the complete title to the farms and their appurtenances, this became a matter for personal settlement later. In the meantime surveying was begun, and records were made by a qualified surveyor of all the purchased property so that the awarding could take place in proportion to the deposited money. I [Scholte] took care of securing the ownership of the purchased claims by paying the government. This was also done to prevent undercutting by corrupt speculators, which was not only possible but very likely. Meanwhile I computed the cost of the land per acre, based on the purchase price and the government's price of free land in order to find out how much each should have as a share. Lots were cast to determine the sequence of owners and section numbers in which they would fall, after which the Surveyor had to do his work to award to each his proper lot. It was arranged that the lots of those immigrants here present would be surveyed and numbered first, so that they would be helped first. All empty farm houses that were not sold to new owners were designated for temporary use by families.[10]

This procedure allowed farmers to begin their work at once. Those who settled on the newly bought farms had to take care immediately of the growing crops in the fields and the cattle. Soon some began to make butter and cheese, to sow winter wheat, and to build barns for cattle, since winter approached.

Fencing the land was a big task. For this, wood was hauled from nearby forests. They used rails ten feet long and about four inches wide, placing them in a zig-zag fashion one above the other about six or seven feet high thus providing a continuous enclosure. In the beginning, the cutting and splitting of trees was cumbersome for the Hollanders. This job was often consigned to others for twenty-five to forty cents per one hundred rails. The less well-to-do who did not have a grove found such a fence too costly. So they erected "quays"—walls of earth three to four feet high and five feet wide—around their fields. In doing this, they followed the practice of their home country, where quays are built on sandy soils. Some of these quays lasted many years.[11]

Various immigrants worked for Americans who also provided housing. Sipma thought that in September, 1848, about one-third of the laborers of the Association were thus employed; the largest part of them made a living in agriculture and cattle raising, either by having their own farm or by working for others.[12] Therefore, the settlement became an agricultural community and still is to the present day. Cattle raising seemed to become of great importance. Many went into the dairy business. A great number were excellent cheese makers. The quality of cheese surpassed American brands and was sold at the highest prices not only around Pella but as far away as St. Louis. By November 1848, the Hollanders "had already delivered five shipments to St. Louis, where it was listed separately as Iowa cheese."[13] Butter was also made, but only for the colony. St. Louis was too far away for shipping butter that would keep its quality. Others raised beef cattle for a ready market "since buyers came from neighboring Illinois to buy and haul them away, and offered reasonably good prices, and paid cash."

In Iowa as well as in Michigan, the economic domination of the young and rapidly growing Chicago affected to a great extent the weal and woe of the farmers, although not yet as strongly as today. In 1848 there was a bumper crop and exporting became necessary. Some farmers experimented with raising hemp and flax, which grew very well. A sample of processed flax was sent to St. Louis to develop a market, and hemp would follow. Colza (rapeseed) also "did very well." The growing of these crops, Scholte imagined, "could foster businesses that would thrive, such as oil extracting, spinning of linen, and rope making."[14]

Farmers and "town folk" busied themselves with gardening. To find a vegetable garden near every house " . . . was a strange sight to the traveling Americans passing through since they themselves usually did little or no gardening." All kinds of vegetables grew very well, except cauliflower, "which problem our gardeners ascribe to the strong air currents." But, " . . . the most delicious melons grow on so-called open ground. Asparagus beds were planted this spring on prairie ground without any more care than well-dug soil, and they look as good as what is expected in Holland in the best tilled beds after two years." Grafted apple and pear trees were planted. Wild strawberries, peach trees, and plum trees were transplanted from the woods. Thus an interest developed in tree and flower nurseries.

Next to farming and cattle raising, other related industries and trade developed. Here, as in Michigan, it was at first on a retail basis, and for years in the form of bartering.[15] A large double log cabin was used by two families. One part of the dwelling was occupied by the only physician among the Dutch, J. Roelofsz, and his family. The other half housed J. Smeenk and family. Soon after the immigrants came, Smeenk and J. H. Wolters opened the first store in this log cabin.[16] It was situated near the shelterhouse and "Straw Town" and therefore prospered, all the more so since the golden "Willempjes" had not yet been spent and since there was no competition during the first months. As building began in town, Smeenk and Wolters built a new place and moved their store. Soon there were competitors—E. F. Grafe, a German, and another one, D. W. Van Sittert, who opened the third store in Pella, a hardware store.

Industry also had its modest beginning. South of town near the Des Moines River, the Americans Welch and Nossaman had a pottery factory, sawmill, and a corn mill. The latter was powered by horses.[17] Because of the increasing demand for building materials, Scholte, a preacher in the Netherlands but also a topnotch businessman in America, suggested "the erection of a stone-breaker and lime kiln" to solve this problem.[18] Success followed, although due to the lack of experience of his workers, the stone and lime turned out to be "somewhat high in price." "The quality of the burnt lime however, is so high that our masons testify that with one mud |one hectoliter| of lime here they can do as much as with three in Holland." Moreover, in the second half of 1848 two brick kilns were in use; one produced two loads at a time and the other, only one, "and all the bricks were sold on the spot."[19]

In addition, Scholte with the aid of a competent American millwright had a good sawmill built on the Skunk River. This mill, operating since the spring of 1848 in conjunction with the already existing American mill, supplied the colonists with all necessary construction material. Scholte wanted a grain mill near his sawmill, known for years as "Elwell's Mill," but he failed to realize this wish because of floods and the death of his partner Elwell in 1851.

Scholte also desired to develop the nearby shallow coal deposits, in view of the winter weather. Scarcity of skilled workers was a problem. "In general, the Hollanders are keen enough to receive American wages but some are not industrious enough to work American-fashion, that is, fast," said Scholte, the entrepreneur. Carpentry in Pella was another busy skill done by |N. J.| Gesman with four or five workers. A blacksmithy flourished due to the demand for farm equipment. Indeed, so great was this demand, owing also to the fact that little farm equipment was imported, that blacksmiths worked night and day to supply the most urgent needs during the early years.[20]

The blacksmith, J. H. Schijf, and his partner, A. Veenman, a cartwright and plowmaker, by their quality workmanship "earned themselves a well-deserved, great name" far outside the colony and also among Americans. Three shoemaker shops "are constantly busy." Their bosses wished that a tannery could be established where hides could be made into leather according to the Dutch process. A few tailors, wooden shoemakers, and house painters were engaged in work in Pella. A bread bakery was under construction and so was a cake bakery, although most people did their own baking at home. A small pastry shop was already well established![21]

One gets the impression that the development of industry in Pella and surrounding areas was more rapid than in Holland, Michigan, and that the Dutch sooner felt "at home" on the prairie—we should be reminded of the asparagus and pastries—than those who lived in the forest. There were various reasons for this more rapid adaptation. Due to the fact that many were well-to-do, people in Pella made money right away, and even the farmers, at least those who had improved farms, could immediately sell and even ship out their surplus, which was good for business and industry. In Iowa a greater number of Americans also lived among the Hollanders, more so than in Michigan. Therefore, the Dutch in Iowa received far more help in their new and unusual way of life. This was all the more so since people could more easily contact one another on the prairie than in the forests. Thus the Pellians saw more of their American neighbors and "profited much from their helpfulness and drew lessons from their experiences in pioneer life."[22]

When the immigrants came to Michigan they still had to build roads, while Pella was platted on both sides of an existing state road. This highway wound its way from Keokuk on the Mississippi River northwestward over the high ridge between the Des Moines and Skunk rivers and several villages were already located along it. Scholte himself declared that this road was easier to travel on than those of the Netherlands, except when the ground was soaked by rain. "Even in winter, when people call it bad, it is better than many roads in the Netherlands."[23] Especially this favorable location on a fine highway brought better conditions to the Pellians and softened for many the rigors of frontier life. This road and the high esteem in which the well-to-do colonists were held, must have contributed to the fact that the administration in Washington immediately gave permission to the request by Scholte and the other members of the Association to reroute via Pella the existing mail route through the valley of the Des Moines River.[24]

The first American pioneers, afraid of life on the prairie, as Beukma had already observed, had settled in the wooded river valleys and from there they slowly moved on to the prairie ridges. The Dutch, however, settled on those ridges right away.

Since the American postmaster had sold his farm to Scholte, his official job was canceled at the same time. The Association requested that it be given to I. Overkamp. The Post Office was set up at the home of G. H. Overkamp, one of the first homes erected in Pella. At first twice a week, but in November of 1848 three times a week, mail was delivered "with a good covered wagon with springs" from Keokuk via Pella to Fort Des Moines and back.[25] Now the colonists could receive mail from the eastern states and the Netherlands. In comparison, Van Raalte's colony received mail only once a week and with what difficulty! In addition, the postmaster in Holland was an American.

We do not wish to give the impression that Pella had no problems. On the contrary! We have seen how many lived in primitive dugouts and sod houses! Some did not even have simple furniture but used boxes and chests for tables, chairs, and storage. Especially toward evening there was the problem of light. Although they made their own candles, even candle light was often too expensive; so they would burn tallow in a saucer with an inserted wick.

Their primitive homes offered poor protection against rain and storms. The totally different life style on the edge of the white man's world, and the radically different climate, were factors that proved too much to endure for many a newcomer. Just as in Michigan, many a settler paid with his life for this human transplantation. Especially those who lived on the low bottom lands along rivers suffered from fevers. The dampness resulting from sod-busting on the prairie adversely affected health also. Some became sick by eating too many blackberries, plums, and other fruit that were plentiful in the groves.

The greatest hardship, however, was caused by the lack of cash. As in Michigan, all their money was spent in a few months; most of it had been used to buy land. In addition, the food supplies taken along on their sea journey—dried beans, peas, and rice—had all been used up by that time. Not a few lacked money to buy food supplies. Moreover, it was 120 miles to Keokuk where the needed goods could be obtained and during rainy weather the road to Keokuk left much to be desired. During the severe winter of '48–'49, from November to May, snow lay three feet high. This was followed by a thaw that made the roads impassable, so that many suffered from a great lack of supplies; they also suffered from the terrible cold during the winter months due to a lack of firewood. Even if someone had a supply of corn or wheat, the mill was hard to reach; as a result, only those who were fortunate enough to own a coffee grinder could afford the luxury of wheat or corn bread—sometimes eaten with syrup.

Cattle were not exempt from much suffering. In summer cattle grazed on the prairie, but when winter came they were congregated in the groves. There was a barn only for the horses and a shed for sheep as protection against hungry wolves. The winter was unusually severe and weeks on end the thermometer registered twenty degrees below zero [Celsius]. People were not at all prepared for such low temperatures, and many of the cattle died of starvation and cold. In May the snow began to melt, causing the rivers to overflow and making the ground so wet that the farmers were unable to prepare the soil. But worse, due to a lack of fodder the cattle were so weak that often these animals became mired in the soaked fields and once caught in the sloughs they did not have the strength to extricate themselves and would "sink down more than half way" and perish miserably. Thus in the spring of 1849 more cattle died than in the winter. That spring two young Hollanders also drowned while crossing a small lake. "So great became the discouragement that many began to think seriously of leaving the colony to find a better location elsewhere."[26]

In later years there were also floods caused by melting snow or continual rains, which brought havoc and great loss. Notorious were the floods of June, 1851, when wide stretches of land along river bottoms flooded and the colonists who lived there were barely saved. "Along these rivers, an awful number of cattle perished and the planted corn was totally destroyed." The fences, built with such effort, floated away and the mill dams were greatly damaged. When the rivers receded, repairs were made, but another flood followed, again causing much damage![27]

The shortage of money was greatly alleviated in 1849 when 250 new immigrants came. They were very well educated and very well-to-do. They came under the leadership of A. C. Kuyper, J. Maasdam, A. R. Dudok Bousquet, J. Hospers, and others, a number of whom had become members of the Association already in 1846. As a group they boarded the sailing ship *Franciska* on May 1, 1849, and arrived in America on June 15.[28] In groups they turned to the West, and traveling on the riverboat *Time and Tide*, one hundred arrived at Keokuk on July 16, 1849. But because of the cholera scare they were ordered to anchor at a spot on the river above the town. An American newspaper made this observation: "The immigrants make a very good impression, seem to be very neat and to suffer from no sickness."[29] Soon they departed for Pella and found lodging there. "The housing of these people was no chore but was kindly offered as a work of love," Van Stigt reported. His father welcomed many of them in his home. Several of these new arrivals remained near the town and bought farms from some Americans. Americans are capricious, one of the immigrants confirmed once more, and "they are ready at any moment to sell the most beautiful farm on which they have worked for years," and to move further westward.[30] Others bought land from Scholte.

Farmhouses and barns had to be built; oxen and horses had to be bought. Oxen were used for sodbusting on the prairie, horses, for less heavy plow work. Proper farm equipment had to be purchased. "In this manner much money came into circulation because not only did they buy, they immediately paid in cash." However, "the greatest number of these newcomers" became town dwellers, which necessitated the building of new homes and also the opening of new stores.[31] Even a jewelry store opened; it had such visible success that soon another followed. Also some loaned out money on interest to those less well endowed who were then able to open a business. Others bought land, not to work it but for sharecropping at one-third of the yearly crop.

Other conditions, somewhat more temporary, influenced Pella in its growth. Pella was favorably located along the highway of travel, especially when news broke about the California gold rush and thousands of adventurers traveled westward. In the spring of 1849 the stream of gold seekers began and major groups of them passed through Pella. This event was described by an eyewitness: "There was from East to West, as far as you could see, a single uninterrupted line of wagons in constant motion. Wagons were drawn by horses, oxen, mules, and some by cows. Some men went on foot, transporting all their earthly possessions in pushcarts. If a wagon broke or if horse or ox became sick, they were shunted aside and the vacant space was immediately filled again. The gold seekers on the roadside hastened to step in line and would keep it filled. When a traveler became sick and died, the body would be buried at the roadside without a coffin or funeral service. When night fell, the wagons would be arranged by the owners to give protection. Most of these people were rough customers. After supper, the bottle and cards appeared, accompanied by shouting, singing, and swearing, which was not soon forgotten. Playing cards were scattered along the whole line of travel. Bottles, when emptied, were smashed against trees, and the broken pieces of glass marked the trail."[32]

The Hollanders really reaped the benefits from these forty-niners and became flush with money. "To these California travelers we sold everything we had," as a farmer observed, who lived on the highway. "To fill the need, we kept buying more supplies from neighbors living further away from this road. We sold corn at $1 a bushel, oats at $1 a bushel, wheat at $1 a bushel, and 100 pounds of hay for $1. Everything for one dollar: that was easy figuring. A span of oxen brought 50 to 55 dollars, and a cow 20 to 25 dollars. The travelers could afford it. Some even had cooks and black servants. A man from Davenport came with a herd of 350 cattle. He had two more droves on the way—1,000 head in all."

Although the stream of fortune seekers began to diminish, it still continued for years and even by 1853, though less than in 1850, it was nevertheless of noticeable importance. Strange as it may seem, only a few Iowa Hollanders followed the adventurers. In 1850 two left but came back to Pella after a period of two years. Again in 1853 three men left; one died in the gold fields, one returned, and the other, Dirk Van Zee, remained living in California."[33]

Sipma wrote in 1848 that "almost daily," transients came through Pella and especially after 1850 great numbers of movers began to search for land, which was productive and cheap in the West. Many of the movers had large families. Picturesquely, they pulled covered wagons with six, eight, or ten yoke of oxen coming from the eastern states going westward.[34] A newspaper in Oskaloosa, a town near Pella located on the same state road, published the following: "From early morning till nightfall, the covered wagons are passing through this place.... We should think, that at least a thousand persons pass through Oskaloosa every week."[35]

This steady stream of westward trekkers provided much diversion and since the Americans were "easy" in spending their money, they contributed to prosperous times in Pella. The settlers could write to the Netherlands: "All the Netherlanders have their daily bread, most of them are content; there is satisfaction with the present, although still more is expected in the future."[36]

B. Transportation Problems

These words underline the great courage that was needed to face life in Pella, because at that time the settlers had to take in stride several setbacks that put a permanent imprint on Pella's eventually very slow growth. This was in contrast to Holland, Michigan, which had been born under much more difficult circumstances and which, as a consequence, had flourished far more slowly, though it eventually achieved far greater importance than Pella. Transportation was worse in the case of Pella than in the case of Holland, Michigan, and this problem was a serious obstacle in the development of permanent markets for its products.

This problem is not always made clear in Scholte's *Stemmen* [Voices]. But one should not forget that Scholte the preacher had become a landowner as well and a merchant and a real estate dealer. Therefore, his letters were characterized by the tone of "an emigration agent's advertisement with a sermon running through it."[37] He speaks of getting high prices for cheese shipments in St. Louis, but as Sipma intimated, after the overhead was subtracted, the price of the cheese was the same as in Pella.[38] In the same letter Sipma wrote that if transportation did not improve "we shall get stuck with the grains"—in spite of the beautiful but expensive state road!

The need for "cheap transportation" caused concern in Iowa even before the arrival of the Dutch. In 1837 the first steamboat came up the Des Moines River, the largest river in Iowa. Another came in 1843 and reached Raccoon Fork, renamed Fort Des Moines for the occasion, and presently known as Des Moines. People thought that now their problem could be solved by making the river completely navigable. With this purpose in mind, Congress in Washington ceded in 1846 all odd-numbered sections of land—five miles on each side of the Des Moines River—to the state of Iowa.[39]

Thousands of dollars, part of which came from the sale of this land, were spent for the "Des Moines River Improvement." But much money was also wasted by state employees and state representatives who were filled with enthusiasm but lacked even the remotest knowledge for this project. Especially the engineer, S. R. Curtis, "prophet and almost poet," fanned this enthusiasm for the development of the waterway. According to him, it would even draw the traffic from the poorly navigable Missouri River, and would turn the Des Moines River valley into the wonderland of the continent.

No wonder that this enthusiasm infected Scholte and other enterprising Dutchmen. This was all the more remarkable since in other parts of the country concentration on canals had already been diverted and was directed more and more towards railroad building. Numerous possibilities opened up for the Pella colony. That is why Scholte speaks about them already in his first *Stem* [*Voice*]: "A start has been made to make the Des Moines River, which passes through our Colony, navigable for boats and steamships; one half of the part to be made navigable has been surveyed to determine where the dams and locks have to be built."[40]

Port cities would, of course, come into existence. Since Pella was located on high prairie ground, thoughts went in the direction of laying out a new town, a port city that could also serve as a county seat. "Several requests" were addressed to Scholte and thus he already declared in his first *Stem* that it was "not unlikely" that he would decide to have such a layout.

Actually, after the surveying of Pella had been completed between May 3 and 15, 1848, the Americans joined in pushing for the development of the new town and the platting was begun. They suggested that it be called Amsterdam, thereby reflecting their high expectations that it "must become the port city for Pella and surrounding territory. The name will commemorate how important Amsterdam once was in the Netherlands, and how important the American 'Amsterdam' (now called New York) is and is becoming. Those are the reasons that this town in Iowa is given the same name; it also is of Dutch origin and destined for commerce. Because of the condition of the river, a dam and locks are necessary on that spot. This is the reason the town is to be built at this location. Also a very usable road runs from it to Pella and is already in use."[41]

The town was plotted on a sharp bend of the Des Moines River between the river and Lake Prairie, a small lake. With the expectation of a thriving town, land on the main streets of Front and Court sold for $100 a lot, just as in Pella on Garden Square. On other streets lots sold for about $40. The names of the "streets" were chosen rather at random: East, Krantz, Post, Scholte, Cherry, Walnut, Lind, Rokin, Pella, Wine, and West streets running north and south. Those going east and west were called: Bluff, Lake, Heeren, Utrecht, Market, Huiden, Beeren, and South streets. In contrast with Pella, Scholte did not take part in naming the Amsterdam streets. "The surveyor and a few others had named and recorded them before I had seen them,"[42] he felt compelled to declare. Did he feel perhaps ashamed about the name Wine Street?

In accordance with his communication to Groen van Prinsterer that it was his will that the settlement "in the full sense of the word (would) be and

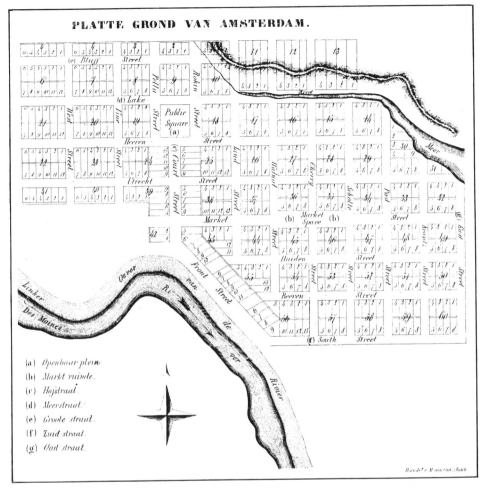

High expectations. A plat map of Amsterdam in Marion County, Iowa

remain a Dutch colony,"[43] lots in Pella were "at first expressly held open for Dutch buyers," which disappointed Sipma and others who thought that Pella would be larger if Scholte also allowed Americans to settle there.[44] However, lots in Amsterdam "are more available also to Americans," although they would not be sold in public, "because then one is bound to assign them to the highest bidder and one would have no control to keep out well-known immoral persons. If sold privately, this was possible, and was already done!"

Anticipating the growth of the commercial town, partially also "because of the beautiful location of same on the river," many bought lots and slowly began to build homes.[45] Slowly indeed, because the bottom land fevers were a handicap. E. F. Grafe and Dingeman De Haan, Jr. opened a store in 1850.

However, Amsterdam became important not through trade but through industry. J. A. Toom built a brickyard and later on a lime kiln. Later on, other brick "works" were started. Amsterdam became the supplier of building materials not only for Marion County but also for the surrounding counties.

Expectations also ran high for [other] industry. Already in his first *Stem*, Scholte called the waters of Lake Prairie "an invaluable opportunity to erect factories powered by water."[46] In addition he pointed out the availability of coal, limestone, and sandstone. According to the *Tweede Stem* [*Second Voice*], there were opportunities for many businesses, first for industry and next for branches of farming and cattle raising, like a beer brewery, vinegar plant, a potato and syrup industry ("since potatoes do extremely well here"), an oil extracting plant, and others. "A distillery I do not recommend since I reckon the increased use of liquor to be bad for society."[47]

According to Cole, the Hollanders thought like real "dikers and canalists"; they wanted to connect Lake Prairie and the Des Moines River with an embanked canal, so there would be a safe harbor for future shipping.[48] Everything depended, however, on the navigability of the river. "Intensely interested," Scholte and his supporters approached the legislature of Iowa with a petition concerning this project.[49]

How very different were the results! The continual heavy rains of 1851—more than 190 cm (76 inches), which was "perhaps the wettest year in the annals of the state"—caused the whole valley of the Des Moines River to flood. These floods sealed the doom of Amsterdam. People found out how fickle Iowa rivers were. This very characteristic limits their importance to this day. Curtis' regulation plan came to nothing after part of the works had swallowed up a fortune and caused a deficit. The contractors declared themselves bankrupt, "probably without any self impoverishment."[50] It is obvious that the Hollanders sustained losses. How much was never mentioned, because it would not have benefited the immigration in any way! But Cole's saying is significant: "Fortunes were wasted, for pathos is born when serious men began [begin] to dream."[51]

Since then, plans to turn Amsterdam into a business town were abandoned. The location, which people envisioned as a metropolis, is now occupied by corn fields dotted with trees here and there. A few farms exist on higher ground, at the crossroads of the highway and a road leading downhill toward a bridge crossing the river, where Scholte had envisioned a country home. This is the hamlet of Amsterdam. This name continues to be used by Pellians, although in 1911 a railroad company christened the nearby stop Howell.[52]

However, the idea of a waterway—a vital necessity—was not so quickly abandoned. The Hollanders themselves now tried to use the Des Moines River for transportation. It was one of the "forty-niners," A. E. Dudok Bousquet, a man who rivaled Scholte as an enterpreneur, who made himself useful in this regard not only for Pella but for the entire valley. In contrast to Scholte, he "deemed it the better part to spend his money in developing the country rather than by buying great quantities of land and making himself rich by advancing prices." Bousquet, rich and very well educated, associated himself with the firm of Smeenk and Wolters, which became the largest business in the region. They built the first known two-story store in the colony. Large supplies of necessities were stocked from St. Louis and traded in the "Old Pella Store" for products from the land. The first large hog packing house in Pella had its beginning there. Also Bousquet had an interest in the Elwell mill.

Just as in Michigan, the businessmen were the ones directly interested in a reliable waterway. Therefore, they initiated a plan. Bousquet, Wolters, Smeenk, Van Dam, and Berkhout had a number of flatboats built. These were loaded with the colony's surplus grain and they instructed the experienced boatmen Kramer, Jot, and others, to make use of the high water level in 1851 and transport the cargo to St. Louis. Soon it became evident that navigation on unknown rivers was dangerous. Some boats became stranded in the Des Moines River, others sank in the Mississippi and caused great loss, leading to the failure of this enterprise.[53]

Bousquet, however, did not quit. Two years later he formed the Des Moines River Steamboat Company with one steamboat. After this boat had made several trips this endeavor also had to be abandoned. Now Bousquet turned his attention to land traffic, which people tried to promote in those days by the laying of wooden plank roads.[54] He started to lay a plank road from Keokuk to Pella. After he had completed twenty to twenty-five miles, it became apparent that here as elsewhere the planks "rotted away in the Iowa mud."

With the rising interest in railroads, this enterprising man tried his best to connect Pella with its great network. This possibility existed already in October, 1847, when Monroe City, located fifteen to seventeen miles northwest of Pella, was being surveyed. It was to be the site of the new state capital. In his first *Stem*, Scholte thought he would write that the railroad from Keokuk to this capital "would almost of necessity run through our colony" and that a second railroad planned to run from Dubuque to Council Bluffs "would have to run through or close to our colony."[55] But neither one of these expectations would, for the time being, materialize.

However, optimism prevailed concerning other matters. People dreamed of making Pella not only into a city of trade and industry, but also into a place of government and, later on, even of science. When it was decided to drop Monroe City as the state capital, in spite of the fact that it had been surveyed, platted, and land was purchased, the Hollanders tried for years to have Pella chosen as the capital of Iowa. They supported their plans with numerous petitions. Scholte even offered land free of charge for the government buildings.[56] As we noted before, the colonists also wanted to move the Marion County seat at Knoxville, south of the Des Moines River, to the Dutch colony north of the river. Neither of these suggestions materialized.

It is obvious that the price of land went up and down with all these "high expectations."[57] All this pie in the sky concerning land speculations, mixed with a good dose of zest for life and entrepreneurship, explains many a dream of the normally level-headed Dutch colonists. Scholte himself felt this atmosphere of elation most clearly, and his own words must have come straight from the heart when he said, " . . . the rapid change from an ominous and oppressive condition in the Netherlands to one of space and freedom caused some dizziness. Therefore the earthly American situation is more appealing than the heavenly one."[58] This was indeed the land of opportunity! However, Bousquet, whose goal was "to make Pella famous and to work for the welfare of all," never took part in "land politics." As he felt compelled to explain: "If I should do this I should be as great a curse to my community as the eastern speculators!"[59]

This land speculation explains also why no other Dutch towns were settled near Pella, in contrast to Holland, Michigan, around which many villages sprung up. Except for Amsterdam, there were around Pella only the few previously mentioned "neighborhoods" with names that referred to the origin of the inhabitants in the Netherlands, just as town names in Michigan. We mentioned the Frisian neighborhood formed at the very beginning of the colony. There, according to Sipma, the Frisians "stuck the most closely together" as far as buying of land was concerned, for their properties formed one single block.[60] There were also the Herwijnen neighborhood [of Gelderlanders], and the one of Kockengen [Utrechters], which is now a part of Pella where a road still bears that name.[61] Thus it remained. However, for years there were thousands of acres available a few miles away that could be purchased not at the squatter's price of $1.25 but for $10 an acre![62]

C. Political and Spiritual Life

The rapid progression of the struggle of the Pellians was not only evident in business life but also in politics. Already in the Netherlands they had formed an "Association" with Scholte as president of the board, which took care of the affairs of the journey and the buying of land. During the first months on the prairie, Scholte was the actual leader. He performed his task "as a worthy president and was like a jewel for the colonists [*voor de Colonisten tot sieraad verstrekkende president*]. He had been appointed by God and men," according to one of his most faithful supporters, L. Van Bergeyk, "and proceeded with diligence, good leadership, and sound judgment."[63] But not everyone was so satisfied. The board members residing in America and other believers tried to form in the consistory a counterweight to Scholte's supreme power. They did not wish to be merely a complaint department, but as in Michigan, they desired to take over the leadership.

After a regular board had been elected according to American law in April 1848, the Association remained in existence for a little longer, seemingly to wind up financial matters. Finances had caused a lot of bickering and also the church consistory struggled with them for many years. Both organizations also dealt with other issues, as can be concluded from Van Bergeyk's *History*, and from the writings by Sipma of September, 1848, when he says: "Whenever in Pella a public meeting is called to consider this or that question an announcement is made, but not a single Frisian attends; by now we know enough about the Association."[64]

One of the first decisions of the ruling board after having settled on the prairie was to invite the proper state official to Pella to receive their petition for United States citizenship. It so happened that Professor [John B.] Newhall, an American author, witnessed the proceedings: "I saw a new breed of beings. Men in woolens and 'jeans' were gone! Instead, a broad shouldered people in velvet jerkins and wooden shoes were here. . . . It was an altogether impressive sight, when about two hundred men raised their suntanned arms heavenwards, relinquishing all allegiance to foreign governments, rulers, etc. And when they all came to the final words of their pledge and answered in their native tongue, '*zoo helpe mij God!*' [so help me God!], not a single one of the bystanders could suppress the response coming from their hearts: '*zoo helpe God hen houden hunnen plegtige belofte!*' [So help them God that they may keep their solemn vow!] They all felt the weight of the responsibility which they had assumed." The Americans were surprised that all signed the documents with their names except two who signed with an X.[65]

Americans greatly appreciated the fact that the first large group of foreigners who settled in Iowa took out their American citizenship at such an early date, September 17, 1847. And it may have been one of the reasons that from then on the state has always been very obliging to them. The officials of the Association approached the government of Iowa with a request that the two townships within which their settlement was located should be formed into one and be called Lake Prairie Township. They also requested that the residents who had become citizens might have the right to vote for township officials and be given the right to hold office. Usually, these voting and election rights are given after five years of residency, as happened for the Hollanders in Michigan. However, as an exception the state granted the request of Scholte and his supporters by special state law. As early as April, 1848, they were allowed to elect their own township officials.

Not only state officials but also the Americans in Pella and vicinity concurred with this decision. The Americans, "of their own accord, recognized that the majority of officials should be elected from among the Dutch, since they formed the majority of the inhabitants. Then it was agreed that we would hold the separate preparatory meetings [primaries] in order to learn on both sides the choice of the people, after which everybody would vote on a single official election day."[66]

On the first Monday of April, 1848, the election was held at Scholte's home with the following results:

Justices of the Peace: G. F. [Green T.] Clark and H. P. Scholte
Policemen: [Stelman] Elwell and C. Van den Berg
Commissioners (Trustees): G. Awtry, A. J. Betten and P. Welle
Clerk: I. Overkamp
School Inspector: H. P. Scholte
Treasurer: J. Rosiersz
Poorhouse Trustees: C. Den Hartog and H. Barendregt
Road Supervisors: W. Nossaman, W. Van Asch, G. Van der Wilt, C. 't Lam,
    P. Van Meveren, and D. Synhorst
Fence Inspectors: A. De Visser and J. Toom

Justices of the peace and policemen held office for two years and all
others served for one year. All could be reelected. At first they had very little
to do, except the Fence Inspectors. "The Judge had only one case concerning the failure to pay a small bill. Otherwise it was only weddings, which he
performs here as part of his duties, and the legalizing of signatures on
personal or mutual documents." In passing I should mention that all documents were recorded in English and, if needed, translated for the Dutch.

Let us refer again to Holland, Michigan, where the first election could be
held only one year later on April 2, 1849. The ten voters were all Americans,
and every single one of them received a public job in an otherwise entirely
Dutch settlement!

Is there an explanation for the difference as to what happened? I do not
know whether Van Raalte, like Scholte, requested an exception to the rule.
The following situation may also have been of influence. The American
neighbors of the Pellians and even a large part of the Iowa population were
Southerners, who were more obliging to foreigners. In Michigan, by contrast, one found among the natives mostly New Englanders, who were more
circumspect and more convinced of their own superiority.[67] Also the Pellians' greater wealth and education must have put weight on the scale.

These various factors may explain why Scholte and other Hollanders
already wielded political influence not only in the township but in all of
Marion County. This was evident when at a public meeting in Marion
County, Scholte as representative of the Dutch colony was chosen as a
member of a committee that was formed to attempt to obtain a change in a
state law. This procedure was followed in spite of the fact that Hollanders
were allowed to partake in county, state, and federal affairs only upon
having obtained full citizenship rights.

Scholte even savored the satisfaction that what he had put down on
paper for that occasion was accepted by the committee and subsequently
by the whole legislature. The result was that the law in question was rescinded. When presidential elections approached, elections in which the
Hollanders could not yet take part, they were nevertheless invited to attend
party gatherings "in order to exert a moral influence on any one of the
parties and thus to swing votes of American citizens." Moreover, some

English-speaking Hollanders were welcomed to attend a campaign dinner, and were introduced "with great cordiality."

When looking at more spiritual matters, we should mention that criticism from the churches in the Netherlands concerning emigration was all too often justified in the settlements.[68] They feared that if people were to be their own unbridled bosses, gross arbitrariness and an "autocratic faith" would result. In Michigan, Van Eijk, together with many others, had this experience. They also feared that many who were said to move for the sake of their faith would be lost to the church. This also happened. Especially those who found employment in the cities on their way to the West joined locally established churches. Even if Dutch Reformed churches were established, as in Buffalo, they slowly died out not only because immigrants moved on but because of the increasing Americanization.

In the countryside, people were also lost to their own church. Wyckoff complained in his report that the many Netherlanders around Rochester were organized as a church but were supervised by the Presbyterians.[69] He felt "painfully affected at the thought that these Dutch brethren who concurred with our church in respect to all the details, in the confession of faith, in doctrine and in church polity, have been neglected for so long by us that they had to fall into the hands of those who were foreign to them as far as their language and customs were concerned." A third objection was that the altogether new environment would leave little room for heavenly concerns. Indeed, in the Michigan colony Van Raalte complained about worldly-mindedness, pride, and unbelief, as we know.

However, it was especially in the Pella colony that this concern of the Dutch home church seemed to be justified. In his first *Stem*, Scholte complains that concerning the religious situation "there is nothing particular to boast about." "Testifying in all sincerity," he had the following to say: "Religious life is not prospering, because in daily conduct it does not become evident that the search for the kingdom of God and His righteousness is foremost, but, on the contrary, the things of this world. Nearly everyone seems to be so busy with his new social and worldly affairs that they live only for them. From some of their actions one would almost conclude that they do not know that God's kingdom is *righteousness, love, peace, joy, happiness in the Holy Spirit*. . . . Self-interest and self-seeking shines forth so clearly in some of them that one would question the reality of their Christianity. . . . It is a fact that the circumstances of the journey and that the newness, strangeness, hustle and bustle and briskness of our present unsettled condition contribute much to distract people's minds; but this is not a tenable excuse."[70]

Apart from this worldliness, the colonists attended church faithfully. From the beginning of their arrival on the prairie, Sunday church services were regularly held, at first partially outdoors near "Straw Town"; later members gathered in the big home of G. H. Overkamp in the new town. The attendance was "usually very good." Soon, in the winter of 1848, the building of a church began and was finished by March 1848. It was used not only as a church, but also as a school building and for all public gatherings.[71]

The church was a plain, solidly-built structure, twenty-five feet wide, fifty feet long, running north and south. The rafters were made from trees chopped out of the woods. The planks forming the outside wall were about twelve inches wide. Inside and outside, everything was rough and unplaned. Only the pulpit was made of some smooth and planed wood. On either side of the north-south aisle were pews—planks nailed on supports. This pioneer building fell under the ravages of time and no longer exists. At present a chapel at that site, belonging to the First Reformed Church, is a reminder of the colonial days.

In this simple church building, services were held twice on Sunday. Morning service at ten o'clock was usually conducted by Rev. [Antonie] Betten and the afternoon service at three o'clock by Rev. Scholte. Before the [first] service, from 8:30 until 10:00, there was catechism for the men, and from 1:30 until 3:00 for the women, while the children went on Saturdays.[72] Not only ministers, but also the overseers H. Barendregt, K. De Hoog, and sometimes also G. H. Overkamp, took turns to lead. Thus Sipma could write: "There are five who preach on Sundays." In addition, in the beginning, Sunday evenings were spent in a short presentation of a part of the Holy Scriptures by one of the believers, and "then they discussed the chosen topic together." Also during the week, such gatherings would be held in the homes by turns "to speak about daily life with God." In the fall of 1848 Scholte initiated Sunday evening services.[73]

Dudok Bousquet, who was highly respected in economics, as we saw, was also very energetic in religious and other matters. He started the first Sunday school in the log house on Garden Square, the home of the Baptist, Post, who had died in April 1848. Bousquet himself instructed the young people in Bible knowledge. "Many children profited highly" from this instruction.[74]

The church organization in the Pella colony was different from those in the settlements of Michigan, Wisconsin, and Illinois. In fact, Scholte had not entertained any thoughts about an organization; it left him cold. Scholte had already shown this independent attitude in the Netherlands. This spirit had led not only to the Secession of 1834 but in addition had caused such bickering among the Seceders themselves that his own brethren suspended him from preaching the Word (1840), as we have noted in chapter 4.[75]

Scholte showed this same spirit of independence even more strongly in America, thanks to its "space and freedom." "This gives us," as he himself declared very frankly, "the most unrestricted freedom to apply all attempts and means God has given us, to develop, to reveal, and to spread God's kingdom."[76] His son-in-law, Jan Nollen, later declared that Scholte really could not be identified with any denomination. God's Word was his only rule. Apart from this, when he showed any preference, he was more Lutheran than Reformed. Independent as he was, he did not want to join the Reformed Church. A few days after his arrival in America he had been approached and strongly urged to do so by representatives of that church. Scholte, however, declared to them he did not care to do this "because I cannot reconcile myself with the Synodical System."[77] Later he also rejected similar attempts made by letter or through personal visits.

Scholte personally wrote in the first *Stem*, "a congregation has been formed again and elders and deacons have been elected."[78] But the "formation" of this congregation, which, it should be noted—and this was typical!—took place during Scholte's absence and without him having anything to do with it, left him—just as typically!—"neither happy nor sad!"[79] This Christian Church of Pella was an independent religious congregation. After the constitution of the Christian Church at Pella had been adopted by five elders and three deacons on November 13, it was incorporated lawfully at the county seat in Knoxville on December 2, 1848.[80]

The church order of Scholte's Christian Church adhered to the "Biblical Reformed Principles," but it did not conform to the Synod of Dordt, 1618 to 1619, like that of the Reformed Church and also that of Van Raalte. It went back to the first century, "to the Apostolic Church," which had received the teachings from Christ Jesus the Lord as the Head of the Congregation: "I am your Master and all of you are brothers."

Article I said: "The Christian Church of Pella is founded on the authority of the complete and undivided Word of God as revealed in the Holy Scriptures of the Old and New Testament. In accordance with these Holy Scriptures it recognizes the doctrinal confessions of faith of the orthodox Protestant Churches as the true standard of faith, and it is ready to practice Christian communion with all denominations that confess the same faith in God the Father, the Son, and the Holy Spirit."

Article II said: "Everyone who believes in God the Father, Son, and Holy Spirit and does not contradict this faith by his behavior can be received and recognized as a member of the congregation with the right to share in the privileges and duties of the congregation. Women are only excluded from voting or speaking on public issues except in cases of recognized necessity. In this matter an exception can also be made for children who have accepted the faith."

Article III said: "In accordance with the prescriptions of the Holy Scriptures, the congregation shall be ruled by elders and deacons, elected by and from members of the congregation who are not under censure due to misbehavior in word or deed."

Article IV lists as one of the duties of elders "to teach with the Word of God, according to the God-given ability that is given to all, in order to prepare the whole congregation to meet the Lord in a spirit of joy and trust, when He comes."

Article V lists the tasks of deacons, while Article VI says among other things: "The elders and deacons shall appoint from the elders for a period of time one elder as Chairman—one as Vice Chairman, a Secretary, and a Treasurer." The total of ten articles, based on "the principles of life depicted so gloriously by the Apostle Peter—I Peter 2:9," were signed by the five elders I. Overkamp, K. De Hoog, H. Barendregt, G. H. Overkamp, and A. J. Betten, and by the three deacons J. H. Meyer, E. F. Grafe (the German) and P. Welle.

We should note that Scholte's name does not appear even though he was an elder too. This shows again his far-reaching indifference toward any church organization. This explains why he was loath to attend any consistory meetings at all. According to Van Bergeyk, he "seldom" attended "because he was busy with colonization duties."[81] Perhaps it was also due to the mutual relationships that left much to be desired. As everywhere else, envy and even worse seemed to rule even in this ultra-Christian circle; if we can believe Van Bergeyk—Judas swayed the scepter. So the status of minister was not recognized in Pella. The elders, trained by Scholte in the Netherlands, all officiated as preachers. But Scholte even refused to be an administrative elder of the church. He went even further and sometimes considered himself completely unattached to this church organization.

Inward Christian life seemed to be improving, however. In the Netherlands, especially among the Seceders, revivals were not unknown; one could mention Uithuizermeeden, Spijk, and Bunschoten.[82] Often in America a revival brought a similar awakening, and Scholte's expectation that this would happen materialized.[83] While only much later, in 1857, '66, and '77, one hears of revival meetings among the Hollanders in the forests of Michigan, a real spiritual awakening arrived on the prairies of Iowa already in 1848. To what extent Scholte's sermons, "always so particularly strong and lively," contributed is not clear. A contemporary declared that this awakening "was not the result of church manipulation but seemingly the work of the Holy Spirit. For this purpose, the Holy Spirit did not use as a tool an outstanding revival preacher, invited for a week or more from elsewhere to do this job. Rather the Holy Spirit used a poor maidservant who could not read or write, but who had a burning heart for Jesus and his service, and who, although she did not possess the least literary knowledge, knew the Scriptures that make one wise unto salvation. She surpassed many of those skilled in literary knowledge of the Scriptures by her way of quoting Bible texts and particularly Psalm verses."[84]

This girl, Grietje Noordtzij, "one of the naughtiest children," was converted and "wherever she was and went, she spread light and warmth through the accounts of her daily communion with Jesus." "From that time on there was a continual, visible working of God's grace. Several children, young sons and young daughters, and mature adults, made public confessions of faith in Jesus Christ as their Savior and Lord. This also stirred former members of the congregation, so that now the situation has changed completely from some months past. . . . It is truly heart stirring for a Christian to hear from the mouths of children the clear and simple confession of how God worked on their souls, and to see how the love of God, poured out in their souls by the Holy Spirit, entices them to look up their former playmates and to invite them to join in their way of life. There is a zeal to examine the beloved Word of God." Scholte wrote: "Now I am doubly pleased to live in Pella, since the Lord has revealed He wants to live in our midst." And he added: "To my many Christian friends I exclaim out of the depth of my heart: 'Come and see!' "[85]

This depicts the religious atmosphere of Pella. But it should be pointed out that the members of the church were closely watched and that joining a church was a serious matter. "They were very strict in the examination of those wanting to join the congregation both as to the knowledge and experience they had of objective and subjective truth that is needed for salvation."[86]

In spite of all this, there reigned nevertheless among the Hollanders of the prairies a greater spirit of tolerance than we noticed in the woods of Michigan. Already earlier I pointed out Scholte's observation that the members of the congregation in the Netherlands had belonged to various religious groups. Also important is his declaration that, "although there are differences of opinion, they do not lead to arguments. Sometimes differences are discussed, without bitterness or enmity resulting."[87]

Of the greatest importance concerning these matters, however, is what the seemingly very well educated Salmagundist wrote about the "*fijnen*" [the ultra-orthodox], that in their daily dealings they are just as easy to get along with as the most liberal Protestants in the Netherlands.[88]

This spirit is more than evident from the fact that Scholte and other members of the congregation cooperated energetically to establish a Baptist College at Pella. They looked with favor upon this project not only for scientific reasons, but in particular for more mundane ones, for speculations in real estate.[89] Characteristic of the Pellians' breadth of mind is, in the end, the answer they gave to the repeated reproach addressed to them, that they not only tolerated a Baptist school but even frequented it: "That it is a Baptist school and not a Reformed one, we have always considered to be of very little importance in the field of scientfic education." It should be noted, though, "that both the board and the instructors are definitely Christians; they are Reformed in their inner principle. But that should be every one's conviction, regardless of the name of the Church organization one carries."

Why was this spirit so different from the one in the colony in Michigan? First of all, the people in Pella were more well-to-do and more educated. Both of these conditions led to greater tolerance in Pella. Moreover, the above mentioned "mundane" considerations that obviously manifested themselves more strongly among many well-off people also contributed to this state of affairs. In the second place, there was Scholte's attitude, who as preacher-businessman influenced through his words and deeds a large section of the colonists; he succeeded in winning over most of them to his religious and general social notions. Thirdly, on the wide prairie they had much more contact with the Americans than the settlers in the forests of Michigan.

The facts we have described so far should not give the impression that everything in Pella was idyllic. Just as Van Raalte, Scholte also had problems with his fellow colonists, and in particular with the consistory. These problems in Pella, as well as in Holland and surrounding areas, often gave rise to vehement episodes. Typical, however, is the fact that church affairs in Michigan were mostly the bone of contention, while in Iowa the causes of discord were of a purely earthly, financial nature. Matter and spirit were joined together more closely in Iowa than in Michigan.

Matter and spirit were united to such an extent that among the colonists two organizations began to be identified: the "*Vereeniging*" [Association], founded in the Netherlands and primarily concerned with business matters, and the "*Gemeente*" [Congregation], organized in Pella and concerned with church matters.[90] The material quarrels were mostly fought out in the church, that is, by the consistory. Article IX of the "Constitution," for that matter, gave cause to such proceedings. For this article declares, among other things, that the expulsion of a member on the basis of false teaching or ungodly conduct may only be decided at a regular meeting of the congregation and when the majority of the attending members has voted on it.

No less a man than Scholte himself was accused of ungodly conduct! What started it all was the fact that as president of the Vereeniging he administered the money that most members had deposited for the voyage and the purchase of land. Once everybody was settled, many people were of the opinion that a statement of account remained too long in coming. By September, 1848, as Sipma wrote, no one yet knew the exact cost of the voyage, "because there is not a single one who has a statement from Scholte."[91] In addition, they accused him of having bought the claims at "much too high a price," and that he asked even higher prices for them. "For one claim, he took $400 too much; for another, $500; and another, $600; even $700 beyond its cost. H. Vierzen had proof: he gave almost 2,000 guilders [$800] too much. The other land buyers, who had not obtained claims, had to pay $2.25 per acre—also one dollar too much. Thus operated the man who like a father should have taken a stand for his children but who now goes out to fill his own purse."

Scholte himself kept almost totally silent about these accusations and does not refer to them in the least in his *Tweede Stem* [*Second Voice*] that appeared one month after the writing of Sipma's letter. While in his *Eerste Stem* [*First Voice*], as we know, he only observed that when the Association did not assume all financial responsibilities, it became "a more personal matter [for the buyers]." His son-in-law, Jan Nollen, merely added that, "for lack of a competent bookkeeper," this became the beginning of financial entanglements, "which later on caused much friction."[92] Van Stigt and Van der Zee remained almost totally silent on this matter. Van Bergeyk, however, placed the blame on the other elders, on the "wolves, the deceitful and sneaky workers who had slipped into the vineyard of our Lord Jesus Christ." He then levels the strong accusation that one of them used $1,200 of the Association funds to buy a larger farm than he could afford and continually failed to remit this money to Scholte. As long as this remittance had not taken place, Scholte reputedly refused to give a financial account.[93]

Meanwhile, Scholte had a hard time justifying himself. "He is now strongly urged by some people to give an account and to hand over to them the proof of purchase of the land. I think he is on the verge of being summoned to appear in an American court. There is much division and confusion in the Association, not among the people, but against the board of the Association. Some support Scholte; perhaps they share in the loot." The Americans say: "He makes all the people poor." One of them said: "You have left behind you the rule of a king to be in a free land, but you yourselves have taken along a king who devours you!"[94] "It reached the point that Scholte and the Association were at loggerheads with each other; each side thought itself to be right and neither side was willing to budge an inch. Satan was really busy to promote gross division."

It is no wonder that several times the conduct of Scholte was discussed in the congregation and at the consistory. Most of the members of the Association belonged to the Christian Church, while elders G. H. Overkamp and A. J. Betten were on the board of directors of the Association. It seems that the congregation mistrusted Scholte too, because in 1849 he was censured and no longer allowed to preach for the time being![95]

With the influx of new immigrants in 1849, Bousquet and others, this tragic situation began to improve. A few, [A. C.] Kuyper and Maasdam, became elders in the consistory. Since the "forty-niners" were not directly involved in this contention and could therefore rise above both factions, they acted in a conciliatory manner both in the Association and congregation.

In the meantime Scholte had received from the land office, after waiting for nine months, the document that allowed him to proceed with the distribution of the deeds. This new development induced the consistory which now had "turned around," to decide "after a few stormy and lengthy meetings," although under protest of some members, to lift Scholte's censure.[96] So, "with an almost general consent of the congregation" Scholte could resume preaching. "On Sunday afternoon Scholte was back in the pulpit. His text was James 5:7,8. He discussed all that had taken place in a frank and wise fashion so that he also gave satisfaction to everybody. . . . No side-stepping that makes people cynical but an open and straightforward discussion, without excluding himself." It seems that the financial account was not given. No one mentions that it took place. Even Scholte's big admirer, Van Bergeyk, does not mention a word about it— and that says a lot. However, in 1898 Nollen wrote that in Scholte's opinion no one was shortchanged; "only his purse had suffered, and he felt bitter when later on he had to hear from no small number of people that he never presented a final account to the Association."[97] Did this refer to the $1,200?

Seemingly, unity was reestablished, but Scholte had lost their trust. Through the charisma of his word many remained his followers. Many felt what Sipma naively expressed: "The worship service is after all the only thing that is fairly good, but for the rest Scholte is very naughty." Not everyone could resign himself to this state of affairs. In 1851 a withdrawal [verwijdering] took place by a number of the members of the congregation. Among them were two elders, K. De Hoog and G. H. Overkamp, and one deacon, E. F. Grafe, "in addition to several of the leading members."[98] At their first meeting at De Hoog's home, the crowd was so large that they had to seek larger facilities. Grafe offered his warehouse. Here they met for a year until their "little stone church" was ready. Both elders and sometimes one of the brothers would preach in turn according to the same teachings as the "groote kerk."

Scholte must not have been the only one to blame. Bousquet wrote on September 29, 1849, "Let's leave aside, for a moment, the question whether the accusations against Scholte were justified or not. Then one can level quite some accusations at the members of the consistory, and this would be the right place to take several of them to task in a thorough manner, but what's the use, especially now that they have had their best time of bossing people around!" Mrs. Bousquet also defended Scholte when she wrote from Pella on November 28, 1852, "For a long time we have accused Scholte of judging local people too harshly, especially those who call themselves believers, but now that things are becoming more clear, he is not so wrong."[99]

The most ardent defender of Scholte, L. Van Bergeyk, "unmasked" some years later (1855–58) those very consistory members and gave us an extremely sad picture of orthodox Christian life. According to him, "a terrible hatred and aversion" were engendered against Scholte through "lies and slander," and all this in spite of the fact that "this respectable man has received from God a heart that is not mean or envious of other people's good fortune in temporal affairs."[100]

In contrast with Van Raalte, Scholte did not want to join the Reformed Church. In Michigan many reproached Van Raalte for joining the church, but in Pella some people resented Scholte's neglect in this matter.[101] From the beginning they formed a separate group, which followed the rules of the Synod of Dordt, 1618 to 1619. Later, because of the constant increase by immigration, they formed an independent church, "The Holland Reformed Church." Thus, in this young colony which had hardly rooted itself, there were already three church groups among the Dutch. This was a reflection of the spirit of its founder, that is, of his great sense of independence—a truly Dutch trait even though not uniquely so. When the struggling years of the first settlement were past, as in Michigan, disputes and divisions would become even more pronounced.

Just as in Michigan, the colonists were interested in education from the very beginning. Among the immigrants of 1847 were two teachers: I. Over-kamp and J. Muntingh.[102] Even before a school building was ready, the latter gave instruction in his large home on Garden Square. In April, 1848, the school was transferred to the church; eight school benches, "patterned after genuine Old-Dutch models," were placed in the sanctuary for this purpose. After three years Muntingh relinquished his dayschool teaching and entered business, just like A. J. Betten, the preacher. For many years he continued to hold evening classes and "in doing so he has, during that time, contributed much, on the scientific level, to those who made serious use of it." Over-kamp remained a teacher, which brought him a measure of fame. When I visited the colony, I was told that the excellent Dutch still spoken by many Pellians was due in part to his instruction.

We know that H. P. Scholte was the elected School Inspector.[103] He was assisted by I. Overkamp, who, as township secretary, was also clerk for the inspector. Scholte divided the township into five school districts. The Pella district was organized immediately and soon after that the Skunk district. I. Overkamp and J. Muntingh were now also acknowledged as "public in-structors," with H. Hospers as assistant instructor. The Pella school re-tained its original biblical Christian emphasis and kept its Dutch character. The Dutch language formed a substantial part of the curriculum. English was also taught since many had already taken up its study while in St. Louis. Reading, writing, and arithmetic were basic well-taught subjects, plus geography, history, music, and others.

The school became renowned for its Bible study, to which Overkamp, who was both elder and catechism leader, devoted much effort. "Every morning," recounts one of his former pupils, "after starting the school day with a prayer and the singing of a Psalm verse, he would explain Biblical History." He did so obviously with great success, because " . . . as a teacher of Biblical History for children and instructor of doctrinal truth for adults he has never been surpassed by anyone who has ever engaged in such service in Pella. In the first 25 years of Pella's existence he has done more substan-tial good than most of the preachers ever did, even if the latter had been at their profession for some 50 or 60 years." Among the pupils there was at first only one American, the son of the Baptist preacher, Post. "Major Post" has always been proud to have been Overkamp's pupil and to have learned Dutch from him.

That in those days the people of Pella already thought of setting up higher education was due to more accidental circumstances. The Baptists desired, as we have noted, to establish a "university" in Iowa. Various locations were considered.[104] The businessmen of Pella, with Scholte as their leader, made a strong bid to have the university come to their town and, as we shall see later, they were successful in their endeavor. Apart from this particular interest in a university, there was a general interest in further education in Pella, education extending beyond church life. The oft-mentioned A. E. Dudok Bousquet became more or less the "soul" of this cultural life. He distinguished himself by giving lectures on physics and history.[105]

Many evenings were spent by gathering to discuss church and "scientific" topics. But there were other social activities which were, although of a lower order, no less significant—visiting neighbors [uit buurten gaan]. These happy evenings of colonial times were later called "wanten parties" [mitten parties]. Anticipating the severe cold weather, the men kept busy crocheting mittens, as they had usually learned to do many years ago. When they went visiting, the men took along their crochet needles and balls of yarn. They would group themselves around the large fireplace where two or three huge blocks of wood were burning. Some of these blocks lay halfway into the room and were used as seats. Others sat on sawed-off blocks. And still others on a kind of "three-block-stack." The women sat around the so-called table by candlelight mending clothes and darning stockings. While enjoying a cup of prairie tea or sage milk, they would discuss the most varied topics. They would begin with the weather, then move on to the happenings of the day, "God's daily care," but especially their talks would be about land and its prices: about "nice forties," "a top-notch eighty," and "the most beautiful quarters [160 acres]."[106]

These evening gatherings must have happened oftener on the prairie than in the woods of Michigan since there was a greater danger of getting lost in the woods. Even though Michigan settlers visited at night, there were mostly morning and afternoon coffee klatches, which led to visiting. As they claimed, "the hospitable coffeepot was the center of social life."[107]

Not everyone felt at home in the community of Pella and its neighborhood. There were some who could not agree with the religious spirit, and there were even more people who had imagined prairie life to be far easier, and who "thought all you had to do was to wave a magic wand as in fairy tales, and a good home would jump right out of the ground." "Four male persons returned from here to St. Louis; everyone was convinced of their wrong principles. After having roamed around for a time slandering the colony, two of them ended up by enlisting for service in Mexico," Scholte wrote in his Eerste Stem. In his Tweede Stem, he added, "We have had enough problems with some of them but are fortunate to be rid of the naughtiest of them."

Thus in the colony of Scholte, as well as in the one of Van Raalte, a kind of sorting out or natural selection ["Auslese"] took place in various areas. On the whole the most energetic immigrants remained, the less energetic ones moved away, mainly to towns. The least religious ones also moved out of the colony. There was still a third selection. Those who were active in agriculture, in general, felt most at home in Marion County, but craftsmen could only make a partial living there. So they also often moved to the towns or, as happened too, while on their way to Pella, they would remain in St. Louis, Keokuk, or other towns along the route and settle there.

10

The Rooting of the Young Dutch Branch in Wisconsin and Illinois

A. The Protestant Colonies in Wisconsin

Besides the colonies in Michigan and Iowa, the fifth chapter mentioned also the religious, mostly orthodox, settlements in Wisconsin and Illinois. These settlements, interesting as they are, never reached the level of importance of the first two. The settling of Wisconsin and Illinois turned out to be easier, in spite of various difficulties. This easier settling explains the curious fact that only a very occasional colonist or descendant of colonists in these settlements felt called upon to write down "memories" or a "history," in contrast to what happened especially in Michigan, but also in Iowa. They seemed to have been far less conscious of making geography and history.

In various ways, the Wisconsin colonization differed from those in Michigan and Iowa. Properly speaking, there were hardly any leaders in Wisconsin. Numerous farmers with their families, mainly from Gelderland but also from Zeeland, were already established when Reverend [P.] Zonne and later Reverend [G.] Baay arrived. Reverend Zonne gave somewhat the impression of being a "manager." He led a number of Netherlanders from Milwaukee to Sheboygan County in 1847. This settlement in Holland Township was called the "Zonne Settlement" and later renamed Cedar Grove.

Just as Van Raalte and Scholte had done, Zonne energetically advertised his colony: "I know several people here who possessed nothing five years ago and others who had only $100 who wouldn't sell their possessions now for 2,000 guilders [$800]. Others who would not sell out for even 4,000 guilders [$1,600] were five years ago totally penniless and burdened with debts. As far as I know, we have only one poor person; he is handicapped by blindness and is given aid. There is plenty of everything, and we have sold more than $1,000 worth of fattened cattle. It is very seldom that one hears somebody complain here." So wrote Zonne in 1852 from Town Holland. For that matter, he openly admitted that he mentioned these things " . . . also with the purpose to draw others to come and live among them

293

since there is room for another 100 families. Why should we not wish to have our fellow countrymen share here with us the blessings that God gives us to enjoy!"[1] Earlier someone had called this colony "a showplace of God's Creation!"[2]

The extent of Reverend Baay's leadership is illustrated by the fact that his group of immigrants left Milwaukee to join the Michigan colony, while Baay himself journeyed on to Alto, Wisconsin, with just two families! We know that many of these colonists rated socially, and to some extent also spiritually, in between the Michigan and Iowa groups. They were neither from among the poorest, as many in Van Raalte's colony, nor from the rich, as many a colonist in Scholte's settlement. In the fifth chapter we noted they were small independent farmers and we saw that this social position was reflected in their choice of land for settlement. The land was not almost all forested as in Michigan or mainly prairie as in Iowa, but it had something of both. Woods predominated in northern Wisconsin and prairies in the southern settlements. According to Zonne, for example, in Sheboygan County there were "many trees." If a farmer bought eighty acres, " . . . all of it would be covered with trees except for a few acres."[3] Concerning Fond du Lac County, which was mostly an old lake plain southwest of Sheboygan County, Baay wrote: "Groves are few, but we have enough trees to screen off the land and for firewood."[4]

The colonization in Wisconsin was very much simplified since many bought established homes, although these homes remained "encumbered" [mortgaged], to be paid off over a number of years.[5] The Americans, just as in all other places, were ready to sell their farms, "this one for $600, another one for about $1600."[6]

For the settlers, Milwaukee, Fond du Lac, and Sheboygan were very near as market places, making trade much easier than in Michigan and Iowa. Due to that happy circumstance, the more inland settlements of Waupun and Alto, as well as the ones of Franklin, Cedar Grove, Gibbsville, and Oostburg near Lake Michigan, all flourished rather quickly. They were primarily farming communities. In 1852 Holland township alone, which supposedly had more than two thousand Dutch residents and to which Cedar Grove belonged, there existed over 200 cleared farms, totaling an estimated four to six thousand acres of tillable land. In five years the number of animals increased from 50 head of cattle to 1,000 head of milk cows and calves, 400 oxen, 500 sheep, 1,000 hogs, 50 hives of bees, and 25 horses. In addition, fishing was important. In 1852, no less than six hundred barrels of fish, each weighing two hundred pounds, were sold for $7.00 a barrel.[7]

Just as in Michigan and Iowa, people were interested in industry. Zonne hoped that summer and winter crops of rapeseed would be a rich source of income, "as soon as here also oil presses could be built."[8] The settlements in Wisconsin were also characterized by a youthful and lively optimism. But peace and quiet did not always reign here either. Just as in Pella, things must have often come to a boil in Zonne's group. Zonne, like Scholte, was a charismatic speaker. Once, when he had spoken to the Netherlanders in Sheboygan, one of them remarked that in his three years in America he had "never heard such eloquent preaching in our language about the Words of Life."[9] It is no wonder that many were simply captivated by him.

However, there were others who had different opinions. They withdrew from his influence and did not want to hear about his religious ideas. Zonne had organized his followers into a church congregation and had a church built on his own property the following year (1848), and had given it to his congregation. No one objected to this. But what was upsetting was that Zonne and his congregation joined the American Presbyterian denomination.[10] In 1849, when Reverend I. N. Wyckoff of the Reformed Church came to visit Wisconsin, he endeavored to have the Netherlanders join this "Dutch" church. It is true that Wyckoff did not have time to visit Holland township, Waupun, and Alto, since he had been detained in Michigan too long—he only came to Milwaukee—but his visit brought some results nevertheless. Some Netherlanders of the "Zonne settlement" desired to join the Reformed Church and founded their own church congregation in Cedar Grove. Zonne's church stood about one mile north of this town.[11]

Thus in the "Badger State" the seed of separatism was also growing and Zonne "who called himself here a '*Dominie*'" lost favor in the eyes of many people. Some even questioned his competence to marry couples. Truly interesting in this respect is a communication that appeared in the *Sheboygan Nieuwsbode* [*Sheboygan News Messenger*] of March 2, 1850, written by P. Groothof and M. A. Zumen of Holland, Wisconsin, saying that they had been married six months earlier by Zonne "but having learned about the presumptuous authority of this gentleman they had followed the example set by many others to do it all over again."[12]

Another notification had appeared in the newspaper several days before: "Most if not all the Hollanders in Town Holland, Wisconsin, wish for a pastor. May they soon rejoice in having a minister and shepherd."[13] It appears that most likely this writing flowed from the pen of one of Zonne's opponents, and should thus be accepted with reservations. However, so many remained followers of Zonne that his church was not only the largest and most important, but in 1853 a second Presbyterian church had to be built four and a half miles north of Cedar Grove along the so-called Sauk Trail. Later on, a Reformed congregation was also established here, as well as in Gibbsville and Oostburg.[14]

There were sharp divisions among the brothers in Holland Township. Contributing to this situation was the fact that the preacher Zonne, in many respects just as Scholte in Pella, appeared to be more "Americanized" than his people and even seemed worldly at times! What must one think of the fact that while in Michigan Van Raalte tried to prevent the sale of liquor, in Wisconsin whisky was sold by—Zonne! "Fellow countrymen! Christians!"

someone in the *Sheboygan Nieuwsbode* questioned, "shall nothing be attempted to replace this unworthy man with a worthy servant of the Lord?"[15]

Also in Waupun and Alto, life in the pioneer years must not have been
idyllic. Van Raalte, who visited these settlements in 1850, found "much
bitterness and division" among our fellow countrymen. Also here some had
initially joined the Presbyterians. Reverend Baay, however, saw to it that his
congregation, spread out over the places mentioned above, joined the Reformed church. They totaled more than thirty families, of which number
forty individuals were confessing members. At the suggestion of Reverend
Wyckoff, Baay affiliated with Classis Holland in Michigan.[16] This was the
cause of all that strife.

It is to be remembered, though, that the first Dutch colonists in Wisconsin did not belong to the Secessionists. Separatists, like Sleyster, Zonne,
and others, came later. Moreover, most of these Secessionists belonged to
the moderate, so-called Gelderland branch. That is why many of these
colonists felt at home in the Presbyterian Church, especially when they
lived among Americans.[17] Others had no difficulty feeling comfortable in the
Reformed Church, and they showed far fewer objections to this move than
did people in Michigan.

Also in religious matters the Wisconsin settlers held the middle between
the far more narrow-minded fellow countrymen in Michigan and the many
even more liberal Dutch in Iowa.

All these circumstances contributed to the fact that these settlements
exerted little influence on the various currents among the Dutch in
America.[18] Thus we have indicated the lack of gifted, highly educated
leaders such as Van Raalte and Scholte undoubtedly were, but there was
especially the tendency to stick to the "happy mean," to the middle of the
road in everything—which has considerably hastened their Americanization
without great shocks! After all, it is the extremes, either good or bad, that
provide leadership.

B. The Settlements in Illinois

The Illinois settlements also lacked leaders like Van Raalte and Scholte.
Apart from that, the villages of High Prairie and Low Prairie showed some
similarities to the Iowa colony. Both villages, like Pella, were prairie villages.
The southerly High Prairie, as we noted, was settled by well-to-do Zuid
Holland farmers in 1847 and the northwesterly Low Prairie was founded in
1848 by Noord Holland farmers, among whom there also were well-off men.

At the start, the Zuid Hollanders lived in tents, while two years later the
Noord Hollanders found housing in a few distant vacated homes until
dwellings could be erected. In High Prairie log homes were built and in Low
Prairie, plank dwellings. The logs were obtained from trees in the Calumet
valley and the planks came from Chicago.

After the first settling difficulties had been overcome, the farmers in both locations, just as in Pella, turned first of all to raising cattle and to the production of butter and cheese, and secondly, to the tilling of the soil. R. A. Gouwens, a descendant of one of the Zuid Holland pioneers, stated: "The experienced dairy men from the Netherlands were endowed with natural aptitude to make rich cheese and pure butter from the milk brought home by their lowing herds."[19] In 1849 a Noord Holland colonist bought three beautiful milk cows and eleven sheep for the sum of $42![20] Oxen, cattle, and sheep were purchased at relatively low prices. Also poultry was immediately acquired and "flocks of ducks and chickens brought new life to the barnyards of the new settlers." In order to grow corn, many a newcomer began immediately to plow his fields with the aid of oxen. Soon after they added potatoes, oats, and hemp.

There were plenty of inconveniences that resulted from this new life of colonization on the frontier. Some who had built their own homes still had to use an umbrella in the house in order to keep dry during a rain storm. Often sleep was interrupted by howling prairie wolves. Many colonists, because of the migrating Potawatomi Indians along the Calumet River, felt insecure. There were also the problems resulting from mixed farming, from raising cattle and crops; cattle would break into the corn-fields and destroy the crops. "When on some September morning a farmer awoke and looked through his little bedroom window at his promising corn crop and discovered his neighbor's cows in the act of devouring it, his wrath was stirred to fever heat, first at the cows, then at their owner." Just as in other places, fencing had to be installed. Wood had to be chopped along the Calumet River and split into "rails." Repeatedly the hungry cattle learned how to destroy the fences. "For any fearless animal with strong horns it was a simple performance to remove a few rails of the fence and make a free for all feast in a neighbor's crop for a drove of cattle.... Such provoking inconsistences [sic] often led to lasting neighborhood grudges."[21]

In one respect both prairie towns were very favored, compared to Pella. The important market place of Chicago was nearby and from there they also received their mail by oxcart. Low Prairie was twenty miles and High Prairie just thirteen miles south of the "Windy City." Going to market in Chicago initially still took much time. After products like potatoes, eggs, butter, a few bags of corn, and sometimes a slaughtered calf or sheep, were loaded, the Low Prairie farmer, in a wagon drawn by a span of oxen, would begin his trip at about ten or eleven o'clock in the evening so that he could reach Chicago by dawn. Having busied himself during the day selling his goods and purchasing needed supplies, he would spend the night in town, and return well-rested the next day, arriving back home in the late afternoon.

Some Low Prairie farmers like Van Vuren and Arentse lived north of the Calumet River; others like De Jong and Gouwens lived south of it. Especially during high-water periods of the river, traveling back and forth was difficult, since there was no bridge in the early years. Not until 1849 was a "frail structure" built.

Not all of the products were transported to Chicago. For both prairie villages the nearest store was in Blue Island, which was located six miles from High Prairie. The prices that could be commanded there were usually the same as in Chicago. These prices, like those of cattle, were low: Butter went for eight cents and cheese for four cents a pound!

For years Low Prairie remained exclusively a farming and cattleraising community. Just about everybody was a farmer, and everybody brought his products to market independently. The "grocery man," so typical in any American town, was not to be found for years. The proximity of Chicago and especially the fact that most of the colonists were farmers explains the remarkable phenomenon that it took until 1855 before the first store was opened—the "first general merchandise store" of L. Van der Bilt—and it took until 1869 before Pieter De Jong was appointed as their first postmaster.

High Prairie, though nearer Chicago, developed from the very beginning in a more diversified way. It was located on a busy highway, the former "Old Indian Trail" to Canada, now called Michigan Avenue. This area's growth was promoted by the town's favorable location for transportation and especially the mixed character of Noord Holland immigrants. There were not only farmers and cattle raisers but also fishermen and some well-educated people among whom a teacher, Piet De Jong, who had assumed leadership for this migration.[22] There was also Cornelis Kuyper, a young, energetic man who became the "business leader," and as often happens, since the two tend to go together, he became also the "leading politician" in the settlement.[23]

Kuyper soon opened High Prairie's first store on Michigan Road. He functioned not only as a "druggist" but even more or less practiced as a doctor. Shortly thereafter Goris Van der Sijde began a second store. Hiram Van der Bilt, who came to Chicago in 1847 and later moved to Calumet, erected a third store. High Prairie was the first to have a post office. In 1852 it was the first [Dutch] settlement to be connected with a railroad, the Michigan and Illinois Central Railroad. The coming of the railroad boosted land prices considerably and its construction provided jobs for many a Dutchman.[24]

Piet De Jong kept taking care of the spiritual training in the colony. For years in High Prairie, he was "their spiritual as well as educational advisor," and as "Meester De Jong," their first school teacher.[25] The church services of both villages were at first jointly held in Low Prairie. As we noted previously, Reverend Wust organized a congregation at Low Prairie in 1848 while High Prairie citizens set up their own congregation in September of 1849. In 1850 people of High Prairie built a church. Reverend Wust left for the eastern states in 1854 and served in turn the Dutch congregations at Buffalo, Rochester, and Lodi. From Lodi he returned to the Netherlands in

1878.[26] In February 1855, a new minister came to the prairie villages from Michigan. His name was Reverend Ypma, who had first served the congregation of Vriesland and then the one of Graafschap. One Sunday he would preach at High Prairie and the next Sunday in Low Prairie.

C. The Roman Catholic Settlements in Wisconsin

In addition to the generally orthodox Protestant colonization ventures in Michigan, Iowa, Wisconsin, and Illinois, the Roman Catholic settlement along the Fox River Valley in "the heart of Wisconsin" is worthy of close scrutiny. Like the first designated colonies, it was also religious in character and thus ranked among the most successful ones. The Fox River settlement resembled the Michigan colony as to the type of people and consequently as to their choice of location. Here we come also in contact with spiritual leaders, Father [Theodorus] Van den Broek and the less-known Father [Adrian D.] Gothard [Godhert], who led a great number of generally poor Roman Catholic countrymen to the first available and suitable territory, the forests in northeastern Wisconsin. Thus forest colonies were established, just as in Michigan.

In some ways there was a difference. The Roman Catholic colonists came to a region where their main leader, Van den Broek, had labored for thirteen years as a missionary among the Menominee and Winnebago Indians. Therefore, he was well acquainted with the region and its people. Also, their location was on the Fox River, which was a very important water transportation channel. The mouth of this river had been discovered by Jean Nicolet in 1634. At this site the French had built a fort in 1721, which later developed into the Roman Catholic town of Green Bay. When the Dutch came in 1848 it was inhabited by some 150 whites, mainly English, French, and German.

Generally, the Netherlanders first came to established places like Green Bay, Bay Settlement, and Little Chute, and from there they proceeded deeper into the forest. Little Chute and Green Bay were almost exclusively inhabited by Indians. Gradually as the whites moved in, the Indians moved out. They were replaced in part by German, French, and Canadian migrants. With their help, Van den Broek, before his departure to the Netherlands, had cleared the land to make it productive and brought improvements and embellishments to the village. He had also built a church "seventy feet long" with a tower, laid out a beautiful cemetery, and erected a house and a school. His congregation numbered five hundred souls.[27] Little Chute, Kaukana [Kaukauna], Wrightstown, De Pere, and Kimberley along or near the Fox River, were no more genuine Dutch settlements than the Protestant towns of Waupun and Alto. The town names generally reflect this fact.

We do well to keep in mind that in those days these towns did not amount to much. The thickly tangled, almost unpenetrable forest reached to the edge of the river. When the Netherlanders came to Little Chute, it lacked all kinds of necessities of life. There were no homes; during the first summer no one had a house; they lived in very primitive huts, just as in Michigan. Jan Verboort, one of the pioneers, reported later, "No one had a stove either and all had to get along the best they could with a kettle or pan brought from Holland to cook and fry the little bit of food they possessed outside over an open fire or baked in the ashes. Usually, bread had to be baked in the ashes or under hot stones and the results were often mediocre. However, if a woman was once in a while so lucky that the bread had turned out so well that when she threw it against a tree and it stuck slightly, or not at all, she would go to the neighbors to display her skills as a miracle of the time, and hear them praise her baker's skill; then she had to tell everybody how she had accomplished it."

As you remember, Holland, formerly called Franciscus Bosch, was the only all-Dutch village. Land in this vicinity was obtained from the government for a dollar an acre and could be paid in installments. Just as in other places, things started out in a primitive way; people lived in huts made of branches. The walls and roof were covered with bark from birch trees. As in Holland, Michigan, they subsequently built a road to connect with the main highway, which ran from Calumet County to Green Bay. "But how powerless they stood there with the few axes and saws brought along from the Motherland. They were facing pine trees and maple trees, heavy and tall, and majestic oaks whose tops were intertwined with the tops of others!" All that magnificent timber had to be destroyed! There were no roads to transport it. The colonists had no wagons or horses at that time. They would not have been able to use them anyway because the forests were so dense that there was not even room to pile up the timber. "Together for two years they chopped and burned the trees until at last through a united effort they had reached their goal. Now they had a road useful for incoming and outgoing traffic." Now they could buy a few oxen and in the winter, when snow was deep, transport logs by sleigh to the highway and sell the most beautiful trees for eighteen or twenty-five cents a piece. Some inventive immigrants designed a wagon with wheels made of thick cross-sections of huge trunks. If someone went to Green Bay for needed supplies these wheels would break as they hit one of the many stumps left standing there as elsewhere. Therefore, equipment was always taken along to make a new wheel on the way. A journey to and from Green Bay could take a week!"[28]

Slowly log homes replaced tents. Potatoes and other crops could be planted among the stumps. Peas were the main dish during the first two years for breakfast, lunch, and dinner. A brew from the peas substituted for coffee. There was an abundance of game but they had no guns. It took three years before they had homegrown corn to bake bread. The nearest house was three miles from the town of Holland. There were no other homes within five miles! After many years a store was set up in Kaukana on the river at a distance of "only" six miles from the town of Holland! Money was scarce and most of the trade was in the form of barter.

Most of these colonists were religious and the church had the important task of taking care of their spiritual needs. A few days after their arrival in Franciscus Bosch, Father Gothard held the first Holy Mass. They used two stumps connected with branches and covered with a white cloth as an altar under the open sky. As soon as possible a simple church was built where they could gather on Sunday. After Gothard left, they were without spiritual guidance but continued to meet there. Then the prayers at Mass were read aloud, after which the rosary or Stations of the Cross followed. Sometimes religious instructions were read from a book. A few years passed by and the colony began to spread out with the coming of a few German and Irish families, and a new shepherd, Father F. Spierings, arrived. He built his own home in the settlement.

The believers in Little Chute attended Holy Mass and Vespers in the existing mission church. Some people who lived further inland often had to travel thirteen to fifteen miles to attend these Sunday worship services.[29] As in Holland, Michigan, this was no problem for true believers!

Education in Little Chute was given in a parochial school. J. H. Wigman, the Amsterdamer, one of the most prominent men among these immigrants, was their first school teacher. At the strong urging of Father Van den Broek he had joined the immigrants and became their loyal friend and advisor. He taught the children in the lower elementary grades and trained them in catechism and prepared them for their first Holy Communion.

In these days of struggling in the forest, where more than elsewhere they needed support from one another, there existed a "spirit of brotherly love." The priests gave a good example and people encouraged each other. They realized that they could not go back, so everyone worked and slaved, and many were happy.

Besides religious affairs, during the first years they found time for fun and playing games. During Shrovetide preceding Lent, for instance, a bird would be carved from pinewood and attached to a pole or tree, and whoever shot it down would be king. For this feat, he would be rewarded with a silver heart or plaque, which he could wear on holidays, and he was obligated to treat everybody. Thus Old World games were brought to the new land and people played them cheerfully; those days were also the occasion for merry dancing.[30] Later, with nostalgia, many a pioneer would think of the good old days, "when all of us were in the midst of the forest, and everybody was just as poor as everybody else; we lived in a far more pleasant and friendlier way with each other than now."[31] But not everybody felt that way. Some moved to cities, while others reluctantly took in stride the misery of those early days.

The leaders, as in Michigan, were conveniently blamed for all that went wrong. In this case it was Van den Broek who was the scapegoat. G. Van den Elsen, who had confidential conversations with many pioneers, found out "that many heaped loads of reproaches on the good shepherd."[32] Only after he had died, three years after settling, did they begin to realize their loss. It was on All Saints Day in 1851 that Van den Broek celebrated a solemn Holy Mass. After the Holy Mass, while speaking to his flock about the glories of heaven and its saints, he suffered a stroke and fell into the arms of young Father [Frans Eduard] Daems, O.S.C., who had recently arrived in Wisconsin along with De Jonge and Nuyts, both Crozier Fathers, and Father Verhoeff. Van den Broek was in a coma until November 5 and then died. His funeral was held on November 9. "Large was the gathering of Netherlanders around the grave and they prayed to God with tears in their eyes for the soul's rest of this worthy, indeed holy, priest." A year before, by a written document, he had willed all of his possessions to the congregation of Little Chute, "for whom he had been a father in the most extensive meaning of this beautiful word." His name is not listed among the canonized Saints. "The Hollanders canonized him in their hearts; vox populi, vox Dei."

Van den Broek had been of importance not only for the Hollanders but even more so for others. "Filled with a burning zeal to gain souls for Christ," he labored among Indians, Frenchmen, Germans, Irishmen, Englishmen, etc., who owe him a debt of gratitude. He is to be thanked for supporting and comforting them in "the Forests" of Little Chute and the Green Bay area.

In 1894, when people did some excavating under the church in Little Chute, they rediscovered his grave. Today a splendid group of statues, representing the Holy Virgin Mother handing a rosary to St. Dominic, decorates his tomb to the left of the Sanctuary and carries the Latin inscription: "In remembrance of the Honorable Th. van den Broek, our first and very beloved Father. Little Chute 1833–1851. His most grateful Children." "If the voices of those whom he assisted could rise from the tomb, they would number hundreds, if not thousands. Wisconsin, at least owes his memory a debt of gratitude which can never be cancelled."[33]

Thus already during these years of rooting, Little Chute and Franciscus Bosch lost their leaders, one through death and the other through moving away. This meant that colonization in this area never was characterized by a personal imprint. Subsequently the following spiritual leaders served Little Chute, each in turn: the Honorable W. De Jonge, Ed. Daems, and W. Verhoeff, and others. In due time the Hollanders spread out from Little Chute, and with the Irish, Germans, and others, formed new colonies, which were at first exclusively farming communities. Green Bay, from the beginning, was the center of trade and industry.

D. Forgotten (Partially Run-down) Settlements

Not all the attempts around 1850 of Netherlanders to colonize by means of village settlements were successful. For example, we think of Bonnema's settlement of Frisia near the Mississippi in western Wisconsin. After a few years it evaporated, so to speak. Its colonists left and spread among the

Americans. The names of some of them we encounter again among Dutch-men who had settled elsewhere. The unifying strength of a common religion, whether embodied or not in a religious leader, was lacking. Mere ethnic ties, so strong particularly among Frisians, were not enough to allow them to tackle in unison the difficulties related to the move from one country to another.

There was still another Dutch settlement that did not take root. This settlement was planted with a different motive in mind than the ones we have discussed so far. These people had not been prepared in the Netherlands to immigrate, neither had they joined more or less spontaneously into one group. This particular case was the brainchild, as would happen so often then and later, of land speculators. At that time, the leader of the group was P. J. G. Hodenpijl.[34] Hodenpijl came to the United States in 1840 and from 1843 to 1846 he was professor of modern languages at New Brunswick, N.J. It is in all likelihood due to his contacts with the Reformed Church that its members appointed him in the Spring of 1847 as "general agent" of the "Netherlands Society for the Protection of the Emigrants from Holland."[35] This society had been organized by members of that church, among whom was Reverend [Thomas] De Witt. Because of this official position, Hodenpijl obviously had regular contacts with land owners. To those realtors belonged one of the relatively many Old-Dutch Americans living in and around Grand Rapids, P. B. Bostwick. He had bought a number of sections of land north of the Grand River on its right tributary, Crockery Creek. He intended to found a Dutch colony there, and appointed Hodenpijl as manager of the project. According to Van Raalte, Hodenpijl "was known as the leader of the Hollanders and member of that Society, so often reorganized and reshuffled, and formed, as the saying went, to protect the Hollanders." Neither did Reverend Baay and others have a good word to say about this Society, also known as the "True Netherlands Society."[36]

Hodenpijl's method of contacting prospects was as shady as his "Society." Many Hollanders were led to believe that his colony was connected with Van Raalte's. In New York, "Dutch newspapers" were printed and in Holland agents were busy to attract the stream of immigrants. "Especially at 'Grand Haven' they attempted to take the emigrants to this place with the Grandville Steamboat. . . . Yet, we have no connections in the least with them," was Van Raalte's statement.

Although numerous Netherlanders did settle in the Grand River Valley— at the end of 1854, there were about six hundred Dutchmen settled around Grand Rapids alone[37] —the planned settlement on the Creek, that was subsequently called Ravenna, failed to grow. Hodenpijl and his wife were among the first settlers. Later others came: J. and A. d'Ooge, [L.] Vos, Winckel [John Winkels], and others. Attempts were even made to have a young minister join this colony, which was a procedure that has been followed until today by land companies in America that want religious Netherlanders to settle on their land.

The well-known, somewhat eccentric Reverend H. J. Budding accepted the invitation to settle in Ravenna. This was truly against the wishes of his Groningen Consistory, but he felt compelled "by inner urgings of his heart and by observation of the ways of divine Providence" to move to America in 1848.[38] He settled in New York and must have become acquainted with the "gentlemen" there. Through his activities, others also came to the Creek, "which was spoken of very highly" and through which ran an important highway to Muskegon. A. Pleune, Sr., was one of them, but at his arrival at the Creek he looked in vain for "a town" or "village." At that time there lived in the "settlement," except for the families already mentioned, only a single farmer, Jan Roelofs. (Roloffsen), on a farm with ten acres of cleared land.

The restless, hypersensitive Budding, who had already roamed around all of Van Raalte's colony, did not feel at home at Crockery Creek either. Already in Van Raalte's colony some of his extreme oddness had been demonstrated: he refused a call to serve the village of Groningen because, although not being present when it happened, he had found out that at meals people had not prayed for him either before or afterwards![39] His departure from Crockery Creek prompted the others to follow suit. Pleune lived in Ravenna for seven years and then moved to Grand Rapids where others had gone. Later a son of a settler remarked that this group should have had the leadership of a clergyman.

Bostwick and Hodenpijl had understood this need. But Budding, their choice of a minister, was certainly the least qualified to fill this need. This erratic preacher bought a farm near Baltimore, Maryland. He "farmed" it with a widow, but when she wanted to marry him he fled taking only a small suitcase with clothes with him. Budding remarked a good many times that "never did I thank God more deeply from my heart then when I saw the coast of Holland again!" He was thoroughly cured of all sympathies for America.[40]

There was yet a third Dutch colony that failed to develop. A young man of the "Lower Betuwe," the sixth and youngest scion of a minister's family, had been trained as a carpenter and made a living as a construction engineer. He thought often about the New World. "But since America at that time was considered to be a land that drew only rogues and thieves I had not dared mention it."[41] After the death of his mother in 1849 he decided to go to America. That same year he left by way of Rotterdam for Boston. He wandered around in America for a few years where one of his jobs was to help build the Union Pacific Railroad.

When a few Netherlanders, among whom was Messchert Van Vollenhoven who later became mayor of Amsterdam, wished to found a colony with some Netherlanders, R. [likely J. H. Redelaar, Jr.], the preacher's son, knew just the right place. It was called Grand Island, surrounded by the waters of the Niagara, and located between Buffalo and Niagara Falls. In 1836 Beukma had already told us that this island had belonged to Noach, a rich

Israelite of New York who was unsuccessful in establishing a Jewish colony there. Finally, he had sold it to the "Holland Land Company, which is now in the process of selling it for a high price, according to what people say."[42] In the early fifties it still belonged to the Holland Land Company. [?] Tallman was its representative in New York, while the lawyer [?] Smit of Buffalo was one of its agents. R. approached the latter.

With the necessary information R. returned to the Netherlands, but the plans of Messchert Van Vollenhoven and associates were finally not acceptable to him. Therefore, R. decided to form his own party of colonists and go to America. About thirty-four Netherlanders joined this group—six families and a few unmarried persons. They left in 1851 with R., who had partly advanced their traveling expenses. R. had bought more than five hundred acres on Grand Island for $17 an acre. So R. established his colony. Wood cutting and the sale of lumber was to be their main source of income. An American was hired to train the Netherlanders.

They prospered and lumber sales increased. R. negotiated contracts with several railroads and other companies to deliver firewood and railroad ties. He even bought a few boats to transport lumber from his own harbor where he had built a pier. Later he bought another 150 acres and subsequently an additional 330 acres, but he paid $30 an acre rather than the old price.[43] In 1852 his two brothers, one a Doctor of Philosophy joined them with forty-five other Netherlanders. Later a brother-in-law with his wife and child also came. This prosperous Dutch colony drew the attention of men like D. Buddingh and O. Van Rees in the Netherlands.[44] However, it did not last in the long run, ironically just like Bonnema's colony in Wisconsin, due to its growing prosperity. Once the Dutch workers were making very good wages and could pay off their debts and save, many decided to leave for the Far West, to invest their savings in cheap land and be their own boss. After all, they had never been true-blooded lumberjacks. Their place was taken mostly by Germans, "who were actually much better workers."[45]

When a school was established and religious training was also given, the number of Germans was already so great that a German Lutheran preacher was called to serve them. As a typical reflection of the spiritual state of affairs, it should be mentioned that the first couple he married were Roman Catholic! In addition to Germans and a few Americans, R. hired twenty Canadians, who were "the best lumber jacks I have ever hired." The island even became a separate township and R. was its chosen justice of the peace. In 1864, R. left for the Netherlands for a few years and returned in 1870. In the meantime the German population had greatly expanded, with an occasional stranded Netherlander among them. A second German church was built. R. and his wife returned to the Netherlands for good in 1875, after having sold his possessions "for a good price, considered at the time even a very high price," to an American of Dutch descent, named [?] Schermerhorn, who was postmaster of Buffalo.[46]

This is a unique example of a colony that after a few years already partly lost its Dutch character due to increasing prosperity. However, it deserves to be mentioned, for it gives us again a good example of Dutch entrepreneurship. It also demonstrates that in those days also the non-religious Netherlanders felt that "westward does the Star beckon!"

We should mention another "Dutch colony" that, however "Dutch" it seems to be at present, never really has made a point of the fact, as far as I know, that it was Dutch.[47] Earlier I remarked that when Van Raalte was looking for a place to plant a colony, he considered the Saginaw Valley in Michigan. But instead, he chose the Black River area. However, there were Netherlanders who did settle and establish homes in the Saginaw Valley at the invitation of interested parties. According to Bercovici, this already took place "early in 1840." The administration of Michigan encouraged this colonization. As Van Schelven wrote, the Michigan government donated five thousand acres in 1848 "for opening and improving the road of Metamora to the Holland Colony, in the County of Tuscola, and for building a free bridge across the Cass River at or near Hurd's mill so-called." One can indeed speak here of a Dutch colony because in 1849 another gift of three thousand acres took place "for the benefit of the Holland Colony *already formed and settled* in the counties of Saginaw and Tuscola."[48]

This colony has rarely been mentioned since, even among the Black River colonists. The reason was probably that those who had settled in the fertile Saginaw Valley were mostly Dutch Roman Catholics, and Calvinists were not interested in Roman Catholics. The colonists of Saginaw did not write about their colony. Very few were educated except for an occasional priest. Most likely they did not realize the significance of their settlement. That is understandable because their settlement did not become a "colony" in the sense of Holland, Michigan; Pella; etc.; that is, an exclusively Dutch colony. Even more than in Wisconsin, other nationalities established themselves among the Hollanders in the Saginaw Valley.

The core of Essexville was made up mostly of Belgians and Frenchmen. The Netherlanders, like real Germanic people who are more accustomed to "*Einzelsiedlung*" [independent settling], lived quite widely scattered around the town.[49] The Roman Catholics from the sandy region of Noord Brabant and Limburg settled mostly in the forests of Wisconsin. The Roman Catholics from the clay soils of the Land of Maas and Waal moved to the Saginaw Valley, which was also characterized by heavy clay soils. As was the case among the Calvinists, there was a certain "sorting out" and selection among these groups too.

In the Saginaw Valley itself, in turn, another selection took place, as happened everywhere else. The farmers, as we know, settled in and around Essexville. Those who were interested in business and industry chose mostly to go to Bay City and Saginaw. Also around these cities farmers endeavored to make a living. It was only years later, because of the religious leaders, [H. J. H.] Schutjens [Schutjes] and [G. Van den] Elsen, that more Dutch Roman Catholics were added to this community.

When Van den Elsen came to visit Essexville, it reminded him strongly of the Netherlands: "Truly I can hardly imagine that I am still in America. One sees Dutch-style ditches and hedges, neat roads, linden, beech, and oak trees, cloudy skies, level ground without hills, sugar beets, heavy-built work horses and farmers' wagons, orchards, and a few gravel roads lined with trees, etc. just like around Zevenbergen or the Land of Maas and Waal. I only see a difference in the way houses are built, all made of planks, and I notice an even greater difference in life style and prosperity."[50] Van den Elsen met several farmers there who had indeed come from the Maas and Waal region in the Netherlands. These circumstances, in addition to similarities of soil and weather that indeed also remind one of the Netherlands, must have made this deep impression on him.

E. Netherlanders in the Cities

Not all immigrants, as we have often noted, settled in the various colonies. Van Schelven wrote that as the immigrants went West, hundreds remained in cities along the way.[51] Some stayed to find work, due to lack of money, but they also often lagged due to lack of energy. Some stayed temporarily to save some money in order to continue their trek; others stayed permanently. That is why one could already find numerous Netherlanders—not always the most desirable ones—in port cities like New York, Baltimore, and others. The better type of folks would be found in towns on or near the highways to the West: in Paterson, Albany, Rochester, Buffalo, Dunkirk, Clymer, Cleveland, and Detroit, and on the highways to Michigan, Illinois, and Wisconsin.[52] Others, as they tried to cross the Great Lakes to those states, would settle in port cities like Chicago, Milwaukee, Sheboygan, and Grand Haven. On their way to Iowa only a few remained in New Orleans, due to the hot climate there. More Netherlanders ended their trip in St. Louis when they came from the East. Numerous Dutch people could be found in cities on the Mississippi that were crossing points from east to west: Dubuque, Davenport, Burlington, and Keokuk.

In all of these cities that were still growing and developing, there was plenty of work and wages were excellent. Especially the manual workers felt at home in those type of cities, but many a farmhand did so too. Yet many of the latter were drawn too strongly to the settlements to remain in these cities permanently. Therefore the Dutch population in several of these towns fluctuated greatly and for the most part even disappeared as time went on.

Besides these stragglers, there were others who reached a settlement but did not like it because of the adverse conditions connected with pioneer life, or because they could not find a job to their liking there. This happened quite often with artisans. Therefore, as we already know, many persons left the colonies and settled in nearby cities. One could find these "colony drop outs" in towns like Allegan, Kalamazoo, Grand Rapids, Muskegon, and elsewhere all around Van Raalte's settlement. Of the Scholte group, one could find some in St. Louis and Keokuk, while those of Father Van den Broek's colony were in Green Bay. Chicago was also the melting pot of "drop outs" from all these areas.

It should thus be stressed once again that a sorting out took place at two levels: psychologically and socially. In general, one could say that in the first place those who were most energetic and determined stayed in the colonies. The result was that they made their influence felt in those colonies and, in turn, in America. In the second place, it must be pointed out that the more well-to-do were able, very obviously, to cope more easily with the pioneering problems that were encountered than those who were less well-off or even poor. Therefore, the latter also dropped out. In addition, circumstances were such that in the colonies, farmers and farm hands were the ones who most readily found jobs. The land owners and those whose livelihood depended on farming generally stayed in the colonies, in contrast to the non-owners, to whom also belonged most of the artisans, who more readily found jobs in the cities. Generally one can say that, taking into account this sorting-out process, no matter how great their economic significance ever became, the influence of the town Hollanders on American society is less than the influence of the truly colony Hollanders.

The religious conviction of the immigrants undoubtedly has greatly influenced this sorting-out process. More than once before, I have indicated that a common faith is the tie that strongly binds. However, one should not overestimate the strength of this tie, and think, for instance, that only or primarily the "believers" were able to cope with the harsh conditions in the settlements. Even faith, no matter how mighty, could not prevent "colony drop outs." This is clearly shown in the remarkable life of Bastiaan Broere, a Zeeland emigrant. It was his religious conviction, influenced by a letter of Reverend Budding, which had led him to go to America in spite of all the supplications of his mother, sisters, brothers, and friends who urged him to stay. As he said, "It seemed to me that the Netherlands were forsaking the truth more and more and abandoning God. This and this alone was the only reason I felt the inclination of leaving my Fatherland. My temporal interests did not in the least compel me to leave. On the contrary, they made me very reluctant because I feared that in America I would have to make a living by farming, which I hated, because since childhood I had been on water. But my desire to be over there and have communion with God's people, who were also my people, overcame this objection."[53]

In 1849 Broere, with a few other fellow travelers, arrived in the "Zeeland village" of Michigan at the home of Reverend Van der Meulen. "We were treated generously, after having received a warm and friendly welcome; and after a few days of rest, people found us jobs and a place to stay." Like so many others, Broere was not satisfied with wages that consisted of "plenty of pork and wheat flour." "Being unmarried and without a home of my own, I declined this offer, and since in that particular location there was not a chance of obtaining a monetary reward, I was forced to look for it elsewhere. And so I moved to Grand Rapids where I was more successful."

As we noted before, many religious people did as Broere did. Their great numbers are shown by the fact that, as we shall see later, in the towns that lie around the settlements in Michigan and elsewhere, there soon were organized religious congregations. Perhaps one would not have expected such a development, but a fact is that most of the orthodox Netherlanders are not primarily to be found in the settlements, but in the cities. The city of Grand Rapids became and still is today the cradle of the orthodox.

On the other hand, as repeatedly and aptly stated by the Reverend Father G. Van den Elsen, many of the immigrants were not generally the best of church attenders.[54] It was the heavy demands and struggles for life in the New World, in addition to the example set by others, that drove them to search for support from a Higher Power. And these initial "unbelievers" became not the least successful among the colonists. The Van der Veen family of Holland, Michigan, is one of the best examples. Thus in the first place it was not religion, but often the psychological and social attitude of the immigrants that determined whether colonists would establish themselves permanently in one of the settlements or in one of the cities.

Those who lived in the cities, and who did not have to struggle with the difficulties of pioneer life, were never considered to be colonists, declared G. Van Schelven a few years ago and with the emphasis of a real colonist.[55] With this statement, he put the spotlight on a contrast which, although it was not sharply defined in every situation, nevertheless was a fact of immigrant life. In its consequences this split manifested itself not only in religious life (greater versus lesser orthodoxy) and in economic life (artisans versus farmers), but also in political life. Even the process of Americanization was shaped by the influence of this duality. Already in the years of rooting, the fast pace of this development was noticed in the settlements. A correspondent in Detroit affiliated with the *New York Tribune* stated in that paper on October 8, 1853, that the Hollanders of the Van Raalte colony not only "persevere under the difficulties incident to Western life with the most unflagging energy" but they also accept Western ideas and lifestyles with "a striking aptitude."[56]

How extremely slowly, and contrary to expectations perhaps, this process developed in the towns, at least in places where the Netherlanders settled in somewhat larger numbers, as for instance in Grand Rapids, is shown by a statement of the American |Alden| Jewell in that city in 1913. Jewell declared that the Hollander, "however ameliorated may be his present mode of living and however much he may have become adapted, is still a Hollander."[57] This fact does not apply only to our countrymen, but is also true for other nationalities, as may be concluded for instance, from Bercovici's *Around the World in New York*. I may not call Dutch city dwellers "colonists," yet we are accustomed to speak of Dutch and other ethnic "colonies" especially when they group themselves more or less on the basis of ethnic or religious grounds.

Religious convictions rather than ethnic awareness soon drew the Netherlanders together. Already before 1849, a church was established by the immigrants in Albany and shepherded by Reverend A. B. Veenhuizen, a brother-in-law of Brummelkamp. In Rochester, an English clergyman who spoke some Dutch, founded a Presbyterian congregation among the Hollanders. Later when Veenhuizen took the call to Rochester, it was his influence that brought about a sharp increase in this congregation. After his departure in 1854, they joined the Reformed Church.[58] Congregations were also organized in Buffalo, Chicago, and Milwaukee. In the southern part of Milwaukee there lived well over sixty Dutch families, mostly Seceders, as was reported on the occasion of Wyckoff's visit in 1848. They built their church near a hill and called "*The Holland Hill*."[59]

However, the most outstanding and influential "colony" developed in the city of Grand Rapids. It had its beginning in 1848 and following years when Grand Rapids was still a very young town. The first white man and founder of Grand Rapids was Louis Campeau,* a fur trader. He established himself in 1826.[60] Later, in 1833, Frederick Baraga, a missionary to the Indians, built a church there. In the meantime some brothers of Campeau joined the budding settlement. The Guild family, with its many daughters, also came in that year. The first election was held a year later, in 1834.

The town grew rapidly until the depression of 1837 hit and stalled its development. A large Roman Catholic church was erected by Campeau. When he had troubles with his fellow believers he sold it to the Congregationalists in 1841. Then the Roman Catholics built their own church. By 1850 the town had 2,686 inhabitants, which included many Hollanders. Frans Van Driele, who was born in Middelburg, Zeeland, arrived in 1848 and found a job as a canal digger. He probably was the first Dutchman who settled permanently here. Also some servant girls from "*de Kolonie*" were engaged to work for the inhabitants of Grand Rapids.[61]

Many Netherlanders on their way to the Van Raalte colony passed near or through Grand Rapids. A newspaper, *The Enquirer*, said in a short news story in September, 1849: "Our streets have been taken by the Dutch." While traveling through, many of the immigrants remained in Grand Rapids, reinforced by those who had left "*de Kolonie*," and, as we have noted, those who came from the Ravenna settlement. Soon some of these Netherlanders desired joint religious services. "Two or three families plus some young men and servant girls felt prompted to have a religious worship together on the Lord's Day. This happened in the month of July of the year 1848."[62] This group grew so rapidly that by the summer of 1849 a congregation was organized. G. Dalman and F. Van Driele were chosen as elders; for the time being they also served as

*The name *Campeau* has since been Americanized to *Campau*.

deacons. This is the birth of the first Dutch immigrant church, which in fact became so important that today in Dutch-American circles, Grand Rapids is known as the Jerusalem of American Calvinism. As we shall see, this Dutch colony also became the most important and influential in spreading orthodoxy to all urban and rural settlements.

In the cities the new immigrants felt more readily "at home" and re-mained Dutch for a longer time. City life caused people to be far less conscious of having become "another kind of human being" than did life in the rural settlements. This may explain why already in the years of rooting, the first Dutch newspaper in America appeared in one of these cities, where also the intellectuals preferred to settle, although not exclusively, as we have seen previously.

Jacob Quintus, who settled in the state of Wisconsin between 1840 and 1850, was the father of Dutch journalism in America. In keeping with what I described earlier about the settling in Wisconsin, he must have found that the conditions were favorable to begin a newspaper in Sheboygan. He published the first issue of the *Sheboygan Nieuwsbode*, the first Dutch paper in the United States, on October 16, 1849. It was read in all the settlements, even as far away as Iowa, and in the towns. It even had a few subscribers in the Netherlands.[63]

A second newspaper, called *De Nederlander*, made its appearance in Kal-amazoo, Michigan. It was a weekly publication and edited by [J.] Van der Wal. A third paper appeared in Allegan, Michigan; it was half in English and later entirely in the Dutch language. The first issue of *De Hollander* was published in September, 1850, by the Americans Hawks and Bassett, with the aid of a few Netherlanders. Later it was published exclusively by the Dutch. Soon the publishing site was transferred to Holland, Michigan, where it was published by H. Doesburg and others. Thus, the city colonies showed from the very beginning to be more or less consciously the focal centers of Dutch ethnic awareness, while at the same time and in close relationship with that awareness they fulfilled that function with regard to Dutch religious orthodoxy.

For the sake of completeness, it should be remembered that the contrast of rural colony/city colony or colonist/city dweller must not be drawn too sharply. Many transitional situations existed. Many a "colonist," for in-stance in Holland, Michigan, or Pella, Iowa, felt more like an inhabitant of a city than did many a "city dweller" in Chicago, Rochester, or elsewhere. In these towns many Netherlanders who had been in truck farming, farming, and cattle raising in the Netherlands saved money and rented a smaller or larger tract of land near the city for growing garden produce or dairying. So the first years of city colonization were already marked by an exodus to the suburbs and a corresponding sorting-out among the immigrants. There were even numerous cities in which emigrated country people formed the majority and not people who originally came from Dutch cities. Chance circumstances, like one or more countrymen already being established in a town and feeling very much at home there, would induce many others to join them, especially if they came from the same province or region.

In this way rural colonies were established east of Rochester in Pultney-ville and Pickleville by Zeelanders. Southwest of Buffalo mostly Gelder-landers settled the lands near Clymer and Clymer Hill.[64] In the first two towns cited, a Dutch church was already organized in 1849 and Reverend Visscher [Johannes De Visser], a missionary of the Old School Presbyterian Church, became their minister. Soon they joined the Reformed Church denomination. The elder A. K. Kasse was ordained by the Classis of Geneva as their minister and shepherd. Elder J. W. Dunnewold was examined by the same Classis and admitted to the administration of the sacraments and called to serve at Clymer.[65]

By a similar chance turn of events, one of the most unique Dutch colo-nies found its origin in the United States. It was the community of oyster fishermen in the village of Sayville on Long Island near New York City. In spite of excellent religious fellowship, Bastiaan Broere, a fisherman by trade, was unable to let down roots in the Michigan colony or in the vicinity of Grand Rapids where he had found employment. He left via Grand Haven for Buffalo, "where I knew many of my fellow countrymen had gone," to work on a canal project. Later, he showed up in New York where he met and married a Gelderland girl. Here he was busy as a bargeman's mate.

In New York Broere learned that good oysters were plentiful at South Bay, Long Island. "From my youth I had been acquainted with this business and did not doubt in the least that I could make a living at it." So, with his wife he moved to Sayville, joining two Dutch families who were already there. After two years, another Dutch family joined them and to the joy of Broere he found out that the head of the family, Jacob De Waal, in contrast to the other Dutch families, "was a man devoted to the fear of God." Several other families followed and they all celebrated Sunday worship, with Jacob De Waal as leader.[66] Broere became prosperous and sold his oysters even in Liverpool. About 1880 he went for a visit to his birthplace at Ierseke. From here and from the town of Bruinisse, other fishermen settled in Sayville during the following years, although Broere did not make any propaganda, as the mayor of Ierseke wrote to me.[67] At present one finds a prosperous, mostly Calvinistic Dutch fishing colony at Sayville.

F. Cooperation

So far we have recorded how and under what circumstances Dutch settle-ments were made around 1850, either as separate, independent colonies or as "colonies" among Americans and others, either in the countryside or in towns. According to the American census of 1850, there were 9,848 Dutch-born living in America. To them should be added those who were born in America from Dutch parents, although this number in 1850 is unknown since the actual count was first made in 1880.* We would estimate their number at about a thousand. Hollanders from overseas and those from Dutch parents form the (Dutch) "foreign white stock." As noted earlier, two thousand of these lived in Holland Township, Wisconsin and three thousand lived in Van Raalte's colony. If one estimates at a thousand each the number in the Roman Catholic colony in Wisconsin and the Calvinistic settlements in Iowa, plus two thousand in the remaining colonies, that would leave about two thousand unaccounted for or not organized. Those unknown individuals, who went their own way, were swallowed up by the masses. Very seldom, if at all, do we hear about them. But the question still remains to be answered how much contact existed between all those Dutch groups abroad and whether any signs of ethnic self-awareness and of cooperative efforts can be perceived.

The questionable interest with which emigrants were received by fellow countrymen, the so-called "runners," has been obvious all along. One met them not only in harbor cities but all along the highways to the West. Even in the quiet town of Albany one had to be on one's guard against them. It was in this city that these crimps attempted to waylay the enterprising minister's son R. in order to rustle his less well-educated traveling companions.[68] Therefore it is no wonder that people became suspicious of their own countrymen. Reverend Ypma went through such an experience when on a trip he ran into a number of Hollanders who were not at all eager to make his acquaintance. When he tried to tell them that he was a minister in Vriesland, Michigan, they jeered in loud voices, and said with meaningful gestures: "Listen to him; how he is a Minister, too." Any further attempts at making contact ceased right there.[69]

We have already mentioned the indifference that the Calvinists showed for the Catholics, in spite of the fact that during the persecutions in the Netherlands Roman Catholics repeatedly stood in the breach for the Seceders.[70] The Catholics, on the other hand, kept showing an interest in the affairs of the Calvinistic immigrants. Scholte of Pella hated the Catholics more than anyone else. Yet *Pella's Weekblad* [Weekly] was read so much among the Wisconsin Catholics that it had a correspondent at Green Bay, Little Chute, and Appleton.[71]

We also mentioned that the mutual jealousies among the "Calvinistic" colonies degenerated sometimes into cunning slander. However, in spite of the fact that everyone needed to concentrate their full attention on the struggle for existence in those rooting years, people were interested in each other and kept in touch. This was evident from the huge amount of correspondence that developed already very early among colonists in the various settlements and elsewhere. This was all the more understandable since relatives were often spread among several settlements. Already in November, 1848, when hardly settled, Scholte declared: "At present we have con-

---

*The 1880 census was the first to report nativity of parents.

tinued correspondence with some old friends who live there [in Michigan]."[72] But with all this letter writing, Pella, Iowa, and Holland, Michigan, did not work together in the development of their colonies, at least not for the time being!

We also mentioned previously the religious ties, the common faith which, due to their great leader, also brought the villages of the Van Raalte settlements into a common Classis at an early date. Of great importance is the fact that this faith united the widespread Netherlanders, even the ones outside of Michigan, and that the inhabitants of the settlements were in continuous contact with fellow Dutchmen in rural and urban "colonies" and thus influenced one another.

This cooperation is due in particular to the great religious zeal and drive of the leaders. In spite of their heavy and difficult tasks, Van Raalte, Van der Meulen, and others still managed to go out and preach in Allegan, Kalamazoo, and Grand Haven, notwithstanding the poor conditions of the roads they had to travel! They even traveled further, for example, when worship services were held in Grand Rapids. Here Reverend Van der Meulen immediately helped the believers. "A father could not have served his children more warmly. Not only on Sundays but also during the week he served us with his advice and instruction through public preaching."[73] Van der Meulen and Ypma constantly mounted the pulpit after a congregation had been organized with the aid of Van Raalte. Van der Meulen traveled to Grand Rapids with a span of Indian ponies, but Ypma walked. The consistory would then meet on Saturday evenings, "often until midnight." On Sundays they preached three times. Not until 1854 did Grand Rapids receive its own minister, Reverend H. G. Klijn.

Our ministers also preached in other places—especially at Milwaukee in Wisconsin, at Chicago and the prairie villages in Illinois, and later even in Pella, Iowa. Also preachers from Wisconsin, like Reverend Klijn, then a minister in Milwaukee, would appear in the pulpits of the prairie villages.[74]

Naturally, this guest preaching led to a closer union in religious matters, as was evident in the classical meetings that we already mentioned. At the classical gathering of October 31, 1849, not only were all the various villages of Michigan represented, but also Grand Rapids, which had delegated its two elders. At the Classis of October 14, 1851, representatives were present also from the recently formed churches of Grand Haven and Kalamazoo; even Milwaukee, Wisconsin, was welcomed as a member of the Classis. A year later Sheboygan sent representatives and at this joint session plans were discussed concerning higher education and a decision was made to have monthly collections for mission work among the heathen. On April 27, 1853, Chicago was also present and the High Prairie church joined the Classis for guidance. In that same year also a fund was started to enable poor families from the Netherlands to come to America.

The common interests of the churches kept on spreading wider and wider, as did their sense of commuinity.[75] What seemed to be purely church concerns, however, did not fail to have consequences that went far beyond them. When these churches joined the Classis they became automatically members of the Reformed Church. This gave them their place in the religious community of the great Republic and promoted their Americanization, though with the previously mentioned reservations. On the other hand, this cooperative effort of the Dutch in America, which later spread to many areas in spite of the fact that they were few in number, would become a force whose influence in various areas was clearly discernible upon closer examination, although it was not necessarily striking.

It may be disappointing to jingoists that the Dutch stuck together not primarily on the basis of ethnicity or nationalism but on the basis of their religion. However, one must admit that this religion was strongly nationalistic in character.

Although the Dutch were indifferent towards fellow countrymen of a different faith, they welcomed numerous Germans and American Calvinists and incorporated them in their community from the very beginning. As an example, the town of Graafschap, Michigan, mostly a German settlement, was represented at the very first meeting of Classis. Later numerous Ost Frisians from Germany were also taken into the Calvinistic church organization. We should notice, too, that in the [eighteen] fifties the language borderline—not to be confused with dialects—between the Netherlands, on the one hand, and Germany (Ost Friesland and Bentheim) on the other, stretched far more eastward into Germany than would be the case after 1870.

How extremely little concern our Calvinists in America showed at times for their fellow countrymen is nowhere more frankly evident than in the confession of Bastiaan Broere about ignoring his neighbors—two Dutch families "who lived very close by." He says: "But from what they said and their habitually loudly taking the Lord's name in vain as if it were a proverb for them, I realized very soon that I was not allowed to keep up friendly relations with them. But this wasn't so easy, for now I had to be careful that my neighbors would not find out that we also were Dutch. Since we were living in the same isolated, unpopulated area it could not miss that they would soon visit us, or rather that they would offend us with their ungodly language. So, to prevent this, I continually had to keep my distance." Although to justify his behavior, Broere, the staunch Calvinist, could quote the following text: "Whosoever will be a friend of the world is the enemy of God" [James 4:4], it seems that later on—and this I mention to his honor—he began to doubt the Christian nature of his attitude. "That I did the right thing at the time, I no longer claim after so many years," he declared almost forty years later in his autobiography.[76] Nevertheless, his attitude and behavior were typical for the people of God, then and later on.

Part Three

The Growth of the Settlements to Around 1895

11

The Material Growth of the Settlements

A. A Comparison

Many are the colonization attempts of various nations that took place in the United States and elsewhere. Even after an initial success, however, many of them failed. The most divergent circumstances have led to either success or failure. One of the prime factors that led to these results, besides the environment in which the immigrants settled, is no doubt the character of at least a core of the colonists.

One of the most tragic failures concerns a number of Hungarians who had fought with [Louis] Kossuth. In 1850, three years after the arrival of the Hollanders, these political exiles tried to found a new Budapest in the state of Iowa where the high fertility was comparable to that of Hungary. A matter-of-fact observer, the Belgian diplomat A. Van der Straten Ponthoz, reckoned this kind of immigrants to belong to the "overstrained part of shocked Europe."[1] A Holland American, Cyrenus Cole, the son of an "overstrained" European, Kool,[2] whom we have mentioned in chapter five, tells us already in typical American fashion of their experiences:

> They selected a beautiful site on the open prairies upon which they laid out for themselves great estates with castles to be. New Buda they planned along the same ambitious lines—a city of parks and public buildings. They did everything in a regal way. But instead of putting their hands to the plow, as the Hollanders in Marion County had done, they dreamed of vineyards growing, and of Tokay wines in rich goblets. They thought of everything that makes men rich and happy—of everything except doing the work that creates everything. They did not come to labor so much as to dream. Their colony was a romance; it never became a reality. It was a conception of medieval Europe on the prairies of modern America. It was fine, but it was not real.

> When they woke up they found themselves living in log cabins and not in castles, and the man who had dreamed of being an American count found himself an American postmaster, distributing intermittent mails. . . . The New Buda was never built. It was a prairie in 1850 and it remained a cornfield.[3]

A number of Hungarians remained in Iowa. Their leader, the nobleman Ladislaus Ujházy, count of Comorn, migrated with a number of followers to Texas, "the big southwestern specimen [among] these United States … where he prospered until he rode into San Antonio 'behind six white mules, all perfectly matched', while they were still plowing with oxen in Decatur Colony."

This "grand opera" not only illustrates the diversity of groups of people who were seeking a home in the United States as the "natural asylum of the oppressed of every clime," but in addition it proves, as one among many more or less intellectual failures, the conviction that homesteading in a new country actually "is the deed of men and nations who are still rugged and primitive, little or moderately civilized. It presupposes simple tastes, and intellectual and esthetic cultural needs that are little developed."[*4]

The success of the Pella Dutch colonization, in which a strikingly large number of educated immigrants participated, proves the relativity of this view. On the other hand, the statement may also serve the purpose of proving why so few Frenchmen are "*une nation émigrante*," [a nation of emigrants], while Germany has become a "*réservoir de nations*" [a reservoir of nations]. Here also it is risky to generalize, for equally numerous are the failures of colonization attempts by the less educated.

For more than one reason, a comparison of the Pella colony with the Decatur colony of the Hungarians is appropriate in this case. Both happened in the same time period and in the same surroundings: on the prairies of Iowa; both had the same soil condition, the same climate, and a previously settled population that received the Dutch as well as the Hungarians with open arms. The colonists were appreciated in America as hard workers from valued agricultural nations whose cradles had been largely in lowlands and whose psychological attitude can be observed to have a certain similarity.[5] In general, both are realistic. Witness, among other things, the fact that Calvinism had also taken hold in Hungary. Both are, in addition, very freedom-loving people. This latter characteristic manifested itself very strongly among the immigrants. Both groups hankered after political, religious, and economic freedom. To both belonged numerous intellectuals as well as men and women of some social standing. I carry the comparison even further: in both colonies the "leadership" once established in America was of questionable value; Count Ladislaus left for Texas, while the Reverend Scholte actually "went into business." Yet Pella became one of the most prosperous towns in Iowa while Buda, on the contrary, remained a dream.

In spite of the various similarities, there were differences between these Netherlanders and Hungarians great enough to have them react so differently in an environment that was similar in all respects. There were differences in their descent and character—"in all people are all tendencies"—but surely in very different proportions! Their social circumstances were different also: the Hungarians must not have had as many golden Willempjes and they were probably less religious.

With these comparisons, I have tried to illustrate my contention made at the beginning of this chapter. We may attribute the success of the Dutch transplantation in Iowa, but also in Michigan, Wisconsin, and Illinois, above all to the character of the colonists, with their leaders out in front! It was proven in their struggle against great odds. Although the characteristics of the environment made a great impact from the very start, it was especially during the further growth and development of the settlements that this environmental factor made itself felt in the strongest way possible. I would like to point out that this concept of environment, taken in its broadest sense, is constantly changing so that one could even speak of its cyclic ups and downs, just as in the economy. Therefore, the simplicity of the truth, just as in the case of the riddle of the egg of Columbus,* will become apparent and has, in fact, already been stressed for some twenty-five years by S. R. Steinmetz. He has stated that in all attempts at colonization, either in the earliest days, or subsequently, the inequality and diversity in character of the people involved, with all ensuing consequences—but also demands—will lead to an interaction with the environment, an endless interaction that continues to vary as the environment changes.[6]

Thanks to their sheer will power, steeled by their faith and by the example of such men as Van Raalte, Van der Meulen, and others, the Dutch colonists could consider themselves to be established after a period of about five years of harsh struggles which at times took on the severity of a life and death struggle. Only after that period of time could they justly call themselves Americans. Many could also call themselves Americans legally after that five-year period. According to the second naturalization law of January 29, 1795, a term of residence of five years was required before one could obtain American citizenship. After having survived for five years, the Dutch could really say that they had conquered their citizenship and not merely obtained it!

But in spite of all the will power, their potential was limited, as we shall see in their further development. The latter would be determined for a large part by the environment. The history of the settlements has the history of the United States as background and is therefore organically as well as materially and spiritually very closely connected with it. For example, al-

---

*A seemingly impossible task is easy if one knows how to do it. When people suggested to Christopher Columbus that he might not have been the first European to discover America, he supposedly challenged the guests at a dinner in his honor to make a boiled egg stand on end. When they all failed, he tapped one end of the egg against the table to flatten it and thus stood it up. Columbus thereby implied that he had discovered the way and now others could easily follow. See Ivor H. Evans, Bremer's *Dictionary of Phrase and Fable*, Centenary Edition Revised, New York: Harper and Row, 1981, p. 260.

ready in the early struggling years of Holland and Pella, the Hollanders intended to turn these towns into industrial centers, making big sacrifices for that goal. Pella has never become an industrialized city, no more than most of the other prairie towns in America. Holland, on the contrary, was an exception, but only after America had become an industrialized nation in addition to being a farm nation. So Holland had to wait until the early nineties before the "Hollanders," with the cooperation of the native Americans, could develop this city into a center of industry. That happened only when economic conditions made it possible. Although the early colonists laid the foundations and indicated the direction in which they wished the settlements to develop, the rate at which this took place depended in a great measure on the environment that at the same time modified, here and there, the original "lines of action" [Richtungslinien].

B. The Development of Transportation

The above-named Van der Straten Ponthoz asserted in his *Onderzoek* [Inquiry], that a good market is not a first necessity for immigrants, but rather the very soil on which they can make a living through manual labor.[7] The farm surplus will certainly be consumed by the subsequent settlers! No doubt there is some truth in this contention, for this also happened in the Dutch colonies. Especially in Pella the newly arrived immigrants were of great importance. In 1849 Van Raalte could still write concerning his colony that, with respect to the products of farming and cattle raising, many found work in the forest and on the water. Because of this and the flow of new arrivals, he wrote, "We need not think of exporting, at least not for the present time."[8] But Van Raalte added that various wood products such as bark, roofing shingles, etc., were exported in increasing quantities. These latter sales point out the relative value of Van der Straten Ponthoz's assertion, which also seems to assume that immigrants display an inordinately passive attitude. Therefore it has a mainly theoretical value. We see in practice that Van Raalte, Scholte, and others, in their choice of a homestead region, not only assessed the potentials of the soil, but also immediately took into consideration future marketplaces.

All colonists, once established, understood that the prosperity of farming, trade, and industry were dependent on the sale of the colonial products in these markets. In order to accomplish this, good connecting routes were necessary and it was precisely these that were sometimes lacking. Hence, our colonists did not rest but tried to change the environment with all the energy they could muster, primarily in the limited geographical sense of transportation demands. The transport problem became pressing, and on its solution all growth and prosperity depended. People felt this especially in the Van Raalte and Scholte colonies, both of which were farther away from business centers than the prairie villages in Illinois, which lay in the near vicinity of Chicago, and the settlements in Wisconsin. Besides, the latter already used the wide, navigable Fox River and had at their disposal a goodly number of harbors on Lake Michigan. In contrast, the Des Moines and Skunk rivers in Iowa and the Lake Michigan harbors in western Michigan, as we know, were hardly usable.

In accord with the basic nature of Hollanders, but also in keeping with the spirit of the times—Ellen Churchill Semple called the years of 1820 to 1860 "the palmy days of water transportation in the United States"[9]—they kept their attention riveted on waterways, both in Michigan as well as in Iowa, in spite of the disappointments they already experienced. This was also despite the gloomy prediction of brother Scholte concerning the Van Raalte colony, that the construction of a good lake harbor would always remain wishful thinking,[10] and in spite of brother Van Raalte's proud contention that the prairies of Iowa, meaning the Scholte colony, were too far away from waterways![11] However, concerning matters in their own settlements, each one for himself was hopefully inclined.

The Hollanders in Michigan not only took the initiative themselves but carried out nearly all of the harbor works independently. After the early failures, people frequently met in Holland to confer on the harbor question.[12] The possession of a good harbor was deemed to be of such paramount importance, not only for "*de stad*" but for the whole outlying area, and primarily the back country, that the deliberations were held with the participation of delegates from the townships of Holland and Zeeland as well as from the later-formed townships of Overisel, and Fillmore, in which lies the village of Graafschap. Costs were estimated at $20,000, for which, because of the various advantages, Holland would have to contribute $12,000; Zeeland, $3,000; Overisel and Fillmore, each $2,000. The voters in the townships accepted these proposals. Results of the voting were: Holland, 292 in favor, 74 against; in Zeeland, Overisel, and Fillmore: in favor, 105, 36, and 56; against, 62,31, and 29, respectively. These figures typify each community's self-interest and also the attitude of the people involved.

Having received a petition to this effect, the state of Michigan passed a special law on February 2, 1858, allowing the involved townships to float loans and to raise taxes in behalf of the harbor. At the same time a harbor board was formed, to which each township could appoint eight members. All of the appointees of the "Haven Board," including Van Raalte, who was selected as chairman, were of Dutch descent, except E. J. Harrington.[13] Already in June, 1858, two piers, each two hundred feet long and twenty feet wide, to be made of woven twig mats and stone and clay, were put out for contract and allotted to Hendrik Zuidweg for $5,000. In the meantime the harbor board appointed L. Schaddelee as superintendent. Jb. Van Putten continued to supervise the construction after he had replaced Schaddelee.

In December of 1858 a second bid was let to lengthen the harbor dams, the northern one to 750 feet and the southern one to 700 feet, "while a sunken protective mattress of 32 feet had to be put on both." The expenses of all this were figured to be $14,000. This time the work was undertaken by a group of enterprising men, among whom the businessmen of Holland were amply represented. The work was finished in the fall of 1861 and approved on January 13, 1862. The expenses were covered to a great extent with the loans that had been floated successfully with the energetic co-operation of one of the contractors, J. Roest. Another contractor, M. D. How-ard, a Michigan legislative representative of Ottawa County, exerted his influence, so that in 1859 the state ceded to Holland and Zeeland as a compensation eleven thousand acres of swampland in the neighboring Ol-ive and Blendon townships. After a few years, these "harborlands" were drained and sold. This largely paid for the expenses incurred.

Now they had a harbor of sufficient depth to accommodate ships drawing eight feet of water. The favorable results were soon apparent, since Hol-land's trade increased fourfold and the population more than doubled soon afterwards. A fleet of numerous sailing vessels, many belonging to the people of Holland, were used as freight carriers. Soon the harbor also became a well-known "port of refuge" in stormy weather and as such was one of the most important harbors on the east side of Lake Michigan.

In 1867 the harbor, as was the case with many others, was transferred to the possession of the federal government. This transfer was the result of policy changes due to the Civil War. The harbor board remained, but it now consisted only of members from Holland Township. The colonists of Hol-land Township in Wisconsin also wanted a harbor and built one of their own to the east of Cedar Grove on Lake Michigan. The pier was of such proportions that big ships could anchor there. A harbor city, baptized Am-sterdam, as in Iowa, came into being and became an important business center.[14]

The Hollanders in Iowa likewise set their hopes on water transportation. Yet they took a less active approach towards this problem than their brethren in Michigan. This is easy to understand, not only because of the previous disappointments but also since making the Des Moines, Iowa's biggest river, navigable was not exclusively a matter of their own interest. In the first place that river's navigability was a matter that concerned the whole state. Otherwise, the Netherlanders were hopeful, especially those who still had land for sale. In 1858 "Een Gelderschman" in Pella related that the work on the Des Moines River "had once more been vigorously tackled by a company from the eastern states and was soon to be finished. When a nation wants a project that pays as well as this one, then people and capital are always found to bring it to completion."[15]

Indeed, the government had entrusted the job of making the river naviga-ble to a new enterprise, the Des Moines River Navigation and Railroad Company. The project gave good returns, although perhaps in a different sense than the Gelderschman had intended. Besides many privileges, the Company received thousands of acres that it hastened to sell. However, nothing came of the river project and the river itself was even further messed up! A new contract produced no better results and only led to a number of lawsuits.[16] The Des Moines River, south of the Scholte colony, was one disappointment after another. However, its silt, time and again, fertilized the fruitful soil of the land.[17] Therefore, people turned to the smaller Skunk River, north of the colony. In 1860, a plot of land was even surveyed that was later to become the town of Leerdam.[18] But that is the way it stayed; people never got around to building the city.

The lack of a good waterway was strongly felt in the Iowa colony. Therefore, its growth was also much slower than that of the Michigan colony. People there had to rely only partially on road transportation with carts—as far as the small towns in its vicinity were concerned—but in Pella people were altogether dependent on cart transportation. One of the chief stagecoach lines, the line from Burlington to Council Bluffs, went through Pella.[19] But all merchandise such as grain and meat also had to be transported via the axle. These transports were a source of income for many carriers who drove wagons drawn by oxen, horses, or mules. But this method of transportation was so poor and expensive that for years the busy road from Pella to the marketplace in Keokuk was strewn with pieces of meat and bacon that had fallen or been discarded from the wagons. In this way there was an enormous loss.[20]

It is no wonder that when in the East railroads found more and more acceptance and competed with waterways, people in the West also looked forward to them and all the more intently since the existing highways left much to be desired. Railway fever was also detectable in the settlements. It was the strongest in Pella where, as we saw, it had already occurred in the rooting years. While the name of the above-mentioned "Navigation and Railroad" company already signaled a turning point, the Scholte settlement paid more and more attention to railroads instead of water transportation. Many railroad meetings were held there. In 1853 the first surveying activities for the building of a railroad took place. It was to pass through Pella's Washington Street. After this, several other surveys were done, but for the time being only plans were made.[21]

The enormous swindle, evidently inseparably connected with the building of railroads in the United States—read Gustavus Myers' *History of the Great American Fortunes*[22]—also showed "the dark side of railroad promotions" in Iowa, according to Cole.[23] This and the "panic year" of 1857, when many banks and other enterprises went bankrupt, and also the Civil War, all contributed to the fact that not until twelve years later, in January 1865, did the colony get its first railroad and the unusual sound of locomotives was heard in Pella. The following year the Des Moines Valley Railroad was completed up to the city of Des Moines.

The consequences were important for Pella, for now it was no longer forced to orient its interests exclusively eastward, to Keokuk, but it could also look westward to Des Moines, which was growing in importance. Pella itself grew in importance. Farm and cattle products from the vicinity were shipped to the town and converted into life's necessities and luxuries, so that it became known as an excellent shopping center. The merchants "shipped" their products by rail. Alongside the commission business houses arose granaries and lumberyards and even the industries expanded.[24] It is true that trade somewhat diminished when in 1875 its southerly competitor, Knoxville, was connected to the rail network. Yet in Pella they had reason to be satisfied because the value of farms and other possessions had doubled in the meantime.[25]

In the older settlements of Michigan the development of railroads had dated from 1830, which coincided with their rush for big waterways.[26] They wanted to join the somewhat navigable Grand River and Kalamazoo River streaming north and south of the Holland Colony to Michigan's east coast by canals, which up to this time, have turned out to be mere "bright dreams."

The Erie and Kalamazoo Railroad, the first in the state, was completed in the forties. Many a Netherlander on his way to the Van Raalte colony made use of it. In 1853 the colony itself contracted the "railroad feeling." Holland at that time hoped to become the terminal of the Oakland and Ottawa Railway.[27] However, the city of Grand Haven, north of Holland, was chosen as the terminal for the newly reorganized company, now named the Detroit, Grand Haven, and Milwaukee Railroad. In 1858 this town was reached by today's well-known Grand Trunk, which in '57 was completed to Grand Rapids. For years, Holland remained outside of the great traffic. Railway passengers on their way to the colony often disembarked at Grand Haven or even sooner at Grand Rapids. Until 1869 a stagecoach went from Grand Rapids to Holland just once per week. The driver at the same time took packages along. Also those who made the trip by boat could, in spite of Holland's improved harbor, reach this town only by way of Grand Haven. A direct Chicago-Holland steamboat service originated around 1870. From Grand Haven people could travel by foot or by stagecoach or some other rented vehicle to their destination.

How primitive passenger traffic still was in 1896 was experienced by a businessman from the Netherlands, A. E. Croockewit, who sailed from Chicago that year and after landing in Grand Haven continued his trip to Holland by coach: a square box on wheels covered with a tarpaulin![28] The trip went along a very bad, sandy road, full of big holes and puddles, across steep hills, and through thick woods to which the many charred tree trunks gave a gloomy appearance. At the halfway mark of this twenty-two-mile-long road was a resting place, at Pigeon River, where a Frisian by the name of Bakker had an inn. An old lady born in Ommen, a typesetter from Arnhem, and a Frisian carpenter, were Croocke-wit's fellow passengers. On their break at the inn, they got some bread and coffee, though "at an excessive price." Two years earlier the immi-grant Bloemendaal had had the same experience at the same place. he had to pay double fare for his dinner! After a tiresome ride of seven hours they arrived in Holland.[29]

In 1870 the Hollanders got their first railway connection when the Pere Marquette Railroad connected "*de stad*" with Allegan.[30] In the same year a second connection was made, so that in 1871 Van Raalte could speak of a "complete system of railway lines" in addition to the "best navigation."[31]

For the Roman Catholic and Protestant settlements in Wisconsin, which generally were favorably located with respect to water traffic, overland transportation was also important. Therefore, it was a step forward for our Roman Catholic countrymen when in 1852 an omnibus service was opened between Green Bay, their main marketplace, and Fond du Lac, also a marketplace.[32] However, the latter was of greater value for their Protestant fellow immigrants in Alto and Waupun.[33] This service passed through Van den Broek's settlements. It must be said that this connection never brought about any rapprochement between Roman Catholic and Calvinist brethren. Neither did the railway connections that were built here in the [eighteen] sixties and following years.

Among these "iron roads," the lines of the Chicago and North Western became especially important for the Netherlanders. The line from Chicago to Green Bay also ran through the Wisconsin settlements along Lake Michigan's shores. Thus, Oostburg and other towns were in turn connected with the Roman Catholic settlements. Because of its location on Green Bay, the town of Green Bay could be compared somewhat with Chicago. It, too, became a railroad center, although on a much smaller scale; yet this promoted its prosperity. The railroad brought new life to the Roman Catholic as well as the Calvinist settlements. Especially in Oostburg and Cedar Grove in Sheboygan County was this noticeable. But not everywhere. The sharp competition between water and land traffic also claimed its victims among the Dutch settlements, for land traffic was preferred due to the dangers of sailing on the lakes. Amsterdam, which, as we saw before, prospered from lake shipping, went into decline once the Chicago and North Western Railroad was built.[34]

However, sooner than all other settlements, the Hollanders in Illinois, at least those of High Prairie, got their railway. They owed this to the proximity of Chicago. Chicago was already the terminal of various trunk lines, which because of its location on the southwest side of Lake Michigan, made it the obvious center for the Midwest. The Michigan Central, which in 1852 reached Chicago[35] and which runs through the Dutch village of High Prairie,[36] is one of the trunk lines. In 1864, therefore also before the Van Raalte and Scholte colonies were included in the railroad network, Low Prairie was included in the rail network since the Chicago and Eastern Illinois was built in that year.[37] Here as elsewhere railroads brought the same results: increased sales of farm and cattle products, greater business prosperity, and rising land and other prices. Furthermore, many a Netherlander found work in railroad construction.

Around 1870 various Dutch colonies were connected by rail, since the rail network had spread itself gradually from east to west. Therefore, direct connections could usually be obtained immediately with the East, and this facilitated the settling of the West. For example, the New York Central and the Erie railroads carried thousands of Netherlanders westward. Moreover, the iron roads connected the colonies *with one another*.

The influences of these developments were felt, sometimes more and sometimes less, but in the most diverse ways. We already pointed out what the results were for economic life. Especially in the business centers of the colonies in Holland, Pella, Oostburg, Cedar Grove, etc., the population immediately increased somewhat. The newcomers were Americans, usually strongly represented in business. Nevertheless, one should not overestimate this increase in population. The settlements were primarily farm colonies that could provide a living to only a small number of colonists. The gradual transfer of surplus labor was taken care of by the railroads, which made economic survival possible in the more westerly, sparsely populated areas. And when the cheap land was gone, the railroads once more carried people from the now overpopulated farm areas to the developing industrial centers such as Grand Rapids and Holland.

With an occasional exception, what Van Stigt observed regarding the Pella colony more than thirty years after it received its first railroad connection was true for all Dutch colonies: "a slow but steady material progress in the social sphere has always been characteristic of Pella, Iowa, and surrounding areas."[38] The establishment of numerous Americans among the Dutch settlers promoted the Americanization of the Hollanders. American ideas, methods, etc., concerning economic and spiritual matters found acceptance in the settlements. The relatively easy traveling facilities, on the other hand, allowed the colonists to visit more readily the surrounding American cities, such as Chicago, etc., to do their trading, go to school, and even to move and live there. In short, all kinds of contacts were greatly promoted.

But here too, one should not exaggerate. Because now that the colonies had easy mutual contacts by rail, the bond between fellow Netherlanders was drawn tighter, at least if they were of the same confession. Under these new circumstances, for instance, a minister could fulfill much more easily a turn as a guest preacher in one of the other colonies, and might even move more readily to a new post. And this tightening of the bonds of faith has, no doubt, strengthened the solidarity of the Dutch element and thus retarded for years the Americanization process. Here, too, one could speak of the end result, of "slow but steady progress," at least from the point of view of the native-born Americans.

The building of railroads has had such a great influence overall on the economic and spiritual life of the Holland colonists that one can speak of a milestone in their development. Next to politics and other happenings, it was the railroads that terminated the "colonial" character of the settlements.[39] Time and environment in the broadest sense of the word have acted similarly as silent forces from the very beginning, that is, for about twenty-five years.

C. Agriculture and Cattle Raising

Agriculture, in the first place, was increasingly influenced by the environment, due to the ongoing development of traffic. We saw how in the very beginning the most varied of crops were cultivated in the Old-Country manner. However, soon experience taught that one has to take into consideration the conditions of soil and climate. Sometimes one or the other factor, or both, prevented the cultivation of certain products. So when people produced more than was needed locally in the various colonies and tried to export them they had to reckon more than before with the demand for certain products. In Michigan, for instance, wheat, corn, rye, and oats were grown as well as barley, buckwheat, potatoes, and hay; but for export the emphasis was on wheat, corn, oats, and barley.[40] In a broad sense, the same held true for Wisconsin, Illinois, and to a lesser degree for Iowa.

The demand for wheat, however, was constantly on the increase, and the prices for this product rose considerably. After the Civil War, they were so high that in nearly all of the Dutch settlements people converted on a big scale to the one-sided production of wheat. Even in Iowa where the soil is better fit for the cultivation of corn, they now raised wheat. Not only the village of Zeeland, Michigan, was described in 1869 as lying "amid luxuriant wheat fields," but the same writer depicted Pella's surrounding area in that same year as follows: "It is a pleasant change to see here and there a few hills of two or three hundred feet, covered to the top with luxuriant wheat or corn or with copses from where farmhomes pleasantly smile at you."[41]

So much money was made in wheat that the Dutch farmers followed the American practice of foregoing the use of fertilizer and they even omitted crop rotation.[42] In the long run, the result of these negligences showed up, no matter how fertile the soil was, and in some places the land was ruined. For example in Wisconsin where, according to |S. F.| Rederus, wheat was also the main crop, the "fresh" virgin soil yielded thirty bushels per acre but in the sixties the yield was reduced by half. Even worse were the consequences of this overcropping in Illinois. In 1881, when C. De Smit, a Zeeland farmer, visited the village of South Holland (formerly called Low Prairie), he noticed that almost no wheat was grown. He was told "that wheat would no longer grow here. . . . Formerly it did well, people said to me, and wonderful wheat was grown. The cause they could not tell me." Yet the land consisted of good clay. However, at other places farmers told him the truth, i.e., "that in the beginning wheat was always sown upon wheat and this depleted the soil for this crop," no matter how excellent the soil generally was. And in Illinois it was the best that De Smit had seen in America.[43]

It seems that Iowa was not spared the bad consequence either, for in the eighties "luxuriant wheatfields" were also a thing of the past. The agriculturist J. P., who also visited a few Holland settlements at that time, even said about Pella that "wheat cannot be grown here." He reiterated this statement in his "*Indrukken van een ooggetuige*" ["Impressions of an Eyewitness"] with the additional comment: "Yet, corn gives an excellent crop."[44] In the nineties Pella had to import the necessary wheat and wheat flour.[45]

Most likely the reduction or disappearance of wheat from the products of the settlements also resulted from the rise of new wheat regions. For example, Minnesota and the Dakotas later became the big wheat belt, famous for spring wheat. Michigan and other states, however, remained the producers of winter wheat. We should be reminded, however, that the initial preference for growing wheat is not typical only for the Dutch; it happened everywhere else, too. It went hand in hand with the continuous improvements in transportation that made Europe into an enormous outlet for American wheat. Thus far, the southern part of the United States had been for a long time the exclusive wheat consumer. Both the faster transportation and the relatively low costs of farm operation—land obtained at a very low price, overcropping, and since 1851, the numerous newly-invented farm machines, enabled the American farmer to compete with his European counterpart.[46]

Since the types of soil in the colonies of Michigan and Wisconsin are very different and show a range of quality, this from the earliest days led to the cultivation of the most diverse crops. Next to wheat, the growing of corn was favored, all the more so as farmers began to notice that uninterrupted wheat cropping exhausted the soil. Various Dutch farmers started to fertilize; in addition, crop rotation became more and more prevalent, and corn was an excellent alternate crop.

In the Wisconsin settlements, Alto and Waupun, wheat did not even remain the main crop but was replaced more and more by barley and corn.[47] The Sheboygan County settlements, located more northward, continued to grow wheat as their chief means of income, although it was largely substituted by rye and barley.[48] This was also the case in Michigan. In this latter colony, oats and potatoes also played a prominent part, while the drained marshes were excellent for the growing of onions that produced big profits for many years. At that time, the surrounding area of Kalamazoo was already famous for the growing of celery, a favorite American delicacy, and many Netherlanders also concentrated on the production of this item.

Initially, the Hollanders were not interested in the all-important growing of fruit in southwestern Michigan.[49] However, when they learned of the suitability of the sometimes very rocky and sandy soil with a moist and not too cold climate, they also applied themselves to fruit growing, after the example of their American neighbors. Thus, many a Dutch native became the owner of a very profitable orchard. For example, Wabeke, the Zeelander we have met before, planted on the most sandy part of his eighty acre farm an orchard of twenty acres, "the most beautiful" that De Smit saw in America. Moreover, he planted three to four acres with peach trees. The apples alone brought Wabeke and other growers $400 to $500 profit per year![50]

In the South Holland settlement in Illinois, after exhaustive cultivation of wheat on the good clay soils, the main crop changed to corn, potatoes, and oats. The so-called marsh soils of blackish muck, which were also found in the Michigan and Wisconsin settlements as well as in the Van Raalte colony, gave rise to a prominent onion cultivation.[51] The most one-sided farming developed when the Pella settlement had to abandon the cultivation of wheat, and corn generally became its exclusive product, although oats, potatoes, and even sugar beets were not wanting.

At first it looked as if Pella would develop large-scale truck farming. Because of its many truck gardens, Americans called it the Garden City.[52] But in the long run there was not enough manpower. It was also too costly when not enough outlets were found to make it a paying proposition. In 1854 complaints were already heard in Pella about the scarcity of vegetables. There were not enough hands to weed the fields. Several farms kept their splendid orchards, but they were not always managed on a sufficiently profitable basis.[53] Pella hung on to the nickname of Garden City because of the abundance of flowers in its various gardens, which had already been observed by Van der Meulen when he visited old acquaintances there, the Roordas. This Frisian poet wrote in his weekly paper in 1882: "The luxuriant flower growth around the homes of these people is strikingly beautiful."[54]

Only in the vicinity of big cities was truck farming and fruit growing profitable. Hence it was near Chicago that a great number of Netherlanders applied themselves with much success to market gardening. For a long time they got the manure of the city free of charge.[55]

Alongside farming, the raising of cattle was taken up in all the colonies and even when at times this slid far into the background, not in the least due to the overcropping with wheat, even in the settlements that primarily consisted of farmers who were originally cattle raisers, as for example, was the case in South Holland and Pella. In the Van Raalte colony cattle raising had always been of great importance, and alongside wheat farming it formed the chief means of income, as shown by the various usages of the soil. Most of the farms, averaging eighty acres in size, allotted forty acres to seed crops, about ten acres of their lesser quality soil served as orchard, while thirty acres were used for pasture and clover fields.[56]

The dairy products were, in the first place, for their own use and for customers in the colony, but in the long run, they thought of exporting them on a larger scale. Sooner than in the Old Country, dairy processing was organized on an industrial basis. Here, as in the Netherlands, the Frisians eventually gave leadership. At the beginning of the eighties (1882) there were already two cooperative cheese factories in the village of Vriesland in the Van Raalte colony. Each had fifty to sixty members who took turns taking the milk to the factory each morning. One of the factories distributed a 40 percent dividend already in the second year of its existence. The very first factory of this kind in the province of Friesland in the Netherlands was founded in 1886, although the earliest attempt at factory cheese processing dated back to the seventies when it was introduced in the Wieringerwaard. However, there was no thought of butter factories in the Netherlands at that time.[57]

Everyone in the Michigan colony praised the beautiful cattle that were well cared for. This was in striking contrast with American practices. Americans usually neglected their cattle, and would for example, give no thought to stall feeding, even in winter. In Sheboygan County, next to wheat growing, cattle raising remained the chief way of making a living for the Dutch.[58] Very early, dairy factories appeared here also, to which farmers brought their milk. However, in Alto cattle raising became a very minor sideline and some farmers did not keep more cows than necessary for their own use of milk, butter, etc. The same practice was seen in South Holland, Illinois.

The situation was different in the Pella colony. Here cattle breeding not only held its own but grew rapidly and changed altogether in character. In the rooting years, the Pellians, among whom were many Zuid Holland cheese makers, specialized in the processing of this very Dutch product for American consumers, and as we have seen earlier, they gained quite a reputation for their brand of Iowa cheese. However, after a few years this changed and farmers concentrated more on wheat and corn growing. The unsophisticated Sipma, more reliable in his letters than Reverend Scholte, already at an early date pointed to the cause for this change: "Cow milking would be better here than agriculture but we lack a good quality of grass. Where herds of cows have been grazing on a piece of land for four or five years, the prairie grass is gone and nothing but weeds are left. The domesticated American grass is not the right kind."[59] They kept dairy cows, because they still needed milk, butter, and cheese in the colony; but cheese processing decreased. In the eighties (1882) there was still a substantial butter factory in Pella.[60]

Meat production became more important than dairy cows. For years, not cattle but hogs dominated in Pella. As corn production constantly increased, but exporting it did not pay because of the poor road conditions, farmers began to concentrate more and more on fattening hogs. Great herds of pigs wandered through the woods and fed on hazelnuts and acorns. In the winter and spring the pigs were fed corn. The demand for bacon and salt pork constantly increased. In the years from 1845 to 1860 the price of hogs doubled in Cincinnati, the "Porkopolis" of those days.[61] This did not go unnoticed in Pella. Big droves of fattened hogs were driven from Pella to Keokuk. It took from nine to ten days to take them to market. "Of course, animals had to be driven slowly, grazing along the way. There was nothing particularly pleasant about the job and often we grumbled: all that for twenty-five cents a day and no lunch,"[62] the 86-year-old pioneer, H. Van Maren, told me the other day.

In the early fifties, the enterprising Dutchmen Wolters and Smeenk, with whose firm Bousquet associated himself, as we have seen earlier, established a hog slaughterhouse in Pella that was the first of its kind. In 1852 already, some five hundred hogs were butchered there. This business grew constantly and so did the fattening of hogs. In this respect it looked as if Pella would become a little Cincinnati. In 1861 the number of slaughterhouses had increased to eleven and in a period of just one week more than two thousand hogs were slaughtered. One could say, therefore, that Pella's welfare in those days came from this trade.[63]

The development of cattle raising around Pella, as well as of farming, was very strongly affected by some general changes. Therefore, one cannot speak of a typical Pella development but rather of a typical Midwestern development. It was the invention and patenting of the refrigerator car in 1868 that made the transportation of fresh meat possible. This caused a steep increase in exports, and cattle raising as well as the meat packing industry were greatly promoted.[64] Pella cashed in on it, too. As in other places, the Pella farmers did not specialize in fattening only hogs, whose numbers kept increasing anyway; they undertook also the fattening of cattle. The latter were brought in from the "Farther West" since its more arid conditions were less favorable for corn growing. Cattle were also bought from states that had sparsely populated areas that lent themselves therefore to cattle raising.

Pella was invaded on September 4, 1872, by W. Rietveld and three other "cowboys" or cattle drovers with some thousand steers that had been bought in Kansas and Missouri, which at that time were known as "cow country." The steers were fattened in Pella and vicinity, which required at least 100,000 bushels of corn.[65] In this way Pella became at the same time an important "home market" for corn growing. M. Witsenburg, one of the most well-to-do cattlemen in the vicinity of Pella, according to Van der Meulen, concentrated on fattening of steers which he sold per pound. In order to weigh twenty steers all at once, a scale was specially built for that purpose behind the barn.[66]

In this way the Dutch farmers took an active part in the development of the Midwest and shared in the general prosperity that prevailed before as well as after the Civil War. Hard work had been essential and an enormous ability to adapt to American circumstances was a must. A shortage of farm labor was the farmer's most difficult problem. In Michigan, for example, generally only two men had to take care of an 80-acre farm, but at harvest time more help had to be hired. In Wisconsin the farms were often somewhat larger than in Michigan, counting 120 to 130 acres, while in Iowa most farms had 160 to 320 acres.

In all these states the shortage of labor was acute. As we saw, the striving for the biggest harvest with the least amount of labor also led the Hollanders to neglect their soil to a greater or lesser extent through the omission of fertilizer and through long periods without crop rotation. On the other hand, this situation induced them to apply the newest discoveries in the area of farming. It was especially Bousquet in Pella who spearheaded the introduction of the first mower and modern threshing machines and promoted their use among the Hollanders.[67] Van der Meulen, who visited Pella in 1881, saw for the first time in his life a selfbinder in operation, pulled by three horses. This machine mowed the grain and transferred it evenly and in a straight line to its upper platform. Each time a kind of arm tied up the lifted grain stalks with a string, which in turn was cut by a knife. After that, the machine laid the sheaf aside and in a wink there appeared a second, third, and fourth sheaf. As soon as there were four sheaves, the platform tipped over and dumped the sheaves on the ground. A farm hand walking behind the machine set the sheaves right side up and against each other. Van der Meulen wrote, "I never saw an instrument that works as beautifully as that."[68]

In the Scholte settlement, where the farms were the largest, the inventions of [Cyrus Hall] McCormick and other equipment pioneers were used first and highly appreciated. They appeared somewhat later in the other settlements. In Bloemendaal's *Amerikaansche leerjaren* [*American Years of Apprenticeship*] (ca. 1867), [it was reported that] many Wisconsin farmers used mowing and threshing machines, but on the low lying "muck lands" Bloemendaal himself had to use a scythe that he still had trouble handling.[69]

About 1880, implements of all kinds, besides the ones already mentioned, were in use in the Van Raalte colony, for example, machines to load and unload hay. To load hay, according to farmer and alderman C. De Smit, farmers attach a certain machine to the wagon and "slowly driving along, the machine heaves the hay on the wagon and two men have their hands full to stack it on the wagon." In that same period, the Schaap brothers who each had an eighty acre farm near the village of Zeeland, already unloaded hay with the help of a machine that they thrust into a load of hay, after which, pressing a spring, a hook would jut out on both sides. "To this device a long rope or line is fastened that runs over some blocks; two horses are hitched and in three thrusts the whole load is unloaded." Corn was planted with a hand machine and the Hollanders dried their apples partly with the aid of machines.[70]

One can not escape the impression that in those years the use of the most modern farm machinery by our fellow Netherlanders in America was far more common than in the Netherlands, although as Dr. [H. N.] Ter Veen explained not long ago, a steam threshing machine was already in use in the Haarlemmermeer [polder] in 1855.[71] However, in our country it was mainly the so-called "model or gentlemen farmers" who imported this machinery, as in the Haarlemmermeer, which was considered to be an experimental farm area, a "vast agricultural school," thanks to such individuals as J. P. Amersfoort or Baron Van Verschuer. The same was found in progressive Groningen.[72] The real point to make, however, is not the exceptional use but the general use of machinery. In America, it was the former

A celery field and old farmsteads near New Groningen and Holland, Michigan. "These are no longer farmhouses, but mansions." (Original photos of Dirk Nieland.)

farmhands and unskilled laborers who used those machines. They too, showed themselves in this regard to be selection material [*selectie materiaal*, that is, sorted out, upward bound people], just as to a lesser degree were the Haarlemmermeer people.

The machines were all the more welcome since the vitality of the vegetation was so much greater than the Hollanders were accustomed to and harvest time arrived sooner. This was observed and pointed out in the Wisconsin settlements by Bloemendaal.[73] "Up to the present, until the end of May, nature was behind, but when the heat began to be felt with full force ... everything began to grow with amazing power; grass and grain shot up from the soil luxuriously, and in the beginning of July wheat had already formed ears. Pasture grass was bountiful and all along the roads there was one big carpet of blossoming wild clover. The cattle were hardly visible and nature revealed itself in its greatest splendor." C. De Smit was overwhelmed by this beauty in Michigan.[74] On May 10, 1881, he arrived in Kalamazoo to see one of his former fellow hometowners; the snow had just disappeared and the wheat stood barely above ground; it was small and had suffered a great deal from the frost and heaps of snow. Already the fourth of July he saw the cutting of this wheat! At his arrival his host, Hollestelle, had just planted potatoes, and eight weeks later they both ate of them!

It seems that this vitality was also present in the animal kingdom. At least it had been observed in Pella that the breeding of all kinds of animals was unusually fast. "So, a pig born in spring often has a litter in the same year and from then on usually twice a year. Often, a horse three years old is seen with a colt alongside, this also goes for cows."[75] This vitality of plants and animals had its problems, but also its great advantages and has certainly contributed to the increase of prosperity, even though the farmers had no time "to let their sweat drip in the dunghill." People are rushed by nature; the psyche of the farmer under these circumstances was not left unaffected.

The farmers' prosperity was noticed by everybody. There were countless examples of those who in the Netherlands were mere farmhands or wretchedly poor day laborers, who, through hard work and perseverance, had lifted themselves in a span of twenty to thirty years from the status of "shabby" immigrants to that of prosperous and substantial farmers. Many weavers, smiths, carpenters, yes, even school teachers, etc., who took up farming in the settlements, achieved great prosperity. However, it goes without saying that those who had been farmers in the Netherlands were usually far ahead and obtained the best results.[76]

The increasing prosperity showed itself in the changing styles of homes. For example, Jan Elsma, the first immigrant in the village of Vriesland, Michigan, initially lived in a tent made of brushwood that was replaced by a log cabin and in turn by a wooden frame structure. The latter made way finally for a "substantial brick building."[77] Hundreds of energetic people, just like Elsma, could afford these changes. As a proud remembrance, some of them built their new building around the former dwelling of planks untouched in another part of the farmyard.

Bloemendaal was already struck in 1872 by Michigan's "beautiful farms." A few years later the well-known Cohen Stuart also noticed them when he made a trip through the colonies and along the fertile fields that were mostly separated from the roads by fences "horse-high, bull-strong, and pig-tight!"[78] The fields were separated from those of the neighbors by small woods maintained for this express purpose and which served at the same time as a shelter against the wind.[79] "Everything bespeaks of prosperity and abundance but without excessive luxury," was the assessment of Cohen Stuart.

De Smit, the farmer mentioned before, drove through the villages of Zeeland, Overisel, Drenthe, and Vriesland almost ten years later and spoke with many farmers there. He said that most of the farmers were making headway. "All may not be rich but many are making out quite well. The farms look neat and trim. Some homes are stylishly built, and where new barns are erected they are much neater and more practical."[80] Many owned a handsome *brikhuis* [brick home], as in the case of Wabeke in Zeeland, whose home even "looks somewhat like a villa!" J. P., who visited all these villages in the same period, confirmed this prosperity. "Here and there especially in Drenthe and Overijssel [Overisel] one sees sizable brick homes. Those are no longer farm houses but manors built of red brick. They are five windows in width, four windows in depth and two stories high."[81] "It is true that most houses are built of unplaned and white painted wood," but everything still looked "nice and tidy." In brief, the whole area around the city of Holland "leaves the visitor with an unforgettable impression of energy."

Similar remarks were made with respect to the other settlements. De Smit found in Low Prairie, Illinois, then called South Holland, "well-to-do farmers who are very successful." Much earlier, in 1867, at the Alto, Wisconsin settlement, even the formerly "poor settlers" had become prosperous farmers. "It is true that after some twenty years they are not yet rich, but as they say here, they are 'well-off.' Their possessions are worth from five to twenty-five thousand dollars. Most of them are living in nice two-story homes, furnished with beautiful furniture. Many own an organ and carriages. Also the clothes they wear are nicer than what they had formerly." In Sheboygan County, Bloemendaal called the settlements "a thriving district" and came across "substantial homes."[82]

The Roman Catholics in northern Wisconsin were also improving, although perhaps at a slower pace, more like the Michigan colonists. The village of Little Chute consisted largely of a farm population that had "the most beautiful estates." Around the village of Holland in this same colony, homes are grouped in an area of three to four miles. "The friendly homes of the farmers with three or four barns on the yard, bespeak of a prosperity that surpasses the prosperity of many a rich Dutch citizen."[83]

However, the Pella farmers surpassed all their fellow countrymen. Even many of those who had left their fatherland in a poor condition and who took up farming in Iowa, were in 1860 the owners "of several thousands of dollars."[84] Here, many farmers had 160 to 320 acres of land and also livestock that on average consisted of some eight horses, two draught oxen, forty cattle, and a hundred hogs, although farming the land, not animal breeding, was their main concern. Otherwise their farmsteads did not leave the same impression of prosperity as they did in Wisconsin, "where better and nicer houses are found," and in Michigan where the environs of Holland City "had a more prosperous look than in the area around Pella."[85]

The cause had probably not so much to do with lesser wealth—on the contrary!—but partly with the circumstance that timber was much cheaper in the former forest states, Michigan and Wisconsin, and partly with the scarcity of labor that Pella and vicinity felt all the more sharply because there the farms were so much bigger. Not only male but also female help was scarce and expensive. Moreover, the maids were even harder to keep than the hired hands. "For a crabby look they quit, and on the slightest provocation they get married." This was the typical general complaint in colonial areas about their shortage of women. Hence the farm homes of Pella exceed many others in soberness, at least in the fifties, in spite of the affluence of their owners, although the interior of farm homes in general has a tendency to look cheerless and far from cozy. One found very few pieces of furniture in those homes; the bed stood in the living room that had no curtains and only bare walls.[86] But sooner than any other settlement, Pella had a bank, where farmers could deposit their savings!

D. Trade and Industry

Commercial success, even more so than industrial prosperity, depended on the progress farmers could achieve. The farmers lived scattered from one another, but the businessmen were concentrated in the various villages from which in some cases cities grew. The thriving of these centers stood in close connection with the prosperity of the rural environment, since trade and industry depended largely on what the land produced and conversely what it needed. The colonies that were predominantly farm colonies progressed gradually. Just as steady was also the growth of their trade centers. This was the case not only in Pella but also in Holland, Zeeland, Oostburg, etc. Moreover, in those towns retailing, not wholesale trade, was predominant. Also, industry would become "big industry" only in the long run and only in some cases, as in Holland! In this society, next to the preacher, the storekeeper played the main role; in a few instances the manufacturer was also influential.

It is obvious that among these centers the forest city of Holland in Michigan and the prairie city of Pella in Iowa are the ones that draw our attention most strongly. The characteristic differences that have existed from the very beginning between the Van Raalte and Scholte colonizations would reveal themselves not only in the rural areas but at times even more strongly in the "cities." In the rooting years this was already noticeable; in the years of development this same trend revealed itself over and over again. For a long time Pellians kept their lead over Holland, Michigan, due to their greater financial strength, their higher level of education, and their broader views in matters of religion and faith. Pella's greater prosperity has been observed by various travelers. For example, in 1869 Pella "in a general sense" made a better impression on A. E. Croockewit than did Van Raalte's city.[87] While in 1882 J. P. found "the town of Pella to be definitely more developed" than Holland City, although most of Holland burned down in 1871, but was reconstructed since then.[88]

To be sure, Pella was located among only a few Dutch "neighborhoods," while Holland was encircled by a number of Dutch villages. But one should not forget that for a long time Pella also served as a marketplace for its American surroundings, and as long as there were no villages farther West, the colonists would ride a distance of twenty to forty miles to trade there. We already saw that the opening of the first railroad at Pella increased its importance as a shipping center. These circumstances also promoted the settlement of many Americans at Pella after the original plan to sell lots in the city exclusively to Holland immigrants had been abandoned. The prevailing broader religious conception made possible the founding of "Central University" at Pella by the Baptists. This educational institution had attracted such a large number of Americans that around 1860 about half the population consisted of Netherlanders and the other half mainly comprised Americans, besides a number of Germans and some large French families.[89]

Because of this growth in population, it was necessary to expand the city. The constant arrival of Dutch immigrants and others had already caused this since 1854. Various farm owners who had land at the boundary of Pella had their estates divided into lots that were quickly sold. The city grew by various additions, first in the south and southeast, after that on the west side, and finally in the easterly and northerly directions.

Pella's character as a shopping center was thus enhanced. In 1855, there were eleven general stores and many specialized stores, including two hardware stores, two furniture stores, three bakeries, one bookstore, two jewelers, and two drugstores.[90] Three years later the business district had expanded to fourteen stores, nine of which were run by Hollanders and the rest by Americans. As we know, many storekeepers specialized in the cattle trade and started slaughterhouses; a few also dealt in preserving and shipping eggs. For a long time the stores accepted eggs in payment of barter transactions, since poultry breeding was so important in Pella.[91] Small industries were also numerous. Although Pella had only five cabinet shops in 1858, the town was oversupplied with carpenters and masons. Furthermore, there were seven blacksmiths, three cartwrights, three saddlemakers, a few coopers, shoemakers, etc. Van Stigt belonged to the last-named occupation. He had learned to speak some English in St. Louis and this brought many American customers to his shop from as far away as ten miles from Des Moines. From that distance, the customers would even send him their measurements: sticks which gave the length and width of the desired footwear.[92] The proportionately great number of craftsmen indicates that they also provided their services for the numerous farmers in the vicinity.

A few branches of industry slowly became big business. Beurkens and Co., the cartwrights, managed to join the big league. In 1872 their vehicles were sent throughout the state by freight train.[93]

Most businesses were based on the raw materials that the vicinity offered, and what manufactured products were necessary in return; this made them self-sufficient. The presence of forests in the area and the continuous house building increased the prosperity of the sawmills. In 1858, Pella had six steam sawmills and one run by waterpower. Three of these sawmills belonged to Netherlanders, H. P. Scholte and Co., H. Hospers and Co., and J. Versteeg and Co. The remaining three belonged to Americans. The venture of Versteeg primarily had also branched out into a shingle business, the manufacturing of wooden roofing tiles.

As the building industry flourished, so did the brickworks and limekilns. Although most homes were made of wood, yet of the more than one hundred homes constructed in Pella in 1855, one-eighth of them were of brick. Versteeg, Aris, Toom, Spaan, and others ran brickyards and had flourishing businesses after some beginner's bad luck. The first of Versteeg's bricks crumbled after cooling off due to little bits of lime not visible in the soil.[94] P. Van Horssen and W. Nossaman, the lime manufacturers, also had flourishing businesses.

The growing of wheat and the demand for wheat flour produced a water-driven flour mill a few miles out of town which, however, left much to be desired. This gave occasion to construct two steam flour mills. A third one, the Washington Mill, was a German undertaking built in 1856 by E. F. Grafe, G. Henckler, and F. W. Waechter; for its time it was one of the best mills in Iowa. This company rose to prominence far beyond Pella or even the state of Iowa; wheat flour was delivered as far away as St. Louis. A great part of the year the mills ran day and night. The export of flour, lard, etc., called for barrels that brought trade to the coopers, particularly B. Ten Broek.

After a decline caused by the depression year of 1857, which also in Pella caused a standstill, if not a recession, industry grew even faster than before with the building of a beer brewery and a vinegar factory, a plant for the carding, spinning, and weaving of wool, a tobacco and cigar factory, a stonecutter's yard, a new lime oven, a hulling mill, etc. Especially the rail service brought great activity everywhere, so that in 1872 there were already four steam flour mills, two woolen mills, an iron foundry, and three steam forges.

The speedy progress found in so many settlements in America, also characterized Pella in the first half of the fifties and created the need for a banking business especially for the benefit of commerce. In 1855, the enterprising H. P. Scholte opened an exchange office in Pella, the first in Marion County, in cooperation with an American [Edwin H.] Grant. A regular banking institution was formed about two years later as the Central Exchange Land Office, initiated by H. P. Scholte, P. H. Bousquet, and Jan Nollen. Soon afterwards, it was continued by the two last-named founders after the institution had been incorporated according to state law as the Pella Savings Institution. In the depression of 1857, many banks failed in the United States; however this young Pella institution, started in the middle of those difficult times, managed to pull through, since it was supported by many people "who had the most implicit trust in Jan Nollen, the cashier, and their confidence was never betrayed." After this crisis, a second bank opened. It is ironic that particularly in those days the businessmen in Pella prospered, for many people no longer trusted paper money and spent it for merchandise in the stores even though the customers had no immediate use for it.[95]

There reigned in Pella an optimistic economic outlook and this inner feeling reflected itself in the appearance of the city. However, we must not overrate either one of them. In the first place, their trade and industry were mainly based on farming and cattle breeding in the immediate area and therefore were limited in scope. The city was thus also modest in appearance! The poetic-minded Gelderschman, filled with civic pride, declared (but at the same time not without the characteristic exaggeration of the realtor): "Pella of 1856 compares to Pella of 1847 as a fairy from the Arabian Nights."[96] Disenchanting, in contrast, were the experiences of A. E. Croockewit who found Pella in 1869 "more than ugly" with "everything there plainly sloppy!"[97] Croockewit himself was not without prejudice either! He had had bad luck with his lodging in Pella's hotel: " . . . the worst hotel I have encountered in all of the United States!" Well considered and therefore more correct seems to me the overall impression Pella made on [M.] Cohen Stuart in 1873.[98] He synthesized in a nutshell the inner as well as the outer state of affairs in a seemingly paradoxical statement: "Pella has a quiet but joyous and prosperous appearance." His judgment is applicable to this very day.

More promising, at any rate more numerous, were the possibilities of Holland, Michigan, because four times as many immigrants had settled in the Van Raalte colony than in the one of Scholte. In contrast to Pella, Holland had from the start immediate use of water transportation, which was so much cheaper. This factor especially made an impact after the improvement of the Holland harbor.

The most important market for the people of Pella was St. Louis via Keokuk, at least until about 1860. Holland had its chief market in Chicago, which was much nearer, even in winter, when Chicago could only be

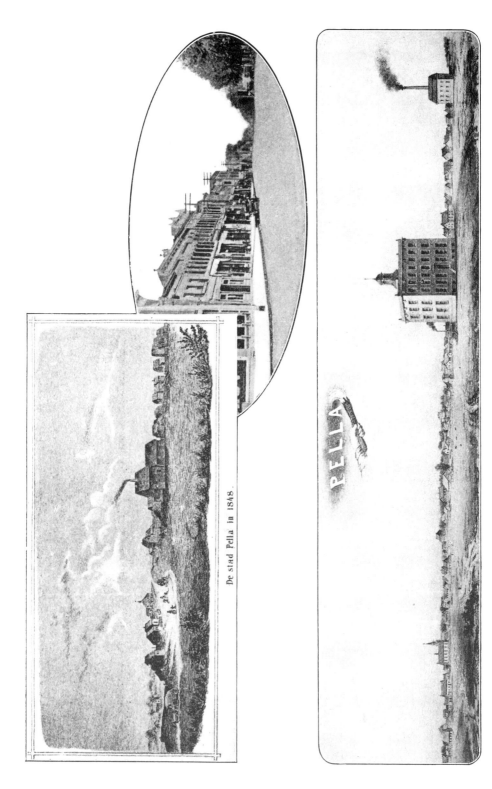

De stad Pella in 1848.

PELLA

The development of Pella. Top: Pella in 1848. Middle: Pella in 1920 (Main Street). Bottom: Pella in 1856. (Een Gelderschman, *Brieven uit Pella*.)

reached by land. In addition to Chicago, numerous other cities could be reached for the sale of its products, such as Milwaukee, Grand Rapids, etc. Holland could develop itself as a trading center and as a harbor town. Surrounded as it was by dense woods, it could ship not only farm products but also wood products. We already know that these woods, at the same time, could give rise to an important lumber industry. Therefore, Holland was far less dependent than Pella on the agricultural pursuits of its surrounding area. Its development could be more diversified: it could be simultaneously a market place, a harbor town, and an industrial center.

Notwithstanding these various beautiful prospects and despite the fact that Van Raalte and his followers had no less will power and enterprising spirit than Scholte, Bousquet, and many others, Holland stayed behind Pella for decades. It was only in the nineties and especially in the twentieth century that Holland was able to catch up and finally greatly surpass the prairie city in importance.

In Holland, the settlers did not lack boldness but, with a few exceptions, the general education left much to be desired and this was a drag on the economic prosperity. Holland was more in need of capital than Pella and this lack usually had a pernicious effect. Only if they had money could the possibilities be developed! Again and again Holland felt this shortcoming and so they sent forth a call to the enterprising spirit and capital in the homeland.[99] But the mother country had already forgotten its sons; it had fallen in a deep sleep that had been continuing for decades and from which it was difficult to awaken in the seventies. The attention of the metropolitan Dutch was nevertheless well focused on America but not on its migrant pioneers. These were outbid by the "real" Americans who were clever enough to attract Dutch capital from overseas for the use—or misuse—of their railroads.

Yet a deeper cause lies at the bottom of Holland's late prosperity, namely the general business outlook. America was above all an agricultural country, and because of agriculture, the prairie states exerted great attraction since people had learned to appreciate their value in the middle of the nineteenth century. All eyes, all interests, were on the prairie; to the prairie went the construction of the railways to transport the abundance of cheap grain, not only to flood America but Europe as well. It was the case with Holland, as with hundreds of other settlements in the woods, that its time had not yet come.

In Michigan the struggle for life was hard because nearly every piece of farmland had to be wrestled from the woods. Therefore, the colony grew only slowly and so did its center, Holland, which grew even slower because of the scanty financial power of its pioneers. Holland became above all a shopping center, like Pella, but its sales figures were lower, although it increased constantly in importance thanks to the dogged tenacity of the colonists. In the words of one of its oldest inhabitants, it and its agricultural hinterland enjoyed "a continuous prosperity, marked not so much by the accumulation of capital or wealth, as by steady and healthy growth."[100]

Holland had nine general stores in 1871. The operation of these stores required some capital. Therefore, several of these stores were in the hands of companies largely formed by Netherlanders. Besides, there were three hardware stores, three furniture stores, four stores for shoes and boots, four meat markets, two clothing stores, two fashion stores, one store for sewing machines, one cigar store, four drugstores, two jewelry stores, two portrait studios, two bookstores, one of which was connected with a bakery, three saddle maker's shops, one barbershop, two bakeries, seven shops that were nondescript, and others. Further, Holland had two hotels, with a restaurant adjacent to one, and in spite of all the struggles by Van Raalte and his followers against alcoholism, no less than three saloons or taverns. Many of the stores were, of course, joined to a small shop where the products were made. Mention must also be made of the five blacksmith shops, one cartwright shop, and three printing shops.[101]

In general, industry found itself, as in many other places, mostly at the sawmill and grainmill stage. It is well worth noting that both industry and business were still for the major part in the hands of Netherlanders. [Alderd] Plugger had a sawmill and a flourmill; W. K. Flietstra had even a steam sawmill. The mill of the American Ferris should also be mentioned. The abundance of lumber had already led to a somewhat more developed industry. In 1871 there were two "shingle, stave and bolt" factories in Holland, one belonging to P. F. Pfanstiehl and the other to Bosch, Mulder, and Volmar; two tanneries, one of Sprietsma and Co., and a large steam tannery of Cappon and Bertsch. In the other branches of industry, mention must be made of the "great and new plane and plow factory" of H. W. Verbeek and Co., a soap factory of H. Mohr, the Holland Brewery, a shipbuilding yard, and finally a "combination plow factory and iron foundry" of Heald, an American.

However, one should have no mistaken notion; these factories were not all that big. So far as I know, there was really only one truly big industry, the Cappon and Bertsch steam tannery. Isaac Cappon who had labored as a common farmhand in his native province of Zeeland belonged to the group that emigrated to America in 1847 under the leadership of Van de Luyster. During the trip, he worked as a cook's mate. In the Van Raalte colony he found work with the enterprising P. F. Pfanstiehl, who not only ran the Grand Haven-Kalamazoo stage line but also made money as pioneer tanner.[102] Cappon learned the tannery trade in Pfanstiehl's tannery, in which he succeeded so well that in the spring of 1857 with the help of Jan Bertsch he dared to start his own tannery, which soon flourished. After a few years, the business grew into a big steam factory that burned down in 1871, but a still bigger business arose from the ashes. During 1881 it employed about one hundred people! In those days a visitor said: "It is almost unbelievable what takes place there. There are three hundred vats and each vat takes up to 125 hides. Many operations take place by machine. When I left Holland, there was a stock of $40,000 worth of [tanning] bark alone."[103] A few years earlier, in 1875, this concern was incorporated as Cappon and Bertsch Leather Co. Before World War I, it was "capitalized at $800,000—the largest concern of its kind in Michigan." In 1914 there were on an average three hundred people employed in the factory of the former Zeeland farmhand![104]

Holland, just as Pella, based its trade and industry in the first place on its own supply and demand, but as we know, a bit of export took place from the earliest time. Timber products were Holland's oldest export, followed by manufactured goods and finally farm produce. When the growing of fruit increased in the colony, much fruit was shipped via Holland to Chicago and Milwaukee. The railways expanded Holland's hinterland.

Here also the economic bustle made a banking institution a necessity. In contrast with Pella, Holland's colonists themselves lacked the needed capital. However, in 1871 Holland had two banking institutions, the Kenyon's City Bank and the American Exchange. They disappeared for good in October of that year when a big fire destroyed the greater part of Holland. Two years later people appealed to Dutch homeland capital, but of course, to no avail! "A trustworthy bank established here, with the certainty of a high interest, would be an infallible means to great usefulness, to awaken new life." Not before 1889 did the First State Bank come into being.[105]

Business life set its stamp also on the outer appearance of Holland. Again it was Cohen Stuart who described this most pertinently when he made a little pleasure trip on Black Lake in 1873: "From our small boat it is a cheerful view; first the wharf of the city, with its sheds, with its factory buildings, and train wagons on the bank of the lake, and then a few slender schooners and some small vessels on the water." Furthermore, he commented that he found the industries in their infancy and made the tragic complaint: "There is no lack of enterprising spirit but a lack of means."[106]

The city's growth was stunted for many years by the 1871 fire and the general depression of 1873 when Holland almost completely lost its hard-earned capital savings. In the words of Cohen Stuart, the lakeside view of the city might not be unfavorable, but the total picture was far from rosy for years to come. In 1881, when De Smit visited Holland, he found that except for the tannery, a couple of sawmills, and "a few pretty shops," the rest of the city was insignificant.[107] The inhabitants of the colony themselves admitted this. Trade was essentially barter: "the farmer makes out best of all, the city and villages do not amount to much."[108]

Among these villages, which consisted mostly of a little church painted white, one or more stores, a blacksmith shop, and a few homes built on a slightly elevated sandy plateau, only the village of Zeeland amounted to something. It was more centrally located than Holland and got the reputation of being a "shopping village." That made it Holland's rival and more than once gave rise to friction not only in the rooting years but also later. In its vicinity was located the brick factory of [Jan Hendrik] Veneklaasen, the oldest large business in the colony. In 1881 Zeeland was pictured as "a nice village that looks very prosperous."[109] And for years it remained a village, primarily an agricultural village.

So Holland and Pella obtained their own character, and they were even mentioned as "cities" by the colonists, though not always without malice. But in none of the other colonies did one of the Dutch centers manage to develop all by itself to a comparable level. With a few exceptions their progress was extremely slow. It is true that in Wisconsin's Cedar Grove and, through the energetic efforts of the Zeelander Peter Daan, Oostburg also rose to importance after the laying of the railroad. In 1867 Daan had started a business in Sauk Trail, but he moved to Oostburg and there opened a store, an elevator, and a flour mill. Both towns up to the present time have remained rural communities.[110]

In the prosperous agricultural colony of Low Prairie in Illinios, a nucleus was so slow in developing that not until twenty-two years after the first settling did it get a post office. The enterprising Pieter De Jong, who had arrived in America with his parents in 1859, had the foresight to open a general merchandise store and was permitted in 1869 to open a post office in his store. At his suggestion Low Prairie was then renamed "South Holland."[111]

Only High Prairie, because of its favorable position on Michigan Avenue, grew into a bustling center and during the fifties and sixties became the leading town in the territory between Indiana and the city of Chicago. The administration of Calumet Township was set up in this town and consisted of a justice of the peace, a mayor, a secretary, a tax collector, etc., all of whom therefore lived there. In addition a post office was established in 1860 in the store of [Goris] Van der Sijde. It was called the Hope post office and consequently the town was renamed *Hope*. In 1875, Hope was renamed *Roseland*.

After the Civil War, High Prairie (as farmers preferred to keep calling it) stood as "a prosperous and beautiful little place."[112] Above all, it was still a rustic spot, mainly populated by farmers, while others found work in the construction of the railroads. When in 1873 a group of new immigrants arrived in town, so I was told by one of them, old Mister [Cornelis Laurens] Clausing, Michigan Avenue—built on an old moraine ridge and old lake shore and therefore a true ridge road—was the only "street," together with some shorter pieces of what are today's 103rd and 106th streets.[113] Good roads and even co-called sidewalks were as yet unknown. Sometimes one had to wade through the mud even up to one's knees, especially if one went to the much lower-lying land by Lake Calumet.[114]

Clausing was the first and for the time being the only painter in Roseland (so far, most people as true pioneers had done their own painting), and he with his family were temporarily put in an empty smithy when no suitable house was available. The blacksmith, unaccustomed to shoeing horses the American way, had had very little to do and therefore had deserted his

business. Old Mister Dalenberg supplied some boards that served temporarily as a table and chairs; thus the new immigrants had to make do and
improvise, just as in the days of initial settlement. The danger of wolves
was past but not that of snakes, which even managed to crawl into Clausing's bed. Since there were no windowpanes, flies, mosquitoes, etc. also
had free access to the home. However, the important thing was that the
newly arrived had found a new home, a "spot."

As one can see, in those pioneer days of the early seventies this small
town and its lifestyle, notwithstanding the hustle and bustle, still had a
primitive character. Even a bank, the criterion of an American town, could
not yet survive there. This was due, it must be said, to the fact that the
people had no confidence in Roseland's first banker, the Netherlander [Wil-
liam A.] Zwart, and consequently this gentleman went broke.

Before it could grow at a faster pace, Roseland, like so many other Dutch
colonies such as Holland and Zeeland in Michigan, and Little Chute and
Cedar Grove in Wisconsin, had to wait for the increase in development of
industry alongside agriculture, which would turn the United States from an
agricultural country into a mixed agricultural-industrial one. Nowhere in the
settlements that were initially almost completely rural has this changing
order manifested itself sooner or more strongly than among the Netherlanders in High Prairie. This village totally lost its own, independent Dutch
character over the years and was, in the end, completely absorbed by Chicago. This development, or rather this turnabout, started already in 1880
with the building of the world-renowned Pullman factories. Especially Marshall Field, the great Chicagoan and real estate speculator, seems to have
been the inspiring, driving force of that enterprise. In the Calumet area he
bought hundreds of acres of land.[115] Although everyone knows these factories, less well known is the fact that they were built on Dutch territory. Even
less well known is the manner in which Pullman managed to lay his hands
on a portion of the Dutch possessions. The sympathetic old Mister Clausing
told me the highlights of it.

The low land lying between the "ridge" and Lake Calumet is an old lake
bottom which lies ten to twenty feet lower than the old shore line. Lake
Calumet itself and many other small lakes are the remains of an earlier and
much larger Lake Michigan. This low-lying land had been bought by Hollanders for a very low price, for $1.25 and up. However, drainage was a
problem because of the sand dunes. One can say that Calumet Lake was to
a certain extent part of a beach lake, a lagoon, and the land was too marshy
to the liking of Americans and others. Since it was too wet for farming, the
Netherlander Jan Ton and others used it as a hayfield. They managed to
drain part of it so that the part near the ridge, which lay a bit higher, could
be used as pasture land. The lowest and least valuable portion was sold by
the Netherlanders to the Dock and Harbor Company, which wanted to give
Chicago better harbors, but which went bankrupt; thereupon the farmers
got the land back. In 1880 a certain "Colonel" Boon came suddenly to visit

one of the farmers, J. De Jong, and informed him that the Dock and Harbor Company would like to have the land back; others were told the same. Since the lay of the land in question was so low, De Jong and other Netherlanders were ready to make a deal and so the "Colonel" ended up with almost all of this land, a total of five hundred morgens [1,125 acres][116] Only three weeks later the first load of bricks arrived for the building of a so-called penitentiary. Indeed, the new construction—the Pullman plant, although later advertised as a "model city," turned out to be a horrible "penitentiary," also for many Netherlanders.[117] Today the complex of Pullman buildings still stands between 95th and 138th streets.

The first houses that were needed were obtained in a similar "noble" manner. Clausing, a Reformed and liberal Christian, continued his story as follows: Colonel Boon used as a middleman a Hollander who was marrying a rich widow and therefore sought a suitable home. The gentleman with marriage on his mind ended up with several houses. However, these were not for himself but for the Colonel!

In retrospect, our farmers were not badly cheated because they still got decent prices for their land. The settling of many fellow Hollanders, but especially the nearness of Chicago that was spreading in such a fabulous way—with today's tramline it is only a short hour's run away—had already raised much of the value of real estate even before the arrival of Pullman. Land originally bought for a few dollars had an average value in 1880 of $50 an acre. Already at the arrival of Clausing, some choice colony property was selling at $200 per acre!

The factories of Pullman, which would employ about ten thousand workers, drew people from all over the United States, even from Europe. These developments and the construction of new roads, railways, etc. increased the real estate prices even more, so that land that Pullman had bought in 1880 at an average of $50 an acre, increased to about $100 to $200 per acre, according to Brennan.[118] Clausing told me that there were people who had bought their land for one or two dollars per acre, and who had sold it during Roseland's expansion and resulting land speculation for $1,000 per acre, and that this was still too cheap!

Today a few building lots even have a value of about $300,000. A new city, named Pullman, sprang up near Lake Calumet. Also other nearby towns such as Kensington, where several Dutch Roman Catholics settled shortly after Clausing's arrival here, were mostly built on the original Dutch property. This new development drew so much attention that in 1882 Charles Boissevain, the well-known Dutch journalist, spent a whole day in this model city, in the company of Pullman and [Todd] Lincoln, the son of Abraham. This town had under construction hundreds of houses, a few hotels, a few churches, a theater, a court of justice, five factories, etc., all "in accordance with the fundamentals of hygiene and with the application of everything that can serve the comfort and happiness of the workers." Boissevain seemingly had no eye for Roseland and his former fellow-Dutch citizens a quarter of an hour away, because no mention was made of it.[119]

These former countrymen, in the meantime had become rich, some of them very rich, through the increased value of their farmsteads that had only been partially sold to Pullman. G. Van der Sijde, Jan Ton, H. Van der Bilt, P. Dalenberg, M. and P. Madderom, C. Kuyper, H. Tien, J., C., and D. De Jong, and many others all became very wealthy thanks to this veritable boom.[120] The Dutch element moved gradually to the cheaper westerly part when property on Michigan Avenue became too expensive. There, for example, a new church was built at a cost of $35,000, inclusive of the property; this purchase was made after the old church and a small adjacent piece of property had been sold for $20,000. They could afford it, couldn't they!

The new era, "the industrial era," had arrived for Roseland. It attracted not only Reformed Dutchmen, but also Roman Catholic Dutchmen, and many more non-Dutch people. C. J. Ton remarks correctly that through this influx the colony threw off its provincial character: "Its commercial, civic and religious lines were broadened." Probably no other family in Roseland experienced this more strongly that the numerous, "famous Ton family," of which "C. J., the historian," was a member.[121]

E. The Industrial Colonies

Industry was the inducement for the Dutch to settle in ever increasing numbers in Roseland but also in other even more advantageously located industrial cities: in Paterson, Rochester, Cleveland, Grand Rapids, Chicago, etc. In Grand Rapids, industry was initially attracted by the rapids in the Grand River, and the sawmill industry had developed a step further into a furniture industry. In 1873, 4,000 of the 16,000 inhabitants were Dutch.[122] By 1882 the population of the Furniture City had doubled, as had the number of our countrymen, which by then was more than 8,000.[123]

Paterson, an older city than Grand Rapids, had become an industrial center much earlier. (Paterson is the most northerly city situated on the "fall line.") The Dutch element was also much older there. Already between 1710 and 1720, Dutch farmers from Bergen County had established themselves near the waterfalls, the "Great Falls" of the Passaic River. They engaged in agriculture, including the growing of buckwheat and tobacco.

Before the War of Independence, six large farms belonging to the families Gerritsen, Post, Van Winkel, Van Houten, etc., were located there. In 1775, a Reformed Church was built after a congregation (called Totowa after the village) had been organized. In 1791, Great Falls of Totowa consisted of about ten houses, which included the well-known store that was run by a Van Winkel. Moreover, the foundations of industry were also laid, because near the falls a small grist mill and a sawmill had been built.

Alexander Hamilton, who had been billeted with Washington at Totowa as his Chief of Staff during the War of Independence, became interested in the town. (Washington stayed with one of the Van Winkels and sometimes with the Van Houtens.) Hamilton had been deeply shocked by the mutiny that was caused by the lack of clothing in the severe winter. Because of this, he founded a company for the manufacturing of clothing fabrics, and considered Totowa the ideal place for this new industry. The Dutch farmers, just as the Roseland ones did later, sold part of their land, and in 1794 the first large cotton factory was founded. From this village of Dutch farmers, a large factory city developed. Hamilton named it Paterson after the then Governor of New Jersey.

Several factories were built, so that in 1824 more than 24,000 spindles were available to the cotton industry, making Paterson one of the two largest cotton cities in America.[124] The iron industry also settled there, similarly attracted by the falls. In 1869, Croockewit found the largest locomotive works in the United States in the city of Paterson. Silk came later, which was the material that would make this city into the Silk City *par excellence*. Many Dutch emigrants who arrived in New York stayed for a while on the other side of the Hudson in the Paterson area, where they usually found work immediately upon arrival. Here also started the trains "to the West."

However, it is striking that despite the work opportunities in New Jersey, only a few Dutchmen settled here initially. This is all the more striking because they found themselves among Americans of Old Dutch descent who still spoke the Dutch language, the old Low German [*het oude Neder-duitsch*]. They not only received them with hospitality and kindness, but also—and this meant so much more to many of them—they sang Dutch psalms with them and often spent the evenings in talk and appropriate singing and closed with a prayer in Dutch!

For the farmers there was plenty of land; even many fertile farms lay fallow. Where the tradesmen were concerned, there was a shortage of them everywhere.[125] Many were attracted by the cheap land; others, like Van Eijk who had found a job in well-known Schralenburgh, New Jersey, where he also experienced "much friendship," were attracted to the West by letters of friends.[126] There was a third consideration, not exclusively an economic or "sociable" [*gezellige*] one, but a psychological factor, which explains why not only Dutchmen but also Germans and others traveled on. They went in spite of the fact that they had just completed a dangerous and miserable sea journey, in spite of the fact that they did not want to become farmers or did not have any friends out West, in spite of the fact that they had job opportunities in the East: it was the dim but compelling urge to go West!

It was this urge, which they felt but did not always understand, that led so many Dutchmen to Grand Rapids. There they found work in the furniture factories, the type of work that Paterson had offered them much earlier. It was this restlessness, considered by the well-known E. A. Ross to be a "mob mind,"[127] that created such an unusual energy in many immigrants. This explains why in a factory city like the so much older city of Paterson only a few dozen Dutch immigrants had remained, while the young city of Grand Rapids, which lay inland to the Northwest and could only be reached via an expensive and dangerous trip, already counted hundreds, even thousands of them.

Only in the sixties, did several Dutchmen remain in Paterson and vicinity after their arrival. This was, of course, after the time that the psychological factor had lost its greatest impetus, and emigration took place practically only for economic reasons. Because of the reduced dangers of improved steamboat traffic and the much lower fares as a result of competition, it was no longer only the most energetic ones who left the Old Country. The lesser risks through the accelerating development of the United States also enticed the less energetic to move. The advance of industry even gave rise, alongside of spontaneous immigration, to an involuntary or supported immigration. This is the reason why an increasing percentage of these immigrants abandoned the idea of moving on to the West. Wages also were a contributing factor as to why they preferred to remain hanging around in the East.[128]

It is of great importance to point out factors like the reluctance to go West, because it makes clear certain traits that have been touched upon earlier when mention was made of the contrasts between the Dutch living in American cities and those living in the countryside. For these factors make understandable why in particular among the Dutch immigrants in the densely populated East of the United States were found those who were the least "American" in their feelings and attitude. And why, for instance, it was notably they who slowed down the Americanization process the most. This category of immigrants have remained Dutch so much longer, in spite of their legal naturalization, not only because they landed in the United States some decades later but because basically they had by nature fewer "American" character traits.

In connection with the remarks just made, it is therefore no coincidence that in the sixties there were a few cities between Paterson and Grand Rapids that attracted the Dutch element more strongly than had been the case previously. The waterfall city of Rochester, New York, in the vicinity of which many Zeelanders had been living since the thirties, now attracted many Frisians and other Dutchmen because of its expanding industry after the Civil War. Cleveland, Ohio, the important port city on Lake Erie, became known to many Dutchmen as they passed through on their journey westward, but only a few dozen decided initially to remain there. A Cleveland Dutch congregation was not founded until 1864. However, once industry rapidly expanded after 1865, the number of Dutchmen increased to a few hundred. Many became prosperous and moved up to foreman in the factories.

In conclusion, we recall the rapidly growing Chicago colony that is located even more westerly than Grand Rapids. Here many were attracted not only by industry but also by trade and even more by the cheap land that lay in its vicinity. The Dutch neighborhoods north and south of present-day Oregon Avenue, in an outlying district of the city, fortunately remained untouched in the great fire of Chicago.[129]

No matter how transient the Dutch element was in the various cities— many who had saved up some capital finally preferred to travel westward— usually a nucleus remained. The custom of the Dutch, as is the case with many nationalities in America, was to seek out each other and live in the same neighborhood. In many cities this was the reason for the development of Dutch ethnic neighborhoods that were even further subdivided according to the provinces of origin. Hence neighborhoods were formed that were inhabited by Groningers, Frisians, and Zeelanders. These exclusive neighborhoods occur in Paterson, Rochester, Grand Rapids, and Chicago. For this reason many a Dutch shopkeeper established himself among artisans not only from the Netherlands, but preferably from his own locale. During these years of expansion, many of these shopkeepers greatly enlarged their enterprise, so much so that a few of them eventually were able to found modern department stores. This will be discussed later.

F. Setbacks

We must not think that the growth of settlements was automatic or without a struggle after the difficult years of growing pains had passed. The extremes of climate, the characteristics of the country, and especially the peculiarities of the inhabitants had to be constantly taken into account. In spite of their proven adaptability, they could not escape the steady strain of these factors. This strain or tension explains the striking nervousness which also shows in the social life of the Dutch immigrants. As previously seen, they showed themselves already in the frontier years to be real Americans.

Ordeals of different sorts made the struggle for survival by the colonists more difficult. For instance, Pella was struck by a cholera epidemic during the hot summer of 1854. Many people were afflicted and the disease carried some sixteen inhabitants to their graves. Two years later the same town was ravaged by smallpox. Again, many people were stricken but only a few died. However, this latter illness had other consequences. Many Americans from the surrounding area, who had become afraid, avoided the city and traveled extra miles to avoid Pella. They refused to trade in Pella, and as a consequence, for weeks and even months, a deadly silence prevailed in the town. This was in sharp contrast to the hustle and bustle of preceding years. After the last patient had recovered, some people were still so much afraid that they preferred to sell their products elsewhere.[130]

The crisis years of 1857, and especially 1873, "the most serious the country had ever experienced," required financial sacrifices also from many a Dutchman, although as already seen, shopkeepers reaped a tidy benefit during 1857—at least in Pella.

No colony was more severely tried that the Van Raalte colony, especially the city of Holland, the greater part of which burned down in October, 1871.[131] For weeks on end the Midwest had suffered from an uninterrupted drought that caused many forest fires in Michigan as well as elsewhere. Holland had been surrounded by forest fires for days, and only through the most extreme efforts had people been able to insure their safety. Eyewitness Van Schelven tells us that the wind turned to the southwest and gradually increased in strength on Sunday, October 8, at 2 P.M. The alarm bell was rung and the afternoon churches were emptied. In vain did they try to stop the enemy's advance; the wind drove the fire into the city. The Third Reformed Church as well as its manse and several surrounding buildings was quickly reduced to ashes and the sea of flames soon reached the tannery of Cappon. The treebark, the hemlock bark, stored there caught fire, and driven by the tornado-force wind, it "showered the city with a rain of burning lumps." This started fires simultaneously in many places and compelled people to flee from everywhere in the city. Everyone took to flight, although many tried to save some of their belongings by burying them in their gardens. All this happened in the middle of the night. Between one and three o'clock in the morning, the bigger part of the city, its center, from Twelfth to Second Street, was gutted. In a span of no more than two hours, Holland had burned down to the ground. More than two hundred houses, seventy-five stores, shops and offices, about fifteen factories and many smaller workshops, the three hotels, numerous storage places, and even five churches were destroyed! Fortunately only one life was lost, that of an old widow, Mrs. J. Holk. However, the remains of more than 250 horses, cattle, and pigs were found.

Van Raalte, after preaching in Muskegon on Sunday, sped home on Monday morning, driving through a blaze of forest fires; he found the railroad bridge near Holland on fire and heard that Holland had been reduced to ashes. "How my heart throbbed! The brevity of this life, and the fact that this fire did not ruin any souls, strengthened me." With much difficulty, he succeeded in reaching his home in the northern part of the city by pushing ahead along the railroad. His house had been spared but was still threatened from the southwest. It was filled with the homeless. The scattered populace was lying around, exhausted or full of anguish, and few had the strength to work in the smoke that burned the eyes and suffocated the lungs.

On October 10 [Tuesday] it began to rain, but the strong wind was still a threat. "The scene is heartbreaking at present," said Van Raalte. "The naked square where once the city stood is filled with people digging for what they had buried. The mass of the curious and interested people milled around. Everywhere around, smoke columns rise and if the wind turns, everything that has been spared will be threatened. What a turn of events! . . . The fruits of some twenty-five years of labor almost totally swept away."

Just as in the early years of settlement, Van Raalte was again able to encourage the despairing: "Do not argue nor complain.... A wipe-out of our goods is often necessary to make us amenable to God's heritage and treasures. Earthly things often have to vanish in a vapor before the souls will ripen for the heavenly good." At a citizens meeting on the Tuesday after the fire, many agreed with his forceful words, so typical for him and many of his fellow colonists: "With our Dutch tenacity and our American experience, Holland will be rebuilt."

Immediately, therefore, people started with the construction of small sheds and hauled in timber and planks. "J. Van Landegend, who had been burned out twice, E. Van der Veen, and many others are already busily at work." What had been spared would serve as landmarks in the reconstruction—the plow factory of Heald, the saw and flour mills of Plugger, the townhouse, the First Reformed Church, the True Dutch Reformed Church, the printing shop of the church magazine De Hope, both railroad stations, and the buildings of the "institution of higher education," Hope College. Especially the fact that Hope College had been spared lifted the spirits of the people in a special way. "We are deeply convinced that this unharmed present is a token of our perseverance, unity, and future prosperity." Indeed, it has worked out that way.

The Dutch, however, have not been able to accomplish everything. More than three hundred families lost their homes, clothes, furniture, food stocks—everything. Fortunately, the sympathy and concern in the surrounding communities was widespread. Food was sent from Grand Haven, Grand Rapids, and elsewhere. State and local committees were formed. Gifts arrived from all sides—from the sister city of Pella and through the mediation of Nicolaas Beets even from the Netherlands. Friends of the Holland colony, who were members of the Reformed Church in the East, gave $40,000. This sum grew to $60,000 and was mostly divided among the victims in Holland, although a small part went to the adjacent townships that had also suffered.

It should not be forgotten that fires broke out in many other places in Michigan and Wisconsin; Chicago in Illinois was destroyed by fire at the same time as Holland. The latter circumstance hindered the rebuilding of Holland to a great extent. In the first place, the ones who carried insurance received only small fractions of the insurance money that was due to them, because the Chicago fire had forced many insurance companies into insolvency. Fortunately in this regard, only $35,000 of the estimated $900,000 of property that burned in Holland was insured.*This shows the conservative spirit of the inhabitants.

The rebuilding of Chicago created such an enormous demand for building materials that prices skyrocketed. This, of course, was also very notice-

*Van Hinte means that the uninsured persons were fortunate in that they had not paid insurance premiums in vain

able in Holland. The cooperation of the railroad companies in transporting Holland-bound materials for free did not offset these price increases. The rebuilt factories, houses, etc., were much more costly than had been estimated, and many people had to borrow money. Those who had sufficient capital to invest in several building syndicates for the benefit of the city were also set back.

The big depression of 1873 was also felt in the Dutch colony. The value of the properties that were built with so much sacrifice suddenly decreased in value by 50 percent, while money to meet obligations had to be borrowed at 10 percent interest. This was too much for even the most courageous tradesmen in Holland. Those who were the most enterprising of the colony and had already lost much during the fire, but nevertheless had cooperated with all their energy in the rebuilding program, now ended up in debt, "a cruel but unavoidable fate." Those "who in the past had contributed to her fair name and prestige" were not allowed to cooperate in the further restoration of Holland. "Brave as they were, they could not outweather the storm, but ultimately were wrecked upon the shores of an honest and honorable ambition."

As I remarked earlier, this fate of financial impotence of these most energetic elements left its heavy mark on the city of Holland for many years. This explains why in 1881 much bartering still took place in Michigan, although by then it was no longer the "Far West." It is these trials that, in addition to the daily struggle for existence, contributed to a kind of selection among the colonists during the years of development. These factors set a stamp on their whole nature, physically and psychologically, that is still noticeable in their descendants.

12

Cultural Change*
Religious Life

A. Local Quarrels

The colonists struggled not only for their material concerns, but as they prospered they also allowed themselves more time for their spiritual development, in the first place in the realm of religion. This spiritual development was also coupled with much strife and led to greater ordeals than were mentioned in the last chapter. In striving to fulfill their material needs, all Netherlanders were, in spite of minor differences, unified in laboring together. But with regard to their spiritual affairs, so much controversy broke into the open that it led to fierce bitterness and eventually even to secession that until now has not yet been bridged.

From what was mentioned in previous chapters it becomes understandable why the difficulties experienced in cultural change were primarily of a religious, or, if one wishes, of an ecclesiastical nature. I need not remind you to what extent their religious conviction formed the fancied, and at times also the real, ideal for the sake of which many had left their fatherland. For many of these immigrants, their religion was even their only, their unique, cultural heritage that, like the Puritans in earlier days, they carried with them across the ocean and that they tried to preserve immaculate like a precious gift. And as far as the immigrants of the forties and fifties took any literature with them, it was by preference of a religious nature.

Emigrants traveling with Van Raalte had, as he mentioned, plenty of Bibles, psalm books, and religious works of [John Angell] James and [Franz Ludwig] Zahn.[1] Those who came later were advised: "Bring large Bibles and at least two small Dutch Bibles for each person...."[2] Only the most educated emigrants, like some of the ministers, also brought along some "art," but these works, too, were by preference of a religious character. Van der Meulen, for instance, at the suggestion of Brummelkamp packed the feast

*In chapters 12–15, Van Hinte speaks of *geestelijke groei,* literally meaning "spiritual growth." However, in the English context a better rendering is "cultural change."

songs of Da Costa, which later on would give him much pleasure and even much consolation.[3]

People in the other Calvinistic colonies also had Bibles, psalm books, and other religious reading matter. When the supply of books ran low the printers would reprint and fill the demand. The well-known Binnenkant of Holland, Michigan, repeatedly reprinted "Dutch works" that, ironically, happened to be of non-Dutch writers such as [James] Milner, *Kerkgeschiedenis* [*Church History*]; Merle d'Aubigné, *Historie van de Reformati* [*History of the Reformation*]; Zahn, *Bijbel en Kerkgeschiedenis* [*Bible and Church History*], etc.[4] But the Bible remained the basic guide for their spiritual life and daily living as it had been in the pioneer years. For many it was the only thing they read.

All colonists strove to be materially successful. Some achieved success from the first, others became more or less successful later, and some did not make it at all. Achieving success caused some settlers to place themselves at a distance from others settlers, especially in the years of development when people had less need of each other's support than in the pioneering years. And, as Bloemendaal repeatedly observed with regard to the Michigan as well as the Wisconsin colonists, those who had "made it," and especially their wives, snobbishly looked down with some pride, at times even with overweening pride, upon their less fortunate fellow immigrants.[5] This did not have to result in a split, though. Because their common ideal remained the same in spite of this difference in "status" that was evident already quite early among our colonists. Since this status was not based on birth but on the number of dollars one possessed, it was very ephemeral.

Things were different in spiritual life, however, especially in church life. Here too, one could find "progress," but frequently not conscious or voluntary progress. In fact it was often the contrary; progress occurred in spite of the fact that people often tried to resist it strongly and even violently! It seems that in this respect most of the newly arrived settlers cherished the same ideal: preservation of the faith of the fathers! The ways in which people tried to realize this ideal varied considerably. On the one hand, there were those who compulsively wanted to hold fast to a "Dutch" Calvinism. For many this attitude expressed itself most tellingly in a no less compulsive attitude that inseparably coupled Calvinism with the maintaining of the Dutch language. In a word, this group wanted a rigid conservatism. On the other hand, there was the group that wished to adapt to the American environment, particularly so as not to cause an aversion to Calvinism among the younger generation.

The more educated individuals, and therefore usually also the more prosperous ones, belonged to the progressives. The less educated individuals, and thus the less prosperous ones, belonged in general to the conservatives. Both these attitudes were in part a consequence of their religious conviction: the latter ones partially because of a more or less conscious love of ease, that is, the continued practice of the mother tongue and of the national mores and customs; the former ones partially because of a calculating outlook, that is, a desire to conquer a good spot in America. So we see that differences, partly of an economic nature, caused a rift not in the economic sector but in the sphere of religion.

Let us look somewhat more clearly at the causes of these religious rifts. One may be convinced that every religion preached among a people must adapt itself to the character and the degree of development of that people if that religion wants to obtain a firm footing and maintain itself. One may also see how our colonists differed in character both individually and as groups, and that their degree of development, taken not only in the sense of knowledge but especially in the sense of life experience, would increasingly diverge over the years. Then one can understand why, due to the additional factor of great variances in susceptibility to Americanization, differences in religious opinions had to arise, or in case they already existed, why they led to great discord, particularly when the peak of the strenuous struggle for material existence was over.

A few factors explain the virulent character into which these disputes degenerated. There was in the first place the fact that adaptation was anathema to a large number of the most rigid Calvinists, since religion was practically their only cultural heritage, so that they concentrated practically all of their spiritual attention on it. And then there was, as we saw, a great tension that arose in the stimulating and even provocative new environment.

The constantly re-emerging religious differences were originally most evident among that group of colonists who were initially, for the most part, strongly orthodox Calvinists of long standing. These differences are still evident today and still result in expulsion and secession. A similar trait can be observed among Calvinists in the Netherlands. It is ultimately the result of human character and the degree of human development. At the same time these differences reflected stages in the Americanization process.

In addition to earlier observations, we can now understand why in the major settlements, notably in their centers of Holland, Zeeland, and elsewhere, the wish for adaptation was the greatest, even in matters of religion—in Pella, despite Scholte!—while among the Netherlanders in the large industrial centers, like Grand Rapids, Paterson, Chicago, and others, as well as in the smallest and most distant rural settlements, people strove to hold on to their rigid Dutch Calvinism.

Thus it is not by accident that, after Van Raalte, Van der Meulen, and others had succeeded in leading the Netherlanders in the Michigan colony to join the Reformed Church, the opposition to this union became the strongest in these industrial centers. It also must be pointed out that this Reformed Church was actually of Dutch origin, but it had been founded more than two centuries before and influenced by a totally different environment. The process of Americanization had not yet progressed far enough to enable the urban Netherlanders and those scattered here and there in rural areas, especially the ones who had not experienced the rugged pioneering years, to feel at home in the Americanized Reformed Church.

Thus it is usually possible to see in the numerous ecclesiastical quarrels, as in the secession in the year 1857—about which more will be said later, a reaction to the Americanization process, which for separate individuals has such a variety of rates of speed. Additionally, one should not forget that the basic and deepest motivating forces are human character and human development, already mentioned. What very often gave rise to these clashes were personal disagreements among the colonists, which in turn were the result of an extreme intolerance, particularly in orthodox quarters, that was closely related to their usually excessively narrow ideology. On the other hand, it would be unfair not to try to distinguish, even in these cases that seem to be purely personal fall-outs, a more deeply lying cause: a clash of characters and at the same time, of particular trends.

Already in the early years of social rooting, when people had their hands full—and their heads too!—with resettlement, we observed rumblings of religious division. In the village of Graafschap, where the brothers were divided into two fiercely lambasting opposing factions, the feud led to a split from the Reformed Church in 1852. A number of seceding colonists, led by R. J. Schepers, affiliated with the Scotch Associate Reformed Church, "the prelude to the dirge."[6] Classis Holland had refused to ordain Schepers, an elder, as a minister!

In the village of Drenthe, inhabited by Drenthers as well as by Staphorsters—both very orthodox groups—each held on to its own views. As a result they stood eyeball to eyeball there too! When Dominie R. Smit, who had emigrated from the Netherlands at a later date, was preaching to his Staphorsters on the holy days, the Drenthe brothers chopped down trees so close to the church that it disturbed the worship services! Also here Classis Holland had to intervene, and ultimately the conflict ended in separation from the Reformed Church. Just like Schepers, Smit and his Staphorsters joined the Associate Reformed Church.[7]

A wayward fanatical zeal and cantankerousness that had nothing to do with church orthodoxy were the factors that turned the scales in both secessions. They give a typical picture of life among the believing pilgrims. A reaction against Americanization was not yet evident, because both groups separated from one American church and joined another American church. However, what seemed worse was that they went from a Dutch-American to a Scotch-American Church. I want to point out that, in the long run, neither group felt comfortable in this Scotch association and later most of them affiliated with a newly created church of secessionists, the Christian Reformed Church.[8] So we see, also in this case, that as time went by, the ethnic background and its close relationship to religion made themselves felt as redoubtable factors, in spite of the fact that perhaps no other denomination stands closer to Dutch Calvinism than this Scotch church, which, however, was already too Americanized for our Hollanders. Thus, in this case too, it was a matter of difference in assimilation.

In other settlements the disputes were no less severe. There also, they were in part personality clashes and, properly speaking, sometimes had little to do with actual religion. In Graafschap a contested marriage caused a rift, in Vriesland a land transaction caused a split, while in Zeeland an elder misused money entrusted to him and this led to secession. In Holland, the rental of church pews—which in itself was quite an event in the rather monotonous life of the colonists—was a source of aggravation for some.[9]

Due to their generally extremely scanty education, these immigrants overestimated the importance of all these events. The fact that nothing very much happened in the settlements, that there was virtually no diversion or amusement, contributed to seeing things far out of their true proportion. A certain provincialism, or some clan spirit, would show itself. In the community of Drenthe it was the Drenthers and the Overijselers (Staphorsters) who were locked in an adversarial position. In Chicago the stumbling block was the contrast between Groningers and "Southern Hollanders" of Noord Holland and Zuid Holland.[10]

The character of the leaders was often far from conciliatory, as in Pella, and was the actual source of altercations. Notwithstanding the high regard one may have for men like Van Raalte and in part also for Ypma and Scholte and others, we should not overlook the fact that, besides numerous good qualities, they nevertheless showed some traits that explain on the one hand why it was these men in particular who became the leaders of the Secessionists in the Netherlands and of the immigrants in America. But on the other hand, it also makes understandable why opposition arose against their sometimes preemptory, imperious dealings, and even made it inevitable.

Pella's Van Stigt, himself a good-natured man and an admirer of both Scholte and Van Raalte, put his finger on this "whole-hog" attitude, this "hard-shell" quality of character in these leaders. Van Stigt also spoke from personal experience regarding Van Raalte, who had sojourned a few times in Pella in order to take care of church business that, believe it or not, pertained to a "secession" no less! A meeting had to be held to discuss the distribution of the church property. This required the presence of all who were involved. Van Raalte requested Van Stigt to make known the scheduling of this meeting in the surrounding community. Van Stigt's refusal, especially since horseback riding "was an uncommon affair" for him—he was a shoemaker—was totally ignored. And "in the mouth of Van Raalte the kind request became an order." So for two days our shoemaker rode a horse and vowed never to ride again. He knew what he was talking about when he wrote that such a relentless character was not always useful and pleasant.[11]

Van Raalte's best friends had similar experiences. B. Grootenhuis, his right hand man in the early years, remarked that the leader "demonstrated

a never-give-up and energetic character," which was at times violent, especially when through their short sightedness or other reasons people contra-
vened his intentions because they did not understand them. He seemed
"sometimes to be somewhat arbitrary, intemperate, high-handed, as if he
had dressed himself up in the livery of a Dictator," Dr. [Egbert] Winter
declared. G. Van Schelven remarked, "The local assembly of representatives
in Holland was Van Raalte, the consistory of Holland was Van Raalte, the
Classis of Holland was Van Raalte.... The inevitable result of all this was
that in these matters, as far as they were concerned with local community
affairs, there was no possibility of appeal whatsoever. So, for the malcon-
tent—right or wrong—there was little else left but secession."[12]

Scholte's character, as we pointed out earlier, was also demonstrated by
his natural bent toward being overly bold and by his arbitrariness. Of Reverend Ypma it was also noted that his character was "not easy to take."[13]
Facing these resolute, strong-willed leaders, the immigrants often stood
marked by little inner and outer refinement and culture. They were "eye-
sores" at times, and yet not mere ciphers or nobodies. "God sent the best,
the most select of human races to our shores to lay down the foundations
of our national existence, broad and deep," wrote Henry Beets almost
twenty years ago. He further asserted, with both youthful and American-like
modesty, that to these chosen few belonged a picked body of Dutchmen. By
this, however, he did not mean the seventeenth-century Knickerbockers, no
matter how much nobility of character was to be found among these old-
time settlers. "No, the best that the Netherlands gave was not the progeny
of Old Holland. It was the children of Young Holland who had come hither
in the middle of the nineteenth century: the Pilgrim-fathers of the West,
guided by divine light."[14]

Indeed, these Dutch formed a select group of people who were not in the
first place composed of believing, theologizing, psalmsinging, quarreling,
snarling, mutually slandering pilgrims. But they were men and women who
had the courage of their convictions, no matter how narrow-minded these
may appear to us. They showed this courage at the risk of losing their
livelihood or of being thrown in prison. They formed a select group of
determined people who consciously or unconsciously broke with the hum-
drum ways and ruts that were indeed prevalent in the very, very old "Young
Holland" in economic as well as in spiritual affairs. Rather than go on
dozing or sleeping, they went forth to meet the dangers of the unknown.
These people, who had a will all of their own, at first submitted to the more
educated and gifted leaders because they felt instinctively to be in need of
them. But it becomes understandable that the longer they breathed the
American air, the more they would rebel in due time against the "tyranny"
of a Van Raalte and the "fanatical zeal" of a Scholte.

Already in the early years of colonial rooting, Van Raalte was called "The
Pope" and the consistory his "Cardinals." In the town of Holland a bitter
and continual fight centered on the question whether the Immigrant mem-

bers of the consistory, who had formed a consistory even before a congregation existed, should relinquish their office after two years in accordance with the church order of Dordt, which was also the wish of the congregation, or whether, according to the Utrecht revision of the Secessionists of 1837, they could remain in office for the rest of their lives, as most of them thought, and initially Van Raalte did too.

The resulting strife and quarrels, which lasted for years, may be seen in part as aimed at Van Raalte. He was "the butt of the dirtiest, most malicious slander," expressed especially in unsigned letters. But in turn, the consistory, which tried to draw slowly away from his overwhelming influence, arrogantly assumed the most intractable official authority in relation to the leader. The struggle became so fierce that when after more than twelve years of a slow, step-by-step progress, the congregation finally won the right to choose its own consistory in March, 1860, Van Raalte at a secret consistory meeting, held shortly afterwards, exclaimed: "Already twenty years ago I should have had a different consistory." Having learned through experience, said Dosker, he had become again a good Dordtian![15]

But the altercations went on, in spite of the change. Very soon after the new consistory had been chosen, it followed the same old groove of tradition and its character did not change.[16] The consistory members felt almighty, which greatly irked many people who rebelled against "the arrogance of the Colonial Elders and the way they lorded it over everybody."[17] In the end, these protestors were even alienated from the church by such highhandedness.

Many other difficulties remained for Van Raalte because, in spite of all the bickering and troubles brought by the Secession, his congregation kept growing. His task, therefore, became increasingly burdensome and his health, already seriously impaired by all the tensions, suffered even more. Van Raalte wanted to split the congregation but his consistory would not yield. In 1862 during a new controversy, an English-speaking church, the "Second Reformed" or "Hope Church," was organized, while those that lived on the "town line" bordering the community also requested an independent organization. Then in 1866, a third congregation, *Ebenhaezer* [Ebenezer] was founded. Bitter jealousy developed among the sister congregations.[18] Finally on July 16, 1867, Van Raalte relinquished his position, as he himself said, " . . . to put an end to the detrimental situation that has characterized the congregation's relationship to himself for much too long a time." Additionally, he said that "numerous activities that God's providence involved him with made it impossible for him, especially since his physical strength was declining, to do those things for the congregation that he would have liked to do for it and which it ought to receive." The consistory was "tenderly moved" and accepted the resignation in anticipation of the confirmation by the congregation that was given shortly afterwards. Van Raalte, although no longer a preacher, remained busy for years as a leader and worked unceasingly for the interests of the people, *his* people, "which he bore in his heart." People felt this especially during critical times when they would turn to him instinctively, as during the great fire of 1871. He remained the soul of the whole colony until his death.

Even more severe than in Holland were the clashes in Pella, where a number of colonists were more educated and an even larger number were well-to-do, and therefore less tolerant of arbitrariness. These troubles were of a totally different nature, although they were turned into religious concerns no matter how earthly they were, as are all concerns of daily life. There was a mistrust of Scholte that dated back already to the time when he had failed to give an account to the Society whose money he administered. He caused new aggravation through his actions as a land speculator when in 1854 he unexpectedly sold, without the knowledge of his congregation, two lots to American businessmen who had made him a "tempting offer." However, these two lots in the center of Pella, on Garden Square, he had already donated to his congregation for the building of a church! Great discontent arose about Scholte's preemptory dealings, and it grew to a generalized feeling of outrage when the leader persisted in his contention that the lots belonged to him because he had not yet tranferred their deeds! He had decided that the lots on Garden Square were a better location for stores than for a church. Therefore, he had set aside a more quiet and suitable place for a church in a recent, newly-platted subdivision of the town. Although according to many church members he was not in the least authorized to do this, he refused "to confess that his dealings were improper, and to redress them." He even told the appointed investigative committee "that it wasn't necessary to go back to this matter again." So they decided "to shun him as long as he persevered in his ways."

Thus the Christian Church in Pella was torn apart. Yet many remained faithful to him, being more drawn by the words of God's man, Scholte, than repelled by his dealings. For a few Sundays he preached to a rather large gathering in a barn of Jacob De Haan's farm, south of town. Later on he used the workshop of I. J. Michmershuizen, the painter. In 1855 he financed and built his own church where he preached every Sunday afternoon, for preaching was his great joy, according to Van Bergeyk.[19] Meanwhile the morning services were conducted in turn by qualified members of his Christian church.[20] By 1858 his church numbered about 175 to 200 members, with no elders or deacons. During the weekly meetings, Scholte was chairman and P. H. Bousquet functioned as secretary. The members were all active and the Bible served as their constitution and Church Order. They were "diligent workers" and paid careful attention to one another.[21]

Thus Scholte as a preacher was yet able to secure for himself some followers, but as a leader of the colony he had definitely had his day. "As far as enmity is concerned, people go on agitating against him and slander and lie against him, and wherever it is possible or allowed they reject his name as evil, and thus they try to cause this honorable man as much unpleasantness as possible," wrote one of Scholte's admirers full of bitterness.[22] Whatever was the truth in these matters, most of the colonists did not trust him anymore; brother Scholte had become too much of a businessman for such trust! When people needed some guidance in spiritual matters they would turn to . . . Van Raalte.

Those that had deposed Scholte now met under Reverend Betten and the elders. In this branch of the Christian Church of Pella, dissatisfaction arose concerning leadership of the elders. It was argued that "no one in the congregation should administer Holy Baptism except those who had been officially ordained as shepherds and teachers, and called to the ministry of the Word and Sacraments."

They also recognized the necessity "to have fellowship with other congregations that profess the same faith." They had in mind the small group which from the beginning wanted to join the Reformed Church and had organized itself as the Holland Reformed Church. They also had in mind Classis Holland in Michigan, with whose members they began to correspond, just as had been done on a permanent basis by this latter small congregation. Finally, this led in September, 1856, to Van Raalte's visit as a representative of Classis Holland. He accomplished the union of the Holland Reformed Church and the Christian Church, now called the Protestant Reformed Dutch Church of Pella, which joined the Reformed Church of America. Two times this new Pella church called Van Raalte by "unanimous vote," but in vain. Finally in January 1859, after having received declines from Brummelkamp and Donner, who preferred to stay in the fatherland, Rev. P. J. Oggel of Grand Haven became their pastor.

Naturally this reorganization did not go smoothly and enjoy unanimous support. Quite an upheaval occurred, and people's minds began to boil over again.[23] Brother J. Maasdam and others disagreed with Van Raalte's demand that "the preaching of the Word and administration of the Sacraments by elders must stop." Consequently, they remained organized as the First Christian Church of Pella. Union with the "Second" one was impossible because of the grievances against Scholte. Maasdam must have had regrets for writing "smutty and slanderous" letters about Scholte, yet he never openly repented of his deeds.[24] After Maasdam's death, his church slowly dwindled and many joined with the Reformed Church, which in 1888 was finally given all the property.

In the meantime the Reformed Church did not remain untouched. As in Michigan, Americanization had its effect upon the church. The fear grew that especially the younger generation, better versed in the English language, would join the English Baptists and other congregations. Therefore, their minister, Reverend Oggel, a capable man of vision, laid plans to establish and organize an English-speaking Reformed congregation. These plans materialized in 1862, in the same year as in Holland, Michigan, but not without opposition! In addition to this new church, two other Dutch-speaking churches sprouted from the First Reformed Church in 1868. One was the Bethel Church on the Skunk River and the other was the Third Reformed Church.

B. The First Split

So far we have written about religious discord usually caused by mutual jealousies and at times also by differences in religious views. This discord was for the most part of a local character. Out of all these disputes among our former countrymen, however, a new church movement came into being, which spread across nearly all the Dutch settlements in the United States. It led to the founding of a new "American" church organization that has contributed, more than any other organization, to the preservation of the Dutch character of the Dutch colonists. I am referring to the Secession of 1857, when many of the Dutch colonists left the Reformed Church. This was also the year when America was struck by a financial depression, which made the otherwise already nervous folk also extremely susceptible to religious influences and led to a time of spiritual awakening and revivals, according to the sociologist [E. A.] Ross and others.[25]

Many different factors primed this secession movement. Their significance is determined, however, by a wide range of opinion, depending on the views of the observer. But whatever those are, the fact remains that personal grievances against Van Raalte as leader played an important role. Yet this seems not to have been the focal point, although the gifted Reverend H. E. Dosker declared that the secession movement was indeed aimed at the policies and the authority of Van Raalte.[26] De Beij and Zwemer, who stressed these personal grievances, also made passing reference to "the popular character and provincialism of the people, which contributed much to the secession that took place there later on, meaning the community of Drenthe."[27]

These differences in social character and their influence on the religious views of the Secessionists had already been plainly evident in the Netherlands, as we know. There, they had already led to strong antipathies between the leaders of the various groups, and had produced "petty bickering." Already in the Netherlands these squabbles had caused division within the Secessionist group itself and two main groups stood in fierce opposition to each other. One, the northern group of Groningers, Frisians, and Drenthers, labeled the De Cock-Joffers-Van Velzen group; the other, the less conservative more broadminded southern or Gelderland group of Brummelkamp and Van Raalte—the Gelderlanders and Overijselers. Since the Secessionists belonged to the simplest, plain people in the country, the personal views of the leaders were a factor that made itself felt more strongly than would have been the case with another class of people.

All these religious concepts, no matter how they had originated, were transferred to America. In the beginning of settlement, when people needed each other, these differences were not so noticeable. But once the rooting period had ended, fierce clashes broke out. These were all the more violent since many immigrants, no matter how well-versed they were in the Bible, did not know what tolerance was.

Besides this we must keep in mind that in 1847 the more broadminded colonists were more strongly represented in the group, while those of the fifties were more narrow-minded and belonged to the "Northerners." It is important to note that also among the leaders one can spot those conservatives of the fifties, those anti-Gelderlanders immigrants, whose general educational background simply could not compare with the background of men like Van Raalte. Most of these men had no university education whatsoever, and this often contributed to their extreme bigotry. Among these leaders belonged Reverend R. Smit at Drenthe, who came to America in 1851 and separated from the Reformed Church in 1853 and R. J. Schepers at Graafschap, who had done so already in 1852. In 1853 a third opponent of Van Raalte arrived in Michigan, Reverend K. Van den Bosch, the minister at Noordeloos, formerly called Noord Holland. He was the promoter of the Secession in that town "due to the abominable and church destroying, pernicious heresy and sins," that, in his views, were prevalent among the followers of Van Raalte.[28] In general, the later immigrant arrivals had not experienced the taxing rooting struggles of the pioneers of 1847. Thus they lacked that broadminded, humane attitude that so often characterizes the true pioneer, the man of vast experience. On the contrary, they outdid the least of these pioneers in bigotry!

Thus we can consider a part of the church controversies among the Dutch in America as a continuation or transposition of the dissent that had already begun in the motherland among the Secessionists. Issues like the term of office of consistory members, the holidays, hymns, ministerial garb, etc., etc. had already been sources of mutual damnation in the Netherlands and were now revived and treated with unusual truculence on American soil. When matters are viewed in this light, we understand Dosker's conviction that the Secession of 1857 was not so much a separatist movement away from the church in the East—since some Netherlanders joined the Scotch Church, the Baptists, and the Presbyterians, while the Secessionists eventually rejoined an "eastern" church!—as it was a separation from the brethren in the West.[29] Subsequently, similar internecine quarrels would occur, both among the faithful in America as well as in the Netherlands.

Time and again this *splijtzwam* [literally, fission fungus; figuratively, disintegrating influence] manifested itself. Repeatedly the ongoing development and progress, the passing of time, caused a conflict between the more conservative and the less conservative factions, and that usually means between the less educated and the more educated Calvinists. This conflict endures to the present time. Seen from that standpoint, this separation, which was merely one among the numberless periodic separations among all orthodox Calvinists—and other denominations, can be distinguished from all the others by the relative weight of its consequences.

I agree with those who separated themselves in 1857 from the Reformed Church and with their followers when they refuse, and rightly so, to see it as merely local and personal differences, in light of the significance of this historical moment so charged with importance for them. They also rightly reject the claim that "there was no soul-stirring principle in their Secession, 'nothing grandiose' of which to be proud."[30] Every religious conflict, when it is a matter of purely spiritual values, of preserving the faith of the fathers, contains something heroic, because of the courage and the conviction with which people try to defend their principles, no matter how narrow they may seem to others.

The Secession of 1857 in America, which was in the first place a church matter, was not exclusively religious in nature. As I have mentioned before, we may see in it also a clash between two "cultures"—Dutch and American. Despite many cultural similarities and even the same Dutch descent and the same Calvinistic religion, the events of the year 1857 showed that "America" had already moved so far in shaping its own character that years of residence would be necessary in order to adapt to it. And how much further back stood our former fellow countrymen from Americans of non-Dutch and non-Calvinistic background!

Therefore, this religious struggle became more than just "an import" from the Netherlands; therefore, it developed a more or less tragic, pervasive tone. People wanted to maintain not only their Dutch Calvinism, but, more or less consciously, also their Dutch customs and traditions, and above all the Dutch language. It was tragic because once they had become American citizens, they could not and should not try to remain Netherlanders. It was tragic too because willingly or unwillingly, they were fighting for a lost cause. They could resist Americanization, they could slow down its progress, but they could never halt it completely! It was finally tragic because all these factors caused such endless heartbreak in many a Dutch-American settlement, or worse, in many a Dutch-American family. There was a lack of comprehension on the part of the more conservative, less-educated settlers for their better-educated fellow settlers who adapted more easily and faster.

Worse, far worse, were the deep misunderstandings that arose between Dutch parents, who still thought in Dutch terms and had their faith rooted in Dutch traditions, and their children who thought in "American" terms and practiced their faith "American fashion," or who had no faith at all! It even happened that they could no longer understand each other; the parents only spoke Dutch, and the boys, having worked among Americans from their early years, only spoke English. Even today, many frantically hang on to the language of the fathers, partly for the sake of a kind of convenience, and sometimes due to a misdirected sense of ethnic identification, but most of all because of their religious conviction.

Therefore, the Dutch-American religious conflicts present a more complicated picture than the ones in the Netherlands. The deep background of the quarrels in America is no longer exclusively formed by either a bit more or a bit less of the same Dutch culture, but what also enters the picture is a bit more or a bit less of that other culture, the American culture. We know that one type of personality adapts more easily than another. It is alleged that the Frisians, who are so individualistic and independent, become "Americans" in their behavior and ways of thinking sooner than the other Dutchmen. This is perhaps due to the fact that they are so independent-minded and have a closer racial relationship to the English.[31]

The differences between the ethnic subgroups were thus accentuated, which further sharpened the conflicts. It is this complexity of the whole immigration picture that in America far more frequently than in the Netherlands causes so many misunderstandings and a lack of mutual comprehension and tolerance. This same complexity also increases the fierceness of the quarrels. That is why we see among the Dutch-American Calvinists the development of both gradual differences and, at a much faster pace, the development of principial differences that lead more quickly to a separation from a particular church organization and a switch to another leader.[32]

It is part of our human nature to idealize a movement to which we owe our origin and existence. This is all the more the case when we are far removed from it in both time and place. Look how the Pilgrims of 1620 have been idealized, and how often in the process the plain truth was overlooked, to the aggravation of Indian lovers such as Friederici. We should indeed keep in mind this constant tendency to idealize, especially in an America that is far less critical and encourages an unadulterated hero worship. This trait enables us to understand and to subscribe in part to the words that Beets, the historian of the 1857 movement, used to bring the perspective of that movement on a higher level, and to protest the matter-of-fact considerations of De Beij and Zwemer and those of Dosker. Beets exclaimed that "something totally different, something deeper, broader, and more fundamental led to the movement of 1857, namely dissatisfaction with the doctrine, worship services, and discipline in the Reformed Church of America that people had joined [in 1850] in what we would like to call a moment of thoughtlessness. Subsequently, they realized that they could grow and prosper better and could achieve their own ideals more easily by standing on their own."[33]

The thoughtful reader will have already perceived from this explanation that more was at stake than merely religious problems, that the real issue was a more generalized cultural conflict. The facts, indeed, the whole development of the newly organized church, prove this. It became a place of refuge for the most common folks who did not yet feel at home in the new fatherland and especially for those who remained attached with heart and soul to the Old Country.

It is, of course, not my intention to write in depth about these continual troubles. Other, more competent historians, especially church historians, have in the past written repeatedly about these events. It is typical both for the significance that is given to this episode in Dutch-American history as well as for the religious, but above all the pugnacious, attitude of the Dutch-Americans—at times Calvinists and belligerence seem to be synonymous—that no other event in their entire colonial history has been written about and is still being written about in such abundance and in such great detail. The religious movement of 1857 is given in the literature in America a notability that is comparable in importance but healthier than the one that is generally given to the literary movement of the eighties ["*de Tachtigers*" in the Netherlands] and which is described in such sickly detail.

The task remains for me, however, to point the reader to the historical moments that have a more pronounced sociographical importance. One of the most typical characteristics of the movement of 1857 is that it was set in motion, like so many other religious and secular movements now and in the past, by vile, sordid slander. In the community of Drenthe, people were literally saying already at an early date: "They sold us out, but whether they can deliver us [to the buyers] remains to be seen," thereby alluding to the Union with the Reformed Church.[34] Also in Zeeland people muttered: "We have been sold down the river without knowing it," while in Holland in the consistory meeting of August 22, 1853, a member was reproached for having said ". . . that Van Raalte had brought the congregation into an impure church for the sake of money."[35]

A second characteristic was that, although personal dissatisfaction sporadically arose in rural churches over worldly disagreements and sometimes got out of hand when church members took sides, the purposeful opposition toward Van Raalte's church did not actually originate among the original pioneers and thus did not come from "*de Kolonie.*" Not any of the agricultural settlements, but the industrial colony in the American city of Grand Rapids became "the actual center of the Secession and at the same time the criterion of the reformation."[36] This circumstance is of great significance as I mentioned in the previous chapter when discussing the city immigrants.

The soul of this movement was the "demagogue" Gijsbert Haan, who was, it should be noted, not a "genuine" pioneer. In Hilversum in the Netherlands, Haan had been a prominent personality among the Secessionists, where, for instance, he led church services and was the main planner for emigration to America. Because of religious convictions, but also, as they said themselves, to make a better living since they were poor, Haan with his wife and nine children, and five other families of Seceders from Hilversum, left for America in 1847. One of them, B. Van Leeuwen, a dedicated, well-behaved worker in a carpet factory, had the prospect of helping to establish such a factory in New York. Two other followers were on leave from the national militia and thus shirked their military service. The influence of Haan was so great that even someone from a well-to-do family traveled with them.[37]

Having arrived in America in 1847, Haan stayed in New York for a short time and then moved on to Albany and Troy. It was not until the fall of 1849 that he settled in the village of Vriesland, Michigan, that is, after the first two most difficult hardship years of pioneering and rooting were a thing of the past. His stay was of short duration due to his altercation with Reverend Ypma concerning the land purchases that we have mentioned earlier. Haan belonged to those who shunned the rigors of rural life of that time because they could not or would not cope with it. Like others, he "dropped out of the Colony" to settle in a nearby town, in this case Grand Rapids. As with many other town folks, he did not participate in any of the rooting struggles; he did not undergo an American baptism. But this spirit of Haan kept blowing through "*de Kolonie.*"

Because of his longer stay in the "East," Haan especially noticed the impurities in the "Eastern" Albany church. He reported that some of its members did not believe in predestination—"Oh, no, God is so good!"— and that they did not have their children baptized but left this matter up to the children themselves, and that they belonged to secret societies, etc. While still in the East, Haan had grown especially suspicious about this church after he had made the acquaintance of some members and teachers of the True Reformed Dutch Church. This Church had been established in 1822 by those who separated from the Reformed Church because they were against its dire neglect of church discipline, the misuse of the Lord's Supper and Baptism, the persecution of those who advocated the true doctrine, and the toleration of false preachers to promulgate further heresy.

Haan was the one who stirred up further unrest in *de Kolonie*; others who had come from the East earlier had already spread unfavorable reports concerning the Reformed Church. "Wherever I came, I was flooded with questions about the Church in America; and to the preachers and people I truthfully told what I thought of it, judging that in my view it had been an imprudent decision to proceed with the union."[38]

Once located in Grand Rapids, Haan kept in contact with his friends in the colony. He wrote letters to those of kindred spirit in the community of Vriesland, depicting secession as the work of God and inviting them to secede. He traveled far and wide, barnstorming in Noordeloos, Holland, Graafschap, and other places, everywhere propagating secession from the Reformed Church.[39]

The growing unrest came to a head at a classical meeting, where since 1852 the theme had been constantly heard: "Why can't we as a people be on our own?" Haan attended as an elder of the Grand Rapids church and often was the spokesman of the dissatisfied faction, raising the subject of "impurities" in the Church. People also accused Van Raalte and Van der Meulen of having published and promoted Baxter's *Call to the Unconverted*, a booklet condemned by orthodox members; later on they accused them of granting Christians of other denominations the privilege of the Lord's Supper. It also grieved the dissenters greatly that hymns were sung. There was a flood of protests and strong controversy arose, especially with Haan. These quarrels reached such a level of intensity that at a Holland classical meeting in 1856 it was decided to have a day of prayer to stem the tide of "this spirit of doubt in the Dutch Reformed Church, this spirit of the devil!"[40]

We should not draw the conclusion that it was due to chance circumstances that this opposition to the Union was centered in Grand Rapids, or to the chance circumstance that Haan lived there. Haan could often be more or less the leader of the opposition also at classical meetings because of the support of his co-religionists at Grand Rapids. Within de Kolonie at Vriesland he had not been able to gather such support; the Vrieslanders did not even deem him to be worthy of a watchman's post.[41] In the factory town, things were different; for there he soon was elected as elder and received the staunch support from leading men like J. Gelock, J. De Jonge, A. Pleune, H. Moerman, B. De Graaf, and J. Gezon.

By 1856 people here and there throughout the colony had resigned from the church for the most varied reasons. These resignations were mostly in Grand Rapids. Here the dissatisfied members met on Sundays, and here two months later, on March 19, 1857, after the preacher H. G. Klijn had openly joined with Haan, Gelock, and others, the mother church of the Christian Reformed churches in Grand Rapids was founded with Dominie H. G. Klijn as pastor. Haan, Gelock, and Gezon were elected as elders and De Graaf, Moerman, and Pleune as deacons.[42] It is also interesting to note that Klijn, who had been called from Middelburg in the Netherlands to Graafschap in 1849, and who labored there for a short time before transferring to Grand Rapids, actually was not an early pioneer, either.

The events in Grand Rapids did not fail to make their influence felt elsewhere. In Graafschap, for instance, many people no longer saw the Reformed Church as being any good and they separated. Typical of this zealotry was the fact that consistory members who had decided to secede, under the influence also of Reverend Van den Bosch of Noordeloos, who was no pioneer either, were making the rounds of the community with letters in their pockets to win anybody who could be moved for the Secession. Even women followed suit and visited homes and read letters to prove that it was now clear that the Lord was leading his people into exodus.[43]

At the classical meeting held in Zeeland, April 8, 1857, the various official documents of Secession were presented by Reverend H. G. Klijn (Grand Rapids), Reverend K. Van den Bosch (Noordeloos), and the consistories of Graafschap and Polkton, Michigan. Thus, April 8th, 1857, became the birthday of the founding of the Christian Reformed Church in America, an historical event of more than religious importance. From a religious perspective, Beets is probably correct when he called this action a return to the standpoint of 1849 that had been abandoned.[44] The plain immigrants of Polkton expressed this more clearly, however, by saying they were again "returning to the point of view that we had abandoned in the Netherlands." In this way they more or less consciously indicated an opposition to the way things had been going in America from the day of their arrival.

The growth of this new organization would indeed prove that its founding rested on more than opposition in church affairs; it was a reaction against the conditions in America. "The Secessionists are totally Dutch and want to remain that way, and our church is a little bit more English," said a Reformed Church member. Another one thought that "the ribbons on the hats of some girls and women of the Reformed Church were becoming too long, too wide, and too worldly, according to those narrow-minded people, and that is why they separated."[45] This observation brings into relevance the developing social differentiation, which played such an important role in many a congregation; it was a far greater role than we usually surmise.[46] How some church members complained when the Van Raaltes, in entertaining a few American families, wore "too much white," was explained to me by Mrs. Gilmore, Van Raalte's daughter.

Such remarks, however insignificant they may be, nevertheless draw a clear picture of the situation and pinpoint the social differentiation. This wish to keep one's Dutch identity and remain the same explains why it took until 1890 before the Seceders joined the True Reformed Dutch Church. By then, in spite of themselves, people had more or less Americanized. From an exclusively religious viewpoint they could and should have done this in 1857, for people continuously corresponded with ministers and members of this church. Even the ultra-orthodox Gijsbert Haan, a "staunch and capable follower" of Reverend [Simon] Van Velzen, had found this church to be pure "in the fundamental doctrines of the Reformed Church, especially in the doctrine of the gracious justification of sinners before God."[47]

Those who thought that the Secession of 1857 had cleared the atmosphere of all controversy and ended it, were sadly disappointed. In 1868 Reverend De Beij accused the new organization and its members of being "schismatics, of harboring injured feelings of pride, diotrefism, personal feuds, of being misleading, pharisaistic, of plucking out the gnat and swallowing the camel, of harboring a spirit of seduction, of being zealots without love, and makers of sects!"[48] These accusations, no matter how harsh they were, were not without some truth. Great controversy raged in the new church, while this time there were no scapegoats, no Van Raalte, and no Reformed Church for its members to attack!

For years they squabbled over a name, until finally in 1864, after having called themselves the "Holland Reformed Church," and the "True Dutch Reformed Church," they took the name of "Ware Hollandsche Gereformeerde Kerk" [True Holland Reformed Church]. There had been so much struggle about this name that even Scholte, who was not a member of the Reformed Church either, spoke of "a community attempting to deceive themselves and others with the title, 'Ware Gereformeerde Kerk', while it is the most wicked district of present-day Babylon, filled with suffocating air, that destroys spiritual growth in grace."

The hassling over keeping or dropping the word *Ware* [True] even led to a new separation! Finally in 1880 it was decided to drop the pretentious word

Ware and call themselves the Hollandsche Christelijke Gereformeerde Kerk [Holland Christian Reformed Church], "in honor of the name of the Dutch Mother, who was to us a rock and fountain head of our birth." In 1890 the word *Hollandsche* was dropped, because the denomination also included English and German congregations and had united with the True Reformed Dutch Church. Since then it is called the "Christelijke Gereformeerde Kerk" [Christian Reformed Church], so that "[we are] completely similar also in name to the Christelijke Gereformeerde Kerk in the Netherlands."[49] This remark characterizes the whole situation!

This name controversy clearly showed the spirit that animated all those involved. However, both the name *Ware* and that of *Christelijke Gereformeerde* also worked as advertisements and produced results. The common run of immigrant people, who knew little about these church differences, already felt drawn to this church simply through these names and would join. On the other hand, the name Reformed Church had an adverse effect on most of these *kleine luyden*.[50]

There were also fierce conflicts about other questions that were often of a very personal nature. Almost every church reported raging conflicts, especially Grand Rapids. The wrangles reached a climax during a meeting of the True* brothers in 1878 in Grand Rapids. They reported to the Classis in Michigan, entirely in the spirit of militant Calvinism, that "the gunpowder smoke of conflict was so dense that one couldn't distinguish friend from foe!" What marked the situation was that differences in religious views, if present at all, usually slid into the background. This became very obvious from the fact that, after "high-flying quarrels," some "troubles," "bickering and dissent," and disbanding of the consistory, numerous brothers would leave the militant organization and join the Reformed Church. Here they would sometimes be aggravated in turn, and go back to the True Church again.

Reverend Klijn, who of all people was president of the first classical gathering of the Secessionists, rejoined the Reformed Church after only a few months. Others, especially in the colony, followed his example. Even Gijsbert Haan forsook his "principles" and returned to the Reformed Church; however, later he defected again! Various preachers, called from the Netherlands, came and went, sometimes twice! "Thus preacher after preacher was a disappointment, and we admire the staunchness of the principles of the followers more than that of some of the leaders," Beets frankly remarked.[51] But he forgot to say that even for a preacher who had seceded two or three times, "the door bolts of this sectarianism" could become too oppressive, the "exclusiveness and slander of this schism-

---

*Van Hinte desired to emphasize the seeming presumptuousness of the word *Ware* [True], so here and occasionally elsewhere he used quotation marks when referring to the "*Ware*" *broeders* or the "*Ware*" *gemeente*. But he was not consistent, so for consistency all quotation marks for the word *True* have been deleted. Historically speaking, it is also difficult to determine from the text if the Dutch-language title "Ware Kerk" or the English-language title "True Church" should apply. Therefore, it is always translated as "True Church" whether or not the reference may be before or after 1880, when the word *True* was deleted from the name of the Christian Reformed Church (ed.).

prone bunch," as one of them declared, could become too overwhelming and such situations finally "drove him away" regardless of any "principle."[52]

As Americanization of the immigrants gradually increased, many reacted against it and thus new congregations arose among the American Secessionists, despite all the conflict. This also happened beyond the borders of Michigan. Again it is characteristic that the [True] brothers experienced a revelation mainly in the cities—Paterson, Chicago, Kalamazoo, Grand Haven, Muskegon, etc.—and separated from the Reformed Church.

The "walkout" among the real pioneers, the "originals" in the farming communities, made far slower headway. For example, in Holland, where there were only a few Secessionists, the brothers were given the advice in 1865 to sell their "church building," which was merely a hut. Nothing was ever heard anymore of the Polkton brothers. In Low [Lage] Prairie in Illinois, a church was established in 1865, which after a year was in dire straights and considered lost. In Gibbsville, Wisconsin, a church joined in 1866 but there were quarrels concerning the psalms, and other continuous troubles, and it disintegrated.[53] Also in the same year, a True church was organized in Pella, Iowa, with an initial membership of over forty.[54]

To what degree the brothers of the Secession reacted against American conditions is apparent not only from the fact that they clung to their Dutch language, but also from their opposition to insurance, and voting by women—both of which were, at least for them, weeds from American fields. These kinds of newly arising American problems formed renewed sources of discord, together with the endless bickering among the True faithful about holidays, baptisms, etc.—in spite of the Secession—and with newly imported problems from the Netherlands, such as vaccination—[which they were against for being an intervention in God's destiny][55] A typical example of the desire to hold on to Dutch church customs, which proves also how much these Separatists, particularly in the cities, belonged to the least Americanized immigrants in contrast to the real pioneers in the countryside, is the fact that the latter, the Pellians, who were no less orthodox, were accustomed to listen in 1854 to Scholte preaching from a farm wagon, "at times wearing a white hat and a light colored vest,"[56] while in 1866 our Secessionists were still wrangling over the issue of whether elders should read their sermon while standing *in front of* the pulpit or *in* the pulpit. And in that same year believers of the factory town of Paterson, New Jersey, requested from the Classis that pastors should, during their sermon, wear full professional garb: a three-cornered hat, a robe with bands, short pants with golden knee buckles, silk stockings, and low shoes with buckles![57]

Let me add that the Classis dropped the matter, although for years the ministerial robes of office were worn in the Netherlands by ministers, until the time probably when undertakers also began to sport three-cornered hats. Then the attachment to that headwear declined, even among the most fervent of preachers. With that decline, the wearing of the robes of office was also abandoned as a "principle."[58]

It was again typical that Van Raalte and all the other pioneer preachers remained loyal all their lives to the Reformed Church. For them the Secession was a great disappointment, which was all the more grating because, according to Van Raalte, they could see in it only "a mixture of ignorance, sectarianism, and a trampling of brothers." It was a "recklessness that would destroy the progeny." But in spite of this more drastic of all their religious ordeals, the pioneers were broadminded enough to let it rest, and to express their wish by way of Van Raalte, "that those who feel they can establish a holier and purer Church than the Holland Reformed Church of this land, may bring us to shame and may bless us through spiritual growth and an active, fruit-bearing Christianity."[59]

Thanks to this broadmindedness and the powerful medicine of time, the rift between the two churches slowly narrowed, and sometimes, due to circumstances, there were mutual transfers of members from one church to the other and even preachers of both churches would take part in ecumenical services. In short, both sides seemed to be able to live amiably next to each other.[60]

Both church organizations grew; but in the first twenty years the Reformed Church grew faster than the True Church. The reason was not only that the pioneer country people and their descendants were more numerous than the townspeople and their supporters in other places so that their growth was more or less automatic, but there were also other influences, both inner as well as outer. To the inner influences belonged especially the revivals that were so stimulating for the spiritual life, and which, as we saw, also made their appearance now and then in the Netherlands. But due to their intensity and relative frequency they must be seen as more Anglo-Saxon or in particular, as typically American phenomena.

It is of interest that the most Americanized among the colonists, the actual pioneers, were the ones most strongly influenced by these revivals. The many trials to which they had been exposed during the exhausting rooting struggle and also later on, had made them more nervous and therefore more susceptible. In contrast to people who have as a dominant function their intellect and will, they became more strongly feeling- and emotion-dominant Christians. Van Raalte and other leaders who were members of the Reformed Church seem to have seen the situation in a similar light and soon if not immediately felt very sympathetic towards these movements that were so unlike the Dutch by their noisiness. They saw in them "the unmerited, surprising, powerful working of God and His blessed presence."[61]

The True Church forbade its members to attend these revival meetings and considered them to be the work of the devil.[62] Being less Americanized and less experienced, people of this church were more will-dominant than intellect-dominant; they were will-dominant Christians.

The religious excitement that swept America in 1857 and 1858 also came to expression among the Dutch immigrants, although perhaps unconsciously for the most part. The Secession of 1857 originated in Grand Rapids but soon after, in 1858, the actual colony of Holland had its first revival. Characteristically, it was of very limited significance; it did not spread to the streets and was conservative in character.

Of greater importance was the second revival, "one of the epoch-making events in the history of our people," as Van Schelven declared. It happened seven years later, that is, when the influence of soil, climate, and people, i.e., Americanization, had made itself felt that much longer. Moreover, it was connected with another religious movement that swept America in the aftermath of the Great Killing, the Civil War.

This second revival was led by a plain stonemason, [Albert] Clapper, an able and industrious worker who was brief and loud in his manner of speaking, and seemingly corrosive in manner, but withal, good-natured, warm-hearted, and with a fiery, earnest spirit. He belonged to the Methodist Episcopal Church and often took turns as a lay preacher, as a hedge-preacher [open-air preacher]. Around January 1st, 1866, he felt "called of God to save Holland," and for that purpose he began to hold religious services in a room above an alehouse there. Initially many young folks attended these meetings to have a bit of fun, while older folks were fuming. But soon a different spirit shone forth among the visitors, and people listened with increasing interest to what the bricklayer had to say. The crowds grew and soon the place became too small, so they had to move the meetings to the Town Hall. Evening after evening the hall was filled to capacity. Many could not find seats, so Clapper asked permission to use the First Reformed Church, Van Raalte's Church.

At first the consistory refused, but at the strong urging of Van Raalte, they finally gave their permission. "Don't you see God's hand in this? That He is telling us something? . . . Are we going to resist God's Spirit any longer?" were his comments. The church building, too, was filled every evening, and even the regular church services under the leadership of Clapper turned, as if all by themselves, into revival meetings. Not only from the city but also from surrounding towns, indeed, from the entire "Colony" people came to listen to him. With his coat off, in shirtsleeves, without a collar, as if he were busy at his daily stonemason trade, Clapper led every meeting and no one felt aggravated any longer. One should compare this with the True brothers at Paterson who demanded at about that same time the full professional garb! The vulgar expressions in Clapper's prayers, so offensive at other times, were not even noticed but rather passed muster. His speeches, always characteristic of the same Clapper, seemed to satisfy an existing need that was strongly felt at that time. He liked to hear Dutch psalms and would always ask someone to suggest a stanza for a change. His services were held in English, but those in attendance would speak about their experiences in Dutch if it so pleased them and it seemed as if all understood each other just as at Pentecost in Jerusalem.

And then, evening after evening, as they were singing the revival hymn, "Come, Ye Sinners Poor and Needy," how great was the number of those who would come forward to accept Jesus! "Every heart, according to Van Raalte, seemed to be open to God's Truth; the lips of God's children overflowed; the things of the world receded into the background. . . . For a better attendance at the meetings, stores closed early; saloons were emptied; at night the streets were deserted, but God's house was filled with people. Left and right, in corners where one did not expect to find it, distress of soul would reveal itself; there was soul-searching and prayerful struggles with God to be saved or the joy through hope in God in Christ. . . . Many of the children of the congregation were brought closer together; even the very aged had their share in the warming fire of God's love."

Continually more people of all classes and all persuasions flocked to these meetings. In spite of severe winter weather, sleighs chock-full with country folk came from all corners of the colony, especially on moonlit nights. After the meeting had dispersed, they would often continue the Clapper meeting on the ice of Black Lake, or Macatawa Bay!

"For twenty years I have labored here among these people and where was the fruit? And now God sends a Methodist to reap where I have sown—and such a Methodist. But I put my hand on my lips and worship," Van Raalte declared at the Communion celebration in his church during the revivals, when new members were confirmed by the dozen. There seemed to come no end to the people around the communion tables. Weeks on end the meetings continued. Finally, in the spring they began to taper off due in part to the busy season of farm work and partly due also to the fanaticism of Clapper, who would pray on street corners and report visions and revelations, which became really too much to swallow for the normally so down-to-earth Hollanders. The deepest cause, however, was that the tide had turned.[63]

About ten years later another wave of spiritual awakening sped across America and once again found a focus in Holland. It originated at a student prayer service. It spread to the First Church of Holland, then to other churches, and also outside the town, across the whole colony, and even through the entire West. Once again, evening after evening, churches were overfilled. Now also sinners became alarmed and witnessed and were converted to God.[64] Again membership in the churches of the pioneers increased, especially in the Reformed Church.

Maybe outside factors conditioned the initial rapid growth of this church in an even stronger way. Earlier I indicated that the opinion people had formed in the Netherlands, and also in Ost Friesland and Bentheim (which belonged at that time partly to the Netherlands on the basis of their common culture, language and religion[65]), concerning the union with the Reformed Church and the subsequent secession, became of great importance for the affiliation of subsequent immigrants with one of the two denominations. This choice also brought about either a faster or slower Americanization of these immigrants and their organizations, depending on the interaction between the members and their churches.

Officially, for the first few decades people in the Netherlands refused to take sides, to the great dismay of Van Raalte who saw in this fence-straddling a recognition of the Separatists.[66] The Netherlands Synod of 1860 decided to recognize all churches that practiced Reformed doctrines and church government and would stick to it. Also, the Secessionists of 1857 were aggravated because they preferred to view the Christelijke Gereformeerde Kerk in the Netherlands as their mother church, but were treated by her as very poor cousins. The Secession in America was received as a "de facto" event and given no further attention. When fifteen years later a deputation from America went to the Netherlands Synod of 1872 to demonstrate the lawful birth of a daughter church, they were informed that no brothers from abroad had been invited to the Synod! Through this artful dodge the True Church was almost disavowed, had not the Synod, in the end and by a majority vote, decided to reverse itself and still welcome the brothers from America. This gesture, however, did not imply any opinion or judgment concerning the American Secession.

Of more importance than this official, "neutral" stand was the fact that most of the leaders of the Seceders [Afgescheidenen] in the Netherlands did not accept the American Secession since they were the friends of the pioneer ministers in America. They were also influenced by the book of De Beij and Zwemer. Brummelkamp, one of the most influential ministers in the Netherlands, hoped that God would spare him the task of ever advising people to join the True Brothers and be dragged along by the Separatists. This is how most preachers felt. An exception was Van Velzen, as quoted before.[67] Still in 1873 most of the Frisians, Overijselers, Hollanders, and Zeelanders, joined the Reformed Church when they entered the United States, while the Gelderlanders seemingly did so as a matter of course. Only the Groningers joined the Secessionists.[68]

Contributing to this latter circumstance was not only the fact that the most orthodox Secessionists were found in the province of Groningen, in accordance with the more down-to-earth, realistic attitude of the Groningers, the so-called Northerners, but also the fact that one of their most beloved ministers, the Reverend [Roelof] Duiker of Niezijl had been called to Grand Rapids.[69] Because of this, many of his parishioners emigrated to America under his leadership in May 1867 via Glasgow, with the intention "to improve their standard of living" in this country and to remain if possible members of his congregation, also in the new homeland. But there were also many other newcomers who left Groningen for Grand Rapids at a later date and who simply asked for Duiker's church—and not for a Reformed or True Church—to insure at the same time a good welcome and further assistance.[70] The flourishing period of the True Church in Grand Rapids dates particularly from the arrival of Duiker, which engendered a strange rivalry between the two churches. As the trains arrived, the immigrants were immediately subjected to a confession of faith: "Where do you come from? To which church do you belong? Answer: From the Secession Church. Then come with us, we are also Secessionists."[71] Thus the Secessionists were led to Duiker's church and the *Hervormden* to Reverend Van der Meulen, the pioneer preacher, who had accepted a call in 1861 to Grand Rapids. Duiker declared that because of this technique his home was often filled with newly arrived immigrants.[72]

Most of the immigrants, except the Groningers, after considering the choice, usually joined the Reformed Church, especially when their chosen church of the Reformed faith called a preacher who was well known to them. Calls to outside preachers from the Netherlands were quite frequent, since the training of ministers in America left much to be desired. We think of Reverend B. De Beij and the Hulst brothers as examples. Also, these ministers sometimes brought along a number of their parishioners or had them join later on.

In general, however, the True Church grew so slowly that people had their doubts about its viability, and when Reverend Van den Bosch died they thought the Secessionists would be finished. Even in the mother church in Grand Rapids, where Reverend Duiker had left the True Church and affiliated with the Reformed Church, it was prophesied in 1879 that the death of this church through sclerosis was imminent. The church was narrow-minded, exclusive, and anti-institutional, as some of the True brothers themselves believed. Thus, a new, young generation, raised in this free and religious country, refused to follow the church on that path. It would not be possible to stave off its slow demise.[73]

The rapid growth of the Reformed Church and the slow growth of the True Church are shown in the following statistics. The totals of the purely Dutch congregations belonging to the Reformed Church are:

> 1851:   12 congregations with 6 preachers and 563 families.[74]
> 1870:   62 congregations with 44 preachers and 4,052 families.[75]

The True Church totals are:

> 1857:   4 congregations with 2 preachers and about 125 families.[76]
> 1875:   26 congregations with 15 preachers and about 1,500 families.[77]

Already in the early rooting years some congregations in other states, such as Wisconsin and Illinois, had joined the Classis of Holland of the Reformed Church. The continued growth of the Reformed Church led to the forming of the new Classes of Wisconsin (1854) and Grand River (1869), which were as purely Dutch in character as the one of Holland. The Netherlanders in the East were joined with the existing "American" classes.[78]

In 1875 the True Church had the Michigan Classis, formed in 1868, with 6,088 members, and the much smaller Classis of Illinois, numbering 1,977 individuals.[79] These 8,065 members (about 1,500 families) were located as follows: in Grand Rapids, 1,400; Graafschap, 720; Paterson, 718; Vriesland, 575; Holland, 475; Muskegon, 430; Chicago, 427; and Grand Haven, 375. The rest of the congregations numbered less than 300 individuals. These numbers clearly show the dominance of the factory towns of Grand Rapids and Paterson, which is understandable in light of my earlier observations. In 1878 two other classes—Hudson in the East and Iowa in the West—were added. Some of the congregations switched to these new classes and withdrew from Classis Illinois and Michigan. Yet the True Church remained of relatively small significance, even when compared with the exclusively Dutch element of the Reformed Church.[80]

C. The Second Split

A number of things happened in 1880 that did not diminish or stop the growth of the Western branch of the Reformed Church, but they greatly improved the growth of the True Church, so that around 1890 the Dutch membership of both churches was nearly equal.

The increasing cultural development closely related to the continued Americanization of the now prosperous pioneers altered their thinking regarding religious matters, and this changed the character of the Dutch element in the Reformed Church. That is why, especially after the seventies, the newly arrived religious immigrants felt at odds even with the "Dutch" element of the Reformed Church and joined the True Church since they felt more at home there because of its stronger Dutch character.[81] The fact that the church members of 1857 preferred to call themselves Seceders was for many of the least unsophisticated immigrants, who were often "Seceders" themselves, reason enough to join them. In fact, the word *secession* rang like a "magic word" in their ears and minds.[82] The changing of the name to "True Church" and subsequently to the "Christian Reformed Church" also helped in increasing the number of new members. Thus the most orthodox immigrants, the common, least sophisticated people, found a "refuge" in the True Church.[83] The less orthodox and usually more educated immigrants joined the Reformed Church. This process of natural selection among new members did not prevent the occurrence of new conflicts in the Reformed Church, although it postponed them. On the other hand, the infusion of this selected Dutch blood in the Reformed Church did not slow down the Americanization process of its Dutch branch to the same extent as would have been the case had all of the Dutch faithful joined that church.

Indeed, for many this process of Americanization went too fast, in particular for two groups in the Reformed Church. One group consisted of part of the "older" immigrants in towns such as Grand Rapids, where as we noted, Americanization proceeded more slowly than in the so-called farming colonies. The other group was the one of "younger" immigrants, especially those who had established themselves in America after the Civil War, and who had not morally earned their American citizenship either through the pioneering rooting struggle or through participation in the War. In these two groups, the townspeople again were generally the least Americanized. It is obvious that the two groups would find each other first in towns such as Grand Rapids where the differences between "old" and "young" immigrants were minimal. This explains the close cooperation between one of the most influential immigrants of the first group, Frans Van Driele, an opponent of Gijsbert Haan in the fifties, and Reverend L. J. Hulst, the main representative of the second group who had arrived in America only in 1874. Both were residents of Grand Rapids.[84] Van Driele was a "highly useful person, God-fearing and friendly with the common people, who dared to stand up to the bigwigs and give them a piece of his mind." Under his influence, Reverend Hulst, who relied on Frans as a trusted advisor, came to the conclusion that in the Reformed Church there were only a few genuinely Reformed people, and that this church "here in the West is rapidly following the path of degeneration of the church in the East." His judgment concerning these facts reflected the conviction of both previously mentioned groups and this led eventually to a new secession from the Reformed Church and a joining with the Christian Reformed Church.

The increase of Americanization among the Hollanders in the West had brought them into Freemasonry. The Hollanders, like "real" Americans, felt drawn to secret societies, which are so characteristic for America, where they fill a certain cultural vacuum and meet a certain cultural need. This is especially the case in small communities, as L. R. Reid remarked, "where the basis of all cultural life is social."[85]

The fact that members of the Reformed Church in the East belonged to the Lodge was suspected by the Dutch in Michigan soon after they affiliated with the eastern church in 1849. At the Holland Classis of 1852 and repeatedly afterwards in various consistory meetings, the question was raised whether this was true. The leaders paid little attention to the questions; they considered the lodge movement a childish and open secret, but finally they could not deny that it did exist in the Reformed Church.[86]

Influenced by this developing conflict between the pioneers of 1850 and many immigrants of a later date, the Classes of Holland (to which Grand Rapids still belonged) and Wisconsin requested the General Synod of 1868 to condemn Freemasonry. But it was in vain. This rejection aroused suspicion, which grew when the Synod of 1877 decided to close the Theological Seminary in Holland where ministers were trained just as in New Brunswick, New Jersey. The reason they gave was the high burden of debt. Now the pastors would be trained only in the East. Those who were less Americanized saw in this closing an attempt to cause the extinction of the Reformed element of the church in the West and thus "bend" them to become easternized.[87] In Holland itself there were opponents, also because the closing of the seminary would reduce the town's cultural importance.

The revival of 1877, mentioned before, strengthened the religious mood and when former Freemasons in Holland and Grand Rapids made disclosures about the abominations of this association, it generated a strong anti-Masonic movement.[88] In the meantime Van Raalte had died and R. Pieters, who had come to Michigan in 1849, took his place as minister. But after one or two years, he "dropped out" of "de Kolonie" and moved to Chicago. He was not truly a pioneer. In the sixties Pieters returned to Holland and became the initial leader in the anti-Masonic campaign.[89] Thus for a short time Holland and its community was the center of opposition in these matters, and from there the compaign spread to surrounding areas.

The Classes of Holland, Wisconsin, Grand River, and Illinois submitted "memorials" at the General Synod of 1880, in which they declared Freemasonry to be anti-Republican, anti-Christian, and anti-Reformed. Those who were the least Americanized thought therefore that the mere fact of being a Freemason was sufficient reason to excommunicate a person from a church membership. Many pioneers, just as Van Raalte earlier, were bitter enemies of secret societies, but nevertheless they thought just as Van Raalte did that being a Freemason was insufficient ground to excommunicate a person; only the sins resulting from Freemasonry, if any, could be acceptable grounds for such a step.[90]

In this latter spirit the Synod dealt with the request for advice in the memorials. The Synod advised the churches "to be very loving and patient and strictly constitutional in dealing with people concerning this subject."[91] Most of the faithful eventually resigned themselves to this view, but not all did, especially not after various leaders in the East had openly declared at the Synod that they were Freemasons. The difference in rate of Americanization is clearly reflected by the fact that Holland was for some time the center of religious excitement and also the starting point from which the revivals spread through the colony. By contrast, the factory town of Grand Rapids was the center where the separatist movement had its origin, just as in 1857. This is, in my view, a clear indication that Americanization in Holland was all that much further advanced than in Grand Rapids, which is understandable after all I have mentioned about this process earlier.

The decision to secede was made on the initiative of the most influential representatives of the two above-mentioned groups who were the least Americanized. The leader of these new separatists, Reverend Hulst, declared in his memoirs: "Although it was not my belief and certainly not Van Driele's intention, it is clear to me in hindsight that God used him to prepare me for our separation from the Reformed Church that took place in 1880."[92] Under Hulst's leadership, the majority of his Coldbrook congregation in Grand Rapids severed from the Reformed Church on September 8, 1881. "Our continual association with the East hinders us, because our people have never had an unqualified trust in the East. It is that same distrust that was the secret root of an earlier secession, in 1857.... Removal of the Theological Department of Hope College shocked the West to the depth of its soul, but the little trust that remained might still have overcome this injury. However, the Synodical protection of Freemasonry in the Reformed Church has completely destroyed that trust."[93]

Initially people thought that many congregations would follow suit, but in the end, it was only a small number. This was due in part to the vigorous intervention of more educated preachers and others under the leadership of Dr. N. M. Steffens, who acted as spokesman for the General Synod and its pronouncements. Saugatuck and Fijnaart (East Saugatuck) led by Reverend J. C. Groeneveld, and a large part of the church at Grand Haven led by Reverend Duiker, and the churches at Graafschap, Montague, and Drenthe were the only ones that severed ties. In various settlements—Zeeland, Overisel, Zoetermeer, Zutphen, Harderwijk, and others, which had often been founded at later dates—varying numbers of members also left the fold. In addition, a large portion separated from the First Church in Holland, formerly pastored by Van Raalte and Pieters. It is significant that those who separated belonged mostly to later arrivals, while almost all those who wanted to stay with the Reformed Church belonged to the early founders.[94] Because of the Freemasonry issue, a total of about three hundred families, mostly all in Michigan and a few in Alto, Wisconsin, separated from the Reformed Church.[95]

In towns such as Holland and Grand Rapids the Secession caused a quandary concerning the dividing of church property. Finally, a secular judge awarded the property to the separating majority. Especially in Holland this decision hurt, for it was viewed as a bitter injustice by the old colonists who had remained loyal to the Reformed Church, although it was legally correct, that is, it concurred with American law. They, as pioneers, had built that church with the hard-earned money they had been able to save despite the tough struggle for survival, and now they had to surrender their cherished building, Van Raalte's church no less, one of the few historical buildings in all of the colony, to the seceding majority of nearly all later-arrived immigrants who had never contributed one penny to the "Pillar Church." It is E. Van der Veen who pointed out in his memoirs a fact that I consider to be of great significance for the understanding of the existing relationships between culture and religion: that among those who no longer wanted to have anything to do with the Reformed Church, there was only one pioneer in Holland, the local leader of the "Seceders," the energetic but ambitious Teunis Keppel.

One can imagine how Keppel felt in those days! Classis Holland had just been scheduled to meet in this historic church building. But the Separatists already called it their property and did not allow the meeting to take place there. Therefore the entrances to the church were locked and kept under guard by members of the consistory. The rest of the consistory and some of their followers stood nearby to prevent the use of their church, with force if need be. Teunis Keppel, dressed in his Sunday best, paced nervously back and forth on the church square, looking searchingly in all directions and with clenched fists as if ready to fight. When the members of the Classis arrived and saw their gathering place occupied, they quietly discussed the situation and finally decided to hold their meeting in another church. With a heavy heart I went home, " . . . surprised to see what selfish men would do in the name of Christianity," concluded Van der Veen.[96] This episode is strikingly similar to the theatrics in the overly-militant Calvinist sister churches in the Netherlands and South Africa. That is the way even God's chosen people were; indeed, that is the way they still are!

Although the Separatists let it be known by way of Reverend Hulst, their "general correspondent," that basically they felt completely in agreement with the Seceders of 1857, they remained initially—and that is typical—all by themselves, expecting others to join them. When they realized that there was no need for a Third Dutch Reformed Church, the schismatic brothers discarded their plan for an organization of their own. It was only now that it dawned upon them "that this could not possibly be of Divine origin, but was rather a shrewd ploy of the devil."[97] Most of the Separatists affiliated in 1882 and following years with the Christian Reformed Church, but there were some who returned to the Reformed Church. The congregation of Graafschap did so in its entirety after their Pastor, Reverend Zwemer, had requested in 1886 "that the separation between Holland Classis and himself and his flock" might end. This request was granted by Classis Holland by a unanimous vote.

By the action of Reverend Hulst and others, the True Church increased both its membership and the number of its gifted ministers. But of greater importance for its growth were other consequences of the anti-Masonic campaign, specifically a change of opinion in the Netherlands. Up to now, church leaders in the Netherlands had refused to get involved officially in the American controversies, although most of the leaders sympathized with the Reformed Church. When Reverend Hulst and others enlightened them about the danger of Freemasonry, there was a change in public opinion. Moreover, when P. D. Van Cleef, who was delegated to represent the Reformed Church in 1888 at the Netherlands Synod of the Christelijke Gereformeerde Kerk in Zwolle, wrote a letter stating that many of the best and most orthodox preachers and members of the Reformed Church were Freemasons, a shiver went through the Synodical assembly when the letter was read aloud—the writer having been unable to be present in person. Thus it was now officially known that many members belonged to "that mysterious order hiding in darkness."[98]

Since an admonishing letter to the Reformed Church had remained unanswered, the Netherlands Synod of 1885, meeting in Rotterdam, not only repeated its admonition but decided, though by a small majority, "to advise consistories of our congregations not to recommend members leaving for America to join the Reformed Church, until such time as it will have turned with firmness against the abomination of Freemasonry."

Now the Christelijke Gereformeerde Kerk in the Netherlands officially stood on the side of the Seceders of 1857 and 1880. Even Brummelkamp was swayed in this respect. Thus, the great stream of immigrants, mostly members of the Christelijke Gereformeerde Kerk in the Netherlands were led from the Reformed Church to the Christian Reformed Church in America. It was just at this time that the immigration of Netherlanders more than tripled!

These various events, it must be repeated, were more important than merely in their religious consequences. The process of Americanization of the immigrants was, no doubt, slowed down by their affiliation with the Christian Reformed Church in America. But for the far smaller number of those who subsequently joined the Reformed Church, the Americanization process was accelerated. More strongly than before, both churches, in particular the Separatists, began to give advice and guidance about immigration. They acted more or less as information offices. The Christian Reformed Church in America even promoted emigration from the Netherlands because they advertised, so to speak, as we shall see, the remaining undeveloped cheap land![99]

The wish to boost church membership played a leading role in this matter. The Reformed Church had been accused earlier that its recruiting of members had become the main goal of its church activities, even to such a degree that the doctrine and the lives of the members were "squeezed and distorted."[100] But among the Seceders of 1857 and 1880 one encounters this evil of "playing church" just as much. I gave as an example Reverend Duiker's case.

This attempt by both churches to gain new membership naturally brought in many true believers, but also the "tares" sneaked in; they were even brought in in good faith. Van der Meulen had already complained earlier about the many worldly-minded people who settled in the colony. They were Sunday saints and weekday sinners, people who only paid lip-service to their creed; the colonists called these quasi-believers "Sunday-Christians" or "Mouth-Christians." The competition between the two denominations greatly increased their number. A woman in one of the Dutch settlements was asked by the minister if her adult but unconverted children had made confession of faith yet. She replied in the negative, adding "We have enough hypocrites."[101]

Nevertheless, total membership grew! It is true that the purely Dutch element remained strongest in the Reformed Church. Immigrants of the Christelijke Gereformeerde Kerk and the Nederlandsche Hervormde Kerk joined the Reformed Church, but the Dutch ratio increased much more in the Christian Reformed Church in America. This church membership was as follows:

1880:   4 classes, 39 churches, 19 preachers, 2,014 families
1890:   6 classes, 79 churches, 46 preachers, 6,833 families.

Just one church, the La Grave Street Church in Grand Rapids, had been Americanized since 1887. In 1890 it had a membership of 97 families, the progeny of the 1857 fathers.[102]

It is difficult to give a comparable total of the Reformed Church since we have to deal here with a far larger group who were Americanized. In addition, such a large contingent tends to make the dividing line between the "American" and the "Dutch" group more hazy. Therefore, the following totals concern only the purely Dutch members of the Reformed Church in the West:

1880:   3 classes, 60 congregations, 48 preachers, 5,187 families
1890:   5 classes, 105 congregations, 75 preachers, 7,324 families.[103]

Thus, the undeniable slow growth of the Reformed Church compared to the Christian Reformed Church is evident. But we must consider the fact that many older congregations that became English-speaking churches are not included in these numbers. Therefore, these numbers on at least two counts are of relative value.

It would be interesting to know how many of the established Netherlanders were "believers." This is difficult to estimate since only part of the Dutch settlers belonged to these two denominations. We have noted how a number of Netherlanders joined other churches, e.g., Presbyterians, Baptists, Methodists, etc. Already in 1871 Holland, Michigan, had different churches: three Reformed churches, one Secessionist church, an Episcopalian church, and a Wesleyan Methodist church. There were also old and new Methodist-Episcopal church buildings.[104] Relatively few native Americans lived here, though. In Pella, Iowa, besides the Reformed Churches mentioned earlier, there were from the beginning Baptist and Methodist churches to which Americans and Hollanders belonged. Besides these, a Presbyterian Church was organized in 1869. Quite a number of Dutch belonged to the community of "The Brethren," or Darbyites, founded there in 1872.[105]

It is hardly feasible to determine how many Netherlanders belonged to the various official "American" churches, because many independent-minded settlers belonged to small "sects" not covered by statistics. Reverend [Jacob] Noordewier was told in Pella that on a Sunday, worship services were held in seventeen different places for a population of about three thousand, mostly Netherlanders![106] In Grand Rapids, besides the two Reformed and American churches there were legions of small sects and groups among the immigrants.[107] It was also this way in Paterson and elsewhere! We know even less about the numbers of Dutch Roman Catholics who spread across America in those years.

Among the Dutch Roman Catholic Churches in northern Wisconsin there existed a much greater unity of faith, at least from outward appearances. Because of the flexible, international character of Catholicism, from the beginning Germans, Irish, French, and Dutch worshiped as one single congregation. There were no small or national differences in the interpretations of their religion. Only language differences led to the formation of parishes grouped according to nationalities, provided the number of parishioners was large enough to justify such divisions, as, for instance, in Green Bay.[108] Nowhere have we come across any desperate attempts to hang on to native Dutch church customs or conflicts between more or less Americanized Roman Catholics; the existing literature mentions very little about it. That does not mean there were no difficulties. Just as among the Calvinists, the Roman Catholics complained about an increasing movement towards worldliness in worship caused by Americanizing influences. Also among the Roman Catholics there were those who left their church and joined American non-Roman Catholic churches. Mention should be made of the fact that the standards of some of the religious leaders left much to be desired; at times not all of them were like Van den Broek and Daems, priests of strong conviction in their faith, men of character and hard workers. A well-known Catholic priest, G. Van den Elsen, said: "It is deplorable that simultaneously with them and after them, men came, who lived and roamed about who were a disgrace to their name and teachings. Because of this there was much backsliding, and abuses arose that the present-day missionaries find hard to overcome even with the best of their efforts."[109] Indifference in religion and morals was the fatal result. *Pastoor* Van den Brandt [Antonius Van Brand], the parish priest of the municipality of Zeeland in Noord Brabant, has not been totally wrong in his writing!

13

Cultural Change
Education and Missions

A. Education

We have reviewed how cultural change evolved through changes in religious convictions. But the rate of this progressive cultural change varied among the immigrants, depending on whether their cultural horizon was more or less broadened. That broadening, in turn, depended in the first place on their natural disposition and aptitude and their social standing (in the broadest sense) upon their arrival in America. Secondly, it was influenced by the duration of their settlement and the environment where they settled. The significance of this environmental factor has been pointed out repeatedly. There was the contrast between settling in towns or in rural areas. And in the latter case, there was the difference between a "howling wilderness" and colonial communities that had been settled for years.

We have seen, in addition, how the differences in duration and tempo of the developmental process, all in keeping with the character of the immigrants and the things they experienced, caused contrasts to arise. Or, in case these contrasts already existed at the moment of arrival in the New World, they were sharpened to such a degree that endless religious conflicts resulted, which usually ended with suspension, dissociation, excommunication, or secession of preachers and church members. Although the religious disputes have continued up to the present moment and have caused schisms that are typical not only for our Calvinist colonists but for the orthodox in general, they nevertheless are not the only manifestation of cultural change.

In addition to religion, the colonists also began to turn their attention to other cultural matters: education, missions, politics, etc. They were able to do so because economic growth generally gave them more time and especially more means to diversify their interests. As they earned more money, they expanded their areas of service. And their preachers led the way by giving the necessary information. Nowhere else than at the classical gatherings is this quite understandable blending of economics and interests more evident. In addition, these gatherings served, in spite of all the discord, to demonstrate to the outer world the unity of the various Dutch Calvinist settlements and their mutual cooperation in many fields.

In the beginning, hardly enough was raised to pay ministers and teachers. These had to support themselves by "farming" on the side, by doing field work for other farmers, by keeping a store, by participating in land sales, or other forms of business. Slowly their conditions improved and it was even possible to provide welfare support to ministers who had become too old or sick, and to their needy widows and orphaned children.

Already earlier, a classical meeting had provided money for missions, higher education, and a weekly newspaper. Later their thoughts turned toward the Motherland and money was collected in a fund to aid poor, believing Netherlanders to emigrate. Each congregation would get a turn, and within the congregation the members would draw lots to designate an eligible family, usually relatives. The sponsored family pledged to settle in one of the colonies that shared in the immigration fund, which would also help to alleviate the shortage of workers, and to pay back as soon as possible and with a small interest the expenses of the crossing to America "so that the same may serve again for the same purpose."[1] Many were helped in this way but forgot to reimburse the advanced money. Even those who subsequently became well-to-do among these chosen children of God no longer paid any attention to this matter.[2]

The interest toward the Netherlands expanded further as large amounts of money were collected to support the Theological School at Kampen.[3] These liberal gifts stood in glaring contrast to the refusal of the many Dutch Secession preachers to accept calls and bring the gospel to their fellowmen in America, even of those who, like Brummelkamp, had urged immigration. Many were the urgent calls that went out to him, but alas, how many were in vain![4]

These decisions were made around 1855, that is, during a period of slow colonial growth. This shows clearly that the horizon of the once so narrow-minded immigrants was widening, that their interests were expanding, and that their care and sympathy for others was intensifying. In all of these activities their deepest wish was to serve God. Sometimes people felt that no sacrifice would be too large. Many a colonist had sacrificed his life for missions; others had done so on the battlefields of the Civil War. In addition, large sums of money were collected. As prosperity increased and as the number of colonists grew, these sums swelled also year after year. Already in 1861 the purely Dutch congregations of the Reformed Church in the West, totaling 1,525 families, collected $11,175 for the church budget and $5,376 for charity. By 1890, 7,324 families of the Dutch-speaking western Reformed Churches—not counting the English-speaking churches, which were usually more affluent—gave $92,793 and $33,090, respectively, for the church budget and charity[5]

A large amount of these monies was used for education. Education was provided nearly from the beginning of the colonies, at first more or less privately by Dutch teachers. Later district schools were organized and became American in style. These district schools caused new problems. Since the school meetings were seldom attended by the Dutch, the school interests were in danger of falling under the control of "unchristian" people. Free Christian schools were one of the ideals at least of the leaders among the immigrants. Therefore Van Raalte, a great advocate of parochial schools, urged the establishment of their own schools in addition to the American schools, as he had seen in New York. The Classis of Holland concurred with Van Raalte and declared at a gathering on Apirl 12, 1854, "that the churches should take steps to educate their children in schools where they will be subjected to specific christian influences, and that as a consequence, since an overwhelming influence of unbelief and superstition is found, it is highly incumbent upon them to establish parochial schools."

But Americanization already made itself felt in a strong way: most pioneers were satisfied with the district schools. So it continued until 1857, when, at the strong urging of Van Raalte, a parochial school was founded in Holland, not because of his narrow-minded prejudices, but because of his principled stand. The consistory even decided that *Nederduitsch* [Dutch] should be taught, that the Bible should be used as a textbook, and that catechism lessons should be given. Within two years, the school proved to be a partial failure. There was no real interest, and even in the consistory there was division, which resulted in serious discord concerning this school. Nevertheless, attempts were made to improve the "Orphanage Building," that had never been used as an orphanage but rather had been adapted for use as a school. In addition to the lady teacher, they added a male teacher. Numerous church members were not enthusiastic about this school. Many were so lukewarm and even refractory that they would not give their financial support to it, and so, after a languishing existence, the school closed on April 1, 1862. Many said this was a blessing for the colony since sectarian schools would have hopelessly delayed Americanization among the Netherlanders.[6]

In Zeeland, where people always went their own way, most of them rejected a parochial school once district schools were established, controlled by parents. Proudly, the Honorable C. Van Loo declared: "It has ever been the endeavor of the settlers in this township to have a free school of the American type. They have never been led off in sectarian or parochial by-paths, not even to the idea of a school taught in the Holland language."[7] And this in spite of the fact that people claimed to have emigrated to America for the sake of a third reason—schools![8] But even the few true advocates of this type of school gave up in the face of the new experiences and environment. Even they had already become too Americanized.

We should notice that the same situation existed among the pioneers in Pella, Iowa. Here, too, district schools were set up at an early date, and the very religious teachers from the Netherlands initially gave them a "biblical" format. But also here, there were people who felt that these district schools were a threat to their age-old faith. So under the influence of Van Raalte, who came to Pella in 1859 and again in 1861 to discuss this matter, which is an indication of his great influence, a parochial school was set up in 1861 with I. Overkamp, H. Neyenesch, and J. Stubenrauch as teachers. But already in 1867, this school closed due to lack of interest! Later, when an experienced instructor made another attempt and started a new Dutch Christian day school, he too had to close it soon afterwards because parents were not even willing to spend 10¢ a week to have their children expertly taught in Dutch.[9]

These developments should not be seen as resulting from a typical Dutch lackadaisical attitude, but as the natural result of circumstances that were inescapable for all colonists, no matter how religious, and thus conservative, they might be. Among the Germans, for instance, parochial schools also failed. "The interest for German private schools among the Ost Frisian Reformed groups in America was never very great and at the present time it is entirely vanishing."* That was the state of affairs a few years back.[10]

It was not by accident that the only place where Dutch Christian schools survived was in Grand Rapids. Already before 1857, Adriaan Pleune served there as schoolmaster for $100 a year. After the Secession of 1857, he used the rear of the Secession Church as a school. Later on, these Dutch Christian schools were found in other towns around the Michigan colony: in Muskegon, Grand Haven, and Kalamazoo, and also in Chicago. In other towns, Paterson, Cleveland, and Cincinnati, they were absent only because people felt strapped financially and were unable to pay for such schools. In other places, especially in the actual colonies, attempts were made, for instance, to teach a few hours of Dutch in the district schools. These attempts succeeded when the majority of the school board was Dutch.

These Christian schools were all characteristically and strongly Dutch, especially since people feared that with a loss of the Dutch language the young people would join the English churches with whose teachings they did not agree. The Seceders, the least Americanized in their way of thinking, also believed that the Dutch language was essential "because home training required it, the existing spirit of the times demanded it, and the welfare of the child made it imperative."[11] This typifies the Dutch spirit in the True |Ware| Church.

Only around 1885 was somewhat less stress given to Dutch and more emphasis placed on the Christian aspect of learning. Already during the rooting years at Holland, Michigan, the basis for higher education had been laid. This was the same in Pella. People in both places hoped to establish a college. The problem was a lack of finances in both colonies, and since the

*"Das Interesse an deutschen Gemeindeschulen ist unter den amerikanischen Ostfriesen Reformierten Stammes nie gross gewesen und ist in der Gegenwart gänzlich am Erlöschen."

interest in such a venture was not strongly evident in their own communities either, the leaders had to look elsewhere for support. Therefore, Hope College was built mostly with money obtained from the eastern Reformed churches. Central College at Pella was organized by the Baptists. Through these circumstances, the rate of Americanization exerted by both institutions has perhaps been greater than would have been the case otherwise.

Thus the "Institute" at Holland, as the colonists called the new educational facility, began in the school building of the district school. Taylor, whom we have mentioned before, was administrator of both schools. At the classical meeting of April 27, 1853, Van Raalte stated that having a district school and a "semi-parochial Academy" operating together was eventually untenable, since "the nature of such an institute demands that it be based on its own foundation" and "sooner or later it will need its own buildings."[12] Therefore, Van Raalte transferred to the Classis five acres of land that he had probably already promised earlier, to be used for the building of a college.[13] At the same gathering the brothers of Overisel offered "to clear the land of the abundance of trees." Large amounts of money were now donated by the East. Elder Samuel Schieffelin of New York donated $7,000 and laid the base for the permanent [operating] fund.[14] Mr. Schaik from the same city gave $500 "for this heartfelt need."[15] Various congregations in the West, although poor, contributed smaller amounts of money. Meanwhile most of the financial aid had to come from the East. In the same year of 1853 the General Synod agreed to take care of this project.

For many years the Institute had all kinds of problems. There was a lack of qualified students and opposition from the colonists, but especially a shortage of money, so that for the time being a building could not be erected. In spite of the contributions, the funds failed to meet the salary of the principal. When Taylor resigned on account of sickness in October, 1853, they owed him $1,800 plus his salary of that year![16] In spite of all this, Taylor fulfilled his duties with great devotion and even felt obligated to instruct from his sick bed. He succeeded so well in preparing two young men, J. Van der Meulen and C. Van der Veen for further education that these first pioneer students of 1854 could continue their higher education at Rutgers College in New Brunswick, New Jersey. To save expenses, since finances were desperate, the Classis asked the Synod for a replacement, one who could also serve as a preacher. In 1854, Reverend F. P. Beidler accepted the double challenge. Now regular English services began in the church of Holland and this increased Americanization considerably. Beidler only brought temporary relief, because in 1855 his task was transferred to a young pastor, John Van Vleck, a graduate from Rutgers and from the Seminary, both in New Brunswick. Time and again one notes this kind of co-operation between Americans of Old Dutch and of Young Dutch descent, especially in church affairs.

Under Van Vleck's leadership, preparatory higher education prospered in Holland. In 1855 he started with eighteen students, of whom two were girls—from the very beginning co-education had been the aim;[17] by 1859, when he relinquished his task, the total had risen to thirty-three. Most of them wished to continue their study at New Brunswick and to join the ministry. Van Vleck had to cope with many adverse conditions and had to shift for himself. First, he taught in the upper room of the public school and later transferred to the "Orphanage Building."[18] Since the "brothers" in the Netherlands left them in the lurch, Van Raalte began to urge others, who were engaged as tailors, carpenters, farmers, etc., to study and alleviate the shortage of pastors.[19] In 1857 there were eighteen young people ranking in age from thirteen to thirty-seven who attended school.

Van Vleck taught on two levels of education. In the classical department, his students studied Virgil, Cicero, Homer, etc. At the primary level he taught twelve boys in 1857. Here, he was assisted by an older student, who later became Reverend John Karsten. In addition, Van Vleck preached, using English in the pulpit, under an appointment that he had received from the Synod. This took place after he had been thoroughly examined by Classis Holland for safety's sake, "because the orthodoxy of the Honorable Gentleman is of great and general importance, due to the position the Honorable Gentleman will occupy at the Dutch Academy." After all, he was coming from that dangerous East! In the meantime, his salary could hardly be met by the brothers because contributions came in so slowly.

Van Raalte supported him mightily, because the great leader was convinced that education "along with God's regenerating influence," was the means "to save this Dutch people and their faith from insignificance." "If they do not want to be the tail end, if they do not want to be swallowed up by foreign influences, if, on the contrary, they want to be a people true to God and influential, then they will have to harbor knowledge in the bosom of some," Van Raalte declared. He was so convinced that these needs should be met that he even threatened to leave *de Kolonie* and to accept a call to Pella if the colonists persisted in their "insignificant . . . heartless and dawdling, unconcerned participation."[20]

Being little impressed by academia in distress, but startled by Van Raalte's threat to leave them, the people of Holland understood they had to do something; so at a congregational meeting they pledged $250 for the academy.* Van Raalte stayed, but the amount was far from sufficient. Again and again he pleaded the interests of the school and tried to collect funds for it. Three times in 1857 he traveled to the East for funds. Finally, he had accumulated $12,000 to build Van Vleck Hall, which is now nearly as "historic" as "The Old First." The faculty was also enlarged. Reverend |Abraham| Thompson and later Reverend Giles Van de Wall alleviated the task of the principal.

---

*The American "academy" can best be compared to the three-year H.B.S. |*Hogere Burger School* (High School)| in the Netherlands; a "college" covers the two highest grades of a five-year H.B.S. and the first years at a Dutch university. The highest "degrees" conferred by a "college" can be compared to our candidate's diploma at the university |Van Hinte|.

Although Van Vleck had been appointed head of the "Holland Academy" in 1855, it was only in 1857, after they had obtained their own building and a strengthened faculty, that the "Pioneer School" changed to a real academy.[21] Soon after, Van Raalte donated another nine acres, which enlarged the campus to sixteen acres. In the meantime some smaller buildings had been erected, e.g., "Zwemer House," which still exists. Van Vleck's successor, Dr. Philip Phelps, educated in the Old Dutch environment at Union College in Schenectady and at New Brunswick, was a friend and admirer of Van Raalte.[22] Under his guidance, the Academy began to expand, outwardly by having more buildings erected and more students enrolled, and inwardly by improving the quality of its education. After 1859 Phelps spent much effort and energy on this education. Some of his students could only read or write, others did not understand or speak a word of English. Some were well versed in the classics but everybody knew his Bible. Phelps succeeded in promoting more uniformity in this situation and in 1862 real "college" education began.

The number of educational personnel was expanded and the faculty was strengthened. It began with one man, the principal, in 1861. In 1863 P. J. Oggel and T. Romeyn Beck were added; in 1864 J. M. Ferris joined them but left already in 1865 to become the editor of the *Christian Intelligencer*; in 1866 Ch. Scott and C. E. Chrispell were added. These were all theologians and, with the exception of Oggel, Americans.

Thus in the year of 1866 Van Raalte's dream became a reality. The Academy changed to an organized college—to which he had often referred in the past as an "anchor of hope"—Hope College—with principal Phelps as president and the ministers, the first faculty, now appointed as professors.[23] Eight students graduated that year with a B.A. degree. These men, too, were cultural pioneers. Indicative of the significance that the academy and college had for the colonists is, in the first place, the fact that seven of the graduates specialized further in theology. The Institute had been called, and not without reason, a school of prophets. With permission from the General Synod, these students could continue their study at Hope College. The professors were instructed to give courses in training for the ministry. Thus the Theological Department had its temporary beginning and lasted until 1869.[24]

Van Raalte and Phelps now raised their sights; they wanted to make Hope College a university! Already in 1867 plans were formulated for a Hope Haven University, and these were proposed to the General Synod the year after.[25] They signal the daring and the youthful optimism that these leaders possessed and thus deserve to be mentioned. Until today these efforts have not materialized. The Dutch element of believers in America is still too divided, and not yet strong enough to be able to support a Free University. The "theological faculty" at Hope was recognized by the General Synod in 1869 after the seven theological students had graduated and had received their "professorial certificates." They were the first classically-educated preachers in the colony.

This center of learning was now recognized as the Western Theological School of the Reformed Church, in conjunction with the existing Theological Seminary at New Brunswick, New Jersey.[26] It was an event that had more than merely religious importance. Now that the future leaders and ministers received their education completely in the West, their religion for a much longer period of time kept its strong Dutch nationalistic character and the Americanization process was slowed down. That was also felt by the colonists, and those feelings became apparent, as we saw before, when they voiced their great dissatisfaction with the closing of the Theological School of Hope College in 1877 by the Synod.

In spite of the great prosperity that existed at that time among the Dutch—"the fat of the earth was enjoyed in a manner unknown before," said an eyewitness[27]—their support of Hope College in general as well as of the seminary in particular was still insufficient. The East was paying for it anyway, they thought. But when a debt of $21,000 had accumulated on Hope College, the Synod thought it necessary to reduce expenses and closed the Theological School of Hope College.[28] This caused the people in the West to fear that Americanization would alter their religious convictions. It was only after they had collected large sums of money to save the school that the Synod, meeting in 1884 for the first time in the West, rescinded the former decision and restored the Western Theological School at Holland.[29] The reopened Theological School was initially still viewed as a part of Hope College, but gradually it became more and more independent. They erected their own buildings and it is now known as Western Theological Seminary.

Since the Seminary was exclusively dedicated to a definite religious persuasion, it was able to maintain a Dutch character more than did Hope College itself, which was completely organized according to American standards. This was most obvious among the faculty of the Seminary. Until 1893, Hope College always had American preachers as administrators. After Phelps, Reverend G. H. Mandeville came in 1879. He was followed by Reverend Ch. Scott. Among the professors and teachers it was the same. Slowly, more Netherlanders joined the American faculty. C. Doesburg, who came in 1866 was the first; later a few graduates of Hope College began to instruct: Reverend Peter Moerdijk and Gerrit J. Kollen, LL.M, since 1871, and Henry Boers, since 1878, etc.[30] As the interest in studying grew among the colonists, which was made possible through the increasing prosperity, the Dutch element among the Hope College faculty increased. But it should be noted that these young people were already Americanized to an extra-large degree due to their enrollment at American institutes of higher education for the completion of their studies that were initiated at Hope College.

There was only one single American among the professors who taught at the Seminary after its reopening in 1884, Reverend J. W. Beardslee. One of the most talented professors was N. M. Steffens, well-known in American Calvinist circles and a native of Ost Friesland. Before 1870 Ost Frisians were usually classified by the Germans in America as Dutch.[31] Generally, most of the theological professors were sons of Dutch colonists, sometimes of pioneer colonists, and they had begun their education at Hope.[32]

The life of the students was sober, as was their education. This life had a strong American flavor, or rather a strong colonial character. One of the oldest fraternities, still functioning, was organized by Phelps in 1863. It was the Fraternal Society, which was a continuation of a similar fraternity that has since been disbanded at the Old Dutch Union College at Schenectady. The "Frats" promoted an "all-around" education through "friendship, love, and truth." This was and still is the purpose of their members. In 1886 Professor C. Doesburg started the Ulfilas Club to promote the study of the Dutch language and literature. It was kept temporarily dormant during World War I, but the Club still exists.[33] Phelps also thought about physical exercise. After the noon meal, students were allowed to leave the premises—most of them were housed according to English-American custom on campus—and spend a half hour in the open air, either "in town" or in the woods. Some of the students kept busy chopping firewood for the stoves, while the younger ones swept and dusted the rooms or made the beds! Between five and six o'clock P.M. they played ball.

The students, guided by a carpenter, also erected a building, or 'gymnasium', which was used for more bodily exercise; it also could serve as an auditorium. During the winter of 1862 these boys, like real sons of pioneers,[34] had chopped and split enough wood for this purpose. Soon after, as a tribute to their proud achievement, the gymnasium was dedicated in a stately manner. They raised the "Stars and Stripes," read a Psalm, sang a hymn, closed with prayer, and ended with three loud-sounding cheers.[35] In this way the typical American student spirit, and with it the "American spirit," was born among the young Dutchmen, just as elsewhere under similar circumstances.

Apart from that, student life in the settlement was rather monotonous. Theater attendance and dancing were considered to be "singularly ungodly practices," if not by the students themselves, then certainly by their usually very orthodox parents. For decades the establishment of a theater group in the colony was not even considered. One of the student frolics was to have once or at most twice every winter an evening ride through the settlement. The older students offered it as a treat to the young ladies of *de Stad*. During the summer they would sail to the mouth of Black Lake, now called Macatawa Park. Here they climbed the "shady hills," the tree-covered dunes, to enjoy the beautiful panorama of Lake Michigan. The most enjoyable of all were the parties held at the home of one of the girls whose parents would vacate the premises and visit some friends for the evening. These evenings were spent in playing games, while nuts, candy, cake and chocolate were served to nibble on. It is no wonder that many a preacher found his life's companion, his "*juffrouw*" [wife] at these get-togethers.[36]

Since the whole institution had initially meager facilities and college life was very simple, I thought of Garfield's definition: "Give me a log cabin with a table and a roughly-hewn bench. Put Mark Hopkins on one end and a good student on the other end of the bench and you have a university." Thus it was in Holland! Here the most qualified students received their education and some later joined the faculty. Those who fell below average were not tolerated.

We owe it in particular to Hope College, to Van Raalte's creation *par excellence*, that the Hollanders of Michigan have not remained "hewers of wood and drawers of water." Thanks to this institution they have been able to develop into a "highly respected element in the population of Michigan," as an Anglo-American confirmed recently.[37] Hope's influence asserted itself not only in Michigan but in all the Dutch Calvinistic settlements of America from which many sons of colonists came to study. A college education for girls, although already recommended by Van Raalte, became popular, at least among the more educated colonists, only at the turn of the century![38] Japanese students, influenced by foreign missionaries, attended Hope College since the seventies. By 1890 there were Hope graduates working in all parts of the United States, some even in Asia and Africa, and the number of alumni, including three Japanese, had risen to 149. They were ministers and missionaries, doctors and lawyers, teachers, and businessmen.[39]

I said that young people came to study at Holland from every Dutch Calvinistic settlement—even from Pella, in spite of the fact that Pella had its own institute of higher education, a "university"! Like Van Raalte in Michigan, Scholte in Iowa was a strong advocate of higher learning. On the whole, however, the majority of Pellians was even more indifferent to such training than people in Holland. The opportunities for advancement on the prairie were evidently still that much greater than in the forests of Michigan, and that was the main reason why education was held to be of little account in Iowa. Many Pellians looked down with some contempt both on those who taught as well as on those who learned. E. J. G. Bloemendaal, a noted immigrant, is wonderfully candid when speaking of his boss: "He was not like many Americans who don't want to work and become teachers or something of that sort just to get out of work."[40] K. Van Stigt, another well known colonial figure, declared: "Many take higher education in order to have an easier life rather than work on farms or be involved in some other kind of manual labor."[41]

Both writers give the popular opinions of the masses—not only of the Dutch but of all immigrants. This generally low opinion of education, plus the many opportunities of making a living without any formal education, are the reasons that such an important part of American education fell into the hands of women. It was only after prosperity increased that appreciation for education also grew. Among the Dutch it grew perhaps more strongly than among other immigrants, even more strongly than among the Americans of old.

Thus in Pella, as in Holland, it was almost exclusively the leaders who propagated higher education. Van Raalte was aided by the Reformed Church, which had entertained for years the idea of providing sound education in the West, and in addition he personally donated land for that purpose. Scholte, who like Van Raalte had studied at Leiden, and who therefore was also deeply imbued with the importance of higher education, was able to persuade the Baptists in 1853 to establish their planned school in Pella, which was incorporated as Central University of Iowa. Like Van Raalte in Holland, he himself donated the land for the school, eight acres. For two years the Baptists had been searching for a suitable site and had four locations in mind, one of which was Pella, where they held a meeting in 1853. Preference would be given to the location [where residents] would help out the institution most adequately by means of financial and other contributions. It is no doubt due to Scholte's strenuous effort, which in turn induced others in the colony, especially businessmen, to contribute "royally with sums of money and land," that the choice eventually fell on Pella.[42]

In 1854 the "university"—modesty is, after all, not a characteristic of young nations—was opened in a two-story stone building on West Washington Street, with Professor E. H. Scarff as the first president. Two years later, a three-story building, majestic for Pella at that time, arose as the institution grew in importance; in 1861 there was a total of 122 students. This growth was largely due to the efforts of Scarff, "a serious Christian man, respected and loved by all," but also with thanks to the constant support of Scholte and other leaders among the Hollanders, such as A. E. Bousquet and A. H. Viersen.

According to J. Nollen, this cooperation between the Baptists and Scholte shows how unmindful the latter was regarding "differing opinions about minor points of religion."[43] J. A. Wormser adds correctly that Scholte even seemed to be heedless of "differences concerning very important points of doctrine."[44] In this attitude we may see a certain broadmindedness which we already pointed out as existing among Pellian businessmen and which was a trait of the preacher Scholte and even more of the businessman Scholte. On the other hand, this cooperation explains why the university was so low in popularity among a large part of the Calvinistic Dutch Pellians, and why these Calvinists, as far as they were interested in higher education, preferred to send their donations for support as well as their sons for study to Hope College in Holland, Michigan.[45] The value of Hope College lay not only in its opportunity for a general education, but particularly in its curriculum offerings for the ministry. It was this latter point that drew the interest and support of many people who had religious concerns, but who could not care less about the usefulness of a broad, liberal education. Central University lacked such a drawing card and, as a Baptist institution, repelled many Calvinists.

The important role that Pella's business world played in the institution was expressed by the membership of two Dutchmen on its executive committee: H. P. Scholte was chosen president and the businessman [J.]

Smeenk, was elected secretary. They expected that the school would increase Pella's prosperity, and this expectation was fully warranted. Especially after the first years of its establishment, numerous Americans moved to Pella and near Pella, drawn by the "university." But the lack of interest shown by the Dutch also became evident. The Board of Trustees, thirty in number, had only two Dutch representatives, the two gentlemen mentioned earlier.[46] Until 1858 the university was nothing more than a very modest academy. The Class of 1861 comprised the first graduates, three in all. One was Dutch, Herman F. Bousquet, whose father was a friend of the Baptists. Only a few Dutch taught at Central. They were Jan Nollen, son-in-law of Scholte, Henry Nollen, Lillian Viersen, and Herman Neyenesch. During the first few decades very few Netherlanders attended this school. Their number was almost negligible. Only after 1890, due to a much further advance in prosperity and Americanization, did their number increase.[47]

For many people this school was an aggravation because some Hollanders of Pella attended not only the Baptist Sunday school but even this Baptist university. Thus, in consultation with the influential Van Raalte, who viewed Central as a thorn in his side, attempts were made in Pella to found a Calvinistic "*Hooge School*."* Those plans were discussed during Van Raalte's second and third trips to Pella in 1859 and 1865. The denominational zeal went so far that this Reformed Church education was "somewhat" begun. But soon it succumbed to the same fate as that of parochial education, mentioned earlier. "The fact that both elementary and higher education in Pella was above average, rendered the duplication of schools in such a rural town altogether unnecessary and superfluous."[48]

But our Calvinists were persistent, as the following events will demonstrate. Prosperity made them affluent and they bought out the "real" Americans, who finally disappeared from the environs of the settlement. Thus, in 1916, they were even able to purchase Central University. More modestly, it was renamed Central College and became an institution of the Reformed Church, going through its second, or Calvinistic, youth and being financed mainly by the Dutch.

Hope College was organized in the first place to train ministers, and from this purpose developed the Theological School in Holland. But the shortage of ministers would lead to the formation of another important institution for higher learning: the Theological School of the True Christians at Grand Rapids. Calvin College, which is an important school today, developed from this, but only after 1890. After the Secession of 1857, the True brothers had at their disposal only one minister, Reverend Van den Bosch. The shortage of ministers had to be filled with calls from the Netherlands.

I have mentioned before, more than once, the psychologically important

---

*By "Hooge School" was meant a college. An American "high school" can best be compared with a Dutch M.U.L.O. school [Meer Uitgebreid Lager Onderwijs (More Extensive Elementary Education)]. The differences between an "academy" and a "high school" are somewhat similar to the differences between our 7 year H.B.S. [Junior High School] and a M.U.L.O. school [Van Hinte].

phenomenon that although the Dutch Secessionists were considered as religious exiles, many fellow-Secessionist ministers had very little ambition to share their "exile." When calls were received from America, these ministers would quote from Scripture for their own benefit, alleging that God did not give them the freedom to respond to the call. Even less was the desire to serve the Seceders from the Dutch Seceders living in America, and consequently, calls for preachers were rejected by the dozen. If it happened that after much urging and willingness to pay the cost of the expensive journey, a preacher would accept the call, then the congregation was not always sure that things would work out as planned and that their minister would indeed stay, as many examples to the contrary demonstrate! It happened more than once that the man of the cloth came and . . . left, came again and . . . left again.[49]

Already at the February Classis of 1861, the True brothers discussed the need for a training of prospective preachers due to "the difficulty of getting ministers from the Netherlands." In July, 1863, Reverend W. H. Van Leeuwen was appointed to do this. With "fear and trembling," he began with one single student, J. Schepers from the village of Vriesland. Monthly collections were held for this cause and so the germ of a theological school began to bud.

Fortunately, there were truly godly men who heeded the call to come to America. Reverend D. J. Van der Werp was one of them and he became the first actual pioneer professor, succeeding Van Leeuwen. For years he educated men bound for the ministry, in his manse, originally in Graafschap and after 1872 in Muskegon. The students would do their practice preaching at his church and instructive criticism and practical advice would be given afterwards. At Graafschap the consistory "would have brotherly discussions about the practice preaching of students to their congregation, and remarks and suggestions were brought to the attention of the minister for the students' reproof and sharpening, both for their own benefit and for the edification of the congregation."

However, students were often deficient in the most elementary subjects of elementary education, and this was a real handicap in their theological studies. To remedy this situation it was decided to have a course in the study of languages. However, minister after minister in the Netherlands declined to cross the Atlantic to teach this course. Thus year after year, following the death of Van der Werp, the task of higher education remained for one man, Reverend G. E. Boer of Grand Rapids. The upper story of a Christian school served as a classroom for the teaching of Boer's seven students of the Theological Seminary. Boer was instructed to add a preparatory department, the so-called "Literature Department," to his higher theological instruction. It included instruction in the Dutch language and composition, Latin, Greek, Hebrew, etc. It is this branch that would grow into a full college later on.

Not before 1882 did Reverend Boer, who taught some twenty subjects, obtain temporary relief through the appointment of the student G. Vos, who resigned after one year, and then from Reverend G. K. Hemkes, who was appointed as assistant instructor. In 1884 Hemkes, who was "a man of study and scholarship," was given a permanent appointment as instructor, and two years later, G. Vos also received a permanent appointment as instructor. He had gone to a preparatory high school [gymnasium] in Amsterdam and had studied from 1883 to 1886 at the seminary in Princeton, New Jersey, where he obtained a scholarship. Thus, he was "a man of renown, even outside of his own church circles." Both Hemkes and Vos had first served as aids. Vos's scholarship enabled him in the meantime to go to Germany where he obtained his doctorate in philosophy. So it was 1888 before he could assume his teaching duties at Calvin College.[50] Now education could be deepened and broadened. Even opponents of this church had to admit that the brothers in Grand Rapids were doing phenomenal work.[51] The number of students increased from ten in 1880 to forty in 1890. During this latter year, the decision was made to secure their own building, and it was not by accident—as I have pointed out repeatedly—that the site came to be in Grand Rapids.

Thanks to the Theological School, culture and education began to spread among the True brothers, as it was experienced already much earlier among their more well-to-do fellow Dutch of the Reformed Church. This cultural trickle-down effect had been initiated and promoted by the one and single holder of a Ph.D. degree teaching among the members of the Christian Reformed Church for a number of years. This cultural development had an almost exclusively theological character and it remained a more or less one-sided, "preacher" culture for many, many years, for much longer than in Holland, Michigan, not to speak of Pella, Iowa. In the Christian Reformed settlements and in many small settlements of the Reformed Church, the ministers were, and still are today, the main promoters of culture, not only in church affairs but often also in politics, indeed in every social area. Of course we must not underestimate the role of the grocerymen and store-keepers in these functions either.

We should point out that it was not exclusively or almost exclusively the children of the ministers who continued their studies. But they were the first ones who would go to college, in addition to children from the store-keepers and some bright youngsters from the usually less-educated class. After their college careers they would enter their life's work, or else continue further studies at a theological school or university, or sometimes at both. Of the first two young men who took higher education at Holland and prepared themselves to go on to New Brunswick, one was a son of Reverend Van der Meulen. Likewise, sons of Bolks and Van Raalte were among the Hope graduates in 1867. The increase in the number of ministers was accompanied by an increase in the total number of preachers' children who went off to college. Examining the statistics of Reverend John Hoekje and his family in Holland, Michigan, one realizes they become record holders of some sort. Hoekje himself had graduated from Hope in 1873 and his six children subsequently did the same. After they had passed their exams, they went on for graduate studies elsewhere.[52]

We should also be reminded of Adriaan Zwemer who, when he was thirty-two years old, began to study at the Holland Academy in 1855 under the tutelage of Van Vleck. Later, his four sons were educated at Hope and they became ministers or missionaries. His only daughter became a missionary of China.[53] And there was also Reverend [Frederick] Lubbers of Cedar Grove, Wisconsin, who had seven sons and one daughter, all of whom studied at Hope.[54]

From the common people it was mostly those who felt "called to the ministry" who went off to college, just as was usually the case formerly in Europe. But from the preachers' families, who were the main producers of the intellectual element in the years of growth, went forth not only ministers and missionaries, but also other future leaders such as doctors, lawyers, teachers, etc. This is a circumstance that can be explained not only from the fact that there existed certain talents for those specialties among these youngsters, but also from the fact that, due to a more ample general educational background fostered in the homes, their interest would be more easily directed to those fields of endeavor.

But there is a third factor that in this respect was of great importance among the orthodox colonists. A greater general education and background caused, and still causes, doubts to arise more easily concerning the divine origin of Holy Scriptures. That is why we see young people, after having begun their theological studies, switch to another field, as was the case with the eldest son, Henry, of the locally well-known minister L. J. Hulst.[55] Henry was a Hope College alumnus, but switched to the State University at Ann Arbor, Michigan, to study medicine. Hulst's youngest son completed his education there too, and became a mechanical engineer. Examples like these were and are typical for the cultural change that took place in orthodox circles. Obviously, this change created a generation gap. It proceeded more slowly among the older people than among the younger set. This would lead, at times, to a mutual lack of understanding and to alienation.

This happened in particular when the younger generation forgot the language of their fathers, or worse, when they neglected their age-old religion and its traditions. Then, painful clashes occurred. Henry Hulst, the doctor, told me in person during a private conversation, that his own father threw him out of the church![56] Instead of becoming a Christian Reformed minister, which was the original intention, he became one of the most well-known medical doctors in Michigan. "His name is synonymous with a good reputation," wrote his old, orthodox, and once so-strict father, not without pride.[57] We could give many more examples of the increase in educational background, in particular through college education, especially among ministerial circles. From these circles, let it be repeated, emerged the leaders for those times. And that is why, also in this respect, one could speak of a "preacher" culture.

What I have written above is in reference mostly, in the first place, to the Reformed and Christian Reformed colonists. However, these observations also hold true for those who, due to the scattering effect in choosing a place to settle but more often due to internecine quarrels, joined the Presbyterians or occasionally the Baptists. Among them the Americanization process usually took place at a faster pace because the leaders would have more contacts with Americans, while these congregations would at times also have Americans among their members. In these "mixed" congregations—and this holds true also for the Reformed and Christian Reformed churches—as in the case of Dutch-German parishes, there would arise a language problem. Which of the two languages, either German or Dutch, should prevail? As a result of overcoming the problem, the introduction of the English language would be accelerated.

There were many more of these mixed churches among the Presbyterians. This was due in part to the fierce propaganda of the Home Missions of the Presbyterians, and in part to the wish of many colonists to join an American church that would be as close as possible to the faith of their Dutch ancestors. Earlier I mentioned that many colonists initially joined the Presbyterians and then switched to the Reformed Church, driven more or less consciously to this decision by their ethnic sense of group-belonging, or through quarrels—which caused secession—or through the intense competition among the churches. Often both factors had an effect.[58] It is obvious that the Americanization process slowed down through all this, and that the Dutch Presbyterian churches remained few in number. Out of these circumstances, a Dutch Presbyterian seminary evolved at Dubuque, Iowa. This is the only Dutch Presbyterian institution of higher learning of which I have knowledge.

In various Mississippi River towns of Iowa there arose small settlements of Dutch people. When there were no trains or bridges yet, the colonists were ferried across the Mississippi by boat and the various delays upon landing on the other side of the river would cause them to settle then and there. Thus in 1856, Keokuk, the Gate City of Iowa, was inhabited by 150 Dutch people. During that year two groups of 25 Dutch families each lived further north in Burlington and Dubuque.[59] Among the Dubuque Netherlanders some rose to prominence. Among them was Adriaan Van Vliet, a preacher in the Presbyterian Church, who established the seminary at Dubuque, where he was active for many years as a professor.[60] Having started out modestly, the seminary became famous and developed into an influential institution. Because here too, prospective ministers came poorly prepared, the school, as in so many other places, had to set up three branches: a preparatory division, a college, and the actual theological school. A full-fledged study in all three divisions took nine years. Besides Van Vliet, other leaders taught there, among whom was the well-known academic theologian, N. M. Steffens of Holland, Michigan. Under strong urging, he later returned to the colony of Holland.[61]

The school at Dubuque never was typically Dutch in character. The number of Dutch students was small, since relatively few calls came for Dutch Presbyterian preachers in the West. There were some who made their livelihood not among their own people but among the Ost Frisians, who were very closely related to the Dutch. One example was Jan Van der Las, who had been at one time a Reformed, door-to-door Bible salesman. Years before he had brought to the attention of the important colony of Ost Frisians in Germany Valley, Illinois, the existence of the Reformed Church in America.[62]

In the early years the seminary was of value especially to the Ost Frisians. In fact it was mostly Ost Frisians who attended the Dubuque Seminary. However, the influence of the Dubuque institution upon the Dutch was greater than has become apparent, so far, from the information mentioned earlier. In the first place, many Ost Frisian settlements were mixed, counting also many Dutch settlers, as was especially evident in Iowa and Minnesota. We have noted earlier also how closely the Germans themselves considered the Ost Frisians to be related to the Dutch. No wonder, therefore, that Americans too considered Ost Frisians to be Dutchmen.

Besides, the religious concepts of the Presbyterians and the Reformed are very close. Therefore, Christian Reformed congregations and their ministers often considered joining with the United Presbyterians, which the Dutch call the "Scottish" church. They also considered joining with the Old School Presbyterians. However, in both cases, their Dutch heritage and the language were obstacles too great to overcome. Not only Reformed ministers crossed over—with or without their congregation—to the Presbyterians, but also the reverse took place. This is evidenced by the Dutch as well as Ost Frisian congregations that switched wholesale—sometimes with their preachers—from Presbyterian allegiance to the Reformed denomination.[63]

The Ost Frisian minister E. Meinders, educated at Dubuque, played a role of importance, even of notoriety, among the Dutch. He was approached to become professor of theology for the Christian Reformed Church in Grand Rapids, and later on, as a minister at South Holland, Illinois, he brought about an important schism in this denomination.[64]

This Ost Frisian character of the Dubuque Seminary did not last, however, even though people, under the influence of the subsequent influx of the German Ost Frisians, called it the German college and seminary. It was precisely the American character of the Presbyterian churches, and their numerous "mixed" congregations, which gave the originally Dutch theological school in the West something typically American: an international flavor. In 1916, for instance, there were thirty-four nationalities among the students. The Germans, not all of them Ost Frisians by far, only formed a minority of 78 out of a total of 260 students.[65] Thus it is understandable that the Presbyterian congregations did not worry about elementary education. People were quite satisfied with the American district schools and the need for parochial schools was hardly ever mentioned.

In the Catholic settlements of Wisconsin the development of education was different again. Almost from the very beginning parochial schools were established, but not as in the Calvinistic settlements, to keep up the Dutch heritage—the Roman Catholic Church was and is too international and too adaptive in character for such developments—but to preserve the Roman Catholic religion. In this respect, we should also keep in mind that the American district schools were mainly Protestant in character, which was absolutely unacceptable for Roman Catholics, at least for those Roman Catholics who had not been sufficiently Americanized.[66] Firmin Roz in his L'Energie américaine may have given the impression that Roman Catholics* submitted to the American school boards: "Soumettre l'établissement au régime américain, quelle que soit la nationalité de ses élèves" [To submit the school to American authority, no matter what the nationality of its pupils might be].[67] It was this way in the East, but certainly not in the West. Western parochial schools flourished among the Dutch, German, and other Roman Catholics to such a high degree that a vigorous campaign by Americans was unleashed against them. "L'expression de son intime harmonie avec l'esprit national" [The expression of its intimate harmony with the national spirit]—which, according to Roz, is the attitude of American Roman Catholicism—is at most evidenced by the neglecting of the mother languages of the colonists. This neglect was, moreover, often a necessity, because in the same parish Dutch, Irish, French, and German immigrants lived together, and it was justified "par raisons d'économie et afin d'éviter des rivalités" [for reasons of economy and in order to avoid rivalries].

If there were enough Netherlanders to organize their own parish and parochial school, they did not only save money, but they contributed unwittingly also to a longer use of their Dutch language. Therefore, in larger towns, where there were many Roman Catholics, the Dutch language was used for a longer period of time than would have been the case under other circumstances. In Green Bay, where the Dutch at first shared their church and school buildings with the Germans, the Dutch grew so rapidly in number that in 1864 they could buy the old city courthouse and renovate it into a "church and school." In 1891 they erected a splendid Holland church; it was, "after the cathedral, the most beautiful Temple of God in the diocese." A new school, which cost no less than $50,000 also was evidence of their growing prosperity.

After the St. Boniface Church was built in 1883 in West De Pere, it also served as a school for many years. Later, besides two public schools, East and West De Pere had four Roman Catholic parochial schools. In 1886 a convent school began. Little Chute also had a parochial school taught by Dominican Sisters. Sometime later, in 1907, high school subjects were added. This was rather an exception among the Dutch colonies at that time!

---

*Roz mentions, by way of precaution: p l u s i e u r s evêques [several bishops]. The spacing is mine [Van Hinte].

In the little Dutch village of Holland [Wisconsin], also inhabited by Germans and Irish, a new parochial school arose in 1869, which was inaugurated in 1871 and led by Franciscan nuns from Alverno, Wisconsin.[68] We notice that parochial schools among the Dutch Roman Catholics of Wisconsin flourished, and they still do, in spite of Firmin Roz's assertion.

In contrast to the Calvinistic colonies, the desire among Roman Catholics for higher education seems to have been minimal. The shortage of priests was largely replenished from the Netherlands and Flanders, and in the mixed settlements also from other lands. We should take notice of this cooperation between the Dutch and Flemish Roman Catholics, which is comparable to the one between the Calvinist Netherlanders and Ost Frisians. As a special case we must mention that P. Van Susteren, who was born in 1865 at Freedom, Wisconsin, of Dutch parents, had the honor to be the first Holland-American priest in the diocese at Green Bay. His education took place in the Saint Francis Seminary at Milwaukee, which was some distance from his own Roman Catholic colony. Van Susteren was ordained to the priesthood at the Saint Joseph Church of West De Pere, and he began to serve as a priest in the Dutch Saint Willibrod Church at Green Bay in 1896.[69]

The already existing training opportunities for the priesthood, and more importantly, the absence of an important social stratum in which priest-producing families could be found—in our case to provide young people endowed with an intellectual interest and willingness to study—explain why it took until the nineties before Roman Catholics built a college, Saint Norbert College, in West De Pere. Another contributing factor to this delay was the absence of leaders who could fully identify with the colony, as was the case with Van Raalte, Van der Meulen, and Scholte. Hope College, founded by the Calvinists, had developed organically from the simple foundations that had already been established in 1851. It had become an inherent part of the colony. But Saint Norbert College was brought in from the outside by the Premonstratensians (Norbertines) who had come from Heeswijk, Noord Brabant, to the United States in 1893. Thus, there were interesting differences in the expression of spiritual life between the Calvinists and the Roman Catholics, just as these were clearly evident before in the Netherlands.

B. Missions

Besides religious worship and education, there was a third closely-connected area of interests that actually proceeded from these two areas—missions. Missions characterized the growth of the Dutch colonists and, through interaction, this activity has broadened their outlook, enlarged and deepened their knowledge, and in general helped them to assume a more broadminded stance in religious matters.

In the beginning the spirit of missions was dormant among the masses;

it originated with some of the leaders, primarily Van Raalte and Scholte. At a time when the mass of common people in the Netherlands was already strongly drawn by America, Van Raalte had wanted to go to the Dutch East Indies, since he was very interested in missions. "Wonderful it would be to labor on Java, also among the Heathen, and to establish there a central source for the spreading of the Gospel, and thus to forget America!" he exclaimed in the well-known brochure that he published together with Brummelkamp.[70]

Again and again the Dutch colonists [of Holland, Michigan] came in contact with the sympathetic missionary Reverend George N. Smith who labored among the Indians, and whose work made such an impression upon them.[71] These colonists themselves became more or less targets for missions, in particular from the side of the Domestic Missions agency of the Reformed Church. When Van Raalte and Van der Meulen traveled to such towns as Allegan, Milwaukee, and elsewhere to preach the gospel to the scattered Netherlanders, what they did, in fact, was missionary work from the very beginning of their arrival in America. Mission work and a missionary spirit were omnipresent. It is no wonder, therefore, that the consistory of Holland's first congregation—Van Raalte's church—decided on November 24, 1851, that 15 percent of the offerings would go to Foreign Missions and 50 percent to Domestic Missions.[72] This decision was made during the days of greatest poverty, during the early rooting years!

Holland's missionary spirit seemed to spread throughout the entire colony, because at the classical meeting of September 1, 1852, the colonists decided to have a monthly offering for missions among the heathen, and ruled that anyone who wished to enter missions would be given an appropriate training. Therefore the pioneer schools—the academy, the college, the seminary and the institutes of higher education—would have to serve in the first place to train missionaries in addition to ministers for the settlements themselves, so that "our children will be molded to be spreaders of the light of the Gospel in the dark places of the earth."[73]

The inference should not be drawn that only the Dutch colonists were moved by this missionary spirit. It was not even typically American, for the missionary spirit had set its stamp on the whole Christian world of that time. With the opening of China and later Japan for import and trade, strong mission emphasis was directed towards Asia. Around 1850 six new mission societies were created in America, Scotland, and the Netherlands (by [O. G.] Heldring!). The Germans also took a large part in this move. Thus the leaders were already permeated with the "missionary spirit" that blew in the Netherlands. They, and now also many of the immigrants, remained in permanent contact with this world-wide spirit, especially through their union with the Reformed Church.[74] This is one of the reasons why those who withdrew from the Reformed Church in 1857 and were, as a consequence, far less influenced in this respect, started foreign mission work only much, much later.

At the time of arrival of the immigrants, some members of the Reformed Church were already busily engaged with those of other denominations to become world-renowned in the foreign mission field. John Scudder, "the pioneer missionary of the denomination," labored in Ceylon since 1819, and later in India near Madras. Reverend David Abeel worked in 1829 near Canton in China. But since he considered his Dutch background and church an asset, he felt it was preferable to establish a mission field on Borneo, Dutch East Indies, in 1839. He labored for some time at Sambas and Pontianak, after the government had grounded him and his coworkers for a whole year at Batavia, with nothing for them to do! He left, greatly disappointed and began a mission post at Amoy, China, in 1842. C. V. A. Van Dijk, M.D., became a medical missionary in Syria at Beirut and was widely recognized. His fame spread so widely that people said of him "after God, Van Dijk," and in this outspoken Mohammedan land, the first monument that was erected in more modern times was a marble bust in his honor.[75]

These were the men of the Old Dutch ranks of the Reformed Church who laid the foundations of missions. The Young Dutch Americans who followed them expanded this basis and in turn earned themselves a world reputation in the mission field. For decades the Reformed Church in conjunction with other denominations had specialized in mission work, and they had centralized their efforts since 1832 in the American Board. They labored among the Indians in the East and in foreign countries. At the urging of many of its members in 1857 the Reformed Church organized its own independent Board of Foreign Missions.* As a supporting group, the Women's Board appeared in 1875.

With this change the Reformed Church began to support and work in the Arcot mission of India and the Amoy mission in China. In the latter field, the Old-Dutch Americans, John Van Nest Talmage, Daniël Rapalje, L. W. Kip, etc., made valuable contributions. Scudder and his son were the pioneers in India. When the Reformed Church in the West entered the field, Young-Dutch Americans—Hope College alumni after their theological graduation—began to contribute their share in the work of missions over there.

Now that the Reformed Church had become independent in mission work, a greater interest for mission work arose among the colonists, especially during the visit of the missionary minister Jacob Chamberlain, shortly before his departure to India in 1859. How the masses were won over to the concept of missions was told by one of the oldest colonists. The youthful missionary, accompanied by Van Raalte as interpreter of his English speeches, visited various churches in Michigan. He told us "what mission work was concerned with, how it was based on the Savior's last command,

*The Americans distinguish Missions as "Domestic" and "Foreign," When it refers to Indians, what do you call it? The Dutch connotation is *Binnenlandsche* [Domestic] and *Buitenlandsche* [Foreign] while *Heidenzending* means "Heathen Missions." In the American sense, "Heathen Missions" refers to Foreign Missions [Van Hinte].

and that it was our solemn duty and our blessed privilege, to be coworkers with God in bringing salvation to our fellow men, who are still bending their knees to gods of wood and stone.... When we had listened to his talks, and had seen, in addition, some of the idols with our own eyes, then came the moment that our Dutch Christian folks were won over to participate in the God-glorifying work of Foreign Missions."[76]

Shortly after, Classis Holland decided to have ministers and consistories of every congregation stress missions, and try to induce members to donate $3.00 a year for missions and education. In 1860 Classis Holland wanted to send their own missionary to South Africa, most likely to strengthen the Dutch mission efforts in that region.[77] However, a suitable man could not be found, so Van Raalte suggested that he himself should go, but since he was indispensable for the colony, they did not pursue the matter.[78] In spite of the setback, interest in missions blossomed and in 1864 one could speak of a new "revival of missionary spirit" among the Dutch in the West. The Particular Synod at Chicago, composed of the Western Classes, wrote to the General Synod of that year and suggested setting up a Professional Chair of Missions as the beginning of a seminary in Holland.

Besides Van Raalte, it was Phelps of the Holland Academy who worked hard for missions. Through his effort the missionary J. Van Nest Talmage from Amoy took part in the keel-laying ceremony of their own mission ship at an old wharf near Holland. It was a very well attended, simple but impressive ceremony that fulfilled the ideal the Dutch leaders had carried with them from the Netherlands.[79] The ship was to be financed by Classes Holland and Wisconsin, but it was never completed. This undertaking was in sharp contrast with the usual levelheaded and practical common sense of the Dutch. It was, nevertheless, characteristic of the change of attitude that had already taken place in their minds. For steadfast Dutch people it is an unusual experience to see these colonists caught up in the true, American "gung ho" spirit of forcefully pursuing an ideal, only to drop it soon afterward with equal alacrity. The keel was laid and that was all! For years it lay there in Black Lake until it rotted away.

Yet, the missionary ideal made many a heart beat faster, and since those early days the ideal has become a reality, a reality of endless selfless deeds. A well-known Holland-American, S. M. Zwemer, a missionary himself, could point out at the semi-centennial celebration of the Michigan colony dozens of men and women of the colony who had become missionaries.* He remarked that "the laying of the keel for a ship that never sailed was indeed a potent auxiliary for the publication of the Gospel!"[80] Indeed, the colonists had built better than they themselves thought.

A young 1867 graduate of Hope College, who had possibly attended the keel-laying ceremony, decided to dedicate his life to missions. An Ost Fri-

---

*Twenty-seven men and twenty-four women of whom thirty-two had studied at Hope College. They were scattered all over China, India, Japan, Arabia, Egypt, and South Africa [Van Hinte]

sian by birth, Enne J. Heeren became the first missionary pioneer of the settlements. His father, a widower with five children from the small town of Uttum in Ost Friesland, had settled near the German Valley colony [in Illinois] in 1855. Later he moved to the nearby village of Forreston.[81] Most of the dwellers of these two settlements had joined the Reformed Church. This young man, Heeren, was sent to Holland, Michigan, to study at Hope College and then at the Seminary. After having been ordained as minister, he journeyed in 1872 to India with his Dutch wife whose maiden name was Vennema. The expenses were covered by the Classes of Holland, Wisconsin, and Grand River. Weakened by the deadly climate, both devoted missionaries had to relinquish their sacrificial task at the Arcot mission in 1877 to return to America and seek recovery of their health in the dry climate of Colorado. Four days after their arrival in Pueblo in 1878, Heeren died. "Born in Europe, he labored in the Far East, and died in the Far West."[82]

Heeren was the first one of a series of idealistic and courageous men and women of the colonies who sacrificed their lives for high mission ideals. Lambertus Hekhuis graduated from Hope College in 1877. Having completed his studies at the New Brunswick Seminary, he sailed via England to India. He labored there from 1882 until 1888 in and near Arcot, and died at his post.[83] Thus he was the second one to die for the mission. John Gerardus Fagg, born in 1860 at Bethlehem, Wisconsin, was busily working in China from 1888 to 1894.[84] He also had studied at Hope College and had obtained a B.A. degree in 1881. John A. Otte, born in 1861 at Vlissingen in the Netherlands, and an 1883 graduate of Hope College, became a famous preacher and medical missionary. In 1887 he began his worthwhile labor at the Amoy mission, accompanied by his wife, a daughter of Phelps. She also had earned a B.A. degree at Hope. Through his effort the first large hospital was erected at the Amoy mission. The Neerbosch Hospital in Siokhe opened its doors in 1889.[85]

After Japan had been opened for world trade in 1858, the Reformed Church and other denominations resolved to send missionaries to that country. Reverend R. Brown went to Yokohama for this purpose. Since Dutch was the only foreign language well-bred Japanese knew—it was "their basis of communication with the Western world and their medium of science"—Brown desired to have an "Americanized Dutchman" accompany him. A young, educated Dutch immigrant, Guido F. Verbeek, volunteered to go. Undoubtedly, he became the most renowned and influential man among the Young Dutch Americans in the mission field.

Verbeek was born at Zeist, the Netherlands, in 1830. His father was the mayor in the nearby town of Rijzenburg. The young man was educated by the Moravian brothers and then proceeded on to the Polytechnical Institute at Delft. In 1852 he emigrated to Green Bay, Wisconsin, a town that was mostly Roman Catholic. He was one of the few Dutch Protestants there. For some time he also worked as an engineer in Arkansas. During a serious illness he decided, if he recovered, to enter the work of missions. When he had recovered, he was urged by his brother-in-law [?] Van Deurs to study theology at the Presbyterian Seminary at Auburn [New York]. So he left for the East. After he had finished his studies, he joined the Reformed Church and accompanied Brown to the Orient. A third missionary named [Duane B.] Simmons also went along. Verbeek's efforts to acquire American citizenship had failed for lack of time; therefore, he left for Japan as a "citizen of no country," since in the meantime he had lost his Dutch citizenship. They left America in May, 1859. The journey lasted 187 days and they arrived in Nagasaki on November 7. Verbeek settled there for the time being.

Verbeek gained numerous friends and admirers as an instructor and missionary and was appointed by the governor to teach at a school for interpreters. A number of distinguished Japanese attended his classes. For some years he even worked in the Japanese government service and reorganized the Imperial University, of which he became the first superintendent. He also was an adviser for Japanese statesmen. Through his efforts a number of Japanese young men were sent to America for studies.The Reformed Church took care of their housing needs. Perhaps this is why we find some Japanese Hope graduates in the Michigan colony already in 1879. Likewise, due to Verbeek's influence, educated young Americans of the Reformed Church were appointed in Japan's educational system.

Verbeek could speak Japanese so fluently that when he was out of sight and could only be heard, one would think one was hearing a native Japanese speak. He was the ideal person for a Japanese Bible translation. Just before he was to present the Japanese Bible to the Emperor, he suddenly died in 1898. With great pomp, he was buried at government expense in Tokyo. A monument for this noteworthy Netherlander was erected, with this inscription: "Claimed by three nations but a citizen of none."[86]

Other missionaries also initially taught in the Japanese schools and took part in Japan's spiritual development. Hope College students found great opportunities to work there. In the first place, the Japanese who were educated in Holland, and later a number of Young Dutch Americans, became valuable educators. Reverend Albert Oltmans, born in Zuidbroek, the Netherlands, in 1855, graduated from Hope in 1883 and from New Brunswick Seminary in 1886. He left for Nagasaki, where he taught just like his colleague Verbeek did.[87] Oltmans was entrusted to guide the "William H. Steele Jr. Memorial School," which grew into a college. Later, he became the President of Gakuin Theological Seminary. Many other "colonists" also made meritorious contributions in years to follow.

In 1889 a fourth mission field, in Arabia, was prepared by some New Brunswick students, among whom was Samuel L. Zwemer, who graduated from Hope in 1887. Zwemer gained world renown in mission circles.[88] Also his brother, Reverend P. J. Zwemer, dedicated years of his life to this cause in Arabia. In Muskate, he erected a school for freed slave children. Undermined by fevers, he was forced to leave his post and return by way of Antwerp to America. On his arrival in New York, he entered a Presbyterian

Hospital and died there in 1898.[89] It was already on the mission field during the years of growth that the Dutch "colonists" asserted themselves both as preachers as well as educators. It was on the mission field that they showed their best Dutch attributes—they were self-sacrificing, devoted to duty, and had tenacious determination. Many, very many, out of the settlements would follow them in this work in the nineties and later.

This is not the place to develop the subject of missions any deeper. We should note, however, that not only was the Gospel spread in lands like India, China, and Japan, but missions were of even greater importance for their social life. Many elementary schools, high schools, colleges, seminaries, and vocational schools were erected; hospitals were established; and all this activity not only spread Christianity but brought the different national groups to a higher level of general education.

I wish to refer to the feedback effect that mission work had upon the settlements in the United States. It enormously widened the horizons and vision of the colonists, especially of those colonists who had a member of the family on the mission field. Great interest arose in this way for lands that were to be Christianized! The circle of interest widened when missionaries visited the settlements and told about their experiences. Sometimes converted Japanese, Chinese, or members of other nations accompanied them and gave their testimonies. There was also the abundant missions literature and documentation that stirred them. Japanese and later also Chinese young people and missionaries' children born and raised abroad influenced their Dutch fellow students at Hope College. The field of vision kept on widening.

Often contacts were made with other denominations through the work of missions. They labored together and admired the good it produced, and in the end they had to draw back from their position of claiming exclusive powers of salvation for their own denominations. Broadmindedness was already at that time the characteristic feature of many a Dutch American.

All this the members of the Christian Reformed Church had to miss for years. Initially they showed little interest in mission work. It was only in 1879 that a minister, T. M. Van den Bosch was appointed to be the first domestic missionary. When he resigned two years later there was so little interest in missions, either in the Netherlands, to which people had turned in vain for the umpteenth time, or in America, that as a result the students who studied in Grand Rapids free of charge were required to give at least one year of service as traveling preachers! How little inner vocation there was for Domestic Missions! Later, Reverend M. J. Marcusse and after him Reverend M. Van Vessem served in the work of "gathering churches."[90]

Even more pitiful—considered from the Calvinistic viewpoint—was the state of affairs of "Heathen" Missions![91] At the classical meeting of October, 1857, the True brothers decided to have a prayer service on the first Monday of each month for the spread of God's kingdom. At that time an offering would be taken for Bible distribution. Thus it remained for years. Even some of the leaders in the eighties thought of missions as "aping the Americans."[92] Here and there, there was talk about missions. At Grand Haven a mission society was establised and sums of money for mission purposes were sent to the Netherlands. In 1889 a decision was made to do missionary work among the [American] Indians and T. M. Van den Bosch was appointed as missionary. But when a year later he tendered his resignation, mission plans were postponed until the second half of the nineties.

One of the True brothers, Jeremias Kruidenier, who had received his B.A. at Holland [Michigan] in 1886, wanted to be a missionary to Egypt. But he found scant support. So he turned to the United Presbyterian Church for aid in this venture and left in 1889 for Cairo, leaving behind his own fellow believers and their bickering over mission plans. The majority of the brothers was opposed to any cooperation with another denomination, and it was at their insistence that the initial support of Kruidenier was dropped.[93] A mission spirit or a call to missions among the Roman Catholic colonists, although they were established in a field of mission themselves, is unknown to me in these years.

14

Cultural Change
Political Life

━━━━━━━━━━━━━━━━━━━━━━━━━━━━━━━━━━

A. Local Politics

During the years of growth our colonists occupied their minds with ideal-istic concepts, such as religion, education, and missions—all genetically related—in addition to material or temporal interests. They paid far less attention to politics. It would be wrong to conclude from an earlier descrip-tion of an election meeting in Zeeland, Michigan, at the time of rooting and struggles for survival in 1851, that the Dutch colonists had any political inclinations. Yet one might expect them to have been politically active, because in addition to a desire for economic and religious freedom, many of the Dutch were driven to emigrate by a more or less conscious desire for political freedom, precisely around the revolutionary year of 1848.

Thanks, however, to the freedom they found in America, all attention was focused on the economic and, in its broadest sense, on the religious as-pects of life, while any political interest, if still present, was satisfied by many immigrants through their voting for local political offices, from police-man all the way to mayor. For many people the interest in these offices was heightened because a person was allowed to enter his candidacy for these offices. Due to the variety of jobs there is "one to fit anyone." This is also true, to a certain extent, for the county-level offices, although higher politics have a stronger influence here. In addition, more knowledge is generally required for county offices, so that initially only a Hollander or two in Pella wanted to run for county offices. More candidates became interested in county offices as the effects of Hope College and Central University took hold. This greater number of candidates for county offices also affected the general interest in these elections.

Temporal interest, more than ideals, are of importance here. This was definitely the case in the Holland Township elections at Zeeland, Michigan. Political passions ran unusually high for Dutchmen, but this was not due to a clash between differing political principles, but to petty personal jealousies; they hated to see others grab the political plums. The election was also influenced partly by economic jealousy—the bitter rivalry between the city of Holland and the village of Zeeland. "People of Holland were more educated and well-to-do, while those of Zeeland and Drenthe were of very low extraction. The 'Hollanders' were thus rather domineering and 'looked down their noses' at the Zeelanders," I was told in excellent Dutch during my visit to the 83-year-old [Cornelis] Van Loo, a pioneer child of Zeeland. In Holland, another pioneer son told me that "one found a lot of 'fanatics' among the Zeelanders." His father had lived in Nieuw [New] Groningen, between Holland and Zeeland, and had been able to observe time and again from close quarters these personal rivalries.[1] Graafschap was another rival of Holland. This rivalry, which also appeared in other settlements, was partly but not entirely an expression of typical American local pride. It was exacerbated by the religious discord that has up to the present time reduced the political influence of the Dutch, who were rather lax in political matters, anyway.

Although it might be thought that the Dutch colonists would vote first of all for capable candidates from among their fellow countrymen, the opposite was generally true. This was confirmed by many conversations I have had. The awareness of race and ethnic bonds should indeed take a back seat and allow higher, more broad-minded considerations to have an influence; yet the jealousy and envy between the various towns and within the towns became most important. Repeatedly, clever Americans took advantage of these local and personal rivalries, since they—the Scotch-Irish or Ulstermen, and currently the Irish—were far keener on the political jobs.[2]

Especially the far greater competition for the higher-level offices illustrated this political wheeling and dealing that was so often the case in local politics. I mentioned the colony in Michigan; but this was also true in Pella, Iowa, which was much more developed during the fifties. Pella developed very quickly during its early period, and this caused a division of interests between the residents of the town and those of the outlying neighborhoods. Having first lived under one government, Lake Prairie Township, the citizens of Pella began to want their own town government. In 1855, after much heated discussion, the incorporation of Pella was decided upon, with 135 votes for and 22 against; a planning committee was chosen, consisting of one American and two Dutchmen. The numbers of votes received in Pella, which at this point was predominantly Dutch, is of considerable interest: the American received 72 votes; Isaac Overkamp, 70; and Pieter Barendregt, 64. And when on September 10, 1855, Pella, with so many cultured Dutchmen, elected a city council, W. J. Ellis, an American, was appointed Mayor![3] A grand total of ten officials was elected: five Dutchmen and five Americans: the "*decemviri*," as Scholte sarcastically called them [after the old Roman administrative body of ten men]. Scholte had been violently opposed to incorporation not because ten new political plum jobs were created—Lake Prairie Township without the city of Pella retained its own council—but rather because the Dutch immigrants who were still steadily arriving would not be able to have any part in the government of Pella until they had become naturalized citizens.[4]

Unlike Pella during its first years, Holland developed much more slowly and here also the American spirit penetrated more slowly. Moreover, the state of Michigan did not give it the sympathetic support that the state government had given to Pella, already in its early rooting years. Therefore it was not until 1867, that is, twelve years after Pella's incorporation, that Holland was finally incorporated and could then rightfully call itself "*de stad*," a title which colonists had used since its very founding.

The separation of both towns from their surrounding townships and their development from town to city, resulted in an increase in American settlers. In Pella, this influx of Americans which was, as mentioned earlier, partly due to the influence of Central University, resulted in Americans and Dutchmen being about evenly represented in 1860. Although it was a little exaggerated, Van Schelven remarked in connection with Holland that "large numbers of citizens of other nationalities began to flock in, increasing the wonderful influx of wealth and population."[5] In this respect one should keep in mind the variety of American churches that were already established by 1871 in Holland.

In spite of this Americanization, the Dutch were able to retain members on the council. In Pella, the American Hamilton succeeded his countryman Ellis; after Hamilton, however, the Dutchmen Isaac Overkamp and Jan Nollen carried this office, the latter even for four years. The succession, after Nollen, went as follows: William Fisher, an American; then Henry Hospers, a Dutchman (almost four years: 1867–1870), then another Dutchman, Herman Neyenesch as deputy mayor; then an American MacCully; the Dutchman H. Neyenesch; a German, E. F. Grafe, etc.[6] Reverend [L. G. C.] Ledeboer, a minister no less, was elected mayor of Holland in 1870. The hamlet of Zeeland became a village in 1875, and was incorporated as the city of Zeeland only in 1907.

Indicative of the slow growth of a rural settlement, South Holland, Illnois, did not receive its own village government until 1893. Pieter A. Anker was elected president of the village board and H. P. De Jong, secretary; the council had six trustees, the majority of whom were Dutch.[7]

B. National Politics: The Choice of a Party

It is important to discover to what extent the Dutch colonists participated in higher politics, which national political party they eventually joined, and why they joined that party.

After 1852, when many Dutch became American citizens, some but not all, by any means, took an active part in politics. Most Hollanders viewed with amazement the "political feeling" of Americans. In the fifties, a Pellian remarked that it is difficult for people in the Netherlands to have any idea of this fervor, and he continued: "It is surprising, especially to us Netherlanders, to see how each and every American, no matter who he is, has a thorough and elaborate picture in mind concerning the social organization and the internal administration of America's government. It is surprising to hear him discuss and evaluate the various branches of government, even in the smallest of details, and to note his gift of discrimination and fine observation in all matters that concern political life. Aside from his daily, routine activities, his main purpose is to be always active in this field." "Politics is his life, his main inclination. Americans will hardly ever talk about the weather, or your health, or other such topics; a laborer does not talk shop with others in his profession; the conversation almost always revolves around government and political affairs."[8]

This same attitude can also be noticed in the more northerly states that have an almost completely northern or Yankee population, as far as Americans are concerned, and not a mixed northern and southern population. Bloemendaal noticed it in Wisconsin: "They are so deeply involved in politics that it seems as if their salvation depends on it. Whoever wants a political job files his petition, goes out and hustles votes of support. You'll find the best political debaters among these people."[9]

This kind of political fervor could not fail to influence even the down-to-earth Hollanders. Of course, we have already noted how the Iowa colonists during the early rooting years, even before they had acquired their citizenship, were introduced by their American neighbors at meetings, even at festive meals, to the intricacies, the highways and by-ways, of American politics.

This introduction to politics by Americans is responsible, to a large extent, for the initial choice of political parties by the immigrants, both in Iowa and in Michigan. The Whigs primarily supported the interests of the capitalistic Northeast, which was becoming increasingly industrialized. The Democratic party combined the interests and ideals of both the agrarian South, that was slowly becoming capitalistic, and of the young, individualistic, agrarian West. This was possible because both parties were afraid of domination by economically powerful New England. Thus, the further west one went, the more the political contrast of North versus South diminished, and in the North, the really democratic principles were the most favored by the common people, who thus called themselves Democrats.

Therefore, when the Dutch immigrants settled in Wisconsin, Michigan, Illinois, and Iowa, they mostly came in contact with Democratic Americans or with immigrants from other countries, especially Germans, who had already become Democrats. This had a lasting effect on the Pellians, while in Michigan this influence was only temporary.

The chronicler of *Pella, Iowa en Omgeving.* [*Pella, Iowa and Surrounding Area*] tells us that most of the American settlers who lived near the Hollanders were Democrats.[10] The most prominent Americans, such as Curtis, the

Hamiltons, Clark, and others, had a strong influence on the Dutch element from the very beginning. In addition, the German E. F. Grafe, who associated with the immigrants as soon as they had arrived in St. Louis, had a strong political influence on the Dutch. Grafe was, as were so many Germans, a Democrat.

In Michigan, the colonists came far less in contact with Americans than did their leaders, such as Van Raalte, Van der Meulen, etc. It is therefore quite important to remember that the Americans, whom we mentioned earlier, and who had done so much to help the colonists get settled, were at that time Democrats.[11] The often-mentioned Th. Romeyn was "brought up in the Democratic school of politics;" N. A. Balch, the postmaster at nearby Kalamazoo, who was so interested in the colony, seems to have been a Democrat, too.[12] The most important person to whom the Hollanders owed a great deal, however, was the very influential judge, John R. Kellogg, a representative of Allegan who served several times as host to the Van Raaltes, and who was an intimate friend of the Democratic candidate for President, General L. Cass, the governor of Michigan. The latter was even called a friend of Van Raalte. Looking at it from this point of view, the offhand remark made to me by one of the local politicians in Zeeland, Michigan, becomes clear: The Michigan Hollanders owed much to the Democrats, and therefore belonged to the Democratic party.

The friendly attitude of the Iowa state government, which acquired a Democratic majority in 1848, is already known to us.[13] In Wisconsin, Reverend P. Zonne supported the Whig ideals, probably because of his Presbyterian connections.[14] Others, specifically [Jacob] Quintus, the Sheboygan publisher of the first Dutch newspaper in America, publicized the political ideas of the Democrats.

However, factors of geography and friendship could not explain everything as the Dutch, and in this case the colonists, were accustomed to make up their own minds. It was very difficult to make a choice in this situation, since the platforms of the Whigs and Democrats, theoretically different from each other, were in reality quite close, so close that many Whigs switched to the Democrats and vice versa; in 1840, [John] Tyler, a southern Democrat and Whig candidate, was even nominated as Vice-President.[15] This may also explain why one of the most prominent Pellians, Henry Hospers, one of the few who had originally joined the Whigs, went over to the Democrats when the former party did not reward him with a county office quickly enough!

But it was Scholte who showed himself to be a master of one-upmanship in this respect, even though he himself mentions, not without sarcasm, Hosper's political desiderata. Scholte announced in 1855 that he was "independent in everything, not bound to any party." But then, he defended the Democrats, who nominated him in 1858 for the job of state bookbinder. That plum eluded him by a 64 to 41 vote. He was chosen as the delegate to the Democratic state convention in 1859; but to the amazement and resentment of many, he did not attend the Democratic convention. Instead, he helped nominate S. J. Kirkwood for governor at the Republican convention.[16] As a colonist once dropped the candid remark to me, Scholte was indeed a bolshevik both in religion and in politics!

If it was very difficult for the leaders, the most sophisticated among the immigrants, to get a clear picture of the political ideals of the Democrats and of the Whigs, one can imagine how difficult it must have been for the simple, common emigrants. Several other factors added to this complex situation. Initially, only a few emigrants understood English; thus their political knowledge was mostly second hand. Then, there was the inherently low level of interest in politics among the Hollanders, while the daily chores of an unfamiliar colonial life required their full attention and effort. All these circumstances help to explain the extreme low level of interest of the emigrants in the elections, even in prosperous Pella.

When the Hollanders were allowed to participate for the first time in the presidential elections of November, 1852, it appeared that the largely Dutch-populated Lake Prairie Township cast fewer votes than in the county elections in August of that same year, from which the Dutch had still been excluded! The state elections in 1854 brought out about the same number of votes from the township as the above-mentioned county elections held without Dutch participation![17]

The Dutch influence first began to be felt in 1855. The issue at hand was not, however, the choice of candidates from any of the parties. Many of our immigrants voted according to their own conscience against a law that would forbid the sale of alcoholic beverages! In Lake Prairie Township (Pella and the surrounding area) 250 votes were cast against the alcoholic blue law, with only 31 supporting it![18]

When making up their minds to vote for one of the parties, the Dutch were not so much motivated by political considerations, but rather by another, even more important factor, especially during the first few years, and that was an emotional factor. I cited earlier the relative inaccessibility and aloofness of the Americans who came from New England, as opposed to the warmhearted nature of those from the South, from the two Virginias, from Kentucky, etc. Both groups were more or less antagonistic toward each other. An interesting example comes to mind. One of our immigrants worked for an American, and he called his employer a Yankee.[19] At this his usually very talkative boss became very angry: he turned out to be an enemy of the Yankees. "The Yankees live in the North of the United States: they come from New England," he said, "and they are haughty people." That is how the Southerners viewed it, and that is also how the Dutch, German, and other immigrants viewed it. Clever southern party leaders both fanned and exploited these sympathies and antipathies. Not only the capitalistic Whigs in the northeast, but also the simplest Whig pioneers in the West were pictured as aristocrats, as dictatorial, etc. The Democratic Party, however, with "people's rights" as their slogan, tried to appear as the party of the *kleine luyden*, even though this became such a difficult image to maintain later on when Lincoln and other men from the lower classes broke into politics first as Whigs and later as Republicans.[20] One should not forget either that the rich plantation owners also were Democrats!

The initial success of the Democrats was due to the fact that it was based in the first place on emotional appeal—*kleine luyden* easily responded to emotional appeal—and only in the second place on rational arguments. And therefore they scored with the Dutch immigrants of around 1848, because these Dutch were particularly sensitive in this matter, having left the Netherlands because of their prejudice against an aristocratic Dutch government. "The most important reason why the Dutch folk of Pella had joined the Democratic party was that people considered the name 'Whig' and later 'Republican' synonymous with 'Aristocratic.' Thus people were deterred from joining the Republicans, since they had so recently said farewell to just such a government when they left the Netherlands."[21] So declared one of the Dutch pioneers in Scholte's colony in Iowa.

In Michigan the Democrats also emphasized this aristocratic nature of the Whigs.[22] The Hollanders in Michigan happened to have met some of the Whig leaders, which no doubt reinforced their conviction that was partly instinctive and partly encouraged by outside persuaders. H. W. Taylor, one of the founders of Allegan, was entirely too much an "old style gentleman" to feel at home in this new country, and he thus left for New York in 1848. F. J. Littlejohn, from the same town of Allegan, although a Democrat at first, was the Whig candidate for governor of Michigan in 1849. He lost that election, which was a good thing for the Hollanders, whose friend he might have been as a Democrat, but who certainly was not a friend as a Whig, as we mentioned earlier.[23]

In Wisconsin Dutch people did not want to have anything to do with the Whigs either, and certainly not when campaigns for this party were conducted on Sundays, and then, of all people, by the Reverend Zonne, who had incurred too many people's displeasure anyway. When this obviously radically Americanized preacher made a political speech in favor of the Whigs on the day of rest, it was seen as "an unprecedented scandal that such activity could take place in the sacred house and on the day of the Lord."[24]

The colonists were strengthened in their prejudiced resolve against the "aristocratic" Whigs by the attitude taken by the Whigs toward the "American Party," nicknamed the "Know Nothing Party," an initially secret organization founded in 1854 to oppose immigrants. The increasing immigration of Roman Catholic Irish, Germans, etc., had initially spawned a relatively local movement against the "foreigners" in the East during the first half of the nineteenth century. This led to the formation in 1837 of the Native American Association of the United States, the purpose of which was to keep the foreigners out of state and federal government, and to revise the naturalization laws.[25]

This movement gained momentum and immigrants were looked upon by many Americans as Europe's "paupers, crminals, convicts, outpourings of the almshouses and her jails." The climax of this "Nativism" was achieved, however, by the so-called "Know Nothings," whose political action was mistakenly seen by some as a merely "No Popery excitement" with a slightly anti-Roman Catholic overtone.[26] The Know Nothings, who owed their name to their secrecy, proceeded to take political action, as so many other secret groups in America did; the Know Nothings even rose to become a political party. Their war cry was "Americans and Americans only should rule America." "Put None but Americans on Guard Tonight," campaigned its members. They wanted to keep foreigners and Roman Catholics out of all public offices, from federal to state to county to township: only after twenty-one years of residency should foreigners be allowed to become American citizens!

The Whigs, and their offspring, the Republicans, repeatedly joined in with the Know Nothings; thus the Know Nothings controlled the elections in nine states in 1855; seven of these states, including New York and Massachusetts, went their way.[27] The Democrats, on the other hand, did not want to have anything to do with "Nativism," and since many of them were Roman Catholics, such as in Maryland, which had been founded by Roman Catholics, they did not take part in anti-Catholic demonstrations.[28] Consequently, Irish Roman Catholics and nationalities of the same religious persuasion increasingly joined the Democrats. That is why the Dutch Roman Catholics in Wisconsin and other areas have remained Democrats to this very day. Protestants also readily joined the Democrats because of the latter's pro-immigrant policy.

Nevertheless, the Know Nothings and the Whigs very quickly gained influence not only in the East, where they had started, but also in the West. In Michigan, the Know Nothing spirit was sparked by the previously mentioned Littlejohn and other residents of Allegan, due to their disdainful comments against not only Dutchmen—after all, they did call the Dutch immigrants "a lot of paupers"—but against immigrants in general. A Democrat from the city of Holland told me that the Know Nothings were so strongly identified with the Whigs that the latter were also seen as being against all foreigners.

The Know Nothings were active from 1850 to 1860 in the Iowa colony, but they met with strong opposition by the colonists there. Scholte in particular raised the roof against the "counterfeit Americans," as he called them. After an election success of the Know Nothings, one of their group made the contemptuous comment that there were not enough wooden shoes in Pella to win the elections in Marion County. Scholte reacted by stating that not only the men who wore wooden shoes, but also those who wore leather shoes and slippers, would without exception continue to vote against them, since they stood far above "those bogus Americans who have the lunatic presumption to maintain that men born upon American soil are the only fit political rulers in our Republic." Scholte stated, not without pride, that "honest Dutchmen have brought too much Republicanism with them from the old country to be deceived or frightened by such bogus republicans." Scholte, who had his eye on an elective office of one sort or another, saw himself opposed by the Know Nothings, who wanted to prevent immigrants from winning government posts. This undoubtedly accounts, in part, for the fact that Scholte, who at first declared himself to be independent of any political party, joined the Democrats and continued passionately to fight the Know Nothings. In 1858, one of his editorials in his largely English language newspaper denounced their "native puppyism" and stated that "the proposed outrage will sink deep into the minds of the Hollanders, and they will take care to resent it." Trenchant as Scholte could be, he called it a singular, misleading concept, as if Republican ideas could flourish only "in the empty heads of the Know Nothing demagogues," and were unknown on the other side of the Atlantic Ocean. Scholte certainly was not afraid![29]

It must have been quite a disappointment for the freedom-thirsting Hollanders when they found themselves thwarted so strongly by some Americans. Scholte was right in pointing out the deep impression that these various events made on the Hollanders. More than anything else, it explains why the newly formed Republican Party that welcomed the Whigs, Know Nothings, etc., gained so little support among the colonists at Pella. It also explains why even in the colony in Michigan, which had received so little help for its harbor development plans from the always stingy Democratic presidents all the way from Polk to Buchanan, the Republican Party's influence grew only at a very slow rate. In 1860 it was a matter of electing as president a man of the *kleine luyden*, the Republican Lincoln, someone who outwardly did not display any "aristocratic" tendencies at all. In that same election the issue of slavery, which the Hollanders abhorred, also was at stake. In Holland Township, the Democrat Douglas received 208 votes, while Lincoln received only 185 votes.[30] In Marion County, which included Scholte's colony, a majority of 99 votes was won by the pro-slavery Democrat Douglas.[31]

These figures point to a preponderant Democratic inclination; however, they also give some indication of an upcoming change in the relationships between the colonial parties, especially in Michigan. The Republicans gained ground in both colonies. This was largely due to the then-current issue: the issue of slavery.

C. The Slavery Question

The slavery issue really dates back to the founding of the American republic. Slavery was incompatible, at least in theory, with the well-known Bill of Rights of 1789;* the ending of slavery was regarded even in the slavery states of the South as inevitable. Eli Whitney's invention of the cotton gin, which made the separation of cotton fibers from its seeds much easier, enabled the cotton industry in the South to expand so tremen-

*Van Hinte erroneously gives the date 1776.

dously; and caused in turn such a need for cheap labor that the South ignored the issue of freeing the slaves.

The North, however, which had fewer vested interests in slavery, wanted initially to prevent the spread of slavery, then to begin to decrease slavery, and finally, gradually to eliminate the whole problem. The North won its first theoretical victory when Congress decided in 1787 to forbid slavery in the recently organized Northwest Territory and in the states that were later to be formed from that territory. This did not alter the fact that in the middle of the nineteenth century slavery flourished in the state of Illinois, which was formed from the Northwest Territory! Further, the Constitution stated that the importing of slaves would at first be discouraged and then would be forbidden after 1808. This did not prevent many states from quietly continuing to import slaves after 1808! The net result of all this can be seen from population figures. Although the United States had a total population of four million people in 1790, among whom were 698,000 slaves (only 90,000 of these slaves were in the North), the total number of Blacks had reached 1,770,000 by 1821, with a total population of 9.5 million!

Although slavery was outlawed in the Northwest Territory, it had to be retained for the Louisiana Purchase area, partly because of the traditionally slave-owning population. This promoted the formation of new states that recognized slavery, alongside of states that disallowed it, so that a real rivalry developed between the slave and free states, especially relative to the composition of the U. S. Congress, where each state is allowed two representatives in the Senate.

Nothing could prevent the rivalry; neither the location of the "Mason and Dixon line," north of which slaves could not be kept—and which does not, contrary to popular opinion, follow the borderline between Pennsylvania and Maryland, but rather runs physically and sociographically further south through Maryland—nor the Missouri Compromise of 1821.[32] Under this compromise the free/slave border was moved toward the south, to the 36°30' parallel, which allowed Missouri to be a slave state. Because of the influence of the immigrants coming from the Northeast down the Ohio valley, Missouri became a free state nevertheless. When in 1848 Mexico was forced to give up an extensive territory which included Texas, New Mexico and California (this was during the settlement period of our Dutch immigrants), the issue surfaced again: for or against slavery.

One should not assume that this conflict of pro and con coincided with the division of South and North. There were many supporters of slavery in the North where many despised the Blacks. K. Jz. Beukma, the oft-mentioned freedom-loving immigrant, was continually aggravated during his trip West by the way Blacks were being treated in the North: "Negroes are not tolerated in the company of whites. For meals on the canalboats they are even relegated, as beings of a lower species, to a separate after-dinner table. In this land of freedom and equality, there is always a stigma attached to anyone with a black skin, even if it had been racially lightened to the lightest brown color; my feelings cannot forgive the Americans."[33] The question of slavery in the free state of Illinois has already been touched upon.

On the other hand, there were many people in the South who were opposed to slavery. While the plantation owners in the lowlands considered slavery a necessity, the common folk in the mountains, "the yeoman element," those in Maryland, Kentucky, Virginia, and in the even more southerly states of Tennessee, North Carolina, South Carolina, Georgia, and Alabama, were either indifferent or opposed to slavery. "Mountain economy found no place for the negro or plantation cultivation in those sterile hillside farms, pathless forests, and roadless valleys," was the comment of Ellen Semple.[34]

Shaler went even further, and saw a relationship between politics and the geological nature of the soil. "The dwellers in the limestone formation where the soil was rich gave heavy pro-slavery majorities, while those living on the poorer sandstone soils were generally anti-slavery."[35] People noted this "geological distribution of politics" throughout the South. Mostly mountainous West Virginia even separated from Virginia because of political beliefs. This phenomenon has special meaning for us, since it was precisely these Southerners who had been the first settlers in Iowa. Scholte and his followers had settled down in the middle of these Virginians.

Opinions were thus divided both in the North and in the South. This division also marked the major political parties. There were supporters and opponents of slavery among the Whigs as well as the Democrats. [David] Wilmot, a Democrat, had proposed as early as 1846 that if the areas given up by Mexico remained with the United States, they should not tolerate slavery.[36] Henry Clay, the leader of the Whigs, was the opposite side of the coin; he was the peacemaker who devised the proposal under which slaves who had fled to the North would be caught and sent back South. In 1848, the Wilmot Proviso was rejected, and in 1850 the fugitive slave law was adopted, although it was a compromise because California would be a free state. Both decisions, however, caused a great amount of discontent, and led to the founding of a new party, the Free Soilers, when neither major party would take a definite stand on whether or not to expand slavery.

In 1848 the Free Soilers, supported by many Whigs and Democrats—all promoters of free land, freedom of speech, freedom of work and free men—presented their own candidate, former President Martin Van Buren, the Old Dutch American. The new party declined after some years, however, and its supporters eventually joined a new organization—the Republicans.

The fact that the Dutch belonged largely to the Democrats, and a few to the Whigs, that is, in Michigan—where a Whig newspaper was even circulated among them—therefore tells us little about the Hollanders' stand in relation to slavery. Some people have mistakenly contended that the Dutch opposed the freeing of slaves because it would run counter to the Word of God.[37] There may have been some who thought that way, and who had, of course, a Bible text ready to support their viewpoint, at least if they were at all religious. They could always fall back on Noah's prophecy, "Cursed be Canaan; a servant of servants shall he be unto his brethren." Besides, during earlier centuries, Calvinism, the slave trade, and slavery had continually gone hand in hand. The Old Dutch Americans in the East, often members of the Reformed Church, had always owned slaves and still owned them, at least if they lived in the South.

The Dutch immigrants of the nineteenth century, however, largely opposed slavery. The sphinx Scholte was the only one whose utterances about this problem were very ambiguous. Chameleon that he was, he seems at first to have been indifferent to the slavery issue, next he supported slavery, and then he opposed it—all based on the Bible. He used I Corinthians 7:21 in support of slavery![38] [Art thou called being a servant? Care not for it: but if thou mayest be made free, use it rather.]

There are several occurrences that point up the anti-slavery spirit of the colonists. For instance, while still in the Netherlands, when various possibilities for colony sites were being discussed, Texas was unanimously rejected, partly because of its support of slavery, which many of the Dutch viewed as unchristian.[39] Beukma, the courageous Groninger, was constantly reproaching Americans in the North for their attitude toward Blacks, especially when people discussed American "freedom" with him. When Classis Holland met in Michigan on September 5, 1855, they resisted accepting several parishes in South Carolina into the Reformed Church on the basis that the "abomination of slavery" existed there.[40] The oft-mentioned Calvinist fanatic Bastiaan Broere, who at first settled on Long Island, but who later moved to Virginia, struck up a friendship with several slaves and allowed his small daughter to teach one of them to read even though it was strictly forbidden to give slaves lessons of any kind.[41]

The general resentment that arose against the Fugitive Slave Act was also evident among practically all Hollanders. At first many individual Americans had been helping these poor slaves; later an organization was formed to help the Blacks flee via various routes to Canada. Eventually this activity, led by Quakers, especially Levi Coffin in Cincinnati, became quite extensive. The members called themselves the Underground Railroad, which counted some of the most distinguished citizens of the country within its ranks; these men and women made sure that the Fugitive Slave Act was outlawed.

The love of freedom—also on behalf of others—among the Dutch colonists was well known to the leaders of this organization, and soon the Netherlanders began to take a substantial part in its activities. Soon the secret routes of the fleeing slaves developed through the Iowa colony and through the colonies near Chicago, Illinois. During my 1921 visit to Pella, I was shown the little white building in which the Blacks going north found a short rest and good food, preparatory to being guided further to freedom.

Cornelis Kuyper, the politician in Roseland, Illinois, helped by Jan Ton and many others, made himself very useful in that town, favorably situated as it was on the main routes northward. Roseland became an important station on the "underground railroad" especially due to the efforts of Kuyper and Ton. The latter had made available a small house on the Calumet River, while at the opportune moment, "Father Kuyper," then the constable, brought the fleeing slaves to the dunes along Lake Michigan. From there, most of the time, the slaves could make their escape to Canada.[42]

It is not surprising, then, given this anti-slavery view of the Netherlanders, that they followed the slavery issue with great interest, and that, already in the days when Whigs and Democrats who were opposed to the spread of slavery organized the Republican party, many of our fellow countrymen joined the Republican party, which was reinforced by the Free Soilers. The statement of Theo. De Veer is thus totally incorrect when he says that many Netherlanders joined the new party only in the days of President Cleveland, and in connection with the latter's policies.[43]

Their better understanding of the English language, due to the slowly increasing Americanization, was a factor which, besides the alcohol issue, and in particular the slavery question, awakened the immigrants' interest in American politics. Furthermore, the newly organized party was actually a creation of the newly developed West, which the Netherlanders themselves helped build. This was in contrast to the Whigs who felt at home in the Northeast, and in contrast to the Democrats who were most active in the Southeast.

The new organization replaced the bloodless, chronically compromising Whig party first in Wisconsin. In Michigan the Republican party was proclaimed under the oaks at Jackson in July, 1854, at the State Convention of the Republican party, and later at a similar convention in Illinois—even though the Union Party was established at a national convention in Philadelphia on July 17, 1856. The fact that Lincoln, such a plain man and raised in the West, was one of its most important leaders, could not fail but make a strong impression. Many immigrants may have withheld their support of the Republicans when the Know Nothings joined (a factor of which the Democrats made political hay). The doubts of others fell by the wayside when Lincoln, as a presidential candidate in 1859, upon being asked about his position on naturalized citizens by the Wisconsin German Th. Canisius, stated that since he deeply regretted the oppression of Blacks, it would be inconsistent "if I were not a supporter of the unalienable rights of white men, whether or not they are born in our country."[44]

The increased interest of the Dutch immigrants in the Republican party dates especially from this year [1859]: Dutch newspapers started supporting the Republican party, following the example of the Sheboygan *Nieuwsbode*, which in 1855 was the first to publicize the Republican ideas. In Holland, Michigan, a new publication was founded for this political purpose: *De Grondwet* [*The Constitution*]. Its owner was Jan Roest from Harderwijk, who had been energetically campaigning against slavery since 1855. With his editor,

[Johannes] Hoogesteger, Roest "converted" many Michigan Hollanders from Democrats to Republicans.

Van Raalte, a great admirer of Lincoln, became and remained a Republican largely due to the influence of his American friends, formerly either Democrats or Whigs, who had joined the Republican party because of their aversion to slavery and their sympathy for Lincoln.[45] One of those friends was the influential Old Dutch American Theodoor Romeyn who returned to Detroit from New York in 1858; he later repeatedly paid prolonged visits to the colony where he supervised Hope College, among other jobs. Romeyn was a strong supporter of Lincoln, especially during the Civil War, when he "stumped the State" of Michigan for the re-election of Lincoln.[46]

To the surprise of many, Scholte became the Dutch champion of the Republicans in Iowa. After all, he had violently stormed against the Republican ideologies printed in the Wisconsin *Nieuwsbode*, which was read in many Pella households. He had done so in his own paper, the *Pella Gazette* (which we know to have first been independent and then Democratic).[47] Scholte even decided to wage his war by writing three columns in Dutch in his largely English newspaper, in which he would, as he announced, "certainly say more good things in that space than the *Nieuwsbode* has ever delivered in a whole issue!" He had also constantly urged his readers to vote Democratic and, when in 1857 a Republican proposal to revise the Iowa constitution was put on the ballot, it was voted down in Lake Prairie Township with 270 votes against 63.

Scholte and the other Dutch colonists were generally against slavery, but they still did not approve of equality for Blacks. In the same year of 1857, in the above-named township, 280 votes were against giving voting rights to Blacks and only 6 for. Scholte had stated earlier "that we must not lose our self-respect and amalgamate ourselves with the black race. . . . We do propose overwhelmingly to vote down the infamous principle of Negro Equality."

Less than two years later, in 1859 (the same year in which Lincoln gave his opinion on the Know Nothings), Scholte, as I mentioned earlier, unexpectedly changed parties. "I should deem it dishonorable to hold fast to principles of government for party's sake, when a man is in conscience convinced that those principles are wrong," was his defense. He added that as a long-time admirer of Henry Clay he could "never become identified with the so-called Democracy, without sacrificing every honorable conviction . . . upon the altar of so-called party interest." Especially the Democratic stand on the issue of slavery aggravated him.

Also among Americans Scholte's about-face did not go unnoticed; people in Iowa as well as in neighboring Indiana reacted to it.[48] They were mistaken, however, about Scholte's political influence on his fellow Dutchmen. The Americans thought that the Iowa Hollanders would follow Scholte, and that they would be the determining factor in the state elections within Marion County; this would result in a gain of two Representatives and one Senator for the Republican party in Iowa. In the gubernatorial election that was held that same year in the colony, 364 votes went to the Democratic candidate and 146 to the Republican.

Scholte himself took a very active part in the political arena, and in 1860 was chosen at the state convention at Iowa City as the delegate to the National Convention in Chicago at which Lincoln was nominated as the presidential candidate. As we already know, however, a majority in the colony voted for the Democratic candidate in the ensuing election. And yet a breach had been made in the Dutch stronghold of the Democrats in Iowa. The *Pella Gazette*, which had ceased publication some months previously, reappeared under the Republican flag. Due to Scholte's newspaper articles in the *Gazette* and an extensive pamphlet he wrote on American slavery,[49] the Republicans acquired "a number" of adherents in Pella.[50]

Also for the Dutch, the days preceding Lincoln's election, especially in Pella, were full of tremendous tension and excitement. Iowa belonged to the so-called "border states," as did a number of other states along the Potomac, Ohio, and Missouri rivers. This was considered the "area of assimilation" of the "conflicting elements."[51] Here more than anywhere else, Republicans and Democrats were closely intermingled neighbors. Since one found the opponents to the spread of slavery in the North—an increasing number of Abolitionists even wanted to get rid of slavery entirely—and since most of the supporters of slavery were in the South, therefore the greatest fence-straddling was found in this middle zone. Pella, with its considerable number of American residents, was typical: people did not want equality for Blacks, nor did they want slavery to spread. Yet to change parties only because of the Blacks was too much to ask for; the voters wavered.

To win over the waverers in Pella, there was a month-long, intense, noisy, real American-style election campaign. "The public rallies that were held even in our small town during the fall of 1860 would surprise the present generation," an eyewitness account stated. "Never since 1860 have there been in Pella such large political processions, which were accompanied by all kinds of performances."[52] Special attention was attracted by "a large wagon pulled by four horses. A fairly large log was on the bed of the wagon. Besides the driver, there were two men on that wagon, each equipped with an axe and other tools necessary to 'split rails,' as Lincoln had done in his youth. As the procession proceeded, they were hard at work amid the earsplitting hurrahs for Lincoln that rose from the mass of people."

The Democrats had their parades, too. Such rallies were repeatedly held by both sides; the closer election day came, the bigger and noisier the parades became, "so that the more staid folk began to long for election day; for then, if previous elections were an indication, overheated feelings would cool off and quiet would be restored." This expectation, however, was only partially fulfilled. The Civil War broke out after Lincoln's election when, following the example of South Carolina, several southern states broke away from the Union and founded a new republic, that of the Confederacy.

Since they were strongly opposed to slavery, the German colonists in the West, under the inspiring leadership of the famous "forty-eighter" Karl Schurz, one of the founders of the Republican party, switched almost en masse from the Democrats to the new Republican party.[53] Many Dutchmen also changed parties, since so many were also against slavery and admirers of Lincoln.

As everywhere else, the number of Republicans increased in the Dutch colonies in that year of 1860. Among those who still called themselves Democrats there were also a number who voted for Lincoln because of their admiration for his personality and ideals. When the Civil War broke out, both Republicans and Democrats in the West declared themselves in favor of preserving the Union. It must not be forgotten that the Democratic presidential candidate Douglas, for whom many Dutchmen in Michigan and Iowa had voted, also had advocated above all preserving the Union; moreover, he felt that people in each state should make up their own minds about slavery.[54] Many who were still unsure about this latter point were nevertheless definite on one point: the Union must be maintained; thus they responded with a strong spirit to Lincoln's call for preserving the Union. Even in politically divided Iowa, there was at that moment only one party, "and that one [stood] for the constitution and the Union unconditionally."[55] To save the Union became the religion of the people.

D. The Civil War

Professor H. T. Colenbrander states that the Democrats began to identify themselves more and more with the interests of the slave owners.[56] This is not generally true, although it might be valid for the Southern plantation owners and for others with a vested interest, especially the politicians in various areas. The people who lived in the southern mountain areas and the western pioneers, both groups Democrats, would usually not hear of slavery. They hated slavery as much as those who lived as far south as Tennessee, where the mountain people called the slave owners "furriners."[57] Neither the mountaineer spirit nor the true pioneer spirit could identify with slavery—or with secession.

The argument that the Civil War was solely a war between the Democrats and the Republicans is untrue, too. Neither was it a war between the North and the South, if one takes the attitude of the Appalachian people into consideration.[58] From the information I have cited above, some things do become apparent. A wave of patriotism swept over the entire country and stirred the members of both major parties and made people in many areas at first forget their party allegiance. In one town in Iowa, the Republicans and Democrats tied their flagpoles together, and flew the Stars and Stripes from the new single flagpole.[59]

It is this spirit and this outlook on life that we see confirmed in the

Dutch settlements. In 1860, however, as far as the Holland and Pella colonies were concerned, there were still definite Democratic overtones. Even if the differences in political ideologies may not always have been clear to them, the shrill tones (too shrill, even) in which [Harriet] Beecher Stowe painted slavery and the threatening rupture of the Union touched their emotions and logic to such a degree that they also took up weapons for the preservation of the Union, and soon thereafter for the abolishing of slavery. Nowhere, so far as I know, did Dutchmen, although largely Democrats, take up service under the leaders of the Confederate States, not even the few Dutchmen who lived in the "Secession State" of Virginia during that time. Bastiaan Broere, whom I have mentioned frequently, was called into Virginia's military service, but tried to escape to the North, regardless of the dangers, rather than to have to fight for the slave owners.[60]

In the Michigan colony it was especially Van Raalte who fired up popular enthusiasm; he saw in Lincoln the ideal American statesman. Van Raalte could be found everywhere—on the streets, at meetings, in homes, at assemblies, near the rolling drums which were encouraging men to sign up— working for the Union.[61] The first Dutch volunteers in Michigan came not from *de Kolonie* but from Grand Rapids. Leonard Semeyn enlisted in the First Regiment of Michigan Infantry. The Dutch youngsters accompanied him to the station with music "as the first one who offered himself up for his adopted Fatherland." Pieter Kloosterman served in the same regiment. In the next regiment to be organized, the Second, two Dutchmen enlisted; there were as many as eighteen in the Third, three of these being sons of the oft-mentioned scholar [Nicholas M.] Steffens, of Holland, Michigan. Although Grand Rapids, Grand Haven, and Kalamazoo all gave volunteers, they came "mostly," however, from Holland and Zeeland in Ottawa County, and from Fillmore and Overisel in Allegan County.[62]

Van Raalte regretted that his own children did not join the service immediately. He wrote to his brother-in-law Brummelkamp that "I am not at all proud of the fact that none of my sons has yet taken up arms against rebellion and treason." His wish was eventually fulfilled: The Eighth Regiment Michigan Infantry had forty-seven Dutchmen among its members; thirty-four were in the Thirteenth; thirty-one in the Twenty-First, including the oft-cited Cornelius Van Loo. However, no less than ninety-one, mostly from Holland and surrounding areas, served in the Twenty-Fourth Michigan Infantry, including G. Van Schelven, later to become an historical author, and many other familiar names—Doesburg, De Kruif, Den Herder, Grootenhuis, Ledeboer, Oggel, Steketee, Veneklaasen, etc., and in addition, two sons of Van Raalte, Benjamin and Dirk B. K. At Kalamazoo Van Raalte said goodbye to one of them with the words: "My boy, you are going to the battlefield. I would rather you come home dead than to have you be a coward and a stain on your family."[63] This is indicative of Van Raalte's spirit and that of the Michigan colony.

A grand total of 410 Dutchmen from the area took part in the war; all but six of these were volunteers. With the exception of one person, all of them were born either in the Netherlands or in those parts of Ost-Friesland and Bentheim which were so closely related both geographically and culturally. Most of them served in the infantry regiments already mentioned, and in others; other young men joined cavalry regiments—five joined the First and no less than twenty-eight joined the Second. Many joined the corps of engineers—forty-four were in the First Michigan Regiment of Engineers, ten were in the First Michigan Regiment of Light Artillery. Only one served with the United States Navy: |John| Van Landegend; about six joined the First Regiment Sharp-Shooters.

Many volunteers came from the Protestant settlements in Wisconsin. Pieter Daan, who lived near Oostburg, Sheboygan County, was one of the first who set an example. He convinced many others to join him.[64] This author does not know anything about participation by Roman Catholic Dutch colonists.

In the Illinois settlements, especially at Roseland, where people were so concerned with the fate of the poor Blacks, many declared themselves ready to follow the Stars and Stripes: Jan Madderom, Jan and Pieter Boone, Jacob and Teunis Munster, W. Anijze, and G. Van der Aa were among those volunteering. Others who were too young, too old, or who did not appear strong enough, were not accepted.[65]

Sixty-three Hollanders from Pella took part in the fighting, as well as twelve, twenty-four, three, and six respectively from the "nearby" Mississippi towns of Keokuk, Muscatine, Burlington, and Dubuque. Lake Prairie Township consistently produced its quota of volunteers; thus when the draft lottery was begun, this township was exempted. Volunteer service was also encouraged here by the collection of funds—a sort of bonus, therefore—while Scholte gave each volunteer a so-called soldier's plot of land just north of the city of Pella. When some Dutch residents of adjoining Mahaska County, including heads of households, were drafted by the army, money was collected in the Pella area to pay for substitutes. To the irritation of many, Lincoln acknowledged the substitute plan, which enabled married men in the generally well-to-do Iowa colony to stay out of the war.[66]

The greater prosperity and the accompanying overall education showed up in still another way. Although only a few men out of the large contingent of Michigan Hollanders, such as Semeyn and Van Schelven, worked their way up in the service to the rank of sergeant, J. C. Klyn, G. Van de Kamp, H. L. Bousquet, and others from the much smaller group of Iowa volunteers, became officers in G. Company, of the 33rd Iowa Volunteer Infantry Regiment, in which many Pellians served, while others were spread over about fifteen regiments.[67] To the best of my knowledge, none of the Dutchmen rose further than the rank of lieutenant. A major factor was probably the lack of complete competence in the English language.

Some Hollanders were killed in battle; others were critically wounded and died in hospitals; still others died of homesickness. Even more—and this included the non-Dutch soldiers as well—died as a result of the poor quality of nursing, sickness, and deprivation; but few died in Confederate prisons. One of Van Raalte's sons was wounded and had his arm amputated; this became a badge of honor his father was able to view for many years.[68] Others were also disabled by the war.

The women performed valuable services and cared for the sick and wounded by sending bandages, clothes, and snacks. Pella sent the most in all of Iowa. This was undoubtedly an expression not only of prosperity, but of typical Dutch generosity. Holland, Michigan, took care of the spiritual needs of the soldiers and also collected money in the congregations to send books.[69] It goes without saying that people in *de Kolonie* followed the events of the war very closely. The war even influenced the sermons, especially those of Van Raalte: "In his preaching and especially in his prayers, the congregation could always hear a tone of triumph or of defeat."[70]

The spirit of unity among the Americans did not last very long, however. "The spirit of the people was right in 1861, but everything else was wrong."[71] Nothing was organized; confusion reigned supreme everywhere; most disgusting were conditions in the military. For one thing money, clothes, food, and weapons were totally lacking for the volunteers who had been so enthusiastic at first. Soldiers were camped unnecessarily for months on end in wretched circumstances, prey to the worst conditions. As a result, thousands died without even having seen the enemy. Only a small part of them went to battle in the beginning. They were dressed in an odd assortment of uniforms, armed solely with "U.S.A. 1829" muskets, and served under politically appointed "officers," often lacking the slightest knowledge of military procedures. They quickly came back to reality; it is no wonder that the old divisions and disunity soon reappeared.

The Confederates stirred things up and managed to build their support especially among the Democrats. This latter group were the so-called Copperheads, who were the Northern opponents of Lincoln. Their name was derived, scornfully, from a kind of snake or from the Indian head on a copper coin that they wore as their emblem.[72] Copperheads were especially numerous in the border states such as Iowa. In this latter state they even started a miniature civil war in 1863 in the Skunk River counties, the "Skunk River War" in which hundreds of Republicans and Copperheads took up arms against each other.[73] Although none of them were Dutch, there were many American residents in Pella, near the Skunk River, who were Copperheads.[74] They could also be found in Michigan, specifically in Grand Rapids.[75] They attempted to spread dissent everywhere. The Hollanders were also contacted by the Copperheads. The unity of these Dutch immigrants was being threatened by another factor, however.

In some Calvinistic settlements, the question of whether or not the spiritual leaders should involve themselves in politics had arisen even before the Civil War. There were some in Holland, Michigan, who were annoyed by Van

Raalte's stand against slavery and for Lincoln. Many of these people were his political opponents; religious beliefs clouded politics and vice versa. Van Raalte, however, would not consider leaving out his propaganda, and stated to his consistory that he had been a citizen before he became a preacher, and he refused to separate his political beliefs from his faith. This position aroused such strong resentment in the hearts of some people that they dared to call him, he to whom they owed so exceedingly much, a "bungler." It nearly became a case for the consistory; I say nearly, because the consistory preferred not to get involved. On April 16, 1860, it decided "because of the profound political changes in which N. N. [Nomen Nescis, i.e., anonymous] and others are so deeply involved, that the business will be tabled."[76]

Except for the period mentioned above, Van Raalte had relatively little political influence—after all, his life's work was not politically oriented.[77] Scholte, however, became much more involved with public affairs than Van Raalte. It is typical, for example, that in 1857, the same year in which Van Raalte visited Scholte's colony for religious purposes, Scholte who was still an ardent Democrat, in turn visited the Van Raalte colony and environs to defend the threatened interests of his party. In his speeches at Holland, Grand Rapids, Muskegon, and Kalamazoo, he strongly recommended to support his fellow Democrat Buchanan as presidential candidate. Only after Scholte had been requested to do so did this virtuoso orator of God's Word also appear as a preacher on this occasion.

Actually, from the day he started the settlements on the prairie, Scholte became so involved with politics that even his son-in-law Nollen had to acknowledge that Scholte's religious influence suffered seriously from it.[78] In contrast to Van Raalte, who was primarily concerned with the salvation of his parishioners, Scholte for many years "did not display the energy that had distinguished him formerly in the fostering of religious life among his fellow-colonists."[79] Politics, which Americans generally view as an occupation, so strongly attracted Scholte "that his active participation in public life brought him into conflict not only with the many classes of people who practiced politics to make a living"[80] —Holland-Americans made these telling remarks—but also with his fellow Christians. They felt aggravated by his business dealings and other projects, the "earthly" affairs, the "temporal" jobs, which he took on, especially during his early years at Pella, and by his "activities in the political arena." Because these activities brought Scholte "into contact with people, and made him frequent circles which were, after all, not very suitable for him as spreader of the Gospel."[81]

During Lincoln's period, especially when it became clear that Lincoln would have nothing to do with the spirit of the Know Nothings, Scholte was a fiery—but now Republican—politician; he even belonged to the thirty-two most prominent Iowa Republicans—"the State's best public talent." This group became the laughing stock at the National Convention in Chicago, when, because Iowa was allowed only eight votes, each person therefore cast one-fourth vote![82]

During my trip through the settlement, it became even more evident how much Scholte was attracted to public life. Although the fact is not mentioned anywhere in pertinent literature, it became clear to me that Scholte, the man of the Secession of 1834, Scholte the man of God, coveted an extremely worldly occupation: that of ambassador; and, of all things, ambassador to the court of the country that was said to have banished him, ambassador to the government against which Scholte had railed so often in bitter terms.

Lincoln, who had appointed the German immigrant Karl Schurz as United States Ambassador to Madrid (to the great aggravation of the Know Nothings), had promised the Dutch immigrant Scholte a similar position.[83] It appears that Scholte had actually been appointed to such a post, not, however, at the Hague, but rather at Vienna. This appointment was apparently rescinded at the last minute, under pressure from the Nativists.[84] Many people, especially Yankee Republicans, felt that the appointment of immigrants was scandalous, both in those early years and even much later. In this manner, Scholte missed out on a second important political post, this time a Republican one. After the war, due to these disappointments perhaps, Scholte returned to what the colonists saw as "the normal occupation" of his life: that of a minister.

Many watched Scholte's involvement in worldly affairs with regret. Not all of them accepted this fact, as did Van Stigt, since also Abraham, David, Luther and other wise and godly men were wrapped in and draped with "the swaddling clothes of all kinds of sins."[85] For it seems that Scholte's political actions were indeed viewed as such. But the times were such that even the churches as organizations, in spite of resistance by some individuals, did not hesitate to take sides. Even the Christian Reformed Church, the most orthodox organization, took sides. In October, 1864, this group decided, in response to a question from Grand Rapids, that those members of a parish who attended meetings at which the government was vilified and at which people were incited to rebellion "would not be allowed to partake of Holy Communion."[86]

These tumultuous events and upheavals caused a certain deterioration in the relationships and general atmosphere of the various settlements. It seems to have been the case, especially in Pella, that the longer the war lasted, the more enthusiasm declined and finally vanished; even loyalty began to waver. This was undoubtedly due to the actions of a group of Democrats. Among these were, especially in Pella, "notoriously active Copperheads." They held a convention as early as July 1861, in Marion County, at which they fiercely attacked Lincoln's administration: "We behold our beloved country distracted at home, and disgraced abroad. Commerce paralyzed! Trade annihilated! The Constitution trampled under foot! Citizens imprisoned! Laws suspended! Legislatures overawed by bayonets!"

Even here, however, the Dutch supported Lincoln, even though many were Democrats. They were so strongly against the Confederacy that, along with Scholte, some even went over to the Republican Party.[87] This staunch attitude of the Dutch must have raised ill feelings among the Copperhead Democrats, who were by and large ignored by the Hollanders. "Various incidents," Van Stigt prudently mentions "took place during those four or five years which in many ways made life and contacts among them restless and miserable."[88] As a result, many Hollanders left Pella, some temporarily, some permanently. Some made a trip to the Netherlands, while others sold everything they owned, goods and chattels, and moved to Oregon; both groups wanted not only to get away from the uncomfortable political situation at Pella, but wanted also to escape the threat of the military draft lottery.

About fifteen families, including the previously mentioned Versteegs, left for Portland, Oregon in 1864; they arrived in that city in the spring of 1865. Sooner or later, most of them came back to Pella after the war was over— the Versteegs returned in 1867. Although their horizons had been expanded, their wallets had become very thin. Some families did not succeed in filling up their wallets again, although the reverse also occurred, so that others, thanks to their wider experiences, now belong to the most well-to-do.[89]

There were colonists in other locales, too, who preferred to leave the country, since they had the means to do so, when it appeared that the substitute plan would no longer be a guarantee of staying out of the war. For instance, the previously-mentioned Dutch leader of the settlement on Grand Island in the Niagara River was able, through the help from "our" congressional representative, to secure his passport in the summer of 1864. And even though he was still eligible for military service, he left for the Netherlands in company of his wife.[90]

Many other Hollanders waited, however, till the war was over before making a visit to the Old Country. Van Raalte, in Holland, Michigan, and |Jan| Berkhout, from Pella, Iowa, are examples. The latter deserves special mention because once he was in the Netherlands, he defended the Confederacy and disapproved of Lincoln's greatest act: the Emancipation Proclamation of 1862 that ended slavery and equalized Blacks and Whites. This is proof that the Copperheads did affect the Dutch element, especially in Democratic Pella; this is also typical for this divided settlement.[91]

Berkhout was not the only one to adopt the Confederate position. Maarten Witsenburg, speaking for others in Pella, voiced the opinion that the Civil War had been "an unnecessary waste of blood and property." "The abolishment of slavery should have been effected more gradually," was the statement made by this practical, yet well-read farmer to T. G. Van der Meulen during the latter's visit to Pella in 1881.[92]

The colonies received the news of peace with great happiness, which was tempered, however, by memories of the many dead and wounded. This was certainly the case in Holland, Michigan, where Van Raalte delivered a speech that made a lasting impression. He addressed himself especially to the returned soldiers, but also to those who had died on the field of battle. Every one of the Dutch youths and men who had gone to the field of battle from *de Kolonie* were cited by him, as he gave their full names, where they were born, and the date and place where they were killed. All of these names and dates were recited from memory and not read from a paper. "The impression on his audience was overwhelming. It was as though he drew a moving, bleeding panorama, in which the entire war passed before the eyes of his listeners, and in which the dreadful cost of the war was depicted as if with the single stroke of a pen."[93] This war, justly called the Great Killing, resulted in the loss of 250,000 men from the North alone; of these, 180,000 died of disease, which was a cause for deep bitterness. The Netherlanders have had their fair share in these losses.

Although it was not at first apparent, the Civil War had far-reaching results for the Dutch, as well as for the Germans and for so many other colonists. The immigrants had again made history, a big chunk of history. This time, however, it was not just for themselves, as it had been when they first settled. This time it was in the interest of the Union, for the sake of preserving the union of the Republic, which in general had accepted them so hospitably. It was only now they felt that they had paid off the moral debt of having accepted this hospitality; now they had paid for their right of citizenship with their own blood. They now felt themselves to be citizens of the United States more strongly than would have been possible through their rooting struggles alone. "I spilled my own blood, was wounded twice, and carry the enemy lead in my body to the grave. Even though I didn't have American blood in my veins, I gave my blood to this country; this makes for just as strong a bond, and nothing but death can destroy or undo that tie." So wrote recently a man in his eighties who had fought in the Civil War for his adopted country—"This huge, good, blessed Country, the best Country on this earth." He had fought three years "for its freedom and for the preservation of the union."[94]

Since this lay in the nature of things, it was the younger people who felt most strongly that they were Americans. Even though they had lived until now almost completely separated in the various settlements, their years-long life in the various camps and garrisons, in a largely American environment, had opened another world with new possibilities for them. When they returned to the Dutch colonies, they formed a progressive element that sometimes refused to stick to the old, traditional opinions, but led in new directions, or had them accepted sooner.

This was especially noticeable in the religious area. Worldliness increased. People even visited the circus in Holland, and the numerous saloons were fuller than ever. "Oh, where will this all end, especially with these, our children, the rising generation, if things continue this way. God is forgotten and deserted," lamented in despair one of the True brothers, Reverend [Douwe] Van der Werp in 1873. And another one, just as orthodox said: "Our children incline toward new-fangled things, and are looking toward American puppets and idols."[95]

As a result of all this, the authority of the once powerful colonial elder, already severely shaken by the revivals, was undermined, even though in general the Americanization process worked together with the mood of the times to further this change.

E. After the Civil War

The return of "our boys" to civilian life after the Civil War has been called a milestone in the development of the colonies.[96] This was not only true in the religious world, but also in economic and political life. In both business and in politics, which are often very closely linked, we can see especially the veterans, honored as old warriors for the rest of their lives, play a role, partly because the future belongs to the young, but also because of the broader view of the world acquired during the war years. Thus Pieter Daan of Oostburg, Wisconsin, became not only the foremost and wealthiest tradesman (we have mentioned that he was the owner of a store, an elevator, and a flour mill), but was also a justice of the peace and a member of Wisconsin's legislative body. In Holland in 1872 the veteran Van Schelven became the editor and publisher of an important English newspaper, The Holland City News. In 1899 he was first appointed as postmaster and later as justice of the peace. One of the sons of Van Raalte already cited, D. B. K., was delegated several times to Michigan's legislative sessions (1875, 1877, and 1909) and even became commander of the Michigan section of the Grand Army of the Republic (1903). Van Loo had become a prominent person in Zeeland. He, too, represented Ottawa County in Michigan's House of Representatives (1881, 1882, and 1883).

The increasing importance of the Michigan Dutch after the Civil War is further shown by the election of J. Roest of Holland as state representative, the first one in de Kolonie (1871 and 1872). He was followed by J. W. Garvelink from Graafschap, (1873, 1874, and 1883), and G. J. Diekema from Holland (1885, 1887, 1889, 1891, and 1902). All of these gentlemen have also been state senators, as J. Den Herder of Zeeland was in 1889.

The Pella veterans, as we shall see later, won permanent fame, especially as leaders of a new colonization. The Pellians had already had local officials for quite some time. During and after the Civil War, they were considered for higher offices—county jobs, for instance. The first Hollander to be so appointed in Iowa was the Frisian Auke H. Viersen—during the early war years he was occupied as county treasurer and recorder. B. Van Leuwen, a Pella merchant and actually of Old Dutch descent, was Marion County's representative to the state legislature in 1865. H. L. Bousquet was chosen as county clerk in 1868 and 1870. Henry Huspers was nominated by the Democrats in 1869 as a candidate for state representative but was not elected. H. P. Bousquet was county supervisor in 1869. H. F. Bousquet and H. L. Bousquet, both veterans, occupied this office, in 1874 and 1877 respectively. Sipke H. Viersen was recorder in 1872.[97] As far as higher politics were concerned, Pella, as was mentioned earlier, remained Democratic. Lincoln in 1864, and Grant in 1868, did receive a small majority, but the elections after that time, especially those of 1875, 1881, and 1885, indicated that in Marion County, Lake Prairie Township voted mostly Democratic. Since 1887, not only this township, but Pella as well is "strongly Democratic."[98]

In contrast, Michigan remained largely Republican, although not as heavily as one might have expected after the Civil War. One of the most prominent Republicans in the colony, the influential owner of De Grondwet, Jan Roest, even became a Democrat, as did so many who were unhappy about the many abuses during the administration of Grant, a Republican.[99] Jan Roest represented the Democrats in 1883 as state senator. Men such as Reverend C. Van der Meulen, Van der Veen and Van Eijk, the latter of whom filled the office of supervisor of the colony for many years, all have continued to consider themselves Democrats.

In de Kolonie the power, however, remained in the hands of the Republicans, even though the Democrats had a strong minority. The election statistics of the village of Zeeland and the immediate area, which along with Holland and Vriesland had once been very heavily Democratic, give us a typical picture.[100] The Democrats received 131 votes and the Whigs received 10 votes in the first Presidential election. In 1876, the Republicans had 296 and the Democrats 147 votes. In 1888, the Republicans had 430 and the Democrats 184 votes.

If one were to wonder why, in spite of the Civil War, so many Netherlanders stayed in the Democratic party, then one should be reminded that under no circumstance must the Democrats be identified with the Southerners and slaveowners. In addition, the Republican party was founded in the West, and this forced the Democrats to "westernize" gradually and to resist the railroad barons, corruption, etc., in defense of the western farmers, while on the other hand, they gave up, at least officially, all opposition to the equality of Blacks and Black voting rights. In addition, it was helpful to the Democrats that after the Civil War the Know Nothing spirit still pervaded the Republican party, so that for instance when President [Rutherford B.] Hayes in 1877 appointed Karl Schurz as minister, a storm of protest arose among the Yankee Republicans against the appointment of an immigrant to such a high office. Finally, simply the name Democrat, had a fascinating influence on the common people, regardless of what the party platform was.

The Republicans, in turn, were able to win supporters among the Calvinistic Dutch colonists, and to keep them by constantly pointing to the many Roman Catholics, and specifically the Irish, who belonged to the Democrats. The resistance of the latter party against alcoholic blue laws—supposedly for the sake of the Irish drunkards who were often the saloonkeepers among them—was another weapon in the hands of the Republicans. "The intense jealousy with which the Zeelanders regard their civil and religious rights and our public school system, all of which they regard in constant danger from the Catholic Hierarchy which together with the liquor interests of the country, form the bulwark of Democracy and is a standing menace to free institutions." So stated the war veteran and Republican Van Loo, by which he also confirms the opinions which I gathered from the Democrats during many discussions.[101]

The fact that the Dutch, as well as the rest of the Americans, often belong to the same religion, and even belong to the same church parish and often have a similar social position, but are nevertheless members of different political parties (even though the parties are constantly drawing closer to each other), cannot be sufficiently explained by the previously mentioned circumstances. For how can one explain that a man like Van Raalte was and always remained a Republican while his fellow parishoner Van der Veen had been a lifelong Democrat? Or even more to the point, why Reverend Van der Meulen, from Zeeland, who was spiritually very close to Van Raalte and as his best friend supported him in everything, has always remained a Democrat? There must be other factors to explain these incongruities.

N. M. Butler, an American and president of Columbia University at New York, once commented that nowhere is the loyalty to the parties and to the party symbols so strong as in the United States.[102] There are remarkable proofs of this among the Dutch-Americans who supported Lincoln and yet, as with so many others, they remained loyal to the Democratic party. The Hollanders in Pella remained Democrats, as did millions of other Americans, in spite of or perhaps just because of the many changes which the Democratic platform went through in 1876, 1884, 1888, and 1892. Butler thinks this attachment and party loyalty are personal expressions of feelings and of a sense of solidarity rather than the expression of political beliefs.

My impression is that, in an attempt to explain these incongruities, one should also mention the herd instinct, which is partly comprised in the feelings of solidarity and the maintaining of old ruts and routines. Both are closely related to a typical lack of personal judgment and sense of spiritual independence, no matter how paradoxical this latter viewpoint may sound. But it must be said that these conditions are found in America as well as in many other colonial countries. These conditions may ultimately be the result of a relatively too low level of general education, a too low phase of cultural development of the mass of the population in these young countries.

These colonial characteristics, which are also found among the Dutch immigrants, explain to a large extent, along with the already cited environment of the Yankee or Southern environment, why the party relationships that were formed shortly before and during the Civil War have been maintained virtually unchanged up to the present time.

How strong this party faithfulness, pull, rut, or routine, and how deeply ingrained this inertia was also among the Dutch colonists, can be shown by the political choices of the largely Democratic Pella area. The anti-trust presidential candidate [Theodore] Roosevelt, who was both ethnically related to the Dutch and a most ideal American—right behind Washington and Lincoln in stature according to many—could not win a majority vote because, no matter how supportive of the western states, he was for the Pella voters first and foremost—a Republican.[103]

There is yet another factor which explains why representatives of both big parties will be found even in the smallest settlements, no matter how homogeneous the population may be, both socially and religiously. It is a factor that explains, at least in part, the tremendous passion of Americans for politics. It also explains the growing, yet still relatively small interest of the Dutch immigrants in this field. Since [Andrew] Jackson (1829–1837), the custom has existed that a newly elected president, if he belongs to a different party than his predecessor, fires all the federal officials and replaces them by persons of his own political party. This procedure is an expression of Jacksonian Democracy: "to the victors the spoils." Thus, a change of president is immediately felt even down to the smallest village, where at least one federal official, the postmaster, must be appointed. That is why even the most apolitical among the Dutch settlers began to be interested in civil government; and thus Republican support in one part of a town almost automatically resulted in Democratic ideals burgeoning in the other part of town—or vice versa.

The American H. D. Post, the political leader of the Democrats in Holland, Michigan, was the postmaster from 1848–1861; yet when the lengthy Democratic string of presidents ended with Lincoln and the new Republican party, this had an immediate effect on the colony. Post was replaced by the local Republican leader Jan Roest.

How much real effect these leadership changes had can be seen from the fact that some disagreements between Johnson, Lincoln's successor, and some of the Republicans in Holland resulted in the firing of Jan Roest. Another Republican, Willem Verbeek, replaced Jan Roest, and has held this office for the last twenty-one years with distinction. But no matter how able he was, and how much he was esteemed by the population, the presidential election of the Democrat [Grover] Cleveland forced Verbeek to resign and J. G. Van Putten became his successor (1887–1891).[104] In Pella, after the pioneer I. Overkamp, the well-paid postmasters were, in order: J. Smeenk, W. L. Boston, P. Barendregt (1856–1861), J. M. Huiskamp, J. H. Betzer who absconded, and A. H. Viersen.[105] Even in such rural townships as South Holland, Illinois, which did not have a post office until 1869, the effect of Union politics was felt. The De Jongs and Gouwens "played musical chairs" as postmaster in this small office.[106]

If we recall the religious character of the settlements, there is one more hypothesis which should be taken into consideration regarding politics among the Dutch colonists. Earlier we have pointed out that one could see the hard-working, sober, partly religiously based life style, described by Ernst Troeltsch as *"reformierte Askese"* [Reformed asceticism], as an expression of the active and aggressive spirit of Calvinism so strongly embodied by Van Raalte himself. This same active and aggressive Calvinistic spirit is manifested in the development of education and missions, whose support became possible only through such a Calvinistic life style. The highest ideal is: "to shape the world for the Glory of God and to bend the reprobates to the recognition of the Divine Law ... a Christian community must be created and maintained with all possible care.*"[107]

One cannot help but wonder if this spirit was the main consideration of the Dutch when participating in American political life. We have perceived very little of that so far. The colonies formed, in fact, a theocracy or—again according to Troeltsch—a bibliocracy.[108] But we saw how the most diametrically opposed convictions sprang up, all justified by Biblical texts, when it came to taking a stand on the most burning question of all, that of slavery. Personal emotions, rather than cool logic, both at times muddied up by self-interest, determined the choice of an appropriate Biblical citation.

The decision to join the Democrats or Whigs, and later the Republicans, rested more upon the sympathy or antipathy toward certain ethnic groups, i.e., toward the Southerners or toward the Yankees (the Northerners). It also depended more upon direct self-interest than on actual political considerations. For instance, the immigrant's self-interest was opposed to the Know Nothing spirit of the Whigs and the Republicans. I already noted that it was very difficult to make a political choice, since really deep, fundamental differences between the two parties did not exist, because essentially the differences between the parties were marked by opportunistic and circumstantial factors.

If the colonists had been completely consistent with Calvinism, then they would have joined up with the Whigs and Republicans—exactly those people whom the immigrants despised due to their aristocratic tendencies. For Calvinism, according to Hans Baron, in its most fundamental depth as far as politics are concerned, is aristocratic, oligarchic in character: *"im Grunde ebensowohl Ursache als Wirkung der in ihnen bestehenden sozialen Verhältnisse"* [basically, just as much cause as effect of the social relationship existing in it].[109] (Republics such as Geneva and the Netherlands, built on aristocratic lines, corresponded with Calvin's religious basic thoughts.) From these considerations we can see how consequential Reverend Zonne had been when he joined the Republicans, the party to which large numbers of American Calvinists belonged.

---

*Die Welt gestalten zur Ehre Gottes und die Verworfenen beugen unter die Anerkennung des göttlichen Gesetzes ... ein christliches Gemeinwesen mit aller Sorgfalt erschaffen und erhalten.

Men such as Van Raalte and Scholte, the most gifted among the Calvinist immigrants, went from the Democrat to the Republican party and remained there.[110] Eventually the majority of the Dutch colonists became Republicans, too, and still is. This final state of affairs in politics finds its most profound explanation perhaps in the Calvinism of these immigrants, coupled with their ethnic characteristics, a Calvinism that was aristocratically colored, primarily through its teachings of predestination.

15

Cultural Change
The Dutch Press

Cultural change, as well as physical growth, is tied to factors that we cannot always view as cultural progress. One such factor is the Dutch press in the United States, at least as far as it uses the Dutch language.

The desire to introduce certain political concepts among the Dutch had as much to do with the founding of weekly and other types of newspapers as did the desire to maintain the strict religious character of the settlements. Because of the character of many settlements and the religious foundation of the civic views of many colonists, it should not come as a surprise to learn that even though some newspapers were mostly political and others mostly religious, both topics often appear in the same newspaper.

It is worthy of note that newspapers that were primarily political in nature usually lasted for only a short time, while among newspapers that were solely religious, a few have managed to continue until the present day, no matter how many had to shut down. Many of them, however, did not appear to satisfy "any particular need"! Several newspapers established a sound financial basis only by responding to one of the baser instincts of the average immigrant: his strong interest in local news, even gossip [nieuwtjes]. "News" papers were read the most, even if some people did not really want them. This, of course, is not a typical immigrant phenomenon or even an American phenomenon. The low moral quality and, for those newspapers that became the most Americanized, the often sensational character of their "news items" were very typical, however.

Even the earliest newspapers can furnish proof of this state of the Dutch press. De Sheboygan Nieuwsbode [The Sheboygan News Messenger], the first Dutch newspaper in the United States, published in Sheboygan since 1849, was forced to reorganize after only six years. The fact that this newspaper was also read outside of Wisconsin, and perhaps even more the circumstance that this initially Democratic newspaper offered its services to the new

Republican party, led to the following change in name: *De Nieuwsbode, Orgaan der Nederlanders in Noord-Amerika* [*The News Messenger, Organ of the Dutch in North America*]. It did not survive after 1858, however. These are facts that have gone largely unnoticed by the writers on these newspapers—the Americans Dr. Beets and Alb. Oosterheerdt and the Dutch journalist Th. De Veer.[1]

The *Nieuwsbode* was relatively religious in character—a necessary condition for survival for a newspaper that was looking for subscribers among such strongly religious Hollanders. However, it was primarily a newspaper, just as the name indicates. The disagreements between Van Raalte and various "revolutionary elements" in his colony, which have been discussed earlier, were printed in the newspaper. It seems that they were eagerly read, because the Wisconsin newspaper had a following among the Dutch in Michigan and Iowa, even when it was no longer "the only organ of the Dutch in North America," as it had called itself, sometimes unjustly, for some years.

De Nederlander, published in Kalamazoo under editor [Giles] Van der Wal in 1850, was a Whig paper, which may have been the reason for its lasting such a short time. Another Dutch newspaper was not published here until 1888. *De Hollandsche Amerikaan* [*The Dutch American*] was a newspaper strongly Reformed in spirit. It was ailing for quite a while; yet later it became much stronger and is still being published.

In 1850 *The Hollander* appeared at Allegan, Michigan, published by two Americans, [Josiah L.] Hawks and [Elisha B.] Bassett, with the support of several Hollanders. Although it was aimed at the Dutch colony, it was started as an English-language newspaper, and called *The Hollander*, because they hoped to make it an official organ, a "county paper."[2] It started out with only a few columns in Dutch, but it became a completely Dutch-language newspaper relatively soon. They even managed to get Van Raalte interested. With his help, ministers in the surrounding villages were appointed as correspondents. Soon after that, the newspaper itself was moved from Allegan to Holland. The Americans were bought out by J. Doesburg and J. Van der Wal (apparently the person cited above), with Van Raalte as the silent partner.

It was decided, right at the sale, that Van Raalte would have complete control over the contents, the purpose of which was "to benefit the people not only with religious articles, but also the events of the day and information about many vital concerns."[3] So said Van Raalte, who actually played a much more passive role in the establishment of this newspaper than his biographer, [H. E.] Dosker, indicates. After all, the initiative itself came from Americans, not the Dutch. In the end, Van Raalte had so little extra time, which was quite understandable, that he never did review the contents as he had originally planned.

Devoted to the Democratic party from the very beginning, *The Hollander* not only espoused Democratic party ideas, but perhaps more importantly, it supported democratic ideals. As was mentioned earlier, it opposed the aristocratic and theocratic inclinations of the great leader of the colony. In a double sense, Van Raalte played in this paper not a leading role, but to the contrary, a suffering, passive role. One cannot deny the idealistic motivations of a democratic nature in the articles against Van Raalte and the consistory, against "the priesthood" that showed itself in Holland in all its "majesty" (that was the way it was expressed). The letters to the editor, almost always anonymous, were usually of a much too violent and too sensational a character, and this made the newspaper completely different from what Van Raalte had wanted; it was "very negative in tone, both in matters of doctrine and of congregational life."

The resultant feud became so severe—as we have already seen—that not only the consistory, but even a colonial church meeting was called to settle the differences. There was so much bitterness on both sides that a church elder, who was not aware of the settlement that had been reached, manhandled the democratic publisher Doesburg in an attempt to keep him from participating in Communion; needless to say this caused quite a tumult.[4] However, Doesburg continued to publish the newspaper, which had now become a completely Dutch-language publication called De Hollander. Half of it was religious, and the remainder were news items, at first mostly descriptions of cattle that got lost in the woods and otherwise missing cows, official notices, and advertisements.[5]

After the publisher moved to Grand Haven, where he was appointed as "registrar of deeds," the paper was successively run by H. Van Eijk and J. Binnenkant (both already mentioned) with Van Eijk continuing as editor under Binnenkant until 1868 when W. Benjaminse and H. J. Slag became the owners. During the great fire of October 1871, the entire printing plant was destroyed. In 1872, however, the newspaper started again and was even larger, being published solely by Benjaminse. It had always been the party organ of the Democrats in the Michigan colony; it ceased publication, however, on December 24, 1895. In Holland, always the core of the Dutch element, several other newspapers have been published since then.

It is my impression that the desire for a newspaper in the mother language could not be reconciled with the financial and spiritual resources of the colonists, both of which were often too limited. Therefore, it was simply too difficult for a newspaper to survive under such conditions. Thus, political considerations coupled with financial support from political quarters (partly American) led to the founding of "Dutch" newspapers rather than any actual love for the Dutch language. I found open proof of this in the newspaper to be discussed—De Grondwet [The Constitution].

The rise of the Republican party encouraged Jan Roest in the spring of 1860, as we have seen previously, to circulate among the Hollanders the Republican ideals in the weekly De Grondwet. This newspaper was "founded from the very beginning" for political purposes, and not out of love for the mother tongue, announced the newspaper in 1897, and it went on to say in a very frank manner that especially "since the Republican victory in 1869, the paper had had better financial support than most newspapers currently receive."

In 1868 Roest got into financial difficulties as a result of the harbor projects he had taken on, and consequently he was forced to sell the newspaper. L. Mulder, born at Goes in 1845, had come with his parents to Holland, Michigan, in 1856, where he became an apprentice at Roest's printing establishment. Together with [M.] Hoogesteger, who was already serving as editor of De Grondwet, Mulder bought Roest's newspaper, and Mulder and Hoogesteger served respectively as printer-administrator and editor.

There were few subscribers at first, even though the newspaper claimed "to exert a not inconsiderable influence" upon them. With the talented Hoogesteger as editor, the number of readers gradually increased so that by March, 1880, the subscription list contained 1,200 names. Hoogesteger had died in 1879, however, and Mulder had become the sole owner. He appointed P. Schravezande as temporary editor until 1880, when the gifted I. Verweij took up this task and served in this capacity for twenty years. During this time period, the newspaper went from four to eight pages, and then to twelve pages. In the nineties, it reached sixteen pages and by 1890 it had a circulation of 5,000 copies.[6] It advertised itself as "The Largest Dutch Newspaper in the United States," an honor which had actually already been claimed earlier, in 1882, by Pella's Weekblad [Weekly].

Although De Grondwet first and foremost became a news and advertisement newspaper, it always remained a Republican publication. Like most Dutch-American papers it also concerned itself with religious matters. About 1880, when religious arguments flared up among the Dutch, the newspaper chose sides against the Freemasons and their supporters. This step earned it a great increase in popularity among the Dutch of orthodox inclination. Mulder himself, who was not actually a pioneer—it is important to point this out—joined the Christian Reformed Church. His children—he had eleven of them—continued to run De Grondwet in the nineties, after their father had died. This newspaper is still considered one of the most important ones in the colony. Over the years, it has become very "Americanized," and is written therefore in anything but pure Dutch; it has also become very sensational.

The church leaders and many of their flock were not completely satisfied with the religious content of De Grondwet. The most strongly orthodox, the True Christians, were especially dissatisfied. They felt there was still room for a newspaper that would concern itself exclusively with religion.

C. Vorst, one of the True brothers in Holland and one of the instigators of the schism within that group and an elder as well, became the pioneer of the religious press. In 1858 he published a religious newspaper, *De Paarl* [*The Pearl*], in Holland. Since the True brothers did not have many financial resources, and since their reading interest was low except for the Bible and psalms, this newspaper lasted for only two years. It does deserve, however, to be called the forerunner of the religious press, specifically of the Christian Reformed Church press.[7] Of *Een stem uit het Westen* [*A Voice from the West*], published by Slag and Benjaminse in 1867 in Holland, "in the interest of the True Dutch Reformed Church in North America," only one issue reached the public![8]

The next year, however, on February 14, 1868, the enterprising C. Vorst started publishing *De Wachter* [*The Watchman*]. This paper has managed to continue publication up to the present time, in spite of many setbacks including the [Holland] fire in 1871 that completely destroyed its printing plant. It came out every two weeks as the church organ of the True brothers, with Reverend D. J Van der Werp appointed as editor. In 1875, Vorst passed the paper on to his church. Reverend G. E. Boer and then G. K. Hemkes succeeded Van der Werp as editors, later with several co-workers. *De Wachter* expanded to a weekly in 1880.[9] Strongly opinionated articles appeared, especially during its early years. They stormed violently at believers of other religious views, but also members of their own church were taken to task. They would "lash out frightfully at times" against the Reformed Church. Calvinism in all its militancy, but also in all its narrow-mindedness, came to its fullest expression in these publications.

Even as the official publication of the True Church, *De Wachter*, like most of the other Dutch newspapers in America, had financial difficulties. A "sinking condition" was even mentioned in 1885.[10] Indifference to a paper in the mother tongue was an additional factor, as well as the extremely limited education of many True brothers, who had been raised with very little attention given to reading newspapers.

J. Tanis, in 1888, at Paterson, put out *De Sabbathschool Bode* [*The Sabbath School Messenger*] as a Christian Reformed paper. Professor G. E. Boer was the first editor and was succeeded by Reverend [Roelf T.] Kuiper. The oldest Reformed press had many difficulties at first, too. The publishing of *De Wekker* [*The Awakener*] by the Holland Colony Teachers' Association began in 1859 for the purpose of upbringing and education, mission work, etc.[11] Interest in this paper also remained limited, and publication ceased after two years. *Het Gereformeerde Maandblad* [*The Reformed Monthly*] also had a short existence.

A religious newspaper for the benefit of the Reformed Church members met with more success. It was J. Binnenkant's *De Verzamelaar* [*The Collector*] which made good progress until it was merged in 1866 with *De Hope* [*The Hope*], a newspaper published by Hope College.[12] P. J. Oggel, whom we already noted in Pella, had been appointed as professor at Western Seminary. He was the founder, with Doesburg, of the still-published religious

Weekblad in het Belang van Maatschappij, School, en Kerk [*Weekly in the Interest of Society, School, and Church*] and served as its first editor. The interests of the Reformed Church were warmly supported and the fundamental beliefs were spiritedly defended by Oggel and his successors, N. M. Steffens and N. H. Dosker.

It is a peculiar fact that in the Pella area, the wealthiest and most developed colony, the need for a Dutch paper was felt later than in Wisconsin and Michigan. The financial circumstances also became favorable there later. The fact that people in Iowa were reading both *De Nieuwsbode* from Sheboygan (Wisconsin) and *De Hollander* from Holland (Michigan) does not explain everything. Neither can it be explained by the fact that the most educated citizens, who were in the minority, read American newspapers such as the *New York Tribune* and magazines such as *Harper's Magazine*. Moreover, these publications were quite inexpensive as compared to the Dutch newspapers. Neither can it be said that people in Pella did not read much; in fact, it was just the opposite. Postmaster Barendregt even reported that "the number of newspapers and periodicals that arrive here regularly for reading, whether daily or weekly, is exceptional."[13]

And yet in 1855, when Scholte offered to publish a "*Hollandsche Courant*" [Dutch newspaper], provided he could be assured of a certain number of subscribers at a cost of $1.50, to be paid in advance—Scholte was first of all a businessman!—there was not enough interest, and nothing came of his intentions. In 1856 and 1857, his renewed efforts to start a Dutch newspaper called *De Unie* [*The Union*] were also in vain because he did not obtain the required number of 700 subscribers.[14] Also elsewhere, all attempts to start a Dutch newspaper from the very beginning on a sound financial footing usually failed. Actually, the reason why Iowa got a Dutch newspaper in 1861, twelve years after Wisconsin did, and eleven years later than Michigan, is due to several factors. The extremely cautious nature of the Dutch, their very materialistic inclinations (except for religious fanaticism), and their limited trust in Scholte all combine with the earlier factors mentioned to explain the late establishment of Dutch newspapers in Pella.

Another paper was planned in Holland, Michigan. It would be published in English and only a few columns in Dutch would have to do. What actually happened, however, was that the English, not the Dutch, quickly disappeared from the paper. In Pella, Iowa, they started with a newspaper completely in English. This paper lasted for several years but then . . . disappeared completely, to be replaced by a paper completely in Dutch! The use of the American language in the schools and the many Americans in and around Pella, "together with intermarriage between native and foreign-born citizens, will leave in a few years but little difference between Pella and other more exclusive American towns."[15] So said the publishers of the first American paper in Pella, the first paper in all of Marion County, and for a long time the paper the furthest west between Pella and the Missouri: *The*

Pella Gazette.[16] Its publishers, H. P. Scholte and E. H. Grant, both notaries public, were however mistaken about the speed of Americanization of the Dutch, just as people in Holland had misjudged this development. After only "a few years" *The Pella Gazette* had disappeared, and *Pella's Weekblad* came on the scene.

There had been great hopes for *The Pella Gazette*—a "two-story building" had been built for it; the motto of the paper was "Independent in Everything," "In Deo Spes Nostra et Refugium" [In God Is Our Hope and Refuge] was the second motto. As with *The Hollander*, this paper had been made possible through joint efforts with Americans; a certain amount of initiative had also come from the outside. Although independent, the newspaper soon declared itself with Scholte in support of the Democratic party. Politics played such an important part in the paper, that when *De Nieuwsbode* from Wisconsin tried to spread some Republican ideals among the Dutch Pella residents, Scholte felt compelled—as we saw—to add some Dutch columns in which he argued vehemently against the new party.

Even this fight against Republican ideals did not arouse a desire among the largely Democratic colonists for a Dutch newspaper of their own. The *Gazette* turned out to be a financial disappointment and suddenly, in September, 1857, it ceased publication; this was due to unpaid subscriptions, not enough advertising income, etc. On July 22, 1859, however, the paper began publication again, this time under the Republican banner, with H. P. Scholte as editor and S. M. Hammond, an American, as publisher. This publication lasted only a short time, the last issue coming out on February 22, 1860. Scholte himself continued to write numerous articles for a variety of American papers in Iowa. The political interest in a paper of their own was simply not strong enough yet among the Dutch-Americans.[17]

In 1861 another effort was made to start a Dutch paper with a Democratic emphasis, which would be primarily a newspaper. P. J. Oggel, a minister, and H. Hospers, a notary public and businessman, managed to get enough money together to buy, among other things, the printing equipment of the *Pella Gazette*. Thus, in the fall of 1861 *Pella's Weekblad* could get started. Except for *De Grondwet* in Holland, Michigan, the *Weekblad* is the oldest existing Dutch newspaper in the United States. When Hospers left for northwestern Iowa, the newspaper became the sole property of the former teacher, H. Neyenesch, the city recorder; he thus became Pella's foremost publisher.[18]

Yet, in the winter of 1864 to 1865, a Republican newspaper was published in English—*The Pella Blade*. After a struggle of many years, during which time it changed ownership at least ten times, Neyenesch acquired it in 1879. He changed the paper from a "radical Republican" to a "positive Democratic paper," which has continued during the last twenty years as the most important English newspaper in Pella. An enterprising Pellian, Gerrit Van Ginkel, had worked as an apprentice for the *Pella's Weekblad* printing plant for some time. In March, 1867, he tried to introduce *De Pella Gazette*, a Dutch newspaper with Republican leanings, but the paper closed down in 1869, and *Pella's Weekblad* took over all the rights and obligations. It should be mentioned in passing that Van Ginkel later became one of the wealthiest Iowa Hollanders. Businesses in Des Moines (Iowa), in Springfield (Illinois), and in Dallas (Texas) enabled him to become eventually one of the richest Des Moines residents.[19]

Even though the above-mentioned papers were important as newspapers and as party organs, many people felt they were greatly lacking in religious content. At the urging of Reverend P. J. Oggel, *Pella's Maandblad* [*Pella's Monthly*] was started as early as April, 1862, in addition to *Pella's Weekblad*. The *Maandblad* was a completely religious paper, as its subtitle indicated: "Christian Voices and Messages Concerned With The Kingdom of God On Earth." When Oggel moved to Holland, Michigan in 1863, the *Maandblad* ceased operations.[20]

In his later years, Scholte had returned to his original calling, to "the ministry," and in September 1866 he began publication of a religious monthly called *De Toekomst* [*The Future*]; he continued this press work until his death in 1868. This newspaper contains important materials for the faithful as well as for the critical observer; in fact it contains Scholte's spiritual last will and testament. Especially an article like "To Put Up for Sale the Word of God" gives sceptics something to think about. This and other similar articles were appreciated by the faithful as " treasures of wisdom passed on to the faithful as if it were a heritage."[21]

It was not until 1881 that another religious newspaper was founded. Neyenesch, already the owner of two news and political papers, printed *De Christelijke Heraut* [*The Christian Herald*] from 1881 until January 1885. As a matter of course, the editing of the newspaper was in religious hands.[22] Dr. H. P. Oggel was the editor of this newspaper with an unusual format, which had as its motto the significant phrase "The Soul without Knowledge is also not good."

It is clear that the newspapers, regardless of whether they were politically or religiously oriented, led a precarious existence, and in the end elicited little appreciation from the people. If they had not already closed down much earlier, they stopped publication, especially after a precarious financial existence, whenever the editor moved away or died. Hardly anywhere have we been able to verify any spontaneous desire for a Dutch newspaper. The only indication of such a need was evidenced by the ten stockholders who met to organize the publication of *Pella's Weekblad*, a meeting called by H. Hospers. It should be remembered, however, that many colonists subscribed, both then and now, to papers published in the Netherlands, and that the more educated colonists were soon reading the American newspapers.

The problems mentioned so far caused the Dutch press in the United

States to lead a marginal existence, which even papers specializing in news reporting could not escape. De Nieuwsbode, published in Sheboygan, was closed down when the editor-publisher [Jacob] Quintus left, even though a large number of Dutch people lived in Sheboygan and in the surrounding area. Apparently, there simply was no need for it any longer. Quintus then settled in Grand Rapids, a town which, as we already know, had a considerable Dutch population that had not been Americanized to any great extent. De Stoompost [The Steampost], the first Dutch paper here, was published by Quintus in 1858.

Since then, Grand Rapids, like Holland and Pella, has become an important area for newspapers. It also became a burying ground for those same newspapers. Several sheets and small papers were published there. Their only importance lies in the fact that they were expressions of particular interests of the Dutch population; none lasted very long. De Stoompost came first, then came De Lantaarn [The Lantern] in 1876, De Honingbij [The Honeybee] in 1879,[23] De Christen Werkman [The Christian Workman], a vehicle for a labor party called "Patrimonium" [Patrimony] and Stemmen uit de Vrije Hollandsche Gemeente [Voices from the Free Dutch Congregation], the philosophy of which was expressed, among others, through Lessing's statement: "The letter is not the spirit, and the Bible is not the religion."

De Stemmen [The Voices] was edited by Reverend F. W. N. Hugenholtz, who was also the publisher from 1886 to 1890, while P. Th. Hugenholtz took care of the administration. As the name indicates, the paper was the vehicle of the religious liberal Dutchmen who had organized the Free Dutch Congregation in Grand Rapids. This group, which counted 316 members by the end of 1889, was supported by the Unitarians in the United States and was acknowledged as a foreign branch of the Nederlandsche Protestantenbond [The Dutch Protestant Confederation]. The Free Congregation had like-minded friends in both Kalamazoo and in Chicago; in the latter city an independent group was established in 1889, numbering sixty members by the end of that year. Because of this De Stemmen reappeared in 1890 as Stemmen uit de Vrije Hollandsche Gemeenten in Amerika [Voices from the Free Dutch Congregations in America], edited by the earlier-cited Reverend Hugenholtz, but now published by the congregation at Grand Rapids. Interesting information about the social importance of the Dutch labor element in the Furniture City appeared. It also took the intolerance of the orthodox Dutch severely to task.[24] A liberal paper that was published around 1890 by [?] Plugge, one of Hugenholtz's supporters, was not successful; Plugge later returned to the Netherlands.[25]

A much older paper, De Standaard [The Standard] was the most important paper published in Grand Rapids among the immigrants; it was put out by [Dennis] Schram and [J.] Van Strien. Primarily a newspaper, it was Democratic from its very beginning in 1875, but became a Republican paper in the twentieth century. As a semi-weekly, it had a readership of two thousand. Several years ago, it was taken over by another company and merged with *The Bulletin*, an English paper; it is currently known as *The Standard-Bulletin*, being partly Dutch and partly English.[26]

A "modern" paper, *De Nederlander*, has been in existence for a long time in Chicago where several hundred Dutch resided during the eighties. H. M. Buhrman, a member of the Free Dutch Congregation in Grand Rapids, was appointed editor of this paper in 1889. However, it flourished to some extent only after the talented Uden Masman had been put in charge. It is no longer in publication. This newspaper will retain historical significance, however, due to an article published February 3, 1893, written by J. Hoddenbach Van Scheltema, a native of Arnhem and a religious immigrant. The article was entitled "*Heeft de Nederlandsche taal eene toekomst?*" ["Is there a future for the Dutch language?"] It was this article which drew a response from the well-known "Greater Netherlander" Hypoliet Meert, and which eventually led to the establishment of the *Algemeen Nederlandsch Verbond* [The General Dutch League*] in 1898.[27]

[John C.] Beeuwkes started a newspaper called *De Telegraaf* [The Telegraph] in Paterson, New Jersey, about 1880; it was later taken over by C. Poelstra. I saw mention of a newspaper called *De Nederlander*, published in New York already in the sixties, but this could not be confirmed.[28] A paper was definitely started in this city twenty years later: *De Nieuws en Handelscourant* [The News and Tradepaper] started in 1883. Jan Van 't Woud, director of the Holland Publishing Company there, was the publisher.[29]

The last newspaper within the Dutch centers was a Catholic newspaper in the mother tongue. The *De Pere Standaard* [De Pere Standard] appeared in 1889 at De Pere in the Fox River Valley. This paper, later renamed *De Volksstem* [The Voice of the People], was published for many years by Heyrman and Kuypers, but ceased publication during the [First] World War.

Though I have called the Dutch press in America an expression of growth, it did not mean progress. It indicated growth because the colonists had attained a certain level of prosperity and an accompanying restfulness, which allowed them both financially and spiritually to enjoy a newspaper. These newspapers contained lead articles in good Dutch, often authored by talented Hollanders such as Oggel, Nollen, Steffens, and others. Contributions by the readers were obviously of a very modest nature. The following is a fragment of a poem, published in *De Hollander* in 1858, and written upon the death of a colonist in Pella in September of that year:

> Oh, day of mourning!
> Oh, hour of sad sorrow!
> A sister whom we loved
> Now lies already bare before us.
> The face disappeared, the voice broke off

*Het Algemeen Nederlandsch Verbond is an organization still in existence for maintaining contact with the Dutch in the diaspora.

> The strength continued to ebb away.
> This caused our tender heart
> To drown in sadness.*[30]

The great majority of the colonists have not been able to raise the quality of their literary effusions beyond this level up to the present day. Therefore, one cannot speak of progress. Another indication of this stagnation—and an indication of the religious mentality of the immigrants—is the fact that the poetic veins began to flow only upon the occasion of a death. Elegies still make up a large part of the newspaper poetry.

It is even worse when lead articles are considered. The quality of these articles did not remain constant, but as we shall see later, in many ways it regressed, both in terms of the purity of the Dutch language and in terms of content. Spiritually the papers became more and more impoverished, even when their financial condition had improved. Those newspapers that had as editors, ministers, or school teachers recently emigrated from the Netherlands, constituted favorable exceptions. This was especially the case among the Christian Reformed, and is still occasionally true. Thus we see the apparently conflicting phenomenon that *de kleinste luyden* [the commonest people] had the best newspapers in Dutch, complete with some really noteworthy editorials, while from a Dutch point of view, the newspapers that served the wealthier and more educated members of the Reformed Church made a decidedly poor impression.

It must not be forgotten, however, that the best and most highly educated people among them were accustomed to expressing themselves in English. They were also the first to read "Dutch" newspapers in English. The end of the Civil War saw the founding of *The Pella Chronicle* at Pella. In 1872 *The Holland City News* was published entirely in English at Holland by the war veteran G. Van Schelven, whom we have met earlier as an apprentice at the printing plant of *De Hollander*. The newspaper was purchased in 1888 by the earlier-cited L. Mulder, whose descendants still retain control.

The younger people, the students so full of promise, published their periodicals in English from the very beginning.[31] *The Central Ray* appeared as early as 1864 at Central College at Pella, while Hope College students have published a paper since 1887, named *The Anchor* (of Hope) in commemoration of the words of Van Raalte.

In the area of religion, the most Americanized citizens read *The Intelligencer* and *The Banner of Truth*, published in the east by the Reformed Church and the True Reformed Dutch Church, respectively. Gradually small religious

---

*   O, *dag van rouw!*
    O, *uur van droeving leed!*
    Een zuster, die ons dierbaar was,
    Ligt nu daar reeds ontkleed.
    't Gezigt verdween, de stem brak af,
    De brachten bleven zinken;
    Die toestand deed ons teeder hart
    In droefheid als verdrinken.

periodicals in English began to appear in the West, for example in the eighties, *The Church Record*, the publication of Grand Rapid's First Reformed Church.

Even though the Dutch press in the United States was doomed to become bastardized from the very beginning (in spite of the peak period after the nineties due to the arrival of more educated Hollanders), this press has not lacked in importance. Besides the influence that this press had upon politics and especially upon religious affairs, the closer bond it fostered or maintained among the far flung Dutch element can be shown.

In this connection we should be reminded once more that, for instance, *De Nieuwsbode* from Wisconsin was read in both Michigan and Iowa. *De Hollander* from Holland, Michigan, could in turn be found among the colonists in Wisconsin and Iowa, while later on *Pella's Weekblad* circulated among the Catholic settlements, as was indicated earlier. The religious newspapers such as *De Hope* and *De Wachter* were also read in the East among the Dutch in New York State, New Jersey, etc. Besides the religious bonds, these newspapers strengthened the bonds of a common ancestry, the awareness of being of Dutch origin. Stories from Dutch history contributed to this bonding as well. Taking just one example, a column headed "*Geschiedkundig*" ["Historical"] appeared in *De Christelijke Heraut*, published in Pella. The June 21, 1882, issue contained an article on "The Arrival of the Duke of Alva in the Netherlands, Egmond and Hoorne." In addition, the newspapers carried extensive news about the Netherlands. These same newspapers, however, often displayed a very militant character which by no means was always very edifying. This was already observed in *De Hollander*. But even the religious newspapers, specifically *De Wachter* of the True brothers was repeatedly below par. Thus its church Synod in 1886 pointed to "the evils of brothers who, forsaking the discipline of love, expose one another in the press as sinner or heretic." In turn the Synod was invited to point out to the editor of *De Wachter* that "under no circumstance could he publish such things."[32]

One favorable exception in this context for a long time has been *De Hope*, under the editorship of Dr. Steffens. His religious opponent, the "free thinker" F. W. N. Hugenholtz, saw in him "a consistent orthodox believer who always shows the courage of his convictions, with whom it is worthwhile to break a lance once in a while because he is a person one can count on," someone whom we "continually and increasingly have learned to appreciate."[33] A strong contrast is provided by the view of an extremely orthodox person, one of the True brothers, as addressed to the Dutch friends who, like Steffens, had joined the Reformed Church: "Come and throw away the golden calves that you have erected at Bethel and Dan. Do no longer whore after other people's gods."[34] This cry, not found in any newspaper by the way, but rather printed in a pamphlet, is characteristic of the spirit that prevailed in some of the most religious broadsides that were put out in addition to newspapers in the Dutch language.

As we have already seen, Dutch books were occasionally reprinted in the United States, especially church literature. The most heavily read Dutch books, also during the growth years, were largely religious works. |Wilhelmus| Schortinghuis's *Innig Christendom* |*Fervent Christendom*| was "a favorite book for more than one" True brother.[35] Besides this and other works mentioned earlier, were J. J. Van Oosterzee's *Het Jaar des Heils* |*The Year of Salvation*| and *Levenswoorden voor iederen dag* |*Precepts for Everyday Living*|; H. Spurgeon's *Volksleerredenen* |*Grounds for Popular Teachings*|; |Pierre Daniël| De Chantepie de la Sausaye's *De Brief aan de Hebreën voor de Gemeente Uitgelegd* |*The Letter to the Hebrews, Explained to the Congregation*|, and other works; |Bernardus| Smijtegeld's sermons; and works by |Louis S. P. (?)| Meyboom. Also among the liberals, people read works by |Laurentius| Knappert and |M. A. N.| Rovers. The Reformed people and liberals both read Hilderbrand's |pseudonym for Nicolaas Beets| *Camera Obscura*; Klikspaan's |pseudonym for Johannes Kneppelhout| *Studententypen* |Student Characters|; the poems of |Isaäc| Da Costa; J. J. L. Ten Kate's *De Schepping* |*The Creation*|, Nicolaas Beets, |Bernard| Ter Haar, W. J. Van Zeggelen and, among the later liberal group, those of |Petrus A.| De Genestet. If we depend for information only on ads, the main things remained "State Bibles, house Bibles, Bibles for the pulpit, church books, four-part singing books, organ books for the Psalms, Neerbosch's songs, etc."

When T. G. Van der Meulen visited Pella in 1881, he remarked that at times much reading was evident. This writer was very surprised by the range of reading and "the solid knowledge" of Dutch history that M. Witsenburg (the farmer we have met earlier) appeared to have. He had a knowledge that enabled him to "draw conclusions and parallels between the rights of nations and the rights of the law."[36] This once more goes to show that not just the least from among the Dutch emigrated to America.

Netherlanders in America

Volume **2**

Leaders of the new colony in Sioux County. Top: The preacher S. Bolks. Bottom: The founder and manager H. Hospers.

Part Four

New Shoots on the
Young Dutch Branch

1

Sioux County, A Daughter Colony in the "Farther West"

A. The Pioneers of the West

In previous chapters I have related how in the thirties and forties immigrants by the thousands from Europe and also from eastern areas of the United States trekked westward and settled there. Although this trek has never come to a complete standstill, the Civil War undoubtedly curtailed this "drive to go West." When peace had returned, the westward movement revived, not only into the Mississippi area but also into the Missouri River basin, the "newer West."

> To the west, to the west, to the land of the free
> Where mighty Missouri rolls down to the sea,
> Where a man is a man if he's willing to toil,
> And the humblest may gather the fruits of the soil.

They moved westward in increasingly greater numbers for two reasons: the railway system extended ever further, which greatly eased the overland journey; and even more importantly, the previously mentioned homestead laws and pre-emption regulations made it possible to acquire excellent quality farmland at very low cost. Those who had fought in the war on the side of the Union were automatically granted 160 acres of land.* What is surprising and noteworthy is that it was not in the first place the immigrants from Europe or even residents of the East who colonized in the new West, but those who were already living in the West.

The oft-quoted American sociologist, E. A. Ross, in his studies on *Chang-*

---

*The Homestead Law of 1862 entitled any persons who were heads of families or twenty-one years of age, and who were citizens or filed a declaration of intent to become a citizen, to enter 160 acres of land that was subject to pre-emption and was surveyed. They could obtain title free after five years by conforming to the residency and improvement requirements of the law. After 1872 Union veterans of the Civil War were permitted to count their military service time towards the five-year residency requirement, but they had to reside on the land one full year.

463

ing America, states: "It was the roomy West, that settled the farther West." This observation is correct in a general sense, if not in an absolute sense.[1] The Dutch colonists established in the United States after the Civil War furnish evidence of this. Most of these new colonies were spin-offs of the parent colonies in Iowa, Wisconsin, Michigan, and other areas. Very few colonies were settled by immigrants coming directly from the Old Country.

The great importance of these older settlements, which we have dealt with so far, does not lie exclusively in their own existence but also in the fact that as mother colonies they gave birth to many a daughter. It is for this reason that I felt it necessary to describe the development of the parent colonies in greater detail, since their distinctive spiritual character, as I have emphasized, carried over into the younger, more westerly colonies and greatly influenced them. This is evident in the fact that they looked toward the parent colonies, where their colleges and seminaries were located, as the sources of their spiritual and cultural nourishment.

It was especially after the Civil War that the already existing tendency to migrate still further west manifested itself strongly in the Dutch colonies as well as in other areas of the West. The younger generation, those who had been born and raised in America and particularly those who had fought in the War, led the movement, but it was by no means limited to them. It included older colonists who had not been able to acquire farms of their own but had hired out as laborers or had rented land. It also included landowners who felt they should go further west because they had large families. The thought that farther west they could find greater opportunities—even better land, even cheaper land, but especially even more land—generated an unrest, a certain "nervousness," which was characteristic of many colonists and kept them trekking all their lives. To obtain the greatest possible independence for themselves and their children was and still is for many their basic ideal. The possibilities that opened up after the Civil War promoted this desire. "To be my own boss" was the watchword, and it was nowhere stronger than among the pioneers of the West. In this connection Ross remarks: "In the pioneer blood lurks too a secret horror of taking another man's orders or pay."[2]

It is an interesting phenomenon that among the Dutch colonists this independent spirit, coupled with continuing urge to trek further west, came to expression more strongly in and around Pella than anywhere else. As early as 1856, before the Civil War and not yet ten years after the town had been founded, Pella settlers were already considering the establishment of another colony in northeastern or northwestern Iowa. Originally they had in mind people still living in the Netherlands who were hoping to migrate and "whose Pella friends (could) be . . . of the greatest help to them" so that "for such a colony the most beautiful prospects (could) open up."[3] In the end it was the Pella colonists themselves who founded the newer settlements.

Those who had arrived in Pella in 1847 with a household of small children (and this was equally true of the other colonies) saw their children grow up to marriageable age. A writer of that period states that also for this reason "they saw more and more the necessity and increasingly felt the desire to find somewhere else in the West another suitable area for a Dutch colony." When the colonists saw and heard about great caravans of wagons, laden with families, cattle and farm tools, daily crossing the Missouri River, headed for eastern Nebraska to find a home on the prairies, plans were made in the Scholte colony to do likewise. Beginning in 1860 prominent leaders in Pella, such as H. Hospers, A. C. Kuyper, W. Van Asch, W. Sleyster, and others began holding consultations and devising plans to raise a common fund for the purchase of land.[4] Because of the Civil War these plans did not materialize at that time, but still "the need to emigrate was felt more urgently and the desire to move grew stronger." We already know that in 1864 a number of families went to Oregon, although unusual motives led to their decision.

In 1867 a Frisian colonist at Pella, Jelle Pelmulder, started another movement to plant more colonies, which led in 1869 and subsequent years to the establishment of what was to become the most prosperous Dutch settlement in the United States: Sioux County, with Orange City at its center, in northwestern Iowa. This creation must be seen as the "daughter" of Pella, which is not a far-fetched biological simile but, just as in the case of the ancient Greeks, is an imagery that forced itself upon them naturally. For, as a Pella colonist tells us, in conversations concerning Pella and Orange City, they used to refer to them as "Mother and Daughter, revealing the close relationship and intimate bond that existed between the two."[5]

Later there were also colonists from Wisconsin and Michigan who migrated to the West or considered plans to do so. In 1865 [sic, 1856] the [Arend J.] Nagel family left the colony of Alto, Wisconsin, and migrated to Fillmore County in southeastern Minnesota and settled near the community of Greenleafton.[6] Especially in 1868 [sic, 1858] and succeeding years, several Wisconsin families followed their example. In Michigan there were several who went to Kansas in 1868 and subsequent years. In 1869 a pioneer by the name of Jan Deters took a homestead at Oak Creek in one of the most northerly counties of Kansas.[7] In the period 1868–1870, Netherlanders trekked from both Wisconsin and Michigan to South Lancaster County in Nebraska where, as in Kansas and other western areas, the vast prairies were made available as homesteads to the colonists by the federal government, especially to those who had fought on the side of the Union in the Civil War.[8]

There are no records of any organization or any specific leadership in these movements, as was the case with the trek from Pella and environs. Each family was usually on its own; at most a few families joined together in this effort. Thus the Netherlanders were in danger of becoming widely scattered. Van Raalte was very concerned about this tendency and made efforts to prevent it. Following the example of Hospers and Pelmulder in Iowa, he endeavored to bring together an organized group to form a new colony in a new place and, oddly enough, he selected a location not in the West but in the South, in the state of Virginia. In contrast with the outstanding success of the Sioux County colony, the settlement of the Michigan Netherlanders in Virginia proved to be a dismal failure.

Without underestimating or downgrading the pioneering spirit of the other Dutch colonies, it remains undeniably true that Pella made the greatest contribution to the development of the Farther West. Other western settlements, which perhaps were not as impressive as Sioux County, were also the offspring of Scholte's prairie colony. This is all the more remarkable in view of the fact that the immediate vicinity of Pella was very fertile and productive while the number of Dutch settlers was not large. There were more Netherlanders living in the less productive, mixed prairie-and-forest colonies of Wisconsin, while the greatest number of our fellow Dutch, who were also the least affluent, had elected to settle in Michigan, the least fruitful area of all. In 1850 there were 1,008 Dutch-born colonists in Iowa, 1,157 in Wisconsin, and 2,542 in Michigan. By 1870 the number had risen to 4,513 in Iowa, 5,990 in Wisconsin, and 12,599 in Michigan. (Regrettably, there are no records of the numbers of Dutch-born in Michigan and Wisconsin for the year 1860, but in Iowa they totaled 2,615.) Thus one would have expected to find the westward movement the strongest in Holland and the least urgent in Pella; yet the opposite proved to be true.

It is important to try to account for this. There were various factors involved. In the first place, as early as 1856, there was no longer cheap land available (cheap by American standards) in all of Marion County, in which Pella was situated. In 1856, one of the colonists wrote: "There is no more unsold land to be found here."[9] This does not mean that all of the land was under cultivation; for many years vast fields lay untouched, displaying "the luxuriant growth sown by the hand of Nature." These fields were owned by land speculators who had observed Pella's phenomenal growth and expected it to continue and spread. In addition, the discovery of coal deposits in various areas and the westward extension of the railroads would make the farmland increase in value, and the wealthy land buyers quickly bought up all remaining acreage.

But the thrifty Netherlanders were not ready to part with their hard-earned money and see it end up in the pockets of land speculators. They found the prices asked for by speculators all the more unreasonable because in 1854 they already knew and commented that "farther west, as far as the Missouri River, with few exceptions, the prairie lay unbroken."[10] The price of land increased more slowly in the Michigan and Wisconsin colonies because these areas were not as productive and also because they were further away from the large transcontinental roads of that time. Both of these two factors were most evident in Michigan. Also, one should not forget that the forests demand much more tedious hand labor than the prairies. This was most clearly demonstrated among the Dutch in Michigan, where Holland was almost exclusively a forest area in sharp contrast to

Pella and also, although to a lesser degree, to the mixed forest-and-prairie character of many Wisconsin settlements. Above all, one must remember that the farms were small in Michigan, larger in Wisconsin, and largest in Pella. In these three areas the farms averaged 80, 120 and 160 acres, respectively. This is another reason why Pella felt more cramped for space than did the other settlements.

We repeatedly observe that among the Dutch prairie dwellers it was not only those who possessed no land of their own who moved but also the owners of developed farms. Repeatedly they were willing to sell their land quickly and go elsewhere; as we have seen, this behavior was also true of many Americans. This tendency, while not unknown, was much less evident among the forest colonists. The well-known geographer, Albrecht Penck, sees in this a deeper, psychological basis, which he stated as follows: In contrast to a prairie-dweller, a forest-dweller feels a greater attachment to his land because of his greater investment of time and hard labor in making his soil productive. "*Der Waldbewohner haftet an der Scholle, die er unter Mühe nutzbar macht, rodet oder abbrennt.*" [The forest-dweller clings to his plot of ground which he has made arable with hard toil by clearing it of trees that he has cut down or burned down.][11]

The influence of the forest is seen in yet another aspect. It hampered travel and isolated the Holland colony in Michigan and to a somewhat lesser degree the Wisconsin settlements even more than they already were because of their out-of-the-way location. How influential this was we already saw in the wanderlust of the Pellians that was strongly stimulated, if not generated, by the sight of many Americans and others moving away. We should, in this respect, remember the forties, which saw so many people move at home and abroad, and the factor of a "mob mind" that can be so suggestive and overpowering: "Everyone is moving. We should be going too." Yet all these considerations do not completely explain why it was a Pella and not a Holland creation that became the most prosperous Dutch colony in the United States and one of its most prominent agricultural centers. In addition to the geographical factors we have delineated and their influence upon the colonists, there are other more fundamental forces at work.

At this point I must refer again to the spiritual differences that became evident among the Pella, Wisconsin, and Michigan colonists. The Michigan colony had comparatively few educated people, but in Pella, there were many. By educated is meant a general outlook and comprehension of life, not formal education and book learning. These qualities seemed to be present in Pella among even the least sophisticated settlers. Examples are the shoemaker K. Van Stigt, a chronicler, and the oft-quoted S. A. Sipma, a laborer and writer of stirring and pithy letters. Such remarkable individuals have not appeared among the Michigan colonists.

I have often said that the immigrants are selection material; it is usually the most stalwart and most enterprising individuals who emigrate. However, there are exceptions. Unusual circumstances often lead to migration, too. In fact, sometimes even a lack of energy does! On closer examination one cannot escape the conclusion that in Michigan, more than in Iowa, there were Netherlanders who left their homeland not as a result of careful deliberation but out of religious fanaticism or driven by the "mob mind" (everyone else is doing it). If in Michigan a certain idealism prevailed— "God wills it!"—in Iowa, by contrast, a majority of the colonists were influenced by more realistic considerations, after having weighed the situation and themselves long and carefully. To select one example out of many, Jan Nollen, later mayor of Pella and a member of the influential Nollen family of both Pella and Sioux County, tells us: "It was only after many years of hesitation and much deliberation that we decided to take the great step" and settle in the Scholte colony.[12]

In many respects the Pellians, more than the Michigan colonists, were a selection, or rather, another product of selection. Their outlook was broader and more matter-of-fact, and they were usually more independent, which becomes apparent in the very different position Scholte had among them, compared with that of Van Raalte in Michigan. The Iowans were religious as well as the Michigan people, but the most fanatical, although also idealistic, pioneers, were found in Holland and vicinity. The fury of raging religious discord swept through the Michigan colony, but at the same time it is here and not in Pella that the love for the missionary movements originated. These contrasts, apparent from the very beginning, undoubtedly were influenced in varying degrees by their environment; however, one should be very cautious in diagnosing and evaluating them.

Although the experiences in America broadened, rather than deepened, the concepts of both groups, their rate of development varied according to the environment. The wide horizons on the prairies seemed to promote broader life-views; the dense Michigan forests seemed to limit them. The strenuous and exhausting battle with the "children of Anak" and the endless labors in the somber woods deepened one's spiritual life and made idealism flourish abundantly, while the so-much-easier existence on the broad, sunny, treeless prairies trivialized (and materialized) the life there. The prevailing opinion in America, that all pioneers are materialists,—"like all pioneers, Idahoans are materialists," said a gifted American recently[13]— was much more true of the prairie colonists than the forest colonists. This is probably the reason why the two preachers, Van Raalte in the forests and Scholte on the prairies, became so divergent, although primarily it was their character: Van Raalte, the spiritual idealist above all, and Scholte, the materialist and politician involved in business.

This is also probably the reason why the new leaders, as far as they developed among the youths in Michigan, felt themselves drawn more to religious, rather than business careers. In the church, the school, and the mission field they found the fulfillment of their ideals. On the other hand, in Pella the young adults became involved in the various local government offices—township, city, county, and others—and the political systems associated with them. This makes it easier to understand why one of their own, "the young Hospers," a born leader, emerged when the first movement to expand began in Pella and many energetic colonists decided to undertake for a second time the difficult and arduous task of pioneering in northwestern Iowa. He was supported by a nucleus of enterprising young men who had gained their experience and made their mark partly by having fought in the Civil War and partly by having gone through the rigors of pioneer life once before. However, once they were established in the new area and looked for spiritual leadership they found it not in Pella but in Michigan—with Dominie Seine Bolks, the founder of the village of Overisel in the Van Raalte colony, and who was now an old man.

In Michigan after the Civil War, many were also attracted by the new opportunities in other areas. But because there were so extremely few intellectuals among them at the time of their arrival in America, there were initially no leaders among these new trekkers who pursued ideals of a somewhat higher order, even though they still became materialistic in the end. So we see that although Van Raalte was now old but still full of energy, he wanted to take in hand the direction of this new movement and raise the general level of colonization. He wanted to make of these newer settlements focuses—ignition points—of mission outreach. But Van Raalte apparently overestimated his physical resources and was finally compelled to stay in Michigan and give up his plans. This was offset by a few young seminary graduates, the first alumni of Hope College, who became preachers in the new settlements and performed courageous and self-sacrificing mission service there. However, a leader with material interests, of the type and caliber of Hospers in the Sioux County colony, did not arise in these Michigan-sponsored settlements, and in consequence, the colonies failed partially in Nebraska and totally in Virginia.

It is characteristic that, in contrast with the settlements established in the forties, there was no longer one general leader in either the spiritual or material realms in the settlements we shall discuss now. This was not only because men like Van Raalte or Scholte no longer stood out among the younger element, but also because the young ones were more Americanized and would probably no longer have tolerated such a type of leadership. Like so many pioneers, they had become too individualistic and, to an even greater degree, too democratic.

When we retrace the origin and development of the fascinating Sioux County colony, which was largely due to the Dutch colonists in Pella and must be viewed particularly as Pella's creation *par excellence*, we are immediately aware that we are dealing here with an exceptional class of people—not exceptional in the cultural sense but in the physical and psychological sense. We may speak here of a selection with more justification than in the colonies that we have dealt with so far. It was the most adventurous and usually the most enterprising people who undertook to migrate further, which is not to say that those who remained behind were less capable. Quite the contrary! Among the latter there were those who had been successful, particularly through their initiative, their energy, and their development; they had "made it," and had even attained a sense of satisfaction and fulfillment that stamped them as spiritually superior. Here, as in every migration movement, we must evaluate those who remained behind as well as those who ventured forth, each according to his worth, and acknowledge with E. A. Ross: "To the wilderness go not the brainiest or noblest or highest bred, but certainly the strongest and the most enterprising."[14]

B. Preparations in Pella for a New Settlement

To "the strongest and the most enterprising" class belonged undoubtedly those Netherlanders who for a second time embarked upon a pioneering venture, this time in northwest Iowa. A businessman from the Netherlands, who sojourned in Pella at that time, attended one of the meetings at which the new pioneers discussed their plans and later said: "One seldom sees such an assembly of vigorous sons of the Netherlands: robust Groningers and Frisians, on whose faces one sees expressed honest character and inflexible will, hardy Zeelanders and Hollanders who still possess the old Batavian facial features. In a word, it is as if the strongest and most energetic element of our nation is present in Iowa."[15] Truly, this was selection material!

In 1855 the above-mentioned Frisian, Jelle Pelmulder, joined the Scholte colony near the Skunk River.[16] He was "a teacher of the second rank" but soon decided to become a farmer instead. He helped to consolidate and carry forward the oft-discussed plans to establish a new colony. In 1867 and 1868, with characteristic Frisian thoroughness, he gathered information from various sources, negotiated with land offices, arranged meetings in Pella, and became the first one to draft definite plans for the formation of a new Dutch colony in northwest Iowa. These meetings were attended by many interested persons. According to the report of a Dutch businessman living in Pella at that time, even in his view the price of land was rising at a "dreadful" rate because of the railroad system stretching ever further westward.[17] (Land that in 1847 cost $2.50 to $5 per acre sold for $40 to $60 twenty years later.) At that price many could not buy land in the area, while the rental of farms also became more and more difficult as the years went by. Those interested in moving often met with H. Hospers, who was for a long time the only real estate dealer in Pella. They appointed a committee of four trusted men, experienced farmers, "who had already weathered many storms of life," to go to northwest Iowa and make inquiry concerning the suitability of the soil there.[18]

At this point it is important to note that of the four committee members, J. Pelmulder, H. Muilenburg, S. A. Sipma, and H. J. Van der Waa, the last two had served in the Union army in the Civil War, while Muilenburg's father had fought in the Napoleonic Wars. Their life on the vast prairies, and even more so the great distances they had to travel to reach the "surrounding" towns, had conditioned their thinking, at least in economic matters, to an equal measure of "hugeness." The geographer, E. C. Semple writes, in confirmation of the views of Friedrich Ratzel: "The small territorial standards of the early European settlers here became profoundly modified by American continental conditions."[19] This applied even more to those who had fought in the Civil War and had crisscrossed the United States from north to south. Especially in them "the bigness of the West was being absorbed into their mental constitution." It is therefore not accidental that although Pelmulder was the best educated, the veteran soldier Van der Waa became the leader of the investigating committee and also later was often given the chief responsibility. Van der Waa, Sipma, and several other war veterans among the Dutch colonists who took part in the conquest of the prairies, demonstrate the accuracy of Ratzel's conclusion which he expressed in his *Politische Geographie* [*Political Geography*]: "*der Krieg doch immer eine grosze Schule der Fähigkeit der Raumbewältigung (ist) geblieben*" [War was and always remained a great school, a training ground, that developed the space-conquering ability].[20]

Van der Waa, a tenant farmer born in Gelderland, like so many others, had not been able to buy any land near Pella. He and his wife decided to move to northwest Iowa and take possession of a homestead at Storm Lake. This decision had brought him into contact with H. Hospers and others of like intentions and resulted in his appointment to the investigating committee.[21]

In April, 1869, the four of them set out on their exploratory journey. Van der Waa had rigged his farm wagon as a covered wagon, a real prairie schooner, for the month-long journey across the plains, and he had replaced his horses with hardier mules. However, the mules were not harness-broken and it took several hours to get them hitched up. For safety's sake they were not unhitched again during the whole trip. They soon came to the end of the marked roads and struck out into untrodden territory, crossing creeks and rivers without benefit of bridges. Most of the time they "navigated" with a compass; at times they followed for some distance the surveyor poles marking the route of a prospective railroad. After several difficult days they arrived at Fort Dodge on the upper reaches of the Des Moines River, where they stopped for their first soil analysis. This proved disappointing and they continued further northwest. They came to a river swollen to flood stage by spring rains and endeavored to direct the mules across it, which proved dangerous to both men and animals. At first the mules were not able to pull the wagon up the steep bank on the opposite side, so they attached chains from the wagon pole to the wheels and dug and pulled the wagon up and across and finally reached a small town, Storm Lake, on Saturday evening. The next day being the Sabbath, they rested. On Monday they continued to Cherokee. They were ferried across the small Sioux River, paying $5 for the service, because the high water had washed away the bridges, as at so many other places. The area they were now in was excellent quality soil and very thinly populated. The committee examined it closely, checking the soil, the subsoil, and the drainage. They decided to try to buy several townships and headed for the land office at Sioux City. They spent Sunday in the village at Melbourne, where they attended church services and listened to a sermon in the German language which, although they did not understand all of it, comforted and edified them sufficiently.

On Monday, two weeks after they had left Pella, they arrived at Sioux City, and the following morning they went to the land office. Here unfolded an American drama that was typical of the times. The land office was due to open at nine o'clock, but long before that time a great crowd of prospective land buyers had gathered before the door, pushing and shoving, each trying to be first in line. Some wanted the same piece of land and this repeatedly resulted in fist fights and races to the desired quarter-sections! The Netherlanders got their turn about noon and presented their applications. They were given an appointment later in the day for a calmer discussion and toward evening were admitted by a back door. They requested that an area from ten to fifteen miles west of Cherokee, on both sides of a projected railroad, be reserved for them. They also learned that large areas in Sioux, Lyon, and O'Brien counties were available for an extensive settlement.

Satisfied with the information, the delegates returned to Pella after an absence of four weeks. A general meeting was called for early June, 1869, and some two hundred interested persons attended. The committee gave an enthusiastic report. Indeed, they could hardly find words adequate enough to describe the attractiveness and fertility of the land at Cherokee. Nevertheless, some of those present rejected the whole idea. They objected that there was no wood there and that it was so far north. According to them it would be too cold to grow corn.[22] Some who had advocated a more southerly location had previously sent a delegation of three men to Texas to look into the possibilities there. However, in New Orleans the three were taken in by a clever con man and lost all their money, so they were compelled to return to Pella without having accomplished their purpose![23]

Among the prospective migrants were some who preferred southwest Iowa, but when it came to a vote the majority were in favor of the northwest, chiefly because so much more government land was available there.[24] Later in June another meeting was held and decisions were made and recorded. As many as eighty-six Pella farmers signed up for the acquisition of homesteads while thirteen others committed themselves to buying at once as much as 80 to 480 acres each—a total of thousands of acres. They agreed to call the settlement to be laid out "New Holland," and also appointed a new committee to take care of that work. L. Van der Meer, H. J. Van der Waa, D. Van den Bosch, and H. Hospers were asked to serve on this committee and to proceed with the plans on behalf of the colonists

Hospers then went to Sioux City by railway, by way of Des Moines and Council Bluffs, to get more information and to study the government land charts and surveyor's maps. In the meantime the other three members of the committee started out again with Van der Waa's mules and prairie schooner—as if there was no such thing as distances! In the land office they learned that the land they had applied for near Cherokee had been bought up by speculators who knew that the Netherlanders wanted the land. They hoped to sell it to them at a pretty profit.

The Dutchmen decided to look into the possibilities in Sioux County. In Sioux City they bought supplies enough for three weeks on the open prairie and set out for Junction City, accompanied by a government surveyor. Junction City (now called Le Mars) consisted of one single building, a store. From this point they headed north along the babbling Floyd River, through territory where only a few settlers lived, until they reached the borderline of Sioux County. Here the land exceeded their expectations. "There were no roads, no homes, no trees. Nothing but gently rolling, magnificent, rich, fat prairie soil. Without any doubt this was the unanimous choice of the committee: 'Here is the place'!" they said, as reported by Hospers.[25] With a state land chart in their hands and with the surveyor's compass as a guide, they traversed several townships, looking for the government's section markers. As they went along they marked their trail with small piles of sand, to help them find their way back more easily. They selected and marked no less than thirty-eight sections, also a town site, and named the future colony "Holland." Only after all this was finished to their satisfaction did they go back to the land office at Sioux City—a veritable boom town, which at that time was the center for all those wishing to settle in the Sioux River area.

Before they left Pella, the committee had been given a mandate to assign in advance to each prospective colonist his piece of property. For that purpose they went immediately to the office of the surveyor, L. Wynn, where took place an interesting demonstration of the method by which pioneers became landowners in the United States. In 1864 Congress had granted to the builders of the St. Paul and Sioux City Railroad all the odd-numbered sections of land on both sides of the projected railroad to a depth of ten sections |or ten miles|. The area selected by the Hollanders included many of the even-numbered sections within the ten-mile limit. We have already seen that the oft-mentioned Homestead Act allowed a would-be purchaser 80 acres (or 160 if he was a war veteran).* However, within the railway grant homesteads were limited to 80 acres. In addition to the 80-acre homesteads, people could pre-empt an additional 160 acres, according to the Pre-emption Act.

The colonization committee wished to make it possible for members of the same family or friends to buy property in close proximity to one another

---

*The Homestead Act of 1862 had always permitted up to 160 acres to all eligible persons, except within the alternate sections of railroad lands.

and to enable homesteaders to enlarge their holdings through pre-emption as one continuous piece of property. To facilitate this arrangement the following method was used: the committee inscribed the numbers of the sections on small tickets and put them together in a box. The names of the applicants were written on other small pieces of paper and put into another box. One of the members of the committee then drew out of the box, at random, a section number ticket and at the same time another drew out of the other box a piece of paper with the name. If the number on the ticket was 37 then the person X., whose name was on the corresponding piece of paper, was assigned the northeast quarter of Section 37 and he might choose which friends or relatives would occupy the remaining three quarters.[26] After having complied with all the regulations, three of the members of the committee started back to Pella, while Hospers stayed behind in Sioux City to fill out the necessary legal papers at the land office, to deposit the sworn statements, and to make sure that the homestead applications were all filled out with the correct names.[27]

In the fall of that same year of 1869, eighteen or twenty horse-drawn wagons, each with four to six men, left Pella for the new unoccupied colony to take possession of their homesteads or pre-emptions. The law required that the property be personally occupied by the new owner for at least two weeks before it became legally his. During the winter of 1869–1870 the new colony was the main topic of conversation in Pella. Many were making preparations for the undertaking in the spring.

C. The New Colony

The first families left Pella in the months of April and May of 1870. For many the farewell was painful. Those who had come to Pella in 1847 and struggled through all the hardships of those early days did not relish the prospect of doing it all over again. The only motive that impelled them was consideration for the future of their growing children. Pella had become very dear, especially to many "of those dignified older people"; to renounce it all and move once more into the hardships of an unfamiliar territory was difficult emotionally as well as physically.[28]

The energetic Van der Waa, who had already made the journey three times, was entrusted with the leadership of the first wagon train. The group, in addition to Van der Waa, was comprised of G. Van de Steeg, Sr., H. J. Luymes, A. Van der Meide, and the Beukelman brothers, together with their mother and sister, the first women of the Sioux County colony. J. Pelmulder led the second contingent, most of them Frisians. A third group was directed by L. Van der Meer and D. Van den Bosch, leaders with whom we became familiar in an earlier episode. This last train consisted of twenty or twenty-five teams, each wagon drawn by two, three, or four teams of oxen. Additional parties followed later in the year, many consisting of fathers and their numerous sons. Some left their wives in Pella for the time being, but otherwise it was a veritable exodus.

A. Van der Meide relates that it took their group nineteen days to travel the approximately three hundred miles, most of it cross-country without roads, through swamps and creeks and across rivers on poorly constructed bridges. The second day of their journey the Beukelman family almost came to disaster. Their horses and wagon fell twelve feet off a bridge into a stream below. Fortunately the stream was only two feet deep and the outfit was not a total loss. The only fatalities were the chickens they had taken along. The wagon had to be repaired, their wet clothing dried, and some minor injuries bandaged. Our courageous fellow countrymen were delayed for a day. Warned by this experience they traveled more slowly—one day they covered only three miles. Every time thereafter when they had to cross water, a slough, a swamp, as a precautionary measure the wagons were unloaded and the freight was carried across by hand and reloaded on the other side. However, no complaints were heard, and no wish to return was expressed. They had full confidence in their leader Van der Waa, who had assured them there was no better or more fruitful land under the sun than that in Sioux County, Iowa.[29]

Having arrived in the promised land, they camped at a spot three-quarters of a mile north of present-day Orange City and the following day they set off to examine the area assigned to them. They had the land office chart as a guide and tried to follow the section lines, but even with that help they almost lost their way on the unbroken prairie. Indeed, Van der Waa had not exaggerated in the least. The following day the other groups also arrived, a total of sixty families, most coming from Pella and environs.

However, not all the newcomers were from Pella. Henry Hospers had strongly recommended the new undertaking in *Pella's Weekblad* and also in other Dutch-language newspapers in America. As a result, families in Illinois, Michigan, and Wisconsin also wanted a homestead in Sioux County. In the spring of 1870 two families, W. De Vos and S. De Bruin, left Chicago in prairie schooners headed for Sioux County. Van der Waa and some friends encountered them on the lonely prairie, during the long and difficult trip, and they helped them go on.[30] That same spring Tjeerd Heemstra with his family of nine children came from Michigan. They left the Van Raalte colony at Holland after having lived there for twenty-three years and came to the new colony in Iowa, where he was destined to play an important role.[31]

From the Wisconsin settlements E. J. G. Bloemendaal first came to Pella, where we have met him before. From there, in 1870 he also went to Sioux County "to take a quick look," with a view to a possible purchase of land. He spent three days there and reported: "The land here was an undulating prairie, rising and falling in gentle slopes, a quarter or half a mile in length and with ascents and descents of forty or fifty feet. . . . When we stood on the slopes an enchanting panorama unfolded before us. As far as the view stretched, we saw flat country. On the far horizon we saw a range of hills. When we stared long at the landscape in the bright and lucid light it seemed as if everything began to dance before our eyes." The soil turned out to be so rich that it did not need any fertilizer for the first twenty years.

In 1871 Bloemendaal decided to move out there. A few farmers from Wisconsin accompanied him and were so amazed at the soil in Iowa that they each immediately bought 160 acres of railway-grant land at $7 per acre. When they returned to their families in Alto, "they had nothing but praise for the region." Many others caught the migration fever and also decided to buy land in Iowa or to apply for homesteads.[32] As a result, in 1871 and subsequent years many Wisconsin colonists trekked to northwest Iowa. Among those arriving in 1871 were the families Van den Berg, Schut, Greevenhof, Franke, Vermeer, Wayenberg, Lagendijk, and others. Most of these originally came from the provinces of Gelderland and Overijsel, while others who came from Pella in 1870 were natives of Holland and Friesland.[33]

To those who came from Michigan and Wisconsin, where they were accustomed to being in the woods, it was far more courageous to adapt to a prairie environment than for those who had come from Pella. They could not get used to the total absence of trees and found the adjustment difficult. It is not surprising, therefore, that one of the Wisconsin settlers, who with three other families was the first to settle in the area west of the West Branch River (one of the sources of the Floyd River), said at his wits' end in June, 1871, "that even if I could scoop up gold with a shovel here, I could not stay!" Others felt as he did, yet they all stayed.[34]

The breaking of the prairie sod under the Homestead Law had already been started by many a settler in 1869. It was pursued by all of them in order to begin subsequently with the sowing of flax, then the most lucrative field crop, followed by wheat, barley, oats, and corn.[35] Everyone was so occupied with farm work that they gave themselves very little time to build houses. Many a family spent their first summer in their prairie schooners. The household activities were performed on the open prairie. The cooking was done on a stove set up outside on the ground, for convenience sake, next to the wagon. Some made dugouts, which were simply big holes in the ground, covered over with some tree trunks and finished with branches and pieces of sod. Somewhat more stately were the sod houses or sod huts, also called mud huts, like those already known in Pella's pioneer days. They built solid walls from chunks of sod. The roof also was made of sod. The huts had usually two openings, a door and a window. Those were the only items requiring a cash outlay, less than $1.50! Such a sod house generally had one single room that served as parlor, kitchen, bedroom, and storeroom. Some built a dividing wall of sod to provide separate sleeping quarters. If the family was large, the beds were stacked along the wall two or three high. The furnishings were also very modest, generally a chest or trunk in the middle of the room in which were stored the household linens and the family clothing. It also served as cupboard and table. The colonists improvised seats from sod. For fuel they used the long prairie grass, especially the grasses from the swamps, which they more or less wove together.

One of the advantages of this type of dwelling, besides its low cost, was that it was comparatively cool during the heat of summer and comparatively warm during the severe winter. For that reason they were generally dug out and built up on the south or east side of a knoll for protection against the ice-cold northwestern storms. Equally primitive were the stables and shelters that were either dug out or "built" in the same way for horses, oxen, and cattle.[36] One problem, even greater here than in Pella, was the lack of trees to provide lumber for building. There were willows growing along the bank of the Floyd River but they were no thicker than ordinary bean poles. Still people came from far and wide to get them and in a short time even these were gone.[37]

Only the wealthiest were able to afford the luxury of buying sawed lumber. The nearest place where this was available was at Le Mars, a distance of eighteen miles, which was a six-hour journey from the colony. Those who could not afford to buy lumber and who found the Floyd River willows inadequate went twenty-five miles northwest where the wider Rock River flowed. The trip to pick up whatever one could find took several days and was also dangerous. Two colonists, G. Kleuvers and D. J. Wesselink, tried to wade through the river to cut a few trees growing on a sandbank. Unfortunately they were caught in a whirlpool and drowned, leaving behind their wives and many children.[38]

When the farm work was finished for the season and winter was approaching, the colonists needed to provide fuel for their stoves. It sometimes happened that one who had gone out with his oxen to get a load of wood was caught in an early snowstorm. The sky might be completely clear. Suddenly—so relates the pioneer, G. Draayom, who had gone several times to get a load of wood,—a small cloud would appear in the northwest or west and an hour later he was enveloped in such a storm "that I could not see more than six feet ahead."[39]

Before the Netherlanders came to the Rock River valley there were Americans already living there. They had been attracted by two factors: first, this land lay outside the twenty-mile-wide railroad grants and they were able to buy homesteads of 160 acres; secondly, there were some trees along the river, the only ones in a treeless region.[40] The Americans now denied the Netherlanders access to the trees, which led to big fights. They used pitchforks to try to drive away "our people" and wounded some with hatchets. They concealed gunpowder in the already cut wood to scare the pioneers and their wives.[41] However, the Netherlanders did not give up the battle. They demonstrated plenty of the pioneering spirit themselves and the wood hauling continued in spite of every obstacle.

All these problems explain why the building of houses proceeded very slowly. When K. Van Stigt came from Pella in October of 1870 to visit his friends and fellow pioneers of 1847 in their new environment, he found only a few in Sioux County who lived in houses built of lumber. Only his host, C. Jongewaard, J. Pelmulder, and a few others were so fortunate.[42] In the spot that had previously been selected and platted for the future "*stad*" of the colony there was not yet a single building. Only a load of planks gave hints of the future plans.

Before the pioneers left Pella they had decided to name the city "New Holland" or "Hope." But after they had arrived and had seen the lay of the land, how the city was laid out, after the example of Pella, on a high ridge between the Floyd and West Branch rivers, they decided to call it "Orange City" instead.

The colonists of 1847 had named their city "Pella." In ancient times, when the conquering Romans were threatening to destroy Jerusalem, the disciples of Jesus fled to Pella, which became a synonym for "city of refuge." The Netherlands colonists likewise thought of America as a place of refuge from the religious persecution they had endured in their homeland. Hence, *Pella*! However, after some years in foreign land the bitter memories had faded. Attachment to the old fatherland revived and was expressed in a single word: *Oranje* [the name of the royal house of the Netherlands]. The new "*stad*" was therefore called "Orange City" and the main street, "William" [after King Willem van Oranje], while the whole colony was divided into two townships, named Nassau [Oranje-Nassau being the title of the Dutch royal house] and Holland.

The original city site comprised a quarter section located in the middle of the colony. The main north-south streets were named William, Sioux, Pella, Washington, and Prairie. In the center of the city a square block was reserved for a future park, as in Pella. The remaining blocks were divided into lots, 50 by 125 feet. One-third of all the lots were given to Henry Hospers as a remuneration for all his labors. Before they left Pella, sixty colonists had each paid $10 down to reserve a building lot in the town site. The buyers were required to plant trees in front of their lots, to which we owe the present-day rural attractiveness of Orange City; it is like an oasis on the otherwise almost treeless prairies.[43]

The first residents of the city were the family of A. J. Lenderink, father, mother, and son. Lenderink, a carpenter, built the first house, his own residence, in 1870, and thereafter a very simple school building. There was yet no store. However, Tjeerd Heemstra had begun a retail business for the convenience of his neighbors on his farm two miles from the city. In the spring of 1871 H. Hospers, at that time still living in Pella, sent a contractor, D. Gleysteen, to erect for him a store building on the north side of the town square. It was almost finished when it was destroyed by a heavy storm but was soon rebuilt. Grits, barley, rice, peas, flour, fish, coffee, sugar and syrup, etc., were available there, but no business was done on credit. Butter and eggs were accepted in exchange. Most of the homesteaders possessed only their fertile fields and anticipated a good harvest, but they had no cash. Therefore, Hospers devised a new medium of exchange. From time to time he issued so-called "store-orders," which in Orange City were accepted as a kind of "fractional currency." For these I.O.U.s [*schuldbriefjes*] he often allowed people to plow the prairies for him, or else he simply waited for them to bring him the cash some day. But he sometimes had to wait a very long time and sometimes forever![44]

Other buildings were constructed about the same time. [Egbert] Van Olst built a sod house with a plank roof and beside it a forge "and soon one heard the blows of his hammer on the anvil." J. Vos opened a shoe store that also served as a barber shop on Saturday to spruce up the men a little. "Mother Mouw" opened an inn, somewhat extravagantly called a hotel. By the end of 1871 there were twenty-four town dwellers. In 1872 more houses were built by H. Hospers, T. Heemstra, and others, and then—so typically American—Hospers opened the first bank, the Orange City Bank. An office was opened by a lawyer, a doctor came in, and in the meantime a parsonage was also completed. With the addition of a second blacksmith and a second tavernkeeper the number of inhabitants rose to fifty. The following year W. Sleyster, C. Hospers, A. J. Betten, and P. Ellerbroek opened stores, while Pierce and Lewis opened a land office and A. K. Webb a law office, etc. The number of homes also increased and the number of residents reached a total of 151.[45]

The environs of the "*stad*" also gradually began to change in appearance. The first winter was unusually mild, and the colonists, who until now had been completely occupied with working the soil and sowing and later on bringing in the first harvest of wheat, "sod corn," potatoes, and vegetables, were now able to concentrate on the matter of house building, except for a few days of severe cold. On the homesteads more houses, however modest, gradually began to appear. When Van Stigt visited the colony for a second time in the spring of 1871, he said he found it "already greatly changed."[46] They had also planted rows of trees to serve as windbreaks against the prevailing northwest winds. On many farms from one to five acres were allocated for that purpose and they received a reduction on their taxes as a stimulus for reforestation.

The second winter and those following were very severe. Several times the thermometer registered twenty to thirty degrees below zero Farenheit, and one time even forty below zero. Nevertheless, wood for fuel had to be obtained and they had to get through the cold somehow, even at the cost of frozen feet! They experienced for the first time those terrible snow-storms—blizzards. One time Bloemendaal was digging a well out on the prairie and was unexpectedly overtaken by such a storm: "It was mild and there was no wind. There were clouds and we heard a kind of buzzing sound. We stopped work to listen for a moment. But suddenly, before we realized it, a snowstorm was raging all around us. We had to start for home as fast as we could. We could not see fifteen paces ahead of us. The wind was fierce and cut like a knife in our faces. It was in one word an emergency situation."

The storm continued almost unabated for three days and with the same violence. Some acquaintances of our informant, on their way to Le Mars to get necessary supplies, were overtaken by the same storm. "They kept as close to each other as they could with their sleighs, yet they could not see one another. Their eyes filled with snow and had to be wiped constantly. Severe cold accompanied the storm. Since it was impossible to see where they were going on the flat prairie, they were at a loss what to do. Suddenly the horses disappeared in a snowbank. It seemed hopeless. As long as they could continue moving they felt they would eventually arrive somewhere but if they lost the horses it would be hopeless indeed! Fortunately, the horses got back on their feet and struggled through. How it happened none of them could explain but after some more effort they reached a farmhouse where they were given shelter. That saved them."

In such heavy snow years even the simplest tasks of the farmer became difficult. During the snowstorm described above many pigs and cattle had to be dug out from under the snow. It was impossible to provide the livestock with the necessary water. The barns and stables had been built a short distance from the house, after the American style. [In the Netherlands, many barns and homes are attached.] In some cases they could not be reached. Many a farmer, trying to get to his barn, only twenty or thirty meters [sixty or ninety feet] distant, lost his way! "Mother Mouw," the innkeeper of the colony, went out with a lantern one night to the stable twenty meters from her house to make sure the horses of her guests were protected. But she did not come back. The guests began to worry so ten or fifteen men went out to look for her. They found her more than an hour later, no more than twenty-five meters from the inn with the lantern still in her hand but her fingers, ears, and toes were frozen. If the search had been made later she would not have survived. Some houses were buried up to the roof and people had to dig a tunnel through the snow to get out![47]

Although the life of the farmer on the prairie was strenuous and precarious, rich harvests rewarded his hard labors during those early years. The soil truly was extremely fertile. In 1871 and 1872 the harvests were so plentiful they had more than they needed. Also, travel and transportation were made easier by the completion of another section of the St. Paul and Sioux City Railroad in 1872 through the valley of the Floyd River in the eastern part of the colony. The Hollanders in Sioux County now had their first railway station at East Orange, four miles east of Orange City. Fuel, building materials, and all kinds of necessities could now be easily shipped in by rail while grain could be shipped out more easily and more cheaply. As a result the price of land skyrocketed, a windfall for those who lived near the railroad, for example, for Bloemendaal. The colony anticipated a great future. Farmers came from far and wide to buy land.[48] By the end of 1872 there were already 1,500 residents

D. Religious and Political Life in Sioux County's First Years

In the founding of the colonies in Michigan and Marion County, Iowa, religious beliefs were an important element. This cannot be said to the same degree of the Sioux County settlements. Better economic conditions for themselves and their children were the basic and only motivations, reinforced by their experiences in America that had promoted an even stronger sense of independence. They were not directed and accompanied by a pastor as were the earliest pioneers, those of the forties. In fact, two years went by before they even attempted to secure a pastor of their own. Therefore, the assertion that was made at the fiftieth anniversary of the founding that the colonists brought with them "a burning desire to extend and promote the Kingdom of the Lord" may be considered as typically American exaggeration,[49] belied by the evidence of many people's acts, even though "faith and crime" can very well go together, as W. A. Bonger showed in the Netherlands.[50]

However that may be, I do not repudiate the sincerity of their convictions. On the contrary I readily accept the statement made by A. J. Betten, Jr., that from the very beginning the majority of the people honored their religious faith and considered the Book of Books to be the indispensable guide and standard for their lives.[51]

The colonists' first worship service, held on the first Sunday after their arrival on the open prairie, must have been a deeply moving experience. It reminds me of the episodes of the treks of the Boers in South Africa: the wagons were placed in a circle and church was held inside the circle, with the open sky for a roof and one of the colonists functioning as leader.[52] Later, services were held in the sod house of one of the brothers, M. Verheul, and thereafter in the school building.[53] In this school building K. Van Stigt from Pella conducted his first worship service on April 23, 1871, on the occasion of his second visit.[54] Occasionally visiting preachers from some other area filled in.

Classis Holland of the Reformed Church now accepted the colony as a mission post and sent Dominie J. Van der Meulen to be their missionary. Church attendance increased and on May 6, 1871, the first Reformed congregation was formally organized with thirty-four members in full communion. The elected elders were T. Heemstra, G. Van de Steeg, and M. Verheul; while S. Sipma, J. Pelmulder, and W. Van Rooyen served as deacons. Twice during the summer of 1871 a preaching service was held. One of the preachers was the seminary student E. Van der Hart, the other was Dominie [E.] Winter. In the autumn of 1871 they resolved to try to call a preacher of their own. It was unanimously decided to invite the old Michigan pioneer, Seine Bolks from Zeeland, Michigan.[55] Although they had not really expected Bolks to accept the call, on account of his age, he was ready and willing to take up again the challenge of being a frontier "shepherd and teacher" and in April of 1872 he came to Orange City. No longer standing in the shadow of the towering personality of Van Raalte, he revealed even more strongly than before his qualities of leadership, not only as a pastor but as a veritable popular leader. He functioned not only as a preacher but as a doctor and counselor, and in so doing he found, "through God's leading, his true life-task—a leader in the fullest sense of the word."[56]

Decades later one of Bolk's parishioners could still see in his imagination the dignified old man—a patriarch with snow-white hair and beard, all dressed in black, standing militarily erect in the pulpit. His eyes spat fire, his balled fist beat upon the Bible until the pages fluttered around, and words rolled from his lips. Without notes, without a timepiece (it was added with dry humor) there thundered across the prairie his warnings about hell, sin, and eternal damnation.[57] It struck home, literally and figuratively.

A spiritual revival followed in the remaining months of 1872, exactly as in Pella and elsewhere before. People came from even the most distant parts of the colony to listen to Bolks.[58] In the school building where the services were held there were not enough seats so the hearers brought chairs and benches from home. The farmers' wagons were placed just outside the opened windows and thus the "seating capacity" was enlarged.[59] The following year, the school directors allowed one side of the building to be breached and a wooden shed was built against the opening "so that everyone could see and hear the Preacher."

In 1872 membership in the church increased by 130 and the following year by 140 more, some by confession of faith and some by transfer of certificates. However, there were also some reverses; the congregation did not have a sanctuary of its own until 1875. That year their building fund was enlarged by "a gift of $3,000" from a lady in New York.[60]

Some members of the congregation found fault with Bolks. He was not orthodox enough, not "Dutch" enough. In 1871 twelve families with a total of fifty persons withdrew and formed a separate Christian Reformed Church. They were without a pastor of their own until 1877 when Dominie J. Stadt came to serve. His abusive prose I have noted in the first part of this book.[61]

On the other hand, there were also those who considered Bolks' preaching anything but stimulating. They too organized a separate congregation, a modernistic church, and surprisingly, they were the first of the two separate congregations to have their own church building already in 1873. Evidently the modernists here, like those in Grand Rapids and other places, were not comfortable in the fellowship of their orthodox countrymen. Their church was later remodeled into a dwelling and was destroyed a few years later in a fire.[62] Although it appears from the available figures that in those years not all the colonists were church members—both Reformed congregations together listed less than 200 members, while the colony totaled 1,500 persons—still it could be said that there was indeed an active, spiritual church life.

Very interesting in this connection is the scene described by M. Cohen

Stuart, who spent some time in America and was invited by Hospers to visit Orange City in November of 1873:

> It was Sunday—a Sunday I shall not soon forget.... What breadth of space— what stillness, what solemnity, what peace!... Around us was the small village of the settlers with some scattered wooden houses. Here and there, in the distance, one saw blue smoke rising from a green field, indicating a farmhouse half hidden among the undulating terrain. But look! Something is stirring! From miles away we see them approaching from all directions, the churchgoers to the morning service; here a fast buggy or an open wagon, yonder a slow ox-cart, or a horseback rider, sometimes a solitary amazon, a stout-hearted, young country woman, galloping across the fields—a pleasure to behold. But fast or slow they all arrive on time. Those coming the farthest seldom come late. We also go to the large "public square," so called with a sort of pride, where the settlers picture in their imagination already impres- sive municipal structures, but where one sees at this time only an empty space, surrounded by a few small houses and some newly-planted trees, overshadowed by *us*. But at the moment it is a very lively place. Horses and oxen are unhitched and tied to posts or are even allowed to run at large in the pasture. Small groups of men and women gather in front of the black- smith shop and church. The church is certainly not the kind of structure one would have expected to see! I'm sure it is the most insignificant place in which I ever preached—a small rectangular building constructed of rough wooden boards, perhaps ten meters long and five wide, with a stove in the middle and benches all around. That is the school part. At the back of the school they have added a shed, shaped like the crossbar of the letter T with rough unplaned boards on props for seats, and against the back wall, oppo- site the entrance, a chair and table for the preacher. The shed and school together constitute the church building.

Though the place was unimpressive, Cohen Stuart had seldom spoken to a more inspiring audience than those before whom he stood that morning: "... men exhibiting calm strength and firmness in carriage and posture; and women, some of whom are holding a nursing infant to their breast with hands folded in prayer in their lap, cradling their heart's dearest treasure, but therefore no less qualified for true praying!" And in the meantime the bleak winter sun sent a playful ray through the one small side window, illuminating the dark partition and "falling upon so many an earnest, silent, and devout upturned face."[63]

Orange City was the economic as well as the spiritual center of the colony. It became also the political center of a much larger area. The Netherlanders in Michigan had always wished their "*stad*" Holland had become the Ottawa County seat in place of the geographically much less favorably located Grand Haven. In the same way, the Pella colonists repeat- edly made serious attempts to have Pella promoted to the county seat of Marion County instead of Knoxville. Where they failed, the Hollanders in northwest Iowa succeeded. After only two years Orange City became the county seat of Sioux County. Various factors contributed to this decision—the scanty population of the area, the unreliability of the then-governing body consisting of a few adventurers interested only in their own advantage, the greater number of Netherlanders, and, more than anything else, the great feeling of self-esteem, the independent spirit of the latter.

E. A. Ross, whom I have repeatedly quoted, speaks of frontier selections, indicating that those who trek the farthest west are the most adventurous and also the most independent: "In the last Westernmost decanting of the pioneering breed, courage and love of independence reach their greatest intensity."[64] Certainly also our countrymen have demonstrated this. Many of the Dutch pioneers in Michigan, Wisconsin, Illinois, and in Marion County, Iowa, were courageous, tough, and tenacious. Yet, as far as this was possible, they were surpassed in all these qualities by the colonists who settled Sioux County. The first pioneers did not know what it meant to found a settlement when they arrived in America. Their perseverance deserves all praise. But those who ventured forth for the second time, knowing beforehand what was involved—men like Sjoerd Sipma and so many others—they were called prairie diamonds and their wives heroines.[65]

Although Sioux County had "already" been officially organized in 1852, it was too remote, too far from the trade routes of that day to attract many immigrants, while the monotony and immensity of the treeless prairies turned them off. In 1860 there were only ten residents in the entire county, in 1867 only 18, and in several of the adjoining counties none at all! But soon thereafter came the homesteaders, among whom were war veterans, and they chose to settle in the river valleys where there was at least some tree growth. In 1869, Sioux County had "already" 110 residents, most living near the Big Sioux and Rock rivers. The neighboring counties of Lyon and Osceola were still completely "empty." By contrast, in the valley of the Big Sioux River, a small town, Calliope, had come into existence and at the time the Netherlanders arrived in the spring of 1870, Calliope was the Sioux County seat, although there was only one organized township (Buncombe) in the whole county.[66]

The coming of the Netherlanders resulted in some changes. Many of these had been American citizens for several years. Their number soon equaled that of the American colonists. Especially after they had organized two townships of their own—Holland and Nassau soon afterwards—they demanded a voice in the county government. In August of 1870, only a few months after their arrival, they succeeded in electing one of their own number, Jelle Pelmulder, as clerk of the district court. Pelmulder held the office by popular choice for seventeen years; it was a longer term than any other Sioux County official has held ever since. Tjeerd Heemstra was elected to the Sioux County board of supervisors in October of 1870 and the following January 1st he became chairman of that board.

However, the Americans continued to hold the upper hand and used their powers for their own advantage. They repeatedly borrowed money in the name of the county and used the funds for their personal businesses. In the fall of 1871, the Netherlanders made a concerted effort to get more representation on the board of supervisors and nominated three candidates, all of whom were elected: Henry Hospers, who had moved permanently to Orange City in 1871, succeeded Heemstra as a member of the board of supervisors; A. J. Betten, Jr., as auditor; and J. W. Greattrax as treasurer.[67]

But when the three officials traveled on a very icy January First, 1872, to Calliope, a sled ride of twenty-three miles, to take their oath of office, only Hospers was allowed to take his seat (which he held until November 1877). The other two newly chosen officials were denied accreditation; their bonds were supposedly not high enough, were not properly signed, etc. Three times they attended a meeting and applied for recognition, but all three attempts were in vain despite Hospers' protests.

This turn of events greatly offended the colonists and increased the mistrust against the "administration" in Calliope. They decided to go there in a body and demand their rights by taking the law in their own hands if need be. One hundred fifty men, most of them Hollanders, gathered at Orange City to go from there by means of horse and ox-drawn sleighs to the county seat. A lawyer from Sioux City accompanied them. Their arrival at Calliope was greeted with alarm, especially by members of the board. The political bosses realized their days were numbered, some of them even attempted to flee to Dakota by crossing the ice-covered Big Sioux River, which was at the same time the border of the county and of the state. The chairman had harnessed his horses to his sleigh, intending to leave, but the Hollanders unhitched them again and tied them in the barn. They invited His Honor to come back to the quickly adjourned meeting and re-open the session and admit the elected officials. Judge Pendleton, supported by Hospers, tried to convince the remaining members of the board to give official recognition to Betten and Greattrax—again in vain. Meanwhile part of the sleigh-riders had grown hungry. In the commissary of the county building they found a vat full of excellent quality ham and bacon and appropriated it.

Finally Judge Pendleton shouted, "Boys, it's all up," and at this signal the Hollanders gathered all the books, papers, and records out of the drawers and files and packed them on their sleds, preparing to return with them to Orange City. At the last moment someone thought of the safe. They could not leave that behind! One of the sleighs was now backed against a section of the wall of the government "palace" where they knew the safe was located and— truly we are here in the Wild West!—with an axe they chopped through the wall, removed the safe and loaded it on the sleigh. Then the Netherlanders— 100 percent American in their actions!—started back across the prairie in a raging snowstorm, arriving at midnight at Orange City, some numb with cold and with frozen ears and noses. However, they had not been able to move the heavy safe across the West Branch River and it was left behind at that point.

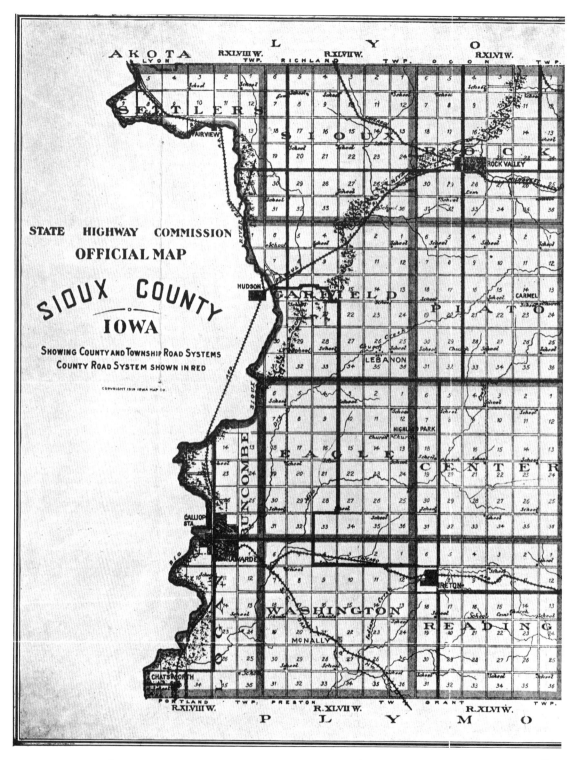

A map of Sioux County, Iowa. The very wide lines (colored blue on the
original) show the boundaries of the county and those of the rural townships.
The narrower, more darkly tinted lines (colored red on the original) show the

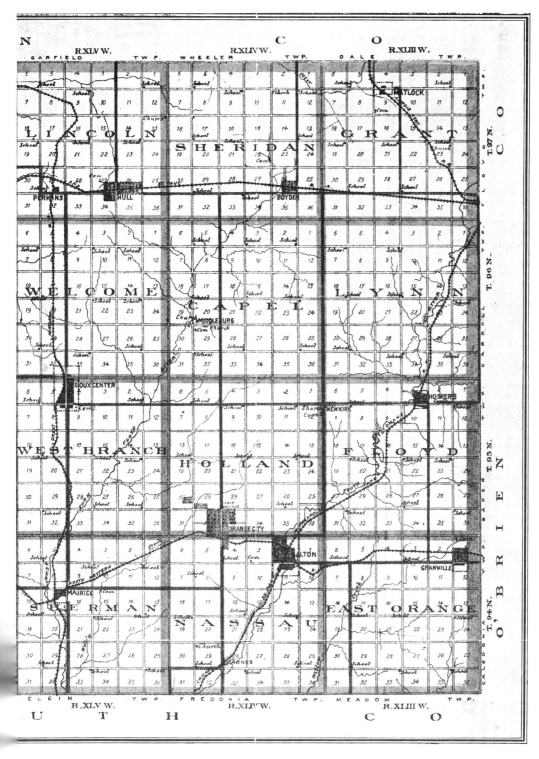

major roads (the county road system). The country roads which separate the numbered sections are shown by double lines.

The following morning Hymen Den Hartog went back and brought it into Orange City. A great crowd gathered to welcome it and fired a thousand shots into the air in celebration.

A few days later the sheriff arrived with the message that Betten and Greattrax had been formally recognized by the board and all disputes had been settled, but also with the mandate to bring back to Calliope the safe, the books, and the records, etc. He brought with him several ox-drawn sleighs. When all the sheriff's papers appeared to be legal and in good order, the Dutch sense of justice prevailed and they agreed to his request. But they also decided that they would continue to use all legal means to move the county seat to their "*stad*," to which the Westsiders, the Americans living in the western part of the county, were strongly opposed, but which the Eastsiders (the Netherlanders) and the Northsiders (the Hollanders, Germans and Americans) supported.

In the fall of 1872 another election was held in which the Netherlanders had a clear majority and as a result the county seat was now officially and legally moved to Orange City.[68] This was an important victory over the clique of "hunters and trappers" at Calliope, whose dealings, it was now revealed, had burdened the county with debt.

On January 6, 1873, the board of supervisors met for the first time in Orange City and Hospers was elected chairman. A few days later the district court also convened and it was learned that a change in administrative control was indeed overdue—the county was threatened with a $10,000 verdict, the result of fraudulent loans contracted by the "rascals" (as the colonists branded the high-minded bosses in Calliope). The debt itself was so large—$37,000—that in May of 1874 it was proposed that an extra annual tax of $10,000 be levied to pay it off. It was defeated by a vote of 194 to 117. The Dutch did not relish providing "atonement" for their American fellow citizens. Instead they voted to issue bonds in the amount of $60,000 for the construction of a courthouse in Orange City. The city itself pledged $15,000 toward that amount. In 1873 the contract for the construction was awarded to G. Dorsman, who erected it in 1874 in the city park area. However, the actual cost came to $100,000 and it is still today the most beautiful building in the city.[69]

Thus, by sheer forcefulness, by energetic initiative, the Netherlanders succeeded in fulfilling their objectives. Similar characteristics were demonstrated in the election of 1873 when, in addition to the previously mentioned county officials, they elected N. Jongewaard, one of their own countrymen, to be the sheriff.

That all these successes in the northwestern area did not go unnoticed in the rest of Iowa and were even considered impressive in the southeastern part of the state, is evident from a Keokuk newspaper, *The Gate City*: "The Dutch have taken Sioux County as effectually as they have Holland. Since going in they have changed the county seat, which the old manipulators do not like. They are building a new courthouse, new bridges, churches, etc."[70]

The transfer of administration led to the development of news media in the colony. On July 13, 1871, the first issue of the *Sioux County Herald* was printed by an American at Calliope. The fiftieth issue was published in 1873 in Orange City and even "began to talk some Dutch."[71]

So we see that the first newspaper in Orange City was not printed in the Dutch language but in English, which was true also of the first newspaper in the Van Raalte and Scholte colonies. It was not until several years after the colonies had been planted that a need was felt for a newspaper in the mother tongue. In all three colonies the initiative for a colonial newspaper was taken by an American and it was "only in Pella that the move was strongly encouraged by a Netherlander—Scholte." And when Hospers started publishing a Dutch-language paper, *De Volksvriend* [*Friend of the People*], it was not primarily intended for the colonists themselves. Its chief purpose was to advertise among Netherlanders in the motherland or in other areas of America the excellent possibilities of Sioux County and to contradict the slanderous rumors real estate speculators in other territories had spread concerning Iowa. But the newspapers soon came to be of equal interest to the residents of Sioux County. The decisions made by the county and state governments were translated and explained in the Dutch language by Hospers. But above all he told his countrymen about the frauds perpetrated by the Americans who had been in control—free-booters, buccaneers of the prairies, robbers—as the otherwise moderate and sedate leader called them.[72] He disclosed all the intrigues by which the dishonest Americans had involved Sioux County in debt and recommended that the debts not be paid. No one more competently defended the rights of the colonists than Hospers. He finally succeeded after endless negotiations in settling all legal claims and charges for $700.

After this, "Wild West" methods of administration no longer had a chance in Sioux County. At election time, Hospers drove his fellow country-men (who were not always such eager voters) to the polls to keep their share of officials in the administration, to the aggravation of the increasing number of Americans. Especially in the 1875 election there was great bitter-ness. The old Know Nothing spirit of former years seemed to revive. "Down with the Dutch" and "No Foreigners in Office" were the slogans, the battle cries of the Americans. But Hospers was happy with the election results. "Well done, Hollanders," he exulted in his newspaper. In the fall election two more Hollanders had been elected, and in 1876, out of the eleven county officials, six were Americans and five were Hollanders: J. Pelmulder, A. J. Betten, F. Le Cocq, S. Kuyper, and H. Hospers. Not a single German or Irishman was elected, although both nationalities had been living in Sioux County for years.

In the more important state political contests the majority of the colo-nists in Sioux County voted Republican, which was not the case in Pella, the mother colony. By way of explanation we should keep in mind that it was predominantly the veterans who had served in the Civil War under

Lincoln who settled in Sioux County. In the election of 1875 a governor was elected in Iowa. The Republican candidate received 275 votes in the colony, the Democrat only 40.[73] With a single exception, as we shall see later, the majority of the Sioux County Netherlanders consistently voted Republican.

E. Setbacks

So we see that from the beginning in the colony there was competence, will power, determination, and a spirit of optimism in the area of economics and politics as well as religion. The colonists seemed able to cope with all the problems associated with pioneering in the newer West, but unexpectedly their will power was again severely tested.

In the first few years the harvests were abundant. With the proceeds they built and improved their houses, bought farming implements and increased their cattle herds. The merchants did good business. Large sums of money were spent on all kinds of things. Optimistically, buyers and sellers alike bought and sold more than could be paid for on the spot—they were counting on the harvest of 1873 as security. But they did not stop there. Like many venturing into new territory they waxed over-confident. Railroad grant lands were put on the market and many a pioneer who owned only his homestead decided to buy an additional quarter-section of the excellent prairie land bordering on the railroad, certain that sooner or later the market value of the land would greatly increase. Many a Netherlander was captivated by speculation fever and bought a quarter-section, planning to pay for it with the 1873 harvest profits.[74]

But grasshoppers descended upon them and destroyed all expectations, bringing misery and woe, and many a one who considered himself a wealthy landowner was made penniless. In the spring of 1873 all the crops, all green growth, stood plentiful and luxuriant—but suddenly in the later part of May grasshoppers rose like a cloud in the northeast, coming out of Minnesota. Bloemendaal was working in the fields and was suddenly surrounded by them. He watched while they devoured all the growing wheat even as they destroyed all the other growing crops in the area.

But after three days they disappeared and everything grew up from the roots again. People breathed easier and forgot all about the grasshoppers, but at harvest time they returned. They settled on the wheat stalks, gnawed through them and the ears fell to the ground. They did the same with the oats and in a moment's time whole fields of the valuable grain were lost. They ate the tassels of the corn and it too was destroyed. Three-fourths of the total harvest in the colony was lost.[75]

And that was not the end of it. In the spring of 1874 they reappeared all over the colony and descended in masses on many fields, again devouring everything that grew. It was to become even worse. In the last of July they returned. It was on a Sunday morning during a worship service in the schoolhouse. Seen through the windows, the approaching insects resembled a snowstorm.[76] It proved to be the grasshoppers again. By Monday much of the vegetation had been eaten. They stayed only a few days, but in the fall they came again. Half of the crops that year were totally destroyed.[77]

This last visit of the grasshoppers in the fall proved to be the most devastating of all, for they left behind their eggs. The eggs hatched in the spring and produced a new generation. The cycle repeated itself for years. People tried in vain to get rid of them by pulling across the fields shallow wooden troughs containing a layer of sticky tar. Multitudes of the grasshoppers were caught and held in the tar. When the trough was full it was emptied and washed and a fresh layer of tar applied. By this means they caught "bushels of grasshoppers" but for every hundred that were caught a thousand returned. The ground was completely covered with them, even the branches of the trees were weighted down by them; 387 grasshoppers were picked off one side of a corn plant! The young son of one of the colonists fell asleep in the garden one warm summer day and when he awoke found himself covered with four layers of grasshoppers![78]

This went on for years. One of the chroniclers of that time records a series of grasshopper invasions bordering on monotony.

1876:   Grasshoppers (appeared) in great numbers and remained about 10 days. The extent of the damage varies greatly. In some areas there is much damage, in others less.

1877:   The grasshoppers of the previous year laid eggs, especially in the sod of the newly broken soil. The following June the young grasshoppers hatched and did much damage. A month later the grasshoppers coming from the north passed by and the local grasshoppers went with them.

1878:   The grasshoppers came in September.

1879:   The newly hatched grasshoppers have appeared and are doing much damage. Later: the small grain is continually ravaged by the devourers. There is not much left of the wheat and oats. In the later part of July the grasshoppers left.
"I warned you, dear reader, that this account would be monotonous."[79]

There were many other adversities. One year there were no grasshoppers and the crops were beautiful, but just before the harvest, smut struck the wheat and oats and it all fell to the ground. "We had to cut the grain with a haymower, gather it in windrows with a horse-drawn rake and afterwards pile it up like a haystack." There was so little profit from this kind of labor that some preferred to burn the whole field.

In another year there were continual dust storms in the spring. The top layer of the soil was very fine, like flour. The wind was strong and carried the dust aloft and filled the air so that one could hardly see or hear. The roots of the plants were exposed and many were destroyed. Still, there was a good recovery and later in the season it all looked fine again. But just after they had cut the grain, it began to rain—the whole month of August.

The rivers rose over their banks and flooded the bordering fields. Haystacks floated away. In early September they tried to gather the wheat, but found wheat, grass, and weeds all sprouted and matted together by the constant rain; they were unable to salvage much of it. What there was, was eaten by grasshoppers and legions of mice.

In addition to the dust storms and severe thunderstorms there were prairie fires in the dry periods of the summer and fall, which increased the misery. Illness spread among the cattle; 1878 was a year of disaster. The farmers lost much of their livestock. According to G. Draayom, this was wrongly ascribed to the smut in the grain. The following year many of the horses were afflicted with glanders. To top it all off, the winters were often severe. Many had no money to buy fuel. Many a pioneer tried to find some willows to cut on the riverbank in "a pitiful scavenging effort." Others burned corn stalks and hay. Coal was too expensive, for it had to be brought in from other areas. Near Pella, coal could be mined locally, but not so in Sioux County. In January of 1876 the county board promised a reward of $2,000, later increased to $3,000, for the finding of coal substrata, but the reward was never claimed. Fuel had to be brought in from elsewhere.[80]

It is difficult to conceive of more hardship and misery than was endured in Sioux County in the years from 1873 to 1879. Those who had arrived in America at a later date, the greenhorns, now also found out what pioneering meant. They were "days of saddened hearts and depression," but also of increasing determination. They were deceived and defrauded by Americans in positions of authority and they reacted in anger and rebellion. The crisis of 1873 and the scandals that were exposed, especially in the "Belknap Affair,"* contributed much to the general distrust. They increased the general uncertainty and destroyed the trust in all business transactions. Even among the colonists themselves there was an increasing distrust. The dishonesty and deceit in matters of land buying involved colonists who professed to be Christians. Even God's children had appropriated more land than they had a legal right to and had not hesitated to commit perjury in the process. Since only those who were legally of age were allowed to purchase eighty acres of government land, "pious" colonists sometimes passed off their minor-age children as adults, "an irreverence towards the oath." In the same manner they acquired land under the Pre-emption Act. One of the pioneers relates: "Indeed, by all kinds of conniving and trickery they got possession of land." If the deception was discovered the deceiver could be dispossessed, which was called "claim-jumping." "Naturally, this caused much dispute and controversy, especially in the first five years," so says our eyewitness.[81]

The many adversities of 1873 and following years weakened the moral standards of the colonists, particularly in the area of economics, according

*William W. Belknap, Secretary of War in the Ulysses S. Grant administration, had accepted bribes to retain an Indian-post trader in office. Belknap resigned to avoid Senate impeachment proceedings.

to Bonger. Perjury was a common occurrence although no one dared to justify it on any biblical basis. Another pioneer states: "When in the days of the grasshopper plagues the creditors made things difficult for us, trust in God was so outmoded that we often did not hesitate to make false statements about our properties and then solemnly swear that they were 'bona fide.' Many paid their real debts in later years but others, even those who later became wealthy, neglected to do so."[82]

That it was difficult under those circumstances to borrow money goes without saying. In the colony there was no money available. A businessman had to go to Le Mars, twenty miles distant, to obtain capital to operate. Woe to the one who had to borrow money. He had to pay 24 percent interest in advance and in addition was required to give the most valuable collaterals.[83] Consequently, in the colony itself the farmers were deeply, even hopelessly, in debt. The merchants also had nothing; the thousands of dollars that were due them from the colonists were uncollectible.

Many a pioneer left the colony in discouragement. Even the landowners, though strongly attached to the soil, began to consider moving. Many sold their farms for a trifle. One man, completely disheartened, sold his 80-acre homestead, including his mules, a wagon and a cow, for $225, although the last two items were worth more than the whole amount. They all left for other areas, in an exodus stimulated by similar movements out of Kansas and Nebraska following periods of extreme drought there. Many who had vacillated for a while now also caught the migration fever—another example of the "mob-mind."[84]

In the fall of 1874 the general discouragement in the Sioux County colony was so great that it would undoubtedly have ceased to exist as a Dutch colony if the invisible God, operating in addition to two men who were supported by a small nucleus of the most strongly spirited pioneers, had not done everything possible to induce the colonists to stay, and for which they owe them everlasting gratitude.[85]

Henry Hospers, the founder, and Dominie Seine Bolks, the spiritual father, were the saviors of the colony. It was at that time that both men demonstrated to the fullest degree the qualities they possessed. Hospers especially was held responsible for all their troubles. He was the general scapegoat. He had attracted the colonists to Sioux County by his glowing descriptions. Now they reviled and cursed him "because he, he alone, had lured them to this land of wind and grasshoppers." They flung bitter reproaches at him. "He no doubt knew about these conditions all the time, they said. A learned man like Hospers must have been aware that these great prairies were subject to repeated invasions of grasshoppers."[86]

This Hospers was an interesting personality, a typical Holland-American of the Midwest. He rose to prominence on the western frontier, on the fringe of the "civilized world," and spent the most important part of his life there. In 1847, at the age of seventeen, he crossed the ocean with many of Scholte's followers on the *Maasstroom* and was one of Pella's first pioneers.[87]

He started out as a teacher—one of the first and youngest teachers in Marion County, but soon saw that America held many other possibilities for an educated person. There was a tremendous demand for land and he wanted to deal in land. First as a surveyor's chain-puller, then as a surveyor in his own right, he acquired seven years of invaluable experience in the Wild West when it was still wild. It was an experience that would not be available at any price again later. He helped build Pella, with all the hardships associated with this. In 1854 he set up a land office and also became a notary public.[88] He was very successful, although the panic year of 1857 also brought him serious reverses. He had ambitions for political office, but because he was foreign born he suffered many disappointments. However, among the Hollanders he was a man of great influence. He started *Pella's Weekblad* and served his city as mayor from 1867 to 1871.

He strongly supported the plans for a new colony. The government of Iowa appointed him to a state commission for the promotion of immigration and sent him to the Netherlands to make propaganda for Iowa. After his return to Pella he closed out all his business interests, resigned as mayor, and moved to Sioux County to help establish the colony there. As we have seen, he was the leader and primary mover. For all his labors he was rewarded with generous landgrants.

In all these activities Hospers, more than either Van Raalte or Scholte, resembled the land locators,* the leaders of the German agricultural colonies of the Middle Ages. They had likewise taken responsibility and leadership upon themselves for a share in the land. Hospers became, as we saw, Orange City's shopkeeper, and as supervisor, virtually its manager, a combination frequently occurring in America as we have already noted previously. He now had to deal with some very serious problems—and he solved them all competently, even brilliantly.

"The young Hospers," as people called him in Pella, arrived a few years before many other members of the Hospers family. He has been described to us as a man "with steel gray eyes and bald crown, whose self-confident carriage and winning manner of speaking exemplified the true diplomat."[89] Thanks to him Orange City won "the courthouse war" (the conflict with Calliope over the location of the county seat). It was also due to him, as we saw, that the colony was absolved of the fraudulent debts. But all this was nothing compared to the grasshopper era when the colonists rose threateningly against him, as the colonists in Michigan had also done against Van Raalte. The more able colonial leaders have always been the scapegoats, blamed by the less competent for everything that went wrong. It will probably always be so.

Hospers had himself shared the difficulties of the pioneers in Pella and

---

Lokator is the German word for the medieval entrepreneur in charge of founding a city for the landowner, and in East Germany the delegate, usually a knight, in charge of distributing land to settlers on behalf of the landowner or lord.

knew by experience the psyche of the immigrant. He knew that the most ignorant were generally also the most unruly, which was experienced previously by both Van Raalte and Scholte. The more competent ones, especially those with previous pioneering experience, understood the heavy responsibilities resting upon Hosper's shoulders as a locator, and they appreciated what he was doing in their behalf. As early as 1873 they acknowledged and expressed the debt of gratitude they owed him.[90] And rightly so, because Hospers, as chairman of the Sioux County Board, fought valiantly. Following the devastated harvests, appeals for help appeared in the leading newspapers of Iowa, and at his suggestion several committees of assistance were organized. Even the state legislature at his urging appointed a committee to investigate the situation and ascertain the facts. They personally visited the area and afterwards strongly urged assistance, "not simply as a matter of humanity, not simply as a matter of duty to a suffering people; but as a matter of justice to men who are engaged in the work of reducing one of the fairest portions of Iowa from the wilderness—as a matter of profit to the State at large." Help came from all sides. The Iowa legislature granted a subsidy of $50,000 for the purchase of grain, seed corn, produce, etc. Mother Pella sent thousands of bushels of corn and many wagon loads of coal.[91]

Thankful for the proferred help, the people anticipated the 1874 harvest with renewed hope. But new setbacks discouraged many and they left, especially the later arrivals who had not yet built up any reserves. It has been ascertained that the majority of those who had lived here since 1870 stayed. It was the latter and not the more recent immigrants who formed the core and kernel of the colony, the selection material we mentioned previously.[92]

How serious their plight was in 1874 can be gauged by the fact that the Union government took note of the situation and temporarily reduced some of the requirements of the homestead and pre-emption acts; residence for some time on the land was no longer required. Hospers stoutly encouraged the troubled people and besought them not to leave the colony. Without charge, he personally saved many from their financial plight and out of obligation to him they stayed.[93] In his newspaper, De Volksvriend, he pointed to the wonderful progress of the colony: in five years, four hundred families had settled there and had brought under cultivation more than 15,000 acres of land. "And now because of some adversity would they leave all this and the friendly Orange City? Consider that it could have been worse. Think of our countrymen in Michigan and Wisconsin, think of the first pioneers of Pella," Hospers admonished.

For several years Hospers went on this way. He had to, because again and again there were grasshoppers, floods, storms, and prairie fires, all testing and challenging the will power of the colonists to an increasingly higher degree. Again there were increasing numbers who left. But there were also many who stayed, encouraged by Hospers, encouraged also by

Seine Bolks, the preacher, who thoroughly agreed with Hospers and "lived in pure harmony" with him. Hospers based his arguments to stay on economic factors; Bolks did so mainly on spiritual grounds.

Bolks was also a typical pioneer, who faced the rigors of the pioneer experience for a second time. In the Michigan woods he got acquainted with this life; there he had helped his fellow pioneers build their houses, had gone into the forest with them, cut down trees and split wood, had given instruction in the English language, and on the Sabbath had preached God's Word.[94]

Restless, full of nervous energy, like so many of the pioneers, Bolks had retained his drive for the migrating life. Perhaps because of the inherent criticism and intolerance of the Dutch church people he had changed pastorates more than once. After leaving Overisel he served churches in Grand Haven, Milwaukee, Chicago, High Prairie and Low Prairie, and Zeeland, Michigan. Although he was nearing sixty he now came to Orange City.[95] Like Hospers, he spared himself no efforts in trying to persuade the colonists to stay in Orange City. It was he in particular who admonished the people to submit to God's will, and to trust in Him who had deemed the grasshopper plague necessary for the salvation of the souls of the colonists. It was Hospers who also aroused the conscience of the faithful brothers, reminding them that it was the penalty for their dishonesty in acquiring land under the homestead and pre-emption acts, and for not paying the debts incurred.[96] Still more serious (and Hospers also pointed this out) many of the devout church members had exaggerated their hardships. Even if their fields had not been affected by the grasshoppers at all, they made pathetic recitals to the authorities in order to back out of their rightful obligations.[97]

On Sundays they streamed into the church. Special gatherings and prayer meetings were held, "to plead with God to help the sorely tried people."[98] And the old Bolks, the sixty-year-old preacher, led many, if not all, into accepting their lot. Through his ministry the power and efficacy of faith was again demonstrated, as earlier in Michigan and Marion County, Iowa. Bolks, "the last of the original pioneer preachers of the Dutch 1846–47 emigration," for a second time convinced a struggling Dutch settlement that it was God's will that they should stay.

There were some who could not make it to church, so Bolks went to them. Day in and day out, neither storm nor rain could prevent the old man from going to visit the sick or comfort the sorely troubled—wading through snow or mud, crossing swollen streams where bridges had been washed away, through swamps, to reach lonely colonists in distant places almost impossible to reach—no obstacle could keep him from doing his duty, doing God's will.[99]

Both Hospers and Bolks demonstrated, for the umpteenth time, as Van Raalte before them, the power of the one over the many, the significance of the heroes in a society. They made hero worship understandable, even self-evident. It was not until the "years of hunger" had passed that the colonists realized how much they owed Hospers and Bolks. It is now acknowledged "that no one did more to relieve the sufferings of the colonists, as far as that was possible at all," than those two men. Those who followed their advice and stayed, became in time the most prosperous. Those who left—approximately one-third of the total colonists—later came to regret it sorely.[100]

Nevertheless, those who stayed in the colony endured an eight-year struggle for bare existence. Sometimes one-third or one-half of the harvest was destroyed; sometimes the loss was total. One of these courageous pioneers who suffered through the eight years of continual ordeal relates in simple words, "There was no question of saving money to pay off any of our debt, we barely had enough to eat. It was enough to make us lose all courage."[101]

Although I stated earlier that there was some mutual distrust among the colonists, there are also countless examples of strong, mutual helpfulness during those difficult years. For example, a certain Maarten Verheul, one of the oldest pioneers, "was always ready and willing to help others, so now why don't we help him?" Accordingly several of his neighbors hitched their horses to their plows one beautiful June morning and went to the homestead of the old man, in an area known as "Pelmulder's wet lowlands," to plow his fields so he would be able to plant his corn earlier.

Another example of prairie life in those years is recounted by our historian, Draayom, who was at one time a hired hand on the farm of a German colonist, Oelrich. One Sunday afternoon he went to visit the Grevenhofs, who, like himself, had come from the province of Overijsel. They had first worked on rented farmland in Wisconsin and then, attracted by the "free land" in Iowa, had moved to Sioux County. As so many others in the early days, they lived in a very primitive home: "Two or three young children sat on stools made of blocks of cottonwood around a cottonwood table, the walls were of neatly stacked pieces of sod, but still, nothing but sod, and in a corner of the room lay the father of the family, ill and helpless." Mrs. Grevenhof told him that their first crop, forty acres of wheat, was ready to harvest but the grasshoppers had come and had eaten a good share of it. Still, they wanted to save what they could. Then Grevenhof fell ill. Something had to be done, so the wife seated herself on the mowing machine with her nursing baby on her lap, "drove the mower the whole day" and cut the grain. The husband and father lost all courage but his wife was convinced it would turn out all right. The baby had been so quiet and contented all day, it was certainly a good omen and she had said, "Look, Gerrit, in Wisconsin we rented land but here we can buy it so cheap and keep everything we raise." So spoke this heroine of the prairie.

That evening Draayom told this episode to Mrs. Oelrich:

"Gerhard, this can't be true!"

"Yes, Mrs. Oelrich, it is just as I said."

She, to her husband: "Carl, there we must help."

Monday on the Oelrich farm they did two days' work in one, doing only what was absolutely necessary. Very early Tuesday, Draayom and his employer went to the Grevenhof farm.

"Gerrit, what are you and that German man doing here so early?"

"What else, Marie, but to bind wheat. We have nothing to do at home today." A few days later, other neighbors also came to help. Grevenhof recovered slowly. And the baby who rode around the grain field on Marie's lap, if she is still living, must be about fifty years old now.[102]

One should not conclude that all those who chose to remain in the colony were equally contented and satisfied, even if Dominie Bolks' church was "always crammed to the doors." They did not all come to church in the same mood. "Humility was lacking in many and even that old dominie could not make a Christian out of a block of wood no matter how hard he hit it, 'that old servant of his Lord.'"[103]

In Sioux County we see the Netherlanders for the first time becoming involved in social movements. This is noteworthy because up to this time our countrymen had chosen to remain aloof from all such contacts; such a large part of our immigration element had always been antisocial.

"The voice of the insurgent West" was heard much earlier than the well-known American historian F. J. Turner claimed, remarkably enough even from the mouths of the Netherlanders, at a time when there was still plenty of "free" land to be had.[104] Turner was of the opinion that the "free lands" (homesteads and pre-emptions) were a "safeguard of democracy." P. L. Haworth correctly agrees with that view and sees in the Homestead Act a kind of safety valve.[105] Those who had settled in the more densely populated eastern states and who found it difficult to adjust to the social and economic order there, were given the opportunity, thanks to the Homestead Act, to breathe more freely in the western hemisphere. In the West they could live out their lives to the full. However, also these truths are only relative.

Indeed, the colonists also found out that as they went further and further west they became more and more dependent upon the powerful railroad companies. For example, the farm products of our countrymen in Sioux County had to be shipped five hundred miles by rail to Chicago, while the Netherlanders in Michigan were much nearer the market, and besides, they had a choice between boat or rail. Because they had a monopoly in the new West, the railroads charged the highest possible rates for both freight and passengers. They refused to acknowledge the moral obligations laid upon them by the government in the matter of land grants; instead they attempted to "charge all the traffic would bear." The operations of the railroads also left much to be desired. Perishable goods were sometimes left on sidetracks!

Two writers of this era have judged the railroads of their time as being less than completely trustworthy. Documenting his view exceptionally well, G. Myers saw in the railroad magnates, swindlers, frauds, and big thieves. I may say in passing that, alas, the "over-zealous and credulous Dutch capitalists" also bled for them when the magnates hauled in millions and tens of millions of "guldens" as taken-for-granted booty through dishonest practices.[106] But also a sedate scholar like P. L. Haworth admitted that men like Jay Gould, the Vanderbilts, T. A. Scott, J. W. Garret, and others, were generally held to be "a band of financial pirates" and were condemned as such by the public at large.[107]

This conviction led to the organization in Washington in the year 1867 of the "Patrons of Husbandry," the purpose of which was to oppose the power of capitalism and to bring some order in the moral chaos prevailing in America at that time. It was only in the panic year of 1873, when the frauds had reached a high point, that opposition by the people took shape with amazing speed in the "Grange Movement," especially among the farmers of the Midwest and Northwest. In a short time membership totaled one and a half million!

Men, women, and children attended the lodges or granges, and while the men discussed their farm problems and politics, the children played and the women held their own club meeting and prepared a picnic supper. They expressed many grievances—for better and less expensive means of transport and for the elimination of the middleman in business transactions. In spite of all the opposition of the railroad companies, in spite of all the intrigues allied against it, some "Granger laws" were passed, bringing those companies under some measure of supervision and setting maximum rates. But soon it was evident that this was only on paper! It turned out already in the eighties that the Grange Movement could not stand up to the "business pirates" and eventually collapsed.[108] Capitalism had been too powerful, too omnipotent. Among the Dutch, for instance, it had been able to convince even the pulpit of its "right." This was the beginning of the end of the Granger Movement, if not immediately, then in the long run.

In the colony the Grangers had attracted especially the young people. They read about it in the newspapers, the *Chicago Inter-Ocean* and the *Iowa Homestead*. The first Granger club was started in Calliope and later others were organized in parts of Sioux County. In Orange City a club, consisting almost entirely of farmers, was started and led by P. Ellerbroek, one of the teachers. However, membership was not limited to the young like Draayom and Sipma; it included several of the older and most influential colonists—M. Verheul, Sjoerd Sipma, Luymes and their wives, the Beukelmans, and others. In short, here as in other areas, the nucleus of the Grange consisted of middle-class farmers.

Dominie Bolks and many members of his church were opposed to the Grange. They saw it as a secret society, worse than the Freemasons. The fact that even members of the consistory belonged, despite all the opposition, illustrates the degree of Americanization of the colonists and the increasing spirit of independence of the colonists the farther west one went.

It should be noted that the Dutch branch of the Grangers has not been

very significant. They attempted to buy farm equipment and other necessities through cooperatives. But they soon learned that although the "greedy"
shopkeepers in the colony were willing to sell to individuals "on tick" [op de
pof], in cooperative purchases they demanded "cash on the barrelhead"
[boter bij de visch, literally, butter with the fish]. Since there was hardly any
money in the colony any more, when people at times tried to buy on credit
they were bitterly disappointed. The buying of "kiplerzen" [an adulteration
of kaplaarzen (top-boots)] is one of those melodramatic cases. The Union
Furnishing Company in Chicago would mail the boots, costing only five
dollars, for a downpayment of only twenty-five cents. This certainly seemed
to be a bargain for the Grangers. Many quarters were collected and sent to
the company, in spite of the warning by Wynia, one of the members. The
boots never arrived and later they learned from the newspapers that the
Union Furnishing Company had never existed![109] The colonists were learning better and better what American "freedom" meant!

But our Dutch Grangers were not entirely without influence. At election
time they were much sought after, and the various political parties solicited
their votes. If the candidates could not gain the support they sought, they
appealed to the preachers and not without some success, both in Orange
City and other communities as well. "We may not judge to what extent the
Spirit of the Lord worked in and through the pulpit," Draayom cautiously
remarked. "But it was certain that those obstinate ones who refused to
confess sins they had never committed were declared anathema."[110] But it
was not the condemnation by Dominie Bolks and other preachers, who
were men of great influence especially in the rural settlements, that brought
the Granger Movement to an end. In spite of Granger opposition the power
of capitalism increased. Exploitation, deception, and rampant corruption
remained triumphant in this land without traditions, and thus without
brakes against excesses. There were other reasons why opposition gradually
was blunted.

After 1879 the grasshopper invasions ceased. In Orange City a community
prayer meeting was held, after which a strong wind arose and carried all the
grasshoppers away, to disappear for good, as told to a visitor from the
Netherlands by good old Dominie [J. W.] Warnshuis.[111] However that may
be, the lean years came to an end and prosperous times began. Years of
blessing, even of super abundance, dawned upon them. "Gold and silver
came flowing toward us and our barns and stables were richly supplied,"
one of the stayers tells us. Since poverty, even more than the sense of
injustice, is the root cause of all social dissatisfaction, when poverty came
to an end even the believers resigned themselves to the moral chaos.

2

The Growth of the Sioux County Colony to About 1895

A. Economic Life

One should not conclude that during the years of adversity all the Netherlanders sat down in despair. Quite the opposite is true. Under Hospers' leadership the colonists in Sioux County and particularly those in Orange City endeavored to make progress. In precisely those difficult years they built a courthouse and a church. At first the colonists had to grind their own grain with a hand-operated coffee grinder or take it all the way to Le Mars, but in 1875 they decided to build a windmill southeast of the city for that purpose.[1] The harvest looked good that year and $800 was subscribed for its construction. Some of the necessary equipment was imported from the Netherlands and it was soon completed. For many years this windmill was a distinguishing landmark, testifying to the Dutch origin and character of the colony; it provided a pleasant and unexpected surprise to many an outside visitor. One such visitor wrote: "You will never guess what we saw on the way to Orange City. Well then, high on a hill, in the middle of the prairie stood a genuine Dutch windmill—a sure sign that we were approaching a Dutch community."[2] Later, steam-operated mills were built and the windmill was dismantled. But people came to regret that the old mill had not been kept intact and preserved as a historic monument of the former years, perhaps to serve as the central point of a recreational area for picnics and festivals.[3] In 1876 a prison and a county almshouse were also built. This should not be interpreted as an expression of the spirit of the times—they were more or less expected and required in all county seats.

More expressive of the spirit of the times is the fact that in 1875 the first Sioux County fair was held and they also began to plan seriously for the erection of an academy or high school.[4]

In the meantime Hospers, convinced that the natural disasters like the grasshoppers were only temporary, continued vigorously to advocate and advertise in De Volksvriend and other newspapers the advantages of settling in Sioux County. As we have seen it was Hospers who invited Cohen Stuart to come and see Sioux County for himself and then go back to the Netherlands and share the information with the people there. In 1886 Hospers also persuaded J. Van 't Lindenhout to visit Orange City as his guest. Hospers was hoping that the colonists in Sioux County would follow the example of the earlier settlers at Holland, Michigan, and form an organization for the promotion of the immigration of Netherlanders. Thousands of acres of excellent farmland were still available and he advertised this everywhere. Naturally, in his enthusiasm he did not mention the grasshoppers and the other disasters the people had suffered. It must be remembered that he was primarily a land agent and realtor, and hence the direct beneficiary of those activities. Hospers' promotions aroused criticism and antagonism, especially among the more conservative people in Pella, which Hospers ascribed to enmity and jealousy. "No," they replied, "honesty is the best policy and you always present the best side and even more than the best side of things."[5]

It is due chiefly to Hospers' efforts that in spite of the unfavorable times, Netherlanders in the mother country as well as in America, continued to show great interest in Sioux County. Hospers succeeded in upgrading his publicity through the supportive testimony of two men of importance, from a doctor and—knowing his own people—from a dominie; this greatly increased his trustworthiness in the opinion of many.

In September of 1875 a committee came from Michigan to investigate the northern part of Sioux County and, according to them, Hospers had not exaggerated the possibilities. In the spring of 1876 a large number of Michigan Dutch settled in the northern part of Sioux County and in neighboring Lyon County. With this in mind, ten thousand acres of land were purchased in Lyon County near the small community of Doon. S. Kuyper went to Michigan as representative of the colony to make more propaganda. In many other states, such as Illinois, Ohio, New York, New Jersey, Indiana, Wisconsin, and Minnesota, Netherlanders were desirous of moving to Orange City and surrounding areas. Even some Netherlanders from the Mormon State of Utah were making similar plans.[6]

The result was that, in spite of the grasshoppers and other problems, the population of Sioux County, which numbered 575 in 1870, rose to 5,426 by 1880. Unfortunately, it is not possible to ascertain how many of these were Netherlanders. The number of those actually born in the Netherlands was comparatively small. By far the greater number had been born in America, mostly in Pella and other midwestern settlements. Orange City and environs were almost exclusively settled by them. In 1875 there were 468 families, totaling 2,500 souls living here.

The now-completed St. Paul and Sioux City railroad brought into being two new towns—Hospers, named for the locator who had also been very deserving and helpful to them, and East Orange. Both railroad stations were located in the Floyd River valley through which the railroad ran. The settlements here resulted in the organization of two new townships formed out of parts of the two older townships, Holland and Nassau. Floyd Township was organized in 1873 and East Orange Township came two years later. In 1875 Sherman Township was organized as a separate entity out of Nassau. In 1876 West Branch Township was laid out, adjoining Holland Township on the west. The greater part of these six new townships was occupied by Dutch colonists. North of the colony the extensive "Township 96" was notoriously known as speculators' territory and therefore avoided for the time being, particularly by immigrants looking for homesteads.[7]

After 1880 the series of natural disasters seemed to come to an end and prosperity came to the colony. The population increased, as many colonists from other areas were attracted to this area. Also at this time many immigrants came directly from the Netherlands. The general agricultural crisis in Europe caused many of the more affluent and very educated farmers to migrate to America. Many of them chose Sioux County as their new habitat.

Between 1870 and 1880 the number of European-born Netherlanders in Iowa, in Pella, Sioux County, and other smaller settlements, increased by somewhat more than two hundred. The disaster year of 1873 weakened the migration movement considerably. In 1885 Sioux County alone had a population of 11,584, among whom were registered 1,818 Netherlanders born in the Netherlands, and a much larger number of American-born "Netherlanders," although exact figures cannot be given. By 1895 the population of Sioux County totaled 21,405, almost doubling in ten years. About one-third of this total had been born outside the United States, the majority (4,325) coming from the Netherlands. Thus, in the elapsed decade, some 3,000 foreign-born Netherlanders had settled here![8]

The next development in the colonizing process was initiated by the children and grandchildren of those colonists who had come here before 1870. They began occupying territory further north into what was called "speculators' land," although this was known to be dangerous. Title to land in this area was difficult to establish and affirm, and proof of ownership often turned out to be false and unsubstantiated! A phenomenon typical of conditions in America at the time was that law offices were set up for the express purpose of examining and advising prospective buyers concerning legal title to their land. The outstanding law firm of Pitts and Kessey did business in Sioux County and soon thereafter some Netherlanders also took up the challenge. It was said of the law firm of Van der Meide and Lohr, "They can tell you many a tale of complicated situations." At the present time there are many young lawyers competent to examine and determine the legality of property titles. In 1924, the aged [?] Pitts, still functioning, was said to be "an expert in this field."[9]

The construction of the Chicago, Milwaukee and St. Paul Railroad through the northern part of Sioux County stimulated the new settlements. In 1878 the small town of Pattersonville was for a time the railroad terminal and became thereby an important marketplace. In 1879, further west on the

Rock River, the town of Rock Valley was born adjacent to the same railroad. As a result many new townships were organized. Two of these were populated chiefly by Netherlanders; the others, located more northward, were settled by American war veterans.

The two townships occupied by the Netherlanders originated out of the notorious "Township 96—the 96 hoodoo—an ominous, dreaded name, a place where lived the prairie wolf, the snake and other evils, imaginary and real." In the 1870s a few Netherlanders were already living there: Pleun De Zeeuw in the eastern section and Jan Van den Berg in the western section. In 1882 Van den Berg suggested the township be named "Welkom" [Welcome]. Some time later M. P. Van Oosterhout named his township "Kapelle" after the place of his birth. In the latter township the church village of Middelburg was established, named in memory of the Zeelanders, although there were in the area mostly immigrants from Gelderland and Overijsel—persons whose names ended with *ink* and *ing*, and also some Frisians.[10]

In the southern part of the county immigration was promoted by the completion of the Chicago and Northwestern Railroad, making East Orange an important rail intersection. In 1882 Orange City became a rail junction and a new town, Maurice, grew rapidly.[11] In 1890 a fourth railroad crossed the colony, the Sioux City and Northern Railway, later known as the Great Northern. Maurice was also now a railroad junction and expanded even more rapidly. In West Branch Township a small church village, Sioux Center, became a town by that name.[12]

Every new rail junction, or the prospect of one, greatly increased the price of land. In 1881 Orange City was hopefully anticipating the coming of a railroad, although the exact route of the rail line was still very uncertain. A visitor to Orange City during this period remarked: "In expectation of the coming of the railroad the price of land around town and especially of building sites in town has already gone up somewhat."[13]

Homestead land was now no longer available. The purchase of a farm required some capital, and therefore the numbers of new immigrant farmers from outside areas slowly decreased. Further developments were vigorously pursued by the children and grandchildren of older colonists, at least of those who had become well-to-do and who had enlarged their holdings, and those were many. Since 1879, rich harvests year after year rewarded the farmers. Prices paid for farm and dairy products in the area also were higher.

More and more colonists began to concentrate on raising corn, since both the soil and the climate were excellent for that crop. It also naturally followed that the breeding and fattening of hogs became important. Hogs were fed primarily on corn and the market prices determined whether the farmer would sell the one or the other, the corn or the animals. Thus he was less dependent upon the state of the market and ran less risk of loss.

After corn, wheat was next in importance, not so much for local use but mainly for the market. Oats were raised chiefly with an eye to the many horses on the farm. Horses were needed to pull the various pieces of farm equipment. Some barley was raised, but in lesser amounts, yet never totally absent. Potatoes and garden vegetables were planted, mainly for the family's own use and sometimes for the local market.

In the earliest years, flax was also an important farm product, especially in recently developed regions being cultivated for the first time. But it gradually declined. Flax was almost always accompanied by an obnoxious weed. The colonists who came from Overijsel called it the "herring blossom" but the more Americanized and therefore more impatient farmers declined to honor it by referring to it as a "blossom." They called it wild mustard. Whole stretches of farmland looked like a big flower garden—pretty to look at but very impractical.[14]

For a short time the colonists tried raising celery. For Americans celery is a tasty snack to be nibbled at every meal and all day long. In restaurants it is displayed in glass vases on the buffet in bunches of a dozen. Kalamazoo and the surrounding area in Michigan provided this article to all of America. Some colonists in Sioux County who had previously lived in Michigan and were familiar with celery culture tried to raise it in their new environment in Iowa and distribute it in the West. An enterprising young Frisian, K. J. Tiemersma, even tried to sell it in Omaha. His celery was much cheaper than that shipped in from Michigan and for a time he did very well. But after a time it was found that the Michigan celery was of much better quality and " . . . the stores could not sell the Iowa product any more. Customers returned it to the stores, complaining that it was too green, and bitter to the taste," and that it was not clear white and crunchy enough. The Kalamazoo variety was the one preferred. "Hotels and restaurants did not dare to put my stuff on their tables."[15]

In the production of livestock, hogs continued to be the most important, with some cattle next, especially for the dairy products—milk, butter and cheese sold at the local markets and for family use. At first these cattle were pastured on the unsold and uncultivated prairies. For a long time the unoccupied Township 96 was considered communal grazing area.[16] Also, after a field of grain had been harvested, cattle were allowed to graze there. In time this became a serious problem, since there were no fences or hedges to mark the boundaries of the pieces of property—wood was too scarce and expensive to use for fences. In October, 1874, in Sioux County an old regulation, the "herd law" began to be enforced: any farmer who found another man's livestock—cattle, horses, hogs, sheep—in his field damaging his crop, between the hours of sunset and sunrise, could seize and hold the animals for himself.[17]

As I have previously stated, a Sioux County farm generally comprised 240 acres. Sometimes part of this acreage was rented land but most was owned. K. J. Tiemersma occupied such a typical farm. Of the 240 acres, 80 acres were in wheat, 65 acres in corn, 25 acres in oats, 26 acres in flax and 11 in barley. The remaining 33 acres were used for pasture, a hay field, garden space, and a tree lot. He also had one hundred hogs, four cows, and six horses.[18]

This will give some idea of a Sioux County farm in the nineties but it must be kept in mind that there were wide variations in crop acreages, depending on the consistency of the soil, whether the land lay high or low, how long it had been under cultivation and the current market prices for the products. For example, Bloemendaal, the farmer I have often referred to, and also many other farmers, stopped raising any flax. Some farmers raised hogs; as many as two hundred hogs were raised on some farms. There were also farmers who, instead of hogs, or in addition to hogs, fattened oxen and sold them after they were three years old.

The size of the farms also varied. Beside the quoted average of 240 acres there were both larger and smaller farms. Bloemendaal began with 80 acres but increased his holdings to eight times eighty! And he was not the only one; "to farm well and to buy more land" was the motto of our people. They bought one eighty-acre tract after another! Many others prospered as well as Bloemendaal. "First I lived in a hut, then in a cottage, after that a house and now I own a castle! In America they continually break down old buildings and put up new ones! I finally had several thousand dollars invested in buildings on my land. One blessing followed another. My table was crowned with eleven children!"[19]

Visitors to the colony confirmed these reports of prosperity. J. P. remarked in 1881, shortly after the "disaster years," "I twice made a tour of the area and all the farms I saw were in excellent condition."[20] Five years later J. Van 't Lindenhout, whom we have already met in Orange City, spent some time in America on behalf of the orphanage in Neerbosch [the Netherlands]. He enthusiastically reported the following: "In the whole area, miles in every direction, the country is covered with magnificent farms, all very neat and attractive, providing the inhabitants with every convenience. The terrain is undulating and the houses are generally built on a carefully chosen high point of land. For protection against the prairie storms they plant trees as windbreaks on the south, west, and north sides of houses but leave the east side open for an unobstructed view of the landscape."[21]

Also in other areas, such as West Branch, the orphanage director was impressed by the many farms "so beautifully laid out." Going southwest in the direction of Maurice he noted the farms were even larger in size than in the Orange City area. Near Orange City land was more expensive and it had also been divided and subdivided among the children of the earlier pioneers. "We saw great prosperity everywhere." Most of the houses were built of sawed timber and compared favorably with many a lordly manor house in the Netherlands, including the furnishings. "The magnificent rocking chairs, neat sofas, and finally the parlor organs, which are apparently indispensable to the American family, immediately give the impression that the prairie farms in America provide a generous livelihood."[22]

From the foregoing it becomes evident that the entire colony was agricul-

Boerderij in Orange City.

A farm near Orange City, Iowa. Most of the farm buildings are concerned, it need not take second place to that of any Dutch constructed of wood. As far as the household furniture is mansion.

turally constituted. Much of the prosperity depended on corn and hogs. Compared with the preponderance of field crops and livestock, industry and manufacturing occupied a vastly inferior place in the economy. Attempts to develop some type of industry met with less success here than in Pella. Pella had the advantage of being situated on a river, providing cheap water transportation. The cost of rail transportation for manufactured goods was too high. Also, labor for manufacturing was not obtainable during the era of free farmland, and later on the hired hand on the farm earned such high wages that the manufacturer was unable to compete.

There were a few small business places serving local needs, such as blacksmith shops, where wagons were made and farm equipment repaired and even manufactured. The Dutch windmill, built by P. Pfanstiehl, who previously had worked in Michigan, was purchased by Hymen Den Hartog (the man who moved the courthouse safe). He dismantled it and changed it to a steam-operated roller mill. Near East Orange was a similar "factory," both of necessity located near the depots (railway stations).

In the eighties, J. Versteeg and N. Snoek built a brickyard, supplying building material for the rapid growth of Orange City. This venture failed. The fuel needed for firing the bricks had to be shipped in and was too costly; wages were also too high. In 1893 B. Van den Aarde and a few associates took it up again and tried anew. By 1895 it was "operating successfully," and known as the Orange City Brick Yard Company. East Orange likewise had a brickyard.

A cheesemaking business, begun by M. P. Van Oosterhout and C. Slote-maker, was discontinued, due to lack of sufficient local participation.[23] A similar plant was built in 1890 at East Orange (called Alton at that time) and was successful for a longer period, although it operated under some-what questionable circumstances: Milk was bought from the farmer by the pound and preferably paid for with groceries, since the cheesemaker was also the community storekeeper.[24] Those who preferred to be paid in cash received a lesser price. In 1895 the cheesemaking process was discontinued and it was then called a "butter factory."[25]

A feeble attempt was made to interest persons in the Netherlands in the business of manufacturing paper from flax stalks,[26] and to build a factory in America for that purpose since there was so much flax straw available, but to my knowledge there was never any response from the Netherlands. The same efforts had previously been made in the Van Raalte and Scholte colonies, also without any response.

Trade—the business of buying and selling—was of much greater significance in the colony than manufacturing. In the first place, in the nineties a good share of the retail trade was still barter and exchange, as we saw at the cheese factory at Alton. Wholesale trade consisted of the sale of farm and dairy products, which were practically the only products to be shipped out of the colony. Goods shipped in were fuel for heating, building materials—especially lumber, and farm equipment and machinery. The buying and selling of land could also be classified as wholesale trade. At times, land was bought and sold in units of thousands of acres. Almost in every community there was a real estate dealer.

B. Elevator Towns and Church Villages

From the foregoing it becomes evident that industry and commerce were closely connected with, and dependent upon, agriculture. Farming dominated the economy in Sioux County, as we also saw earlier in Marion County. These factors also determined where, how, and why the towns and villages originated.

Characteristic for the colony—indeed, for the entire Middle-West—were the widespread, isolated farms, the so-called "*Einzelsiedlungen*" [lone settlements]. However, the business of buying and selling made some trade centers necessary and resulted in the formation of small business towns, the so-called "*Verkehrsiedlungen*" [traffic settlements]. Orange City was designated as such a trade center before it was built. Its location on a high prairie ridge was selected to preclude any flooding from the small prairie rivers. In later years the water flow was better controlled and regulated, and the valleys became desirable territory. Some of the colonists with whom I had personal conversations about the location of Orange City mentioned that these early flooding conditions were often forgotten by less grateful people.

As the colony expanded, new trade centers were needed. The locations of these new towns were determined by the layout of two railroads, built some years after the founding of Orange City. However, the railroads were not built on the ridges but followed the valleys, partly because the construction and operation was easier and partly because the farmers and merchants in the valleys needed the shipping points. The railroad stations were intentionally spaced about three hours driving time apart, along the same rail lines. Exceptions were made in certain cases, notably in behalf of the already-existing Orange City. For the rest, the regularity of distance between these rural stations is noteworthy, even between the stations on different rail lines. This was not accidental. It is obvious they were carefully planned to expedite as advantageously as possible the movement of grain and, incidentally, also passengers.

The depot (station) became the starting point of many a town—the nucleus, as it were. Near the depot they built the tall grain elevators where the grain is stored, ready for shipping. It is these tall structures and not the railway stations that dominate the landscape. They emphasize the importance of agriculture in the area and together with the extensive corn fields project the cultural symbol of the prairies. Near the station are also found

the lumberyards, stacked with piles of imported wood for building, especially in the rapidly growing towns. Occasionally one sees a pile of coal that
was shipped in, or a stockyard or two for the temporary confinement of
livestock to be shipped out to the meat packing plants, or a buttermaking
plant, a grain mill, or a brickyard. On the road to the station, or on the
town's main thoroughfare, generally called Main Street, which almost without exception runs parallel to the rail line, are found one or more hotels,
banks, business offices, and a great variety of stores, in particular the general stores. The churches are more removed in a quieter, rustic setting, in
the residential area. Even at the present time most of the towns being built
in the new West follow the same pattern, although the garage and the
movie theater now play an important part.

The oldest towns of this type in the colony are Hospers and East Orange,
founded in 1873, on the first railroad leading through the Dutch settlement.
Both towns immediately took away a large part of Orange City's importance,
due to its wholesale trade. All commercial activity was still in its early
stages and wholesaling was concentrated at that time chiefly in the railroad
town of Le Mars, in the more southerly located Plymouth County, where
there were many Netherlanders—three hundred residents in 1890. In the
nineties there were about five hundred inhabitants in Hospers. There were
three elevators, where "awfully much grain" was stored and sold, and an
important lumberyard. There were also a hotel, a few hardware stores, a
drugstore, and grocery stores, and others.[27]

East Orange became immediately more important because of its location
near Orange City, the official county seat, which lay an hour's driving time
to the northwest and at that time still without a railroad. Therefore, East
Orange became the railroad station of Orange City. It was also the first
town in the colony to have its own governing body. It was incorporated in
1881, two years *before* Orange City and thus became independent of the
Nassau Township board. Its name was then changed to Alton, shorter and
less confusing (East Orange and Orange City were too similar). The Americans in the area had proposed that the town be named after the son of an
American, Wilfred, the first child born in the town, but the Netherlanders
had preferred Delft. They compromised on Alton, a totally meaningless
name and a spiritless, typically American solution. The name Alton was
chosen for no better reason than that there was not yet any other post
office in Iowa by the same name.[28]

Two years later a railroad was also laid through Orange City. This did not
diminish the importance of Alton but increased it since it was now a rail
junction. In the nineties it had four elevators, two lumberyards, two stockyards, and the previously-mentioned steam flour mill and brickyard, in addition to three hotels and many stores. At that time it was the busiest and
most active town in the colony. The farmers all took their wheat, and other
grains to the mill to be ground into flour. However, most of the grain went
into the elevators and was bought by the wholesaler, who paid the farmer

with a check on the local bank, an indispensable link in the commercial transactions. At the bottom of the elevator the grain was weighed and evaluated and then transferred to the upper storage bins where it was kept until it could be sold at a profit, according to the prevailing market price. When the wholesaler in turn sold the grain and it had to be shipped out, railroad cars were brought alongside the elevator and the grain flowed down a long sloping pipe directly into the car, filling it in short order. The lumberyards, covering large areas in and around Alton, did business on a big scale, shipping in quantities of material from the sawmills for the carpenters who, especially in rapidly developing areas, were an important part of the citizenry.[29]

Wherever the railroads went, similar activities developed and small towns grew up all through the northern part of the colony. One of these towns is Hull, a much shorter name than Pattersonville, as it was called formerly. In 1890 Hull had five elevators, two lumberyards, a flour mill, a butter factory, two banks, four general stores, etc. At Rock Valley in the same time period there were four elevators, a flour mill, two banks, three hotels, and a great number and variety of stores.[30]

It should not be concluded that the only population and growth centers in Sioux County and elsewhere on the prairie were the railroad centers. We could call them the typical "elevator towns," thereby indicating their location on a railroad line, while a railroad town was not always an elevator town. There was, however, another type of population center whose origin was not economic but spiritual. I refer to the so-called "church villages." [F.] Von Richthofen describes the church villages in the Alpine valleys as being the social centers for the widely separated farms and huts in the mountains.[31] Church villages are also found on the prairies and in the forests of the United States among the Netherlanders, Germans, and other nationalities as far as they are religious colonists.

Several of the Dutch villages in the Michigan woods could be called church villages. There also the farms were widely scattered and isolated, although not in such a regular pattern, due to a greater variety in soil conditions. However, a mill or a store could also be the starting point for a town. In the Van Raalte colony in Michigan there were no railroads at the time of settlement, so there could not exist at mathematically calculated distances along the rail line the railroad towns we saw on the prairies. Only the harbor town of Holland was called a "town." In contrast with Sioux County, there were more villages than towns, due partly to the original forest terrain and partly to the usually lesser fertility of the soil. In Marion County, north of Pella, near the Skunk River a small village or rather hamlet came into being in 1866 when a Reformed congregation organized and built Bethel Church there.[32] The German writer K. Hassert would have called it a "Kleinsiedlung" [small settlement].[33]

Although the church village was characteristic of the forest colony in Michigan, and the small town was typical of the prairie colony in northwest

Iowa, yet the strong religious convictions of countless colonists brought about the formation of church villages also in Iowa. We have learned about the Reformed Church in Orange City. For years it was the only congregation of the Reformed Church in the colony, even after the colony had spread over a series of townships. Many colonists walked for hours, from eight to twelve miles, wading through swamps, the sloughs or even the West Branch River, to attend the Sunday church service. On the other hand, old Pastor Bolks visited distant portions of the colony and preached on weekdays in the schools when Sundays did not give him the time to do so. This ensured that everyone could hear God's Word and hopefully understand it.[34]

The increasing population and the prosperity that followed the grasshopper era made the organization of new congregations and the building of churches both necessary and possible. The new congregations were organized before the "disaster years," but the new buildings were erected afterwards. In May, 1877, Dominie Bolks helped organize two new congregations: West Branch, northwest of Orange City and East Orange, southeast of the city. Their memberships were respectively 26 and 27. The East Orange church prospered and in 1878 obtained their own pastor, the very gifted Dominie J. W. Warnshuis. He had previously been a missionary preacher among the Ost Frisians and had helped organize many a pioneer congregation. On the other hand, West Branch, a completely rural area, secured their first pastor, Dominie J. De Pree, in 1880. Both men grew up, not on the western prairies but in the eastern forests, and mention of this should be made in relation to what I have discussed on this subject previously. Warnshuis came from New York state; De Pree, like Bolks, from Michigan.

In 1879 Bolks had asked for emeritus status so that he might still enjoy a few years of well-earned rest. His successor was Dominie Ale Buursma. He organized three new churches out of the mother church: in October of 1882 North Orange, to the northeast; in October of 1884, Maurice to the southwest; and in July of 1885 Bell's Lake to the north of Orange City, with memberships of 26, 25, and 29 respectively.[35] To complete the record I should add that in the towns of Pattersonville, Hospers, Boyden, and Rock Valley in the years 1885, 1886, 1888 and 1891, respectively, new Reformed congregations were organized, demonstrating the continuing expansion and influence of the Dutch element. The congregation of West Branch was renamed Sioux Center in 1881; North Orange became Newkirk and Bell's Lake became Middelburg. Each of these places became a church village, of which the nucleus, the pith and kernel, was and still is the church.

The real estate company of C. L. Davidson and Company donated five acres of land to the North Orange congregation. A lady in New York gave a gift of $500. With this assistance the Netherlanders built their first church and in September of 1883 they welcomed their first pastor, Dominie L. Dijkstra, from the forests of Michigan. In the nineties there were 80 families, with 162 recipients of the Lord's Supper, all living in the immediate area. For their convenience large stables were built near the church, as was done at all the other churches, in which to tie their horses during the worship service. This drew some small business places, which were built nearby. In the nineties there were two grocery stores, a blacksmith shop, and in a short time a post office and twelve residences. Several of these homes were occupied by senior citizens whose ideal it was to live near the church so they would not miss any of the services.[36]

The Bell's Lake congregation was also given five acres of land by the Davidson company on which to build a church and a parsonage. A church, like a railway station, attracted new colonists, often people of high quality. By becoming members of the church they also became landowners and permanent residents. This increased the value of the land, which in turn was advantageous to the real estate dealers. In 1885, another church, the Free Grace Church, was built and included a house for the sexton and stables for the horses. The following year they also built a parsonage and the first occupant was Dominie A. Zwemer and his family, from the forests of Wisconsin and Michigan—take note! Later the church and the horse stables were enlarged and a store was started in the vicinity. In 1890 a post office was established and the name of the village was changed to *Middelburg*. More houses were built, a shoemaker's shop was opened, after that a blacksmith's forge, etc. The store was enlarged, the postal service became a daily service, with the exception of Sunday, and a telephone connection was obtained. By 1892 the church had a membership of seventy families, most of whom lived on large farms in the vicinity.[37]

The church village of Sioux Center had an unusual development. After the first church was built in the late seventies, they began, with the co-operation of the pastor, De Pree, to lay out a planned community in the spring of 1881. The church property comprised 20 acres. They divided it into four square blocks with five building lots in each square.[38] Since the church was already there the "village" would surely grow. They had great expectations for it, especially since it was located in the middle of Sioux County, therefore the name—*Sioux Center*. Like Orange City it was located on a high ridge of the prairie, a location preferred by all the church villages. J. P. visited the village the same year it was begun. There was the church building, the pastor's residence, and one store. He remarked: "The location of the parsonage is not particularly attractive, on the top of a hill in the middle of the prairie."[39] Five years later, Van 't Lindenhout, the director of an orphanage, came to the church to speak in behalf of his orphans. In the meantime the church had been replaced by a larger building, seating six hundred persons, and the village had grown rapidly. Now, beside the "rather large" church and "good" parsonage there were several houses, a couple of stores, a blacksmith shop, a wagonmaker's shop, a school, etc.— in short, "the rudiments of a city."[40]

Apparently Sioux Center was about to become the largest church village in the colony. However, as I related previously in another connection, in 1890 the Great Northern laid their rail line extension three-quarters of a mile north of the village, built a station there, and laid out their own city. The merchants soon moved their places of business to the new location. It grew so rapidly that when the articles of incorporation were drawn up it absorbed "the old town," the old church village. Several of the streets, notably Main Street, extended into and through both towns and it became an organic whole. By 1895 Sioux Center had four elevators, two lumberyards, two banks, and a great many stores. The population totaled 650 and it was already one of the busiest places in Sioux County.

Due to the rapidly increasing migration, the First Reformed Church of Sioux Center gave birth to a second congregation in 1895. The new congregation was organized northwest of the city for the benefit of those who were traveling from five to ten miles to attend the services in Sioux Center. This new church developed into another church village by the name of Carmel.[41]

The colonists were contemplating building another church southwest of the city at the urging of Dominie Bolks—"We must do something in the southwest," he repeatedly said—when the railroad built another station in that area, and this confirmed their decision. The town of Maurice thus owes its origin not so much to the church as to the railroad. In 1890 it became a junction where two rail lines crossed, and it grew even faster as a railroad town rather than a church village. By 1894 it had already four elevators, a great number of stores, and a bank building.[42] The bank prospered to such an extent that in our time a couple of bank robbers thought it was worth a visit. The reception they were given by the Dutch colonists demonstrated that the sons of those who had been involved in the "courthouse war" knew how to deal with this type of American situation in the American way.

From the above it is evident that there were significant differences between the two types of population centers in the West. On the one hand there was the elevator town that dominated economic life. This was observed and stated also by the French writer, Vidal de la Blache in reference to the prairie states: "c'est la ville qui régit les relations entre ruraux" [It is the town that determines the rural relationships].[43] And then there was the village, reminiscent of Europe and colonial America, which saw itself deprived of an important part of its reason for existence, namely its economic "raison d'être," by the railroad station with its elevators, stockyards, lumberyards, banks, etc.

The first observable difference is usually in their location, their site. The railroads on the whole follow the valleys, and therefore the stations were erected in or against the hills: Alton, Hospers, Maurice. The church villages are found instead on the high points of the landscape, on the prairie ridges, where they were not menaced by flood waters from the rivers.* The church on the hill was visible everywhere, not merely as a symbol, as is customary in hilly or mountainous country, but also for practical purposes. In the early

---

*The railroad companies had money at their disposal for flood control and in 1872 drainage canals were dug in the valley of the Floyd River [Van Hinte].

days getting lost on the endless prairies was not the exception and there was no more appropriate landmark than the church steeple. Van 't Lindenhout experienced this himself in 1886 when he and his companions left Maurice for Sioux Center through an area with only a few farms. The colonization pattern had progressed, as we have seen, with the formation of new church congregations radiating from Orange City. Quoting our orphanage director: "From Maurice, we rode for two hours in the general direction of Sioux Center but on the uncultivated prairie with hardly any roads to follow we had to pursue our journey at random while keeping an eye on the steeple of the Sioux Center church to find our destination."[44]

As these two types of towns and villages differed in their location, so they differed also in their constituency, both according to social standing and descent. The railroads and the businesses that followed close at their heels attracted many Americans but also Irishmen and Germans and other nationalities. Many of these small railroad towns, especially in the early years, had a very mixed population; the Netherlanders were even in the minority. In Alton and nearby Hospers, in the very center of the colony, there were so many Irishmen and Roman Catholic Germans that in both towns a Roman Catholic church was built, while in most of the other towns we have described, congregations of Congregationalists, Baptists, and Presbyterians existed alongside or prior to the Reformed and Christian Reformed churches. In Rock Valley, for example, with about 1,500 inhabitants in 1895, six denominations were represented: Methodists, United Presbyterians, Lutherans, Roman Catholics, Reformed, and Christian Reformed—all with their own church buildings except the latter.[45]

The Americans were attracted by the commercial opportunities. At first the Germans and Irishmen generally worked on the railroads. Netherlanders were involved in commerce, retail shops, and railroads. The railroad workers were mostly those on the lowest social and economic level. They were often harshly treated, practically like slaves. They were even forced to work on Sunday, against their convictions. Especially the foremen of the work gangs behaved at times like barbarians. This was personally experienced by G. Draayom, a capable and highly respected historian, who was compelled to work on the railroad during the disaster years. In his later writings he described "the inhuman treatment" he endured. To get to his job on time he had to ride his horse through the swollen Floyd River and then he went to work, soaking wet and shivering with cold. He had no choice; he needed the money and could not afford to lose this job. Years later, in his writings, he compared the treatment of the railroad laborers with the Roman domination over the Kaninefaten, a tribe in the Low Countries, recorded in Van Lennep's novel Brinio![46]

K. J. Tiemersma was also bitterly disillusioned concerning the American concept of "freedom" by the same kind of hard physical labor. He too was compelled to work for the railroad in order to eat and to feed his family. His foreman was a very crude fellow who seemed to think that only blasphemous cursing would compel respect for his authority. Except for the fact that they could take leave of their boss if they wanted, the workers "looked like a slave gang, working under an overseer," without hardly any rest periods. He wrote: "I pity those who for the sake of their families had to work here like slaves and who had the misfortune of being under a tyrant as we had."[47] Tiemersma worked for days on end on the open prairie in icy cold weather, in snowstorms; then, after a thaw, in wet snow. Many Netherlanders, like these two I have quoted, truly came to assess the value of the promised land by such experiences.

To some degree it was the railroad workers who gave the elevator towns their international character. For example, at Alton many Italians worked on the railroad. Most of them lived here only temporarily, although several tried to move on to a normal human existence and managed to acquire permanent homes in this or that small town. The resulting heterogeneity of the townspeople was in sharp contrast to the homogeneity of the population in church villages. In the colony the latter were populated almost exclusively by Netherlanders—some shopkeepers, small business operators, and the elderly, usually retired, all belonging to the same church, the Reformed Church, sometimes also to the closely-related Christian Reformed Church. Indeed, there was no sharper contrast than between the industrial activity in the towns and the rustic quiet of the villages.

Though the population of the church villages was more stable and that of the elevator towns more fluctuating, yet it was the towns that grew most rapidly. An intriguing example of this is the contrast between the church village of Sioux Center, founded in 1881, and the railroad town of Maurice begun two years later. Van 't Lindenhout visited both places in 1886 and remarked that Sioux Center, strictly a church village, was not as large as Maurice. In the latter, "several houses already stand next to one another and regular streets are being built."[48]

Among all these towns and villages Orange City occupied and still occupies a unique place. As we have seen, the whole town was designed and the streets planned before there was a railroad, even before a church was thought of. Hosper's store and later on his office next to it, which was also the first bank in the colony, were the nucleus of the city, reminding us of the "colonial" days when the country store was the focus of the community, as in the case of Holland, Michigan, and Pella.

The church began only in 1872, and the school building served for church meetings. In 1875 a church was built. The town was already the county seat then. However, because it was on a high ridge of land, its location was less suitable for the building of a railroad and it was not included in the railway system until 1882. After that Orange City grew rapidly and like other railway towns it also attracted Americans and others. In 1881 its population was 500. By 1886 it was approximately 1,300 and four years later the total was about 2,000. The boom that the colony experienced between 1880 and 1890 contributed to this growth, but was no doubt also the result of better traffic connections.

One year after its inclusion in the railway system, Orange City was incorporated as a city and became independent of Holland Township. This indicates how rapidly its character and interests had changed, from the rustic environment. In the nineties it had two banks and a large number of stores; it "looked very nice with excellent wide streets with many neat and even impressive homes," we are told by a visitor to Orange City, and he was not one of Hospers' personal guests.[49] By 1894 there were electric lights and a countywide telephone system. Even church life was influenced by the railroad. In April of 1885 an English-speaking congregation, the "American Reformed Church of Orange City, Iowa" was organized for the benefit of those, especially Americans, who did not understand the Dutch language. Thirteen members of the Dutch congregation affiliated with it.[50]

We have observed that in the colony Orange City lost some of its significance in the fields of business and finance and to some degree also in religious life. On the other hand, it gained influence in the area of education.

C. Cultural Life

From the very beginning in "de nieuwe Kolonie" elementary education was provided, as had also been done in the Holland and Pella settlements. But there was a difference. Since many Netherlanders had been American citizens for years, the instruction in the schools here was on an American footing from the first day on, contrary to what had happened in the Van Raalte and Scholte colonies. The public school was among the first buildings in Orange City. Soon others were built in the area. In July of 1873 the builder, [A. J.] Lenderink, had six school buildings under construction; in 1875 there were seventeen scattered around the colony. The official language was English. The Bible was used if requested. The prairie colonists were above all a practical people and they wanted their children to learn good English. It was characteristic of their highly advanced degree of Americanization that they did not sufficiently appreciate Christian and Dutch education in their schools.[51]

But they did retain high ideals. When the city was still in the planning stage, they included in the plans an academy or high school which they thought of as a necessity. Many of these colonists were optimists, and as pioneers for a second time they had to be optimists. They even dared dream of a university!

When they were laying out the plans for Orange City it was agreed they would set aside one-fifth of the amount of the sale of building lots for education at the secondary level. One of the reasons why Dominie Bolks had been asked to come from Michigan to be their pastor was this very thing; in Michigan he was familiar with, and had been active in, the setting up of secondary and higher education and they wanted and needed his help to set up an academy that would develop into a college. In 1875 serious thought was given to an academy but doubts arose about the possibilities in view of the natural disasters they were encountering. "That's how the grasshoppers flew away with it [the academy]," Bolks said regretfully.[52]

However, in the fall of 1882, after several years of prosperity, all the Dutch preachers, led by Bolks (by that time retired) and supported by a few businessmen, decided to proceed with the building of an academy. The city of Alton, which grew so rapidly that it seemed likely to surpass Orange City, took an active part in the planning; as a result it was decided to build the academy halfway between the two cities.

As it turned out, that decision was not carried through as agreed. Orange City actually became the seat of the institution. Hospers, following the example of Van Raalte at Holland, Michigan, and of Scholte at Pella, Iowa, donated the land for the building, located on the city limits.[53] The instruction was to be basically Christian in character, again following the examples of Holland and Pella. A preacher, Dominie J. A. De Spelder, was appointed the first principal and was officially installed in January of 1884. The actual teaching had already begun in the preceding fall, under the leadership of the principal of Orange City's public school and the pastors, [J. W.] Warnshuis and [Ale] Buursma. There were twenty-five students the first year. It was soon realized that the academy building, known as the Pioneer School here also, was too small and for some time classes were held in an abandoned skating rink bought for the Pioneer School. In 1890 Dominie J. F. Zwemer became the principal, and he successfully headed a fundraising campaign. In 1894 they built a fine three-story building, costing $25,000.

The school, known as the Northwestern Classical Academy, had close ties with the Reformed Church and was intended as a preparatory school for students intending to attend Hope College and the Theological School at Holland, Michigan. Although preacher education had not been the primary objective in the beginning, it became an important one. By 1895 NWCA had had among its pupils three ministers, twenty theological students preparing for the ministry and thirty other students, and twenty teachers; meanwhile eighty young people had been admitted as students in that year.[54]

The university was less successful. Doctor A. F. H. De Lespinasse, who had studied at Utrecht, was the moving spirit of higher education. He opened a medical school for nineteen-year-old youths and set up a preparatory curriculum. He intended to add a law school and theological school later! The general feeling was that the excellent location of Orange City, the healthful climate, the inexpensive living, all among the predominantly Dutch population, made it an exceptionally advantageous place for a university! Seven young men enrolled in February of 1875 and in late October of the same year the first examinations were held.[55] However, the university did not continue beyond that point! Though the university remained only a dream, Orange City continued to be the intellectual center for the Hollanders because of the academy, the courthouse, and the newspapers.

De Volksvriend, previously referred to, became a power in the colony. The early years of the paper were difficult. During the disaster years the readers neglected to pay their subscriptions, but even after the years of prosperity arrived the publisher found it necessary to send a man on horseback through the colony to collect the bills. In spite of their continuing Americanization, the Dutch colonists remained frugal and somewhat tightfisted. A sum of $200 of outstanding subscriptions fees had to be collected, but after a ten-day round trip the collector was able to collect only $36. Somehow the paper was able to survive and its circulation and influence increased. Among the editors were Dominie K. Tietema, A. J. Betten, Jr., and at a later time H. P. Oggel, already well known in Pella as the publisher of De Christelijke Heraut [The Christian Herald]. Primarily a Christian paper, it dealt with religious issues—and of course also the controversies! In politics it offered a Republican point of view, which to the present day it still maintains and supports. In addition to colonial news items it included news from the Netherlands and a growing number of advertisements. Especially its Calvinistic Reformed basis attracted many readers. The number of subscribers grew from 120 in 1874 to 400 in 1881 and to 1,000 in 1891. In 1881 H. P. Oggel, a teacher at the academy, became the owner and chief editor. Under his leadership in particular, the influence of the paper increased and he secured the contributions of many—of Jan Nollen at Pella and Van Driele at Grand Rapids, Michigan. Four years later, in 1895, it had 2,000 subscribers.[56]

But by that time De Volksvriend also had competitors. In the various Sioux County settlements there were many English papers and two in the Dutch language. In 1892 at Orange City, M. P. Van Oosterhout began printing a Democratic newspaper, De Vrije Hollander [The Free Hollander] and in the same year at the rival town of Sioux Center a Republican paper was started and is still extant, Het Sioux Center Nieuwsblad [The Sioux Center Newspaper.][57] These two Dutch papers and De Volksvriend also had readers in more westerly areas, the Dakotas, etc. Especially the Democratic paper, De Vrije Hollander, with its enthusiastic editor, stimulated political interest that had started so actively in the colony.

The liveliest interest was not in "high level" state or national politics but in local politics. Twice, in 1891 and again in 1896, an attempt was made to have centrally-located Sioux Center made the county seat. Later the same efforts were made in behalf of Alton, but both were in vain. Orange City has remained the county seat until the present day.[58] Such a controversy concerning the location of the county seat is typically American.

Indeed, it seemed that all the areas of colonial life were characterized by controversy, especially matters pertaining to the church. In spite of their increasing Americanization, when it came to religious convictions the Netherlanders retained their Dutch stubbornness. As soon as a new congregation was organized and the location of the building had to be decided upon, the arguments began. At Maurice the problem was settled when it was learned that the railroad was coming and a station would be built; then "the location of the church building was determined at once." The dissension at Sioux Center was worse. Everyone wanted the church in their own neighborhood. No two agreed—"many men, many minds." Feelings were so strong that some brothers pulled out of the newly organized congregation, deeply grieving many fellow believers and not the least old Dominie Bolks who had worked so hard to bring it together.[59]

There was rivalry between the various denominations, especially between the Presbyterians, Reformed, and Christian Reformed, who were close at one another's heels. At Hospers there existed a Dutch Presbyterian congregation even before there was either a Reformed or Christian Reformed church. Christian Reformed congregations were organized at Orange City in 1871, at Sioux Center in 1890, at Rock Valley in 1891, and at Hull in 1893, but not in Hospers until 1894. Finally, there was also enmity between the Protestants and the Roman Catholics. Especially at Alton, around 1890, there was so much bitterness between the two, it was called a religious war.[60]

The immigrants in Sioux County were more Americanized in their religious attitudes than those in some other Dutch colonies and thus the controversies in the area during the years we have been discussing never reached the dimensions we have observed, for example, in Michigan. Here people were more tolerant. Perhaps the greater prosperity made them more relaxed, more lighthearted, less worrisome. Some of the sharp corners, the stern convictions of the Dutch orthodoxy wore off, at least for many. The services in the churches became a bit more informal. For example, in 1886, when Van 't Lindenhout visited Orange City, the musical society of the city serenaded his arrival to the tune of the Netherlands national anthem and escorted him to Dominie Buursma's church, where they gave a brief concert in the church! Compare this with the strict Hollanders in Michigan who were initially opposed to an organ in the church, who considered a piano a sacrilege and permitted a flute only if it played psalms—not hymns!

On the prairies people enjoyed various festivities. At Holland, Michigan, the church elders spied on the church members to check if any attended the forbidden horse races, but at Orange City they celebrated the American national holiday, July 4, with all the various forms of public amusement: races, pole-climbing, racket games, fireworks, etc. One of those present reports: "Our little town had huge crowds of people. The festivities continued until late in the evening."[61] Also in late September they celebrated for some three days a county-wide agricultural exhibition and the city was again crowded.

So we see that on the prairies in northwest Iowa there was a completely different atmosphere among the Netherlanders than we find among the forest dwellers in Michigan and even those in Marion County, Iowa. No doubt in Van Raalte's colony the contrast was due to the forest environment as distinct from the prairies. In the case of both Van Raalte's and Scholte's colonies, the circumstances of the early years also had an impact.

The immigrants who came to Sioux County in the eighties and subsequently had not lived through the critical time of the Secession in the forties. Socially they stood at a somewhat higher level. Even so, in comparing the situations in these three colonies during the same time period, one cannot escape the conclusion that the Netherlanders who settled Sioux County were an exceptional breed. They adjusted to the American lifestyle more readily, and they exhibited great will power and vitality; in addition, they were selection material. In spite of the fact that Americans were rather envious of the Dutch, they conceded, as one of them expressed it, that the Dutch through their great will power had made Sioux County into "the best part of the best State in the Union."[62]

3

A Colonization in Virginia that Failed

A. Why Did Van Raalte Choose the East?

How very different from Pella's daughter colony in the further West was the experience of the Holland, Michigan, attempt to establish, around the same time, a colony in the East during the seventies! There is no sharper contrast than between prosperous Orange City and its environs on the prairies of northwestern Iowa and the new settlements, already bloodless from the very beginning, in the forests of Virginia.

Little was heard in Michigan of men such as "the young Hospers," Sipma, Pelmulder, Van der Waa, etc. Undoubtedly there were some—one thinks of the aforementioned Heemstra—but it was impossible to get them to cooperate, to act. Divisions, such as we have noticed in church matters, also were evident in matters of settling new colonies. There was a need for expansion and additional lands just as there was in Pella but perhaps not to such a marked extent. Through lack of young, enterprising leaders, the Michigan Hollanders had scattered so much that one could speak of a dispersal.

It was Van Raalte, already advanced in years, who became concerned. Since no younger men came forward, again he undertook to give leadership to the emigration, especially because he wanted the colonists to remain in the church; indeed, he even proposed to make them participants in missionary work. As early as 1868 he had called the attention of Classis Holland to the necessity for new "focusing settlements." People were too concentrated in one area and it was feared that a "swarming" would take place, resulting in scattering. The classis charged Van Raalte "to give direction to the emigration and to those constantly seeking new settlements in order that their congregational life, etc., might be preserved." The experienced leader courageously accepted the heavy task "to be a blessing for tens of thousands, if it pleases God to accept," he wrote to his friend Muntingh in Pella—whom he had considered as a coworker.[1]

523

Van Raalte was to be bitterly disappointed. Still more serious, it was largely his own fault, and possibly the result of too much idealism. Just as in the forties, Van Raalte again had a vision of establishing colonies in the East. More than anything else, he wished to have mission stations. However, the stream of immigrants during the later sixties, just as twenty years earlier, was directed to the West; and just as then, their primary goal was not directed at high missionary ideals but at more down-to-earth objectives: the chance of a better station in life, a better way of life.

The refusal of the Dutch government to allow him to establish a religious, completely independent colony on Java had protected Van Raalte from worse disappointments in the forties. Undoubtedly, his coreligionists who had already been caught in the emigration stream to America, to the West, would have followed him only in very small numbers to the East Indies. Van Raalte was forced to go westward too—to follow the stream. That is why, even though beset by tremendous difficulties, he was able to establish a colony—secular and spiritual ideals could intermesh.

After the Civil War there was a new migration to the West, to the farther West. As we have seen, Michigan Hollanders established themselves, like so many others, such as Yankee Americans, in Kansas and Nebraska. Others had even gone to Oregon. I consider it a fault of Van Raalte's not to have followed up on this mainstream of renewed migration. In all the years of struggle he had become well acquainted with his people; he knew the power of an idea, and he himself had experienced the feeling of "Westward ho!" But instead, his mind was set on the East, even if it was only the Southeast. It is even strange to see that while homesteads were available for virtually nothing on the extremely thinly populated and very fertile prairie plains, Van Raalte, nevertheless, made propaganda for Virginia. The lands there had been exhausted through cannibalization of the soil; and they were even more devastated by the Civil War, which had also thinned out the population so that parts of the land had fallen in the hands of speculators.

These factors explain why there was in Holland, Michigan, so little interest for Van Raalte's plans, whereas in Pella the undertaking of Hospers evoked great enthusiasm. From the outset there were signs of distrust in Michigan concerning the new colony in the East. "The old settlers had no faith in it; sympathy for the plans was followed almost immediately by antipathy toward them."[2] Thus the attempt to win over a cadre of older and more experienced colonists miscarried from the beginning.

It is worthwhile to consider what circumstances caused Van Raalte, who had proven to be a generally clear-minded and practical individual, to select an area of land that was described even by Van Raalte's biographer and admirer, H. E. Dosker, as a choice that was "perhaps less than fortunate."[3]

It is regrettable that nowhere in the literature and archival materials, etc., that are available to me is mention made of the advisers who doubtlessly influenced Van Raalte's choice. However, the number of facts that can be reported make Van Raalte's plans understandable, if not acceptable. The Civil War had particularly ravaged the southern states and many former well-to-do planters had been reduced to poverty. The possessions of many an individual had been wiped out. Where the war had swept through, everything had been burned down at times. In these years the population was sharply diminished. Many had been killed in battle, others had died from illness, and still others had left the South to settle in the West. The population of the South in 1866 was 9,568,709, or 690,308 less than before the war![4] There was a great lack of labor, especially after slavery had been officially abolished. It was expected that after slavery had been eliminated it would be less objectionable for whites to settle here. It was now even reckoned that "the most important stream of immigration (would) flow toward the Chesapeake."

Interested parties tried by all means to attract immigrants to the coastal and adjoining states, an area geographically termed the Coastal Plain and the Piedmont. Thus, the directors at a January 1869 convention of southern railways, meeting in Atlanta, decided to issue excursion tickets—until July 1, 1869—at two cents per mile on all railroads in order to encourage northern landowners to investigate the soils of the southern states. Actual emigrants would only have to pay 1 cent per mile and they were permitted an eighty-pound baggage allowance.[5]

Even before this, in 1868, Van Raalte had visited "the South" and particularly Virginia, where he had seen three "well-situated areas" connected via canals with central markets. The area around Richmond, Virginia, had a special appeal, but he also liked an area in North Carolina that desired Dutch immigrants. East Tennessee and northeast Alabama were also considered; the latter area even seemed to him to be the best and the most productive, but it was too far away.[6] In this enumeration we can easily see the results of publicity put out by the South. It was the result of a campaign pushed both in America and in the Netherlands.

It is significant that only after his trip to the Netherlands in 1866—after the Civil War—did Van Raalte become convinced that settlements should be nearer the ocean.[7] His motivations, as reported by Dosker, seem altogether illogical to me. He is reported to have found the South particularly suitable because the settling of altogether new colonies |in the West| would require too much time, while settlements along the Pacific Railroad stood under the control of Roman Catholics and speculators. There certainly were still other areas, apart from the South, with greater fertility of the soil and a healthier climate that were suitable for settlement! For is it not true that the South had also been disqualified in earlier days not only because of slavery but because of its climate?

In the first place we can conclude from the foregoing that Van Raalte, impressed by his trip to the Netherlands and carrying with him that deep impression for years to come, was mainly thinking of potential emigrants from the Netherlands for his venture in Virginia, and only secondarily of the younger generation growing up in Michigan.

There is more. At that time in the Netherlands there was an interest for Virginia in general and in the port city of Norfolk in particular. The renowned American nautical authority, T. H. Maury, born in Virginia, had written a book about his native state that was also read in the Netherlands, thanks to his "bosom friend" M. H. Jansen, a retired Dutch navy captain.[8] The latter was carried away to such an extent by the local patriotism of his American friend that he became a powerful propagandist for a Dutch "Bridge Across the Ocean." This bridge would extend from Vlissingen (Amsterdam and Rotterdam were still not modern seaports) to the Chesapeake Bay area, to Norfolk, Virginia, and not to New York. "Vlissingen," wrote Jansen, "which is not yet a commercial town, will initially have to specialize in attracting emigrants, and the voyage to the Chesapeake will probably be speedier than that to New York." According to Maury, in the words of Jansen, Norfolk was the most expeditious route for emigrants from the east coast to settlement centers. Not only was it shorter but Norfolk was also better situated in relation to the railways and especially the waterways.[9] Even if the emigrants arrived in Norfolk during the winter, they would find a temperate climate, etc., etc. In his brochures, Jansen also called attention to the Virginia area itself as being fit for colonization.

It is extremely remarkable that at the same time Van Raalte was asserting in America that there should be colonization nearer to the coast and that "Norfolk, rather than New York, should be the port of entry."[10] It is very likely that an exchange of ideas between Van Raalte and Jansen took place. My research in this area, however, has not produced any positive results. In Jansen's papers concerning his seafaring plans, which are deposited in the Dutch Economic-Historical Archives in The Hague, no items are found concerning Dutch colonization.[11] Nor do Jansen's recently published memoirs refer to the matter.

There is still the other possibility that Van Raalte was sponsored by interested parties to visit the southern states and was informed by them about the shipping plans. In the South people were very pleased with the projected communications. Virginia was still under military rule, but the government of North Carolina stated that it would like to see Norfolk develop a direct trade "with a Government and people as favorably known and as highly esteemed as those of Holland." A trade convention held in Memphis, Tennessee, in May 1869, greeted "with great satisfaction the movement inaugurated in Holland by Captain M. H. Jansen for direct trade with Norfolk."[12] As we have noted, North Carolina as well as Tennessee had been considered as a colonization site by Van Raalte. He even spent some time in Knoxville, Tennessee, for that purpose.

Finally, there is third consideration that was probably the decisive one. I refer to the union of the nineteenth-century Dutch-Americans in the West with the descendants of the seventeenth-century Hollanders in the same church organization—the Reformed Church. Already in the seventeenth and eighteenth centuries, settlements by American descendants of the seventeenth-century Dutch had been established in some of the southern states such as Virginia, Kentucky, and South Carolina.[13] Earlier we noted that, as members of the Reformed Church, the Dutch immigrants in Michigan had to consider in 1855 the possible membership of the slave-holding congregations in South Carolina. So already then their attention was directed to the South. But there is more. There were New York financiers, members of the eastern branch of the Reformed Church, who bought lands in the war-devastated South. Among them was a certain |Elder Samuel| Scheffelin who was an admirer of higher education in the Van Raalte colony.

Surprisingly, it was the large tract of land purchased by this man in the area west of Richmond that was chosen for the new Dutch colony.[14] We have noted that Van Raalte had been attracted to the Richmond area. It would be extremely interesting to know if Scheffelin himself already owned the land or if he had bought it at the urging of Van Raalte. The latter is less likely because, according to Dosker, the settlement in Virginia was not at the place originally selected by Van Raalte.[15]

Whatever the case, once again we see the great significance of the "Union" of the Dutch immigrants with the Reformed Church in "the East." Just as in the case of Michigan, eastern capital, although not responsible for the settlement, certainly made it easier. If this capital did influence the choice, then it is also coresponsbile for the eventual failure.

B. Amelia County

Amelia County was the chosen area—one of the so-called "Southside" counties—situated south of the James River in Virginia.[16] Physiographically it belongs to the Piedmont Plateau, east of the Appalachians. According to the geographer Bowman, the name Piedmont Plateau can only lead to erroneous conclusions with respect to the form, morphology, and geology of the area.[17] It is at a much lower height than a real plateau, particularly in relation to the much higher mountainous areas to the West. From west to east it is 400–160 meters |1,312–526 feet| above sea level. It can be termed a plateau only when compared to the much lower Coastal Plain, from which it differs not so much in height but in composition and in the age of the earth and the rocks.[18]

The term Piedmont is misleading for those who interpret it as land "at the foot of the mountain," which is the meaning of the name, and therefore assume it has a diluvial and alluvial geology. The area was formed from very old (archaic) crystalline rock—a coagulate, residual and metamorphic, particularly granite and gneiss. As we know, gneiss is composed of quartz, feldspar, and mica and the latter is found, especially in gneiss, in a layered form. In the ensuing paleozoic or "primary" epoch, limestone and coal were formed. In 1822, about 54,000 tons of coal were mined near Richmond![19]

In various places, particularly in the Dutch settlement area, the oldest rocks were covered in the mesozoic—or "secondary" epoch—with triassic sandstone. The flowing water, together with erosion, especially during the tertiary period, has ground down the old rocky area into a peneplain. It is this low, rolling peneplain that dominates the morphology of the area, although an upsurge at the end of the tertiary erosion cycle has given a "younger" character to it. This youthfulness and its accompanying restlessness are particularly noticeable in the transitional zone between the Piedmont Plateau and the Coastal Plain. It was of importance to the Netherlanders who established themselves in this transitional area and to the west of it. This zone, from one to twelve miles in width, is characterized by an abundance of waterfalls, rapids, and gaplike river valleys—better known as the "fall line," or "fall belt," or "fall zone" as more appropriate names, which separates the very old and somewhat higher "plateau" from the lower and much younger Coastal Plain that was built up from alluvial deposits.[20]

The fall zone, which marks the upper limits of shipping, caused Van Raalte to advise his colonists to settle near the boat canal that would connect them with Richmond. But most did not follow this advice, which made the shipment of their produce and their efforts at colonization all the more difficult. According to Dosker, this circumstance contributed to the final failure.[21]

Of even more significance than this fall belt were the various soils and sub-soils formed from very old rock formations through erosion and interaction with the type of vegetation determined by the climate. This eroded material, much of which remained where it was formed (it therefore had a residual character in contrast to the "alluvial" soils deposited by the rivers) created the red clay soils. They were given that name because the sub-soils were composed of red clay; they turn more and more greyish in color when the sand content increases. Some of these lands, insofar as they were formed from granite erosion, are well known as loams rich in gravel. There, the sub-soil is formed of heavy, mica-laden, red clay-like loam also rich in gravel. This latter circumstance makes this type of soil a relatively easy prey to erosion, the wearing down caused by the rushing waters.

Some varieties of cedar, short-needle pines, and hickory trees are typical on these soils. The finer loamy, red-sand soils, containing more sand than gravel due to the wearing down of crystalline schists and slates, were generally rich in oak trees and some of the trees already mentioned, and identifiable by the experienced colonist; that is, of course, where the drainage was good. The Triassic rocks generated the most striking "red soils," the Indian or purplish soils that dominate in Amelia County. Sometimes they were sandy, sometimes gravelly, and sometimes a purer kind of loam. Especially these soils promoted tree growth, such as chestnut trees, oaks, etc. These and even the more stony areas are excellent for orchards.[22]

All of the above is reflected more or less in the account that Cohen

Stuart gave of his trip of Virginia, and explains to a great extent his writings. He undertook the trip at the strong urging of "our friend" Scheffelin in order that upon his return to the Netherlands he could report that Amelia County was an undertaking of Holland, Michigan, just as much as the settlements in Sioux County were a creation of Pella.

Cohen Stuart was welcomed at the Richmond station by the young Reverend J. Huizinga whose "typical Dutch face" immediately struck him.[23] Both proceded to another station from where they left for the colony, an hour's journey by rail from the capital. They reported: "Once again [we passed] through a beautiful and rich area of stone quarries and coal mines until we got off at a little station—Mattoax," which is in the easternmost part of the new "planting." "There we found a wagon with a handsome team belonging to a Mr. De Vries, the most well-to-do farmer in the little colony. We rode for a good hour through a fine, largely forested and hilly area of splendid beeches, oaks, pines, and cedars. The curious bright red color of the clay soil impressed us as a characteristic of the area. The thought occurred to me that that must have been the type of soil with which the earliest colonists in Virginia filled a whole ship and sent it to England in the mistaken idea that it was gold ore."

The next day Cohen Stuart rode to the little church in the settlement. "The route was nature's own but the scenery is glorious. Everything one sees along the way testifies to the luxuriant vegetation, the fertile soil, and the mild climate. Stately timber trees with heavy trunks and widespreading crowns are set off by cherry and peach trees as well as wild grapes in such abundance that one can have all the fruit one wants just for the picking."

Cohen Stuart wandered about a good deal, encouraged by the most agreeable weather—it was in February—"at times it might be cold for half the day, comparable to the late March and early April weather in the Netherlands but here without treacherous harshness; it is mild and balmy as on a radiant May day in Holland." On rare occasions snow falls and one would have to don a winter coat, as had happened during the exceptional previous winter. "The wooded undulating landscape and its variety reminds me of Gelderland's Wolfheezen region, but it is more majestic and wider and, in general, more luxuriant. And then, there are no moors and heaths but a soil swelling and bursting with fertility. Rich mineral deposits are everywhere. At times it looks as though the surface of the earth is covered with small glittering pieces of broken glass. This gives evidence of mica deposits. One need only dig a few feet to uncover a veritable mine of that remarkable natural substance, found in big chunks which can be split and sliced to the thinness of paper and with the transparency of glass."[24]

It stands to reason that this red earth, with its numerous mica deposits, must have made an unusual impression on the colonists, especially on those who had recently arrived from the Netherlands. But nowhere have I been able to find any trace of enthusiasm for the new settlement. Even worse, upon becoming more familiar with the area, people felt even more turned off. For no matter how glorious the climate of the Piedmont might be, the fertile soil turned out to be rather treacherous in many places! Cohen Stuart did not exaggerate about this climate, mentioning that it was a "most agreeable climate, soft and gentle";[25] it did not have the tropical heat of the Carolinas, Florida, or Texas, nor the stinging cold and long winters of the northern states. It also did not matter that the Virginians accepted the Netherlanders extremely hospitably and treated them cordially.[26] It was "a gentle dominion," as Virginia was termed,[27] precisely since Virginians are afraid to displease others. They "have inherited a certain consideration for the feelings of others." In the end however the odds outweighed the advantages.

The colony was established in an area of former tobacco plantations that became dominant northward up to the James River. Two and a half centuries of tobacco culture had depleted the soil, for the tobacco plant, as Russell Smith has indicated, is notorious for being a soil destroyer.[28] The first Dutch settlers must not have been spared some bitter disappointments. Even Cohen Stuart had to acknowledge that an unnatural, one-sided, and thoughtless cultivation, which did not heed the vitality of the soil, had so weakened some of the most fertile fields and cannibalized them that they would have to lie fallow for years and be heavily fertilized before they could regain their former productivity. It is remarkable that Cohen Stuart later exclaimed, as though he had not understood that his previous observations had condemned the area: "But in general how unusually well situated this place seems to be for colonizers and agriculture!" He wrote as if the colonists had sufficient time and money for the restoration of the land.[29]

Even if the land could be rejuvenated, tobacco was the obvious crop, but with few exceptions the Netherlanders were ignorant of its cultivation. In addition, tobacco cultivation required a large labor force, which was totally lacking. Corn production, with which the Michigan colonists were familiar, could have been started, but it did not offer much promise because the Midwest was ideally suited for its production. Wheat, which was usually the preeminent farm product in the new settlements since it did not require close attention, could not be produced in Virginia without some risk. Russell Smith, in his new book, *North America*, states that the James River is the southernmost limit for wheat production and the Netherlanders were settled even further south than this, where the damp warmth in the early summer would mitigate against successful wheat growth because of fungi tendencies and other plant diseases.[30]

The Dutch colonists had to experience all of this. Attention must also be called to the cheerless, neglected aspect presented by many a formerly prosperous Virginia region. Even today, one gets the impression when traveling through this tobacco country that everybody had walked away. This may be no more than an appearance and be related to the particular demands of tobacco growing. Only three to eight acres out of a hundred can be used and the sight of all this is discouraging—"a disheartening sight to the traveler who is accustomed to well-kept fields and a neat countryside."[31]

How much more discouraging the general aspect must have been around 1870, shortly after the Civil War that had so devastated those areas around Richmond. Unwittingly, Cohen Stuart causes one to reflect upon the scenes he describes: "It is as though the houses that are there try to go into hiding.... Viewed from a distance, these old residences half hidden by the trees, still appear grand and stately. But—alas, do not look too closely.... An aura of fallen grandeur hovers over these houses in which a gracious gentility formerly prevailed, surrounded by luxury, comfort and a liberal hospitality probably unequaled anywhere in the world.... What they have they graciously offer to you. But there is little of that way of life left and it is heartbreaking to note the gap between the polished, cultured manners of the residents and the sad condition of the houses and the furnishings; the house with its decaying steps, crumbling columns, and broken trellis work. In the interior there may still be fine pieces of antique furniture but in poor repair—tapestries, drapes, and furniture coverings on chairs and sofas that are faded and worn out." Everything seemed to be in a state of collapse; even the most necessary tasks remained undone; "the dripping hole in the roof becomes in a short time a large gaping wound that can no longer be healed, and a window blind, with a broken latch, rattles in the wind until it falls off its hinge."[32] Thus we see that there was not a stimulating atmosphere for the Dutch colonists who by nature were not optimistic, and who had to endure their share of worries and disappointments.

C. The Failure

It is no wonder that, within a few years, this new colony was abandoned as practically a total failure. In addition to the factors previously described, the basic cause was the lack of strong, no-nonsense leadership. Originally, Van Raalte had planned to settle in Virginia with his family. His wife, though in poor health, was still living and the mild warm area would be beneficial for her. If the Muntingh family of Pella, Van Raalte's friends, would have gone along, it would have been of considerable comfort, especially for the women, and they would have been better able to withstand the new difficulties and disappointments.[33]

Little came of these intentions. A number of colonists, both from the older colonies and also from the Netherlands itself, settled in the new area in the spring of 1869. Since many of them were of a religious bent, they reported to the Classis of Holland in August, 1869, about the possibility of establishing four churches in Virginia.[34] In addition to the Reformed element there were also some of the Christian Reformed persuasion who wished to organize as a church with their own minister. They called J. Brilman from the village of Rijsen in the province of Overijsel, and in September, 1869, he accepted the call. He had not yet arrived at the time of Cohen Stuart's visit.[35]

The Van Raaltes did not go. The poor health of Mrs. Van Raalte, the decision of the Muntinghs not to go, and the little enthusiasm among the colonists must all have been factors. The difficult and thankless task of serving as spiritual leader for the new colony was entrusted to a younger man, J. Huizinga, who had been born in the Frisian town of Kollum and educated as one of the first at Hope College and the Theological School in Holland.[36] Van Raalte lost all desire and interest after the death of his beloved wife in June of 1871 and the burning of Holland in October of that same year; his strength had been seriously undermined by these past events.

According to Dosker, "Van Raalte was still in favor of the project but he no longer had the verve for it; something in him had snapped and he desperately wanted rest just like the laborer looking forward to the evening."[37] There was little or no enthusiasm and trust that are so necessary for colonization. It was a difficult beginning for the young Huizinga. In 1870 he and his young wife and children took up residence in a former plantation house, or at least in a part of it. One of the other colonists, named De Vries, occupied the other half with his family.[38] His own parsonage would have to be built later. The least educated among the colonists, who were also the least able to withstand the difficulties, already wanted to leave. I referred to this phenomenon earlier in connection with a brother of the Seceders' church. Classis Michigan of the Christian Reformed Church—not to be confused with Classis Holland of the Reformed Church—felt themselves "called upon" to help these people leave Virginia due to their "deep poverty."[39]

The Reformed faction, in general a better educated group, displayed more energy. In the center of the colony, at Amelia Courthouse, an institute for education was established, although it existed only on paper at first. Due to Van Raalte's efforts in 1870, it was commended to the Michigan church for prayer and financial support. In 1871 the church at Amelia Courthouse had only five families and was obviously too weak to sustain itself. The church in the railroad town of Mattoax, which because of its more favorable traffic location had attracted more Netherlanders, had nineteen Reformed families and twenty-five members in 1871. It united with the church at Chule [Chula]. I know nothing about the fourth congregation. During the following year no report of the Virginia churches was brought before Classis Holland. Colonization was dwindling and the immigrants were leaving. Scarcely any newcomers arrived; the panic of 1873 caused immigration to virtually cease. In this crisis year of 1873 Classis Holland even deleted the Virginia churches from its rolls.[40]

It was in this same year—as we are aware—that Cohen Stuart sought out the daughter colony that had been abandoned by Classis Holland and preached to his fellow countrymen just as he had done in Sioux County and elsewhere. De Vries, previously mentioned, brought him in his wagon to the little church, which appeared quite picturesque in an apparently wild nat-ural setting. "In an open place, among the trees, stands this building that functions as school and church and that can hardly be imagined more humble. It is a plain four-sided, rectangular structure, twelve paces long and eight in width, with a door in front and three windows on the side, fur-nished with loose pews and a small pulpit chair. This was the church where I preached in the morning to about forty people. Yet it was good, even though my own Dutch sounded strange as I saw through the open door or the windows the wagons and saddle horses among the trees."

In the afternoon Cohen Stuart preached again—this time in English—before a larger audience that had come from afar and filled the little build-ing. In the evening there was a small gathering at the house of De Vries. "The old family Bible was brought out and there the twenty of us sat about the table and the large blazing fire—old Mrs. De Vries with her children and grandchildren, the young wife of the minister with her baby at her breast and little deaf-mute Johnnie, with a huge dog next to him on the floor, with a friendly, roguish look in his eyes. One must be an Evangelical preacher to feel what it means to speak in such a small circle."[41]

Cohen Stuart spent some further time in the colony and joined in the celebration of the king's birthday on February 19, at which time he joined in singing with them "at the top of their voices" the Dutch national anthem, and so the "Appomattox River heard the Wilhelmus of Nassau" ["Wilhelmus van Nassauwe" is the title of the Dutch anthem, from the initial words of the first line]. A few days later, on a Sunday afternoon, he baptized Huizinga's second newborn child, Maaike, as well as another young girl named Antje Woelding. It was on the Sunday afternoon after he had had lunch with [?] Geerling, a baker from Dordt, whose arrival in the colony had been an important event, "a real social step forward for the group." Geerling's wheat bread and raisin cakes made it unnecessary to prepare these at home, and so this was considered a step forward that would undoubtedly be followed by others, particularly the sale of butter cakes. Cohen Stuart was the first to taste these and he declared them to be of excellent quality. Cohen Stuart understood the situation when he said: "One should not laugh at such little things! Small things sometimes are important. Those first butter cakes were the beginning of some luxury and enjoyment in the society of the Dutch 'backwoodsmen' of Virginia and surely that is not trifling."[42]

But even Geerling's butter cookies were not enough to save the colony. More and more it went into decline. It is true that in April, 1874, the church congregations, at Van Raalte's request, were transferred to the more pros-perous Classis New York, but it was to no avail. Little or nothing remained of the Chule congregation and the combined congregation at Mattoax and Amelia Courthouse, which, according to the report of Reverend Huizinga, totaled only 22 households, 33 members and 50 Sabbath School pupils. By 1876 these figures had dwindled to 19, 29, and 35 respectively.

Huizinga left the colony in discouragement to work among the pioneers in Nebraska and continue his mission work that had known such a difficult beginning in the East. He served as pioneer and minister nearly his entire life. Beginning in 1877, reports concerning the Virginia colony ceased. In 1885 their names were dropped from the synodical records. Did they survive? I have not been able to uncover any trace of their existence.

It has been said that this last idealistic goal of Van Raalte ended in complete disaster.[43] Where does the blame lie? Who can say? It was a combination of many factors, most of which I have mentioned—largely worn-out soil, an unfavorable climate for wheat production, the lack of strong, centralized leadership—a Hospers should have been here!—etc. In particular we must refer to the people themselves, but we have learned so very little about them that it would be unwarranted to make any final conclusions. We have enough evidence to say, however, that no matter how religious the colonists may have been, they did not have the stamina, steeled and supported by high religious ideals, that motivated the immigrants of 1847. The warmer South and all that is involved in that, which would later witness other disastrous Dutch colonization attempts, tells something—but not everything. In North Carolina, situated still further south, Netherlanders from Michigan and Illinois had also established themselves. In addition to all the other vicissitudes, they were here defrauded by state officials, scandalously swindled in the purchase of state-owned lands.[44] This is all that is known to me about this colony.

A new settlement in the East, in Virginia, could have been the crowning achievement of Van Raalte's work—a fitting culmination of a full life. It was not to be. In addition to the frustrations already mentioned, he did not escape the total collapse of this last effort. Cohen Stuart, who visited Van Raalte in Holland, Michigan, in 1873, described him as a martial looking man: "He seemed much more like a pensioned general rather than a retired minister," but now his strength had been completely broken.[45] H. P. Scholte—his rival in Pella—had passed away August 25, 1868, and the Reverend C. Van der Meulen—his old comrade-in-arms—had died August 23, 1876. The following November 7 Van Raalte joined them in death. His passing made a profound impression on his followers. He was buried a few days later with great marks of sympathy. The entire colony flocked to Holland on that day and many came all the way from Wisconsin and Illinois.[46]

Among the numerous Americans in attendance, the most notable was the Honorable F. W. Ferry, at that time Vice President of the United States.* As a long-time Michigan resident, he was well acquainted with Van Raalte's great pioneering efforts. The funeral was an impressive ceremony, although the deceased had requested that it be kept as simple as possible. Each one present realized that a great Hollander, as well as one of America's best citizens, had departed.

---

*U.S. Senator Thomas F. Ferry of Michigan, served as president *pro tempore* of the Senate during the mid-1870s, and became acting vice president of the United States in 1875 when Vice President Henry Wilson died in office.

4

Daughter Colonies in Michigan, Nebraska, Kansas, Minnesota, Wisconsin, and Illinois

A. In Michigan

Following the disappointments in Virginia and North Carolina, the Michigan colonists turned away, at least temporarily, from the South. But they kept a predilection for wooded areas—a predilection that was dictated by their not always rosy economic status, and caused them to seek the cheapest areas that would provide quick profits. Since Michigan was still a wooded area, many remained in this state, especially those least well-off. As was indicated previously, the forests—although not the easiest areas in which to live—provided the least expensive opportunities for settlement.

The railroad companies in particular, owners of huge land grants, tried to exploit this general attitude by means of their agents, and not without success. The organic expansion of the old Van Raalte colony led to many new settlements in the neighborhood—Fijnaart (East Saugatuck), Beaverdam, Harderwijk, etc., which were mentioned earlier in connection with the establishment of Reformed congregations in 1869, 1870, and 1880, respectively.[1] In addition, other Dutch settlements were created at greater distances, and indeed those were usually located on or near most of the rail lines built around 1870. Thus we find the settlement of Hamilton, in Allegan County, situated near the railroad bridge where the Pere Marquette line between Holland and Allegan crosses the Rabbit River. G. Dangremond, from the Netherlands province of Overijsel, who had been educated at Hope College and the Theological School at Holland, Michigan, was a pioneer preacher there since 1869, and the following year a Reformed congregation was established.[2] In that same year the Spring Lake congregation was formed and in 1882 it numbered 130 families. Spring Lake was located on the Grand Trunk near Grand Haven.

Grand Haven also became a mother colony for other settlements. As we have noted previously, many Hollanders resided there from the beginning and the Reformed congregation there numbered 360 families in 1882; there

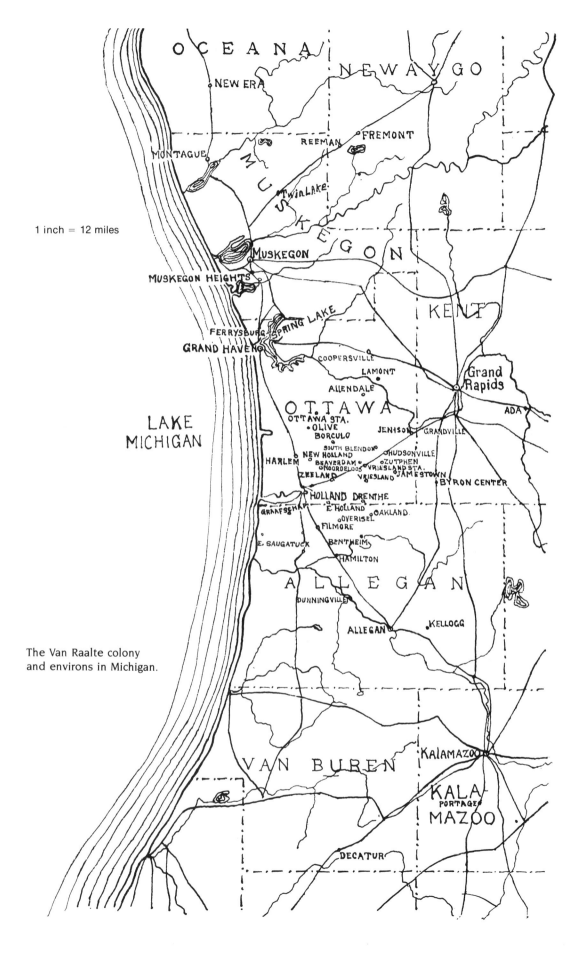

1 inch = 12 miles

The Van Raalte colony
and environs in Michigan.

was also a Christian Reformed congregation. The Dutch settlements stretched out especially along the Pere Marquette Line in a northerly direction, because the further north one went, the cheaper the lands generally were.

In Muskegon County, W. Meyer, P. Vos, and J. Bennema were the first settlers in the port of Muskegon and in 1852 there were numerous Hollanders there, particularly Groningers.[3] Although the Dutch settlement at Ravenna had failed, there were settlements at Montague and Twin Lake—on the Pere Marquette Lines. Reformed congregations were organized at both places in 1875; in 1882 they had twenty-six and forty-one families respectively, but they dwindled after about 1885. Church enmity was probably not foreign here. In 1881 a congregation of the True |Ware| brothers was organized in Montague and it is still in existence.[4] In Twin Lake, however, the Reformed element regained the lost ground.

To the north of Montague there was a settlement at New Era, in Oceana County; since 1884 it has had a Christian Reformed congregation, and since 1894 a Reformed congregation, both of which are still in existence. Northeast of Twin Lake, settlements came into being in Fremont and Reeman, both in Newaygo County. In 1870 a Reformed church was organized at Fremont and in 1882 it had forty families.[5] In this latter year a Christian Reformed congregation was started probably as a consequence of the anti-Freemasonry movement; in 1914 a second congregation began. In spite of various religious clashes which here, like elsewhere, frequently disturbed the rural peace, these three congregations have survived. Reeman had its first church—a Christian Reformed congregation—in 1890.

To what extent either Muskegon—which in 1882 had a Reformed Church numbering 350 families as well as a Christian Reformed Church—or the Van Raalte colony served as parent settlements, from which radiated the new colonies along the Pere Marquette Lines, is not always entirely clear. The English names of most of the settlements indicate that the initiative came from the railroad promoters.

A colonization attempt directly out of the Van Raalte settlement had taken place earlier, in 1868, when moving was the order of the day. It was made in cooperation with a railroad company and it seemed that this endeavor would lead to a really new Dutch settlement, a more homogeneous unit than the ones mentioned so far, somewhat like the forest settlement of 1847. I am referring to the |Vogel Center| settlement in Missaukee County, much more to the north and located midway between Saginaw Bay on the east coast and Grand Traverse Bay on the west coast of the Lower Peninsula—an area at about the same latitude—about 44½ degrees northern latitude—as the Fox River Valley in Wisconsin. The latter was the northernmost Dutch settlement in America to date. It was Jan Vogel, who had been born in the Dutch province of Zuid Holland and was living at Noordeloos in the Van Raalte colony, who moved in 1868 with three households to the south bank of the Clam River—a tributary of the Muskegon River—and

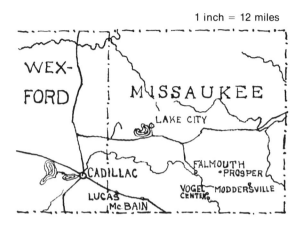

The forest colony in Missaukee County, Michigan.

settled in the so-called Clam Union. He became the founder of Vogel Center, which in 1881 already numbered seventy Dutch families.[6]

An increasing scarcity of timber in the southern areas was the cause for the migration to this heavily wooded area. The area is of a moraine type, as I have previously described. There are numerous hills in this Missaukee County area, some reaching a height of up to 500 meters [1,650 ft.].[7] In this region north of the Grand and Saginaw river valleys the soil is of a very sandy composition, occasionally interspersed with clay lands and boggy deposits among this land of numerous lakes and swamps.

The great value of the forest riches of these areas—"the native habitat of the white pine," says Chase—were recognized in the years after the Civil War. Consequently railroads were constructed to carry the gigantic timber loads to the south and bring immigrants for a low fare to the districts of the north that had to be deforested.[8]

Lumbering was the primary occupation of the early colonists and only after that could thought be given to working a piece of land. Reverend R. T. Kuiper visited this new forest colony for a few days in 1881. He found his way along deer trails and cow paths in the largely undeveloped area and twice he found it necessary to wade through a stream. It seems that in this heavily timbered area, bridges did not generally exist. The poorest elements had come here, but many of them by lumbering and reclaiming the deforested lands had then already become well-to-do.[9]

It was Kuiper's opinion that, "although extremely isolated, it was an excellent place of settlement" for farm laborers. But they had to be hardened because life there was rough, especially in the notorious American lumber camps, with their international population. In addition, the distant location was for many a serious objection. Cadillac, originally called Clam

Lake, was situated on the Grand Rapids and Indiana Railroad. It became the market center for the new settlement and is now a railroad center, but situated twenty-two miles west of Vogel Center. In 1877 the enterprising |Wijnand| Modders established the colony of Moddersville, east of Vogel Center and it still exists although the locator moved to Grand Rapids.[10] The Reformed Church there has scarcely ten families.

In the early eighties when there was a renewed urge for emigration just as in the sixties and seventies, and also because of the coming of age of the children, plus the arrival of many family members from the Old Country, committees were formed at Holland and elsewhere in "*de Kolonie*" to seek other suitable lands. In Holland such an inquiry was entrusted in 1881 to the preacher R. T. Kuiper—the church remained a significant factor in colonization matters—as well as to a farmer named |Wiepke| Diekema.[11] The next year Harm Lucas of Graafschap and J. H. Eppink of Allegan—both places in Allegan County—were requested to perform a similar inquiry. As a result of a visit of R. T. Kuiper to Vogel Center, which had impressed him, both of the latter men journeyed to Osceola and Missaukee counties "nearly in the center of the state." The border zone between these two counties impressed them most; nowhere had they found "such good land, such valuable timber and so well and favorably situated for progress" as here.[12]

It appears that Lucas and Eppink were appointed by the above-mentioned railroad company and by land speculators to be their representatives and encouraged the founding of a Dutch settlement. Twenty thousand acres were set aside—half by the railroad and half by the speculators—about six and a half miles southeast of Cadillac and five miles east of the nearest railroad station at Hobart. Separated only by a very thinly settled township from Vogel Center, the new settlers wanted "to establish a large Dutch settlement on a par with Holland, Zeeland, and Vriesland. This we, and also many others, would like to see."

The land was reported to consist of mixed clay, sand, and gravel and was said to be fertile "to an unusual depth" and was covered with a growth of trees "splendid to behold."[13] Maples, elms, ashes, linden, birches, beeches, etc., were found. The gentlemen neglected to mention the pine woods, probably for "business" reasons. It was evident that we are here in a transitional area from the more valuable hardwoods to the more exclusively prevalent pine woods or softwoods to the north, in connection with the changes in soils.

The construction of a second railroad, already well underway, running east and west through or near the colony would increase the value of land even more. Even so, the price of the land was low, it was claimed; a minimum of forty acres could be bought for $7 per acre—one-fourth down and the remainder payable within five years at 7 percent interest. Prospective purchasers of the railroad lands were offered a refund of their round-trip fares between Grand Rapids and Cadillac if they wanted to pay a visit to see the land themselves. They would also receive free transportation for their families, if they bought and settled on the newly-opened lands. The land agents called it a "free crossing," perhaps still under the influence of the ocean voyage. This offer would hold only until January 1, 1883. Developed lands, which had been homesteaded and initially obtained for free by those who had worked it and now owned it, were also available but at a much higher price. These did not concern Lucas and Eppink.

It is true that not everyone was in favor of the established "favorable" terms, but in the end many Hollanders did settle here. In this connection, however, we must consider the "rushing in " of colonists and their "on the spot" purchases as figurative language that even the most orthodox land salesmen were accustomed to use. The fact that there was a Dutch settlement, Vogel Center, which already at that time had a church and school, post office, general store, etc., must certainly have contributed to this new influx. Thus, Lucas and McBain came slowly into existence in connection with the construction of a new railroad.

At Falmouth, north of Vogel Center, a few Dutch families had also already settled in the early eighties.[14] In addition there was the establishment of a settlement around nearby Prosper. Thus slowly, an interesting Dutch settlement grew here. The inhabitants, largely farmers, sold their farm produce and meat and dairy products initially to the timber merchants, loggers, and miners and then later found markets in the surrounding towns. The Missaukee settlement certainly did not develop into as rich a colony as Sioux County, Iowa. Especially after the area had been deforested, the soil was not sufficiently productive and the area not important enough. Millions of acres of infertile, unproductive land are still lying around, deserted by the small population that was once there. Naturally, this was detrimental to the Dutch colonists who had hoped to sell their produce locally.[15]

Living an out-of-the-way and isolated life, our colonists have religion as the dominant force in their lives. Reformed and Christian Reformed factions clashed with each other and this helped, at least somewhat, to break the monotony of daily life! In 1873, a Christian Reformed congregation was organized in Vogel Center and in 1881 it numbered fifty Dutch families with J. Schepers as their minister, while the remaining families were mostly Reformed.[16] Only in 1890, did a Reformed church come into being and in 1892 they had their own preacher—S. Vennema. When he left in 1900 the congregation declined to the point where it became a mission station.[17] Vennema had also preached in Falmouth and Moddersville; in both places there is still a Reformed church today, but in Vogel Center the Reformed could not survive against the Christian Reformed and were dissolved in 1907. In Lucas, the Rehoboth congregation was established in 1890 but it is temporarily holding its own today as a mission station. Other Christian Reformed congregations were established in 1883 in Lucas, in 1894 at Prosper, and in 1917 in McBain.

It is due to men such as Vogel, Modders, Lucas, and Eppink that many

Dutch and Dutch-American families established themselves here. Their efforts, as the latter two expressed it, to be of help "for the welfare of our fellowmen in body and soul" may be considered to have been successful.[18] The first three towns, called after these men—Vogel Center, Moddersville, and Lucas—are a permanent and, we hope, a thankful remembrance of this achievement.

B. In Nebraska and Kansas

We have seen how already after the Civil War the Michigan colonists dispersed in different directions—to the forests of Virginia and North Carolina, but even more so to the woods of northern Michigan. There were also those forest colonists who now tried their luck on the open fields and prairies. We encountered some of those in Sioux County, Iowa. Many of these courageous and enterprising colonists followed the mighty stream of emigrants, "home seekers," that flowed from the northern states. They went with those who had fought in the Civil War on Lincoln's side and who wanted to take advantage of the freely obtainable homesteads in the blooming state of Kansas (no longer the "bleeding" state of Kansas as before the War) and in the state of Nebraska, opened up by the first Pacific Railroad in 1869.

It was not poverty that originally prompted these Dutch emigrants to move and neither was this usually the case in several of the settlements that were made in 1868 and in succeeding years. Least of all can we speak of "*Armutsemigration*" [poverty emigration] on the prairies. More so than elsewhere, the prairie colonization of the farther West was an expression of one of the results of the Civil War, so "successfully" waged by the North. In the neglected and decadent surroundings of the settlements in Virginia we could feel the results of a lost struggle that reduced the confidence and enterprise of the residents, according to [S. R.] Steinmetz.[19] The resulting collapse and decay, no doubt, had a discouraging affect on the Netherlanders. How different, however, is the aftermath of a victorious war. "The prestige of the nation is enhanced, new sources for the general prosperity are exploited, the increased self-confidence endows all actions and enterprises with a vigor unknown before, all of life is lifted to a higher plane; the nation comes into full blossom and the population increases substantially."[20]* Whatever one's views may be in this matter, one major fact stands out after the Civil War, and I repeat it: the mighty Pacific Railroad was completed in 1869 and the Northerners went in huge numbers to the new, to the farther West.

*Das Ansehen des Volkes wird erhöht, neue Wohlfartsquellen werden geöffnet, das gehobene Selbstbewustsein verleiht allen Unternehmungen einen ungekannten Schwung, das ganze Leben wird auf einen höheren Plan gestellt, das Volk gelangt zu heller Blüte, die Bevölkerung wächst kräftig.

The Dutch Americans participated in relatively large numbers in this outreach, as we have seen in the case of Sioux County, giving expression to this feeling of self-assertion and vigor [Schwung]. And they prospered! Also many of those who settled in Kansas and Nebraska did well even though these states were even more subject to prairie fires and grasshoppers than Iowa.

They settled, as I indicated earlier, in Lancaster County, Nebraska, in 1868, drawn from Michigan and Wisconsin by the Homestead Act and the relatively cheap railroad lands. The Union Pacific runs through Lancaster County, and the state capital, Lincoln, situated near the middle of the county, lies on the railroad. Our fellow countrymen settled in an area somewhat milder than the American continental climate they had heretofore experienced. It was south of Lincoln, in the southernmost reaches of the county, in the fertile Missouri valley that forms part of the endless prairie plain. It is "a rolling, alluvial plain, growing gradually more sandy toward the West." Nebraska has short, severe winters, stormy flower-laden springtimes, long, hot summers and splendid falls which last until Christmas: "a season of perpetual sunlight, blazing blue skies, and frosty nights, the season of beauty and sentiment, as spring as in the Old World," according to W. S. Cather in an unusually fine account of Nebraska.[21]

In 1868 the first hardy individuals arrived with their households in covered ox-drawn prairie schooners—typical immigrants. Just as in Sioux County, living quarters were dug into the earth—the so-called "dug-outs"—and so a "prairie-dog village" came into being. Later came the sturdy sod houses that were very warm and even comfortable. The prairie sod was so tough and strong due to the interwoven prairie grass roots, that it could be

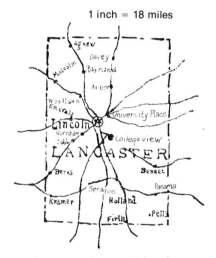

Lancaster County, Nebraska.

dug and cut out like peat. The first settlement was named Holland, after "*de stad*" in Michigan.

Jan W. Te Winkel, born in Winterswijk in the Netherlands, assumed the difficult task of being their first minister in Nebraska, just as the young Huizinga had ministered earlier in Virginia. Te Winkel had been educated at Van Raalte's institution, "Hope," and its affiliated Theological School in *de Kolonie*, where he had been one of the earliest students and builders of the gymnasium. He had served at Oostburg, Wisconsin, before going to Nebraska. Since most of the homesteaders were religious, they had organized a Reformed Church in June 1870, the year previous to Te Winkel's arrival. As was the case elsewhere, Te Winkel conceived it as his task to attract additional settlers in order to strengthen the church organization. He encouraged many to settle in Nebraska and soon a "substantial" church and parsonage were erected. Te Winkel proved to be a strong leader.[22]

At the same time they were not without difficulties. The land was fertile but the hot dry winds often destroyed the harvest, so that here also many left disheartened. Just as in Sioux County, others took their place, coming not only from Michigan and Wisconsin, but also from Marion County, Iowa. A settlement was established southeast of Holland by people from Pella and was given the name Pella after the mother colony. Pella first had a Reformed congregation in 1884, but it did not have its own minister, J. J. Dragt, until 1895.[23] He also preached in the third Dutch settlement, Firth, situated south of Holland and west of Pella, which was a much more lively town than the other two very rural communities, since a branch of the Chicago, Burlington and Quincy Railroad made it a railroad town.

I do not know if Kramer, also in Lancaster County and west of Firth, was inhabited by Hollanders or not. It appears that some Hollanders settled about 1880 near Hastings in Adams County, but I have not learned whether any Hollanders lived in Roseland, also located in the county.[24]

About the same time numerous Hollanders joined the stream of Yankees to Kansas, which had become a state in 1861. Even before the Civil War many anti-slavery people had settled there. They were true crusaders, men and women who were intellectual and social pioneers, with much idealism, and they had set their stamp on the land. Those who had fought on the Southern side lost out on the homesteads, and so the Yankee element, using homesteads and cheap railroad lands, had become dominant, "covenanters of various sorts."[25]

Several Michigan Dutch settlers were scattered among the Yankees throughout the middle of Kansas, as in the western and eastern parts. Van Raalte, concerned about their welfare, called the attention of Classis Holland to these pioneers and, invited by the Classis to do so, decided to pay a visit to them. His declining health prevented this for the time being, but finally in late 1871 or 1872 it seems that he made the trip, and the climate in this more southern area apparently benefited him. It was probably due to Van Raalte that the emerging congregations in the Sunflower State came into being.[26] In 1871, two Reformed congregations were organized. Somerset, situated south of Kansas City in Miami County, was served by a missionary named [Joseph] Mayou, who had been trained at New Brunswick. He served there from 1872 to 1876, after which the congregation no longer existed. I am not aware if there were any Old Dutch or Young Dutch in addition to the colonists among them. The hamlet named Block and possibly the very international name Koch, at that time the name of a well-known Dutch land speculator in America, might indicate that both had Dutch ties but no more than that.[27]

A true Dutch settlement existed along the boundaries of four counties in the middle of northern Kansas near Oak Creek, mentioned previously. The Rotterdam congregation was organized there in 1871, which now belongs within the town of Dispatch, in Jewell County. Rotterdam had a difficult time during its first years due to the drought that lasted until 1878; then they could support their own minister, the Reverend [John] Hoekje, and he served until 1891.[28] At present the congregation numbers sixteen families. In 1880 a Christian Reformed congregation was established and this now numbers sixty households. The settlement was served by the Missouri Pacific Railroad and this was a definite advantage to its growth. Colonists from Pella settled here and Rotterdam was considered a virtual creation of Pella.[29]

Perhaps it could more justly be said that Pella was responsible for the origin of the more westerly Prairie View, situated in Phillips County and

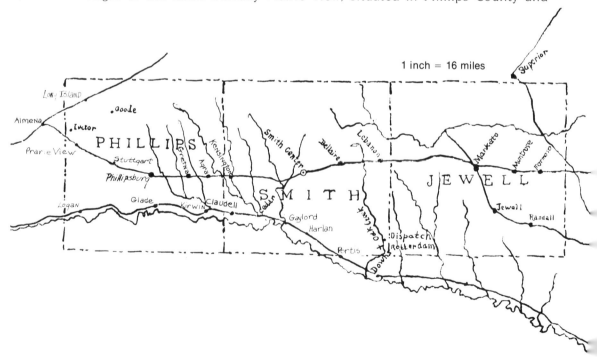

Settlements in the northern districts of Kansas.

served by the Chicago, Rock Island and Pacific. Hollanders from Michigan, smitten with "Kansas fever," settled here early also. The nearby hamlet of Goede is probably also indicative of Dutch colonization. This was also true of Holland, situated on Holland Creek, and Zutphen in Dickinson County. This was all the more remarkable since none of the three were railroad stops, which would have indicated participation of railroad capital. It is possible that these settlements, just as the German-sounding town of Winkler in Riley County, were established by Dutch companies operating in America, as so many were and a few still are. Prairie View also suffered from drought. The entire state suffered from it in the early seventies and it occasioned a momentous exodus following closely upon the hopeful entry. The Hollanders in Kansas were given aid by Sioux County, itself in great difficulties, in the spring of 1875.[30] But it was true here as elsewhere that as some left, others came. There were some who did not feel at home in Lancaster County, Nebraska, and went to try their luck in Kansas.

In the spring of 1878 a group arrived in covered wagons, drawn by twelve yoke of oxen and a team of horses and settled in Phillips County, Kansas, to homestead the land and to break ground as a requirement of the Homestead Law. Among them were P. Smit, A. J. Kip, and B. Kappers—all born in Noord Holland (Krabbendam and St. Maartensbrug in the [northwestern] Zijpe region)—and B. Roland, a French-American married to a Dutch woman.[31] Then, as true Americans disdainful of distance, they returned to their homes in Nebraska to harvest their crops. In the spring of 1879 they settled permanently in Phillips County, Kansas, and soon they were followed by others and established a new colony—Luctor. In 1885 a Christian Reformed congregation was organized and in 1924 it numbered 73 families.[32] In that same year of 1885 a Reformed congregation also came into existence, as was so often the case elsewhere. The Reformed group obtained their own minister, D. Scholten, in 1886; the True brothers had to content themselves during the first years with Bible reading services and an occasional sermon from a passing missionary. When E. Bos arrived during the nineties they had their first preacher. Those who lived around Prairie View organized a congregation in 1915, which has now only six families, while the Reformed church there, dating from 1907, has 61 families.

The prosperity of these Kansas settlements was furthered not only by the railroads but also by the "Pike's Peak, Ocean to Ocean" highway. Nearly all the settlers have automobiles, which in America is the rule rather than the exception. Seldom did the Netherlanders in Kansas and Nebraska fare as well as the Sioux County colonists. But what profited from this condition was their cultural, or rather religious life, that is, the ultra-orthodox viewpoint. W. A. White in *These United States* has termed the Kansas population in general a "puritan survival." This also seems to apply to the Dutch inhabitants. Dr. Beets, who spent a portion of his youth there and who preached there several times in 1924, noted that spiritual life was better among the Kansas Dutch than in many other Dutch communities. Old and young spoke

Dutch and English, but above all the language of Canaan. Their secular as well as their spiritual life was difficult. Perhaps because of this there was more coming and going here than elsewhere. They were not attached to the soil as was the case in the Old Country. They were restless, looking first of all for material progress, just like the American farmers, even like the Puritan farmers.

There were peculiar "trekkers" who remind us a good deal of the men of the South African Transvaal for whom they held a feeling of affinity. But one should not conclude that these wanderers were a typically Dutch phenomenon. These roving, restless people were found and are still found wherever undeveloped land is available. Drought and the hot winds caused colonists to move often, now here, now there, especially in the more western states. Bloemendaal ran into them repeatedly, and at one time a group, coming from Nebraska in their covered wagons, told him that the hot winds had scorched everything.

These wanderers roamed for years, especially in the western areas that constitute a portion of the Great Plains and which, because of their aridity, Russell Smith has termed "the land of tragedy." For two and a half centuries the whites had been moving steadily westward, conquering the land, developing it, setting up farms that brought into existence prosperous towns. The colonists in triumph followed this route from the Atlantic to central Kansas and Nebraska. But their triumphant march came to a halt in the Great Plains, which at first glance appeared to be as fertile as the prairies—the grass was luxuriant and the dark soil indicated fertility. Only after their arrival did the colonists learn how different was the transitional area between the Mississippi valley and the Rocky Mountains—the rainfall decreased the farther west they went and this was coupled with the dry, hot winds. Here the army of colonists first met defeat and hundreds of thousands were thrown back, time and time again.[33]

There were numerous Hollanders among these "fighters," also among the defeated ones. Some had accumulated some capital in Iowa and left, full of hope, for Kansas, Nebraska, and Oregon, where they expected to become landowners. But they were bitterly disappointed in this "drought-ridden land." They lost everything and, profoundly disappointed, they returned to Pella, down and out, almost totally defeated.[34] I said "almost" because there was still a glimmer of hope among a few and this grew into a new drive to revive the struggle once more, not against other people but against nature. They were heroic warriors, although these men did not announce their deeds ahead of time and left no monuments to celebrate their "feats of arms." Thanks to the firmness and tenacity of a determined small group— they were selection material!—the Kansas and Nebraska settlements pulled through and are now a permanent reminder of the heavy struggle.

About the same time—around 1870—the Iowa Dutch established colonies in Texas and Colorado, also named Pella after the mother colony; but these had to be given up after forty years of struggle.[35] They no longer existed after 1911. In Texas there was drought and heat and in Colorado the land was too unfamiliar for the Dutch.

C. In Minnesota and Wisconsin

Many new communities were formed by settlers from Marion County, Iowa, as well as by those from Ottawa and Allegan counties in Michigan. In both areas there were colonists with more initiative (in Pella) or less initiative (in Holland) who took up leadership. They were driven by the relative poverty of many settlers in the forested areas and attracted by the great prosperity of others on the prairies. The prairie prosperity was an additional incentive to the motivations I have mentioned earlier, the incentive of land speculation.

Thus both poverty and prosperity drove people to act, and their actions resulted in the Dutch migration to Sioux County, Iowa and to Missaukee County, Michigan, and elsewhere. Again, it is significant that among the Wisconsin Dutch, little is noticed of such an initiative or leadership. We remarked earlier that little initiative, personality, and originality marked the Wisconsin Dutch settlers, which is more or less the result of their being of average quality among the Dutch immigrants. Another setback in their case was the fact that they had spread out too thinly from the very beginning and lacked great leaders.

Already in Sioux County we have met Wisconsin Hollanders from Alto, Waupun, and Fond du Lac County, while those who settled in Holland and eight miles further in Pella, Lancaster County, Nebraska, had largely come from Sheboygan County; most of them were Gelderlanders. Thus there was an impulse toward dispersion. For that matter, we have already encountered the Nagel family, originally from Alto, who were in Fillmore County, in southeastern Minnesota as early as 1865 [sic, 1856] and a large number of Hollanders from Alto subsequently settled there, probably under the influence of the Chicago, Milwaukee and St. Paul Railroad Company, whose tracks run through both Fond du Lac County in Wisconsin as well as through Fillmore County, Minnesota. In those days Minnesota was virtually a battleground for railroad companies and experienced a tremendous boom period, which was interrupted only by the Panic of 1873.

According to the geologists [Th. C.] Chamberlin and [R. D.] Salisbury, Fillmore County was part of "the driftless area." There [Oepke] Bonnema and his Frisians had settled but on the Wisconsin side of the Mississippi. They were preceded by some who had settled on the Minnesota side of the river in present-day Houston County. Insofar as I am aware, these were the first Dutch colonists in Minnesota. Since Fillmore County adjoins Houston County, the thought comes to mind that the Frisians must have been the first ones to plan settlements in this region. The fact, however, that Fillmore was colonized by Gelderlanders, rather than Frisians, casts doubt on any connection. Whatever the case, the driftless area, which is composed of eluvial soils caused by the erosion of the underlying rocks and which, through the centuries of drainage, is free of swamps, had attracted the Frisians.[36] Now the Gelderlanders established themselves.

One does not hear of leaders in these colonies. Here it was just as we noticed in so many other places: the arrival of a single family—in this case perhaps the Nagels—caused a settlement to come into being as westward-bound settlers were attracted to their fellow countrymen and preferably to people of their own province, sometimes through a single conversation or letter, and because they were already restless Americans, always ready to pack up and go.

This is why Bloemendaal met many Alto acquaintances there, after he had first gone to Sioux County, and then in 1870 traveled to Fillmore County where he remained for five days.[37] About eighty Holland families were residents there, clustering around the church village of Greenleafton. According to Professor |A.| Raap, of Holland, Michigan, it was named for a Miss |Alice| Greenleaf of New York who had donated money for the building of a church; a portrait of her is still to be seen there. The settlement is very rural and so small that it even lacks a post office. If one wishes to receive mail, it is necessary to go to Preston or Harmony—both located on the Chicago, Milwaukee and St. Paul lines. Bloemendaal found the area "a good region but hilly and twenty miles from a market," adverse conditions that still exist. The water table was low and water could only be obtained by the use of windmills, which our Geldersman saw in "huge numbers."

Bloemendaal visited the area again twenty years later and observed some progress. The total number of colonists had not increased considerably because several had left—the normal American symptom. In 1869 a Reformed Church was organized—the first in Minnesota, and P. Lepeltak, a Hollander who had studied at Rutgers College and New Brunswick Seminary, was called as pastor. In 1924, this congregation numbered 111 families, and so it is evident that the colony grew considerably after the nineties. There is no Christian Reformed congregation since the people from Gelderland, as was previously noted, were attracted to a far lesser degree than, for instance, the Frisians and Groningers, to this denomination.

There are several retired farmers living around the little church at Greenleafton; others, more secularly inclined, have established themselves in the nearby little railroad towns such as Spring Valley and others. The farmers have spread more widely up to Bristol Township.[38] Still it is difficult to refer to this as a real Dutch settlement since, from the very beginning, other ethnics were present. During Bloemendaal's first trip, the settlement was already "very cosmopolitan." No subsequent Dutch settlements were founded in the "driftless" area; the more chalky and fertile, old-time glacial and moraine lands had a greater attraction.

If Alto residents went to Greenleafton, the Netherlanders from Sheboygan—also largely Gelderlanders—went to Baldwin, St. Croix County, which was situated near, but not in Minnesota, where the twin cities of Minneapolis and St. Paul constituted a desirable market for their dairy products. Also here, the Chicago, St. Paul, Minneapolis and Omaha Railroad that cuts through the settlement must have taken the initiative; after a few had settled there, more came. At present (1924) there is a Reformed Church with 116 members and since 1888 there has been a Christian Reformed congregation, counting 72 families.

The only colonizer, or "locator" as it were, whom I heard of when I was in Wisconsin, was a Frisian, T. Tillema, who prospered greatly. Insofar as the Dutch Protestants in Wisconsin were largely Gelderlanders and in Sheboygan County also Zeelanders, it was Tillema who was largely responsible for attracting the Frisian element to Wisconsin. Tillema had journeyed to America in April, 1854.[39] He had lived with his parents—ordinary working-class people—at Hiaure in Westdongeradeel, the home country of Worp Van Peyma. Originally the Tillemas, like so many others from the Dongeradeel region and the rest of Friesland—one thinks of the Van Peymas, Koopmans, Dijkstras, Zuidemas, etc.—had settled near Buffalo. The following year the Tillemas went to Milwaukee, Wisconsin. The parents remained there while the younger Tillema, with some others, traveled to Michigan to work on the farms in the summer and in the lumber camps in the winter. The young Frisian continued in this manner until 1861; he then married a Frisian girl born in Blya and settled in Columbia County, Wisconsin, southwest of Alto, where two Dutch families had previously located. Tillema became wealthy. Through his efforts several Frisians settled in the vicinity and the hamlet of Friesland came into being.[40] A branch of the Chicago and North Western line facilitated communication and encouraged the general prosperity, which condition has increased sharply during the last twenty years. Friesland has a Reformed Church now numbering ninety-one families.

Some of the residents bought land in the vicinity and a new colony came into existence in and around Randolph, Dodge County. Randolph Center, near Friesland, also attracted some settlers. Randolph has a Reformed Church of sixty-five families, and a Christian Reformed Church—begun in 1908—had sixty-eight families in 1924. Already in 1893 Randolph Center had a Reformed mission station.

Tillema was a staunch Republican; he voted twice for Lincoln and for every subsequent Republican presidential candidate and went to hear men such as Karl Schurz and others. He served for many years as justice of the peace in Friesland as well as mayor (supervisor) and as a member of the school board. He lived in Friesland for thirty-two years. In 1893 he moved to Milwaukee where he served as an elder for nine years in the Reformed Church. In 1911 he returned to his colony and this time settled in Randolph. Here the founder of Friesland, Wisconsin, and his equally sturdy wife, S. Van der Velde, celebrated their sixtieth wedding anniversary in 1921 among their countrymen and fellow Frisians, many of them natives of the Dongeradeel region.

After this Frisian colony, some Dutch settlements were established much further north in Wisconsin around Vesper in Wood County and Plover in Portage County, both small railroad towns. In Vesper a Christian Reformed Church was started in 1898 and in Plover, in 1909, counting forty and twelve families, respectively, in 1924. In addition, Vesper has a Reformed Church of twenty-nine families.[41]

D. In Illinois and Indiana

After the Civil War some new settlements also came into existence in Illinois, but it is difficult to speak of them as daughter colonies of already existing settlements. As we are aware, the colonists from High Prairie and Low Prairie—later known as Roseland and South Holland—first spread out over the area of the Little Calumet River in Thornton Township in such villages as Dalton [Dolton], Thornton, Phoenix, Riverdale, and especially Lansing, southeast of South Holland. The rapid growth of Chicago had attracted many nationalities to this area and so it cannot be accurately stated that these were Dutch settlements. Since Lansing was furthest from Chicago, land prices remained "bearable" there, while closer to the metropolis they soared. Therefore, many Hollanders settled in Lansing, having left the increasingly expensive Roseland area. An example is that of a branch of the famous Ton family that came to have considerable influence in Lansing. One of the members of this proliferating family—the American progenitor of this house had twenty-two children!—was Jan Cornelis Ton, a well-known figure in the Calumet district. He served as postmaster in Lansing for many years and also engaged in real estate transactions. In the latter capacity the Tons must certainly have encouraged the settlement of Hollanders in Lansing.[42] In 1875 a Reformed Church was started, which numbered 128 families in 1924. In 1919 a Christian Reformed Church came into being and it numbered 85 families in 1924.

Some Hollanders settled even further eastward in the Calumet area, going beyond the borders of Illinois and settling in Lake County, Indiana. Many located in and around Munster on the ridge south of the Little Calumet, while others settled further eastward, on the same ridge in Highland. The [S. P.] Schoon family is a typical example of those who went into this more easterly area.[43] The family had come from the province of Noord Holland and was originally attracted by Roseland, which had drawn many from Noord Holland. In 1856 they settled in Fernwood, north of Roseland. Later they moved to Riverdale, a half-mile eastward and more distant from Chicago; therefore the land was less expensive. They lived here, on the banks of the Little Calumet, for about twenty years and when this land also increased in value they moved in 1884 to Munster, in Lake County, Indiana. Many had preceded them in this trek. There was already a Christian Reformed Church in Munster by 1870 and the Schoon family affiliated with it. In 1924 this congregation had one hundred families. In 1908, eighty-eight families joined the congregation of this same denomination in nearby Highland, on the same ridge road.

In addition to truck gardeners and onion growers, many factory workers settled in both towns. Two new industrial centers came into being in the area traversed by the Calumet River, which runs parallel to the Little Calumet over a great distance. They were the world-famous iron and steel city of Gary to the northeast and the lesser known, but no less important Hammond, situated northwest of Munster and Highland. Industry attracted so many different ethnic groups and in such huge numbers that the Dutch element was scarcely noticeable, and so one cannot speak of Dutch communities.

The earlier Illinois colonists tended to remain in the Calumet area also because their holdings continued to increase in value. They broke up their holdings into smaller parcels and sold them at high prices and then moved further from Chicago to buy and occupy cheaper lands, but still within the Chicago area of influence. A shortage of land did not constitute such an impelling motive for moving to the Far West, since the land continually increased in value. On the other hand, the proximity of Chicago engendered an increasingly intensive cultivation of the soil and actually changed farming to a truck gardening operation. The Windy City and the light sandy soils at the foot of the dunes, which were comparable to the Dutch *geestgronden*, encouraged the production of garden crops, especially of onions and white cabbage. Thanks to the German element in America, there was a constant demand for sauerkraut, and this truck gardening was very profitable.[44] Relatively little land—but much more labor— was needed for this activity. A segment of the labor force was engaged in factory work at Pullman and elsewhere. Prior to 1893 Pullman paid rather high wages.

It is even more difficult to identify the remaining Dutch settlements in Illinois as having originated from High and Low Prairie, but that is not to say that in those settlements there are no original High and Low Prairie residents. Toward the end of the seventies there was a settlement around Danforth, situated south of Chicago in Iroquois County on one of the Illinois Central lines but this "city" had only a few houses in the seventies! In 1869 a Reformed Church was organized and Reverend |A.| Duiker served the church from 1872 to 1874, after which he was followed by the well-known Reverend L. J. Hulst, who had been called from the Netherlands.[45] Groningers, particularly from the bog and peat areas |*veenkolonin*| such as Stadskannal—Hulst's last charge in the Netherlands—settled here apparently because the foundations had been laid by Hollanders from Chicago and environs. When Reverend Hulst arrived, the congregation numbered

1 inch = 15 miles

MICHIGAN

LAKE

PALATINE

ARLINGTON
HEIGHTS

MAYWOOD
OAK PARK

Chicago

ENGLEWOOD

EVERGREEN
PARK

FERNWOOD
ROSELAND
KENSINGTON

Mt GREEN
WOOD

DOLTON
PHOENIX   RIVERDALE
S. HOLLAND HAMMOND
HIGHLAND
THORNTON   MUNSTER
LANSING

JOLIET

CHICAGO HEIGHTS

MANHATTAN

W I L L

WILMINGTON

BRAIDWOOD

K A N K A K E E

BOURBONNAIS

CLARKE CITY

MOMENCE

KANKAKEE

KOSTER

WICHERT
ST. ANNE

CHEBANSE

CLIFTEN   MARTINTON

DANFORTH

GILMAN

ONARGA

WATSEKA

I R O Q U O I S

MILFORD

INDIANA

Settlements near Chicago, Illinois.

scarcely forty families; with the comings and goings it remained at about this figure. In 1924 the congregation consisted of forty-two families.

The Danforth settlement in this very productive area consisted almost entirely of farmers engaged in raising corn. Corn production, just as in Iowa, was so dominant here that on Sundays the ultra-orthodox church members were more inclined to discuss corn than the Bible. "Scarcely were we out of church when talk concerning corn and related matters resumed again." This secular concern, so typical for America, deeply disturbed the still "green" minister and he gave this as the reason why there were so many quarrels among the orthodox.[46]

To the south, in Jasper County, but also on the Illinois Central line, is located the town of Newton. In and around this town there are Dutch settlers, most of them belonging to a Reformed Church, which has forty-eight families. I am not aware as to whether the nearby hamlets of Boon and Boos are Dutch or not.

Nearer to Chicago, about two hours travel via the Chicago and Eastern Illinois Railroad, is the town of Kankakee, located in Kankakee County. A settlement was founded on the less fertile, mostly sandy soils east of Kankakee in such towns as St. Anne, Wichert, and Koster. There has been a Reformed Church in Wichert since 1893 and it now has seventy-two families. It is not a prosperous colony; the farmers rent the land or work it on half-shares for others. Corn is the chief crop, followed by onions and sugar beets.

How did the settlement come into existence? The name of Koster—the Kosters are related to the Tons in Roseland—indicates capital from Roseland. After a few had settled there we note the usual pattern—newcomers arrive and others leave. "We have worked hard and we had quite a struggle but we make progress and are content," was the comment that colonists made to Mr. Raap, and in three days they gave him $750 for the benefit of Hope College.[47] In this little congregation, too, faith is the power that leads to deeds.

There are some older settlements west of Chicago in Whiteside County on the Mississippi River. A Reformed Church was organized in Fulton in 1867 and it now has 235 households; a second Reformed Church was started in 1917 which now numbers 124 families. Numerous Seceders arrived from the Groningen town of Warffum under the leadership of [?] Van der Meulen. There has been a Christian Reformed Church there since 1886 and it now has 109 families. On the whole it is a considerable settlement. East of Fulton, and also on the Chicago and North Western line is the town of Morrison with a Reformed congregation of 201 households; to the north—and between both towns—is the town of Ustick which has a Reformed Church of thirty families.

The settlements in Whiteside County seem to have been influenced by the larger and older related Ost Frisian colony of German Valley in Stephenson County, one that spread into Ogle County. Netherlanders live among

Whiteside County, Illinois.

the Ost Frisians in the colonies at Baileyville, Meekin, and Ridott in Stephenson County and at Forreston in Ogle County.[48] The close relationship between these Ost Frisians and the Hollanders was indicated earlier. They both use the Dutch language in their Reformed and Christian Reformed congregations, while for the Ost Frisians Hope College is also significant. We have also seen that Ost Frisians took an early part in missionary work.[49] Finally, in Logan County we find the community of New Holland. The proximity of the Ost Frisian colony of Emden |12 miles distant| testifies to the close relationship.[50] I shall take up the Hollanders in and near Chicago in another place.

We hear little of colonization leaders or locators in Illinois, just as was the case in Wisconsin. I have mentioned the name of Van der Meulen. A colonizer of more significance—in some respects to be compared with the young Hospers of Pella—was the previously mentioned real estate dealer, J. C. Ton, who, just as in the case of Hospers, acted as a realtor in establishing Dutch colonies elsewhere without settling there himself; thus he really cannot be considered a locator in the medieval sense of the term.

Wealthy as the Tons were through the sale of their increasingly valuable lands, caused by Chicago's growth and the establishment of the Pullman works, they specialized in this tempting speculation. Thus, the young "J. C." bought considerable swampy and wilderness lands in Jasper County, Indiana, where in 1894 a Reformed congregation was organized in and around the city of De Motte |Demotte|; it now has seventy-three families. Out of this church an "American" congregation was formed which now has forty families. For a time an effort was made to found the new Dutch colony of Newland, also in Jasper County.[51] Some fifteen miles from the town of Jasper |in southern Dubois County| is still found today the town of Holland,

The Tons encountered adversity with their purchase of low-lying Mississippi River lands near New Orleans. Experienced in the drainage of low
ground, first near Calumet and later in Indiana, they constructed dikes
around the Louisiana lands and then tried to persuade Hollanders to settle
there. However, the polder lands were too expensive and the mosquitoes
made a Dutch settlement virtually impossible; so their efforts at a third
settlement came to naught. The entire enterprise was a large financial loss
for the Tons.[52]

E. A Postscript

From the foregoing it can be observed that from the older settlements in
Michigan and Iowa, just as in Wisconsin and Illinois, a "swarming" took
place, resulting in the establishment of numerous new colonies, in a few
cases entirely new settlements were created. The nuclei consisted of those
colonists who had become acquainted with pioneering in the older settlements. They were the ones who knew how to cope with the difficulties and
reverses posed by the new areas. They conquered them and, tough and
determined as they were, stayed. Those who left were in most cases the
"greenhorns"—those who had but recently left the Old Country or had
come straight from it and had worked as laborers for a while in the older
settlements but were independent-minded and desirous of having lands of
their own. When they moved westward they learned for the first time what
real frontier life was like. Although courageous enough, they did not always
have the stamina to overcome the setbacks; they returned to the more
populated areas and often spent the rest of their lives as tenant farmers or
went even further west to try their luck again, strengthened by the acquired
experience. That was the case of the hardy P. Smit, who in 1874, with the
Seceder families [Pieter] Klerk and [Jan] Slot—originally from the province
of Noord Holland—was attracted to Holland, Nebraska, but in 1878 departed for northwestern Kansas.[53]

It is of some import that nearly all the settlements that have been
mentioned were of a definite religious and in particular of a Calvinist character. This, plus their common ethnic origin, held the people together. The
two factors, faith and nationality, interacting together were the binding
forces, in which process their faith, particularly Calvinism, was of considerable importance. Calvinism seemed to awaken a driving force for which one
looks in vain among Roman Catholics and those of other beliefs, as far as
they were Dutch. In some cases, this Calvinism was more important to them
than nationality or ethnicity, as shown by the frequent quarrels between the
Reformed and Christian Reformed factions. But these controversies also
revealed its weak side, Calvinism's dark side.

The greater virility of Calvinism, in distinction from Roman Catholicism,
as a factor in colonization among the Netherlanders becomes evident when

we inquire into the new settlements that came out of the old Roman Catholic settlement in the Wisconsin Fox River Valley. The answer is clear—none of any significance; its achievements are little known. Earlier it was noted that there was little activity among the Roman Catholic immigrants and it is evident again. Where are the Roman Catholic daughter colonies? Where is there a Roman Catholic Sioux County or even an aborted Virginia colonization? Where are the Roman Catholic Nebraska and Kansas settlements? They are unknown. Why? Undoubtedly there were fewer Dutch Roman Catholic immigrants than Calvinists. Those who left for America never displayed the energy of the Reformed colonists. The establishment of a Hope and a Calvin College, with the hope of a university in the future, is an ideal unknown to them.

This seems also to be true of the drive for new colonies. Some Roman Catholics did settle further west and north. G. Van den Elsen, who sojourned for a time in the Fox River Valley and more northward in Wisconsin and Michigan, met some on his journeys in the far North but he found them as individuals, not as groups of coreligionists or fellow countrymen. There was but one exception; Van den Elsen commented that the Hollanders whom he had met in northern Wisconsin and Michigan had earlier lived in De Pere.[54] "Now that this town has been developed and built up, the sons and daughters of these Hollanders search out the waste areas to do, in turn, what their parents had done in De Pere." But Van den Elsen does not anywhere mention the establishment of colonies, let alone real settlements. He does mention the prosperous shopkeeper, A. Muthey, whose parents had come from Horst, in Limburg, and had settled in De Pere. Two sons had gone northward to Michigan's Upper Peninsula and had settled in Trenary, Alger County. The one was a storekeeper and the other a farmer.[55] In Munising, in the same county, Van den Elsen met a Dutch woman who had been born in Sevenum, Limburg, and who had married a Frenchman here and was now living among Swedes and Finns. In Ishpeming, Marquette County, he met an old man from Winterswijk who was well-off now after having worked in the mines for twenty-five years.[56]

But there was no trace of any settlements except possibly one—Gouda, in Lincoln County in northern Wisconsin. It was in an area of thin and sandy soil, comparable to the poor Dutch "Peel" region. It had been settled about 1900 by Roman Catholic colonists—not from Wisconsin but from Illinois. They had come from the tiny Roman Catholic community of Kensington, near Roseland. They had worked in the Pullman shops but the monotonous life and the deafening noise in the "model" factories proved too much and so they left and switched to agriculture—potatoes, oats, and even some corn production. There were a few who had their own farms of from ten to fifteen *bunders* [twenty-five to thirty acres] of land. Van den Elsen preached and read masses for them in a small chapel they had built themselves. It lacked a confessional and so Van den Elsen had brought one with him from a neighboring town![57]

Some Wisconsin Roman Catholics did migrate westward as far as Nebraska, but no trace of any settlements can be found.[58] On the one hand, the number of Roman Catholic emigrants was smaller, on the other hand they were prolific and frequently had very large families. Many remained close to home under the ministrations of a priest while the growing industry also provided jobs or else the existing enterprises were intensified. Bercovici corroborated this among the Roman Catholic Hollanders in Essexville, Michigan, when he asserted that "most of the children of the older settlers have remained in Essexville, expanding, reclaiming more land from the marshes, intensifying the culture."[59]

On the other hand, the international character of Roman Catholicism must have weakened their national identity and ethnicity, making our former Roman Catholic fellow countrymen more easily inclined to live among the Roman Catholic Americans, Irish, French, and other coreligionists, just as had been the case from the beginning in the Fox River Valley. This was in contrast to the much more nationalistic Calvinists who with their religion occupy a far more secluded position.

The efforts of Lambert Kniest, a Dutch Roman Catholic in Dubuque, Iowa, who tried to establish a colony of fellow countrymen and coreligionists in the West in 1870, failed probably because of the above reasons. Lands were purchased in Carroll County, Iowa, and they laid out the towns of Mount Carmel in Kniest Township, and more to the northwest, Breda, on the route of the Chicago and North Western Railroad. By 1885 a total of eighty-five Dutch Roman Catholics had settled, scattered over Kniest and Roselle townships and in the "stad" of Breda. In 1895 the total was sixty-two, but this had dwindled to only fifty-two in 1905.[60] Later colonization efforts of the Roman Catholics were not originated by the older settlers or their descendants, but by their priests, and not on behalf of those already settled but of expected emigrants.

In matters of colonization effort, the contrast between Calvinist vigor and Roman Catholic lukewarmness becomes even more marked when one recalls that already in the eighties a new drive for expansion took place from the Reformed and Christian Reformed daughter colonies themselves. Sioux County, Iowa, became too expensive and too populated for the Calvinists. New lands were sought where those who were still independent-minded could begin a new and freer career. Truly, Calvinism proved to be a real force!

5

Granddaughters in the Dakotas and Minnesota

A. In South and North Dakota

We must march, my darlings, we must bear the brunt of danger,
We the youthful sinewy races, all the rest on us depend,
    Pioneers, O Pioneers!

Walt Whitman

We can indeed compare these new departures with a military campaign full of dangers, as had been the case with the migrations to Kansas and Nebraska. Similar dangers threatened those who came from Sioux County, Iowa, in 1880 and subsequent years and who settled in what was then the territory of "Dacotah."* In 1889 the territory was divided into the states of North and South Dakota. Like Kansas and Nebraska, the Dakotas lie astride the 100th meridian of west longitude—a transition area between the Middle West and the Far West and a land of hazards. This is the area that receives the bare minimum of 50 centimeters |20 inches| of annual rainfall needed for agriculture and forms the transitional zone between the prairies and savannahs and the treeless steppes. Most dangerous is the northwestern part of the area that is subject not only to searing heat during summer but in particular to bitter cold in winter. It led to a real life and death struggle, a struggle for bare survival, and more pioneers succumbed here than anywhere else.

Here also the glorious westward movement came to a standstill, and several times it was thrown back, but only to go forward again:

Conquering, holding, daring, venturing as we go the unknown ways,
    Pioneers! O Pioneers!

In 1876 and 1877 thousands of fortune hunters were attracted to the area by rumors of rich gold strikes in the Black Hills. The area belonged to the

---

*An old American variant of Dakota.

Sioux Indians, but the many dangers of this trek, one of them the danger of being scalped, did not serve as deterrents. This was not an imaginary danger; there were many battles with the Indians. In one of them General* [George] Custer and all his men were slain.[1]

Just as many of those who participated in the 1848 gold rush went through Dutch Pella, so this new onslaught went through the town of Hospers, in Sioux County. Crop failures in southern Minnesota fueled this trek. According to one eyewitness: "Therefore, large groups went through Hospers already in the early summer to join with others in Sioux County enroute to the gold fields in the Black Hills."[2]

If all this trekking and hustle and bustle already drew the attention of the Sioux County Hollanders to the farther West, it was accentuated by the discovery of new, very rich agricultural lands, just as had been the case in Australia and America—in California and the Klondike! Dakota turned out to be ideal for wheat production and this was the chief result of the new "craze."

Railroads made the new lands accessible; the fiercely competitive Chicago and North Western and the Milwaukee and St. Paul spread networks of tracks in the southern part of the region; the Northern Pacific Railroad completed its line in the northern area in 1883.[3] The government promoted settlement indirectly through its land grants to the railroads and directly through the Homestead and Timber Culture Acts. The latter legislation provided for a grant of 160 acres of free land provided that at least ten acres of it was planted to trees within a ten year period. Land could also be acquired under the Pre-emption Act—160 acres at the very low price of $1.25 per acre if the land was more than ten miles from a railroad (the so-called "minimum lands"). If the land was within ten miles of a rail line it could be obtained for $2.50 per acre (the "double minimum" lands). Thus, one could obtain 320 acres virtually free or for very little through a combination of a homestead and a tree claim or a tree claim and a pre-emption.[4]

It was therefore not surprising that in Sioux County, where the rapid population increase had boosted land prices, people felt attracted to the Dakota plains, a couple of hundred miles westward, especially since they knew that free government lands were available. Within a few years about one hundred families from Hospers had migrated thither.[5]

Thus about twenty years after the establishment of the first colonies in Michigan and Iowa, thought was given to founding daughter colonies. But scarcely ten years after the settling of the daughter colony in Sioux County, new pioneers trekked further westward to face pioneer life anew in dugouts and sod huts and to battle the bitter winter weather. [E. A.] Ross' comment, that "in the last Westernmost decanting of the pioneering breed, courage and love of independence reach their greatest intensity," is quite in order.[6] Here also the driving urge was to become an independent owner, possibly

*Custer had the rank of colonel at the time.

of 320 acres of land, rather than a tenant. This was possible because Americans had no sentimental attachment to the soil; land was only an object of trade.

Droves of homeseekers from Minnesota, Wisconsin, and Iowa, as well as newly arrived European immigrants, especially Norwegians and Germans, settled during the "experimental eighties" (at least for those regions) in present-day South Dakota, "the heart of the North American prairies"—"the essence of prairieism!"[7] The settlers from Sioux County and later the Hollanders from Alto, Wisconsin, besides those having arrived directly from the Old Country, were as everywhere else part of a mighty stream.[8] They felt in themselves the wanderlust that had often been fanned by the railroad companies and land agents, and took up the difficult task of breaking the tough prairie sod and of substituting the endless grazing lands with fields of waving grain. Our countrymen contributed mightily to make this the "spring wheat region"—the world's wheat granary, even though they did not join the ranks of the typical Dakota "bonanza farmers," owing tens of thousands of acres.

Walt Whitman's lines also apply to them:

O you youths, Western youths,
So impatient, full of action, full of manly pride and friendship,
   Plain I see you Western youths, see you tramping with the foremost,
      Pioneers! O Pioneers!

      O, resistless, restless race![9]

Originally these colonists established themselves in Lincoln County, separated from Sioux County only by the Big Sioux River, and then in neighboring Turner County. Thus they moved, ever westward, into adjoining Douglas, Charles Mix, and Bon Homme counties—the Missouri River constitutes the southern border of the latter two. According to Bowman, Charles Mix and Bon Homme counties belong to the Dakota glacier strip bordered by the Missouri. It is of considerable economic significance because of the fertile chalky soil that had been created by the glaciers. Hollanders also settled in McCook and Aurora counties, situated north of these areas. Others went even further northward, establishing homesteads in Campbell County, a part of which was later included in Emmons County, North Dakota, and another part in South Dakota.[10]

During the nineties and especially in the twentieth century, the number of Dutch settlements in the Dakotas increased rapidly. In various South Dakota counties bordering on Minnesota—the most easterly and thus not as arid—our countrymen settled in such places as Valley Springs and Colton, in Minnehaha County; Aurora and Volga in Brookings County; Gary and Bemis in Deuel County; Estelline and Castlewood in Hamlin County; and Twin Brooks in Grant County. Yet one cannot refer to these as real settlements.

Most of these Hollanders lived among pioneers of other nationalities. However, a homogeneous Dutch settlement did come into being in the northern part of Charles Mix and Douglas counties.[11] A. Kuiper, Sr., a former peat bog worker in the Dutch province of Drenthe, fancied himself called of God to serve as a leader. The agricultural center of New Holland, where many Geldersmen from Sioux Center and environs settled, as well as Friesland and Overijsel, came into existence. But only New Holland survived; the other two dwindled and disappeared when railroad towns developed along a "feeder line" of the Milwaukee and St. Paul Railroad.[12]

These disappearances of small towns are due also in part to the departure of a number of discouraged colonists—the usual phenomenon—although the arrival of others assured the survival of this Dutch colony, as had been the case in Iowa's Sioux County, and in Kansas and Nebraska. Thus Platte, in Charles Mix County, and Corsica, in Douglas County, both on spurs of the railroad, served as business centers and elevator towns, but New Holland and Harrison are the spiritual centers, the church villages. Harrison was established by the Le Cocq family, originally from Amsterdam. This Secessionist family worked as commission agents and formerly resided in Pella, then part of the family moved to Orange City, and then again to Harrison.[13]

Just as was the case in Sioux County, the first two or three years were prosperous ones—the very fertile land produced a rich harvest of wheat. But that was followed by five or six years of adversity occasioned by drought and hot winds. In 1886 it was particularly dry and this drought continued for some time, so much so that the Hollanders considered their settlement to be a complete failure. Just as many others, they had large debts to pay so they mortgaged their land. "Then they let it lay and surrendered it to God's mercy," after which they left. Usually the creditors took over the land.

It was difficult, too, for those who remained. The summer heat was unbearable: "It was as though we stood in front of a burning baker's oven." That was countered by the intense cold of the winters. In North Dakota there was sub-zero weather for about seventy days. Those who remained had to be helped; funds were collected for them in the churches and in the railroad stations. Generous amounts of money and corn were given. Wagon loads of grain were forwarded to the pioneers. Difficult as the times were, they never suffered actual starvation. To remain was only a question of determination. It developed that, just as in the case of Sioux County and elsewhere, those who left did so prematurely. After the years of drought there were abundant harvests that rewarded the die-hard "stay putters," particularly in 1892.[14]

For some time the growth and prosperity of the Dutch colony in Charles Mix was hindered by its distance from the railroad; the nearest line was thirty miles north at White Lake in Aurora County. The mail had to be delivered from Running Water, seventy miles southeast of the colony and

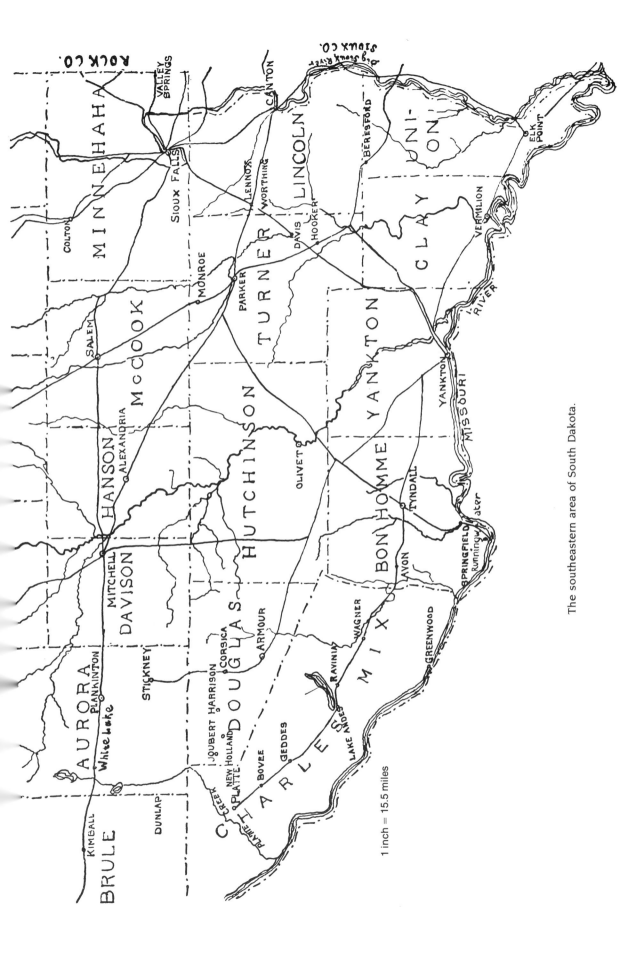

The southeastern area of South Dakota.

situated in Bon Homme County, where the Missouri River was navigable. From here the mail was delivered by stagecoach to the local post office, which was still eight miles from the place where the first Christian Reformed Church was established, the Overijsel congregation. With the construction of feeder lines, the settlement began to prosper.[15]

In his panegyric on the prairie, Hayden Carruth, who had spent much of his life in South Dakota, wrote some striking thoughts: "The Prairie is the world in its calm, serene, beautiful old age, meditative, unhurried, unafraid, approaching Nirvana. . . . Every spot on the Prairie is a High Place whereon may be offered sacrifices to Truth and Beauty. The Prairie is but the desert watered, and, as hath been said, 'The desert is of God, and in the desert no man may deny Him.' "[16]

It is very difficult to ascertain to what extent the cultural and religious life of our countrymen were affected by this prairie environment. Many of the pioneers came from very religious homes and this "godliness," in Kansas, Nebraska, and elsewhere, flagged far less than in the older colonies where Americanization and the spirit of the age were much more powerfully manifest and also continued for a much longer time. Personally, I believe that although the prairies, those endless plains, may have been conducive to a contemplative view of life, in reality the colonists had little time for that. Especially during the first decade but also later on, the lack of a labor force meant that the colonists must have had very, very little time for such contemplative activites. I think that it must rather have been the loneliness and monotony of their daily existence and the low level of education in general, just as had been the case in the wooded areas of Michigan, where not the enormous expanses but rather the oppressive encirclement had its effect. It contributed to a flourishing of orthodoxy, with all its consequences. It should not be overlooked that the Dutch element, especially in the homestead settlements, was constantly augmented by an inflow of usually very religious new settlers often sponsored by the churches in the Old Country. Thus, a religious outlook was usually present from the very beginning.

It is not surprising, therefore, that from the very beginning first mission stations were established in the settlements and then churches. In the Reformed denomination there were, in particular, the Reverend H. W. Warnshuis and the preachers F. J. Zwemer and S. J. Harmeling, who distinguished themselves as missionaries. Warnshuis was active, beginning in 1890, at the mission stations of Lennox in Lincoln County, and Centerville in Turner County. Many Netherlanders settled midway between these two towns, among the Ost Frisians already present there. The first of these had arrived in 1873 and the majority of them came between 1879 and 1885.[17] In 1882 a mission post was established north of Centerville at Van den Berg, later known respectively as Turner, Holland, and Hooker. A Reformed Church was founded in 1892 at Davis and in 1900 at Worthing, east of Lennox.

In the most northern part of Turner County a congregation was also established in Marion, now known as Monroe, which at that time was called the Sandham Memorial Church. S. J. Harmeling served here from 1883 to 1894, while to the north, in the area around Salem in McCook County, F. J. Zwemer was active; Salem obtained a mission station in 1884. Somewhat earlier, in 1880, Douglas County received a mission station and in 1883 Harrison had its own minister, A. Stegeman. A second station was established in Armour in 1885, while preachings took place since 1884 in the now defunct congregation of Castalia in Charles Mix County, which later moved to Platte. Immanuel Mission was located at Springfield on the Missouri River in Bon Homme County in 1884; the Ebenezer post at Scotland in the northern section of the county came into being in 1893. These mission posts are not only significant at the church level, but they also indicate the dispersion of the Dutch element on the prairies.

From the location of these posts it appears that the settlement of the northern part of the Dakotas, in Campbell and Emmons counties, took place at a somewhat later date. Not until 1885 and 1886 were mission stations founded at Hope and at Van Raalte (later named Thule) in South Dakota's Campbell County. These missions no longer exist. Especially F. J. Zwemer and S. J. Harmeling were active here also.[18] The Hollanders in Emmons County, North Dakota, have had a continuous existence to the present. There are now Reformed congregations in Westfield and Strasburg as well as at Marion and Litchville in the more easterly Lamoure County. Neither at Hague in Emmons County, which has a Russian Catholic group, nor at Zeeland in McIntosh County are there Hollanders, although both these names are Dutch.

In addition to the Reformed denomination, the Christian Reformed also tried to "gather up" churches. Their first missionary, Reverend T. M. Van den

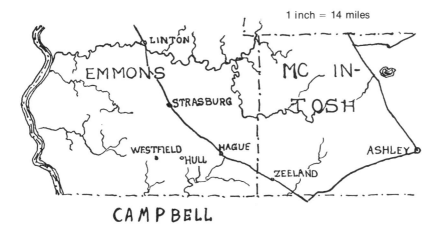

Emmons County, North Dakota. The river on the west side is the Missouri. The south side forms the border of North and South Dakota.

Bosch went to Dakota with Reverend H. Bode in 1880 "to see what possibilities there were for the Church" and the possible establishment of new settlements. A small congregation of nine scattered members was formed at Turner (now known as Centerville) in Turner County, and placed under the jurisdiction of the Orange City congregation in Iowa.[19] Both denominations were close upon each other's heels. Instead of cooperating they strove against each other, sowing dissension, and thus depriving the colonists of the unity that would have given them a far greater capacity to cope with the odds they were already facing without the added religious imbroglios. There were also Methodist and Presbyterian zealots who, according to one pastor, caused an "often unholy competition" between the various religious groups and generated a spirit of divisiveness and bitterness among the Hollanders and the Ost Frisians and thus weakened what ethnic solidarity existed between the Dutch and the Ost Frisians.

No matter how unsympathetic we may feel towards this interreligious jealousy, which was more destructive than constructive, credit must be given to Van den Bosch and those who followed him in mission work: Reverends H. and C. Bode, R. T. Kuiper, E. Broere, and others, since they did their work with much self-denial on their part. They traversed the boundless, pathless prairies to reach their people, undeterred by unmarked roads, often riding through streams both summer and winter, at unseasonable hours, through storms and blizzards, and sometimes getting lost in the dark. They rode out on horseback after having reached their mission base by night train, lying down on the hard, wooden benches to save the $1.50 that a Pullman sleeper would have cost. And if in the end they did not

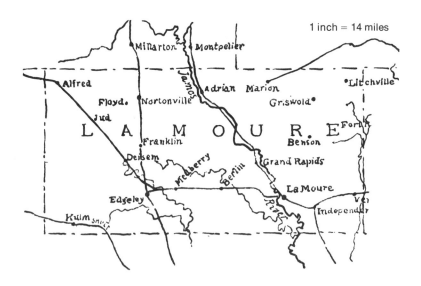

Lamoure County, North Dakota.

succeed in developing "promising stations," they had to endure mistrust and calumny from the ranks of their "brothers."[20]

But these men did achieve some positive results through their devoted work. In February of 1883, Reverend H. Bode succeeded in establishing a Christian Reformed Church called Overijsel, near a townlet then called Edgerton. There were twenty members in this church, the eighth one established west of Chicago. Two years later a small 24 × 18 foot church building was constructed. Previously they had met in one of the sod huts or in the schoolhouse where one of the elders read the Bible. They did not have a minister of their own until sixteen years later, when Reverend F. Stuart arrived in 1901. During all those intervening years their services consisted of Bible reading and during the summer there were sermons by some theological students or an occasional minister.[21]

The same held for Friesland, which even had to share some of the students with Overijsel. During this same period, New Holland had had five pastors. The New Holland congregation in Douglas County had been established in May of 1883, a good two months after the one in Overijsel and it consisted initially of twenty-two families and eight unmarried members. In August of that same year, the Reverend T. M. Van den Bosch took up his charge there. In the meantime a 32 × 33 foot church had been erected. Van den Bosch, whom we have met before as a missionary, left one and one-half years later to accept a charge in neighboring Harrison in the same county; a church had been organized there in 1884.[22] The first True |Ware| congregation was established in 1889 at Hull, in Emmons County, North Dakota.

The fact that it took eighteen years before Overijsel had its own minister, while New Holland had had five during that same period, gives some indication of religious life and the related mentality of our fellow Dutchmen in the Far West. Most of the ministers served only for a few years in Overijsel and considered it as a stepping stone that they preferred to bypass. In one instance, twelve calls had been declined before there was an acceptance. A shortage of ministers in one congregation and a surplus in another actually stemmed from the same cause—the endless disputes that here, as elsewhere, characterized the church life of the most orthodox, of the True brothers. In many cases this was the result of a total absence of the virtues of brotherly love and tolerance that should distinguish true Christians in the first place. The very low level of general education, the atmosphere of irritability resulting from the many adversities, and the fanaticism of the pioneers, explain much. It was said of New Holland that "there were many disputes and divisions in the congregation as well as great discouragement because of the drought and poor harvest." Yet, ministerial candidate A. W. Meyer was called to New Holland in 1889 and remained there for five years before he left.[23]

In Overijsel there was a good deal of argument as to where the church should be built, which was a matter that had very little to do with faith. But in such a scattered settlement it mattered to those who wanted it conveniently situated. This had also been the case elsewhere, such as at Sioux Center in Sioux County. The mutual bitterness was so strong and resulted in so much dissension that there was no way in which they could support a minister of their own. This was all the more true when financial worries began to plague them.

Finally, the arrival of a railroad solved the question just as had been the case earlier in Maurice, Sioux County; the resulting trading city of Platte became the most appropriate site for the church. A new church, five times as large as the previous one, was erected and the dissident elements reached a measure of accord under the direction of Stuart, who proved to be a "great harmonizer." Later on, the remnants of the former Friesland church were taken into the church at Platte and, as a result, in 1924 this congregation totaled 110 families.[24] In this area as in others, struggle meant growth. Today the New Holland church has 140 familes and the Harrison church has 65! In 1907, a group from the latter congregation organized a new church in Corsica, which has now 80 households.[25] The Christian Reformed group in Hull, North Dakota, has 58 families today.

Professor Raap, who visited the area frequently as a fund solicitor for Hope College, related many striking anecdotes to me concerning the religious life of these pioneers.[26] In Westfield, Emmons County, North Dakota, where many Michigan Hollanders lived, they traveled twelve to fourteen miles (nineteen–thirty-three kilometers) on foot or by wagon in order to go to church. Therefore, they set out on Saturday afternoon. Today, as owners of 160–320 acres of land, they go much more easily by automobile. One found and still finds in South Dakota a similar attachment to the church. More than once in those early years Raap would join small groups of those living around Tyndall who would set out on Saturday in order to "church" on Sunday in Springfield, located southward on the Missouri River. It was this spirit of determination that enabled the settlers to stay during those early difficult years. Here again, faith proved to be one of the mightiest of supports, necessary for the success of any colony, wherever it might be.

B. In Minnesota

If Charles Mix can be considered a "granddaughter" colony of Pella, although other colonists settled there too, as was usually the case in colonies, other "granddaughters" grew up in the more northerly state of Minnesota. In addition to the previously mentioned settlements of Wisconsin colonists in the southeast area, many settlements came into existence in the southwest especially during the nineties and in later years. Efforts had been made to establish a Dutch colony in this state as early as the sixties. Not until the eighties was a very modest success achieved when Dutch-Americans—not native Hollanders— began to show an interest. Attempts to form Dutch colonies here after 1847 practically all miscarried, but Dutch-American colonies were able to succeed. (I shall comment on this later.)

The first successful colony—excepting that of the Gelderlanders in Greenleafton—centered around Prinsburg in Kandiyohi County. In 1885, the Chicago-based land company, Prins and Koch, obtained title to about 100,000 acres of land in Kandiyohi and neighboring Chippewa County to the west of it. The firm tried to attract Dutchmen to the eastern part and German settlers to the western portions of their holdings.[27] Since the area was but thinly populated, the land speculators seemed to have preferred that experienced pioneers come at first, since they would be able more easily to cope with the attendant difficulties and disappointments. In any event, the most glowing accounts of these areas began to appear in the newspapers in Michigan, as well as Illinois and Iowa.

A German Ost Frisian colony was established in Chippewa County in Rheiderland Township, a name indicative of its Germanic influence, and it became very prosperous in spite of tremendous setbacks. Many were under the impression that they had purchased good land only to find that it was swamp land. Other lands had not been properly surveyed and in the beginning there was a shortage of almost everything. There was not a tree or a bush to be found for miles around. The nearest railroad station, Renville, was eighteen miles distant and provisions, as well as timber and firewood, had to be transported from this station. Except for a few Norwegians, there were no residents in the vicinity. In 1888, the Great Northern Railroad laid tracks through the colony and a "town" came into being. It was not called Bunde after the city of their homeland, as the Ost Frisians desired, but Clara City, for Koch's wife.

Here as elsewhere, Hollanders settled among the Ost Frisians. Reformed and Christian Reformed churches sprang up for Dutch and Ost Frisians alike. The Christian Reformed Church of Bunde was organized in 1887 and that of Emden in 1890. In the latter group twenty-four of the thirty-four families are now of Dutch origin.[28] After a bitter struggle between the Presbyterians and the Reformed elements, a Reformed Church was organized from an initial Presbyterian church in 1899, which now numbers only 13 households.[29] A new Presbyterian congregation also came into being later on.

In the meantime, according to the original plan, a purely Dutch colony was laid out in 1886 in Kandiyohi County, reputedly by the Netherlands Land Company. The town was named Prinsburg after the two businessmen—Prins and his friend and possible shareholder Zwanenburg. Both of these gentlemen had been active in the emigration business in the Netherlands and were known as representatives of the *Nederlandsch-Amerikaansche Stoomvaartmaatschappij* [Holland-American Steamship Company]. Among the Dutch Americans, Prinsburg was even considered to have been founded by these two gentlemen, Prins and Zwanenburg of Harlingen, who were agents of the Holland-American Steamship Company.[30] Being good

Kandiyohi County, Minnesota.

businessmen and paying close attention to their immigrant "wares," they took particular care to have church facilities available; a Christian Reformed Church and a Reformed Church mission station were established the very first year. Surely that would attract immigrants!

However, the largest stream came in the nineties, mainly from the Dakotas, where many were forced out by the droughts and "fell back" eastward, as we are already aware. Many colonists from Dakota joined with those from Sioux County to settle near Prinsburg, and to the east a second center, Roseland, came into being.[31] Still others settled in the vicinity of Olivia in Renville County. Today the Prinsburg-Roseland Christian Reformed Church has 110 households, while the Prinsburg mission station [of the Reformed Church], founded in 1894, is now known as the Roseland church, numbering 42 families. However, the "post" at Olivia has been abandoned.

Northwest of these Prinsburg and Roseland colonies lies Kerkhoven, in Swift County, on a track of one of the Great Northern lines. It is erroneously assumed that it had been founded by Messrs. Kerkhoven of Amsterdam.[32] Kerkhoven and Company, as was true of other financial houses, were agents for American railroads and raised capital for them. They were able to obtain funds for the subsequently notorious St. Paul and Pacific, which had laid a line to the town of Breckenridge in the Red Valley. One of the towns along the tracks was named Kerkhoven—as thanks for their aid in making our capital disappear into the pockets of the American swindlers.[33] In the same manner many other Dutch bankers were memorialized in town names by grateful American railroad barons who grew rich with the help of those bankers and their speculating clientele. They suggest, but falsely, that they are related to Dutch colonization attempts, whereas they only remind us of Dutch speculation ventures!

It was not the Kerkhoven firm but the bishop of St. Paul who established a purely Roman Catholic colony in Swift County. It was bisected by the railroad and, in addition to Kerkhoven, three other railroad "towns" belonged to it. This was called to the attention of Dutch Roman Catholics but without any significant results.[34]

In the nineties and subsequently, many other settlements, primarily of Sioux County colonists, were founded in Minnesota. The question could well be asked as to why colonists from Sioux County had not settled there earlier, because Minnesota was an older state, having obtained statehood already in 1858. The primary reason was that when people in the area around Orange City were thinking of migration, the Dakotas were enjoying a boom at that time and so it drew everybody's attention, while during the Minnesota boom period, around 1870, Sioux County itself was still emerging. In addition, a goodly portion of central and northern Minnesota was covered with forests, and prairie dwellers had little interest in that. Moreover, those parts of Minnesota, as well as the southern Minnesota prairie lands, were largely held by the railroads and speculators. Therefore, there is little mention of homestead settlement and colonization here. In addition, Minnesota had the reputation of being as cold as Siberia.

It is a remarkable fact, therefore, that the settlement attempts in Minnesota were largely undertaken directly from the Netherlands. Settlements originating from Sioux County and other Dutch-American centers had a far less spontaneous character than was the case before. This was evident in the founding of Prinsburg, and it was also true, to a greater or lesser degree, in other settlements that will be discussed. The homestead era quickly passed, at least in those areas where the soil and climate were favorable. Prinsburg is a good example of this, as is the Leota settlement [Nobles County].

In the nineties, then, as was mentioned earlier, the attention of the Sioux County residents was more strongly drawn to Minnesota than before. In the meantime they had spread into neighboring Plymouth and especially O'Brien and Lyon counties in Iowa, but now Minnesota lured them. As said earlier, the impulse came not from themselves, but rather, from the railroads and their closely allied land companies. They were more successful in offering their lands for sale after the droughts had hit the Dakotas.

E. J. G. Bloemendaal was one of those who investigated the opportunities in Leota and he has left an account.[35] According to this pioneer, "after the harvest in late August 1891, some land agents came to our colony who tried to interest the people in founding a new colony in Minnesota, sixty or seventy miles north of us, where fertile land was available for ten dollars per acre." Homestead lands must have been gone by that time. "Soon the agents had nearly two hundred men ready to go northward." They traveled to Luverne in neighboring Rock County via Worthington—a roundabout route—and then were taken by carriage to the undeveloped lands fifteen miles further away. Considerable difficulty was experienced in assembling the necessary transportation. "When we finally drove through the streets of Luverne in twenty-five carriages, the Hollanders from Orange County attracted much attention, and were the topic of conversation." For seven miles outside Luverne the land was cultivated, "but then we saw vast stretches of prairie where large herds of cattle, at times numbering three or four hundred heads, were grazing. They were tended by boys mounted on Indian ponies. The land was level and fertile. The area seemed auspicious for settlement." Many miles were covered in showing the excursionists the land that was available.

Many Hollanders purchased lands here and settled on them and a gradually growing and flourishing colony came into existence where wheat, oats,

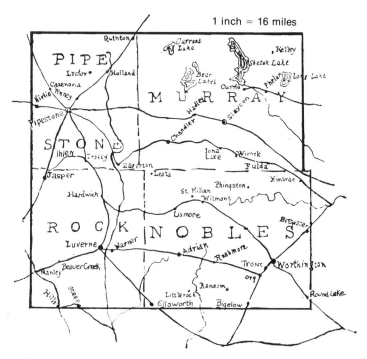

Southwestern Minnesota. Bordering states on the south and west side are Iowa and South Dakota, respectively.

etc., were the main crops and not corn as in Sioux County. "Corn does not grow as well here as in Iowa"—it was too far north—"but grain flourished," Bloemendaal knowingly remarked. He may have meant to include corn, since he mentions "corn and grain." Many, such as Bloemendaal, were elated with the land, consisting of forests and prairies, and Luverne appeared to be a good marketplace. "To sum it all up, the area is wonderful!" Bloemendaal does not mention what settlement was actually established;[36] he apparently had in mind Leota in Nobles County, bordering on Rock County. His brother-in-law settled there too, as a farmer and storekeeper, at whose place "everything, including medicine, could be obtained."

In Leota, the mission post of Bethel was organized in 1891 by the Reformed Church and this was served between 1893 and 1895 by G. Dangremond and later by H. J. Pietenpol. When Bloemendaal traveled through the area in the fall of 1895, while enroute to visit his brother in South Dakota, there were a hundred Dutch families living there and the value of the land had increased to about $20 per acre. There was a Dutch colony to the north, in Pipestone County, called Holland; in 1895 it had about fifty families living there.[37] It was not until 1897 that a Reformed mission station, called Churchville, was established there.

In 1891 the Great Northern Railroad sponsored a second excursion to the Red River Valley, which was the former Lake Agassiz area, bisected by North Dakota and Minnesota, with the Dominion of Canada to the north. No colonization resulted from this.

Bloemendaal, who had been invited to participate in the expedition, asserted that the land offered for sale was "unusually fertile, of inexhaustible heavy black clay; I have never seen more fertile land." However, the valley was subject to occasional floods. In addition, the summers were so short that the grain would freeze. The winters were too long and there were many places lacking in good drinking water. For these reasons—although the land could be bought for only *fl.* 50 [$20] per hectare [2.471 acres], none of the Hollanders decided to settle there.[38] No Dutchmen would settle in the region until the twentieth century.

Through repeated colonization efforts from the Netherlands, a few scattered Dutch immigrants lived especially in the area north of St. Paul, in particular around the Mississippi River town of St. Cloud. A few had settled in Wright County in 1867 to the south of St. Cloud in and around Silver Creek.[39] Some Sioux County and Dakota colonists settled at Maple Lake in the nineties; the Silver Creek Reformed Church was organized in 1894 and it now consists of 47 families. In Mille Lacs County, east of Benton County, the town of Pease was settled by Sioux County residents. A Christian Reformed Church was organized in 1895 and it now has 120 families. An attempt at Dutch settlement there in the sixties failed. Colonists also journeyed northeasterly to Pine County and a Reformed Church was organized at Friesland in 1896.[40] North of Friesland, also on the Northern Pacific line, the village of Groningen arose and to the east of both

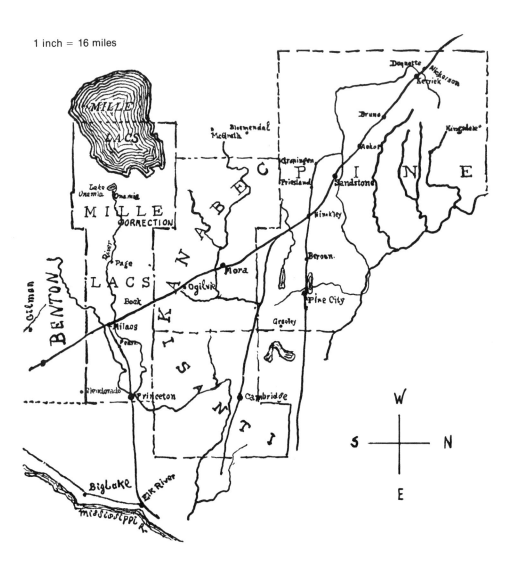

Settlements in mideastern Minnesota and Pine County.

towns, a settlement took place around the Great Northern station town of Sandstone. A Reformed Church was started there in 1903 and it now numbers 25 households.

Others from Sioux County went to Goodhue County, south of St. Paul, where the settlement of Spring Creek grew up on the Chicago, Milwaukee and St. Paul. A Reformed Church was begun in 1902 but it numbers only five families at present. They eventually had to share their minister, T. Hibma, with the Reformed Church that developed in 1921 in Bejou, which lay much further northwestward in Mahnomen County. In 1915 a Christian Reformed Church had been organized there which now consists of 16 families.

Each one of these colonies also had elements from other older and younger settlements, as well as from the Netherlands. But the majority of those in the Dakotas and Minnesota were "daughters" from Sioux County, and thus "grandchildren" of Pella. Although these "family" relationships weakened, they are still felt. We still find similar relationships between young settlements that originated from the Michigan and Wisconsin areas and their "parents."

Part Five

Plants That Did Not Take Root

Emigration and Colonization Since the Second Half of the Nineteenth Century

6

Emigration Since the Second Half of the Nineteenth Century

A. 1855–1880

1. Social Conditions in the Netherlands

In the first part of this work we considered the causes and motives for emigration from our country until approximately 1855. This movement had a distinctive character because next to economic considerations, which were of primary importance, religious and, to a far lesser degree, political factors also played an important role.

It was especially the religious impulse—the desire to worship freely without government interference—that led many people to leave the country in groups rather than individually. At times this took place more or less en masse under the aegis of ministers. A feeling of religious solidarity not only led to immigration in groups but also to colonization. What held the colonies together was the powerful bond of religion—a bond that showed itself to be stronger, in many aspects, than the one of ethnic identity. It was the power of religious conviction that must be credited for the success of nearly all of these colonies and that made them into the foci of the Dutch presence in America. This was to change after about 1855. Theological and political considerations faded far into the background, henceforth only economic forces—with a few exceptions here and there—led to emigration.

The consequences of the revolutionary years of 1848 and 1849 also affected our country. More than had been the case before, consideration was given to the will and the wishes of the people. The gradual development of a popular government within the framework of a constitutional monarchy had become possible and this tended to abate some of the earlier widespread political grievances. After 1850 voting rights were granted, based on certain proofs of affluence—the payment of a rather large amount of land taxes, taxes on personal property, or license fees. Proportionately, the number of voters increased more than population growth. From 1850 to 1887

579

the population increased by 43 percent, but the number of voters between 1853 (the first year for which statistics are available) and 1887 rose by 61 percent. After 1887 suffrage was liberalized again and the number of those eligible to vote for members of the Tweede Kamer |the Second Chamber or the lower house of the legislature| increased as follows: 83,561 in 1853; 134,987 in 1887; 292,613 in 1888; 302,021 in 1896.[1]

Due to the growing awareness of new values and norms, changes were also made in government economic policies, particularly in the tax structure, thereby reducing much popular criticism. Excise taxes, previously referred to as one of the incentives for migration, were gradually abolished for the benefit of the poorer classes, but also for the benefit of industry which needed cheap labor. Provincial excise duties were abolished as early as 1850, but they continued in the municipalities until 1865. In 1852 the State abolished taxes on mutton and pork and this was followed in 1855 by the abolition of rates on milling |flour|; in 1863 taxes on peat and coal came to an end. Out of similar considerations, import duties on grain were continually reduced, especially by the law of 1853, in order "to encourage the importation of grain and other foodstuffs." In 1877 these duties were abolished completely.

Consideration was also given to religious grievances. In 1841 the government arrived at an accommodation with the Seceders by a royal decree "concerning the recognition and sufferance of the Christian Seceder congregations." With the passage of time this decree was enforced with increasing leniency and in 1868, a royal decree officially abolished all unequal treatment of the Seceders. Restrictive regulations concerning other religious communities, notably the Israelites, had already been rescinded previously.

It should not be assumed that all political and religious desires had thus been fulfilled. On the contrary, with freedom-loving America as an ideal in their minds, there were many dissatisfied people whose desires remained unfulfilled. When even a noted scholar like R. P. A. Dozy wrote in one of his articles in De Gids in 1870 that he saw the United States as a state that had taken over the good aspects of Europe and discarded the bad or obsolete ones, one can imagine how the average Hollander viewed the Union.[2] According to Dozy, "there is no frivolous or ignorant nobility, no church that persecutes those of other beliefs, no enormous standing armies. Popular sovereignty is an undisputed fact. The school system is her darling—free of cost and all dogmatism banished. Even the lowest classes, with the exception of the Irish, show a great degree of development and relative good breeding." These sentiments were eagerly quoted in emigration literature. In 1871 both Dr. H. Hartogh Heys van Zouteveen[3] and infantry lieutenant J. A. Obreen referred to Dozy in their exhortations to encourage emigration to America. Obreen, following Dozy, asserted that there was a freedom and an equality never known in Europe and that the excellent educational system was not designed to mold submissive underlings or regimented, obedient soldiers, but rather to produce educated and enlightened citizens.[4] Settlement in America was thus desirable not only for material reasons but also on the basis of higher ideals.

However, to an increasing degree, economic considerations came to be decisive. Economic conditions in the Netherlands, particularly in the rural areas, had improved remarkably since the fifties. The industrial development of Western Europe, closely coupled with more and more free trade, created a great demand for our agricultural and cattle-raising products. As a result, the 1850–1877 period has been described as "exceptionally favorable" for our farmers.[5] Good harvests and very high prices, due to constantly expanding trade, brought great prosperity to farmers and cattle breeders.

People spoke of the champagne years, the golden age of our peasantry, especially in the clay soil areas.[6] As we have pointed out earlier, market fluctuations were felt far more rapidly and sharply there than in the sandy soil areas. It is obvious that during those years there was little inclination on the part of independent farmers to leave the Netherlands. Consequently, there were comparatively few emigrants during that time, since the rural areas usually contributed the most emigrants.

However, one should not be misled and assume that all was rosy. Dutch wholesalers and industrial firms were extremely slow in developing. Especially in the more affluent circles there still prevailed a spirit of indolence and dormancy, the spirit of *Jan Salie* [the good-for-nothing character in Everhardus J. Potgieter's previously-quoted poem, "Jan, Jannetje en hun jongste kind"]. A full subscription of the loans for the construction of the North Sea Canal [to open Amsterdam to ocean vessels] even failed. King Willem III subsequently refused to pay his annual visit to the capital of the country [Amsterdam] until the project was completely underwritten.[7] Amsterdam's capitalists would rather speculate in American railroad securities than further their own country and it took this "royal cuff on the ears of the Amsterdam financial magnates" to bring forth the necessary funds.

The insignificance of our shipping trade in those days is evident from the fact that in 1863 Amsterdam's IJ-port was depicted not as a forest of masts as in former times, but rather as a port with only one fishing barge and one boat, as Jan Ter Gouw wrote in this bit of doggerel:

> A pleasant little scene—The babbling IJ,
> A fishing smack and a boat
>   Outlined against the big city!
> But—it is all so quiet and dead!*

This characterized the spirit of Amsterdam—the heart of the nation! Even eleven years later, in 1874, Ter Gouw wrote, "We can see the decline of the IJ; no fleets are coming in."

---

*   *Een lief gezigtje—'t kabblend IJ,*
      Een vischschuit en een boot,
    En in 't verschiet de groote Stad!
      Maar—'t is zoo stil en dood!"

However, slowly a new era dawned. The first to sense this revival were our Jewish countrymen and, as so often happens, it was sensed by them in the literary field before moving on to the commercial field. Symptoms of this revival were the founding of the firms of Sarphati and Mendel in Amsterdam, and that of Pincoffs in Rotterdam—the latter was encouraged by the king's brother, "Prince Hendrik, the Sailor."

For a time conditions in industry were as bad as those in commerce. In a few provinces, like Friesland and Drenthe, what little industry there was, lost ground. This was all the more regrettable since at the time there was a strong population increase: 3,056,879 inhabitants in 1849; 3,579,529 inhabitants in 1869; 4,012,693 inhabitants in 1879. Thus, between 1849 and 1869 the annual increase was 26,133 and from 1869 to 1889 it was 43,316.[8] Some found employment in the rural areas, while industry offered only a very limited number of jobs—usually with preference given to women and children. Consequently, wages were extremely low and poverty was widespread. And this poverty increased constantly due to the rapid increase in population and the very sluggish development of an enterprising spirit among the "leading" men. As late as 1870 it was still considered such a politically dangerous situation nationwide that to alleviate it in cases where religious and other charitable organizations had been unable to cope with the popular misery, the government consented that the civilian authorities might intervene, but only "in case of absolute inevitability, that is, what police controls make necessary, not what charity makes desirable."[9]

One can well imagine what "maximum misery" developed with such a "minimal concern." Greatly neglected was the development of lower class children, the next generation. Not much education took place. For example, according to an 1860 report dealing with Leiden, there was a large decrease in school attendance among children aged eight through fourteen. A more acute manifestation of this poverty was reflected by the military draft statistics. In a ten-year period, of 3,636 conscripts, 1,366 were deficient in height and 422 were unfit for other reasons! This is not surprising when one considers that as children they had done strenuous work in the factories day in and day out for twelve to fifteen hours.[10]

In some Frisian areas wages in 1860 turned out to be lower than in 1841, probably because of the increase in labor supply. However, the twenty-hour work day was a thing of the past.[11] Wages were also low in Twente, where an excessive number of child laborers worked in the very unhealthy atmosphere of the textile mills which were "always filled with fine cotton dust." According to a report of 1861 these poor drudges worked twelve-hour days without sufficient rest periods. "In addition, their health is sapped by a lack of fresh air and this, coupled with their food, clothing, living quarters, and lack of proper sanitation makes them susceptible to scrofula, premature burn-out, and so forth. These children in our factory work force—in 1861 some 600 of them out of a total of about 4,500 factory workers—made a very sorry impression."[12] It is not surprising that later on many of them sought a better life in America, and today one is repeatedly struck by the large number from Overijsel and Gelderland, the "Achterhoekers."*

Conditions were the worst in the Roman Catholic "dark South" where there was even opposition to an investigation of working and living conditions. The industrialists there, particularly the well-known P. Regout, tried to avoid the spotlight with the motto: "Let Nature have its course." In 1861 the police commissioner of Maastricht [Limburg Province] "ruefully" reported that, "Here one can see the young factory workers looking like wraiths, completely devoid of upbringing, roaming the streets like brute animals. This is no cause for wonder, since very many children, beginning at nine years of age, have been working far too many hours daily in the glass, pottery, and other factories. Some of them do not leave the factories until midnight or even two hours later, only to be replaced by other children of their own age at those hours. The lax concern of parents in providing for their childrens' welfare is scandalous; they use their children from the earliest possible time to obtain all kinds of advantages for themselves and very often to give themselves over to idleness, sloth, and despicable immorality. In addition, I cannot deny that greed on the part of the factory owners is also a contributing cause."[13]

It was not until 1874 that Van Houten's Childrens' Law put a stop to child exploitation, after the national conscience had been stirred especially by the novelist J. J. Cremer, also a favorite among Dutch Americans, in a discourse entitled "Factory children, a plea, but not for money."[14] It should be expressly stated here that this kind of exploitation was not a specific Dutch phenomenon but was common to all of Europe. It showed perhaps its worst excesses in England at that time. When in Europe the social conscience opposed it too much, then it spread elsewhere and was perhaps found to be worst of all in the factories of New England, since the exploitation of children and women is like a weed that proliferates in lands of unbridled big business.[15]

As is evident, social conditions in the fifties, sixties, and seventies left very much to be desired in the Netherlands. This was particularly true in the cities, but it also applied to the rural areas, even though considerable prosperity was found among the farmers. It should not be overlooked that in the clay provinces, there was a laboring proletariat as well as a landed aristocracy. This labor proletariat, although it flourished in times of agricultural and stock-raising prosperity, nevertheless remained dependent to a considerable extent, due not in the least to their numerous progeny. For the many children accrued to the labor force, and eventually supply exceeded demand, since in the rural areas child labor in the fields also occurred very frequently at the cost of general education.[16]

For many people economic conditions remained as bad as they had been

---

*The Achterhoek is the most eastern "back corner" of the Netherlands; it was often equated with backwardness, comparable to Appalachia in the U.S.A.

in the forties. Exports of all kinds had increased, but food costs had consequently risen sharply and the removal of excise taxes had not been sufficient to compensate for the difference. The lack of daring and of entrepreneurial spirit on the part of the affluent people further increased unemployment, which was already growing due to the ever increasing population.
"Prospects for the working class become increasingly bleak. The cost of
foodstuffs rose but wages were not raised. Even some of those on the
higher rungs of the social ladder could maintain themselves only by the
greatest of efforts. Individuals were pushing and shoving to obtain positions and jobs, also in industry." These sentiments were expressed in 1857
by J. J. Hasselman, a former high official of the Dutch East Indies. He had
observed that many had gone to America for a better life and that emigration was becoming common, "particularly among those elements that are
not altogether penniless."[17]

Men like Obreen, who were irked by the stupor that kept the Dutch
nation paralyzed, vigorously encouraged emigration and in 1871 loudly
called upon farmers and tradesmen to go to America. "Go thither and begin
a new life, flee from the murderous competition, the poorly paying employer, the cramped and unhealthy housing, the perilous spirit of the age
that encourages hedonism when means are lacking, the wars of the kings,
the strikes of the workers, and the agitational influence of the Internationale [Marxism]. Prepare another home for yourself where you can
work, not merely to survive, but to be well-fed, well-clothed, and well-
housed. Choose yourself a second fatherland where the principles of freedom and equality are more widely practiced, where all can have a voice in
government, where all are eligible for any office, where you are not
hampered by a spirit of lethargy [slender- en jansaliegeest] in the development
of your strength and talents and in the pursuit of your good inclinations."[18]

Here too one hears a protest against the spirit of the age, though it is an
open question as to whether Lieutenant Obreen's protests were based on
love for his nation or on his interest in an agricultural and emigration
organization.[19] More on this later. This undertaking, too, was a protest
against the existing lassitude that mentally cramped the Netherlands and
at the same time it suggested a slowly emerging resolve to act.

I wish to stress the latter point because observers tend to generalize far
too much while analyzing the national spirit of our nation during the first
three-quarters of the nineteenth century, particularly among the laboring
classes. To the period under discussion applies, no doubt, the judgment I
made earlier and which was recently confirmed by I. J. Brugmans.[20] He
described the Dutch laborer of that period as "someone who resigns himself to his shabby existence in dull submission, one who lacks the physical
energy and temper to pull himself up by his bootstraps and whose general
education is too meager even to think about the possibility of improving
his lot, in general as someone who is still completely unemancipated." This
picture can be accepted but with one reservation, as I have noted previ-

ously: Not everyone resigned himself entirely; there were some who strove to improve their station in life; there were some who rebelled against the spirit of the times and who therefore left the country, as a sort of (usually) silent protest. Once more I stress this idea of a *silent* protest, because it apparently totally escaped Brugmans' attention; he does not make mention anywhere in his important study of these departing laborers. Yet, hundreds of them left.

2. Emigration

The emigration flood that was unleashed all over Europe in the forties continued to flow also from our country. Emigrants were, so to speak, flushed out of their homelands but also attracted by the increasingly faster development of America. The panics of 1857 and 1873 and, especially, the Civil War caused only temporary interruptions. This is evident from the following Dutch emigration statistics which, because of our own inadequate records, are based on American sources:[21]

Year	Number	Year	Number	Year	Number	Year	Number	Year	Number
1856	1,395	1861	369	1866	1,613	1871	993	1876	855
1857*	700	1862	339	1867	2,598	1872	1,909	1877	591
1858	1,201	1863	349	1868	718	1873	3,811	1878	608
1859	168	1864	520	1869	1,134	1874	2,044	1879	753
1860	342	1865	572	1870	1,066	1875	1,237	1880	3,340

Crisis years served as high water marks in the statistics because the economic crashes affected only potential emigrants—not those already enroute to the promised land or those who had already sold their effects and booked passage. Thus, in comparing emigration with the movement of the tides, the "neap tide"† took place *after* the crisis years, in 1859 and in 1875, and in the years immediately following. People knew years ahead that the Civil War threatened and were thus cautioned, as we have already pointed out before.

The well-known geographer Fr. Ratzel once commented that *"der Kampf ums Dasein im Grunde immer um Raum geführt wird"* [the struggle for survival is basically always carried on as a struggle for space].[22] There is perhaps no better proof for this observation than the emigration to America in the pre-Civil War years and, even more, after that conflict. One need be reminded only of the Homestead Act, the Pre-emption Act, and the Timber Culture Act, all of which also lured many Hollanders to the United States even in the very years that were so favorable for agriculture in our own country. Many a tenant with some financial resources grasped the opportunity to become a landowner in the United States.

*The number for this panic year is only for a six-month period, and thus gives an inexact picture [Van Hinte].

†The neap tide is a tide of minimal range occurring at the first and the third quarters of the moon.

Ratzel's comment is also applicable to those who settled in industrial cities and tried to make a living in a factory job at least temporarily. Some of these laborers strove to accumulate a bit of capital that would enable them to obtain a farm in the West or to occupy a homestead. Even those who remained in the factory towns had and still have as their highest ideal the acquisition of a small plot of land with their house on it. That many of the Dutch, like other Germanic emigrants, achieved this ideal is seen in the industrial centers of Paterson, Rochester, Grand Rapids, Chicago, etc. Since this "*Kampf um Raum*" |struggle for space| carried many dissatisfied Europeans across the Atlantic Ocean, one can interpret this particular struggle as the deepest cause for emigration, provided one considers Ratzel's "space" as being not only physical and geographical but also spiritual. This "space," then, is identical with the striving for freedom in all its meanings.

This emigration became easier over time because so many relatives, friends, and other acquaintances, who were usually fellow-believers, had already settled in the New World. They received the newcomers hospitably and in many cases made their journey possible in the first place. In many towns, such as Holland, Grand Rapids, and Grand Haven, there were organizations of members paying annual dues and who yearly drew lots to designate who might sponsor a family, related or not, that was ready to emigrate.* This was especially true in Holland, where the event was of some importance in the first years of the life of the colony. Developments in both steamship and railway traffic also considerably diminished the fear of travel that formerly had deterred many.

It is not surprising that the optimistic reports from acquaintances resulted in an easier and quicker decision-making process than had previously been the case. It is especially these letters that still caused so many to leave in spite of improved conditions in the countryside. One single letter could swing the opinion of numerous villagers to make the fateful decision, as was related by |George| Schnücker concerning Ost-Frisians from the village of Neermoor.[23] He related that an "America letter" in the thirties and forties was considered so unusual that it would be printed and distributed—like the letters of Sipma and Van Malsen—for the benefit of all the neighboring people. Later, as postage rates decreased and the letters became more numerous as more friends settled in America and prospered there, they were almost taken for granted. Only land, steamship, and railroad companies would print excerpts from the letters for advertising purposes.

G. Bonwetsch relates how numerous these America letters were also abroad. For example, in the town of Norka among the old Baptists on the Volga River |in Russia| in 1877, one mailbag might contain as many as fifty America letters, written by fellow Baptists who had settled in Wisconsin and

---

*This kind of credit union or savings club helped to speed up the emigration traffic, since a family could be brought over every year from the very start, without having to wait for one individual's accumulation of savings.

elsewhere.[24] The impact these letters had on emigration can not be underestimated. This is evident from the fact that in the sixties the Austrian government burned all such America letters, without exception, "so that they would not spread the desire for a better fatherland or for freer institutions!"[25]

Of greater significance, particularly after the Civil War, was the growing number of visits to the home country by colonists who had become successful. Bloemendaal, whose acquaintance we have previously made, was urged by such a visitor—a certain V.—to leave his birthplace of Vorden and to emigrate to Alto, Wisconsin, because, as V. had reported, "everything was so good there."[26] Later, Bloemendaal and several of his fellow countrymen returned twice for visits to the Netherlands. His influence on emigration was obvious and typical of hundreds of similar visits.

Driven by an "inner desire," Bloemendaal and five others visited the Old Country in November of 1870. "They did not come as little American peasants but as real dandies, traveling in first-class and finely dressed because they wished to astonish their friends in Holland and let them see what had happened to them in America! One young man in our group derived particular pleasure from this prospect, 'for,' as he said, 'when I left, people laughed at me, ridiculed me, and said I was crazy but now I will laugh at them and say they are crazy because now I have money in my pocket!' and at the same time he jingled the dollars in his pocket." Having arrived in the Netherlands, this young man painted a picture of America that was a bit too rosy. Bloemendaal, with a greater concern for the truth, asserted, "This was a fault from which many people suffered." But this "fault" contributed in no small way to more migration.

Bloemendaal himself was overwhelmed by the many questions by numerous inquisitive villagers in his birthplace, " . . . and since this repeated itself day after day, and was the same all the time, it became pretty annoying." What were the results? In the spring of 1871, when Bloemendaal planned to return, many wished to accompany him. He was not the least intent upon discouraging them, even less so since a few already had relatives in America. As a consequence, in spite of the "boom times" in the rural areas, a "sizeable group" accompanied him, anxious to find "room" in the New World—something which the Netherlands could not offer them.

Bloemendaal shared Ratzel's conviction: "When there is overpopulation and poverty in a country and there is no possibility of owning a house or land, one turns his back upon it in search of another place where there is bread and living space." He was so convinced of this necessity that he advanced a portion of the fare to some of the group who were too poor to finance the complete cost themselves. "Much of that money I never got back," Bloemendaal commented, which was not an entirely unique experience.[27]

In 1901 Bloemendaal once again visited his birthplace. The aforementioned V. had made this trip three times. It can readily be understood that the steamship and railroad companies profited from these visits; it is also obvious that increased emigration was another result. Because of these letters and visits, emigration increased until it became a natural stream that continued to flow. It was a "natural" stream because it was encouraged not so much from the outside as from the inside, as a result of what people heard and saw about their relatives and friends.

A somewhat artificial stimulus to emigration was exerted by the letters and visits that lacked in part or altogether this family character. These were the letters and visits that were primarily meant to serve "business" purposes. These were, therefore, less concerned with the particular needs of the would-be emigrants.

In this connection it should be noted that the steamship, railway, land, and other companies printed and distributed more or less fabricated colonists' letters and they sponsored visits with the special intent of recruiting emigrants. Even from the outset, they vigorously promoted an artificially-stimulated emigration that increasingly developed along with the spontaneous family emigration and that resulted at times in "assisted emigration." Just as fast as this type of company-promoted emigration rose, the caliber of a number of emigrants dropped.

To the numerous "recruiting" ["werf"] letters previously mentioned should be added among others, those printed in the *Nederlandsch-Amerikaansche Gids en Tolk* [The Dutch-American Guide and Interpreter].[28] To the "recruiting" visits, belong especially those that were made to the Netherlands by the young Hospers from Pella, Iowa, in 1870.[29] Hospers, at that time the mayor of Pella, can even be considered as a real, although distinguished and high-minded, recruiting agent who had been officially deputized as such. He was a member of an Iowa government commission to promote colonization of that state. Since he had, as we already know, just planned a new colony in Sioux County and since his interests as a land dealer were closely related to the need for colonists by Iowa, he was the obvious person to go to Europe, and specifically to the Netherlands and beat the peaceful recruiter's drum there.

As a member of the State Board of Immigration, Hospers arrived in his native country in October of 1870 and opened a recruiting office in his former place of residence, Hoog Blokland, near Gorinchem from where he canvassed the entire country. He announced his arrival and his willingness to give information on Iowa in numerous newspapers—*De Heraut, Het Nieuws van den Dag, De Provinciale Friesche Courant, De Wekstem, De Bazuin, De Heusdensche, De Haarlemmer,* and *De Nieuwe Rotterdamsche Courant.* He received hundreds of letters of inquiry and he answered them with a thousand copies of a freely distributed pamphlet "Iowa: *Zal ik naar Amerika gaan verhuizen . . . "* [Iowa—Should I Emigrate to America . . .] and at the same time he distributed 5,000 copies of a brochure translated from the English, entitled "*Iowa: Het Land voor Emigranten"* [Iowa: The Land for Emigrants].[30]

Hospers traveled throughout the country from November 1870 to January 1871 and addressed gatherings that often lasted beyond midnight, since there was a great and growing desire for emigration in spite of a flourishing agriculture. Hospers spoke five times in Gorinchem, four times in Rotterdam, three times in Amsterdam, twice in both Utrecht and Heerenveen, as well as in Genderen, 's-Hertogenbosch, Dordrecht, Klundert, Axel, Leeuwarden, Dronrijp, etc. People from all classes of society were interested. According to Hospers, individuals worth from $10,000 to $40,000 thought about emigration especially for the sake of their children. Many immediately followed Pella's burgomaster; others were delayed because of the American Panic of 1873, but went after it had passed. Most of them, as noted earlier, went to Sioux County where Hospers had settled permanently after he had submitted his resignation as mayor of Pella—in part to reap the fruit of his tour to the Netherlands.

Although we cannot speak of religious impulses as having been pertinent to this emigration, yet even after 1855, religion had not remained altogether without influence, for the simple reason that this family emigration, especially of the Seceders, largely involved common people [*kleine luyden*] who, in many cases, felt more at home among their coreligionists in America than among their neighbors in the Netherlands. That is why Hospers had advertised particularly in the religious papers, although for him as a businessman, the "unbelieving" elements among the emigrants were worth just as much, as was evident from his reports in the Nieuwe Rotterdammer, Nieuws van den Dag, and similar papers.

A curious reason why many Dutchmen emigrated in those years was simply the departure of some pastor or other for the New World. It should be remembered that calls were repeatedly sent to pastors in the Netherlands by the Seceders in America and even more so by the True brothers who had seceded from them. In most cases these ministers declined, "instead of going to a foreign country and help us in our need," as was observed [in America], not without bitterness, in a recent comment.[31] But next to the dozens who, after having heard God, thought they should stay in the Netherlands, there were those who heeded the call from across the ocean, whether driven by a sense of religious duty or by the additional concern for the future of their children, as for instance, Reverend R. T. Kuiper declared with somewhat unusual candor when he and his wife and seven children left for America in 1879.[32]

Among those who "crossed the Ocean"—in addition to "those teachers who had been 'duds' [*"Waar een steekje aan los was,"* i.e. with a screw loose somewhere] in the Netherlands (but seemed) still good enough for our country"[33]—were the following ministers, all of whom had received a call: D. J. Van der Werp, 1864; W. H. Frieling, 1866; R. Duiker, 1867; H. R. Koopman, 1867; B. De Beij, 1868; F. Hulst, 1868; W. P. De Jonge, 1871; W. Van der Kleij, 1871; N. M. Steffens, 1872; F. Rederus, 1872; N. H. Dosker, 1873; G. E. Boer, 1873; L. J. Hulst, 1874; J. Kremer, 1876; G. K. Hemkes, 1876; R. T. Kuiper, 1879; H. Van der Werp, 1881; H. Beuker, 1893, etc., etc.[34] So the departure of various of these pastors caused some members of their con-

gregation or village also to take the big step, since they considered themselves to be safe under the leadership of their shepherd. Sometimes there
would be a strong personal attachment to the pastor and his personal
convictions, as in the case of the nestor of the Christian Reformed American preachers, J. Noordewier. When his former pastor, R. Duiker, from Niezijl
in Groningen, decided to go to America, he said to him "Jake, I have
received a call from North America and if I go, you will go with me, won't
you?" To this Noordewier replied, "For sure, I will go with you."[35]

Many in Niezijl prepared to accompany the Reverend Duiker on the
journey. "There was a great deal of activity and hustle and bustle in our
small village," and no wonder because no less than seventy emigrants
followed him to Grand Rapids, in hopes of improving their lot.[36] At about
the same time, Reverend De Beij left Middelstum with a large group also,
attracted to the fertile farmlands of Michigan and Illinois.[37] Reverend G. E.
Boer—who, like Duiker and De Beij had served in the province of Groningen—moved with a part of his congregation to Grand Rapids.[38]

The importance of this minister-led immigration is enhanced when it is
remembered that, as previously mentioned, they not only took some of
their parishioners with them but later these were followed by many others.
Surely their minister would find employment for them! At times Duiker's
house held so many new arrivals "that there was scarcely sufficient room
for him and his family."[39]

3. The Mormons

During the period under discussion, the only emigration that was purely
religious or at least free of materialistic incentives was that of the spiritual
heirs of the Zwijndrecht Brothers, the so-called New Lighters. We have
previously sketched their beliefs. Following the death in 1832 of their
leader, the peat barge captain Stoffel Muller, a number of disagreements
arose in the Zwijndrecht Brotherhood, particularly concerning the status of
women, and as we already know, a few of the dissidents left for America.
After 1848 there was no longer any independent organizations among stragglers, derisively called the "sulphur sticks" ["zwavelstokken," i.e., "stinkers"].
They continued to lead a life of poverty without any mutual contacts, scattered over the villages of Zuid Holland until 1863. After that, most of them
emigrated to the New World—remarkably, however, as separate individuals,
not in organized groups of congregations.

It was in 1863 that many of these New Lighters were convinced of the
imminent downfall of European society of that time—a conviction that had
often prevailed before, in the forties, as I have mentioned. This belief additionally motivated them to emigrate to America. Some of the more or less
educated Zuid Hollanders, in the Linge village of Heukelum were regular
readers of the *Nieuwe Rotterdamsche Courant* and were therefore also convinced that this doom was certain and believed that God would establish

with the world a new covenant—the seventh. The news spread from one village to another, wherever New Lighters were found, that the Spirit was calling them to go to the Mormons in North America, where that seventh covenant was supposed to be a fact and where it would become a physical reality. A bargeman who traded by barter and was known as "Swop-belly" ["ruilebuik"], [W.] Heystek, served, so to speak, as the traveling agent for the New Lighters; he urged everybody on.

Therefore, a strange and indescribable excitement overpowered these New Lighters. A smoldering fanaticism burns into a flaming inferno. "We are being called," they said. "Everything in this damned old world is coming to an end. But there will be salvation among the Latter Day Saints in Utah. There love and equality reign. There everyone is a worker. Whoever does not go there is lost!" Even well-to-do farmers were convinced. One of their village ministers, [Abraham Johannes] Oort, asserted that "the rich will cry and lament because here the cup is full." He related all this to Professor [H. P. G.] Quack.

More than thirty left to join the Mormons in Utah. They came from Heukelum and its vicinity—the region that had furnished so many fanatical Seceders to America—as well as from Boskoop and Waddinxveen, all located in the province of Zuid Holland, from Polsbroek in the bordering province of Utrecht, and from Vuren and Dalem in Gelderland.[40] One or two returned and some succumbed along the dangerous route over the Rocky Mountains; the Central and Union Pacific railroads had not yet been built. Most of them merged with the Mormons, but a few, who found the situation in Utah undesirable, went to Hosper's colony in Sioux County, Iowa.[41]

This New Lighter emigration is of interest not only because of its exclusively religious nature but also, as was the case with many of the Seceders in 1846 and 1847, because of what I would like to term a "doomsday" and "search-for-equality" incentive. Not only did these play an important part in the emigration but they also accounted for some of the consequences. Ever since that time, an increasing number of Hollanders settled among the Mormons in Utah. Not in the least was this due to the moral commitment of every Mormon—and therefore of every Dutch Mormon—of going "on mission" at their own expense for at least four years. Naturally, they preferred to work in their native land. Only after having fulfilled this obligation does a Mormon have any standing, any significance. It could well be that the exodus of 1863 was a result of some of these missionary efforts, although neither the Reverend Oort nor Professor Quack mentions this possible connection. This is all the more surprising since the Reverend Oort was living among the New Lights.

Even at this time there were a few Netherlanders living among the Mormons in Utah. One of them was a Frisian, A. W. Van der Woude, born at Franeker in 1812, who was baptized into the faith of the "Saints" in 1852 by an elder named Taylor. At the time of the 91st [sic, 31st] annual April Conference of the Latter Day Saints held in 1861 in Salt Lake City, he was "set aside to be a missionary to the Netherlands"—the first Hollander to be deputized "for missionary work" by the Mormons. Van der Woude traveled to Rotterdam in the company of a German-born elder, P. A. Schettler, who had relatives among the Moravian Brethren in Zeist [the Netherlands] and who had also been deputized for mission work in the Netherlands. They arrived at Rotterdam on August 5, 1861, "and, being plentipotentiaries and possessors of the keys of the Kingdom, opened the Door of Salvation for the people residing in the Low Countries by the sea."[42] Upon his arrival in Rotterdam, Van der Woude went to visit his relatives in Amsterdam and Schettler went to be with his relatives and numerous friends in Zeist. Later the two men met again in Rotterdam. Neither of them had much success, either with relatives or acquaintances or wherever they had tried. The local pastors had warned their people against these "terrible Mormons, who had come to seduce the people."

Van der Woude next visited his relatives in Workum. In this Frisian town he preached to a few well-attended gatherings and created quite a stir. From there he went to Leeuwarden and then to Dokkum and its vicinity where he addressed several large audiences "in chock-full barns" and proclaimed the tidings of salvation from America; here, at last, he met with a measure of success. There were at least three converts—G. W. and B. Van der Woude and E. Wolters, all residing at Broek near Akkerwoude in Dantumadeel; they let themselves be led to the watery grave [the ceremony of baptism] on October 1 in order to bury their old nature there. On December 23 Schettler performed his first baptism service in Amsterdam; among the initiates was H. Van Steeter, who, before going to Utah, completed a missionary tour in Holland. Thus, in 1861, a total of six persons were converted. This was "the historical initial number [of members] of the Church of Latter Day Saints in the Netherlands." In May of 1862 their first congregation, called a "branch," was organized in Amsterdam with a total of fourteen souls, all members of the "very poor" element in the city.

Schettler translated a few small tracts into Dutch and subsequently the *Book of Mormon*. However, he was transferred to Switzerland since Mormonism in the Netherlands grew extremely slowly due to the resistance against it. Even a visit to Amsterdam by the president of the European mission, G. Q. Cannon, had little noticeable effect, although according to [Frank I.] Kooyman, he instantly healed an aged, sick sister who had experienced much suffering, by anointing her. By the end of 1862 the first Dutch branch had only fifteen members.[43]

Elsewhere their number gradually increased, particularly in Zuid Holland. It must have been during this period that Heystek became familiar with the beliefs of the Mormons, influenced either personally by Van der Woude or Schettler, by their followers, or by the reading of their pamphlets. The New Lights also held to a notion of the "final days" and the belief in a speedy return of the Lord, which they adduced from the foreshadowings of war, revolution, great poverty, etc. Thus, they must have felt themselves to be kindred spirits of the Saints. Even the orthodox among the Dutch believers prepared themselves for this second coming and took pains about being saved when the great and terrible day of judgment would arrive. For this reason there were many among them who liked to listen to the Mormons.

It was thus not fortuitous that the first important gathering of the Dutch Mormons—the first so-called convocation—took place on October 22, 1865, at Gorinchem, with Dutch Saints from several areas present. Note that this took place in the region where the Newlights were most numerous, in the center of the most orthodox Seceders whom we have seen depart for America much earlier, since 1846 and 1847. Gorinchem also was the center of an area which, even to the present day, is marked by its ignorant population, addicted to superstition and even the belief in sorcery! Are these evidences of the same spiritual attitude?

At this Gorinchem conference, the Saint P. J. Lammers was ordained as an elder and deputized to carry on missionary work for more than three years in the Netherlands. After this job was completed in 1869, he left for Utah.[44] He returned to the Netherlands several times "on mission"; from 1875 to 1877 and again from 1882 to 1884 he acted as head, as president, of the mission to the Netherlands. Next to Van der Woude he was one of the most important of the Mormon missionaries to the Netherlands. He translated several Mormon publications into the Dutch language and distributed them. As a preacher he was so effective that Dutch papers warned their readers against him, particularly because, as is still the case in Christian Reformed circles today, Mormons were considered first of all to be polygamists.

After Lammers' departure, J. W. F. Volker headed the Dutch mission. Since that time the number of missionaries has steadily increased; nearly all were lay preachers, and most had been born in the Netherlands. The combined Dutch-Belgian mission territory has since been divided into four Dutch and two Belgian conferences. Today these exist in Amsterdam, Arnhem, Groningen, and Rotterdam; the latter includes branches at Rotterdam, Schiedam, Dordrecht, the Hague, Delft, and Leyden. At the head of each conference there is a conference president, with a number of missionaries under each.

The number of missionaries has steadily increased. In 1911, eighteen operated in Amsterdam, eleven in Groningen, thirteen in Arnhem, and twenty-two in Rotterdam; in addition there were several assistants.[45] In 1921 there were twenty-four salvation deputies working in Rotterdam alone! They come and go almost weekly. One cannot read an issue of the Dutch-American Mormon weekly, De Utah-Nederlander, without finding an item detailing the celebrations in honor of Dutch Mormons going "on mission" or returning from it. These parties are very lively and jolly since the "Saints" love to dance, in sharp contrast to the Seceders.[46]

In essence, these missionaries also became emigration agents, for the ultimate goal of the Saints was to live in the ideal state of Utah. This particular Zion seemed to exert a most powerful attraction on women as, for example, on "Mother" Berend who emigrated in 1900. A year later "Father" Berend also felt that "the old fatherland had become too confining."[47] Therefore, Utah is the only state in the Union that has more Dutch women than men; in 1920 there were 1,024 and 956 respectively—a phenomenon most unusual for a "colonial" area.

The missionaries also influenced young people. For example, our vice-consul, E[vert] Neuteboom, at Ogden, Utah, had once listened to one of those "degraded, terrible, Mormons" in the Netherlands when he was fifteen years old. "No one seemed to take an interest in the old gentleman, as to what he had to say, except the boy Evert. I took in every word he had to say and I knew he was telling me the simple truth of the Gospel of Christ." Although he had attended Sunday school and catechism classes faithfully, up to this point religion had had little impact on Evert. "Now when the true religion came to me I knew it was true and have known it ever since until now." Since that time Neuteboom has been active for many years as a missionary and "traveled a good many thousand miles," converting his parents and many of his relatives to the faith of the Saints. In time they all moved to Utah, where they belong to the "most contented, happiest Hollanders in the State."[48]

One repeatedly notes that, although converts temporarily continue to live in the Netherlands, after a year or two the "spirit of get up and go" affects them and they emigrate. Undoubtedly they are influenced by the contrast between their life in the Netherlands and what the missionaries portray about life in Zion. As a result of the preaching of Van der Woude, hundreds settled in Salt Lake City and in Ogden; in recent years they have also gone to Los Angeles where they have settled among the many nationalities there and engage in a wide variety of occupations. There is no separate settlement whatsoever. But they do have their own organizations, the most important being the one of the old-time missionaries. The concept of missions as an expression of religiosity still characterizes them. It was above all this religiosity that brought them to Utah. "It was not a desire for money or gain that brought you to these distant places but it was your faith in the pure and holy gospel," declared the highly respected Levi Edgar Young, one of the First Seven Presidents of the Council of Seventy, in July of 1921 on the occasion of a celebration by the Utah Netherlanders at Salt Lake City, commemorating the work of Van der Woude's mission, that had sent such a constant stream of Dutch emigrants to Utah.[49]

B. 1880–1895

1. The Agricultural Crisis in the Netherlands

The statistics on Dutch emigration shown previously in this chapter indicate a sudden increase from 753 in 1879 to 3,340 in 1880. Emigration continued to increase even more strongly in the following years, with a peak in 1882 of 9,517 Netherlanders who settled in America in that year! Although emigration has always remained important, that number has never been surpassed since. The figures are as follows:

Year	Number	Year	Number	Year	Number
1881	8,597	1886	2,314	1891	5,206
1882	9,517	1887	4,506	1892	6,141
1883	5,249	1888	5,845	1893	6,199
1884	4,198	1889	6,460	1894	1,820
1885	2,689	1890	4,326	1895	1,388

This rapid increase is all the more remarkable because during the late seventies conditions changed in the Netherlands. Thanks to the surge in German prosperity, Dutch commerce and shipping increased sharply, assisted by the opening of the North Sea Canal to Amsterdam and the New Waterway to Rotterdam. This in turn even led to the formation of some steamship companies. Very gradually, heavy industry began to develop in the Netherlands, encouraged by the growing Dutch rail network and especially the extension and improvement of Dutch waterways. At first growth was extremely slow. According to an 1892 article in *De Economist*, "no significant new sources of prosperity had been developed" since the publication of a report in 1857 pertaining to this matter.[50]

Population increased at a faster rate than trade and industry. Between 1879 and 1889 there was an annual population increase of 49,872; between 1890 and 1897 the yearly gain was 69,540 souls. In 1889 the population totaled 4,511,415 and at the end of 1895 the figure was approaching the 5 million mark! It was no surprise that this awakening new life resulted in a new spirit of action that was especially evident in the writer movement of the eighties among the intelligentsia and in the rise of socialism among the masses. This new spirit was expressed among the common people by an increased urge to emigrate; they hankered after more room in every area of life.

During this time there was not only a heavy emigration from the Netherlands but also from Germany, England, and the Scandinavian nations. These nations also sent record numbers to America in 1882—250,630 from Germany, 179,419 from England, and 105,326 from Scandinavia!

Year	Germany	Great Britain & Ireland	Denmark, Norway and Sweden (Scandinavia)
1881	210,485	153,714	81,852
1882	250,630	179,419	105,326
1883	194,786	158,082	71,994

Emigration to the United States reached a spring tide in 1882, with a record number of 788,992!

It thus appears that there was no unique reason for Dutch emigration;

the same conditions prevailed in other West European countries. At this time trade and commerce were flourishing in Great Britain and Germany and industry in the island kingdom was at its peak. Industrial Germany was developing even more rapidly. So it is obvious that the forces for emigration in the eighties existed not only in Europe but also in the United States, with its attractive factors.

Perhaps we should look for an interaction from both sides, for that was indeed the case. Between 1878 and 1895 there was a terrible crisis in all of western Europe, caused partly by agricultural conditions in America. It must be emphasized that American conditions were only *partially* responsible because the crisis would not have been so severe in the eighties if the West European and in particular the Dutch farmers had been more educated and energetic, and if they had changed a little faster with the times. More than one competent source affirms that the Dutch farmers of the sixties and seventies, to use an overdrawn image, had become rich while "asleep"—not because of their own efforts and will power but almost entirely because of a combination of very favorable conditions, mentioned before.[51] America jarred the drowsing farmers into wakefulness.

Influenced by the widening railroad network, particularly in the second half of the nineteenth century, immense regions of virgin soil were turned over to agriculture and cattle raising. This took place first in Russia and the United States, followed by British India, and then by Argentina and Canada. But nowhere did the development of agriculture move at such a fast pace as in the United States, where railroads had developed so rapidly. From 37 kilometers |23 miles| in 1830 it had grown to 201,881 kilometers |126,180 miles| at the beginning of 1885. Also, both the government and private companies offered extremely fertile land for sale on the most favorable terms. It was almost given away. All these factors contributed to a surge to these rich western lands not only from the American eastern areas but also from overseas. Beginning in 1850 about 250,000 emigrants came annually; this number increased to more than 450,000 in 1880, to nearly 670,000 in 1881, etc.

Therefore, agricultural production increased enormously but "mining" of the land led to soil exhaustion, as we also saw taking place in the Dutch settlements. In those years little thought, if any, was given to the use of fertilizers. Because America was rather thinly populated, a large amount of its agricultural products was exported. This was particularly true of wheat; about 5.5 million bushels were sent out in 1830 and this rapidly increased so that 50 million bushels were exported in 1870 and 180 million bushels in 1880! Next to America, British India and Argentina became increasingly important, as well as Russia which, just as America, exported in addition to wheat also rye and barley and, in lesser quantities, oats.

Land in these countries had been acquired at relatively little cost and it was exploited by overcropping. Therefore, Europe, with its expensive land, high rents, and backward practices, simply could not compete when prices were depressed. As in the rest of Europe, grain prices fell in the Netherlands, as was reflected in the prices quoted in Groningen (per hectoliter) |2.84 bushels|:

Years	Wheat	Rye	Barley	Oats
1871–80	*fl.* 10.98	*fl.* 8.11	*fl.* 6.76	*fl.* 4.55
1881–90	7.46	5.79	4.92	3.75
1893–95	4.50	3.50	3.30	2.50

In Amsterdam the price of wheat dropped to *fl.* 4 per hectoliter in 1895.[52]

All of western Europe, where cereals were still the main agricultural product, was seriously hurt by these declining prices. One could speak of a real grain panic. Many farmers were almost reduced to beggary, particularly those who had expanded their holdings at great expense in the golden days or who had to pay high rents. Backwards as our people were, they were helpless in the face of this flood of grain. This backwardness was already manifest at the International Agricultural Exhibition held at Amsterdam in 1884. The period of material prosperity was contemporary with one of intellectual malaise in agriculture, according to |C.J.| Sickesz van de Cloese and |F. B.| Löhnis.

Agriculture deteriorated still more when traditional staples lost their importance due to new inventions; madder |the roots used for red dye| did so completely and rapeseed |for lubricating and lamp oil| partially. Meanwhile, due to increased and better means of transportation other agricultural products, such as tobacco, were imported from overseas, which in turn heavily damaged our sandy soil agriculture. In general, prices declined to less than half the levels of the previous years of opulence. As a result, many farmers turned their farmlands into grass meadows and raised cattle; those on the sandy soils devoted themselves more than before to the fattening of animals, especially hogs. Consequently, the prices of cattle, dairy products, and meat went down!

The prosperity of former days gave way to poverty. Those who had formerly been the best customers of the goldsmiths and silversmiths and the stockbrokers could now no longer pay their mortgages and rents out of their income and so were forced to sell out at great loss on a depressed market or to vacate their rented farmstead. Many were completely ruined while others were able to keep their head above water only through the most drastic economies. Many experienced heavy financial losses and "indescribable suffering."[53]

It was the professional pride of these farmers, who had formerly been well-to-do, that caused many of them to escape their cramped fatherland and flee to America where they could begin a new life with their now rather limited capital. In the Old County, it would have embarrassed them if they had worked with their own hands, after having been the masters over many employees. They might even have been shunned by their former farmhands.

But these matters were of no concern in America and they could breathe more freely in all respects. In addition, they would escape the heavy Dutch taxes of that time. There was a flight of capital—just as there is at present. More noble motives also played a part; they were concerned about the future of their children who had been brought up in luxury.

A Frisian writer, T. G. Van der Meulen, gave an interesting account of many things found in the clay soil area of the province, setting them forth in the April 15, 1882, issue of the *Weekblad voor het Kanton Bergum* |Weekly Paper of the Canton of Bergum|. The farmer—so says this friend of the emigrants, more or less in the following terms—is a member of a variety of clubs and organizations and his wife, when she sits next to the notary public's wife at the meeting of the Society for Public Welfare and Charity is addressed as "*juffrouw*" |Mrs.| and when on Fridays, she goes shopping with her husband at the fashion stores in the provincial capital of Leeuwarden, dressed in her best finery and with jeweled pins in her *muts* |traditional Frisian lace cap|, she is even called "*mevrouw*" |Madame|. The farmer is called "*mijnheer*" |Sir|. He prides himself in running a horse in the trotting races and when it comes to drinking he knows how to propose "high-faluting" toasts, real "ripsnorters" |*die slaan als een klok*, i.e., ring like a bell|! His sons are habitual frequenters of the pubs where they play billiards and down a drink or two, they ride their super-de-luxe "chais" |the Frisian "*sjees*"|*to show off their horsemanship, and belong to the local amateur theater club, etc. They sport gold watches and chains across their vests and wear gold rings on their fingers. Each of his daughters is quite a lady, dressed to kill and cutting a dash with an exquisite hairdo. "They pick and choose with refined taste stylish gowns, hats, collars, and laces in Friesland's largest stores. '*Oars is er sa it rejuchte fatsoen net oan*' |Otherwise they are not in the height of fashion|, as they say in Frisian."

Then came the depression in the price of grain and subsequently of dairy products, occasioned by the competition from America and Denmark. The fat years were followed by lean ones for which no provision had previously been made. The proceeds from many a tub of butter had been left behind in the stores of Friesland's capital. The farmer notes how everything is going wrong and is worried for months by the threat of insolvency and bankruptcy. He finally proposes to go to America where a former laid-off farmhand had gone and prospered. "To reef one's sails here, to abandon one's position and career here in order to take up a lesser one, that is too hard to digest, and in fact is a no-win situation, since taxes are now going up every year." The children approve of the decision; the daughters instinctively feel that they will remain spinsters here and the young men fear being forced to become mere farmhands. So everything is sold and it still nets the former well-to-do family some *fl.* 20,000. They leave for America where their immediate concern is to avoid at all cost the clutches of the unscrupulous land

---

*A tilbury or two-wheeled light horse carriage.

speculators who, having been informed of their arrival, will converge on them like ravenous sharks.

Leafing through the pages of the *Weekblad*'s issues during these crisis years, one comes across numerous reports concerning this type of emigration—reports of fine people whom "destiny smote" and who were obliged to emigrate.[54] On his 1881 trip through the United States, Van der Meulen met many of these kind of people who had been forced to exile themselves from the Netherlands and who had found a refuge in America. In northwestern Iowa, near the village of China in the vicinity of Le Mars, he paid a visit to R. Feenstra and his family who "had been for a number of years one of the most highly bracketed poll-tax payers in the village of Beetgum, and who was now a farmer in free America."[55]

Numbers of these "genteel" farmers from the clay soils of Noord Holland, Friesland, Groningen, and Zeeland settled especially in the Sioux County, Iowa, whose Dutch-born population increased by three thousand souls between 1885 and 1895.[56] There they rose again to great prosperity due to the relative greater breadth of vision that still characterized them. Today their children, thanks also to their education, occupy important positions in Iowa and elsewhere. One of them, a well-known and highly esteemed attorney, has been for a number of years mayor of Orange City.

It was these people of the eighties who brought a more liberal spirit to the typical orthodox and rather narrow-minded atmosphere of the Sioux County settlement. Their more cosmopolitan attitude caused the social and spiritual life of Sioux County to stand in marked contrast to the staid spiritual and social life that characterized Holland, Michigan, and Pella, Iowa.

The crisis did not only affect Dutch agricultural circles but spread to other areas, and caused a general depression. Numerous farmhands had already been laid off as an "economy measure" and this step boosted the rate of agricultural unemployment even further, since it was already high as a result of the chronic over-population of the rural areas. This unemployment could only have been reduced by transfers to the cities or abroad. This depression was experienced not only by small businessmen and artisans in the rural districts but also in the cities, whose growth depends, after all, also on a prosperous farmer class. As a consequence trade and industry were likewise affected by the agricultural crisis and the advantages of very low prices of foodstuffs did not make up for the high unemployment. In fact, wages were brought in line with food prices, and therefore they were scaled down to such a degree that they continued to be virtual starvation wages. These sorry labor conditions of 1860 were still manifest to a large degree in the eighties, although some legal protection had been provided for women and children.

Even the pope had to recognize the deeply sad state of the laboring class and declared in his encyclical "Rerum Novarum" of 1891 that "a yoke had been imposed on the masses of the proletariat which was but little different from slavery." So it is no surprise that many common people, both rural and urban, not without a feeling of bitterness in their hearts again turned to America, since in that country agriculture and cattle raising, industry, and commerce grew with a feverish speed even though these enterprises were temporarily disrupted by the panic of 1893, just as had been the case in 1857 and 1873.

In our little fatherland there were now thousands of emigrants, in contrast to the hundreds of previous years. Everywhere people prepared to leave, particularly in Friesland, where in 1880 and subsequent years, conditions among the laborers were worse than anywhere else. "There was almost no work to be had and those who did have employment worked regularly from five in the morning until eight in the evening during the summer months; many worked even longer hours and the wages were frightfully low," according to R. Van Zinderen Bakker.[57] "Field and forest laborers in the area where I lived* were content to receive forty or fifty cents per day in the winter months; carpenters and masons were put off with a dime or eleven cents an hour. Each year, in March or April, the peat cutters staged their very poorly organized *"bollejagerijen"* [strikes] to prevent the bosses from 'nibbling still more from their meager wages as had been repeatedly attempted in times past and sometimes successfully. This was true for eastern Friesland, but it was not any better in the western clay areas, according to W. Giezen. He remembered a strike in Het Bildt by the laborers who were tired of working for nine cents an hour (five or six gulden per week) except during winter, when they were unemployed, or when they received only sixty cents a day, working the flatbrake machines [to remove the woody part from the flax stems], harvesting the wealth of the land to fill the coffers of the rich farmers and landowners."[58]

Although numerous Frisians were attracted by the newly emerging socialism—perhaps more so here than elsewhere—many others chose to go to America and these were often followed soon after by the militants. Many "Biltkers" from the so-called "Parochie" villages† left the country; indeed this America-fever threatened the continued existence of many a small town. For example, the hamlet of Firdgum, which had only 250 inhabitants, lost more than twenty when they left for America in April, 1881. Twijzel, in the eastern part of the province, reported: "Our village is breaking up to make America great."[59] At that time, there must have been many episodes like the one that took place at Bergum where R. Weeber and his wife— "honest and able people"—prepared in 1882 for the ocean trip. "At the farewell, our village gave evidence of their general respect in which

*At that time, R. Van Zinderen Bakker, born in Kortezwaag, was an alderman of the municipality of Opsterland, in which Kortezwaag is located. In 1895 he became a member of the Provincial States of Friesland [Van Hinte].

†Het Bildt (meaning "territory formed by silt deposits"), is one of the oldest polders of Friesland, lying northwest of Leeuwarden. Three of its villages, Sint Annaparochie, Sint-Jacobiparochie and Vrouwenparochie are often referred to as "de Parochies" or Parishes.

R. Weeber and his wife were held by riding out with them. Many eyes were wet at the time of the final handshakes."[60] Great numbers of Frisians left from Bergum's vicinity.

It should be mentioned that once they had become successful in America, those who were of a socialistic bent greatly changed their political ideas and and many even abandoned socialism altogether. More concerning this later. From a letter of G. Van der Veen, a native of Hardegarijp, we get an idea of the spirit of these energetic and very interesting fellows whose thirst for freedom played a role in their lives even though they did not take part in the socialistic movement. Bamboozled by land speculators in Iowa, Van der Veen finally found work in a Missouri coal mine. "I hope to work without interruption underground through the 1882–83 winter and then in the spring of 1883 I hope to exchange the black element for the shiny white element, to go from the coal mines to the mountains of nature's wonderful Colorado in order to extract gold and silver instead of coal from the earth."[61] At the time Van der Veen was earning six to nine gulden per day, which helped to sweeten the hard labor that involved working on his knees or bent over in cramped quarters. "But all this crawling is not as difficult for a free person who earns more than his bread with manual labor, than the crawling of so many a Dutch slave groveling before the worldly gods to secure a morsel of bread for himself and his family." Thus wrote this stalwart Frisian of the eighties, who on the other hand, never ceased "to praise and love my native land, my beloved Netherlands." Truly, great human resources were lost to our country when such individuals left! But not all emigrants went to the United States; thousands left for South America.

2. *Trafficking in Human Beings*

Unusual circumstances, quite independent of the agricultural crisis, encouraged emigration in these years. It took on huge dimensions that cannot be explained, even in these abnormal times, by solely American or European causes. As a result of improvements in steamship and railroad traffic, the trip to America had become much more comfortable and the ocean crossing had been reduced to about ten days. Numerous new laws and regulations, the establishment of emigrant hotels, and the opening in New York of the well-known American disembarkation center of Castle Garden— later, Ellis Island—meant that emigrants were better protected than previously, although not yet as much as should have been the case.

Fierce competition between the steamship lines and, at the same time, between the American railroads, had made traveling so exceedingly cheap that even for the poorest persons, costs were no longer an obstacle. Since these traveling costs were lower than they had even been and would ever be again, these charges were often paid or temporarily advanced by other interested parties.

The Cunard Line—the first steamship line between England and America—had begun operation in 1840 and sparked an intense rivalry. Soon there were also ships sailing from German, French, and Belgian ports. Since 1872 ships also sailed directly to America from Rotterdam on a regular schedule. "The steamboat war" of 1885 reduced the cost of steerage passage to $10 or $12. Just before the [First] World War it was *fl.*80 to *fl.*90 [$32 to $36] and afterwards about *fl.*370 [$148]. At one time emigrants were transported from Hamburg, via England, to New York for a fare of seven, indeed, *seven* dollars![62]

At about the same time competition between American railroads was at its peak. A vigorous rate war raged for years; competition was so keen that in 1888 one could ride from New York to Chicago for $5. At one time a passenger could travel from Chicago to San Francisco for $5 and, on another occasion, the Pennsylvania Railroad reduced to a mere $1 the passenger fare from New York to St. Louis—more than a thousand miles distant![63]

Whatever significance these low tariffs may have had, there was another factor that was far more permanent and whose consequences for emigration have been far-reaching to a much greater extent. It resulted from the mutual competition in the transportation field and reared its head until the present day, sometimes openly, sometimes less openly—the institution of immigrant agents. The very existence of several transatlantic steamship lines—in 1871 there were four operating between Liverpool and the United States alone!—depended to a large degree on the transportation of emigrants. For both the British and the continental lines the promotion of emigration thus became a matter of survival. The emigrant himself became more and more a mere item of merchandise, a mass product, "bulk cargo"; only those more well-to-do emigrants who traveled first or second class were treated as "general cargo," as individuals.

The firms stationed agents in various European cities to encourage emigration by whatever means and in whatever ways. This kind of emigration "business" was not new; we have already called attention to its occurrence in the Netherlands, namely in Winterswijk. However, it had never been practiced on such a large scale as in the eighties. The Imman Steamship Company alone, sailing between Liverpool and New York, had 3,500 agents operating in Europe during the eighties. They had an equal number operating in the United States and the job of these agents was to sell—and to promote!—prepaid tickets to the colonists for the purpose of enabling relatives and acquaintances to cross the ocean. In little Switzerland alone there were four hundred agents operating in 1885, and this was only after they had been given permission by the Swiss authorities, who did not give it to just anybody![64] These "gentlemen" pictured the New World in the most tempting terms, in the rosiest of colors. Young and old, married or single, fit or unfit, they were lured into selling their goods and making arrangements for passage. At times the agents, eager for a commission, would advance funds for passage against a mortgage or simple lien. This practice led to serious abuses.[65]

Emigration from the Netherlands was encouraged in no small measure by these developments and practices. At first many Netherlanders traveled to America via England and Germany, but with the establishment of the limited partnership of Plate, Reuchlin and Co., in October of 1871, who organized the departure on October 15, 1872, of the steamer *Rotterdam*, the first regular direct steamship route was inaugurated between the Netherlands and New York.[66] Already during the first trips, so many emigrants were transported that the firm was enlarged and, in April of 1873, the previous limited partnership became a limited liability company, the Nederlandsch-Amerikaansche Stoomvaart Maatschappij [Netherland-American Steamship Company]. This enlargement enabled the company to increase its fleet by several ships. Naturally, many Dutch emigrants made use of this newly opened line. In 1873 Cohen Stuart traveled on one of these new ships, the W. A. *Scholten*. Of the 200 emigrants on board, 150 of them were Netherlanders; most of the rest were south Germans.[67]

This "dreadfully large number of steamships" plying the American routes in the eighties, according to one of the reports of the N.A.S.M., helped to keep fares extremely low because these companies had to face not only foreign but also domestic competition. In 1881 the Koninklijke Nederlandsche Stoomboot Maatschappij (K.N.S.M.) [Royal Dutch Steamship Company] began to sail some of its vessels from Amsterdam to New York and thanks to "a heavy emigrant traffic and in spite of lower prices"[68] it did an excellent business, so good indeed that the company considered the construction of new vessels. These developments, in turn, prompted the N.A.S.M. to sail its largest vessels out of Amsterdam in 1882. This local competition between the N.A.S.M. and the K.N.S.M. caused a further drop in both freight and passenger rates between Amsterdam and New York, as observers have emphatically pointed out. In 1882 the fare from Amsterdam to New York was less than *fl.* 60 [$24][69] This low price benefited not only emigration *via* the Netherlands but especially also emigration *from* the Netherlands, or rather, it strongly promoted such emigration.

How sharp this competition was and how eager the companies were for a "load" may be gathered from the fact that the Amsterdam company transported not only a large number of foreigners and residents of the northern parts of the Netherlands but also residents from the southern parts of the country—groups that would ordinarily embark from Rotterdam. In May of 1882 a writer for the *Handelsblad* visited an emigrant waiting room erected by the Royal Dutch Steamship Company in a customhouse warehouse. There he found, besides a number of Poles, Germans, Swiss, Norwegians, Swedes, etc., not only families from Noord Holland but also farm families from Zeeland wearing their picturesque local clothing; and it was noted in passing that the clothing "was as colorful as that of the Poles" but looked "more prosperous and clean."[70]

Both steamship companies used recruiting agents to grab the booty from each other. The Royal Dutch Steamship Company had secured the services of the firm of Prins and Zwanenburg, located in Harlingen; this firm specialized in rounding up emigrants. In 1883 an agreement was reached by the two competing shipping companies; the Royal Dutch Steamship Company for a consideration, canceled its connection with New York and neighboring ports for a ten-year period, while the Netherland-American Steamship Company took over a number of Royal Dutch Steamship Company commitments, including those with the Harlingen firm.

This firm (Prins and Zwanenburg) continued to do business in an "unscrupulous manner;"[71] one of its inducements was to point out the "boon" of exemption from the military draft and this practice almost led to political problems. So the N.A.S.M. felt obliged to take the emigration business completely in its own hands again. This is not to say that this step put an end to the abuses in the system, since foreign companies also had their recruiting agents in the Netherlands. Recruiting was carried on more actively than ever before; it was not concerned only with emigrants going to the United States but also to other countries, like Brazil and Argentina. The N.A.S.M. placed a few ships on the latter run in 1888 after the Argentine Immigration Commission had guaranteed the fares of 10,000 emigrants.[72] Well-paid "runners" were more than willing to help, which resulted in a real trafficking in human beings. In this connection one should read the article "Argentinië" [Argentina] by the Reverend Dr. J. Van Lonkhuyzen.[73] In 1889, more than 4,000 Hollanders had been expedited to South America, chiefly to Argentina; between 1888 and 1891 just the Belgian and Dutch agencies arranged for the transportation of 17,765 persons. Brazil paid recruiting agents 120 francs for every adult, 60 francs for every child, plus a premium of 100,000 francs to the shipping company that would bring in 10,000 immigrants per year.[74] All these new arrivals would have to serve as "cultural fertilizer!"

It is quite clear that under such circumstances, the quality of the emigrants changed. In the eighties and nineties they were strong-willed and self-confident, but later they often totally lacked will power and let themselves be shunted from one country to another. In several western European countries, especially in Germany, but also in England, Belgium, France, etc., powerful organizations were even formed to export the nation's paupers by providing them with free tickets to America. That was one way of getting rid of the "dregs" of society! This type of "export" reached such proportions that in 1882 America began to initiate restrictive measures, and in 1889 immigration regulations were tightened up considerably since many of the unfit or poorly prepared immigrants became public charges.[75] In 1887 the state of New York alone was supporting 34,100 aliens in its almshouses.[76] Even Dutchmen were found among these "undesirables." As early as the seventies there were organizations in the Netherlands devoted to furthering the emigration of indigent elements to Minnesota.[77] This was repeated during the nineties—not for the sake of aiding paupers but rather to help those who were poor and willing to work, and yet lacked all means of pulling themselves out of their social impasse.[78]

The Dutch emigrants of 1885 were usually of a different type than those of the forties and fifties who often left their native country full of confidence and amid the singing of psalms. It has already been noted that the emigrants of the eighties were often no more than items for export, without even the slightest faith in their own ability and without any hope for the future. The *Handelsblad* reporter, mentioned previously, noted that when he visited the emigrant building of the K.N.S.M. at Amsterdam in 1882 he found "an overall easy-going atmosphere, and on the faces of the emigrants there is an expression of seriousness and even somberness rather than an expression of joyous expectancy concerning a better future."[79] Ten years later W. F. Andriessen remarked that, considering the dejectedness of many Dutch emigrants, one must conclude "that the present Dutch generation is not the real race of emigrants."[80] In my opinion this applies to only a few select groups.

What were the results of this emigration? Hundreds arrived in the New World and wandered aimlessly about until they finally called on the Dutch consuls for assistance! According to the 1890 annual report of our consul-general in New York, the number of Dutch emigrants that asked for help at this consulate "was again unusually large"; many had been misled "by committees or agents" with prospects of a beautiful future. The report for 1891 stated that an "unbroken stream of immigrants from the Netherlands and Luxemburg" had applied also during that year to the consul-general for assistance, having been duped by beautiful promises or thoughtlessly sent off by well-meaning elders or family members. In 1893 there was "again a large number of needy Netherlanders" asking for help, and in 1896 "a large number" of our countrymen who "had been reduced to poverty."[81]

An even more dismal picture of the quality of these Dutch emigrants is presented by the Reverend G. G. Haan, a Dutch-American missionary. A group of these poor wretches had gone to the Far West and were eeking out an existence there in hopes of improving their miserable lot, thus proving what [W. F.] Gevers Deynoot, a member of the Dutch Chamber of Deputies, had said in 1859 in New York when he made a trip through the United States: "Whatever is good for nothing is shunted as much as possible to the Far West."[82] During his missionary work, Haan repeatedly encountered these wanderers and described them in anything but a loving and brotherly manner in the January 26, 1898 issue of the True church weekly, *De Wachter.* He described them as "gullible, ignorant, ill-bred people, loathesome scum" that in the past few years had come "by the shiploads" and spread themselves all over the West. According to this man of God, they were "irreligious and unmannerly, with a look of insulting godlessness on their faces."

Later Haan was forced to retract some of these words for being too strong, but H. Beets maintained that there was some truth in the description. "No one who is acquainted with the situation can deny this," Beets said.[83] This agreed with the outcome of a prediction by the Netherlands Minister of Internal Affairs and reported in his Inquiry of 1860 dealing with child labor. This stated that the result of the then-existing labor conditions in the Netherlands would be "that these children would grow up without guidance or control and, even if they did not fall into crime themselves later on, their unmannerliness and immorality (would) still be transmitted to their children."[84] So it is not surprising that among the American vagabonds (tramps) one would always meet some of Dutch ancestry; they had come not only from the laboring class but sometimes were descendants of wealthy families—all of them castaways on the ocean called Life.[85]

From the foregoing one must not conclude that the steamship, railway, and land agents were the cause of all the misery, that they were merely "traders in human souls." Nor were all the real estate speculators "land sharks." What a noble man was, for instance, Henry Hospers, who nevertheless was above all a true real estate man, a true realtor! Men of noble character could also be found among the agents of steamship lines and other companies, particularly those associated with the N.A.S.M., and especially those living in Groningen and Oisterwijk (Noord Brabant) in 1888, who operated under very strict supervision of district inspectors.[86]

At times a steamship company agent was definitely viewed as a trusted advisor and a source of information for those seriously contemplating emigration. One of the most remarkable and sympathetic examples of such a man is that of Tjibbe Geerts Van der Meulen (Tsjibbe Gearts), the Frisian poet and writer and one who had seriously considered going to the United States but who remained in Friesland for the sake of his parents. His brother |Bastiaan| and a group of men and women from the vicinity of Bergum, thirty in number, crossed the ocean in 1853 and most of them settled in Iowa; Van der Meulen himself, at Pella; a number of them later on moved from there to Nebraska.

An exchange of letters between Tsjibbe Gearts and his friends in America gave him some insight into American conditions and contributed to his decision to be an agent for emigration. The visit of his brother in 1866 gave him a still better picture of American life. He assisted many would-be emigrants with words and deeds and provided them with references in America; many of them were thankful for this aid.[87]

How serious Tsjibbe Gearts was about his work is shown by the following case. About 1880 and in the years following, "American" land agents tried to promote the sale of land in various underdeveloped states. He solemnly warned his Frisians: "People, investigate first. Put your money in the bank, learn to farm in a foreign country, and inspect carefully before buying any land." He steadfastly refused to serve as an agent in Friesland for American land companies even after having made a trip to the United States, no matter how attractive some of the offers were. Instead, he violently criticized the practices of the land agents and publicly exposed their methods. "America is a Wonderland (*Luilekkerland*), but before one arrives there one has to eat one's way through the mountain of rice pudding [i.e., obstacles], and there many perish. Many swindling agents are active; they stir in the rice pudding and many newcomers have their eyes smeared shut. Many weep when they finally realize where they have actually landed. Oh! that rice pudding mountain." "Whoever desires to earn lots of money should become a recruiter," is the title of an article by Tsjibbe Gearts, in which he mercilessly exposed the activities of the land sharks.[88]

He constantly harangued against the "Messrs." Kuipers from the village of Steggerda, who represented a land company in Iowa and wished to found a settlement of "Kuipers City" there and then later in "Dacotah." Tsjibbe Gearts described these efforts as "a web of impurity chiefly aimed at enriching themselves at the expense of others."[89] In passing, I should mention the further details in order to characterize this sort of "enterprise." The attack on the Kuipers was strongly supported by Hovens Greve, director of the *Steenwijker Courant*. The Kuipers were so stung by these attacks during the winter of 1881–82 ("emigrant campaigns" were usually carried on during the winter) that they wanted physically to attack Hovens Greve![90] The Kuipers, finally, had to leave the country!

Tsjibbe Geart's efforts more and more incurred the displeasure of the firm of Prins and Zwanenburg, which had been functioning as land agents. At one time our Frisian had been an agent for the firm to encourage emigration to America among his fellow Frisians in the "Wouden" region.* He had dared to give assurances "that Messrs. Prins and Zwanenburg had always set the goal of more than satisfying everyone of the emigrants transported by them. But now that the Amsterdam-New York line was opened, their promoting of this line is proof that they want to foster the happiness of the emigrants!"[91] However, he became so indignant about the "scandalous" manner in which the firm in the end housed and generally treated the emigrants that he no longer wanted to have anything to do with the company, in particular since it was becoming involved in American land sales.

So it is understandable that Tsjibbe Gearts was no longer interested in serving as an agent for a Dutch company; he had no more use for the Rotterdam shipping line than for the Amsterdam line that had employed Prins and Zwanenburg at first. But he did support the Red Star Line of Antwerp and sold passage tickets for them; in his *Weekblad voor het Kanton Bergum* he gave it as much publicity as possible.

When he made his 1881 visit to America he used one of the ships of this company. One of his sons informed me that especially after this voyage he supplied traveling maps, etc., as agent of the Red Star Line "to very many

---

*De Wouden [the Woods] is a region south of Dokkum, northeast of Leeuwarden.

from all parts of Friesland." During the depression years he personally escorted many Frisian groups to Antwerp for the Atlantic crossing! At about this same time this agent, with a bent for poetry, wrote one of his most famous poems, his "*Lânforhuzerssang*" [Emigrants' Song], which is still sung by many Frisians up to the present day.[92] It was with this song on their lips that many Frisians left the "heitelân" ["fatherland"]! It should be said that two sons of the poet were among the emigrants (Lândforhuzers):

> Farewell, William, your eyes ever upward.
> If at first your spirit is still tied to the parental farmstead,
> America, the land of fortune and blessings,
> Will give you a morning in the coming of our evening.*

Tsjibbe Gearts published this in his weekly for the benefit of his son Willem[93] and later wrote regarding his oldest son, Geert:[94]

> Farewell, my child, Farewell! Farewell!
> You, the eldest of my sons.†

Apart from all that, Van der Meulen also promoted emigration to America because he needed to make a living. Upon his return from the New World, according to Gearts' son, he gave some "exceedingly good talks" and displayed some of its products both inside and outside of Friesland. Soon after his return he advertised the lectures that he would deliver—at Harlingen on October 27, 1881, at Midlum (in the Frisian tongue), on October 28, at Franeker on October 29, at Birgum on November 1st, at Adjerk on November 3rd, at Aldtsjerk on November 4, etc. The lectures would be "*alles mei printen en kaerten fardudelike*" en "*yn 'e twade pauze sjen fen Foarwerpen út de nye wrâld.*" [Everything clarified with prints and cards and during the second intermission he would show objects from the New World].[95]

Those who could not hear Tsjibbe Gearts in person were able to read his series of articles, "Van Bergum naar Amerika," in the *Weekblad voor het Kanton Bergum*,[96] and these travel descriptions undoubtedly influenced many other Frisians to leave, especially those living in the poor forest villages around Bergum. There were also many clandestine departures from Friesland that later turned out to have taken place via Antwerp. These did not detract in the least from Van der Meulen's good intentions; on the contrary, it added to his reputation, in particular in Friesland's Wouden region.

In those days the True Church was an extremely reliable recruiting agent and financially totally disinterested. As we already know, the Christelijke

---

*   Far Willem wol, it each altyd omheagen
    Is eerst dyn geest oan 't aldererf yet boun,-
    Amerika, it lân fen lok en sègen,
    Yowt dy in moarn, yn 't kommen fen ús joun.

†   Vaarwel mijn kind! Vaarwel! Vaarwel!
    Gij oudste van mijn zonen.

Gereformeerde Kerk in the Netherlands in 1882 recognized the Christian Reformed Church in the United States as the true Reformed denomination and advised its followers to join the True brothers there. |G. M. W.| Jellinghaus reports to us something especially noteworthy: that during the eighties in some English village parishes the ministers read the most important announcements from the Emigrants Information Office that had been organized in 1886.[97] The church in our country was just as effective in promoting emigration. On February 5, 1884, a letter was sent by the Synodical Committee of the Holland Christian Reformed Church in America "to the Honorable Consistories of the Christelijk Gereformeerde Gemeenten in Nederland" |Christian Reformed Churches in the Netherlands| calling attention to numerous promising, new settlements, where cheap lands were still available and where churches had already been organized. As a result, settlements well-known to us—Fremont, Allendale, Vogel Center, Richland (Lucas) and New Era in Michigan, as well as New Holland and Charles Mix in South Dakota, Rotterdam in Kansas, and East Friesland in Nebraska—were highly recommended. It is obvious that the intent of this writing was to give "leadership" to emigration. The fact that emigration was thus also promoted is obvious, all the more so since now immigrants were assured of spiritual aid that, as we have seen before, would often extend also to material aid.[98] The effect of newly arrived Dutch immigrants on the growth of the new settlements has been repeatedly pointed out.

The fact that in the first place this American church group tried through its activities to prevent immigrants from joining the Reformed Church or perhaps going unchurched and falling prey to demoralization, and that it wanted above all to establish as many churches as possible, all this does not detract from the significance of its entirely disinterested support of Dutch immigrants, at least as far as financial support is concerned. These considerations, it was felt, promoted not only emigration from the Netherlands but also encouraged colonization in America.

The "American" ministers—in the Reformed Church as well as in the True Church—worked tirelessly for this goal, usually in real competition with one another. Since the eighties the True brothers had sent their preachers to the Dakotas to investigate the possibilities for their church there, "as well as for a Dutch settlement."[99] We have already called attention to the results. With these initiatives the True Church achieved its main objective, according to H. Beets—the large stream of Christelijk Gereformeerde immigrants was channeled into its fold.[100]

From this it must be concluded that the above-mentioned characteristics of the emigrants of the eighties were very atypical for many of them. The Reverend Haan's account may have been influenced by the setbacks encountered in "organizing" churches. The importance of many of the "eightyers" for the further development of Sioux County, for instance, has already been described. But also among those who traveled much further "into the West," one did not necessarily find solely the outcasts. On the contrary, a party of two hundred Colorado-bound Hollanders was described by the newspapers in St. Louis and vicinity as "the best looking and most able immigrants that have ever passed through here."[101] Generalizations are always very dangerous, especially in matters of emigration, because motives for it were always extremely varied and so were the causes and grounds, although usually these were of a preponderant economic nature.

C. Since About 1895

It should not be assumed that emigration came to an end when conditions in our rural areas, beginning in 1895, gradually began to improve. The farmers managed to recover and benefited from a continuing demand, and consequent higher prices, for their products. They also benefited from agricultural research and from the increasing use of commercial fertilizers and crop rotation. They also paid more attention to world markets. Those on the clay lands, particularly in Friesland and in Noord Holland and Zuid Holland, replaced grains more and more with root crops such as potatoes, sugar beets, etc. At the same time the farmers on the sandy soils redirected their agricultural efforts towards stock breeding; what grain they did raise was used to fatten hogs. In other areas, low lying heath and moor lands were converted to pasture lands and farmers specialized more in dairying. All in all, the farmers prospered after 1900 and the World War surely did not have an adverse effect upon them.[102] Not until after that conflict was there again mention of a "crisis."

In the meantime, following a small decline after the Panic of 1893—a "crash" seems to occur every twenty years or so in America—emigration from our country to the United States increased again considerably. This was all the more remarkable because, next to agricultural, horticultural, and stock-raising activities, also trade and commerce grew considerably. In fact, after 1889, our country, that traditionally had been a trading and agricultural nation, became also more and more an industrial nation. The census of 1909 showed 34.6 percent active in industry, 28.3 percent in farming and fishing, and 18.1 percent in trade and commerce.[103] At present 40 percent are engaged in industry, 26 percent in fishing and farming (in its broadest sense), and 18 percent in trade and commerce. In the period between 1898 and 1914 there was also a "great blossoming" in trade and industry.[104] During this period our entire economy was in a "general period of prosperity" and was described by C. Te Lintum no less enthusiastically as an "almost veritable golden age."[105]

Why then, during this "golden period" did thousands again leave the country? The United States was no longer the prime objective for our emigrants;[106] thousands also went to the developing industrial nations of Belgium and Germany. But even so the United States attracted many:

Year	Number	Year	Number	Year	Number	Year	Number	Year	Number
1896	1,583	1901	2,349	1906	4,946	1911	8,358	1916	2,910
1897	890	1902	2,284	1907	6,637	1912	6,667	1917	2,235
1898	767	1903	3,998	1908	5,946	1913	6,902	1918	944
1899	1,029	1904	4,916	1909	4,698	1914	6,321	1919	1,098
1900	1,735	1905	4,954	1910	7,534	1915	3,144	1920	5,187

An analysis will show that the terms *blossoming* and *golden age* are theoretical and vague; they rest entirely upon one's point of view, upon the vision one has of life in human society. If one accepts unemployment of thousands and the emigration of thousands of others year after year as "normal," only then can one designate these times as a continuing "period of prosperity," even though in addition every year about 60,000 people temporarily left our country for Germany!

To understand the condition of the masses during this flourishing period, one should read K. Reyne's *De Uittocht der Plattelandsbevolking* [The Exodus of the Rural Population] (1904).[107] In this work he calls attention to the following conditions: a class of heavily mortgaged landholders (the true farming class), a class of tenant farmers for whom the day of tomorrow remains a big question mark despite their hard work, a class of field laborers, the rural proletariat, working for the most frugal of wages and continually threatened by unemployment. "This is the state of the country folks, whose life and lot has been glorified in so many pastoral ballads. It is an endless drama of human misery; a world where the restlessness of life and the hard realities of existence belie the peacefulness of the fields and the abundance of the harvest. . . . And from this welter of misery, suffering, exploitation, and scantily paid toil an almost unbroken stream of humanity flees to the cities—to the centers of trade and industry," and it might be added, to foreign countries as well.

But the centers of trade and industry to which many rural folk were attracted since about 1860 were not idyllic, either! In spite of labor laws and many other social improvements, much was left to be done. As small enterprises gave way to large enterprises in commerce as well as in industry, there was often unemployment. Times were hard for many of the common people. Professor H. Brugmans recognized this, particularly in Amsterdam, where like anywhere else times of prosperity alternated with periods of depression, only more vehemently so.[108] This came about precisely at a time when the workers became more and more conscious of their human dignity. They came in conflict with existing conditions with an unprecedented fierceness that often resulted in their being "turned into the streets" with their wives and children, a prey to hunger.

It would be too simplistic to attribute the cause of all these troubles to "capitalism"! The question is warranted as to whether perhaps an imbalance existed between the growth of agriculture, commerce, and industry on the one hand, and a large population increase on the other. The population did increase more rapidly all the time. Between 1830 and 1840 it grew .91 percent, from 1889 to 1899 1.24 percent; and from 1909 to 1920 1.39 percent [these percentages are yearly averages]. In the latter year it totaled 6,841,155 and today it has already passed the 7,500,000 mark. Some, such as Jonkheer J. C. C. Sandberg, felt that before the World War the growth in population paralleled the growing demand for labor; however, this opinion is mainly based on anything but reliable figures.[109]

If one heeds the "spirit of the times" when consulting the emigrant literature, one cannot escape the conviction that in the rural areas as well as in the urban centers, in agriculture and commerce as well as industry, there certainly was more supply than demand for labor. The "cheerful, buoyant" life in the Netherlands of the past fifty years has also shown serious depressions. In 1908 Dr. J. Van Lonkhuysen, an American Christian Reformed minister who was at that time still a pastor at Aarlanderveen, visited some Hollanders in Argentina and reported "that there was *work* and *bread* to be had, that there the life of the industrious did not need to succumb to the burden of poverty and debt, that there the father did not have to cast sad looks over his children and wonder what the future would portend for them, and that there the son did not descend almost systematically on the social ladder to a point lower than the father; but that there for those who are able and willing whole fields lie fallow.... We must rid ourselves of the weak-kneed notion that causes men to destroy each other over one small clump of earth rather than to seize the opportunity to swarm out over God's wide world and cultivate it.... "[110] That was the picture of our "booming times" by someone who did not restrict himself to mere *words* but who *acted* and who moved first to Grand Rapids, Michigan, and then to Chicago, Illinois! Men of all callings followed this example—office clerks with no chance of promotion, commercial agents who had been eliminated by competition, retailers who had been squeezed out by big enterprises, factory workers, and especially the day laborers in rural areas.[111] This enumeration shows the widely diverse reasons for emigration, even in our own times.

[H.] Blink is biased when he suggests solely agrarian motives for this emigration: "... the existence of large or reasonably large land holdings with little possibility for land redistribution, the occurrence of much cultivated soil with a large number of farmers." He assumed that during a period, 1904 to 1913—still a "period of prosperity"!—emigration appeared to be quite heavy. At this time, however, numerous small farmers and market gardeners emigrated due to harvest failures, but especially also because of "too great a subdivision of the soil"! J. Maurer, a friend of the farmers, said that "everyone toiled hard for the prosperity of the mortgage companies that now left them in the lurch."[113] It is therefore only a half truth that the extreme subdivision of land holdings would nevertheless curtail emigration, as alleged by Blink, since in that case everyone is more closely tied to the soil due to the fact of owning it. Reverses of many

Langendijk truck gardeners forced them to go to America about 1910. Also a depression in the culture of flower bulbs caused many a tulip grower to emigrate.

Emigration is really much more complex than is generally accepted, especially in our days, now that the wanderlust spirit is more prevalent than was formerly the case. People are much more easily convinced to pack up and go, less resigned to their fate, and more self-aware, as is the case with the laborers of today. Better transportation and improved conditions in the United States, which are no longer as forbidding as they were in former days, contributed to this. The phenomenally rapid growth of industry in the United States and the high wages paid there are the reasons, in spite of the lack of available cheap land, that a very great attraction is still exerted on the most diverse groups of the Dutch, particularly on the laboring class.

Therefore, there was a sharp increase in the natural, or more or less spontaneous emigration, that is, an emigration undertaken through a free choice, although abetted by relatives who had already prospered in the new country and who now sent over money or prepaid tickets to other relatives to join them. This type of emigration contrasted with the emigration that land agents and ship company agents promoted. And this was even the case at a time when their own country was prospering, simply because prospects in the United States were much brighter. This explains why, in spite of uncontestable progress in the Netherlands, a continual exodus took place, because this progress could not keep up with the prospects in the United States and elsewhere.

Much more so than formerly, these development differences or geographical and economic differences reflected themselves in emigration. One could even say that emigration had become their mirror image. However, thanks to a great simplification in transportation, Blink's striking comment that emigration is more or less a barometer of economic conditions[114] was more applicable than ever. And this was true in spite of the fact that fares were now set by the railroad and steamship companies for their "mutual benefit," and that so-called "pooling" arrangements were made by the steamship companies so that fares never again reached the low point of the eighties.

The great difference in travel conditions experienced by the working man in the middle of the nineteenth century, when the voyage sometimes took months and was considered to be a huge obstacle (one need only recall the account of Bonnema), and of the present time was clearly shown to me in a letter from an artisan, C. J. Van der P., who had come from Ierseke. Acquaintances in Grand Rapids, who had done well, had sent him an advance. In June of 1923 he traveled to America by second class aboard the *Nieuw Amsterdam*. He was full of praise for the ship where there were so many activities "that a person had no time for any worrisome thoughts whatsoever." In the morning he usually took a stroll on deck with his fellow cabin passengers until the bell rang for breakfast. "That sure was a nice event—a bowl of oatmeal, followed up by bread with two fried eggs and ham, bread and smoked beef, and coffee and sugar and milk, as much as one desired, followed by an orange or sweet-sour apple. I would be so filled that I would have to loosen my trousers or else lie down for a bit, you know. Then another stroll on deck and at about 10:30 we would go to the ballroom to hear some beautiful musical selections. There were two violins, two bass-viols and a piano. It was most wonderful, you know; I must say again that one was scarcely aware of being aboard ship. The days sped by, thanks to the wonderful music and the antics of the clowns.... I split my sides laughing on this ship and I had to hold my stomach several times and sometimes my face was tired from so much laughing. . . . Well, Dear Parents, and Relatives, I wish that soon you all could experience and enjoy this too, because I can assure you that I have certainly had a great time myself all those days."[115] If not the typical emigrant, he was certainly a modern one!

This is the way in which the unskilled laborer of today travels, thanks to his American friends. It is also an interesting example of the influence of Hollanders already in America on those relatives who stayed behind, because the above case is not an isolated instance. Jonkheer Sandberg commented recently that an increasing number of emigrants are traveling second class, people who, considering their financial means and general education, would have felt more at home in third class.[116] This was confirmed for me when I traveled to America aboard the *Rotterdam* in 1921.

To some extent one can see the influence of America on the newly developing mentality, on the "awakening consciousness and self-awareness" of Dutch laborers, as it was expressed by our native of Ierseke further on in the letter quoted previously. "Our acquaintances should not travel third class, for I can assure you that that is a mess." This observation need not have resulted exclusively from the new spirit among the working class, or from a certain over-evaluation of their position. It could have been based on observed facts as supported by testimony of the director of the Nederlandsche Vereeniging "Landverhuizing" [Dutch Emigration Society], [117] that "third class travel on some ships is inhumane" and even on Dutch ships (in 1920) "conditions in part of the third class quarters . . . (are) not compatible with present day standards of human transportation."[118] These data again point up the fact that one has to be very careful in establishing "permanent" causes for emigration under continually changing economic conditions. One should be aware that emigration is far more the result of a coincidence of circumstances and therefore also of certain arbitrariness. It is precisely the previously mentioned barometric function, i.e., that emigration reflects economic conditions, which reveals this randomness and unpredictability.

This arbitrariness is especially evident in the American tariff laws, which directly led to the emigration of numerous Hollanders to the United States. During the Civil War, tariffs were increased because money was needed to carry on the war. The rapid growth of industry, however, raised the call for more protective rates and this led to the McKinley tariffs that were highly protective.[119] Many Dutch enterprises—commercial, industrial and agricultural—were harmed by this protectionism. As a consequence, many Hollanders were even reduced to beggary. The high tariffs made exports to America prohibitive. Some goods were even refused entrance point-blank by the American government, and as a result, many Dutch businesses dependent on the American market were virtually bankrupted. One need only think of the Boskoop nurserymen whose chief market was in America! The same applied to the flower bulb growers. There was little alternative for these ruined people than to proceed to the den of the murderer: to settle in America!

The growth of the American cigar industry and the accompanying difficulty of importing foreign cigars resulted in many Dutch cigar makers settling in the eastern states in the sixties and particularly in the eighties, especially in Boston and New York. The |Soloman| Gompers—a family of cigar makers—settled in New York about 1863, and one of their sons, Samuel, of whom much would be heard later on, went into that business too. Some of these tobacco workers were induced to go to California by "anti-Chinese men" to replace the unwanted Chinese workers. However, these Hollanders as well as other Caucasian cigar makers were not able to compete with the "yellow men" and so were discharged within a few weeks.[120]

In the East they seemed to feel at home. J. Jansen noted that at the beginning of the twentieth century in Boston "many cigar makers were in evidence" and he mentioned that he thought many of them had come from Rotterdam and Zwolle.[121] They remained devoted to Holland; since many of them were above all tipplers of Schiedam's whoopee water!*

The diamond workers constituted the best example of those driven to America by the latter's tariff laws. A few of them had settled in America about 1860, encouraged by the depressed conditions of the Dutch diamond industry. Thanks to them a diamond industry has since developed in the United States. The sharp tariff increase of 1890 on polished diamonds caused not only a growth of this newly-established industry in America but also a real exodus of Dutch diamond workers, in many cases even under the leadership of their financially strong employers. Since that time there has been a significant colony of Dutch diamond workers in New York, as well as in other places. More about this later.[122]

It need scarcely be mentioned that many non-Dutch were also affected by these tariff laws, causing them to settle in the United States, too. In November of 1906 the British embassy in Washington noted the large emigration to America, which it considered to be caused in part by the protectionist tariff rates that induced manufacturers of certain products to settle in America.[123]

Some unusual and unexpected circumstances also resulted in emigra-

*Schiedam was the center of the Dutch distillery industry, producing particularly gin.

tion. A few examples may be cited. The ending of the Boer War in 1901 brought many South African Hollanders to the United States, particularly those who had been working on the railroads, in addition to a number of "irreconcilable" Boers. In that year our consul-general in New York, J. R. Planten, reported that nearly every N.A.S.M. ship brought over a few of these Dutch Afrikaners.[124] These former railroad officials had been unsuccessful in finding employment in Holland and thus many of them came to America to settle among their fellow Dutchmen. I am not aware to what extent the Cronjé settlement near Holland, Michigan, or the settlement of Joubert near the Dutch colony in South Dakota, were influenced by this Afrikaners emigration or whether these names were a reflection of the strong sympathies for the Boers among the Dutch Americans.*

In addition to the above example of emigration, which are more or less based largely on personal initiative, irrespective of basic causes, one must still distinguish, up to the present day, the artificial and directly stimulated emigration based more often than not on false presentations: the activities of the land, steamship, and railroad agents; in short, the whole business of "emigrant recruiters." These traders in emigrants were responsible for very many totally unfit immigrants going to their doom in America, provided these misfits had not been "caught" by the Dutch consuls and sent back. In 1906 our consul-general in New York thought that he saw some improvement, even "a noticeable change for the better" in the quality of the Dutch immigrants. A year later this same official noted that there were still too many Netherlanders coming to America "who must be considered unsuitable in almost every respect for this country."[125]

Restrictions should have been imposed particularly also in our country on the dubious business of those who engaged in the selling of souls. They were even worse in the Netherlands than the crimps abroad and they were as notorious as the "land sharks" in the United States. Even today they are not regulated. As late as 1912 it was pointed out that the amateur and professional recruiters in our country, assisted by an army of sub-agents, among whom there were many with an apparently elastic conscience, applied themselves "with redoubled zeal" to the recruitment of those with the wanderlust. Interviews were scheduled with them, exhibits and lectures organized, movies shown, stories run in the local press, brochures distributed, etc., all with this "business" in mind.[126]

The situation is still the same today. The recruitment system still exists, often, according to Jonkheer Sandberg, because of the fare generated for the rail and steamship lines who mislead and trick many of our countrymen.[127] As late as 1925 there was an "unusually large" and "undesirable interest" on the part of the recruiters, the real estate men, etc., in our emigrants. In the spring of 1925 there were twenty of these recruiters independently

*Piet Cronjé was a Boer commander and Petrus Jacobus Joubert their commander in chief against the British.

active in our country and many of them worked with large numbers of agents scattered throughout the country.[128]

It is true that there has been some improvement since the enactment of the still entirely inadequate emigrant law of 1861. There are government committees for the supervision of emigration in the port cities but they exercise jurisdiction only over emigrant housing and the emigrant ships and much improvement is still necessary in the latter, as we saw before.

In contrast to regulations in Italy, Switzerland, Hungary, etc., the Netherlands offer no protection against the practices of the recruiters. Last year a justice of the peace dismissed charges of sharp practice against some recruiters.[129] It is difficult to unmask the real intent of these men and their coworkers; they often have an uncanny knack of instilling confidence in their victims and are very slick and cunning, as is proven time and time again. Some Netherlanders who, due to their professional status, would be least expected to participate in such practices, nevertheless belong to this "noble" guild! It must have come as a surprise to many when, in the eighties, a Christelijk Gereformeerde minister made propaganda in the interest of a particular steamship company.[130] A few years ago, many were deeply disappointed when a Roman Catholic priest turned out to be a "seller of souls."[131] And what must one think when very recently an inspector in the Department of Justice was unmasked as one of them!?[132] Now that immigration has been restricted by the United States, these "gentlemen" have had to adopt new methods; today their activities are more often directed toward Canada than was formerly the case.

There were two groups in the United States that were most interested in curtailing immigration and by cooperating they were finally successful, following vetoes by Presidents |Grover| Cleveland, |William Howard| Taft, and |Woodrow| Wilson, the latter even twice. In the panic year of 1893, when there was considerable unemployment throughout the United States, American labor first became strongly aware of the serious competition from cheap immigrant help. In former times disgruntled laborers, dissatisfied with their wages in the East, could go to the West, where land was still available. But free land was virtually gone by 1890 as a result of the Homestead Act of 1862. No longer could the West serve as a "safety value" for the dissatisfied Eastern elements. Now they felt more than before that they had to compete "with the slums of Europe." The leader of the American machinists union declared that, "Our living is gauged by immigrants."

It is true that various laws prohibited the entry of criminals, prostitutes, the handicapped, etc., but a literacy test, which would have reduced the total number of immigrants by half or two-thirds, could find no favor in the eyes of the presidents previously mentioned. A few Chinese exclusion acts were passed. For the time being, America stuck to its tradition of being "a haven of refuge," although American labor ridiculed this and similar "high sounding expressions."[133]

As a result of the World War, America became more nationalistic than ever; everyone had to be "100% American." The Americanization of hundreds of thousands of foreigners, particularly from southern and eastern Europe, was well-nigh impossible as long as they were reinforced by hundreds of thousands more from the Old World. The Know Nothing attitude, which has been described earlier, manifested itself again, as evidenced by a kind of hatred of foreigners and a suspicion against the "hyphenated Americans," against the "pseudo" Americans, that is, the foreign-born Americans. It was felt that if immigration were restricted, the Americanization of those already here could be hastened.

Under the influence of an ever increasing number of proponents of eugenics in America, there was a movement to use these emigrant restrictions for the improvement of the American racial type. A somewhat altered Nordic type, preferably Protestant, was the ideal.[134] But the mass immigration from southern and eastern Europe threatened to dilute this type, particularly since the "new immigrants" belonged to the poorest classes and this was happening just when, according to [S. R.] Steinmetz, the so-called "new race in America" was doing well and expanding because of the disappearance of the pauper type.[135]

There is evidence that the immigration restrictions of 1917, 1921, and 1924 were directed against the non-Teutonic elements, but Teutons were also affected.[136] Although the act of 1921 established a quota of 3 percent of those who had settled from each country in the base year of 1910, according to census figures, it was superseded by the act of 1920, the notorious Johnson Act, which limited them to 2 percent of those resident in 1890 according to census data when the "Old Immigration" from northwestern Europe was still dominant. As a result, the reduced Dutch quota of 3,607 under the 1921 law was further reduced to 1,648. These limitations were not without influence upon the Americanization of those already resident in the United States.

At present there is such a cooperation between labor and the nationalistic eugenists that in spite of all the beautiful traditions, these measures have been passed with overwhelming majorities by both political parties. Even employers relinquished their opposition due to a Soviet phobia. According to Siegfried, it appears to be "*l'expression d'une volonté nationale* " [the expression of a national will].[137] Lothrop Stoddard goes so far as to assert that the Johnson Act is merely "the first step in the re-forging of America.[138] It is true that a further limitation to 150,000 Europeans per year after 1927, based upon the "national origins" of the American population, was delayed for a year, but since that time a bill has been introduced in Congress that would ban all immigration.[139] In defense of this, Justice [Horace] Gray has said that America is perfectly entitled to such a right; it is an "acceptable maxim of international law."[140]

All that remained thereafter was clandestine immigration, which should not be underestimated. Until recently, it amounted to about 400,000 annually and there are still 50,000 to 100,000 clandestine entries per year until authorities find a way to stem that flow as well.[141] The results of all these limitations are already highly evident in our own country and have turned the whole emigration question into one of the most important ones of our own time. Whither now? That is the question faced by thousands in our country.

7

New Attempts at Colonization in Minnesota, Directly from the Netherlands

Adding up the immigration figures that have been noted earlier, it appears that between 1841 and 1855 there entered 13,195 Netherlanders, most of whom became the founders of the settlements in Wisconsin, Michigan, Illinois, and Iowa, which were the settlements of lasting importance. Other statistics indicate the following entries: 1856–1860, 3,806; and 1861–1865, 2,149. Following the Civil War there was a rapid increase:

Year	Number	Year	Number	Year	Number
1866–1870	7,129	1886–1890	23,451	1906–1910	29,761
1871–1875	10,394	1891–1895	20,754	1911–1915	31,392
1876–1880	6,147	1896–1900	6,004	1916–1920	12,374
1881–1885	20,350	1901–1905	18,501		

Between 1856 and 1920, "official" emigrant figures show that 192,212 Netherlanders settled in America.

The question arises: Did the arrival of so many Netherlanders result in the formation of new colonies directly from the Netherlands rather than merely a strengthening of already-existing settlements? An investigation discloses the important fact that there were indeed a few spontaneous attempts in the Netherlands to found new colonies but that these attempts, in most cases, did not go beyond the paper stage, as far as they originated from the emigrants themselves. Most of the plans originated from self-serving land companies and a few from "philanthropic" societies. A few even resulted in the temporary founding of new "cities" but, in the end, they all failed.

The earliest of these attempts goes back to the immediate post-Civil War period and is related to the rapidly expanding rail network in the North. A "boom" developed in Minnesota when the large railroad companies, such as the Great Northern, tried to sell their land grants to the immigrants. A significant amount of Dutch capital aided in the construction of American railroads in general and of those in Minnesota in particular and resulted in several Netherlanders being employed by these railroad companies, especially those of Minnesota. It was the Netherlanders who worked in the "land departments" of the Great Northern, then known as the St. Paul and Pacific Railway, who drew the attention of Dutch emigrants to Minnesota.

We have already noted that Bonnema, a Frisian, together with a few others from his area, had purchased land in 1853 in Houston County, in the extreme southeastern part of the territory. This was thought to be the first Dutch colony in Minnesota, although it should be remembered that their original settlement was the town of Frisia in Wisconsin, east of the Mississippi River.

About 1860 "several farmers, originally from Zeeland" settled in Dodge County, also in the southeastern area.[1] Minnesota was about seven times as large as the Netherlands; it had become a state in 1858. In 1860 its population included about 18,000 Germans, 12,000 Swedes and Norwegians, and 3,000 other Europeans, among whom were a couple of hundred Hollanders, some of whom lived in and around St. Paul, the capital.[2]

To the northwest of St. Paul, located on a high bluff along the Mississippi River, was situated the "city" of St. Joseph, ten miles west of St. Cloud. St. Paul was beautifully located, spaciously built, and had very wide but as yet unpaved streets. Gevers Deynoot had visited it in the course of his American trip in 1859.[3] He called it the most scattered and most spacious town he had seen. The town had been founded in 1840 and in 1859 it already had seven thousand residents of all kinds of nationalities. According to Pelz, it had "a unique conglomerate of interesting elements that attracted and repelled one another and among whom were found the full range of colors from bronze natives to the pale Caucasians."[4] To repeat, in the sixties to the northwest of this town, which had soon become notorious among the speculative financial groups in the Netherlands, and near the "town" of St. Joseph, "near" the Mississippi and west of St. Cloud, some Frisian families had settled. They had taken with them 250 gulden each on their trip to Minnesota, and already by 1872 they owned their own farms.[5]

J. H. Kloos, an engineer with the St. Paul and Pacific Railway, became acquainted with these families living in the Sauk River valley near St. Joseph, and this circumstance must have motivated him to acquaint the Dutch financial world with the lands his company had for sale. According to him, they could be paid for in the most profitable manner with securities of his company that could be bought in Amsterdam. In addition he made special efforts to encourage a settlement by some of his countrymen. To this end he spent some winters in our country.[6]

To further these plans, he published a brochure in Amsterdam in 1867, entitled Minnesota (V. St. v. N.-A.) in zijne hulpbronnen, vruchtbaarheid en ontwikkeling geschetst voor landverhuizers en kapitalisten [Minnesota (United States of North America)—Described as to its Resources, Fertility and Prospects for Emigrants and Capitalists]. The brochure apparently was successful, for in that same year a second edition was printed in a larger number of copies. By then, a group composed largely of Dutch artisans and laborers had already arrived in the cosmopolitan St. Paul and the foundation had been laid for a Dutch colony, "which no doubt would eventually prosper just as much as the settlements of our countrymen in Michigan and Iowa." At least, that is what Kloos and all land agents thought, filled as they were with optimism.[7]

In order that the group might have some better knowledge of the land before making a permanent settlement, the St. Paul and Pacific Railroad gave it sixty-four hectares [260 acres] of rich and wooded land located northwest of St. Paul in Sherburne County, five hours away from the Big Lake railroad station. A part of this land had already been under cultivation. Assisted by their neighbors, the Netherlanders immediately began to plow the earth. Corn, potatoes, and vegetables were planted so that there would be a harvest in August or September. According to Kloos, a certain well-to-do farmer named Tenvoorde, who had lived for years "in the neighbor-hood"—actually it was several hours closer to St. Cloud—would be a big help to them.

Apparently, not much came from this effort. Lured by Kloos' account of the high wages in St. Paul—three to four dollars (fl. 7.5 to fl. 10) a day for skilled laborers—mainly city folk responded to this appeal, hoping that they could take up farming after a year or two of work.[8] The change from urban life in the densely populated Netherlands to the lonely and inhospitable "Big Woods" of Minnesota, especially in winter, proved to be too much for them; at the same time there was a lack of able leadership.

Some of them settled to the northeast of Sauk Rapids, located in Benton County, near the hamlet of Gilman, where a certain J. J. Pas, together with a "few Hollanders," had bought some railroad land. They tried to attract affluent farmers' sons from the Netherlands to settle in the area. In all fairness they warned that initial difficulties would be encountered such as poor roads and here and there lands made infertile by prairie fires. Four to five thousand gulden [$1,600 to $2,000] would be necessary, since the St. Paul and Pacific sold the land for $ — [amount omitted] per acre cash or $6 to $7 in installments with interest at 7 percent. Pas indicated that the land was suitable for sugar beet production and that a sugar refinery should be built by Dutch farmers with enough capital.[9] A tobacco factory could also be built. It seems that there was a good response to this call; some farmers' sons came from the Haarlemmermeer area; the two Knibbe brothers, with their sister, left in 1872 for America and settled in Benton County.[10]

Dr. S. R. J. Van Schevichaven wrote about Minnesota in 1872 for the benefit of emigrants and also for the benefit of the holders of railway securities. He mentioned the Netherlands colony in Benton County and described the colonists, living partly in the woods and partly on the prairie, as being "in prosperous circumstances." Of greater importance was his comment that the colonists did not stay together. "The bond that united the members of the group does not appear to have been strong enough to keep them together." Since that time almost nothing has been mentioned concerning this colony unless the description in the Minnesota *Kompas voor Landverhuizers* |*Guide for Immigrants*| of "an unusually pleasant sight—a company of Hollanders who will soon increase in number!" was meant to describe the Benton County colonists.[11] Referring to Kloos's efforts at colonization, E. J. G. Bloemendaal noted that "he was not successful."[12] Some of the "colonists"—urban residents from the beginning—had settled in St. Cloud.

In his *Aanteekeningen* |*Notes*| written subsequent to his visit to St. Paul and its environs, |W. F.| Gevers Deynoot wrote: "The profits that can still be realized from the purchase of land in this Far West are unbelievable."[13] This comment by a member of parliament, of all people, coupled with the advice of Kloos and Van Schevichaven, must have attracted the attention of Dutch capitalists not only to the railroads but also to the railroad lands in Minnesota. The latter commented that a Dutch firm bought large tracts of land near Albion (a hamlet no longer on the map under this name) in Wright County located south of St. Cloud and west of Minneapolis, with the seeming intent of founding a colony.[14] I do not know whether this ever materialized. Some Netherlanders did settle in Wright County. But, as was previously noted, such places as Silver Creek and Maple Lake were settled first by Dutch Americans, although it is possible that at that time a Netherlander or two had already settled here, and that Albion might even be identified with present-day Maple Lake.

Kloos had already called attention to the importance of the Red River Valley, which he described as "a thick layer of top soil resting on heavy clay."[15] Because of a lack of timber, colonization would be possible there only after railroad tracks had been built. Van Schevichaven reported that a few Hollanders had purchased 800 hectares |324 acres| of land in this valley in Becker County, near the railroad to Fargo on the Northern Pacific.[16] But as far as we know, a Dutch settlement did not materialize here; at least, there is no mention of one even by Bloemendaal who, as we are aware, later accompanied an exploration party to the Red River Valley.[17] The only Hollander he encountered there was a tenant farmer who lived much further to the south, near Morris, in Stevens County. The latter said that during his three years' stay he "had never seen a Hollander."

Many attempts were made to steer Netherlanders to Minnesota. Kloos, Pas, and Van Schevichaven—particularly the latter—sang its praise. He said that he had actually come to love the state, "a land which need not take a back seat to any other with respect to its healthiness and fertility, . . . where the rights of all are respected, where education is at a high level, . . . where the climate contributes to the energy and welfare of the people, where agriculture, one of the main sources of the prosperity of any nation, is carried on with good results and profit, . . . where property steadily appreciates in value, and where everyone has a voice in determining the governmental policy under which he lives. . . . "

As though this were not enough, there was also a pamphlet written by the banker G. Hewitt and published by the State of Minnesota.[18] There was even a German-language "Guide for Emigrants to Algiers, the Cape Colony, Australia, South and Central America, the United States of North America and Canada," which had been translated into Dutch. This translation was probably due to the fact that the compass needle pointed primarily in one direction—to Minnesota, where things went "remarkably well" for immigrants and where many became rich in six to eight years. Some day "the power of this continent will be concentrated here." It pointed in particular to the land holdings of the St. Paul and Pacific Railway, centering around the twin cities of St. Paul and Minneapolis, where "the seat of government for this great continent" would be established, sooner or later![19]

A monthly journal, *De Landverhuizer—ter bevordering der Emigratie naar den Noord-Amerikaanschen Staat Minnesota* [*The Emigrant—For the Promotion of Emigration to the North American State of Minnesota*] was widely distributed in 1872. Societies for promoting this emigration were organized, appeals were made for support by Dutch communities, provinces, and even the central government itself.[20] These activities took place under the influence of interested railroad companies that were represented in the Netherlands by their agents and sub-agents. For example, the chief agent of the Northern Pacific was G. P. Ittman, Jr., at Rotterdam.[21] Judging from the number of societies and publications, Amsterdam was particularly interested in sponsoring emigration to Minnesota. Especially the firm of Kerkhoven and Co. "invested" a good deal of Dutch capital in the American railroads. As a memento of this, "a token of tribute," the hamlet of Kerkhoven was founded in Chippewa County, although it was to leave a bitter aftertaste!

The attraction of Minnesota for the Netherlanders declined in the seventies, not least because of the Panic of 1873 and because of the way in which the Dutch venture capital had been squandered and was lost to the Netherland speculators. But during the eighties a growing emigration from the Netherlands revived interest in the "Bread Basket State." In the seventies the Red River Valley had already been described as "the future granary of the United States;" now these lands were advertised to the Dutch public "as veritable gold mines."[22] A former Dutch officer, J. Knuppe, now a farmer in Crookston in the Red River Valley, advocated settlement there. People could deal with him not only in his capacity as a land agent but also as an agent for a few steamship companies. For some time Knuppe had been in the employ of the St. Paul and Pacific, charged with the administration of its land sales. In this way he had become acquainted with the area at an earlier date and he had seen its value rise. In 1877 there were no settlers living around Crookston, but within a few years the land was worth from twenty to fifty dollars an acre! Apparently Knuppe had learned from experience, because he had little desire to create a purely Dutch colony. According to him, at most two or three families should settle together and mingle immediately with the Americans or other neighbors, in order to learn from one another.[23] Because of their faith, Dutch Roman Catholics could probably settle in the exclusively Roman Catholic but otherwise very multinational settlements founded in Smith County by the bishop of St. Paul. To these settlements also belonged the "town" of Kerkhoven. Those wanting to go here could also apply to Knuppe.

A few years later, the company of Prins, Zwanenburg, and Koch tried to establish a colony on land they had purchased in Kandiyohi County. In the Netherlands there was a certain skepticism regarding this plan, in part due to the warnings by the poet-author |Tjibbe Geerts| Van der Meulen. As a result, Prinsburg was not populated primarily by Dutch emigrants but by Holland Americans who had previously lived in other parts of the United States. Direct colonization from the Netherlands failed here also.

Later, F. G. Geerling tried to influence Netherlanders in Amsterdam to settle in the Red River Valley of Minnesota and in the southwest, especially in Murray, Swift, Stevens, Wilkin, Clay, Norman, and Polk counties, where he offered 300,000 acres of land for sale.[24] It was a tempting offer; the soil there made it possible "to lead a carefree life and to become rich after a shorter or longer time." A single harvest could repay "the entire cost of the land and its development"! No more beautiful land was to be found in the world. . . . It was a land of wheat and corn where the eye and the soul never tired of viewing the gently sloping land, the lovely and fruitful valleys that make this desirable part of the earth one of the most fertile areas. . . . There never was a more beautiful land![25]

It is doubtful that many Netherlanders settled in this paradise; Geerling preferred to sell his land sight unseen for hard cash, in which case he deducted 75 cents to $1 per acre from the sale price![26] "If people object to buying the land sight unseen they can make a conditional contract with me and close it with one of my agents in Minnesota after having seen the soil." Were many "contracts" closed? There are so many secrets in the real estate business! There is little evidence of any noticeable emigration to this area and even less of colonization.

On the whole, efforts to establish Dutch colonies in Minnesota miscarried, largely because of their speculative nature. As early as 1874, N. J. Den Tex had warned in an article in *De Gids* against "the embellished accounts" about America and the attempts that were made to bring inflated statistics "with a certain calculation under the eyes of the public." At the same time he pointed out that a "Society for Promoting the Emigration of Indigent People to the North American State of Minnesota," organized on March 13, 1873, by "philanthropists" and even endorsed by a K. B. |*Koninklijk Besluit*, Royal Edict| on October 30, 1873, apparently was influenced by American railroad firms because, by coincidence, these "philanthropists" happened to be also "freight brokers or agents of the Northern Pacific Railway Company"![27] He publicly warned against the agents of these companies in the Netherlands, whose funds were gathered largely in the Netherlands themselves—and for the St. Paul and Pacific even exclusively in the Netherlands. Tsjibbe Gearts termed these Minnesota proposals "a fraud" and during the eighties he continually reminded the people of it: "Trusting individuals went there, wasted thousands, suffered from hunger and cold in a State where there is winter weather for about nine months, and so they all but succumbed from want."[28]

These tragic results can not be attributed solely to the speculators. There seem to have been too many difficulties for the Netherlanders to overcome on Minnesota's undeveloped soils. The demands, as far as courage, will power, and stamina were concerned, were extremely high. In his book dealing with the Ost Frisians, Schnücker gives striking examples of this. The preponderant numbers of Norwegians and Swedes who have settled in Minnesota and who achieved great political power—six of the last nine governors were Scandinavians!—caused the well-known author Sinclair Lewis to refer to his native state as "the Norse State."[29] These conditions prove that this state, sometimes referred to as an American Siberia, is really quite suitable only for individuals coming from countries with a more rigorous climate and a less cultivated soil than the Netherlands.

We have already pointed out that numerous Dutch Americans settled there and succeeded with their settlements. However, they too went to Minnesota only after the cheap and fertile lands situated further south and west were gone and suitable homestead grants were no longer available. Most of all, these people were united by the strongest bond possible—their faith.

8

Colonization Attempts in California

A. Netherlanders to the Gold State

At the time of the American boom, when colonizing the American "land of a thousand lakes" was on many lips, settlers also considered trekking to a state with a totally different climate and a totally different soil, both entirely unlike those of the Netherlands, namely California. Even before going to Minnesota, Netherlanders had established themselves here, attracted by gold. However, it was much later, twenty years later, before the first serious attempt was made at colonization. It came so much later precisely because the soil and the climate were so entirely different.

The news that gold had been found in California in the valley of the Sacramento River spread "with the speed of a flaming cross" throughout the world. The gold seekers streamed in from far and wide "with unbridled passion." They also came from the Netherlands, lured by the most fabulous reports. One only had to stir in the soil with a spade and pickax to find gold, said C. L. Plasberg in his description of California in 1849.[1] "Gold is found there in tremendous quantities," and "more than 100,000 people can dig here for a century without fear of running out of work"! Someone else, an anonymous writer, declared that one did not even need any capital, nothing "but a spade to dig and a metal pan to wash the gravel sand."[2] In the second volume of *Onze Tijd* |*Our Times*| of 1849, it was noted that in the Netherlands also the dailies "are filled with advertisements of those who ask for participants in their plans to emigrate there or who try to find a ship to take them to California."

Is it any wonder that even in the Achterhoek, the outlying part of Gelderland, these reports stirred simple people to move to this El Dorado? The story is still told of a farmer who walked to Amsterdam and sailed via England to New York thinking that he had already reached his goal! The poor man had still to travel 5,000 kilometers |3,000 miles|! First he went by rail to the Mississippi River; after that his journey took him over the prairie;

629

then through the Rocky Mountains and the deserts. Unlike the thousands of gold seekers of all kinds of nationalities who perished from exhaustion on that dreadful overland journey, that farmer managed to reach the land of gold. But after a few years he returned to his native country, bitterly disappointed and poorer than before, with only a pair of golden earrings as a remembrance. "The gold digger," as he was called in mockery ever since, spent the rest of his life on a small sharecropper farm.[3]

There were more than ninety thousand gold seekers already in 1849—therefore called forty-niners—who had come from all parts of the world. They were a wild bunch of adventurers who cared not the least about the land rights of the "German" owner, J. A. Sutter, on whose land the gold had been found. He himself fell into poverty.[4]

San Francisco originated as Yerba Buena in 1835 and was located near the San Francisco de Asis mission of 1776, which was secularized in 1835, and now is better known as the "Mission Dolores" after a small neighboring brook.[5] For years it was a poor settlement of mostly "Yankee Californians"; in 1848 it had no more than two hundred dwellings. But in the gold year of 1849 its population suddenly jumped to fifteen thousand inhabitants.[6]

An enormous demand for food, building material, etc., developed. Netherlanders who had been stirred up by Het Handelsblad and Onze Tijd also tried to meet this demand and profit by it. A great many ships were rigged out in the harbors of Holland to carry the most unheard of variety of articles via the Strait of Magellan to California, where initially everything was bought up regardless of price.[7] In the harbor of San Francisco nine Dutch vessels arrived in 1850, twenty in 1853, and nineteen in 1854. From 1850 to 1855 the total of ship arrivals reached as much as ninety! Butter, white lead, cigars, linseed oil, coffee, salt and bricks, all sorts of things, were shipped in the beginning; even a few big shipments of wooden shoes at which the adventurers would gape with curiosity and wonderment, and which were finally sold as fire wood![8] Originally diggers earned at least $10 to $15 per day, and a ferryman who took people across the San Joaquin River for $2 per person earned from $500 to $1,000 in a single day![9] But when the earnings in California slowly became less, it turned out that supplies could be brought cheaper from New York, and as a consequence these "tramp ships" became less frequent and finally disappeared entirely. People had kept on blindly chartering ships and great financial losses were the end result. For instance, a cargo of Java coffee turned out to be smothered and musty when it was unloaded! Consequently no more ships under the Dutch flag arrived at San Francisco in 1861 and 1862.[10] Later on, ships would occasionally dock—six ships appeared in 1864 and five in 1872—but in 1888 our consul reported, among other things, that in that year the Dutch flag was entirely absent in the San Francisco harbor. "Indeed, this was most often the case"; in fact the shipping traffic from the Netherlands to California had stopped entirely.[11]

It is well to recognize here the importance of this California shipping, even though the official sources are silent, because emigration must have been fostered by it in no small degree. In 1849 the pay of sailors on the California run was raised to *fl.* 200 [$80] per month in order to prevent them from deserting the ship![12] Yet there were those, notwithstanding their obligations, who towards evening jumped overboard and swam ashore, if indeed they had not already deserted or had possibly been paid off![13] And how many paying passengers would have been on board those ships? Plasberg tells of many shipowners in the United States and also in the Netherlands who chartered their ships for transporting victuals *and emigrants.* Although the trip around Cape Horn took five months, yet it was the best way. Many preferred this route rather than to go around the Cape of Good Hope, or to take the trip via New York and through the isthmus of Panama, not to mention the dreadful "land journey" through prairies, mountain terrain, and deserts of the American continent![14]

So it is no surprise that in 1864, in what to my knowledge is the first report from our first consul James De Fremery and our first vice-consul W. C. B. De Fremery at San Francisco, mention is made that "very many Netherlanders" are found among the population of California and neighboring territories. This was five years before the opening of the first transcontinental, of the first Pacific railway. Most likely there were many forty-niners among them. Also the report points out that many Netherlanders already lived in the United States before their arrival in California. Therefore, quite a number of these immigrants must have trekked by land to the Far West. Among them there must have been people from the "colonies" of New York, Albany, Chicago, St. Louis, etc. and additionally from the settlements in Michigan. We already know some people who came from Pella, Iowa.

According to the De Fremery report, some Netherlanders were in California because of interest in "trade and factories." However, most of them were artisans, mineworkers, or truck gardeners.[15] A few of them had already prospered so much that they could send money to their poor relatives via the Dutch consulate, while "many Dutch families" invested in one of the foremost savings banks, the San Francisco Savings Union, of which James De Fremery was the founder and president, while the rest of the board consisted of Americans.[16] They prospered from charging the prevailing high interest rates—10 to 12 percent and in the beginning even 2 percent per month—which at that time were asked and paid. That is indeed the case in every new country and is a characteristic colonial feature.

Through the intermediary of an employment agency, the California Labor Exchange, founded in 1868 and for which a Dutchman worked first as assistant and then as secretary, "a number of Dutchmen" were able to obtain jobs. In 1874 our fellow Netherlanders at San Francisco even established a "Dutch Mutual Aid Society" to promote the spirit of brotherhood among them, especially in case of sickness and adversity. In that same year this first Dutch society in the Far West was already "active in giving welfare benefits that met with great approval."[17]

Despite the "depression" that seemingly also prevailed here in 1873, the Netherlanders felt at home in San Francisco. The delightful and, according to Russell Smith, the "most amazing" climate of the city and its immediate vicinity must have contributed in no small degree to this feeling. Due to the contrast between the cold ocean water on the west side and the hot valley on the east side of the city, a fresh sea breeze blows during the summer. Thus the average July temperature stays as low as 59 degrees Fahrenheit and turns the city into a real "holiday resort."[18] This "summer climate," which some interested parties have sometimes unjustly ascribed to all of California, was a strong drawing card that continually kept the attention of the emigrants riveted on this Pacific Ocean state.

However, of more importance were particular circumstances, namely California's development as a farm and truck-garden state. Under Spanish and Mexican rule, California was every bit a land of cattle raising and ranchos. Hides were the largest export of this very thinly populated land where aridity as well as the scanty population made farming of minor importance. Hardly had California become "American" when gold was discovered there.

Yet, gold would not become the greatest source of riches. Already in 1849, an anonymous writer of the preface in the equally anonymous *Gids naar California* [*Guide to California*] made the observation with reference to the latest news that the region was "fortunately marked by a lack of crime," and that once the gold fever would be over, "then perhaps the greatest treasure will be found where it is least expected."[19] This is the way it happened: many a forty-niner who got tired of looking for gold applied himself to farming, especially when he had access to river water. Many a prospector ended up possessing sometimes several thousand acres of land, either obtained from the government or bought from ranch owners. They became wheat growers or bonanza farmers, shipping their wheat around Cape Horn to England by sailing vessels. The opening of the first Pacific Railway, however, offered new possibilities and in 1882 the wheat growing business reached its peak.

B. The First Colonization Plans

In the Netherlands, completion of the first Pacific Railway, which was truly a world event, strongly drew attention once more to California. In a series of articles in *De Gids* in May, June and July, 1871, no less a person than Professor R. Dozy pointed out this wonderful country of the future.[20] This was "more by chance than by choice," since he could consult "new and detailed reports." And behold, already one month later a reaction followed on Dozy's eulogy—"California had the certainty of becoming the most prosperous state of the Union"—and plans were considered for a Dutch agricultural colony in this land of high expectations!

It is a rather peculiar phenomenon that these California plans involved above all the more-educated Dutch colonist candidates and that interested parties addressed themselves in particular to this class of people. The result was that the colonization plans of this period, as well as twenty years later, were marked by a more or less aristocratic and intellectual character. This was already evidenced by the first announcements in the distinguished *Haarlemmer Courant* and in the no less fashionable *Nieuwe Rotterdamsche Courant*: "I think that emigration must benefit us in many ways besides and beyond our mere purses and pockets"—[Charles Flinders Jr.] Hursthouse. "To respectable families in the possession of some capital who might wish to emigrate and who possess sufficient culture in order to regulate in a rational manner their conduct and the moral leadership of their subordinates, is hereby offered the opportunity to enter into negotiations with similarly inclined families who wish to emigrate to a section of the United States of North America which is richly endowed with beautiful scenery and has a very healthful climate and where, because of its location, population, etc., much is coming together in order to insure the speedy prosperity of a settlement through farming, cattle raising, commerce, or any other branch of industry.... Further information will be given to those who meet the above specified requirements and who will identify themselves in a satisfactory manner as to their social position."[21] It is obvious that the use of an English quotation [by Hursthouse] and the choice of newspapers in which to run the advertisement were meant to catch the eye of an intellectual audience. In short, this was meant for the "select"!

Therefore, on October 14, 1871, the first meeting of candidates was held at Utrecht in the Bellevue Hotel and a committee to design a colonization plan was formed, consisting of Messrs. Dr. H. Hartogh Heys van Zouteveen, first infantry lieutenant J. A. Obreen, and B. Van der Feen. However, Van der Feen withdrew. In succession two plans were drawn up. In the second one, however, they dropped the initial idea that the emigrants and the partners of the association who would remain in Europe would jointly own property; this initial idea was considered "inadvisable." In addition to an agricultural and cattle-raising colony, the Dutch-American Agricultural and Emigration Company would be established at the same time. It had occurred to the committee that the purpose should be "bigger," because due to overpopulation there was a need for large scale emigration. According to Heys van Zouteveen this large scale emigration was "the only rational solution" of "the so-called social question."

For us the following draft articles are of importance:

1. Thirty or more families will establish an agricultural colony in the State of California.
2. The Dutch-American Agricultural and Emigration Company is founded in which emigrants of means and Dutch capitalists will participate. The company buys an extensive tract of favorably situated land in California, preferably in the Sacramento basin or the

central coast districts and if possible in the immediate vicinity of a
railway.

3. The Agricultural and Emigration Company sells enough land at cost
(buying price plus reimbursement of expenses) to every family mentioned in Article I, so each can develop a big farm after a few years.
Thus will be formed the first nucleus of a large scale Dutch agricultural colony on the company's soil.

The articles of the association would have to be further developed and
"later formulate the means that would open the possibility of indigent
emigrants to travel inexpensively to California, and if need be, to advance
their fare against sufficient security." Furthermore, an additional statement
is important: in case the total subscription should be less than fl. 500,000
[$200,000] the company would not be established.[22] According to this first
plan, it was the intention to invest part of the money available for dividends
in the San Francisco Savings Union.[23] Thus we may assume that at that time
they consulted our consul in San Francisco, J. De Fremery, who was president of this bank.

The designers were fully confident. Dr. Hartogh Heys van Zouteveen especially had high expectations of the colonization, considering his generally
very business like brochure: "If we succeed, then it is my conviction that we
have achieved a great and good thing, indeed, that we have perhaps laid
the first foundation for a new and greater Netherlands prospering there on
the coast of the Pacific Ocean. And if a foreign superior power should seize
the European fatherland, former Netherlanders will be offered in California
a safe haven and freedom."[24] It is difficult to say to what degree this contention reflected the conviction, which was widespread among the emigrants,
that the doom of the Old Country was at hand—the French-German war
had just come to an end. It is also difficult to say to what extent interested
parties played on those feelings. Yet it is feared that the designer of the
Agricultural and Emigration Company already shows his hand as a
businessman, in view of the manner in which Professor Dozy's articles were
exploited. Indeed, the impression was even given that Professor Dozy had
written down words that were not his own, but those of Hartogh Heys van
Zouteveen. "California needs only one thing to become one of the richest
countries in the world, perhaps the richest of all and that one thing is—
people," said Dozy. To this, Hartogh Heys van Zouteveen skillfully added,
but without quotation marks: "The Netherlanders who settle in California
will help to provide that one necessity. They have the certainty that their
descendants are headed for a glorious future and that they will be citizens
of a powerful world empire when perhaps the old Fatherland will long
before have gone down in one of the many big wars of which the future of
Europe is pregnant, and will have been obliged to sacrifice its freedom and
independence . . . ."[25]

Because Dr. Hartogh Heys van Zouteveen brought similar considerations into play, it is a rather fortunate phenomenon that the public's interest in his company was not as big as the gentlemen had hoped for: not everyone wanted to flee from the threatened fatherland for these reasons! Obreen confirms this public attitude when he speaks of the futile attempts "of a few people" to launch a company for the purpose of emigration that would also give the shareholders a good profit, while a philanthropical society to promote emigration had had no chance of success either. In the Netherlands people have neither "ear nor eye, heart nor mind for such things," grumbled Obreen and he added that despite all that, the Dutch-American Agricultural and Emigration Company had been founded, though still informally. When the second meeting was held at Utrecht on February 10, 1872, not one-fifth of the required sum had yet been raised; not even *fl.* 100,000 [$40,000]! Nevertheless, the representatives intended to go to California and buy land. It seems that things did go no further than these good intentions, although in the meantime "some capable men" had joined the "temporary Company." In general, however, people remained too skeptical about the enterprise and warned against making the plans for the agricultural venture too ambitious because it was a "somewhat risky business." In *Onze Tijd*, a certain H. B. Van Daalen urged great caution and, although full of praise for the brochure of his "esteemed friend Dr. Hartogh Heys van Zouteveen," he warned that the latter's estimate of the expected wheat harvest in the intended colony was too rosy, "too high in view of the facts," and that the barley yield was even "much too high," at least as a basis for calculation.[26] Since then no more has been heard of the plans. Neither do the consuls' reports from San Francisco make any mention of the project, even though, no doubt, De Fremery had been informed about the situation. The crisis of 1873 must have put an end to these plans, just as well as to the intentions with respect to Minnesota.[27]

C. Vorden

A Netherlander in California undertook an altogether different colonization attempt, which has to be viewed as a big success in the technical and economical sense, although the Netherlanders were not able to make a nationality foothold. I refer to the land reclamation project of P. J. Van Löben Sels in the Sacramento Valley. Dr. Hartogh Heys van Zouteveen in his *Californische Hulpbronnen* [California Resources] had repeatedly pointed out the swamps and the lands subject to flooding along the Sacramento and San Joaquin rivers and their tributaries.[28] At the time around 1870, these lands were sold for only one dollar per acre, of which only 20 percent had to be paid within fifty days while the rest was carried at the legal 10 percent interest rate; moreover, the whole amount of the purchase would be used in damming up the land for the benefit of the buyer. Once these tracts of alluvial land had been "diked in," especially those in the delta region, they ranked among the best in the state and were excellently suited for farming, truck gardening, and cattle raising. Some land reclaiming of the fifties had already indicated this. Since Californians were not familiar with the diking up of low-lying land, "inpoldering" progressed slowly and many mistakes were made. For example, the dikes were built too close along the river, which resulted in repeated dike breaks and earthslides during high water times. In 1912 when Professor J. F. Niermeyer visited the Sacramento delta, which reminded him so very much of the Rhine delta that he called it the California Netherlands, he noticed in several places these wrongly built dikes and their fatal consequences. Dikes were undermined by the river stream at the hollow banks and also by the ripple effect caused by steamboats.[29] Therefore, as he observed, dikes were under constant repair.

One of the first who avoided these mistakes was Van Löben Sels, a Netherlander who had been in America since 1877. As he recalled, "In November 1881, I was assigned to drain 8,800 acres covered with fourteen feet of water. Under my supervision a big dike and a big steam-driven pumping station were built."[30] This is what this pioneer, who had returned to Europe in his later years, was so kind to write me. The soil turned out to be very fertile and the climate was ideal for the growing of farm products. "This led me to buy approximately 4,000 acres, later increased to 5,100 acres," so Van Löben Sels wrote very simply, concealing the real pioneer work he had done with the drainage and exploitation of the swamp. Neither did he mention the risk he took in view of the fact that until 1880 flooding occurred nearly every year. After 1880 other lands were still repeatedly flooded, especially those where farmers had neglected to follow "his excellent example of dike building and his manner of land reclamation." So tells J. F. Niermeyer after his visit to these so-called Netherlands.[31]

The 1887 report of the Netherlands' consul at San Francisco drew attention to this work. P. J. Van Löben Sels had been chosen as chairman of a polder committee and had successfully diked in the Pierson Reclamation District and taken care of the building of "two beautiful steam-driven pumping stations."[32] Van Löben Sels himself took charge of his polder, which was named "Vorden", after his provincial birthplace in Gelderland. He applied himself to truck farming, particularly growing white beans and asparagus, and also to general farming. Among other things he concentrated on beet culture, which since about 1870 appeared in California when a couple of large sugarbeet factories were built near San Francisco. He also cultivated alfalfa, which at that time was called chiliclover; it was an excellent cattle fodder and did well on alluvial soil, giving three to four cuttings per year.

In 1902 Dr. H. P. N. Muller visited the Vorden polder, which is a couple of hours' traveling time from the city of Sacramento and lies on the river of the same name. Dr. Muller wrote: "Dutch landscape surrounds us. It is low, even altogether level, with much water and many small dikes. A tiny post office carries the name of the settlement. Then we find ourselves on the ranch, on the farm of the former Netherlands' consul.... This year the harvest of *spergels* alone, the word used by our |Dutch| forefathers for asparagus, amounted to $40,000 or equal to a ton of gold. Japanese workers are busy cutting this vegetable at a feverish pace, because hardly have they cut the stems when on the same row other stems peep out of the ground."[33] A young Dutchman, M. Jongeneel, hailing from the agricultural school of Wageningen, was charged with the business, which he managed in a scientific manner. Not all of the polder was used for this purpose. Large pieces of land were subleased to Holland and Frisian farmers.

By this leasing, a significant Dutch settlement could have come into being, although this had not been the specific purpose of the venture, so Van Löben Sels specifically wrote to me. This was fortunate because the settling of our fellow countrymen has, generally speaking, not been successful, although the reclaiming had contributed to Dutchmen settling there. Only a few were successful, such as, for example, the |?| Pijlman brothers who as poor little Frisian farmers settled near Vorden at Merrit Island in about 1890. Fifteen years later they were the owners of a ranch worth about $30,000. There was also W. De Back who became the head of an important carpentry firm at Vorden.[34] Wherever colonization was attempted "our fellow countrymen proved themselves to be too stubborn and too unsuited to adapt to foreign circumstances and ways of operating," Van Löben Sels stated to me bluntly, which was a significant statement, because it reflected thirty years of experience![35]

Since non-Dutchmen rented parts of the land, the population of the polder developed an even more strongly mixed character than was already the case through the use of laborers from the most diverse countries, especially Chinese and Japanese. "Silently, the workers of the most varied of nationalities sit down for the hearty meal by which a Chinese cook unites us all," writes Muller.[36]

Vorden is now supplied with electric power and remains in possession of Van Löben Sels. Jongeneel was not only entrusted with responsibility as superintendent of Van Löben Sel's actual agricultural business, he was also the manager of the whole polder, which was considered one of the best managed in the state of California. The situation in 1923 looked "very favorable" in spite of the stress on the operation due to the low prices of farm products. Fully one thousand acres of sugar beets were grown that year by a company that ran a sugar factory.[37] Asparagus and sugar beets still played an important role, as they had during the first years.

It seems that the example of Van Löben Sels did tempt others of our countrymen. At least, many Netherlanders in California in 1905 tried to get their hands on the riverbank lands, the so-called reclaimed lands. Land speculators, indeed, urged them to do so and sought to give priority to our countrymen, assuming that they were acquainted with the building of dikes for these riverbank lands. For only after such dikes had been built did cattle raising become possible as a first step toward dairy farming.[38] Any successful ventures in these attempts at individual colonization have not come to my attention. Keeping in mind Van Löben Sel's previous statement, this lack of success will surprise no one.

D. The "Great Valley"

In the meantime, a totally different kind of cultivation, that of tropical and subtropical fruit and grapes had conquered California, and this also drew dozens of Netherlanders. The Spanish monks had settled "Alta California" in the second half of the eighteenth century by establishing missions ["*zendelingschappen*," as the Dutch call them], that were defended by presidios, i.e., small military detachments. They had introduced a great variety of tropical and subtropical fruit, attracted as they were by the mild climate that reminded them of their home country. Thus within a few years time the mission buildings were surrounded by orchards that were already in "flourishing condition" before 1786, while in that same year people in all of the southern posts were actively engaged in wine cultivation, according to G. Wharton James.[39] After the secularization in 1835 and the transfer to the United States, these wine and fruit cultures, however limited—since they were for domestic use only—were kept up and drew the attention of many adventurers, including German forty-niners. Some of the forty-niners were originally from the Rheingau, the German wine growing region par excellence. It was those Germans, so A. B. Faust tells us, who already in the sixties had taken an important share—"*ein starker* Anteil"—in the spreading of the wine culture.[40] And it was especially the German undertakings, in particular their colony of Anaheim founded in 1857 near Los Angeles, that aroused general interest, also among the Netherlanders.[41] Only after California had been connected to the American rail network could sales of tropical and subtropical fruit and wines begin. Thus it was not until the seventies that a strong expansion of these cultures took place, opening up new prospects for many job seekers.

The consul's reports of 1885 made mention of "a number" of Netherlanders living in California who had applied themselves to the growing of beans, "some already for several years." As we already know, Van Löben Sels likewise grew beans. The 1888 report emphasized the importance of the Golden State for the growing of "fruit and tubers" whose cultivation, preservation, and trading are such a "truly Dutch industry that this cultivation seems to be very attractive for Netherlanders who take up residence in California." For years, according to the report of 1889, the cultivation of fruit was practiced by the Netherlanders in California.

It is this growing interest in the cultivation of tropical and subtropical fruit that called into being a colonization attempt which, because of the "standing" of the colonists and the great fraud that victimized them, belongs to the most notorious scandals in the history of Dutch emigration.

The now famous Great Valley of California lying in the center of the state, with the basin of the Sacramento River, flowing from the north, and the one of the San Joaquin River, flowing from the south, has now developed into the greatest export region of fruit and produce in the world, thanks also to the bitter experiences by many Dutch pioneers. They were *Kulturdünger!* [cultural fertilizer].

The Great Valley, just like the low-lying plain of the Upper Rhine, had originated during the beginning of the Tertiary Period as a *"Grabental"* [trench valley]. However, unlike the Rhine "Valley" this was not the result of the sinking of bottomland but, according to F. L. Ransome, the result of the constant rising of the surrounding landscape forming the coastal mountains, so that these ranges as well as the much older Sierra Nevada, constantly became higher.[42] This valley, then is not a real collapsed valley, no *"Grabenversenkung"* [sunken trench] but belongs, according to the geographer [W. H.] Obrutschew, to the type of valley he distinguishes from the former and which he calls *"Disjunktivtäler"* [disjunctive valleys].[43]

The many tributaries flowing especially from the Sierra Nevada to the Sacramento and San Joaquin rivers have for centuries been carrying masses of debris from the mountains and have deposited it at the base of the foothills. This process formed the alluvial plains, the so-called fans, through which the tributaries, especially in the southern arid region, flow with difficulty to the main rivers. These circumstances caused the formation of inner deltas, the low confluent alluvial fans.[44] They are the so-called valley flats and flood plains that have become very important for agriculture and truck gardening. They were obviously built up from finer material, while the more sandy and coarse or even rubble-like alluvial "rock" (rough, bouldery material) was deposited closer to the foothills, lending itself more to the cultivation of tropical and subtropical fruit, and in particular olives, especially where the ground is very porous.

Just like the low-lying plain of the Upper Rhine, California is also protected by mountains from the cold winds from the north and the east. Thus it has an unusually mild climate, despite its northern latitude. It has winter temperatures in which oranges and olives grow even in the northernmost region of the Sacramento Valley, located at the same latitude as New York. In wintertime, the warming influence of the Pacific Ocean is also a contributing factor. However, the capriciousness of the American climate makes its influence felt here also. The Dutch colonists who were not in the least prepared for frost, even those who settled in the southernmost part of the Great Valley, that is, the San Joaquin Valley, to their amazement saw frost patterns on their window panes when waking up in the morning. More than once there was freezing weather of minus 1 to 4 degrees centigrade! [about 30 to 25 degrees Fahrenheit][45]

In summertime, however, it is unusually hot in the Great Valley. According to Hilgard, the heat is "very intense," often above 100 degrees Fahrenheit. In Fresno, the surroundings of which carry very unpleasant memories for the Netherlanders due to those high temperatures, the *average* July temperature reaches 100 Fahrenheit at its warmest part of the day. Fortunately the nights are cool, thanks to the dry climate, and average a minimum of 64 degrees Fahrenheit. In the valley, going from south to north, the precipitation measures from 12.5 to 62.5 centimeters [5 to 25 inches], of which 50 centimeters [20 inches] already fall during the period from December to May.[46] It is this meager precipitation that accounts for the lack of trees in a great portion of the valley, in addition to its late use for agriculture. First there was cattle raising, and after that came wheat and barley growing, since these crops can grow with a small amount of rain. It is the lack of precipitation in the southern parts that caused the San Joaquin Valley to come into consideration for more intensive colonization only after settlement of the Sacramento Valley and only after people had succeeded, or rather were trying to succeed by means of irrigation works in remedying the shortage of water. Irrigation opened up many "opportunities" for tropical and subtropical fruit cultivation, since the climate is excellent for it.

In the seventies, when great parts of the Sacramento lands had already been sold to individuals, the San Joaquin lands were also offered for sale. Along the main river, however, the land tracts were too swampy and therefore they first had to be diked in. Between the branch rivers the land as a rule was too dry. The properties along the Merced and Fresno rivers, branch rivers of the San Joaquin, which territory later would bring so many Netherlanders to poverty, were at that time already depicted as being "a most rich soil, consisting of sandy, alluvial loam, fertilized for centuries by the heaping up of decaying plant material and the accumulation of minerals, washed down from the hills and mountain sides." In spite of their "various excellent qualities that seemingly could not be surpassed anywhere in the world," these lands initially found no takers among the colonists and only a handful of buyers among the speculators.[47]

Only with the opening of the Southern Pacific Railway did interest increase in the San Joaquin Valley. Then organizations were formed that especially tried by means of sprinkling systems to turn "the arid wasteland" into a valuable agricultural and truck gardening territory. In Fresno County, a "sand desert," people had already started with irrigation in 1874 and fifteen years later one could find a "paradise" there.[48] Fresno County was described as a sand desert in the various descriptive pamphlets, because interested parties always highlighted one particular aspect, the one best suited to their own advantage; in this case irrigation was stressed.

After the completion of the railway, others followed the example. Many "Land & Water Companies" were formed which, through the construction of irrigation canals and other facilities, attempted to improve and sell these lands that they had acquired at very low price. Very active land dealings and speculations sprang up and agents attempted to find their victims, especially among the Dutch who had the reputation of being rich. These agents turned their attention to the people of the Netherlands who had always shown a willingness to invest their hard cash in America. We already know of the Dutch capital with which American railroads were built!

Dutch "middlemen" tendered their services for these land dealings. By preference, a choice was made from those who had already lived a few years in America and had had some "experience." With their cooperation and often upon their initiative—they were no philanthropists either!—separate companies were organized that exclusively handled the American land sales in the Netherlands. Around 1890, California in general and the San Joaquin Valley in particular experienced a boom. At about the same time our country found itself in a general depression due to the prevailing agricultural crisis and therefore Dutchmen had not much to look forward to. This situation gave the land speculators an excellent field of activity. No less than four large companies were formed at that time to canvas their Dutch "territory." The names of these companies were as follows: the Holland California Land Company, founded in 1899 and located in San Francisco; the Fresno Land Company, a Dutch company approved by Royal Decree on September 21, 1890, founded at Amsterdam but located in Rotterdam; the South Riverside Land and Water Company, located in San Bernardino County, with an office in Rotterdam; and the First Netherland Fruit and Land Culture Association of Humboldt County.[49]

E. The Merced Drama

Of these four companies the Holland California Land Company deserves most of our attention, not only because of the daring manner in which it operated and perhaps made the most victims, but because it made an honest effort to establish a Dutch settlement. It even founded a "city" named Rotterdam, while a second city, Amsterdam, was projected. From 1883 to 1888, Messrs. Ch. Crocker, Sr. and C. H. Huffman ordered a canal dug for the irrigation of their extensive possessions in Merced County in the San Joaquin Valley. It was dug through the famed Yosemite Valley, creating the no less famed Yosemite Lake. After that the Crocker-Huffman Land and Water Company provided the necessary irrigation water without which it could not have sold the land. One of the land tracts was located near the lake and had originally been intended for a four thousand-acre "pleasure park." It was, of course, "the very best part of their entire possession." Through the Holland California Land Company this tract was offered for sale to prospects in the Netherlands.[50] Messrs. W. A. Nijgh, who had already resided for sixteen years in San Francisco, and J. H. De Veer, "who had traveled through America for the past three years," acted as the "representative directors" of the company in the Netherlands. They left for the Netherlands in 1889, the year the company was founded, to recruit prospective buyers for the "planting" of the colony.

For establishing the small town of Rotterdam, 200 acres were set aside and the remainder was divided into 20-acre tracts, which were big enough for a fruit farm. The land directly surrounding the town was sold for $200 per acre; the adjoining 1,060 acres were sold for $160 per acre, the next 1,080 acres at $175 per acre, and the most outward region of 1,280 acres at $200 per acre. Payment would take place in five installments as follows: 60 percent in advance to the principal agents, C. L. Schepp & Son in Rotterdam, the remaining 40 percent to be paid immediately upon closing of the contract in America, or in four annual installments at 8 percent interest per annum. Included in the sale was the right to use the necessary irrigation water from the Crocker-Huffman works at the rate of one dollar per acre per year to be paid to the Crocker-Huffman Canal Company.[51]

This was not exactly what one would have called a give-away operation! But the soil was supposed to be the very best available: "an inexhaustible rich arable soil that at the same time is very easy to work. No matter which agricultural crop was grown in this area, its harvest has been gigantic."[52] In addition, the buyer enjoyed all kinds of privileges. Those who wish "to create a happy home" on these lands will not have to go it alone or without a guide. "They will find their best friend and support in the Holland California Land Company from the moment they leave Holland until, of their own accord, they wish to become totally independent." No sacrifice would be too great for the company to insure the success of every single colonist or investor. The company could even take care of providing a furnished house and all kinds of farm equipment, all depending on the payment, while everyone received the land plowed and ready for immediate cultivation.[53] Those who were not yet acquainted with farming could work under the supervision of the instructor and agricultural advisor of the company "who would give advice and help without charge." "For not even one service given by the company to the colonists will a commission be charged or wages demanded; everything is either free or at cost."

The growing of grapes for raisins would be the main activity in this El Dorado. There was a huge demand for this product. "Therefore, overproduction is not to be feared." Olives, oranges, and lemons could be additional crops, all for export. For the local market one could plan on growing vegetables and alfalfa. The Southern Pacific Railway was willing to run freight cars with cooled air or ice from Merced to San Francisco—a six-hour trip—for the transportation of choice vegetables and dairy products. Finally, for the first few years people would have to concentrate on the raising of chickens and the growing of various fast-maturing crops for their own use.

How attractive it all sounded, how simple. The work on a farm in the irrigation districts runs calmly throughout the whole year, they said. "No waiting for rain in the plowing and seeding season and no fear for water from the skies during harvest time." And in addition, not *one* but *two* harvests and still lots of free time in between that could be spent on one's cultural development. All this in the midst of an hospitable, cordial, mature and very well-educated population, in fact, "a very particular sort of

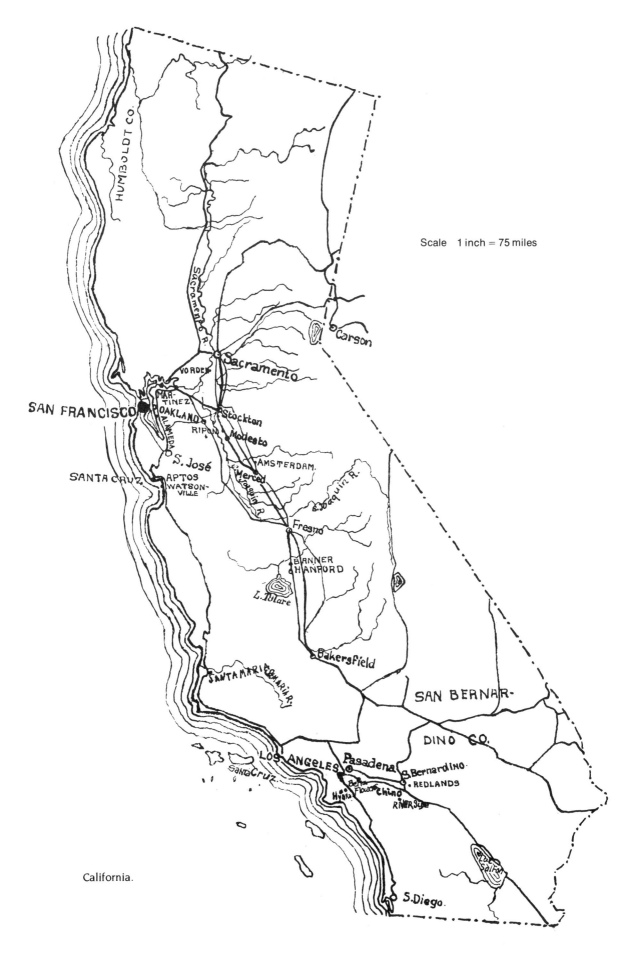

Scale 1 inch = 75 miles

HUMBOLDT CO.

Sacramento R.

Carson

Sacramento

VORDEN

SAN FRANCISCO
MAR-
TINEZ
OAKLAND
ALMEDA

Stockton

RIPON Modesto

AMSTERDAM.

S. José

SANTA CRUZ
APTOS
WATSON-
VILLE

Merced
San Joaquin R.

San Joaquin R.

Fresno

BANNER
HANFORD

L. Tulare

Bakersfield

SANTA MARIA Maria R.

SAN BERNAR-

DINO CO.

LOS ANGELES
Santa Cruz.
Pasadena
Behr
Hyatt Flour
Chino
RIVERSIDE

S. Bernardino.
REDLANDS

California.

S. Diego.

farmers" who had grown up in California under these circumstances.[54] Hence, Nijgh and his aides addressed themselves to a selected group of farmers, just as Hartogh Heys van Zouteveen had done before. Russell Smith called fruit cultivation "a rich man's game" and this was also the opinion of Nijgh and De Veer: "We do not wish to see the actual farmers go to Merced but rather the younger generation who have been educated and have attended agricultural schools and other institutions for secondary and higher technical training to run a better kind of farming enterprise than formerly. Another category is the broader stream of young men from good families who possess ability, but not enough means to develop these abilities under the present economic situation in the Netherlands. We also strongly advise middle-aged people with not too large a family and enough energy to consider our proposition. In short, everybody should come who feels that California promises more with less effort than the Fatherland."[55] There was no doubt about it; it would become an elite colony. That was guaranteed by the price of $200 to $160 per acre! A farmer of the "everyday type" would surely not pay this amount of money! On top of this, a working capital of at least *fl*.7,500 |$3,000| was required.

The wonderful prospects did not fail to make the desired impression. Also the lectures given in many towns in the Netherlands by the zealous Nijgh had the desired effect, as well as the displays of California fruit at the exhibition of the Holland Company of Agriculture, at Haarlem, no less. Those fruit samples were obviously no measuring stick for the significance of the Holland California Land Company's lands, no more than Betuwe cherries or full-fat Gouda cheese would be proof of the fertility of the sand soils around the Veluwe village of Ede! (The observation is from Van Löben Sels.) But who would normally stop to think of that? "Let's go to California!" became the slogan, especially among the theater and concert-going elite of aristocratic Holland. In California people could lead a pleasant and rich life without knowledge of the business—instructors were appointed for this—and with less effort than in the Netherlands—all help was available for this also. So irresponsibly rosy was the situation in California painted— and that by someone who had already lived there for a period of sixteen years—that dozens of people flocked to the Rotterdam office of the company, that soon became known as the *"klepkooi"* |trap| that "lured people with its honey-sweet bait," scattered with a liberal hand![56]

As early as the end of 1889, already 320 acres of land had been sold in Merced County and a year later more than a thousand acres, and all of that without the buyers having ever seen a glimpse of the land they had bought; they knew no more about it than what the speculators had told them. Even businessmen and highly educated persons bought land this way for $200 to $160 per acre, land that subsequently would turn out to be worth no more than $10 per acre. Why did all those people not stop and think for a moment? They could have known what awaited them! Yet, full of courage and pep they set out for the land of great expectations. On December 10,

1889, the first group departed for the Rotterdam colony. In March of 1890 more followed. In May of that same year an even greater group left, among whom were persons with names of great reputation, like Du Celliée Muller, Van Outeren, Jonkheer Ridder De Stuers, Thieme, Torchiana, Van der Dussen, etc. Still later Bannier, Frohwein, and others departed.[57]

With curious interest, and partly also with admiration and awe, people observed the departure of all these men, many accompanied by their wives and children. A sympathizer noted the following: "Most of them show not a single sign that bespeaks of poverty; on the contrary, we see many proofs that the emigrants are accustomed to a life in which luxury plays a great role." And he continued somewhat pompously: "Those fine and well-groomed hands will have to handle the plow over there and under California's skies those white-as-snow collars will be drenched with the sweat of their brows. However, there was respect for these men who could not keep up their high standard of living and therefore went to America rather than close every year with a deficit!"[58]

Hundreds were awaiting the experiences that these first colonists would have. Naturally, they met with all kinds of problems, in spite of the fact that everything was supposed to have been perfectly organized. Since the region was treeless, there developed an immediate shortage of wood for the building of the many houses that were needed. The climate, no matter how mild it generally was, initially was a disappointment, although Hilgard had noted that night frosts were rare. They even had to struggle for weeks on end with constant thick fog and rather sharp cold weather, which showed the need for cattle sheds they had thought to be superfluous.[59] On the other hand, the summer was hotter than they had expected; temperatures of 110 degrees F. occurred repeatedly. This was extremely annoying, because they had no running water, which was one of the first and big grievances. This was contrary to the promise that the colonists, like the inhabitants of the city of Merced, would have running water from Yosemite Lake.[60] Thus, in addition to houses, they had to build sheds and dig wells. The company cooperated by buying the woods along the banks of the Merced River in order to supply the colonists with firewood during the winter.[61] In addition Dr. G. Eisen, a German American and reputedly a competent agriculturist and truck garden specialist, was appointed to supervise the land of the Crocker and Huffman Land and Water Company and act as an advisor.[62]

In July of 1890 alarm spread among the colonists due to financial problems of the Holland California Land Company. Nijgh seems to have been involved in a less than reputable way in this affair. But the Crocker and Huffman Land and Water Company intervened and reportedly assumed all obligations; it also reorganized the management of the Holland California Land Company. These steps restored the shaken confidence, although not entirely, because the immigrants had become too suspicious, especially now that they were in California and realized that they had paid too much for the land.[63] This had also drawn the attention of J. De Fremery, Dutch consul in San Francisco. It must be noted that he had been the person who earlier had advised not to become an on-the-spot landowner in America but first to work for others for a while. In the meantime, the immigrant should deposit his money in a savings bank.[64] How few had taken his advice!

Nijgh's criminal intent to lure wholly unskilled emigrants to California also backfired from the start. Besides the many serious-minded colonists willing to work, there were also elements who were not fit for truck farming and even lacked the desire for it altogether. They became a hard to handle group who were difficult to satisfy, and one of the members of the administration complained by saying: "But honestly, many of your young country-men who have come here seem to care more about their beer mugs and tobacco pipes than about sustained work."[65] It was an outcry that provoked a protest from Van Outeren and his friends, but it seems that it contained a nucleus of truth, in view of the very carefully-worded remarks of consul J. De Fremery.[66] Already in 1880 he had clearly pointed out that "a total lack of experience, often combined with a lesser physical fitness required for manual labor, does not contribute to a speedy success of the colonist, and in any case not to thrifty management."[67] In 1890, he declared without mincing words that some who had come to California "stayed reluctantly and lacked the ambition necessary to succeed in their newly chosen trade.... Neither did they see the necessity of economical management nor the need for labor with their own hands."[68] Also there were "those who turned out to be physically unfit for the work." These observations mainly referred to the Merced colonists, although at the same time they applied to all those who were making a new beginning in California.

Apart from such groups of discontented colonists, who were not only present here but can be found in nearly all colonizing ventures where people tend to react against brand new and especially unfamiliar circumstances, there were others who dedicated themselves completely with heart and soul to the new life style. These were the quiet workers, but not less worthy! So it seemed that the colony of Rotterdam still would become a reality and a thriving achievement, in spite of and perhaps also in part thanks to the discontented individuals. The fact should be pointed out here that there were plenty of reasons for all the discontent, while among the ungrateful elements there were also men who later on developed an unusual energy. T. J. Van Outeren, the leader of the malcontents, is an example; his "tremendous energy," although in another occupation and after hard experiences, was highly praised by former consul Van Löben Sels. Others also, after being branded as failures, reached high stations in life.[69]

Fine homes were built in and around Rotterdam. The home of C. D. Canne, the former governor of Sumatra's Westcoast, especially caught attention. Even though he was already middle-aged, he had ventured out with his big family, as had so many others. Roomy verandas heightened the attractiveness of this cozily furnished home. Jonkheer De Stuers' home was no less eye-catching. It was an elegant building with a dome-shaped roof; and next to the home stood a big barn that could house six horses. Others also built big houses, an indication of their plans for the future.[70] A public school was erected on the boundary of Rotterdam and neighboring Yosemite Colony. A public bus took care of transportation between Rotterdam and the city of Merced located on the Southern Pacific line. The trip to Merced was not ten minutes, as had been advertised, but actually took fifty minutes.[71] This was one of those "little" mistakes that so often happen in the business of land dealings!

Different attempts at cooperation were tried out in hopes of making progress. Among the "influential" and "well-disposed" colonists the Neerlandia Society was founded to stimulate an interest in problems of truck gardening.[72] G. Lotman was chosen as president and H. A. W. Torchiana served as secretary of the society. Dr. Eisen lectured every week on subjects dealing with horticulture such as raisin-grape culture and the benefits of olive cultivation. These discussions had far-reaching consequences and, in fact, hastened the debacle. Another form of cooperation was caused by the arrival of "a multitude of Chinamen" who would take care of the heavy work of planting. A number of Netherlanders united to form a limited liability company for the purpose of collectively hiring these Chinese.[73] For sociability the younger set came together at least once every two weeks at which gatherings they usually had a great time. The malcontents especially belonged to this group.[74]

In general, the Dutch settlement in Merced County must have made a pleasant impression. The venture itself was located on the edge of the foothills where the colony was lying partly on low land and partly on high land. The laying out of vegetable and flower gardens by many a Dutchman, which neighboring Americans thought to be uneconomical, would have created a pleasant view, provided enough water had been available.[75] The colonists themselves were kindly disposed. [?] Wood, the mayor, stated that the Holland colony "promised to become one of the most beautiful places in all of California," thanks to the colonists who "generate much energy." G. Eisen, the specialist, predicted that Rotterdam had a good future since it was excellently located on high sloping ground. He also seemed to be pleased with the colonists, whom he described as "intelligent and well-educated people," the best kind of people one can wish for the state. Eisen did not commit himself about the nature of the soil, as he expressly stated later on.[76]

Many trusting Dutchmen, however, must have come to the conclusion from the impressions of this man that the soil was "excellent." His opinion and that of Mayor Wood were exploited in the Netherlands in order to draw more and more colonists to California. For that purpose W. A. Nijgh was still busy in the Fatherland, and now frequently accompanied by an accomplice, E. J. Brul, who had bought land from the Holland California Land Company and thus praised it sky-high. Later the company admitted it had made a mistake by becoming involved with this man. However, Brul was too smart for them; he skipped out, leaving a great deal of company debts behind. He left after having ordered a windmill, and "presumably" had enjoyed a commission from Nijgh.[77] Also the Company sent to Holland for propaganda purposes a beautiful cluster of muscatel grapes from the farm of J. L. Verwey Mejan, one of the first colonists. In retrospect, it was found out that the whole harvest had consisted of that one bunch, which was immediately preserved in brandy. That there had been "several big clusters" was pure fantasy![78]

An even bigger form of propaganda, no doubt, must have been the establishment of the "Rotterdam Company for Land Exploitation in California" in the spring of 1890 in Rotterdam. A relative of Nijgh, J. C. Nijgh, was chairman, and "bought" four hundred acres from the Holland California Land Company, to have this property developed.[79] Most likely this land was a share that W. A. Nijgh had bargained for as the commission for his activities as "agent." Later this share of the loot was alluded to by our consul Van Löben Sels.[80] People's confidence must have been won when men of note, no doubt with entirely good intentions, declared themselves to be available to provide information. They were men such as C. D. Canne; Jonkheer F. Van Citters, alderman of Rotterdam; Dr. Th. Van Doesburgh, director of the Rotterdam Municipal Gas Company; J. Van der Hoop Az. of Rotterdam; and L. J. du Celliée Muller, retired head engineer of the *Waterstaat* [the Department for Canal Maintenance] at Nijmegen.[81]

In any case, one expedition after another left for California; however, the promoters took good care to sell the expensive land before anyone left. And if some had been smart enough to wait with their purchase until they had arrived, it caused so much worry that "those slippery fish might slip away" that the company saw to it that these prospects would not be left alone for a second until the deal was made.[82]

On April 4, 1891, the sixth group of Netherlanders consisting of twenty-six persons already left for Merced County. They arrived twenty days later.[83] In the meantime, six miles north of the Rotterdam colony on a railway from Merced to Oakdale, the Amsterdam station had been projected. This was in the center of the Crocker and Huffman Land and Water Company property. There the company built a big grain depot with a capacity for six thousand tons of grain.[84] The Rotterdam colony kept on growing. In October of 1890, the population count was more than 100 souls and in the same year the number grew to 135. The total land sold amounted to fourteen hundred acres. The Rotterdam Company possessed four hundred acres of this land; V. P. Smissaert, eighty acres; and the rest of the colonists sometimes had forty acres but mostly twenty acres, which was the average size of a fruit farm.[85] Also five Netherlanders from Michigan had joined the settlement.

The largest part of the grounds, but not all, was planted and the prospects looked good, especially for those who with "deliberation and diligent zeal dedicated themselves to fruit culture," explained the Netherlands con-

sul, De Fremery. But he added cautiously that the success of the colonization and other ventures would be evident only after the trees had borne
fruit. This was rightly said, because disaster struck soon afterwards, causing
this colony as well as others to fail totally.[86]

What had happened? The roots of the plants, in particular the olives so
strongly recommended by Eisen, upon pushing deeper into the soil, had
eventually struck a stone-hard underground layer called hardpan. This is a
notorious occurrence in arid and semi-arid alluvial regions, where an almost totally impenetrable layer of clay or similarly impermeable conglomerate of debris was supplied by the rivers. This debris often occurred in
more than one layer. In April of 1891, [?] Van Dulken, representative of the
Rotterdam Company for Land Exploitation in California, notified J. C. Nijgh,
chairman of the company, of this hardpan evidence: "Now that progress
was made with the planting of olives, hardpan was found in many places."
In the meantime great consternation was manifested in the colony itself,
which was only partly allayed by the assurances of Eisen that the company
would take steps to dynamite the hardpan. The situation became worse at
the beginning of April when Eisen tendered his resignation as of May 1st
because of the shameful treatment he had received from the Crocker and
Huffman Land and Water Company. The assurance of Huffman that to a
depth of six to seven feet the soil was holding moisture and was free of
hardpan, turned out to be a great big lie! The soil proved to be of much
poorer quality and hardly worth from $10 to $70 per acre. People in the
Netherlands could hardly believe this debacle, but the Rotterdam company
for the time being decided to continue with its payments. The bigger Holland California Land Company seemingly did not dare to continue recommending their holdings; at least in the thirty-first and following issues of
the company's publication, "Californie," their advertisements no longer
appeared.[87]

Bowman explained in his *Forest Physiography* that by using irrigation water,
the hardpan would slowly become soft but that it "normally" is impenetrable to plant roots.[88] The truth in these matters was also demonstrated in the
Dutch colony. E. M. Ehrhorn, a specialist, who at the request of Van Dulken
in consultation with W. A. Nijgh had examined the four hundred acres of
Nijgh and their partners, stated that they comprised a good and rich soil,
suitable for all cultivation. Examination of the soil of others was not mentioned. In some parts, however, hardpan was present in strips that were not
considered damaging in the least. On the contrary, after a few years of
cultivation, the hardpan would crumble and then prove to contain the
richest nourishment for the trees. At the bottom of the irrigation ditches,
the hardpan had already become very soft.[89] This conviction was seemingly
shared by our consul J. De Fremery, who tried to encourage his fellow
Hollanders with this information.[90] In his consular report, in which he obviously tried to reassure interested relatives and other participants in the
mother country, he wrote: "The hardpan is a layer of solid soil and can be

found in many regions; the color is sometimes grey, reddish or yellow; it is sometimes clay, sometimes rocky, a mixture of various kinds of soil. At times it is difficult for water to soak through hardpan, which is as hard as rock and yet easily crumbles. Much hardpan soil is being condemned that through later experience and proper treatment can be cultivated and used for the successful cultivation of some kinds of fruit and other crops."

No doubt, the relative truth of all these opinions was confirmed in years to come. In most instances it took not a few years but a good many years for hardpan to soften up, which was a length of time that for many spelled doom. It was only those who came later and started to cultivate the soil anew, who reaped the fruits. Not all the colonists, however, had confidence in Ehrhorn's report, not even after the Dutch consul's inquiry and report in which he gave his judgment that was not unfavorable concerning the hardpan. At a meeting of the consul with colonial representatives and the Huffmans, all kinds of proposals were considered, and four colonists were even given other land in exchange.[91] However, the credibility had been shocked too much. Many colonists could not be persuaded to stay; they left, abandoning all their possessions. Some of them had been embittered right from the start, since development costs turned out to be much higher than had been originally suggested and this had gotten them into debt.[92]

The principal agents of the Holland California Land Company tendered their resignation in July of 1891, which must not have strengthened trust in the future either. The fifty-second number of the weekly publication of the company, at the end of September, was the last to appear. As a result, further recruitment was discontinued, since the company realized that doing business had become impossible.[93] They were not the only ones to have this dubious honor conferred on them. They had a competitor who shared this notoriety of having rashly brought many to poverty.

F. The Fresno Drama

The Fresno Land Company, using similar tactics, had tried during that same time to bring Netherlanders to the already developed Fresno County, bounded on the north by Merced County. The owners there were also Americans. The "directors" were P. J. Koch at San José and Rob. Mack at San Francisco, both Californians. They, too, organized an independent company in order to win the patronage of the Netherlanders. They even obtained Royal approval in the Netherlands and tried, so to speak, to outdo the America-based Holland California Land Company by being more reliable.

In Rotterdam, the Fresno Land Company, originally known as the Fresno Land Syndicate, had the support of the Rotterdam Consignment Company which acted as proxy for its directors. Supervising directors were M. G. Van den Arend, director of the Tobacco Company at Arendsburg, W. F. H. Van Peski, director of the Rotterdam Consignment Company, and the lawyer J. B.

Roelvink, managing partner of W. B. Blijdenstein and Company, which is the Twentsche Bank Society. These gentlemen were a match for the associates of the Holland California Land Company. Both Van den Arend and Van Peski lived in Rotterdam and Roelvink lived in Amsterdam. The company, although founded in Amsterdam, located its headquarters in Rotterdam, and Geldersche Kade 12 became "the trap." They sold "choice fruitland" in Fresno County in central California. They also handled the planting of trees for third parties and floated limited amounts of 6 percent bonds with security. Information could be obtained from M. Bolte in Haemstede, R. Van Heyst in Kampen, Noordhoek Hegt in Zutphen, etc.

Propaganda was also made for the Fresno project, apparently aided by the author W. F. Andriessen. At any rate, he wrote a pamphlet about California with the Dutch immigrants in mind. He mentioned Fresno as well as Merced but told only of the many good things in Fresno: "In general, Merced does not look as flourishing as its competitor," meaning of course, the town of Fresno. At that time this city already counted 14,000 inhabitants, and the town of Merced had only 2,500 people. Fresno was a real business town with two sizable first-class hotels in addition to various smaller ones, well-stocked stores, etc. It is obvious that this comparison between the two cities—correct as it was—was taken by the emigrants as also applying to a certain degree to the territory surrounding both towns that was ready for colonization. The promoters further stressed the advantages of Fresno over Merced by adroitly quoting De Fremery's observation about the high prices asked for the Merced lands![94]

Still the Fresno Land Company seemed not to be able to get the better of its competitor. One important element was missing: a man like W. A. Nijgh. With great cunning, he tried to demonstrate why his land had to be approximately $100 more expensive than that of the Fresno Company. The previously mentioned Brul served for that purpose! It was claimed that before settling permanently in California he had also visited the Fresno lands, in particular the colony of Perrin intended for Dutch settlers.[95] It was said that during Brul's visit to Perrin Colony No. 2, not much of the colony was yet in evidence; there was only a boarding house and the home of one colonist, Crans. The quality of the soil there was much inferior and it still had to be worked (the advertising spoke of soil ready to plant), and there was no water. Hence it could be sold for $100 less! Merced, also according to Brul, had heavy clay whereas Fresno had only sand. Moreover, it was much hotter in Fresno County in the summer and colder in the winter. Therefore, it would be fit only for raisin cultivation which, it must be admitted, was not altogether a fabrication because even today Fresno is known as the raisin-growing country par excellence; it is the home of Sunmaid Raisins.[96]

Furthermore, it was later discovered that the nitrogen content was wholly insufficient in the Fresno soil, as was the content of phosphoric acid. Potassium was also lacking, that is, if one wished to grow strong plants.[97] In this manner, Nijgh and his men enticed the entranced majority to Merced instead of to Fresno. Besides, there even seemed to be gold-bearing quartz in the Merced soil, indeed, it appeared that the whole Rotterdam colony was gold-bearing![98]

The consular report of 1890 mentions that "a great number of Netherlanders," many with wives and children, established themselves as fruit growers in California.[99] "A number" went to the Perrin Colony No. 2 in Fresno County under the guidance of the Fresno Land Company. "Most of them went to the Rotterdam Colony in Merced County, which until now is the foremost settlement of their countrymen." This occurred despite the much more expensive land in Merced. One realizes what a man like Nijgh meant in the land business!

Just as in Merced County, the Perrin Colony in Fresno County had similar problems. Here also development costs had been far higher than anticipated and there was a lack of water. But all these disappointments were surpassed by the hardpan disaster. Many colonists left Fresno County.[100]

Initially, as in Merced County, many colonists also remained in Fresno County. As in every colony, these were the most energetic ones, the core of real settlers, as we have seen them in Michigan, Wisconsin, and elsewhere. Those who pulled up stakes belonged to the normal number of "losers," a "normal" selection phenomenon. Not much good was said of those who left. Among this group there were those who "lacked stick-to-itiveness, judgment and ambition and who demonstrated little or no fitness for farming or truck gardening." Some allowed the weeds to take over the field! Just to get rid of the whole mess, one of them burned the weeds; that was the easiest way out! But as told by De Fremery, a number of young fruit trees were burned or scorched at the same time and he was set back a whole year.[101] De Fremery's successor, the well-known P. J. Van Löben Sels, also pointed out that there were many who were unsuited. The pie-in-the-sky idea had spread that if anyone invested *fl.* 8,000 to *fl.* 10,000 [$3,200 to $4,000] in an orchard, it would turn into a goldmine. Many a father or guardian had bought twenty acres for his son and promised the young man a salary of $75 per month to administer the property. But that was not enough to live on. There were those who straightforwardly acknowledged: "We spent too much for luxuries and munificent living and also too much for wages." Many of these young men found it to be "so vulgar" to be working side by side with a farmhand. There were also those who liked "to toss off a stiff drink or two, or three, or four."

In addition to these thoughtless young people, blame attached primarily to the Dutch land agents, according to Van Löben Sels. He exposed the shady practices of the latter and indicted men like Nijgh. However, this consul goes too far when he blames the Dutch settlers for not appreciating the liberality and fairness of the American landowners.[102] The hardpan phenomenon was not unknown to them, as is evident from the incident when Eisen blamed Huffman. Anyway, they were the ones, first of all, who should have investigated and convinced themselves whether or not any hardpan was present on their property.[103] So all the blame is theirs! This has also been proven by the later development of the settlements. Because in the final analysis, their failure was not caused by the nature or character of the colonists, but by a natural phenomenon, the constitution of the soil and also partly by the climate.

We have already mentioned that a good nucleus of settlers remained in Merced as well as in Fresno. Their future did not seem altogether dim. De Fremery wrote in his last yearly report that the transfer of land to more vigorous and more experienced hands was considered to be beneficial for the colony, "which was yet thought to have good prospects." In his first consular report for the years of 1892 and 1893, Van Löben Sels mentions that the news from the Dutch settlements was "not entirely unfavorable." The active colonists, especially the natural-born farmers, "are not altogether dissatisfied." At the beginning of January 1893, there were still fifty-two people left over in the colony of Rotterdam and that was months after the discovery of the disaster. They figure on being successful, people thought, because the nature of the soil was not disappointing, provided it was cultivated in the right manner. In many places, the trees did well and the scare of hardpan had even disappeared.

A similar reserved optimism seemed to reign among the Fresno colonists. They also were "not discontented," especially now that many young people, the "carpet knights" [salon loopers], had left the colony, thereby improving considerably the quality of colonists.[104] With a few exceptions, however, this better quality of colonists in Merced and in Fresno were not able to bring it off. Hardpan was too much of a drawback. In reality, those who had stayed a few years longer had simply "wasted" those years. According to a conservative estimate, besides the valuable time that was lost, the Netherlands wasted one million guilders [$400,000] of Dutch capital in the Merced County colony alone! In the end most colonists had to leave their "farms," their well-kept orchards. Properties that had cost them $13,000 to $14,000 were disposed of for $100 to $200. One syndicate alone lost fl. 400,000 [$160,000]!

The much trumpeted orchard land reverted to its old state of affairs, "that of undeveloped land for grazing and sheep raising." Any buyer willing to pay $10 per acre would be taken in, so Van Löben Sels said in his 1898 yearly report.[105] This was the same man who not so long before had been of the opinion that the Netherlanders had shown themselves ungrateful to the American landowners!

G. Still More Deception

Even more reckless than the Merced and Fresno settlements was a third undertaking, this time in the mountainous northern section of California in Humboldt County, which received ample precipitation, thanks to the prevailing southwesterly ocean wind. Here was planted a settlement of plainer folk such as families of the working class. In 1890, just for a starter, ten Dutch families were transported to fruitland Hollandia. Every immigrant family received a cow and two pigs besides the use of a house. For a meager monthly wage, the families pledged to labor five years for the First Netherland Fruit and Land Culture Association of Humboldt County. Only after these five years of service would they receive a four-year old, five-acre orchard.[106]

Already a few months after the arrival of the colonists, the whole settlement came to nought. The planners had insufficient funds to carry on. And only then did the colonists learn that the land was heavily mortgaged and that in case of a sale the mortgage holders had priority. These circumstances forced the immigrants to vacate the land and since then they have scattered. Fortunately, most of them found work at a large lumber company that did both cutting and sawing in the same county, one of the most timber-rich areas in the state, owing to the heavy rainfall. Lumbering was just becoming increasingly important there. The earnings of our lumbermen were now $30 per month; with free firewood and free living quarters, for which the Merced and Fresno people could have envied them.[107]

A fourth undertaking that was at work in the Netherlands was the South Riverside Land and Water Company, which in 1890 opened an office in Rotterdam. From there they tried to induce interested parties to emigrate to southern California, to San Bernardino County, which had a relatively low rainfall. More cautious than the previously mentioned companies, it closed contracts only at the place of destination.[108] This particular circumstance and the fact that mostly farmers had settled here, perhaps explain why this most southerly of the settlements was the only one mentioned in the annual reports as "doing well." The Netherlanders there were thriving, at least during the first few years. Later on, however, no further mention was made about this colonization, either. Irrigation was a necessity there due to the very long and hot summers because, first of all, rainy seasons were all too short and only occurred during the winter months. Secondly, the amount of rain, 30 c.m. |12 inches|, was also too little for a county at this elevation, 350 meters |1,155 feet|.[109] And although there was less night frost, the circumstances were such that in the long run, farming by the Dutch settlers—alfalfa, grains, and sugar beets in the valleys, and fruit trees along the mountain slopes— must have held little appeal.

A number of Netherlanders shrank back from settling in Merced County because of complaints about the Holland California Land Company published mostly by T. J. Van Outeren in the *Arnhemsche Courant*. These Dutchmen, who were also averse to Fresno County due to public dissatisfaction there, settled in other parts of California. Later on, various Merced and Fresno victims who still had some capital left, joined them. Thus a few

Netherlanders settled south of San Francisco in Santa Cruz and Santa Clara counties, which had a wonderful and favorable climate. Because this is a fruit land—the Santa Clara Valley is one huge orchard—the settlers concentrated on fruit culture here also. With only a few exceptions, however, they had little success.

In January of 1893 it was reported that fifteen farmers who had settled in Santa Cruz County found the price of $35 per acre for really good soil still too steep to make ends meet. In Merced and Fresno counties, it was $160 to $200, as we remember! This is understandable when one realizes that a newly-planted orchard produces little or no fruit the first four or five years, and that there were many who could not remain without an important source of income for that long.[110] The fruit growing enterprise, *Berg en Dal* |Hill and Dale| near Aptos, around which the above-named compatriots had settled in 1892, was one of the few "successes." It was operated by a very knowledgeable colonist who had lived there since 1890 and who had also worked in the Netherlands as an agriculturist.

Others settled in southern California in the Southland of Los Angeles County and also applied themselves to fruit growing.[111] This Southland can also be reckoned to include the coastline counties located north of Los Angeles, Santa Barbara and San Luis Obispo. At the boundary of these counties lies the Santa Maria Valley. This was one of the many valleys with limited sources of income; therefore it was very sparsely populated but still highly recommended by land dealers. This valley contained rich alluvial soils that were described as "pre-eminently fit for the cultivation of apricots, peaches, walnuts, and plums."

J. H. De Veer, the man who helped found the Holland California Land Company but has since resigned, called the attention of the Netherlanders to the Santa Maria Valley. In 1891 he tried to gather a capital sum of at least $25,000 to put into operation a fruit growing undertaking.[112] As with so many projects, it must have remained in the planning stage, because no further mention is made of it. Perhaps this was the consequence of a situation, according to De Veer, which made "it difficult to eliminate the fearfulness" with which people are beginning to look at California, now that many are faced there with a "less brilliant career," even with total failure. These poor results are "constantly throwing a shadow on the high expectations" that people have of California's development in the area of agriculture and horticulture. This man did eventually reap the fruits of the light-hearted Merced venture.

Finally, there is still one other colonization attempt that resulted from the Merced drama. An endeavor was made to found a "Queen Wilhelmina Colony" in the southern part of the Great Valley, in the fertile Tulare region. This section is known for its constantly shrinking Tulare Lake, which is due to reduced rainfall, irrigation, and polder developments. The polders have turned into farmland large parts of the bottom of Tulare Lake, which is isolated from the San Joaquin River by alluvial fans.[113] Vast 2,000 and 3,000-acre ranches were found here during the Merced and Fresno debacle and parts of some were being offered for sale.

Two of the colonists from the Rotterdam colony, A. Slotemaker, who had warned the Dutch public against the evil practices of Nijgh, and L. C. Lens bought three hundred acres of land at the end of 1890. This land was near the city of Hanford, north of Tulare Lake in today's Kings County, which at that time formed one single unit with the section lying east of it and which is still called Tulare County. A. Bannier, who as we know left for California later than the other two gentlemen, showed little interest in buying land in the Rotterdam colony, no matter how kindly he was received by M. S. Huffman. But Bannier took over a small part of the land purchased near Hanford. Others followed so that a settlement arose, especially after the hardpan episode at Merced and Fresno.[114] Lens became their leader or director. Especially in 1892 he sold various pieces of his land, each ten or twenty acres in size, to Netherlanders and also to Americans. The colony was located in the fertile Lucerne valley, six miles north of Hanford in today's Kings County, which is still indicated by Lens as Tulare County. Now that he had become a land speculator, Lens advertised it to be "the best known and most desirable county for fruit growing."

However, the director of this Queen Wilhelmina Colony was not cheap. He sold the land for $125 per acre, including the use of irrigation water, while it had the advantage of being near one of the Southern Pacific Railway lines. Young people also qualified as colonists and could count on Lens's guidance if needed. They could obtain board and room at $25 per month in a boarding house. This seemed like a small-scale repetition of the Merced colony! However, in this case there was no hardpan, because Lens made it expressly clear that the Lucerne valley was altogether free from hardpan, as well as "badrock." But here and there the colonists did find alkali in the soil. In a brochure Lens said in 1893 that his colony "has already a populated look."[115] Since then no more mention has been made of it. Seemingly the whole affair was unsuccessful. We will meet Lens again as director of a Dutch industrial undertaking in Spokane, Washington.

H. Postscript

All of the above-related attempts at settling Netherlanders in California turned to failure. In his annual report of 1898, our consul in San Francisco testified "that they failed miserably."[116] This admission is all the more valuable because Consul P. J. Van Löben Sels, a landowner himself, was closely acquainted with colonization efforts. Some colonists found work elsewhere; many drifted to the big cities as had been also the case in Michigan and Iowa.[117] In 1900, California had 1,013 Dutch-born immigrants, of which 244, almost one-fourth, lived in San Francisco, 33 in nearby Oakland and 86 in

Los Angeles.[118] Many of them led a poor existence. A few of those who had been able to salvage some of their capital returned to the Netherlands, some others returned with the help of their relatives.[119]

The number who made out well in California was extremely small. H. A. Van Coenen Torchiana, an "eighteen-ninety-er," was one of those few who made headway. Already in the Rotterdam Colony his farm earned the distinction of being "one of the most beautiful" in the colony, and he even obtained a first prize at an exhibition in Merced.[120] Later on he was appointed consul-general of the Netherlands at San Francisco. In October of 1904 he wrote from Watsonville, California: "It is so very seldom, that we meet young men of Dutch extraction here in the U. S. to whom we can point with pride." Not only did Netherlanders "lay far behind with the Americans," "our countrymen as a general rule |were| far out-classed" by almost all Northern European and most Latin descendants.[121]

Later I hope to show that this opinion was incorrect because it covered all of the Netherlanders in the United States, while Van Coenen Torchiana remained for years practically unacquainted with these elements outside of the Far West.[122] He could only speak for California, and in the case of this state, his judgment was affirmed, remarkably enough, by the protest against his words by P. J. Van Löben Sels, "ex-consul," and "also in the name of the rather strong colony of Netherlanders settled on the coast." In this protest, it was conceded that Van Coenen Torchiana had said many things that were true but that he had greatly exaggerated. Nevertheless, Van Löben Sels, who, as the successor of De Fremery, had been a close observer of the disintegration of the settlements, went even further than Van Coenen Torchiana in his assertion, to the point even that one gets the impression he understated the situation. The ex-consul stressed that the colonists "almost without exception were people who could not stick it out in Holland;" they were "weak in body and spirit," and "most of them were unfit for any type of heavy manual labor, in other words, failures."[123]

It is obvious that after a similar protest, Van Coenen Torchiana stuck to his statement, although in the protest mention was made of forty outstanding Netherlanders. These were from the "immediate vicinity" of Van Löben Sels and were selected "from a greater number" than those Van Coenen Torchiana had been writing about. Still, the latter acknowledged having mainly the West in mind.[124] This is, therefore, not only a confirmation of what I have mentioned above, but at the same time it is very acceptable in connection with what was said formerly about the Netherlanders in the Far West.

The fact that a Belgian, G. J. G. Marsily, rather than a Netherlander, looked after the Dutch interests in California for many years after Van Löben Sels's resignation as consul, also gives pause for thought. This fact is proof once more of Van Coenen Torchiana's argument that almost all Netherlanders in California, with some exceptions, were found "in the more humble walks of life."[125] Hardly anywhere were they leading; they were serving instead.

Moreover, this has been confirmed by the late C. V. Gerritsen, town councilor of Amsterdam, who in 1904 visited California for over a month and talked with a great many people, but not with Netherlanders! There was one exception and that was Van Löben Sels, who was at that time a kind of celebrity because his polder, Vorden, in the Sacramento Delta, belonged to one of the few pieces of land that had not been flooded that spring by the huge masses of "mountain water." This was pointed out to Gerritsen as a great event when he traveled on the boat downriver from Sacramento, which years later Professor Niermeyer would do with the Netherlands Line. "I met here Swedes, Danes, Russians, Englishmen, Germans, Swiss, Italians and, of course, also Americans, who after a few years of persistent labor, are now substantial citizens of California. Only Netherlanders I did not meet on my trip." Nowhere did Gerritsen hear any mention of a Dutch colony or of Dutch capital in the fruit-growing business, nor even in the dairy business, which was such a Dutch specialty. "It is remarkable how few Dutchmen are to be seen in central California's farming and cattle breeding. One finds here very prosperous Swiss, German, and even Russian colonies, but a Dutch colony, for which these farming endeavors are so eminently suited, is not as yet found here," was Gerritsen's justifiable complaint.[126]

Not the Dutch "immigrants" but the Dutch-Americans would discover California as a land of cattle breeding and dairy industry. But this was not until the twentieth century, which was rather late, since Dutch cattle had already been in California for several decades. Frisian cows had been imported on a wholesale scale here in the eighties, not directly shipped from Holland but from the eastern states. Formerly called "Holsteins," they were now in great demand as "Holstein-Frisians" because these heavily-built cows furnish excellent milk and were gentler than other breeds.[127] In California, Dutch cattle as well as Dutch people were seemingly successful only after having been Americanized in more than one respect.

Why direct colonization from the Netherlands to California did not meet with success has already largely come to light, especially with respect to the Nijgh dealings. No matter how one looks at the latter, they were set up in an irresponsible manner, even to the extent of being criminal. I have gathered abundant information about this colonization from one of the "well-disposed elements" from the late Rotterdam Colony because the opinion of the "discontented faction," of T. J. Van Outeren and followers, is already sufficiently known to us. H. A. Van Coenen Torchiana, when he was still our consul-general at San Francisco, assured me that the Merced colony ended as a "total failure" because of several reasons:

1. The land was entirely unfit for the fruit culture for which it was sold. Some of the land was ordinary grazing land, while some was good wheat land. But the hardpan, that is, a hard shale of undersoil, was so close to the surface and so impenetrable for the roots of the fruit trees, that no success in fruit farming could be expected thereon.

2.   The land was sold for too high a price.

3.   The class of Netherlanders brought out there did not belong to the agricultural or horticultural category and were totally unfit to become fruit farmers.

After his judgment had had a chance to "mature and settle" for thirty years, Van Coenen Torchiana summed it up in the following pithy manner: "The wrong people were brought to the wrong land at wrong prices. Therefore that Colony had from its very inception, within its own bosom, all the elements of failure."[128]

No wonder that practically nothing reminds us of this tragic episode of Netherlanders in America. Yet something was left; when one studies the map of California and more in particular of Merced County, one will search in vain for the name of Rotterdam, yet one will spot the name of Amsterdam. This is the railway station where Huffman built his elevator and where a second Dutch city was supposed to have come into existence.[129]

In Fresno similar factors were at work as in Merced but the prices of the Fresno land were lower and thanks to irrigation the land was generally of better quality. That is the reason why not all Netherlanders left. In spite of the fact that Gerritsen did not meet any Netherlanders in Fresno, which is evidence enough that they did not go far there, still there were a few left.[130] In the Fresno public schools in 1917, there were fifteen children who were listed as "Dutch" and whose fathers had been born abroad.[131]

Earlier we have commented at length about how important it was that the Netherlanders in the Midwest settled in locations whose soil and climate were not altogether foreign to them. This is clearly evident when one compares the Midwest experience with that of our countrymen in California and in particular in Fresno County. Except for the hardpan here and there, the soil was not bad. Russell Smith even called Fresno County "the second richest agricultural county in the United States."[132] But it was altogether different from soils in the Netherlands. Thus, the Netherlanders were too unfamiliar with California soil, all the more so since many among them, also the farmers, hardly knew what was involved with fruit growing.

In 1918, the schools of Fresno taught youngsters of forty-six nationalities, not counting the American and Black children.[133] Two years later in the Fresno County schools of these forty-six nationalities thirty-three were represented by at least one hundred pupils each. The fact that Armenians were in the majority, numbering five thousand souls, followed by Mexicans and Italians, each counting more than three hundred, indicates once more, except for the Danes there, that next to soil conditions the climate is also a big factor. People from southern nations seemingly feel better at home in this dry climate and summer heat, and they can also cope with a lower standard of living. This is also the reason why Chinese, Japanese, and even Hindus make a good and comfortable living in California.

In the final analysis let us not forget that in Merced, Fresno, and all other colonizations of the nineties in various parts of California, real pioneer work still had to be done. With regard to California fruit growing, people were still in the experimental stage. Only in the long run, often after very expensive experiences and many disappointments was it possible to establish the suitability of a specific area for a particular kind of culture. Only after long and sometimes bitter experiences did Santa Clara become almost exclusively the land of plums, did Watsonville and vicinity (Torchiana's haven of refuge) become that of apples, Fresno that of Sunmaid Raisins, and Southern California the land of oranges and lemons.

The excessive prices of the land and the exorbitant freight rates charged by the mighty and all-powerful Southern Pacific Railway of those days made a profitable business almost impossible for the most hard-working colonists and even for the specialists among them. Even today, distribution, outlets, and the danger of overproduction of California fruit still form the greatest and most difficult problems of the Golden State. Growers try to solve these problems through cooperative efforts of large organizations such as the Raisin Growers Association, the California Peach Growers Association, the California Prune and Apricot Growers Association, and many other such organizations. Even then, they often meet with dubious success.[134]

If one considers all this, and also looks at some other facts, then one sees the Dutch attempts at implantation in California soil in another light, and then our judgment becomes milder. For we must not forget that even in 1925, of all the California orange enterprises only one-third were profitable, while one-third of the orchards were worthless because of poor soil, water shortages, or night frost problems. And the remaining one-third suffered from neglect due to lack of knowledge or carelessness of the growers. All this was despite several decades of experience.[135] It is obvious that the mildness of our judgment cannot extend to the land speculators who pictured everything in terms that were too rosy and too glowing, but it does extend to their victims. Among them were those who like their countrymen in Michigan, Iowa, and elsewhere tried to fulfill their thankless pioneer task with great will power, a task that in the end proved too much for most of them.

Not all of the "ninety-ers" were "failures" from the outset or became so. A few were able to work themselves up in America, but proportionally their number was very small. I will name a few, borrowing from P. J. Van Löben Sels's previously-mentioned protest against Torchiana's report. At the same time I am giving the occupation of these immigrants, in which they were employed in California in 1904: H. A. Beekhuis, superintendent of a canning factory in Hanford where Lens had tried to establish a colony, and where the Banner station reminds us of the previously mentioned Mr. Bannier; J. H. Smissaert, who became a real estate expert and who apparently obtained extensive knowledge of soils and geology and as a "$300,000 man" was in great demand; E. C. Willekes MacDonald, owner of the *Berg en Dal* fruit farms near Aptos, Santa Cruz County; and B. Van der Dussen, superintendent of the Sheldon Ranch at San José, Santa Clara County. These were, in a broad sense, concerned with agriculture.

Others applied their talents in an altogether different direction. These were: H. A. Van Coenen Torchiana, who became an attorney-solicitor and notary public at Watsonville, Santa Cruz County; T. J. Van Outeren, who pursued a "very fine and promising career" with the Dining Car Service of the Southern Pacific Railway Company at San Francisco; A. F. Groh, who became superintendent of one of the biggest California hospitals; G. J. E. M. d'Aquin, who developed into a "special reporter" for the Hearst papers; and H. Dijkmans, who became a music teacher and concert singer at San José, Santa Clara County.[136] Other "ninety-ers" not mentioned by Van Löben Sels are R. Insinger, who tried his luck in Canada, after which he went to the northwestern part of the United States and became one of the "builders" of the Inland Empire, the city of Spokane in the state of Washington. The previously named L. C. Lens also became one of the "builders" of Spokane.

9

Settlements in Colorado and New Mexico

Next to Minnesota and California, a third area in America, that of Colorado and the bordering state of New Mexico, attracted the attention of Dutch capitalists and through them that of Dutch emigrants. This was at the peak of the economic cycle around 1870. Many had become interested in Colorado since the discovery of gold, especially at the well-known Gregory mines in May, 1859. Because of this the population grew rapidly, and the city of Denver was founded on the upper reaches of the South Platte River.[1] The coming of the Union Pacific Railroad, in particular its so-called southern or Kansas route, opened up new possibilities, especially in farming. Now the railroad directly connected Kansas, organized as a territory in 1861, with the cities of New York and San Francisco.

Characteristically, there are broad and far-reaching plains near the southern Rockies that are suitable for agriculture and the raising of cattle. They are depressions among the high mountains dating back mostly to the beginning of the Mesozoic or second age in the Triassic period. In Colorado these valleys were often labeled "parks" [level valleys between mountain ranges]. The headwaters of various rivers flow through these valleys and in time of drought are useful for irrigation purposes. I. Bowman called these regions "broad intermont structural depressions."[2] Two of these "parks" are located on the borders of Colorado and New Mexico. One of these valleys is located to the west and the other to the east of the Sangre de Cristo Mountains. This is one of the eastern ranges of the Rocky Mountains and is still called the Sierra Madre Mountains. These two areas became of particular importance for the Dutch immigrants and colonizers.

In the same way that emigration to Minnesota was encouraged mostly by interested railroad parties of that state, it was the railroad speculators in the Netherlands who pointed out to their fellow countrymen the importance of Colorado and New Mexico for settlement purposes—or they saw to it that others pointed out this importance. F. W. Oewel, the well-known bank director and promoter for American funds at Amsterdam, was the "mediator" who called the attention of the money men of Holland to these new possibilities.[3] At about the same time, Professor R. P. A. Dozy published an article in De Gids of May, 1871, in which "more by accident than by choice" he pointed out to Dutch intellectuals the great importance of Colorado for cattle raising.[4] Colorado was considered to be even better suited than Texas for this purpose because of the abundance of grasses that were on a par with oats and the mild winter weather that required cattle to be fed indoors only twenty days. Colorado supposedly experienced stormy weather very seldomly and above all "the climate was pure, healthy, strengthening, and mild."

Due to this publicity, people in our country became very interested in two land companies that wished to exploit large tracts of these two "parks." These border areas were located partly in Colorado and partly in New Mexico. The latter area had belonged to two Mexicans, Miranda and Beaubien, while the first area had been the sole possession of Beaubien, who was a Frenchman by birth. A part of the "Beaubien and Miranda Grant" had been sold to the Maxwell Landgrant and Railway Company and has since become known as the Maxwell Estate, an area of about two million acres. At Rotterdam and also at Amsterdam, in 1870 and in 1872, loan subscriptions could be made to the Maxwell Company for settling this area, which was pictured as "extremely rich" in minerals, timber for building, and fertile soil.[5] With the help of the loans these riches would be exploited and this would also encourage emigration.

The "Beaubien Grant" at that time was also known as the Sangre de Cristo Estate, located in the San Luis Valley, the "park" west of the Sangre de Cristo Mountains, lying between these mountains and the Sawatch Range, and the largest in Colorado! Part of the Sangre de Cristo Estate, the so-called "Costilla Possession," had been obtained by the United States Freehold Land and Emigration Company. It was an area of more than 500,000 acres, whose riches, especially in minerals, were "highly touted." The company wished to develop its holdings and extract these minerals and also offered small pieces of land for sale. In December, 1870, loan subscriptions to this company were opened in our country. In 1872 F. W. Oewel was even appointed as director for the Netherlands. After he had visited the "Estate" and had also become acquainted with the board members and the dubious practices of the board of this land company, Oewel resigned at the end of that same year.[6]

In the meantime the "Land- en Emigratie-Maatschappij der Vereenigde Staten van Noord-Amerika" [Dutch-American Land and Emigration Company of the United States of North America], known in the Netherlands as the "Colorado Land- en Emigratie Mij." [Colorado Land and Emigration Company], kept promoting emigration also in the Netherlands. G. J. Rollandet of Leiden had written a brochure in which not unexpectedly he praised the abundant fertility and mineral riches of the land and also declared that in order to settle on the company's land only fl. 250 [$100] to fl. 300 [$120] were needed for travel expenses.[7] That was a claim that is hard to believe! Upon arrival in New York, a representative of the company would lead the emigrant to Colorado by railroad. Besides, the company would furnish all necessities at cost on credit, such as a home, food, land, cattle, necessary equipment, etc. The stipulation was that this advance should be paid back over ten years in installments at 10 percent interest.

Did many Netherlanders make use of this seemingly tempting offer? N. J. Den Tex declared in 1873 that he did not know "if the plan of luring Dutch settlers to this area had succeeded or how much response was obtained."[8] Their numbers must not have been large, otherwise mention would have been made of it. Twenty years later a new settlement attempt by Dutch colonists was made in the area of the former Costilla Estate. At that time there was only one Dutch family living there. It was the T. Te Linde family that had lived there for "a number of years."[9] Tonie Te Linde, the father, spoke the language of his homeland poorly and wrote it even worse. It

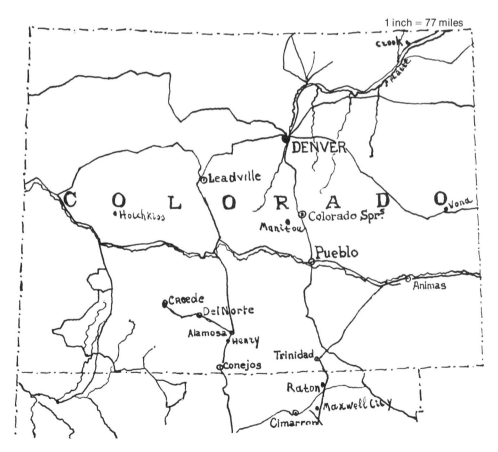

Colorado and part of northern New Mexico.

showed that he was either poorly educated or that he had not associated with his countrymen for years, or both. Other names I am not acquainted with, except one, the brochure writer's name. This man, G. J. Rollandet, settled in Denver and was still known in 1920 as a competent lawyer and very well-disposed towards his fellow Netherlanders.[10] Whether Dutch settlers went to the Maxwell Estate at that time is not evident anywhere.

In 1874 another attempt was made to draw Netherlanders to settle in Colorado. A. J. G. W. Van Motz was a civil engineer at Manitou, Colorado, just like Kloos was in Minnesota.[11] One can assume that he spoke from his own observation and experience when in that same year he said that numerous valleys were very suitable for agriculture and cattle raising. A "large amount" of land was still "easily obtainable," especially for cattle raising, for which this state offered "unparalleled advantages." In a number of counties "thousands of our countrymen can still find a pleasant and happy hearth"—provided one comes with some capital, this writer claimed. He highlighted in particular the beautifully located Manitou region that, with its many cold water springs, presented a bright future. This prediction was fulfilled. Recently, a well-known traveler, W. J. Van Balen, LL.B., corroborated this fact, saying that now this place is "the most popular summer resort in all of the Rocky Mountains."[12] Nowhere did I find any evidence that at that time many Netherlanders followed Motz's suggestions. His brochure came just too late.

The oft-noted crisis of 1873 must have affected plans concerning settlements in Colorado and New Mexico, just as it did in Minnesota and California at that same time. The boom period in America around the nineties, when Dutch immigration increased rapidly, gave them new life, as we saw in California, but after having made numberless victims, these plans also came to naught. After 1890, first mention is made of a few settlements attempted directly from the Netherlands and located on the land of the previously mentioned companies.

Actually on May 3, 1890, the Maxwell Land Grant Company was founded with the help of, among other people, F. W. Oewel, with a capital of $fl.$ 12,000,000 [$4,800,000] for the exploitation of the Maxwell Estate and to promote settlements in northeastern New Mexico. At various locations they appointed representatives, in particular in the existing Dutch settlements and from there they even organized excursions to their land holdings. They advertised it as "the largest Dutch possession in America" consisting of "one and a half million acres of the most beautiful and most fertile soil in Colorado and New Mexico." "Large Dutch colonies are already being formed." A free journey was promised to all those who purchased 160 acres. For information they could see, among others, J. R. Van Dam, land agent at Grand Rapids, Michigan.[13] In spite of this free travel offer, they seem not to have been very successful.

E. Bos, the Dutch-American missionary preacher of the Christian Reformed Church, wrote in the church weekly, De Wachter, about the settlement at

Maxwell City, one of the creations of the company. The "manager" of this "colony," however, lived in Raton, thirty miles north of Maxwell City in New Mexico. The colony never grew big, numbering only ten families.[14] The Christian Reformed Church in America was concerned about the fate of these families and tried to establish a church there. Reverend I. Van Dellen became its pastor, and was also the director of the Christian Reformed tuberculosis sanitarium at this place.[15] In the long run, the church element was not vigorous enough, but it made a special mark. It established the first "modern" Christian school for the Dutch at Maxwell City, and it is from there that this private education began its triumphal march through all the other Dutch colonies. Finally, the Christian Reformed congregation became defunct due to lack of membership, and the sanitarium was moved to Denver. This colony has never been mentioned as flourishing. The type of land and arid climate, which necessitated irrigation, added to this situation. The Netherlanders were too unaccustomed with all the new circumstances to feel at home in this location, so they finally decided to move elsewhere. This land company still exists with H. A. Hartogh as director. In 1905, the company sold a large portion of its land for mining purposes, and now it is being liquidated, although it still owns some 400,000 acres.[16] The company never prospered.

Greater attention was drawn at this time by an attempted colonization in the San Luis Valley. Over the passing years, this valley had become more important due to the fact that the Denver and Rio Grande Railroad had finally been completed. During his colonization attempt in 1873 Oewel had already mentioned the prospect of this railroad line. Therefore, the Dutch-American Land and Emigration Company wanted to try its luck there with the help of many Netherlanders.[17] This effort led to a scandal that greatly surpassed in magnitude the scandal of Nijgh and his henchmen. This time the failure was not due to highly touted "aristocratic" plans but to the rigorous religious and philanthropic character that the promoters tried to give to this venture. Every single social group in our dear fatherland by turns experienced the exploitation by "American" land salesmen. One is amazed by their inventiveness and inexhaustible energy, up to our present times, thanks in particular to their "Dutch" partners!

This Dutch-American Land and Emigration Company was organized in 1892 by [Albertus] Zoutman and C. W. Van der Hoogt who had been able to obtain cooperation especially from the strict Dutch Reformed groups in the Netherlands. No one else but Professor M. Noordtzij of Kampen* became the chairman of the board of this new organization. He was attracted by the "pure" philanthropic purpose of this organization that wanted to be of service particularly to its orthodox constituents. If land was sold, the company would be satisfied with a "moderate interest" for its shareholders from "slimmer profits."[18]

---

*Maarten Noordtzij was a respected professor of theology at Kampen Theological Seminary, and a man of some influence in the Reformed Churches (Gereformeerde Kerken).

The two other supervisory directors, J. Den Boer and |Karel De| Vidal were also very respected and well-known men in their circles. As in so many similar cases, it was the names of these directors that inspired confidence, and therefore the plans of this organization were supported by many Christian newspapers. Even the liberal press was sympathetic towards them.[19] Plans were to establish a Dutch colony of farmers, preferably with a Calvinistic background, in the San Luis Valley in Colorado, where the Land Company claimed to have purchased fifteen thousand acres of outstanding land from the Empire Land and Canal Company. The Company distributed a brochure that promised a very attractive future to buyers of its lands. A farmer with only eighty acres could, of course, make a substantial living for his family and meet all his obligations. In addition, he would make a net profit of six or seven thousand guilders per year. In short, within a few years he could very easily be wallowing in wealth! And all this was possible in "the Italy of western North America" among "the grandiose beauties of nature" to which "the most ignorant heathen would bow down in adoration."

"After a long, careful and competent inspection," as the directors of the organization called it, they were fortunate to buy some of this paradise land that was so eminently suited for Dutch colonists. The director, Zoutman, "agriculturist and state observer of the United States of North America, stationed at Alamosa," had personally led this investigation "without considering the pains nor expense." This land would be offered to the Dutch immigrants not only ready to be cultivated but also ready for habitation and for the price of only $26 per acre, a price that was so low that it had soon to be raised to $30 an acre.[20]

It is no wonder that where such splendid promises were made and broadcast by such trusted and highly regarded men as Noordtzij and others, prospective settlers flocked from every corner of the Netherlands in order to share in this felicity that was beaming down upon them from Colorado "under the high protection of the government" there. It was a time when the raging agricultural crisis in Europe threatened many with a reduction to beggary. Interested people came daily to the office of the company in Utrecht, where it was "at times very busy." The "directors" themselves went to great lengths to travel extensively across the country to enlighten further the brothers, and their prospects as described in the brochure were further blown up. Thus, for instance, the net gain of six and a half thousand guilders was only a "minimum." That brochure also put certain words in the mouth of the only Dutch farmer in the San Luis Valley, the aforementioned T. Te Linde: "I won't do it for that amount, the land can produce more."[21] As appeared later, these claims were totally unjustified.

As a result, numerous small farmers decided to establish themselves in the San Luis Valley. In that same year the company made arrangements to send about two hundred emigrants to Colorado. The date to sail was set at October 15, 1892, while a second group of another two hundred would leave in early February, 1893. The initial success of this venture could really be described as extraordinary. But the proposed journey of the second group never took place, since by that time the Utrecht organization had already been unmasked as a fraud.[22]

The series of disappointments began already before the first group had embarked; their departure had to be delayed for four weeks, due to an outbreak of cholera. Most of them had sold their household possessions and now their homes had been rented out to others. This coupled with many other difficulties became a costly affair for them, since they had to do without any income during all that time. Besides, many became more and more concerned about the additional delay because the late date of departure meant that they would arrive in the promised land in the dead of winter. Those who had been more careful had held off on this account and did not report for the first trip.

Saturday morning, November 12, 1892, the emigrants boarded the ship at Amsterdam, led by J. Van Boven, publisher-editor of the small paper *De Oranjevaan* [*The Orange Banner*] in Zuid Beveland [Netherlands]. In good conscience he had accepted for this journey, although conditionally, the job of administrator with the Dutch-American Land and Emigration Company. Because of his position he was later able to unmask the designs of this "philanthropic" organization. Zoutman, who had promised to lead them personally, was not on board their ship, the *Dubbeldam*; but strangely enough and to their dismay, he had boarded another ship, the *Veendam*, which left on the same day for New York.

After a terrible stormy voyage they arrived at Hoboken on November 26 and director Zoutman showed himself again to be anything but a leader. He declined to accompany his colonists to Ellis Island. Being steerage passengers, they had to go through an inspection as required by American law. Originally, he had promised to be there to speed up this inspection. This disappointment was all the greater for colonists meeting for the first time their newly chosen "father" land, because they received bad treatment from the inspectors, whose dishonesty was blatant, a common everyday thing. Without flattery Van Boven wrote: "They engage in under-the-counter dealings as much here as elsewhere.... With money and hard liquor one can accomplish much here also."[23]

Sunday afternoon the Netherlanders left Jersey City by express train for St. Louis. There they had to transfer to continue their journey to Colorado. St. Louis, as well as Chicago, are inland terminal stations—the only two in the United States—where all passengers must transfer. After a long, tiresome train trip they arrived in Alamosa on November 30, 1892. The citizens of that small town gave them a hearty welcome. The arrival of immigrants was a considerable boost for this area that was still very thinly populated in spite of all the publicity. The citizens gave the newcomers an "excellent dinner" at the "Concert Hall." Besides, many received free lodging on that first night among the people.

They were fortunate, since the houses for the immigrants were not entirely completed in the new colony about seven miles from Alamosa when the colonists arrived. Thus they had to get along with difficulty in their new location. After a short train ride from Alamosa, they arrived at their destination on December 1. "How busy it was! The arrival of all these people was quite something. It was quite a job to unload the boxes and chests and move them into the buildings so that each would have its proper place. What a noise—you could hardly hear or see. It was bewildering."[24] After this period of busy work, they investigated their surroundings and were greatly dismayed by the first meeting with their El Dorado.

The date of the formation of the San Luis Valley is of a later period than the other "parks" in Colorado. It was formed by the sinking away of the subsoil and produced a trough, which was not exclusively composed of igneous rock as claimed by the geologist [F. V.] Hayden,[25] but sandstone, according to Bowman.[26] For a long time this depression had been a large lake collecting sediment during the late Tertiary Period and Pleistocene or Ice Age. The mountains surrounding the valley were covered with glaciers that brought down additional rubble. At the same time the Rio Grande cut its way through the depression and changed the lake into a vast alluvial plain covered with glacial debris.

It is important for us to know this, because this information disproves Hayden's statement, widely spread in publicity brochures, that the San Luis Valley was constituted exclusively of volcanic—igneous—material that is generally very fertile. The Utrecht organization in its brochure also considerably overrated the availability of minerals in the soils of the San Luis Valley. The latter description of how the valley was formed agrees better with the reality and helps us to understand better what Van Boven wrote about the land of this colony: "As you view the land it is far from being enticing. Around the immigrant homes it looked like an arid plain without end." The soil, which had not been cultivated, as was the case with a large part of the land intended for the Dutch settlers, was covered in winter with all kinds of yellowish, dry growth—sagebrush, chico, and rabbitbrush. According to the brochure the soil was composed of a seven-foot layer of fertile clay, and therefore fertilization was totally unnecessary. But it was nothing more than a thick layer of drift sand, at times no more than a few feet deep. It might be possible to grow a small crop during the first years, and then the soil would be exhausted and useless. In short, the soil that they had bought for $26 an acre turned out to be, according to experts, not worth $5 an acre.[27]

Another important factor was the lack of trees. "There wasn't a tree in sight on the whole monotonous dry plain. Only along rivers and creeks near the mountains you would find some. Elsewhere in the valley there is nothing. That is perhaps the main reason why it has such an uninviting and lonesome appearance. It is always the same. In the distance there are mountains but they are too far away to enjoy their beauty."[28] Neither was the climate desirable. Zoutman had said that cold weather was unknown and overcoats were not needed. Therefore, they suffered unnecessarily and very heavily during the month of December when the temperature often dipped far below zero. On the 17th of December it even went down to 30 degrees below zero Fahrenheit.[29]

The atmosphere of irritation, almost always present among colonists, grew to open dissatisfaction due to the irresponsible management and extremely deficient leadership of the directors. The colonists' attitude changed to plain disgust when it was realized that the heating of the houses was deficient, that there was a lack of firewood, that drinking water ran short because it had to be brought in in drums, and that several times food ran out. "The first Saturday we spent there, the bread wagon came only at five o'clock P.M.. The children cried for bread and the parents were embittered and grumbled about the poor administration. Some colonists threatened to leave on the spot if conditions did not change immediately." [Jan] Zwier, one of the most level-headed men, "was so disturbed since there was no food for his children, that he decided to leave at once."[30]

This was the spirit in the colony, but those conditions also showed the mettle of the colonists. Especially if one compares this situation with what Van Raalte and his followers faced, one sees the difference, which can be ascribed only in part to the different tenor of the times. Now we can also understand why the San Luis Valley colonization finally came to naught; greater misfortunes than the late 5 o'clock bread wagon would plague them. Truly, continually darker clouds formed over the colonists. They became acquainted with T. Te Linde and others in the valley, who enlightened them about the San Luis soil. Then it became plain they had been swindled. The brochure of the Utrecht organization was nothing but a bunch of lies and proved to be a "mockery of the truth."[31]

Zoutman himself, the "agricultural engineer" and "state observer," became unmasked as an adventurer. For a few years he had worked at the office of the Holland-American Steamship Company at Rotterdam and then left for America and found work in Denver, Colorado, again as an office clerk. Here he met a Dutchman named [?] Zelle who built irrigation works. His job consisted in carrying the surveyor's measuring chain "as boys in the Netherlands do for a surveyor!" This director had declared in the Netherlands that he had lived in the San Luis Valley "for several years," but now it became evident that he had never been there before February, 1892. Besides, his investigation of this outstanding land had neither been done for a "long time," nor "thoroughly," nor "expertly." It was not even worthy of the word *investigation*.

Even more grating was the outrageous profit of at least *fl.* 57.50 [$23] per person that the "philanthropic" organization had made on the traveling cost of the emigrants. The "Messrs." Van der Hoogt and Zoutman also declared before God and their conscience that the price of $26 per acre was in keeping with the Christian philanthropic principles of the organization, since they had had to pay about $23 an acre. Afterwards it became clear to the colonists that the promoters could have bought the land for $11.25 per acre. Thus, they would have made a huge profit here also. I expressly said, "could have bought," because it finally turned out that the Utrecht company only held an option on fifteen thousand acres but lacked the capital to pay for it! Even in installments they could not pay for it! In addition, the land was not level and therefore it was not suitable everywhere for irrigation purposes. Not a single artesian well was present, and harvesting in July, as the "experts" had claimed, was out of the question. Only by September could a mere twenty-five bushels of wheat per acre be brought in, and not thirty or forty as promised. It was like the experiences of the Hollandia Company in Humboldt County, California.

The Utrecht company did not have enough capital to swing the deal! So few bonds had been sold that money had to be borrowed to transport the first colonists to Colorado. Still there was a shortage of money. During the middle of December the directors in the Netherlands tried to obtain $2,000 from the administrators in the San Luis Valley. But in the valley there was even less money available. The directors had to pay the carpenter $2,500 for erecting the immigrant homes. To T. C. Henry, president of the Empire Land and Canal Company—one of many such land companies that had taken over bits and pieces of the former Costilla Estate of the United States Freehold and Emigration Company—they had to pay a sum of $5,000 cash on December 1st as a second installment for the option on the land. Well, this money was not available. By a slippery maneuver, Zoutman and Van der Hoogt tried to cover the bill by having the colonists sign their drafts and entrust these to them; only a few had refused to do this. An inquiry at the bank in Alamosa revealed that the money of the colonists, about $11,000 to $12,000, had been deposited in Van der Hoogt's account the day before and then somewhat later in the account of the Dutch-American Land and Emigration Company.

When Messrs. Van der Hoogt and Zoutman failed to pay the $5,000 due to Henry, even after he had waited many days, he finally decided not to transfer the land to these "administrators." This caused a shock among the colonists and especially among those who had handed over their signed drafts! Four colonists—J. Zwier, A. Heersink, G. Van Dalen, and J. De Kruijter—who risked losing the most money, went to Alamosa that same evening, December 10, 1892, to confer with the lawyer McDonald as to what could be done. Immediately the account of the Utrecht Company at the First National Bank of Alamosa was blocked by court order. The following Tuesday, Zoutman and Van der Hoogt were forced to transfer the money to the account of the colonists who could either cash in their money or leave it in the bank.[32]

The deal was still hampered because Henry refused to give the land to Zoutman and Van der Hoogt, as he confirmed in a telegram to J. Van Boven who was more or less in charge since the "administrators" were not available. Naturally, the administrators complained, as if they were being victimized and they did not refrain from calling the land owner, T. C. Henry, a scoundrel. He in turn called Zoutman and Van der Hoogt "scoundrels and swindlers"! A very tense meeting was held by the colonists, the "gentlemen," and the mayor of Alamosa. The mayor wanted to protect the Dutch farmers and assure them of his and the citizens' sympathy. They could come to no agreement and even some fist fights broke out!

But to the astonishment of the colonists that same afternoon, after Henry had tried in vain to sell land directly to the farmers at $15 to $20 an acre, he was seen again in the company of "Messrs." Zoutman and Van der Hoogt. Then at a new meeting, Henry declared that the "misunderstanding" had been cleared up and everything was completely in order. The board of directors had assured Henry that there was plenty of money, which he believed. He again considered the Utrecht gentlemen as his friends. After all, Henry tried to get rid of some land that was not of the best quality! Shortly thereafter, Van der Hoogt and Zoutman left the colony and the latter never returned. But again, they could not meet their obligations to Henry, who finally declared that he refused to cede the land to the Utrecht Company.

One can imagine how upset the colonists were. Now they were completely left to themselves and hardly knew what to do. Their misery increased and was worsened by the severe cold weather. There was an outbreak of communicable diseases, especially scarlet fever and diphtheria. Many children suffered from it, but also adults. A total of eleven children died in the homes of the immigrants and many remained sick. "It was a terrible situation in the homes." It was so terrible that the citizens of Alamosa called a few meetings and laid plans to help the Dutch in their dire distress.[33]

Van Boven, however, thought it was going too far, "that others were preparing to work for us, decide about us, and take care of our interests, all without our participation." He feared "that our independence would be endangered and also the unity in the colony, especially should the Americans come to settle our affairs." At Van Boven's suggestion, on Sunday morning, December 18, before the worship service, a "Committee of Farmers" [*Boeren-Comité*] was chosen by the heads of families to administer the affairs of the colony. It consisted of L. Verburg, D. Sjaardema, J. Zwier, F. Zijlstra, and A. J. Van Lummel. Their first act was to send a telegram to Professor Noordtzij at Kampen about the circumstances: "Neglect of our affairs and those of Company necessitates dismissal delegate and director. Otherwise liquidation and dispersal. Request immediate empowerment of Braamse and Van Boven."[34]

Moreover, the committee decided that they would act independently of the Utrecht Company and that they would not first await Noordtzij's announced arrival. Various land companies offered land for sale to the committee and they went to investigate the various offers. Finally, they chose the so-called Empire Farm five miles south of Alamosa. This land also belonged to Henry and his Empire Land and Canal Company. With the permission of the heads of families of the colony, Van Boven, Zijlstra, and Van Lummel made a deal with Henry at Denver, which everybody acknowledged as being "very fair." The Dutch could buy the land of the Empire Farm that had been cultivated, partly plowed, and was completely ready for irrigation at $17.50 per acre. This included enough homes for the various families, the perpetual water rights, the barns, and the fences. On the property there were also four extra large buildings with barns for which they had to pay $1,200 separately. For the maintenance of the canals, they would pay at most 10¢ an acre per year, a very small sum compared to the 50¢ per acre per year the Utrecht Company had wanted to charge the colonists.

Payment would be made in five yearly installments. The initial payment could be made after the first harvest, if so desired. In this way, those who had no money could also buy land. The company went out of its way to furnish to those who had nothing at all a set of horses, a cow, hogs, chickens, needed equipment, enough money for food until the harvest, and household equipment. Naturally, in time it had to be paid back. In case of a crop failure or other reverse beyond the fault of the buyer, payment of the installments could be delayed one year.[35]

Already on Old Year's Day [New Year's Eve] a few families moved to their new homes. Then on January 4, 1893, the rest of the families with their household goods, etc., were moved by special train to their new location without cost. "There was thankfulness because of the turn of events" and with renewed faith they entered the future. Despite the urging of Van der Hoogt, only three or four families decided to await the arrival of Professor Noordtzij, while others, due to the sickness of their children, were forced to remain for the time being in the immigrant homes.

Thursday, January 12, 1893, Noordtzij arrived in Alamosa and examined the original immigrant homes and on the following day the new colony. As chairman of the board of the Utrecht Company, he launched an inquiry. After hours of discussion and of listening to the complaints, he finally refused, to the dismay of the colonists, to acknowledge any fault and would not dismiss Zoutman and Van der Hoogt.[36]

At the request of the Dutch government the American authorities investigated the complaints of the colonists and confirmed them. The American authorities pointed out that the articles of incorporation of the Land and Emigration Company were faulty and that they owned no land, as Noordtzij had claimed they did, even after the meeting. All they had was an option and in nearly all cases the Company had lured the colonists to Colorado under false pretenses. They had not fulfilled their obligation of furnishing land and work, as they had promised to the colonists before they left the Netherlands, etc., etc.[37] Noordtzij called the report biased and challenged its correctness, while his company continued to spread lies! It is no wonder the colonists refused to have any further connections with the Utrecht Company and completely lost faith in Noordtzij.[38]

Some farmers, however, remained loyal to Noordtzij and his aides and settled at Crook in the valley on the Platte River in northeastern Colorado. The governor of "the Centennial State" (Colorado had become a state one hundred years after the Declaration of Independence of the United States) had drawn the attention of the colonists to that region because there was still government land available, "enough for a large colony." Noordtzij and Van der Hoogt held an "investigation" and "right away" moved their people to this place. According to Van Boven, this was even more reckless and irresponsible than what they had done to the San Luis Valley colonists.[39] Van der Hoogt and Noordtzij tried in vain to persuade the remaining colonists to settle in this very arid region. Most of them remained on the Empire Farm where they would never become rich but where they could make a decent living once they had paid off their debts after a few years. In any case, the land was much better in quality than they could have obtained for $26 an acre from the Utrecht Company.

The future did not look too dark. The valley afforded a fairly good living. Therefore, they put forth efforts to encourage other Netherlanders to come and settle in the new village named Rilland, in remembrance of Zuid Beveland's Rilland.[40] A school was established with Zijlstra as principal and — above all—a Reformed congregation. The Christian Reformed Dutch Americans had helped to organize that church, in particular A. J. Van den Heuvel, the preacher of the True brothers at Rotterdam, Kansas. He had become acquainted, through news items in an American newspaper, with the plight of the colonists in the San Luis Valley. He promised to help and received permission from his consistory to go to the Colorado colonists for three weeks and give material and spiritual aid where needed. Many times he preached for them in the school building and led them to organize a congregation. L. Verburg, A. J. Van Lummel, and H.|arm| Mulder were chosen as elders; J. Van Dalen, and D. Sjaardema as deacons. In all things Van den Heuvel was "a true friend" for whose coming they could not be thankful enough.[41]

Later a second congregation, named Bethel, was organized, most likely by those who had settled in the dry Platte River valley voluntarily or through nice promises and threats. They also tried to strengthen their colony by urging Netherlanders to join them. Thus two competing colonies were established, besides the one in and around Maxwell City, New Mexico. J. Zwier had moved here where he became one of the most influential colonists among the Dutch. However, the colonists became bitterly disappointed also in their new expectations. If I may use the expression, they did not "take root" since they spent only a very short time in Colorado.

Because of the spiritual labors of Reverend Van den Heuvel, a better feeling was brought about at Rilland. However, troubles further undermined their hope for a better future, so that in the same year of 1893 they decided that only a move somewhere else would ensure their future. The soil around Rilland also proved to be too poor and there was no guarantee of enough water. Besides, there was only one market center where they could sell their products, at Alamosa, and there was only one buyer there, the Alamosa Milling and Elevator Company. Industry hardly existed there, so the Dutch had no other choice but to work the land. Moreover, their American neighbors gave them a very hard time by driving their horses, cows, and hogs on the land of the Netherlanders, which would be eaten bare in no time at all.[42]

Through *De Wachter*, the weekly church paper, members of the Christian Reformed Church learned about the plight of their Colorado kinsmen. Already in January, 1893, this paper mentioned how they had been misled and fooled. Through the efforts of Reverend Van den Heuvel a closer contact was established. After Van den Heuvel, it was especially Reverend H. Bode, reared in Ridott, Illinois, and appointed in August, 1892, as an itinerant minister in the West, who became concerned about their welfare.[43] Also his brother, Reverend C. Bode, stood up for them. In an article in *De Wachter*, "Distress in Alamosa," he asked for help for the colonists there who "had been brought out of the Netherlands in a shameful manner."[44] Thanks to these two ministers, people in Sioux County began to sympathize and money was collected in Orange City to move them there from Colorado.[45] Through Reverend H. Bode, a number of these unfortunate people were settled in and around Sioux Center and Rock Valley, both in Sioux County, Iowa.[46] Others went to Luctor, Kansas, and still others returned to the Netherlands.[47] Most of them, as can well be imagined, had no possessions left. *De Wachter* openly reported that one family which had "fled" to Luctor, Kansas, had been swindled out of *fl.* 3,000 [$1,200] by Zoutman and Van der Hoogt.[48]

Thus the colony in Colorado completely disintegrated. When considering the reasons for this failure one thinks in the first place, just as in the case of California, about the recklessness in organizing the whole enterprise. This enterprise was all the more loathsome since it was conducted under the cloak of religiosity. The Utrecht Company was considered, in essence, to be "an association of very unreformed Hollanders operating under a Reformed flag."[49] So be it. Already in the Netherlands people had questioned Zoutman's "religiosity."[50] But that does not remove the fact that it was the Reformed [*Gereformeerden*], although with good intentions, who through their participation, contributed to a great degree to the initial success, but also to the debacle that soon followed, even though this was due to their irresponsible gullibility and stiff-headedness, to put it mildly.

The Utrecht Company was reckless to start with a greatly insufficient amount of capital, in their choice of land, and in their timing of the colonists' departure for America. They were reckless practically in everything—everything, that is, except one thing, their choice of colonists. They were careful to choose mostly farmers with at least some capital. In general most of the Colorado colonists belonged to the lower middle class and some farmers were even well-to-do. As they traveled through St. Louis, it was evident that they were "respectable and suitable" men.[51] Reverend C. Bode also noticed that they were people of some means. He wrote in *De Wachter*, that "they came from various provinces, from Noord Holland, Zeeland, Drenthe, Overijsel, Friesland, Groningen, Gelderland, and Noord Brabant; they [the women] went to church with golden helmets [traditional cauls under their lace cap] and golden corkscrews [traditional, spiral, head-ornaments worn at the side of the temples]."[52] Neither should we forget the $11,000 or $12,000 that Van der Hoogt tried to deposit in his personal bank account!

These Netherlanders—leaving aside one or two exceptions—belonged to a desirable class of pioneers who could be expected to succeed, after the Committee of Farmers was formed, and especially after they had settled in Rilland. In contrast with the California Netherlanders, they were professionals and surely not "softies." One can read in *De Wachter*, that "some walk around with a big open-blade knife in their pocket."[53] That certainly is an indication of stalwart men. The fact that neither Zoutman, Van der Hoogt, nor Noordtzij ever had an encounter with those knives also indicates that these men had self-control, will power, and a certain amount of breeding. These were all good qualities to insure success. Indeed, our own consul in St. Louis spoke about an "encouraging future."[54] Especially, since after the initial disappointments caused by the "inexperience of the directors"—Oh, such diplomatic language!—they had reorganized themselves under "other leaders" (the Committee of Farmers).

Yet, already in 1893 they were hit by adversity. Their will power had already been undermined by too high expectations followed by deep disappointments. Now the last straw broke the camel's back. The Netherlanders were too unfamiliar with the Colorado soil and the Colorado climate. The dry climate made irrigation works necessary, but they knew very little about this. They were forced to use agricultural methods entirely new to them. Again it shows us how important it is to settle in areas whose land and climate, at least on the whole, are similar to those in the motherland.

It was not just the land and climate in themselves, but rather the colonists' inexperience with these new circumstances that prevented a permanent settlement in the San Luis Valley. This is clearly demonstrated by the fact that at the beginning of the twentieth century a new contingent of "Netherlanders" arrived at Alamosa and settled in Rilland. But they were Dutch Americans with years of experience in American practices.

In 1893, only one family remained in Rilland, namely the family of C. [actually Adolph] Heersink. It had been one of the most well-to-do, but because they had spent a large part of their capital for buying farmland, they remained attached more strongly to the San Luis Valley than others.[55] The presence of just one single Dutch family has repeatedly triggered other families to come and establish a colony, the oldest "example" being that of Beukma at Lafayette, Indiana. This happened in Colorado also. In a short time the Heersinks had company. Several came and went, for indeed the land and climate were hard on farmers and farming, although the geographer Russell Smith labeled the San Luis Park as "a fine agricultural valley" and Van Boven expected "thousands upon thousands" to settle in the valley. At present, the total number of inhabitants in the valley is no more than 30,000, and the small number of Netherlanders included in this number threatens to disappear completely, especially in times of drought.

No matter how many Netherlanders left, the Heersinks remained. Then others would come again and strengthen their numbers, attracted by that same too dry and repulsive climate. A particular circumstance would then be the deciding factor: the healthful mountain climate. Earlier [W.] Blackmore, Professor [R. P. A.] Dozy, and others had not exaggerated in this respect; Blackmore had even predicted correctly that Colorado had a bright future and would one day become a health resort because of the dry air that was a boon for many health seekers. Many Holland Americans came for health reasons and settled temporarily or permanently near the Heersinks. At present there are about twenty families and a few singles, some of whom suffer from tuberculosis or asthma. But in spite of this adverse condition, they have been able to achieve a certain prosperity although they did not become rich. For this they would have had to go to Iowa. Nearly all have possessions.[56] The Heersinks rented part of their property to others. They were mainly engaged in farming and grew wheat, oats, barley, peas (so-called "field peas"), and especially alfalfa, also known as lucerne. Near the rivers the growing of hay was also important.[57]

Only a few live in the small town of Alamosa, "the Hub of the Valley," which has now a population of 3,500. It is their marketplace and has thus no less than three banks. Most of the Netherlanders live in the "country," where a Christian Reformed congregation of twenty families was organized in 1904.[58] About nine miles from the town a church was built and in 1923 also a parsonage. At present G. Zijlstra is their pastor. The congregation calls itself Alamosa; the name Rilland has gone into oblivion. Nearby lies Henry, a railroad station, which is the only geographical name that reminds them of the bitter conditions of 1892.

10

Settlements in the Northwest

A. In Washington and Oregon

A familiar phenomenon in newly developed countries is the lack of capital, resulting in very high interest rates. An example of this phenomenon is seen in the development of the United States, which already previously had drawn the attention of Roscher in his *Onderzoekingen over het Koloniewezen* [*Investigations Concerning Colonization*].[1] Indeed, this fact had also been noted by European financiers, in particular those in the Netherlands! Dutch capital had played a role in the development of the East and after that of the Midwest, which was notorious for its railroad swindles! In the nineties this Dutch capital was also sought after for the development of the extreme Northwest, the Pacific Northwest, and for the South—the new South; and it was offered in generous amounts. A part of these loans were made, however, through the newly-formed mortgage banks that were established for this purpose.

Interest rates in the United States are still at the present time very high, depending upon the distance westward or southward from the centers of capital in the Northeast. In December, 1918, they were 6.5 to 7 percent west of the Mississippi; 7 to 8 percent west of the Rocky Mountains; going south to South Carolina and Tennessee, 7 percent; in Florida, Louisiana, and Texas, 8 percent; and in New Mexico and Arizona, even 9 percent. Since then, these figures must not have changed much, since interest rates drop "extremely gradually," according to J. C. Kempees, from whom I took the above data.[2] This observation is confirmed, for instance, in the annual reports of mortgage banks currently operating in America. Thus, the average mortgage rate of one of these banks in the Northwest was 7.88 percent and 7.84 percent in 1922 and 1924, respectively. However, the amounts of the loans outstanding were usually not very large.[3]

It is the great difference in interest that one can earn in America compared to what one must pay in Europe—the latter averages 5 percent—that primarily made the mortgage business in the "newer" American states so attractive for English, Scotch, as well as Dutch, investors. The above-mentioned American bank, in the years 1922 and 1924, respectively, paid an average of 4.90 percent and 4.94 percent on mortgage bonds.[4] The bank also earned commissions and profit on real estate. In October, 1883, the first Netherlands bank for this purpose was established in Amsterdam, the Nederlandsche-Amerikaanse Land Maatschappij [Netherlands-American Land Company], which in the beginning sought a field of operations in Canada. After that it operated especially in Minnesota, from St. Paul, and later also acquired "interests" in Iowa, Indiana, Dakota, Montana, etc. It even became involved in the cotton plantations in the South.[5]

The extreme Northwest (formerly the Territory of Columbia and now Washington State) was opened by the Northern Pacific and the Great Northern, which railroads reached their Seattle terminal in 1883 and 1892, respectively, and by the Union Pacific, which made Portland, Oregon, one of its end stations. Soon afterwards, the attention of Dutch capital was drawn above all to this very promising area. H. A. Van Valkenburg became our financial pioneer there. In 1885 there was founded in Washington's capital, Olympia, the Northwestern and Pacific Mortgage Company, which was headquartered in Spokane Falls City—later shortened to Spokane—with Van Valkenburg as director.

American taxation policy, which among other things demanded high fees from similar companies founded and operating in America, led to the dissolution of the company and in 1889 to the establishment of the Northwestern and Pacific Hypotheekbank [Mortgage Bank] in Amsterdam that took over all the rights and obligations of the "N. and P. Mortgage Company." This mortgage bank had difficult years, just as so many other pioneer businesses. Above all, the crisis of 1893 made heavy demands upon it, due particularly to the management in America that was at first disappointing. "Foreign management" is always the weak spot in this kind of mortgage banks. In this case it led to bankruptcy in 1898, but it ended in a settlement.[6]

After its reorganization, however, the Northwestern and Pacific Hypotheekbank became a flourishing institution. This was not surprising because, to cite but one example, in the depression year of 1893 the scarcity of money was so severe in the Pacific Northwest that, according to the testimony of the Dutch businessman, G. O. Van Wijk, who traveled there at that time, farmers and storekeepers had to pay the bankers 4 to 6 percent interest *per month*, plus 2 to 3 percent commission.[7] Hence, in that same crisis year of 1893 a third mortgage bank was established despite the risk of doing business. Since that time many others have been formed, including three in 1911 and seven in 1912. There was a total of twenty Dutch mortgage banks headquartered in the United States and in Canada in 1918, of which there were five in Spokane, three in Seattle (four in 1920), and one in Portland. All these cities were in the extreme Northwest.[8]

However interesting it might be as an expression of the Dutch spirit of enterprise, it lies outside the scope of my study to explore the development of this business in America. I refer those who are interested in pursuing this topic to Van Oss' *Effectenboeken* [*Securities Books*], among others. Suffice it for me to point out that these banks fulfilled their none too philanthropic task of providing capital with varying degrees of success. But there were great differences. The Holland-Texas Hypotheekbank paid a dividend of 15 percent in 1923.[9] Over against that, the North-American Hypotheekbank was recently threatened by "forced liquidation" and has since gone into bankruptcy.[10] Meanwhile, the Hypotheekbank voor Amerika [Mortgage Bank for America] has been liquidated, as well as the oldest of this type of bank, the Ned.-Am. Land Mij. [Netherlands-American Land Company]. The results of the Netherlands-American Hypotheekbank were "very discouraging" in 1926.

Of utmost concern to us is the question as to how much the mortgage banks influenced the settlements of Netherlanders and possibly even the founding of specific colonies. In spite of my efforts, I would not presume to be able to give an altogether satisfactory answer to this question because a nebulous atmosphere surrounds everything that has to do with trading in land and in people, with emigration and colonization. The annual reports of the mortgage banks, as far as I know, tell us almost nothing concerning our subject. As a matter of fact, according to Kempees, who was closely involved with this business, they "often reveal as little as possible." At most, these reports lead to certain conjectures.

Therefore, my direct questions addressed to several directors or their representatives in America are of greater importance. Had their business furthered emigration to America, aside from the resettling of a few of their directors or managers who were in charge of the operations of their banks? "The settling of Netherlanders has always occurred indirectly," E. J. Everwijn Lange wrote to me, and he confirmed this orally.[11] "The Dutch mortgage banks that operate in the United States have no influence on the settlements," J. C. Kempees declared to me in an interview, as distinct from those—and that is significant—"that have their sphere of action in Canada." Several directors graciously complied by providing answers to other questions, but they neglected to answer my main question. One writer definitely aroused my suspicion when he wrote "that we cannot provide the information that would be relevant to your purpose."[12]

Due to the very nature of their business, mortgage banks are closely related to the real estate business, if not from the beginning, then surely as time goes on. However, by now several states of the Union had denied foreign companies the right to own land unless it was obtained through repossession of mortgage property or to settle a claim. These American restrictions explain the difference in operation between American and Canadian banks. Sometimes, but not in Washington State, companies had to divest themselves of such possessions within a specified time. Now the oldest mortgage company, the Ned.-Am. Land Mij. [Netherlands-American Land Company], as the name indicates, was originally closely involved with land affairs in Canada.[13] Later on it stood in very close relation with the Maatschappij voor Landbezit in Amerika en Canada [Company for Land Ownership in America and Canada]; already in 1895 G. O. Van Wijk spoke of its "possessions."

In that same year the Northwestern and Pacific Hypotheekbank seems to have been forced to change partially into a real estate company.[14] Especially after lean harvest years, banks came into possession of land, some more and some less. Repossession occurred all the more frequently since, as we have seen earlier, Americans are easily inclined to move and abandon their homes and land. Very often they also do so without having fulfilled their obligations. The numerous annual reports of banks are an eloquent testimony to these matters. And whenever a bank was forced to hold abandoned farms for years—one also reads of these complaints—it is very understandable that fellow countrymen were sought. The banks favored them because, aside from a few bad apples [kwaden], they generally had better success cultivating the soil, they were less inclined to abandon it quickly, and they were more thrifty and more reliable in fulfilling their financial obligations. It was precisely for these reasons, too, that Netherlanders were less frequently compelled to take out mortgages than were Americans.

Van Wijk, who was himself a holder of several mortgage bonds of the "Northwestern and Pacific" company, became well aware of the contrasts between American and Dutch farmers during his "inspection" trip in the Northwest. He even spoke of "the stupidity, laziness, and recklessness of the American farmers," in contrast to the diligence and good judgment of the Dutch farmers, who combined land tillage with cattle-breeding.[15] Thanks to this "mixed" farming, they suffered far less from the grain crisis of 1893. So sharply does this "interested party" accentuate that difference that one may see it as a direct "hint" to the directors of his mortgage bank, in addition to the other ample advice Van Wijk's letters usually contained.

What must one think of an obscure monthly, Van Overzee [From Overseas], distributed in our country in 1919 and 1920, which contained all kinds of information about Canada and the United States?[16] Especially the front page illustration is eye-catching: a harvest scene, so abundant—with the enticing Statue of Liberty in the background!—that the message is plain. The "effect" of it could hardly be surpassed by any real estate paper. The mortgage banks made its publication possible and placed advertising in it. It is thus uncertain to what extent one can speak of a "direct" promotion of emigration, also because the meaning of the word direct is variously interpreted, as I found out. But the mortgage banks had an interesting "indirect" influence on Netherlanders settling in the Northwest.

With regard to the Northwest, one must distinguish between two quite different areas. There is first the mountainous, deeply indented coastal area, of which Puget Sound Valley forms the center. It is a "valley" that drowned for the most part due to its sinking and the scouring action of the "piedmont" and "valley" glaciers. A deep fiord was formed, now Puget Sound, in which the unsubmerged mountain tops and ridges formed numerous islands. One of these, Whidbey Island, gained a special significance for the Netherlanders, as we shall see later. The rivers that discharge into the fiord have formed small but very fertile deltas that enhance the significance of the "valley."[17]

Next to the fiordland there is secondly the remarkable basalt plain that lies east of the Cascades and is surrounded by them and the Rocky Mountains. Since the miocene age, this ground has been formed of volcanic rocks, especially lava, according to the most recent "thorough" studies of J. C. Russell.[18] These strata have greatly weathered, and formed in some places fertile, clay-like layers 20 meters |66 ft.| deep. This was formerly called the Spokane plain but is known now as the Columbia plain.

It is this latter land that first drew the attention of the Dutch financiers. It has a dry climate because it is set apart from the very rainy coastal area by

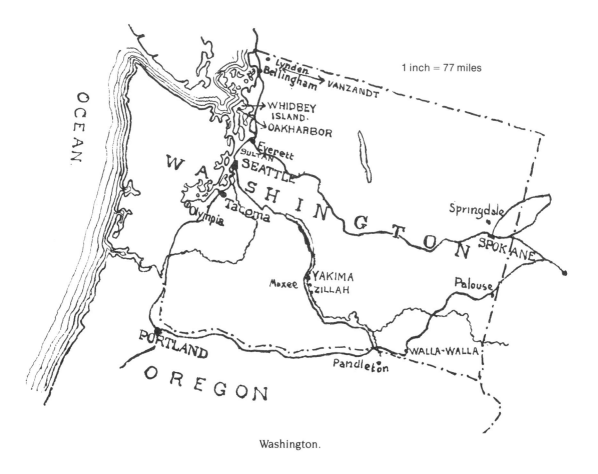

Washington.

the mountains surrounding it. Apparently the financiers' interest was due to the fact that the opening of the territory by the railroads, in which Dutch capital already had a long-time interest, proceeded from the East. Eventually, however, farmers and artisans from the Netherlands felt more at home in the Puget Sound Valley, because the sea climate there, although gentler than in the Netherlands, was more like the climate of their home country. This made it easier to adapt to the new environment.

It is difficult to discover who were the first Dutch colonists in the Northwest; a pioneer is seldom a recording historian. It is very likely that victims of the California colonization efforts settled here. Later on we will encounter several of them, and not the least worthy ones! The first Netherlanders one encounters in the extremely scarce literature are those in the Spokane plain. In 1839, Spokane was no more than a mission post of the Presbyterians, who had come here to compete with Roman Catholics and Methodists. The celebrated Flemish missionary [Pierre J.] De Smet visited this area in 1846.[19] Although he was full of praise for the valleys, he had little praise for the great plain; he called it "arid, undulating, covered with scrub grass, wormwood and cactus, and at the same time stony in many places." He did find "remarkable the volcanic and marble-like formations that stretch across that whole area."

Besides De Smet there were a number of other members of his order, the Jesuits, who preached here, e.g., A. Boeken and others. It must be this missionary spirit that explains why among the earliest Dutch residents of Spokane there were two parish priests, [Alphonsus M.] Verhagen and [Johannes H.] De Kanter. A third Netherlander, judging by his name, was probably the lawyer Tiel. These gentlemen lived there at the time of Van Wijk's visit in 1894.[20] Spokane, which in 1880 had no more than 800 inhabitants, was by then already a center of seven railroads and had grown to 30,000 souls. There were probably few Netherlanders among these, but in any case no fellow Dutch of any significance. In a sense this is substantiated by the fact that the representatives of the Northwestern and Pacific Hypotheekbank were the American-born, Messrs. [?] Binkley and [?] Taylor. The first Dutch resident of Spokane, probably the previously mentioned H. A. Van Valkenburg, who in any case lived there already in 1885, remained only briefly in Washington State, and could not properly be considered an "immigrant." Everwijn Lange assured me that there were very few there of our stock. When he traveled to Spokane in 1894 on behalf of his bank, he met only one Dutch family.[21]

There were already at that time several farmers of Dutch blood in the Palouse Valley, southeast of Spokane. I do not know to what extent their settlement was related to the Northwestern and Pacific Hypotheekbank. In any case, they were free of mortgages in December of 1894. It was these farmers for whom Van Wijk was so full of praise: "I visited one of the unencumbered farms, and it was wonderful to see how prosperous the owner was, and how much luxury he could permit himself even after the drought year of 1893."

From this it is clear that the description given to us by Van Wijk is completely different from the writings of De Smet fifty years earlier, probably because Van Wijk kept his eye almost exclusively on the valleys: "On one sleigh trip across the land, I saw fields covered with green, prepared for the following harvest. The soil is very fertile and without a single stone; the plow can be pulled by two horses."[22] One hears nothing of "aridity" here, which is understandable since Van Wijk traveled in winter, which in this area is the rainy period. Moreover, the writer was an optimist, apparently under the influence of numerous conversations.

Van Wijk comments further on the great significance of the flour industry for Spokane, and mentions a factory which operated day and night and still could not meet all the orders, especially from China. In spite of the poor times the mills earned 50 percent regularly, "and a flour mill in Spokane is a profitable venture, especially when the mill is operated by water power and nothing has to be spent on coal."[23] This was something to make the mouth water, also among Dutch capitalists! They took the hint to heart, although not at once. In 1901 in Amsterdam there was established a limited liability partnership, the Spokane Meelmolens [Flour Mills], a predominantly Dutch business with a capital of $fl.$ 10,000,000 [$4,000,000] in the spring of 1922, of which $fl.$ 2,452,500 [$981,000] was underwritten and paid in full. The company, the pride of Everwijn Lange, has experienced a period of great returns. It also operated "mills" in Seattle, the important outlet on Puget Sound, and in Pendleton in northern Oregon. The director of this business, L. C. Lens, was a man rich in American experience and with whom we became acquainted earlier in California. In 1922 there was already a change, and business diminished as a result of the economic crisis following the [First] World War. Heavy losses, far more than a million, were incurred. The mill in Seattle had to be rented out, and to prevent worse losses, the Spokane Meelmolens was made into a new "American" business, the Spokane Flour Mills, that attempted to save what could be saved.[24]

Van Wijk also mentioned the significance of waterpower for sawmill operations in which, reputedly, very great profits could be made. There was a follow-up to this hint also: a new enterprise arose. In April of 1898 there was established in Amsterdam a venture called the "Phoenix" sawmill, with a capital of $fl.$ 75,000 [$30,000], which in 1901 was increased to $fl.$ 500,000 [$200,000]. All the shares had been sold in 1903. One mill was rented from the Washington Water Power Company in Spokane. Initially the business prospered; in 1900 it produced a 12 percent profit and in 1902 even a profit of 30 percent. After that, however, reverses came so that the profit in 1904 had decreased to 2 percent.

One thing and another led in 1906 to the reorganization of the business,

in consultation with E. F. and P. M. Cartier van Dissel. Both of these gentlemen had come to California in the nineties through the efforts of Nijgh.
Later they moved to Washington State and became owners of extensive
timber lands and tillable lands, a total of approximately 10,000 acres, which
had originally been exploited by the Springdale Lumber Mill. With their
cooperation the "Phoenix" sawmill was reorganized as the "Phoenix Lumber Company," for which preferred capital of $100,000 was raised, and a
debenture loan of $200,000 was transacted, guaranteed by the Cartier van
Dissels who submitted their timber lands in Stevens County, Washington,
as collateral. E. J. Everwijn Lange in Amsterdam became director of the new
enterprise, and "ninety-ers" R. Insinger, E. F. and P. M. Cartier van Dissel
became supervisory directors. This new business, however, never prospered,
and since 1919 it has been in liquidation.[25] The "cream-skimming" stage
was past even sooner for this business than for the flour mills!

We wish to point out that these enterprises induced a great number of
Dutchmen to settle in the Northwest. In the first place, as we noted, the
"superintendents" (directors) and also the bookkeepers were Netherlanders. The same was true for a portion of the factory workers who "are
making a good living there," according to J. P. Guépin, director of the
Northwestern and Pacific Hypotheekbank, in a letter to me.[26] Although no
workers were recruited from overseas, still these enterprises "undoubtedly
contributed much to the immigration of Netherlanders," said Everwijn
Lange. He noted some striking examples, which I reported earlier, how the
presence of a single family or person led many others to join them in a sort
of "snow balling" effect in which one person is attracted by another. This is
genuine immigration because it occurs naturally.

When one considers the numerous Dutch mortgage banks that had their
main offices in Spokane, then one understands why this city in time became an important Dutch center. It was a trade and working man's colony
that counted only 24 Dutch-born persons in 1900 but had 168 already in
1910 and 183 in 1920. Dutch capital played a big part in the "making" and
development of this area, which Americans advertised optimistically and
with pride as "the Inland Empire." It was, above all, our mortgage banks
that furnished this capital.[27] Along with these we must also mention the
Holland Bank, established in 1896, which conducted a banking and credit
operation; it worked with an original capital of fl. 1,026,000 [$410,000], but
since 1906 this has been increased to fl. 4,000,000 [$1,600,000]. This banking
institution arose out of the reorganization of a companion company that
had been established with Dutch capital in 1890: The American National
Trust Company in Spokane. As a result of the depression of 1893, it had
suffered great losses and it had been reorganized under the same conditions as the previously mentioned mortgage company. Out of the Holland
Bank, whose board of directors included R. Insinger in Spokane, a new
organization was formed in 1924, the Holland Land Company, with a capital
of $5,000. Its purpose was to take over the real estate that through foreclo-

sures had been repossessed by the Holland Bank in connection with the agricultural crisis of the previous years. Henry Crommelin and Ch. A. O'Connor were the Spokane representatives on the board of directors of this most recent Dutch enterprise in this area.[28]

The Northwestern and Pacific Hypotheekbank, out of which a second bank developed since then, remains one of the most important institutions. R. Insinger was the managing clerk of both banks in Spokane. This Insinger is a characteristic figure, a typical Holland American who, just like Lens, the Cartier van Dissels, and so many others, came to America thanks to Nijgh's efforts. He endured much hardship, as is seen in the deep lines that mark his sharp features; I had the pleasure of briefly meeting Insinger. For ten or eleven years after his California "greenhorn time," he farmed in Canada, and after that, as did so many other Netherlanders, he went "down" to Washington State where he was naturalized as an American citizen.

It is through this person that the significance of the Dutch capital in the Northwest came to expression and was recognized by Americans. For years Insinger was chairman of the Chamber of Commerce in Spokane where he, like no one else, was seen and acknowledged as the financial leader. Along with Everwijn Lange in Amsterdam, who managed their affairs there, we may consider Insinger as one of the builders of the city of Spokane.[29]

The swift development of the "Inland Empire," of which Spokane is the capital, has now come to an end. Above all, the sparse rainfall sets limits that even the greatest optimism cannot overcome. This was seen in the case of the Spokane flour mills and the sawmill. The last census [1920] for Spokane and surrounding area revealed an extremely slow population growth of less than 5 percent. In eight neighboring counties the population figure even went down. The future seems anything but hopeful: "Scarcity of water is its greatest limitation," geographer Russell Smith tells us in his book *North America*.[30] Scarcity of water is probably the reason why this area had slight significance for any colonization by Netherlanders. I have found no evidence that more Netherlanders settled in the Palouse Valley, where Van Wijk encountered such hardy Holland farmers.

Even though the above-mentioned Dutch enterprises did not "directly" further immigration of nationals, yet E. F. Cartier van Dissel attempted to set up a Dutch colony on his property in Springdale, Stevens County, north of Spokane. This settlement seems to have had some significance for the dairy business—if one can take the word of a railroad agent.[31] Other than that, I have no further information about that colony.

Finally, there was yet a rather important colonization effort southwest of Spokane in the Yakima Valley of Yakima County. In 1920 there were, according to consul Kempees in Seattle, not less than about three hundred Dutchmen who settled in and around North Yakima and were mostly active in fruit growing. The Yakima Valley is one of the "famous Apple Valleys," thanks to an elaborate irrigation system, but also thanks to an extensive advertising campaign. This publicity at first victimized hundreds of settlers, all of whom had hoped to see a five to ten acre farm turn into a gold mine, but who instead received a piece of arid land that only became of any value after an exceptionally great effort by those who took over the land from these cheated farmers.[32] This was one of the countless examples of the most unscrupulous large scale flim-flam and that reminds us of California, but which was also so characteristic of American colonization methods elsewhere!

Netherlanders lived not only in and around North Yakima and Yakima, of which the little town of Van de Water reminds us, but one finds many more to the southeast, in the same valley around the town of Zillah. How sharp also was the difference here between what people expected and what they found. Five families (and one "bachelor"), full of hope, bought land here and settled on it. Soon this paradise revealed itself to be a desert, covered here and there with tough scrub, and plagued with sand storms! Especially the women despaired and threatened to leave with their children. Yet they remained. Their husbands had bought the land. If they moved they would lose everything! This was, after all, God's will! The little colony remained and survived, thanks to much heavy labor, which was usually very poorly paid.

There was at work here also a single great power, their faith, which bound all settlers together and speedily led to the organization of a Christian Reformed Church in 1901. Recently the church commemorated its twenty-fifth anniversary. Other colonists of the same faith settled near them, but many also left again, frightened away by the dry climate and arid surroundings, unless there was irrigation. The Rammermans, the Harkemas, and the Oords remained; they formed a nucleus, just as the Heersinks had done near Alamosa, Colorado, as we mentioned earlier. Around this nucleus many others grouped themselves later on. Eventually, the land became better suited for living and working, which led to the arrival of new settlers. Thus in 1925, the originally insignificant congregation counted 44 families, 107 "members" and 239 "souls."[33]

The Netherlanders around Yakima also organized a church and formed a Reformed congregation, with a church building in the town of Moxee, where its minister, J. B. H. Van Lierop, was installed. This church has 53 families (111 members), spread out over the entire valley, for which reason the congregation is called Yakima Valley. Also here in this isolated valley people demonstrated their religious zeal, although through different denominations. But this did not exclude mutual appreciation.

In other places in this "dry" area, scattered Netherlanders must also be living. Town names such as Vader and Van Ess, both on the same railroad line, seem to indicate this, although one must exercise extreme caution in drawing such conclusions, as we shall see later on. Their number cannot be large, for if that had been the case, they would have organized ecclesiastically or otherwise.

In spite of the promotional efforts of our representative in Seattle in 1911 and 1913 in favor of the Yakima Valley, our fellow countrymen felt drawn much more toward the Puget Sound area, where they finally settled in much larger numbers.[34] The ocean climate, comparable to the climate of southern England, made businesses feasible that were similar to the ones in the Old Country; this was a strong attraction. These favorable circumstances were confirmed to me by Kempees in Seattle.[35] Here the farmers could farm in almost the same way as in the Netherlands, and equally well in agriculture as in dairying. This was a powerful attraction for many; for this particular reason farmers felt immediately at home!

In addition, there was the rapid growth of cities in and near the Puget Sound. Seattle, which at the time of Van Wijk's visit in 1894 had 50,000 inhabitants, already had 315,000 in 1920. Furthermore, cities such as Tacoma, Everett, Bellingham, and others, developed.[36] These drew a number of artisans and numerous farmers who established themselves in the environs and found an important market for their agricultural and animal products in these cities. Primarily the dairy business became important, after that vegetable growing and poultry. Poultry caught on so well that large shipments of eggs were going to New York. Through these various circumstances, there arose an important workingman's colony in Seattle, where, as we noted before, there was also a significant Dutch mortgage business. Around Seattle a farming settlement formed, similar to those around Everett and Bellingham.

More characteristic were the settlements established by Netherlanders on Whidbey Island in Puget Sound and at Lynden, in the extreme north of Washington State, north of Bellingham in Whatcom County, where also the villages of Van Zandt, Van Brockline, and Van Wijck are located. Originally, most of these areas were covered with dense forests. Indeed, Washington State still belongs to the category of states rich in woods. Strips of land from which most of the timber had been removed, although the stumps remained, were sold to the farmers as "stump" land, which the farmers would further clear with axe and dynamite during the winter months. This sort of task was taken for granted in the forties and fifties, but it is a task that American farmers of today dread so much that they prefer not to settle in Washington's countryside. This explains the small rural population and the large number of city dwellers that are found in this state, which gives it the label of "the land of cities." Here, as in so many other places, the heavy pioneer labor was done by foreigners, namely by our fellow countrymen. Both this heavy labor and the damp climate scared off Americans. It is "a worker's climate, not an idler's," notes R. Whitaker.[37] But he did not doubt the coming of better days, "the dawn of a tomorrow."

It seems that around 1895 a considerable number of Netherlanders settled in this area. Already in June, 1896, Reverend J. W. Brink organized the first Christian Reformed congregation at Oak Harbor on Whidbey Island, the first such congregation near the Pacific.[38] After some time, however, this congregation with its pastor transferred to the United Presbyterian Church: poverty and the long distances were listed as causes for this decision.

Apparently here, too, the denominations were close upon each other's heels! Along with that, not all the colonists were God-fearing, and in this respect the "missionaries" had far from pleasant experiences! We recall the reports of Reverend G. G. Haan and his none too flattering judgment concerning the "shiploads" of Hollanders who at that time were scattered all over the West.

What became of all these people? Who knows? Apparently they were the ones who laid the foundations for various workingman's colonies whose members, as Kempees confirmed to me, had largely come directly from the Netherlands. A number of them must also have settled on the farm lands. According to the testimony of the same consul, a large number of colonists came directly from the Old Country to Oak Harbor and Lynden.

Alongside these "Dutch immigrants" in the Northwest, one finds two other groups. First there was a group that had already been established in the United States for many years. It was composed of factory workers, artisans, etc., whom the crisis of 1893 had rendered unemployed, and who had left the cities for a new start in the Northwest, some in the "Sound cities" and some on the farms. In this group were also numerous farmers who had been impoverished by succeeding years of drought in the Dakotas or "farther West" in Montana, Idaho, etc. They attempted to start anew in the rain-soaked Pacific area. In addition to this group came also the Canadian Netherlanders. Hundreds of our countrymen were and still today are led in an irresponsible manner to Canadian homesteads where sometimes the drought and at other times the extreme cold made life virtually impossible. Finally, in desperation, they forsook their land and homes and did what R. Insinger had done; they settled down in Washington State on the other side of "the line." Time and again one reads in Holland-American newspapers news items from Lynden about the arrival of these "Canadians." I was struck by the Dutch families there that had originated from Saskatchewan. Lynden especially drew like a "magnet" and thus a great deal of construction work was generated and "a brisk real estate business arose."[39]

Hundreds of these "refugees" settled not only in Lynden, but also elsewhere in the Pacific Northwest. J. J. Leys, who in 1923 visited a number of Canadian settlements and also those in the Northwest of the United States, states that the colonies on Whidbey Island, in Lynden, Everett, and Seattle flourished because of the "entering Canadian" fellow countrymen, not only from among the "homestead" colonies but also from the environs of Winnipeg.[40] The future looked too dark to them; there was too much persistent unemployment, and moreover the climate was too severe. Compared with that, the northwestern United States seemed like a paradise; Seattle had a climate comparable to that of London and Portland to that of Paris.

A great deal was required of them here, too, especially of those who settled in wooded areas or on "stump-lands." One finds among these settlers spirited fellows who came directly from the Netherlands, from "the

East," or from Canada. Listen to what the people of Lynden said about the first colonists: "It was a noble band of settlers, our heroic and faithful pioneers! Untrodden wildernesses were their first surroundings. The work of clearing the ground was very arduous. But the Lord heard their prayers and caused the work of their hands to prosper and many a psalm or thanksgiving resounded through the tall firs and cedars of our woods."[41] Is it not as if one sees Van Raalte and his followers of fifty years earlier?

It was not the least worthy who around 1900 settled in the woods instead of in the tempting cities! In 1913, the judgment of J. C. J. Kempees, still a vice-consul at that time, concerning these largely Frisian colonists, was favorable but matter-of-fact, as befitted a genuine Netherlander.[42] He called them "earnest, hard-working people, who have achieved a certain degree of prosperity." Most of them, Kempees told me seven years later, were free from mortgages. Kempees' banking institution had placed only one to two mortgages among Netherlanders. This unencumbered state of affairs existed in spite of the fact that they also suffered reverses and had to contend with considerable hardship due to the long-lasting rains. One gets a notion of these circumstances from an account from Lynden in one of the Holland-American newspapers in October 1921.[43] For six weeks already the rain had been pouring down; the potatoes rotted in the fields, and the shocks of grain left on the land to dry for threshing, turned green. The pastures were as beautifully green as in May, although often too wet for access. Does a report like that not sound downright Dutch? In 1920, approximately two thousand "Netherlanders" lived in and around Lynden. Outwardly, the town itself has an entirely American appearance, although one can use the Dutch language everywhere. Moreover, it distinguishes itself by its prosperity and exceptional neatness, both of which, needless to say, are ascribed to the Dutch element.

In 1920 Whidbey Island, about half the size of Zuid Beveland in the Netherlands, had more than eight hundred Dutch inhabitants. Most of them were farmers who originally engaged primarily in dairying and later went into truck gardening and poultry. The long and narrow island, hilly and sometimes rocky, is covered with lovely forests of heavy timber including many conifers. It has such a mild climate that a number of deciduous trees retain their leaves during the short and mild winter.[44] The village of Oak Harbor takes on more and more the character of a town with its electric lights and cement sidewalks. Our fellow countrymen live primarily in the valleys.[45]

In contrast to these agricultural colonies, one can speak of a working-man's colony in Seattle; it numbered 77 Dutch-born in 1900, 317 in 1910, and 525 in 1920. Except for the representatives of the mortgage banks and a "businessman" or two, most of these were manual laborers, primarily carpenters and masons, bakers, tailors, cigar makers, etc., who on the whole were doing extremely well.[46] According to the consular reports, our trade with Seattle, even though it increased after the [First] World War, does not amount to very much yet. The representative of the "Royal Dutch" [Shell] in Seattle is an American. One finds also a similar workingman's colony in Portland, Oregon, with 365 Dutch-born in 1920, compared to 52 in 1900 and 223 in 1910. The colonies in Everett and Bellingham are more mixed and have a predominant farmer element. The small colony in Sultan, east of Everett, is also mixed. In all these "colonies" there is a busy coming and going, since many settlers are restless and have already gone through a "lifetime" of experiences. When they have earned a few hundred dollars, they often attempt to begin a new enterprise elsewhere and "start out again on a new adventure," say the Americans.

That this restlessness is not conducive to godly living is obvious. That is possibly the reason why so many in the Farthest West lost their faith. Worthy of note, and at the same time moving, is the complaint of an old Dutch father to his dominee.[47] He had lost $25,000 by coming West. Still he did not find this as bad as the fact that through all this wandering his entire family had fallen away from the church.

Under such circumstances it may come as a surprise that both the Reformed and Christian Reformed congregations are still relatively large in numbers; some are even flourishing. It need not surprise us that these are found in the agricultural colonies, since farmers are most conservative also in godly things. So one finds in Lynden two Christian Reformed congregations, organized in 1900 and in 1920, numbering at present 190 and 44 families respectively (1,062 and 196 souls). Besides these, there is one Reformed congregation of 95 families. In Oak Harbor one finds a Reformed congregation of 60 families and since 1902 a Christian Reformed congregation also of 60 families—the latter with 286 souls. Since 1914 there has been a Christian Reformed congregation in Sultan, counting now 21 families (87 souls).

That orthodoxy is much weaker among the city dwellers in the Northwest is demonstrated by the fact that neither Spokane, Seattle, nor Portland, with their large numbers of Dutch inhabitants, have either a Reformed or a Christian Reformed congregation. In Spokane one does find a Dutch Church, however, and in Seattle an organization was recently set up, the Immanuel Reformed Church. However, the latter was made possible only by the financial support of J. T. Cremer* and former prime minister [Hendrikus] Colijn.[48] This congregation still did not have its own pastor in 1920. They were helped out by Reverend A. Klerk who would travel for eighteen hours by railroad car from Spokane for services. Among these Dutch city dwellers there must have been members of American churches. However, from the preceding data we must conclude that many Dutchmen, even if they had not become irreligious in the broadest sense of the word, must nevertheless have been living outside any organized church.

---

*Jacob Theodoor Cremer (1847–1923), a Dutch entrepreneur, colonial expert, and liberal statesman, Netherlands Ambassador to Washington.

In "mixed" Everett, on the contrary, there has been a Christian Reformed congregation since 1911. Its continued existence was often threatened by departing members, but today it has 64 families and 328 souls. Noteworthy about the structure of the Everett colony is that one encounters in this congregation carpenters, a shoemaker, a tailor, a butcher, store clerks, office workers, factory workers, bakers, farmers, etc. Many of these, and this is confirmed once more, came over from various states of the Union and from various provinces of Canada.[49]

The census of Netherlands-born is as follows: In Washington, 632 in 1900; 2,157 in 1910; and 3,097 in 1920; and in Oregon, 324, 618, and 917, respectively.

B. In Montana and Idaho

In the Northwest of the United States we can consider, besides Washington and Oregon, three other states that geologically and morphologically form a unit with them: Idaho, Wyoming, and Montana. Although the nature of their rocks and the form of their soil is largely similar to those of Washington and Oregon, their location is such that they are differentiated from the Pacific Northwest as the Interior States.

It is precisely this interior location with its consequently dry climate—still dryer because the Cascades and Rocky Mountains prevent the flow of moist air—which explains why it took until the twentieth century before these states were considered for agricultural colonization. This colonization occurred when, at least according to the American conception, the more humid and consequently better areas elsewhere became too populated, which in turn made land prices too high.

As land prices rose, people had already considered earlier ways to increase the yield of the land, which up to this time, due to drought, had only been used for extensive cattle-breeding or ranching, in contrast to dairying. They hoped to be able to make it suitable also for agriculture and fruit growing, and thus more valuable. How this led to the development of irrigation works to water the land is already known to us from the experience in California and Colorado. According to the American geographer, R. H. Whitlock, there were already 54,000 farms "under irrigation" (3.6 million acres) in 1889.[50] It is obvious that for this purpose they selected the most suitable lands that could be irrigated with the least cost.

The federal administration attempted in several ways to encourage irrigation, among others, by the so-called Carey Act [1894]. This is a law by which the Union government gave large tracts of federal land to the states containing desert lands, with the provision that they would irrigate the land and sell it in units of up to 160 acres to actual settlers. The states in turn would let private companies develop irrigation systems. Also irrigation districts were set up under specific state laws and were controlled by the water users. The Interior States have especially used this Carey Act and are known, together with Oregon, as the "Carey Act States."

Irrigation by private owners was encouraged by the Desert Land Act [1877], which in fact was an extension of the homestead laws. In areas of scanty rainfall, the serious settler can take up 320 acres of land at favorable conditions, namely, at 95¢ per acre cash. If within four years he has succeeded in bringing water to the land and has one-third of the "homestead" under cultivation, then he can get title to the 320 acres of land for $1 per acre.*[51] Finally, since the Reclamation Act of 1902, by which the U. S. Reclamation Service was established, the Union government itself took up the construction of expensive waterworks that were funded from the proceeds of land sales. Earlier the federal administration had acted directly in this matter when it set up the United States Indian Service for the benefit of the Indian reservations. This is mentioned only for the sake of completeness.

All these regulations eventually led to the fact that in 1909 irrigation water was provided for a total of 13,738,485 acres.[52] Meanwhile a tremendous publicity campaign touted all these lands and a land rush was expected from the ranks of land seekers. Especially Montana, third in size among the states of the Union, hoped that it would become more than a land of miners and cattle ranchers, for both groups only brought unrest and often bitter fighting. Only through farming would it obtain a settled population, and along with it a certain stability.

Still another circumstance made Montana and the other arid states more attractive. It was the increasingly popular system of "dry farming" in areas where irrigation was too costly. The precipitation of more than one season must be preserved in the ground since one season was insufficient. To that end farmers carefully work the ground, they harrow it several times after plowing, and after each good rainfall they loosen the top layer to reduce evaporation. As a consequence, farmers must leave large pieces of land lie fallow and preferably use crop rotation. Because dry farming requires much time and labor, it is especially attractive to large families that have many hands but little money, and therefore are unable to pay for the expensive "irrigation rights."

In this way irrigation and dry farming seemed to offer a future to both the well-to-do land seekers and the less well-to-do. The federal government helped to create new "opportunities which would go far to allay social discontent," Whitlock acknowledges. The states, railroads, land companies, the banks, etc., also helped to strengthen that belief. Everyone was con-

---

*The specifics of the Desert Land Act of 1877 were that settlers could take up to 640 acres by filing an application and paying 25¢ per acre; three years were allowed to complete the improvement of irrigating the land, after which time the balance of $1 per acre was due, and the settlers secured title.

vinced that "in the land of the copper collar," farming would finally gain the upper hand.[53] Thus a new safety valve would be provided, similar to that in the Midwest years before. Numerous Netherlanders thought so too, especially the leaders of several mortgage banks, who therefore no longer limited their field of operations to Washington, Oregon, etc., but extended it to the Interior States.

One of these banking institutions even moved its headquarters to southwestern Montana, to the mining and market town of Bozeman, the capital of one of the most fertile valleys in this state, the valley of the Western and Eastern Gallatin rivers, which along with the Madison and Jefferson rivers form the headwaters of the Missouri River. The Gallatin Valley, northwest of Yellowstone Park, is the joint name given to the two Gallatin River valleys. They are both closed in by high mountain ranges and owe their significance for farming primarily to soils that have been formed from weathered volcanic materials. These materials are rich in nutrients and, according to physiographer Bowman, originated from the volcanic breccia that partially form the Gallatin Range.[54]

Of almost equal significance is the circumstance that people in this "valley," which strongly reminds us of the "parks" in Colorado and New Mexico considered earlier, do not have to struggle so strongly with the shortage of irrigation water as is the case elsewhere in this state, where they are afflicted with drought. These areas are on the prairies of the eastern foothills of the Rocky Mountains, in the Great Plains. Thus it must not have been accidental that when this territory was "opened" by the Northern Pacific Railroad with the customary accompanying publicity, a Dutch colony developed in and around Bozeman. In the eastern Gallatin Valley, northwest of Bozeman, lay the town of Manhattan, also located on the eastern Gallatin River and on the Northern Pacific line. In and around this town a greater number of Netherlanders settled than anywhere else in Montana. They were preceded, however, by Dutch settlements in the Yellowstone River Valley, as we shall see later on. In Manhattan, where especially many Groningers settled, the first Christian Reformed Church was established in 1903 and in spite of the reverses that the colonists experienced since then, it now has 115 families with 615 souls. A Reformed congregation came into existence here in 1910 and at present has 13 families.

Of less significance is the Dutch settlement that came into existence about 1908 in and around the "town" of Conrad, located on the Great Plains in the northwestern part of Montana, northwest of the small Missouri River town of Great Falls. Conrad is served by a feeder line of the Great Northern Pacific, a great competitor of the Northern Pacific Railroad. It was especially the Carey Act that had induced colonization here, but subsequently it led to bitter disappointments. In spite of an existence that was constantly imperiled by drought and cold weather, people were unable to

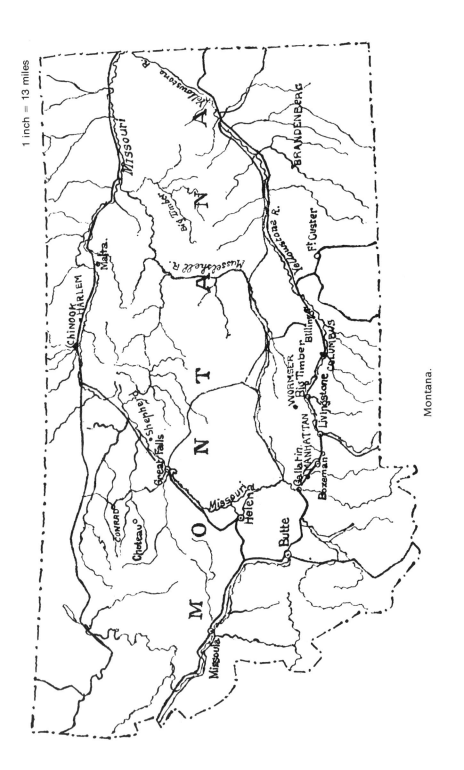

1 inch = 13 miles

Montana.

come to a spiritual unity. Both "Dutch" congregations followed each other close at the heels, so that in 1908 the first and still existing Reformed congregation in Montana was organized here. It is still called "Montana First" and has twenty families. Already in 1909 a Christian Reformed congregation was also formed, with seventeen families and 121 souls.

Nowhere has the spiritual disunity of Dutch colonists wreaked greater havoc than in Conrad, Montana. The support of two church buildings and two ministerial families, which in the early days of relative prosperity did not seem impossible even for this small colony, became much too burdensome in the long run when lean years followed for these more than thirty families, even though they were willing to make great sacrifices in matters of faith. Both churches became destitute after several poor harvests. The great poverty that ensued made it difficult to pay off mortgages, etc. Some forty churches in the West collected $5,000 to keep the Reformed Church in existence and to ease the distress.[55] The equally-burdened Christian Reformed congregation also had to call upon its more prosperous brothers and sisters for help. The continued existence of the latter congregation was so seriously threatened that recently, at his wits' end, one of the True leaders advocated a merger of the two Conrad congregations.[56] That speaks volumes!

While Montana still appeared to be promising, thanks to several good harvests, a small colony was founded near Choteau in 1916. These settlers organized a Christian Reformed congregation that numbered only nine families in 1921, and has since been dissolved. Of not much greater importance than the Conrad settlement were a few colonies in the valley of the Yellowstone River in southern Montana. The Northern Pacific connected this valley earlier with the Midwest than the Gallatin Valley and it was viewed as very fertile because of its rich deposits of alkali salts, especially in the vicinity of Billings.[57] Only recently, this town was advertised as "the center of a very fertile farming country."[58]

So it does not surprise us that, as far as I know, in this valley the initial attempt was made to form a Dutch settlement. This oldest Dutch settlement in Montana was called Wormser City, after Reverend A. Wormser, with whose help it was established. In 1896 he organized a congregation of Reformed persuasion [kleur]. Unfortunately, the congregation languished, apparently plagued by drought, so that already in 1897 it declined into a mission post. Wormser served then as a classical missionary but could not stop further decline. In 1900 he left, apparently at the "end of his rope." Three years later the post was officially abandoned. The name Wormser City, or more simply Wormser, which still appears on some maps, is therefore for us of no more than historical significance. I do not know whether all the colonists left. One or two may have remained. In any case, in 1911 the Reformed Church established a new mission post south of the old colony and closer to the river, in Big Timber. It was called Hope, but up to the present time has not yet broadened into a congregation.[59]

There exist, however, several small colonies of Christian Reformed Netherlanders closer to Billings. These established a congregation in Shepherd in 1908, now counting twenty-two families and 122 souls. Besides that, a "branch" of this congregation was established in Billings, with seven families and 43 souls at present.

As is obvious, these Yellowstone colonies are not large and several, like Shepherd, for instance, were "distressed." This was no wonder, because however fertile the valley might be, the alkali salts became a major nuisance in times of great drought. And drought also ravaged this valley, which belongs in part to the "plains." Drought was then so bad that even the expensive irrigation works could bring no relief because of lack of water.

Besides the more or less orthodox brothers, and very probably also many "pagans," whose voices were seldom or never heard because they did not live in communities, there was in northern Montana also a number of our Roman Catholic countrymen. The town of Harlem, among others, reminds us of this. At that time the vicar-general of the bishop of Montana's capital, Helena, was a Belgian, Victor De Brabander, who made repeated visits to his native land, and encouraged large numbers of Belgian and Dutch families (especially from Brabant and Limburg) to settle in Montana in 1913. A number of Netherlanders settled farther north around the town of Chinook on the Great Northern Railway, where about sixty of them reportedly obtained work for three or four dollars a day. Thirteen others took homesteads of 320 acres south of the small town of Malta on the same line. So "happy and satisfied" did the Netherlanders at Chinook seem to be that others followed. This additional immigration was boosted by the fact that in that same year a Belgian-Dutch colony came into being at Williams, west of Conrad.

It was especially the Dutch parish priest J. M. Vermaat who gave his support to the colonization of 1913. Early in 1914, he made a trip to Belgium and the Netherlands as agent of the Great Northern to recruit new colonists, while he had, at the same time, connections with the Valier Farm Sales Company. This explains his determination to set up a Belgian-Dutch colony at Valier, also west of Conrad, where some Belgians already lived. There and at Conrad, the land was provided with the necessary irrigation water at decent prices by the Valier Montana Land and Water Company. In a number of lectures given in the Noord Brabant village of Roosendaal and elsewhere, the good pastor praised the Montana land, where according to him plenty of work was available. He praised especially the land around Valier, where the possibilities of fruit growing were even illustrated with pictures; but he completely forgot to mention the indispensable irrigation works and their cost. A large number of Belgians and Netherlanders followed "Father Vermaat" to Valier, where to their bitter disappointment there were no fruit trees to be found and no work either. There was cheap land available from the state, thanks to the Carey Act, at 50¢ per acre; but to this had to be added $40 per acre to the "water" company for the indispensable irrigation water, to be paid in installments. Nobody had counted on this. Is it any wonder that when in 1915 our vice-consul [F. E. H.] Groenman visited the Netherlanders in Valier all of the colonists were full of bitter complaints?

How great was the number of Roman Catholic Netherlanders and what became of them? Leedy, an agent of the Great Northern, speaks of "thousands" of Netherlanders and Belgians. But the same agent also speaks about Montana, the "treasure State," as the paradise of farmers! Vermaat soon said farewell to this "paradise" and went to North Dakota, where he took up his shepherd's functions and perhaps found more tractable sheep.[60] About these colonists I have since then learned no more. Undoubtedly they experienced what their Calvinistic fellow countrymen also experienced: with difficulty they may have been able to maintain themselves. He should consider himself lucky if he is able to make "little more than a living for his labour," is what Whitlock said about the average farmer "under irrigation."[61]

Because the total cost of water is difficult to calculate, varying also according to the nature of the more or less porous soil, Americans themselves are reluctant to settle on irrigated land; they prefer to let foreigners and "greenhorns" take the risk. This explains the great amount of advertising for these lands among immigrants. For that reason our consuls and others concerned with immigration have the duty to warn immigrants not only against settling in dry-farming districts, which are not suitable for Netherlanders either; consuls also must warn them against irrigation lands. Apparently we have not yet paid sufficient "apprentice dues" in California and other places!

Settling in Montana presents still other difficulties. The tremendous unreliability of the climate causes fatal consequences that apply here more strongly in time of drought than elsewhere. The average rainfall from 1914 to 1916 was approximately 40 centimeters [15.7 inches]; during the following four years the average dwindled by one-half, which wrought havoc everywhere. Over against a maximum summer temperature of 117° Fahrenheit. in the valley of the Yellowstone River, stands a winter record of minus 63° Fahrenheit. in the same state, only eighty miles farther west! Why does a man like First Chamber member [J.] Westerdijk fail to mention this when in a pre-advice he incidentally points to the fertility of the Gallatin Valley?[62]

The well-known American [Henry] Mencken calls Montana "largely uninhabitable," and thus concurs in the judgment of his fellow countrymen not directly "interested" in this matter.[63] Rightly so. For the correct information, one should not study the prospectuses of real estate men, nor even ask for the opinion of our mortgage banks and their respective directors. One should ask the colonists themselves, and if that is not possible, one should read their reports in papers like the Dutch newspapers of the Midwest, in *De Volksvriend*, *Pella's Weekblad*, *De Grondwet*, *Onze Toekomst*, etc. Then one finds out that, for instance, in the Gallatin Valley, specifically in the Dutch colony of Manhattan, the winter of 1919–1920 lasted seven and a half months, whereas in the two preceding years, they had hardly had any winter weather at all. But in those two years they suffered from such a severe drought that there was a total crop failure; there was not even any irrigation water. Then one also reads that in 1920, due to massive snowfall and apparently through the warm wind, the snow-eating Chinook, the other extreme prevailed: floods tore large holes in the roads and washed away large sections of them. An even worse misery is implied in the following report from this same "most fertile" and most important Dutch colony in Montana: "Here it is a region of going and coming. Every year people *leave* for Washington and California. This spring (June 15, 1920) there are still some families coming from the Netherlands."[64]

In the Yellowstone River colonies things were not better, particularly in the Dutch settlement near Columbus. From there it was reported that in June, 1924, the Hollanders had lost their best properties due to the bad times, which they regretted all the more because later on, through the drilling of oil wells, the land increased greatly in price.[65] Also the picture of Conrad and environs was a sad one, even in 1926, when some improvements had already set in. So badly had they suffered from the period of drought, but also from grasshoppers, that many had moved away, and a number of houses and stores in Conrad and adjoining villages stood empty, while in the countryside many farms were abandoned. Solidly built, prosperous, outstanding houses, which testified of the faith that the builders had in the land, now stood empty. The dwellers had moved to the more densely populated East or to the mild and green Pacific area—"like Elimelech and Naomi once left Bethlehem for the fields of Moab," we were told by a Holland American, well-versed in the Scriptures.[66]

The mortgage banks themselves, sometimes on the verge of liquidation, had to acknowledge to the mortgage holders that Montana farmers had moved elsewhere by the thousands; thousands of homes stood empty.[67] Whole counties, says A. Fisher, have fallen into bitter poverty and can no longer fulfill their obligations; one bank after another is forced to close.[68] That is a characteristic cultural picture of the "Farther West"!

And let no one say that this depression was of a temporary nature. So far it has lasted quite long (five years) and even climatological and economic "bearish" factors contributed to it. Depressions can be expected to happen again and again, especially to the extent that they originate in climatic factors. Climatological fluctuations of longer or shorter duration, of the sort the Russian geographer A. Woeikof purportedly determined for Russian Turkestan, are also found in America.[69] They are obviously felt sooner and more sharply in those areas, just as in Turkestan, where rainfall is exceedingly scanty to begin with. Russell Smith speaks of "variation in rainfall," an expression that is somewhat too weak; elsewhere he more correctly mentions "cycles."[70] Such a "cycle" we noted earlier, in the nineties in the Dakotas, with all its consequences—a true exodus, a throwback of the legions of scarcely established land seekers, a first "HALT!" that rang out to the Westward-ho!

It is these fluctuations that made so uncertain the existence of the farmers and everyone who depended upon them in the Interior States, and that led repeatedly to migrations and subsequently to a depression. Some areas of the Great Plains have been colonized three times in a row after having been abandoned twice, an American once noted. Will that be all? One of our mortgage bank directors recently declared that American farmers are well on their way to overcoming serious difficulties.[71] This is a judgment, so far as it concerns the arid states, that once more can lead to too high expectations. The American federal government understands this now, and seems to realize that the promotion of colonization in the Interior States is not the correct thing to do, even though in "normal" times dry farming and irrigation make farming possible. Presently federal authorities are beginning to see in their homestead acts, which eventually in 1916 made possible the possession of 640 acres of "desert" land, an "unjustifiable encouragement for the use of new lands," as the Department of Agriculture in Washington honestly acknowledges. It is seriously considering modification of its land policy, especially the abandonment of the homestead laws.[72]

A similar modification would also benefit our fellow countrymen. They have repeatedly formed small "homestead settlements" in the farther West, as for example, as recently as 1911 in Elgin, near Vona in Colorado, nineteen miles away from the nearest railroad.[73] Great believers as these settlers are, they built their Christian Reformed Church in the middle of the colony.

Every climatic fluctuation of the last forty years has taken its toll of victims, also among our countrymen. Since then, rain-rich areas, that is, those with rainfall of at least 75 centimeters [29.5 inches], have all been sold to private owners, while semi-arid lands with an average rainfall of 50–75 centimeters [19.7–29.5 inches] (this is taken as the minimum for agricultural purposes), have been hard to get, so that only arid or "desert" lands remain available. In both latter areas the rain shortage is a constant handicap. This is not a hopeful outlook, no matter how earnestly one uses agricultural know-how to overcome this difficulty by planting varieties suitable for the climate.

We already noted the fate of Wormser City and Choteau. A study of the yearbooks of the Reformed and Christian Reformed Churches in the United States—practically our only source materials—informs us of many another "death." There is, for example, the folding of the colony of Amsterdam in Idaho. As far as I know, there exists in that state no other "colony" of any significance, even though our mortgage banks also operate there, and the Internationale Hypotheekbank has large interests in Burley County. There are a few Netherlanders in Nampa, a town midway between Idaho's capital, Boise, and the border of Oregon. There are also a number of Sioux County people who live in the Apple Valley, about 30 miles away from Nampa, where they have bought apple orchards.[74] In neither settlement has a congregation developed, which in most cases, is an important yardstick. On the other hand, a Christian Reformed Church was organized in Amsterdam in 1913, but the church dwindled during the drought years after 1916 and had to be abandoned in 1920. Even though other Netherlanders have subsequently arrived there, such as from the colony of Shepherd in Montana, the settlement in Amsterdam is for thé time being of little interest.[75]

Finally, we give a few figures concerning the number of established Dutch-born: in Montana, 316 in 1900; 1,054 in 1910; 1,675 in 1920; in Idaho, 50, 261, and 439 respectively; and in Wyoming 18, 87, and 130 respectively.

11

Colonization Attempts in the South

A. In Virginia and Maryland

Earlier we have seen how after the Civil War the heavily devastated South tried to draw capital and manpower from the North for its reconstruction. The total failure of Van Raalte's colony in Virginia illustrates the results of these attempts. The increasing shortage of manpower was due to the continual emigration of Blacks, among whom a "pioneering spirit" seemed to awaken too slowly. Therefore, attempts increased to replace them with whites.[1]

People in the South also began to realize the risk of a one-crop economy, in this case, raw cotton. They attempted to grow food crops to put an end to this situation, but this increased the demand for white workers. The expansion of the railroad network and the resulting land sales were the factors that kept the interest of northern investors going, although not very strongly.

It was only the increased realization and fear of drought problems in the West that made Northerners turn their thoughts anew to the South in the nineties. The army of homesteaders that had continued to pour into the West swerved and turned to a large extent to the "new" South. In 1893 our consul at St. Louis, Missouri, B. B. Haagsma, ascertained this new trek for the first time, which was particularly strong among native Americans.[2] This trek was directed toward Arkansas, Texas, and Louisiana, states which had a shortage of farmers; their "high" regions with a "fairly warm but healthful climate" promised good results. The importance of this migration was shown in the year 1895 when people fled the drought in the Northwest and more than 100,000 families arrived in Missouri. Haagsma confirmed that they came "mostly from the cold and dry northwestern states" and that many of them were on their way to the more southerly states; some of them even traveled too far south into Texas and Mississippi, where it was too hot.[3]

Among these Americans there were some of Dutch descent who had fled from Dakota and from Iowa, because even in the western part of Iowa, for example, in Sioux County, the livelihood of many a colonist appeared to be threatened.[4] From the small town of Hospers a number of Reformed families moved to Arkansas.[5]

For that matter, aspiring colonists in the Netherlands had earlier centered their attention upon the South. In 1882 the very well known journalist Charles Boissevain sang a song of praise about the southern Atlantic area, "America's Italy."[6] "Nothing that I have seen in America drew my attention more than this region, which, because of its climate, location, and products, is the France and Italy of the United States." It "will become one of the richest parts of the Union." It is very likely that Boissevain read Cohen Stuart's *Zes Maanden in Amerika* [Six Months in America] and knew about the Dutch colonization effort of Van Raalte in Virginia, but he carefully avoided mention of its complete failure.[7] On the contrary, it was in particularly Virginia that he strongly recommended for colonization, for there "the Chesapeake is the natural waterway to the heart of the Republic." Most likely he considered this region as an important market for farm products, since he even prophesied "that on Chesapeake Bay will be established the Marseilles, the Liverpool of America to rival New York's position."[8]

Boissevain strongly recommended Dutch colonization in the Piedmont country, at the foot of the Appalachians, but only after a careful inspection of the location. However, I do not believe that Dutch emigrants followed this suggestion during the first forty years. Maybe they knew better! What the colonists of 1870 had experienced seemed to have become more widely known.

A fact that draws our attention is the opening of a New York branch office by the banking firm of Adolph Boissevain around 1880 under the leadership of Charles Boissevain. This firm became interested in the construction of various railways. A. A. H. Boissevain was able to have a large amount of Dutch capital participate in the building of the Norfolk and Western Railway in Virginia, and in the reorganization of that railroad company. The town of Boissevain, and probably also the town of Holland, west of Norfolk, are reminders of this Dutch participation. Norfolk is located on the Chesapeake Bay which, as we saw previously, the journalist Boissevain had envisioned to be heading towards a prosperous future. One tries to establish relationships between various events and I have tried to do so. It seems that the people involved in these matters thought the moment inopportune to give any details and therefore my requests for further information received unsatisfactory answers.[9] I surmise that here also "land" interests were at stake.

Indeed, the firm of Boissevain at New York had acquired various "interests" around Norfolk, as a result of their participation in the development of the railway. At various points along the Norfolk and Western, Boissevain and Co. made investments to further the development of the region. At these places blast furnaces, sawmills, and other factories were built. Near towns that had suffered from a great developmental lag after the Civil War, large tracts of land were purchased. This was in particular the case in the environs of Norfolk where on the purchased land all kinds of modern improvements were made. This land is now part of the port city of Norfolk and explains why the journalist Boissevain wrote such laudatory articles about events there.

The firm of Boissevain sent the young J. P. André Mottu, an alumnus of the O.H.S. [Openbare Handelsschool] at Amsterdam, to Virginia to send reports concerning the new enterprises. The result was that André Mottu was entrusted with the directorship of the new Norfolk territory. Since then this gentleman has lived there and for a number of years has been consul of our country there.

After the arrival of André Mottu, the firm of Boissevain sent ten other young Hollanders to Virginia with similar aims. However, these young men later moved to other states. Some of them have already died. In time a brother of J. P. André Mottu established himself in Baltimore where he also became Dutch consul. A nephew of Adolph Boissevain stayed only a few months in Virginia and then moved to New York. H. J. Van Hemert later moved to Colorado and now lives in Colorado Springs. J. Van Hall married one of the daughters of Charles Boissevain, lived in Virginia for a few years, and then returned to the Netherlands.

J. P. André Mottu declared to me specifically that the firm of Adolph Boissevain (now Pierson and Co. at Amsterdam), where he labored a number of years, "never [has] bought land in Virginia with the purpose of establishing Dutch colonies."[10] Be that as it may, many Netherlanders did not settle here and the growth of Norfolk, as prophesied by Boissevain, took a little longer. I already became aware of these various trends from a letter by André Mottu published in 1906 in the organ *Hou en Trou[w]* [*Loyal and True*]. In this letter, André Mottu strongly urged graduates of the O. H. S. not to come to the seaport of Norfolk.[11] This surely does not point to prosperous growth. In addition, it is of interest to us that in a list of categories of Netherlanders in America he never mentions farmers, and only mentions one single agriculturist in Virginia, E. H. Storm van 's-Gravensande.[12]

An attempt was made to establish a Dutch colony further north in Maryland but this was a total failure, even though a Christian Reformed church seems to have existed there for a short time.[13] For some time C. W. Van der Hoogt, who was a former Dutchman, had headed the State Bureau of Immigration in Maryland. We already met this Christian gentleman at the Colorado colony and at that time his reputation was none too good. Since he was especially interested in Dutch immigrants, it makes sense to try to establish a relationship between the Maryland colony and this "gentleman," also because both prided themselves on being "Christian." But here too further details were lacking. However, Van der Hoogt was appointed by his "friend" Paul Krüger to be a diplomatic representative of the Republic of

South Africa. The ways of many a Holland American are odd! Later he withdrew from the immigration "business" and became known as an honorable and important businessman in Philadelphia.[14] As head of a "Holland Importing Company," he is listed in 1909 as one of the "representative Hollanders in America." The number of Dutch-born in Maryland totaled 220 in 1900, 203 in 1910, and 314 in 1920. In Baltimore alone there lived 98 in 1900, 106 in 1910, and 193 in 1920.

B. In Texas

More interest seem to have been generated for the region around the Gulf of Mexico, Texas, and states "beyond," than for the southern Atlantic area. Charles Boissevain had also elaborated in his letters to the *Handelsblad* about the future importance of the southern Mississippi and Gulf States.[15] He mentioned in particular Missouri: "Yet no state in the Union has a better climate and more fertile soil. Everything thrives and grows there." However, his descriptions are hardly encouraging when he mentions "the City of the Dead," a part of New Orleans, the seaport of the South.

It was especially our consul at St. Louis who years later stood up for this part of the South.[16] Time and again Haagsma, in his annual consular reports, mentioned its importance, also for Dutch colonization attempts. In his annual report of 1893 he said: "I always regret the fact that venturesome Hollanders begin colonies either in the extreme cold of Dakota, or in the arid regions of Colorado, or in the too-highly praised lands of California, when there are 1,000,000 hectares [2,471,000 acres] of land in the South of which many are exceedingly fertile and partly covered with the heaviest and the best kind of trees." A year later he again made known his wish that immigrants should go south, at least to southern Illinois, southern Missouri, or northern Arkansas, etc.[17]

It is difficult to determine the influence of Boissevain's letters in the *Handelsblad* or of Haagsma's consular reports. Boissevain pointed out that there was a great lack of capital in Kansas City, the shipping port for midwestern crops from Kansas, Colorado, and a part from Texas.[18] And since there were no capitalists or bankers to "handle" all of the harvests of the Midwest, Kansas City lost out on part of them. No doubt, there were also other informants for the Dutch investors concerning this lack of capital in the South, just as we have seen previously in the Northwest.

At any rate, we have seen how the banking house of Boissevain lent help to the Norfolk and Western Railroad in Virginia. In the nineties plans were devised to establish a railroad from Kansas City to a port on the Gulf of Mexico, in order to connect the "big Middle West" with the sea by means of a shorter haul than via the established railroads to the Atlantic coast. At that time, the promotor of this line, Arthur E. Stillwell, found mainly Dutch financiers ready to support it, along with a few Americans and Englishmen.

Banker J. De Goeijen became the big Dutch financial backer of this project. Especially with his help, the building of the Kansas City, Pittsburgh and Gulf Railroad was made possible. When the company was reorganized as the Kansas City Southern Railroad, it was also with Dutch money that the line was further enlarged. In this connection J. Van Tijen wrote to me from Port Arthur: "In developing the line, Holland capital was interested to a great extent."[19] Because of this, from the beginning, a Netherlander, H. Visscher, was the treasurer of the Kansas City Southern at Kansas City.[20]

This line, which was equal to the distance from Amsterdam to Marseilles [France], was also subsidized with land grants, just as were so many others. For this reason more than ever, attempts were made to start colonies "along the way." In 1897 and 1898 many towns were mapped on the "land-grants" and Dutch names were given to a number of them, either to recognize the Dutch financial support or perhaps to encourage Netherlanders to settle there. After all, settlers would feel at home more quickly in a town with a purely Dutch name. For this reason—although I mention this in passing—a town in Canada has been baptized Edam!

The terminus of the Kansas City Southern Railroad was christened Port Arthur, after its promotor, since it was also being built as a port city. The first town north of the seaport intentionally received the name of Nederland because it indeed had to become a "colony" of Netherlanders. Other towns along the line have Dutch names like De Ridder and Zwolle in Louisiana, Bloomburg in Texas (named after the banker E. B. Bloembergen of Leeuwarden), De Queen (after De Goeijen, phonetically written in America as De Queen), Janssen (after De Goeijen's father-in-law), Vandervoort, and Mena (after Mrs. Mina De Goeijen) all in Arkansas, and Amsterdam in Missouri, which "town" is about two and a half hours by rail south of Kansas City.[21]

In none of these towns, as far as I know, have Netherlanders settled in large enough numbers so that they could be called colonies. Most likely, the Dutch did not look forward to pioneering in this barely developed region in spite of its mostly fertile and reddish yellow soil that covers this part of the tertiary peneplain. In addition to the climate, the dense woods especially must have held them back, since Dutch farmers have a natural antipathy toward forests.

This "wilderness recently come to life," thanks to the Gulf Line, looked beautiful, especially to people who like R. P. J. Tutein Nolthenius had the privilege of traveling through it by rail in a "private car."[22] The Coastal Plain is somewhat different in the area near the Gulf of Mexico. There one finds vast stretches of flat prairie, occasionally broken by a strip of woods where rivers have deposited sandy banks slightly higher.[23] On such a prairie the "town" of Nederland was plotted in 1898 on the 46,000-acre land grant controlled by the Port Arthur Land Company that was set up for that purpose.[24] De Goeijen and other Netherlanders had paramount interests in this land company and J. Van Tijen, a Netherlander, was for years its manager. This may explain why a Dutch colony was established in such a

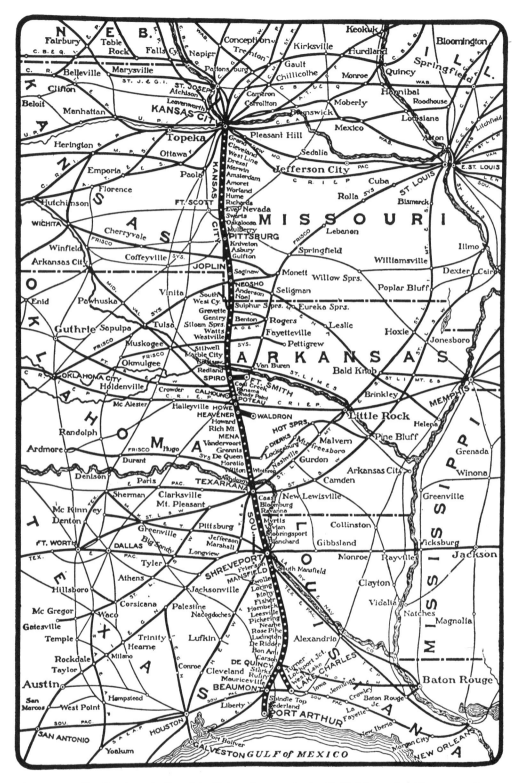

The Kansas City Southern Railroad, built to a large extent with Dutch capital. Numerous town names are reminders of this involvement.

southern part of the United States. The warm, damp climate was a handicap, but the fresh sea breeze made it bearable.

In addition, there was an expansion of rice growing, which until now had been important in South Carolina and Georgia. Since 1892 it had spread across the borders of Louisiana and Texas, in particular also in the vicinity of Port Arthur where the level land was just right for it and offered a good future for many farmers. This old occupation was performed by totally modern methods.[25] Thus Nederland would become a rice-growing colony, especially since the flat land prevented the drainage of the irrigation water, while the clay bottom stopped it from sinking away. As a safeguard an irrigation company was established to supply water should a shortage occur.[26]

There were other reasons that made it likely that a colony could be successful here. Next to rice they might grow vegetables and fruit on the sandy soils that were scattered here and there and that were better suited for this crop. The colonists could find a market for some of their products in the nearby harbor town of Port Arthur, less than half an hour away by train. Produce could also be sold in the region along the Neches River and Sabine Lake that could be reached by boat. The rest of the products could be sent from Port Arthur at small cost. This was an advantage, compared to the situation of the farmers of western Montana, who had to send their products to Chicago by rail and had to pay 13 percent of the value for freight shipment.[27]

The future was promising and the chance of success was great, especially since the Port Arthur Land Company had subdivided the land into 20-acre lots. If a person did not wish to buy a quarter section of 160 acres, he could get a 20-acre tract or even a 10-acre tract next to a road. The cost seemed also to be fair. Depending on location it was only $20 to $35 an acre, with a third down and the rest in installments at 7 percent interest. Ownership papers (deeds) were furnished after paying the one-third down in cash.

Extremely fertile—"deeply rich and fertile"—as the soil was, it gave promise of two or three harvests per year. The climate, moreover, was described as being uncommonly healthful, "purified by the fresh salt winds from the ocean." In addition, a very mild "winter" meant inexpensive living! Surely these circumstances would even draw nonfarmers, all the more so since an "experimental farm" had been established for the benefit of buyers. It served "for profit and for furnishing to purchasers improving their lands, the best varieties of nursery stock at reasonable prices, and also for furnishing practical agricultural and horticultural information useful in their improvement."[28] When we are reminded that around the same time these "splendid" offers were made in 1896, the grain crisis reached its peak in the Netherlands (1893–1895) and business and industry felt the after-effects of it for years, then it is understandable that hundreds were ready to establish themselves in De Goeijen's colony.

It is most likely that in "recruiting" colonists, De Goeijen engaged the services of J. E. Kroes, whom we shall meet later as the "soul" of the celebrating colony. He had been "district inspector" for the northern United States of the Ned.-Am. Stoomvaart-Maatschappij [Holland-American Steamship Company]. By accident I "discovered" that this gentleman had also worked as an agent for the Red Star Line at Harlingen.[29] Thus he was someone who knew this type of "job" thoroughly! I mention this particular skill because it is strange, if not totally incomprehensible, that every Tom, Dick, and Harry [Jan en alleman] was accepted for the colony. Among the colonists, whom I estimate at six hundred, there were in the first place farmers from Groningen, Gelderland, (especially from the neighborhood of Hattem), and Noord Holland (particularly from the neighborhood of Alkmaar and Schagen), etc.[30] There were also a few nurserymen from Boskoop. But others were mainly manual laborers, office clerks, small shopkeepers, teachers, and even ministers.[31] In other words, this was a group of people who could not be considered as the best choice for a farming and vegetable gardening colony.

At the outset, it seemed that the colony had some chance to succeed. Although the Dutch farmers had no experience in growing rice, it appeared they had somewhat good results. According to Van Tijen, they made "quite a success of the crop."[32] Since the Christian Reformed Church in America is very active and always "quick at hand," it organized a church for the believers among the colonists. The well-known Dr. H. Beets traveled south especially for this purpose. This church planting most likely pleased the "Company," because a church congregation would give "stability" to the venture.[33] So the future seemed bright and promising. In Nederland, Texas, they were even in the mood to celebrate on a large scale the crowning of Queen Wilhelmina, which took place on September 6, 1898. It is somewhat strange that Kroes was the "pivot" on which the feast hinged, also in a literal sense, because Kroes was the secretary of the festival committee, and also the chief speaker and the leader of the village ball.[34] Maybe the colonists were in need of some "recreation"! Kroes, after all, knew his people and really understood his job!

The celebration may also have had an adverse effect on many a settler. Many people did not feel at home in the colony of Nederland and became homesick for the fatherland, in spite of having their Koningspark and Oranje Hotel, and in spite of the nearby town of Oranje, east of Nederland. Anyway, as H. Visscher wrote me from Kansas City, many "very soon" returned to the Netherlands because they were dissatisfied with "conditions" in the settlement.[35]

When a year later R. P. J. Tutein Nolthenius, probably as an "interested party," visited the town of Nederland, all he could say was that the settlement was "not yet a going operation." His status may have been indicated by the fact that during the coronation at the colony there were "splendid fireworks" consisting not only of Goeijen's (Queen's) golden rain with Hornbeckers, "Stillwellers," etc., but also a "pinwheel with Tuteiners."[36]

As a gifted writer Tutein Nolthenius gives us an interesting picture of this colony. Standing on the ramp of the railroad station at Nederland he gave a description that coincides with Bowman's description of the physiographical peculiarities of the land. All we have to do is listen:

> The prairie stretches as far as one can see. In the distance on one side a long row of trees breaks the horizon, giving evidence of a river. The silence is broken only by the buzzing of the cicadas and now and then the chirping of a bird very high in the air, distant and invisible. In the direction where Port Arthur is located, there rises nebulously a square monster like the Dordt tower out of the Biesbosch swamps. It is the newly-built elevator. Around it, at low level one sees the white flicker of homes. Nearby dust billows up sky-high. It is a farmer sitting firmly in a Mexican saddle who joyously gallops his horse down the road. The sun has already sucked up the shimmering of the dew drops. The air is rarefied, without clouds, and fresh with the sea breeze. Still, something holds the eye in this vastness. Right before me lies the double line of train rails, which disappear in the distance. Above them endless rows of telephone and telegraph poles line up, becoming smaller and smaller. In the depot, still closed, the telegraph apparatus ticks a joyfully rhythmed dance. It is some evidence of human life because the homes scattered here and there in the flat plain, without flowers, without trees, without anything but some grass, still sleep their morning sleep.

"Whether the Dutch farmers who have settled here enjoy this solitude, I really doubt," said Tutein Nolthenius in a concluding remark, and he was right.[37] Not once does the writer speak about the non-farmers. As we saw before, they had mostly moved away. Some had returned to the Old Country; others had settled in the nearby town of Port Arthur. Still others had moved northward to cooler regions, to the growing towns of northern Arkansas and Missouri and a few even went to Canada.[38] Even most of the farmers moved away so that the church congregation had to be disbanded. Growing rice was too unfamiliar and did not appeal to them over the long term. Also difficulties arose with the Irrigation Company; it finally stopped operating, which caused a lack of irrigation water.

All these setbacks did not imply that the land was unfit for growing rice. On the contrary, in the border region between Louisiana and Texas, according to Russell Smith, due to the "wonderful levelness" of the land, one finds "the newest and most interesting of all the world's rice fields."[39] Credit must also go to the pioneer labor of these Dutch settlers, although it is their successors who benefited from it, because the locale of Nederland in Jefferson County is now one of the two greatest rice districts in Texas. There are no Dutch farmers here anymore, but it was Dutch capital that partly made all this possible! The Port Arthur Rice and Irrigation Company, founded through this Dutch capital, takes care of no less than 125,000 acres of irrigated land.[40]

Although the town of Nederland increased in importance, the number of

Netherlanders there waned. When [Dutch Vice-consul F. E. H.] Groenman visited it in 1914, there were only four families left![41] Only one, G. Van de Weg, was really prosperous; he gradually bought more land. The two brothers Koelemaij also did well. One of them, P. K. Koelemaij, had been a member of the Queen's celebration committee. This points to optimism, an important and needed quality of pioneers, which often insures success. Both of these brothers were still operating farms, but they had difficulties with a poor market, and they were mostly dependent on storekeepers who wanted to make big profits. J. Van Tijen wrote to me: "The soil is clay and produces very heavily"; but he adds cautiously, "if the season is right."[42] Maybe this is precisely what hampered them once in a while! Nevertheless, the colony continued to grow because a few colonists had remained due to the high farm prices during the war years, and especially it was influenced by the increasing growth of Port Arthur. In addition to being a lumber seaport, it became more and more an important oil port and industrial city. Also the growth of the oil town of Beaumont had a beneficial influence.

Because of this development there were in January, 1920, about eighteen Dutch families living on their own farms ranging from twenty to two hundred acres. Some were engaged in cattle raising and others in dairying and gardening. This latter enterprise brought about the founding of the Southeast Texas Truck Growers' Association, of which D. G. Reinstra was secretary. Port Arthur and Beaumont, which expanded rapidly after the discovery of oil in 1901 and subsequent years, became the most important market places for truck-garden crops and cattle products.

As we have seen, Port Arthur was the terminus of the Kansas City Southern Railroad, but also of a line of the Southern Pacific. The city was founded in 1895 on Sabine Lake, a characteristic part of the lagoon coast of the Gulf and part of the partially "drowned" Sabine River. Port Arthur is connected with the Gulf by this river mouth. The middle course of the Sabine River, which is navigable, could enlarge the hinterland serviced by Port Arthur, although to a far lesser extent than did the railroads, provided also that more care is taken of the waterways than has been the case up to now.

For us as Netherlanders it is interesting that Port Arthur was built largely with Dutch capital. In 1895 a second organization, the Port Arthur Townsite Company, was formed out of the above-named Port Arthur Land Company. It had a capital of $600,000 and was given the sole task of selling 4,000 acres of land of the Port Arthur Land Company. The land was designated especially for the development of the town of Port Arthur. From the Port Arthur Townsite Company, the Holland-Texas Hypotheekbank [Mortgage Bank] was born in 1911. It had a capital of $1.5 million, with headquarters in Amsterdam and a branch office in Port Arthur. This banking institution, after it had liquidated the Port Arthur Townsite Company in 1912 due to financial policy considerations (just as earlier in Washington State), was split into three divisions—land sales, home construction, and mortgage lending. Later these divisions were reunited, Everwijn Lange wrote to me, and the bank has "facilitated the settlement of thousands, of whom several were Netherlanders."[43]

The Americans acknowledged the importance of the Holland-Texas Hypotheekbank for the town of Port Arthur and call it "one of the city's valuable assets,"[44] which reminds us of the Holland Bank in Spokane. Besides the companies that have already been mentioned, Netherlanders are closely involved with the still existing Port Arthur Land Company, the Port Arthur Farm Company, and the American Land and Oil Company. These companies are controlled to a large extent by the "International Land Syndicate" established in Amsterdam in 1901, of which at first J. De Goeijen, Jr., and since 1903, E. J. Everwijn Lange, was the director.[45]

The city owes its rise to the opening of the Kansas City Southern Railroad in 1898.[46] In that same year the city was incorporated. It became an important transport harbor especially for lumber. With the discovery of oil near Beaumont in 1901, not only this city but also Port Arthur became more important. It not only became an oil harbor but an oil industry center. Large refineries have been established since then, which are connected with the oil fields in Texas and Oklahoma by pipelines. The oil lands rose to $100,000 an acre and were too expensive, while around Port Arthur land was obtainable for about $100 an acre. One of the two large refineries, the Texas Company, is directed by a Netherlander, L. F. J. Wilking, who is responsible for 2,500 employees. Of these a few are fellow countrymen. These Dutch workers are highly valued in Port Arthur, as is also the case with Dutch workers elsewhere in the United States. At present Wilking is also our consul there.

In 1920, about 150 Netherlanders from thirty families lived in Port Arthur. In part they came from the settlement of Nederland, in part from Winnie—about which more later—and in part also from runaway sailors and other seafarers, which is an element we often meet in big seaports.[47] In addition to these groups, mostly factory workers, one finds the small but interesting nucleus of businessmen closely connected with the above-named companies. What R. Insinger and J. P. André Mottu have been for Spokane and Norfolk respectively, so in a somewhat lesser way J. Van Tijen was for Port Arthur until his recent return to the Netherlands. However, they all were managers who ran companies according to directives from their headquarters in Amsterdam. One of the great Amsterdam leaders was E. J. Everwijn Lange, who built Port Arthur and Spokane out of his office in Amsterdam! It was De Goeijen, Everwijn Lange, and Van Tijen who have made Port Arthur—which advertises itself now as an important summer fishing resort with "tarpon, fresh and salt water fishes of all kinds!"[48]—into an important place of business and industry. It is also a pleasant place to live, which is a combination of things rarely found in the United States. The Dutch promoters saw to it that the Port Arthur Americans could proudly say: "Verily, citizenship in Port Arthur, the 'Pan American Gateway,' means something."[49]

In general the true Dutch immigrants did not show much interest in settling in Texas, although in the days of Van Raalte and Scholte there was already talk about it and articles about Texas repeatedly appeared in our various provincial newspapers. They appeared, for instance, in the *Weekblad voor het Kanton Bergum* [*Weekly of Kanton Bergum*], which in 1884 tried to explain that the name Texas may have originated from "Ta has," i.e., "here is everything."[50] Could a more suggestive interpretation be found? In spite of that "everything," all attempts at Dutch colonization in Texas have failed. To the continual astonishment of our consul Haagsma at St. Louis, Dutchmen seemed to be turned off by the possibilities in Texas.[51] In 1902 he was irked again that so many Dutch were moving from Iowa to North Dakota with its "nearly Siberian climate," while among the many Americans moving from the North to Arkansas, Missouri, and Texas, there was hardly a Hollander.

Some years later new attempts were made to settle Netherlanders near the Gulf of Mexico in a similar, though perhaps somewhat less fertile, region but with a larger hinterland and better market opportunities than the colony of Nederland had. But it also failed. In 1900, a West Indian tornado, a "hurricane" accompanied by a "tidal wave," devastated the town of Galveston, and six years later a Dutch company was involved in rebuilding the town. Did its activities draw attention to the importance of Dutch workers once more? At any rate, somewhat later around 1909, the Holland-American land dealer Koch—maybe the same one we met in Minnesota—tried to have Netherlanders and Dutch Americans settle on his real estate east of Galveston at Winnie and later on also at a location five miles further, at Hampshire.[52] Both places were in Jefferson County between Galveston and Port Arthur, fifteen miles from the coast. Land was advertised at $40 an acre among our fellow countrymen, and initially not without success, since many a Dutch American was quite ready to move on a moment's notice.

Also here, as in Nederland, the Christian Reformed Church hastened to lead church life in the right channels. They organized a church that was at the same time a recommendation for Koch's land company. Making full use of this additional publicity, the company raised its price to $50 an acre!

E. J. G. Bloemendaal, who had so much success with the farmers in Sioux County, Iowa, visited the new colony sometime after it had started.[53] He found his countrymen in a very good mood and full of confidence for the future. "They expected that the land would rise to $300 an acre." Obviously a certain speculative attitude, in addition to a dose of optimism, was not lacking among them. Especially, the elders of the Christian Reformed Church tried to convince Bloemendaal about the great fertility of the soil. In doing so they showed themselves to be allies of the land dealer, although moved by quite different motives. What they were after was a strengthening of their church. One elder declared that one could make a living on five acres. Another elder, the very first Hollander who had arrived a year and a half before, spoke of sixteen-foot corn stalks while twelve feet would already be quite good. Most of the Hollanders were gardeners, truck farmers. Due to mild winters, they could make a good profit on early vegetables and fruit, all the more so since they expected to grow two crops per year. They grew potatoes, tomatoes, cucumbers, all kinds of melons, and even cotton, alfalfa, and rice, all of which promised much for the future. The rice fields offered an especially beautiful sight. "Stretching endlessly and surrounded by a small dam, the water was pumped over the land by the company." It cost $6 per acre and the water had to stand on the land for one hundred days.

No matter how beautiful things looked, Bloemendaal did not dare to urge anyone to settle in Winnie. "I cannot urge them not to do it either," he added. The soil was so much different than in the North. It was "a mixture of all kinds of colors, including white, and a small amount of sand." This careful farmer wondered whether such soil would remain fertile as time went by. He finally concluded: "Everyone must consider for himself, and must examine, before he does anything." This was extremely wise advice, because great responsibility rested upon anyone involved with promoting this colonization. Already a few years later this settlement that had started out so beautifully was nearly finished and the colonists had spread all over the United States; some had landed in Port Arthur.

When the one million-acre ranch of a certain Mrs. King was sold, perhaps the largest ranch in the United States, Koch tried to sell part of it (around 50,120 acres) to the Netherlanders; he was only partially successful. This may have been due also to the fact that our consul at Port Arthur, who visited this colony of Riviera in Kleberg County, did not have much confidence in the project because there was too little rainfall and people had to rely on artesian wells.[54] And yet, the power of publicity did wonders! A number of Netherlanders dared to undertake this venture and several lost much money there. The land was good but too expensive, considering the drought that could last six months and longer so that half of the land is unworkable!

The land agents failed to mention these dry conditions, although they dared to ask $200 to $300 an acre for what they called fruit land and where fruit growing was done. Beware of land agents, warned one of the Texas colonists, J. Zandbergen, who had settled in the Rio Grande Valley near McAllen. A number of Netherlanders who had lived for a while in America, some already for a very long time, had settled in and around the village of Idenburg. Too many, however, were defrauded by Americans and left in disappointment. A few went to the oil fields of Tampico, Mexico, drawn by the higher wages paid there by fellow Dutchmen in charge of the Mexican operations.[55] Often these harassed roamers, these land seekers, were restless. Does the town of Harlingen in southeastern Texas remind us of them? Perhaps it does, but certainly not the town of Holland in Belt County; not a single Netherlander dwells there.

Finally, I wish to mention an attempt around 1915 to draw Netherlanders to northeastern Texas, to the neighborhood of the town of Paris, northwest of the hamlet of Bloomburg on the Kansas City Southern Railroad. Here the earth was heavy black prairie soil, part of the black belt. In addition to cotton they were expected to grow grains. I do not believe that "Colonel" J. S. Williams succeeded in this effort.[56]

The Dutch day laborers felt more at home in Texas than the farmers, at least in the big cities where "first class" carpenters, masons, and painters could usually find plenty of jobs. Therefore, one finds some in Dallas (28 in 1920) and some in San Antonio, where until recently the Holland-Texas Hypotheekbank had a branch office. In 1920, 59 Netherlanders lived in San Antonio; most were manual laborers plus a few office workers. The total of Dutch-born living in Texas numbered 261 in 1900, 424 in 1910, and 554 in 1920. The Americans of Dutch descent are obviously greater in number.

C. In Arkansas, Oklahoma, Louisiana, Alabama, and Florida

Earlier we have already noted that some Holland Americans left Sioux County, Iowa, and moved to Arkansas. A number of other Dutchmen settled here in 1910, especially in the extreme northwest, in the well-known tourist region of Arkansas along the rims of the Ozark Mountains. They settled in and around towns like Decatur, Gravette, and Gentry, where they especially engaged in fruit growing, while others became chicken farmers and still others storekeepers.[57] In Decatur, where the Holland-American Fruit Products Company was established, they received recognition through the fact that a "Hollander," G. Brusse, became secretary of the "Commercial Club" in 1917.[58] The fact that all three towns were located on the Kansas City Southern Railroad showed a certain relationship between the part played by the Dutch in establishing the rail line and these towns. So far, these towns have not been "privileged" by a Reformed or Christian Reformed Church, since the Dutch element there was either not strong enough or not religious enough. For that matter, the number of Dutch "Arkansawyers" has never been great. There were 69 in 1900, 145 in 1910, while it went down to 116 in 1920. One should remember that these numbers do not include those who were born in America of Dutch parents, for those are listed as "native born" Americans.

Equally insignificant, numerically speaking, is the Dutch element in Oklahoma, the state that was originally intended for the Indians and was the last one that was partially opened to the white landseekers in 1892. This was the state where, according to Mencken, "the American frontier is gasping out its last breath."[59] Also here Dutch capital took part in "the making of the State." This was not only the case with the Kansas City Southern, which helped to open up the eastern part of Oklahoma, but it was also the case with financial support the Dutch gave to build other railway lines. S. F. Van Oss became interested in establishing a branch line of the Atchinson Railroad. Therefore, the town of Van Oss appeared and since 1919 is inhabited mostly by Blacks.[60]

As far as I know, this financial support did not lead to colonization. Nor did the Dutch "petroleum interests" in the state bring in any of our countrymen, except for an occasional Dutch engineer and laborer.

Yet there have been some Dutch settlements in Oklahoma by fellow countrymen who had first settled in Pella, Iowa, and surroundings. These settlements were most likely due to the influence of mission work by the Reformed Church among the Indians and other inhabitants, and which made this land better known in Dutch circles. Mission posts of this denomination were found in various towns since 1900. Later, they were organized into congregations and were even joined together as the Classis of Oklahoma. One thing and another led to the founding of a Dutch settlement at Moore, in Cass Township, where in 1906 a congregation was formed and a small church was built in the hills, the Sandham Memorial Church.[61]

It seems that as time passed the Dutch farmers did not feel at home because of the climate, or because of social conditions that still strongly resembled those of the Wild West. Maybe it was both. Anyway, after a few years the church congregation disintegrated "because our people wished to leave that community."[62] This is the only very sparse information about this colony that came to my attention. The Reformed Church also left Oklahoma. This was understandable since this state was described by someone who had lived there for years as "the worst possible place for an idealist"; it is a "boomer state" that is mostly inhabited by land speculators instead of land seekers.[63] In 1911 the Reformed Church transferred all of its congregations in this state to the Presbyterian congregations. In these "churches" the predominantly southern people felt more at home than in the "Dutch" church organization, whose diligent missionaries had started so hopefully.[64]

As far as the small folks of Dutch stock were concerned, they never took root in a state whose governing body was fully corrupt due in part to "oil." It was declared that there "graft [is] so prevalent and inalienable a feature of State government that the only citizens who are not partaking of it are the stupid or unlucky."[65] Thus it is understandable that the number of Dutch colonists has never been great in Oklahoma. There were 85 in 1900, 230 in 1910 and 176 in 1920. But all the greater were the Oklahoma interests of our oilmen, of our stockholders of the "Koninklijke," the "Royal Dutch" [Shell].

While Reformed influences were noticeable in the Oklahoma colonization, the many Dutch Roman Catholic priests working in the state of Louisiana in 1911 led to an effort to have Dutch Roman Catholics settle there. The former archbishop of New Orleans was a Netherlander, Monsignor [Francis] Jansen [Janssens], who would always be remembered as a "benefactor of the whole congregation," according to our ambassador in Washington. In the diocese of Alexandria alone there were twenty-three Dutch priests in 1911 while the bishop himself, C[ornelius] Van de Ven, was also a Netherlander.

Cotton growing in the South had suffered so much from the boll weevil that many a planter had left his plantation. The land was divided into forty-acre tracts and offered for sale to the colonists. These "forties" were advertised as outstanding for gardening and farming, in short, for "diversified agriculture." The warm climate made possible the growing of early vegetables which obviously commanded higher prices on American markets than the vegetables becoming more plentiful later on in the season.

People did not have to fear the Blacks in the South since they were a peaceful lot. Neither did people have to be afraid to be equated and treated like Blacks, declared canon J. B. Bogaerts, who was chairman of the "Bureau of Colonization in the State of Louisiana." This gentleman tried to give colonization a more idealistic character by emphasizing not only preservation of the faith but also the spreading of it.[66]

Indeed, an earnest attempt was made to get a Dutch Roman Catholic settlement in Louisiana. Father [Pieter M. H.] Wijnhoven, a Dutch priest connected with the archbishopric of New Orleans and known for his practical charity work, tried to start a Dutch farming colony near New Orleans.[67] But he was not successful.[68] As I have pointed out before, there never was a great desire to settle in the southern states. The climate and the Black population were two great hindrances that no brochure writer, even a canon, could fully invalidate. In this special instance, this "diocesan" attempt, although supported by the archbishop of New Orleans, J. H. Blenk, and by the bishop of Alexandria, was opposed by mightier if not higher Roman Catholics. It seems strange and gives much food for thought to see other Dutch-American priests at the behest of other archbishops warn people against small Catholic undertakings and against "Diocesan Bureaus" that recommend their own state at the expense of other states who sometimes have available a greater variety of land.[69] More about this later.

What would Dutch emigration candidates think of such internecine competition between their honored priests, bishops, and archbishops in this land of promise, in America? Is it any surprise at all that they began to have doubts and finally rather went their own way? Here are a few figures that show that "Madame de la Louisiane" had but little charm for Dutch settlers; she drew 78 in 1900, 113 in 1910, and 260 in 1920. About half of these people were settled in New Orleans, the great transit center, which had 27, 43, and 149 Dutch-born for the respective years.

In the adjoining state of Mississippi the number of Netherlanders is even less. In 1900, 11 Netherlanders lived there and in 1910 none, while in 1920 they numbered 31. As far as I know, colonization was never tried here.

In the beginning of the twentieth century, Dutch capital and promotors took part in the industrialization process in neighboring Alabama. The Dutch managed the Cullman Coal and Coke Company that worked a mining area. A Dutch firm and Dutch engineers built a railway for this company and even the town of Juliana would arise.[70] In 1913, a small Dutch colony of fifteen Holland families was located in and around the town of Foley in southern Alabama, and was doing well.[71]

In the spring of 1918, new attempts were made to recruit Netherlanders for this state, but the well-known Nederlandsche Vereeniging "Landverhuiz-ing" [the Dutch Association "Emigration"] pointed out with emphasis the two great hindrances of the South: the climate and the Black population.[72] In the largest city of Alabama, the industrial center of Birmingham, there were only 3 Netherlanders in 1900, 18 in 1910, and 13 in 1920. In the seaport of Mobile there were 15 in 1910 and 21 in 1920. For the whole state the following numbers are given: 42 in 1900, 127 in 1910, and 83 in 1920.

Finally, we come to the most eastern Gulf state of Florida, bordering on the Atlantic Ocean. Although colonists had settled in this "Riviera" of the United States since 1870, it took until the nineties before colonization became more important, when a few large railways were built and numer-ous land companies started their "work."[73] At the dawn of the twentieth century those companies also attempted to draw Dutch settlers to their lands. They used the good offices of a Rotterdam company to promote Florida lands and awaken Dutch interest in them. Their publicity called attention to the fertile northern area and the mild climate as ideal for truck gardening. Both conditions were also very favorable for growing tobacco.

So it is not by accident that the first Dutch colonists who settled in Florida at the dawn of the twentieth century were a few "planters" who chose the northern part of the state around Monticello, Jefferson County, for the growing of tobacco. They seemed to have been successful, for they mentioned in 1912 "being satisfied with the results obtained so far."[74] These results were obtained in spite of the high-priced land, varying from $50 to $150 per acre!

Around the same time (between 1911 and 1912) a small Dutch settle-ment must have been started on the land of the Womanada Land Company in the area of Crawford, northwest of Florida's port city of Jacksonville. This organization went bankrupt and so the colonists had to leave, just as in California. When in 1914 our consul Groenman went to look for his fellow countrymen around Crawford, the honorable gentleman did not find a single one. They all had left![75] In 1914 the "Florida Company" advertised this area among our fellow Dutchmen.

Swampier than the Atlantic coast are the Florida lands along the Gulf of Mexico. They are part of the lagoon area mentioned before. This explains why it was only later, in 1919, that an attempt was made to have Dutch farmers settle along Florida's Gulf Coast near the phosphate harbor of Tampa, which had become important through the Atlantic Coast Line Railroad.

The Tampa Bay Land Company was clever enough in 1919 to get a number of Frisian farmers, who had already lived for some time in the state of New York, to settle three miles south of Tampa, in South Tampa. The Frisians bought land from this company in portions ranging from ten to twenty acres. First they had to clear the land of trees and then they became successfully engaged in their familiar dairy business. [?] Julsingha Blerick, our vice-consul at Tampa visited them in 1920 and found them satisfied and well-established even though they had performed strenuous pioneer labor.[76] The land was made ready for dairying, and they had built barns and homes that were not there when they came. These colonists were full of optimism and their numbers grew steadily thanks to the publicity that appeared in the Holland-American newspapers through the intermediary of J. M. Vos of Newark, New Jersey, on behalf of the Tampa Bay Land Company.[77]

The Frisians were determined to develop a prosperous Dutch colony and to prove to Florida that their land was fit for something better than the growing of grapefruit and oranges. This unique dairy colony in Florida was to be named "New Netherland." One will search in vain for it on the map. As so many others, this Dutch-American venture also went up in smoke. Again the Netherlanders must have trusted others too much. Here more than anywhere else, they had to depend on their own insight and their own initiative; because precisely here, like in all of the southeastern United States, the "land sharks" were on the lookout for suckers.[78] And yet, as Julsingha Blerick wrote to me, the Tampa Bay Land Company seemed to be a favorable exception to the rule.[79]

In most recent times, a new group of Netherlanders who had generally lived in America for years, settled in Florida. A few went to Jacksonville in the north, but most of them came to Miami in South Florida. The tremendous speculation in land and the big plans to make Florida a "world playground," etc., in short the "boom" that surpassed everything that had ever been seen in America in this respect, brought colonists, including a number of Netherlanders, from all American states to this land of sunshine.[80] Now that this "boom" is over and without having made too many victims among the generally speculative Dutch element, increasing numbers of them have settled in Florida. This is particularly the case as ever larger parts of the swampy Everglades are drained and turn out to be good land for truck farming. Classis Muskegon of the ever-active Christian Reformed Church showed concern for the welfare of these Dutch "Floridians" and sent the preacher B. H. Spalink to them.[81]

A mission post, or if you will, a Society of the Christian Reformed Church, had been established for the Hollanders in 1926 in the famous town of Miami, one of the most important seaside resorts near the Everglades. A few times they made use of the Presbyterian church building. Thus religion may be able to help in the establishment of a Dutch colony in Florida, aided by the great publicity that the mission preacher Spalink purposely aims at the religious element of his fellow Dutchmen. This is an important support for land companies who, as we have often seen, do not underestimate the church as a colonizing factor! Desperate cases of rheumatism are cured in Florida due to the sun; there are only two days without sunshine! Spalink declared further that there are excellent types of soil that are able to produce three or more harvests per year. Spalink is firmly convinced that after some more growth the Society of the Christian Reformed Church can found a full-fledged congregation. Is not this a beautiful example of co-operation of realtors and church interests?

However, the church does not always have the strength to hold on to its Dutch members in the South, as we have noted in Nederland and Winnie in Texas, and in the Oklahoma settlement. In one respect the Florida colony has now a greater chance of success. The Netherlanders on the whole do not live among the "Southerners" who are more foreign to them, but among the more familiar "Northern people." Florida is the only southern state with a predominant number of northern people.[82] With a variation on [Israel] Zangwill's words, Florida calls itself the "meltingpot of the States." In and around Miami, where most of the Netherlanders live, Northerners form 75 to 85 percent of the population. This is a good reason to feel more quickly at home in this sunny South. Besides, during the winter months they meet a number of their fellow Dutchmen who temporarily flee the northern cold. In this "Gulf and Atlantic" state there lived only 52 Nether-landers in 1900. This number in 1910 is unknown to me, while in 1920 it had increased to 357. In view of the preceding, their number must be far greater now.

D. In Virginia and North Carolina

Again we come to the Atlantic coast where our attention is drawn to three colonization attempts, one in Virginia and two in North Carolina. These were the states on which Cohen Stuart and later Charles Boissevain had focused people's attention. According to the Nederlandsche Vereeni-ging "Landverhuizing," these states, as well as the southeast in general, were suited for colonists who think they must go "farming in America," even though they are from business or administrative circles and have enough money to pay the price of an "apprenticeship" in the new situation should this be the case.[83] Thus what happened here was somewhat like in California where "intellectuals" also colonized and totally failed.

Of such an "intellectual" character was the small settlement that L. J. De Balbian started in November, 1912, in Basic City in the well-known Shenan-doah Valley of Virginia on land that he had bought from the Shenandoah Valley Apple Lands Company. Nearly all of the Dutch colonists became members of the Algemeen Nederlandsch Verbond [General Dutch Alliance] and Balbian was the director for the Nederlandsch-Anerikaansche Fruitteelt Maatschappij [Dutch-American Fruit Growing Company] called "Virginia." He was also deemed to be the "locator" of this colony and became the representative of the Alliance in Basic City.

Something new in the area of land publicity also happened, because a beautiful write-up appeared in the Alliance organ, *Neerlandia*, which must have inspired unusual confidence. The fruit growing colony was not large. It

numbered six Dutch families, a few administrators and laborers. The Fruitteelt Maatschappij operated two farms called Gelderland and Drenthe. The
colonist families each owned the following farms: Holland (50 acres), Richmond (15 acres), Claerbergen, Utrecht, and Sumatra (30 acres each) and
Salland (40 acres). In 1912 the Hollanders had a total of 350 acres on which
they had planted mostly apple and peach trees, but where they also grew
other fruit: pears, plums, grapes, cherries, etc. Meanwhile beneath the trees
corn, tomatoes, potatoes, etc. could be grown. Besides, cattle raising,
chicken raising, and apiculture kept them busy. The whole framework of this
settlement, in keeping with the Alliance spirit, had a real Dutch national
character as was shown by the names of the company and the farms. Last
but not least, the Dutch character came to expression in the tricolored
Dutch flag on the office building of the Fruitteelt Maatschappij "Virginia."[84]

Must it not have been a delight for an ardent fatherlander to live in a
similar national community where they also thought about establishing a
Dutch school? In one of the schools there was already a Dutch teacher;
however, that turned out to be a report based on a "misunderstanding."[85]
Moreover, this venture was launched in a valley that was considered as "the
golden spot of the world," the historic granary of the United States.

Great plans were in the making. Once additional Netherlanders had settled here, they would start a "Cooperative Association of Dutch Plantation
Owners," with their own building near one of the stations in Basic City.
Together they would buy spraying equipment, tools, packing materials, etc.,
which would result in enormous savings on expenses. It would be the kind
of cooperative that Boissevain had also staunchly recommended and which
according to him "would bring about wonders."[86]

These wonders never came to pass in Basic City. Groenman visited this
patriotic colony in November, 1914, and found a number of disappointed
colonists. It appeared—as often happens—that the brochure's presentation
of things had been far too beautiful and based on "misunderstanding" and
on "mistakes." The soil was not as fertile as claimed, the trees did not grow
as rapidly, and the operating costs were not that low. The only thing that
was calculated "liberally" was the price of undeveloped land that sold at
$75 per acre.[87] This explains why Basic City is not mentioned anymore in the
A. N. V.'s organ *Neerlandia*.

Although the official consular reports made repeated, emphatic mention
of the "possibilities" in Virginia, particularly the regions around Norfolk and
Richmond were strongly recommended as "very suitable" for the settlement
of "solid" Dutch citizens,[88] as far as I know no specific settlements were
made, even though, as we saw, the banker André Mottu still lived in Norfolk. The total number of Netherlanders in Virginia was 72 in 1900, 99 in
1910, and 335 in 1920, and of the latter 118 lived in Norfolk.

Meanwhile two other colonies failed, both initiated by the North Carolina
Truck Development Company. They were located in the nearly flat coastal
lagoon region a few miles north of North Carolina's largest seaport, Wil-

mington. Already in 1909 the above-named organization had tried to start a Dutch truck-gardening colony at Castle Haynes about fifteen kilometers [10 miles] north of Wilmington. Herman Vogels, who as the former director of vegetable auction organizations was familiar with garden produce, seemed to be its originator and driving force. This soil was sour, the so-called Norfolk sandy loam. It first had to be sweetened before it could be used, but then it was good vegetable growing soil. Also the climate was ideal for truck farming. Because of the generally low, flat land and the heavy rainfall, the organization dug a system of canals, etc., to rid the soil of the excess water.

Numerous growers settled in Castle Haynes and at first most of them were rather successful. But others were disappointed about the soil since they showed little inclination to sweeten it first. H. R. Jolles, who was then our consul at Savannah, visited the colony in 1912 and found most of the colonists in comfortable circumstances. Many were engaged in growing trees, shubbery, and flowers for which it was not difficult to find a market in Wilmington and in the larger cities like Baltimore, Philadelphia, and New York. With great expectations for the future they hoped to make Castle Haynes the "Boskoop"* of the United States.[89] They also grew fruit, so that in 1913 Vogels could declare: "Four years ago there was hardly a fruit tree in Castle Haynes and now there are acres upon acres planted with fruit. Vogels even grew some wheat successfully, a product "that within living memory had never been seen there before."[90] Other colonists also showed satisfaction and appreciated their freedom. "For myself I'm happy to be here and prefer a free life with somewhat less money rather than much hard work and plenty of money," declared L. De Wildt, who was optimistic about the "future" because of the rapid developments of Wilmington and surroundings.[91]

That explains why the North Carolina Truck Development Company decided, a year after the beginning of the first colony, to start a second one ten kilometers [about six miles] further north. It was called Van Eeden, after the well-known Dutch writer Frederik Van Eeden,† a name not accidently chosen. This is not the place to elaborate on Frederik Van Eeden's social ideas. It is sufficient, however, to recall his attempt to realize his social ideals in the colony of Walden near Bussum [in 1898 in the Province of Noord Holland], which attempt ended in failure. The basic idea of this utopian experiment was that land ownership was cooperative and there would be relative equality for all; this combination of factors, it was hoped, would lead to a more or less harmonious society. But Van Eeden was sadly

---

*Boskoop is today a town of some 11,000 inhabitants, half-way between Leiden and Utrecht. Since the fifth century it has been a renowned center for arboriculture, and produces more than half of all Dutch trees and shrubs of which 90 percent are exported.

†Frederik Willem Van Eeden (1860–1932) was a versatile Dutch poet, prose writer, essayist, playwright, and medical doctor. He led the literary renewal movement of the 1880s and is considered one of the greatest and most controversial Dutch authors of his age.

disappointed and he was equally shocked in the trust he had put in his workers. Subsequently he declared in a talk with E. d'Oliveira that "they are not even able to take sufficient care of a small undertaking."[92] The official socialists viewed Van Eeden's attempt as mere swaggering and showing off, and not devoid of a desire for publicity. By way of their party member at that time, "J. Saks," they commented that the colony was "neither financially nor morally a well-run, paying operation by a philanthropic gentleman farmer who could not even manage his people."[93] Van Eeden, in turn, accused these socialists of a lack of communal sense, which was an especially remarkable allegation concerning people "who call themselves socialists."

In spite of his shaken confidence, Van Eeden did not abandon his ideals, ideals he did not try to put into practice in the Netherlands but in America, the country of his hero, H. D. [Henry David] Thoreau, and his idyllic Walden. Did Van Eeden remember Owen's experiments in New Harmony, Indiana, and those of so many other world reformers? In any case, there was plenty of space and seemingly also plenty of interested people. Van Eeden visited America three times in 1908 and 1909 to exchange ideas with a number of Americans and gave a few lectures explaining his plans. [?] Hoggson of New York became Van Eeden's coworker. Also [?] Mac Rae of Wilmington, North Carolina, seemed to be strongly inclined toward these ideas. This was a fact of importance since Mac Rae was the director of the North Carolina Truck Development Company and therefore a pragmatist who saw "something" in Van Eeden's aims. Therefore he reserved part of the land of this company for the beginning of Van Eeden's colony. However, as a good businessman, he demanded proper security!

It may seem strange that an idealist like Van Eeden got so closely involved with a real estate man, the type of man who in America is considered to be the epitome of levelheadedness and materialism (although this need not always be the case). Obviously this was because of circumstances. How else could one obtain land? Besides, by that time Van Eeden was no longer shunning high finances and capitalists, among whom he thought he was perceiving more idealism and a greater sense of community than among the men of "the party." In addition, he had come to the insight since the failure of Bussum's Walden, "that machines have no power but that the machinist is the power. The co-operatives must be led by shrewd, experienced men of business with commercial or industrial genius or talents. In short, guidance must come from the top. Whether they are capitalists or socialists doesn't matter," thus commented Van Eeden.[94]

Such conceptions made the working together of Van Eeden and Mac Rae not only understandable but also possible. So it must have been the "views" of Mac Rae that further changed the already altered ideas of Van Eeden concerning cooperatives. In the Netherlands Van Eeden had started out with cooperative land ownership; now in America cooperative production would be considered first. And that approach would be followed after the producers had first bought a few acres for themselves at the very substantial price of $50 per acre. This was a price which our consul in Savannah intimated "cannot be called cheap under the circumstances."[95] Yet Mac Rae must have known this better than Van Eeden!

However this may have been, the new colony of 3,000 hectares [7,413 acres] was advertised on a large scale. A few colonists from Castle Haynes helped in this effort. Herman Vogels, one of the pioneers from Castle Haynes, declared that the soil in Van Eeden was "surely very good" and "better than at Castle Haynes." That statement came after our Dutch consul in Savannah had investigated the soil and found it to be not so good, too "sour," and lacking in humus. Vogels remonstrated also against the consul with respect to the conditions set by the company; their payment conditions were "as fair as could be," Vogels insisted. He was also of the opinion that the climate was excellent, living costs low, and the possibility for marketing the products very great. "Potatoes and greens that in Holland would be called hog food are considered first quality produce on the local markets here," he pointed out to Van Eeden's idealists! Finally, he urged all those interested in North Carolina to contact himself, Vogels, since he was fully confident "that it was in the interest of president Mac Rae as well as of the company to have people succeed."[96]

And what about the writer Van Eeden? In word and as well as in writing he encouraged the colonization at Van Eeden. He hoped that more well-to-do people, the so-called "five-percent philanthropists" would provide some investment money on reasonable terms, so that also less well-to-do people could become members of the "Association of Co-Producers," that Van Eeden, Hoggson and Mac Rae expected to set up. So it came to be that Willem Rond and his family took possession of Van Eeden's first house. The Dijkers family, overly blessed with children, and later the family Leeuwenberg, etc., all settled in the new colony. Is it possible to view already in these prolific families part of Van Eeden's required idealism? Surely with a large number of children they were bound to succeed since, for pragmatic reasons, big families were ideal colonist families. Yet, Van Eeden demanded more and set out to write down his altered ideas for the benefit of candidate colonists. He was convinced that just ownership was only that amount one could use for oneself through one's own labors. Furthermore he saw [prevalent] ownership to be the power to prevent others from making use of any goods. The only way to free oneself from the "terrible grip of owners" would be to live completely independently, that is, from one's own production on one's own soil. But under present conditions this was impossible—this was the lesson from Walden. However, a group of people could pledge to work cooperatively and produce cooperatively on their own soil, so that the most cunning methods of owner control would have no power over them, according to Mac Rae's coworker!

It should be everybody's wish to become rich in an honest way, to produce as much as possible of what people need and to satisfy real human needs. Under such conditions, people could form a community with "group ownership" that would guarantee in a much better way than in our present society that all that belonged to the community would really remain in the hands of the community, and that private ownership could never become a tool to rob the weak. Everyone would be allowed to join the cooperative and remain lord and master of his own house and land. Private ownership was acknowledged under certain conditions, namely, that it was put under cooperative supervision. The owner might leave it as inheritance to his children, but he had to promise not to alienate it, or to neglect it, or to have other people work it and pocket the profits from their labor. As soon as any property is abused, it reverts to the cooperative. These "limitations" were offset by the benefits of cooperative buying of supplies and cooperative selling of the products. They even thought about their own cooperative industry: a cooperative dairy, canning factory, bakery, etc., where wage laborers might be employed provided they would not be treated as wage-slaves but where they would receive decent pay for decent work. Here also a man of some experience is speaking!

Let us understand Van Eeden correctly. He did not wish to have a community of saints, but of people who did not have to be more well-behaved or stronger than they were now. "They have to be a little less greedy and short-sighted, and become a little less childish—that is all."[97] But even this was still asking too much. Again Van Eeden misjudged mankind, because this model colony did not come to any good either, in spite of the fact that in many respects it had adapted more to everyday circumstances, that its future looked rosy, and despite the initial busy activity at Van Eeden. Yet the colonists earned nothing. On the contrary, they saw their capital melt away and felt cheated. The scenario came to its usual end. Van Eeden has since remained totally silent.

The warm South was too much for the Dutch; the unaccustomed soil and Mac Rae's land prices that were none too low must have been contributing factors. The cooperative idea, which really could have been so valuable here and which had been advocated by businessmen like Boissevain, De Balbian, and others, was not the only cause of this failure. This is shown by the fact that in spite of the self-confidence of Herman Vogels, the American "Boskoop" at Castle Haynes came to practically nothing either. Therefore, it is not strange that when in 1915 M. N. Beeking tried anew in Hilversum to awaken an interest among the Dutch for the North Carolina Truck Development Company, this time for its older colony of St. Helena, just between the two Dutch settlements, he did not breathe a word about the Netherlanders who lived in the Great Winter Garden or—more likely—had lived there.[98]

Our vice-consul at Tampa, Florida, who cherished a lively interest in Dutch colonization in America, has confirmed to me that the failure of the North Carolina colonies was mostly due to quarreling and dissension.[99] And he added, "[it was] especially due to a leader who wasn't fit for the job," which demonstrated the correctness of Van Eeden's allegation "that it all depends on leadership." In 1920 only 115 Netherlanders remained in North Carolina. Among these was the Van Noppen family from Zeeland, which brought with them their son Leonard Charles. As we shall see later, he became famous even beyond the borders of the United States and the Netherlands.

J. P. André Mottu mentioned to me that there are still some Dutch families living near Castle Haynes.[100] In 1925, the Broad Acre Ranch, Inc., even established a new Dutch colony at Terra Ceia, Beaufort County, North Carolina, for which the Netherlander A. M. Welling of Albany tried to recruit Dutch-American colonists.[101] By a clever, indeed cunning maneuver, the Broad Acre Ranch people unofficially called in the help of semi-"official" Dutch civil servant, Dr. N. Van Aken, who was connected with the Dutch Chamber of Commerce in New York. It hardly deserves any mention to say that the "report" of this gentleman contained the usual, trite song of praise about the land in question.[102] In the meantime more than ten families have settled in Terra Ceia.[103]

Virtually all of the Dutch colonizations in the South have failed. This fact is not without importance for us, because for centuries there has been propaganda among Netherlanders to settle in the Dutch East Indies, with the same lack of results. Obviously, the reasons for failure were many, as could be observed in every colony. We do not have to repeat these reasons here. Of paramount importance for us is the fact that the colonists in most southern settlements gave the climate as the main reason for their failure. To be sure, a few Netherlanders are still living in the South, for example at Nederland, Texas, where they have become acclimatized. There are also some in Arkansas and elsewhere, but they live by preference in towns and not in the countryside. If one asks landseekers about this, they give the same answer as they did to Groenman: "Our constitution needs cold winters" and "The hot weather is not good for us."[104] Everywhere one can observe the debilitating influence of this hot weather, which increased the burdens of the colonists. Therefore, it should be pointed out that those who nevertheless have succeeded in the South were a few select ones, those who came through the first most troublesome pioneer years in the United States and because of this were more adapted. This is confirmed by T. Van Tijen who testified in one of his consular reports at Port Arthur, Texas: "I know from experience that most of the Hollanders who live in these regions came from the North after they had lived there in the Midwestern states for some years." Therefore, coming directly from the Netherlands and settling in one of the southern states is in most instances to be strongly discouraged, even in spite of "reports" like those of Dr. V. Van Aken and similar propagandists.

12

Roman Catholic and Miscellaneous Settlements

In the previous chapter we mentioned a Roman Catholic settlement that "Father [Pieter M. H.] Wijnhoven" tried to establish in Louisiana, but he encountered opposition from apparently more influential fellow believers. The latter consisted of a group of priests who intended to aid their coreligionists and prevent their dispersion. With that purpose in mind, they founded in 1911 "The Catholic Colonization Society U.S.A." (C.C.S.) with a Chicago Hollander, Julius E. De Vos, as its president and no less than two archbishops, J. Glennon of St. Louis, Missouri, and S. G. Messmer of Milwaukee, Wisconsin, as influential patrons.[1]

Such top-notch sponsorship obviously ruled out any speculative practices. "No speculation" was therefore one of its slogans, one of the basic rules of this reportedly completely nonprofit organization. The group wished to be viewed above all as a "not for profit society." It only made a study of areas considered suitable for colonization, negotiated with the companies—although it had no capital and did not buy and sell any land—and obligated the company whose land was chosen for a settlement to guarantee for three years the support of the leader-priest of the settlement, who would be designated by the C.C.S. Naturally the C.C.S. was to be compensated for its efforts, which would be in the best interests of the land company. The Catholic Colonization Society noted that the designated priest "is the main factor in bringing and keeping the people on the place." (This is an example of American practicality.) Thus all parties would profit. With the cooperation of the priest, care was taken to insure that the land company obtained first-class colonists for the lands because, according to the C.C.S., "it is a select class of people that go to Catholic colonies; people of deep faith and sterling character, of high aims and noble enterprise."

According to the Catholic Colonization Society, colonization was in turn made easier for the settlers. The C.C.S. provided "a society and a market," because these settlements " . . . created ideal Christian communities; each was a paradise by itself in a world that was indifferent to religion." They formed model communities where people could enjoy all conveniences of modern times and where there was concern for both body and soul, and where both temporal and eternal concerns were looked after. In short, "Catholic colonies as planned are full of progress, high intellectual development and pleasant in societal life."[2] Thus, the C.C.S. served the church in various ways; it promoted the faith and in this way worked hard for church extension, all with a disinterest, at least in a higher sense, which nevertheless did not exclude mutual competition in Roman Catholic circles. This competition within the creed itself was shown by the way in which it opposed equally disinterested colonization efforts that originated among other Roman Catholics. Some of these efforts even came from the diocese level, as in the above example where the archbishop of New Orleans gave his support.[3] So we see, once again, that everything that has to do with colonization is filled with enigmas, even in cases where the church gives its sanction.

It was not surprising that a Netherlander headed the C.C.S. This was due to the fact that, although it aimed to help Roman Catholics of all nationalities, it was mostly Dutch and Belgian priests who had taken the lead already at the very beginning of the colonization efforts. As early as 1907 a "Priesterbond" [Priests Association] had been organized in Chicago by the Dutch and Belgian clergy with the two-fold purpose of promoting the spiritual interests of Dutch and Belgian Roman Catholics living in various parts of America and also to aid their countrymen upon their arrival in America.[4] Indeed, the Catholic Colonization Society had been born out of this association of Belgian and Holland Priests; at its founding, nine different nationalities were represented among the priest-members. These priests openly admitted the preponderance of Netherlanders and Belgians. As they declared: "The Belgian and Holland Priesterbond has made the greatest progress in the colonization movement; it has a special and efficient department of colonization, which has given the idea and impulse to the formation of the National Society."[5]

Indeed, it was so. By 1909 the Priesterbond had formulated plans for a settlement at Butler and at Onamia in Minnesota, which were realized the year after. In that same year the settlement of Wilhelmina was started in Missouri. All three attracted mainly Dutch and, in addition, Belgian-Flemish groups. Therefore, they merit our full attention even though there were already more predominantly Belgian settlements elsewhere, such as Spalding in Nebraska and Ghent in Minnesota.

Negotiations between church prelates and large landowners in Minnesota, in the northeastern portion of Otter Tail County, led to planning for the Dutch settlement of Butler in the area. Land was made available to Dutch Catholics on "moderate" terms—$20 an acre with $3 down and the rest in annual installments with interest at 6 percent. The land was fertile black loam, most of it covered with trees and shrubs. As a temporary measure a parcel of developed land would be made available by the land company at a rental fee of $2 to $3 per acre, thus enabling individuals to begin cultivation and cattle raising at once, and to build up some reserves.

A. A. Van den Heuvel, pastor at Loretto, was authorized by the bishops of Duluth and St. Cloud and the archbishop of St. Paul, all of Minnesota, to go to the Netherlands as "chaplain of colonization" to recruit interested parties for the new colony, or rather to assist in any way possible potential Catholic emigrants. Thus, this leader should not be put on a par with ordinary, run-of-the-mill recruiters. Van den Heuvel was "active" in our country for three months and selected those who "might be inclined to try their luck in the New World," as the well-known Crozier Father H. W. IJzermans, informed the readers of *Het Centrum*. He, another priest, and a brother from Van den Heuvel's native Uden, where he was born and educated, would accompany the elect to the American paradise. They were "elect" because not all those who applied turned out to be fit. Therefore, many had to be turned down. Candidates had to be not only "good and faithful Catholics" but they had also to possess at least *fl.* 2,000, which would be needed as a downpayment for land, for the purchase of cattle and equipment, and especially for the passage that would be in second class. About ninety colonists met these qualifications and, accompanied by the priests, embarked at Antwerp on March 12, 1910, on the *Lapland*, "the largest and most luxurious steamer of the Red Star Line."

After a favorable voyage and an equally pleasant overland journey via a special train with sleeping cars, a diner, etc., during which the immigrants were repeatedly treated "to beer, cigars, and sweets," they arrived at Butler or, rather, at the nearby station of New York Mills. Here they were met by carriages and so rode to the new colony where Dutch and American flags welcomed them. How different from Van Raalte's arrival at the Black River! The colonists were graciously and hospitably greeted at the model farm of the land company. They were housed in some comfortable temporary houses and in empty homes, and during the next few days busied themselves with inspecting the surrounding lands and making arrangements for possible purchases.

Busy days lay ahead; there was hard work to do. The purchased land had to be cleared and cultivated and houses had to be built. Within a few months many were able to make a living. By the fall of that year, most of the colonists owned eight or nine cows—one owned fifteen—and a large amount of milk could be delivered to a nearby creamery.

It was a fairyland for the children. There were many of them—Van den Heuvel had chosen large families—and, following the American custom, schools were not in session in summer and so the children enjoyed a wonderful freedom. However, IJzermans decided to give them a few lessons, including English, so that they would be somewhat prepared when school opened in September and not feel as strangers in their new school surroundings. At the same time they would be somewhat prepared for the Americanization process.

Everyone, both young and old, seemed to feel quite at home, aided by the welcome extended to them by the predominantly Protestant population of Butler. According to IJzermans, these latter seemed to be very pleased with the "new Dutch colonists" and considered them to be "very fine people," perhaps because the Americans assumed that the Hollanders had large sums of money with them. The fact that the colonists were of the "rather affluent urban and rural classes" and that some of them had come from large Dutch cities, which thus made them *crème de la crème*, plus their travel in second-class accommodation, must have helped to foster this impression.

In any case, they also profited from this impression. The Hall, the community building, could be used free of charge by IJzermans for his preaching; he was pleased that Protestants also attended. This friendliness went so far that the Protestants even cleaned the hall and when the Catholic church was completed they donated a clock for it. In addition, a good deal of support was given by the land company, which extended all possible help in the matter of building, procuring provisions, etc. In a letter, IJzermans testified that the colony had become a success during its first year, and he invited especially men with large families and possessing some capital to locate in the new settlement.[6]

In the meantime, Julius E. De Vos, whose attention had also been drawn to Mille Lacs County in Minnesota, investigated the area around Onamia, accompanied by his countryman Father [F. X.] Van Nistelrooi, pastor at Kimberly in the Wisconsin Fox River Valley. He was also accompanied by an American, F. Murray, who served as the general manager of the colonies established with the support of the bishop of Duluth, Minnesota. The Mille Lacs area greatly appealed to him. It was a typical moraine landscape: gravely hills covered with thick forests interspersed with numerous fertile black loam valleys formed by the melted snow and ice. The area turned out to be ideal land for grass and clover, and was praised as a "fine dairy country."

A Roman Catholic colony was planned to the southwest of the lake region, where we have already noted many settlements. Once again Van den Heuvel was commissioned to go to the Netherlands to assemble the needed colonists.[7] The "chaplain of colonization" established an "office" at Ginneken, near Breda, and in May of 1911 left for America with a group of Hollanders.[8]

Meanwhile the Catholic Society went on publicizing the colony as being well-situated, near a branch of an important railroad—the Minneapolis, St. Paul and Sault Ste. Marie Railway ("the Soo Line"). There the soil was "a strong producer of all vegetations, grain and root crops," but more than anything else, thanks to the "luxuriant" grasses, a beautiful pastureland, "the paradise of the dairy cow." It will be noted that the Colonization Society understood the power of advertising. This second settlement was named New Netherlands; Van Nistelrooi served as the manager and Father William Van Dinter of Onamia was assigned as its pastor.[9]

Still, matters in these two settlements—Butler and New Netherlands—did not go as well as had been hoped. It seems that too much attention had been paid to the "pennies" [duitjes] and not enough to fitness, and so disappointments could not be avoided. A hint of this already appeared in a letter of IJzermans written from Butler on August 31, 1910.[10] In it he noted casually that the prosperity of the colonists made their adjustment "somewhat more difficult" and he further remarked that young unmarried people were the least desirable. In retrospect, it appeared that these were the first who left the colony! Four years later, when IJzermans was transferred, he honestly confessed in *Het Centrum* that initially the Butler settlement had not worked out well at all. Within the first year two large households had returned to Holland; the women had become homesick and one of the men asserted that he had not come to America to work. Had the New World been presented to him as too much of a lazybones utopia? The other man was making a good living but returned to the Netherlands because of his wife. Almost all of the "singles" who had not purchased farms—and so were not tied down—had moved elsewhere in hopes of earning more than $25 a month. Other families had moved to Montana, etc.

In the autumn of 1914 IJzermans was again in Butler, on a visit from his parish at the "city" of Verndale, and he found that only a few of the original families were still there. Fortunately other families had moved in, replacing those who had left. It was the same experience as that of the Protestant settlements; advertising continued to be effective. It is also interesting to note that the Protestants left Butler, making room for the Catholics; eventually it became a truly Roman Catholic community. When IJzermans visited there again in 1915, there were thirty Catholic families and the settlement appeared to be a success. Economic conditions were, "if not rosy, at least not dark either." The woodlands had been cleared and made partly into pastures while the other part was devoted to corn, rye, wheat, oats, and potatoes. Any and all Hollanders were welcome there provided they left their "dreary complaints" behind in Holland.[11]

The colony of New Netherlands, near Onamia, must have had a similar experience. IJzermans conceded that in both colonies there had been some carelessness in the choice of colonists. "Based on the experience we have had in both of our colonies, I would be more hesitant than I was originally, even with regard to the genuine farmers." Now, the Reverend Father's advice was very cautious: "I would not dare advise anyone in Holland to settle here, either for religious or moral reasons or because of unemployment." Still, he did not discourage the arrival of stalwart laborers, although he preferred Hollanders or Belgians who had already lived in America for a few years.[12]

The disappointments experienced by these early colonists did not remain a secret. Our consul-general in Chicago felt compelled to report on it. From this report it becomes clear that there had been far too much carelessness in recruiting. It is true that several of the colonists knew a trade but they knew absolutely nothing about agriculture. What could such people do with the land they had bought? Therefore, the consul-general, [George] Birkhoff, strongly urged non-farmers not to settle in Minnesota.[13]

In the meantime the energetic De Vos had planned a third colony to be located in Dunclin County, Missouri; it was to be named Wilhelmina, after the popular Dutch queen. Earlier the archbishop of Missouri, J. J. Glennon, had founded Glennonville on a tract he had purchased in southeastern Missouri in the swampy, but very fertile, Mississippi and St. Francis river valleys. De Vos, accompanied by his nephew, a farmer from Spalding, Nebraska, and Father [Vincent] Tesselaar of the Service Order in Chicago, decided after a few visits in 1909 and 1910, that this alluvial soil, ten to thirty feet deep, would be very well suited for Hollanders, accustomed as they were to watery land. The archbishop offered this land very inexpensively, at "pioneer prices," and in an area, according to De Vos, where the harvests were "enormous" and both corn and cotton grew "to the highest perfection" and these harvests could be followed by a potato crop—all in the same year.

Originally the Reverend F. F. Peeters was in charge during the reclaiming of the first part of the land. Then Father Tesselaar, a native of Noord Holland, and according to De Vos, the ideal man to convert the marshy land into good crop and pasture land, was designated as both "director" and "pastor" at Wilhelmina. Both Peeters and Tesselaar were fully qualified and hailed as experts "in machinery and in devices of all kinds to start new enterprises." When one further realizes that the land is traversed by "a splendid navigable river," that there are two railroads nearby, that it is unusually suitable for farming, truck gardening and cattle raising and is a "paradise for poultry farmers," and that St. Louis and other cities are eagerly awaiting the products of the colony—four harvests in a year!—then one must agree with De Vos that Wilhelmina "had to become the queen of the Catholic Dutch and Flemish settlements."

It appears that it was also the intent to have Netherlanders, who had already lived for some years in America, move to the new paradise, where a small church was soon to be established. Specially low-priced, round-trip excursion tickets for landseekers were made available in Green Bay, Milwaukee, Chicago, Moline, and Grand Rapids; all towns where Roman Catholic Netherlanders and Flemings lived.[14] I am not aware how De Vos' predictions turned out or if many bought land at fifteen to twenty-two dollars an acre. But I must report that in a 1915 directory of Dutch settlements in the United States, there is one single item for Missouri—Wilhelmina.[15] And that is saying a lot; it must have survived the first difficult years.

These Dutch examples gave rise to the Catholic Colonization Society as a further development of the colonization division of the Priesterbond. There was first of all the Dutch-Belgian bureau and secondly an Italian bureau.

It can thus be seen that in spite of the strong zeal for Americanization that made such ethnic colonies no longer desirable, nevertheless the religious interests were given higher preference, although the founders of these colonies were quick to assert the "desire [for] the quick and full amalgamation and merging of such races in the American nation."[16] "Our principal object [was] to surround [the colonists] with the helps and safeguards of Catholic faith and practice." At the same time another aim was realized, although this was more openly admitted among the Protestants: the establishment of new centers from which the faith could be spread. In this regard there are similarities between the Roman Catholic and the Calvinist colonial policy, although the Roman church appeared to be more active here, at times even in quite a "*kaufmännisch*" [mercantile] way. Butler, New Netherlands, and Wilhelmina remind us somewhat of the way in which the colonies of Van Raalte, Scholte, and Van den Broek were founded, but with the big difference that there is more planning now, while in the forties there was the pressure of circumstances. To a certain degree one may compare persons such as IJzermans, Tesselaar, and others, with the pioneer preachers of the forties and especially of later years, but I do not know of a recruiting minister like the recruiting priest Van den Heuvel, who came to the Netherlands specifically to induce colonists to come to America and who was especially appointed to perform that very particular task. From the standpoint of Roman Catholic extension policy, Butler, New Netherlands, and Wilhelmina constitute interesting contributions also.

In addition to these three, numerous other Catholic colonies were established under the aegis of the Catholic Colonization Society. De Vos reported that they were in the most diverse places in the Union—in Washington State and Montana, as well as in Florida and Texas.[17] In this latter state Calvinists were also urged to settle on the lands of Theodore Koch at Riviera in Kleberg County. I am not aware as to how many Hollanders are living in all those settlements where non-Catholics were also admitted. In any case, they were welcome at Spalding and Humphrey in Nebraska and at Ghent, Graceville, and elsewhere in Minnesota. These were all "havens of security for the tired-out city people, who long to go to the country." My research in these latter areas was usually fruitless, especially because the C.C.S. informed me that, much to its regret, it could not enlighten me.[18]

Thus we approach the end of the colonization efforts known to me. "Known to me," I must say, because much remains secret, classified; there remain many projects that people prefer not to talk about. In connection with this whole subject of colonization, I have often noted that there was "something rotten." Is that perhaps the reason for the above-mentioned powerlessness to enlighten me regarding the Catholic colonies? Is that perhaps also the reason that other attempts that came to my attention were hushed up? For example, there was the firm of H. Oyens and Sons that also informed that to its regret it could not supply me with information, so they wrote, "which could be of assistance to me in the task I had undertaken."[19] From other sources I learned that the projected undertaking was "not a success." It went out of business.[20]

A curious colonization effort was undertaken by the Nederlandsche Handelmaatschappij [Dutch Trading Company], the founding of a tenant farmer colony. Years ago this organization commissioned A. Colijn, Jr., the well-known mayor of Nieuwer Amstel, to purchase extensive acreage in Stark County, located in the southwestern part of North Dakota. Contrary to the recommendation of Colijn, as he informed me, the organization settled at its own expense a number of Dutch tenant farmers on its land holdings situated west of the city of Dickinson, along the railroad line of the Northern Pacific. However, the youthful colony had to cope with reverses due to recurring periods of drought and so there was little if any talk of "profit." The company finally followed the advice of Colijn and, as much as possible, let the colonists farm for themselves.[21]

Some of the farmers bought land and others followed the American custom of working as tenants for a third of the harvest for a newly and independently organized group, known as the "Holland Dakota Landbouw Compagnie" [Holland Dakota Agriculture Company]. This "Company" was organized in Amsterdam on May 19, 1910, and it is still located there. It has as its purpose the purchase of lands in the United States and the clearing, cultivating, leasing, and selling of the land, the selling and buying of farm products and implements, the extension of credit to farmers, etc. The firm was organized with the intent of purchasing land in the vicinity of Dickinson, Eland, South Heart, and Belfield, all in North Dakota. At the same time the company acquired $20,200 of the $25,000 capital stock of the First National Bank of Belfield, North Dakota. These shares became available in 1912. In 1925, the firm held 14,400 acres of land, of which 12,994 acres were farm land located in Stark and Billings counties; it also had 290 building

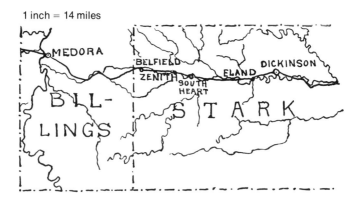

The field of activity of the Holland-Dakota Agricultural Company in North Dakota.

lots in Belfield and 18 lots in the business section plus the bank building as well as other lots in South Heart. The company, under the direction of A. Colijn and F. H. De Kock van Leeuwen, had a capitalization of *fl*.1,500,000 [$600,000].

Those who devoted themselves to cattle raising were doing well, according to a report of Colijn issued during the winter of 1920. For agriculture, however, the very fertile, volcanic soil was too dry. In 1920 fifty Dutch families from all parts of the Netherlands were located in the area west of Dickinson, in and around Eland, South Heart, Zenith, and Belfield.

The company itself is still operating with a deficit because of years of drought. A large number of tenants left during the drought years and as a result only 1,132 acres of its holdings were cultivated in 1920, as compared to 2,355 acres in 1919. As a consequence the wheat and oat harvests were very small and this resulted in a deficit of *fl*.64,353 [$25,741] in 1920. The subsequent years were not much better and one reads in the reports of the "large number of abandoned farms and the many sales by mortgage holders"—a cultural phenomenon which we already learned about earlier, especially in Montana. Conditions improved somewhat in 1924 and have continued to do so. As a result the company's deficit in 1925 was reduced from *fl*.171,246 to *fl*.170,232 guilders [$68,498 to $68,093]. The latter report gave its asset as *fl*.1,030,802 [$412,320] in farms and farm structures as well as *fl*.152,202 [$60,880] in building lots in towns like Belfield and others which no longer grow very much. Its debts were *fl*.100,952 [$40,380].[22] Consequently, one cannot speak of a "flourishing" enterprise.

The attempt of an American firm, the "Danaher Holton Company" of Minneapolis, to establish a Dutch settlement in Orchard Valley in the extreme northwestern portion of Wisconsin, fairly near the city of Superior, was not a success. In the beginning "twenty sturdy Dutch families" settled there in the expectation that the region was "frost proof" during the growing season and that even tobacco could be grown there! This proved to be "erroneous" so that most of the colonists felt they had been deceived and left. Only a few—all of them complainers—remained.[23]

Thus I have reviewed many colonies of the most varied types. Some were religious in nature, others neutral. Some were founded under Protestant auspices, others under Roman Catholic direction. Only one or two were of a genuinely philanthropic nature; most were of the so-called "5% philanthropic" variety. Most of them can be justly considered as business ventures, with a smaller or larger percentage of "ethics" mixed in. In most cases the land companies were the chief beneficiaries. It was in particular this entrepreneurial spirit, with its primary motive of turning a profit, which caused so much disappointment, since it brought so many to America who did not belong there. In the end this resulted in a total loss of capital, which was not made up by private profits.

I will conclude, therefore, by relating the account of a colony in which disappointments were at a minimum and where there was no talk of deficits, a colony that may be regarded as a model and one of considerable interest for the future because no promoters in the usual meaning of the word were necessary. There were no governmental involvements or any important or self-important emigration committees. It was the kind of settlement that entailed a minimum of expense and which led to no subsequent criticism. There were no "official" scapegoats because each member held himself individually responsible or, at the most, could only hold a single friend here and there responsible.

This ideal settlement was the Frisian colony in Whitinsville, Massachusetts, located midway between the big cities of Providence and Worcester. We already became acquainted earlier with this type of settlement, although in a less conspicuous way. A few affluent residents in this beautiful village of Whitinsville—despite the many factories, its hilly diluvial landscape reminds one of Bussum and Zeist [in the Netherlands]—had some Frisian cattle shipped over between 1880 and 1890 to stock their model farms because the American cattle were very small and inferior. At the same time, this cattle transfer created a demand for some Frisian farm hands, and the first one went to work at the Castle Hill Farm. He liked it so much that he urged his friends and relatives in Friesland to join him; it was at a time when conditions were deplorable in the Netherlands. Before long a few of his friends came over, also unmarried. They were followed by several families from the southwestern corner of Friesland and a few from the Wartena area. Following up on this I found such family names as Bosma, Fennema, Visser, De Boer, Feenstra, Frieswijk, Plantenga, Glashouwer, Werkman, and Kooistra. By 1904, after about a ten-year period, the settlement had increased in number to about seven hundred.[24]

They found employment on the farms, and others earned a good living in the machine shops of Whitinsville, etc. Since they were well thought of because of their faithful performance they began to work for a weekly wage of $7.50 immediately after their arrival straight from the Netherlands, even though they were still "plenty green." As a result, many a worker was able to send money back for passage tickets. The travel expenses were repaid later on and then others could have relatives and friends come over. There were always openings for them in the factories, rather than on the rocky, infertile soil. A similar "settlement" had been made at Lafayette, Indiana, in the 1850s but there was this difference: the colony at Whitinsville grew far more rapidly due to the much-improved transportation facilities.

But even these more "modern" immigrants still had some unusual experiences. For example, one family made the ocean voyage in third class and arrived destitute in Worcester, having spent all its money on travel; not a penny was left! The family found itself in a foreign environment without funds and totally ignorant of the language of the country. Finally, at his wits' end, the head of the household decided to walk to Whitinsville! After many hours he arrived at the factory town, totally exhausted "with only one shoe left."

Enroute he had been treated like a common "tramp." "He had been snubbed as a dog and chased away like a vagrant, even when he asked for a drink of water," so tells us the Reverend J. Jansen, who was later his minister.[25] Once he had arrived in the village, all his troubles were over; relatives arranged for his wife and children to come from Worcester.

Many of the colonists were of a religious bent and soon gatherings were held where sermons were read and psalms sung in the Dutch language. The Presbyterian Church building was made available to them, at least its basement, and later also the town hall for evening services. By coincidence the sending of some money to a Seceder church in Wartena led to correspondence with the leader of that little church, F. J. Drost, which resulted in his arrival at Whitinsville in 1895. Here he again met some of his former villagers. Drost succeeded in influencing his new congregation to give up their original intention of setting up an independent church and instead to affiliate with the Christian Reformed Church there. Drost himself, who had formerly been a catechism teacher in the Hervormde Kerk, was later ordained into the ministry by Classis Hudson of the Christian Reformed Church, after having first served the new congregation as a "preaching elder."[26] At its inception, thirteen families joined this Christian Reformed group. In 1898 the congregation had its own building and Drost served until 1902; in that year he was called to the church in Eastmanville, Michigan.[27] Dr. J. Jansen, who had come directly from the Netherlands, followed Drost and he served from 1904 to 1906. The church had four hundred members—four-sevenths of the total number of seven hundred souls in the Frisian colony. Jansen found it to be a pleasant place to work although there were some restless and troublesome elements. But Drost had established the church on a firm basis and that made Jansen's work easier, as the latter gratefully acknowledged. Jansen returned to the Netherlands and years later, reminiscing about his time in America: "Yes, I found Whitinsville a pleasant place to work! How inspiring was the sound of the Dutch psalms echoing in our simple but friendly little church. Our services were conducted entirely on the Dutch pattern and were very impressive; they caused many a parishioner to be one in thought with their relatives and fellow believers in the old home country, which most of them would never see again."[28]

Following Jansen, F. Fortuin and L. Trap served this isolated congregation. A Harvard student, (now Dr.) C. Bouma, led the first English evening service.[29] Since that time it has been a bilingual congregation. Now in 1925 it numbers 162 families and 752 souls. If the ratio between the Christian Reformed congregation and the other churches and the non-churched has remained the same, which is very likely, the colony should number about 1,300 settlers of Dutch descent, i.e., those born in the Netherlands or born in America of Dutch parents.

There were 993 Dutch-born settlers living in Massachusetts in 1900; by 1910 there were 1,589, and in 1920, there were 2,063, most of whom lived in Whitinsville. There was also a small number in Boston, largely cigar makers, to whom reference was made earlier. This once Puritan city had 391 resident Hollanders in 1900, 486 in 1910, and 691 in 1920. There were only a few in the industrial towns of Fall River, Lowell, and Worcester—3, 9, and 8 respectively in 1910. The famous town of Cambridge had a total of 18 in 1910. In 1920 these last four cities respectively had 6, 17, 69, and 20 Hollanders.

Part Six

The Contemporary Significance of Dutch Americans

13

The Economic Development of the Settlements Since About 1895 and Their Present-Day Significance

---

A. General Economic Trends

1. *The Spreading Out of the Settlements*

There were a significant number of attempts at colonization that we may consider as having almost totally miscarried, while in other instances settlements could scarcely be called successful. Inevitably, our thoughts go back to those colonies that were founded during the fifties and seventies and that flourished so wonderfully in spite of the fact that in many respects there were far greater difficulties to overcome in those times. So, once more I turn my attention to the colonies in Michigan, Wisconsin, Illinois, and Iowa and to the accomplishments of Van Raalte, Van den Broek, De Jong, Scholte, and Hospers.

I am quite justified in calling attention to these men simply because they contributed in such a high degree to the success of the colonies. It is not an overstatement to assert that the present status of the Michigan colony and Sioux County, Iowa, colony could not have been achieved without the efforts of Van Raalte and Hospers. Perhaps the same can be said, but not to the same degree, of Scholte's work in Pella.

Van Raalte, Hospers, and to some extent Scholte also, were for their settlements what Thomas Carlyle termed the Great Men: "the leaders of men, . . . the shapers, the modelers, and in a larger sense the creators of what the great mass had managed to achieve."[1] We certainly agree with the author of *Heroes, Hero Worship, and the Heroic in History* that they were the ones who in this case put their stamp on the colonies. Especially from the numerous conversations I have had, I could detect, even during the short time that I was able to spend in the various settlements, that the spirit of Scholte still pervades Pella, that of Hospers is still present in Orange City, and that of Van Raalte pervades not only Holland in the Michigan colony but nearly all the settlements I visited, both in the eastern and midwestern United States.

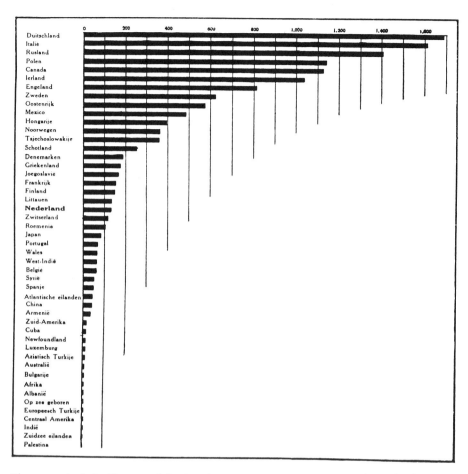

The numerical significance of the Dutch in America. An overview of the foreign-born
population of the United States in 1920 according to the country of birth. The figures
are in thousands (from the Fourteenth Census).*

Hardly any of the later settlements knew such men. They had to make do
with such individuals as Prins, Nijgh, Zoutman, Van der Hoogt, Vermaat,
Kroes, and men of that ilk who were themselves in part instruments of big
business but never under the sway of a noble thought. The idealism that
animated and strengthened such men as Van Raalte, Van den Broek, and
their followers was totally foreign to these hucksters.

The significance of the "forty-ers" and also of Hospers in the seventies
manifested itself immediately in the choice of places for settlement, and as
we now know, those locations were of paramount importance.

*The data in this chart cannot be confirmed in the published volumes of the Fourteenth Census of
the United States, 1920. Cf. Vol. 2, *Population*, p. 893.

Thus the wrong choice of areas too far south and therefore too hot spelled disaster for many a colony, while the droughts in the West doomed other colonies. But I hasten to add that both with respect to the location of the area to be colonized and the nature of the soil, which was a second cause for many disappointments, the men in the forties and again in the seventies had a much wider choice than was the case later on. As a result, their responsibility was even greater.

This difference in choice is the reason why the accounts of developments of the older colonies that were so successful did not go much beyond 1895. The period of 1890–1895 was a landmark in their history. From that time on there has been a continual change in their growth and consequently in their sociographic appearance and economic significance, which has continued practically undisturbed until our own time. This modification is closely related to the rapidly changing sociographic structure of the United States of that same period, from a predominantly agricultural nation to a nation in which industry did not play a less important role. This latter development was in part due to the world-wide progress of technology, and in part due also, and more in particular, to the fact that the homestead lands in the Union at the disposal of the landseekers were running out. Many a would-be homesteader saw himself compelled to spend the rest of his days as a factory worker.

With the end of "free" land around 1890, there came an end to the two and a half century-old colonization of the "West" in the old sense of the term, that is, to the extensive exploitation by pioneers. There was not much, if any, further possibility of expanding the "borders." With few exceptions, such as the Oklahoma territory that was initially put at the disposal of the Indians, frontier life or pioneer life had come to an end. F. J. Turner called this coming to a standstill of the "border" shifts, "this final rush of American energy upon the remaining wilderness," "the closing of a great historic movement."[2]

This occurrence was quite evident in the Dutch settlements. Earlier I pointed out that when the land in the Pella area became too expensive, a "homestead" colony was established in Sioux County. In addition I mentioned that when the price of land in Michigan, Wisconsin, and elsewhere increased, new homestead settlements were established further west, at a distance of several days travel, in Kansas, Nebraska, and the Dakotas.

Thus the Hollanders, by the swarming out of many families, scattered across America just as the Germans did and as the Chinese had done in East Asia, as Count Béla Széchenyi had pointed out after his scientific journeys of 1877–1880.[3] Did not Jan Nollen already in the fifties consider Pella, Iowa, a beehive? This phenomenon had been taking place for years in the "new" America, while it had lasted for centuries in ancient China. Groups of colonists with their wives and children and a minimum of household goods, all packed in a covered wagon, would go father west to seek and settle on land that was as good as what they had left but much lower in price.

This swarming lessened after 1890, when most of the land became more expensive as a result of falling into private hands. Men who wished to remain farmers as well as their own boss were faced with the choice of settling in the less productive but cheaper lands of the arid Far West that also were largely in the hands of land companies or agents, or of purchasing much more expensive lands nearer their homes. The latter alternative resulted in the spreading of the existing settlements like "oil slicks." Therefore, we can observe after 1890 a more rapid growth than before that date of the colonies of Holland in Michigan, Pella and Sioux County in Iowa, etc.

This expansion resulted in an even stronger emergence than before of the exceptional qualities of the Netherlanders, especially after 1890 when extensive cultivation was more and more intensified and required more advanced skills. Then the farmers could enlarge their holding only when they had sufficient capital to buy out their immediate neighbors. Only under these circumstances did it become evident that Dutch character traits such as industry, patience, thrift and a love for and great knowledge of farming, led to a farming element of considerable significance in the United States. Indeed, in many respects they not only excelled over the Americans but over other nationalities as well.

In the contest between Americans and immigrants of the various nationalities, the latter were usually the winners, as far as farming was concerned. This did not take place immediately but after the difficulties of the first settling had been overcome and roots were put down in the new area, that is, after a selection process had taken place and the most able had managed to survive.

This type of victory was gained also because of the restless nature of the Americans who were quite prone to sell out "lock, stock, and barrel" and start anew elsewhere, as we have had occasion to point out frequently. This restlessness made it difficult for Americans to concentrate and to dedicate themselves exclusively to farming; they totally lacked the patience for it. The immigrants, once established, still felt for years like outsiders in their "American" surroundings. American culture also remained especially alien to them and in their "isolation" they consequently concentrated all their forces on their material task—to work for themselves and their family, to clear the land of debt and keep it that way, and also if possible to expand their holdings for their usually numerous children. Compared to such steady endeavors, Americans, who usually partook of the fullness of life, gave the impression—often wrongly—of being lazy, and this was in some cases even established without mincing matters. The life style of many colonists was religiously oriented, especially that of the Calvinists, but also that of the Mennonites, Roman Catholics, etc., and this strengthened them in their more or less ascetic life.

So it is understandable that already in the 17th and 18th centuries,

French colonists who had left their homeland for the sake of their religion (Protestantism) and had settled in New England and South Carolina, achieved greater prosperity than did the "American" neighbors around them. This is all the more remarkable because the French have on the whole been praised far less as settlers than their Germanic counterparts. [Gilbert] Chinard comments: "There is no doubt that the French quickly surpass the English settlers who lack perseverance and who seem rather ignorant to them."*[4] He supports this view with regard to the Huguenots in Massachusetts (New Oxford) and the Santee River colony in South Carolina where his fellow countrymen produced larger crops and achieved greater prosperity than the "English."

We should not ascribe these results mostly to the power of Calvinism, as Max Weber wanted to make us believe when he stressed above all the asceticism and capitalistic spirit of the Protestants and particuarly the Calvinists,[5] because Weber overlooked the fact that the French Roman Catholics in America (the French Canadians) are now more and more driving the American Puritans out of their very stronghold—the Boston area. "*Zeitvergeudung ist also die erste und prinzipiell schwerste aller Sünden*" [The wasting of time is thus the first and in principle the greatest of all sins] is a characteristic Puritan conviction, Weber asserted, basing this view on [Richard] Baxter's works.[6] This conviction also existed with so much vigor among Roman Catholics that the French Canadians, for example, have increasingly overtaken and in many a case even squeezed out the Puritans not only in the New England cities but also in the rural areas there. However—and this should be made perfectly clear—other factors also played an important role, as for example, the large families of these Canadians. As a result there are now thousands of French Canadian farmers in New England and the ideal of many thousands of others is to "*s'emparer du sol américain qu' abandonne le Yankee*" [take over the American land that the Yankees abandon]. The English Protestant element is being replaced more and more by the French Catholic element. In his *La Tragédie d'un Peuple* [Tragedy of a People], Emile Lauvrière writes that "*les Puritains disparaissent de leur vieil habitat jadis si durement acquis*" [the Puritans disappear from their old habitat which they had acquired with such great pains in days long ago]. He views this as one of the most remarkable demographic phenomena, "*un juste retour des choses humaines ou une intervention quasi providentielle*" [a just reversal of the human situation or an almost providential intervention].[7]

Would not the "isolation" here play as great a role as religious conviction? To this should be added the fact that the common man, who in a material sense is accustomed to a difficult existence, works harder than his neighbor who has reached a certain level of prosperity and who lives under

*"Il n'y a point de doute que les Français n'arrivent rapidement à surpasser les colons anglais qui manquent de persévérence et lui [Sic] semblent assez ignorants."

better circumstances. This is a phenomenon that has also been observed among the Dutch, and which manifests itself, for instance, in the constrast between the clay farmers and the sand farmers, the latter being the hardest workers, known as the toilers or plodders.

It appears that the Frenchman has not been considered very highly as a settler—in many cases unjustly so, in my view—and does not play by far the most important part in immigrant history. The Ost Frisian agriculturist [Fridrich] Arends, who lived for years in Missouri, portrayed them there and elsewhere as "usually poor rural economists."[8] Thirty years later, an anonymous but apt judge of immigrants commented that no nationality was less suited for immigration than was the French.[9] However, in my view we must be careful here to distinguish between "suitability" and "necessity." It is overlooked that the high productivity of the French soil in particular has created a local prosperity that mitigated against emigration and has even made it mostly unnecessary. Birth control was also a contributing factor, a factor that often went hand in hand with prosperity. "*Le peuple normand disparaît sur place: il n'émigre guère*" [The Normandy people vanish while staying put; they rarely emigrate], according to C. Vallaux and in this connection he quotes the well-known words of [Leopold] Mabilleau about "*la pléthore dont meurt la Normandie* [the overabundance of which Normandy is dying].[10]

It is entirely different with the Germans who were of tremendous significance in immigration and were considered to be unusually desirable colonists. Poverty forced tens of thousands of Germans to America. It was a real "*émigration de la faim*" [emigration of the starving]. Even more strongly than the French they demonstrated their dominance and drove out the American farmers. The well-known Karl Lamprecht was full of praise for their significance in American agriculture after he had visited the descendants of seventeenth-century German emigrants in Pennsylvania as well as those of the nineteenth century in Wisconsin.[11] According to Lamprecht, only one American state is well-cultivated, and that is German Pennsylvania, while in Wisconsin those parts that excel are inhabited by his fellow countrymen. There the great scholar even found "an improved Germany, an area of which the poet prophetically said that the land appeared like a garden; it is German farmland, a land of German diligence."* A. B. Faust, the author of one of the best books about the Germans in the United States, even considered his countrymen to be the best farmers in the Union. "For over 200 years the Germans have proved to be the most successful farmers in the United States. Statistics prove that the later German immigrants of the nineteenth century have upheld the age-old reputation of the German farmer."† Faust calls attention to the industry and thrift of the

---

*"ein verbessertes Deutschland, eine Gegend, von der der Dichter ahnend sagte: Und wie ein Garten war das Land zu schauen, das ist deutsches Farmerland, Land Deutschen Fleiszes."

†"Ueber zwei Jahrhunderte hat sich der Deutche als der erfolgreichste Landmann der Vereinigten Staaten bewährt. Aus den Statistiken geht hervor, dasz die späteren deutschen Einwanderer des 19. Jahrhunderts den alten Ruf des deutschen Landwirts aufrecht gehalten haben."

German farmers in the East as well as in the Midwest that enabled them to enlarge their holdings by constantly purchasing the lands of their non-German neighbors, especially of the Irish during the 18th century. And during the 19th century they caused *"die eingeborene Bevölkerung ständig zum Weiterziehen"* [the indigenous population constantly to move on].[12] They even displaced the energetic Scotch-Irish!

Since a writer may be inclined, even though unconsciously, to overrate the significance of his compatriots, we must read the German-American Faust as critically as the French-American Chinard, and in this light it is therefore all the more significant that French writers also acknowledged the great worth of the German farmers in America. For example, [R.] Gonnard agreed fully with his countryman [Achille] Viallate that the German element "has been one of the best among those that contributed in forming the contemporary United States"* and that its greatest service (*"le plus grand service"*) had been to give America "that class of agriculturists who have established themselves in the footsteps of the American pioneers"† in the Midwest.[13]

It is regrettable that Faust did not mention the Hollanders. Perhaps he included them with the Germans, as we have demonstrated on several previous occasions, as he did for example with the Mennonites and as Americans were so inclined to do. Perhaps he did not consider them separately but lumped them together under the heading of *"Andere Länder"* [Other Countries].[14] That is unfortunate because careful research indicates that whatever was said of the German farmers concerning their importance for America could be said to an even greater degree of those of Dutch blood. The Dutch tillers of the soil in the successful settlements were even more prosperous than were the Germans. Therefore we see in their colonies after the 1890–1895 period a greater evidence of expansion than in those of any other nationality. I compared this phenomenon with the spreading of an oil slick, which from a biological standpoint can be better compared, as Vidal de la Blache did, with the spreading of coral reefs.[15]

G. Schnücker, a German-American minister, who, although he had come from Hesse in southern Germany, had lived for years among the *Plat-duitschers* [northern Low Germans] (known to us as the Ost Frisians and closely related to the Dutch), was repeatedly impressed by their great prosperity. He frequently pointed out how they steadily grew, buying out their surrounding non-Frisian colonists. In numerous places the truth of the Frisian-American saying was *"aufs glänzendste"* [most conspicuously] demonstrated that where the Frisian obtained a foothold he stayed and gradually displaced all non-Frisians.[16]

The same held true for the Dutch Frisians, who were of the same stock and came from a similar area. It also applied to the other Hollanders, at

---

*"a été un des meilleurs parmi ceux qui ont contribué à former les Etats-Unis contemporains"
†"cette classe de cultivateurs qui sont allés s'établir à la suite des pionniers américains"

The expansion drive of Dutch-American farmers. 1, 2, and 3: The "capturing" of Hudsonville in Michigan — new celery farms and a celery field. 4: The "capturing" of Doon in Lyon County, Iowa — the Christian Reformed Church and parsonage, powerful allies (1-3, original photos by Dirk Nieland and others; 4, *The Banner*, Dec. 9, 1927).

least in so far as they were of Calvinistic conviction, as I was able to ascertain. Because of a lack of source material I dare not give a final judgment concerning the non-Calvinists, although I want to point out once more the definitely non-religious but still energetic element that established itself in the eighties and nineties in Sioux County, the most flourishing of all the colonies.

In most cases race and religion (asceticism!) were responsible for the striking degree of prosperity of our countrymen. This was first evident in the Van Raalte colony in Michigan, where most of the common folks had settled. Here the Dutch-American families spread out more and more to the villages in the area that had previously been entirely American. In another connection I wrote previously how this development could be traced in the successive establishments of Reformed and Christian Reformed churches. Let me remind the reader that the colony of 1846 and subsequent years mostly comprised the southern part of Ottawa County and the northern section of Allegan County and was generally located around Black Lake. In Allegan County there were originally the Calvinist Dutch-Bentheim (in short "Saxon") hamlet of Graafschap and four "Dutch" towns: Overisel (Overijsel), Hamilton, Fillmore, and Laketown. Since then, but especially after 1895, the Hollanders spread southward over Manlius and Health townships and then over Salem. Their spreading continued and now they are settled in large numbers in Allegan, Leighton, Wayland, and Martin.[17] In all these towns they built churches. One need only consult the church statistics.

In the same manner the Netherlanders spread to the north of Ottawa County; for example, the originally entirely American town of Jamestown has become a true "Dutch" enclave. In the course of several decades the "true" Americans had all been bought out. Already in 1894 a Christian Reformed Church was established in Jamestown—notice the date in relation to what I have observed previously. Eight years later a congregation came into being in Hudsonville to the north, while another one of this denomination was set up already in 1875 in Jenison, where a "colony" had formed as the result of "swarming." G. Van Schelven, a justice of the peace, and G. J. Diekema, a former member of the Michigan House of Representatives, both of whom live in Holland, Michigan, gave the same reasons for this spreading in conversations I had with them.[18] Both "Honorables" were convinced that the Hollanders lived more frugally, and therefore less expensively, and worked harder than did the Americans; they also more often did without. In addition, they were less inclined that the Yankees to move to other states, and they hankered less for city life.

The Dutch sense of family life is also greater. T. G. Van der Meulen related how strong these Dutch family bonds were in his account of the Johannes Witsenburg family which in the eighties had settled in the Pella area on a beautiful, "well-situated" farm and was doing very well and therefore had no reason whatsoever to move.[19] However, two of his children settled on their own farms in Nebraska at a time when fertile "free" tracts were still available. They were able to convince their father and mother and the children yet at home also to emigrate to Nebraska! A similar close family attachment was also evident in Michigan, where at that time all the free land was gone. But instead of the elders moving "farther west" with the children, it was the children who settled near their parents; there was no "swarming" here but rather an agglutination, with people remaining in or near the old family homestead. Many times Americans took advantage of this typical Dutch trait by asking higher prices for land they offered for sale to the Dutchmen, who would gladly pay $50 an acre more in order to have their children nearby.

The same thing took place in other settlements, although sometimes the circumstances were different. In the Illinois colonies, in South Holland and particularly in Roseland, expansion was difficult because of the high prices. Prices rose enormously because the lands had fallen into the hands of speculators as Chicago grew rapidly. In general the Netherlanders were not victimized in those locations because they were the first ones to own property there. And particularly in Roseland, which was nearest to the Windy City, they sometimes sold their lands at great profit to the real estate dealers and others who divided the farms and meadow lands into town lots or building lots for resale. Even so, many Netherlanders here bought out the Americans, as for example in Evergreen Park, a suburb of Chicago. Around 1870 it was still a rural town and many Germans had settled there. Ten years later the Hollanders began to arrive and bought out a large number of Germans. Consequently, today more than half of the population of this suburb is "Dutch" and it is striking to notice the many Frisian and Groningen names, as I did during a walk through the town. The colonists engage in truck gardening on the one hand, and on the other hand, work in Chicago. An example is Albert Oosterheerdt, a warm friend of the Netherlands, the representative of "*Nederland in den Vreemde*" [Holland Abroad], whose hospitality I had the pleasure to enjoy.[20] The strongest evidence of this expansion drive is found in the prairie state of Iowa where there were hardly any large cities to absorb many rural people, as in the case of Michigan and Illinois. In Iowa people had to stick to agriculture while a conversion to the more intensive truck gardening that can be done on smaller tracts has remained of lesser importance, as we shall see later, due to the lack of dense population centers.

At this point I also want to recall that in 1846 H. P. Scholte founded Pella in Lake Prairie Township, in Marion County, and following the Civil War the Dutch swarmed from this "beehive" to the northwestern tip of Iowa, to Kansas, Nebraska, "Dacotah," Colorado, Texas, etc. After the nineties they tended to stick closer to home. By then, as we already know, the good and very cheap lands, the free lands, had all been sold or given away. In the meantime, the settlers of Pella had achieved such great prosperity that they were able to buy the surrounding lands, even at higher prices, from their less successful American and other neighbors who then moved elsewhere.

In this fashion the well-to-do Hollanders took possession of all the land between the Des Moines and Skunk rivers. By diking the bottomlands, the low river banks, they were able to make them far more productive than anyone else. Then they spread north of the Skunk River and south of the Des Moines River as well as to the northwest and southeast of Pella, between these two rivers. Having originally settled in Marion County, they gradually took over large parts of neighboring Jasper and Mahaska counties. In 1911, all of the land within fifteen miles of Pella was "Dutch," and if one went to New Sharon, twenty miles northeast of Pella, or to Oskaloosa, eighteen miles to the southeast, scarcely any American farm could be found along these highways.[21]

Just as in Michigan and elsewhere, this expansion was reflected in the organization of Reformed and Christian Reformed churches. For our study, the dates of their founding are of particular significance. Here are but a few examples. Already in 1889 Otley, northwest of Pella, had a Christian Reformed Church; to the west lay the cheapest land. Then there was Peoria, in Mahaska County, northeast of Pella and just north of the Skunk River, which got its church in 1892. Leighton, to the southeast and also in Mahaska County, built one in 1893. Sully, north of Pella and Peoria, in Jasper County, got a church in 1896. Tracy, south of the Des Moines River obtained one in 1903 and Prairie City, northwest of Pella, in 1904, etc. Near Bussey, even further to the south, our countrymen also settled, but as of now no church has been organized there.[22]

Naturally, this expansion did not go unnoticed even in wider quarters. In 1909 an article appeared in one of the newspapers of Iowa's capital city, Des Moines, with these headlines: "Hollanders are the Boys. They buy up overflow Land and are getting rich." The first part of this article is of particular interest to us because it states more or less in these words: "It will not be many years before the Hollanders are in possession of all the land between Pella and Oskaloosa and between the Des Moines and the Skunk rivers. They buy thousands of acres each year and it is axiomatic that, once a Hollander has bought a farm, he never lets it go. They especially buy the less costly lands and make them fertile; they 'make it blossom like the rose'." The Americans finally had to admit: "The Hollander also is an intensive farmer and it is no unusual thing for one of them to make a [single] crop pay for the land."[23]

Even more interesting than in the area of Pella is the continuous expansion of our countrymen in the northwestern part of the state, where we find Iowa's greatest concentration of Dutch settlers, in Sioux County and the surrounding areas. We recall that this began with the founding of Orange City in 1870 by Hospers. This Sioux County development is interesting because here the Hollanders had to compete not only with Americans but also with Irish, Norwegians, and especially Germans.

Following the original colonization of the Orange City area in Holland Township and elsewhere, the increasing price of land here also caused a

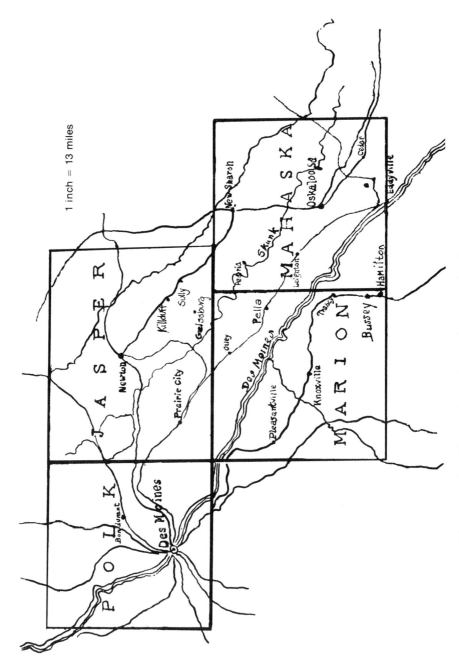

1 inch = 13 miles

The expansion drive of the Netherlanders around Pella, Iowa.

"swarming" to Minnesota, South and North Dakota, and even to the state of Washington—Lynden, Oak Harbor, North Yakima, etc. Along with this took place a more intensive colonization of Sioux County by more well-to-do or rather more "successful" stay-at-homes who hoped to expand their holdings in behalf of their children by buying out their foreign neighbors.

The result was that in 1911 the townships of Holland, Capel, Welcome, and West Branch (all in Sioux County) were all in the possession of the Dutch, except for a few sections.[24] In Lynn Township, the Dutch invaded from the southwest and "conquered" the largest part from Americans as well as Germans, who still "occupy" the remainder today. The western portion of Floyd Township is Dutch but the eastern part is still German. It is also a fact that the town of Hospers, originally German, is now largely Dutch, while the German businessmen have gone elsewhere, thus proving Dutch penetration also into this area.[25] The pioneer G. Draayom relates in a gripping manner the departure of a German shopkeeper and grain dealer named Bauman.[26] The latter had lived in Hospers for seven years and then moved to Pattersonville (now Hull) in northern Sioux County, where few if any Hollanders were living at the time. The Milwaukee Railroad had only recently reached the place. Mother Bauman especially urged the departure. "If we want a good place to live then we must be there first"; she herself "drove" the household goods to Pattersonville!

Nassau Township and the town of Alton are largely Dutch but East Orange is predominantly German. J. Van der Zee notes the peculiarity that the Chicago, St. Paul, Minneapolis and Omaha Railroad forms the demarcation line in all these townships in southeastern Sioux County between the Dutch who live north and west of the railroad line and the German residents who live south and east of the line.[27] It is obvious that this author did not recognize that this railroad mainly followed the valley of the Floyd River and that it is in particular this river that was for a long time the boundary between the two nationalities, especially when there were no bridges yet or very primitive ones.

The Hollanders, most of them children and grandchildren of the first Sioux County settlers, in the long run crossed the Floyd River (which as a borderline Draayom had compared with the IJsel River in Gelderland) and settled among the Germans, although the latter were reluctant to accept them. These "Germans" in Floyd Township, largely from Luxemburg, had arrived about the same time as the Dutch and showed the same determination, industry, and thriftiness. Draayom, who lived among them for fifty years, termed them "excellent citizens of the Union."[28] Just as our own countrymen, they wanted to expand their holdings and were just as reluctant to sell even at a good price. Consequently, in the long run, the holdings remained far more stable here. The proportional numbers of both nationalities also remained stable, for when finally the owners had become prosperous and began to rent out their farms, both the Dutch and the Germans preferably did so to those of their own nationality.[29]

Dutch expansionism moved faster where our colonists faced Americans, as in the most northerly townships of Sioux County where this movement is still going on. Hollanders settled in parts of Grand and Sheridan townships and by 1911 they owned half of Lincoln Township; Americans and Germans held the rest. Pattersonville, later renamed Hull, which was originally "strongly American," has become almost all Dutch and is now even a cultural center for our Christian Reformed brethren. The hamlet of Perkins has also become almost entirely Dutch as well as a large part of Boyden, in Sheridan County. All of these locations have been previously mentioned in another context.

Not only did the Netherlanders expand to the north and west but also to the east and south, confronting not only Americans and Germans but especially the Irish. Reading Township, as well as the hamlet of Ireton, were originally American and Irish; now they are almost totally Dutch. Particularly the Irish were quite ready to sell their land for $100 to $150 an acre! About half of the townships of Center, Plato, and Rock fell into our hands although Germans and the no less esteemed Norwegians were there.[30] Flourishing settlements are now found far beyond the borders of Sioux County in the nearby counties of Lyon, Osceola, and O'Brien and also here and there in Plymouth, particularly around Le Mars where the hamlet of Oyens reminds us of the investment of Dutch capital. This situation is most pronounced in Lyon and Osceola counties where, since the eighties, enterprising Ost Frisians from Illinois and central Iowa had settled. South Germans, Irish, and Scotch had settled there even earlier.

The Scotch had settled in Lyon County along the small Rock River, which awakened such memories of "Ye flowery banks o'bonnie Doon" that they named their settlement after Burn's poem "Bonnie Doon," and later simply Doon. About 1900 some orthodox Dutch settled here and organized a Christian Reformed Church in 1902. Their numbers grew to such an extent that in 1908 a Reformed Church was also organized. Then the Scotch Americans began to leave. They could not maintain themselves no matter how hard they worked.

But the Dutch had to face even more serious partners. Foremost among them were the Ost Frisians, who were no less Reformed than the Netherlanders. They continually spread out "*in ihrer jugendlichen Stärke und kraft ihres Wohlstandes und der in ihr wohnenden Energie*" [with their youthful strength and thanks to their well-to-do position and the energy that was in them].[31] In numerous villages such as Sibley, Matlock (in Sioux County), Melvin, Rock Rapids, and elsewhere, we now find Ost Frisians and Hollanders who came in later, living side by side. Both elements crossed over into Minnesota where at the present time we find Dutch settlements at Hills, Steen, Bigelow, and others, and also an occasional Ost Frisian settlement.

The expansion here also is reflected in the organization of Reformed and Christian Reformed churches. One need only consult the church statistics, of which I will mention a few of the most recent ones. For example, a

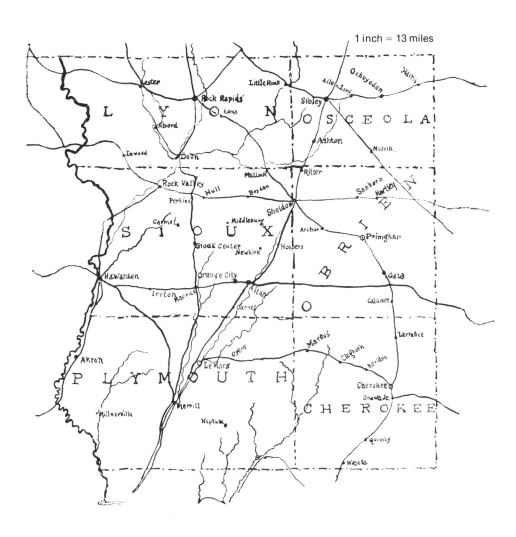

The conquests of the districts around Sioux County, Iowa.

Christian Reformed group was organized in 1911 at Sanborn in O'Brien County. The one at Ocheyedan in Osceola County was formed in 1913 and in Rock Rapids, Lyon County, in 1922. The strength of the Dutch element is shown in the fact that Little Rock, Lyon County, near the Minnesota border, is being taken over by the Dutch. According to Schnücker, Little Rock was to become *"eine der ostfriesischen Hochburgen und Leuchten"* [a highlight and shining center of the Ost Frisians].[32] The Ost Frisians had a Reformed Church here in 1895 but the Hollanders organized a second one in 1919 and—according to a characteristic news item in De *Volksvriend*—took over the church and parsonage of the Methodists whose church had been disbanded.[33] If this news item testifies more to the departure of Americans than of Ost Frisians, who in Iowa were largely Presbyterians, Reformed, Christian Reformed, Lutherans, and sometimes Baptists, it still indicates how the Dutch are threatening the Ost Frisians in their "stronghold." The much older Ost Frisian congregation had eighty households; at present the Dutch, with the Groninger E. Furda as minister, have already fifty-three families.[34] Our countrymen are breathing down the necks of the sturdy Ost Frisians!

One could well ask if this rapid expansion of the Dutch element led to envy and thus to friction. Envy is found everywhere; it is a general human trait. Therefore, it is of interest only as a characteristic of a group and then only if it leads to ethnic and racial confrontations. It goes without saying that some envy must have developed among the Dutch colonists, particularly when people no longer needed each other so much, that is, after the initial pioneer days. But even then it was present, as we recall the friction between Holland and Zeeland in Michigan. A similar friction, of a rather harmless nature otherwise, developed between the prosperous Hollanders in "uppity" Orange City and the simple Gelders farmers who had settled in and around Sioux Center and on whom the former looked down as real "greenhorns."

On one occasion some inhabitants of Orange City erected a sign with the words "Here mankind comes to an end" on the edge of Sioux Center near the West Branch, a tributary of the Floyd River, which served as the border-line between the "Gelders" and the "Holland" areas.[35] (Even in modern times rivers play a larger role as borderlines than is commonly assumed, also in America.) The Gelderlanders had a splendid revenge. Coming from areas of poor sandy soils, they were hard workers and progressed rapidly. Sioux Center became an industrious center and, as the name indicates, it is located in the middle of the county. The name has a larger connotation—it indicated the aspirations of the colonists who had prospered and who had hoped that Sioux Center would become the county seat. On two occasions, in 1891 and again in 1896, the Gelderlanders tried to realize this ambition but without success, as we know.[36]

Since there was some mutual jealousy, which showed itself most strongly in religious matters, one would surely have expected friction with "alien" neighbors. I have found no evidence of this as regards the Germans and the Irish. On the contrary, when Draayom in 1924 looked back upon the last fifty years of colonization, he referred to the Irish as "friendly fellows."[37] These Irish should not be confused with the unskilled laborers of the same nationality. It should be noted that the Irish and the Dutch, especially in Sioux County, were united in their hatred of the English, particularly during the Boer War, and they demonstrated this also, as will be shown later, at the ballot box. The Dutch were also on the very best of terms with the Germans; many of them had spent their first years in America together, in Wisconsin, Iowa, and elsewhere.

So it happened that various Wisconsin Germans, who had emigrated to Sioux County in Iowa, met their Dutch friends from Wisconsin again![38] That formed a bond. Our countrymen had respect for their German fellow colonists. This is mentioned repeatedly in Draayom's account of the early days of Sioux County in which he asserts "that they do not take second seat in comparison with our compatriots."[39] He called them "high grade citizens [who] showed in word and deed that they were exemplary Americans and had helped to make this beautiful part of the state what it is now."[40] No one was in a better position than Draayom to observe this, because in his youth he had worked for a German, Carl Oelrich—one of the very best! In addition, Hollanders and Germans (particularly the Ost Frisians) sometimes professed the same Reformed faith and thus, besides a racial kinship, there was also a close bond in religious affairs. Moreover, they felt that they were all comrades in arms sharing the same fate—strangers on American soil.

Naturally, there must have been some jealousy. This usually manifested itself most strongly at election time. For example, the Germans and the Dutch in the Chicago area were and are the best of friends. But in local elections to public office, in Evergreen Park, for example, they often opposed each other; this was also the case in other places. People understandably prefer to capture the political jobs for their countrymen, whereas this was often where the Dutch showed great indifference.

The attitude of the Netherlanders toward the Americans, their hosts so to speak, was somewhat different. In agricultural matters they greatly surpassed them, and the Yankees and Southerners did not particularly appreciate this. Thus there was, on the one hand, a great sympathy and benevolence, but on the other hand, a certain amount of envy among the great mass of people, the mob. That feeling could at times turn into intense hatred, as happened during the [First] World War. An alleged inclination toward Germany or, even worse, a purported lack of patriotism, were grounds for threats, even death threats, against the Hollanders. Their barns were burned down and this happened even in one instance to their church and Christian school. These hateful actions were most strongly motivated, however, by the prosperity of our countrymen, which contrasted sharply with the relative poverty of their American neighbors, and that often resulted in forced "sell outs."

These events must not be construed as anti-Dutch sentiment. The manifestation of such a "mob mind" was also directed against other nationalities and it occurred in earlier times as well, even centuries before. It was a type of xenophobia that was often evident in Europe also, even more than once in the Netherlands, and frequently the result of prosperity among the "newcomers." In the Old World it often manifested itself as pogroms against the Jews and during the last few years, in both Germany and France, against foreign travelers taking advantage of favorable rates of money exchange. This same type of attitude, which was certainly not an exclusively American phenomenon, nevertheless often came to expression even in normal times. The lynching of Blacks and even pregnant Black women and the growth of the Ku Klux Klan testify to this nativist spirit.[41] As early as the seventeenth century the "English," moved by the same spirit, laid waste the French neighboring colony of Frenchtown in Connecticut. Life had also been made miserable for the French in South Carolina where they had been persecuted under so-called political pretexts which in reality, as Chinard asserts, were a cover-up for *"une jalousie assez mesquine"* [a rather petty jealousy].[42] The Germans of the 18th century did not fare much better, and attempts were made to stop their colonization efforts. Faust said with great emphasis, *"wofür die geheime Ursache in der bekannten Ueberlegenheit des deutschen Ackerbaubetriebes zu suchen ist"* [that the secret cause of these attempts can be found in the well-known superiority of the Germans in agriculture].[43]

With the above examples in mind, it is understandable that the "mob mind" and its expression, the "lynching spirit," manifested itself nowhere more strongly against the Hollanders than in Iowa, because there they had become the most prosperous. In Sioux County difficulties were prevented, at least in later years, in part because here the Dutch had already rung down the curtain on the Americans at an early date; the strongbox "war" comes to mind. In most places they had been replaced by Germans and Hollanders and therefore the foreign-born element is still predominant there. In part, altercations were prevented also due to the tact of the leaders of our countrymen, in particular, Gerrit Klay, former mayor of Orange City and Sioux County's delegate to Iowa's House of Representatives.[44]

Things were different, however, in the vicinity of Pella where the Dutch had consistently expanded almost totally at the expense of the "real," or "100%" Americans. When one considers that here more than anywhere else many settlers had remained Dutch—"Pella is still Dutch to the backbone" [*in hart en nieren*, in heart and kidneys]— then one has all the ingredients for sharp frictions in the already hypersensitive atmosphere of the wartime period.

In fact, there had been friction in the Pella area already for years before the World War. The general complaint of American farmers was that the Hollanders caused land prices to escalate; they paid prices that the Americans could not possibly afford and so the latter were forced to move. Relations were further aggravated because it was also keenly felt, just as earlier in the case of the Huguenot French colonies, that the Dutch held themselves somewhat aloof as came to expression, for instance, in the establishment of Christian schools. In Sully, Jasper County, at a school picnic in 1914 or 1915 the Dutch flag was flown over the schoolhouse and the people refused to comply with the mayor's request to fly the American flag next to it. The Hollanders seem to have been nettled by the attitude of the Americans, but they themselves also showed a lack of tact in this case. In 1918 the American farmers tried to burn down this "Dutch" school. However, the fire was extinguished and the damage was relatively minor.

Even more polarized was the situation in Peoria, Mashaska County, which the Dutch had "conquered." In the eyes of the Americans there were too many Hollanders—most of them of the Christian Reformed persuasion—who were exempted from military service largely due to the activities of their minister. The bitterness grew to such intensity here that some of the Americans—the less successful ones—tried to kidnap this minister from his home at night with the intent of lynching him. One of the older Americans warned him at the last moment and a lynching was averted. As a precautionary measure, the minister was arrested and taken to Ottumwa where he was released on a $10,000 bond. Later the church and the Christian school at Peoria nevertheless went up in flames. This was the revenge of the American farmers who tried to obtain "justice"(?!) by taking the law into their own hands. Thus the lynching spirit was rampant in Peoria both as an after-effect of the pioneer days, but also of the war years. The parsonage was saved in the nick of time and for months it was guarded by armed Dutch farmers, just as was the Christian school at Sully.[45] It was a return to the years of the Wild West.

These events should not be ascribed to a lack of tact on the part of the Hollanders, at least not in the first place. The true and chief cause was an economic one, particularly professional jealousy [*broodnijd*, bread envy], as was shown in New Sharon, Mashaska County, where the Dutch farmers had taken over. In Peoria it was the Christian Reformed farmers who had remained the most Dutch, who had to bear the brunt of the attacks. But in New Sharon the Americans directed their attacks at the generally more Americanized Reformed element, although no fault whatsoever could be found with the actions of the minister in this town. Yet the Reformed Church was set ablaze and dynamite was discovered under the windows of the parsonage. A defective fuse that went out prevented worse consequences here! Reverend S. De Bruine, who lived in the vicinity of Oskaloosa and who witnessed these events, wrote me while still in America that it was "some parallel of the lynching parties of the South that could have had even more serious consequences."[46]

This broad-minded minister described these events as "an explosion of excitement." It could better be described as flames bursting forth after decades of a smouldering fire because the wartime psychosis was only a pretext, not the cause which lay much deeper. In the area of New Sharon, which was the area of the most violent frictions since it was the one most recently "conquered" by the Dutch, the American farmers openly admitted that they wanted to get rid of the Dutch who surpassed them in agriculture. Thus the Americans responded with violence against the danger of being "bought out." Many Dutch farmers around New Sharon received threatening letters warning them to leave or they would be "burned out." Several Hollanders found out that the Americans meant business. A big barn of one of the church elders, who was born in America and had two sons serving in the army, was burned down and totally destroyed during the night. He was a man who could not be blamed for anything but his prosperity. Another colonist in the same manner lost a house that he was ready to occupy. And who was responsible time after time? It was American farmers who wanted to drive out the Hollanders, to force them to sell their land, and thus to obtain for a song a farm they would otherwise be unable to obtain! In some instances, American farmers had hired fellows to set fire to the churches, schools, houses, and barns of the "damned Dutch," paying $50 to $100 for each "job."

The fact that even native-born Holland Americans were among those who suffered indicates that these actions were not directed against specific individuals, not even against the Dutch in general, but only against the more successful of them. We could concur with [S. R.] Steinmetz's view of it as "punishment," as more or less a group revenge, the explosion of feelings of revenge of the "have-nots" against the "haves," between the more and the less successful.[47] The conflict was between groups rather than between individuals. But here, as in other situations, it must not only have been an attempt at intimidation, but also a way to gain satisfaction by revenge and to bolster one's own hurt feelings and sense of inferiority. Just as with lynchings in general, one should see all these cases as reflex actions, despite a certain factor of "premeditation." This is extremely characteristic of people like Americans, many of whom believe in primitive brute force. A lack of tradition and of higher education—as I have said before—made "mob psychology" so much more significant. Also "judicial" America has considered, more or less consciously, all these cases of mob violence as psychological phenomena of a passing nature. Since they were motivated by the temporary flaring up of tempers, rather than by permanently ingrained feelings of hatred, they did not have to be severely controlled. Seemingly, the courts have also perceived, although not always clearly, that in many respects American behavior can be compared to that of savages and that of children. Americans can be very vindictive but their thirst for revenge, being a direct, psychological impulse, can just as easily and quickly vanish.

The criminal courts handled all of these arson cases. A few rather light sentences were imposed and many cases were postponed, some because of illness of the people allegedly involved. In the meantime, elections were coming up, "and then strange things sometimes happen," as Reverend S. De Bruine wrote to me in April, 1920. He was one of those who had no great faith in the proceedings. And he added: "The closer to November, the less chance for a fair hearing." The state's attorney-general was a candidate for governor of Iowa and wanted votes. Other judicial candidates also wanted some position or other and so would certainly take into consideration the patriotic(!) feelings of their voters.*

---

*Van Hinte stresses this judicial "subjectivity," since in the Netherlands judges are appointed for life by the Monarch from a slate of candidates, and thus are not subject to political pressures. In the administration of justice, the Netherlands also do not use a jury system but leave judging completely to the "experts."

Indeed, De Bruine had the right view of the situation. Everywhere and at all times "justice" has been a very elastic concept, but in America justice is one of the most odd things. This was proven again in 1920 at the court hearings concerning the attacks on the Hollanders. This was particularly true in the handling of the case of G. Vos, who lived near New Sharon and whose barn was burned down on the night of September 27, 1919. The entire area held its breath. "The case attracted considerable attention of people from all over Mahaska during the ten days that it was in progress. Every day the courtroom was packed with spectators anxious to get in on all the proceedings," according to a newspaper clipping sent to me.[48] It was revealed that one of the chief offenders, paid by Americans, one Davis, had suffered a fall in 1912(!) and had "sustained injuries to his head which have apparently wrought great changes in the conduct and character of Davis." Yet, he had been able to serve as a soldier during the war, but at the time of the hate campaign against the Dutch it was claimed he had no "will power" anymore and on these grounds he was found "not guilty"!!

In all fairness it must be acknowledged that there were also Americans who felt aggravated by this kind of "justice" meted out by a jury. "Does the attorney general of Iowa have a right to hire men of this class and keep them on the payroll?" one of them asked. His chief concern, however, was that this form of "justice" was so expensive.[49] This case alone cost Mahaska County between three and four thousand dollars and thus this American especially wished that "all the taxpayers in the county could have heard this proceeding!"

2. Other Consequences of the Disappearance of Free Land

The expansion of land holdings into adjacent areas was not the only result of the disappearance of free lands after the years 1890–1895. A second result was the breaking up of holdings. Earlier we have observed that the less prosperous colonists in the Van Raalte colony in Michigan owned on an average 80 to 120 acres; the Wisconsin farmers of moderate circumstances worked 120 to 160 acres but the more prosperous ones who went to Iowa had a quarter section—160 acres, and many even bought 320 acres. The same was true in Sioux County, in the same state, where many owned a half section—320 acres, and in the course of time quite a number of people, usually through purchase, became the possessors of an entire section or more. Recently, one of the pioneers there, Pleun De Zeeuw, was feted on his fortieth wedding anniversary. In a poem recalling past events, he was lauded for having expanded his homestead to 800 acres:

> "Eight hundred acres and then some
> Were entrusted to you by God's will"*[50]

Although this elegy did not give evidence of high poetic talent, it is of interest for recalling some history.

---

*   "Acht-honderdakkers, en daar komt nog al wat bij,
    Dat werd U toevertrouwd van Godes zij."

Another pioneer, E. J. G. Bloemendaal, began with 80 acres and finally had a holding of 640 acres. P. Mouw, well known in America as a hog raiser, also began in the seventies with an 80-acre farm in the Orange City area, but at his death in 1922 he left no less than 1,400 acres![51]

Although there are many 640-acre farms in Iowa, and they belonged to the biggest, even larger ones are found in the Dakotas, some of them held by our countrymen. In the vicinity of Colton, Minnesota County, in South Dakota, there are Hollanders with holdings of 800 acres.[52] This is of significance when one recalls that in the Netherlands a 100-acre farm (around 40 hectares) was unusual and holdings of 10 to 20 hectares (25 to 50 acres) were "common."

Gradually these large holdings became rarities and nowadays in northwestern Iowa, a 320-acre farm is considered to be a considerable enterprise.[53] In the "older" Pella area, such big farms are still found, but the average size farms run to 160 and 240 acres. Here also the splitting up went so far that there were many farms of "only" 120 and 80 acres, especially near the "cities" where the land was obviously more expensive.

A former farmer, B. Mouw, wrote to me from Sioux Center that "there is no longer a prairie here. It is all developed and there are large farms everywhere, but they are gradually decreasing in size."[54] What so many older farmers, such as Pleun De Zeeuw, had built up through years of hard work is now being divided up among their often numerous children, although some of the children had gone off to study. They did this all the more easily since they no longer trekked further west as in former days, due to the fact that both good and cheap land was no longer available there. But, as the very sympathetic seventy-year-old Orange City pioneer, P. Mouw, complained to me, these developments are due also to the fact that the desire of the younger generation to go west is no longer so great anymore. "They have no desire to do so anymore and wish to begin where we left off. There is no more glamour in it," he grumbled, and he went on to relate how he had to haul timber from the Rock River valley, which was a very different situation than that faced by the youth of the present.[55] This is a complaint we should not take too seriously since it is repeated by every generation. Memories of "the good old days" or of "our times" have been uttered by the older generation of all peoples and all times!

It is evident that this subdividing went even further in the older states of the Midwest—Illinois, Michigan, Wisconsin, and others. It was particularly true near the metropolis of Chicago. Formerly worthless marsh land fetched more than $1,000 an acre; other lands, purchased for $1.25 an acre increased in value to over $1,500, thanks to the growth of Chicago. The same could be said of Milwaukee, Wisconsin; Rochester, New York; etc. Everywhere the land was becoming too expensive! Thus, expanding one's holding was not possible for every family. We see repeated instances of partitioning. In 1850 W. Anker had bought a 400-acre farm near South Holland, Illinois, for four dollars an acre; he divided it among his eight children. Others saw their farm holding ultimately divided into 10- or 20-acre tracts, necessitating more intensive cultivation if the plots were to prove sufficient for a livelihood.

The proximity of large cities, especially for the Netherlanders near Chicago, but also in Michigan, led automatically to a change in land use from general farming to truck gardening or dairying, depending on the nature of the soil. An additional factor for both truck farming and dairying is that, especially on the east side of the lakes where in winter the tempering influence of the large water mass is felt most strongly, the land was ideal for both gardening and stock raising. It is significant that killing frosts come a month later in the Michigan settlement, east of Lake Michigan, than in Sioux County, Iowa, that is, in November rather than October.[56]

The increasing price of land had still another result, which is related to fractionization but differs in that it also deals with the purchase of neighboring area by the most successful settlers. Both the fractionization and the buying of land caused a supply shortage. The later arrivals who above all wanted to live among their fellow countrymen, which was a very important factor, were forced into tenancy through a lack of capital. This was also the case for those who had inherited a tract but who felt it was too small and did not have the money to buy additional land.

In the beginning most of the farmers, particularly in the Midwest, were landowners. But in the 1890 to 1895 period the tenant category increased steadily and today in Iowa tenants are the largest population group. The war speeded up this process. It caused the prices of farm products to double and even triple. No enterprise was more profitable than agriculture. Everyone, it seemed, wanted to be a farmer, and it must be remembered that this could be accomplished much more quickly in America than in the Netherlands where there is a far greater difference between the agricultural and factory worker. Those who were already farmers, whether tenant or owner, were now making so much money that they tried to buy the rented farms or to increase their holdings. We have already seen how this was particularly true of the Dutch and the Germans. "Be good farmers and add to your land" has always been the motto of the colonists; indeed, it was the gospel for the most Christian of brothers and led to a veritable passion which, after the war, degenerated into a wild speculation that raged perhaps nowhere more strongly than in the Iowa Dutch settlement.

This was not an accidental occurrence, because in addition to all of the earlier motives that were mentioned, an inclination to speculation has long been a weakness of Hollanders, even though that trait seems to be in stark contrast with their usual matter-of-factness. We need only recall the tulip bulb craze of the seventeenth century, the stock-jobbery of the eighteenth that the Dutch call wind trading [*windhandel*], and the railway scandals of the nineteenth, to be able to understand also why the land dealings of the twentieth century got out of hand.

Previously undreamed of land prices were being paid. In pre-war times

$100 to $150 per acre was considered such a high price that only Germans and Hollanders would pay it. Americans, Irish, Norwegians, and Scotch were also ready to sell to them at such prices. However, during and after the war these prices leaped to $200, $300, and $600 an acre. P. Mouw informed me that much land around Orange City was sold for $700 an acre. In some instances it even reached $1,000! There are many accounts in De *Grondwet* and De *Volksvriend* about these enormous prices. A few examples follow: A farmer named Verploeg sold his 53-acre farm located two miles west of Leighton, in Mahaska County, Iowa, in the spring of 1920 for $620 per acre![57] In Sioux County, similar prices were frequently paid, as happened in Sioux Center, Hull, Rock Valley, and other places.[58] One mile east of Orange City, forty unimproved acres sold for "only" $330 an acre while the slightly improved so-called "Van Zijl ten acres," a quarter mile east of the town, found a buyer at $1,000 an acre.*[59]

According to those who were informed about these matters, $1,000 an acre was undoubtedly a record since around Orange City the average price was $500 an acre. Because of such rapid price increases, land became a choice item for speculation. With money or without it, everyone wanted to deal in land. The most ludicrous examples were brought to my attention. Young and old participated in it. Even the most staid persons were sucked into this maelstrom. One of the most respected citizens of Orange City, the publisher of the most important newspaper and an aged and extremely prudent man, could not resist the temptation and told me himself that he had purchased a ten-acre plot at $500 an acre and sold it shortly thereafter for a total price of $6,500, and the buyer, in his turn, made a profit of $750 reselling it!

I was told of a Hollander who had purchased 1,100 acres of land when suddenly the disillusionment came and the prices began to decline, although not as rapidly as they had risen.[60] But the fall in prices was fast enough to cause large losses, especially among those who had not purchased the lands with their own money but had borrowed it and then had to come up with cash. They were the first ones who were forced to liquidate. Thus, a farmer from Rock Rapids in Sioux County, who had purchased a farm for $600 an acre, had to sell it for $430 an acre when the bear market overtook him![61] Others experienced even greater losses. It was said that one Hollander had lost $150,000! During those days of crisis I made an auto tour through the area where speculation had raged and

---

*As a comparison of some sort, it should be noted that according to the *Weesper Courant* of December 31, 1927, in the Netherlands a farm of 12 hectares, 12 ares, and 75 centiares—over 30 acres—with buildings and land in the municipality of Nederhorst den Berg, was sold at auction for 46,010 guilders [Van Hinte]. In U.S. currency, this would have been $18,404 or roughly $613 an acre, including the buildings.

came to the farm of Van den Berg, the owner of the 1,100 acres that were mentioned. He had to surrender most of it because he had fallen behind in his payments. One fortunate thing for all these speculation victims was a homestead provision in the American law that entitled them to keep their houses, regardless of their value, forty acres of land, their tools, a team of horses, etc., to aid them in starting over again. Our countryman mentioned above, with a debt of $150,000, was, thanks to this provision, cock of the walk again the next year—living on a richly furnished farm in Minnesota![62]

It is understandable that with prices as high as those mentioned, the purchase of a quarter or half section was impossible and that people were happy if they could just buy forty acres, while others, yielding to the temptation of high prices for their large holdings, sold part of them or sometimes subdivided them entirely into parcels; thus, there was a splintering of property. It is also understandable that many did not have the money to give free rein to their gambling urge, no matter how easily the banks usually provided loans. As a consequence, even more than formerly, it was necessary to rent. Renting increased more rapidly after these events, no matter how high the rents rose, since they kept in step with the increases in land prices. If tenants paid $8 an acre rent before the war, this increased to $15 or $18 dollars, while the rent in the Orange City area was predicted to reach $30 an acre. The number of tenants increased rapidly because after the crisis many who had bought a farm with borrowed money could not meet their obligations at the bank; the farms were foreclosed by the banks or by their former owners. The transactions turned out to be mere "paper sales," except for those who were still able to remain the owners but were encumbered with a heavy mortgage. This was so common in Iowa that this most productive of all states in the Union was termed a "mortgaged Eldorado." Through economic necessity so many farmers were forced into tenancy, that is, renting from the original owners who had sold their lands at high prices earlier, or at yet higher prices in the speculation years and who had resisted the urge to buy again, that Iowa was one of the states of the Union with the highest percentage of tenant farmers. This was a process that began in the nineties but accelerated during boom times. Americans admit it themselves and in the words of one of them, J. J. Smertenko: "One of the purest landholding communities in the world has been transformed during the past thirty years into as bad a tenant-farmer State as any north of the Mason and Dixon line."[63] And the landlords—many of them Hollanders— were now in Los Angeles, California! Various pioneer settlers from Orange City settled in the Sunshine State.[64]

The sharp increase in tenant farmers had consequences in another area. The tenant was much more inclined than the farmer-owner, to abandon farming and to live in town where he could find a job in industry that would provide him a living that the farm could not do or not to a sufficient degree.

The high prices of land had earlier deterred others from settling on the land. Before 1895 industry was faced with a continual shortage of labor, often in spite of the high wages that competed with farm wages. But after 1895 this shortage sharply diminished and industry could then grow faster and also spread to the rural areas. Up to now industry had located in the most favorable cities, for instance in the cities on the fall-line. Because "free" lands were no longer available, a diminishing percentage of the hundreds of thousands of immigrants streaming into the country could hope to find employment in farming, and they were therefore available for industry. The development of technology all over the world—note the numerous inventions—and the increasing lack of land resulted in a flourishing of American industry, which, after 1895, for the above-mentioned reasons, began to spread also to the Dutch settlements in Michigan, Wisconsin, and elsewhere. Holland and Zeeland in the Van Raalte colony, Cedar Grove in the Protestant Wisconsin region, and De Pere in the Roman Catholic Fox River colony in the same state became industrial centers of importance, as we shall see later. Especially the fortuitous location of Chicago with respect to these Dutch colonies, and also their local raw materials, such as are found in the woods, fostered the growth of many important industries. The surplus rural residents, augmented by the newly arrived immigrants, constituted the labor force.

The size of this new migration to the centers of industry, especially during the crisis that followed after the years of feverish land speculation, especially among the tenant farmers, is indicated by news items in the Holland-American newspapers. Rents were far too high in comparison with the rapidly declining prices of grain and other farm products in the autumn of 1920. Prices were so low that in some Dutch settlements, such as Sanborn in O'Brien County and Doon in Lyon County, the farmers refused to sell their grain to the grain dealers.[65] In the largely Dutch Sioux County a rent strike was considered in such places as Middleburg, Maurice, Rock Valley, and other towns.[66] Due to falling product prices, rents were 50 percent too high! In the more northerly situated Lyon County the situation was just as dire and one of our countrymen in Rock Rapids complained about his lack of money: "Two years ago we were struck with blindness and most of us were attacked so severely by the speculation fever that 75% of the farmers will go nearly or entirely bankrupt."[67]

There was a first movement following the boom years that drove many farm families to the cities because of the high land prices and rents, especially in Michigan and Wisconsin, which had far more factories than the almost completely agrarian Iowa.[68] Now a second movement followed in which many farmers gave up their trade, especially in Iowa in such settlements as Ireton in Sioux County and Rock Rapids in Lyon County and elsewhere.[69] It is true that many a landowner came down a peg or two and lowered the rent; in Middleburg rents were halved and in other places the contracts were changed so that, in Sioux Center for example, two-fifths of the harvest (a half in Ocheyedan, Osceola County) would be for the land-lord. This brought things back to normal proportions; nevertheless, the trek to the cities continued for a number of years.[70] The trek from the farms to the factories was of such a size that when many Iowa Dutch left to join their compatriots in the factory city of Grand Rapids (the Furniture City), people in that city, in 1924, felt they had to advise their "friends in the West," suggesting that easy does it and that they remain where they were because in Grand Rapids, too, both the surplus of manpower and the general de-cline in industry had resulted in lower wages and scarcer employment opportunities. "Anyone still considering coming here should realize that there is no certainty at all of finding steady employment at a high wage."[71]

Hollanders also departed from other states in the Midwest. Many left Goshen, Indiana, to go to Grand Rapids and many also left for the silk city of Paterson, located near New York.[72] As time went by, the Dutch were no longer deterred by great distances either! How great the flight from the land had been already before the crisis, even in a state like Michigan, where specula-tion in land never even approached the levels it reached in Iowa, is reflected in the report of the Michigan State Farm Bureau in the spring of 1920. According to this report, this Midwestern state had 11,537 farms lying fallow. In Kent County, partially Dutch, there were 471 abandoned farmsteads; in nearby Allegan County, largely Dutch, there were 394.[73] On the other hand, the industrial city of Grand Rapids saw the construction of 1,051 new houses and 2,046 garages in 1923. In addition, 1,175 houses were remodeled![74] Can a greater contrast and a better evidence be found of the transition! It is obvi-ous that the change caused at the same time another imbalance, a dearth of farm help in the rural areas. In the Dutch settlement of Waupun, Wisconsin, there were serious complaints about the scarcity of farm help.[75] In the Dutch settlements of Michigan thousands of bushels of fruit were lost because of a lack of pickers.[76] America is indeed a land of contradictions. The move to the cities, once it had started, continued strongly, especially because of the still relatively high wages, even when the rural areas began to recover economi-cally and still had to buck an increasing shortage of labor!

Nevertheless, we still find the largest number of Hollanders in the older farm states where the oldest settlements are located. The 1920 census statistics indicate that most of the Hollanders were living in Michigan and Illinois; Iowa and Wisconsin were exceeded only by New York State and New Jersey. It will be recalled that in New York State the Hollanders had settled earlier along Lake Erie, while the industrial state of New Jersey provided a living to many immediately upon their landing in the New World. The statistics also indicate, naturally, that the largest numbers of those born of Dutch parents also resided in the same states but that Iowa exceeds New York and New Jersey in this respect. The following figures are abstracted from the Fourteenth Census (1920):

U.S. and States	Dutch-born	% of Total	Dutch-born or of Dutch Parents	% of Total
United States	131,766	100.0	362,318	100.0
Michigan	33,499	25.4	98,705	27.2
Illinois	14,344	10.9	37,759	10.4
New York	13,772	10.5	32,841	9.1
New Jersey	12,737	9.7	30,892	8.5
Iowa	12,471	9.5	35,587	9.8
Wisconsin	7,473	5.7	24,744	6.8
Minnesota	5,380	4.1	15,007	4.1
California	4,592	3.5	9,829	2.7
South Dakota	3,218	2.4	9,074	2.5
Washington	3,097	2.4	7,517	2.01
Ohio	2,529	1.9	8,055	2.02

I have listed only those states where 2 percent or more of the Dutch-born or Dutch "natives" [born in America] reside. The figures clearly indicate that the younger emigration turned to the industrial states. The high figures for Michigan, for example, are due not only to the Van Raalte colony but also— and since the eighties even more so—to the industrial city of Grand Rapids. The same holds true for Illinois where many were attracted by industry in and around Chicago.

B. The Settlements Around 1925

1. In Michigan

In what follows it should be noted that in the various Dutch settlements as we find them around 1925, the cultural image is initially the result of a development whose basis had been laid in the forties and in the seventies. Furthermore, this development, as indicated in the chapters dealing with the period up until around 1895, was more affected in one place and less in another by the disappearance at that time of good and extremely·inexpensive "homestead" lands. These changes, which I outlined above, were the expansion of land ownership in their own areas and the subdividing of the land and a more intensive agriculture that led to truck gardening and cattle raising. There was, in addition, the shift from ownership to tenancy, the move to factories by farm laborers who no longer saw an opportunity to become farm owners, and the consequent increasing industrialization, etc. Except for one single instance, all these changes that took place during and after the speculation years with an increasing speed have not altered the basic character of the colonies. They continued primarily to be what they had always been—either predominantly agricultural colonies or industrial colonies, not to mention an occasional commercial settlement. It is true that in some settlements industry eventually became of greater or lesser importance in addition to agriculture. Some examples were already mentioned in passing, although they could not be called real industrial colo-

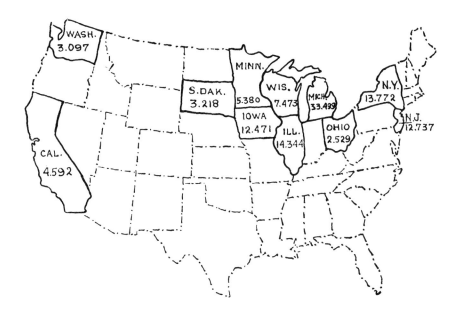

The American states with the greatest number of Dutch-born, 1920. The numbers are actual totals. The total in the U.S. is 131,766.

nies. The one settlement whose character was completely altered, Roseland in Illinois, owes this to a very particular circumstance, in part related to the increasing industrialization. It owes it to the amazing growth of Chicago, the metropolis that swallowed up Roseland. In fact it is now already officially an integral part of Chicago.

Of all the settlements, the oldest—the Van Raalte colony in Michigan—is still the most important and at the same time the most interesting. This is mostly due to its economic and spiritual capital, the city of Holland, the largest community in the United States almost exclusively built and inhabited by Netherlanders. In 1920 it had 12,166 residents. The colony originating from the nucleus in the Black Lake area straddling the borderline between Allegan and Ottawa counties, steadily expanded north, south, and eastward, growing because of its own natural population increase and the continuous arrival of other immigrant Hollanders. Thanks to an ever-increasing prosperity, they bought out the less prosperous Americans. The cities of Grand Haven, Allegan, and Grand Rapids delineate this Dutch territory, with Muskegon to the north and Kalamazoo to the south as outposts. These five towns have a large and sometimes preponderant Dutch population.

The colony is what it has been from the start, above all an agricultural settlement. The oldest settlements such as Vriesland, Zeeland, Drenthe, Overisel, and Graafschap as well as the newer settlements such as Noordeloos, Borculo, Zutphen, Haarlem, and Harderwijk, as well as the "captured" American towns such as Hudsonville, Jenison, Jamestown, and many others, have mostly continued as agricultural villages. The farm products, initially mostly corn, wheat, oats and barley have gradually been replaced, to a considerable extent, by more profitable crops. The soil, basically formed by the glaciers during and after the ice age, is sandy with occasional stretches of clay and marshy peat lands but almost all of it is light soil, especially along the shores of Lake Michigan where very sandy soils (*geestgronden*) and even sand dunes are found. This typically hilly moraine territory is ideal for truck gardening.

The local climate, although generally continental with severe winters and hot summers, is also conducive to such gardening because, as we saw earlier, it is tempered by the proximity of Lake Michigan. Compared to other parts of the Midwest it can even be considered to be a more or less maritime climate since the colony lies on the east side of Lake Michigan and has cooler summers and warmer winters thanks to the prevalent south-westerly winds. Through these circumstances, the Dutch colony is part of the important orchard belt that stretches along Lake Michigan in the south-western part of the state. Although some fruit was already grown by early settlers and also by the Dutch, orchards developed and became important. Much fruit is exported from the port city of Holland to Chicago and Milwau-kee across the lake. The division of the land into smaller and smaller parcels compelled farmers to use increasingly intensive agricultural meth-ods to which the Hollander with his patience, care of detail, etc., was more peculiarly adapted than the restless Americans. Thus, in the vicinity of Holland, strawberries and currants are important crops and cherry orchards are found there also. In other localities, apples, pears, and peaches are important.

The significance of fruit growing for farmers who have only a small acre-age is shown by a news item reporting that in 1920 a farmer in the Holland vicinity netted $2,000 from two acres of strawberries, while another picked 150 crates from less than one acre of land.[77] However, further developments are hampered by a number of drawbacks. There is in the first place the climate that may at times revert to the full harshness of a continental climate; for instance in the winter of 1919–1920 many currant bushes died from heavy frost. There is also a shortage of pickers at harvest time. In that same year of 1920 there was such an abundant harvest in Allegan, causing a shortage of pickers, container materials, and transportation, that anyone could get a bushel of peaches for a dollar if he would bring his own basket and pick the fruit himself.[78]

Even more important is the cultivation of celery, one of America's favo-rite vegetables, and of onions. From the beginning the marsh lands, "the heavy, well-drained muck lands, with a subsoil of hard stiff clay," had been used for such production, as L. A. Chase observed in his book, *Rural Michigan*.[79] In addition, various vegetables such as beans, carrots, cauliflower, etc., are grown, and around towns like Zeeland there is at present a flourishing tomato culture; the consumption of tomatoes in America is even greater than it is in England. Among all these crops, celery ranks first. The Kalamazoo area is renowned throughout America for this product and celery growing is largely in the hands of Dutch farmers.[80] Celery is also grown by a small group of Dutch more to the south, in the Decatur area, located in Van Buren County—a region known for its production of peppermint and spearmint. Much celery is also grown more to the north, just south of Zeeland, and the low, former swamp lands around Vriesland and Hudsonville are simply covered with it. So it is not by chance that after Kalamazoo, the very Dutch Ottawa County became the main celery county in Michigan. In 1919, they raised 790 and 730 acres of celery respectively.[81] Florida is now becoming an important "celery state"—the "celery delta" near Sanford is, according to Russell Smith, "the greatest celery-producing and shipping point in the world."[82] In spite of this growing competition, celery growing is also constantly increasing in the Dutch colony. Hudsonville, for example, had its greatest celery harvest ever in 1920.

Other products are also of increasing significance, such as potatoes and sugar beets. Both are well suited to the type of soil and climate, as well as to the nature of the Dutch, since both crops require constant close attention and care. These are no longer garden crops but farm products, while potatoes can be considered as an in-between or transitional crop. Both crops can endure a colder climate than fruit, but they put higher demands on the soil and therefore flourish in Michigan. In 1920 the total of sugar beet production in Michigan was 10 percent higher than in the previous year and this was due principally to the activities of the Dutch and German growers. A 1921 report stated that "sugar beet production is steadily increasing in the Holland area."[83]

Next to agriculture, cattle raising is becoming more important. This is also due to the greater care that is now given to dairy products and for which, thanks to good means of transportation and surrounding large cities like Grand Rapids, Chicago, etc., more ready markets have been found than in earlier times.

The phenomenal success of the Dutch farmers is also due to another factor. It is the organizing of farm cooperatives, a movement that is slowly gaining momentum in America through Dutch initiative and support. In the eighties the hamlet of Vriesland already had a co-op. Cooperation of all sorts among farmers and cattle raisers led to the creation of Farm Bureaus in many states following the [First] World War. These organizations are similar to our Agricultural Companies [Maatschappijen van Landbouw] in the Netherlands. Especially in Michigan they caught on among the Dutch. In January of 1921, at its first annual meeting, 2,446 Dutch farmers were members of the Allegan County Farm Bureau and 1,700 were listed in February in the Ottawa County organization.[84] While these bureaus distribute information through salaried agricultural specialists, exhibits, brochures, etc., numerous other organizations are engaged in the buying and selling of various products. In 1922 only 7.9 percent of the farmers in all of the United States sold through cooperatives but this figure was much higher in states with large Germanic populations. Thus Minnesota, with its large Scandinavian population, was in first place with 43.9 percent of its farmers selling through cooperatives.[85]

Unfortunately, I cannot supply the statistics for Michigan; Chase asserts that reliable figures are not available. But it is a fact that cooperatives are strongest among the "foreigners"; true Americans are too individualistic for such an enterprise. Chase recognizes this when he says: "As a businessman, the Yankee farmer does not take kindly to cooperation, and it is apparently chiefly among the more alient [sic] elements that cooperation flourishes best."[86] Chase greatly emphasizes the role of the very numerous Finnish cooperatives in northern Michigan. If he had been better acquainted with the Dutch, he would surely have included them. Our countrymen have organized numerous sales organizations. One of the best known is that of the celery producers in the vicinity of Zeeland and Vriesland. Thanks to this Celery Growers Association, the Hollanders obtain the best prices in the Chicago market because of the care they devote to preparing and shipping their product and the regularity of supply, a factor that prevents the flooding of their market. Thus, their celery obtains "the choice quotation in the Chicago market each winter."[87]

The Michigan Potato Growers Exchange is also an influential organization with 123 branches in 1921.[88] This indicates the importance of the potato in the Peninsular State. Many of the branches are in Dutch areas. For example, one was established in Holland in 1919 with an exclusively "Dutch" board.[89] In addition, there are many exclusively local sales cooperatives, as in the predominantly Dutch community of Hudsonville, where the Hudsonville Produce Association was established by our countrymen. In the fall of 1920 it shipped out more than 70,000 bushels of onions.[90] In some areas the farmers cooperatively own an elevator. In other areas they control milling operations; in Jamestown the Hollanders run the Jamestown Co-op Milling Company.

In the dairy cattle business, this same united spirit is spreading as evidenced by the establishment of increasing numbers of cooperative dairies, although as of yet they are far from having attained the significance of our Friesland creameries in the Netherlands. In all of Michigan—five times as large as the Netherlands!—there were only seventy-four cooperative creameries in 1921.[91] This should be compared with the fact that the village of Vriesland had already two co-op cheese factories in 1880.

More and more purchasing cooperatives are also being organized. For example, in Holland there is the Holland Cooperative Store which had five hundred members in 1921 and sells exclusively to its farmer-members; it was able, recently, to construct a $6,000 building. Farmers Cooperative Stores are now also found in numerous villages with a Dutch population.[92]

Farming and cattle raising also move in new directions technically and commercially. The old methods based only on experience are gradually abandoned, to the extent that they are no longer up to date. More than ever, science has made inroads into the world of the farmers. Our fellow countrymen are very open-minded to these new trends; one only needs to read "De Boerderij" ["The Farmstead"] column in De Grondwet, the colony's paper. Even better, one should visit some of these farms and see for oneself. Most of them are of forty or eighty acres; the farm dwellings, sometimes veritable villas, are set completely apart from the barns; and everything, especially the barns and stables, is well painted. And then one should recall that in 1846 the immigrants who settled in the Michigan woods were from among the most common and unpromising of the Dutch. Can one imagine anywhere a greater contrast than between that former wilderness and present-day central western Michigan? It is Chase who articulates the Yankee gratefulness to the Dutch for having made this area "one of the most highly developed farming areas of the State."[93]

Various factors promoted the prosperity of the colony. First there was the development of industry, especially after 1890, when the labor force increased. Since that time Holland has become more of an industrial center because many of the larger factory towns lacked sufficient hands. The favorable location on Black Lake, near Lake Michigan and opposite Chicago, contributed to this industrialization. Perhaps of even more importance was the favorable reputation that was particularly ascribed to the Calvinistic Hollanders. They were deemed to be very suited to factory work, since they were highly trustworthy, they had a strong sense of duty, and they almost completely lacked any tendencies toward class struggles.

Dutch capital, although frequently solicited to develop industry in the Dutch colony, had persistently declined to take advantage of the "opportunities" in western Michigan. But once the colonists had come to some prosperity, they accumulated the necessary funds from their own resources to establish various industries. In addition to the "Hollanders," it was especially the Americans from elsewhere who started industries in the Van Raalte colony. I. Lippincott comments that especially after 1880 American industry grew rapidly and completely new industries began to flourish.[94] In 1860 industrial America ranked fourth, lagging behind England, France, and Germany, but by 1894 it had surpassed all of them and ranked as number one. In addition to being an agricultural nation, the Union had then definitely become an industrial nation.

This development was mirrored in the Dutch settlements, especially in Holland, where numerous new industries sprang up. I shall mention several types and as much as possible give the date of establishment. I can thus show how Holland's time had come and how its economic growth closely paralleled that of America, and how Holland outdistanced its rival, Pella. I have used the names of directors (as of 1914) because they reflect, to some extent, the Dutch-American participation in the various enterprises.

Holland, Michigan: Commerce and industry. Top and middle: One of the main streets before and after "Fordizing"; bottom: The leather tannery of Cappon and Bertsch. (Middle photo, original by J. Van Hinte.)

One of the oldest business activities in Holland, due to the presence of large woods and cattle raising, was that of leather tanning (1857). It became one of the most prominent industries largely due to the efforts of I. Cappon, a former farm laborer from Zeeland.[95] As we have seen before, he was able to build up his enterprise, the Cappon and Bertsch Leather Company, to a large-scale industry. It averaged about three hundred employees and was "one of the largest tanneries" in the United States. A second tannery also came into existence and both firms later gave rise to shoe manufacturing. The Holland Shoe Company produces three thousand pairs of shoes daily!

Even earlier, the vast forests had given rise to sawmill activity. Just as was the case in Grand Rapids, a furniture business developed from this pioneer sawmilling, under the influence of that nearby large industrial center, which had reached a later and higher scope of industrialization. Although Grand Rapids was the chief furniture center, Holland also got its share and has now eight large firms producing furniture. The oldest of these, the Ottawa Furniture Company, specializing in "high grade" dining, bedroom, and library furniture, was founded in 1887, financed in part by capital from the colony and in part by American capital. Arend Visscher, whom I mentioned earlier as a student at Hope College and the son of a poor pioneer, became president. However, an American became plant manager, while A. A. Visscher was the treasurer of the firm that employs about 150 hands. This largely "Dutch" undertaking specializes more particularly in English style furniture (Chippendale, Sheraton, etc.), although the American Colonial style is not overlooked. But a strictly American company, the Ch. P. Limbert Company, with about 250 employees, specializes in furniture based on Dutch patterns and therefore it calls itself Limbert's Holland Dutch Arts and Crafts Furniture. Another American firm is the West Michigan Furniture Company (1889) with about 300 workers. The Thompson Manufacturing Company has both American and "colonial" origins; C. E. Thompson served as manager and treasurer and C. Verschure as vice-president. An entirely "colonial" firm is the Holland Furniture Company, established in 1893 and specializing in bedroom furnishings. J. A. Van der Veen serves as its president, with J. Veneklaasen of the well-known brickmaking family of Zeeland as vice-president, while Dr. A. Knooihuizen is the administrator of the factory; it is considered "one of the largest and most prosperous of the Holland industries," employing approximately 150 hands. The Bay View Furniture Company, founded in 1898, employs about 125 and produces mainly extension tables; it is an entirely "colonial" enterprise. H. Van Ark is its president, H. C. Pelgrim, its vice-president and H. Pelgrim serves as administrator of the firm, which produces one hundred tables a day for national distribution; its products are termed "of the finest grade."

The furniture business in turn led to the establishment of two other industries: the Bush and Lane Piano Company, an "American" company with approximately 200 employees, and another "American" firm (1892), the C. L. King and Company, with about 175 workers producing veneers. There is also an American-organized glass and mirror company, employing about 50 hands, and which produces mostly for the furniture manufacturers. The Holland Furnace Company, established in 1908, is another predominantly "colonial" enterprise and its kitchen-ranges complement the wooden furniture. It is a firm "that is second to none in the United States." It distributes its products directly and through thirty agencies all over the United States. In 1920 it had 320 employees. It is headed by A. Visscher, president, the American W. H. Beach, vice president, I. Marsilje, bookkeeper, and A. H. Landwehr as treasurer and manager. Almost completely "colonial" is a second heating firm—the Home Furnace Company—with an all-"Dutch" management in 1921.

In 1906 the locally sponsored De Pree Chemical Company came into existence in Holland. The Holland Gelatin Works, with an annual capacity of one million pounds of "pure food gelatin," is noteworthy. There are also the Holland Chemical Company producing disinfectants, the Holland Aniline factory, etc.

Of markedly greater significance are a number of businesses closely related to the surrounding agricultural and truck gardening pursuits. In part they owe their founding to agriculture and in turn they strongly stimulated agriculture and truck gardening. There had long been some grain mill activity that had been completely modernized by, among others, W. H. Beach, one of the older American industrialists in the colony. After a 35-year history the firm was reorganized in 1902 as the Beach Milling Company and belongs now to "the live industries of the city." Five years later a Hollander, J. Muller, formed the Standard Milling and Grocer Company, also a flourishing business.

The above industries were based on cereal production, but truck gardening brought the well-known German-American, H. J. Heinz, the Pittsburgh pickle purveyor, to Holland, where he located one of his numerous ancillary factories on the shores of Black Lake, now known as Macatawa Bay.[96] Of the sixteen large factories scattered throughout the United States and Europe, the branch in Holland was advertised as "the second largest of the H. J. Heinz plants." The universally known "57 varieties," as Heinz advertises, are also shipped from Holland throughout the world. One can say without hesitation that it is a world industry, the largest of its kind. The company has about seventy "pickle salting stations" and one-tenth of their pickle growers are Dutch farmers in the colony.[97]

Financed by both American and "colonial" capital, a sugar refining industry has come into existence in Holland. According to Chase, the first Michigan sugar refinery was founded in 1898 at Bay City in the well-known Saginaw Valley, while the second refinery was set up at Holland on Michigan's west coast in 1899.[98] This latter plant is owned by the Holland St. Louis Sugar Company, organized by both American and "colonial" investors. It has also located sugar refineries in St. Louis [Missouri], in Gratiot County (Michigan), and in Decatur (Indiana). It is interesting to us that the management is American but several of the directors are "Dutch." For example, in 1914 we find, among others, such names as J. J. Cappon, G. E. Kollen, A. Visscher, A. Lahuis, and others. So far, this is information about the company management. The plant itself in Holland had the American S. R. McLean as manager but two Hollanders, O. G. Kan and H. Van Eyck, functioned as superintendent and chief engineer, respectively.

It is not necessary to comment on the significance of such a factory for the city and the surrounding area. Large tonnages of sugar beets are brought in annually by rail, electric interurban, and trucks. Consequently the production of sugar beets in the area strongly increased. In 1919 the Holland St. Louis Sugar Company alone paid out more than a million dollars to the growers for their beets. In 1920 the firm contracted for 21,000 acres of beets at $13 per ton. The average yield that year was about ten tons per acre. In the 1920 to 21 season the three factories of the Holland St. Louis Sugar Company processed nearly 200,000 tons of beets into 46,000,000 pounds of sugar; they paid the growers more than $2,135,000.[99]

Biscuit and rusk baking is another important Holland industry, brought over from the Netherlands, and many large firms are engaged in this activity. Most important is the Holland Rusk Company, "the largest concern of its kind in the world," according to the unpretentious firm's advertising. It employs about sixty people. The firm was established originally in Grand Rapids by the Arendshorst family from Friezenveen [Netherlands], but the manufacturing was transferred in 1897 to Holland, bringing with it "the experience and skill of a hundred years of rusk baking." The result was marvelous: "success was immediate," first among the Dutch element in America and then among the Americans. This "conquest," that is the acceptance by Americans, was described in this somewhat turgid, bombastic style: "Little by little the American neighbors took a liking to the rusk and gradually the sales spread until today there are few places where you cannot find the progressive grocer selling this daintiest of Dutch bakings, 'The Holland Rusk.'" It is not surprising that especially through this branch of industry "Holland is rapidly assuming rank as a food producing city." As such, Holland is thus receiving a more general recognition. Because of the neighboring dairy farms there is also a large creamery. There are also various other enterprises—cigar production, umbrella manufacture, automobile "bows,"* a printing plant, one making "paper" boxes, etc.

In 1919, Holland had sixty-four plants with a total work force of 2,748, consisting of 2,268 men and 480 women.[100] Steadily, other industries are being established. The Holland Maid Company was recently organized to produce electric washing machines, ironers, and dishwashers. The community itself raised the necessary capital; therefore the "Netherlanders" A. H. Landwehr and G. J. Diekema are the company's president and vice-

---

*"Bows" were likely the wood support arches between the exterior roof and interior ceiling of early automobiles.

president, respectively, and a German is serving as general manager.[101] Indeed, seeing all this activity, there is some truth in the conviction of many colonists that Holland is "the coming city of Michigan."

But all the industry was not concentrated in Holland. Zeeland had its share, although a smaller one. If Cappon's tanneries were the pride of the Holland colonists, those in Zeeland also prospered with their pioneer industry—the brickworks of H. H. Veneklaasen, which has several branches, including one in Hamilton, Allegan County. In Zeeland, which is situated closer to the Furniture City than Holland, there are also several furniture plants. It also has a creamery and just as in Holland in the past few years a canning factory where especially women and also school children can earn some money.[102]

The building of these canneries in addition to the creameries are an indication of an increasing production of truck-farming commodities next to dairying. Just as dairying began first on the farms and led to the creameries, so canning plants are now found in the smallest villages, as Chase points out.[103] Faust's comment that the canning industry in the United States is *"hauptsächlich in den Händen Deutscher"* [largely in German hands] is erroneous, or, at least, dated—unless, like R. Cronau, he includes the Hollanders among the Germans, which is seemingly the case.[104]

Zeeland with its 2,275 residents has retained the characteristics of an agricultural center much more than did Holland. It is an unusually prosperous town; in 1920 the two banks there had combined deposits of nearly 3½ millon dollars.[105]

Aside from being an agricultural and industrial town, Holland has also become a commercial center of significance. The shipment of lumber had long been of importance and remains so, next to the shipping of agricultural products, thanks to several enterprising lumber companies. This commercial importance is due in part to railway connections of the Pere Marquette going in five directions, to such towns as Chicago, Muskegon, Grand Rapids, Allegan, and Ottawa. In addition to these lines, the electric interurban is of very great importance. The Grand Rapids-Holland and Chicago Railway or "Interurban," makes round trips between Grand Rapids and Holland every half hour, transporting not only passengers but also goods. Just as in our country, the bus lines and interurban tramways are competing increasingly with the railroads. Numerous bus lines connect Holland with outlying communities and are a factor in local transportation. Finally I call attention to another extremely important means of transportation, the Graham Morton Line, a large American enterprise that operates numerous ferries on Lake Michigan. Twice daily there are round trips to Chicago, carrying passengers and goods in close cooperation with the Interurban, which even runs special boat trains. The ships themselves are well-appointed and especially popular for summer travel; I journeyed on one from Holland to Chicago. Although the usefulness of this line is limited to the period from the middle of March to the beginning of November—

Holland, Michigan: Its traffic. From bottom to top: The wharf of the steamships going between Holland and Chicago, located on Black Lake at Holland and at "the mouth" at Macatawa Park on Lake Michigan; Black Lake (Macatawa Bay); a gas station near Holland. (Original photos by Dirk Nieland and others, and from "Holland the Gateway.")

because of the dominant continental climate and resulting freezing over of the lake—in Holland it is nevertheless gratefully considered "one of the ruling factors of the city's commercialism." And rightly so!

Because of this steamship line Holland has become the shipping point for many products destined for Chicago. However, Holland became even more the center for many summer residences and an important departure point for summer trips. I can testify to this myself. On a beautiful summer evening, I boarded a ship for Chicago with many others who had been vacationing on Macatawa Bay (formerly Black Lake) and who returned now to their busy occupations in the Windy City and its environs. The fervent Christian pioneers of 1846 could not have imagined at the time that the place where they had landed, the western Michigan area at "the mouth" where so many of them had succumbed through fatigue and exhaustion almost within sight of the yearned-for Zion, would one day be a pleasant hyper-modern and elegant resort area. Black Lake has indeed a picturesque setting amid the dunes through which a passage to Lake Michigan had been kept open with difficulty by the vigorous efforts of the Dutch colonists. This idyllic spot was eventually discovered by the inhabitants of Chicago who during the summer were desirous of fleeing the hot city, the "city next to hell," in order to vacation on the other side of the lake.

Many summer resort villages came into being, such as Central Park and Macatawa Park on the south side of Virginia Park, a lake six miles long and two miles wide. Later on, Central Park was dubbed "Saints Rest" because of the many ministers who rented cottages in the area. On the north side of Virginia Park arose Evanston Beach, Waukazoo Beach, and Ottawa Beach. The entire area thus became an important health resort. In relation to this development, the very simple name of Black Lake was changed to the more attractive name of Macatawa Bay. It had been called Black Lake because it was always of a very dark color due to the peaty swamp water. This new name like those of Ottawa and Waukazoo, recalls the days of the Indians whose trails through the rather thick dune forests have now become modern concrete paths. Along these paths are found a whole series of the most diverse bungalows and cottages, some of which are very attractive and others extremely eccentric.

Once the resort was in vogue, Americans arrived from all parts of the Union, even from distant places such as Missouri, Kentucky, and elsewhere. They rented cottages or built their own splendid residences. While I was visiting these lake resorts, various villas in the $20,000 to $50,000 price range were in process of construction! On the north side of Black Lake, where many wealthy Chicago Jews reside in the summer, there are numerous elegant summer homes. Somewhat more modest are the houses on the south side of the lake where the Christians, many of them Hollanders, live. In addition to the ministers, there are many Dutch and other industrialists from Grand Rapids and Holland who live here in their summer residences amid those from Chicago and Indiana. This is indicated by the names on the gates of the villas rather than by the architecture, which does not resemble ours in the least. Others spend their vacation in splendidly located hotels. I mentioned the Waukazoo earlier; Pine Lodge is another one.

It is unnecessary to add that this seasonal population brings extra business to Holland. When one considers that the Holland area population increases by about 10,000 during the summer, not to mention those who come by train and boat for only one day, it is obvious that during the summer months there are considerably increased sales of garden and dairy products; the construction of hotels, houses, etc., also benefits the building contractors and workers of Holland. In addition the various shopkeepers prosper from the increased traffic. In short, the lake resorts bring in considerable revenue, according to what the Honorable [G. J.] Diekema told me repeatedly; in summer he himself goes to a cottage in the resort area.[106]

Thus prosperity, resulting from many factors, has come to Holland. As in the case of Zeeland, this is shown in the first place by the outer aspect of the town. Especially in summer it is one big flower garden where one looks in vain for slums. In Holland, the bank deposits tell the story even more eloquently. All three banks are almost completely locally owned; the oldest is the First State Bank, organized in 1889 and the modern successor of previously mentioned pioneer enterprises. Later on the Holland City State Bank and the Peoples' State Bank were established as Holland prospered. At the end of 1919 these three banks had total assets of $5,299,545.65 and in 1922 these had increased to more than $7,000,000 as a result of the uncommonly great prosperity.[107] It may be of interest to note that by the end of February 1921 the two banks first mentioned had savings deposits of $1,686,524.17 and $1,151,743.74, respectively.[108]

If we wish to ascribe this prosperity to the energy, determination, and thrift of the Dutch colonists in general, we must also consider, in particular, the importance of the leaders who, more than any others, helped to build Holland. We noted earlier that there was a small core of businessmen who constituted the driving spirit for trade and industry among the pioneers. Later there was a young, largely American-born or in any case American-raised generation that, also thanks to the founding work of their fathers, Van Raalte's Hope College, was better prepared to participate fully in American business life. Yet they wished to continue to live in Holland. Naturally, they saw even more clearly than their elders, whose energies had first of all been absorbed by the hard struggle for survival in the new environment, what opportunities *"de Kolonie"* provided for a truly American-style development by taking precise advantage of its peculiar Dutch characteristics.

The rise of this new group of enterpreneurs around 1890—the older element had been virtually ruined, as noted previously, by the fire of '70—coincided with the change of America into a truly industrial nation. This was not in the least surprising, for the rise of this new group was closely

Zeeland, Michigan, and its environs. Top: Main Street. Bottom: A celery farm.

connected with the new direction America was taking. That is also why the younger group concentrated primarily on industry, while the pioneer element of a generation before had been more oriented to trade. They realized that there were opportunities for success in those particular branches of industry that not only used the raw materials of their own area or found a ready market in that same area, but which, despite the high degree of mechanization, also required workers with those exclusive abilities that are more particular to the Dutch than to any other group or nationality.

Thus it was not a mere accident that in Holland and Zeeland, as well as in the very Dutch-like city of Grand Rapids, the furniture business flourished to such a high degree. For centuries the furniture industry has been a preëminent Dutch branch of industry, which nowhere else reached greater periods of prosperity, also because our patient and painstaking nature is particularly suited to it.

The same can be said for some other industries as well as for certain areas in agriculture, particularly in sugar beet production—"real" Americans prefer not to be involved in that. As a result, the refining of beet sugar also became not an American but a typical Dutch undertaking, in the sense that the Dutch achieved top results in this industry. To have achieved those economic insights has been the great merit of Holland City's captains of industry. A certain number also became its "financial geniuses," since in America, industry and banking are even more closely related than in our home country. In Holland such promoters of industry as Visscher, Verschure, Landwehr, Pelgrim, Diekema, and others were also board members of the banking firms and especially therefore they were considered the biggest boosters of the town.

From a sociographic point of view one of the most significant of these leaders was no doubt Arend Visscher, who passed away in 1921.[109] We previously noted that his father, J. Visscher, who had come from one of the Zuid Holland islands, was the baker in the pioneer colony, although he had very little to do. Arend was native-born, an American, since he came into this world in Michigan's city of Holland in 1850. He graduated from Hope College in 1872 and was the only graduate of Hope that year, being the only member of that graduating class! He graduated from the University of Michigan Law School in 1875 and returned to the city of Holland to engage primarily in business. He met with success! In his later years he was president of some of Holland's most important firms, such as Ottawa Furniture Company, Holland Furnace Company, Holland St. Louis Sugar Company, Holland Aniline Company, and also People's State Bank.

A figure of even greater significance is the Honorable G. J. Diekema, also native-born.[110] His father was a farmer in the vicinity of Holland where the young Gerrit was born in 1859. Just as in Visscher's case, the young Frisian studied at Hope College, graduating in 1881, and then studied law at the University of Michigan at Ann Arbor, after which he returned to Holland to establish a lawyer's practice. Diekema also became interested in Holland's industrial development, although not to the degree of Visscher, and succeeded Visscher as president of the Holland St. Louis Sugar Company after the latter's death. He was also, as we saw, vice-president of the Holland Maid Company, a producer of electric washing machines; in addition he was president of the First State Bank of Holland.

Both men, whose careers were so similar, are for various other reasons the most characteristic representatives for us of present day "colonial" business life. They had a great desire for the material and spiritual growth of their city in the widest meaning of the word. Visscher, for example, found enough time to serve his Holland as a town council member and as an alderman from 1893 to 1897, and for seventeen years he was a member of the board of public works, serving as its president for many years. He was its moving force and he was mainly responsible for the excellent waterworks and the "first-class" illumination of the town, both of which were self-supporting. He was also interested in Holland's surrounding area: for six years he served as Ottawa County's prosecuting attorney—a typical unmistakably American combination! Diekema had a similar career. He was Holland's city attorney and then even its mayor. Visscher was primarily interested in industrial life and was more attracted by technology; Diekema, on the other hand, was more interested in the general welfare and was to become a member of both the Michigan state legislature and of Congress.

Both men deserve our attention in still another area of human pursuit. Both had been brought up in the Reformed Church and notwithstanding their breadth of view, maintained their memberships throughout their lives. In spite of their demanding activities, they both found time to serve their church and occupy various posts. Visscher belonged to the Third Reformed Church and Diekema is presently a member of the First Reformed Church of Holland. Visscher even served as superintendent of the Sunday School and was active on the board of Hope College; Diekema functions in the latter capacity at present.

Visscher's younger fellow citizens have acknowledged his service in these grateful memorial words: "His business integrity, his high moral worth, and his keen interest in the community's welfare and progress, paved the way for his entering actively into the industrial, civil, social and religious growth of the city, and in each he made his influence strongly felt. His earnest efforts for the city stand today as a monument to his memory."

Thus it is evident that these business leaders contributed not only to the material prosperity but also the flourishing spiritual life of their city. In many respects Diekema is the moving spirit of Michigan. Although a member of the Reformed Church, he is also one of Michigan's most prominent Freemasons. With our tribute to this outstanding Michigander we do not want in the least, as will be shown later, to diminish Holland's greatest glory—Hope College. After all, was not Diekema one of Hope's most successful alumni and does he not owe part of his status particularly to Hope

College's outstanding education, which was unique in America? The many-sided nature of Holland's spiritual development, thanks to the contributions of the business leaders, teachers, ministers, and professors, is evident not only from the numerous elementary and secondary schools, among which is "a $100,000 high school," but also from its Western Seminary that sends its ministers all over America and even to Asia, Africa, etc.

The spirituality becomes even more evident from the multitude of Holland's church denominations. However, this particular Holland phenomenon should not be seen primarily as a schismatic mania, as we have observed earlier in Pella, because denominational differences are indeed often too great. In addition to eight Reformed and six Christian Reformed congregations there are also Methodists, Wesleyan Methodists, Lutherans, Adventists, Christian Scientists, and Baptists. And amid all of this there is a flourishing Freemason lodge![111]

It is Holland's numerous and varied sources of income and its heterogeneous economic character, its many-sided economy, that is reflected in its spiritual life and more particularly in its church life. Economic friction also causes spiritual friction and leads to exchanges of ideas not only on the material level but also on the spiritual level. Thus, we can see Holland's buoyant spiritual life as a reflection of its many-faceted economic flourishing, while both of these glorious human manifestations have also been the result of longstanding influences that emanated from the greatest monument of the pioneers: Hope College, Van Raalte's creation. It was Hope College that helped develop men such as Visscher and Diekema from the mass of "unsightly" immigrants of 1846 and later years, as Van Raalte himself had characterized them. It was Visscher who provided Holland with its most flourishing industries, while Diekema rose to preside over Michigan's legislature. That was how *de Kolonie* had gone; that was where it stood now after a period of less than eighty years! One cannot help but view it as one of the most splendid results of spontaneous emigration, as compared to the government-subsidized kind.

As we have seen, following the Civil War, a small daughter colony of the Van Raalte settlement was formed in Missaukee County in the north of Michigan's Lower Peninsula. It has continued to remain a real forest colony but is gradually changing to an agricultural one, with practices—intensive growing and cooperatives—that had been used in the Holland area. Oats, rye, and wheat are more suited to the northerly climate and have been traditionally the most important agricultural products, but in addition or as replacements, more and more potatoes and sugar beets are being produced. Vogel Center and Moddersville are the most rural of communities but Falmouth, at the end of a spur of the Grand Rapids and Indiana Railway, has become the trading center. Here one finds, due to the increasing potato culture, the storage houses of the Falmouth Cooperative Marketing Association as well as those of private firms such as M. Boersma and Son.[112]

2. In Wisconsin

Three distinct colonization areas can still be found in Wisconsin: the Calvinist settlements in Sheboygan County and in Fond du Lac County (which are even somewhat older than the Van Raalte colony in Michigan) and the Roman Catholic element in the more northerly Fox River Valley.

It will be recalled that the soil characteristics in the Wisconsin colony are similar to those in Michigan; both came out of the old glacier age. In Wisconsin there is even more water than in Michigan and so there are more clay soil areas, as well as low lying lands and swamps. This is one reason why Wisconsin has developed more of a cattle industry than Michigan; it is known as the "Dairy State."

Wisconsin, lying on the west side of Lake Michigan, has more of a continental climate than Michigan because it does not experience the tempering influences of the southwesterly winds blowing across the lake. Although the soil, consisting mostly of mixed varieties, is suitable for orchards, the cold weather and night frosts are a deterrent. Winters are too severe here. For example, in 1919 Alto had a December temperature of 20 degrees below zero.[113] Winters also last too long; the farmers around Waupun complained even in the latter part of May (1920) of the cold weather that caused delays in the farming activities.[114] But some fruit is produced; there is a rich yearly harvest of strawberries in the Fond-du-Lac settlement of Waupun.

Of more importance are farming and particularly cattle raising. Farming is even made increasingly subservient to the cattle raising needs and therefore specializes in hay and corn growing. Especially in the last several years, in all of America and in Canada too, corn is raised and then cut and stored in huge silos as silage to feed cattle. Corn for silage can be brought in a few weeks earlier and so corn growing is practical at that northern latitude in America. Wheat, oats, and rye are also produced and, especially around Waupun, hemp. In addition, potatoes are produced in large quantities for the Chicago market. However, the pride of the Dutch farmers is their cattle. This is true not only in the Frisian villages of Friesland and Randolph but also among the Gelderlanders in Alto and Waupun, which are separated from the younger Frisian settlements by Fox Lake. The situation is the same in the communities of Oostburg, settled by Zeelanders, and Gibbsville, settled by Gelderlanders, and in Cedar Grove, Hingham, Sheboygan Falls, etc. P. K. Dame, who visited most of these towns in the winter of 1920–1921 on behalf of a Christian sanitarium, has commented on the prosperity of our countrymen there. He had previously heard of the wealth of the farmers in these settlements, but he was nevertheless amazed at the neat barns filled with cattle: "It is certainly something wonderful." In his own quaint American-Dutch vernacular he expressed his admiration at the "magnificent" facilities of the farms. "Many farmers have electric lights in their stables and barns and this is preferable to the constant walking around with a lantern as there is not so much danger of fire. The cows have

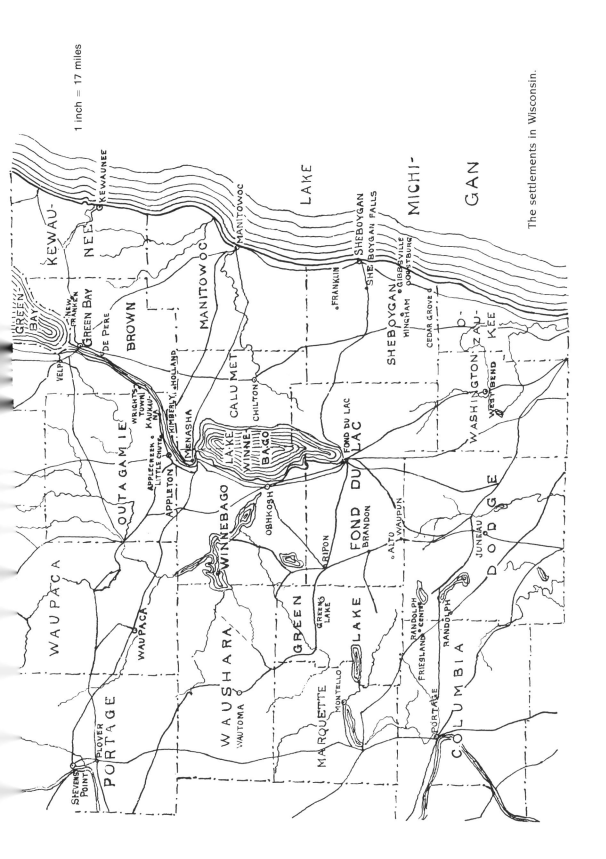

1 inch = 17 miles

The settlements in Wisconsin.

drinking containers in front of them and can drink whenever they wish because the water is piped in. Everything is equipped for neatness, cleanliness, and convenience. I must honestly confess that I had never seen anything like it. Progress is evident everywhere, in the country as well as in the cities."[115]

As we have noted, in that same year there was a crisis in agriculture, although it did not cause as many victims in Wisconsin as it did in Iowa. Land prices never rose as high as in Iowa, although in 1919 land around Alto was $190 an acre.[116] The situation in Wisconsin never became so serious because of various factors. There was a combination of farming and cattle raising and so the vulnerability, as in the case of cropping only, was not as great, and dairy prices were not as strongly influenced by world trade prices either; consequently reverses were far less serious here. That is why already in 1923 there were many farmers in Sheboygan County who could retire, while the settlements were described as "a rich area of neat and splendid farms" varying in size from a few acres to 40, 60, 80, 120 and 160 acres.[117]

The industrialization of America is also evident here. Industry is related to the farming characteristics of the area. There is a creamery in Alto, which at present is a town with a declining population of 1,132 souls; there is a creamery in Brandon with a population of 682 (in 1920 they had populations of 1,211 and 684, respectively). Although a rather constant population is characteristic in an agricultural area, where the surplus always flows off in order not to cause unemployment, the above decline points up the drawing power of the factory town of Waupun that now has 4,400 residents (3,362 in 1910) and thirteen factories producing hemp products, butter, and canned goods. In September of 1920, for example, seventeen families left Alto to settle in Waupun where especially the three or four Van Rens hemp factories and a "$150,000 canning factory" gave employment to many, as did the J. Hinkamp creamery.[118] Randolph, a younger Frisian settlement of 1,183 people, has three canning works in addition to a wagon factory that employs 75 hands.

In Sheboygan County we find Cedar Grove, a rural community of eight hundred residents, which has become quite industrial thanks to its location on the Chicago and Northwestern Railroad as well as on interurban lines to Milwaukee and Chicago. There is a stove factory, a steel foundry, a shoe factory organized by "Hollanders" with M. De Meester as manager, a cement plant, canneries, creameries, etc. At present it is also a small trading center, thanks to the rich surrounding farmlands. Naturally, there is a bank and also a Farmers Cooperative Exchange.[119] It has also become a minor spiritual center and for the benefit of these largely Calvinist Dutch there is a high school, the Wisconsin Memorial Academy, whose graduates go on to Hope College in Holland, Michigan.

In addition there is the prosperous large industrial city of Sheboygan with 31,000 residents. As in other port cities of Wisconsin, many residents are Hollanders, mostly of a religious bent, but there are even socialists here. The city constitutes a market for the farm produce of the Dutch settlers in the surrounding area, especially to the south.

The Roman Catholic settlement in the Fox River Valley, just as most of the other settlements mentioned thus far, has remained largely agricultural in nature. A priest, W. H. H. De Haan, who seems to be knowledgeable concerning his co-religionists and countrymen, wrote me in 1926 from Wisconsin, stating that 90 percent of the "Netherlanders" were engaged in agriculture and that as a typical indication of their prosperity, about 90 percent owned their own farms. Indigents are not found among them; even the least advantaged have two or three cows. Most of them have automobiles and work with tractors; in short, "there are few farmers in the Netherlands who possess houses, barns, and stables such as are found here."[120]

Some of the settlements, such as Holland in Brown County, have continued to remain almost exclusively agricultural villages. The hamlet itself consists of a few houses belonging to tradesmen and others. There are a couple of grocers, a blacksmith, and a few retired people; together with their priest they constitute the entire populace.[121] But spread for miles around the town are flourishing farms.

Other communities along the Fox River—such as Kimberly, Little Chute, and De Pere—set up various forms of industry because of the available water power from the falls and rapids. Especially the paper industry developed because of the available timber supply from the neighboring woods. Little Chute, with its two thousand inhabitants, nearly all Dutch, is connected to nearby towns by interurban and rail lines; it also acquired some large paper mills. Yet this settlement retained the overall characteristics of a farming community. The village of Kimberly lies across the river from Little Chute and subsists almost exclusively from the paper industry. A large part of the village belongs to the paper mill, where many of its inhabitants—especially new arrivals from the Netherlands—try to make a living. The significance of De Pere (originally known as Rapides des Pères) was also altered by the swift waters of its rapids and, more than the other villages, became an industrial center with about five thousand inhabitants. In the twin cities of West De Pere and East De Pere on each side of the river there are brickworks, iron foundries, and related to the latter, boiler works and machine foundries. Since 1895 there has been an "enormous" paper mill.[122]

The port city of Green Bay, already connected for a long time with De Pere via a Dutch-owned steamboat service, became a trading center but also an important industrial city. It had paper mills, iron foundries, and textile mills for linen and damask, etc. The city has a modern and lively appearance. It is laid out in the American pattern with straight, and at present broad, well-paved streets and has been considerably beautified during the last few years. Numerous electric streetcars criss-cross through the city and various railroads have their terminal there.[123]

However, not Green Bay but De Pere became the spiritual center of our countrymen. In De Pere, Dutch clergymen founded St. Norbert College and today it has a flourishing business school. Following the |First| World War the Roman Catholic press disappeared, but prior to the War first *Onze Standaard* |*Our Standard*| and then *De Volksstem* |*The Voice of the People*| had been published in De Pere. J. Kuypers, who had come from Oeffelt in the province of Noord Brabant and who had been mayor of De Pere for many years, was the proprietor of the latter paper and also of an American paper, *The Brown County Democrat*. Thus Kuypers, just as Wigman who settled in Green Bay, was one of the few lay persons who played a leading role among the Roman Catholic Dutch in Wisconsin.

To sum it all up, it may be said that our Roman Catholic fellow countrymen in and around Green Bay, De Pere, Freedom, Little Chute, Kimberly, Kaukauna, Appleton, etc., who have become interested in some branch of industry, have achieved prosperity, although they have not become nearly as significant as the Calvinist Hollanders. I have found no evidence that industry in the Fox River Valley is controlled by Hollanders, as is the case in Holland, Zeeland, Waupun, etc. Some Roman Catholics have become lawyers, doctors, etc., in cities such as Green Bay, but their number is far less than among the Calvinists. Dr. G. Rijbroek of the Holy Convent in Alverno, Wisconsin, wrote to me in 1925 that on the whole the Roman Catholics are very "prosperous" and "some have become rich."[124] The numerous county seats along the Fox River in and around Wrightstown—an area of retired people—are visible proof of this.

3. In Illinois

Of the two early settlements in Illinois—Roseland and South Holland—the latter has retained the characteristics of a farming community. Industry, although not insignificant, does not play a large part. Here are established the Chicago and Eastern Illinois Railroad yards, a coke plant of L. L. Simmer and one large Dutch undertaking, the Cement Block Works of Jacob Meeboer. In addition, this town has mainly stores and, naturally, a bank—the South Holland Trust and Savings Bank of Waterman and Holmes, a largely Dutch enterprise. There is also the important lumberyard of J. L. Vinke and numerous typical onion warehouses. South Holland is governed entirely by "Hollanders" as in the case in most of the Protestant Dutch settlements (but not in the Roman Catholic settlements, which are more intermixed with Germans, French, and Irish).

Among the Dutch settlements, South Holland is the onion town *par excellence*. Onion production has become the chief agricultural pursuit, having replaced the initially preponderant grain farming and the cattle industry. The onion dealers Van Deursen, Pals, Van Baren, and a few others, are located here. The onion growers and dealers of South Holland and surrounding area are men of consequence. In 1920 Pieter Peerbolte shipped out $175,000 worth of onion sets and in the course of one single season paid his employees $10,000 in wages. Functioning as both producer and distributor, he ships his product throughout the United States, especially to Texas, Oklahoma, and Arkansas. Through his cooperation a new "onion colony" is being established at present (1927) at South Quincy Gardens. C. E. Waterman is really the Onion King among the growers; at the same time he is a dealer and, as we have seen, a banker. For us, this is a most unusual combination of vocations, but not for an American![125]

The onion-producing area extends far beyond South Holland's territory and so do our countrymen. In the neighboring Riverdale, S. P. Schoon became one of the largest onion growers, after having completed elementary school with "high honors." He now has a tract of 225 acres on which onions, onion sets, and sugar beets are produced. At the same time he is a banker—vice president of the Dolton State Bank.[126]

Nearby Lansing was platted in 1865 by J. Lansing, an Old Netherlander from Greene, New York, and the town was named after him and his brother. Both had already settled there in 1846. One of the important men in Lansing is Jan Meeter who set up a sauerkraut works in 1892 after contracting with the neighboring farmers for onions, etc. Meeter's firm, now headed by his sons Anton and Maarten, has steadily expanded and now comprises many warehouses and canneries, covering three acres of land in Lansing alone. In one season alone, 3 million bushels of onion sets were processed. J. and W. Jabaay assist the Meeters; Anton is the technical director and Maarten the sales manager. These enterprising fellow countrymen have established a second plant in Onion Grove, Wisconsin, employing fifty to sixty hands. They are also engaged in important hay dealings and both are known as "balers of hay" and manufacturers of sauerkraut.[127]

South Holland now numbers about 1,300 inhabitants and there are seven De Jong families! Among them the first—Pieter De Jong—was the most interesting. For years he served as postmaster and justice of the peace. His pride was his son Frederik—an important lawyer, a "$15,000 man" who was in a partnership with some others. For some years this Frederik was the judge of the circuit court in Cook County but, as a good Republican, he had to give it up when [Woodrow] Wilson became president.[128] The first De Jong, "Zwarte Piet," [Black Pete] has passed away. Among the public-spirited men of South Holland must also be mentioned postmaster R. A. Gouwens and mayor P. A. Anker, the president of the village board.

This settlement has remained more typically Dutch than any other, in spite of the proximity of Chicago, and therefore the only congregations are a Reformed and a Christian Reformed church. Being almost exclusively agricultural, and having specialized particularly in truck gardening, it practically excluded all others from competing, except perhaps for a few Germans. American farmers in the surrounding area and a very few American businessmen in the village, were bought out; this was prompted by their not feeling at home among the Calvinists.[129] When I visited South Holland in 1921, I found it to be a peaceful, prosperous village. I will consider Roseland and Chicago together, because Roseland has been absorbed by Chicago.

4. In Iowa

The Netherlanders in and around Pella in Marion County and Orange City in Sioux County have become even more prosperous than those in South Holland and other settlements. Earlier I have discussed the reasons for this prosperity and compared Pella with the Wisconsin and Michigan settlements. When Pella celebrated its 75th anniversary, the Reverend H. M. Bruins of Alto, Wisconsin, gave an address that confirmed my conclusions, although with a differing emphasis. His father, who was born in Deventer, had left the Netherlands in July of 1847 and had gone to Wisconsin. According to Reverend Bruins, the rapid and significant development of the colony was encouraged by the fact (notice again the curious [i.e., old fashioned] kind of Dutch he uses) "that the class of people were neither of the poorest, who would have been unfit to assume leadership, nor were they of the kind brought up on velvet cushions, because they would not have been energetic. Rather, most of them were of the middle class who had been well educated but were dependent on the reward of diligence and the exercise of practical frugality." In addition, he said, "The soil here and the climate reward with twice the return in rich harvests the wages of the farmer's sweat. In Michigan also the hand of the industrious immigrant found its reward in the fruit of the field; the land in Wisconsin was not of the poorest type either, but it was in Iowa that nature was most richly endowed by God. This is the prime portion of the Mississippi Valley."

Who could better testify to this at this diamond anniversary than those who had come with their parents to Iowa in 1847? There were P. Ten Hage, S. H. Viersen, A. Van Stigt, Mrs. H. Wormhoudt, Mrs. G. Van Horsen, [?] Hasselaar [likely Adam P. Hasselman], H. Van Maren, Th. Van de Pol, G. Van Zee, Mrs. A. Van Sittert, J. Ten Berge, Mrs. D. Van Zante, all of Pella, as well as A. De Reus from Otley, H. J. Van der Waa (the baker's son from Hattum and an Orange City pioneer), and W. J. Curtis from San Bernardino, California.[130]

Pella has continued to be a peaceful and prosperous little city with a largely Dutch population of 3,500. It has become the economic and spiritual center (Central College!) for the expanding Dutch agricultural area. Much more so than in Holland, Michigan, Pella's prosperity is dependent upon the surrounding farm population. Although for many decades Pella surpassed the other Dutch settlements, it lost that place when America's industrialization made Holland an industrial city. Like most of the settlements west of the Mississippi River, Pella remained predominantly agricultural; thus Holland eventually greatly surpassed Pella economically.

This is not to imply that Pella, the Garden City, has no industry whatever.

Quite the contrary! From the beginning there has been some industry to meet the needs of the farm population and the products of their harvests. There was the long-established Beurkens cart factory that has twelve employees today. There is also a carpenter's yard. Of more importance is the Garden City Feeder Company that manufactures farm machinery and particularly parts for threshing machines. It employs one hundred to two hundred workers, depending on the ups and downs in the prosperity of the farmers. The processing industry includes a creamery, plus a cannery where women and girls form the majority of the employees. There is also an "egg and poultry business" that H. Rhijnsburger has developed into a highly prosperous enterprise.

Less directly involved in filling solely the local needs are other branches of industrial activity. There is a factory that makes the typical American overalls and especially a window blind factory that moved recently from Des Moines to Pella. This Rolscreen Company employs fifty to one hundred men. Arrangements are being completed for the establishment of a factory to manufacture washing machines; at present the firm is located at Newton in Jasper County, Iowa, but it has been bought by Pella residents. This is a matter of importance because the firm will provide employment for one hundred to three hundred workers. It should be noted that there is a constant pressure of westward moving industry, in spite of a shortage of labor and the lack of cheap transportation, e.g., waterways. The increasing buying power of the population is largely responsible for this new industrial development, and usually compensates for the above-mentioned negative factors.

From this it appears that there is a dependence on agriculture, as was explained to me by G. G. Gaass, an attorney at law and spokesman for Pella's chamber of commerce. He informed me that "Pella depends largely on the farmer trade." The many prosperous stores in the city—three drug stores, a "very large department store," and two jewelry stores—rely for their trade to a considerable extent on the farm populace. This also applies to the eight garages and the banking firms. The Dutch-managed Pella National Bank had a capitalization of $110,000 in June of 1926 and the assets totaled $1,106,862.69.[131] The Dutch-owned Security State Bank had a capitalization of $100,000, and then there is also the Farmers National Bank, with a largely Dutch management, that had resources of $751,516.39 at the end of 1919.[132]

If the name of the last bank indicates the developing cooperative spirit of the farmers, then this may also be said with regard to the Farmers Cooperative Union. The farmers began to join this Union particularly after the crisis years. The Sully Cooperative Exchange was also founded by our ethnic kinsmen in Sully, more to the north, and in 1920 it shipped out seventy-nine car loads of animals, including 3,541 hogs, which brought $162,314. In addition, the Co-op acquired the local grain elevator.[133] As a consequence, their prospects after the reckless speculations and consequent disasters of the past have gradually improved. Corn is the chief product, followed by small grains such as oats and wheat. The soil here is so fertile that magnificent harvests average forty-five bushels of corn per acre, which is five bushels over the Iowa average. Forty bushels of oats and twenty of wheat are harvested per acre. Little of the corn and oats are brought to market; they are largely used to fatten hogs and steers. A good deal of corn goes to the canneries and this is also true of pumpkins and such orchard fruits as apples, etc.

To what extent the prosperity of the farmers has been increasing after 1923 is reflected in land prices which, in general, have not declined to pre-war levels. Although they did decline during the crisis years, they still remained high. Thus, the land around Pella is again being sold for $100 to $300 an acre; before the war it was $100 to $150, as was previously mentioned.[134]

Pella is inhabited largely by Hollanders, but being an increasingly important center, some Americans also live there and this is reflected in the church bodies. There are three Reformed and two Christian Reformed congregations but there are also a Baptist and a Methodist church. There is some variety, but it cannot rival by far the situation of Holland, Michigan. This is in contrast with former times, when particularly in Pella the religious differences were the most numerous, but for quite different reasons as we have seen earlier. Now there is also a certain economic homogeneity in Pella, which is reflected in the spiritual and religious sphere.

This is also true in the countryside, which has become more and more Dutch. Tracy, Leighton, Peoria, New Sharon, Otley, Sully, etc., have almost completely been taken over by our fellow Dutch and they have established Reformed and Christian Reformed churches and Christian schools. Just as in Michigan, the surrounding towns have many Hollanders. Examples may be found in Oskaloosa and Knoxville, the county seats of Mahaska and Marion counties. There is even a Reformed Church in Oskaloosa. However, Pella is the ideal residence for the elderly. The Garden City is for them the place for retirement. They prefer to live there. A Holland Home has been established there and forty older people reside there now. Many others live by themselves. The park in the center of town is the gathering place for all. Gossip is exchanged there and memories of the Old Country are recalled. No other spot in the United States is as "Dutch" as Pella's Central Park!

But an even more prosperous and pleasant place is the settlement in Sioux County, in the northwestern part of the same state. In previous pages I have dealt at great length with the founding and growth of the "New Colony." It is amazing to notice the numerous changes there since the seventies. B. Mouw, a 75-year old Geldersman who had settled in Sioux Center in 1871 (but who had not yet forgotten his Dutch), wrote me in 1925, responding to my request that he supply me with some reminiscences. Actually, he dictated his thoughts to his son, P. B. Mouw, who apologized: "You must look over [*overzien*, literally, *look over*, but meaning to "overlook"] the errors in this letter because I never attended no Dutch school. In earlier

The farm of Otto Van Roekel near Orange City, Sioux County, Iowa, in 1921 (Original photo by J. Van Hinte).

Orange City, Sioux County, Iowa. Top: First Reformed Church. Middle: Main Street.
Bottom: First National Bank [building with pediment].

Sioux Center, Sioux County, Iowa. Top: Netherlands [Nederduitsch] Reformed Church. Middle and bottom: Main Street — notice the very wide streets so typical of colonial areas.

times we rode behind cows and oxen and later, horses, but now it is almost nothing but automobiles. . . . In those days there were no public roads; we just drove across the prairies and since the streams were not bridged, we forded them. Now there are good roads everywhere. There are now gravel roads between the towns and we fly over them in our cars. When I arrived here there was little or nothing to be seen, but now I can sit in front of my house and see a stream of cars coming and going, back and forth."

Yet, in spite of all these changes the characteristics of Sioux County, once it had become a totally agricultural settlement, have changed but little. They did not even change after the rapid American industrialization that is felt in this farther West, though to a lesser extent than in the East. This was in spite of the fact that this area was ready and willing earlier than others for the consumption of America's newest industrial products. The most modern of farm equipment—the "combined harvesters" that both reap and thresh—are found here as well as corn pickers and hay loaders, which stack the hay on the wagons; machinery also puts it in the barns. In addition there are cultivators and "iron ponies"—Fordson tractors. There are also a greater variety of automobiles—America's most distinctive factory product—than in any other Dutch settlement. If the Ford is the car of the working man, the average resident of Sioux County has a second one to serve his pleasure. In 1921 while visiting various settlements, I did not have a more beautiful car trip and did not ride in a finer automobile than in Sioux County. The Cadillac of Mr. Klay was one of the newest models and furnished with all the available optional accessories.

The countryside also shows its prosperity by means of the building styles and the care lavished on nearly every farm. In typical American fashion the home is entirely separated from the barns and stables and sometimes it is a veritable villa. In the cities the prosperity is evident from the appearance of every single home. Since 1895 the cities of Orange City, Alton, Sioux Center, Hull, Hospers, Maurice, etc., like the countryside, have not changed in character either. They have only grown somewhat in size, contain a few more buildings, and sometimes boast an additional elevator and a few more well-supplied shops. Sometimes a bank was also added. In 1923, the Northwestern State Bank of Orange City had a capital and surplus of $125,000; at the end of December, 1922 the Orange City National Bank had a capital of $220,856.22.

The wealth of the farmers is reflected in the increasing value of their land. As in Pella, prices have gone up again following the crisis of 1923, and now land costs about $225 per acre.[135] This increase in wealth is also reflected in the growing bank deposits and the goods displayed in the store windows. Not only do the automobile showrooms evidence this but also the furniture stores, which advertise in this "peasant" country "Queene Anne" and "Heppelwhite" furniture, items which in the Netherlands are usually advertised only in the largest cities.[136] Other examples of this affluence can be observed in small but nevertheless no less characteristic details, such as the sales of silk shirts for $9.50 plus war tax in small towns comparable to the villages of Muiden or Diemerbrug [in the Netherlands]. All these sales are made to our once so poor, small sand farmers from the Gelderland Veluwe and Overijsel and to their wives, who have now become the prominent ladies and gentlemen!

A peaceful industriousness characterizes all these "elevator and store" towns. Among them Orange City and Sioux Center attract especially the retired farmers, although many of the latter also go to California and even Florida. None of these towns have much significance as industrial centers although in addition to some trade, there is some industry directly related to farming. Corn growing is most important—Iowa is the chief corn state in the Union—but wheat and oat production are also of significance and cattle raising is gradually becoming more important. Fattening cattle has long been practiced but now attention is being given to dairying, although the scarcity of labor poses a problem. This dairying leads everywhere to the establishment or enlarging of creameries.

In this area, cooperatives are also finding more and more acceptance, although they are still in their initial stage. There is in fact an increasing pressure to set up these co-ops so that farmers will no longer be considered barely good enough to foster millionaires at their own expense, as one writer put it in a depression-year issue of Orange City's *Volksvriend* [*Friend of the People*], adding that the individual farmer was standing "alone in the fog" between "trust" and "organization."[137] P. B. Mouw wrote me that in Sioux Center, to cite an example, there is a farmers' cooperative trading center that purchases and sells on a wholesale basis for the benefit of the farmers. In this way building materials are bought, grain is shipped, and also 135,000 hogs per year are sent to market by this organization alone.

In addition it should be noted that, since the Iowa farmers suffered more than any others after the speculative years, American farmers also are moving in the direction of co-operatives. Thus, the Farmers Grain Dealers Association formed the Iowa Farmers' Marketing Association, a buying and sales organization, with branches all over the state. In 1920 some Hollanders, for example, [?] Huibregtse from Hull in Sioux County, were on its board.[138]

Corn rules supreme in Sioux County, followed closely by cattle and hogs. Therefore, these animals are given a great deal of care, especially with an eye to fattening them up, while dairying is gaining ground, thereby enhancing the importance of milk cows next to meat cattle. Thus, it is not merely by chance that Sioux County is famous not only for its highly developed agriculture but also for its slaughter cattle and hogs. Its breeders are known far outside the county; they even have a state-wide reputation. Pieter Mouw, who passed away in May of 1922, was one of the foremost of these stock-breeders. His "biggest Poland China" hogs and "Big-type Hereford" cattle were his pride and glory and helped to put Orange City on the map of America. This stalwart Gelderlander regularly took first prizes at the Chicago exhibitions where his "breeders" attracted crowds of admirers. "You got the

The late Piet Mouw and his business — the pride of Sioux County, Iowa. Top: The barns and silo, Mr. and Mrs. Mouw and Mayor Klay in the foreground. Middle and bottom: Mouw's famous "biggest Poland China" hogs. (Original photos by J. Van Hinte and from catalogs.)

crowd around you all the day, Mr. Mouw; stick to it," one of his admirers once exclaimed. He was an individual who realized Mouw's significance for Sioux County. It was Mouw who set the trend to replace smaller types of hogs and cattle by larger ones and so he was credited with having accomplished "an enormous task" that was highly successful; it made him a "nationally known character by swine men of all breeds."[139]

Corn, steers, and hogs have accounted for the prosperity of Sioux County. It sounds sober enough but it is not without import. The structure of the economy is even simpler here than in Pella. We notice also that spiritual culture is more uniform here. Still, the Northwestern Classical Academy of the Reformed Church, located in Orange City, and the Christian Reformed Western Academy at Hull, bring some life to this otherwise all too peaceful spiritual climate. The two strongest churches at present, the Reformed and the Christian Reformed, also see to it that some friction is generated to keep things hopping.

In this connection it should be mentioned that Sioux County has not produced any writers of note, as was the case in Holland, Michigan, and in Pella in Marion County. Yet the most typical of young Dutch Americans are found among the Sioux County colonists; they are pioneers one generation after another.

Have these colonists become too materialistic? (In this regard Smertenko ironically commented that "rural Iowa—more than a million souls—has no interests beyond bread and butter.") Are they too prosperous? Whatever the case, materially they stand head and shoulders above the other Dutch settlements and have achieved the greatest success, although external causes independent of the colonists themselves have been contributing factors. A Hope College alumnus, G. F. Huizinga, with the Sioux County colonists mainly in mind, wrote as follows: "The extensive scale of their operations, the easy circumstances of the people, and the general and remarkable prosperity of their communities prove the Dutch in Iowa not only the best farmers among all the Dutch, but among the best in the United States."[140]

5. Smaller Settlements Elsewhere

Although not as typically Dutch as the large settlements previously noted, I should also mention the younger settlements of the eighties in southern Lancaster County, Nebraska, where the hamlets of Pella, Holland, and Firth more or less constitute one joint colony. In addition there are Prairie View and Rotterdam in the northern Kansas counties of Phillips and Smith, respectively, and which are spiritual centers for the Dutch. The first is a railroad stop, the latter is away from the railroad but it is a pleasant rural village, well-located on Oak Creek. Charles Mix and Douglas, adjoining counties in South Dakota, have generally continuous, larger Dutch developments in and around such towns as Harrison, Corsica, Armour, Joubert, New

Holland, and Platte. Platte is the terminus for the feeder lines of the Chicago, Milwaukee and St. Paul and it especially has become a trading center, the marketplace for an area more than twenty miles round about. This is an agricultural area exclusively, producing wheat, corn, alfalfa, and cattle, either for slaughter or for dairying. As elsewhere, the latter is growing in importance; there are four creameries in Platte. The busy trading explains the presence of three banks in this small town.

Platte is also a church center with seven churches, two of which are Dutch; there are several schools, including a Christian Reformed school and a high school. Chiefly because of the churches, Platte has become a popular retirement town for the farmers who here also have achieved prosperity after years of adversity.[141] This has not been true in all cases; some became discouraged and left, as in the case of the colonist [Adriannus] Bliek who had settled near Harrison. After having harvested only one good crop in thirteen years, he left for Iowa, and resettled first north of Leighton and then at Pella where I met him, serving as director of the Holland Home. Therefore, the splendid harvests that marked the later South Dakota period have not been witnessed by this gentleman. They did come, however, as they did in so many other places for the benefit of those who had stuck it out. This had been the case in Sioux County also where settlers had to face initial years of reverses followed only later by years of prosperity.

Finally we should mention the oldest and also the least characteristic Dutch settlement among the larger ones: the fruit growing colony in Wayne County, New York State. It will be recalled that it had its origins with colonists from Zeeland who had settled in Pultneyville (even before the arrival of Van Raalte and other immigrant leaders) and they served as a model for many others. Without any previously worked-out plan, a vast community developed very gradually. In particular, Zeelanders from Kadzand and its environs have been in control up to this day. The descendants of these Zeelanders even comprise 80 percent of the population of Sodus and its neighboring area, also in Wayne County. They are numerous in and around Ontario, Williamson, and East Williamson, as well as in the more southerly communities of Marion, Palmyra, and East Palmyra.

Real leaders, men of some education, were not found among them. For this reason and also due to the gradual growth of the area we have heard and still hear so little of this settlement. This lack of leaders also explains why these Hollanders, who at times settled amid the descendants of their seventeenth-century fellow Dutch, nevertheless kept so little of their Dutch characteristics, but have become Americanized largely due to the New England element that arrived and soon outnumbered the Old Dutch. Yankees settled in these Old-Dutch areas, which as the domain of the Holland Land Company in the early nineteenth century had once again become "Dutch." The American element was located particularly in the cities where they dominated business life, while they left the countryside to our Zeelanders. The latter exclusively engaged in agriculture, particularly in fruit growing.

1 inch = 9 miles

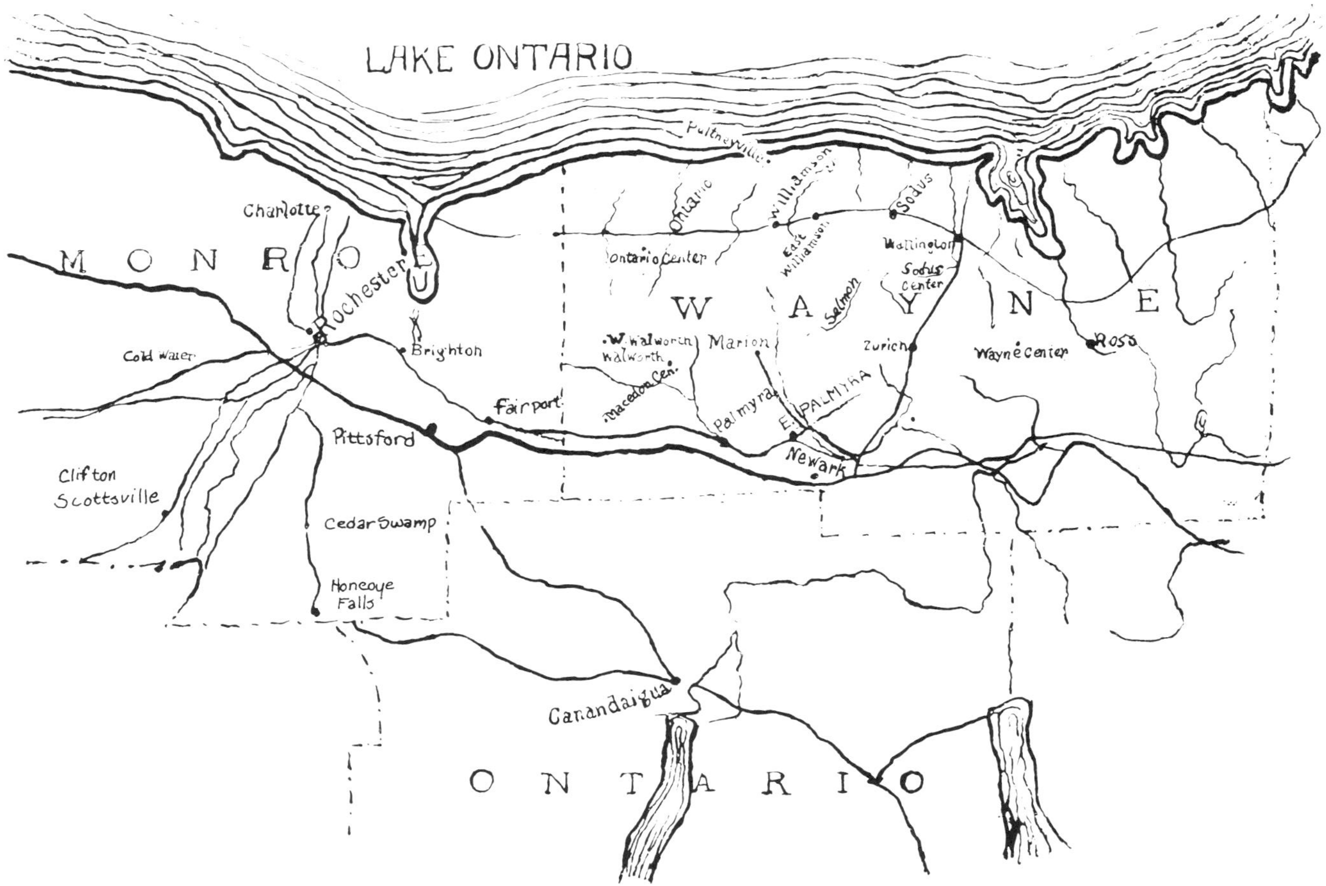

LAKE ONTARIO

M O N R O E

W A Y N E

O N T A R I O

Charlotte

Rochester

Brighton

Cold water

Pittsford

Clifton

Scottsville

Fairport

Cedar Swamp

Honeoye Falls

Canandaigua

Fultonville

Ontario

Ontario Center

Williamson

Sodus

Wallington

Sodus Center

East Williamson

Salmon

Zurich

Walworth

Marion

Walworth

Macedon

Palmyra

E.PALMYRA

Newark

Wayne Center

Ross

Zeeland settlements in Wayne County, New York. Zeelanders and Frisians at Rochester and environs.

Thanks to their industry, Wayne County has become one of America's foremost orchard areas. This area is magnificent, particularly in spring when the peach, plum, cherry, apple, and pear trees are in full blossom. Numerous residents from "nearby" industrial Rochester travel to Sodus or Marion by car, rail, or trolley to enjoy the beauties of nature. Very few, even among the Dutch visitors, are aware that descendants of Hollanders, who already had such an excellent reputation for that highly exacting fruit growing and gardening specialty in Europe, are responsible for these splendid showplaces.

The bankers, manufacturers, tradesmen, etc., in all these "garden cities" are American however, in contrast to the larger settlements dealt with in this survey where businessmen have largely come from among the colonists themselves. For example, in the overwhelming Zeelander town of Sodus there is scarcely a Hollander "in business." To a considerable extent this situation can be ascribed to a lack of spiritual leaders, which resulted initially in a dearth of good educational facilities. This lack accounts also for the fact that many believers—more than anywhere else—were lost for their old native church, the Reformed Church. They associated instead with the English-language Presbyterian Church, the church that comes closest to the Reformed Church. This, in turn, hastened the process of Americanization. But then, one wonders why these most Americanized fellow country-men stayed the farthest away from business. One wonders all the more strongly because many of these Zeeland colonists, who are portrayed as frank and candid people, had come from the so-called "fourth district" of Zeeuws-Vlaanderen and were descendants of the Huguenots who had set-tled there in the seventeenth century. As a result of the constant transplant-ing, it might be expected that they would be a mobile and active element. Or is it possible that the vestiges of French character traits would be, in the long run, a deterrent to such activity, as seems also to be the case among the French Canadians?

It is also possible that where Dutch orthodoxy helped to drive out the "real" Americans in the various settlements, the latter felt more at home among the somewhat more fickle and frivolous "French" Zeelanders—although the number of these "French" among the Zeelanders should not be overestimated—and that therefore Americans were less inclined to pack up and leave. In any case, it is a remarkable fact that although among the Zeelanders in Wayne County there are nine Reformed churches in addition to the Presbyterian church, the Christian Reformed Church, which is the most orthodox, has put out very few roots there. Only one Christian Re-formed Church exists in East Palmyra and it may well be asked if its founding [openbaring] in 1907 was due to its orthodoxy rather than to the convenience of its quite frequent use of the Dutch language.

Be that as it may, the colonists in the West themselves feel that they are "different" from those who arrived in America at the same time and settled in the "eastern" Wayne County. This was made clear to me by some most

important news items in the "western" *Volksvriend*. From his new home in
Sodus, Wayne County, B. W. Lammers wrote literally: "Whoever comes here
from the West will perceive that there is quite a difference between the
West and the East." Later he wrote: "There is a significant difference between the Hollanders here and those in the West.... Business here is
largely in American hands. Furthermore, the Hollanders here are not as
attached to the Dutch language as is the case in most of the western
settlements. Even Dutch older adults who arrive here prefer to speak English. There is usually little difficulty in introducing English religious
services."[142] Lammers ascribed these peculiarities to the fact that "*ons volk*"
[our people] settled among Americans, which forced them to learn "the
Language of the land." However, this does not explain everything, for even
to this day, there is a numerical majority of Zeelanders in Wayne County.
Why are there so few businessmen among them? There should have been
far more, considering the dominant Zeeland element and their strong
Americanization.

Undoubtedly, the greater weight of the much older American culture in
the East, when compared with the situation in the West, must explain the
important fact that the prosperous Zeeland colony in Wayne County is the
least original and is in all respects the least self-governing among the larger
Dutch settlements.

In addition to these settlements, which the colonists themselves considered as colonies, there are throughout the Midwest, and even in the
entire United States, numerous smaller settlements that were sometimes
established as Dutch colonies according to well-defined, preparatory plans.
Very frequently, they bear Dutch names (Prinsburg and Roseland in Minnesota, and Nederland in Texas, etc.) and in many cases they sprang up rather
spontaneously, due to the chance circumstance that a Dutchman was already living there. In the latter case the Hollanders usually live among the
Americans or among other nationalities and frequently the settlement has
an American name. There are many examples of both, as I have previously
pointed out.

The Hollanders in America, more or less unconsciously, differentiate
among themselves between these "settlements" and the larger colonies.
Some of these settlements are scattered over Minnesota. Hollanders have
established themselves now even in the most northern part of the state at
Crookston in Polk County, in the Red River Valley where land speculators
had earlier tried in vain to sell land to Bloemendaal and his followers. A
genuine Minnesota "colony," as the ones in Michigan, Iowa, etc., did not
come into being in spite of all the efforts I previously related. The latest
attempt in this area, that of the Payne Investment Company, has not yet
produced any results in this respect. This firm had earlier operated in
Freeborn County in southeastern Minnesota where in a former glacier area
it had drained a swamp of about 15,000 acres around Lake Geneva, a
moraine lake, and made excellent muck land available for sugar beets and

potatoes. A big advertising campaign was launched in the Dutch-American press and Dutch-American children were even encouraged to come up with a suitable name. The colony would be completely Dutch. Thus, Hollandale—one of the many contest answers—was chosen as the most appropriate name for the new "town" and streets such as 's-Gravenhage, Rotterdam, and Zuiderzee Avenues were laid out. The name of Hollandale was also a success in the publicity campaign. Around the town various farms were established—Neerlandia, Hollandia, Zeldenrust [Seldom Rest], Arbeid Adelt [Labor Ennobles], Geduld Overwint Alles [Patience Conquers All], Eendracht Maakt Macht [In Unity is Strength], Standvastig [Steadfast], Meerzicht [Lake View] etc. Through the company's cooperation a Reformed Church building was erected. The company called attention of native Hollanders to the new settlement in the pages of the *Handelsblad* and the *Leeuwarder Courant*.[143] In spite of this, the cautious Dutch were slow to take the bait. They were so slow that the land company opened the area to other nationalities and so the original plan—to have a colony with only Dutch characteristics—was abandoned.

Minnesota is going to surpass Wisconsin as the "butter" state. But no matter how suitable it is for the Dutch specialty of dairying and for agriculture, the majority of Dutch farmers want nothing to do with the "bread and butter state." It is too cold for them and so these days they prefer to go to California.

Since about 1910 Dutch farmers went to California and its wonderful climate. Numerous settlements have sprung up. Many Hollanders are swarming in, coming from Michigan and Illinois, Wisconsin and Minnesota, but especially from Montana and Canada, and even from South Africa, South America, and last but not least, from the Netherlands itself. They are taking up dairying and truck farming near the large cities.[144] In 1904, the Amsterdam councilman [C. V.] Gerritsen sought in vain to find Dutch farmers in California; now they are encountered everywhere, but especially around San Francisco and Los Angeles. The best evidence of this newest trek is found in the establishment of numerous Christian Reformed churches; in fact, a separate Classis California was set up. These churches are found in Redlands (1911), in Hanford[145] (with many people from the Haarlemmermeer as well as many Roman Catholics) (1913), Los Angeles (1914), Ripon (1918), San Francisco or rather its suburb Alameda (1924), Stockton (1926), Chino and Bellflower (1927). Clearly, California is on the map.[146]

None of these is a specifically Dutch settlement. Perhaps by buying out Americans a completely Dutch settlement may evolve. This may materialize particularly in the Los Angeles area. Originally rich Iowa farmers moved there; the suburb of Hynes, twenty miles distant from the downtown area, is now attracting so many Hollanders that it is already referred to as "Little Netherlands." Many Frisians reside in nearby Clearwater.

In Hynes, situated near Bellflower, one hears more Dutch and Frisian spoken than English. At the cattle sales these two languages are used exclusively![147] Dairying is the principal California activity and, as mentioned earlier, the (Holstein) Frisian animals that were imported already much earlier are ideal for that purpose. The number of Dutch farmers is steadily increasing; "more are coming in every day." What this really means is that most of them do not come directly from the Netherlands but from the northern and western states. Most of them are of a religious nature; they are "the stauncher church folks that leave the colder East for the mild Southwest and settle here."[148] They constitute the backbone of the church and so are a more or less permanent nucleus in each of the various Dutch settlements, although they sometimes "backslide and collapse" as, for example, in Afton.[149] Obviously, also in California, the number arriving directly from the Netherlands has been curtailed by immigration restrictions. For a survey of a couple of hundred other settlements scattered throughout the United States, I refer in this concluding overview to the church statistics.

14

Dutch Colonies in the Cities

A. In Paterson, Rochester, Grand Rapids, and Chicago

No less prosperous than those who located in the rural areas were those of our countrymen who settled in the large American industrial and commercial centers, although their significance was of an altogether different nature. Their total number has always been smaller, even after 1890 when the "free" lands were largely gone. By then America's industry had gone through its early period and had become the first in the world, the "youthful giant in industry," which constantly demanded more employees.[1]

No matter what statistical data may say, to all intents and purposes the greater part of the Dutch immigrants live in the rural areas and the smaller part is found in the large cities. With this assertion I have in mind the numerous "suburb farmers," the dairy and truck gardening farmers who live near Rochester, Chicago, and other cities. They are officially counted as inhabitants of large cities but in reality these farmers live *near* the cities, as so many do in Nieuwendam and Buiksloot around Amsterdam [in the Netherlands], and so they are really country people. This ratio seems to be changing constantly. Depending on economic conditions, people migrate from the cities at one time—the year 1893 was typical—but then later there is a reverse migration from the countryside such as after the agricultural crisis of 1920.[2]

In spite of these changes and due to the steadily increasing cost of land, a permanent shift to the cities may be observed:[3]

	1900	**1910**	**1920**
Dutch immigrants in the U.S.	*94,931*	*120,063*	*131,766*
In cities of 25,000 and more inhabitants	36,328	50,211	59,204
In rural areas (country)	58,603	69,852	72,562

In America all incorporated towns of 2,500 or more inhabitants are considered as cities. (In Massachusetts, Rhode Island, and New Hampshire, the term *town* is used.) Looking at it this way we get an even less accurate picture, because it would seem to indicate that the majority of the population lives in cities. In 1920, according to these criteria, 74,424 (56.5 percent) of the Dutch-born in America lived in urban areas and 57,342 (43.5 percent) resided in rural districts. The number of native-born in America of Dutch parents living in urban areas was 118,101 (51.8 percent) and in rural areas it was 109,988 (48.2 percent). The totals are 194,557 (53.7 percent) urban and 167,761 (46.3 percent) rural [these figures do not jibe (ed.)]. Since those born in the Netherlands generally were late-comers, these figures indicate a shift to the cities, too.

Cities that have long been of importance for the Hollanders are Grand Rapids and Paterson and the commercial centers of Chicago and New York. Paterson itself has many satellite industrial areas such as Passaic and Clifton, and numerous Hollanders also live in these two towns. In addition, industrial centers such as Rochester, Cleveland, and Detroit (thanks to Ford) each have more than a thousand Dutch-born, while Salt Lake City (because of the Mormon missionary effort!), Los Angeles, San Francisco, Boston, Milwaukee, and Seattle each have more than 500.

City	Dutch-born			Dutch-born plus native-born of Dutch parents
	1900	*1910*	*1920*	*1920*
Grand Rapids	11,137	11,891	11,422	30,846
Chicago	8,555	9,632	8,843	22,136
New York	2,608	4,193	4,750	9,552
Paterson	4,893	4,929	3,604	9,448
Rochester	927	1,220	1,891	4,677
Detroit	397	584	1,861	4,230
Cleveland	804	1,076	1,039	2,778
Salt Lake City	57	443	874	1,525
Los Angeles	86	408	797	1,807
San Francisco	244	500	788	1,452
Boston	391	486	691	1,313
Milwaukee	606	615	528	2,026
Seattle	77	317	525	1,143

Among American cities with 25,000 to 100,000 inhabitants in 1920, Kalamazoo and Muskegon, Michigan (because of the nearness of the Van Raalte colony) had more than 1,000 Dutch-born, while Clifton and Passaic—both in the Paterson industrial area—each had more than 500, as did the port city of Hoboken; all the latter are in New Jersey. Ogden, Utah, (because of Mormon propaganda) and Sheboygan, Wisconsin, (because of the proximity of the old "Zonne settlement") also had more than 500 each.

1920	Dutch-born	Dutch-born plus native-born of Dutch parents
Kalamazoo, Mich.	3,483	8,389
Muskegon, Mich.	1,752	5,761
Clifton, N. J.	919	2,224
Passaic, N. J.	910	2,548
Hoboken, N. J.	767	977
Ogden, Utah	749	1,501
Sheboygan, Wis.	530	1,231

It must be understood that the total number of our ancestry in these towns is actually much larger. Those of Dutch descent are found not only in New York and New Jersey, where one finds so many descendants of the Dutch who originally settled there in the seventeenth century, but also in the newer states where sometimes four Dutch generations have lived since 1845. Grand Rapids and its suburbs had approximately 150,000 residents in 1920; the city itself had 137,664. The Hollanders belonging to the "foreign white stock" (Dutch-born plus native-born of Dutch parents) constituted two-ninths of the total population or 38.4 percent of the total foreign white stock of Grand Rapids. However, the total Young-Dutch element is estimated at a third of the total population. An important trend indicated by these statistics is that immigrants who had been city dwellers, as well as the rural element, settle mostly in the West, drawn by family connections and the high wages. This may also be partially due to the old urge to go west.

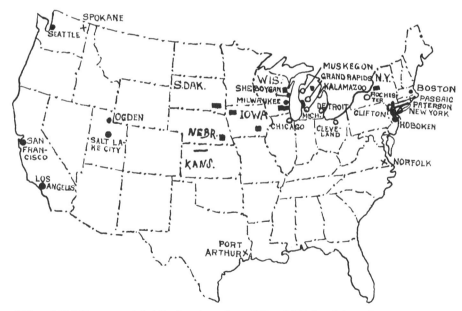

- Cities of 25,000 or more inhabitants, where from 500 to 1,000 Dutch-born live.
○ Cities of 25,000 or more inhabitants, where more than 1,000 Dutch-born live.
■ The true Dutch settlements.
✗ Cities built with Dutch capital. Spokane with 183 Dutch-born, Norfolk with 118, and Port Arthur with 150.

Geographical distribution of the Dutch settlements.

It was not due to chance that the city element tended to settle mostly in the industrial centers. The large majority of this group of immigrants made a good living as factory workers, especially in Paterson's silk mills and the furniture factories of Grand Rapids. They did well in all other places, too, and also in other industries. In the twenty-one largest industries, less than 1 percent of the employees were Hollanders and, when one considers the small total number of Dutch immigrants, this is not surprising. Already before the [First] World War, according to Jenks and Lauck, the Dutch formed the largest group of workers in the American furniture industry— 18.6 percent; an additional 7.1 percent were "native" workers whose fathers were Dutch-born, giving a total of 25.7 percent. (The Swedes came next with figures of 14.7 percent and 1.8 percent, for a total of 16.5 percent.) In the silk industry (dyeing and weaving), Hollanders made up 8.6 percent and 2.0 percent, respectively, of the total number of employees; of the native-born, 1.6 percent and 3.1 percent, respectively, had a father born in the Nether- lands. They were only outnumbered here by the Germans, Italians, and Irish.

Several specific Dutch attributes stood them in good stead; these were the same virtues that accounted for the success of the farmers. Also in industry they distinguished themselves as hard workers, although we should not overrate them, for the Germans and the Czechs were just as hard-working. Their accuracy—just as in Holland—adapted them to preci- sion work. The Dutch especially were largely responsible for the finishing touches in the Paterson silk mills where also many women and girls were employed, while the men were engaged in machine work. The very exacting task of "degumming" the silk was usually assigned to our countrymen. It involved the boiling of the raw silk in a soap solution to dissolve the layer of sericin, which process imparts a beautiful softness and sheen to the silk. This was a very hot job requiring close supervision to prevent part of the sericin from sticking to the silk. Before the war the average pay was $12.50 per week but that figure has now risen to about $25 and there were some who received about $35. I was informed by more than one source that our workers in Silk City are tops and quite a number of them had risen to become foremen and they earned even more.[4]

We find a similar situation in the furniture factories of Grand Rapids. Even though many and varied machines are used, individual work is still required for the final finishing touches. So once again it is the Dutch employee—often a fine cabinetmaker by family tradition—who adds the personal touch. Grand Rapids has seventy furniture factories employing some 14,000 people and many of these are Hollanders. They are also found in other Grand Rapids factories producing ice boxes, carpet sweepers, clocks, automobiles, etc. Others are found in the steel factories, textile mills, etc. In 1920 more than 37,000 workers were engaged in these indus- tries; more than 7,000 of them were women and girls. In 1917 they earned an average wage of $15.90 weekly but this had increased in 1920 to $30.84— and most of these pay checks went to our former "little guys in wooden

Why the Dutch at Grand Rapids have little interest in socialism. A furniture factory at Grand Rapids where most of the employees are Dutch: 1 and 3: Parked cars of the factory workers during factory hours. 2 and 4: Workers coming out of the factory at the end of their shift. (Original photos by Dirk Nieland and others.)

shoes" [*klompenmannetjes*].[5] I say "former" because this very deeply ingrained Dutch habit of wearing wooden shoes was initially continued at Grand Rapids, despite the derision it evoked, but it finally gave way due to the increase in prosperity and Americanization. As a result, both of the wooden shoe manufacturers in Grand Rapids went out of business.

J. Steketee, Dutch consul in Grand Rapids and one of the city's prominent citizens, informed me that "the Dutch workmen in the Furniture City are very highly rated," a fact I kept rediscovering no matter with whom I would discuss the point. This is also true in Chicago and its suburbs of Roseland and Kensington, where thousands of workers of Dutch ancestry are employed in the Pullman shops, the Piano Manufacturing Company, etc. J. Vennema, our consul-general in Chicago, assured me that our people "enjoy the reputation of being industrious and law abiding."[6]

There are other reasons for this reputation; one of them in particular is the reliability of our countrymen, who are reputed to be less restless than Americans. When the Yankees become dissatisfied they may unexpectedly leave to seek another job elsewhere. Typically American in this regard are the actions of an emigrant from Zeeland who had worked during the winter at a Grand Rapids automobile plant for 45 cents an hour—in 1925 the work week was 50 hours.[7] But he could earn 65 cents an hour during the summer as a mason and so he left the automobile plant. The foreman at the plant cordially shook hands with the Zeelander, expressed his great pleasure with the work he had performed and said that he was welcome to come back at any time. They prefer Hollanders; "I had given a week's notice and they like that, you know. The typical American does not do so. When he takes a dislike to his work at a quarter of nine he is gone by nine o'clock without bothering to inform his boss."

How "Dutch" things often are in such a factory appears in another letter written by the same immigrant to his parents. His foreman was J. Labbezoo [Lobbezoo] from Krabbendijke [Netherlands]: "quite a fine fellow for me, you know." There were also quite a number of employees from Ierseke: "Jaap Glerum, Den Hoed, a son of Joris Koster, and two sons of Jaap Glerum from Ierseke, who liked to drink bitters. There is also a son of Boone from Ierseke and Bobbel [son] of Piet Muus. That's pretty cozy, isn't it? It is just as though I were sitting in Ierseke but the work and the food are better and that is all a laborer needs."[8]

Although all Hollanders were generally looked upon as desirable employees, employers preferred brothers of the Reformed and Christian Reformed churches because these workers believed strikes to be in conflict with their religious beliefs. They are even less inclined to strike than other Netherlanders, much as our letter writer and his comrades referred to above, who were more or less "worldly" because they attended Salvation Army meetings for their spiritual relaxation. Until recently, these churches considered membership in a labor union if not a sin, at least terribly wrong; and so only very few Hollanders were members of unions. Union members were not permitted to partake of the Lord's Supper, as A. Couwenhoven found out years ago when his church consistory delegated the minister and an elder to inform him, considering his union affiliation, that this Communion privilege was henceforth denied to him.

How great this preference of employers is was made evident to me in Paterson where a well-known manufacturer hired only employees who belonged to these denominations. It was said of that factory that "if you are not a member of the other community, you cannot work there." This factory is mockingly referred to as the "Holland Home." It is obvious that hypocrisy is encouraged by this state of affairs.

This was very much the case in Grand Rapids, as was told to me by old Mister [?] Plugge, who had served as a factory foreman there before returning to the Netherlands.[9] Many became members of a particular church merely out of self interest; then they would be assured of employment. "In order to move ahead here, religion is a first requisite," an early settler stated previously to a certain "L" when the latter left for America to try his luck.[10]

It should not be inferred that this condition was found only among the Netherlanders in North America. It was also evident elsewhere. "To what church do you belong?" was also in earlier days the oft-asked question among businessmen, as Max Weber once remarked: "Those (and in general *only* those) would rise in business or profession who belonged to the Methodist, Baptist, or some other church (or sect-like conventical)."*[11] In the Netherlands we see something similar but perhaps not to as great a degree and certainly not so openly. It is moreover a characteristic of human nature.

Something else should be noted. In many industrial towns such as Whitinsville, Massachusetts, the manufacturers build houses for their employees. It will be recalled that in this city the Dutch element is composed almost exclusively of religious Frisians and they are much in demand and appreciated as employees. When Dr. J. Jansen asked the Reverend [John Albert] Thurston for an explanation, the latter answered: "They pay their bills."[12] On the other hand, Poles and Italians live six months in a town, work there and make all kinds of purchases, and then vanish. America is so big, they cannot be located or even traced [by bill collectors]. Yet these immigrants also usually belong to a church—the Roman Catholic church. What should one think then of those who do not belong to any church? Not everyone is inclined to agree with W. A. Bonger, who maintains that religious faith—or lack of it—is of rather little importance when it comes down to the problem of crime.[13] Max Weber once talked with an American traveling salesman who said that he would not give fifty cents credit to an "unbeliever." "Why pay me, if he doesn't believe in anything?"[14]

But it would be unfair to the Dutch factory worker to place too much emphasis on this religious factor. Other traits have also contributed to his prosperity—his very great thrift, and closely related to that, his tightly-knit family life. If Harvard professor T. N. Carver can be believed, thrift is increasing so fast among American laborers that they "are growing rapidly in

*"Es kamen diejenigen (und im allgemeinen nur diejenigen) geschäftlich hoch, welche methodistischen oder baptistischen oder anderen Sakten (oder sektenartigen Konventikeln) angehörten."

financial power" and this trend is promoted not only by the government savings campaigns but also by the rapidly increasing number of workman's savings banks.[15] In the ten years from 1914 to 1924, savings deposits more than doubled, the number of depositors tripled and the average account increased from $89 in 1914 to $186 in 1924. And savings banks are only one of the many ways in which accumulated savings can be made to yield interest. Hollanders seem to surpass Americans and nearly every other nationality in America in thrift.

How far this has gone may be seen in the case of the Marinus Maas family in Grand Rapids who had won in 1922 a prize of $100 for being the most thrifty family in Michigan. In 1921, the family had earned $887 and $395 of this was deposited in a savings bank. The husband, wife, and seven children had lived on $492. They live in an eleven-room house and have an organ that can be played by each of the children (8–17 years in age). However, none of the children had ever attended a "movie." Mrs. Maas did all her own baking and served few sweets and never "desserts and salads."[16] I call attention to these details, in the manner of |Pierre Guillaume Frédéric| Le Play, because this situation—although not always to the same degree—is characteristic of the Dutch laboring element in American industrial towns.

The results are clearly evident everywhere. Although the Italians, Poles, etc., live in the inner city, "downtown," or in the "slums," usually in the large run-down tenement houses, the Hollanders can afford the luxury of living in the suburbs of the city, "uptown," occupying their own house, and often they have their own automobile—even though it may be "only" a Ford—which they drive daily to and from their place of work. In Holland, as well as in Grand Rapids, I was indeed struck by the numerous vehicles parked near the factory buildings. But that was the normal thing! Even more impressive were the nice, almost villa-like, single-family homes in the suburban areas of these towns. For example, the city of Paterson is surrounded by boroughs such as Prospect Park, West Paterson, Hawthorne, and Haledon, and many Hollanders live there as well as in Paterson's residential quarter.

This is also true of Grand Rapids. I was assured that 60 percent of the Hollanders there live in their own houses. They had helped to make Grand Rapids the "home city"; among the large cities it is "second in the United States in percentage of home ownership." It is primarily due to the Dutch furniture industry employees that the city makes such a special impression and that it is such a "homey" city: "That is why Grand Rapids, the city and the homes of its citizens are the neatest and the cleanest you will find anywhere in America."[17] H. Beets, who knows his people at Grand Rapids perhaps better than anyone else, finds "that this is easy to understand because it is mainly due to Dutch thriftiness."[18]

Already before the |First| World War the housing standards of even the poorest Dutch families were higher than those among most other nationali-

Dutch blue-collar districts in Grand Rapids, Michigan. Top: Baldwin Street, where the better-off workers live. Middle: Van Dine Court, where the least well-to-do workers live. Bottom: Worden Street, a residential section of workers who have made some progress. (Original photos by Dirk Nieland and others.)

ties of immigrants, with the exception of the Scandinavians. A study was
sponsored by the Immigration Commission, involving 15,127 foreign-born
families—including 144 Dutch—living in the poorest sections of New York,
Philadelphia, Chicago, Boston, Cleveland, Buffalo, and Milwaukee.[19] The results are noted below:

Nationality	Number of Respondents	Average number of person per:			Number of families with:	
		house	room	bedroom	boarders	per 100
Netherlanders	144	5.68	0.97	2.34	9	6.3
English	461	4.52	0.87	1.89	59	12.8
Germans	948	5.19	1.02	2.15	154	16.2
Swedes	485	4.90	0.92	2.02	58	12.0
Roumanians	77	12.47	2.57	3.72	60	77.9
Serbians	69	9.62	1.97	2.89	64	92.8
Total Number "Foreign Born"	15,127	5.81	1.38	2.53	4,978	32.9

It is obvious that one should be cautious in drawing inferences. But these
statistics do indicate the economic head start that the English had because
of their language, which assured them higher wages than the non-English-
speaking elements. In the meantime, since the World War the situation has
already changed.

Carver, referring to his 100% Americans, states—perhaps with some exaggeration—that "laborers are rapidly becoming capitalists as well as laborers" and "prosperity is being more and more widely diffused."[20] Without
doubt, the same thing is true among a large segment of the Dutch element.
But some of the poorer elements who still live in downtown Paterson (their
number is small) appear to be without any church affiliation! The same
condition exists in the nearby woolen-mill town of Passaic where, in general, the Hollanders are somewhat less prosperous.

Even though the factory employees have done well, their prosperity
should not be overrated. "Single-family houses" are frequently purchased
with mortgages. For example, the Grand Rapids Housing Corporation (with
a capital of $400,000) assists in the financing.[21] As we have seen, nominal
wages seem to be high. The average annual wage of an employee in the
Grand Rapids furniture industry was $1,549 in 1923. The Rev. S. J. Menning
wonders where all this money went and concludes "that the workers with
all those good years of high earnings have not become rich in our big city,
as was also true of workers in the West."[22] M. G. Levenbach, LL.B., explains
this, citing Professor [Paul] Douglas; he points out that when one takes into
account the many price increases of food, etc. real wages, even though they
rose again after 1917, are less than they were at the end of the nineteenth
century![23]

It is also a striking fact that, in spite of the esteem the Dutch workmen
have enjoyed since the 1840s, a relatively small number have advanced

Dutch neighborhoods in Grand Rapids, Michigan. Top and bottom: Wealthy Street in the suburb of the Groningers. The stores shown all belong to Netherlanders. A flower nursery of Freyling and Mendels, a Groninger butcher shop, etc. Middle: Van Dine Court, a "poor" residential section. (Original photos by Dirk Nieland and others.)

beyond the rank of foreman. Scarcely any have become manufacturers themselves. In Paterson I was told that Jan Van Buiten built two factories but leased them to others. In Grand Rapids, where our finest furniture craftsmen are employed, one and only one manufacturer with a Dutch name, Van den Berg, was mentioned to me from among the numerous furniture firms. There was also a man named Otte, who was the proprietor of a large laundry firm.

It should be well understood, though, that the Dutch workers enjoy "a high esteem" primarily in the eyes of the employers. Thanks to our countrymen, few "floaters" are found in the furniture industry. It is also due to the Netherlanders that the Grand Rapids furniture industry can boast of something that is exceptional in America. That is, that in most factories, the employees continue to work in one and the same factory for their entire lives. They are "well paid, satisfied with their work and their bosses. . . . You cannot find in all America more prosperous and more contented workingmen than those of the Grand Rapids woodworking trade."[24] As good taxpayers and as people who only rarely are in conflict with the law, as law-abiding citizens, our workers also enjoy a good reputation with the authorities.

But it must be said that for a long time they were but a small minority and of no great account. Since they were willing to work for very low wages, American workers considered them as scabs who depressed wages. Many of the more well-to-do viewed them as dumb work donkeys [arbeidsvee], easy targets for exploitation. With them it would never come to a strike—and if need be the preachers would see to that! The end result was that in Grand Rapids—and perhaps elsewhere too—no group was more thoroughly exploited than the Hollanders. And by whom? By previously established Dutch-Americans who had become rich, "who had become rich by the ruthless exploitation of their own simple countrymen," asserted R. P. J. Tutein Nolthenius.[25] And it was done in such a manner that Americans sympathized with the "little guys in wooden shoes" and had nothing but contempt for their exploiters.

A "modern" minister, F. W. N. Hugenholtz, did his best to bring about changes in this situation and tried to develop some self-esteem among the laborers. During his ministry wages were also extremely low in Grand Rapids. A re-migrant who was mentioned earlier, [?] Plugge, received $8 a week in 1891. His highest pay was $12, and that when he was a foreman. Wages remained at this level for years. When Tutein Nolthenius visited Grand Rapids in 1899, wages were 75 cents a day, which was "an amount no American would work for."[26] But not so our "guys in wooden shoes" who, as "non-union men," everywhere slipped into the jobs Americans had quit. This happened even more when the Americans demanded an eight-hour work day, while the Netherlanders refused to fight for it and go on strike; that is, the Calvinistic Dutch workers who were checked by their church acting as a policeman. It is obvious that the original American sympathy turned to rancor and contempt.

It may have been balm to the orthodox soul that during strikes in Michigan—particularly in Muskegon—"our compatriots during those long weeks distinguished themselves by their spirit of modesty, tolerance and peacefulness—so much that an American newspaper called it to the attention of the various nationalities living there."[27] But the modern spirit of Hugenholtz felt aggravated by these Dutch sneaks who caused our countrymen "to be even more despised by the general public and to be even more the target of kicks and insults by the American workmen while losing their self-respect in the process."[28] This courageous man loudly exhorted his orthodox fellow Dutchman: "In the Kingdom of God one does not earn his bread by the death of his brother."

This same Hugenholtz had conceded earlier that the Hollanders, although they were not least in the qualities of diligence, ability, and reliability, were "still frequently treated with the least of respect." As a step in improving their lot, he considered in 1890 the organization of an association of Dutch factory workers that would become a division of the Furniture Workers Protective Association. "It was a good sign."[29] However, it was mostly the more liberal element that joined the association; the Calvinists stayed away and continued to work for low wages.

That wages have increased during our lifetime is not the fault of our countrymen. Other branches of industry established themselves alongside the furniture manufacturing firms in Grand Rapids as a result of America's increasing industrialization. In vain did the furniture manufacturers try to keep them away. Now they were finally forced to pay higher wages; and because of price rises during the war, wages have considerably increased even further. In the war plants $10–$12 per day was not unusual. Later on, wages declined to the previously mentioned "good average" of around $25 |per week| although some men received less, as will be recalled in the case of Maas!

What remained was a certain enmity on the part of American workmen, and this increased, just as we noted among the agricultural element, because of the obviously growing prosperity of the Dutch workers. To this very day, few Dutch workers are affiliated with labor unions. In 1917, out of 152 Dutch-born workmen, only 3 were members of a trade union; out of another 36—all of whose fathers had been born in the Netherlands—not a single one belonged![30] One of the officials of the Chamber of Commerce assured me during my visit to Grand Rapids: "The Dutch seldom belong to them."

In my view, this state of affairs accounts for the contempt and hatred that manifested itself during the |First| World War against the Dutch in Grand Rapids, Paterson, and elsewhere. This cannot be simply attributed to a war psychosis and an alleged pro-German attitude. It is precisely at such times of national arousal that the most deeply felt feelings emerge. The Dutch in the industrial cities were hard put to it. Woe to those who did not purchase Liberty Bonds or would not hurry to become naturalized citizens; they were called "yellow dark |dogs?|"[31] This is the other side of the "high esteem" image.

It must be admitted that this animosity was not directed against Netherlanders as such, but rather at foreigners who worked for less and achieved greater prosperity. At the same time they were blamed for the rather limited success of the labor unions in America, which [M. G.] Levenbach not unjustly termed "guerilla organizations." When Carver views the limitation on immigration as the beginning of an even more glorious period for his already glorious fatherland and considers the memory of the years 1870–1920 as a nightmare because of the stream of cheap labor—how thankless can one be!—his views apply not only to immigrants in general but also to our immigrant factory workers![32]

These factory workers are thus partially responsible for the fact that one of America's most unsightly factory towns, Passaic, New Jersey, which contains people of many nationalities including many Netherlanders from the area especially around Uithuizen in Groningen, witnessed in 1926 a parade of more than 5,000 children demanding better living conditions. The banners read: "We are fed up with constant illness and hunger, you bosses and murderers." "In Passaic 50 percent more children die than in the rest of our country. Why? Because of the night work of our mothers, the lack of food, and the low wages."[33] That slogans such as these should be paraded in Carver's "glorious country" even during our own time, is due not only to the despised "cheap," southern European factory hands but also to Dutch orthodoxy that contributes to it.

Arthur Feiler in his interesting travel guide, *America—Europe*, states that there were people who marked the period around 1890 as the beginning of a tragedy—America's increasing industrialization.[34] It was the time following "the great turn in America's destiny ... the end of free land."*

Unconsciously, perhaps willy-nilly, our Dutch immigrants have contributed to this tragedy and even in a significant way in the industrial centers of New Jersey and Grand Rapids. For the sake of the truth, this significance of the Dutch element in the United States must not be overlooked either.

The factory workers are not the only Dutch element in the American industrial centers; they are not the only working segment of the population. In many of these cities such as Paterson, Rochester, Grand Rapids, and Chicago, there are Dutch building trade workers such as carpenters, painters, and masons who very often work for Dutch bosses. This is particularly true of those who had learned their trade in the Netherlands; they are much sought after because their craftsmanship is superior to that of the "Americans." The laying of the streets, sewer systems, etc. is often entrusted to Dutch contractors. And it is remarkable how often one finds the names of Dutch artisans embedded in the sidewalks and walking paths of Paterson and Grand Rapids. In the pavement of Grand Rapids I found such names as Van Oosten, Kooiman, etc.

Thus, it must not be mere chance that in the city of Rochester, as I have

*"die grosze Wende des amerikanischen Schicksals ... das Ende des Freilandes."

been told, many of our people are employed in the public works department. Nor is it by accident that among the Netherlanders in America, building contractors are flourishing. They seem to have a natural talent for it. Many contractors have made a name for themselves in Chicago, such as George Birkhoff, Sr., who emigrated from Ooltgensplaat, located on the island of Goeree Overflakkee in the most southern part of Zuid Holland. In 1869 he and his wife and seven children left for America and settled on the west side of Chicago where many Hollanders were living. He became a man of great standing in his trade of carpenter and contractor. He was even an honorary member of the Chicago Carpenters and Builders Union. He passed away in 1911. For several years one of his sons served as our consul-general in the Windy City.[35] The Feenstras, Tiemstras, Joukemas, etc. are well-known names in the Chicago building and contracting industry. "A Frisian," who knew these men, visited them in 1925 and admired the structures they had erected: "There were long rows of new houses erected by them. In addition Joukema had built several stylish middle-class homes as well as entire blocks of rental apartments (flats)."[36] These homes, built at his own risk, were often sold within a month of completion. Some of the contractors, just as some manufacturers, rose from the laboring class.

I should also call attention to another group—the house servants. Among the Dutch and Flemish who settled in America during the 1911–1912 fiscal year (ending June 30), there were 5,964 skilled and unskilled artisans and in addition 282 carpenters, 160 bakers, 161 gardeners, 102 painters, 1,595 farm laborers, 438 farmers, 777 laborers, 195 tradesmen, and no less than 733 house servants![37] Our countrymen seem to have also an inborn talent for this kind of a "job," which requires qualities such as neatness, trustworthiness, and it seems, a lack of excessive pride. Manufacturers prefer to choose their household personnel from among their Dutch employees. Other well-to-do families also give preference to Dutch servants not only as gardeners, etc., but also as housekeepers, instead of the all too expensive work princesses.

Who make themselves most often available for such lowly, though honorable, professions? None other than our proud and independent Frisians! Now admittedly, every human society is a complex organism and the various ideals one encounters there are quite different. But does not this type of employment conflict with the innate sense of freedom of the *Stânfries* [Frisians]? This was my question, for I felt somewhat disappointed. My friend, the Frisian poet and orator Sjouke De Zee, who had lived for a number of weeks with his brother in Rochester, answered that such was not at all the case. Many a young Frisian farmer's son, who did not do so well in Friesland and was too proud to work for others in the Old Country, would go into service of a gentleman in America. He cited several examples. Being a "gentleman's gentleman" provided an easy life and much leisure time. In Rochester very many Frisians hold such jobs, in addition to those who are gardeners or factory hands.[38]

Dutch shopping streets in Grand Rapids, Michigan. Top and bottom: Eastern Avenue, the heart of the Groningen neighborhood. Middle: Leonard Street, the center of the Dutch neighborhood. (Original photos by Dirk Nieland and others.)

Dutch store magnates in Grand Rapids, Michigan. Top: The large department store of Paul Steketee and Sons. Middle: the largest retail furniture store of Van den Berg Brothers. (Original photos by Dirk Nieland and others.) Bottom: the home of America's largest Dutch bookseller, W. Eerdmans (original photo by J. Van Hinte).

The same situation is found in other places. In Grand Rapids some Dutch are engaged as janitors in office buildings. In the factory of the previously cited Van der Plasse, a certain M. M. fulfilled this humble task: "He is well liked there, he works in the boss's office—just a bit of scrubbing and polishing, etc."[39] One should not think that all emigrants went to America with the same high goals; this was certainly not true during the last fifty years! This could not be expected and one should be on guard against idealizing. In so many cases reality is very down to earth, and presumed greatness is nothing but tinsel. In any case, let us not understimate the importance and "the high esteem" also of these workers, for they too help us gain a "view" of the complexity of the emigrant population.

In addition to the workers there are other Hollanders who are quite prominent on the American industrial scene. In addition to the "lower middle class," the label that by now fits the laboring class, there are a relatively large number of shopkeepers. Many of them have come a long way and made a name for themselves, provided that they belonged to one of the church groups. A storekeeper in Paterson named [?] Radersma, who has a large family, simply cannot prosper—the poor man is a Socialist and does not belong to any church. Both factors combine to keep away his religiously inclined fellow countrymen. Many others are luckier. A stroll on Paterson's Main Street gives striking evidence of Dutch entrepreneurship. The stores of Schoonmaker (Schoenmaker)—the "largest and most select clothing store in New Jersey"—and of Vroegindewey remind us of our fatherland and even of the ultra-orthodox Goeree Overflakkee, the land of the city of Middleharnis.

The same holds for Grand Rapids. The Dutch tradesmen here are even more numerous. The Steketees are among the foremost of the Dutch businessmen. They have prospered much more than the mass of their fellow immigrants. We call to mind the first of the Steketees, Jan, who was one of the many Steketees to emigrate in 1847 from the island of Zuid Beveland in Zeeland with Van de Luyster and Van der Meulen. Jan was in charge of one of the three ships filled with Zeelanders that left for America. The "old" Steketee became a timber dealer in "*de Kolonie*." Five of his six sons went into merchandising and some became very rich. The father of our consul in Grand Rapids, my informant, became a notary public and land dealer; Paul founded a large store, a skyscraper, on the busiest shopping street in Grand Rapids. Another Steketee [George G.] became the first Dutch mayor there (1881).[40]

Many Frisians in Grand Rapids have done well as storekeepers, in contrast to those in Paterson and Rochester where they largely function as factory hands and day laborers. Although he spent weeks among the Frisians in Rochester, Sjouke De Zee did not meet a single one who was well-to-do. It was different in Grand Rapids. I personally stayed with one of the most prominent Frisians there [William B.] Eerdmans, who owns the largest Dutch bookstore in the United States, originally known as the Eerdmans-Sevensma Company. It is located in Grand Rapids' banking district. For some time there was a branch in Paterson but it was discontinued as the result of the increased Americanization resulting from the [First] World War. Other well-known names are Schaafsma, Hoeksema, Spoelstra, etc. It is not surprising that a Frisian, G. P. Tilma, rose to become mayor (1916–1917).

Among those who have done very well in the Grand Rapids merchandising field are such men as Trompen, Buth, Van Zoeren, Ritsema, Van den Berg, Hekman, Van Rossum, Van Stensel, Buys, etc.[41] In the banking community are such men as Idema, Daane, and Verdier, although I do not know of a specific Dutch bank, as is found in Holland, despite the thriftiness found among our countrymen. The Kent State Bank—with resources of $16,000,000—which handles the financial interests of many Hollanders and which for a long time was known as "The Dutchmen's Bank," ("The Home for Savings") still does not have much Dutch capital invested in it.

Just as important as in Grand Rapids is the Dutch (especially Frisian and Groninger) mercantile element in the Chicago suburb of Roseland and the other outskirts of Chicago. Roseland, situated on a very busy highway, was from its beginning well suited for trade. The large sums of money that our countrymen acquired as a result of selling their lands that kept rising in value constituted an excellent starting capital for trading. Among the enterprises is the Boersma Company, one of the largest department stores located at the intersection of busy Michigan Avenue and 111th Street, in the center of old Roseland, in "the loop," "the Heart of the Calumet." It is currently managed by [J. C.] Bovenkerk from Weesp, Netherlands. The firm was founded in 1882 and is a most important and modern organization with many departments in its large building—clothing, on a "daylight clothing floor," shoes, men's furnishings, a boys' department, and the newest wrinkle, a "self-help basement," which uses such slogans as "A New Departure in our Line of Business. No Long Waits. No Salesmen. Help Yourself. Save Money. Prices and Sizes Marked Plainly So You Can Select What You Want."[42] It is obvious that this firm understands the art of American advertising no less than do Schoonmaker and Steketee.

In Chicago, just as in Paterson and Grand Rapids, there are many different Dutch shops, mainly in the Dutch neighborhoods. Only the largest firms can succeed in doing business in the "downtown" areas, like the firms of Schoonmaker, Steketee, and Boersma, as I have already related. But especially in Roseland, in "the loop," there are more Dutch firms (for example, J. H. Jansen's Furniture Co.), because this part of Chicago started out as a Dutch community, completely built up by our fellow Dutch. In Roseland they also have their "own" bank, the Wiersema State Bank founded in 1891. Today it has a capital of $350,000 and resources of $3,500,000. "Dutch" is also the Roseland Home Building Association with a capital of $1,076,148.67 in October of 1923. H. Teninga was secretary of this largest savings and loan association in Roseland. In addition there is the Netherlands Building and Loan Association which in April of 1926 had an entirely Dutch board—E. H. Wieringa, G. Ottenhoff, H. Bierma, and J. J. Zandstra. At that same time the Hollandsche Bouw -en Leenvereeniging [Holland Building and Loan Association] of Chicago was controlled by A. Danhoff, E. Nienhuis, H. Bierma, and E. Van Herik.[43] It is obvious that these organizations attest not only to our commercial initiative but primarily to our thriftiness. The Frisian acumen for business is shown not only by the strikingly large number of Frisian names but also by the fact that J. Broekema is one of the chief officers in the world-renowned Marshall Field Company, directing a personnel force of 12,000.

In these cities there are also Dutch groups that are much smaller in size but not in influence. I am referring to the intellectual and semi-intellectual element. Among the third- and fourth-generation descendants of the poor devils who emigrated in the middle of the nineteenth century, we now find quite a number of alumni from the academies, colleges, and universities. Dutch dentists, doctors, lawyers, notaries, etc., are becoming more numerous. Except for a few cases in the olden days, their greater reliability has brought them large practices. Their advertisements already fill several columns of the Dutch-American press; for example, in Chicago's Onze Toekomst [Our Future], this "Guide to Professions" is continually growing. Last, but not least, I merely mention the most influential group of all—the ministers. More than any other group, they characterize the Dutch community.

In the countryside near the large cities are numerous Dutch dairy farmers and truck gardeners who provide dairy products and fresh produce for the city dwellers. These truck gardeners and farmers constitute an interesting group. In an administrative sense, and to some extent in a sociographic sense also, they are a part of the urban population and are some of the most industrious residents. Frequently they got their start in America as factory hands. In the nineties, when wages were still very low, many of them—such as Plugge—worked the parcel of ground around their home during their free time. In the early morning before the factories started up, the garden stuffs were quickly sold—in this case on the Grand Rapids market where, incidentally, many Hollanders were initially defrauded.[44]

Many of these combination factory worker-gardeners, who are also found in our own country (where they are viewed to be in transition from farm hand to factory worker), gradually switched completely to agriculture and used their factory earnings to increase their land holdings or to rent a larger tract. Thus in America the development was reversed—from factory worker to agriculturist. An interesting "Auslese" [Selection] occurred here. For many the factory years were merely a stepping stone and adaptation period for entering into the American way of life. Those who had always been farmers preferred their old way of life and went back to it. They simply had an inborn love for the land. The constantly increasing value of land was also an attraction. Those who were innately industrialists usually continued in the factories.

Nowhere is this "distillation" process better illustrated than around

Grand Rapids, Rochester, and Chicago. Numerous Hollanders are engaged in truck gardening around the Furniture City and have met "with outstanding success," according to many witnesses.[45] The presence of a large number of dairy farmers in the city's proximity gave an enterprising Frisian, H. Soet of Grand Rapids, the stimulus to establish a creamery in the country where the butter was made in the Frisian fashion. Thus, the result was superior to the American product.

A similar situation may be found in and around Rochester. Although there are many Dutch factory employees living in the residential areas of the city itself, the numerous dairymen and truck gardeners are found to the east of the Flower City in the town of Brighton that is already partially incorporated into the city. In Brighton there are numerous nurseries employing many Zeelanders. Hollanders are so numerous in Brighton that it is referred to as "the Holland settlement" and even as "the Dutch town."[46]

We became acquainted with some truck gardeners in Evergreen Park, which is near Chicago. They are also to be found to the west and the south of the Windy City. "Very many Hollanders around Chicago" are engaged in farming, although their farms are not very large. They are most often gardeners who cultivate ten, twenty, or forty acres of land and sell their produce on the Chicago market. Ten years ago they drove a horse and wagon to get to market; now the automobile or truck is in common use, according to an account written to me by a Frisian woman living in the Chicago area.[47] Since many of them are religiously inclined, they eventually formed a belt of Dutch settlements around the metropolis with their churches as centers; many of them were immigrants who first built up some capital as laborers and then began truck gardening. Others, particularly several from Broek op Langedijk [Netherlands], have done this from the beginning. Douglas Park, Summit, Archer Avenue, Gano, Oak Lawn, and Mount Greenwood can all be termed, to a greater or lesser extent, truck gardening settlements. The many means of communication such as railroads, electric streetcars, etc. are making these towns more and more American. Mount Greenwood is a good example of this.

B. In New York

The New York colony is unusual among the city colonies. If anywhere, one can refer to this as a "very miscellaneous" Dutch settlement. Although I mentioned earlier that 4,750 Hollanders found a permanent home here, there are also many who have not become naturalized citizens but remain here only temporarily, though that time may stretch to many years. Among these one may include the office staffs of various Dutch enterprises—the Holland-America Line, the K. W. I. M. [Koninklijke West Indische Maatschappij], the banking house of Boissevain and Co. (Pierson and Co.), and various import-export firms. Then there are employees from the consul-general's office, the Dutch chamber of commerce, as well as a number of musicians, a few engineers, professors, etc. These also form a "colony" but in a different connotation than has previously been used. The Netherlands Club (3 Gramercy Park) is their (seldom used) meeting place, serving as a restaurant and place of relaxation.

But this colony in a strict sense gives an impression of restlessness that is different and more restless than what we encountered in other areas. Life is fast here and there is no feeling of oneness, chiefly because there is not that single powerful bond of unity: the church. A very small group of the New York Dutch belong to the Reformed or Christian Reformed Church, but it must be understood that I am not referring here to the descendants of those who settled New Amsterdam.

How difficult it is to get information about this loosely formed group is evident from the fact that, in spite of our ambassador's request on my behalf to the consulate-general and to the Dutch chamber of commerce, neither was able to provide me with any information.[48] It is true that there are a number of run-away seamen among the New York Dutch and that they could scarcely be expected to report to the consulate-general. But this can only be a very partial explanation for the odd fact that Dutch officials on Beaver Street are barely aware of Dutch life and characteristics in the world's largest city. This "official" disinterest was echoed by some of the largest businessmen whose motto of "make money" left them no time to concern themselves with their fellow Hollanders in New York. In Greater New York I found a feeling of Dutch ethnic solidarity only among the Hollanders who were not so greatly blessed by earthly goods. In this connection, my first thought is of F. E. H. Gebhardt, whose rather uncertain calling as a music teacher still enables him to find time in ultra-materialistic New York to promote the Dutch cause. The same may be said of the elderly J. Van Twisk, who was one of Hoboken's oldest settlers and the moving spirit behind so many St. Nicholas celebrations on American soil.[49] There was also J. Schenk, as well as others.

Hollanders are found scattered all over New York City; they live in all five boroughs. There are many in Brooklyn, in the most northern part of the borough on Long Island, and others in Long Island City in the borough of Queens on the same island. There are others in the Bronx, located between the Harlem and East rivers. Most of them live in New York itself, in Manhattan. There are others on Staten Island (officially known as the borough of Richmond), particularly in New Dorp, the birthplace of the old Van der Bilts.

New York City and Boroughs[50]	Dutch-born in 1920	Dutch-born plus those with one or both parents of Dutch birth (foreign white stock) 1920
New York City	*4,750*	*9,552*
Bronx Borough	471	1,146
Brooklyn Borough	1,672	3,519
Manhattan Borough	2,164	3,837
Queens Borough	329	851
Richmond Borough	114	199

Hoboken and Jersey City, west of the Hudson River, also are a part of Greater New York. The Dutch element is so strongly represented in Hoboken that a person would think he was somewhere in the Netherlands. The fact that here on this side of the Hudson are located the piers of the Holland-America Line explains certain things, such as the grade of "Hollanderdom" one finds here. In Brooklyn there are many who have white collar jobs—office workers and skilled craftsmen, especially diamond workers, but in Hoboken there are many Dutch dock workers as well as a small middle class group of upholsterers, bakers, shopkeepers, etc. In 1920, 767 Dutch-born lived in Hoboken; there were 274 in Jersey City and 272 in Newark. If one adds those born in America of Dutch parents the total rises to 977 (in the other two cities to 563 and 658, respectively). Among the Dutch-owned stores I found a cigar store, a hairdresser, and especially several restaurants. One of them, if the advertisement is to be believed, was "the oldest and coziest Dutch cafe-restaurant with 'Real Dutch Cooking,'" but if one desires "a good Dutch meal" one should patronize the establishment of H. W. and J. T. Names such as the Amstel Hotel, Café Hoek van Holland, and particularly the Holland Seamen's Home attest to a sailor's environment that is as international as it is Dutch and that gives rise to very mixed nationalistic feelings.[51]

An indication of the dispersal in Greater New York of those who still feel that they are Hollanders is shown by the members' list of one of New York's most important and oldest Dutch organizations—"E*endracht maakt Macht* " [Unity Builds Strength]—a group formed back in 1864.[52] In March 1921, the organization had 76 members, of which 21 lived in Hoboken, 18 in Brooklyn, 16 in New York, 5 in the Staten Island communities of New Dorp and Livingston, 4 in Jersey City and Jersey City Heights, 1 in Long Island City, etc. Neerlandia, an organization of generally less well-to-do individuals, had approximately 100 members, concentrated in "Hoboken and environs." A third group, *Vriendenkring* [Circle of Friends], had 80 members, largely active in the harbor; it is located in Hoboken also and operates health and life insurance programs. So it is obvious that Hoboken is of importance to the Dutch element. As I mentioned before, the New York Dutch element, generally speaking, is not religiously inclined, but in Hoboken, which because of its harbor quarters has long had a notorious reputation, there is a small Christian Reformed congregation that provides a good reception to the newcomers on their way westward.

In his travel account, *Around the World*, Konrad Bercovici stated that New York had its Syrian and Greek quarters, a Chinatown and a Little Italy, a Negro section, a Czech one, and many others, even "Gypsy-quarters."[53] Although he was well-informed about the New Amsterdamers, the nineteenth and twentieth century Dutch eluded him. He was under the impression that the 11,000 New Yorkers of late Dutch immigrant extraction, as well as the more than 100,000 Scandinavians, did not congregate in such a group "that I could have been able to visit them." This may be the case in

New York City but it does not reflect the real situation of Greater New York. A segment of Hoboken's State, Third, Fourth, and Bloomfield Streets, and even Washington Street, form a more or less homogeneous Dutch neighborhood where one can meet one's fellow countrymen in such places as Schenk's cigar store or in one of the restaurants. In this neighborhood many immigrants found their first American home. Also, those who do not want to put up with a dry [Prohibitionist] America can find here what they want!* We need not be too proud of this Dutch quarter. What Bercovici probably could not have realized strikes the Hollander as a typical Dutch characteristic—the shopkeepers command high prices. This is particularly true if the conversation turns to national affinity; often an extra charge is made to help speed up the financing of a trip in the near future to the beloved fatherland!

If Hoboken then is characterized by a Dutch port settlement, the so-called commercial colony has its seat in New York City. Many Dutch dealers have their offices here and some Dutch jewelers run their own shops. The jewelers are especially found in Nassau Street, while the dealers are located in the skyscrapers along Broadway. J. H. Duys is the big tobacco importer; G. Schilperoort is a grain exporter. I have already mentioned the Boissevains who are active in banking. On Beaver Street, a side street of Broadway, we find (at number 44) the offices of the consul-general and the Dutch chamber of commerce on the same floor. There is also a display room devoted to samples of Dutch and East Indian products. So one can speak of this as a sort of Dutch trade center, but this should not be overrated. It is obviously not possible to make a sharp distinction between this "trade colony" and the more or less permanent colony of Hoboken previously considered.

In addition to this group of temporary business people there is another element of more permanent residence. Some of these commercial firms have recruited a number of their personnel from the permanent Dutch-American element, for example, from Paterson. Some of the merchants, such as Duys, have become naturalized citizens and are almost completely Americanized. This is not to say that all bonds with the old country have been severed. On the contrary many American-Dutch patrician homes often reflect on the inside, if not on the outside, a Dutch spirit according to Jo Van Ammers-Küller, the Dutch woman novelist, who spent some time as a house guest of John and Birdy Duys.[54]

This Duys family resides in a mansion north of New York City on the wide Long Island Sound; others have rented or purchased a residence in "nearby" Mount Vernon and still others occupy deluxe apartments in the city itself, such as on Riverside Drive. Others have established homes in such New Jersey commuter towns as Summit or Montclair. In the latter town there were twenty-nine Dutch-born residents in 1920, and including native-born of Dutch parents there were sixty-six of our stock.

---

*Van Hinte visited America in 1921, during Prohibition.

While the total number of these merchants is small the great distances between their homes further militate against a feeling of solidarity, which is even more reduced by their wide diversity in personal interests. There is little of real Dutch life to be found among them. One or two are members of the "E*endracht maakt Macht*" Club, but they seldom if ever attend its functions, except such rare men as D. G. Verschuur. Only on the occasion of a reception for a visiting official does the commercial element show some unity and then mostly because of the well-provided dining table. These gentlemen would certainly not pass up occasions like these. That is why the only information that was available at the Dutch chamber of commerce of New York concerning this Dutch colony was a list of those present at a testimonial dinner in honor of [orchestra conductor Willem] Mengelberg.[55]

Much more interesting for more than one reason is the Dutch colony that acquired an international significance—the diamond workers colony. At first it appeared that the diamond industry would develop mainly in Boston. Earlier I related how depressed conditions in the Dutch diamond industry around 1860 drove several diamond workers to America. Some settled in Detroit and others in Boston and New York. A resident of Amsterdam, A. Keizer, sought to build himself a new life in Boston. At the end of 1870 he entered by chance a store of the Crossby, Moss and Foss firm. Suddenly he heard a familiar sound—it seemed that someone was busy polishing diamonds. Indeed, it turned out that on a wooden disk one of the partners—Moss—was trying to polish diamonds that one of Crossby's kin in Kimberly, South Africa, sent over in exchange for food items. It is obvious that the results, using this primitive equipment, were not impressive.

The firm commissioned A. Keizer to set up a Dutch-type workshop for them, using metal disks and other more modern devices. Keizer was to receive $60 a week for this task. He decided to find a few artisans for the new undertaking. He became acquainted with two former diamond workers, G. Van Herpen and [J.] De Boer, both of whom had also come from Amsterdam. They had opened a clothing store in Detroit and occasionally traveled to Boston for goods and it was there that Keizer met them. The men indicated that they were willing to resume their former calling for $40 per week and so they sent for their families in Detroit to come to Boston. But Keizer did not stop at that. He himself was a cutter; the two newly hired men were polishers. He still needed an adjuster and found one in Boston in the person of H. Wiener, an older man. Later on N. Van Volen and H. Cohenno were hired as polishers and M. Streep as an adjuster. All were Hollanders.

Thus an entirely Dutch diamond industry developed in Boston. The only difference between the way of carrying on here and the industry in the Netherlands was that the boiler that provided the power for the mills was located in the same room. The enormous Boston fire of 1872 also damaged part of the shop of Crossby, Moss and Foss but the business was resumed. Van Herpen had been able to save the diamonds that were in the workshop, as well as the tools.[56] The children of Van Herpen, De Boer, Van Volen, and

Keizer were apprenticed in the business and one of the partners, Moss, also learned the polishing art. Occasionally a New York jeweler, such as I. Herman, would have the Boston firm work up stones he had acquired in South Africa.[57]

However, the diamond industry in the Netherlands went through a tremendous revival—the so-called "Cape period"—and enormous sums were earned in Amsterdam. Consequently, most of the Dutch diamond workers—work or no work, they were paid $40 a week [in America]—returned to the Netherlands after the expiration of their two-year contract. Only a few, such as Cohenno, remained and this meant the decline of the Boston diamond industry. Cohenno later left for New York and when he later returned to Boston, he was the only polisher there. The difficulty in obtaining raw diamonds, because of monopoly control, contributed to the difficulty in reviving the industry in Boston.

The industry then gradually developed in New York, and P. De Bruyn and a certain [J. H.] Groen were the pioneers. They were the first Dutch polishers in New York in the early years beginning in 1872, and were particularly adept in jewelry repairs for jewelry stores; they also followed their Boston colleagues in getting the required tools from Amsterdam. They repolished many stones, using the best methods available. De Bruyn was a particularly skilled craftsman—the best of the polishers—and taught many apprentices. Thus it was that the diamond industry slowly grew in New York, in part because the New York importers maintained the most and best trading contacts with London. This relationship became particularly important once the South African diamond monopoly had chosen London as the center for the uncut diamond trade.[58] A temporary abolishing of import duties on raw diamonds was also a factor; later these duties were levied again.[59]

A rapid growth in the industry took place beginning in 1894. The Wilson-Gorman tariff act of that year lowered the general tariff duties on raw materials on average from 49.5 percent to 39.9 percent but the duties on diamonds were increased and a sharp distinction was made between the raw and the finished product. The latter, being a manufactured product, was subject to 25 percent import duties [25 percent is an error; it is perhaps 75 percent].

As a consequence, many importers wanted to have their own polishing shops and by offering high wages they tried to attract diamond workers from the Netherlands and Belgium. The Amsterdam industry felt itself threatened to such a degree by this American initiative that a few of the strong firms in the town on the Amstel decided to move part of their enterprise to the Hudson shores. Thus occurred a veritable exodus of both employers and employees.[60] In 1894 alone, about 150 Dutch diamond workers moved to New York.[61] Still, the American diamond industry in New York did not soar as high as was originally feared. The thought that New York would become the center of the industry has, as yet, not been realized.

The high tariff on polished diamonds created such a smuggling problem that in 1897 the American government again reduced the duty to 10 percent. In addition, raw diamonds that formerly had been bought on long term credit now had to be paid for in cash in New York as well as in Antwerp [another diamond center], while the labor costs had to be paid on the spot. Furthermore, other less valuable items had to be worked as well as the choice stones [since only "mixed" lots were offered for sale by the diamond monopoly].[62] Thus, for these several reasons, Dutch diamond exports to America increased again, especially due to an enormous demand that developed as a consequence of the existing high prosperity. A desire for primping, which is stronger among colonial folk than anywhere else— Roscher already commented on this trait—has no doubt further contributed to these developments, just as it brought prosperity to the silk industry. America became the prime market for Amsterdam's diamonds, especially after 1908, following its recovery from a severe crisis. North America bought 90 percent of Amsterdam's production. In 1925 the total value of raw and polished diamonds sent from Amsterdam to America totaled $30,000,000. Most went to New York where the product was distributed to other cities.[63]

On the other hand, the increasing demand also stimulated the diamond industry in New York. Not only increasing numbers of employees but also a few employers as well as importers and representatives from Belgian and Amsterdam diamond firms established themselves in New York. Especially after 1914 many of these representatives went to New York. It remains to be seen how permanent this will be. In any case, a certain international division of labor took place that actually made the New York industry more important than it seemed on the surface. In particular, the purest and highly expensive raw stones are processed in America. The smaller and cheaper items are handled in Amsterdam and Antwerp because manufacturing costs of these stones, especially labor, are too high in the United States. A few dollars more per carat does not make much difference for the expensive stones but it does for the cheaper items. In addition, many more employees are needed for working the mixed lots of diamonds than the small, select, higher priced assortments. Due to all these factors, the most expensive stones are polished in New York, the average ones in Amsterdam, and the cheapest and more common stones in Antwerp. But there were some notable exceptions [some of the most famous large diamonds were specifically cut and polished in Amsterdam].

There is some difference of opinion about the number of Dutch diamond workers in New York. Just as in the case of musicians, they are usually quite mobile. They go here and there, migrating back and forth several times depending upon the state of the industry, an industry where unemployment is not unusual. This is particularly true because it is a luxury business. According to Dr. F. Leviticus, in 1908, 90 percent of the New York diamond workers were from Noord Nederland (the Netherlands) and Zuid Nederland (Belgium). Mr. [?] Diamant told me that in 1919 there were about seven hundred employed in the New York diamond industry. In 1920 Henri Polak estimated that the total number of Hollanders in the industry was about two hundred.[64] In 1926 there were approximately three hundred Dutch workers, of which a small percentage were Flemings.[65] Most lived in Brooklyn, but part of them work in New York City on Nassau Street, where one finds many jewelry stores. On this street, which is a veritable stone canyon due to the gigantic buildings, one can often hear our language spoken. In 1912 the New York correspondent of the *Nieuwe Rotterdamsche Courant* asked: "Do you wish to hear Dutch spoken on Nassau Street? Then go on a Saturday afternoon to the corner of Nassau and John Streets, and stand near 'Ye Olde Dutch Shop House' and you will soon hear the weal and woe of diamond workers in your mother tongue."[66] The diamond workers are organized in the Diamond Workers Protective Union; in 1908 Andries Meyer was its president. On their part, the employers have formed the Diamond Manufacturers' Association.

Among the Dutch employers in the New York diamond industry was the late and well-known Eduard Van Dam who in addition to his large Amsterdam establishment, opened a shop and office in New York in 1894 and thus he was enabled to increase considerably the sale of his products in the New World.[67] Since that year he traveled regularly between Amsterdam, Antwerp (where he established another branch), and New York, just as some of his colleagues. The enterprising Van Dam passed away in 1920, but his sons continue the international operation, also in New York.

The Zilver brothers arrived in New York about the same time as Van Dam. The firm of S. M. Van Wezel was set up by the brothers of the recently deceased and well-known A. S. Van Wezel. D. S. Granaat arrived later but his enterprise in New York was of brief duration; the same was true of J. Hoedenmaker who was associated with Mr. [?] Roe; the firm of S. Konijn was also of short duration.[68] The Van Wezel firm is at the present time the most important diamond house in New York and employs more than seventy workers. This is a large number for a concern engaged in working rough diamonds, and large sums are at stake. A. S. Van Wezel, the founder of the company and a generous person, had first come to America early in the twentieth century.[69] For the sake of completeness, I should mention that, in addition to those in New York, there are Dutch diamond polishers in small firms located in Cincinnati, Chicago, and Los Angeles. They receive very high wages, as is generally the case in New York.[70]

Because of their constant contact with the Netherlands and with their Dutch colleagues, the diamond people did not assimilate readily. But their children did, especially those who have not followed their fathers' craft, which happened often despite the high wages. Their adherence to the Dutch language and customs allows us to reckon this group in New York to be a typical Dutch colony. This colony is all the more unusual because, so far as I know, the diamond workers are the only ones who have influenced the American language, even though it is only through the technical language of their industry. This cannot be said of the much more numerous silk workers in Paterson nor of the even greater number of furniture workers in Grand Rapids.

C. In San Francisco

I have mentioned that Hollanders may be found as residents in practically every city of any significance in the United States. But in the cities I will only speak of a "colony" if through a visible bond of some sort—in most cases a church congregation, but sometimes a more secular organization—the Hollanders as a group are aware of their heritage, that is, if they show a certain group spirit. It is not my intention to treat the smaller, numerically less important urban colonies because they reflect, to a lesser degree, the same image as the colonies that have already been considered.

However, there is one exception—San Francisco. There were 244 Hollanders residing in San Francisco in 1900, 500 in 1910, and 788 in 1920. Including native-born, those of Dutch parents, there were 1,452 of Dutch descent. In most cities our people form an industrial colony but, just as in New York, the San Francisco Dutch element is quite mixed. Although there are no diamond workers, there are several elements that are missing in New York or not represented there to the same degree. In San Francisco one finds more people from the oil business and industry, and in connection with this an East Indies element.

Most of the Dutch in San Francisco are *kleine luyden* [common folk] employed as shoemakers, bakers, clerks in stores and offices, etc. There are also waiters and especially harbor workers and near the city are some farmers. About half of all these people live in San Francisco proper; the others are found in the suburbs, on the opposite side of San Francisco Bay, in Oakland, Alameda, etc., where the residence areas are located. There is a small non-sectarian Dutch church that has occasional services when a traveling minister is in the "Frisco" area. The most orthodox element have had their own Christian Reformed congregation in Alameda since 1924 and it has now twenty-two families (one hundred souls).[71]

In addition to the workers colony one can also find a commercial colony here. Many are dealers who have become naturalized citizens. Others have retained their allegiance to the Netherlands. Among the recent Americans of Dutch ancestry is the well-known Van Coenen Torchiana family. H. A. Van Coenen Torchiana is our consul-general. There are also the De Fremerys who have been long-time residents. The Willekes MacDonald family arrived in the nineties, as did the Van Coenen Torchianas.

In addition to the firm of MacDonald and Co., other "Dutch" companies in San Francisco are the San Francisco Trading Corporation managed by L. H. Hymans; the G. E. De Vries Trading Co., the Ph. Van Ommeren Co., and Van Geuns and Co. These companies generally employ Americans. There are also representatives of the Holland-America Line in Frisco. In addition to these, there are other influential individuals such as W. Van Asperen and A. Binneweg, both of Oakland; L. J. Van Beusechem of the G. E. De Vries Trading Co.; C. D. De Jongh with the Seaboard Branch of the Anglo-California Trust Company; B. Van Dyke, manager of the States Restaurant; J. C. H. Ferguson; J. H. Van Hoboken, secretary of the Holland-American chamber of commerce and head of the Dutch trade museum; M. Jongeneel, director of the California State Land Department and E. Van Jones—all residents of Frisco.[72] In addition there is Jonkheer C. J. Strick van Linschoten who is connected with the U. S. Post Office in Oakland.

The "floating" nature of this colony can be seen when comparing the membership rolls of the Dutch-American chamber of commerce which symbolizes its "group-spirit," albeit a very economic one.[73] A more or less separate group in this organization are the oilmen (as far as they are members) who are connected with the *Koninklijke* [Royal Dutch] Shell Company of California. For years the head of it was J. C. Van Panthaleon Baron van Eck, LL.B., and others associated with it were B. A. Van der Linden as geologist, D. Pijsel as mechanical engineer, E. Hepner as engineer, [?] Van Senden as superintendent, etc., all of San Francisco. It is apparent that this is also a colony of transients. As far as I know, the activities of this company, either at its refineries in Martinez, or at any other "Royal Dutch" establishments in Oklahoma and elsewhere, have not led to Dutch settlements. They have mainly hired American employees.

The Holland Club in San Francisco was intended as a relaxation center for these Hollanders of "standing" but, just as with the club in New York, it is of little importance. Surely Dutchmen are not jingoists! Only on St. Nicholas Day and the 31st of August [Queen Wilhelmina's birthday] do they remember that they are of Dutch descent, and sometimes on the occasion of official visits such as the recent visit of the [Dutch] warship *Sumatra*. But they show their Dutchness through their Benevolent Society, which was organized in 1919 to aid "stranded" fellow countrymen. The long distances between the various Dutch homes in the "Metropolitan Area of San Francisco" also militate against a uniquely Dutch way of life.

During the [First] World War numerous Hollanders arrived in San Francisco, originating both from the mother country and especially the Netherlands East Indies. Many were only temporary residents, merely passing through. This trek reached a high point in 1918 when our consul-general in San Francisco issued 3,505 visas while many others acquired their visas in New York.[74] Many resided temporarily in San Francisco and even brought some of their capital with them for investment purposes, which were generally successful. In the purchases of land they often had less pleasant experiences, just as elsewhere.[75] It is not easy to ascertain the number of the former Dutch residents of the Dutch East Indies [oud-Indisch-gasten] in the San Francisco region. Many have left; only a few remained in California. There are some retired pensioners attracted by the mild climate; others began a new life. The Dutch A. Tigler Wybrandi family is a typical example of one of the more well-to-do, old-time familes of the Dutch East Indies. He was formerly director of the International Credit and Trading Company "Rotterdam," in Berkeley. C. M. Pleyte is another example; he was formerly director of the Bataafsche Petroleum Maatschappij [Batavian Petroleum Company], since located in Oakland.

If we cannot speak of a typical "Dutch East Indies" colony now, we may be able to do so in the future. The increasing trade relations between the Dutch East Indies and America's west coast are pointing in this direction. Elsewhere in California there are other indications of a closer tie between these Pacific areas. Some Indies planters have already settled in the "Golden Poppy State." Paul Addens at Galt, Sacramento County, is an example. Various retired civil officials and an occasional military official from the Indies have purchased generally small businesses in the area, such as Baron Van Heeckeren Molecaten, a former cavalry captain in the Indies army who has settled in the Sacramento Valley.[76] In the meantime, interest in the area is increasing. Our consul-general in San Francisco has received "very many" inquiries not only from the Netherlands but also from the Netherlands East Indies on the part of individuals who are considering residence in America, many by preference in one of the cities.

Thus the Indies are sending a contingent of Dutch emigrants principally (and understandably so) to America's west coast, just as Japan and China had done in former years. Bad times in the Indies—as has been the case recently—make America look like a good safety valve, provided America does not keep restrictions on immigration. The increasing significance of the Pacific Ocean as a unifying force between its bordering countries is thus also evidenced in the little contingent of Netherlanders from the Indies who settled on America's west coast.

15

Cultural Life in the Settlements

A. The Church Denominations

In his book, *Our Country*, which was widely read during the eighties in America and also among the Netherlanders, the writer J. Strong stressed the fact that the first permanent colonizers were those who left an imprint of themselves and their character upon the future.[1] Powerful influences might bring about important changes in later years, but it was the first influence that reached farthest and was usually decisive. This is even more generally acknowledged in our time, as expressed, among others, by W. McDougall. In his book, *The Group Mind*, he declared that every community is dominated by the dead as well as by the living, and the part played by the latter in determining the manner of its development is only of minor significance in comparison with the part played by the former: "Society consists of the dead as well as of the living, and the part of the living in determining its life is but insignificant as compared with the part of the dead."[2] Both Strong and McDougall point out in particular the great importance of leaders. In the work already quoted, McDougall pens a special chapter about them and is of the opinion that every nation "to them owes in chief part its existence," although he additionally acknowledges that the influence of personalities is surely greater in the first stages of a civilization than in the later ones.[3]

These views are corroborated in the various settlements of Netherlanders in the United States, perhaps more than anywhere else. I have pointed out previously how the spirit of the pioneers, in particular that of their leaders Van Raalte, Scholte, Van den Broek, and others, is still felt as very much present. The psychological atmosphere created by these men through their close cooperation especially also through their mutual conflicts, is still found to be very much alive there. It is almost totally inviolate in its deepest essence, no matter how great the outward changes.

Nowhere is this more plainly demonstrated than in the spiritual lives of the descendants of these pioneers. Their lives have remained spiritual above all. The church has remained central just as seventy-five years before. It rules their lives and keeps the Netherlanders together, and provides more than common descent for a "group mind," although both descent and religion are closely related. What has also been maintained are the contrasts among the various groups, as I have developed earlier. This spirit of the leaders and their followers is strongly felt in the communities they created: in the great rural settlements. By dint of the "after-effects" of their influence, one finds here the most "broadmindedness" in church matters. On the other hand, in the urban colonies, due to the initial lack of great leaders, orthodoxy still reigns supreme; there one meets with the strongest kind of fanaticism and zealotry, resulting in continuous religious quarrels, secessions, excommunications, etc.

Broadmindedness in religious matters is still found in Van Raalte's colony of Holland and its surrounding area, and to a certain degree also in Scholte's project of Pella, and in the one of Orange City of Hospers and Bolks. These are all bulwarks of the "western part" of the Reformed Church in America. The centers of the younger, "seceded" Christian Reformed Church in America, that is, the towns of Grand Rapids, Paterson, Chicago, Muskegon, etc. are foci of orthodoxy, indeed even of hyper-Calvinism. Especially Grand Rapids, the Jerusalem of the Christian Reformed Church as may be recalled, has earned itself a certain notoriety even among Americans due to the quarrels that resulted from this hyper-Calvinism. They shrug their shoulders somewhat contemptuously concerning these endless disputes in the Dutch-American churches and say more or less mockingly, "That is the Dutch of it."[4]

It proves a point: this kind of quarreling is considered un-American. This becomes better understandable when one sees that contemporary American churches often set aside their doctrines, and draw less of a principled line, and take on more and more a social character. Completely in accordance with the utilitarian nature of modern Americans, the churches degenerate into "useful," "socializing" institutions where music and dance increase their attractiveness and where the sermon is replaced by a show, a "play," though on a fitting topic. This even happens in such an outspoken Holland-American community as Kalamazoo, Michigan![5] In circles like those, agitation about doctrine, etc. is a thing that is simply not done.

So we notice these kinds of old-fashioned disputes most often in the Christian Reformed Church, which had remained the most Dutch or rather the least Americanized; but we hear about them seldom if ever in the most Americanized Reformed Church. Thus one notices here a stability, which in part is the result of a certain selection process. In general, people remain members of the church in which they grew up, partly due to a certain inertia and because of convenience. Therefore, church membership is in many instances the result of chance and tradition. But those of an independent nature, those who in the long run no longer feel at home in their own church, join another church, one which is more in keeping with their convictions. Thus numbers of Holland Americans who no longer felt comfortable in the Christian Reformed Church for being too doctrinal, have joined the Reformed Church, which was less rigid at least in practice, or the Presbyterians, or other American denominations. Already for a number of years, Dr. Beets estimated that every year about 5 to 10 percent of the young people left the Christian Reformed Church and that number has now sharply increased.[6]

On the other hand, there are also those, although obviously fewer in number, who think that the American denominations are not steadfast enough in upholding their principles and who therefore join the Christian Reformed Church or even more strongly fundamentalist small church groups. It is due to this differentiating selection process that each denomination retains its own character for a longer period than would have been the case otherwise. This outspoken conservative character is further enhanced by the "group spirit" that, thanks to tradition, is often continually reinforced. Gifted men promote confidence in their own strength, in particular in the Christian Reformed Church. This denomination, which for such a long time had been practically totally isolated, is clearly aware, more than ever, now that it is coming more in contact with other groups, of its own "group consciousness": a |great| solidarity through |mutual| agreement in religious convictions.[7] In the Reformed Church, one notices the same trend, especially with respect to missions. The herd instinct, which is more or less present in each and every one, promotes a grouping together of people who think alike and keeps us from joining others who are not like-minded, in particular if, in addition, the latter speak another language.

These factors, plus the upholding of their old character, explain why both Dutch church groups in America continued to grow primarily within their own circles despite increasing Americanization. The growth of both groups was first and foremost of an internal character, which was due not in the least to the generally very large colonial families. In the second place both denominations went on growing as a result of the continued immigration of their fellow countrymen. Those who were strongly orthodox affiliated with the Christian Reformed Church while those who were less orthodox joined the Reformed Church. In America, the "Gereformeerden" Netherlanders became Christian Reformed and the "Hervormden" Netherlanders and many that were "indifferent" joined the Reformed Church.

There is still a third source for growth that is very important, especially for the Reformed Church. The increasing Americanization of this denomination has weakened its original Dutch character to such a degree especially in the past twenty-five years, that many who are not of Dutch descent have joined it. The Reformed Church, although one of the oldest in the United States, was still looked upon as a foreign church until the nineties. That was the experience of a gifted Dutch American who observed that the "English congregations" of this church in the West languished to the extent that they

Cultural life in Holland, Michigan. Top: A Reformed church. Bottom: Hope College and its campus.

consisted not of Americanized fellow Dutch countrymen but of "full-blooded Americans." As was said at that time, "The conservative Dutch and the more fickle American character did not seem to work well together even in God's church."[8] Now it seems that at least in the East, particularly in large cities such as New York, this has changed. The Reformed Church in this city even has a few Italian congregations!

We should not forget that the Reformed Church is really divided into two parts. The "Eastern" part was built up in the seventeenth century by the Dutch and their descendants and is therefore the most "American," and the "Western" section, embraced mainly the nineteenth-century "Young Netherlanders" in the Mississippi Valley region, although many of these "Young Netherlanders" were also found in Paterson, Rochester, and other places in the "East." One of their leaders, Reverend S. Van der Werf, stated that many of these younger western Dutch Americans also "realize our tremendous responsibility toward the souls in our communities, whether they are Hollanders or Americans or any other nationality."[9]

How very "Dutch" the Reformed Church really still is, is shown by this same leader when he stated that there is no place for this church in the thoroughly American South, such as Oklahoma, New Mexico, Alabama, etc. "The South is not our proper field. Experience in Oklahoma has taught us this lesson. The South does not know us and we do not know the South intimately enough."[10]

Since 1890, as we remember, the Christian Reformed Church has also had an Old Dutch "Eastern" branch. Then a number of the very orthodox Old Dutch congregations joined them and were organized into Classis Hackensack. Just as in the Reformed Church, this union of the old East and the young West has had its consequences and has not remained without influence on the development of church life and the Americanization of our orthodox fellow countrymen. It brought about the use of hymns in the Christian Reformed Church, which had until now met with such strong opposition and which contributed in 1857 to the secession. It was also this Classis Hackensack that continually urged the use of English, also at the Synods. It gave to the West its first Christian Reformed English-speaking minister. Naturally he was received with strong objections from the Dutch-speaking and believing brothers!

In spite of the accelerated Americanization, a result of this union, only a very few non-Dutch have joined the Christian Reformed Church so far, although city missions have been bringing about some change. Just as was the case for her older sister, those non-Dutch who joined the Christian Reformed Church were mostly Ost Frisians and Bentheimers, which means that in the end they were still members of the Greater Dutch racial stock. Here the same thing happened as in the "Gereformeerde" churches in the Fatherland; in both American churches these "German" believers, who originally spoke Dutch, belonged to separate Classes. In the Reformed Church they were "Pleasant Prairie" and "Germania," and in the Christian

Reformed Church, "Ostfriesland," with 22, 17, and 18 congregations respectively in 1925. These all existed in the West, mainly in Illinois, Iowa, Minnesota, and the Dakotas.

The total strength of both denominations in 1925 is shown below:

	Congregations	Pastors	Families	Professing Members	Total Souls*[11]
The Reformed Church in America:	730	808	81,537	145,373	—
The Christian Reformed Church in America:	251	250	21,430	47,873	103,668[12]

It should be pointed out that the western part of the Reformed Church, which is not only divided into a number of Classes, but which is also organized into two "Particular Synods," the one of Chicago and the one of Iowa, is about even in strength when compared with the mainly "western" Christian Reformed Church. In 1925 both of these Synods totaled 256 churches which, as in the Christian Reformed Church, had developed from the so-called "immigrant churches" of 1847 and the years following. The importance of the Young-Dutch branch of the Reformed Church for the growth of this Old-Dutch denomination is generally acknowledged, not in the least by the "eastern section." [E. T.] Corwin mentions these two elements that constitute his church and he characterizes their influence as follows: "In general it may be said that the older element contributed the spirit of democracy and breadth of vision to the united Church, and the newer element has contributed respect for authority and intensity of devotion. Both have vied with each other in consecration to the Master whom all Christians acknowledge as their Lord."[13] No less than 52 percent of the missionaries of the Reformed Church came from the West, although it included only one-third of the congregations.[14] With the exception of the theological seminary at New Brunswick, New Jersey, Reformed higher and secondary education is found exclusively in the "western section" of the Reformed Church. Already numerous gifted Young Netherlanders from the West serve as preachers or as professors in the East. Therefore the Reformed Church would not like to lose its youthful branch. An interested outsider observed: "The west is proving to be too good a feeder to the east."[15]

How great the influence of this Young-Dutch branch already is, is demonstrated by the fact that thus far the West has refused to let the Reformed Church in America amalgamate with its somewhat more liberal sister church, "The Reformed Church in the United States," built up by German Americans. It is a "union" that is strongly advocated in the East. Could this refusal be an indication that, aside from a greater or lesser piety, the "Dutch" character, at least that of the western part of the Reformed Church, is rearing its head? Whatever the true cause may be, this union, which has

*The Christian Reformed Church distinguishes communicant (professing) members from non-communicant members. Both are designated as "souls."

been strongly favored for thirty-five years, has not yet materialized. There are well-informed people who firmly believe that this union would have resulted in a split between the eastern and western Reformed Church.[16] Therefore, to strengthen the bond and to recognize the strength of the West, the highest church gatherings of the Reformed Church, the General Synods, were held several times in the Young-Dutch colonies at Grand Rapids, at Holland in Michigan, at Englewood, which was the "Dutch" part of Chicago, Illinois, and even at Pella, Iowa.

Since it was the West that blocked the amalgamation with the German Reformed, we should be surprised that thus far it has not seen its way clear to bring about a union with the Christian Reformed Church. But we should immediately add to this observation that the cause of this inability is to be found mostly in the latter denomination. Even for unchurched but nevertheless racially conscious Netherlanders, it reflects a very interesting phenomenon: the fact that the two Dutch and orthodox-Calvinist churches of the Reformed and Christian Reformed denominations in the United States live *alongside* each other but not *with* each other. The reasons that originally led to the split of the Young-Dutch orthodox immigrants into two denominations have been discussed earlier. It was not only caused by religious differences but also included a cultural and economic aspect. The often fancied contrasts between the two denominations have practically vanished since the nineties. This is especially so because the True [*Ware*] brothers now also have an "eastern" branch, and because the English language is used more and more in their church services and the old Dutch habits are gradually discarded. For example, in many churches they did away with a *voorzanger* and established their churches in American style, etc. Corwin declared that next to their Dutch roots, the main point, indeed what counts most heavily, is their similarity of creed: both churches are "identical in doctrine and polity."[17]

How very trivial the earlier contrasts often were was already experienced about thirty-five years ago by A. C. Rink, a former principal of a Christian school in Rotterdam. He had emigrated to America and settled in Grand Rapids. Although he had been Christian Reformed in the Netherlands, in the Furniture City for three months he visited in turn the Reformed and then the Christian Reformed churches but could not detect any difference: "The only thing is that one minister preaches better than another; but this is true in both churches."[18]

Where the worship service may have shown differences in other respects, those have since practically disappeared, as I have previously noted. The Reformed minister S. De Bruine from Oskaloosa, Iowa, wrote to me about this: "I have been here now for more than thirty years and in this time the Christian Reformed Church has made remarkable progress in many respects, but today they also do many things that they used to object to in us."[19] The Christian Reformed Church has also become "worldly," at least in its worship service. This is due to the influence of its social and geographic environment which, according to Franz Boas, "*stets nur eine umgestaltende, nie eine unmittelbar schaffende Wirkung hat*" [always has merely a transforming effect, never a directly creative effect].[20] Initially in this denomination, hymns were considered to be of the devil, yet in 1920 the singing of hymns was fostered; indeed, even the performing of an orchestra, a choir, and soloists were defended! Everything was proper, it was emphasized, provided it was not used for artistic purposes but served only to create a "devotional spirit," or at least would insure such a spirit.[21] For that purpose, the believers in Grand Rapids by 1919 had already begun to organize a musical organization, a "city mission band," "bringing the Gospel to the wandering and down-trodden" in the Valley City.[22] Also elsewhere, especially at the mission fests of the most orthodox brothers, a band is now used to accompany the singing of psalms. That happened, for example, at the fest at Cutlerville in 1919, when the small organ that had been placed on the platform really did not fill the bill![23] Even such a worldly instrument as a piano is now found in many a Christian Reformed Church. In 1923, the strict orthodox brothers at Sheldon, Iowa, began to use one.[24]

There is now hardly any difference between the services in the Christian Reformed Church and the Reformed Church in the West, and at least in this respect, the contrasts between the West and the East are also waning. As we remember, in the East Dr. Cohen Stuart already observed the use of a "band" during worship services in the seventies. A typical American noisiness, somewhat reminiscent of the Salvation Army, already characterizes church life in the most distant and thus still very orthodox Dutch settlements. To give just one example, in 1923 at Pella, Nebraska, the new Reformed minister, [T.] Hibma, was greeted with trumpet blasts by his enthusiastic parishioners after which the meeting was opened with a prayer.[25]

It must also be this real absence of differences in both creed and worship services that gives rise to the somewhat odd phenomenon, the ease by which ministers switch from the Reformed Church to the Christian Reformed Church and even more frequently the other way around. There are even some who have repeatedly served the one and then the other church. We have already come across such examples, but this "running back and forth" now "really begins to look like a rule," as one of the orthodox brothers commented, who then concluded that there is a lack of "church loyalty."[26] Others ridicule this phenomenon and speak of a church indifferentism, or more sarcastically of a "leap frog game."[27] This is the situation in Michigan, but it happens much more often in Iowa and other places west of the Mississippi.[28] For that matter, not only preachers, but—just as significant—also congregation members, are given to this evil. It happens especially during a vacancy at one of the very intensely competitive Reformed and Christian Reformed Churches. A case in point is Ogilvie, Minnesota, where in one year's time twenty families transferred from the Christian Reformed Church to Reformed Church.[29] That is why old Mister [H. P.] Oggel earnestly warned in *De Volksvriend* of January 25, 1923, "Henceforth we must no longer build small churches in the shadow of other small churches." It is good advice that is quite to the point, as we have had an opportunity to point out more than once, as for instance in the case of Conrad in Montana. For that matter Dr. Beets, speaking for the most orthodox sector, urged sister churches, especially in small settlements, to strive for greater unity.[30] Why not unite then, since both sister churches are Dutch and so orthodox?

Cooperation is already evident in various fields. Mutual exchanges of preaching engagements often take place. Reverend S. De Bruine, who is Reformed, has at times filled the pulpit in the Christian Reformed Church. In other places this happened more often. Especially on national holidays both sister denominations work together and sometimes also on mission fests. Also, Christian schools in a number of towns are supported by believers from both churches. For example, in Lafayette, Indiana, it is reported that "members of both Christian congregations work together in brotherly fashion."[31] By mutual cooperation in a number of towns a "Holland Home" for the aged was established. We can cite the example of Muskegon, Michigan, where twelve churches of differing orthodox color support such a home.[32] Both denominations jointly finance a mental institution in Michigan and a home for tuberculosis sufferers in Colorado. Jointly both churches publish a mission magazine, De Heidenwereld [The Heathen World] and eagerly advocate a closer cooperation on the production of religious literature.

Already for years mutual appreciation has replaced the bitter wrangles and internecine friction of former days, even though disagreements still occur here and there. The Christian Reformed members who developed a grudge against Van Raalte when he united with "the East", and because of this could no longer see any good in him, are now beginning more and more to understand him and acknowledge the fact that he was a great leader. "Above all he was a man of God who served his generation well."[33] In one respect the Christian Reformed believers were even better followers of Van Raalte than his own church people: in the field of Christian education, some of the strongest support comes from the Christian Reformed people. It is in accordance with Van Raalte's wishes that they further develop this type of education. Not only with respect to Van Raalte, but also toward the Reformed Church as a whole, the True brothers are showing a change of attitude. They are fully aware of the great obligations they have toward this denomination and they have openly acknowledged this state of affairs by way of Dr. Beets, their spokesman.[34] They have even done better and expressed their warm thanks in a speech, entitled, "What we as Christian Reformed Denomination owe you and What I hope for both our Churches." This "broad-minded" leader of the True brothers said to his own fellow believers: "We owe the Reformed Church in America more than most of us realize."[35]

The Reformed Church members from their side are likewise showing more interest and respect for their younger sister denomination, which for a long time they used to view merely as a dissenters' church built up by quarrelmongers, pathologically schismatic firebrands, and uneducated provincials. Dr. H. E. Dosker first began to show more respect.[36] After him, another leader, Dr. J. E. Kuizenga, did the same, while at present more generally, by way of Reverend G. De Jonge, it is admitted that the Christian Reformed Church "is now strong and flourishing, up-to-date, and progressive."[37]

It is obvious that under such circumstances the recurring thought of unification presented itself. Already in 1884, the Reformed Church made an attempt.[38] Still today, this denomination openly voices as its conviction: "For the sake of the advancement of Christ's Kingdom the disagreements of an earlier generation should be forgotten and the two denominations should become one."[39] Similarly, Christian Reformed men, such as Reverend [E.] Bos and his followers suggested a possible reunion in 1885. Their preference was to unite with the "western section" of the Reformed Church. This brother wrote at that time: "If ever people belong together, these two [groups] do. May God give to us, Dutch descendants here present, the understanding that in union there is strength."[40] Up to this present time there are many who fervidly wish for such a unification. Not long ago Dr. H. Beets gave a "hint" in this direction, based on geographical considerations.[41] The Young-Dutch Reformed and Christian Reformed faithful live generally in the same regions, together designated as "the West." How Dutch many of our fellow countrymen still feel, in spite of their Americanization, is clearly reflected in these efforts to form a union. They are hesitant to affiliate with the Old Dutch, for instinctively they feel them to be too American and therefore too liberal, and also too non-Dutch. But the Christian Reformed faithful keep hankering for a confluence with the "western" Reformed Church, the most typical Dutch part, and they can no longer leave this issue at rest: "The hearts of the western Dutch brothers and fellow believers were beating too strongly for that," frankly declared one of them who was an enthusiastic American, but in heart and soul a Netherlander.[42]

However, the western Reformed people, who are really in a more advanced stage of Americanization, will not hear about "a break with the East"; they feel too much obligated toward the Old Netherlanders. For that matter, they have never regretted this Union. On the contrary, they view it still as "a blessing for the West."[43] "We find many reasons to express our appreciation to the Church of which we are a part for its help and encouragement.... After 75 years, we are grateful to God for his providential guidance and for the blessings we have enjoyed in the fellowship of the Church."[44] After such an outpouring it should be plain to anyone that a "break" is not even considered. This is further supported by the explicit declaration of a "western" Reformed church member that the churches that belong to the Particular Synods of Chicago and Iowa, that is, the "Western Churches," are an integral part of the Reformed Church.[45] This is a declaration that brings out something of rare importance, since it comes from a side that cooperates more than any other with Christian Reformed people, and in fact counts some of their best friends among them.

I have described this situation in detail so that the most indifferent observer will note the particular significance of this "occurrence." We have here two groups of people from the same ethnic background and nationality, who came to America at the same time and who have gone through nearly the same experiences. They adhered to the same religion in nearly the same orthodox manner and initially differed only in worship services, a difference that has now practically disappeared. Facing impinging forces all around them that were somewhat strange to their mentality and that in particular threatened their faith and creed, they longed for unification, sensing in the deepest recesses of their being a certain herd instinct that drove them to it. Again and again the best members of both groups have tried to bring this union about, but thus far in vain.

Taking note of this state of affairs, we are inevitably led back to reconsider the words of Strong and McDougall at the beginning of this chapter: it is the dead who still manifest themselves, and even the noblest among the living stand powerless in face of that power. The traditions are still too strong, are still too vital. In fact, they are still so pervasive that many well-intentioned group members resign themselves to the situation, although they are deeply saddened by the existing division. They simply cannot cope with the dead. Therefore they say that both denominations should live together in peace and harmony, alongside each other like an older and younger sister. They even go so far as to assert, perhaps unconsciously and against better knowledge, that it would be foolishness to put an end to the duality that has developed historically.[46] Younger leaders will have to break these traditions as far as they have become worthless. For them we must wait; that is also the feeling of Dr. H. Beets, who is broadminded enough but still unable to overcome this obstacle.[47] Laymen and spiritual leaders of both churches must come together again and again to pursue this goal: [with] "meetings steeped in prayer, with the sincere purpose of trying to see eye to eye . . . and if ultimately, why not *now*?"

Looking into the future, Beets sees both churches joined together. But this Christian Reformed leader also declared that too hasty a unification is undesirable and that it is better to live side by side as good friends, as has been the case so far, "a great deal like the twin streams, Euphrates and Tigris."[48] But do not these tributary rivers finally flow together and become a single mighty stream?

However, one should not carry the conviction that, should this union ever materialize, it would end all the religious discord among our orthodox fellow believers in the United States. Neither should one believe that if Van Raalte and his followers had not sought a union with the Old Dutch in the East, one single Young-Dutch denomination, comprising all the orthodox immigrants, would have been formed. The facts prove otherwise. For these show that among those who separated from the Reformed Church in 1857 such a spirit of "rule or ruin" existed that from this True Church numerous small groups seceded in turn over the course of the years. Each of these small dissenter groups again formed their own mini-denominations or in some instances they went their own way fully independently. As I noted in the introduction of this chapter, this schism syndrome, regardless of its cause, is still going strong in the Christian Reformed Church of today. And what is particularly striking for these cases is that the more orthodox a schismatic group is, the more Dutch it is, and the more adherent it is to the language and customs of the Old Country. On the other hand, the excommunication of a person, as also happens among the True brothers, may be due to views that are considered too liberal, which have resulted, in turn, from a too rapid Americanization of that person in comparison to the developmental growth of the mass of church members.

These splits stem from too great a gap between "conservatives" and "progressives" in the True denomination. As we have observed earlier, in all these cases there appears to be a close connection between religious practice and cultural development as they relate to the level of Americanization. This trait is very evident in relation to the geographical spread of the separatist sects. Obviously, the most Americanized ones were the real pioneers, the men and women of 1847 and their descendants, who settled in the true colonies. Less Americanized were those who settled around these colonies in the neighboring towns and in large factory centers, as I have tried to explain earlier. Less Americanized were obviously also those who came later and who, in spite of the hardships frequently encountered in making a living, had not experienced the "Wild West Years," and thus were not permeated with the "pioneer spirit."

Around 1880, the "Netherland[s] Reformed Churches" (Nederduitsch Gereformeerde Kerken) left the True brothers. There are twelve such churches, in particular in the factory towns of Paterson, Passaic, Grand Rapids, Chicago, etc.[49] They are organized into a Western and an Eastern Classis. Since then, a secession from this church took place, the so-called "Vrije Gereformeerde Gemeenten" [Free Reformed Churches] at Passaic and Kalamazoo. Closely connected with both groups are a few "Oud-Gereformeerde Gemeenten" [Old Reformed Churches] at Kalamazoo, Sheboygan, Sioux Center, and Rock Valley.[50] Sometimes these are identified as one group.

In addition to numerous subsequent small breaks from the Christian Reformed Church, which are documented in the works of Beets, one secession of importance was the excommunication of Reverend H. Bultema at Muskegon in 1919. Bultema believed in premillenianism and expected the "Thousand-Year Reign." He formed the "Berean Reformed Church," which drew away a number of members from the Christian Reformed Church, in particular in the smaller and larger industrial towns. Besides the one in Muskegon, there are now six churches: in Grand Rapids, Grand Haven,

Holland, Paterson, Chicago, and Moline. This young denomination in turn had break-aways at Chicago and Paterson, and the latter group separated practically completely from the Bereans.

A difference of opinion concerning "Common Grace" led to a third large break from the Christian Reformed Church in 1924. The hyper-Calvinistic preachers H. Danhof and H. Hoeksema, respectively from Kalamazoo and Grand Rapids, refused to believe in "Common Grace" and they broke away, forming still another orthodox denomination calling themselves the "Protesting [Protestant] Reformed Churches." These churches are located in Grand Rapids, Kalamazoo, Hull, Sioux Center, Doon, etc. In the meantime, this youthful denomination has experienced a further frittering away, when Danhof left Hoeksema; the results are that Christian Reformed Church life in Sioux County, Iowa, finds itself entangled in a hopeless confusion.[51]

Finally, there exist a few totally independent churches that are ultra-orthodox. One such church is found in Paterson, called the "Vrije Kerk" Ebenhaëzer [Ebenezer Free Church], ordinarily called the "Flakkeesche" Church. It is so named because many of its members hail from Goeree-Overflakkee, the island south of Zuid Holland and belonging to that province. Such a church also exists in Grand Rapids, and primarily Zeelanders belong to it. In Sheboygan there exists a "Ware Gereformeerde Kerk" [True Reformed Church], etc., etc. As one can see, there is tragic division among our brothers, which is only surpassed in numbers in the Old Country, where one finds at least seventeen variants and shades among the Reformed faithful. This is not much consolation for our Americans!

In contrast to the schismatic mania among the ultras, we find relative unity and peace in the Reformed Church, although there, too, new interpretations command people's attention while the Americanization process steadily continues. But here also not everything is "hand in glove" as was demonstrated at the last General Synod, when an unexpected "flare-up" of younger members caused a certain commotion. "We can no longer express our religion in terms of three-hundred years ago," exclaimed D. Van Strien and his followers; thereby they gave notice that the Reformed Church, too, should adapt more than it has done so far.[52]

A separation was averted, however, when a few that were dissatisfied left the Reformed Church but did not try to develop a "following" and thereby cause division, as is often the case in the Christian Reformed Church. The "rule or ruin spirit" is practically foreign to the more broadly educated Reformed leaders. On the contrary, "a prevailing spirit of charity, 'liberty of prophesying' makes us dwell together in unity," declared S. Van der Werf with a certain pride,[53] while his friend Beets of the Christian Reformed Church had to admit that "the absence of such a spirit accounts for a good deal of our denominational troubles in recent years."[54]

But again, the deepest reason, in my view, is the difference of Americanization in both denominations. "We feel the difficulty at the present time of applying our Calvinistic principles to our American life," admits the Christian Reformed Reverend J. J. Hiemenga.[55] The Reformed members have either completely gone through this stage, or moved ahead at this stage, and Americanization became easier when they joined "the East." Those who no longer feel at home in the Reformed Church have usually been Americanized to the point that they can join an American orthodox denomination such as the Presbyterian Church. In this church there are a number of Dutch ministers, even among their intellectual leaders in the seminaries, while in Wayne County, New York State, and in Wisconsin some Presbyterian churches were totally developed by Netherlanders, as was mentioned previously. American churches serve therefore more or less as an escape hatch for the "dissatisfied" in the Reformed Church. The Reformed Church, in turn, serves the same purpose for the most progressive members of the Christian Reformed Church, while its too conservative members join the Christian Reformed Church. (This is in part also an explanation for the "leapfrog game.") We should also mention what is often forgotten, namely that those of the Christian Reformed Church who are too conservative have no place to go except to leave and begin their own church.

The detailed description I gave of these aspects of Dutch life in the United States I feel to be completely justified because, as far as one can still speak of Dutch contemporary life in the United States, all that is left is in fact what is found in orthodox Calvinistic circles.

Dutch Modernists, the more or less "ethical" Protestants, as we know had originally only two congregations in America: the Free Church of [F. W. N.] Hugenholtz in Grand Rapids and its branch in Chicago. Dutch Modernism does not flourish in America, while in sharp contrast our Calvinism does. Dutch Modernists are far more inclined to join an American church than the Calvinists are. Their feeling of solidarity is much less. As far as I know, the Modernist church in Chicago has vanished and as I have been told the one in Grand Rapids has affiliated with the American Unitarian Church. Hugenholtz organized it; later it was led by Pastor [B. Van] Sluyters, with a membership of three hundred. They were supported by the Unitarians. In 1916 they called Klaas Oosterhuis as preacher. He was an orphan from Leeuwarden who had come to America five years earlier. He had studied at Meadville Theological College in Pennsylvania, the school that acquired such a reputation under [Frederick] Huydecoper [Huidecoper]. By then the church had already been somewhat Americanized. One Sunday a month the sermon was delivered in English and for the rest, Dutch was used. It was then known as the Holland Unitarian Church.[56] After this time Americanization increased more rapidly due to America's participation in the [First World] War, when nationalism was greatly strengthened.

As far as the Roman Catholics are concerned, there is even less to write relating to Dutch life, since Roman Catholicism has an international and cosmopolitan character by nature. Although there are some 40,000 Dutch Roman Catholics in the United States, they are so widely scattered that only twenty-five Dutch congregations were established, and they had no mutual connections. In sharp contrast there are five hundred Calvinistic, well-organized churches of the Young-Dutch branch. As we know, most of these Roman Catholic Churches are in the Fox River Valley in the heart of Wisconsin. The rest are scattered in different parts of the Midwest—Michigan, Minnesota, Missouri, etc. Initially, the Roman Catholics began an important church in Grand Rapids called St. Joseph; but in time only a "handful" remained. Now there are only a few Dutch Roman Catholics in the Furniture City. Of greater interest is the church at Essexville near Saginaw Bay in the same state. Of still greater importance is the church of St. Willebrordus in Kensington, the only Dutch parish in Chicago, led by the spiritual leader, J. A. Van Heertum, O.P. [Ordo Praedicatorum or Order of the Dominicans]. Van Heertum was born in Gemert [Noord Brabant] and was for a long time a Norbertine at Heeswijk. Later he became the rector of St. Norbert College at De Pere. Around 1913 he was named pastor of the Kensington parish in one of Chicago's suburbs. This parish at Kensington-Roseland now totals about two hundred families. The older families were mostly from Noord Holland and Zuid Holland, and the younger ones, as far as they were not born in America, hailed from Waalwijk and other Noord Brabant towns.[57]

Furthermore, a number of Zeeland Flemish Roman Catholics live in Rochester, New York, closely intermingled with fellow Flemish believers just as in Moline, Illinois, and other places. The spiritual care of these churches was usually entrusted to Norbertines or Crozier Fathers, who came partly from the southern part of our country, but a number also had already grown up in Wisconsin. However, their bond with the Netherlands is so very minimal that Van Heertum was recently able to declare that of "all non-English-speaking people, the [Roman Catholic] Dutch settlers, and especially their children, have more rapidly learned and adopted the language and customs of the United States."[58] This explains why, in addition to the numerous Dutch Calvinistic newspapers in America, there is only one Roman Catholic newspaper that still appears in the Dutch languages, the *Vlaamsche Gazette* [*Flemish Gazette*] of Moline, which actually is a Southern Dutch [Belgian] paper but is also read by Roman Catholics from the Northern Netherlands.

B. Education

1. Higher and Secondary Education

Once again we shift our focus to the Reformed and the Christian Reformed denominations. Although we may regret that these two groups are not yet united, nevertheless we must recognize that the existence of these two strong Dutch Calvinist denominations has given rise to a healthy spirit of mutual competition which, except for such excesses as for example the race to "establish new churches," has in general been very fruitful. Truly, an urge to excel is not only found in every person but it plays a very important role in every society. It is found "in many of the most serious activities of life," according to W. McDougall, and he confirms that in "the collective life of societies it plays no small part."[59]

This is the way it was among our pious brothers, who by evaluating each other were better able to recognize their own shortcomings and ascertain their own weak points. It is in particular the Christian Reformed Church that is critical if not jealous of her older sister, and time and again it compares the growth of both organizations, time and again it reviews the development of both churches. In this way it urges its own members not to slacken in their Christian duties. This is evident in the area of the missionary outreach but particularly in the field of education. For example, "while the Reformed brethren call one missionary after another and budget large sums for Church Extension Work, we neglect one field after another and thus drive hundreds of households permanently from our churches," exclaims the Christian Reformed Dr. Beets regretfully in the latest Christian Reformed yearbook, and he then goes on to compare the seminaries of the two denominations.[60] Especially the publication of these yearbooks provides a ready occasion for comparison. The Reformed element, in turn, likes to compare its Hope College with the much younger Calvin College of the Christian Reformed group.[61]

On the other hand, I would not be spilling any beans by pointing out that the financial sacrifices that were needed in order to found Calvin College eventually were made when the advocates of Calvin kept hammering on the great significance of Hope College of the Reformed Church. B. K. Kuiper, one of the Christian Reformed leaders, particularly commented on the "great educational impact" exerted by Hope College. "Unquestionably, Hope has done much to bring the Dutch people in the Reformed Church to a higher level," declared this True brother.[62] And so he greatly admired Van Raalte, the founder of Hope College, and viewed him as "a truly great figure, one to whom all people of Dutch descent in America, both Reformed and Christian Reformed, are very highly indebted." It is indeed mostly due to Van Raalte's work, according to Kuiper, that "generally the level of social life is higher among the Reformed than among the Christian Reformed," and that in the former denomination " . . . more outstanding men are found than among those of the Christian Reformed Church. Why is this so? The simple answer is: Hope College." Thus we see that this jealousy led to a sober but also well-intentioned self-criticism and that is why I think I can speak of a *healthy* jealousy.

To what extent this self-criticism has now progressed among the True brothers is reflected in the first place by this same Kuiper who comments on the "contrast between the broad vision" of Van Raalte, a "man with an *academic* background" and the views of our earliest leaders, who were "men devoid of practically any education."[63] Therefore, it is to the lack of a complete college education that Kuiper ascribes the fact (in 1918) that "his people" still consisted mainly of common farm hands and factory workers: "a small and feeble bunch of people in the midst of a gigantic America." Kuiper blames this condition not on the relatively small number of Christian Reformed members but on the absence of this educational opportunity. Due to this lack, as Kuiper commented, "We occupy an altogether and completely insignificant position in the whole of American life.... Who, outside of our own small circle, has ever heard of us?... Indeed, what perceptible influence have we ever exerted or are we exerting right now on the intellectual life of America?"[64]

Kuiper was not the only self-critic among the True brothers. Others were also convinced that the favorable reception that Americans generally accorded Hollanders was due largely to what Americans learned about us from [John Lothrop] Motley.* From him Americans also learned what they owe to the Dutch. Americans were indebted not in the first place to those Hollanders who had come to America but much more to those who had remained in the Netherlands [and who had helped the young republic in its fight for independence]. Beets remarked: "We are still like the moon, shining by means of reflected glory—the brilliancy of the Old Dutch sun," and he added: "We have yet to make our mark in America, we the sons of the pilgrims of 1846 and following decades."[65] How much greater the significance of the Reformed group already was became evident from our discussion of the economic growth of the city of Holland which, as we have seen, was fully recognized by the True brothers. It was this realization, as I pointed out, and the mutual comparison and strife that were born from it, that brought the True brothers to such a level of self-knowledge and that also prompted them to strive for a higher "social standing." The constant disputes between both groups have since given way to mutual emulation. This "tendency of emulation" that more and more replaced the combativeness prevalent among Calvinists and through which, in Professor [William] James's words, "nine-tenths of all the work in our world is accomplished" has, as a result of its individual and collective significance, contributed to raise education among our countrymen to a higher level.[66]

Earlier I presented a detailed account of the origins and subsequent development of this education, primarily among the Reformed element, the followers of Van Raalte. It has developed since, but their ultimate goal—their own university—has not yet been realized. It is remarkable that while Rutgers College and the seminary at New Brunswick are the institutions of this sort in the East—Union College at Schenectady has become independent—it stopped at that. On the other hand, in the West where we formerly saw only Hope College and the Western Theological Seminary in Holland, and subsequently the Northwestern Classical Academy in Orange City as

---

*John Lothrop Motley (1814–1877) was an American historian who wrote seven volumes of Dutch history: *The Rise of the Dutch Republic* (3 vols., 1856), and *The History of the United Netherlands* (4 vols., 1860).

Reformed institutions, the strong growth of educational facilities has resulted in two college and three academies, with flourishing Western Seminary as the "capstone." The spirit of Van Raalte and his followers still permeates these western institutions, and to them apply more than to any other institutions the comment of F. J. Turner: "The democracy of the newer West is deeply affected by the ideals brought by these immigrants from the Old World."[67] When considering all this, it should not be forgotten that the old "Eastern Church" is twice as large as its young western branch; thus the significance of this |smaller| West for education is therefore even greater.

The growing cultural development of the colonists was also shown in the changing leadership at Hope College. At first "Eastern men" such as Dr. |Ch.| Scott, who was the first permanent president, directed the college. It was not until 1893 that for the first time a son of the pioneers was chosen—Dr. G. J. Kollen, a son-in-law of Van Raalte. Like so many capable instructors, such as |John H.| Kleinheksel, |H.| Yntema, |Henry| Boers, |J. B.| Nykerk, and |M. J.| Hoffman, he was born in the village of Overisel, Michigan. Hope grew under Kollen, as well as under his successor Dr. A. Vennema.[68] How greatly the desire for higher education increased among our countrymen is reflected in the statistics. In the years 1908–20 as many students (761) graduated as in the previous 42 years.[69] Today (1925) 487 students are enrolled in the college itself while its "preparatory school" has 74 and there are 123 in the school of music! The total number of alumni has increased to 1,100 already! The three schools have 21, 6 and 5 faculty members respectively. Dr. E. D. Dimnent is the current president.

The campus has ten buildings, some of them quite monumental.[70] The most important are Graves Library with more than 23,000 holdings and Winants Chapel, both named for their generous donors—the Honorable N. F. Graves and Captain G. E. Winants (1893). There is also Van Raalte Memorial Hall, which serves as the main building and contains laboratories and classrooms. It was given in 1903 by the pioneers and their descendants in the West as a memorial to Van Raalte's work. E. R. Voorhees Hall was financed by a $100,000 "gift" from the R. Voorhees family and is in the traditional Dutch stepped gable design and has served since 1907 as a dormitory for women students. There is also Van Vleck Hall for male students, as well as Carnegie gymnasium, given through the munificence of A. Carnegie, etc., etc.[71] An endowment fund of more than a half million dollars contributes to the support of Hope College and its faculty. Following an American custom, a "financial agent" of the college solicits the Reformed constituency both in the West and the East, as far as they are of the Young-Dutch branch, in efforts to increase the size of the endowment. Charitable donations from the faithful maintain and expand the institution, which is one of the finest results of the efforts of the colonists.

The city of Holland is just as proud of the existence of Western Theological Seminary as it is of Hope College. The seminary has made Holland the highest spiritual center of the colonists of Young-Dutch origin in both East

Distinguished pioneer children of Holland, Michigan. Top: The late Dr. G. J. Kollen, former president of Hope College. Middle: The late Dr. A. Vennema, former president of Hope College. Bottom: The late A. Visscher, promotor of many branches of industry.

and West; students come from Yakima, Washington, and from Paterson, New Jersey, as well as from the "German" German Valley, Illinois. In 1925, a total of thirty-nine young men were enrolled in the seminary and this grew in 1927 to "an unprecedented total" of forty-five; at the same time there were only fourteen in New Brunswick, which served the older and twice as large eastern branch of the Reformed Church.[72] In 1927 there were five chairs [professors] at each school, but Western Theological Seminary now has six. It is an interesting fact that all the professors hold the [Honorary] Doctor of Divinity degree and that all of them are descendants of the pure pioneer Dutch element. They include E. J. Blekkink, J. E. Kuizenga (the current president), H. Hospers, S. C. Nettinga, J. Van der Meulen—a son of the pioneer Cornelius, and A. Pieters. In addition, M. J. Hoffman, born in the village of Overisel, was the first "Westerner" to hold a professorship at the New Brunswick Seminary. All these facts are striking evidence of the increasing significance of the Young-Dutch Americans.

The physical plant of Western Theological Seminary consists of four buildings: the "$6,000 Semelink family hall," the "$15,000 Beardslee Memorial Library" with approximately 12,000 holdings—both structures are named for their donors—a $20,000 dormitory, "and a $7,000 power plant." A substantial portion of the funds for these structures and the maintenance of the professors was raised by Reverend J. F. Zwemer, just as he had done for Hope College and Northwestern Classical Academy in Orange City. The endowment of the seminary is more than $110,000 and is growing.[73]

Whereas Hope College grants the Bachelor of Arts degree, it can also grant, upon recommendation by the seminary, the Bachelor of Divinity degree. These degrees may be compared to our Dutch degree of "candidaat," although it should be noted that the B.D. degree is awarded after three years of seminary study following four years of college studies. The divinity degree makes one eligible for the ministry. Thus there is a close connection between Hope College and Western Theological Seminary, although the latter also attracts students mainly from Central College in Pella, Iowa.

Central College, as we have noted before, was established as a Baptist "university." Still, many Young-Dutch people from Pella and neighboring areas attended it. This led the Reformed Church to take over the university in 1916, once the number of its congregations in the West had grown sufficiently and with it the prosperity of the population. (We should recall the practice of "buying out" Americans.) This acquisition was done, according to the Particular Synod of Chicago, not only "for the training of ministers and missionaries but also for the development of higher ideals of life and service, to hold and promote the loyal interests of the coming generations of our prospective physicians and lawyers, teachers and businessmen."[74] In accordance with this, and the laws of Iowa, Central College grants Bachelor degrees upon successful completion of four-year curricula in three areas—Bachelor of Arts, Bachelor of Science, and also the one of Bachelor of Music, since a music school is associated with the college, known more grandiloquently as the "conservatory of music."[75] The bravado attitude that I have already described earlier as being so characteristic of the psychology of the young West is also evident from the name of the four-year preparatory school related to the college and known as Central Academy. This is a terminology which is tame in comparison to that adopted by Hope and Calvin colleges, but these are illustrations that indicate the differences in spirit between the older Michigan and the younger Iowa. Of course, we also should not overlook the fact that the Old-Dutch element manifested itself much more strongly in Michigan and still does today.

Under the leadership of President M. J. Hoffman, Central College grew rapidly and became a new center for Christian higher education in the Reformed Church. But it was not a competitor of Hope in the sense that it took students away from Hope. On the contrary, 90 percent of Central College's students have come from settlements that, up to this point, have not "steered" students to the Reformed schools. In short, Central developed "new fields" in the farther West. Central has about twenty professors and an enrollment of 267, a number of whom are studying both at the college and the conservatory. The respective enrollments in the academy, college, and conservatory are 48, 170, 106.[76]

The campus of Central College encompasses eight acres "of lawn and trees nicely laid out." The administration building, "Old Central," one of the oldest and most monumental buildings in Pella, recently burned down, probably at the hand of arsonists whose love for this sort of activity we have encountered earlier. The other buildings—Jordan Hall (1906), the library with nine thousand volumes, the gymnasium, and auditorium ("a real asset to the life of the college"), the ladies dormitory, etc., cannot meet the demand for space.[77] Therefore, there was a cry of distress from the board of trustees: "Central College desperately needs its new building," and more money. Central's endowment is only $200,000 and according to everybody's conviction it should be expanded at least to half a million dollars.[78] The "wonderful growth" of Central justifies these convictions. With Hoffman's departure to New Brunswick, his successor, Reverend J. Wesselink, had the challenging task of getting Central up to Hope's caliber and, if possible, exceeding it. That is the spirit of the farther West.

In addition to the seminary and the two colleges in the West, the Reformed Church also has three institutions of secondary education (academies) that may be compared to our three-year high schools (H.B.S.) [Hoogere Burgerschool], although the American schools are more "classical" in orientation and offer Greek and Latin, as do the colleges. The academies serve as preparatory schools for the colleges but they also offer terminal degrees.

The oldest of these academies is Northwestern Classical Academy, founded in Orange City in 1882. On its eight-acre campus a second "Science Hall" has recently been opened next to the "Old Main" building.[79] The

864

school has seven instructors, including a female assistant for music, and an enrollment of 104 students—65 young men and 39 young women. There are three curricula. The "classical" track offers Greek and Latin. The "modern classical" track offers Latin, but French has been substituted for Greek. The third track is the "normal course." The first track is a preparatory study for college, the other two provide terminal degrees. The normal track confers, under certain conditions, the competency for elementary school teaching, just as the college B.A. degree confers the right to teach in academies and similar institutions of learning. At least, this is the modern practice.[80] Pleasant Prairie Academy was established in 1893 in the center of the German Valley (Illinois) area for the benefit of its Ost Frisians and formed a second independent academy. There are now four instructors—including the rector—and 43 students.[81]

The most recent of these Reformed academies was founded in 1900 in Cedar Grove, Sheboygan County, Wisconsin, at the suggestion of the board of trustees (council) of Hope College. This school also has four instructors

- • Academy or high school
- ○ College
- ◎ Seminary and college
- ◉ Seminary, college, and high school

N. B. Grundy Center and German Valley are mostly Ost Frisian; North Brunswick is mostly Old Dutch.

Dutch-American institutions of secondary and higher education.

and in 1920 it had sixty-six students, "by far the largest number in the history of the school."[82] Thus there are a seminary, two colleges, and three independent academies; all are denominational, that is, they are supported by the members of the Reformed Church in the West. It is a flourishing achievement of which they can be rightfully proud. It is also a testimony of the energetic activism of the Reformed principle.

Let us now consider our countrymen of the Christian Reformed persuasion. According to a former president of the State University of Iowa, the development of American education in general is best indicated by the saying "that in the kingdom of education, as in the kingdom of heaven, the movement is from above downward."[83] Nowhere is the confirmation of this statement more obvious than among our most pious fellow countrymen for whom both kingdoms are, indeed, so closely allied to each other. Just as in the Reformed denomination, the Christian Reformed constituency was first of all concerned with the education of ministers. The latter group is a good example of education beginning first at the top level with higher education, and then continuing with secondary education, since they did not have at their disposal a New Brunswick. Subsequently, and contrary to the Reformed practice, they pursued their educational goals even more forcefully and increasingly concerned themselves with elementary education.

Their ambitious desire was also to have "a university where all sciences are taught." This was an ideal of such magnitude that in 1918, according to the ever-matter-of-fact B. K. Kuiper, it was an ideal "that no one then living would ever see anything of but some relatively feeble attempts at approaching it."[84] This was an opinion in which he could well have been mistaken, because since then the desire for a complete system of higher education has increased tremendously. It is "an ideal worthy of the hearty support of every lover of the truth." Nearer to home, the younger element already envisions their own Calvin University, an ideal "big enough for united efforts of the next fifty years," according to one of them, J. J. Hiemenga, the first president of Calvin College.[85] These comments are of significance because they show the spirit that animated the Christian Reformed people in their furtherance of education.

For the present the crown of this educational system consists of the Theological School at Grand Rapids, which so far is the only faculty of the future university. The beginnings of this seminary have been sketched earlier. It initially offered tutorial instruction, as a sort of "school in the parsonage," and then in 1876, class instruction was given in "the upper room," an upper room of a Christian school. This year of 1876 is considered as the founding date of the Theological School. Since that time it has grown considerably in many respects, as was portrayed enthusiastically at the recent semi-centennial of its founding. The seminary has six chairs now, held by representatives of the Young-Dutch American element and one "German" fellow classman—L. Berkhof, B.D.; S. Volbeda, Th.D. (the rector in 1927); C. Bouma, M.A., B.D., Th.D.; M. J. Wijngaarden, M.A., B.D., Ph.D.;

H. Schultze, B.A., B.D.; and B. K. Kuiper, B.A., Th.D.[86] Recent emeriti professors are F. M. Ten Hoor and W. Heyns, both of whom belonged to an older
guard who held other traditions. In 1925, the school had forty students but,
in contrast to what took place in Holland, Michigan, this number dwindled
to twenty-seven in 1927, which was "the smallest number in many years."[87]
Time will prove to what extent this decline is permanent.

Some of the professors have spent a shorter or longer period of study at
the Free University in Amsterdam. Volbeda, for example, obtained his degree there. These facts have been of some cultural significance. As a result
the scholarly level of the school has been enhanced, despite the departure
of the gifted Dr. G. Vos, who accepted an appointment to Princeton Seminary in 1893. As a result of their study at more than one university, some
professors have broadened their outlook, which must be considered to be
of great value both personally and in a scholarly sense. This "broadness"
did not find immediate acceptance among the True group; initially at the
Theological School it was not tolerated and even viewed as an "error." This
was experienced by Dr. R. Janssen, one of the most gifted of the professors,
who in 1923 was put off the ship for good [blijvend aan den dijk gezet] for that
very reason.[88]

From the "literary department" that was associated with the Theological
School in 1894, a college developed that is now considered to be the heart,
the center, of Christian Reformed life and—how ultra-modern!—as the
"broadcasting station" of the Christian Reformed people in America.[89] A. J.
Rooks, an alumnus of Hope College and of the University of Michigan at
Ann Arbor, Michigan, and K. Schoolland were the first "literary professors."
Schoolland had obtained his "candidaats" credentials in the Netherlands
and had replaced the famous G. Berkhof, who had died shortly after his
appointment. It took until 1900 before two more instructors were added to
this department and Rooks was appointed as chairman. With the increase
in prosperity, slowly but surely the urge for more and better education also
grew among the generally poorly educated True brothers. This urge came to
expression when the literary department was changed into a "junior college" which was already named "John Calvin Junior College" two years
before it came into formal existence. P. Hoekstra, H. Meeter, J. Mulder, and
J. Van Haitsma were in 1908 the first to graduate. Meeter was also the first
student to receive a B.A. degree from Calvin (1913) although Calvin was not
a truly four-year college until 1920. The year before, the first college president—Reverend J. J. Hiemenga, M.A., B.D.—was appointed and Rooks was
named as dean (and also vice president and college secretary).[90]

The significance of Calvin College grew by leaps and bounds both inwardly and outwardly. At present there are twenty-one professors, all from
the Young-Dutch American group. Just as Hope, Calvin also had a "department of music," and until recently it had a "preparatory school." The latter
was allowed to "die out" when the decision was made to establish an
independent Christian high school. In view of the increasing number of

Christian schools that were being set up, Calvin inaugurated a "normal department" in 1922 to train teachers, following the failure in 1919 of a Christian normal school based in Grand Rapids. In 1925, the college had 249 students and in 1927 this number had increased to 320.[91] Once aroused, the love of study among the *True* brothers and sisters increased rapidly.

The growing number of students created a need for more buildings. Time and again "campaigns" were launched and as a result, Calvin now [1928] has a twelve-acre campus with a magnificent main building on it, estimated to be worth $300,000, which is double the cost of its construction. In addition there is a sizable boarding school, a gymnasium, etc. The latter two buildings are also very efficiently equipped and "thoroughly modern in every respect."[92] The Hekman family in Grand Rapids donated a library building that is nearing completion. The other buildings also, thanks to the campaign efforts of Reverend J. Van der Mey, were erected and maintained by the charitable gifts of the faithful. And still people are not satisfied. Education must be upgraded constantly: "Only men of the highest type, morally and scholarly," may be appointed as professors. They also wish to have more buildings, particularly one to be used separately for the seminary. This all costs money, however. At least one million dollars is needed as a basic sum. We must "and we can do these things," declared Hiemenga who had made his mark in these campaigns.[93] The new president of Calvin, J. Broene, M. A., had the task, however, of raising this million dollars and thus come nearer to the goal of a Calvin University! There you can witness an example of Dutch-American idealism! There you can witness the driving force of individuals who still had to be urged in 1918 by one of their leaders to "no longer be content with a situation in which we are only hewers of wood and drawers of water."[94] And now there are already more than three hundred college students at Calvin alone!

There was even a second college and also another seminary at Grundy Center, Iowa. The Ost Frisian fellow clansman and fellow believer Dr. W. Bode had already started a sort of academy of his own. With the assistance of Classis Ostfriesland, he opened in 1916 a college and seminary at Grundy Center, which was primarily for the purpose of training Ost Frisians to be ministers. When the Christian Reformed Church refused to support a second seminary, thinking that even a second college would be overdoing it, many discussions finally resulted in a sort of compromise. The seminary was discontinued and the college became a junior college—to all intents and purposes it was reduced to an academy—and was placed not under the jurisdiction of the Christian Reformed Church but of a specially created association of Ost Frisians, Netherlanders, and other parents—provided they were orthodox. Today Grundy Center College has about a hundred students, both Ost Frisians and Hollanders.[95]

The Christian Reformed group in Sioux County, Iowa, also had big plans. They hoped to found a Western Calvin College when it appeared that they could not join with their Dutch Reformed brethren. The more level-headed among them did not want to hear of it, feeling that it would be superfluous to have a college in addition to the existing academy in Orange City.[96] The stubborn element—the "fanatics"—would not give up and so in 1919 Western Academy was opened at Hull, to the north of Orange City in Sioux County. It has now about a hundred students and is a competitor of the much older "Northwestern." Thus, the competition that existed in Michigan between Hope and Calvin was found to a lesser degree in Sioux County between the Reformed and the Christian Reformed academies. "Now we stand further away from the Reformed brothers than ever before," was one of the remarks made in the heat of the struggle, which is a sorry picture of the division in two groups so closely related.[97]

Grundy and Western Academy are by no means the only "feeders" for Calvin College in Grand Rapids. In other places the Christian Reformed elements did not lag, either. Restlessly and with increasing energy—that has to be admitted—they spread their propaganda for Christian Reformed education, and they adapted to the new pedagogical practices and breakthroughs among the Americans.

In 1918 MacLean stated that there was "an increasing feeling that the systems must be reconstructed from bottom to top."[98] Already earlier, in many areas of the United States a second kind of secondary school—the high school—had come into existence in parallel with the academy. The precise difference between the two is seldom spelled out; even Dr. M. C. Van Mourik Broekman does not do so; incorrectly he views the high school as a five-year Dutch H.B.S.[99] The high school and the academy both offer four years of course work. My view is that the difference exists primarily in the "atmosphere" in the two schools. The academy is generally an exclusive, even a somewhat aristocratic preparatory school, having often developed alongside a college and radiating the same spirit. It develops its own "school spirit" that manifests itself at Northwestern Academy in Orange City in its own type of "student life." A practical difference is that Greek is taught in the academies, but this has been abandoned in most of the high schools. To all intents—and here I rely on Dr. H. Beets—both preparatory schools are practically alike.[100]

The Christian Reformed people, who were formerly so backward but are now so progressive in many respects, have established many similar schools, naturally all with a strong orthodox color. Within three years, four came into existence—in Chicago, Paterson, Grand Rapids, and Holland. They are supported by independent associations and are also concerned with preparing students for Calvin College. In these instances, too, one marvels at the energy displayed since these schools demand large sums of money. In Chicago, they erected a $225,000 structure, and in Holland one of $200,000. The personnel are preferably college graduates! One is amazed at the sacrifices of the faithful, who still must pay taxes for the support of the public schools! [This is contrary to the established practice in the Netherlands where private and public schools are fully financed by the state.]

In addition to these "Christian Highs," our fellow countrymen have established junior high schools in various towns such as Grand Rapids and others, in conformity with standard American pedagogical practice. They may be compared to our M.U.L.O. schools [Meer Uitgebreid Lager Onderwijs (More Extensive Elementary Education)] that bridge the gap between elementary and high school education but serve especially, according to MacLean, "to afford more opportunity for adaptation of courses to the abilities and life work of the pupils."[101]

According to Dr. J. L. Snethlage, there is in America a growing movement for this type of vocationally oriented education and this is also found among the True brothers.[102] Therefore, in addition to an academic section, the "Christian High" in Grand Rapids also has a commercial department, while in Chicago there is a "general course, a teacher's course, a scientific course, and a two-, three-, or four-year commercial course;"[103] there is indeed "something for everyone."

It is obvious that this type of education is in sharper contrast to the more sophisticated academies and preparatory schools, even though some academies offer the same type of courses. This is particularly noticeable between the practical high schools and the more cultural academies, as when one compares the Christian Reformed high school in Chicago and its numerous courses with the much older Reformed Northwestern Classical Academy in Orange City. In the latter there is a climate as in all older American schools that does not primarily prepare pupils for a trade but is rather concerned with the development of character, in short, with the "harmonious development of the individual."[104]

This is specifically spelled out in the latest (1920–21) catalog of Northwestern. "The aim here is not directly utilitarian or vocational; that is, we do not propose to prepare directly for any of the vocations of life, but our aim is rather cultural, seeking, by developing the whole man, to lay such a foundation, that upon it may successfully be constructed the necessary technical knowledge for any of the professions or vocations of life."[105]

We can see that both streams of development in the American educational system are well-represented among our countrymen. There is the older and more culturally oriented stream among the most Americanized and most highly educated Reformed group. In addition, there is the younger, more practical stream among the present-day very progressive Christian Reformed people who until recently were the least Americanized and least sophisticated. This is understandable because when the older academic schools were at their peak, the True brothers were not yet concerned with secondary education. Therefore, one should not make unwarranted conclusions!

There is no doubt that, considering all these developments, the Christian Reformed have abandoned their former "splendid isolation" in many areas;

they have adopted American ways of life and form an integral part of the American nation, even though a modest one. That is the way these ortho-dox brothers feel about it themselves and they speak of "the break of our isolation and the bursting of the shell of our self-containedness."[106]

2. The Elementary Education Problem

The fact that the faithful felt increasingly motivated by high ideals con-cerning education in their adopted fatherland is even more apparent in their fostering of elementary education. I have pointed out earlier that, although the Christian school problem was one of the motives for emigra-tion, such a school could not put down roots among Van Raalte's followers, and even among the seceders of this group it led a marginal existence. This was even the case when the emphasis was shifted from the Dutch to the Christian character and when subsequently English was used more and more as the language of communication. In the eyes of many, such schools were sectarian schools and this was felt especially by the most Americanized emigrants to be un-American, particularly because the church controlled them and so they were viewed as parochial schools. It was felt that the use of the Dutch language would automatically cause the schools to fail. In America the Christian school was seen as "outlandish" and "foreign."[107] But they did not fail. Quite the contrary. When numerous educated, orthodox Netherlanders settled in America during the 1890s, they also brought with them the educational ideas of A. Kuyper. Therefore they too were convinced that education was not the exclusive concern of the state or of the church, but rather of the parents. In other words, independent Christian schools should be established by specially created associations not limited to Christian Reformed members but also open to other orthodox Reformed and Presbyterian believers.

Independent schools thus became the goal; they were first promoted in Chicago in 1894 by P. R. Holtman. The schools existing under church spon-sorship were turned over to newly organized associations and new schools were set up by school associations. People even wanted to separate Calvin College from the church but to this day that has not succeeded. Abraham Kuyper himself warned Americans against imitation of the Dutch schools, urging that "good American schools" be established where the children could be molded into solid, truly American Calvinists. "If the Dutch element is to be a blessing for the American nation, they would do well to renounce once and for all any attempt to remain Netherlanders, organized into unique groups." Kuyper wrote this comment using the Algemeen Nederlandsch Verbond as a model. Men such as J. Veltkamp, B. J. Bennink, P. Van Vlaan-deren, K. Kuiper, and other Dutch-Americans adopted these ideas and worked hard for independent Christian schools.[108] Today, just as here in the Netherlands, a large number of these schools have come into being in America. More than eighty Christian elementary schools are found among the Christian Reformed in America and more than three hundred teachers instruct more than ten thousand children in them.[109]

In some centers, such as Chicago, the school associations have organized "alliances." In 1921 the National Union of Christian Schools was formed with M. Fakkema as its secretary. Its purpose was to promote standards in Christian education and to extend the movement also among other denominations. At an earlier date, brochures about the Free Christian School by Reverend [George] Hylkema, and others were already spread.[110] Today it has its own publication, the *Christian School Magazine*, edited by G. Heyns, principal of Western Academy in Hull, Iowa.

In America, which is becoming more and more secularized, the True brothers are convinced that they have an important educational task to fulfill. How they propose to fulfill that "task" is not a matter of unanimity among all the believers, no matter how much the proponents try to represent private education as being fully "American." Its supporters claim that it developed "from Dutch to American, from parochial to free."[111] But insiders know better.

Even Beets, when at a given moment he was cornered by Reverend J. Bovenkerk of Muskegon (a Reformed minister born in Weesp in the Netherlands), had to acknowledge, despite the fine words of M. Fakkema, that the independent American school was actually the same as the former sectarian school: "They certainly belong to the same genus, even though they might be called a different species, although we would not even grant that in reality. They are essentially the same under a new name, that's all."[112] Other True brothers who strongly champion the Christian school movement from the depth of their heart also view the Christian school nevertheless as a "transplanted institution" that, according to J. G. Van den Bosch, "had to be domesticated even among our own people."[113]

This American school problem is of considerable sociographical interest because it is closely related to the Americanization process and the progress Americanization has made. Protestant America—just as earlier the Protestant Netherlands—was strongly in favor of public schools and, according to Van den Bosch, had "a very reverential regard" for them. It is interesting to note that the Reformed element, who are in general the most Americanized of the Hollanders in America, want nothing to do with private schools but feel that it is their duty to see to it that there is a Christian atmosphere in the public schools. Therefore they are convinced that public schools may not be wilfully abandoned. To do so, according to J. Bovenkerk, would indicate a lack of civic responsibility and "I repeat *civic neglect is sin*."[114] (Hear ye, hear ye, also ye Calvinists in the Netherlands!)

The Reformed church members generally view the Christian schools as "sectarian" or even as "opposition" schools that have no place in America. From this it follows that Bovenkerk could state solemnly: "I am not ready to abandon civic duty and to surrender our public institutions to the devil—

not until the case becomes hopeless. There is a world of difference between Calvinism and Separatism."[115]

It is this very widely shared opinion that accounts for so little support for Christian schools among the Reformed members. This attitude also explains why until recently for example, in Holland, Michigan, of the children from Reformed Church families enrolled in secondary schools, 90 percent went to public schools and scarcely 10 percent to the preparatory school of Hope College.[116] It is again this conviction that explains why only exceptionally few Christian schools, such as the one in Boyden, Iowa, have been established by the Reformed group.[117] It also explains why the total number of children from Reformed households sent to such private schools—with exceptions such as Chicago—is "not numerous."[118] Some of their ministers are even opposed to any cooperation despite the fact that the schools are not sponsored by churches but by independent associations; thus their support might be possible. It was in view of this kind of support that the transfer of school stewardship from the public authorities to the associations was promoted.

In this connection it is interesting to note that also among the Christian Reformed people there are many who will have nothing to do with private schools. For them it is not only a material motive (the heavy expense that is attendant upon such private schools), but above all it is also a matter of personal conviction, closely related to the greater or lesser degree of Americanization. "The remarkable fact is, that especially among the older element in our denomination (and that does not simply mean our oldest American churches, either), there is not that enthusiasm for schools of a Christian character which we happily find among the people whose forbears reached our shores in later years."[119] As I see it, this remark of Beets is not so remarkable in view of what has been noted above.

In addition, it is somewhat unpleasant for the supporters of the private school that the more sophisticated—usually also the most Americanized—of their own fellow believers are not in sympathy with the movement. And these public school supporters, who are "some very fine Christian Church members," are at times, and not without tact, called more or less to account by their brothers![120] It is decidedly painful for these partisans of private education that the pride of the Christian Reformed Church, Ate Dykstra, LL.B., who up to that time was the only True brother who had made it to the level of legislator in Lansing, Michigan, really wants nothing to do with the independent school either. More than 92 percent of the children in Michigan are brought up in public schools. "Can any Christian citizen be indifferent about the kind of education given to ninety-two out of every one hundred children of school age in Michigan?" asks this really True "representative"; and then he exclaims, "Shall we, as Christian citizens of a great State, earnestly contend for the faith which was once for all delivered to the saints?"[121]

No matter how carefully Beets and his colleague, Reverend E. J. Tanis, wish to sail around this "reef," they cannot deny that the Honorable Dykstra is for all practical matters entirely on the side of Reverend J. Bovenkerk and the latter's Reformed Church. Dykstra asserts that in many Michigan public schools, classes begin with an opening prayer and Bible readings are part of the curriculum. Indeed, both Beets and Tanis acknowledge that there is "a growing demand today for such religious teaching in the public schools"; it is even an "insistent and ever growing demand."[122] Beets also concedes that it is criminal "to be lukewarm regarding such interests,"[123] but meanwhile he continues unabated to promote his private school: "a school with the living Christ in it, as invited Lord, and not simply as a great rabbi, tolerated by majority consent. A school with the Bible in it—not simply as Hebrew literature, but as the sword of the Spirit. And praying people back of all this."[124]

Thus we have seen that our countrymen took their school controversy with them to America. For others, however, private schools were no problem. In larger numbers, the Lutherans, and particularly the Roman Catholics, have their own parochial schools. Among the Calvinists in North America, insofar as I am aware, only the Christian Reformed faithful have set up their "free" schools which are also open to those of Reformed, Presbyterian, and other closely related persuasions. In Los Angeles as well as in Chicago the [True] brothers have been somewhat successful with their propaganda. In Los Angeles, they were already active at an earlier date due largely to the talented Reverend J. Groen.[125]

At the present time these "free" schools are attended almost entirely by young people of Dutch descent. Through this "Dutchness," even though there is no longer a language barrier—as English is generally spoken by all young people—a certain kind of "isolation" is fostered once again. This becomes remarkably plain when one comes across the fact that these schools are praised for certain social advantages that they offer: they are a force against worldliness but more in particular these schools counteract mixed marriages. "By having our boys and girls attend our Christian schools we naturally promote acquaintance among young people who are guided by the same principles. . . . " I am not aware how much *pénétration pacifique* [peaceful penetration] has taken place in Grand Rapids between the Dutch and the Poles. After the Dutch, the Poles are the largest ethnic group in the city. However, it is a fact that in Paterson already many a young Hollander has won the heart of one of the numerous Italian beauties there. For various reasons this is not to the liking of the True brothers because they are convinced that "on the whole the marriage of folk guided by the same principles, with the same historical and ethnological background, is apt to be the happiest, the most satisfactory in the long run."[126]

It is evident that the old "clan spirit" is still alive and well even after a sojourn of three-quarters of a century in this spacious land of America, despite increasingly rapid material and spiritual development. The faithful deny that a complete Americanization is hampered by these types of educa-

Religious and political leaders of the Reformed and Christian Reformed Dutch Americans. Top to bottom: The late Dr. H. E. Dosker, church historian and biographer of Van Raalte; Dr. H. Beets, church historian, journalist, and mission director of the Christian Reformed Church; A. Dykstra, Christian Reformed politician, Grand Rapids; G. J. Diekema, Reformed ex-Congressman, Holland, Michigan.

tional preferences, but outside of their circle the opposite viewpoint is generally held. This situation explains why the most nationalistic Americans view with increasing mistrust the development of the "free" schools of the Christian Reformed people, as well as the even more numerous parochial schools of the Lutherans and especially those of the Roman Catholics. Citizens in Oregon and Michigan have repeatedly tried to make the operation of private elementary schools impossible by stratagems such as revision of the respective state constitutions making attendance of public schools mandatory. Up to this point this has not been successful despite the all-out campaign of support by the extremely anti-Roman Catholic Ku Klux Klan. The school burnings in Iowa that were mentioned earlier could be viewed in part as a consequence of this social climate. Among our fellow countrymen, this struggle over the schools has manifested itself in three ways. As in all conflicts, their group identity was strengthened; they even say that the school has become "the center of our group consciousness."

Opposition to women's voting rights was initially very strong among the Christian Reformed—only a few years ago, their women in a number of towns refused to vote.[127] This opposition has now subsided. When in Michigan it appeared that in 1924 a proposed legal amendment threatened the existence of private schools, the ladies were urged to get out and vote. Thanks to their additional votes, the proposed amendment was defeated, 451,410 to 257,095. Still, this danger for the private schools was real, for in the outspoken religious city of Holland only 2,591 votes were cast against the proposal and 1,116 for it. In the equally orthodox Holland Township, the respective figures were 492 against and 130 for; in largely Dutch-populated Grand Haven, they were 7,330 against and 790 in favor.[128]

Even more remarkable is the totally altered attitude toward the Roman Catholics, at least among the leaders. Earlier we have noticed repeatedly how great the aversion was to the Roman Catholics, even of such men as Scholte. This anti-papist feeling came to a climax in 1924 on the occasion of the Eucharist congress held in Amsterdam in the Netherlands. This assembly irked many Americans of Dutch ancestry. Acting as their spokesman, Hans Hansen queried: "Who gave you the right, O Roman Prelate, to paint the ancient free nation of Orange with your crimson and to offer it your wine of harlots?"[129] B. K. Kuiper said, however, that in educational matters the Roman Catholics and Calvinists had similar interests and stood "shoulder to shoulder."[130] Even Beets, who knew full well that his brethren were anything but pleased at being mentioned in one and the same breath with Roman Catholics, was aware that the anti-Catholic sentiment, as in the case of Hans Hansen, "has been bred into the bones of a number of us." Nevertheless, Beets urged that their hatred against the "yoke-fellows" be permitted to lapse.[131]

Calvinist leaders felt that henceforth their cause and that of the Roman Catholics, at least on the school issue, was a mutual one and so they attempted constantly to erase the old hatred. "We appreciate whatever

good Rome has done and whatever truth it has stood for and still pro-
claims." And then at least the truth was out: "We grant that in the great
fundamentals we stand nearer to it than to the liberals who reject the Holy
Trinity and the authority of the Bible."[132] However, in this matter Beets
considered it safer to refer to the stand taken by the Reformed leaders in
the Netherlands! Reverend E. J. Tanis went even further: "Let us remember
that there are many vital things wherein we agree."[133] Tanis went on to
express his admiration for those who plead for Roman Catholic (one could
as well substitute Calvinist) education: "Hats off to the good judgment and
common sense of this Roman Catholic!" As is evident, they are hand and
glove [*koek en ei*, literally cake and egg]—all for the sake of "the principle."

In the meantime, J. H. Hoekstra (alias Hans Hansen) and so many other
Dutch Americans eschewed "Rome's shackles," either due to their family
background or to the stories of authors such as [Eduard] Gerdes that were
great favorites among them. They had witnessed how in the Windy City
itself "the papal parade on dike and path" passed "with the communion
wafer by the gates and through the streets." They had seen them groping
for Protestant America.[134]

3. *Results of This Education*

Of more immediate interest, evidently, are the results of this educational
system. In this light it must be said that both Hope in Holland and Calvin
in Grand Rapids have very high reputations in America. It is generally
acknowledged that both are among the best colleges in Michigan. Professor
R. M. Wenley of the State University at Ann Arbor [University of Michigan],
where many Hollanders pursue their studies, was quoted by Dean Rooks in
1920 (and he related it to me) that Calvin was "the best small college in the
State." Since then, the significance of this college has increased so much
that Dean [John] Effinger of the University [of Michigan] declared: "If all the
small colleges in the United States equalled Calvin College in its thoroughness and in its ability to put the scholarly emphasis upon its work, there
would be cause for rejoicing throughout the land."[135] Others also admire the
"splendid standing" of Hope and Calvin, a "standing" that is reflected in
the numerous awards received by the Dutch students in American universities and seminaries and in the many fellowships and scholarships they
receive. Thus, many are the Young-Dutch Americans who, after having
studied at an American university, have completed their studies, thanks to a
Rhodes scholarship at Oxford or Berlin, Heidelberg, etc. Several have also
gone to the Free University in Amsterdam or to "famous Leyden."

As I have remarked before, our countrymen have a healthy critical disposition, and therefore they do not overrate the significance of their educational system. Professor [Albert] Raap, who escorted me around Hope College, admitted that, compared to the Dutch educational system, their's was
superficial. How well he remembered the thoroughness of his boyhood

textbooks in the Netherlands! For that matter, people at Calvin are also convinced, as far as "thoroughness" is concerned, that "America can learn a good deal from Europe."[136] A Dutch-American pedagogue and professor told me: "We are waging a strong fight against superficiality and we try to teach more and more in depth at both Hope and Calvin."

Numerous are the Dutch-American youth who already have gone, via one of their colleges, to positions of importance in the Dutch-American community and in a few cases elsewhere. Naturally they have gone first of all as men of the cloth, either in America itself or in one of the many mission fields abroad; others have made a name in the general cultural and economic spheres—in politics and industry. In this connection the latest statistics from Hope College are interesting. A total of 1,058 have graduated from Hope and 945 of these are still living. Among them are 310 clergymen and 27 clergymen's wives; 95 have gone into mission work—3 in Africa, 17 in Arabia, 27 in China, 18 in British India, 20 in Japan, 3 in South America, and several in other places; 10 are theology professors, 6 are college presidents, 249 are principals or teachers at an elementary or secondary school, 52 are professors; there are 44 medical doctors and 20 lawyers; 65 are theological students and 76 are engaged in other areas.[137]

Similar statistics from Central College in Pella and Calvin College in Grand Rapids point up the religious nature of these institutions. In 1921 Calvin had graduated 336, of which 305 were still living. Among them were 186 ministers, 9 missionaries, 11 professors or high school teachers, 19 were principals or elementary school teachers, and 40 were theological students.[138]

From this it appears that for the time being the cultural value of our colonists lies in the area of theological pursuits. This cultural contribution consists of their efforts to Christianize the American people, so far mostly by way of the ministry, in an increasingly greater measure through missionary work, and now more and more through education. Theologians, missionaries, and pedagogues—all closely related to one another—are primarily the "men of culture" that the settlements supply in increasing numbers to America. There are in addition a few politicians. We have already seen that the professorial chairs in the Holland and Grand Rapids seminaries are held exclusively by "our own men." We also saw that the West has sent one of its own, Hoffman, to New Brunswick in the East.

Recognition is also given to our colonial theologians outside their own circles. Since 1893, Dr. G. Vos of Grand Rapids has taught with great distinction at Princeton Seminary. Dr. H. E. Dosker, who passed away recently, was a professor at Holland, Michigan, from 1893 to 1903 but then became associated with the Kentucky Theological Seminary of the Presbyterian Church South at Louisville, a sister institution of "northern" Princeton.[139] At the same school Dr. J. M. Van der Meulen, a grandson of the pioneer Cornelius, is still serving as a professor. Our countrymen are esteemed not only as scholarly theologians but also as preachers, as is demonstrated by the rather large number of them that serve the Presbyterian Church, among other denominations. A few years ago, Reverend Louis Van den Berg, a Hope graduate, was called by one of the leading congregations of Louisville, Kentucky; they offered him very enticing terms. At the time he was serving the First Presbyterian Church of Paterson, and at the insistence of his own congregation, which raised his salary to $6,000, he declined the call.[140]

C. Missions and Scholarship

1. Mission Work

The influence of our "Dutch" missionaries extends already far beyond the borders of America. From the statistics cited previously it is evident how important a role the missionary movement plays in the Reformed Church and, increasingly, also in the Christian Reformed denomination. Earlier we took a close look at the birth of the missionary idea among the immigrants and we noted that it grew the most vigorously among the most Americanized of them. And so it has been to this day. The True brothers, who were less Americanized, concentrated their energies primarily on private education and secondarily on mission work; with the Reformed element it was just the reverse. "Our great responsibility in foreign missions has formed the center of our group-consciousness," declared the Reverend S. Van der Werf.[141] Indeed! And in this respect the Reformed Church in the West has already outmatched the East. Sixty percent of the Reformed missionaries in China have come from the West. The other fields—India, Japan and Arabia—have respectively, 40, 64 and 49 percent from the "Western branch." The average is 52 percent! One can go back to the previously given absolute numbers. It should be noted that 45 percent of the cost of missions is borne by the Western churches and the remainder by the Eastern ones, though the latter are twice as numerous. In 1924, despite the growing agricultural crisis, the West contributed $155,920.85 for foreign missions.[142]

Our countrymen fulfill a grand task in Asia as well as in Africa, driven by a noble and enviable idealism. Along with H. Ten Kate, we may be skeptical of the results of missions, or we may with Fr. [Brother] Nansen be opposed to their efforts.[143] We could even agree with [Eduard] Pechuël Loesche that missions are not recommended for the Negro nations. But it cannot be denied that they brought an end to many barbaric conditions, and that they accomplished much in the way of practical work, and so the work is not without social significance. Ten Kate expected the greatest benefits from medical missions. This has indeed been the case, because next to education, it is these kinds of missions that play an important role among our practical Dutch Americans in most of their mission fields. In addition to their work in hygiene, their "practical" bent comes to the fore, particularly in a land such as India, where many natives are reclaimed from the pernicious caste system, and in Arabia, where they try to reduce the flourishing institution of slavery and, if possible in any way, to eliminate it.

At present, the Amoy mission in China, with 47 missionaries, runs 5 hospitals. In addition to Neerbosch as the first hospital, which we have already mentioned earlier, the talented Dr. |J.| Otte, with the assistance of his friends in Holland, founded two more hospitals "Hope" and "Wilhelmina." Since then also "Fagg Memorial Hospital" and "Elisabeth Blauvelt Memorial Hospital" were built, and all are directed by Dutch-American physicians, at present, Dr. R. Hofstra, Dr. T. Bosch, Dr. C. H. Holleman, and Mrs. M. Van de Weg (Vandeweg), respectively. In 1924 they treated 39,680 patients. In addition, this mission has 23 churches, a college and theological seminary headed by the Reverend H. P. De Pree, 6 boys boarding schools, 6 girls boarding schools, and 3 women's boarding schools, and 60 day schools—a total of 75 schools with 4,839 students.

The Arcot mission in British India, with 53 missionaries, has 7 hospitals that treated 60,316 patients in 1924. It also has 17 churches, 7 boys boarding schools, 5 boarding schools for girls, a theological school, and 226 day schools—a total of 239 schools with 8,869 students. Among these schools are an agricultural and a vocational school!

The mission in Japan with 37 missionaries numbers 17 churches. There is also the famous theological school, Meiji Gakuin, with the former member of parliament, D. Tajawa as its president. As we noted earlier, Dr. A. Oltmans had done important work at this school. Since he had reached "retirement" age he was succeeded by the Reverend H. V. E. Stegeman. This area also has two seminaries and an academy in cooperation with the Presbyterian Church U.S.A. The work of the mission is concentrated in Tokyo, Yokohama, Shimonoseki, Saga, Oita, Kagoshima, and Nagasaki.

The Arabian mission, with 40 missionaries, has 4 hospitals or rather, for the time being, policlinics, that treated 59,413 patients in 1924. In addition there are 5 churches, a boarding school for boys, and 10 day schools. This mission has posts at Amara, Basrah, Bahrein, Kuwait, and Masqat. At present (1924) a new mission field is being opened in Mesopotamia, which is a cooperative effort of the Presbyterian Church U.S.A. and the Reformed Church in the U.S.[144]

It is through these fields of missions that the Holland Americans have already achieved a world-wide reputation. Well known in missionary circles are such names as the recently deceased Dr. J. Otte in Amoy, |Guido F.| Verbeek and |A.| Pieters in Japan and Reverend A. Oltmans in Tokyo. Then there was Samuel M. Zwemer who, as we remember, was one of the founders of the Arabian mission and is currently stationed in Cairo. S. M. Zwemer is considered (also by |Christiaan| Snouck Hurgronje) as one of the best experts on Arabia and the Mohammedans in general; thanks to him there is a considerable literature available.[145] How highly our Reformed Holland Americans are appreciated in these countries appears from the fact that of the two secretaries of the International Missionary Council—a body that provides advisory leadership to the whole missionary work of the Protestant world and particularly to the English language churches—one of them, Dr. A. L. Warnshuis, is a Hope graduate, who was recognized for his work on the Amoy field and who is now in London filling his new position.[146]

In America itself the Reformed Church naturally engages in church extension primarily among our countrymen. The Board of Domestic Missions is not only concerned with this but also works, as I mentioned, among the "new Americans" in the East—among the Italians and Hungarians. The Board is assisted by the Women's Board of Domestic Missions, which since 1899 has been working among the mountain folk of Kentucky. They also worked among the Winnebago Indians of Nebraska. Mission work in the Virgin Islands has nearly ceased with the return of the Reverend P. Jonker.[147] Mission work among the Southern Blacks does not seem to have been a success. The maxim "as the people are, so is their worship" is clearly in evidence here. Without mincing matters, it is acknowledged that Dutch Calvinism is not suited for everyone. "It did not take long to demonstrate that the type of worship in the Reformed Church was not attractive to the rank and file of the Negroes, who preferred the more emotional service offered by other churches. Only the better educated were reached by our churches."[148] If the last part of this quotation points up the rational character of our Calvinism, the statement as a whole means that mission work is partly condemned and can be seen as a partial confirmation of H. Ten Kate's opinion. In this connection, I commented earlier about the ill-fated efforts among the "Southerners" of Oklahoma.

As I mentioned earlier, there was originally little missionary zeal among the Christian Reformed but this attitude changed as they became more Americanized. Naturally, "Domestic Missions" were their first and greatest concern; they wanted to extend themselves among their fellow Hollanders. We have already learned of their zeal and rivalry! As the True brothers became more sophisticated they broadened their view and also their "missionary vision." In 1896 the Christian Reformed Synod decided to send missionaries among the Indians in the western states. A previous attempt to do so had aborted. Now they were to have more success. The Reverend H. Fryling and laymen [Andries] Van der Wagen and [James E.] De Groot, with their respective families, were the first missionaries here of the True Church.[149] They left for New Mexico to work among the Zuni and Navaho Indians. Curiously enough, fourteen years earlier another Hollander, Dr. H. F. C. Ten Kate, Jr., had visited and studied these tribes, which fact was unknown to the True Church until they were apprised of it recently by the writer of these lines.[150] Despite the rivalry of some competing Roman Catholic brothers, the True brothers expanded their field, especially later on through the efforts of their missionary, the Reverend L[eonard] P. Brink. The True brothers now "work" among 8,000 to 10,000 Navahos and 1,600 Zunis.

They established posts at Rehoboth, Crown Point, Farmington, Toadlena, Tohatchi, and Black Rock. In the latter place Reverend H. Fryling, after a short interlude, is still active. Since our Americans are so practical, they have established numerous schools and so far one "hospital" in the area.[151]

In addition to the missionary efforts among the "Heathen," the Christian Reformed Church is especially engaged in mission work among the Jews in Paterson and Chicago, where the Paterson Hebrew Mission and the Chicago Jewish Mission carry on the work. The Reverend J. I. Fles, himself of Jewish background, was one of the early pioneers in the 1890s.[152]

Mission work among the Mormon fellow Dutch of Utah was also undertaken in the 1890s at the insistence of the Reverend [A. J.] Van den Heuvel but it was not successful, "due in part to organized opposition from the side of the Mormon hierarchy," and so was abandoned.

There were better results from evangelization in the large cities to which America's growing industries attracted large numbers of poor immigrants. Brother P[eter] Stam, who was the director of the Star of Hope Mission, preached in "dark, godless Paterson" about 1920.[153] As noted previously, city evangelism had also been begun in Grand Rapids. The most successful of these efforts was in Chicago where the late Reverend P. J. Hoekenga helped to found the Helping Hand Gospel Mission. [John] Van de Water and his assistants have since served here for several years. They seek the down and out in the slums of Chicago and turn many to the paths of peace. A similar city mission is functioning among the "forgotten men" in the industrial city of Hammond, Indiana, "the dumping ground of Chicago."[154] The obvious sociological significance of such efforts need not be detailed here.

Of a similar special nature is the work of the Christian Reformed brothers among the immigrants and seafarers in Hoboken, New Jersey. This is "the most important work of eastern home missions," and is an effort that deserves more attention and should be better supported since it is closely related to our own country. Here more than anywhere else, the Netherlands, and particularly its shipping companies ought to cooperate better than before. As early as 1867 the Christian Reformed brothers contributed for work among the immigrants, and this increased after 1910 when the church took over the work. Upon their arrival in America, very large numbers of immigrants received a friendly welcome in Hudson Street, Hoboken, and were strongly encouraged on their way westward. Today the church provides spacious rooms (until recently at 322 River Street, then at a roomy corner building nearby) where many longshoremen also find a welcome and, among other amenities, find a reading and writing room at their disposal. In the meantime the question arises as to what extent the Netherlands should help and why it could not be more "royal" than it has been so far. My brother [Jan E. Van Hinte] and I have both experienced what a fine piece of work the Christian Reformed Church is doing here and the broad manner in which they receive and assist those who come to them, regardless of their religious affiliation—or lack thereof. It appears that we may be mistaken with regard to the "narrowness" of the True brothers and that there is more narrowness on *this* |Netherlands| side of the ocean, even in the so-called "enlightened" circles.

In connection with this program, Dr. Beets asked: "Churches in the Netherlands, do you think, that we get what President Roosevelt used to call 'a square deal' when for our work at Hoboken, although especially and specifically helping Dutch citizens, we get next to nothing from you, even though twice your General Synod endorsed and recommended the matter?"[155]

While awaiting some form of cooperation, which the Reformed Church has also declared that it is ready to offer, the Christian Reformed brothers continue to support the work of welcoming our fellow Dutch in the most generous manner.[156] The good that they do, even among non-believers, was brought home to me recently in a letter that I received from a young woman who was a servant. She had married and was moving to America with her husband. Mr. |A.| Visser of the mission took charge of the couple "and that gentleman did not turn us over to anyone else but kept us with him and all was nice and reassuring."[157] Everything they needed to continue on to Chicago was freely provided "and there a short prayer was mumbled for us and a little hymn sung and then we were brought to the train." She added the thankful thought: "It is such a wonderful organization for people and they so much want to help their fellowmen."*

Thus it can be seen how widely the Christian Reformed brothers interpret the concept of "mission" and how closely it is related to the most varied kinds of social work. In time to come, with their further development and Americanization, the Christian Reformed brothers would have an even wider concept of the "missionary vision." For years they have supported Dutch congregations in Argentina that had been formed there about 1890. The increasing prosperity also among the True brothers, caused such an increase in their contributions for missions that they are now thinking of their own "foreign" missions or rather are beginning to work on them. There had already been considerable thought given to it. As the Reverend |W. R.| Smidt commented about the Mohammedans: "I mean, those people understand us best. . . . Allah (God) wills it; this is enough to convince them. Their daily confession is that God is God. Is that so far removed for our Calvinism?"[158] The same patriotic ideas that motivated the missions to the Indians—a mission in their own country—caused them to think about Cuba when in 1898 it became American.† When in 1918 "the opening of a new field" was definitely decided upon, they quickly obtained $75,000—they had hardly dared hope for $50,000—and settled upon China as a field. Six reasons contributed to this choice, of which number six—for us the most

*This is brought to the attention of the Netherlands in general and the *Royal* Dutch Steamship Company in particular for further consideration |Van Hinte|.

†The United States liberated Cuba from Spanish misrule in 1898 and occupied the island until 1903, when the independent Cuban Republic was established.

interesting one—said that the Chinese were conservative and intellectual in orientation "and hence fit our people's type of character more than the African, who is emotional."[159] It is evident that in their preparations they had gone for advice to their Reformed brothers who were more experienced in this respect. Were the brothers also acquainted with Pechuël Loesche's work?

In any case, on October 30, 1920, the first three foreign missionaries—J. C. De Korne, L. S. Huizenga, and H. A. Dykstra—left San Francisco where a last church service was held and they embarked on the *China* that transported them to Shanghai.[160] Jukao, a town of 50,000 to 100,000 inhabitants situated north of Shanghai, became the first foreign mission station of the Christian Reformed brothers and here they began medical and educational work, even though they were "only handmaids to the higher calling of the church to preach the Gospel."[161] Since then the number of missionaries has more than doubled and young men and women prepare at the Nanking Union Language School for their selfless task. A second post is about to be opened in Ching Kiang, a town of at least 25,000 located fifty or sixty miles from Jukao.[162]

The mission projects developed so much that since 1920 there has been, in addition to the Christian Reformed Board of Missions, an executive director or "secretary of missions" to oversee the day to day operations.[163] The mission director, Dr. H. Beets, also has to promote the work in various ways and "to enlighten and enthuse the people on the subject of missions in all its branches."[164]

The extent to which the mission spirit, as far as it is not already present, is captivating more and more of our religious fellow Dutch is manifested by the increasing number of young men at Hope and Calvin who dedicate themselves when still students to serve in missions and so become members of the Hope Student Volunteer Band. Since 1915 there has been a branch of this organization at Calvin, with branches throughout America. In 1921 the Christian Reformed brothers in Chicago, Illinois, even founded for the benefit of lay people a "missionary training school" primarily to promote city missions. The missionary fervor has grown to such proportions that many of our religious countrymen accept missionary work in the service of other denominations, and even convert to these other denominations. Earlier I mentioned the Reverend J. Kruidenier who went over to the United Presbyterian Church. This Dutch American, born "on the Itsert" in southern Bavaria, recently passed away in Tanta, Egypt, where he had been serving for decades as a missionary.[165] Another one of the most popular Dutch-American missionaries is Miss Johanna Veenstra, who works among the Negroes in the Sudan region of Africa. Others such as Miss M. Van Vessem work in South Africa for the South African General Mission. More than ever before we can characterize the religious Dutch Americans as a missionary-minded people.[166]

I mentioned earlier the social consequences of these missionary efforts for our fellow Dutch and how, among other things, they resulted in a wider outlook and a tuning in to world events. We in the Netherlands can hardly imagine the magnitude of these events. For example, the most ordinary among the Calvinists follows the developments in China as they are reported with great detail in their church paper because his missionary is also laboring there to spread the kingdom of God! Mission festivals are held where missionaries back for a vacation in America are preferably featured as speakers. These festivals encourage not only the zeal for missions but also promote geographical knowledge among the hearers. In addition missionaries visit even the smallest towns to deliver a "lecture" and people become familiar with India, China, Arabia, etc. As an example, when the Reverend and Mrs. Dykstra returned from Arabia in 1920, they gave many illustrated lectures with slides in the towns of Sioux County, Iowa. A simple Hollander in Ireton wrote that it was a strange experience "to sit on the floor in true Arabian fashion, and be served Arabian refreshments by Mrs. Dykstra."[167]

2. At *the* Universities

It appears from the foregoing that the educated colonists were primarily active in religious affairs and that their chief significance lay in this field, but they also were increasingly active in areas outside the church.

Even the most pious began to spread their wings. One of the leaders of the Christian Reformed younger crowd declared: "It seethes and surges in the hearts of the younger generation, while the older generation looks at us with astonishment or with distress. . . . From a poor immigrant group, our people are developing into a strong and self-assertive body that has become sufficiently strong, materially and spiritually, to occupy all kinds of positions in city and state, in trade and industry, in the sciences and in the arts."[168]

It was understood that for that purpose, more knowledge was necessary first of all, and consequently there was a yearning for more and better education even in the most out of the way places. In 1923, as isolated a place as Holland, Nebraska, sent eight students to various colleges and universities.[169] An increasing number of students from Hope and Calvin continued their studies at the University of Michigan in Ann Arbor or elsewhere to graduate and make a living as doctors or lawyers or to serve education or science. In 1920 at Ann Arbor there were no less than seventeen Calvin alumni pursuing their studies. As an indication of their increasingly widening interest, there are six in medicine, three in philosophy, three in economics, and one each in psychology, sociology, literature, zoology, and engineering. It is also interesting that in that same year, nine Calvin alumni were engaged as instructors or assistant professors in eight different departments at the University of Michigan.[170] Dr. Albert Hyma, who has also studied at Leyden, is a professor of history and has the reputation of being a "splendid scholar." Other esteemed professors there are J. Kuiper, O. Bouwsma, G. Van der Lugt and Dr. [John] Muyskens—all Calvin alumni.

Calvin alumni are also found as students and instructors in other parts of the United States. [John] Ramaker teaches at Hartford, [Theodore] Kreps at Yale, and A. Van den Bosch is a professor of history at the University of Kentucky.[171] Dr. J. Van Ek, since 1927 a professor at the University of Colorado, has recently been named as Dean.

Hope College, being that much older, has produced an even larger number of young scholars. Dr. H. Keppel was appointed professor at the University of Florida (where Dr. J. C. Th. Uphof also teaches) and Dr. G. Droppers at the University of Tokyo in Japan. In 1921 Dr. J. E. Winter was appointed as professor of philosophy at the University of West Virginia. Dr. J. Van der Erve as professor of physiology at the State Medical School in Charleston, South Carolina, and Dr. H. Yntema as a lecturer at Columbia University, etc., etc.[172]

Then we must mention with honor Professor B. Vos at the renowned Johns Hopkins University, and L. Ch. Van Noppen—a son of one of the South Carolina colonists—who, for years, held the Queen Wilhelmina chair at Columbia University in New York. He has gathered a cadre of eminent, young, and largely Dutch-American students about him.

More and more graduates of Pella's Central College are attending the State University at Iowa City. Others, particularly from Orange City's Northwestern Classical Academy, go to Grinnell College or to the well-known Agricultural College at Ames, north of Des Moines. In 1912, thirty-five students from Sioux County alone were enrolled at the State University of Iowa; seventeen of them were from Orange City which, at that time, had a population of only 1,500. No other locality in Iowa of similar size sent so many students to Iowa City. The capital, Des Moines, with a population in excess of 100,000 sent only twice as many![173] I have frequently cited the historian J. Van der Zee, who is an associate professor at the University of Iowa. No matter how incomplete this listing, it is apparent that our people have excelled in other areas than that of theology and faith; our people are not of insignificance in the field of scholarship.

It is also evident that our brethren have been of primary importance in the field of pedagogy; a considerable number of them function as principals of elementary and secondary schools. We have already mentioned the presidents of Hope, Central, and Calvin, but there are others who are similarly active outside our own circles. For example, B. H. Kroeze was president of Whitworth College. J. S. Nollen, who had studied at Iowa City, became the head of Lake Forest College and is now president of the very important institute of higher learning, Grinnell College.[174] G. Droppers rose even further; for years he was the president of the University of South Dakota. Dr. [William] Masselink, of Christian Reformed origin, is the head of Ferris Institute in Big Rapids and—as is so common among college and university presidents—is active in the political field.[175]

D. Political Life

1. *Participation of the Dutch in Government*

Here we come to an area in which Netherlanders up to this time have been of much too little influence. As late as 1912, someone who had then already lived among the Netherlanders in America for twenty years described their political influence, at least where they lived among Americans, as "insignificant." They followed one of the two major parties with "servile docility" and "reprehensible submissiveness," while they were usually enlightened very one-sidedly by their Dutch papers. Although the Netherlanders were very well qualified for public office, they were excluded from the "closed circles" of the parties and were kept and remained shut out from almost all influence.[176] In as far as the Christian Reformed were concerned, it was established even six years later that political life among them consisted mainly "in casting their ballot." Even this function, however, could not be fulfilled by all of them, because many of them had not yet taken the trouble to try to become American citizens.[177] As a result, the political influence of our people has remained very meager for decades even in towns like Paterson and Grand Rapids. There is a noticeable change at present, however.

It is obvious that towns like Holland, Zeeland, Pella, etc., almost exclusively or predominantly inhabited by Hollanders, are governed by our countrymen. Thus, in 1920 the following were elected as mayors: of Holland City, Mr. |Evert P.| Stephan, born in Harderwijk in the Netherlands (his predecessor was named |Nicodemus| Bosch); of Zeeland, M. C. Verhage; of Pella, |Henry J.| Van den Berg; etc. At De Pere, Wisconsin, J. Kuypers, a native of Oeffelt in Noord Brabant, was mayor for years. Gradually the Dutch also occupied government offices in towns with a more mixed population. Even in the Far West the necessary ambition has been developing during recent years. As late as 1921, people in Platte, South Dakota, complained that although a few Netherlanders had been placed in government, their number was proportionately insufficient.[178] But at that same time, the most important offices at Prairie View, Kansas, were already filled by fellow countrymen,[179] while in November, 1923, people at Edgerton, Minnesota, were able to rejoice: now the entire city council was Dutch, headed by Dr. H. De Boer as mayor.[180]

The same process of development is noticeable now in the large factory towns and in their surrounding villages. Now that Netherlanders are becoming more and more Americanized, they also demand their share in the local governments. Up to the present, in addition to the real Americans, the Irish and Poles had a great deal of influence, not in the least thanks to their oratorical talent and political inclinations; the former also with thanks to their knowledge of the English language

The great trustworthiness of the Netherlanders explains why, now that they have committed themselves to the slippery path of politics, they have also been able to garner many a non-Dutch vote. More and more it appears that the reliability of the otherwise so stern Dutchman can overcome the glibness of tongue of the most amiable Irish or Polish American. As a result, a Hollander, F. J. Van Noort, could be elected mayor of Paterson in 1919 all the more easily since his Roman Catholic religion was that of the Irish and Poles.[181] And the same holds true for neighboring Prospect Park, where the Hollanders have also been proportionally more numerous. Up to the present time the recently created office of mayor has been filled without a break by a fellow countryman, respectively by A. Struyck, L. Touw, under whom the "borough" grew and prospered, and C. Bosland. In Passaic County, F. W. Van Blarcom, a Hollander, has chaired its board of commissioners for years.[182]

Something similar is noted in Grand Rapids, where the Poles trail the Netherlanders as the most numerous among the non-Americans. The Furniture City has been governed for the last ten years by a city commission that performs mainly the legislative work and sets the main policies of government, and by a more technically educated city manager. In short, the Valley City has a "commission manager government." The mayor who heads the city council is an Old-Dutch American: E. Swarthout. Among the remaining six members are two Young-Dutch Americans: J. D. Karel, president of the commission, and W. Oltman. They reflect quite well, therefore, the population proportions, when one is reminded that one-third of the city is of Dutch descent. However, the powerful man, the city manager, who heads the service, welfare, and safety departments, is no Hollander. His name is F. H. Locke. But one of his immediate subordinates is Dutch: J. Slinke, who heads the safety department, i.e., police, fire department, traffic, etc. Significantly, also Dutch are the municipal tax collector, E. De Vries, who was appointed by the city commission and as city treasurer also heads the finance department, and comptroller R. Doornink, who was directly elected by the citizens. As one can see, money matters in the heterogeneous city of Grand Rapids have been entrusted to the careful, trustworthy Dutchmen!

Among the principal officers are two other Hollanders who also occupy offices of trust: E. De Ruiter who is among the assessors appointed directly by the city commission, and W. Geldersma, sealer of weights and measures, whose duties fall under the safety department.[183] Among the court officials of Grand Rapids are judge [L. D.] Verdier and prosecuting attorney [Stuart] Hoffius. At Kalamazoo, C. Verburg had been mayor since 1920, after having been alderman for years. He died in 1923.

Also in a world metropolis like Chicago our people demand their share of offices. Naturally, Hollanders because of their comparatively small number are less prominent here. However, here also they have some local politicians of prominence. Especially Guy Madderom is their man here. He has had a seat on Chicago's city council for years and is the representative (alderman) from the 9th Ward, a section of the Windy City where many of

GUY MADDEROM

Kandidaat voor herkiezing als Alderman der 9de Ward

Ter eere der Negende Ward is het noodzakelijk dat wij allen, mannen en vrouwen, Dinsdag, den 22sten Februari, naar de stembus gaan en onzen stem uitbrengen op onzen gewaardeerde landgenoot, **Mr. Guy Madderom**, thans Alderman der genoemde Ward.

Mr. Madderom gaf van zijne bekwaamheid en geschiktheid bewijs. Hij staat manmoedig, eerlijk en trouw voor de rechten van het volk. Hij vertegenwoordigt alle gedeelten der Ward, hetzij dichtbij of verre, en is door en door met alle gedeelten der Ward bekend, daar hij sedert zijne kindsche jaren inwoner van dit gedeelte der groote stad was.

Mr. Madderom is alleszins vertrouwbaar, en zal getrouw allen terzijde staan.

Dus Waarde Stamgenoten, stem aanstaanden Dinsdag, den 22sten Februari voor Guy Maddderom en plaats hem terug in den zetel in den Stadsraad.

Election Feb. 22, 1921

Polls Open Erom 6 A. M. to 4 P. M.

Guy Madderom's election campaign advertisement in Chicago's *Onze Toekomst*, February 18, 1921.

GUY MADDEROM

Candidate for Re-election as
Alderman of the Ninth Ward

For the sake of the Ninth Ward it is necessary that we all, men and women, go to the polls on Tuesday, February 22 and cast our vote for our esteemed fellow countryman, Mr. Guy Madderom, presently Alderman of this Ward.

Mr. Madderom gave proof of his ability and fitness. With manly courage, honesty and loyalty he stands for the rights of the people. He represents all areas of the Ward, whether nearby or far away, and is thoroughly acquainted with all parts of the Ward, since he has been a resident of this part of the great city since childhood years.

Mr. Madderom is trustworthy in every way and will stand by the side of everyone faithfully.

**So, fellow countrymen, vote
next Tuesday, February 22, for Guy
Madderom and return him to the seat
in the city council.**

Election Feb. 22, 1921

Polls Open From 6 A.M. to 4 P.M.

English translation of Guy Madderom's election campaign advertisement in Chicago's *Onze Toekomst*, February 18, 1921.

our fellow countrymen live. "Mr. Madderom gave abundant proof of his ability and fitness. He stands up manfully, honestly, and faithfully for the rights of the people. He represents all sections of the Ward, whether nearby or far away, and is thoroughly acquainted with all sections of the Ward, since he has lived in this part of the great city since childhood.... So, Worthy Fellow countrymen, next Tuesday, February 22nd, vote for Guy Madderom and return him to the seat in the City Council." So stated the election appeal in 1921, an appeal that was not in vain.[184]

The Holland Americans do not limit themselves any more, however, to local and district or county politics. Their active participation extends also more and more to state government; they even send their countrymen to the House of Representatives of the Union in Washington, D.C. More than heretofore they get involved with big-time politics; they had already succeeded, as we have seen previously, in sending some of their fellow Dutch Americans to various legislatures, namely in Michigan, Iowa, and Wisconsin.

The more general participation of our people in political life is related to their continuing Americanization and with their increasing economic and cultural development that widens their horizon continually. Americanization is apparent, for example, in an increasing sense of eloquence, a talent or gift that nowhere but in the West is thought of so highly. "The West has never lost its early admiration for oratory, whether from the hustings, the pulpit or the lecture-platform," declares the writer of *The Valley of Democracy*.[185] To become an orator is now also the ideal of our Holland Americans, so that a beginning is being made in the elementary schools of the settlements for the development of this skill. Contests in oratory are being organized in the schools, in which at times, as at Melville, Iowa, the local ministers serve as judges. Similar contests between the schools of a given county are held annually. In 1920, the Sioux County Declamatory Contest was held in Orange City, in which the schools of Boyden, Hospers, Hawarden, Ireton, Orange City, and Sioux Center participated; the silver cup was won by Ireton.[186]

In the high schools eloquence plays an even greater role, naturally, and also in the Christian high schools. With regard to the colleges, one gets the impression that oratory is one of the most important subjects. Every self-respecting college, therefore, has several of its own debating teams, for which the professor of public speaking functions as coach. These teams and coaches are among the most popular among students and professors. They occupy a position that can best be compared with that of the soccer teams and their trainers in the Netherlands.

That young women occupy a prominent place in this field, even at our own denominational colleges, is an interesting phenomenon that should not be surprising. So it happened that in 1920 Miss Tena Holkeboer, now a missionary in China, won first prize as representative of Hope College in a contest in public speaking with an oration, "A Century of Centuries," in which contest all colleges of Michigan participated.[187] A year later, Mr. J.

Stapelkamp and Miss Vera Keppel were oratorical representatives of Hope College. "Certainly a proof that Holland produces great speakers," it was reported—characteristically!—in a news item.[188]

From these details it is clear how important a place eloquence occupies among the otherwise very staid Hollanders; they are already beginning to surpass the Americans in this regard. It is shown still more clearly by the following news item of March 6. 1923, which is also a good example of the typical cultural image at the time: "Hope College students were excited Friday night and residents who were already in the arms of Morpheus were awakened from their sleep by their boisterousness, when the news reached here that Hope had won first place in the oratorical contest at Hillsdale. Hope was in second place in the ladies contest, Miss Nellie Kole won the second prize, and in that of the men Simon C. Heemstra won the first prize. . . . Miss Kole's subject was "The Cross or the Cannon" and Mr. Heemstra's was "The Challenge of the Ideal." Today, Monday, was "Glory Day" for the students of Hope and excitement reigned as if the Jubilee Year had dawned. We congratulate Hope College."[189] It is clear from the chosen topics that these contests do not only promote future pulpit eloquence at these dyed-in-the-wool orthodox colleges, but definitely also promote political acumen. That was the case in a 1922 debate between students of Central College at Pella, and Parsons College at Fairfield, both in Iowa, about the proposition "That the United States should take steps toward granting the Philippines immediate independence."[190] Hope's debating teams in 1926 had both to defend and oppose the proposition: "Resolved that the United States recognize the present government of Russia,"[191] while ultra-orthodox Calvin College at Grand Rapids won a double victory in 1927 with the proposition: "Resolved that this house shall endorse the governmental principles of Mussolini"—thanks to the "fine criticism" and "severe training" by the coach also present.[192]

Should anyone still doubt the political results of an education in public speaking such as this, let him be convinced by the fact that in 1920 Hope students organized a Harding-Coolidge Club and a Cox-Roosevelt Club that publicly defended the Republican and Democratic platforms.[193] And at about that same time, Miss Jessie Hemmes of Hope College delivered in the Knickerbocker Theater of Holland "a fiery address in which she gave ten reasons why she would vote for Republican candidates."[194]

However, the training in public speaking did more. It also stimulated the ambition of the Hollanders and paved the way for them to function as leaders themselves, rather than as my American friend J. H. Hoekstra had expressed it, "to serve others as camp-fighter," and then to be rewarded with at most a postmastership or, as in the case of our aforementioned friend, with a small assessor's job.[195]

In America, it is also desirable for political leaders to have a good education; oratorical ability as an integral part of that education is indeed a first requisite. In this connection, G. Timmer, head of Orange City's frequently

Announcing

Calvin Intercollegiate Debates

at

Calvin College Auditorium

Affirmative: B. Kruithof, C. Veenstra, alternate;
P. Holwerda, C. Van Dyk

Issue: Resolved that this house shall endorse the governmental principles of Mussolini.

Negative: L. J. Ligtenberg, M. Bolt, T. Yff, alternate;
J. Postma

Calvin College vs. Mt. Pleasant
Thursday Evening, Feb. 10, at 8 p. m.

Alma College vs. Calvin College
Friday, Feb. 25

Your presence will be greatly appreciated.

Price 25c
The same ticket will admit to both debates.
On sale at the door.

Advertisement for Calvin Intercollegiate Debates (*The Banner*, Feb. 4, 1927).

mentioned Northwestern Classical Academy even pointed out "that it has been shown by investigation that an 'education' increases one's chance to become a leader of the people 400 times!"[196]

We now have the situation that many an orthodox, even ultra-orthodox, Dutch American dreams of "becoming a leader of the people," thanks also to the special training in public speaking. Not only at Hope but also at Calvin College, there are those who as pre-law students are already preparing themselves to go to one of the larger universities to study law, which is *the most* ideal path for a future statesman. Such a path was followed by the most prominent representatives of Dutch descent in Michigan: by G. J. Diekema as well as by G. W. Kooyers, both alumni of Hope and of Ann Arbor.

We became acquainted with G. J. Diekema earlier as prosecuting attorney and mayor, as bank director and promoter of various industries in his native city, Holland, the city of "Hope." As a member of the Republican Party, Diekema was delegated as state representative year in and year out (1885, 1887, 1889, 1891, and 1892) to the Michigan House of Representatives. In 1889 he even held the chairmanship of this House of Representatives. From 1907 to 1910 he was also the Representative of Michigan in Congress at Washington. Even before that, his importance was recognized by the U. S. government and Diekema was appointed as a member of the Spanish Treaty Claims Commission at Washington. This Commission had to finalize the settlement of various Cuban affairs with Spain. For a number of years he has also been chairman of the Republican State Central Committee, and performed a number of other tasks, such as chairing the Committee on City Corporations, "one of the most important committees of the State Legislature," serving as president of the committee that regulated Michigan's participation in the exhibition at Buffalo in 1900, etc., etc. And all that in spite of a busy career as lawyer and banker; as such he was also president of the Association of Bankers in Michigan. In short, he was the pride of the liberally-minded Dutch Americans. I emphatically say the liberally-minded, because it was the lesser brethren of the same Dutch descent who have seen to it that Diekema did not become still more influential. It has been his own fellow Dutch Americans who have allowed him to go thus far and no farther, because Diekema, although Reformed, was at the same time a friend of the Freemasons, which was a vexation in the eyes of the *kleine luyden* [small or common folk], who were small also for being narrow-minded.[197]

Gerrit W. Kooyers, a descendant from Dutch parents, was born in 1876 in Fillmore Township, Allegan County, Michigan, and attended public schools in Holland, then Hope College, and finally the University of Michigan, from which he graduated in 1899. Since that time he has been occupied in the practice of law, real estate, and insurance in Holland. Here he was elected as supervisor in 1912 and again in 1914, and was also justice of the peace. As a Republican he was a member of the 1915–1916 Michigan legislature and was re-elected in 1916.[198]

A third Hollander in public life was Ate Dykstra. Like Diekema he was of Frisian descent; however, he had been born in the Netherlands and not in America like Diekema and Kooyers. Diekema rose to prominence in the Reformed circles at Holland. Dykstra achieved his leadership among the Christian Reformed in Grand Rapids, after having studied law in Ann Arbor, just like Diekema and Kooyers, although in another manner. In the Netherlands Dykstra had worked on a farm; after his arrival in America in 1890 at age twenty-five, he worked initially in the furniture factories at Grand Rapids. Later, however, he entered the retail business, managed a grocery and dry goods store for twenty-five years, and used part of his free time to study. Just as so many grocery men in America, Dykstra also become highly respected. He was appointed as a member of the board of supervisors of Kent County and held that office for five years. In Grand Rapids itself he served three times as alderman, and in 1910 he was even a candidate for mayor. In 1922 he was elected as a Republican to the legislature of Michigan and was re-elected in 1924 and 1926.[199] Dykstra is among the influential members of the House in Lansing, where he is a member of a number of important committees, among others the Committee on Education and the Committee on Religious Societies. Like Diekema before him, he is even chairman of the all-important Committee on City Corporations.[200]

One cannot escape the impression that among the Dutch element in Michigan, Dykstra begins to come more and more up to the level of Diekema, politically speaking that is, provided he does not become too liberal either. For we already know that Dykstra is an advocate of public education and as such he is skeptical of the private schools of his fellow believers. They are proud of him but at the same time he worries them. Will political disgrace also await him sometime? In any case his service is striking proof of the increasing influence of the True brethren, who support more and more the much older, more educated, and more thriving Reformed folk.

It is striking that both of the most influential representatives, Diekema and Dykstra, are of Frisian descent, which confirms the frequently observed phenomenon that Frisians, who consider themselves to be closely related to the English, can so much more easily adapt to American life than any other branch of the Dutch nation.

In addition, there are still more people of Dutch blood in political life in Michigan, for example, A. H. Bosch, who was born in 1869 in Holland. He attended the public schools, "took a business course," was a teacher for fifteen years, and then went into farming. Later he became—in typically American style!—something like a process-server (notary work and auctioneering) and later on in Jamestown he held a few secretarial jobs. Just like Kooyers, he was elected as a Republican representative in 1915 and re-elected in 1916.[201]

The following is a summary (complete to 1917) of Netherlanders who have served Michigan as state representatives, delegated by Ottawa and

Allegan counties (including "*de Kolonie*") and Kent County (including Grand Rapids): *Ottawa*: J. Roest, Holland, 1871–72; D. B. K. Van Raalte, Holland, 1875, 1877, 1909; C. Van Loo, Zeeland, 1881–83; G. J. Diekema Holland, 1885, 1887, 1891–92; I. Marsilje, Holland, 1895, 1897–98; A. Lahuis, Zeeland, 1907, 1909; G. W. Kooyers, Holland, 1915–16; A. H. Bosch, Hudsonville, 1915–16. *Allegan*: J. W. Garvelink, Graafschap, 1873–74, 1883; J. Kolvoord, Hamilton, 1891–92. *Kent* (Grand Rapids): J. Killean, 1887, 1889; H. B. Van der Cook, 1901, 1903; J. J. Van Zoeren, 1901, 1903; H. Vander Veen, 1907, 1909; L. D. Verdier, 1909, 1911; W. De Boer, 1915; A. Dykstra, 1922, 1924, 1926.

Detroit in Wayne County, a town about which we usually hear very little as a center of fellow countrymen, has (at least when we consider the names) delegated many a Hollander, namely: E. Kanter, 1857; P. Klein, 1869, 1870, 1875; M. V. Borgman, 1881–82; H. Klei, 1881–82; W. E. Molster, 1897–98; H. J. Eikhoff, 1897–1900; J. P. Mas, 1913. In addition, Branch County delegated G. W. Van Aken in 1873–75 and Montcalm County delegated Cornelius De Young in 1909.

The following have been state senators: J. Roest, Holland, 1883; J. Den Herder, Zeeland, 1889; S. Wesselius, Grand Rapids, 1889; J. Nagel, Detroit, 1889; J. W. Garvelink, Graafschap, 1891–93; S. Van Aken, Ida, 1903, 1905; L. Lugers, Holland, 1907; J. Van der Werp, Muskegon, 1911; L. D. Verdier, Grand Rapids, 1913, 1915; and E. Hofma, Grand Haven, 1915. As presidential-electors the following men were chosen: J. Den Herder, 1876; G. G. Steketee, 1884; J. Cappon, 1888; J. A. S. Verdier, 1900; G. T. Haan, 1912; J. Van der Laan, 1912.

In the settlements of Illinois there were a number of local politicians. Only a few of these, however, became state officials. One who deserves to be mentioned was Frederic R. De Young. He was the son of P. De Jong who named South Holland and was its first postmaster. Frederic received his early education at South Holland, and later went to Chicago to study law. He also settled in Chicago as a lawyer and was associated in this capacity with a few others. He had a busy practice. With a great deal of pride his father told me that in 1921 Frederic was then a "$15,000 man"![202] His fellow countrymen in Roseland called him "a brilliant young man"; he was also very well known as a competent Republican party speaker, in the English language as well as in Dutch. The Republicans also elected him in 1914 as representative in the General Assembly of Illinois. Here De Young made himself known as "one of the most valuable as well as the most capable of the first-termers of the Assembly."[203] "As head of the Judiciary Committee he made a particularly efficient record," declared the Legislative Voters' League in 1918 and recommended Frederic for a position as Probate Court judge. De Young sat as a judge for a few years in the Circuit Court of Cook County, until a change in the presidency deprived him of his occupation.[204] De Young is a man of the future.

We have previously heard about the Zeelander P. Daan in Wisconsin, a "self-made man" and a member of the legislature there in 1873. Daan died in 1914. I do not know of a single state politician among the Protestants nor among the many Roman Catholics there. It is somewhat strange, however, that the number of politicians is not greater in Iowa, where so many educated Hollanders have settled and where on the whole there is such great prosperity among our countrymen. At Pella and environs several of them succeeded in winning a township or even a county office; only two have advanced as far as state representatives. These are the Democrat H. Rietveld, who was elected to that office in an off-year election in 1898, to be defeated only a year later, and now his fellow party member and fellow townsman N. Gesman, whose grandparents had arrived in 1847 on the sailing vessel *Nagasaki* and were among Pella's founders.[205]

The younger and more fervent Sioux County made its influence felt in a more energetic way. Henry Hospers has been the representative here several times and later was a two-term state senator. He was highly regarded as a leader also by the non-Hollanders in northwestern Iowa "because he possessed the qualities of integrity, determination and courage." And when he died in 1901, Americans acknowledged that "he was one of the men who deserve foremost places in the history of a great State."

After Hospers, only one other Hollander in Sioux County reached the State House of Representatives: G. Klay of Orange City. Klay, a descendant from affluent farmers, came to Sioux County with his parents in 1883, as will be remembered. At first he engaged in farming, later—we are in America—he went to study law. In 1897 he was admitted to the bar, engaged in local politics, and was elected to the General Assembly in 1908 and again in 1910. In the same year of 1908, N. Balkema of Sioux Center was chosen state senator. Balkema was born in Sheboygan County, Wisconsin, and in 1884 he moved to Sioux County where he made a great deal of money in business.[206]

At present Sioux County has no Dutch representative in Iowa's capital, Des Moines. In the last election (1924) they won numerous county and township offices, as they had done formerly, but for representation in Des Moines they did not even have their "own" candidate.[207] This is a symptomatic occurrence that can be considered favorable only if one wishes to view American politicians, as M. G. Levenbach does, merely as seekers of cushy jobs and patronage.[208]

However, none of the fellow countrymen mentioned thus far are "professional politicians." Nor are those whom I will now mention, such as Cyrenus Cole, a gifted journalist and witty historian, who at present represents the people of Iowa as Congressman in Washington, D.C. This was not due to the "Dutch" but to the "American" voters, because Cole quickly associated with Americans after having studied at Central University. I was privileged to visit Cole's parental home in 1921. It is a simple grocery store in Pella, where his brothers still call themselves Kool [the Dutch word for cabbage and pronounced like cole] and continue to run the business of their father. His writing ability attracted the attention of newspaper people, who gave him a job on a Des Moines daily. Later Cole settled in Cedar Rapids, Linn County, where he edited two papers which he himself published and in which he propagated Republican ideas. The Toledo district, situated west of Cedar Rapids, later delegated him to Washington, D.C. As a reporter of Iowa's happenings, he attracted so much attention that he was chosen by unanimous vote to be a member of the committee on foreign affairs.[209] Although he switched so completely to American life and has such little association with his fellow countrymen that in contrast to Diekema he is known scarcely if at all in Dutch circles in America and is completely unknown at our embassy, yet he does not deny his Dutch ancestry.[210] On the contrary, he speaks of Holland as "one of the oldest and proudest civilizations of Europe," for it was also the native country of his beloved mother whose maiden name was De Booy.[211]

Another "Pella man," G. R. Hagens, also an alumnus of Central, has become a famous politician in the state of Wyoming. In 1921 he was vice-chairman of the Republican party there and the man designated for chairman of the Republican State Committee.[212] In the East, Dow Drukker of Passaic became a representative to Congress. Later he was appointed, among others, as a member of the grand jury in Passaic County. Additional information about this leader I do not have, however.[213]

A number of Hollanders have won for themselves for a longer or shorter time a place in some of the legislatures, whereas others have exhibited their leadership in the executive branch. Just as we have learned about mayors and county officers, so some others have advanced to state governor. "Captain [Samuel Rinnah] Van Sant" has been governor of Minnesota and Frank Steunenberg of Idaho, the state where Wild West conditions have prevailed longer than elsewhere. That is why Idaho is called "A Remnant of the Old Frontier."[214] Steunenberg, who had been considered incorrectly as German-born, became more or less a victim of the old "pioneer spirit."[215] After having been at the head of Idaho's government from 1896 to 1900, he was murdered by a bomb attack in 1905 in front of his home at Caldwell. This was allegedly in revenge for his attitude toward the mine workers during his governorship, when he called out the National Guard against the workers. Not "genuinely American," but indicative of the spirit of the Dutch governor's family, is the report, carried in the papers later, that the widow of the murdered man spent her days reading the Bible, having forgiven the destroyer of her family happiness.[216]

In Michigan, a descendant of the seventeenth-century Dutch colonists, A. Groesbeck, frequently mentioned before, is seemingly a most powerful governor; at any rate, if one can believe A. Dykstra, he runs a real "boss government." Recently the Christian Reformed Dr. Masselink, mentioned earlier, president of Ferris Institute of Big Rapids, was casting an eye on the office of lieutenant-governor, which is additional proof of the growing importance of the True brethren.[217]

Finally I will mention here also "Colonel" Cornelius Gardener, United

FOR PRESIDENT

FOR VICE PRESIDENT

Het Amerikaansche Volk Wacht Met Ongeduld op de Overstelpende Republikeinsche Overwinning in November.

Het volk weet bij jammerlijke onder-vinding, dat ons land verandering noodig heeft van slecht tot goed be-stuur en zijn besloten zonder uitstel dit te bewerken.

Omdat:

Ze dood moe zijn van de schandelij-ke profiteering, hooge prijzen, crimi-neele verkwisting en drukkende be-lasting gedurende de zeven jaren van Democratisch bestuur.

Omdat:

Ze van de Republikeinsche partij verwachten een eind te maken aan die vloek en opnieuw de fabrieken in vollen gang te zien en de boeren in staat stellen beloond te worden voor hun werk en 't Amerikaansche werk-volk vast werk geven en de gebruikers beschermen tegen afzetten.

Omdat:

Zij walgen van de luimen en gevaren van een onbekwaam een-man gouvernement en herstellen een vertegenwoordigd gouvernement volgens de constitutie, van het volk, voor het volk en door het volk met volle toepassing van de constitutie, vrijheid van vrije speech en vrije pers.

Omdat:

Ze sterk tegen vreemde allianties en verbindingen zijn, die onze jonge mannen over de zeven zeeen naar den oorlog zou zenden niet om de Amerikaansche belangen te beschermen doch om het Buitenland te dienen op bevel van gouvernemen-ten van vreemde potentaten.

Omdat:

Amerika moet zijn als van ouds, vrij, vooruit strevend, welvarend, gelukkig, vrede in huis en recht, sterk en milda-dig tegenover andere landen.

De Amerikaansche stem-mers, vrouwen zoowel als mannen weten wat te doen. Ze zijn verlangend hun heilig-ste plicht te doen als burgers uit 't buitenland herkomstig en hun stem werpen met de verzekering dat hun wil zal zegevieren.

Victorie staat geschreven in de sterren. Wij gevoelen het rondom ons. Het is in de lucht, die we inademen. Het is zoo zeker als de Drieeen-heid.

Republican National Committee.

An election advertisement in *De Telegraaf* of Paterson, New Jersey, October 13, 1920.

FOR PRESIDENT

Warren G. Harding

FOR VICE PRESIDENT

Calvin Coolidge

The American People Wait Impatiently for the Overwhelming Republican Victory in November

People know as a result of sad experience, that our country needs a change from bad to good government and are determined to accomplish this without delay.

Because:

They are dead-tired of the shameless profiteering, high prices, criminal waste and oppressive taxation during the seven years of Democratic government.

Because:

They expect the Republican Party to put an end to that curse and see the factories operating full-time again and farmers rewarded for their work and the American laboring class fully employed and consumers protected against being fleeced.

Because:

They loathe the moods and dangers of an incompetent one-man government and want to restore a representative government according to the constitution of the people, for the people, and by the people, with a full application of freedom of speech and freedom of the press.

Because:

They strongly oppose foreign alliances and agreements that would send out young men across the seven seas to wage war, not to protect American interests but to serve foreign powers at the command of governments of foreign countries.

Because:

America must be as of old — free, progressive, prosperous, happy, with peace and justice at home, strong and generous toward other countries.

The American voters, women as well as men, know what to do. They desire to perform their most sacred duty as citizens with foreign backgrounds and to cast their vote with the assurance that their desires will triumph.

Victory is written in the stars. We feel it all around us. It is in the air which we breathe. It is as sure as the Trinity.

Republican National Committee.

English translation of an election advertisement in *De Telegraaf* of Paterson, New Jersey, October 13, 1920.

States Army, who had distingushed himself in the Spanish-American War, and who as governor of Tayabas, Luzon, in the Philippines, had attracted a great deal of attention for "having made the first true report of atrocities in the Philippines."[218] He was a son of the Zeeland minister W. Gardener of Kalamazoo, a former student of H. P. Scholte, and who died in 1855.[219]

In view of the above facts, one cannot deny that the Dutch element gradually exercises an increasing influence. And they work especially in favor of the Republican party, the party indeed that almost all of these leaders served, with the exception of Rietveld, Gesman, and Steunenberg. As A. Siegfried remarked, "*L'armée républicaine se recrute pour des raisons d'intérêt, mais aussi de race et de sentiment national*" [The Republican army is recruited for the sake of interests, but also in the interest of race and national sentiment]. Siegfried continued by saying that the Anglo-Saxon and Nordic elements of the population generally make up the essence (*le fond*) of it.[220] Our fellow Dutch prove this "rule," with still one well-known exception, that of Pella. Most of the immigrants of the 1880s also later joined the predominantly Protestant Republicans, whether as J. H. Hoekstra did, "with well-considered reasons," or in imitation of others.

Party membership among the Netherlanders has been indicated even more clearly by election results than by the chosen leaders listed previously. In addition, it should be noticed that there has been little or no change in these party attitudes over the years. If anywhere strong political traditions are upheld in American party life, it is also the case among the Dutch Americans (as stated before), even though more and more the two major parties—also according to Dr. M. C. Van Mourik Broekman—are coming closer together in actual politics.[221]

Here follow some statistics for the presidential election in 1920 in the various settlements, respectively:[222]

	Harding (R)	Cox (D)
Ottawa County, Mich.	10,566	2,396
Holland City, Mich.	3,144	644
Grand Haven, Mich.	1,729	478
Zeeland City, Mich.	556	120
Orange City, Iowa	609	75
Holland Township, Iowa	228	29
Nassau Township, Iowa	407	228
Welcome Township, Iowa	175	1

With regard to the Hollanders in the East, it is reported that there also Republicans dominate and that, for example, in Prospect Park there were 7 votes cast for Cox and 20 for Harding. Still more numerous are the Republicans among the Hollanders in the Dutch suburb of Clifton, where 667 voted Republican and only 5 Democratic. Especially the administration of Wilson had caused much antagonism here.[223]

That Pella and environs have remained predominantly Democratic became clear to me in the election of various representatives and officials in

1922. The results of the election, which was held at Pella for that town and Lake Prairie Township, indicated the ruling power of the Democrats. Their candidates for the office of U. S. Senator, representative for Congress, governor, and secretary of state received in Pella a majority of 313, 614, 191, and 199 votes respectively; the candidate for state representative even had a majority of 897 votes.[224] With the exception of the last candidate, N. Gesman,* who we already know was a "Netherlander" and resident of Pella, which circumstance influenced the number of votes, none of the offices mentioned was won by Democrats, because in the meantime Iowa, in the midst of "the whirligig of politics"—see also Cole[225]—had become predominantly Republican. Even in Marion County the Republican candidates won a majority for the county offices. Therefore it is all the more remarkable and certainly an evidence of tenacity that in almost entirely Dutch Pella and environs, "naturally"—so it is reported—"all the Democratic candidates [are] elected, although it is very interesting this time, because the Republicans also had candidates for all of the positions, except for assessor."[226]

That people everywhere are not equally party-bound and that national origin as well as religion can be of influence is shown in several election results. The Pella people, as we noted before, voted against their "compatriot" [Theodore] Roosevelt, because they were Democrats and he was a Republican. Probably it came about also because Roosevelt was very progressive and belonged to the "most progressive Republicans." In contrast, predominantly Republican Sioux County, starting in 1891, elected for twelve consecutive years the same Democratic sheriff—because the candidate was a Hollander.[227] In predominantly Republican Ottawa County, Michigan, Republicans were also elected for all offices in 1922, with one exception. Evidently for the same reason as in Sioux County, people elected a Democrat for sheriff, F. H. Kamferbeek, the first Democratic sheriff in the past forty-six years.[228] His Republican opponent was an American, while Kamferbeek was strongly orthodox, being Christian Reformed. And when in the last election he had an equally orthodox Dutch Republican as an opponent, the editor of *The Banner*, although himself a Republican, saw fit to promote both candidates and thus blunted all political considerations.[229] Therefore in this case religion influenced the political attitude.

With how little seriousness politics are sometimes regarded and to what degree the candidate's choice of party is determined by "the soft job," we learn from the history of a postmastership in South Holland, Illinois. The second presidency of [Grover] Cleveland forced P. De Jong to surrender his job and R. A. Gouwens became his successor. But when the Democrat Cleveland was succeeded by the Republican [William] McKinley and then by Roosevelt, the South Holland Democratic postmaster also had to be replaced by a Republican, just as everywhere else in the United States. The

---

*As far as I know, Gesman, after Rietveld, who only substituted, is the first Hollander to represent Pella and environs in Iowa's House of Representatives [Van Hinte].

farmer, C. Dalenberg, a Republican, took over the office. However, since he lived a mile from the village, he had the duties performed by the Democrat R. A. Gouwens, whom he had appointed as his "assistant." The gentlemen shared the booty! Finally, however, the government put an end to "this exceptional arrangement" and appointed Gouwens to be postmaster because Dalenberg was willing to assume the benefits but not the duties of the office.[230]

In contrast to this lack of seriousness there is "the holy fire" with which many Dutch women went to the polls when they had received the right to vote in 1920 through the 19th amendment of the Constitution. It is true that initially people in ecclesiastical circles were against this right and we noticed that the orthodox folk gave up their Biblical objections only when this appeared to be necessary for the sake of their private schools. But in Reformed circles, as everywhere else among the Protestants in America, people had already given up their opposition out of fear of the Catholic threat. Roman Catholic women were urged to vote, so we had to do the same. "Otherwise we will soon be ruled by Rome," were more or less the terms in which *De Volksvriend* in Sioux Center put it, which warning many took to heart.[231] The women voters even gathered in the courthouse to determine jointly their position. Octogenarians among them such as Mrs. [Grietje] Van den Bosch, Mrs. [?] Aalberts, Mrs. H. J. Van der Waa, etc. cast their votes.[232] In a number of other towns women also voted heavily. In Pella even the 95-year-old Mrs. [H.] Nyenesch voted.[233] Just as formerly, by way of spokesman [Cornelis] Van Loo in Zeeland, Michigan, the old suspicion against the Roman Catholics by our Reformed folk was expressed anew in this election.

That the number of votes cast by the women nevertheless was still far less than the ones cast by the men is understandable. In the year 1920, as mentioned before, 503 men but only 153 women voted in Holland Township. In Holland Township of Sioux County, Iowa, the figures were then, respectively, 188 and 70, and in Orange City 515 and 117.[234] Let it not be forgotten that at that time the Christian Reformed folk still directed their Biblical quotations mainly against women suffrage and only recently selected new quotations from this rich source in behalf of that same voting right.

That election campaign days in a number of towns take place just as boisterously as in the 1860s indicates how little change has occurred in the character of the American people in spite of the millions of immigrants. On the other hand, our people are still as skeptical as previously about all that noisiness. At Edgerton, Minnesota, "a genuine street carnival" was staged in honor of the election of 1920, and two airplanes, a ferris wheel, races, a parade, etc., were necessary to attract people to come to listen to the speech of the Republican candidate. Two bands from elsewhere added to the festive mood. The Dutch band had declined the "honor." To the aggravation of the Hollanders there was a public dance in the evening on a platform on the main street. The greatest vexation for our compatriots, however, was the fact that in the morning a minister had opened the "whole caboodle" with a prayer![235]

Regardless of how influential Hollanders may already have been here and there in the so rambunctious campaign days, the American element still predominated, even when numerically, as we have noted in Pella, it was in the minority. For the rest, the days of passive attitudes on the part of the Hollanders seem to be over. With steadily increasing success, they demand their share in the distribution of the various offices; more and more they are coming out with their own candidates. Indeed, they are at present considering the organization of a new American party, a Christian party.

2. "Third" Parties and Social Issues

There have been numerous "third" parties in the course of the nine-teenth century. They seldom seem to have been viable in the long run, however, because their programs, as far as the essentials were concerned, were often taken over by either the Democrat or Republican party, no matter how much the latter lost their individual character in the process. These parties have now become so colorless that one can no longer com-pare them anymore with our [Dutch] political groups, according to Sieg-fried, since they include so many elements.[236]

Hollanders had also joined these different parties. We should be re-minded of the movement among the farmers in the West in the 1870s, when especially in Sioux County many a colonist joined the Grangers. Later, around 1880 in that same West, the Greenback movement arose, which favored the increased issuance of paper money, after whose green color this effort was named. Still later, about 1898, the Populist move-ment sprang up, which revived old grievances, especially against the land speculation of the railroads, by which many a Hollander had also been duped. Then still later, in 1912, Roosevelt organized the "Progressive Party," which this time did not originate in the West, which was the usual seat of political unrest, but nevertheless it attracted the most ad-herents there—at least relatively speaking. This new party, which strove for a genuine government by the people, for social and industrial justice, and for a limitation of the power of the trusts, etc., "was not the least heartily welcomed by many Hollanders in this country," according to [Alb.] Oosterheerdt.[237] Yet it definitely found much support again among the colonists in the West, especially in Sioux County, where the Nether-landers had previously belonged to the "progressive wing" of the Repub-lican party.[238] In 1916 the progressives were once more included in this party, until in the crises years around 1920 a new party of dissatisfied people was organized once more in the West, namely the Non-partisan League. Numerous Dutch farmers joined this party. Indeed, in the perennially progressive state of Wisconsin numerous Hollanders were even delegates of the "non-partisans."[239]

Not a single one of these third parties, however, could find favor in the eyes of the most strictly orthodox, especially the orthodox ministers. How old Mr. [Seine] Bolks had already previously thundered against the Grangers! They also spoke vehemently, particularly in Grand Rapids, against the Progressive Party—the party of their fellow countryman—because it was rooted in revolutionary principles and invoked the sovereignty of the people.[240] Also because of similar considerations the orthodox wanted to have nothing to do with the Non-partisan League, especially since the League paid no attention to the Sabbath. Therefore, a great deal of indignation prevailed among the Hollanders at C[r]ookston in Minnesota when [A. C.] Townley, president of the League, landed in an airplane on a Sunday to address the populace. "We Hollanders cannot support such a party of Sabbath-desecrators," an orthodox brother wrote to De Grondwet,[241] when he had recovered from his initial fright.

We now see the orthodox people themselves busy organizing a "third" party! Indeed, the two main parties, which Levenbach compared to strong drums that were "naturally empty but could be filled with anything and everything," have become so colorless, due to continual additional "mixing," that any so-called Christian tints can scarcely be detected anymore.[242] It must also be said that from the very beginning attempts were made to keep religion out of politics.

It is clear that a similar lack of color and character must displease the principled Dutch believers, who have such strong characters. Just as in the Netherlands they wish to make religion itself the origin of all politics. Now they bring the antithesis* to America in the form of the Christian school.

The first efforts to this end date back many years, when the orthodox people in Grand Rapids organized the society "Fas et Jus." The leaders, who in the Netherlands had belonged to the Antirevolutionary political party, attempted to make propaganda for their principles by means of meetings and through their paper, De Calvinist. They were the ones who especially opposed the Progressives. Except for that, "Fas et Jus," according to B. K. Kuiper, "has never been able to develop sufficient strength to take a somewhat important part in a political campaign under its own banner."[243] The society ceased to exist during the [First] World War. A second effort, also in Grand Rapids, which led to the organization of the Christian Civic Association, had no success, and neither did a third organization.

It looked as if the Calvinists in Chicago would have more success. In the fall of 1920, a "lively action" was waged there for the organization of a

---

*Antithesis is the Reformed theological tenet of the absolute distinction between Christians and non-(anti-) Christians, derived from Genesis 3:15. The Dutch Calvinist followers of Abraham Kuyper especially stressed the sharp philosophical and societal division between Christians and non-Christians.

Christian party. The Hollanders formed the center of this activity, in which, however, also German, American, and Bohemian churches cooperated. They drafted a "program of principles" that acknowledged "the sovereignty of Almighty God in every realm of life," and accepted without reserve the Word of God "as revealing the Christian principles for our political, societal-pedagogical, and public-moral life." The program further declared that by "supporting our democratic form of government, we would oppose all auto-cratic interference and anarchistic agitation."[244]

Of late we do not hear about this "party" anymore unless we identify it with the "Fifth Congressional Christian Political Organization," which in December, 1920, chose a number of Hollanders as board members but afterward shrouded themselves in secrecy.[245] So we can only subscribe to the conviction that the Holland American H. J. Van Andel harbors: "If we may trust the rumors in the papers first, and the lack of rumors later, we must conclude that also this movement has not had the success expected."[246]

The Hollanders began to realize that even though they took the initiative, it was still not their privilege to lead. America would have none of that "because we were too hurried, too unsympathetic, too particularistic, too foreign. Let us acknowledge that we have been too Dutch and too Christian Reformed." Notice again the self-criticism so typical of these Calvinists. Not entirely correct, however, as I see it, is Van Andel's conviction that, "We did not fail because of America, but we failed because of ourselves." Similar experiences of so many other parties, some of which were thoroughly American in character prove that at least a part of the failure is definitely chargeable to America. Think of the Progressive Party of the most idealistic American [Theodore] Roosevelt.

Since 1922 the Hollanders in Grand Rapids have ranged themselves quite willingly under the leadership of the Young Men's Christian Association. The members of the various church denominations formed a joint fraternal organization, the Protestant Laymen's Union, to which each delegated two members. The ministers Beets and [F.] Stuart promoted this organization among their people. This time they did not proceed in a Dutch manner, but as Van Andel desired, they followed the "American historical development," seemingly with as little success.[247]

But our Calvinists would not have been Dutch Calvinists if they had stopped there. Since 1925, the Honorable Ate Dykstra, the well-known rep-resentative, urged the organization of the militant believers: "We as Chris-tian People in Grand Rapids are not using our influence for good as we should, and if united, are able to do."[248] A Christian political party is thus essential "to look after law-enforcement and matters of similar character." The liberally-thinking Beets was also convinced that the time had arrived "to line up our people in a Christian party." If well organized, the Calvinists in Michigan would wield the "balance of power" between the two major political parties, Beets had already declared for many years. An American

A. Kuyper* is necessary "to lead us like a Moses out of present conditions." Well, this Kuyper is there already—A. Dykstra?—but followers are still lacking. Beets therefore challenged them in his weekly, *The Banner*, that "we need a *Christian political party*. . . . United we stand and *do* something. Divided, politicians 'do' us."† Thus we see in this regard that a great task still lies ahead for the Dutch Calvinists.

Although the Hollanders still belong predominantly to the Republican party, and only a minority belong to the Democratic party, there are also those, though not many, who consider themselves to belong to another group, the Socialists, who have never really taken root in America. Socialism does not thrive in America. The possibilities that are offered to everyone in this country, the relatively high wages and standard of living among the actual American workers have not been able, up to the present time, to generate any class consciousness and consequently any class struggle. The most poorly paid work is done by the millions of immigrants who often were worse off in Europe and therefore are hardly conscious of their misery. Should they wish to organize, it would be difficult because of the different languages of these immigrant laborers. In the same factory there are sometimes thirty to forty different languages being spoken!

As a result socialism only became somewhat more effective after about 1890 when America became more and more industrialized and the farming West became increasingly dependent upon the industrial East. More remarkably, "the new doctrine" received the greatest following among the small farmers in the West, namely in German Milwaukee and in German and Dutch Sheboygan, both in Wisconsin. Sheboygan even got a socialistic city government. Previously, we already became acquainted with the West, espe-

---

*Abraham Kuyper (1837–1920) Dutch Reformed theologian, editor of the Anti-revolutionary daily, *De Standaard*, which he had founded. Representative in the Dutch Lower House (*Tweede Kamer*), Professor at the Vrije Universiteit that was founded in 1880 in Amsterdam through his initiative, Prime Minister and Minister of the Interior from 1901 to 1905, subsequently also a member of the Upper House (Eerste Kamer), he was known as "Abraham the Mighty." The Anti-revolutionary party was the first formally organized political party in the Netherlands. Although Kuyper was sympathetic to modernism at first, he was essentially a conservative (a proponent of a corporative structure of society, of a conscious cult of the national myth, of a strong and independent royalty, of war as a national stimulus, of special regulations for the political and social position of the Jews). His leadership of orthodoxy led to the Secession of 1886. Still he saw the need for adaptation to modern circumstances. He promoted the doctrine of common grace to help the Reformed, especially the "common people" ("kleine luyden"), to break out of their spiritual and social isolation. He abhorred the secularization of Europe's scientific thinking. His idea of "antithesis," i.e., that all Christians should cooperate against the godless forces in politics, enabled him to form the "Coalition" of 1888 with the Roman Catholics which made possible the formation of a great many cabinet ministries. The anti-strike laws (the "throttling laws") that he initiated in 1903 after the first general railroad strike lost him his popularity as a democratic leader. This loss of power was also due to the lagging of social reforms that he had always propagated, but that for various reasons beyond his control did not materialize. After 1905 he gradually faded into the background.

†One cannot escape the impression that Beets, however, preferred to have a separate Christian party because cooperation with others could lead to a "watering down." However, Van Andel and other outspoken "progressive Calvinists" regarded this cooperation as a primary necessity for success [Van Hinte].

cially the Farther West—the Dakotas and neighboring territories—as the center of political unrest, as the birthplace of so many an "ism."[249] It was not until 1920 that socialism seemed to be a "power" for the first time, when the talented E[ugene] V. Debs, the socialist candidate for the presidency for the fifth time, received 900,000 votes. But that was also its high point, because the party itself was at that time very divided due to the influence of the World War. The Socialist Labor Party had already separated itself from the Socialist Party. Thus in the same year of 1920 the city of Sheboygan, among others, "flip-flopped" and went back to the Republicans.[250]

The two major parties had indeed followed the old tactic and taken over "some of the strongest planks of the Debs party": the eight-hour workday as well as the five and a half day workweek, women suffrage as well as the abolishment of child labor, etc. As a result, socialism lost its reason for existence for many people.

How did our fellow Dutch feel and still feel about this socialism? "Official" orthodoxy was initially totally opposed, since it opposed all progressive parties. As late as 1912 the Synod of the Christian Reformed Church declared itself against socialism and it allowed no adherents among its believers, since socialists were considered to be underminers of public authority.[251] In the settlements, socialists were therefore poorly represented. In the Dutch neighborhood of Clifton, near Paterson, there was in 1920 only one socialist among the 773 registered voters; among the 4,500 registered male and female voters in Holland, Michigan, there were only 47![252] There were probably more in progressive Sheboygan and environs, but I do not have any figures.

That socialists are barely tolerated by the believers we have already seen in Paterson. The Dutch have been earning high wages in recent years, at least high in comparison to the wages of other immigrants in Grand Rapids and even, as I was assured recently, in comparison to wages paid to Americans.[253] Thus they are too well-off to associate themselves with the socialists even though they do not belong to orthodox groups. They consider themselves to be much too fortunate even to consider such a step. So, for example, [C. J.] Van de Plasse, originally from Ierseke, who worked at an automobile factory in the Furniture City said: "Furthermore I have a fine job, I tell you, I go to the factory in the morning well dressed, I wear the grey suit, and I work all day in it, and in the evening I am as clean as in the morning and I am no more tired than in the morning."[254] A mentality like that obviously does not breed socialism.

The same must be said regarding the small bosses and their wives. The cousin of P. Bleeker-Vos would be called a "common carpenter" in Holland, so this immigrant wrote from her new residence in Chicago to her former mistress in Amsterdam in the Netherlands. "But here it is different. The working class is respected here, especially skilled tradesmen, and their work is well paid; my cousin has his own home with a garage, a deluxe car, two beautiful rooms, three bedrooms, one bathroom, one kitchen, one pantry with ice-box and cellar . . . and then they have food and drink as not one working man in Holland has. Therefore, Madam, believe me that I will get used to it here, since everybody is as well-off. The little silk dresses are so beautiful here and something from Hirsch for $15, $18, and $20 is wonderful . . . and that alone makes life very pleasant."[255]

It need not come as a surprise that people who in the Netherlands and elsewhere in Europe had been the most ardent adherents of socialism have no time and no interest left for it once they have established themselves in America. "*Und von einer irgend in die Tiefe gehenden sozialistischen Bewegung ist heute gar keine Rede*" |Today there is not the slightest inkling of any solid socialistic movement|, states A. Feiler. We now understand why. We have in the Dutch industrial colonies the confirmation of the declaration that a labor leader made to Feiler: "Our laborers are not permanent beggars," as in Europe.[256] Therefore, the disappointment of the random genuine idealist from among our "Reds" has been particularly bitter in America. He had witnessed and even participated in the struggle in our country and firmly believed he should "propagandize" the "new idea" in America. Even former friends who had come over to America with him largely deserted him in the new country.

We must include G. Elferink among these "idealists."[257] It was under |G.| Bennink that he had participated in the struggle in Twente. However, he had been born in Lonneker |Overijsel| and later took refuge in "Holland," and from there he went to America where friends in Rochester provided shelter for him. Since that time Elferink has remained in that city, and there he found former sympathizers among the many Frisians, especially followers of |R.| Van Zinderen Bakker, whose sayings were still frequently quoted in America, particularly by one of these Frisians, old Mister K. Velsing, who had participated in the socialist movement in Friesland and had even listened to the first sermon of |Ferdinand| Domela Nieuwenhuis.*[258] Elferink organized a Socialist society at Rochester that on the whole only caused him disappointment and soon ceased to exist. People were too well off materially here in America: "the people are better fed here" but spiritually they are "covered with mold" |*onder de schimmel*|. A Rochester benevolent society, called the "Domela Nieuwenhuis Club," did not have a long existence either, even though it had some initial success.

---

*Ferdinand Domela Nieuwenhuis (1846–1919), a Dutch politician, started as a Lutheran minister at Harlingen in 1870. He left the church in 1879 and dedicated himself entirely to socialism. He edited *Recht voor Allen* |Justice for All| from 1879 to 1897 and was prosecuted for least-majesty (insulting the monarchy) because of an article—not of his hand—in 1886. Condemned to a year of prison he served seven months. He founded several political action organizations and was a member of the Lower House (*Tweede Kamer*) from 1881 to 1891. This turned out to be a fiasco since Domela Nieuwenhuis was a fiery apostle but no politician. He was not tactical, a muddled thinker, a rambling speaker, and poor debater. After 1891, more and more disillusioned, he broke with his own party and paper. He founded *De Vrije Socialist* |The Free Socialist| in which he advocated anarchism but lost more and more of his followers. Only during the 1903 railroad strike and the summer riots of 1918 in Amsterdam did he briefly reappear in print.

It seemed that the socialist movement among the Dutch in the West would become more important, at least in the factory towns. When strikes broke out in 1894 as a result of the shameful wage reductions at the Pullman factories near Chicago (read G. Myers),[259] Netherlanders, even though a small number, also fought in the front ranks among the strikers. However, it appeared as if socialism was headed for a permanent stay among our people in the centers of Holland and Grand Rapids. In Holland, Michigan, Dutch "party" members in 1908 even published their own weekly organ, De Volksstem [The Voice of the People]. But it had only a brief success, as did a later effort to publish a biweekly paper, the Voorwaarts [Forwards] in 1914.[260] A federation of Dutch socialists in America never actually materialized; True brethren were lacking. There were not even enough leaders to be found, no matter how "educated" a few might have been, because, as Elferink expressed himself sadly, many who had taken part in the struggle in Europe remained entirely aloof in America. They were now owners of their own homes, were they not?

N. A. De Vries had similar experiences during his trip through America in 1923, when he accused "good Dutch socialistic veterans" of having lost their ideals. "Leaning backward in a plush armchair, they point to their possessions ... a fine home, a car, the opportunity to see something of the world, to be able to bring up their children better. That is what we have always suffered and fought for, isn't it?"[261]

That is the way it happened also in the case of the German and other party members. And what was the end result? "In America, the country of the most highly developed industrial and financial capitalism, there is to-day practically no socialism that carries any weight."*[262]

That Debs as a candidate for the presidency in 1920 received almost a million votes does not detract from these conclusions. These votes were not cast primarily for Debs as a Socialist, but for Debs himself. From the beginning Debs had opposed the war with Germany and by his strong character and attitude he had won the respect of even his most fierce opponents: the Dutch orthodox folk. "There is no question but what this reformer's motives were pure and his ideals very high. . . . we ought to pay him our tribute of respect," wrote Reverend E. J. Tanis in The Banner. This rigid minister even extended his appreciation to the entire party movement. He acknowledged that a number of social reforms, which have now been introduced in various states of the Union, were first expressed in Socialist party planks. These Socialist contenders however, are too one-sided, too materialistic, and too neglectful of the spiritual well-being of humanity, Tanis believed.[263] Apart from that, socialism does have a reason for existence—note well, it is one of our orthodox people who said this—because "it represents a protest against existing evils."

*"Es gibt in Amerika, dem Lande des höchst gesteigerten Industrie- und Finanzkapitalismus, heute keinen praktisch irgendwie ins Gewicht fallenden Sozialismus"

These expressions are of the greatest importance for us. They indicate that broader insights are breaking through among the orthodox, and that here also the "social conscience" speaks. Years before, the gifted minister J. Groen, born in Vriesland, Michigan, under the influence of the works of Kuyper and [H.] Bavinck, had tried to arouse the interest of his people in political issues in general and in social-political ones in particular. He participated in the founding of a Christian political party and attempted to cooperate with other church groups to that end. He also attempted to spread milder opinions among the True brothers concerning labor unions, prohibition, and women suffrage. Although he was viewed with some suspicion by many of his fellow ministers—it seems that they kept him from being on the Board of Calvin College and Seminary, Groen's opinions gained acceptance more and more as a result of increasing education and Americanization.[264]

Professor L. Berkhof even made a special study, *The Church and Social Problems*, and pointed out that the church in addition to its spiritual task had secondarily to perform a special task; it must cooperate in the "moral uplift of social life," but without overdoing it as in the case of other churches. The Bible, which was also a mighty weapon in the hands of the progressives among the True brothers, points in numerous places to the social task of the church. As Berkhof remarked as a good Calvinist, "social injustice, social sins, social misery may find no fertile soil, no congenial atmosphere in her midst." Lay organizations of a positive Christian character, of course, are most desirable for improving wrongs.[265]

The question of voting rights for women indicated how slowly but surely opinions about social-political issues were influenced by men like Groen, et al, and by the times and circumstances. This is also true of the labor issues. Originally the Christian Reformed Church opposed the labor movement very vehemently and (for example in 1881) warned earnestly against joining labor unions, which "are usually un-Christian." The Order of the Knights of Labor was definitely condemned (1886) and all members were warned by the Synod to avoid these and other orders, and factory supervisors were advised "to warn against them with sympathetic earnestness."

The Synod of 1904 still dared to speak of "degenerate Unions" in addition to "tolerable neutral Unions." Membership in the former was not condoned, but the Synod had not dared to go further,[266] because it was already convinced then, just as was Reverend R. B. Kuiper later, that it must establish as few rules as possible, especially with reference to issues about which the Bible does not speak or does not speak fully enough.[267]

Meanwhile the position of the True brethren has become much more liberal, especially after they had studied the position of their fellow believers in the Netherlands. The majority is now convinced that "every Christian must be entitled to work freely together with his neighbors in every lawful area of society, and that as a member of society he has the perfect right to participate in such mutual endeavor or that he may unite with others in that kind of organization." At least this was the judgment of the Synod of 1926, although a final statement was delayed until 1928. Meanwhile, Representative Ate Dykstra called people's attention to the favorable side of unions and Beets brought this point of view into a wider circle. All of this pointed to a continuing change for the better in Christian Reformed circles.[268]

All the many efforts that have been made since 1892 to organize a Christian labor union in Grand Rapids, to establish a "Patrimonium," have after original successes failed in spite of abundant good advice such as by the Synods of 1904 and 1916.[269] A Christian Laborers Society, which in 1918 formed a sort of evening school, and studied the political and social principles of Calvinism, I have not seen mentioned since. Neither have I seen further mention being made of the Christian Labor Union that was organized in 1918 at Grand Rapids "to fight Socialism, Bolshevism, in fact, all revolutionary ideas wherever they confront and attack us."[270]

Much simpler was another issue that had kept the minds busy for years, that of prohibition. Dutch settlers in the main have never been averse to the use of strong drink and least of all the orthodox among them, as is also the case in the Netherlands. A stiff swig was imbibed since the pioneer years, especially in the East, although people in the West were not opposed to it either. And that is the way it has remained. Nevertheless, it is noticeable that in contrast to the East, the West in this regard is gradually becoming more moderate. This runs completely parallel with the East (New York and New Jersey) remaining wet and the Midwest becoming in the main steadily "drier".[271]

Years before universal prohibition, many compatriots in Michigan were members of the "Prohibition Party" and even published their own organ. Saloons were not found in Zeeland or in Holland, but they were heavily frequented by our fellow Dutchmen in Paterson, New Jersey, and Rochester, New York.

It is interesting in this connection to study the advertisements in festival programs of the Dutch immigrants. A similar program of a "Dutch Festival" held in 1910 at Newark, N.J., was teeming with gin advertisements. "Hulstkamp Genever" seemed to be the greatest recommendation for every hotel, cafe and restaurant: "*Vraagt een Hulstkamp borrel*" [Ask for a Hulstkamp drink] is the way it was said in a recommendation of "Hotel en Café the American." A Hulstkamp ad even covered a whole page![272] In contrast, in a festival program in the year 1914 of the Roseland division of the Algemeen Nederlandsch Verbond, I came across only one such advertisement, namely by Peter Martens, in whose place of business "Genuine Holland Gin and Brandy" was sold. Instead of a whole Hulstkamp page, I found here a full-page advertisement of Jansma Brothers "Manufacturers of High Grade Biscuits, Chicago, Ill."[273]

The correctness of the conclusions I had drawn from this study of advertisements was proven to me by the well-known Frisian Sjouke De Zee. He stated that on his trip in 1920 the Frisians in the West favored Prohibition much more than Frisians in the East. In fact, in Paterson there were many violent opponents of this law among the Frisians and also in Rochester there were many who would have nothing to do with it.[274]

The well-known prohibitionist N. A. De Vries declared that in America the fight against liquor is the main social concern of the churches and of church people.[275] As far as our Calvinists are concerned, this is only partly true. We should be reminded of the minister P. Zonne, who aggravated many people by selling whiskey himself in his store! It is true that there were among the spiritual leaders of our believers those who favored moderation. Still it is significant that it was reported as something unusual when the Christian Reformed minister, J. Groen, in the beginning of his career when he served for nine years at Zeeland, Michigan, *openly* defended moderation in the use of strong drinks. More significant still is the remark that "through his [Groen's] experience in the congregation he soon became a confirmed abstainer and a leader in the fight for local prohibition."[276] We have already seen the final result. Now it was well recognized that Groen rated as a white crow among his people, as an extraordinary person, as a progressive man who was spied upon with utmost suspicion.

As for the East, the moderate people were found especially among the socialists, although there were also some "wets" among them. The socialist Elferink attempted in Rochester to limit the abuse of strong drink, but his organizing efforts failed.[277] Originally, in the mostly liberal Frisian society, "Ny Fryslân," in that town a stiff drink was also imbibed, according to Sjouke De Zee. The arrival of the [?] Van Apledoorn family from Winsum in Friesland, however, brought about a change. The three sons, Jan, Maarten and Hein, had come to Rochester with genuine blue-ribbon convictions. And they changed the situation for the better. Prohibition did the rest.[278]

It was the federal prohibition law that first provided our leaders in the United States with a firm direction. Now all opposed the consumption of strong drink in the United States, not however because they were convinced that alcohol presented a danger—"No Calvinist will say that it is a sin to drink wine," Reverend E. J. Tanis admitted recently[279]—but because the federal constitution forbade it. Obedience to the law is the first duty of all Calvinists, provided this law does not conflict with religion. For the rest I have been able to ascertain personally that, when it comes to evading the prohibition law, the Dutch are in no way less adept than the Americans and other nationalities.

It would carry me too far afield to relate where the Dutch stand with regard to other important issues, movements, etc. Let me simply add that they will have nothing to do with the so-called nationalistic, but self-righteous Ku Klux Klan, which claims that it protects the people against injustice and defends the Constitution of the United States, no matter how anti-Roman Catholic this movement may be. The fact that the members of the K.K.K., as well as they themselves, mostly belong to the Republicans (typically!), makes no difference. They regard this movement, which in our opinion is so typically American, as "un-American" and un-Christian.[280]

Involvements with Europe, that is to say, international treaties, etc., are equally rejected. This explains their criticism of [President Woodrow] Wilson. The World War had also caused our fellow Dutch to realize "the folly of seeking any good from international alliances," wrote E. J. Tanis, one of *The Banner* staff members.[281]

It is somewhat different with regard to their attitude toward America's imperialistic policies. A. F. Pollard is of the opinion, expressed in an interesting study, that since 1898 half of the American people accept "imperialism" as a deliberate policy, but in as far as this also means annexation of territory, the people since that time are quite a bit less "imperialistic" than were the Democrats before the Civil War and the Republicans afterward.[282]

The correctness of the first statement is also evident among our compatriots. One finds, regardless of party, ardent imperialists among them and just as ardent opponents. But at the same time the relative and even doubtful character of the second proposition becomes apparent. What must we think of the fact that in 1921 in a Holland-American paper published by Republicans, territorial expansion was advocated? This paper proposed no less than that England and France sell their West Indian possessions to America, although for a good price, as part payment for the war debt, "while we will also give assurance that there will be no suffering or humiliation for the inhabitants who do not wish to change their citizenship."

Although such a statement should not be overrated—it may even have been well-paid "political" copy—it is still interesting, especially because among the Hollanders in the same town where the quoted paper *De Grondwet* [*The Constitution*] was published, namely in Holland, Michigan, there were colonists who owned sugar plantations in Cuba. It is also a symptom of how "American" they already considered themselves to be.[283] Among the opponents we must also include J. H. Hoekstra of Roseland in Chicago, who could be called the "public conscience" and also the "*enfant terrible*" among the Holland Americans. "Modern politics are, however, especially in America, matters of mood and tense," was the opinion of Pollard.[284] In an interesting manner one sees this proven by the Frisian-American Hoekstra. Seemingly our Frisian belongs to Pollard's "strong body of public opinion" that wants to give the Philippines their home-rule. Just listen: "And now Sam lives in deed and law like Johnny Bull and Marinet and thinks that on earth there is no longer a Judge living as Supreme Lord, who soon will hale him before the court of justice for atrocities. . . . Yes, Uncle lives so cruelly, so unrestrainedly, and fills the poor pagan land with children of sin and shame, and gives those souls accursed evil and makes them a prey to famine and hellish death."[285] [The rhymes were lost in the translation.] As we see, besides Gardener, it is again a compatriot who exposed America's political "idealism" regarding the Philippines, although he reached a much smaller circle—the readers of *Onze Toekomst* [*Our Future*] in Chicago and of

Het Oosten [*The East*] in Paterson. So one can see reflected in *De Grondwet* and in *Onze Toekomst*, both Republican papers, the opposing tendencies that existed among the Dutch, just as among all Americans, with regard to "imperialism."

E. The Press

It is especially in the press that one can readily trace the increasing involvement of the Dutch element in American life. The press has for a long time been a kind of mediating agency in the continuing Americanization. By means of the press, Americans also try to exercise influence upon the Dutch and indeed upon all other nationalities, especially in political matters. On the other hand, our people also attempt to exert influence on non-Hollanders by means of the press.

To reach their objectives, the Americans sometimes support—especially during political campaigns—the American papers appearing in the Dutch language. In 1912 A. Oosterheerdt went so far as to ascribe the reprehensible docility of many Hollanders in times like that to the "very partial" information in many Dutch papers, a partiality that was "often bought with money."[286] Indeed, campaign advertisements, too, were often paid for liberally. All of this probably helps to explain why despite the rapid Americanization of the last ten years so many papers still appeared in our language in America. Indeed, financial support played no small role since the beginning. Let it not be forgotten either that in America there is no end to elections and every interested person, even the candidate for the political office of policeman (constable), must advertise his candidacy extensively!

Naturally, we do not wish to minimize the political opinions of the owners of the weeklies. For we should not forget that many a publisher is at the same time a "politician." This was true of C. Poelstra, publisher of *De Telegraaf* in Paterson, who had been for more than forty years an active member of the Republican Party and an admirer of President [Warren G.] Harding. Poelstra had become better acquainted with Harding when he had met him as a delegate to a "meeting of ethnic groups speaking foreign languages" at Marion, Ohio.[287]

However, one should not exaggerate in any way this supposed political "support." Critical as Dutchmen are and often more inclined to be negative in their criticism than constructive, they often do not spare their own party members. Fierce, for example, was the criticism in the Grand Rapids *Christian Journal* by Republican Ate Dykstra against governor A. Groesbeck, who was not only a fellow party member but even a fellow Dutchman.[288] He accused him of high-handedness and financial extravagance in running the government. We also recall the manner in which the Republican Hoekstra pictured the imperialist policies of his party members for the readers of *Onze Toekomst* in Chicago.

And if one would like to know how independently *Het Oosten* in Paterson viewed the election in 1920, one should read one of its editorials of that year, in which it is admitted that both candidates for the presidency at that time had very little advantage over each other: "The so-called most enlightened nation on earth and the freest people in the world will soon go to the voting booth in darkness in order, as free men, to be led by the hand by their political bosses to choose their candidate."[289] Therefore, these independent papers are not primarily dependent on politics. Like virtually all newspapers and advertising papers in the colonies, they have with only one or two exceptions primarily a religious, even a strongly orthodox character. This is still at present a matter of survival for this press. They cannot afford to leave out religious opinions and comments.

The fact that there are, especially among the elderly in America, hundreds who read only the Dutch language and thousands who read it by preference is obviously the main reason why periodicals still circulate in our language.

An automatic and gradual decline is inevitable, now that immigration and therefore the strengthening of the Dutch element is being restricted to such a great degree. This slow death is noticeable in the diminishing number of subscribers as well as in the shrinking size of some papers and especially in the increasingly deficient Dutch language used in them. *De Telegraaf* in Paterson, *De Volkstem* [*The Voice of the People*] at De Pere and *De Vrije Hollander* [*The Free Hollander*] at Orange City experienced a continual decrease in the number of their subscribers. *De Hollandsche Amerikaan* [*The Dutch American*] in Kalamazoo, which for years had been appearing three times per week was forced to go back to its initial semi-weekly format.[290] Indeed, even as such it is still a remarkable exception in the Dutch press in America that normally has only weekly and monthly papers. The *Sioux Center Nieuwsblad* [*Newspaper*] originally had eight pages; now it only has four. In most of the "colonial" papers, such as *De Grondwet* and, in a lesser degree, also *Pella's Weekblad* [*Weekly*], our language has become more and more a caricature.

The fact that the more successful, or rather the least financially troubled, Dutch-American newspaper businesses are being carried on in a few of the larger population centers, which have remained mostly Dutch and therefore also the most ultra-orthodox, is a further result of what has been mentioned above concerning Americanization. That is why we find these papers still appearing in a few factory centers: in Paterson, Grand Rapids, Holland, Kalamazoo, and Chicago. They also appear in the West, in the settlements, in the comparatively isolated rural areas whose isolation has prevented their Americanization also with regard to language, such as Pella, Orange City, and elsewhere.

A few of these latter papers were even able to grow, which again shows how dangerous "conclusions" can be. *De Hope* in Holland, for example, has increased the number of pages from eight to sixteen, although at the same time the page format was reduced. *Onze Toekomst* in Chicago has grown from four to eight pages, and as a result I think a special Chicago edition of *De Grondwet* at Holland has become superfluous. At Salt Lake City, where previous efforts had been made to found a "Dutch paper," a completely new paper *De Utah-Nederlander* was started in 1907.[291] It should be noted in this connection that all these papers had a more or less religious character.

Meanwhile many papers died. Even before about 1895 many a paper had perished. A still greater number failed than were established after that date when more "intellectuals" settled in America. Causes that contributed to these failures were too high an expectation regarding the competency of our kinsmen where other than ecclesiastical ideas were involved. The same was true with regard to their level of development and their Dutchness. At Holland, Michigan, alone, a half-dozen Dutch papers were born after 1895, only to disappear usually within a year. This happened in 1896 to *De Volksstem*, an organ of the dissatisfied Hollanders who had joined the Populist third-party movement, and who worked hard among other things for the use of paper and silver money. The same happened in 1901 to *De Heraut* |*The Herald*|, a Democratic paper and successor of the pioneer paper *De Hollander*, which had died years before.

A more lengthy existence seemed to be the lot of *Ons Vaandel* |*Our Banner*|, a paper that, in imitation of *De Standaard* |*The Standard*| in the Netherlands, attempted to promote A. Kuyper's antirevolutionary views in America. It appeared in 1901 in Holland initially three times per week. Its publishers even attempted to make it into a daily paper in consultation with the Synod of the Christian Reformed Church. Nothing came of these plans and within a few years the paper ceased to exist. Still shorter, as we have seen, was the life of the socialistic weekly *De Volksstem* (1908) and of the red biweekly publication *Voorwaarts* |*Forwards*|, the latter having appeared from 1914 until January 1915.[292]

The life of *De Gereformeerde Amerikaan* |*The Reformed American*|, a monthly, was longer because it was strongly orthodox. It had been published since 1897 in Holland and was originally edited by a few Christian Reformed ministers: H. Van Hoogen and F. M. Ten Hoor and by Professor H. Beuker. These gentlemen also formed a consortium that was later increased by still a few more ministers. However, when in 1906 the gentlemen disagreed, they sold the magazine to the publisher H. Holkeboer, who since 1897 had been a "shareholder," and who now became the sole owner. Of the old editorial staff, Ten Hoor, as editor-in-chief, remained responsible for the leadership. *De Gereformeerde Amerikaan*, which intended to be more or less "scholarly," was forced to simplify its material soon afterwards. In spite of this, in 1899 the number of subscribers had not reached a thousand. In 1907, however, it numbered 1,400 readers. But religious differences led to the failure of the paper in 1916.[293]

A similar fate as that experienced in Holland befell many periodicals in Grand Rapids. In 1905 *De Schoolbel* |*The School Bell*|, a weekly, was started there in the interest of Christian schools. Two years later it numbered more than 1,000 subscribers.[294] In 1907, De Getuige [The Witness], a monthly, appeared in opposition to the opinions that were being propagated in De Gereformeerde Amerikaan. It had about 1,000 readers. Both papers have since been combined along with a third one, De Gids [The Guide], a weekly by J. Pas that had attempted to promote Calvinistic principles in politics; in 1907 it numbered more than 1,500 readers.

The new combined weekly, De Calvinist, was purchased by the Eerdmans-Sevensma Company, which continued the paper as The Christian Journal in the service of the progressive younger set among the Christian Reformed. In spite of the English name, it was mostly written in the Dutch language. At first B. K. Kuyper was the editor-in-chief, and after him H. J. G. Van Andel. In an extremely interesting series of articles, "We and the World," the latter had already reported under Kuyper's editorship what was happening among the young folk who wished to arouse their people out of a "slothfull sleep": "Spring is coming into the hearts of our young people. More light, a growing desire for more education and culture reveals itself. . . . The minds are profoundly moved and there is a mysterious motive power that propels us continuously. . . . The future is ours! The flood swells in school and church and society." Thus Van Andel wrote with youthful zeal, inspired by the works of A. Kuyper and infinitely more by those of Bavinck.[295]

Having become responsible himself for the writing of editorials, Van Andel continued the struggle. However, the majority of the True brothers, especially the older generation, would have nothing to do with the progressives among them nor with their neo-Calvinism. Therefore, The Christian Journal could not continue to exist as the banner of the younger folk; after a few years it was sold to the more conservative M. Berghage, who also owned the formerly-mentioned bilingual Standard-Bulletin. Continued as the weekly Christian Journal and edited by Dr. Y. P. De Jong, A. Dykstra, and Reverend A. Keizer, it generally contained the same articles as the Standard-Bulletin. Sooner or later both of these orthodox and Republican papers will very likely be combined.[296]

Meanwhile a few other brain-children had succumbed: Een Stem des Volks [A Voice of the People], published by G. Roelofs as the organ of the teetotalers (1898); De Kerkbode [The Church Messenger], De Geestelijke Wandelaar [The Spiritual Wanderer], De Republikeinsche Vrijheidsbanier [The Republican Freedom Banner] of W. Verburg (about 1898), the bilingual The Yankee Dutch and the monthly De Zendingsbode [The Mission Messenger] of M. Berghage. H. H. D. Langereis has for a time published a richly illustrated monthly, Het Ideaal [The Ideal], at Grand Rapids, having in 1907 a total circulation of about five hundred copies. Langereis also published a sternly religious monthly De Huisvriend [The Friend of the Home] and a trade paper for farmers De Hollandsche Farmer. Again it is a typical fact that in 1921, of these three periodicals only the orthodox De Huisvriend was still in existence. It absorbed De Gereformeerde Amerikaan and also De Boodschapper [The Messenger], a monthly that contained sermons by

Christian Reformed ministers and that was the property of Reverend R. L. Haan, the editor of De Huisvriend.[297]

In addition there have existed in Michigan at Battle Creek a small paper in the interests of Adventism; in Muskegon a weekly, De Volksvriend [The People's Friend]; and in Chicago, Illinois, besides the formerly-mentioned Nederlander, there existed the De Bazuin [The Trumpet] and De Batavier [The Batavian*]. On the other hand, the little religious paper, Onze Toekomst, the organ of the Reformed Young Men's and Young Women's Societies, begun in 1897, grew to be a sizeable weekly, thanks to the veteran journalist H. Masman, whose work was later continued by L. Holstein.[298] At Fulton, Illinois, the paper De Boodschapper [The Messenger], which was published there around 1898, succumbed.

K. Van Stigt, for a time (around 1912) in Pella, Iowa, published a religious monthly De Christelijke Uitdeeler [The Christian Dispenser]. Later (around 1915) this paper became De Uitdeeler, the monthly organ of the home for the aged in Pella. Since that time I have not come across it any more. Beets was able to report to me recently only the fact that De Christelijke Uitdeeler no longer existed.[299] A weekly paper at Harrison and De Bode [The Messenger] of J. Hospers at Springfield (about 1898), both in South Dakota, have not been able to survive the competition or their fellow Dutch papers in Iowa. A weekly that was begun around 1895 at Port Arthur in Texas had to be discontinued soon after.[300]

At Rochester, New York, with a sizeable Dutch population, [?] Graskamp published The Holland-American (around 1907), a religiously liberal paper in the Dutch and in the English language. As such, however, it did not have the ability to survive and for that reason it came successively into the hands of the ministers [P.] Van Vlaanderen and [A. J.] Van den Heuvel, who gave it, according to my socialist informant "an exaggerated ecclesiastical flavor." "I have read the paper only a few times," Mr. Elferink wrote to me, "and then laid it aside, since it was in no way useful to me except to arouse anger." In Rochester, however, De Grondwet from Holland and De Hollandsche Amerikaan from Kalamazoo were read a great deal. Seemingly The Holland-American was not able to compete with these orthodox-tinted papers either, and it was finally sold to a few Roman Catholic kinsmen in Rochester, to a certain [?] Hille and someone else. However, under the management of these men the paper declined still more and finally ceased to appear.[301]

In Paterson, New Jersey, De Oostersche Kerkbode [The Eastern Church Messenger] could not survive, nor could a small socialist paper. However, a strict orthodox weekly Het Oosten has circulated here with a great deal of success since 1904. The oldest paper in Paterson, De Telegraaf, with about two thousand readers in its "heyday," was discontinued upon the death of its editor-

---

*The name "Insula Batavorum" (Batavia) was the Latin name for an island between the Rhine and Waal rivers in the Netherlands where a Germanic tribe, the Batavi or Batavieren, had settled in Roman times. Thus Bataafs has the meaning of "pertaining to the Netherlands or the Dutch."

publisher, C. Poelstra, a few years ago. He had tried in vain toward the end of his life to sell his paper to others.[302] After having gone through forty-two yearly volumes, it could not find a serious purchaser, probably due to the continuing rate of Americanization that further accelerated after the [First] World War.

This Americanization process has indeed had the effect not only of causing many a paper to become bilingual, such as the Grand Rapids papers, but it certainly caused the demise of a few important ones.[303] In Wisconsin, at De Pere, the solid, very conservative and strict Roman Catholic weekly *De Volksstem* [*The Voice of the People*], which had attained at one time a circulation of about 2,500 copies, could no longer get a sufficient number of readers and was discontinued in 1919. So also was another Roman Catholic weekly there, *Onze Standaard* [*Our Standard*], as Dr. G. Rijbroek reported to me.*[304]

New efforts to establish a "Dutch" periodical in this rather thickly populated Dutch Roman Catholic colony seem not to have been made. At any rate, the priest W. H. H. De Haan of New Franken, Wisconsin, informed me in 1926 not only that the Dutch Catholic papers had "ceased to appear during the war," but that there were "no Catholic daily or weekly papers in that language" to be found.[305] This was true for Wisconsin, but elsewhere we find a Flemish paper that was either unknown to De Haan or was not included by him among Dutch periodicals. Remarkably, none of my other Catholic spokesmen reported regarding this paper.

However, the comparatively untimely disappearance of *De Volksstem* was caused by still another circumstance; at least it was hastened by it. When American nativism was in bloom during the war days and later, full-blooded Americans tried to buy up the Dutch papers. *De Volksstem*, as W. Eerdmans told me, was purchased by them and it appeared later as an American paper in the English language.[306] This is information that does not exclude the explanations given to me from the Catholic side.

Indeed, the Americans bought out still another paper, probably the most nationality-conscious Dutch paper that ever appeared in the United States: *De Vrije Hollander* [*The Free Hollander*], a Democratic paper that appeared semi-weekly in Orange City.[307] It seems that this paper, which numbered a thousand readers, could not survive the competition of the Republican *Volksvriend* in overwhelmingly Republican Sioux County. This was sad, for how courageously *De Vrije Hollander* defended the Boer cause at the time of the Boer War; how fiercely it stormed at [Leander Starr] Jameson, [Cecil J.] Rhodes "the great bandit," and also [William] McKinley and [Theodore] Roosevelt, who allowed mules and horses to be exported for the benefit of the English army. Never have the Hollanders in America been more conscious of their "*Dietsche*" [Dutch] ancestry than at that time, not in the least due to *De Vrije Hollander* and its first publisher-editor

---

*Dr. A. Kuyper lists in his *Varia Americana* (1898) on p. 92 still another Catholic paper, *De Gids* [*The Guide*]; however, it seems he did not see it. I have not come across this paper anywhere else [Van Hinte].

Maarten P. Van Oosterhout.[308] This, however, makes it understandable precisely why this paper had to succumb.

However, Americanization during these years should not be exaggerated, for even during the springtide of American nationalism a few new papers were able to start in the Dutch language in the United States. In Kalamazoo in 1917 a new monthly was published with the meaningful name *Teekenen der Tijden* [*Signs of the Times*]. About 1922 this paper, which was naturally a strictly orthodox periodical, could even be converted into a weekly! The Zeelander and journalist J. Van Boven, well-known to us from Colorado, who later worked as a school principal in Michigan, in such towns as Grand Haven and elsewhere, had returned to his first love and became the publisher-editor of this Christian weekly.

Still more orthodox is a second, even an entirely post-war paper, *De Bereër* [*The Berean*] published since 1919 by H. Bultema, et al., who had seceded from the Christian Reformed Church. It is now published in Muskegon. Exclusively a church paper and quite voluminous, although in book format, it appears semi-monthly.

Finally there is still a third orthodox paper that is published since 1924 by the formerly-mentioned protesting churches: *The Standard Bearer*, a "Reformed semi-monthly." In spite of its English title it appears as a bilingual paper, most of it in the Dutch language. G. Van Beek, co-editor, known to us from *De Gereformeerde Amerikaan*, would indeed not wish to write in another language. The Reverend H. Hoeksema and G. M. Ophoff make up the editorial board with him, to which originally also belonged Reverend H. Danhof, who has since withdrawn.

So it is a matter of coming and going in the Netherlands-American press. Only after a careful examination can one speak of an extremely slow decline. As far as I know, the following papers still exist:[309]

In Michigan:

At Holland:

De Grondwet, 1860. A conservative Republican news and advertising weekly, 8 pages. Publisher: Mrs. L. Mulder; director: J. B. Mulder. Circulation about 7,000.

De Hope, 1886. A Republican, Reformed Church weekly, 16 pages. Publisher: The Reformed Church in America; editors: Reverend S. Van der Werf, Reverend G. De Jonge, and T. Welmers. Circulation around 4,000.

De Heidenwereld [*The Heathen World*], 1896. A monthly in the interest of missions, 32 to 48 pages. Publisher: De Heidenwereld Publishing Company (actually the Reformed and Christian Reformed Churches jointly); editors: Dr. H. Beets and Reverend S. Van der Werf. The paper originally appeared in Orange City, Iowa, where it was started by F. Overkamp and was moved to Michigan in 1920 where it became bilingual.

At Grand Rapids:

De Wachter [*The Sentinel*], 1868. A Christian Reformed Church weekly, 16 pages. Publisher: The Christian Reformed Publishing House (The Christian Reformed Church); editor: Reverend H. Keegstra. Circulation over 9,000.

Standard-Bulletin, 1875. A Republican and Christian Reformed news and advertising weekly, 8 pages. Publisher and editor: M. Berghage. Circulation about 1,500. Bilingual.

Christian Journal, 1887. A Republican and Christian Reformed news and advertising weekly, 8 pages. Publisher and editor: M. Berghage. Circulation about 1,000. Bilingual. The content is generally the same as the articles of the *Standard-Bulletin*. The *Christian Journal* is illustrated however.

De Huisvriend, 1893. A religious monthly, 16 pages. Publisher and editor-in-chief: H. H. D. Langereis.

Holland Home News, 1893. A small religious monthly in the interest of the Holland Home, a home for the aged, 4 pages. Publisher: Holland U. B. Association. It appears in the Dutch language despite its English name.

The Standard Bearer, 1924. An orthodox semi-monthly paper, organ of the Protesting Churches, 16 pages. Published by the Reformed Free Publishing Association, editors: Reverend H. Hoeksema, G. M. Ophoff and G. Van Beek. Circulation about 700.

At Kalamazoo:

De Hollandsche Amerikaan, 1889. A conservative-Republican and ultra-orthodox news and advertising paper that appears twice per week, 4 to 6 pages. Publisher: Dalm Printing Company; editor: G. Van Beek.

Teekenen der Tijden, 1917. A Republican, Christian news and advertising weekly, 10 pages. Publisher: J. Van Boven.

At Muskegon:

De Bereër, 1919. An ultra-orthodox church paper that appears twice per month with about 30 pages. Publisher: Bereër Publication Committee; editor: H. Bultema. Circulation about 1,000.

In Illinois:

At Chicago:

Onze Toekomst, 1897. A Republican and predominantly Christian Reformed news and advertising weekly with a strictly orthodox religious Sunday edition, 8 pages. Publisher: Christian Literature Publishing Company; editor-in-chief: Dr. J. Van Lonkhuyzen. Circulation about 3,500 (in 1922).

At Moline:

Gazette van Moline, 1908. An independent Flemish Catholic news and advertising weekly with a "Detroit section," 12 pages. Publisher: Moline Gazette Publishing Company (C. L. Cozijn, president; J. L. Van Lancker, secretary-treasurer and manager.*

In Iowa:

At Pella:

Pella's Weekblad, 1861. A Democratic and religiously oriented news and advertising paper, 8 pages. Publisher: Boland and Dieleman; editor: J. Dykhoff. Circulation about 2,000.

At Orange City:

De Volksvriend, 1874. A Republican and strictly orthodox news and advertising paper, 8 pages. Publisher: H. P. Oggel and Son; editor: H. P. Oggel.

At Sioux Center:

Sioux Center Nieuwsblad, 1892. A Republican news and advertising paper, 4 pages. Publisher: H. Brandes.

In Utah:

At Salt Lake City:

De Utah-Nederlander, 1914. A Republican, religious news and advertising paper. Organ of the Church of Jesus Christ of Latter-Day Saints, 4 pages. Publisher: Associated Newspapers; Dutch editor: W. J. De Brij.

In New Jersey:

At Paterson:

Het Oosten, 1904. An independent, ultra-orthodox news and advertising paper, 8 pages. Publisher: Lont and Overkamp Publishing Company; editor: F. Overkamp.

A study of the above review indicates that there is still only one Democratic paper appearing in the Dutch language and that the others, to the extent that they are not "independent," promote Republican principles. Furthermore, all of them, without one single exception, have a religious, even a more or less orthodox, character. In both respects they generally reflect the attitudes of the immigrants. Indeed the daily life of the colonists is mirrored in their press and obviously most completely in their newspapers.

Newspapers had as their main purpose the reporting of the "gossip" that people are unable to share personally because of the great distances. People live spread out over an area that is several hundred times the size of

---

*Only once I saw mention of a Flemish paper in Detroit. As far as I know there is no independent, *Gazette van Detroit* in existence [Van Hinte].

Geographic distribution of Dutch papers in the United States. If there is more than one paper in a place, the number is indicated.

our country.* What interesting insights these little "gossip" items give us of the life of the immigrants and their children in the Far West is evident from an October issue (but also from others) of *De Volksvriend*. From Melvin, Osceola County, Iowa, it is reported that the busy time of threshing oats is over and most of the people have also finished plowing. But it is still too early to pick corn. So the minister and his elders went family visiting during this interlude. From Bemis, South Dakota: "Many could not attend the mission festival because threshing has not been finished." From Hotchkiss, Colorado: "Rev. [John William] Te Selle filled his silo with sunflowers and corn. This seems to be very good for milk cows." From Westfield, North Dakota: "We saw G. Van Vugt bring a small load of corn for the cows of the minister. Threshing is done here with many small machines driven by a tractor."[310]

De Volksvriend, just like *Pella's Weekblad*, gives us a glimpse of life in the country; the Grand Rapids papers and *Het Oosten* in Paterson naturally reflect factory life. Thus in *Het Oosten* of January 7, 1921, it is reported from

*The Netherlands has an area of 41,200 square kilometers (including 7,158 square kilometers of water) or 15,900 square miles, of which two-fifths lie below sea level. The country measures 190 miles from north to south and 160 miles at its greatest breadth. By comparison the state of Ohio has an area of 41,222 square miles and measures 220 miles north to south and 225 miles in width, or roughly nearly three times the size of the Netherlands.

Midland Park that, among other things, the workers in the Granite Linen Mill there, the large majority of whom were Hollanders, "have again experienced a blood letting," the second in two weeks. "Last Monday they were obliged once more to drop 10% of their wages, otherwise the mill would not run. Of necessity, the majority signed the new contract, some under protest." A view of an entirely different sort is a report in *De Grondwet* from Muskegon, in which it is claimed that Herman Havinga from that town "is, to say the least, a sound sleeper: His car went off the road into a deep excavation. Sheriff |?| Matthews, upon arrival, found Havinga sleeping in the car and had to pull him out through the door. 'I could not get out and so I just went to sleep,' said Havinga. He will have to answer to the police for driving a car while in an intoxicated condition." And that happened in a "dry" county![311]

Even the smallest happenings are reported; thus it was learned by the Hollanders in the farthest West as well as in the farthest East of the United States that in Leota, Minnesota, "little Harriet Hofkamp celebrated her ninth birthday with her little friends. The mother had provided for delicious refreshments, and the children had a pleasant afternoon." From Ogilvie in the same state they read with the greatest interest that "Mrs. C. Hoitinga returned in good health after her visit in Sioux County. That Charley was happy about this goes without saying."[312] In separate sections it is frequently reported who "in the settlements" was born, married, and died, especially the latter.

In addition to their church organizations, it is through these chatty columns that the Dutch kept informed about one another throughout the whole United States. By keeping abreast of other Hollanders' activities, they constitute, so to speak, one gigantic family from the Atlantic to the Pacific Ocean, from Mexico to far beyond the borders of Canada. It must not be forgotten that besides church papers, also *De Grondwet*, *De Hollandsche Amerikaan*, and especially *De Volksvriend* reached out over an enormous territory— several times the size of Europe!

These papers contained besides the neighborly "gossip" a number of other features, domestic and foreign news, etc. A major feature column, "Nederland," occupied a special place. Sadly enough one found here also— with a few exceptions—only our "miscellaneous news," which was mostly borrowed from some small Dutch provincial paper, preferably from a paper in the district from which the majority of immigrants themselves had come. For the rest, chance sometimes also played a part. Old Mister |H. P.| Oggle in Orange City, for example, although himself a Zeelander, got his Dutch news, as he told me, from *De Graafschapper*, the religious Achterhoek newspaper that had existed for fifty years.

Only *De Utah-Nederlander*, usually the least original among the papers mentioned, often took over important articles from the Dutch press. Although they carried items of local interest, they were of minor importance. But as a rule one comes across major articles that were reprinted from *De Nieuwe Rotterdamsche Courant*, *De Telegraaf*, *De Amsterdammer*, *Het Vaderland*, *De*

Correspondentie

EDGERTON, Minn. — Mooi weer; er wordt naar regen uitgezien.

Mrs. K. Kooiman en zoon van Boyden waren hier op fam.-bezoek.

Mr. en Mrs. J J. Kallemeyn van Castlewood, S. D., waren de gasten van E. Hofkamp en fam.

De Chr. Ger. gem. werd weer teleurgesteld: Ds. A. J. Russ bedankte voor de roeping. — Student P. De Koekoek trad Zondag 3 keer voor haar op; 's avonds in de Eng. taal.

Vrijdag, 2 Juni, werd er een picnic gehouden door de ouders en kinderen van de Chr. School. Bij deze gelegenheid liet de Vr. Vereen. der C. G. gem. eenige gemaakte kleeren verkoopen die $129.10 opbrachten. Eenige artikelen vervaardigd door de schoolkinderen brachten $44.00; de winsten der cantine waren $167.32; dus alles te samen, $340.42 en ten bate van de Chr. School. Zoo ziet gij dat hier nogal een cream check gebruikt wordt ten bate van het Chr. Onderwijs.

Mr. en Mrs. B. Broekhuis van Brooten zijn hier op fam.-bezoek. — Mr. en Mrs. J. B. Doornwaard bezochten Sioux County.

WORTHINGTON, Minn. — Nog altijd droog; erg wordt naar regen uitgezien.

Mr. en Mrs. Hofwegen en dochter Grace bezoeken fam. en kinderen te Hull en Sioux Center. — Henry Tuininga is met zijn gezin op bezoek naar Hull en Rock Valley.

Bij J. Adema te Org bezochten ze Zondag nacht een vreemde ontmoeting. Terwijl er een vrachttrein aan het switchen was, werden ze wakker door iets waardoor de hond erg begon te blaffen en in de store en later jankende deed neervallen. Toen ze het licht voor den winkel opdraaiden, merkten zij dat de hond bewusteloos was gemaakt door choloroform, doch later weer bijkwam. De Adema's zijn verder opgebleven en hebben niets meer vernomen. Wij hopen maar dat dit de laatste poging is. Adema heeft al eerder roovers in zijn winkel gehad, te Carnes, Iowa, daar kwam hij nog zoo goed niet af.

Er zal een program gemaakt worden voor 4 Juli; eenigen zijn gekozen om dat op te maken, en dan in een van de mooie plaatsen hier rond te vergaderen. Waarschijnlijk weer bij Zevenbergen. Alle vrienden van Bigelow en omstreken worden uitgenoodigd. Voor een cantine zal gezorgd worden.

PEASE, Minn. — Een mooie regen verl. week, tot blijdschap van mensch en vee.

Wm. Kalsbeek was te Estelline, S.D.

Decoratie-dag was het stil; bijna alle burgers waren naar de Lakes.

P. Van de Veen en vrouw van Prinsburg bezochten hier fam. en vrienden.

H. Nagel rijdt met 'n nieuwe Ford.

Vandaag, Maandag, Children's Clinic in het schoolhuis. Een dokter van Mpls. onderzoekt de gezondheid der kinderen; alles vrij. Dit gaat uit van het Roode Kruis. Heden avond houdt hij een rede in de kerk.

Woensdag staat het huwelijk voltrokken te worden van Ed De Witt en Miss Dora Groen, in de kerk. Mr. De Witt is principal van de Chr. School te Prinsburg.

BROOTEN, Minn. — Ds. en Mrs. Wassink en J. Luppinga en vrouw waren in Ferges Falls om Mrs. Van der Molen te bezoeken; zoo wij vernemen maakte ze het redelijk wel. Deze week hoopt Mr. v. d. Molen er heen te gaan met den Corr.

Velen gaan uit visschen en rapporteeren goede vangsten.

Mr. en Mrs. Broekhuis bezoeken Edgerton. De fam. Van Dyk is naar Leota. — Een broer van Floegman was met zijn vrouw hier van Prinsburg. — Henry Te Brake was met Decoratie-dag hier van Roseland, Minn., om zijn verloofde die daar op bezoek was, weer op te halen.

Mrs. Gt. De Young was weer ter kerk.

S. Blauw is naar Chandler.

Herman Dykstra en vrouw en kind en een paar kinderen van TeBrake bezoeken Ocheyedan.

Bij Gt. Jansen, 'n dochtertje.

Zondag a.s. hoopt Ds. Paauw van Hancock hier op te treden.

STEEN, Minn. — Echt corn weer. De boeren zijn allen druk met cultivateren, en dat gaat goed, omdat 't te genwoordig droog is.

Mr. en Mrs. Willem Sneller van Sioux Center waren hier ter kerk. — Ook Miss Eggink van Sioux Center en Miss De Jonge van Doon waren alhier. — Een zuster van Piet Appel van Denver, Colo., is bij haar broer op bezoek, en zal hier eenige dagen vertoeven.

Zoo als ik in een vorig nr. hebt gemeld, zouden wij een reisje doen naar Bemis, S. D. Wij zijn dan nu terug en hebben een aangenaam bezoek afgelegd. Wij bezochten de fam. Buyert, Nagelhout, Ds. Reurdink van de Presb. gem., en meer anderen. Ik dacht zoo, men vindt toch overal goede menschen in de wereld. Maar jammer was het, die menschen konden ons niet helpen op onze terugreis, toen wij ongeveer 50 mijlen door de modder moesten rijden. En wij waren maar erg blij dat wij weer tehuis waren.

Ds. Bosch van Leota preekte Zondag te Hills, Minn.

Mrs. Crangle viel van de porch en brak haar been.

John Bosch en A. Fikse verzonden een carload vee naar Sioux City.

Henry Bosch en gezin zijn naar Sioux County.

Harm Timmer is thuis gedurende de vacantie.

Blyenbes van Edgerton was bij vrienden op een kort bezoek.

CROOKSTON, Minn. — Groeizaam weder; alles groeit dat het een lust is. De eerste snee alfalfa en sweet clover wordt gemaaid. Best gewas. Aardappels en corn komen mooi op. Veel aardappels geplant hier.

De "relay race" tusschen de Crookston High School en Grandforks werd gewonnen door de Grandforks boys, die de 25 mijl aflegden in 2 uur, 22 min., 20 sec.; een van de Crookston boys liep een mijl in 4 min., 48 sec.

Dick Goodyk kreeg 500 kuikentjes van Mr. Wyngaarden van Zeeland, Mich., een afstand van 862 mijl; er waren slechts drie dood.

Bij W. Stoub 'n zoontje. Ook bij R. Epema.

Mrs. Sip LaFleur is onder de dokters handen. — Mrs. John Achtien blijft sukkelend.

Eise Kooi en Jacob Haan hadden 30 Mei al 450 acres in crop. Haan neemt nu een paar week vacantie, haalt zijn auto die hij in Wisconsin had; en wil ook de Hollanders in het zuiden van den Staat bezoeken.

20 Mei clean-up day; 25-duizend "cans" (blikken bussen) werden opgenomen, en daarvoor aan de jongens 10c per 100 betaald.

$300-duizend werd hier dienstbaar gesteld voor State Highways, in de Co. Daarbij komen dan nog de county roads.

Hemelvaartsdag was er dienst bij Ds. Meyer; een flinke opkomst.

De Amer. Legion tracht op Zondag, 18 Juni, hier een speed carnival te houden. Velen zijn er tegen om dat op Zondag te hebben en protesteeren. Het is ook tegen de Staats-wet van Minnesota.

HOLLANDALE, Minn. — In dubbelen zin feestdag alhier. Ds. Mansen van Middelburg, Ia., was tot ons overgekomen, en leidde den dienst. 53 personen waren hoorders van zijn ernstige woorden. Bereidwillig wordt ons de zoo schoon gelegen bungalow der company afgestaan. Een fraai eikenhouten orgel werd de jonggeboren gemeente cadeau gegeven, terwijl wij de eer hadden den gever, Mr. Payne, dien dag in ons midden te hebben. Driemaal hadden wij het genoegen den dienst bij te wonen. Des avonds sprak Ds. Mansen in het Eng.; na den dienst varia: zang, enz. Alles bracht bij, dat die dag een dag van veel genoegen; ja meer, een dag van zegen werd. Warme dank aan de Classis van haar sympathie.

BEJOU, Minn. — Prachtig weer; alles groeit welig; rogge staat al in de aar; corn en aardappelen staan goed, en vlaszaaien in vollen gang.

Bij J. Post, 'n dochtertje, No. 1.

R. Van Essen heeft een zeere hand. Dr. Kersen heeft er geducht ingesneden.

S. Boekhout huurde een farm te Little Rock, Ia., en gaat ons dezen herfst verlaten.

De S. S. in de Chr. Ger. gem. is weder begonnen met 4 onderwijzers: W. Van Eps, Mrs. Fred De Vries en Mr. en Mrs. Geo. Reitsma.

Geo. P. v. d. Plaats was te Mahnomen.—Clara v. Essen bezocht P. Osinga. — J. Wiersma was naar Iowa.

De Primary verkiezing nadert, 19 Juni. Nog nooit zooveel candidaten in deze County als ditmaal.

Bredasche Courant, Het Dagblad van Soerabaja, etc.[313] Relying solely upon these articles, one could even conclude that the most educated immigrants of our nationality are found among the Latter-day Saints. Indeed, the other papers, even in the very well-educated towns of Pella and Orange City, would soon find this material to be "too heavy stuff." Readers of these papers had no patience for such features. An article of three columns, for example, was "a bone on which the present generation would rather not nibble," said the *Volksvriend* editor while he threw a lengthy article of that sort about California in the waste basket.[314] He was convinced "that the large majority of subscribers have neither the time nor the desire to read it."

The newspapers often also contained one and sometimes several religious articles. However, a column, "Literature and Arts," was unknown to all of them. A few, for example, *De Grondwet,* did contain such columns as "The Farm"; others carried a medical column, "Health Service or Hygiene," as did *Onze Toekomst* and *De Gazette van Moline.* The political column "Civil Government," run in both bilingual newspapers in Grand Rapids, is also interesting. This column (and that is characteristic!) was written in English, while the religious column "Leer en Leven" ["Doctrine and Life"] appeared in Dutch in both papers. Of course serials were not lacking either; sometimes they were stories translated from English; however, often they were Dutch stories mostly of a religious and historical character. In particular the stories of L. Penning* were favorites, just as previously were those of Gerdes and also the historical stories of [W. F.] Andriessen.

To mention just a few examples, *De Wachter* in 1920 ran a story about the life of Dutch fishermen by L. Penning, *De Eilanders* [*The Islanders*]. *Teekenen der Tijden* in 1924 published a story by the same author entitled *Onder de Vlag van Jan Pz. Coen* [*Under the Flag of Jan Pieterszoon Coen*].† However, especially stories about the Boers in South Africa drew the attention of the immigrants and "won the hearts of thousands."[315] *De Grondwet* readers had indeed enjoyed Boer stories earlier, such as *Jan Van Dijk, Lotgevallen van een Nederlandschen Kolonist in de Transvaal* [*Jan Van Dijk, Adventures of a Dutch Colonist in the Transvaal*] by S. H. Ten Cate. Stories by Johanna Breevoort and other likeminded writers are also presently found in the colonial press.

A special weekly leading article is actually found only in *Onze Toekomst* and in none of the other papers. In this editorial column, "From Week to Week," Dr. J. Van Lonkhuyzen showed his great journalistic talent, as at times did [James J.] Van Pernis. Van Lonkhuyzen wrote his editorials in a concise manner and allowed his readers to share in American national events, then again in world events. He stimulated their interest with one issue after another.

The lead articles of H. J. Van Andel in *The Christian Journal* were also

---

*William Levinus Penning, Jr. (1840–1924) was a Dutch poet, whose specialties were epic poems such as *Benjamin's Vertellingen, Tom's Dagboek.*

†Jan Pieterszoon Coen (1587–1629), who established Dutch power in the Indonesian archipelago, was governor-general and founder of *Batavia,* the capital of the (former) Dutch East Indies. He was a talented warrior and administrator.

interesting. But as we have already noted, this talented editor and promotor of neo-Calvinism was muzzled, as were all Bavinck worshipers. In addition, Van Andel was no minister and his writings against "churchism" threatened the authority of "the profession." "Playing church and dominie has as its result that the pastor is the leader of all meetings, that he is the only one who may speak with authority," thus Van Andel wrote spitefully in one of his commentaries. He wished to give professors, doctors, lawyers, and other cultured people a place as leaders, in addition to the clergy.[316]

Two other papers that were the most original and probably also the most independent ones, went on attacking the all-powerful *"dominee,"* although for entirely different reasons. In contrast to Van Andel's broadly Calvinistic *Christian Journal*, they are the ultra-orthodox *De Hollandsche Amerikaan* and *Het Oosten*, with their respective spokesmen G. Van Beek and J. H. Hoekstra (the latter using the pseudonym of "du Fond"). In a usually biting and destructive manner, they warned the ministers: "Shoemaker, stick to your last." According to their pre-Kuyperian opinions, ministers should busy themselves exclusively with church matters and should very definitely not get involved with a worldly press, even though it is Christian. "We do not know so very much dear brother," Van Beek called out sarcastically to a like-minded companion. "Many dominees know much more, and there are some who think that they understand everything, and that as newspaper writers they have also received a kind of Pauline call."[317] No wonder that *De Hollandsche Amerikaan* is known among the men of the cloth as that "wretched, barbed Dutch rag" that is always "picking on us ministers." Nevertheless, the broadminded H. Beets praised it as one of the best papers of our press in America as far as originality is concerned.[318] He is right.

"I do not know much, but this I have noticed in my full life, that ministers want to think, speak, and act for me," remarked "du Fond," no less scathingly in one of his "Carpettacks" in *Het Oosten*.[319] He was still more malicious in another one: "When one observes the teachers, one notices that God calls them all to beautiful churches with a good salary. One could not help thinking that God takes notice of Mammon just as we do."[320]

May the above suffice to provide an image of the content. It also tells us at the same time something about the unpolished Dutch language in which these papers were written. Previously, *Pella's Weekblad* ranked as the best Dutch paper in the United States, as far as the Dutch language was concerned, at least according to K. J. Van den Bussche.[321] Both Dr. J. Te Winkel[322] and J. Van Ginneken[323] simply repeated in a doltish way what he had said, without having studied the "American" press themselves, however. There is every reason to doubt their judgment, strange as it may sound, because it is precisely in Pella that a purer Dutch is spoken than anywhere else in America. Much, however, depends upon the editors, and it must indeed be admitted that living conditions attendant on newspaper jobs were of such a nature that, again apart from exceptions, it was seldom possible to attract good talent. It is for this reason that in matters of diversity of contents as well as richness of language most of the "colonial" papers, such as *De Grondwet* and *Pella's Weekblad*, no matter how "typical" they may have been, were precisely the least significant ones. Singularly odd is the Dutch that one encounters in these papers, especially in *De Grondwet*. That of *De Volksvriend* is better, and so was the Dutch in Van den Bussche's days in the *Christelijke Heraut* [*Christian Herald*] which appeared at that time.

Both of these latter papers were also a bit more orthodox and up to the present moment one could almost go by the rule: the more orthodox the paper, the better the Dutch that is used in it. For one generally also notices that the more orthodox the people, the closer is their relationship with the Netherlands. And this relationship is usually also of a more recent date. It is for this reason that the Dutch language in *Het Oosten* and in *De Hollandsche Amerikaan* is generally much better than the Dutch in *De Grondwet* and in *Pella's Weekblad*. For this same reason also the language in the Christian Reformed Church's *De Wachter* is purer than in the Reformed Church's *Hope*. The best quality Dutch, however, one will find in Bultema's *Bereër*, which is indeed hyper-orthodox. However, in this case also, generalizations remain hazardous. *Onze Toekomst*, for example, although first of all a *news* paper, may well be considered, as I see it, as the best in its class. This must be ascribed in part to its talented editor-in-chief, who moved to America at a relatively advanced age and who had had a broad education in the Netherlands. His coworkers also contributed to his success.

Due to their non-typical Dutch "gossip" columns, which are genuinely American (originally Anglo-Saxon), the *news*papers much more so than the *church* papers have acquired for us an un-Dutch character. The *Gazette van Moline* and *De Grondwet* have the strongest American style. The *Gazette* looks American especially because of its many illustrations and heavily printed headlines, and the *Grondwet* does so because of its sensational headlines that appear somewhat odd in an orthodox media. To name only a few: "Costly Fire"; "Chicago Widow Commits Suicide"; "A Million-Dollar Fire"; "On the Scaffold on his Nineteenth Birthday"; "Poor Chinese Babies are Sold for One Dollar"; "Desperado, Murder and Suicide"; "Wishes to Die, Wish Satisfied"; "Woman Poisoner under Arrest, Suspected of Six Murders"; "Sleeping Boy Attacked by Rats"; etc.[324] As can be seen the concocting of catchy headlines, which has almost become the most important part of journalistic work (according to Huizinga), is diligently pursued by our kinsmen, while in our country, with the exception of *De Telegraaf* and similar papers, journalists resort to it only reluctantly.[325]

More American still, because they are louder, more blatant, and more clamorous, are the advertisements in the Holland-American press. They are often gigantic in size and frequently include appropriate photos of the advertisers. Of special value are the real estate and land rental advertisements. Many a Dutch settlement has come into being and has even flourished as the result of such an ad in *De Volksvriend* or one of the other papers.

In this connection we should be reminded of the carefully prepared and long-term advertising technique of the Payne Investment Company of Omaha, as a result of which the settlement of Hollandale, Minnesota, was started.[326] There was also a clever campaign carried on for a number of years to persuade our kinsmen to settle in Crookston in the same state.

For us Netherlanders, the overabundance of announcements by "Undertakers and Embalmers," especially in the weekly *Het Oosten*, is striking. This may indicate a special concern for the deceased, a concern that had already struck the Dutch settlers previously and from which "Coaches for rent for Weddings" (in the same advertisement) do not detract.[327]

One notices enormous automobile advertisements, ads of steamship companies and their agents, and announcements of excursions to "the Old Country." All of these are indications, even in a small press like this, that among that part of the Holland-American population that has remained most Dutch, a material prosperity has been attained for which many a Dutch "intellectual" only yearns.

One must not come to the conclusion, though, that the journalistic work of our people in America is restricted to the "Dutch" press. On the contrary, their periodicals and newspapers written in the English language are becoming continuously more important. Not only in the completely Dutch cities and villages, but also in the "mixed" settlements, they often control the local "English" press, thanks to their better education.

In Dutch-American circles, people read almost exclusively *The Leader* and *The Banner*, which are respectively the organs of the western branch of the Reformed Church and of the Christian Reformed Church. *The Leader* we already learned about previously. *The Banner* was originally *The Banner of Truth* which was published in the East and later moved to Holland, Michigan, in 1903 and to Grand Rapids in 1906, where since that time the presumptuous *of Truth* was deleted.[328] One can now call *The Banner*, thanks in part to its active, progressive editor-in-chief, H. Beets, the most informative weekly paper appearing in orthodox "colonial" circles. It also looks the most prosperous and contains news items concerning missions that are of extreme interest for non-believers too. Recently the paper added a few new sections, notably one for women. This did not seem to be a success and was (characteristically) discontinued temporarily. *The Banner* has at present sixteen pages, which is the same number of pages as *The Leader*, the paper of the much more developed and numerous Reformed Church. It must be remembered at the same time, however, that in the East a much older Reformed weekly, *The Intelligencer*, still appears. Since 1922 it was combined with a mission paper, *The Mission Field*, while the Reformed folk in Somerset County, New Jersey, since 1906 also have *The Somerset Church News*.[329]

Among the Christian Reformed Church organs must also be included *The Instructor for the Sunday School*, a paper that is published in Zeeland, Michigan. There is even a separate little paper for the very young believers. Both are very widely read and are replacing more and more the *Sabbathschool Bode*

How the land speculators advertise among "our people."

Many a settlement came into being and grew with the cooperation of the ministers as a result of advertisements in De Volksvriend and other Dutch newspapers in America.

[*Sabbath School Messenger*] mentioned before.[330] Part of the more or less official church press includes the yearbooks of the denominations, and also the yearbooks and the bulletins of the colleges and academies that appear a few times each year.

The students themselves have their periodicals also, as will be remembered. *The Central Ray* at Pella and *The Anchor* at Holland have now even been converted into weeklies. At the so-much younger institution at Grand Rapids, *The Calvin College Chimes*, a monthly, is published. However, the journalistic inclinations of our younger kinsmen are carried still further. At the colleges as well as at the academies and the high schools, they annually publish yearbooks. The outstanding finish of these yearbooks would be amazing in the eyes of students at Dutch universities, at least with regard to the externals if not the intrinsic value. The *Milestone* of Hope, the *Pelican* of Central, the *Prism* of Calvin, *Cullings* of the Academy at Orange City, and, if I remember well, *Memoir* of the Christian High at Grand Rapids, all give evidence of prosperity and of a very active school life.

These yearbooks as well as the monthly publications strongly accent a vigorous activity of student clubs and student life among our young kinsmen, an activity that is stronger than is the case in our country. What one observes among the Anglo-Saxons and also among the Germans comes to expression here: There is not only a "school spirit" but above all a "club spirit." From this student press, one learns to know, too, the general mentality of young Dutch Americans. Thus, a new section was included in the orthodox student organ, *The Calvin College Chimes*, called "Athletic Department."[331] It was introduced as follows:

"Nine Rah's for Calvin! Hip, Hip!

"Rah, rah, rah,—rah, rah, rah,—rah, rah, rah.

"Calvin!—Calvin!—Calvin!—"

I think that this would certainly be too much for our most worldly students, to say nothing about those at the Free University [in Amsterdam] or at Kampen [the Theological School]. They would mumble something about "American hysteria," which could at best be condoned on election days but not in ordinary times and most certainly not among the orthodox. Indeed, it is already evident from the press that American Calvinism is certainly of a different type than Dutch Calvinism, or that it is becoming so.

Another periodical written for young people but not by them is *The Young Calvinist*, the official organ of the American Federation of Reformed Young Men's Societies. It has appeared since 1920 every month under a completely "Dutch" editorial staff in Grand Rapids, Michigan.[332] It has an orthodox character, just like *The Christian School Magazine*, to mention it once more, which has appeared since 1922. The mission periodical *The Christian Indian* that appears in Farmington, New Mexico, is also orthodox.

Most of these real orthodox papers have a few thousand subscribers, almost all Dutch countrymen. Very seldom, however, do they acquire subscribers from outside their own circles. In addition to these more general publications, we find growing numbers of small local church and school papers. A few of them have been mentioned previously. Thus, Reverend A. J. Benjamin of Milwaukee has published *The Wisconsin Christian Advocate* for more than thirty years.[333] Supporters of Christian education in Rochester, New York—all Netherlanders—publish there a monthly, *The Rochester Christian School Chimes*, etc., etc., so they all have more or less a propaganda purpose.

An effort to publish a strictly scholarly magazine has failed. The scholarly element of the colonists, who are also on the whole the most Americanized part, has access to a large number of American journals for publication of their articles. The necessity of having a periodical of "their own" arose again, as in most of the above-mentioned cases, in Christian Reformed circles, in particular among the progressives. Indeed, in May 1919, a tri-monthly magazine *Religion and Culture* was published exclusively in the English language by the Van Noord Book and Publishing Company at Grand Rapids (temporarily in Holland). Reverend E. J. Tuuk, H. J. G. Van Andel, R. B. Kuiper and W. H. Jellema were the editors of this extremely interesting periodical that originally—and very promisingly!—appeared in the format of our *Gids*.* It aimed to be "an American quarterly," but above all a Reformed one. But it was to be "in no sense a church affair," according to the "editorial preface."[334] Although the ideals were the same as those of the *Christian Journal* at that time, in this orthodox "Gids" they proposed "to publish essays with some scientific merit and productions of some literary value."

Even though some Reformed contributions were included, the make-up of the editorial staff, as originally intended, already points to a Christian Reformed origin. The articles in the early years contain valuable material. They give evidence of an increasing development and of a continually growing interest, but also show the courage, willpower, and high idealism of these most common folk. I will mention a few of those not directly religious: In issue No. 1: "The Meaning of Architecture in Relation to Church Buildings" (B. W. Hertel); Poetry (Gertrude Mulder). In issue No. 2 (in addition to a continuation of Hertel's article): "The Dutch Stadhouder a Prototype of the American President?" (P. Hoekstra); "Walt Whitman" (Prof. J. G. Van den Bosch). In issue No. 4: "Emerson from a Calvinist Point of View" (A. Ooster-heerdt); "Alsace Lorraine and the Peace Treaty" (A. Van den Bosch). In issue No. 6: "The Psychology of Religious Revivals" (J. C. De Korne); "Reconstruction a la Kant" (H. J. G. Van Andel). In issue No. 7: "The Native of the Ozarks" (W. Smitter); "What is Personality?" (C. Bouma), etc., etc.[335]

Still it seemed that they had overestimated the intellectual capacity of the *True* brethren, and in addition it happened that they did not receive the interest and cooperation that they had expected from the Reformed side. If

---

**De Gids,* a literary publication, started in 1836 by publisher Beijerinck as a competitor to *Vader-landsche Letteroefeningen*, published by the bookseller Yntema. It has been published up to the present time with changing emphasis on culture, politics, and social life, under editors of renown.

I am not mistaken, the number of Reformed contributors gradually decreased. The third volume already was different in character. *Religion and Culture* thus became a monthly with shorter articles of a popular-scientific nature. But this too was still too heavy for many readers and the editors became convinced that "the great mass of our people may not care for such articles."[336] The common people desired only religious contemplations. The publication soon became so theological that the appearance of an article about Anatole France [a modern French novelist] had the effect of being somewhat strange.[337]

The publication began to look more and more like the late *Gereformeerde Amerikaan*, although it was much more progressive. *Religion and Culture* also threatened to deteriorate into a religiously polemic pamphlet, which seemingly was the only possible way to continue its existence. It made a stand for the doctrine of Common Grace. "We heartily disapprove of constant quarreling, faultfinding, and suspecting," the editors confessed, however.[338] But on the other hand, they realized that simply for that reason the magazine suffered "a moribund existence, because it was gradually losing its spirit and its color." One of the readers admitted outright—and this typifies "our people"!—that he now had "really enough of this colorless periodical. To me, it was not worth the money or worth reading!"[339] So, the number of readers declined and amounted to only two or three hundred in 1924.

Meanwhile the paper had also been undermined by *The Witness* in the same way as its above-mentioned predecessor. The most orthodox brethren came out in December, 1921, with a competitive magazine, *The Witness*, written largely in Dutch, that was even distributed for a number of months free of charge thanks to a few affluent ultra-conservatives. Its purpose, "to stand guard over the principle," was achieved to the extent that in the end *Religion and Culture* was not able to continue.[340] Just as the former *Gereformeerde Amerikaan*, the periodical also succumbed as a victim of its defense of the doctrine of Common Grace. Therefore, the periodical was considered by some people as "ethical" [non-scriptural (?)], however unjustified this was. Just like *The Christian Journal*, the paper now came into orthodox hands, into the possession of those who would have nothing to do with the doctrine of Common Grace. A more liberal-minded person was at best tolerated now and then. Also the name *Religion and Culture* had to disappear, because many people seemingly were violently opposed to "Culture."

Because of "editorial" considerations, *The Witness* also ceased to exist. Both papers were united into the *Reformed Herald* of which the first number appeared in June, 1925.[341] The "merged" editorial board, however, seemed to have been purged of its most progressive elements. One man missing was the energetic Van Andel, from whom *The Christian Journal* had already been taken away and who had busied himself so courageously in *Religion and Culture*. Also ousted was the talented E. J. Tuuk, whose articles about Van Raalte had given evidence of unusual breadth of vision for his circle, and who probably for that reason was considered "suspect."[342]

The Reformed Herald lived for only one year. In May 1926, the twelfth and final number appeared. Although the original plan had been to make it a biweekly paper, it soon became evident that its coming on top of so many other religious papers was superfluous, to say the least.[343] Against whom were they to fight? In addition, the main purpose of silencing Bavinck's followers in America had been accomplished! Hadn't it, "brethren"?

It is more difficult to trace the part our people played in the "worldly" press. At Holland the gifted A. Mulder edits the *Holland City News*. The [Van] Koevering brothers publish *The Zeeland Record* at Zeeland. [Cornelius] De Vos heads the *Coopersville Observer* at Coopersville. At Grand Rapids, W. J. (Van) Etten edits the *Grand Rapids Spectator*, a biweekly. There may be other names to mention in Michigan, however these came to my attention.

In Wisconsin J. Kuypers (at least in 1908) published not only the now defunct *Volksstem*, but in addition *The Brown County Democrat*, as may be recalled.[344] More numerous are our newspaper people in the Northwest and other parts of Iowa. In 1912 I. Hospers edited *The Sioux County Herald*; J. F. D. Aué: *The Alton Democrat*; W. C. Muilenburg was the owner of *The Grand Chief*; J. W. Van der Burg and Company: *The Sheldon Mail*; G. H. Vos: *The Southerland Courier*; J. Van der Mast: *The Monroe Mirror*; D. Tollenaar: *The Marne Free Press*; J. De Wild: *The Waukon Standard*. The frequently mentioned politician C. Cole even headed two papers at Cedar Rapids, Iowa: *The Evening Times* and the *Cedar Rapids Republican*.[345] In South Dakota J. W. Bordewijk edits the *Springfield Times*.[346]

Our kinsmen are also involved in the "big press." A. H. Van den Berg is one of the influential editors of *The Grand Rapids Press*. Among the "colonists" who had moved to California, J. C. Klein around 1905 was editor-in-chief and manager of the influential daily, *The Oakland Herald*, in Oakland. [G. J. E. M.] d'Aquin, one of the victims of the notorious colonization of 1890 was a well-known reporter in the chain of Hearst papers. A. W. Voorzanger was editor of the periodical *Emanuel*.[347] In 1909 at San Francisco, M. H. De Jong was the owner of the *San Francisco Chronicle*.[348] In that same year our kinsman G. F. Goldsmith was appointed as business manager of the *Philadelphia Ledger* and J. E. Italie became a member of the editorial staff of that paper, both in Philadelphia.[349] The well-known S. M. Zwemer is still the editor of a tri-monthly periodical, *The Moslem World*, a magazine that, also according to Snouck Hurgronje, is not without merit.

Incomplete as this summary may be, it provides us at least some idea of the Dutch press in the United States. Numerous are the Dutch co-workers on the most varied American papers and magazines, and especially on the scholarly periodicals. My information about these, however, is too incomplete and would therefore lead to an incorrect and unfair image.

How important a role our orthodox brethren wish to play in the present-day press is indicated by their efforts to begin a large American daily on Calvinistic principles. It is remarkable that a paper such as *De Standaard* [of Kuyper], does not exist in all of America, as seemingly "Puritanical" as this

The "Netherlandic" press in the United States: Papers appearing entirely or mostly in the Dutch language (original photo taken from a complete collection in the possession of the author).

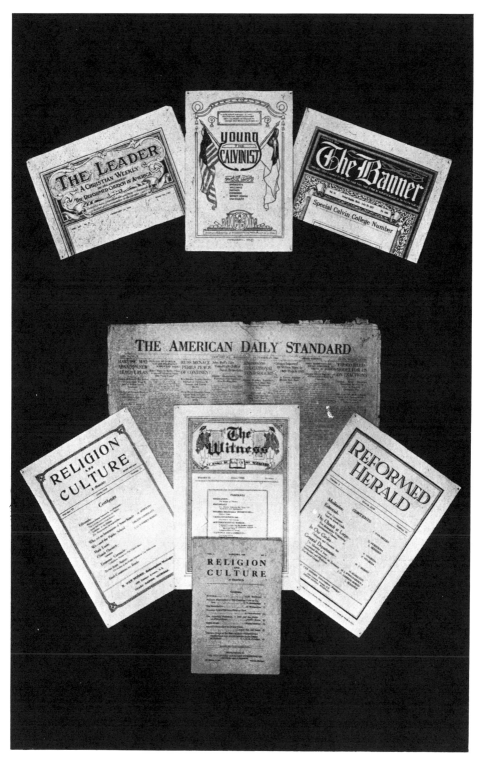

The "Netherlandic" press in the United States: Top: The leading church papers in the English language. Bottom: Those that failed in the struggle for more culture. (Original photo of papers in the possession of the author.)

country is. On the contrary, everyone knows how sensational and worldly, sometimes almost pornographic, the American daily press is.

This state of affairs impelled millions of Roman Catholics in the United States to bring out their own daily paper in 1917, the *Daily American Tribune*. This is the national Catholic daily, which is also widely read by our Roman Catholic kinsmen and in which the frequently mentioned priest W. H. H. De Haan of New Franken, Wisconsin, wrote a series of articles, "Miracles of our Lord Jesus Christ."[350] If tens of millions of Roman Catholics in America saw their first chance of publishing a daily paper only in 1917, and I mean *one* and no more, then we must acknowledge the courage and enterprising spirit of our orthodox Calvinists to attempt the same thing.

The Christian Reformed minister J. Clover Monsma had that courage. "Swept away by the enthusiasm of his faith and sometimes surprised by glorious results after a fearful struggle," as this typical Midwestern believer testified later, he drew up great plans.[351] Four million dollars would have to be collected to publish a national Christian daily in Chicago as well as in New York, Philadelphia, and San Francisco.[352] With a great deal of energy the dominie began to work to that end. In the first place it was his own fellow believers and fellow "Dutch" who were challenged to support "this work of God" by subscribing and placing advertisements. He chose coworkers in part from his own circles. Monsma named himself editor-in-chief, and chose as correspondents the Reformed gentlemen Samuel Zwemer "of Cairo, Egypt, the greatest authority on the Near-East and all Moslem lands"; Prof. J. E. Kuizenga and J. Dosker; and the Christian Reformed missionaries Dr. L. S. Huizenga and Reverend J. C. De Korne in China. Monsma traveled around Europe to organize a "news service" there also. Arrangements were made for a special cable and correspondence service in England, France, Germany, and the Netherlands. Representatives were even appointed in Poland and Russia. In addition to regular staff-correspondents, such as Y. G. Kuiper in Rotterdam in the Netherlands, he engaged "special writers," "men of renown." Monsma had interviews with a number of "prominent" people during his stay in Europe; he even visited Krassin and Kameneff* in London.

Meanwhile a large high-speed press was purchased in America and all kinds of other arrangements were made. Full of confidence, Monsma headed into the great endeavor. "God has again paved the way. His name be praised."[353] The first issue of *The American Daily Standard* actually appeared at Chicago on December 22, 1920; it was a Christmas edition. For weeks a high quality paper was produced in "home" and "national editions" with "Saturday night specials." But it betrayed its Dutch background, despite its American appearance (catchy headlines and many pictures), by the names of coworkers and advertisers, by its religious character, and by the nature of the

---

*Leonid Boisovich Kraisin (1870–1926) was a Soviet diplomat and Lev Borisovich Kamenev (1883–1936) was a Russian politician who went through ups and downs in the new revolutionary governments and occupied important positions in them. Kamenev was executed in 1936 during the first Stalin purge.

articles and especially by the type of news that was not printed in it. There was an editorial on "Revolution or Reformation," a "Daily Sermonette" by T. W. Muilenburg, a Reformed minister at South Holland, Illinois; a serial "A Demoiselle of France" by C. Atwater Mason; news from the Netherlands by Y. G. Kuiper; and an "Open Forum" in which a [?] "Terborg," a [?] "Cooper" etc., etc., wrote. All this pointed to the Dutch background.[354]

It is a pity that the paper was unable to continue, in spite of its urgent appeal to the American public. "This paper does not believe that a daily newspaper should be only a mirror, a faithful mirror of life as it is. It looks upon the daily newspaper as the greatest means of the modern age for spiritual, moral and intellectual uplift. This paper means to be a radical departure from present day newspaper habits and customs. . . . Do you want a newspaper that will not massacre reputations, that will not glorify the mud in the gutter, that will not taint the pure and sweet atmosphere of the home? . . . Do you want a newspaper that is a newspaper every inch, but that never, never forgets the sacredness of its trust, and that would rather go down to utter defeat than in even one instance pander to the scurrilous forces of evil, or rummage in the offal of humanity for the purpose of finding a few trinkets of gold? Do you want such a newspaper?"[355]

The mass of more than a hundred million Americans, the mass even of the millions with a Dutch ancestry, apparently did not feel the need for a "clean paper." Also for many Puritans that kind of paper was too dull. Great were the difficulties with which Monsma had to cope and greater still the disappointments that awaited him. $4,000,000 had been needed, $500,000 for a start. The new pilgrim had been able to collect only $120,000 on his journeys. It had been possible to secure only 5,000 subscribers, the 12,000 copies of its largest edition were not even sold out. Also its street sales were very disappointing, and so was the number of advertisers.[356] In addition to all this, opposition came from all sides, not the least from his own circles. *Het Oosten* and *De Hollandsche Amerikaan*, for example, considered it offensive that Reverend Monsma mixed religion and the worship of Mammon, and borrowed money at high interests in the name of God.[357] *The Grand Rapids Press* also undermined the new undertaking, because it had considered having "editions" for Kalamazoo and Grand Rapids in addition to those already mentioned.[358] Moreoever, the paper swallowed up a minimum of $8,000 per week. No wonder, therefore, that on March 19, 1921, publication had to be discontinued. It is surprising that the paper was able to continue as long as it did.

However, a storm of indignation broke loose. "Woe and Alas" was lamented by the stockholders, among whom there were many small farmers, in Ogilvie, Minnesota, and elsewhere. In the hubbub of defeat, the losses of the members of the board, one of whom lost more than $20,000, were even completely disregarded. "This cause was God's cause," had been the assurance, a cause begun by God, and that cause gone to pot. If that is not blasphemy against God, the most pious brethren asked, what is it then?[359] And Monsma, for whom many had originally had "the greatest admiration,"

"Why the American Daily Standard Failed," an advertisement placed in *De Hope*, weekly of the Reformed Church.

"Why the American Daily Standard Failed."

We have been obliged to discontinue publication of our Christian daily.

Many guesses will be made; many will say "Financial difficulties", and, as usual, many will say, "I told you so!"

The real reasons why we had to discontinue the publication are of an entirely different nature than most people will imagine. An enumeration of the reasons is impossible for us in the limited space of a "brief statement."

Furthermore, in a report of the reasons, we would be obliged to relate many things that are [so] shocking and startling in their nature that this paper would not be able to print them.

We have decided to write a book, to relate our experiences therein, from the beginning to the end. We will have to publish that book ourselves, because no publisher would venture to place a work with that content upon the market.

We hope to have it finished within only a few weeks. For the time being, the edition is going to be limited; if one wishes to obtain a copy, let him write directly to the undersigned. We ask for no more than the cost to us: 50 cents. Enclose 50 cents in your letter. If one wishes to have two copies, he can enclose a dollar bill in the letter; this makes sending the money easier than when one must send coins.

The title of the book will be *Why the American Daily Standard Failed.*

We have already corresponded with all readers and shareholders.

And finally, let no one think that the cause of a Christian daily paper is lost! We do not give Satan the victory so easily! We will continue personally to devote all of our time to this glorious cause.

But before we can do anything else, our book must make its appearance — a book, just as *Max Havelaar* at one time in the Netherlands, and just as *Uncle Tom's Cabin* in America, will tear away the veil from much that is now covered; a book for which we will "be answerable only to God; a book which will at all costs expose the truth, the full truth, the undisguised truth.

For tactical purposes, we have remained silent about many things thus far. Now the paper is down and out. Enemies and false friends rejoice. Now the time has come to sweep away all pretenses and to say just what is what.

Only the truth can and will bring about future victory to the cause of a Christian daily.

J. CLOVER MONSMA.

Send your orders for the book to:
Rev. J. Clover Monsma
441 WEST 63RD ST.   CHICAGO, ILL.

English translation of "Why the American Daily Standard Failed," an advertisement placed in De Hope, weekly of the Reformed Church.

was forbidden by Classis Zeeland of the Christian Reformed Church, acting altogether on its own authority, to preach within its area.[360] This enterprising man found himself compelled even to resign his office as a minister of the Word. Still he did not surrender his ideals; on the contrary, he organized a Christian Press Bureau and immediately wrote—and this was typically American—a book about the reasons for the failure of *The American Daily Standard*.[361] Since that time he has been barred completely from preaching in the Christian Reformed denomination; in fact he was cast out; he joined the Presbyterian Church, which he has since served as clergyman somewhere in New York state.

"From the beginning it was a boastful, blustery endeavor, spouting religious twaddle," declared *Het Oosten* in retrospect.[362] This is indeed partly true; one need only read the somewhat boasting "At Home Again" by Monsma in the Holland-American papers to agree.[363] However, it must not be forgotten that in this regard a considerable amount of sinning was done in America; it is often the only way to accomplish anything.

In my opinion the undertaking was in the first place a *feat* of no mean importance. "We must be a lighting light and a salting salt, not passive, but active: alert, awake, working!" was the spirited slogan of the younger people as formulated by Van Andel.[364] *The American Daily Standard* has been up to the present time the most impressive, but at the same time the most curious expression of the idealism of Calvinistic Dutch Americans. It reflects their determination to be of influence in their adopted fatherland in the best sense of the word.

F. Colonial Literature

For years our people have had a definite influence through their writings. They were less sensationalistic, but probably because of that they had a greater influence, or in any case a more permanent one. In addition to the press, colonial literature already existed. This is a far greater indication of the increasing importance of Dutch Americans than writings in the newspapers. At the same time this literature also shows that for many the rooting struggle has been completed. In short, the people have been victorious over the last stage of this struggle; they have made it. Once they had become in a material sense the equals of Americans, a psychological peace set in that made scientific work possible. At the same time the increasing prosperity led to artistic achievements, at least it made them rewarding and thus promoted them.

Although these writings were originally in the Dutch language, now they usually appear in English. Therefore, with a few exceptions, the scientific and artistic value of the colonists must be measured primarily in terms of their work published in English because the most educated are also the most fluent in this language. That does not alter the fact that for us the works written in the Dutch language, even though they may not be the most important, are in any case the most interesting because they not only indicate a certain level of scientific or artistic achievement but, in addition, they indicate the various steps in the process of Americanization. These works, aside from their intrinsic value, take on special importance not only for sociographers but also for linguists, for those who want to study the mutual influence of the English and Dutch languages upon vocabulary and sentence structures. Of course, in this situation the impact of the social environment on the language and the changes that are thus brought about or, if you wish, the language disintegration or degeneration, are far more evident in Dutch writings than in the English literature. However, it is not incumbent upon me to go into these details, because that is the task of linguists.

That the writings, whether in Dutch or English, initially dealt almost exclusively with religious subjects hardly needs to be demonstrated. Even today religious literature still occupies the most important place among the Holland Americans and this literature in particular gives them their significance, although not as exclusively as formerly. The circumstance that until some decades ago ministers were practically the only intellectuals—earlier I spoke of a "dominie-culture"—has been a contributing factor. But the laymen also wrote and still write even today in part by preference about religious questions, about contemplative as well as more historical problems. In 1905, a series of "*Opstellen mijner Jongelingsjaren*" ["Essays About the Years of My Youth"] by A. Oosterheerdt appeared in Holland, Michigan. These essays, which had already appeared before in various Holland-American papers, covered historical, political, and religious topics. These latter topics, however, are considered to be the most important part.[365] Yet the writer was no minister, but an office clerk in Chicago. A second example is the postmaster at Holland, Michigan, W. O. Van Eyck, who wrote a book in 1922, *Landmarks of the Reformed Fathers or What Dr. Van Raalte's People Believed*. This work deals purely with church history matters and explains for the umpteenth time how unmotivated had been the secession of 1857—a subject that already gave us a slew of literature.

It would take me too far afield to enumerate writings of this kind. Each new secession or new quarrel gave rise to another stack of related brochures or books. If they were written by Reformed ministers, they can be found in the second volume of *Corwin's Manual*, where the most important "Publications of the Ministry of the Reformed Church" are listed. Concerning the writings of the Christian Reformed ministers or laymen, at least the laymen who graduated from Calvin or were connected with it, Prof. R. Stob has provided a complete listing in the commemorative book of the Theological School and Calvin College that appeared in 1926.

Proof of the importance of the Dutch-language religious literature in America was evidenced by the fact that when the Calvinistic church in Hungary—the largest Reformed Church in Europe—wanted to have a solid handbook about the doctrine of the Calvinists, a Dutch work was chosen from among a whole list compiled by a committee. It was the work of a Holland American, Professor G. Heyns, born in the Haarlemermeer, who had been connected until recently with the Theological School in Grand Rapids. His *Gereformeerde Geloofsleer* [*Reformed Doctrine*], published in 1916, was translated into Hungarian and is at present read and studied in Hungary in theological circles. An English translation of the same work was published by the W. B. Eerdmans Publishing Company of Grand Rapids. Heyns also wrote a series of other theological publications.[366] As a second important ecclesiastical work in the Dutch language, I mention here the book of Dr. H. Beets, *De Chr. Geref. Kerk in N.A.: Zestig Jaren van Strijd en Zegen* [*The Christian Reformed Church in North America: Sixty Years of Struggles and Blessings*], to which I have referred previously several times. It appeared in 1918, also in the Furniture City. It is a book that must certainly be of interest not only to believers but to every Netherlander who is interested in the life of his compatriots in America.

From the beginning, therefore, a steadily increasing flow of theological literature has been published. For the sociographer it would be of value to investigate when and where there developed an interest in "other areas of life," because that would provide a measuring stick of the extent to which the increasingly general development had progressed.

In addition to the theological literature, there developed in close connection, as is evident from the above, a few historical, especially church history writings. The pamphlets by De Beij and Zwemer (1871), N. H. Dosker (1888), G. K. Hemkes (1893), J. Nollen (1898), etc., are all of this nature. All of them, just like the *Gedenkboek van het Vijftigjarig Jubileum der Christelijk Gereformeerde Kerk* [*Memorial Book of the Fiftieth Jubilee of the Christian Reformed Church*] (1907), are written in the Dutch language. For the sake of completeness, it should be stated that the respective church histories by H. Van der Werp and Dr. H. Beets appeared in English in 1924. In these histories an interest was shown for various church figures as part of the subject. But soon afterwards, booklets appeared that had one of these figures as a main topic. They were the men who in early colonial life had played a more or less important role; initially almost all were ministers. In 1876 a collection of sketches appeared in Grand Rapids, *Ter Nagedachtenis van Rev. Cornelius van der Meulen* [*In Memory of Rev. Cornelius van der Meulen*], while in 1893 the talented H. E. Dosker published his *Levensschets van Rev. A. C. van Raalte D.D.* [*Life of Rev. A. C. Van Raalte, D.D.*], although (and this is significant) it was not published in America but in the Netherlands. Here [in the Netherlands], equally significantly, also appeared an interesting biography of a minister, the "reminiscences" by Rev. L. J. Hulst, *Drie en Zestig Jaren Prediker* [*A Preacher for Sixty-Three Years*] (1913); while at the same time G. K. Hemkes published in Grand Rapids *Een Man des Volks* [*A Man of the People*], a biography of Prof. G. E. Boer (1904); and also the reminiscences of the Nestor of the Christian Reformed ministers, Rev. J. Noordewier, *Een Tachtig-Jarige* [*An Octogenerian*] (1920).

After the ministers, a few orthodox brethren had their turn. H. De Vries presented a *Korte Beschrijving van het Leven en de Wonderbare Leidingen Gods met Bastiaan Broere, in Nederland en in Amerika* [*Short Description of the Life and the Wonderful Guidances of God with Bastiaan Broere, in the Netherlands and in America*] (Amsterdam, 1889). In 1900 reminiscences of the Christian Reformed elder Francis Van Driele, were published in Grand Rapids. In 1911 there appeared the reminiscences of the colonist E. J. G. Bloemendaal in a little book *Naar Amerika* [*To America*].

If all this denotes an historical context, people have also become more conscious of the fact that the settlements of colonies by themselves were acts of great importance, worthy of continued remembrance by their descendants. That this consciousness first became apparent in the most important colony, in Hólland, does not appear to me to be accidental. In 1886 D. Versteeg collected a series of pioneer reminiscences and wove them mostly into a story, *De Pelgrim Vaders van het Westen* [*The Pilgrim Fathers of the West*] (Grand Rapids, 1886). Only years later, from 1897 to 1900, K. Van Stigt published at Pella the *Geschiedenis van Pella, Iowa en Omgeving* [*History of Pella, Iowa and Environs*], which has remained incomplete, however.

A desire for a better understanding of the epoch of the pioneers brought D. Van Schelven to collect still more accurately and more broadly than D. Versteeg had done, sources for the history of *"de Kolonie"* in Michigan. They were published in two series, *"Wat bracht U hier?"* ["What Brought You Here?"] and *"Historische Schetsen uit het Koloniale Leven"* ["Historical Sketches from Life in the Colony"] from 1908 to 1915 in *De Grondwet* in Holland. Extremely important as these are, however, no publisher was ready to publish them in a single volume. This valuable material, therefore, is threatened by loss: only one or two people have a complete collection in their possession.

Sources for the Sioux County colony were collected in 1895 in a jubilee issue of *De Volksvriend*. In 1908 there appeared in Chicago, Illinois, a still more complete collection of source material, now in the English language, in the *Standard Historical Atlas of Sioux County, Iowa*, frequently mentioned by me. During the last few years, there appeared in *De Volksvriend* a long series, *"Schetsen uit het Verleden. Herinneringen van vroeger Dagen in Sioux County"* ["Sketches from the Past. Reminiscences of Early Days in Sioux County"] by G. Draayom. All of those sources frequently have a very simple, even naive character and must therefore be used very carefully. A truly scientific history first appeared in 1912 in Iowa City, Iowa, written by J. Van der Zee, *The Hollanders of Iowa*, in which Pella as well as Sioux Center are dealt with not only during their pioneer days but into the beginning of the 20th century.* All of social life— agriculture, trade and industry, church, school, press, and politics—find a place in it. I consider this book to be an interesting symptom of the cultural height that has now already been reached by the colonists.

*The text erroneously states "19th Century."

It is somewhat surprising that a similar work about the Dutch in Michigan or about those in other states has not yet been written. However, A. J. Pieters published a study in 1923 at Grand Rapids, A Dutch Settlement in Michigan, but he writes almost exclusively about "de stad" Holland and then only in the pioneer years. About the important settlements in Wisconsin, as far as the Calvinistic colonies are concerned, there is only one short magazine article by S. F. Rederus. A real historian has not arisen among the Calvinists there, nor among the Roman Catholics.

That we must not overrate the colonists' sense of history is further indicated by the circumstance that until now there is not even the simplest study in existence about the very populous industrial colonies at Paterson, Rochester, and Grand Rapids. Only very recently there appeared some articles in the weekly papers about the Hollanders in Chicago by A. Van den Bosch, while H. Beets intends to write about the Hollanders in Grand Rapids. Our colonists have not yet reached the point where they could produce a sociographic study of all of the Dutch people in the United States. The writer of these lines has intended making an attempt at this.

Among the masses, the interest in their own life is still so limited that W. O. Van Eyck of Holland, Michigan, as well as L. Holstein of Chicago, have had to give up their intention to write a study about the Hollanders in the towns where they live. The former received information that was too unreliable, the latter, who had sent questionnaires to two hundred families, received only a half-dozen replies! Indeed, my own experiences among the colonists were not much better. Only among a few of the most educated and strongest Dutch sympathizers did my request for written information bring a response, although it must be acknowledged that Holland Americans respond far more easily when it is a matter of giving oral information—many and profitable were, therefore, the conversations I have had—than of providing elaborate information in writing. Also here one must be extremely careful in drawing conclusions. We only need compare these experiences with similar experiences in the Netherlands.

It is nevertheless in the historical area, after that of religious issues, that Dutch-American writers have the most to say. Increasingly broader interests continue to be in evidence here. H. Beets wrote two popular histories, Leven van President McKinley [Life of President McKinley] (1901) and Abraham Lincoln, zijn tijd en leven [Abraham Lincoln, His Life and Times] (1909), with the purpose of creating a better understanding among "ons volk" of America's political relationships and to arouse a love for the adopted Fatherland. With the same purpose in view, A. Meijer produced De Geschiedenis van het Amerikaansche Volk [The History of the American People] (1915).

A History of the People of Iowa by Cyrenus Cole (1921) is very scholarly, but still sympathetically written. We already became acquainted with Cole as a journalist and politician. In this work he reveals himself as an historian of importance and a literary man of note, in short a unique, many-sided figure among the Dutch Americans; his work may well be considered to be of importance for the entire United States. No other work by a "colonist" has impressed me personally so particularly as this one. How moving is the last chapter "A Personal Postscript," in which the writer recalls the very difficult pioneer life of his parents and more particularly that of his mother. How thoroughly Dutch must have been the family life of the Kools: "The mother of whom I have been writing, and of whom I am still thinking—and there were many such in Iowa then—was happiest when her children were gathered around the evening lamp—and one lamp served all—each one with a book or slate. All idleness was waste, and all waste was sin."[367] In this way a Senator of the United States remembered his youth and his Dutch mother.

Interest, however, was not limited to the history of the new Fatherland. Many an educated Holland American felt attracted to "*het oude land*," especially to a study of its spiritual life. F. De Vries wrote *Dutch History, Art and Literature for Americans* (1912), and *Holland's Influence on English Language and Literature* (1916); H. E. Dosker, the biographer of Van Raalte, also published *John of Barneveldt* (1898) and *The Dutch Anabaptists* (1921), in addition to a number of theological studies. According to the American D. M. Smeets, D.D., *The Dutch Anabaptists* "received cordial commendations from the religious press and made a tremendous impression at the time of its appearance."[368]

H. Vreeland, under the leadership of the talented L. C. Van Noppen, at that time professor at Columbia University, completed a study entitled A *Life of Hugo Grotius* (1915). A. Hyma, also a pupil of Van Noppen, wrote a work about Geert Groote and his followers, entitled *The Christian Renaissance* (1924); it is a thick book that has attracted attention and is gratefully used not only in America but also in our Fatherland.[369] Very recently, the same author wrote a "source book" about Luther.

H. A. Van Coenen Torchiana, already well known to us, published two works that admittedly do not meet strictly scholarly standards like the above-named works, but I mention them because of the love that they express for the Old Country and because they are not without importance for America, or rather California, if you wish: *Holland, the Birthplace of American Political, Civic and Religious Liberty, An Historical Essay* (1915) and *Tropical Holland, An Essay on the Birth, Growth, and Development of Popular Government in an Oriental Possession* (1923). Still less pretentious, and again of a different character, is the small work (really a reminiscence) of Cornelia De Groot, *When I Was A Girl in Holland* (1917), a small book that intends primarily to give Americans a picture of the Netherlands.

Although in some of these works cited, the influence of the Netherlands upon America is traced, the mutual relations are presented more particularly in a study like *Thirty-Seven Years of Holland-American Relations* (1917) by P. Hoekstra. This work, which examines trade relations between 1803 and 1840, demonstrates the increasing interest that our most orthodox circles also show in purely economic subjects. This indicates an increasing expansion of their cultural horizon.[370]

This broadening of interests revealed itself also in the rapid increase of mission literature. This sort of publication appeared up to the present time primarily among the Reformed folks. Samuel M. Zwemer, for example, wrote a number of books about Islam, *Arabia the Cradle of Islam*, *Islam a Challenge to Faith*, *The Mohammedan World of Today*, etc. Widely read today is a book by the highly esteemed missionary Johanna Veenstra, *Pioneering for Christ in the Sudan*. Also the Christian Reformed, who are now applying themselves with great energy to missions, give their missionaries in the various fields the opportunity to publish their works. The significance of these studies goes far beyond immediate religious purposes; they have a general anthropological value. J. Van de Water wrote a book about the slums of Chicago, entitled *The Street of Forgotten Men*. Conditions in China were already covered by J. C. De Korne in *Chinese Altars to the Unknown God*, by L. S. Huizenga in *Unclean! Unclean!* or *Glimpses of the Land Where Leprosy Thrives*, and by Dr. R. H. Pousma in *An Eventful Year in the Orient*. Needless to say, such studies greatly advanced the knowledge of foreign peoples.

Economic development increases the interest in the most varied subjects. How far this interest reaches is probably most clearly indicated by the studies of Mrs. C. Hulst-Steketee, M.A., M.Pd., of Grand Rapids, Michigan. She had already written earlier *St. George of Cappadocia*, [*in Legend and History*, London, 1909] and *Balder's Death and Loke's Punishment* [Chicago, 1918]. Now in 1926, this author, one of the few Dutch women who have applied themselves to writing in America, published *Homer and the Prophets* or *Homer and Now*.[371]

It should be noticed, I repeat once more, that all of these works appeared in the English language so that they could reach a much larger number of readers. On the other hand, a work in the Dutch language appeared a few years ago that was of a more or less sociographic character, *Ons Opmaken en Bouwen* [*Our Spending and Building*] by B. K. Kuiper (1918). This work had a real American spirit that is also found in the *Memorial Book* of 1907. The purpose was to make the Christian Reformed people more conscious of their own importance and especially to help them concentrate on a definite task. Finally, there have appeared, partly in Dutch and partly in English, some works in the area of tales and narratives, mostly fiction. In one instance one may even speak of a novel.

In addition to a number of writers on religion and history, one finds among the Dutch colonists one artist, a novelist: Arnold Mulder. The fact that this author is making a living in Holland, Michigan, one can regard as incidental or one can ascribe it to the fact that Holland is the largest colony. As I see it, it must be a contributing factor that Holland is obviously the most multifaceted and most developed settlement. One recalls that it is a colony involved in agriculture, cattle-raising, business, and industry; it is the site of Hope College, etc., etc. Economic diversity leads to breadth also in the cultural realm, because this diversity makes possible an exchange of ideas that results in an animated cultural life that in the end must lead to creative art. In this case it led to Arnold Mulder's works: *The Dominie of Harlem* (1913), *Bram of the Five Corners* (1915), *The Outbound Road* (1919) and *The Sand Doctor* (1921).

The proof for my conviction I discovered during an interview with the young writer. Mulder grew up in rural Zeeland but studied at Hope College in Holland, from which he graduated in 1907. Subsequently he attended successively the universities at Ann Arbor and Chicago, and received his M.A. degree at Chicago in 1910. He feels himself to be so closely related to the "colonial" atmosphere, however, that he has created a position for himself as editor in the thriving city of Holland, in which role we had already become acquainted with him. Only his living and working in the "*de Stad*" can inspire him to any creative work, a phenomenon that the Dutch author Felix Timmermans* observed also upon his return to Lier from the Netherlands. Mulder was also strongly influenced by Knut Hamsun's† *Hoe het groeide* [How It Grew] and other authors.

All of Mulder's works breathe a "colonial spirit." This spirit is obviously the strongest in *The Dominie of Harlem*, a story that reflects the difficulties of a young, dynamic minister who, although living among the colonists, is nevertheless not in the strictest sense orthodox. With a very keen eye he depicted the sanctimonious piety that many a colonist indulged in at times, and this was one of the reasons why the book was received in *de Kolonie* with very mixed emotions. Although it is now sold out, it had for that reason been unable to find a publisher for a second edition. American critics received it favorably and W. E. Lovett mentions that he found it to be written "with clever originality and keen perspective." The remaining works also attracted attention to such an extent that, although the first two were published in Chicago, both of the latter were handled by the well-known publishers Houghton-Mifflin Company of Boston and New York.

To sketch the contents of these works would carry me too far afield. It is, however, extremely interesting to notice how one can discover in them the entire development of "colonial" life, the increasing adjustment to America, together with all the major and minor conflicts that were inevitably caused by the interpenetration of two life-views differing in so many respects. It is therefore obvious that the main theme is formed especially by the change from a strictly intellectual and theoretical Calvinism to a real American practical Christianity with all the difficulties pertaining to such a "blurring" of life goals. For the rest, one rediscovers the entire cultural development of the colonists in this "cycle" of novels.

Thus it is not incidental that in the first work, *The Dominie of Harlem*, a minister, Reverend Van Weelen, played the leading role. After all, in the various settlements the minister was still the most dominant figure for a long time and in many respects. Neither is it by chance that in the second little work, the main character, Bram, refuses to study for the ministry, while the minister, Van Wijnberg, occupies second place here. And in the third

---

*Felix Timmermans (1886–1947) was a Flemish writer, painter and graphic artist, born in Lier, Belgium. His works were translated in twenty-five languages.

†Knut Hamsun (1860–1952) was a Norwegian novelist and Nobel prize winner (1920). His novels were translated in many languages; some were made into movies.

book the hero is an artistic young man, Teunis Spykhoven, who attempts to free himself more and more from his strictly orthodox environment, while the second place in this case is no longer occupied by a minister but by a professor named Bakkezeel. In the last work, religion retreats even further into the background, while the main character, as a typical evidence of cultural progress, is now a doctor who is entirely absorbed in his scientific studies. The Americanization process had then already gone so far that the main characters no longer bear Dutch names but are baptized Dr. Quentin and other names. What has remained, however, in all of these works is the very characterisitic dune landscape of western Michigan as a background. Mulder is so thoroughly acquainted with this landscape that his description of it in his last work *The Sand Doctor*, is compared to [Thomas] Hardy's description of England's countryside.

The third book is considered to be an autobiography of the writer. In it he says things that he must have experienced deeply, very deeply. In relation to what I remarked before, one will find very striking the conviction that Mulder expresses here via one of his characters: "A writer of stuff to be printed may live anywhere; usually the farther he stays away from New York and the closer to the soil and the traditions and the spirit that produced him the better for his work."[372] This is truly the justification of his decision to continue to live among the colonists, even though his work caused them to feel "intuitively that he is not in sympathy with their religion," and although in his earliest works he had portrayed his compatriots to the Americans as "backward, ignorant, and bigoted folk."[373] Actually the entire cycle of novels can be viewed in the light of what Mulder told me: "I sketch the people and conditions as I saw them and sensed them when I was a child."

In short, the novels are not only an autobiography of Mulder, but of the entire younger generation of Holland Americans. Their difficulties and conflicts with the older folks who Americanized at a much slower rate were described by him, thanks to his artistic soul, in a most poignant way, although others may have felt that change in an even more searing way. As a reflection of the Americanization process of the Dutch colonists, Mulder's works thus have for us, besides their literary value, also a very particular importance. In that part of the Holland-American circles in Holland City to which Mulder belongs—he is a member of the Reformed Church—this process is now fairly well completed. In many respects, these people are already thoroughly American. Probably as a result, Mulder's own conflicts relating the Americanization process have been overcome, which may explain why since 1921 no new work by the young artist has appeared. Seemingly he has expressed himself completely in these matters.

There are still others who have chosen as the subject matter of their particular interest the Americanization process of the colonists, and who have produced sketches and rhymes. These are not of a caliber that compares with Mulder's work but they are still not without importance, although more for their sociographic than literary nature.

Van Zinderen Bakker once remarked that when Domela Nieuwenhuis in

Friesland predicted a better future for mankind, the new gospel stimulated even simple laborers, "from whom no one had ever seen anything remarkable," to write pieces in the newspapers that really hit home.[374] This same thing can be observed among the colonists who saw an entirely new perspective opening up in America. I have already mentioned the Groninger A. Oosterheerdt. A fellow Groninger is Dirk Nieland of Grand Rapids, who as an ordinary youth from among the common people left for America and after "twelve trades and thirteen failures," ended up there in an insurance office. Presently he is a notary public. His work brought and brings him constantly into contact with his compatriots in Grand Rapids and environs so that he has ample opportunity—the talent for this he has by nature—to notice the "weaknesses" of his people. Especially their lack of balance as a result of Americanization forms the subject of his observations.

In contrast to the great earnestness with which Mulder portrays for us this Americanization process as basic conflicts over life-styles—which they indeed are for many, especially when the faith of their ancestors is at stake— Nieland sketches these difficulties for us in a humorous manner. What he really does is to deal mainly with outward aspects, viewing them preferably from the comical side. Nieland has thus far had no time to write a book but his sketches and rhymes have appeared in part in *The Christian Journal*, and later they were bound and published under the title *Yankee-Dutch*.

As the title already indicates, most of these little pieces—partly in "Dutch," partly in English—dealt with the difficulties resulting from the use or non-use of the English language; and as such his contributions contain interesting information. One of the points he makes—and it is a very significant phenomenon—is that especially women, particularly the young girls who think that the use of English sounds very distinguished, are the first ones who prefer to forget the language of their fathers (which usually happened to be mostly dialect anyway). In my opinion the three most clever sketches from this collection are: "It's Always Something," "Dutchiness," and also the one known by some people in the Netherlands, "Zwaantje spreekt geen Hollandsch meer" [Zwaantje No Longer Speaks Dutch]. All three have this language aspect as their theme. Interesting also and not without importance is his "Geen Nieuws" [No News], which relates in a really cute way the plodding thought process of the phlegmatic "slow Dutchmen," at least in the opinion of the much more lively Americans. Although the little collection does not have any literary pretentions, nevertheless, it has attracted the attention of the talented American critic H. L. Mencken and is mentioned in his *The American Language*.

We give here the text of the poem.

Zwaantje Speaks Dutch No More

Dutch throughout the centuries
Has always been recognized as a language fair.
Nevertheless, many of Holland's children

Have turned away from it with disdain.
One example I want to tell you here;
It is the one of Zwaantje Van der Scheer;
In America only for two years, [and]
Already Zwaantje speaks Dutch no more.

And therefore—does anything come more naturally—
She has seized upon English for helping her out;
At least, that is the name she likes to give
To that language monstrosity of hers.
It is a terrible thing to hear
How she murders it, time after time;
But it is pardonable because after only a few months
Zwaantje already speaks Dutch no more.

And although her sailor from the coal barge
Understands quite well a better language,
That does not bother Zwaantje in the least,
As long as people let her speak.
"You bet your boots" and "Quit your kiddin',"
She has to use repeatedly;
And "sure Mike," is her preferred language padding,
Because Zwaantje speaks Dutch no more.

And if she has to talk with her mother
Who does not even understand "yes" or "no,"
—Whether it be in a streetcar or in a store—
Then she avails herself of whispering;
People must not hear her speak Dutch,
That would injure her pride too much.
That language may be suitable for a "Dutchman,"
But Zwaantje speaks Dutch no more.

However, the best of things may also fail at times;
That was indeed shown in Zwaantje's case.
But for that she is not to blame;
Who of Adam's seed is perfect?
But alas, she suffers from the ailment of many,
And that is certainly not to her credit,
Because although she makes a mess of English,
Zwaantje simply speaks Dutch no more.

It happened during the Christmas season
That Zwaantje's mother once asked her
To go and buy some red baize [fabric]
That her father always uses for his shirts.
She went and entered a shop,
Where she immediately sat down on a chair,
And chattered away in English with the ladies,
Because Zwaantje speaks Dutch no more.

"I vant to see red baai |baize| for fader,"
She boldly tells the shop girl.
"All right, I'll call him," answers the latter,
And immediately sends a boy.
While Zwaantje sits there waiting,
And grouses about the cold weather,
She obliges the company with her English,
Because Zwaantje speaks Dutch no more.

Soon the errand-boy is back again
To Zwaantje's seat, he comes running.
A smile is playing upon his lips.
With humor he is richly endowed.
"Vesuvius is coming, lady,"
Is the answer of the young man.
She thanks him with a "T'ank you, mister,"
Because Zwaantje speaks Dutch no more.

Immediately thereupon, a big fellow
With hair red like carmine
Politely approaches Zwaantje,
And asks her if she is looking for him.
"I vant to see red baai for fader,
Dat's all I vant to day, meneer,"
She answers him in English,
Because Zwaantje speaks Dutch no more.

"Then I must be the one you're seeking;
I am the only red-haired boy,
In all the years this firm existed,
Who ever was in their employ."
That is what the ruddy merchant said. But our Zwaantje
Now said: "It is for onderweer;
I no vant boy, but 'baai' for fader."—
Because Zwaantje speaks Dutch no more.

But now all seriousness came to an end,
The seriousness for which the merchant was well-known;
He laughed uproariously with the others,
And made Zwaantje feel deeply ashamed,—
She got her baize, but remained aggravated;
Still, it was a good lesson for her;
That is obvious now from her conversation,
Because Zwaantje speaks Dutch once more.*

ZwaantjeSpeekt Geen Hollandsch meer

* Het Hollandsch is door d' eeuwen henen,
   Steeds als een schoone taal erkend.
Toch hebben veel van Neerlands kind'ren
   Er zich met smaadheid afgewend.
Eén voorbeeld wil ik hier verhalen;
   't Is dat van Zwaantje van der Scheer;
Slechts in Amerika twee jaren
   Spreekt Zwaantje reeds geen Hollandsch meer.

En daarom—wat is meer natuurlijk—
   Heeft zij bij 't Engelsch hulp gezocht;
Ten minste zij betitelt gaarne
   Met dezen naam haar taalgedrocht.
't Is echter vrees'lijk aan te hooren
   Hoe zij het radbraakt, keer op keer;
Maar, 't is vergeef'lijk, want sinds maanden
   Spreekt Zwaantje reeds geen Hollandsch meer.

The poems of the Frisian J. H. Hoekstra of Roseland are much sharper and sometimes definitely malicious, but often strikingly true. Hoekstra was a former baker's employee from Hallum in Friesland, whom I was privileged to meet just as I met Mulder, Oosterheerdt, and Nieland. Some of his short poems have appeared in *Onze Toekomst* and *Het Oosten* and have been collected under the pseudonym of "Hans Hansen." Hoekstra by no means restricts himself to his own people; on the contrary England especially takes the brunt of his sarcasm in some of his short pieces. Yet he provides us with descriptions of the social life of the Holland Americans, which for us are the most interesting. I have already cited some of this and therefore merely refer to it.

Just like Oosterheerdt and Nieland, Hoekstra is no less conscious of his nationality than they, and writes preferably in Dutch. It is obvious that the work of these three is appreciated the most in Dutch circles and is important mainly in those circles. Naturally their circle of readers is much more restricted as a result. At this time, the only Dutch fiction writer in our language seems to be the self-educated G. Schmidt, whose *Hij die Staar of Uit het Leven van een Predikant* [*He Who Stands* or *From the Life of a Preacher*] is a rather pleasant story based upon Holland-American folk life. Just like the style of most other colonists who write in the Dutch language, this storyteller also sounds

En of nu 't steenkoolschuit-matroosje
 Ook veelal bet're taal verstaat,
Dat hindert Zwaantje niet in 't minste,
 Zoolang men haar maar spreken laat.
"You bet your boots" en "Quit your kiddin',"
 Gebruikt zij dan ook telkens weer;
En "sure Mike," is haar liefste stopwoord,
 Want Zwaantje spreekt geen Hollandsch meer.

En moet zij met haar moeder spreken,
 Die zelfs geen "yes" of "no" verstaat,
—'t Zij in de streetcar of in winkels—
 Dan neemt zij 't fluisteren te baat;
Men mag van haar geen Hollandsch hooren,
 Dat krenkt haar hoogmoed al te zeer.
Die taal mag voor een "Dutchman" passen.
 Maar Zwaantje spreekt geen Hollandsch meer.

Maar ook de beste kan soms feilen;
 Dat bleek bij Zwaantje inderdaad.
Doch daarom is zij niet te laken;
 Wie is volmaakt uit Adam's zaad?
Maar ach, zij heeft de kwaal van velen,—
 En dat strekt weinig tot haar eer.—
Want schoon zij 't Engelsch moest verknoeien,
 Spreekt Zwaantje toch geen Hollandsch meer.

't Gebeurde in de Kerstmisdagen
 Dat Zwaantje's moeder haar eens vroeg,
Om toch wat roode baai te koopen,
 Waar vader steeds een hemd van droeg.
Zij ging en trad de winkel binnen,
 Zett' dad'lijk op een stoel zich neer,
En babbeld' Engelsch met de dames,
 Want Zwaantje spreekt geen Hollandsch meer.

"I vant to see red baai, for fader,"
 Zoo spreekt zij stout de juffrouw aan
"All right, I'll call him," antwoordt deze,
 En laat direct een jongen gaan.

Terwijl nu Zwaantje zit te wachten,
 En moppert over 't koude weer,
Geeft zij haar Engelsch druk ten beste,
 Want Zwaantje spreekt geen Hollandsch meer.

Weldra kwam weer de boodschapsjongen
 Bij Zwaantje's zitplaats aangedraafd.
Een glimlach speelt hem om de lippen;
 Hij is met humor rijk begaafd.
"Vesuvius is coming, lady,"
 Is 't antwoord van den jongen heer.
Zij dankt hem met een "T'ank you, mister,"
 Want Zwaantje spreekt geen Hollandsch meer.

Onmidd'llijk daarop komt een heerschap
 Met haar zoo rood als karmozijn,
Die, Zwaantje met beleefdheid nad'rend,
 Haar vraagt of zij bij hem moet zijn.
"I vant to see red baai for fader;
 Dat's all I vant to day, meneer."
Geeft zij in 't Engelsch hem ten antwoord,
 Want Zwaantje spreekt geen Hollandsch meer.

"Then I must be the one you're seeking;
 I am the only red-haired boy,
In all the years this firm existed.
 Who ever was in their employ."
Zoo spreekt de koopman. Doch ons Zwaantje
 Zei nu: "It is for onderweer;
I no vant boy, but 'baai' for fader."—
 Want Zwaantje spreekt geen Hollandsch meer.

Doch nu was ook de ernst ten einde,
 Waarvoor de koopman was befaamd;
Hij lachte luide met de and'ren,
 En maakte Zwaantje diep beschaamd.—
Zij kreeg haar baai, maar bleef geërgerd;
 Toch was het wel een goede leer,
Dat blijkt thans uit haar conversatie,
 Want Zwaantje spreekt het Hollandsch weer.

somewhat naive, as is the case with the work of a few scholars. The minister R. H. Hoeksema has dared to write . . . a play. He has, however, immediately reconciled his fellow believers with this project by casting a minister as his main character! *Dominee Kouwenaar of Zedelijk Dualisme* [*Dominie Kouwenaar* or *Moral Dualism*]. To give some idea of the "style" I include only the dream of Schoonbeek, one of the main characters.

> "I dreamt—it was a dark night—
> And terribly raged a hellish power,
> A hellish power in a dark night.
>
> Stretched I saw a black cloth,
> On which burned beautifully a hellish curse;
> A hellish curse on a pitch-black cloth.
>
> That curse was by Satan so beautifully
> [Shaped] in flaming gigantic figures;
> Flaming so beautifully in letters gigantic—"*

Whether up to this time any poets of renown should have arisen from among the colonists, I do not know, but this is not to say that no poetry is being written. To the contrary! It is again the ministers who once in a while venture out in this field. H. J. Van der Werp must be given some credit in this respect. Hoekstra wrote in this connection: "Although there is on this shore no Bilderdijk who planted his feet; still H. Van der Werp does not hang his lyre on the willow of the river of tears, but he plucks it lovingly and softly in beautiful Dutch songs of rejoicing."† That even men of renown, who came to America already as children and who have spent the major part of their lives among Americans, felt the need in later life to express their most tender feelings in the mother tongue, is shown to us in a collection of poems entitled: *Spiegel der Genade* [*Mirror of Grace*] by the well-known Gerhardus Vos, professor at the famous Princeton University.

Whatever the judgment regarding all of this Dutch work may be, one cannot deny that it all points to a certain amount of culture, to a Holland-American life becoming more complete. However, one should not judge our compatriots, at least not primarily, on the basis of what they wrote in the mother tongue, but on the basis of the fruit of their pens in English. Here partly lies the tragedy of their existence. Their importance for America lies almost exclusively in what was produced in the English language and that is no small amount, as we have seen.

---

* "Ik droomde—'t was donkere nacht—   Die vloek was door Satan zoo prachtig
En vreeslijk woedde een helsche macht,   Gevlamd in figuren reusachtig;
Een helschen macht in een donkeren nacht.   Gevlamd zoo prachtig in letters reusachtig. . . . "

Gestrekt zag 'k een zwarten doek,
Daarop brandde prachtig een helsche vloek;
Een helsche vloek op een pikzwarten doek.

†Al is het dan dat aan dit strand geen Bilderdijk zijn voeten plant; toch hangt H. Van der Werp, zijn lier niet aan de wilg der traan-rivier, maar tokkelt hij haar lief en zacht in Hollandsch jub'lend lied'ren pracht."

For us Netherlanders, the spiritual work of our kinsmen has a very special importance in still another way. The history, the cultural life, indeed our best intellectual products are presently spread among the English-reading public more and more through the intermediary of Holland-Americans. This is now done by works that our kinsmen have translated, which because of their intrinsic value deserve to be included in world literature. I want to mention, for example, [the dramatist-poet Joost Van den Vondel's] *Lucifer*, that L. C. Van Noppen translated so excellently into English. What this means for us Dutchmen is indicated, for example, by the fact that the great importance of Vondel's work is now recognized so generally that *Het Leven van Vondel en zijn Tijd* [*The Life of Vondel and His Time*] has even been translated and published from English into Hindu. Under the influence of Van Noppen several other translations have also appeared, partly by Americans originally of the Old-Netherlanders generation, partly of the Young-Netherlanders generation, and partly also by "English" Americans. *De Sevenste Bliscap* [*The Seventh Bliscap*] was transposed into English poetry by [?] Gilmore. [Gerrit] Kalff's *Geschiedenis der Nederlandsche Letterkunde* [*History of the Literature of the Netherlands*] is known today by many an American through Miss [?] Franke's abridgement. Even the *Brieven van Kartini* [*Letters of Kartini*]can be read today in English, thanks to Mrs. [Agnes Louise] Symmers.[375]

Naturally, and entirely independently of Van Noppen, believers have translated into English some works of Kuyper and Bavinck. I have already indicated elsewhere the great importance of this kind of labor, and the large task that rests upon our compatriots. I wrote as follows: "Now that the colonists have reached a degree of cultural development and prosperity that place them in a situation where they can participate in the cultural life of America, they are the ones to bring over into American society and make it part of American culture that portion of Dutch thought, of Dutch culture, that is worthy of being included in world thought, that is worthy of becoming world culture."[376] The translations noted here indicate that our compatriots eagerly take this task upon themselves.

G. Comparisons

The foregoing gives us first of all some concept of the cultural level that has at present been attained in the various settlements. Secondly, it points up the significance that the Dutch Americans have already reached as contributors to present-day American society. However, the picture of this latter development is by no means complete. Actually, the importance of the Dutch element in the United States is much greater than we have so far observed. It should be remembered that we have recorded chiefly the development of those Netherlanders living in the settlements. There are many others, indeed a far greater number, who live among Americans entirely outside of any Netherlandic connection or structure. It is a noteworthy phenomenon that although some Netherlanders achieved positions of prominence and influence in the various colonies, yet great numbers of those who had from the very beginning merged into American life, came to much higher and more influential positions.

There are examples of this assimilation and excellence in every area of society. Steketee and Van den Berg became the most important merchants in Grand Rapids. The Frisian F. H. Kuipers, born at Akkrum, became one of the most powerful merchandisers in the United States. In his early youth he had worked in a drapery business in Leeuwarden where he learned several languages, to some degree at least. In 1866, at the age of twenty-three he left our country and went to America where among other people he found employment with one of the Van Peymas. Later he got a job as a sales clerk in a store in Buffalo. Here he met A. De Graaf, a young lady from Zeeland [Netherlands], and they were married. She did tailoring, making men's vests; he sold them and continued as a store clerk. At first they made only a scant living but in time their profits increased. After years of hard work they had saved enough to start their own business in Toledo. Here the young wife died. Kuipers in the meantime had changed his name to Cooper.

After a brief period of wandering, Kuipers started yet another, bigger business at Peoria, near Chicago, and entered into a partnership with [Henry] Siegel, a German-born drapery businessman. Together they started a huge department store. According to some, it was the first business of its kind in the center of Chicago. In 1887, with an investment of $125,000 the majestic store was opened. The business was so profitable that when the buildings were destroyed by fire, the partners were able to build even larger ones. In time they also built a similar structure in New York. Cooper became wealthy and annually went back to Akkrum for a vacation. When he died in 1904, his children did not choose to carry on their father's business. But for many years the names "Siegel-Cooper" could still be seen on the buildings in Chicago; the buildings in New York had been sold earlier.[377] During the [First] World War, Dutch names were generally considered to be German and because of strong anti-German sentiment the Siegel-Cooper name, though carved in stone, was cut away!

In the area of finances there are similar examples. In the colonial settlements we have encountered many bank directors, but their influence was chiefly local. However, the financiers Ch. Boissevain at New York, and [Arthur] Van Vlissingen at Chicago were far more widely known. And anyone interested in railroad shares became familiar with the name Van Sweringen. Two of the most important names among the railroad magnates are those of O. P. and M. J. Van Sweringen at Cleveland, Ohio.[378]

Many publishers and editors of large and small newspapers and magazines grew up in the Dutch colonies. However, the most prominent one among them, Edward Bok, lived among the Americans all his life, although he was born in Den Helder and came with his parents to America in 1870 when he was almost seven years of age. He had a thoroughly American education and pursued a thoroughly American career. Subsequently, as the originator and publisher of the *Ladies' Home Journal* at Philadelphia, he became world-famous both as a writer and business executive. Even President [Theodore] Roosevelt was one of his contributing writers. One can read about all this in *The Americanization of Edward Bok: The Autobiography of a Dutch Boy Fifty Years After*, which was published in September, 1920, exactly fifty years after his arrival in America. In November of the same year, scarcely two months later, the second printing was made and in 1923 it was still one of the four most widely read non-fiction books in the United States. In 1923 a Dutch translation (or rather, an adaptation) was printed. The year 1926 saw the 37th American edition of Bok's *Autobiography*. Thereafter three special editions were printed for England, three for the Netherlands, one German edition, and one in Braille for the blind. In the meantime several other writings by Bok appeared: *A Man from Maine* (also widely read), *Two Persons, Twice Thirty, Dollars Only*, and *America, Give Me A Chance!* Bok exercised considerable influence upon America's mentality through all these books.[379]

However difficult it may be to evaluate this, one cannot escape the conclusion that Bok the journalist exercised more influence in America than all the "colonial" journalists together. Evidence of this, I believe, is seen in the fact that even in scientific circles, men like [Horace M.] Kallen and [Thomas Nelson] Carver took account of Bok. According to Kallen, Bok was too willfully American,[380] but according to Carver (a 100-percent American) he was still too European in his way of thinking and behaving.[381] At the age of 56, Bok retired from many of his former activities. This was considered as being un-American and was condemned as a dangerous European example for America.

There are some comparisons to be made also in science. First of all, the engineer [?] Pieck, has achieved fame in the electro-technical field in the United States as no colonist ever has. The physician Dr. H. Hulst of Grand Rapids is known far beyond his home city, indeed, beyond his home state of Michigan, as a respected writer on medical subjects. The bacteriologist, Dr. Paul H. De Kruif, the son of an Amsterdam family that, like the Bok family, settled among the Americans, is even known in Europe. Although people in the Netherlands first came to know him through what was written by and about him in Sinclair Lewis' *Martin Arrowsmith*, his own book, *Microbe Hunters*, was translated into the Dutch language under the title of *Bacteriënjagers* and was widely read in the Netherlands. Recently he participated in a "pro- and anti-kissing" debate and as a "pro" he set the whole "civilized" world at ease. The photograph of this "authority" also appeared in the newspapers in the Netherlands, a distinction not shared by any "colonial" physician, as far as I know.

As I mentioned before, the Dutch immigrants are also making contributions particularly in the realm of history. The Netherlander H. W. Van Loon is one of the most widely read historians of our time in America, and even in the whole world. Unfortunately, he is not one of the most reliable. Van Loon was born in 1882 at Rotterdam and at the age of twenty went to

America where he studied at Cornell and Harvard universities. He then became a journalist for the Associated Press and for several years traveled through Europe as a foreign correspondent. Meanwhile he also took courses at Munich and Paris. At Paris he received his doctorate and subsequently became famous for his book *The Story of Mankind*, which is one of the most-read books in the United States. Within six months after its publication, 40,000 copies had been sold and a special edition was printed in London. Dr. C. P. Gunning translated it into the Dutch language with the cooperation of the author. However, Prof. Dr. J. Huizinga, in an interesting article in the *Gids*, questioned the usefulness as well as the value of both the original and the translation and considered it "an ominous sign for our civilization."

A second book by Van Loon was also translated into Dutch by Rector Gunning and appeared under the title of *De Bijbel naverteld* [*The Bible Retold*]. A third book by Van Loon, entitled *De Vrijmaking der Menschheid* [*The Liberation of Mankind*], was translated into our language [Dutch] by J. L. Gunning, L.L.M., in 1926. Of more scientific value are the works of the historian A. J. F. Van Laer, who was also an "individual immigrant." As archivist of the state of New York at Albany, his writings, especially his translations of Old-Dutch documents, are of interest to us.

In the area of politics, I would like to remind my readers finally of the labor leader, Samuel Gompers. He was born in 1850 in London to parents who were natives of the Netherlands. Sometime during the 1860s the family emigrated to America.* Samuel rose from the job of apprentice cigarmaker to president of the American Federation of Labor. For many years he occupied this responsible position and exercised greater influence than any politician in the Dutch "colonies." It was asserted quite recently that he did more than any other American, "native-born or naturalized, to raise the average material standards of American life."[382]

Even in the realm of religion some of the most influential leaders are found among the "individualists." This is especially true of Roman Catholics. So far as I know, no "colonial" Roman Catholic has yet become a bishop. Neither F. Janssen, the former archbishop of New Orleans, nor C. Van de Ven, the present bishop of Alexandria, Louisiana, nor A. J. Drossaerts, the bishop of San Antonio, Texas, grew up in any of the colonial settlements; they belong to the more than 150 Roman Catholic priests of Dutch ancestry actively functioning in the United States.

In addition to many of the outstanding leaders who are known not only

---

*The United States ship passenger lists report the arrival at New York of the Soloman Gomper(t)s family on July 7, 1863, aboard the ship *London* from London, England, steerage class. The father Soloman, age 35, gave as occupation "cigarmaker" and the accompanying family members were his wife Sarah, 36, and children Samuel, 11; Henry, 9; Alexander, 5; Louis, 3; Harriet, 2; and Jacob, 1. All of the family members, including Samuel, reported Holland as "country of origin." See Robert P. Swierenga, comp., *Dutch Immigrants in U. S. Ship Passenger Manifests, 1820–1880: An Alphabetical Listing by Household Heads and Independent Persons* (Wilmington, Del., Scholarly Resources Inc., 1983), p. 336.

in America but also in Great Britain and Europe, there are other immigrants who could be named, who are not as well known as most of the gentlemen mentioned earlier, yet they have also performed meritorious services for the United States. I mention only a few of these. In the first place there is the chemist and geologist G. Troost. In the first half of the nineteenth century he lived in Robert Owen's well-known colony, New Harmony [Indiana], and was a technical adviser there. Later he was a professor at Vanderbilt University at Nashville, Tennessee.[383] Then there is the marine artist A. Van Beest, who was born in Rotterdam and spent a lonely life in the eastern United States and died in New York in 1860.[384] At Indianapolis the Van Camps founded an important packing [canning] industry, and at Pittsburgh G. A. Samuels set up a butter processing plant, while J. R. Planten, for many years the Dutch consul-general at New York, successfully established a business for making capsules for the medical profession. At New York H. H. Vreeland, the son of a Dutch preacher, was a renowned railway engineer, having laid out the municipal rail system of New York City. J. O. Schimmel founded a cannery at Jersey City; and [?] Bosman and [?] Lohman, who operated a similar plant in Boissevain's Norfolk, may also be mentioned, although [A. B.] Faust claims these were Germans. In contrast, the many Dutch-owned "canning works" in the colonies are comparatively minor in size.

M. Goedhart became one of America's most competent builders of harbor works. He constructed the facilities at Galveston, Texas, and was known and recognized everywhere in this particular field. In Idaho a certain [Joseph R.] De la Mar advanced from mineworker to multimillionaire. In 1879, a prominent businessman in Rotterdam, [L.] Pincoff [Pincoffs], was compelled to leave the Netherlands and go to America where he made a meager living as a cigar retailer. He also wrote magazine articles, etc. He died in 1911. One of his sons, A. Pincoff, became a prominent lawyer in New York.[385] H. Vos became famous in New York as a portrait painter. There are also many musicians among the Dutch immigrants to America. However, because they are frequently on the move—as required by their type of work—they should be classified as cosmopolitans rather than exclusively as "Americans." In New York the name of [?] Kriens is familiar and the fame of W. Van Hoogstraten has spread from the Atlantic to the Pacific, from New York to Portland.[386]

From all these examples one feels involuntarily inclined to conclude that the immigrants who settled among the Americans developed more rapidly and fully and made greater progress than those who settled in colonies among their own kind. This is an important question because both H. Beets and the A.N.V. [Algemeen Nederlandsch Verbond] have both raised the question: Should immigrants come in groups or as individuals?[387] National [ethnic] background and common religious convictions may make the former way of settling preferable. On the other hand, individual interests of most of these immigrants and particularly the differences in the states to which they wish to go, often make a wider dispersion desirable. However, we should be cautious here and not draw unwarranted conclusions from my list of "immigrants who succeeded."

In comparing the successful "colonists" and "individualists," we must bear in mind that the number of Netherlanders who are scattered is much greater than those who live in the various colonial group settlements. However, exact figures of the ratio would be most difficult to obtain; in fact, they do not exist. The statistics of the membership of the Reformed and Christian Reformed churches do give us some clues. The "western" part of the Reformed Church, plus the Christian Reformed Church, total at present more than 200,000 souls. The assumption is that these are Young-Dutch Americans. If we estimate at 100,000 the number belonging to the smaller Reformed groups, to the Presbyterians and to the Roman Catholics and who probably live in groups, then we come up with a total of 300,000, counting four generations.

However, it is estimated that the total number of all Young Dutch belonging to the four youngest generations stands at almost one million. According to these figures only one-third, or more accurately one-fourth to one-third, of all the Netherlanders in America live in nationality groups. Taking these figures into consideration, a "Who's who?" research would be more in their favor than we might have expected. Besides, we must reckon with the fact that the more educated Netherlanders were more inclined to migrate as individuals then were the less educated persons. One can thus expect that the percentage of "intellectuals" among the "individuals" would have been greater.

It remains a fact, as I have remarked during my discussion of Mulder's writings, that settlement among Americans leads to more friction and therefore to a more rapid and intensive development of latent powers than does living among countrymen.

Finally, the question may be raised whether the total number of Netherlanders who achieved distinction in America is relatively greater or smaller than that of other nationalities. Here also we lack any adequate basis for comparison, although my impression is that such a comparison would certainly not be to our detriment, at least at the present time. At the beginning of the twentieth century, Van Coenen Torchiana offended many by giving as his opinion exactly the opposite view.[388] We must never forget that great numbers of our most energetic youth, willing to leave our country, have found rewarding work, whether it be in the Orient or in the West. On the other hand, the same can be said of the Germans, Swiss, Danes, etc. The records prove that they too have achieved gratifying careers.

Nevertheless, we should not consider all the Netherlands immigrants as being faultless. Among them are some less desirable elements. Many have hanging over them a "shady past." During the nineteenth century, many a Netherlander chose to seek a safe haven in a free America rather than to face something worse. Several times I have thus called attention to the fact that the greatest danger menacing the colonists came from the least expected source, namely from their own countrymen. This was not confined to the inexperienced newcomers, the "greenhorns" who were duped by "runners." Even those who had spent a great part of their lives in America continued to be threatened. [?] Heineken, who had lived in Kansas City for eighteen years told me that both he and the Dutch consul there had been victimized by a Dutch swindler.[389] That is why especially in the large cities the Netherlanders prefer not to associate with their own kind. No doubt it was for that reason that the Dutch consul in Kansas City, Missouri, wrote to me in 1920: "In this city there are no Hollanders to speak of, except a few naturalized ones."[390] But the records show that in this "busy, boasting and Babbit-ful"* city at that time there lived 107 immigrants born in the Netherlands and 247 whose parents were Dutch-born, a total of 354 of Dutch origin! That was probably also the reason why, when I asked Prof. J. A. De Haas about the Netherlanders in the U. S., he replied "I have met very few."[391]

Statistics regarding the number of Netherlanders involved in various types of crimes are not available to me. However, my impression, which is derived from various sources of information, is that the total is extremely small. Our people are generally known as "law-abiding." This does not deny that they are sometimes guilty of transgression. For example, they sometimes break the liquor laws (I quoted a striking example) and are fined for speeding.

In reference to these matters it is not appropriate to speak of "crime." A more exact word is "mischief." And when it comes to mischief the young Dutch boys go all out. To engage in mischief, in "monkeyshines," seems to be a genuinely Dutch trait. Heineken told me that "even the street kids in America are more restrained than those in Holland." For example, in winter they would not think of pelting passers-by with snowballs. Obviously my informer was less familiar with the American youths of Dutch blood. They throw not only snowballs, but eggs! Except for these youthful monkeyshines, the Netherlanders on the whole conduct themselves very properly.

Discerning Americans have high regard for the Dutch immigrants, especially our farmers. The government of North Dakota evaluates them as "industrious, progressive and cooperative citizens." South Dakota is convinced of their success sight-unseen. Even in the more southerly states where they were not as successful, they are nevertheless esteemed. In New Mexico, where we have previously studied a Dutch settlement, they are the most highly valued of all the farmers, as is also the case in Mississippi.[392]

That it is not only the farmers who are successful but also the Dutch intellectuals is evident from the many responsible positions that are continually offered to Dutch engineers. At Albany I met the hydraulic engineer, Quarles de Quarles; other Dutch engineers are working on the railroads. Hollanders are also instructors at various universities. I think of the profes-

---

*George F. Babbitt characterized the striving middle class businessman in the 1922 novel, *Babbitt*, by Sinclair Lewis.

sors [Adriaan] Barnouw and [J. A.] De Haas at New York. The first was appointed a lecturer at Columbia University but soon thereafter was promoted to a professorship by the governing board. On a train between Chicago and Washington I talked with a college student who spoke enthusiastically of Professor De Haas' excellent teaching. A well-known geologist, [Willem Anton Joseph Maria Van] Waterschoot van der Gracht, worked for many years for a firm of oil magnates. However, not all of these professionals became naturalized American citizens. Several remained citizens of the Netherlands. S. C. Bosch Reitz, who for twelve years (from 1915 to 1927) has been curator of Oriental art at the Metropolitan Museum of Fine Arts [in New York City], is planning, like so many others, to return to the Netherlands.

How highly the Dutch immigrants, taken as a whole, are esteemed, was expressed to the Reverend [T.] Jongbloed by an official at Ellis Island, the admission station for immigrants. Pointing to a Dutch family he said: "Give us one such family and you can take fifteen others away." Rev. Jongbloed, who at that time (1920) was charged with the supervision and guidance of incoming immigrants from the Netherlands, received from the American Immigration Commissioner, F. Wallis, the following message: "We have been receiving some interesting Dutch immigrants. As I said to Mr. [?] Veenstra, I wish you would bring your whole country over. The Dutch have prior claim on Manhattan Island and I am sure no better representatives of the great continent of Europe could come to us than those from historic and picturesque Holland."

Very recently Lothrop Stoddard released figures showing that between 1820 and 1920 there were admitted to this country as immigrants 33 million Anglo-Saxon and Irish, 5 million Germans, and 2 million Scandinavians. In comparison he mentioned only one-fifth of a million Netherlanders, which nevertheless was "the only other stream of real importance in the Old Immigration." As evidence that these statements were not merely "words" or opinions but concrete facts, it has been proposed that immigration be reduced overall, but that the quota of immigrants from the Netherlands be increased by 1,400 above the previous number, which is possible only with a proportionate decrease in the quotas of other nationalities.[393]

H. The Significance of the Dutch Americans for the Netherlands

It is difficult to evaluate the effect that all these thousands of residents have had on our mother country. What was their significance for our Fatherland?

Obviously they left more space for those who stayed behind. The increases in the cost of buying and renting land, if not stopped, were at least slowed down and in many areas unemployment was lessened. This emigration also provided a kind of safety valve for the release of bitterness over certain situations, especially the social conditions. Particularly in Friesland, where there existed such abuses as large tracts of land owned by absentee landlords, many of the most energetic left for America. This, in my view, eased the tension.

Not without significance is the alteration in the ratios of young people and old, of men and women, etc., brought about by emigration. Generally speaking, those who emigrated were in the prime of life. Therefore there were now a greater number of older people left behind, some of whom were unable to provide for themselves. For instance, the writer [R.] Kjellen tells of a similar situation in Sweden where, due also to a lower death rate, there is "*eine unverhältnismaszig grosze Menge von alten Leuten*" [a disproportionately large number of old people].[394] Here again we must proceed with caution, because many an immigrant, having become prosperous in America, sent for his old parents to join him, which was an evidence of the strong family ties among our people. A good example of this is "Pake" Velsing, who at the age of seventy-two left the Netherlands and went to live with his children at Rochester, New York.

I do not have exact figures on the ratios of young and old left in our country. However, I do have quite precise data on the ratios of males and females who emigrated. By 1920 there were in America 75,510 males who had been born in the Netherlands and 56,256 females. To put it differently, for every 1,000 female immigrants there were 1,342 males. In 1910 the ratio was 1,322 males to 1,000 females. The disproportion has increased slightly between 1910 and 1920. The women left behind in the Netherlands thus had fewer opportunities for marriage but greater influence in the voting booths. Only one of the American states attracted more women than men—the Mormon state of Utah. In 1920 there were in Utah 956 men who had been born in the Netherlands compared with 1,024 women. Apparently the women were greatly attracted by these Latter Day Saints!

Has the emigration brought American influence to bear upon our country? We can detect very little of it. We could have expected that friends and relatives in America would have told us about American farming methods and practices and this would have changed ours. Recently there appeared a series of letters in the *Leeuwarder Courant* written by "a Frisian" in America describing American farming methods. But the Netherlanders are usually too tenacious and stubborn to change.

I know of only one instance of American influence. [Klaas] Beukma, a farmer in Groningen, went to America in 1836. In 1847 he returned to visit his birthplace and brought with him a threshing machine to demonstrate to the "Genootschap van Nijverheid" [Association for the Promotion of Industry] at Onderdendam. According to a report by C. Borgman, "It was still being used seven years later by G. Reinders at Warffum with excellent results."[395] E. Borgman, a brother of the above reporter, began to construct similar treadle machines powered by six to eight horses for the farmers of that province.

The use of silos is not finding any acceptance by our farmers. The few that can be seen are mostly found on experimental farms that are operated "scientifically," so-called, and that often means very uneconomically. Various farmers who had returned to the Netherlands after having worked for a few years in the United States, confirmed to me that the Dutch immigrants in America had made very little impact upon the agricultural methods in their homeland. At the present time tractors and other types of farm equipment manufactured in America are promoted here only by salesmen from import firms.

H. W. Heuvel, who died recently and who was probably more familiar with the "Achterhoek" of Gelderland than any other region, wrote me that he was unable to discern any influence from America upon the life-style, the farming methods, etc., of his fellow citizens, even though it was particularly from this area that many of the first immigrants left for America.[396] The power of the old Achterhoek milieu was too great to be displaced. Heuvel did acknowledge that the departure of immigrants had produced wider spiritual horizons. I myself have also observed this phenomenon here and in other areas. But this widening of the local outlook also had the effect of encouraging more inhabitants to exercise their freedom of choice to leave.

Incidentally, there are a few reminders of the emigration. A few of the emigrants, having become wealthy, wanted to share their prosperity with the residents of their birthplace. Thus, in 1901 at Akkrum, the well-known American merchant Cooper (Kuipers) built an old peoples' home, called "Coopersburg." There are forty-four residents spending the evening years of their lives in peace and comfort.[397] There are other instances, such as the "American" preacher who returned to the Netherlands and donated his library to the University of Groningen; the millionaire |B. A.| Bierman, who had acquired most of his wealth in Canada, invested part of his fortune in the digging of a coal mine in Vlodrop, the village of his birth. There is also the memorial window in one of the churches of Delft, given by Edward Bok on the occasion of the jubilee year of Queen Wilhelmina's reign.[398] Finally, here and there one sees on the graves of old parents a beautiful tombstone, revealing the piety of their children in America. On one such stone near the little village of Firdgum in Friesland are chisled these words: "In thankful remembrance this iron fence has been placed around these graves by their son, R. R. La Fleur, residing in New Amsterdam, Lacrosse County, Wisconsin, North America, Sept. 30, 1882.[399]

Since so many people had migrated to America because of deep religious convictions, we might have expected some discernible religious influences to rebound in the Netherlands. However, these also appear to be very minor. I am not aware that many "American" concepts in the spiritual realm have penetrated our churches through the emigrants. Unquestionably there have been, and will continue to be, some such influences. For example, in Reformed circles in our country people read church newspapers printed in America in the Dutch language and sometimes also secular newspapers. Leaders of the Christian Reformed churches of America regularly visit the

Expression of attachment to the Old Country. The late Frisian American F. H. Kuipers (above), who had a mausoleum built for himself in his native village of Akkrum (middle), and who founded an old people's home, Coopersburg (below).

Netherlands and some have studied there. At the present time, two American preachers, the Reverends E. Woldring and C. Van Reenen, both of whom received their training at Calvin College and at the Theological School in Grand Rapids, are serving two Gereformeerde churches here. There have also been preachers who spent years in America and then returned with a very broadened outlook to occupy pulpits here. One of the latter is Rev. S. De Bruine, to whom I have often referred in my writings.

Finally, there are typical street scenes that can be observed, particularly in recent years in many a Dutch village or town. Dutch Mormons from Utah and elsewhere have temporarily returned to the Netherlands as missionaries of Mormonism. They try to win converts and preach their religious convictions, frequently in open-air gatherings, and in public auditoriums in larger towns. They have made, and continue to make, many converts. This has led to a new wave of emigration to America, which is portrayed as a virtual Zion. The Mormon churches in Rotterdam and Amsterdam, designed in a friendly American style, exist only through the help of American financing, although not exclusively Dutch-American financing. They receive funds from the Mormon church in its entirety.[400]

Though there are numerous traces of "Americanism" to be found in our Fatherland, yet compared to other countries they are often remarkably small. Consider Italy where many immigrants, after having acquired wealth in America, returned preferably to the vicinity of their native villages, bought land, and spent the rest of their lives there living as "Americans." Consider Sweden where, according to Kjellen, American influence was very strong in matters such as religious controversies and alcohol prohibition. In Sweden there is an increasing number of Baptist and Methodist churches which Kjellen interprets as "a direct spiritual exchange along the lines of a close relationship that the emigration fostered between Sweden and America."*[401] The emigration is also bringing about more Anglo-Saxon influences in Sweden, which has a political impact as well.

We must also keep in mind that in a numerical as well as in a relative sense both Italy and Sweden surrendered to America a far greater number of their citizens. So great was the exodus, in fact, that they began to speak of "de-population" and formed organizations to work against the emigration movement. But there was also an important remigration. It was quite considerable, especially to Italy, since Italians are strongly attached to their home country. In many villages it was an embarrassment, something to be ashamed of, for the relatives who had stayed behind, if those who had gone to America never returned, so say the husband-wife authors [Carel Theodorus] Scharten and [M. Scharten-] Antink. It was the remigrants who brought American influences to Italy, rather than the letters that came back.

But in our country the ratio of returning immigrants has always been very minor. However, during the [First] World War, many immigrants returned

---

*"einen direkten geistigen Verkehr auf den innigen Verbindungslinien, welche die Auswanderung zwischen Schweden und Amerika gezogen hat."

because they were reluctant to be drafted into the American army. Also many European immigrants were criticized as foreigners during the war and grew weary of the constant suspicion and harrassment. For others, it was not possible to go back to a homeland in Europe until after the war. But after the war had ended there was a veritable exodus, not only of Dutch people but of the most varied nationalities—Norwegians, Swedes, Italians, etc. Heavy taxes, prohibition, and other governmental regulations raised the number of remigrants to as many as one thousand per day.[402] Both Germany and Sweden tried to promote the return movement.[403]

[J.] Maurer is of the opinion that at the present time many Netherlanders emigrate to America, fully intending to return after having made a fortune.[404] "Who goes now, goes not for good but with the hope of returning sooner or later." This may apply particularly to the intelligentsia, to musicians, and to engineers but not the majority, I believe. A. Van C. P. Huizinga maintains that the total of Dutch remigrants is "negligible."[405] I do not agree, although I think the percentage would not go above a few percent. I do not have complete statistics.

Some idea about the remigration may be formed by figures compiled by [Jeremiah W.] Jenks and [W. Jett] Lauck:[406]

	1911	1912
Emigrants leaving the Netherlands	8,358	6,667
Immigrants returning to the Netherlands	461	564

The percentage of returnees would then be 5.5 percent of the emigrants in 1911 and 8.5 percent in 1912. These percentages are further reduced when one takes account of the fact that many of the remigrants later went to America a second time. How homesick they had been for the Old Country, but how different it actually was when they came back! How restricted, how small, how cramped! Besides, many of their relatives and old friends were no longer living. More than one returned to America disillusioned, with a new sense of reality. For example, J. Sleyster had lived in America for twenty years but wanted to spend the evening years of his life in the Netherlands. He went back, but found he no longer felt at home there and returned to Orange City, Iowa.[407] The Van Beek family returned to Waupun, Wisconsin. They also had too greatly idealized the Netherlands and when they went back there they found the situation to be different from what they had imagined.[408]

Especially after the war the returnees found conditions in the Netherlands had changed. They were greatly disappointed and went back to America as soon as possible. For these various reasons it is even more difficult to get an accurate count of the number of remigrants. Their actual influence is therefore also less significant than the known figures would indicate.

There yet remains for me the appointed task to ascertain to what degree and extent the Netherlanders have become truly integrated Americans, or have remained genuine Netherlanders.

16

From Netherlander to American

A. To What Extent the Colonists Became Americans

In August of 1907, the sixtieth anniversary of the founding of *de Kolonie* at Zeeland, Michigan, was celebrated. One of the many speakers at the event was Reverend M. Kolyn, and he expressed his conviction that the colonists "have entered fully into every part of the broad and pulsating life of the great American people. We are part and parcel of a great and prosperous nation."[1] Ten years later the prominent G. J. Diekema spoke and also wrote about the "complete Americanism" of the colonists of his town, Holland.[2] But in the colonies in the large metropolitan areas, things were different. In the spring of 1927, the correspondent of the *Nieuwe Rotterdamsche Courant* visited Grand Rapids in western Michigan and had "a hard time finding any trace of genuine Dutch influence," except for the large number of Dutch names in the telephone directory and the Dutch language services in a few of the churches. "It seems as if people of Dutch ancestry have deliberately chosen to ignore and abandon their Dutch traditions and customs."[3]

There is indeed a great deal of truth in these observations. The only traces of Dutch heritage and background that a visitor sees in the various colonies are the Dutch names over many of the shops and on the mail boxes in the residential sections. Aside from these, a casual observer notices very little evidence of their Dutch origin, neither in the layout of the cities or villages, nor in the architecture. Our seventeenth-century ancestors established themselves in other foreign lands and founded cities there. Gothenburg in Sweden, Frederikstad in Holstein, etc., were built by Hollanders after Dutch models. Earlier still, parts of Hamburg and Danzig evidenced the Dutch touch. Kaapstad in South Africa is another good example. Even in the tropics [Jan Pieterszoon] Coen built Batavia after the example and pattern of his home town of Hoorn in the Netherlands. In the first half of the nineteenth century New York, Albany, and Schenectady were still thoroughly Dutch in appearance, while Beukma commented on the "*grachten*" [canals], so characteristically Dutch, in Buffalo.

Two centuries later there were but few traces of Dutch architecture in the colonies. Some colonists in Michigan did attempt to follow the pattern of the Old-Dutch, centrally located village [*komdorp*]. To that end, the settlers in Overisel set apart a portion of the purchased land for the intended village, while in Graafschap several colonists bought an acre of land in the planned village area.[4] However, the plans did not materialize. Since the farms were larger and the distances greater, the farmers preferred to live each on his own land. Only the church, the school, and a few stores identified the area where they had expected to establish the typical Dutch-Saxon type of village green or village commons [*brinkdorp*]*

Those immigrants who had farmed on clay or bog in the Old Country were accustomed to living further apart; and in America they immediately did the same, even though they felt and maintained a kind of unity. It was natural that for them especially the church and the post office, located in one of the stores near the church, should be the center of the settlement, although this would not be comparable to the built-up area [*de kom*] of a centrally located village. As early as December 15, 1847, the Zeelander J. Van de Luyster Jz. wrote: "Three villages are already being built. They are measured and laid out according to the American plan."[5] Later other businesses were established in the "villages" or "towns," especially banks, giving these settlements the typical American appearance—generally one very broad street.

The larger communities, the real "cities," were laid out by American surveyors׳ and therefore from the beginning they had the typical nineteenth-century (or rather, the typical "colonial") right-angled streets. It is known that Holland was laid out after the pattern of Allegan but is differentiated by a beautiful park, called Centennial Park, also laid out rectangularly of course. However, in Holland one does not find the business district literally in the center of the city as in other United States cities. Its location on Black Lake, which drew industry and business, explains why the residential areas lie mainly south of the shopping streets.

In Pella people had planned to make the church the central point of the city, as is the custom in many of the small towns in the Netherlands (although this is not true of larger cities, as demonstrated by Dr. [C.] Te Lintum[6]). But also in this instance the American idea triumphed and it was eventually the real estate speculators who won out, as happened in Chicago, Cincinnati, and St. Louis.[7] Business interests captured the centrally-located building lots that were intended for the church. This led to some very strong clashes between Scholte, who inclined toward American methods, and those among his followers who still clung to the Dutch style. The church finally ended up somewhere else.

---

*A *brinkdorp* is a village built around a common meadow or public square or park, in contrast to a ribbon village built along an existing road and lacking a "focal point."

As I wrote in a previous chapter, Orange City was a copy of Pella, its mother city. The layouts of the cities, therefore, are not reminiscent of the Netherlands. They are completely American. This becomes more understandable when one bears in mind that in America people did not have to cope with the Dutch "polders" or with fortifications; by contrast, they had unlimited acreage for expansion.

Also the architecture of the houses, whether in the city or on the farm, does not indicate the Dutch origin of the inhabitants. This latter fact is striking because it is especially the farmer who clings to the traditional forms in this respect. When walking or cycling through our Fatherland anyone will observe this; the West Frisian builds a West-Frisian farmhouse even though he may be living in the Horstermeer [Noord Holland Province]. On the [northern] island of Texel one immediately recognizes the small houses but very large barns of [southern] Zeeland settlers. A Groninger who moves to De Krim in Overijsel builds a house there in the Groningen style. For a long time the Haarlemmermeer [polder] was a remarkable hodge-podge, a sampler, of the various farmhouse styles. According to [M.] Gevers van Endegeest, there were tabulated in 1860 some 365 large and small farms "of varying types because the farmers who come from all parts of the country brought with them the architectural style of their former homes to their new location in the Haarlemmermeer." H. Ter Veen tells us that after the new land area was populated one saw four different house styles, the Noord Holland-Frisian square farm building with a pyramidal roof [the Noord Holland "*stolp*" or Frisian "*stjelp*"], the well-known Zuid Holland T-shaped structure, and the long Brabant and Zeeland farmhouse types.[8]

In the American colonial settlements one rarely sees a building resembling a Dutch one. But there are some notable exceptions such as Voorhees Hall on the Hope College campus at Holland, Michigan, with its Dutch gabled roof. But nowhere did I see an authentic Dutch-style farmhouse. There must have been at least a few. However, Prof. [Johan Hendrik] Gallée exaggerated considerably when he claimed that in Michigan he could identify Frisians by the Frisian-style houses they had built.[9] It is true that insofar as attempts were made to copy the architectural styles of the Netherlands, the Frisians were the most ardent. In Frisia, Wisconsin, the colonists under the leadership of [Oepke Haitzes] Bonnema did build their new homes "more or less after the Frisian manner."[10] And when [C.] Borgman visited a colony of Frisians near Lancaster in New York state he was struck by the Groningen- and Frisian-style cow stalls in the barn of J. Z.[11] while T[jibbe] G[eerts] Van der Meulen, when visiting Pella, Iowa, and vicinity, spent many a rewarding hour and day in the home of a Frisian, M. Witsenburg, in his "*dwarshuizinge*" [a red brick, Frisian-style house, in which the ridge of the roof runs at a right angle to that of the attached barn].[12] In addition to these Frisian examples, there was a farmer colonist from Ruurlo (so writes Gallée[13]) who in 1875 built himself a house in Grand Rapids after a distinctly Dutch model. In 1921, another Gelderlander, P. Mouw, proudly showed me his home near Orange City, which was supposedly a copy of a wholly uncharacteristic dwelling at Apeldoorn in the Netherlands.

From these meager examples it is apparent that we are here reviewing exceptions. This is all the more strange considering the many carpenters among the immigrants. A genuinely European-style farmhouse is so seldom seen in the pioneer settlements in America that recently at Ogilvie, Minnesota, when a German colonist, contrary to the American model, built a house and barn under one single roof, a Frisian wrote in the weekly paper, De Volksvriend: "Such a building makes a funny impression in America. Many a passerby shakes his head and mockingly mutters, 'He's going to regret that!'"[14]

In the seventeenth century Netherlanders migrated both to America and South Africa and there built their homes according to the pattern of the homeland.[15] No doubt the huts of the Hottentots in Africa and the tepees of the American Indians did not appeal to them! On the other hand, those who migrated to America in the nineteenth century built their houses after the [white] American models.

Also in their daily activities and living arrangements, our fellow Netherlanders appear to be thoroughly Americanized. In 1914 Sjouke De Zee visited many Frisian families and was very disappointed to observe that they had so radically changed their native life-styles, especially as it was manifested in their homes. Even though they had sofas, they did not actually use them. All the more, they used instead their rocking chairs in the house and their swings on the porches. De Zee was surprised, and many times so was I, to see that the housewife did very little of the housework.[16] De Zee not only saw men pushing baby carriages, he even saw men changing the baby's diapers, while the wife looked on or was out of the house! This Americanization was evident even in the most orthodox circles of "true-blood Dutch" Grand Rapids. Recently one of my friends in Grand Rapids wrote me about "the rapid, the much too rapid Americanization" that was taking place in the Dutch community during the war and especially after the war ended.[17] They all want a bathroom in their home, which does not necessarily mean that they use it. They also have pianos, bookcases, gramophones, radios, etc. These items are for the most part decorative. They want them because "it is the thing to do," the neighbors have them, and it demonstrates that they are truly Americans. Of course, the automobile is not lacking, even when they cannot really afford the payments.

This new spirit, this new attitude, comes to expression even more strongly in social affairs. We see that it is not merely "modern" but genuinely American. For example, consider the father-and-son banquets, the mother-and-daughter banquets, and even the mother-and-son banquets that are held several times annually in towns like Holland, Zeeland, Pella, and others. At such a banquet a toast such as "What a son wishes to see in his father" or "What a father wishes to see in his son" strikes us as being somewhat bizarre.[18] Similarly, a banquet of the firemen in Zeeland, described as being "one of the most pleasant affairs ever held here,"[19] and a "businessmen's dinner" in Holland, etc., seemed equally odd.

Also typically American is the desire for "pomp and splendor." Uniforms are much admired in America, whereas in Europe we dislike them and would like to abolish them altogether. We consider them as displays by people who long for outward ostentation and who are still children at heart. I have never seen more colorful uniforms than in Holland, Michigan, on the occasion of the groundbreaking for a Masonic lodge hall. Many Freemasons were walking around in gala outfits wearing uniforms and the three-cornered hat with white plumes. Also band players love to dress in livery. The music corps of the American Legion at Holland, under the direction of Major [John] Van Vijven, consisted of more than thirty members, "all decked out in very attractive uniforms."[20]

That this "pomp and splendor" is not limited to "secular" events was demonstrated in the Sunday worship services of some of the very orthodox Reformed churches I attended. The American flag is prominently displayed in spite of the objections voiced by some of the brothers, but it is another outward evidence of the highly advanced Americanization of the Netherlanders and their commitment to their new country. Many Reformed churchgoing ladies are preferably dressed in rustling silks and flamboyant colors, not always in the best of taste. Also in many Reformed churches the "program" is very American in style, as is evident from the accompanying program of a church service I attended in Holland in 1921. The entrance of churchgoers for a service and their exit once the service is over are even more typical to behold. There is often no expression of spiritual meekness or humility. Indeed, the people coming to the service at the First Reformed Church in Holland and leaving afterward made one think of a theater performance rather than of a religious service. It all seemed very mundane and worldly, due to the sumptuous automobiles and the fashionable clothes and modern coiffures of the ladies. The services of the Christian Reformed churches are also changing. Many consider the Dutch-type services "too dry." Also here there is a "growing sentiment for a better order of worship," including the introduction of such elements as the "word of reconciliation," an "offertory" prayer, and worse.[21]

The part that the Dutch women play in the American women's club activities is also significant. This need not surprise us. We have seen them performing various types of public service, for example, in mission work and even in politics. Many a young woman from the Netherlands served with the Red Cross on Europe's battlefields during the [First] World War. It is not surprising that they have their clubs, even in many of the smaller communities of the West. Holland has its Women's Literary Club, Orange City its Women's Federated Club, etc. The corresponding secretary of the Business Women's Club in Grand Rapids is Dutch, Jane Van Domelen [Dommelen]. Mrs. E. B. Van Etten is president of the Michigan Federation of similar clubs.[22] In all Holland-American towns, society life and socials take on

Hope Reformed Church

West Eleventh Street, Holland, Michigan

Organized 1861

Rev. Paul P. Cheff, B. D., Pastor
Parsonage, 79 West 11th St.

Rev. Willis G. Hoekje, Foreign Missionary
45 Shimo Tatsuo Cho
Kagoshimo, Japan

G. Van Schelven, Treasurer, City Hall
John J. Riemersma, Clerk, 355 River Ave.
Willis A. Diekema, Mus. Dir., 134 W. 12th St.
Harris M. Meyer, Organist, 318 Central Ave.
Mrs. C. V. R. Gilmore, Pres.Women's Mis'y Soc., 30 E. 12th St
Mrs. D. Van der Haar, Pres. Women's Aid Soc., 216 River Av.
Hon. G. J. Diekema, Supt. Bible School, 134 W. 12th St.
Ernest Van den Bosch, Pres. C. E., 87 W. 14th St.
A. H. Lordahl, Sexton, 356 West 15th St.

For Week beginning August 7, 1921

N. B.—Dr. J. M. Van der Meulen, of Louisville, Ky., will serve our pulpit thruout the present month.

Announcements

We are pleased to announce that next Sunday the new Hymnal of the Reformed Church will be used in our Worship.

Tho' truths in manhood darkly join,
  Deep-seated in our mystic frame,
  We yield all blessing to the name
Of Him that made them current coin;

For Wisdom dealt with mortal powers,
  Where truth in closest words shall fail,
  When truth embodied in a tale
Shall enter in at lowly doors.

And so the Word had breath, and wrought
  With human hands the creed of creeds
  In loveliness of perfect deeds,
More strong than all poetic thought;

Which he may read that binds the sheaf,
  Or builds the house, or digs the grave,
  And those wild eyes that watch the wave
In roarings round the coral reef.

From Tennyson's "In Memoriam."

10:30 a. m. Morning Worship

Opening Voluntary—"Larghetto" (2nd Sonata)
           Guilmant

Processional

Opening Sentence - - -

Doxology

Invocation, Closing with Lord's Prayer } All standing

Salutation— - - -

Violin Solo—"Meditations" (From "Thais")
           Massenet
    Miss Ruth Keppel

Psalm 91 } All standing
Gloria Patri

Hymn—No. 321 (All standing)

Reading of Scripture

Prayer

Response—"Bow down Thine ear" - *Shelley*

Hymn—No. 71

Anthem—"Why art thou cast down?" *Spicker*

Sermon Our Faith in God.

Prayer

Hymn No. 322

Benediction (All standing)

Three-fold Amen

Organ Postlude—"Fanfare"   *Lemmons*

7:30 p. m. Evening Worship

Opening Voluntary—"Vison"   *Rheinberger*

Hymn—No.   (All standing)

Reading of Scripture

Prayer

Pater Noster (Choir)

Hymn—No.   (All standing)

Offertory - Anthem—"The Eternal God is thy
           refuge"   *West*

Sermon An Impersonation of Judas Iscariot

Prayer

Hymn—No.

Benediction (All standing)

Organ Postlude—

Noon—Sunday School Classes for all ages, in the Chapel and Auditorium.

A bulletin of the Hope Reformed Church in Holland, Michigan, August 7, 1921. The author attended the evening service.

increasing significance. Now that many of the immigrants have become prosperous and even wealthy, we can detect an increasing ambition for social posturing and swaggering, accompanied by an increase in class distinction. One only need read the accounts in the newspapers! The *Grondwet* printed an account of the wedding of M. A. D. There were no fewer than 125 guests and, according to the reporter, it was "one of the most attractive weddings" he had ever witnessed.[23]

Although Beets recently stated that in America little attention is paid to social status and to the expense of maintaining it,[24] my observations during my short stay in America were often very different and I noticed an increasing differentiation. I conclude that this is a modern American trait. In Europe it is waning, although people being what they are, it will never completely disappear here either. Several times I heard condescending remarks made about persons who had not attended college and therefore were not very highly respected. Since the beginning of the twentieth century there has been in Grand Rapids a "Knickerbocker Society," with membership limited to persons of a certain social standing. The differentiation in standing of American churches is also striking. No doubt this came about because they are neighborhood churches, and in American cities each social class has its own neighborhood. For example, in Holland, the First Reformed Church is the "elite" church and many of the prominent families have their private and reserved pews, the Diekemas, the Keppels, the Van Schelvens, etc. This lifestyle appears to be even more puffed up the more westward one goes, no doubt because this part of the country is the most Americanized. This is shown, for instance, by the headline of an article in the *Pella Chronicle* reporting a reception given by the president of Central College and his wife: "Rank and Dignity have Festivity; Dr. and Mrs. Hoffman entertain Authorities at Dunn Cottage."[25] The report was signed by "One of them."

It strikes me there is something childish in all this, something juvenile. Indeed, in many respects the spirit of America is exactly that. It comes to expression not only in the cities but perhaps even more so in the countryside where there are fewer diversions and thus these "socials" acquire even greater importance. They obviously play an important role in social life. These social gatherings are often of a very naive character. Especially is this true of the so-called "surprise parties" or "farewell parties." The use of these English words in the Holland-American newspapers attest to the un-Dutch character of these events, at least in the circles in which they are held. When in the latter part of February farmers prepare to move to a new farm, their stay-put neighbors pay them a surprise visit in the evening, bringing along refreshments and possibly some beautiful parting gifts. They do not knock or ring the bell, but simply shout, "Surprise!" Then they spend a pleasant evening together and the uninvited guests bring with them coffee and sandwiches.[26] Similar parties, as described by Hamlin Garland,[27] occur quite frequently, especially in view of the migrating fever among our

Dutch clansmen. Sometimes an oyster party is organized, or a newly-married couple will be given a "surprise-shower," or a "chicken party" or a "hen party," to which the generous neighbors will bring the chickens to fill up the chicken coop.

Especially the family of the "dominie" in these predominantly orthodox settlements is often entertained in this fashion. The guests bring their own refreshments. I will give a few examples, which also serve as specimens of rural social life. The first occurred at Ogilvie, Minnesota. "It is Wednesday evening. All is quiet and peaceful in and around the parsonage of the Christian Reformed Church. Suddenly, unexpectedly, there is a knock on the door of the parsonage. 'Come in!' The door practically falls in followed by five men and their wives. The men are the members of the consistory, and they have come for a surprise visit. On March 1st, Dominie De Bruyn had turned forty-nine and now they have come to honor him. They spent a very pleasant evening together. The diligent wives had brought a generous supply of refreshments. They presented the preacher and his wife with a sum of money as a token of appreciation, which the latter received with thanks. They sang and they prayed and precisely at midnight the guests left for home, very gratified."[28]

Needless to say, the "American-ness" lies especially in the unexpectedness of these affairs. This was demonstrated even more strongly at Ringle, Wisconsin, on the occasion of the twenty-fifth wedding anniversary of their pastor, Dominie L. "Monday evening they were surprised when suddenly a group from the church, young and old, came to their yard to congratulate them and spend the evening together. After it quieted down a little they sang a psalm and one of the elders, M. Abma, offered a prayer. They then presented the dominie and his wife with a generous purse full of silver."[29]

The various American holidays are enthusiastically observed by our kinsmen. They commemorate the important historical events, the foremost of which naturally is July 4, Liberty [Independence] Day. They observe Decoration or Memorial Day in May when they commemorate the Civil War, Labor Day in September, Columbus Day on October 12, Armistice Day on November 11, and finally Thanksgiving Day on November 4.* It is interesting to us to observe the military shows that are associated with many of these holidays, also in the Dutch settlements. There is generally a parade in which veterans of the various wars participate—the Civil War, the Spanish-American War, and especially the [First] World War. All these members of the American Legion are preferably in uniform. Even a salvo of gunfire is included! These parades are certainly not typically German, but typically American, and according to L. R. Reid they form an "integral part of American life."[30]

A day of thanksgiving, a well-known observation in the Netherlands†, is

---

*Thanksgiving Day is the fourth Thursday and not November 4.

†Also often held after a military victory, and accompanied by a Te Deum, a religious service with the old hymn "Te Deum laudamus" (We Praise Thee, God) being sung.

TON FAMILY,
Largest On Record

The renowned Ton family in Netherlandic circles in America. The first of the Tons, J. Ton, who came from the region north of Alkmaar in 1849, settled south of Chicago where High Prairie, now Roseland, was founded. The C. Ton family soon followed. The Tons, originally farmhands, have become very rich, because of, among other reasons, the increasing land prices around Chicago. Branches of the family have since spread all over America. Once a year the members of this family, which has grown to a very great size, like to gather in Roseland for a family reunion. Among all American family reunions, that of the Tons in 1920 set a record: about seven hundred members took part in it (E. P. Beaudette-Neil, *Thornton Township, Cook County, Illinois*).

usually held in Dutch-American circles as a family reunion that may also be held on other holidays or on New Year's Day. These family reunions as such cannot be considered typically American, for we have them also in our country where they are known as "*gastdagen*." However, in America they take on a different dimension because of their large size and the great distances often traveled by family members who attend. One of the most renowned reunions is that of the Ton family of Roseland, Illinois. In 1920 seven hundred members of the Ton clan from all parts of the United States were present. Many families, like the Tons, have a complete board of directors—president, secretary, and treasurer, to make arrangements for these reunions.[31]

The fact that families are separated by such great distances evidently accounts for these reunions. Family members do not meet often enough, if at all, in their day-to-day routine. Parents, too, seldom see their children all together. Therefore they schedule definite dates for reunions and hold them on those days even after the parents have died. Since almost all the members of such a family live in the midst of people of other origins, it is hard to prove, and can only be surmised to what degree there is a need for family solidarity, for a sense of belonging, of togetherness, even a herd instinct.

Festivities such as reunions help break the monotony of life in the countryside, as do events like fairs and market days. Although these exhibitions, called "fairs," are regarded with suspicion by many Dutch Americans—for example, read Mulder's *Outbound Road*—they are becoming increasingly popular also in the Dutch settlements. A fair is held annually at Holland, Michigan, and in 1920 J. Arendshorst was its secretary. It was advertised as "Ottawa County's Greatest Fair, Bigger, Brighter, Better than Ever" with "Wonderful Exhibits in all Departments, Band Concerts Daily," etc., etc.[32]

Other diversions in rural areas are what they call chautauquas—small choral groups, musicians, and orators. In various towns they put up tents for a few days and give concerts and presentations. In both Holland, Michigan, and Orange City, Iowa, chautauquas were held during my stay there. According to Mencken (*Americana* 1925) they form "the chief arena of American 'idealism.'"

However, peak events are the celebrations held in commemoration of the foundation of various colonies or settlements, in Zeeland in 1907, at Orange City in 1920, and at Pella in 1922.[33] They are organized and promoted chiefly by associations of the first settlers and can be considered as large-scale family reunions. They are also supported and encouraged by the Chambers of Commerce and the so-called Boosters Clubs, which are comparable to our V.V.V.'s [Verenigingen voor Vreemdelingen Verkeer (Tourism Associations)]. At Pella the Chamber of Commerce vigorously advertised: "75th anniversary of the founding of Pella, Iowa; Sept. 5, 6 & 7, 1922. This will be the biggest and best celebration ever held in Pella. Speakers of National Reputation, 5 Bands, Free Attractions, Ball Games, Historical Pre-

BIGGER, BRIGHTER, BETTER THAN EVER

OTTAWA COUNTIES GREATEST FAIR

TO BE HELD AT

Holland, Mich. September 14-15-16-17

1920

WONDERFUL EXHIBITS IN ALL DEPARTMENTS	MORE AMUSEMENTS AND ATTRACTIONS THAN EVER BEFORE	RACING DAILY--LIBERAL PURSES

FISH HASKELL--Michigan's Best Known Airbird--will Exhibit WEDNESDAY, THURSDAY and FRIDAY Take a Ride with this Airship King--15 Minutes--$15.00. Reservations now Booked

Fisher's Exposition Orchestra In the Grand Stand Every Day Worth the Price of Admission	*Midway* Crowded with Interest Fun and Mirth	*America's Greatest Aeronauts* Will make an Ascension Daily--Wednesday 1 Parachute Drop--Thursday 2 and Friday 3

Band Concerts Daily--The Best Free Attractions Money could buy

We can not tell you everything--But there will be something Doing every Minute.

Come Every Day--Your Friends will be There! They Expect You!

For Premium List or other Information Write the Secretary, J. ARENDSHORST, Holland, Mich.

Advertisement for the Ottawa County Fair at Holland, Michigan, in *De Grondwet*, September 14, 1920.

sentation, Parade."[34] Many feel that the formal memorial celebration is exploited and banalized by all these extras. It is thoroughly American and not at all reminiscent of the Dutch background. It is "small-town realism." The parades, family reunions, fairs, etc., etc., are an integral part of American "small-town life." According to Reid, these are all part of basic American culture, which is thoroughly provincial.[35]

Although it is evident from all the preceding that the process of Americanization is far advanced, in fact, almost completed, it is naturally most strongly expressed by the younger generation and is accompanied by an equally strong secularism. Modernization and Americanization are practically synonymous and are observed with fear and trembling especially in religious circles. Even in the most orthodox churches they cause great uneasiness and bring to mind, not only in the cities but also on the prairies, serious doubts about the future, even about the continued existence of the Christian Reformed Church.

The young people have their own special festival day (or rather, evening): Halloween, the last evening of October, which is dedicated to mischief. The young people go through the area, ringing doorbells, throwing grain through the windows, hauling away unattended wagons, etc., etc. These are customs supposedly related to the change of season, warning the tardy to harvest their last field crops and to hurry up to finish the late field work.[36] More plausible is the old folk belief, derived from pagan beliefs, that during the night of October 31-November 1 all kinds of evil spirits fly overhead and must be driven away by loud noises and tumult. At the same time one sees in these customs an expression of fear. Halloween was probably brought to America by the Scotch-Irish; it is still celebrated in old Scotland and was immortalized by [Robert] Burns in his "Halloween—a picture of rustic merrymaking." Among the Germans, particularly among the Paltsers, the practice was unknown.[37] Halloween has since spread all over America, including the Dutch settlements, and has become a genuinely American custom, although it has degenerated into lawlessness in some areas. The young people, especially those in the orthodox settlements, seem to use these opportunities to express their adolescent rebellion. It is as if, for one night in the year, even the children from strictly disciplined religious families remain indifferent to everything the church and religion have taught them, to all that has to do with the simplest principles of good breeding. Halloween seems to be a reaction to normal life for which the more or less "normal" Saturday evening rowdiness in many towns seems to offer no sufficient outlet.[38] In the first week of November the local papers and especially *De Volksvriend* and *Pella's Weekblad* in the more over-excited West are full of accounts of Halloween vandalism. In 1920 the *Volksvriend* printed a report from Ireton, Iowa, that at Halloween much damage was done, and at Doon the vandalism was not limited to the youths.[39] In *Pella's Weekblad* one often reads that even the police were unable to control the situation. As time went on, efforts were

75STE

VERJAARDAG
PELLA - IOWA
5-6-7 SEPT. 1922

Dit zal de grootste en beste feestviering zijn die Pella ooit had.

Sprekers van Nationale Reputatie:
Smith W. Brookhart, Rep. Candidaat U.S. Senaat, Clyde L. Herring, Dem. Candidaat U. S. Senaat, Pat Haley van Ft. Dodge, een der grootste redenaars van Iowa, Ben G. Gibson, Algemeene Advocaat van den staat Iowa, en andere voorname sprekers.

5 Muziekcorpsen 5

Vrije Aantrekkelijkheden

Opstijgen van Ballon, Wolkenzwaai, Koorddansers, Sterke Man, Hansworst, Dixie Quartette.

BALSPELEN:

5 September, Pella vs. Winterset; 6 September, Pella vs. Victor; 7 September, Pella vs. Milo. Telkens om 3:30 p.m. op genoemde datums

HISTORISCHE VOORSTELLING

300 Personen nemen deel aan het voorstellen der geschiedkundige gebeurtenis van het stichten van Pella en den groei der stad - Een grootsch product.

:-: PARADE :-:

Een mijl lang, gekenmerkt door Ossenwagen, Sierlijke Vlotters, Muziekcorpsen, Am. Legion.

TOELATINGEN:- Draaimolen, Ferris Wiel, Spelen, overvloed van eten en drinken.

SPORT GEBEURTENISSEN:- Athletische Wedstrijden, Hardloopen, enz.

:-: Denk om de datums :-:

5, 6, 7 September

*Wees een goede "Fella"
En kom naar Pella.*

Alles is ingericht om u te ontvangen. Kom met het geheele gezin en geniet het goede.

Pella's 75th birthday notice in *Pella's Weekblad,* September 1, 1922.

75TH

ANNIVERSARY
PELLA - IOWA
SEPT. 5-6-7, 1922

This will be the biggest and best celebration
Pella has ever had.

Speakers of National Reputation

Smith W. Brookhart, Republican Candidate for the U.S. Senate, Clyde L. Herring, Democratic Candidate for the U.S. Senate, Pat Haley of Ft. Dodge, one of the greatest orators in Iowa, Ben G. Gibson, Attorney General of the state of Iowa, and other prominent speakers.

5   BANDS   5

Free Attractions

Balloon Ascension, Weight Lifter, Clowns, Parachute Jump, Tightrope Walkers, Dixie Quartette

BALL GAMES

September 5, Pella vs. Winterset; September 6, Pella vs. Victor; September 7, Pella vs. Milo. Daily at 3:30 p.m. on above dates.

HISTORICAL PRESENTATION

300 participants involved in an historical pageant portraying the founding and development of the town of Pella—A great production.

:-:   PARADE   :-:

A mile-long parade; wagons drawn by ox-teams, decorated floats, music bands, American Legion.

BY ADMISSION FEE: Merry-go-round, ferris-wheel, games, plenty of food and drink.

SPORTS EVENTS: Athletic Competition—Races, etc.

:-:   Remember the Dates   :-:

September 5, 6 & 7

Be a good "fella"
and come to Pella.

Everything is ready; bring the family and enjoy the goodies.

English translation of Pella's 75th birthday notice.

made to turn the "custom" of Halloween into a civilized evening of festivity, preferably an indoor activity.

The young people present still other problems. Many who had a Christian Reformed background and upbringing no longer have qualms of conscience regarding dancing, card playing, smoking, and wearing bobbed hair and knee-length skirts. Even among the older Netherlanders there are some who agree with H. H. Bosch at Stockton, California, that such "novelties" as bobbed hair and short skirts are no longer incompatible with their religious standards. Even the Christian Reformed preachers are no longer unanimous in their condemnation of these newer and more modern lifestyles, although there are some who, with E. J. Tanis, deplore the increasing worldliness in orthodox circles that is expressed also in a far-reaching trivializaton of life: "the absorption in material things—beautiful homes, elegant furnishing, high-priced automobiles, innumerable banquets—accompanied with a sad indifference to lectures that stimulate the intellect, sermons that feed the soul, and prayer meetings for mutual edification."[40]

Already during the World War years, the Christian Reformed Rev. B. K. Kuiper pointed out that since the past few years, starting with 1915, there was an "alarming" increase in the evidence "that the Hollanders were possibly undergoing a change not only regarding their ethnic origin but also regarding their basically Reformed character."[41] In the following years conditions degenerated still further, at least from the Christian Reformed point of view. A stormy decade followed. H. J. Kuiper warned that with the Americanization process "a swelling tide of worldliness" was undermining the faith of the fathers and boded ill for the future. In addition to the sneaking in of the aforesaid sins, Kuiper deplored the neglect of the Sabbath observance and the weakening of respect for parental authority.[42]

Although the great independence of young people is a generally modern phenomenon, in some of its manifestations it is typically American. In this respect, the sons and daughters of the Dutch immigrants have also been "Americanized" almost completely. How else can one interpret a news item in *De Volksvriend* in Orange City in 1921? "The students at the Northwestern Classical Academy have decided to again observe Saturday as their day off instead of Monday"![43] The students in the various academies and colleges in the settlements indeed play an important role in their local communities. I have already referred to their public debates. They provide additional evenings of recreation for the local population by their choral groups and band concerts. It is a singular contrast that the parents show adolescent traits while the children of school age reflect oldish traits in their behavior. Very early the young learn the hard facts of life; they must often work to earn money to pay for their own college expenses. Many others, even though financially not compelled to do so, prefer to earn their own money because of the drive to be self-sufficient. Many young women, planning to attend N.W.C.A. in the fall of 1923, advertised in advance in *De Volksvriend* that they were "desirous" to earn their room and board by doing household jobs outside of school hours.[44]

The same thing could be observed in the Michigan colony. While I was in Holland, Prof. [J. B.] Nykerk of Hope College invited me to dinner at the Waukazoo restaurant, which is most attractively located on Black Lake. When the waitress brought us the menu, my host first introduced me to her, before we ordered anything. She was a student at Hope College who, together with a friend, worked in fashionable Waukazoo during the summer months. I met several Hope students working as waiters in Holland restaurants. It goes without saying that their studies suffer to some extent. Prof. [E. D.] Dimnent, president of Hope College, told me of one of his students who worked outside of school hours twenty-two hours per week in an eating place in Kalamazoo.

One should not conclude that our Dutch clansmen were merely imitating the "real" Americans, even though "imitation" always plays a great role in the life of the masses. This was by no means the case. Their circumstances as immigrants, beginning very often at a very low economic level, brought it about through sheer necessity. When A. E. Croockewit traveled in 1869 from Grand Haven to Holland, it turned out that the stagecoach driver was a young immigrant from Herwijnen who was a seminary student in Holland studying to be a preacher![45] Thus it becomes apparent that also in the Dutch colonies these customs were the natural result of circumstances and that the immigrants, at least in this respect, became Americans by the most organic process.

B. To What Extent the Colonists Remained Netherlanders

Should one conclude from all the foregoing and from statements I made previously in other connections that nothing Dutch has remained among the colonists, or that as the aforesaid correspondent of the *Nieuwe Rotterdamsche Courant* stated, referring to Grand Rapids and the entire "Dutch" community of Michigan, "They have done away with everything that could be called typically Dutch"?[46] In my view, the answer is no, far from that. But then one should take a closer and more critical look at people and places. Especially on the Sabbath day the contrast between the Dutch settlements and the genuinely American cities and villages becomes very evident. In the former, one is struck by the rural peace and tranquility, while the latter are more noisy and tumultuous on that day. In the Dutch settlements both husbands and wives attend church services twice a day, while in the American communities only the women attend church while many of the men enjoy themselves on the sports fields.

Other differences keep coming to one's attention. The Dutch settlements, not only in Zeeland and other Michigan areas but also on the prairies and in the Far West, are extremely neat and tidy. The well-known Swedish writer, Pieter Kalm, extolled the Dutch housewives of Albany in 1749 as "very good housekeepers, exceedingly tidy about their floors."[47] This is true, and the

Young Hollanders maintain that reputation. How attractively Holland and Zeeland are laid out, and likewise Pella and Orange City. How nicely all the houses are painted and especially the churches, many of which remind one of the village churches in the Netherlands! This Dutch neatness is so evident that, as I drove through the northwestern areas of Iowa, through Sioux and Lyon counties, I could rather accurately ascertain which villages had been "conquered" by our countrymen in the continuing process of further farmer colonization. In Doon, Lyon County, in part "taken over" by the Netherlanders, I was greatly struck by the marked contrast. One could clearly distinguish the Dutch homes, with their clean, bright and attractive exteriors, from the homes of the Scotch-Irish, which were generally unkempt and neglected!

If among the Dutch colonists there should chance to be a somewhat untidy homeowner, a committee of local women (such as there was in Orange City) would take it upon themselves to have the streets and alleys made spic and span and charge the cost to the negligent resident. The aim was "to make our locality the neatest, handsomest, and most attractive place in this part of Iowa"; this is also a typical expression of civic pride.[48]

In most of the settlements a movie theater is also definitely absent. There is one in Holland, Michigan, but it leads a marginal existence. Attempts to set up a movie theater in Pella and Orange City failed. In most of the smaller settlements, such as Zeeland, there are no dance halls, billiards, smoking and soft drink parlors. Also absent is the Masonic Lodge hall (Holland is an exception) or any group of a secret society. According to Reid, the secret society is characteristic of the American small town and reaches its ultimate in the Ku Klux Klan,[49] which the Dutch settlers abhor. A demonstration of the extent and the method by which the Netherlanders imposed their standards upon a community not founded by them can be seen in Valley Springs in South Dakota. When about 1917 a few Netherlanders settled there one of them declared that Valley Springs was "the ungodliest place they had ever been in." There were movie theaters, dance halls, and various lodges, and the Sabbath was outrageously desecrated. But gradually more Netherlanders moved in and as a consequence many of the "loose runners" packed up and left. The Dutch settlers bought the large dance hall and used it as a store for farm machinery. The "show" was compelled to close, etc., etc. Five years later, in early 1922, the town was completely dominated by the Netherlanders in spite of all their Americanization and to the chagrin of the many "real" Americans.[50]

More traces of Dutch influence can be seen in the store window displays. The obviously Dutch names on the store fronts lure the onlooker to a closer scrutiny and, depending on the type of store, one often sees tucked among the American products various Dutch items: Verkade's honey-cake, Dutch rusk and windmill cookies, Droste's cocoa and once in a while Blooker's cocoa, Lambermont's ginger-bread and citron bread, Wouterlood's plain or sliced green beans, Spoor's mustard, Holland herring, and "Dutch" Java tea!

In many a store there are numerous books in the Dutch language for sale; others have wooden shoes! As we may remember, in Grand Rapids the Netherlanders were known for a while as "the little wooden-shoe guys" [*klompenmannetjes*]. The use of wooden shoes has since decreased in all the Dutch settlements, not only because the wearers became more Americanized in their dress styles but chiefly because of the nature of the soil. They continued to be worn on sandy soil but on clay they were soon found to be impractical.

The clothing the colonists wear is also sometimes reminiscent of the Old Country. More than once it was confirmed to me that the immigrants arrived here in the garb of the province from which they came, including the wooden shoes. They continued to wear them for several decades. As proof of this one need only examine the many photographs in the 1907 anniversary booklet of the celebration in Zeeland. Not only in Michigan but in many other areas, even under the smoke from New York's chimneys, the Dutch immigrants held to these traditions and customs of the Old Country. The Frisian writer T. Greidanus was astonished while visiting Paterson around 1907 not only to hear men and women speaking Frisian, but to see women—it was on a Sunday—still wearing the traditional Frisian head ornament ["*oorijzer*"].[51] Indeed, I myself observed many years later in 1921 in the Dutch suburb of Paterson many a working man still wearing the blue blouse and black waistcoat and the silk cap on his head. And when on a Sunday in the same town I attended two church services, one in a "Zeeuwsche" and one in a "Frisian" church (note the provincialism!), I saw several elderly women wearing the Dutch lace bonnet and a few wearing the Frisian head ornaments. Indeed, in 1927 an eighty-three year-old woman, Ytsje De Oude-Van Dyk at Paterson, well-known among the Frisians as "*Beppe*" [Frisian for grandmother], was still wearing the complete Frisian costume [*de volledige "Fryske dracht noch brûkt."*] She was the only one in the Silk City still dressed in the Dutch fashion.[52] "Born a Hollander, you die a Hollander," said the president of Hope College in a conversation with me later. Recalling what I had heard and seen at these church services I gave full assent. However, one will look in vain for Dutch clothing now in America, because of the restrictions strongly limiting immigration. Also in our own country the strictly provincial type of clothing is worn less and less.

The characteristics of the Netherlanders are more fully and strongly evident in home life than "on the street." As W. McDougall states, "It is a general law of imitation that modes of doing persist more obstinately than modes of thinking and feeling."[53] In my view, this is strikingly demonstrated among our colonists, not so much in "public" as in the privacy of the home. This can be seen in the arrangement of many interiors, for example, in the disproportionately large kitchen. Many families—and this is not limited to farm families—carry on all the family activities in the kitchen after the Old-Country custom and use *de mooie kamer* [the parlor] only on special occasions. Often a Dutch home is more appealingly *gezellig* [cozy] than an

American one. There are usually rugs on the floor, a painting or engraving on the wall, preferably a Dutch landscape, and on another wall next to it the family portraits. There will also be a small book collection, often made up of religious books, in the first place a Bible, then books by Abraham Kuyper, at times works by [H.] Bavinck and frequently by much older writers than these two.

Imitation is expressed even more strongly in home usages. During my sojourn in the United States I was often a guest in Dutch-American homes and had opportunities to observe how the everyday routine was carried on. It struck me that breakfast, which just like all the other meals was generally begun and ended with a prayer—and those prayers in the Dutch language, started off with a soup-plate of porridge. At eleven o'clock they had coffee and cake or gingerbread, at twelve o'clock in many families a hot lunch, tea in mid-afternoon, and after that the evening meal (open-faced sandwiches). I witnessed a few times the popular Old-Dutch habit of slurping hot coffee from the saucer, which together with steaming deep plates of genuine Dutch soup, reminded me of the Fatherland. Once in a while in the evening I drank a cup of hot chocolate.

Naturally there are some who deviate from the old habits. On the other hand, I saw the old customs maintained in sophisticated families in which both husband and wife had been born in America and had never seen the Netherlands. Obviously they had been accustomed to these usages from their childhood, the years when the "power of imitation" is strongest. Sjouke De Zee had the same experiences when he visited Frisian families in the United States. We read of his irritation concerning the Americanization of many a colonist, but he also wrote of having been surprised by the thoroughly Frisian lifestyles in other families. De Zee saw farmers using the familiar one-legged stool while milking their cows. It is a device that is totally unknown to American dairymen. Also, many a Frisian tied the hind legs of his cow together during milking, which the Americans never do. It does not seem necessary since American cattle are much quieter and not as restless as the Dutch breed. Some still feed their cattle with a pitchfork as in the Netherlands and give them real Frisian names. However, the farmers in the vicinity of Grand Rapids, Rochester, and elsewhere had to give up their endeavors to do their work in the Frisian manner because it was simply impossible.[54]

In a few instances one gets the impression that a custom, which had practically died out in the Old Country, was revived in America, or at least was kept alive, although as we have observed so often in other areas, in an exaggerated and even in a wild, disorderly form. This is seen, for example, in old customs associated with weddings. According to [L.] Knappert, the popular custom in times past was to celebrate a wedding in a noisy way, "with singing and cheering so that the whole world would know there was a wedding being celebrated."[55] However, in the last half of the eighteenth century persons of higher social standing preferred to be married quietly and this tendency gradually spread to all levels of our culture. However, it had very little impact in the countryside where various old customs lingered longest. There the bride "was danced to bed" and often the bridal pair was plied with music and levity all night, if one may believe [Johann Wolfgang von] Goethe.

The colonists of the seventeenth, eighteenth, and nineteenth centuries brought these usages to America with them. The Germans in Pennsylvania still carry on all kinds of wanton mischief at weddings as they formerly did in Europe.[56] According to [J.] Schrijnen, "*ketelmuziek*" [a mock serenade with kettles, pans, horns, tin cans, etc.] would only be used in the Netherlands when there was reason for public aggravation, when something was not right.[57] But in America it accompanies all weddings without exception, even in the middle of the night, as was done in the Netherlands in the fifteenth and sixteenth centuries. [F.] Vulpius, who had lived for many years in Missouri where many of his fellow Germans had settled, tells us that in 1840 and 1841 in Weston, Missouri, every wedding, in spite of efforts to keep it secret, was treated at night to frightful caterwauling: "With blackened faces and dressed up in every imaginable outlandish disguise they would assemble at the home where the bridal couple was spending the night and would fill the air with an appalling din, howling and yelling, blowing fifes, beating on drums and old cans, and using speaking-trumpets to amplify their voices—everything that would make a loud racket. They would keep it up until they had forced the bridegroom to come out to give them some money to go and buy drinks. Even in cases of extreme poverty there was no exemption."[58]

Similar customs have survived to the present time in the orthodox Dutch settlements, particularly in Michigan, where they have taken an even more wanton form, to the point of being insulting. This was experienced in 1920 in Drenthe, east of Holland in Ottawa County, by a newly married couple, Mr. and Mrs. Z. According to the "rural custom" they were serenaded by loud and raucous music. The musicians demanded $20. When the bridegroom refused to pay that amount the troublemakers invaded the home, damaged the furniture and even cut the telephone wires. Six of the trespassers, all Netherlanders, were arrested and later severely penalized.[59] This was not an isolated incident. In 1921 Mr. H. and his bride were married at Olive, northwest of Holland, also in Ottawa County. They were likewise serenaded by Dutch youths. When these "gentlemen" received only $4 instead of the $10 they had demanded, they pelted the bridal couple with eggs and chased them up the road.[60] Mischief had again turned into misdeed and a court case was the end result.

In more distant western states there were equally eccentric incidents. In 1919 at a wedding in that very proper and orthodox community of Pella, Iowa, there occurred behavior that was just as aggravating. Windows were broken, the door damaged, etc., all this despite the presence of two policemen.[61] In 1921 in Sioux County, Iowa, at the wedding of Mr. and Mrs. E., many uninvited guests—the so-called "charivaries" or "shivarees" as these mock musicians are sometimes called—appeared at the party and stole ice cream, let air out of the automobile tires, etc.[62]

In this way the Dutch in America still pay a toll to the old customs that survive. In this "mischief" one can trace to a certain extent the tendency of the Dutch toward unruliness, monkey tricks and even hooliganism [kwajongensachtigheid]. This is all the more strongly expressed when it is a reaction to the strict orthodox regime, a "bursting out of the bonds," which is also observed quite often in the Netherlands. But part can be traced to the American nervousness or hysteria that plays such a significant role at lynchings.

There is no doubt that through a more intensive study, more of these "survivals" could be traced. The foregoing may suffice to demonstrate once again the tenacity of the Dutch "customs." Professor Dimnent assured me that in the city of Holland, so visibly Americanized, one still finds in most households the same customs that one would find in the Netherlands.[63] Only after three or four generations do they undergo profound changes. Nevertheless, the Americanization of the Dutch in Holland City had already progressed to such an extent that when Governor [John Judson] Bagley of Michigan visited Holland in 1875 he requested, after having spent two days in the city, to be finally introduced to a "Dutchman," so G. J. Diekema informs us.[64] The preservation of customs depends mostly on the mother in the family. If the father is Dutch but the mother is not, that spells the quickest loss of the old usages and also of the language.

When comments are made concerning the rapid Americanization of the immigrants, invariably the subject of loss of the Dutch language is brought up. However, one should be very cautious in this area. There was a time when language was considered synonymous with race and thought to be an unchangeable as the color of one's skin. But we now know that language is very changeable. [H.] Schurtz states in his book *Völkerkunde* [*Ethnology*], that entire tribes of Negroes changed their language in one generation![65] [S. R.] Steinmetz supports [Johannes] Lepsius in a similar statement. It is generally known that some business languages are quickly learned; we have examples of such *lingua franca* as Malay [in Southeast Asia] and pidgin English, while basic English and plain English have been universalized. Again we must be cautious despite examples of Germanification, Russification, etc. The dialect geographers, [Jules Louis] Gilliéron, [Edmond] Edmont, [A.] Dauzat, [E.] Fischer, [Jacob] Ramisch, [J.] Van Ginneken, [Gesinus Gerhardus] Kloeke, point out how tenaciously a people will cling to their native tongue, which is a tendency not limited to the countryside. This can be observed not only when one primarily pays attention to the actual words but to the pronunciation, the sounds, the sentence structure, the turning of a phrase. There are many language islands, for example, the German enclaves in eastern and southeastern Europe, and in the Netherlands the rural-type Frisian, of which Kloeke says, "It has remained substantially pure."[66]

Our language has maintained itself in the United States longer, much longer, than Van Raalte, who was so farsighted, could have suspected. In a letter dated November 27, 1846, this leader wrote to his brother-in-law, [A.] Brummelkamp: "I fear we shall have to work harder to keep the Dutch language alive than to learn English."[67] How wrong Van Raalte was is proven by the fact that in 1927 there were still nineteen newspapers in the Dutch language being published in the United States.

Still there appears to have been some basis for his concern. In the beginning there was so little to be earned in his colony that many of the young people went to neighboring cities, such as Grand Rapids, Allegan, etc., to make a living. On July 12, 1847, C[ornelia] M. Van Malsen at Holland wrote: "Yesterday we sent a number of housemaids and laborers to Kalamazoo, a small town. They were immediately received with open arms." In the same letter this lady stated that if the young people understood English "there were excellent prospects for them."[68] But in the cities where they knew no English at all they had many difficulties. [D.] Versteeg shares with us some amusing incidents that these greenhorns went through.[69] For example, several young men became very angry when their employer told them they would sleep "upstairs." They thought he meant *onder de sterren* [under the stars], out of doors. Others were very distrustful when their boss told them they would be paid in cash. They thought they would get nothing but *kaas* [cheese]. Clearly, a worker who did not know what he was being told to do was unemployable. The Netherlanders in the Michigan cities, as well as those in St. Louis on their way to Pella, tried to learn some English as quickly as possible.

There was a second reason. Most of the Dutch colonists came from the countryside where a great variety of dialects is spoken. Even among themselves they had difficulty understanding one another. This led to much misunderstanding that was sometimes amusing and often downright painful; it was "the cause of much trouble."[70] Schrijnen is of the opinion that the unity of dialect ultimately rests on the solidarity of people who are enclosed by a tight cultural bond.[71] Since dialect and local ethnic character are closely interwoven, it must have been the solidarity resulting from this close interconnection, in addition to the "convenience" that is also immediately derived from that pairing of spoken word and ethnic character, that led our colonists to settle in the United States very often according to their provinces of origin. We saw this happen on a larger scale in Michigan and on a somewhat lesser scale in New York State, Iowa, and other areas. The colonists were so much more comfortable in areas of familiar dialect that any Gelderlander who applied to Hospers for a piece of land would be sent on by this well-known land dealer at Orange City to Sioux Center where there was a settlement of Gelderlanders, even though that was further away.[72]

However, in a community like Holland, where colonists from the various provinces had settled, they more quickly felt the need for a language or dialect common to all. The logical choice was English, but it did not cause them to forget their native tongue.

On the other hand, at Pella, where there were so many educated residents, they obviously did not feel any need for English. Therefore, the classic, pure form of Dutch has been able to survive to the present day in Pella. I still remember how old Mister |G. G.| Gaass at Pella, who still had such a fine feeling for the language, felt obliged to correct immediately a person who pronounced the "a" somewhat too much in the affected "Den Haag" style, a mannerism that turns Dutch long "aa" sounds, more or less, into "è" sounds.

In 1921 I spent some time in America and at that time there were still several Dutch dialects being spoken for reasons as detailed previously. It may be recalled that Prof. |A.| Raap visited all the Dutch settlements on behalf of Hope College, and he told me that in the village of Overisel settlers still spoke a great deal of "Overijselsch," the European Overijsel dialect. Also at Drenthe and Graafschap at that time people still spoke the Old-Country dialect in spite of the wave of |American| chauvinism that swept the country due to the |First| World War. At Zeeland in Michigan the "Zeeuwsch" |Zeeland dialect| was still so powerful that immigrants from Groningen and Drenthe who had come to live in Zeeland eventually adopted "Zeeuwsch" even though it was not native to them.[73]

The distinguishing characteristics of the various dialects are more evident in the colonies located further west in the thinly settled areas. In West Branch, Sioux County, Iowa, there are many colonists with a European Gelderland or Overijsel background. To the present day they *write* the classic Dutch but *speak* in the idioms of Gelderland and Overijsel. As recently as May, 1924, the elderly Mister |G.| Draayom at Hospers, Iowa, wrote concerning his "mother dialect": "How attentively we listen when we hear someone pronounce the 'ie' |ee| and 'oe' |oo|".[74]

One should not conclude that it is only in the countryside that the Netherlandic dialects have survived. They are found likewise in the great industrial cities and, in view of what I have previously stated, this should not be surprising. In the Groningen neighborhoods of Grand Rapids, Chicago, and especially Muskegon, much "Groningsch" is still spoken as well as in the countryside. When Dr. H. Bouwman visited Muskegon in 1910 he heard the "Groningsch" in all of the Dutch neighborhoods.[75] |Cornelis| Van Loo gave as his opinion that the Groningen dialect survived longest in Michigan.[76] Its "power" was confirmed by publisher |William B.| Eerdmans at Grand Rapids in a communication to me in which he states that even some Blacks living in the Groningen neighborhood of Grand Rapids had adopted "Groningsch."[77] How strong the attachment of the Groninger is to his "*moudertoal*" |mother tongue| is shown by the accompanying poem by Groninger Dirk Nieland of Grand Rapids:[78]

My Mother-Tongue

When my heart is heavy with a weighty matter,
And does not become lighter through sighing,

Then by means of a little rhyme I often try
To lighten that depressing misery.

And then you, my mother-tongue, comes to mind,
My mother-tongue, which first I learned to stammer,
And in which I still am a mere stammerer,
When it comes to express praise for you.

Still, you have well deserved praise from me,
For how much haven't I enjoyed myself through your tones,
—Somewhat harsh and boorish perhaps, but well-meant,—
That gently and fairly issued from my mother's mouth.

And amidst the playful learning during youth
You were the vehicle for all our thoughts.
In youthful grief or in youthful joy,
We could often expect sympathy through you.

At a riper age also, although far from home
And far away from all those who knew me once
Grönnegers always brought me into an ecstasy
Of joy, where'er I heard it from joyful mouths.

For, no matter what, that language I'll ne'er forget;
Whether I travel to the East or West:
Where "Uncle Sam" his starry flag unfurls,
Or where the "Union Jacks" guard their citizens.

Whatever language I hear from people whom I meet
Civilized or wild, of many diverse colors,
None of all those languages sounds so sweet,
Or is, as you, able to cheer me up.

And so I've dedicated this little poem to you,
My Mother-tongue; to you, so oft downtrodden,
So oft ridiculed, disparaged and defiled
But always again, like a hero, arisen from the slime.*

The great purity with which the children of the colonists were able to
adopt and preserve these dialects of their fathers was further demonstrated

---

* **Mien Moudertoal**

As 't haart mie vol is van 'n zwoare zoak,
  En 'et gemoud nait roemer wordt deur zuchten,
Den tracht ik deur 'n riemke nog al voak
  Dei dompe noarigheden op te luchten.

En den kom's doe, mien moudertoal m'ien 't zin:
  Mein moudertoal, woar 'k eerst ien leerde stoamlen,
En woar 'k nog moar 'n stoameloar ien bin
  As 't geld om lofsproak veur die te verzoamlen.

Toch, lofsproak hest doe van mie wel verdaind:
  Want wat heb 'k dien deur klanken nait genoten;
—Wat stroef en boersch meschain, moar welgemaind—
  Dei zacht en goud de moudermond ontvloten.

En onder 't speulend leeren van de jeugd
  Wast doe het voertuug van al onz' gedachten.
Ien jongessmart, of wel ien jongesvreugd,
  Kon wie deur die voak sympathie verwachten.

Op rieper oller ook, schoon ver van hoes,
  En ver van allemoal dei ains mie konnen,
Brocht 't Grönnegers mie altied ien 'n roes
  Van vreugd, woar ik het heurd' oet gulle monnen.

Want hou 't ook gait, dei toal vergeet ik nooit;
  Ik mag noar 't Oosten of noar 't Westen trekken:
Woar "Uncle Sam" zien steerenvlag ontplooit,
  Of woar de "Union Jacks" heur börgers dekken.

Wat toak 'k ook heur van mensen dei 'k ontmuit,
  Beschoafd of wild, van allerhande kleuren,
Gain van al dei toalen klinkt zoo zuit,
  Of is as doe, geschikt mie op te beuren.

En doarom heb 'k dit dichtje aan die gewaid
  Mien Moudertoal; aan die, zoo voak vertreden,
Zoo voak bespot, bemodderd en beklaid,
  Moar altied weer as held oet 't sliek geschreden.

to me by a communication from J. Kuiken of St. Anna Parochie [in Friesland]. A couple of his friends and their three-year-old daughter had migrated from Het Bildt [Friesland] to Paterson. Seventeen years later their daughter returned on a pleasure trip and called on him. She had practically no recollections of her birthplace, and yet despite the seventeen years of absence Kuiken could not detect in the least from her language or way of speaking that he was dealing with an American. Even her Bildt dialect had been preserved faultlessly. She explained to him that at home they always spoke "Bildtsch." At school and at the silk manufacturing plant where she worked, nothing but English was spoken. Whenever other "Bildtkerts," who had lived for a long time in America, would visit Kuiken, he noticed the same thing to be true, although they would throw in an English word here and there.[79]

As tenaciously as all these dialects maintain themselves, the Frisian language, according to some observers, does so even more strongly. I have given examples of how Frisians adapted faster than others to the American language and culture, but there are as many cases in which Frisians maintained longer than others their own distinctiveness and especially their language. The independence of their spirit was demonstrated in the middle of the nineteenth century, when the 1856 census was taken in Lake Prairie Township, Iowa. Of the residents, 1,480 gave simply "The Netherlands" as the place of their birth, but forty-four registered Friesland as the land of their fathers.[80] Their independent spirit is also demonstated by the love they have for "kaatssport" [a distinctively Frisian ball game]. It is played in New Jersey in the East, and in Sioux County, Iowa, in the West. A "kaatspartij" is often announced on the printed program of various festivities. That independence of spirit is also shown in their organizations where they practice—sometimes more, sometimes less—the Frisian language by presenting plays in Frisian, by singing Frisian songs, etc.

Frisian organizations can be found in the following towns:

Location	Name	Organized	Members in 1927
Paterson	Utspanning troch Ynspanning [Relaxation through Exertion]	1893	120
Rochester	Nij Fryslân [New Friesland]	1906	80
Grand Rapids	Friso [Legendary Frisian Forebear and Namesake]	1909	140
Chicago, Roseland	Ut en Thús [Out and (at) Home]	1923	120
Chicago	Nocht en Wille [Fun and Pleasure]	—	80
Hebron, Ill.	Friezenforieniging [Frisian Club]	—	40

Later additional Frisian groups were organized at Clearwater in California, with sixty members, and at Holland, Michigan, with seventy members.

It must be acknowledged that initially none of these groups led a flourishing club life. They did perform some services, however. The Grand Rapids organization provided the public library with three hundred items of Frisian literature. Among them I saw writings of Waling Dijkstra, the book of Frisian songs by [Pieter Jelles] Troelstra and [P. H.] De Groot, booklets by [J.] Veltman, [Joh. A.] Noordebos, [Justus (Joast) Hiddes] Halbertsma,* [Franke G.] Looyenga [Luijenga], etc. There were also copies of "*Sljucht en Rjucht*" [Plain and Straight], a very old and very popular Frisian magazine. Nevertheless, use of the Frisian language steadily declined. The Frisian book dealer, Eerdmans, continued to import Frisian literature and advertised it in the Holland-American papers, but by 1920 many Frisians were still ignorant of this opportunity. Also at Rochester and vicinity Frisian was used less and less and one seldom heard it spoken any more. The Frisians had become Americans. Yet, there still were many Frisian parents who had continued to teach the old, familiar language to their American-born children. For example, [Toussaint (?)] Bokma, the secretary of Friso, the Frisian organization at Grand Rapids, was born in America yet he knew more about Friesland and its history than many a native-born Frisian.

How deep and strong the emotional attachment was to the old Frisian language and culture became evident in 1920 when Sjouke De Zee spoke in Paterson and people came from forty miles away to hear Frisian once more spoken from his mouth.[81] From De Zee's presentation and those of Y. C. Schuitmaker and B. S. Hylkema, who traveled to various areas in America and spoke and sang about *Fryslân* in the *Fryske tael* [in Frisian], it was clear how little had changed in the hearts of many American Frisians:

> Fryslân, Fryslân, dy forjitte
> Kin 'k allinne yn 't tsjustre grêf.

> "Friesland, Friesland, to forget thee,
> I can do only in the dark grave."

So we see that the native dialects are still strongly adhered to, not only among those born in the Netherlands but also in the second- and sometimes third-generation descendants of the immigrants in America, who learned it at home as children or rather absorbed it without effort in a playful manner. No doubt this is the reason why the authentic, classical Dutch generally no longer occupies the position in Holland-American culture that one would have expected. The dialects have indeed accelerated the use of the English language.

Children learned the classic Dutch at their parochial schools. But, so they wondered, what was the use of it all? They could not use that language in their own villages and even their parents who all the time spoke a provin-

---

*Most prominent of the Halbertsmas. His brothers, Eettsjes Hiddes and Tjalling Hiddes Halbertsma, are also noted literary figures and writers of folk tales. They are usually referred to as the *bruorren* [Brothers] Halbertsma (like the Brothers Grimm).

cial dialect could not understand them clearly in Dutch. To the present day many of the colonists and their descendants are reluctant to speak to other Netherlanders in the Dutch language because their Dutch has been corrupted so much by dialect that they are afraid it will make them ridiculous. I have often personally observed in both Holland and Grand Rapids that intellectuals, teachers, doctors, lawyers, although they were the descendants of fairly recent immigrants, would soon give up their effort to talk to me in Dutch, even when I had specifically requested it. They apologetically explained that their Dutch was so "fractured" they were actually ashamed to speak it.

This accounts for the fact that I have talked to many people living in the Netherlands who visited Holland, Michigan, spent some time there and never heard a word of Dutch! In this respect there is no greater contrast between Holland and Pella. This also accounts for the attitude of the children and young people toward the Dutch language. They have no taste for it nor even much respect. Respect and love for the language of their parents and grandparents is totally lacking in Michigan and in the cities in other states. Several parents said to me, "They [their children] don't think much of Dutch."

In the public schools the children learned only English and later also in the Christian schools, although they were given at most a few hours of Dutch per week as in the Christian colleges. As youngsters at home they had learned either their parents' dialect or formal Dutch. After they became older, more mature they learned "the language of the land," the language of the mass of people among whom they lived and worked and with whom they had most of their contacts.

It is not surprising, then, that in time the Dutch language was supplanted, be it ever so slowly. Many of those who in their youth had learned to speak a very pure form of Dutch gradually lost that ability. [W.] Wundt points out that in the changing process ["Sprachmischung," the mixing of languages], the newly acquired [target] language changes relatively little but the mother tongue of those who learn the new idiom changes all the more so.[82] First one mixes in the words, then the syntax and word derivations, and lastly the sounds. In Michigan and in other areas there was a deterioration of the language of many immigrants from Noord Holland, Zuid Holland, and elsewhere, who originally spoke a pure form of Dutch. This "language conflict" can also be detected in the newspapers.

It is obvious that the first intrusions or adulterations concern words that designate matters that are not current in the Netherlands and for which the user does not know the Dutch term or does not know it well enough. This resulted in an odd kind of Dutch. Matters pertaining to politics, social activities, clubs, schools, and sports were expressed in English. Many of the English words were "Dutchified" and became compound words, partly Dutch and partly English. Examples are: *auto-drijvers* [car drivers; in Dutch *autobestuurders*], *stijlen* [styles of clothing or *costuum-modellen*], *najaarsschoonen* [fall housecleaning or *najaarsschoonmaak*], *rollend land* [rolling country or *heuvel-*

achtig land], *mijners* [mine-workers or *mijnwerkers*], *helpvol* [helpful or *behulpzaam*], *een kostelijke brand* [a costly fire or *een zware brand*], *een tijdige kwestie* [a timely question or *een actuele kwestie*], *gecande en ingezette vruchten* [canned and preserved fruit or *ingeblikte en ingemaakte vruchten*], *het nummer zendelingen* [the number of missionaries or *het aantal zendelingen*], *publiek notaris* [notary public or *notaris*], *onmogelijk met den storm de haven te maken* [impossible to make the harbor in the storm or *onmogelijk om de haven te bereiken in de storm*], *wat is de troebel?* [what is the trouble? or *wat is de moeilijkheid?*], *hij verwacht te blijven* [he expects to stay or *hij hoopt te blijven*], *het is deftig persoonlijke kleren te dragen* [it is fashionable to wear personal (custom-made) attire or *het staat deftig maatkleding te dragen*], *de band leverde een schoon programma* [the band delivered a beautiful program or *het orkest speelde prachtig*], *zij verloor het bestuur over haar auto* [she lost control of her auto or *zij verloor de macht over haar stuur*], *een X-ray onderzoek* [an X-ray examination or *een Röntgen onderzoek*], *een wandeling genomen* [took a walk or *een wandeling gemaakt*], *H.C. is op een hevige wijze om het leven gekomen* [H.C. died a violent death or *H.C. is door geweldaad om het leven gekomen*], *order uw weekblad bij G.L.R.* [order your weekly paper from G.L.R. or *bestel Uw weekblad bij G.L.R.*], *O. en K.(kleermakers) "offeren den kooper een combinatie van elegante snede en langdurige dienst"* [O. and K. tailors "offer the buyer a combination of elegant cut and long wear" or *O. en K. "bieden den klant een combinatie van elegante snit en duurzaamheid"*]. A final example is a report in De Grondwet of May, 1921: "*Holland is een van de weinige steden, w. i. municipale publieke utiliteiten met profijt worden beheerscht. Beide de electriek licht en de waterwerk inrichtingen zijn meer dan zelf onderhoudend geweest in de laatste 10 jaren, wel een bewijs dat de inrichtingen door bekwame personen worden bestuurd.*" [Holland is one of the few cities whose municipal public utilities are managed with a profit. Both the electric light and the waterworks installations have been more than self-supporting in the last 10 years, evidence that the facilities are being directed by competent persons. In Dutch, *Holland is een van de weinige steden waar de openbare nutsbedrijven met winst worden beheerd. Zowel de electriciteitscentrale als de waterleiding hebben in meer dan eigen behoeften kunnen voorzien in de afgelopen 10 jaar, wel een bewijs dat de bedrijven door competente personen worden geleid.*][83]

It is therefore easy to understand that many a Dutch American is reluctant to speak his mother tongue and prefers to speak and write in English. Inevitably then, sooner or later the Dutch language will disappear. Indeed we had already observed this among our clansmen in the seventeenth century. The American H. E. Dosker wrote in 1893: "Slowly, irresistibly, inch by inch overcoming all opposition, the language of the land pushes back the foreign import language. At first, this happens in the schools, then on the streets, then in the households, and finally in the churches."[84] Dosker asserted that the churches were the last to capitulate. This demonstrates how great a part the churches play in preserving the native language of the colonists, since for many there is an intimate connection between faith and language, especially in the ultra-orthodox churches. This is also true in the

Reformed churches in spite of the fact that (as has been pointed out in an earlier chapter) the process of Americanization was accelerated by the union with the Reformed Church.

Up to the present time there is still in many Reformed and Christian Reformed churches an ongoing controversy over the language question. It gave rise to the most unsavory incidents, to the most vehement disagreements that often resulted in a split. How important a role the Dutch language played in colonial Calvinism can be assessed to some degree by the fact that even in the German Christian Reformed churches in America the Dutch language was used for a long time. The dispute over Americanization was preceded by an equally bitter dispute over Germanization when about 1870 and subsequently the German unification movement made itself felt and the German language began to dominate in the area. The German congregation at Ridott, Iowa [sic; Illinois], used the Dutch language continuously from its organization in 1866 until 1882 when the controversy began. It continued until 1893 when, due to the increasing number of new German immigrants, the final decision was made in favor of the German language.[85] A similar sequence occurred in many other congregations. The church at Steamboat Rock, Iowa (later renamed Wellsburg), organized in 1867, used the Dutch language exclusively at first, then Dutch and German together were used until the winter of 1916 when Dutch was discontinued and German became the official language in the pulpit. At the present time German and English are battling for supremacy.[86]

When one considers that the Dutch language was so tough to beat, even in the German churches, it is understandable that it fought tooth and nail for its life in the Dutch churches. We know that the first "American" Christian Reformed congregation was organized in Grand Rapids in 1887. By 1907 there were only seven, all located in Michigan with one exception, the one in Chicago. There were none in Iowa, which is understandable in view of the previous discussion.[87] During the [First] World War preaching in a foreign language was forbidden and the number of English-speaking churches in Iowa increased. However, in 1920 there were still only twenty-eight, representing one-eighth of the total membership of the denomination.[88] In addition, many churches became bilingual, although that also caused much trouble. In most churches the afternoon service remained Dutch, in some also the morning service. In a few others, for example at Denver, Colorado, and at Midland Park, New Jersey, people tried to solve the problem by appointing two preachers, one English-speaking, the other Dutch-speaking. In very many churches an obstinate faction refused to compromise and as a result a separate parallel "American" congregation was organized out of the Dutch congregation.[89]

In the Reformed denomination, the transition obviously was accomplished somewhat more rapidly due to their union with the older Reformed churches in the eastern states. However, this statement must be taken with caution. Those who vigorously promoted the "Americanizing" did so partly out of fear that the young people would desert their own churches and go over to the "American" (English-speaking) ones, as had occurred years before in the Reformed churches in the East. However, Americanization often had a reverse effect; the older members often "dropped out" and went over to the Christian Reformed churches if Dutch was spoken there! These considerations all slowed down the "switch," the language-change process. The important town of Orange City, for instance, organized an "American" church only in 1919, and then only because of an aggressive but very small minority who forced the issue. A congregational meeting was held to decide the matter. Out of 183 members of the existing First Reformed Church, 142 voted in favor of retaining the Dutch language and only 41 voted for English! They also rejected a bilingual compromise.[90]

Thus there are Reformed as well as Christian Reformed churches in which the Dutch language is still used. But there is already a much larger number of bilingual churches, in addition to "American churches." Exact figures are not available. In November, 1927, I wrote to Dr. Beets asking about this matter and he replied that in the countryside Dutch "is still predominant," but in the cities it is English.[91] It is probably that in both the Reformed and Christian Reformed churches approximately one-half of the congregations use the Dutch language, the other half "more or less exclusively" use English. In the Berean churches (as stated previously) and the *Nederduitsch Gereformeerden* or *Oud-Gereformeerden* [Low-German] only Dutch is used. In these churches one can still hear the Dutch psalms being sung in the versification of Dathenus!*

Keep in mind that many of those who attend Dutch services speak English in everyday life. But they apparently feel that the Bible can be read and understood only in Dutch and that psalms can only be sung in Dutch. Therefore, they have misgivings concerning American churches. A *Banner* correspondent at Lynden, Washington, states: "Many of our people . . . [use] the American tongue" six days a week "but tenaciously cling to the Holland in the divine services."[92]

In many homes the use of the Dutch language is limited to the reading aloud of a section of the Bible and the singing of psalms in family devotions. That is the reason why the Dutch of so many Holland Americans (and this is not limited to the preachers) has such a Biblical ring! People living in the Netherlands who entertain fellow countrymen from America sometimes have surprising experiences. A friend living in Amsterdam shared the following with me. They once had an American houseguest who spoke only English, until they sat down for dinner, upon which he offered a prayer in Dutch and also read a chapter from the Dutch Bible. Still more surprising,

---

*Petrus Dathenus (ca 1531–1588) was a Calvinist pastor of Dutch refugee congregations in Germany, where he wrote his popular psalm versification, *De Psalmen Davids ende ander Lofsanghen uit den Francsyschen dichte in Nederlandsche overgeset* (1566). He was active in the rebellion against Spain and served for a time as advisor of William of Orange. He presided over the Council of Wezel (1568) that laid the basis for the Reformed Church in the Netherlands.

when they all attended church, he also spoke Dutch but upon leaving the building after the service, he reverted to English. Apparently this was the force of habit. Another resident of Amsterdam had a missionary as his guest. He seemed to know no Dutch either, but when they began to sing Psalm 42 he suddenly joined them in excellent Dutch, and later also in Psalm 68. No doubt, he remembered because they are two of the best-known and most popular of the psalms.[93]

We are dealing here with language remnants and "relics." The language itself will certainly disappear now that it is loosing its last bulwark, the thoroughly Dutch Christian Reformed Church. Dr. Beets reported that at the most recent national Synod of that denomination "hardly any Dutch was used."[94]

The reading of Dutch books has also decreased considerably, which is comprehensible in view of the above. Such material as is available is mostly church literature. The leading importer of books from the Netherlands, the Eerdmans Publishing Company at Grand Rapids, has been doing a flourishing business in Dutch literature for fifty years and recently expanded into a new, ultra-modern four-story building. In September of 1920 Mr. Eerdmans told me they had sold thousands of the books of Dr. A. Kuyper. Indeed, Kuyper still enjoys so great a popularity that Eerdmans ordered one thousand copies of the Kuyper biography by [Reverend W. F. A.] Winckel [*Leven en Arbeid van A. Kuyper* (1919)]. The Eerdmans Company (formerly Eerdmans and Sevensma) sold hundreds of copies of the books by Dominie J. Van Andel, Dr. H. Bavinck, Dr. B. Wielenga, Dominie G. Wisse, etc. A thousand copies of the *Bijbelverklaring* [*Bible Commentary*] by Mathew Henry, published by Kok at Kampen, were sold.[95] [H.] Ten Have said (and it was confirmed by Eerdmans) that twelve sermons by Dominie W. H. Gispen, combined into one volume and printed under the title, *Wet en Genade* [*Law and Grace*], exported by Van der Laan at Zeist, had many readers. The writings of almost all the Reformed theologians were in demand.[96]

In addition to this religious, or rather, theological, reading matter, the Grand Rapids company, which had a branch store at Paterson for some years, sold thousands of narratives by [Jacob] Van Lennep, [Anna Louise Gertruida] Bosboom-Toussaint, [Eduard] Gerdes, [Pieter Jacob] Andriessen, [P.] Louwers, [Hendrik Jan] Van Lummel, [Reverend Jan] De Liefde, and later also works of Johanna Breevoort, G. Schrijver, Marjorie Bowen—in short, all the literature published by Daamen, Callenbach, Kok, Bredee, and Bolle.

Approximately between 1910 and 1920 the writings of [Frederik] Van Eeden, [Willem J. T.] Kloos, [Albert] Verwey, Fiore della Neva [pseud. M. G. L. Van Loghen], [Lodewijk] Van Deyssel, [Abraham Elia Jessurun] d'Oliveira, etc., were sold in small lots to public libraries and to students at Hope and Calvin College. In 1920, in spite of the damaging influence of the [First] World War on our language, the continuing interest in Dutch literature was nicely demonstrated when an award was given at Hope College for a study paper on "De mannen van '80" ["The Men of '80," i.e. writers such as Van Eeden, Kloos, Verwey, Van Deyssel, etc.][97]

However, our modern literature was not always to everybody's taste. American Puritanism and especially Calvinism, which supported and complemented each other, rejected certain writings as being "too obscene" and these were returned to Eerdmans-Sevensma.[98]

I made some inquiries at the Ryerson library at Grand Rapids. In 1920 they had on hand 2,451 items in our language. In comparison with other foreign languages it was surpassed only by German with 3,500 items. In 1919 to 1920 the number of Dutch books lent out totaled 6,672, which is 1.45 percent per year. In 1918 to 1919 the percentage was 1.73. Although these percentages appear small I thought they were high when compared with the number of books in other foreign languages that were lent out. The German, French, Italian, Norwegian, Polish, Swedish, and Spanish books lent out in the same time period totaled, respectively, .18, .09, .03, .00, .52, .01 and .01 percent of the available books. The Frisian writings previously referred to were not included in these statistics.[99]

I visited the Ryerson library in the first part of August, 1921, and the most requested Dutch books in the first seven months of that year were: [F. J. Heeris and W. Toose, compilers] *Aangename Uren met Toose* [*Pleasant Hours with Toose*], 30 times; [J. H. Been] *Het Leven van Admiraal Dubbelwit* [*The Life of Admiral Dubbelwit*], 24 times; [Frederik Willem] Van Eeden's *De Blijde Wereld* [*The Happy World*], 23 times; [Everhardus Johannes] *Potgieter's Poëzie* [*Potgieter's Poetry*], 23 times; [Jan Rudolph] Slotemaker De Bruïne's *Sociologie en Christendom* [*Sociology and Christianity*], 13 times; [Willem] Kloos, *Nieuwe Literatuurgeschiedenis III* [*New History of Literature*], 12 times; [Jacob Van Lennep's] *De Roos van Dekema* [*The Rose of Dekema*], 7 times; [Edward B. Koster, translator] *Uren met Shakespeare* [*Hours with Shakespeare*], 7 times; [M. F. Van Lennep's] *Het Leven van Jacob van Lennep* [*The Life of Jacob Van Lennep*], 6 times; [W. F. A. Winckel's] *Leven en Arbeid van A. Kuyper* [*Life and Work of A. Kuyper*], 6 times; [Jacobus Jan Cremer's] *Novellen van Cremer* [*Short Stories of Cremer*], 4 times, etc.[100]

However, Mr. [Samuel H.] Ranck, the head librarian, said that a comparatively greater number of religious books were taken out by our countrymen. Nevertheless, the books listed above show a wide range of interest. This was also true of the periodicals I found on the racks, viz: *Het Boek* [*The Book*], *De Gids* [*The Guide*], *De Hollandsche Revue* [*The Dutch Review*], *Het Huis* [*The Home*], *Neerlandia* [*Land of the Netherlands*], *Op de Hoogte* [*Informed*], *De Prins* [*The Prince*], *Stemmen des Tijds* [*Voices of the Times*], *Wereld-Kroniek* [*World Chronicle*], *Repertorium op de Nederlandsche Tijdschriften* [*Repertoire of the Dutch Magazines*].[101]

In addition, many colonists are subscribers to a Dutch newspaper. Before the war Eerdmans was receiving two hundred copies of Dr. Kuyper's *De Heraut* [*The Herald*] for clients, although that number has since greatly decreased. A smaller number were subscribers to *De Standaard* [*The Standard*], *Gereformeerd Tijdschrift* [*Reformed Review*], *Stemmen des Tijds* [*Voices of the Times*], *De Spiegel* [*The Mirror*], *De Bazuin* [*The Bugle*], and *De Prins* [*The Prince*].[102] Mr. Kuiken of St. Anna Parochie wrote to me in 1917 that there were about eighty copies of the *Bildtsche Courant* currently going to America and although the addresses frequently changed the number of copies was quite stable.[103] In Iowa many Gelderlanders read *De Graafschapper*, while the Frisians read the *Franeker Courant*. [Sietse] Hepkema informed me that the most popular Frisian newspaper in America was the *Leeuwarder Nieuwsblad* with at least one thousand subscribers. The more distinguished *Leeuwarder Courant* had only ten subscribers, according to the manager. There probably were many more provincial papers that people read, depending on which province the immigrants came from. All of this sufficiently indicates that the ties with the Old Country have not yet been broken. On the other hand, there are also subscribers in the Netherlands to the Dutch-American papers.

To what extent the interest in Dutch reading matter has declined is shown by figures given me by Eerdmans. Before the war his company was selling 80 percent Dutch and 20 percent English books, but afterwards the percentages were exactly reversed. Mr. A. Van C. P. Huizinga is even more gloomy about the prospects. In 1921 he wrote me: "There really never was a great interest in the language in America, but now that it has disappeared the very existence of the newspapers is threatened."[104] And we indeed saw some newspapers disappear although in some areas new church papers came into being.

There is much truth in the statement that "there really never was a great interest." A chair in the Dutch language, art and history set up at the University of Chicago in 1912 and occupied by Prof. T. De Vries has since been discontinued. Efforts to establish a similar position at the University of Michigan at Ann Arbor failed, notwithstanding two supporting factors, viz., a committee organized for that very purpose in Grand Rapids and the largest population of Young Netherlanders anywhere in the United States. The lectureship at New York was actually established and promoted by the Netherlands. The Americans even failed to contribute their share of the expenses (fl. 35,000)! After the [First] World War the lectureship became a professorship, the chair occupied by Dr. [Adriaan] Barnouw. To the best of my knowledge, even to the present time the major portion of the expense is borne by the Netherlands.[105]

The majority of the Dutch Americans seem equally indifferent to the Algemeen Nederlandsch Verbond, branches of which were formed after Abraham Kuyper's inspiring addresses in various areas during his visit here in 1898–1899. Branches of this Verbond were organized in two main areas, the Eastern branch in New York, the Western branch in Grand Rapids. The first had only a brief existence. The second was divided into three subdivisions, Grand Rapids, Chicago, and Roseland.[106] Since then it has become six units, including Boston and Minneapolis. After the first group in New York disbanded, it was reorganized into a group of smaller societies called the North American division of the Verbond. In spite of these efforts, genuine and enduring interest appeared lacking. In vain the energetic overall secretary of the Verbond, F. E. H. Gebhardt, professor of music at Yonkers, New York, has tried to breathe life into the organization.[107] No doubt the Verbond will eventually disintegrate and the various groups will go their own way. Any real interest is lacking here [in the Netherlands] too. In the opinion of the membership the basic nature of the Verbond is too intellectual and therefore "too high" for many. Besides, those who are also affiliated with churches are sufficiently involved in their Christian organizations.

It must be admitted that an organization like the Algemeen Neder-landsch Verbond, the purpose of which is to promote and perpetuate every-thing native to the Netherlands and which wants to have its members remain Netherlanders, actually has no legitimate place among naturalized Netherlanders in America. In the first place their language should be "American." As Netherlanders we would not be pleased either if naturalized citizens in our country organized themselves into separate nationalistic organizations according to their origin, such as German, English, etc.

As *Groot Nederlanders* [Greater Netherlanders, i.e., Netherlanders spread worldwide], we should be able to share the feelings and convictions of someone like Dr. H. Beets who, though strongly attached to the Nether-lands, desires above all to be a good American. Hence, he could write with true dedication, referring to the above-mentioned Synod meeting, that he "hails with delight the news that the official language of our Synod has been made to all intents and purposes the language of our beloved land."[108] Recently in an article in *Neerlandia* he irrefutably justified this posi-tion: "If anyone can continue to use in parallel the Dutch language, or any language of their Fathers, one is free to do so but not at the expense of the language of the land. Mentally speaking, for many it is simply impossible or at least impracticable in our busy country to master two different languages and keep up with them. If one of those languages must suffer, it should not be the language of the land in which one lives. . . . Therefore we insist that preference be given to English. That is our patriotic duty."

Even if a few Netherlanders should succeed in the future in preserving the Dutch language as a "luxury," in reality our language is doomed to die, though it be a natural death.[109] "There lies a language in its death throes," exclaimed Dr. Beets in 1902 at the much-publicized literary and philological conference at Kortrijk [Belgium]. He was referring to the Dutch language in the United States. Since then, however, the language has by no means been discarded. This has been repeatedly demonstrated. In 1917 our ambassador to Japan, Baron D. Van Asbeck, on the occasion of Her Majesty's birthday received a number of guests, among them some American missionaries, all of whom spoke fluent Dutch and expressed great attachment to the Netherlands. Yet they were members of the Re-formed Church, the most Americanized church among all the immigrants and were all former students at the throughly Americanized Hope College.[110] In a basketball tournament they cheered for the Dutch colors by shouting Hope's battle cry in Dutch:

Tik, tak, tol [Tick, Tack, Toe]
De boer die nam een knol [The farmers took a turnip]
Van de wagen [From the cart]
Zonder vragen [Without asking]
Tik, tak, tol!
At the end came a long drawn out "Keeesje!"*

In the same year, 1917, the American A. S. De Jong was utterly amazed to hear in Minnesota not only older folk speaking Dutch but young people, even those whose parents had been born in America. They were using the language exclusively, not only when they were talking about matters pertaining to the church or family life but about school activities and sports, and their games. "That's strong [*sterk* or remarkable], I said to myself.—Stronger yet," even persons who had had a very good education, including some preachers, seemed able to converse more easily in Dutch than in English.[111]

I myself on my journey among our clansmen through the various settlements in Michigan, Illinois, and Iowa almost never found it necessary to speak English in my contact with them, regardless of their educational background. Some would answer me in English out of embarrassment over their Dutch dialect. How proud many were in Pella and Orange City of their Dutch mother tongue. Lose it? Never! To be able to speak good Dutch was highly appreciated everywhere in Pella. A preacher who preaches in good Dutch lures members away from other churches of related denominations!

How far this love for the language is carried is repeatedly demonstrated. J. Ellerbroek, who came to Iowa as a child with his parents, testified a few years ago in *Pella's Weekblad* of his love for our language. In 1923 he wrote: "I am now seventy-nine years old and could very well use some extra money but I would not want to sell my Dutch at any price." That this was not just a hollow phrase is proven by the fact that he made sure his seven children learned English first but also Dutch. They all knew their Dutch as well as their English, in spite of the fact that five of his sons were the first Netherlanders who settled in Sibley, Iowa, in the midst of Americans. But the Iowa Netherlanders are not ashamed of their Dutch origin in contrast to so many of their clansmen in the large cities. Ellerbroek's sons are proud of their Dutch ancestry and are determined to keep up their use of the language. Because of it they were respected. Of his eight grandsons, all born of "American" parents, there are still three who write excellent English *and* Dutch. One of these grandsons had a daughter (the fourth generation in seventy-five years!) who knows her Dutch and her English equally well.[112]

---

*"*Keeesje*" (pronounced Kays-ya) is derived from the male name Kees (an abbreviation of Cornelis), which, according to old Dutch dictionaries, is used in an old colloquial saying—"Hij is een regte kees" [he is a great blockhead, a clumsy fellow]. Hence, Keesje in the college cheer is a term of derision, or at least a term of (friendly) reprimand, for a misdeed or blunder. One can imagine the Hope students all shaking a forefinger at the opposing team and supporters as they yelled "Keeesje," emphasizing the "je," and perhaps shaking their heads as well.

I have since observed that these are not isolated cases. For example, Dries Bosch at Steen, Minnesota, sees himself as being first of all an American. He sees his adopted fatherland as being above all the land of freedom; he expressed it somewhat naively as follows: "It is a country where many are released from tyranny.... Here one is not obliged to tip one's hat to Mister Bigwig just because the fellow is simply living off his money." He had many critical things to say about the Netherlands but finally he wrote to his friend, F. Van der Stoep at Piershil: "Be assured that I think a great deal of the Netherlands. I am proud to be of Dutch blood, and that my ten children can read Dutch just as well as English and write Dutch almost as well as English. I taught them myself because there is no Dutch school here."[113]

One senses that these people, by a resolve of their will, have intellectually made a firm decision to be Americans, but emotionally they are still very much attached to the Old Country and to the old language. To relinquish them is so very difficult. The separation of nationality and ethnic heritage does not just happen, it is not a matter of course. On the contrary this break is very painful, although people try to conceal it with a little cynical smile or a humorous little rhyme.

Finally, here is one last example. In 1927 the same correspondent from the *Nieuwe Rotterdamsche Courant*, who could find so few traces of the Dutch in Michigan, made the acquaintance of the preacher of a small Dutch church in Albany, New York. It turned out that he was of Dutch descent too, four generations removed, but nevertheless he spoke "good and fluent Dutch." Neither the preacher nor his wife had ever been in the Netherlands but often talked Dutch to each other and were teaching it to their little daughter. Both parents came originally from Sioux County, Iowa.[114]

In the Midwest, especially in Iowa, Dutch hearts seem to beat most strongly in spite of all the Americanization. This is repeatedly demonstrated not only by means of the language, although it is spoken in its purest form here, but by the behavior of the colonists. They were the most typical pioneers, the most independent of our countrymen and from the very beginning they rebelled against American pressures. They continued to raise the flag of the Netherlands over their Christian schools even in times and places when no one else dared speak a word of Dutch, when others Anglicized their names so no one would notice them as the "dirty Dutchmen," akin to the Germans. We saw that Pieter Mouw and his family did not tolerate the displaying of the American flag in their church while elsewhere our clansmen raised the Stars and Stripes over their homes and wore them over their hearts as a testimony of their loyalty.

No doubt the tenacious survival of this spirit was promoted by the fact that where our Iowa farmers settled down, the Americans made room for them and as a result the Netherlanders could live in closer proximity to each other. Another factor that contributed much to the long life of Dutch culture on the prairie was the inadequacy of the rural public school system at that time. The many and long vacations and the poor quality of the instructors reduced the influence of the American schools while it strengthened that of the Dutch family.[115] However, both of these phenomena are more the result of what seems to have been the extremely strong vitality of the Dutch spirit here, which we have earlier recognized as being the "crème de la crème" among all the immigrants.

Thus we see that the Dutch language has not yet died and the Dutch lifestyle has not yet lived its last, not even among the young people. The many young men's and young women's associations, the adult men's and women's organizations, almost all associated with the church, testify to this. So long as the young people maintain their "Deborah" and "Dorcas" societies, needlework guilds such as "Draagt elkanders lasten" ["Bear Ye One Another's Burdens"] at Roseland, "Weest een Zegen" ["Be a Blessing"] at Kalamazoo, "Onderzoekt de Schriften" ["Search the Scriptures"] at Holland, one need not doubt the continuation of Dutch culture. There are also more secular organizations such as "Neerlandia" at Hoboken, "Eendracht maakt Macht" ["Strength in Unity"] at New York, "De Harmonie" and "Tot Nut van het Algemeen" ["For the General Benefit"] at Paterson—all in the eastern states; a Dutch Athlete's Club, "Hercules," a soccer club, and a group of Dutch-descended Mormons who are very avid dancers and who devote themselves to amateur theatricals at Salt Lake City and Ogden, Utah, in the Far West. All these guarantee that the Dutch language will not be forgotten.

There are many who feel that the loss of the Dutch language would be an impoverishment. Mrs. [J. E.] Struyck at Albany made a curious observation in this connection. She was born in America of Dutch parents but still understood the Dutch language perfectly and spoke it clearly although with some dialect. She had in her home an exceptionally beautiful painting and she had noticed that when she had Dutch visitors they would stand in admiration before the portrait and express their feelings with six or more different Dutch adjectives such as, how beautiful, how clear, how nice, how sweet, etc. On the other hand, American visitors almost without exception merely said, "How pretty!"[116]

Our language is still so influential that others living among the Dutch colonists have found it to their advantage to learn it themselves, especially in business affairs. Examples of this can be can be found in Muskegon, Holland, and Pella. In the seventeenth century the Hollanders living along the Hudson River saw and heard the same language exchange.

Even foreigners who dwell among Dutch Roman Catholics have fallen under the sway of the powerful Dutch ethnicity, although the Dutch Catholics are generally not the ones who hold on most strongly to their Dutchness in lifestyle and language. Bercovici, who recently visited the Roman Catholic Dutch colonists at Essexville and Bay City in Michigan, mentions that their French and Belgian neighbors "spoke a Dutch that was much better than their English."[117] Apparently the Netherlanders themselves used Dutch exclusively.

So far as I know, in spite of this vitality of the Dutch language, one does not encounter many—or any—words of Young-Dutch origin in the "American language." This is naturally due to the fact that the Dutch Americans are a small minority in the total American population. Words that have been adopted from the seventeenth century are boss (from the Dutch *baas*) |a master|, a boodle (*boedel*) |property, possession|, pinxster flower |"*pinkster bloem*" or Pentecost flower, the American cuckooflower|, hooky (*hoekje*),* cooky (*koekje*), high stoop, |*hoge stoep*, or a raised platform at the entrance of a house with steps and usually seats|, to snoop (*snoepen*).†[118] A word appearing often in American literature, "trek" (a noun as well as a verb), was introduced by |Rudyard| Kipling and borrowed from the history of the "Great Trek" of the South African Boers. This is also an example of how very cautious one must be in tracing the origin of "influences."

Now that |Arnold| Mulder's writings and that of other Netherlanders are being more widely read, and Americans are beginning to write about Dutch-American life, such as Quick's *Vandemark's Folly* and Edna Ferber's *So Big*, it is likely that more Dutch words will be assimilated into the American vocabulary, especially since many of our fellow countrymen are beginning to occupy positions of influence in American cultural life.

I must call attention to one exception. The Dutch diamond workers in New York have transposed Dutch terms of their craft to the American language and thus "grafted a new Dutch twig onto the English language." The American diamond worker does not ask for a "disk" or a "wheel" as the English do, but for a "skive," clearly an adaptation of the Dutch term, "*schijf*." This is even more exceptional when one considers that the American craftsman has available English words like "sheave" and "shive." The "American" plant manager at New York sends an order to Amsterdam or Antwerp; "Send immediately verstelpitten, doppen and tangen" |Dutch words for specialized parts in diamond polishing|.[119] This is purely craft idiom, but it also shows evidence that our language is still vital.

In all this competition between the two languages, an interesting question may be asked: What part do men play in all this and what part do women play? |A.| Dauzat states in his *La géographie linguistique* |*Geography of Linguistics*|, "*à âge égal, une femme sera, en principe, plus archaïsante qu'un homme*" |"A woman of the same age as a man will, in principle, be the more conservative of the two"|.[120] My time in America was too short to confirm this statement with regard to our colonists, and the literature I have gathered is not sufficient for such a study. The above remark made by Mrs. Struyck reveals a conscious insight into the significance of our language and at the same time her sympathy for it. Other women whom I was privileged to meet showed a similar sympathy, especially the mothers of families at a more advanced age. I was told by Dr. Hulst that his wife Mrs.

---

*Hooky means "to hook it" or to run away. It is probably not a Dutch derivative. *Hoekje* is a corner.
†Snoop means "to spy on" and is probably not a Dutch derivative. *Snoep* is candy.

Hulst, nee Steketee, during the [First] World War demonstrated her love for our language so openly that she got into great trouble (this is in "free" America) and was threatened with imprisonment. I regret I did not have the time to interview her. Dr. Hulst, urgently requested me, on behalf of his wife, to compile a list of some of our more recent Dutch literary works.

On the other hand, the only person in Pella I was not able to converse with in Dutch was a young woman who was a daughter of H. P. Scholte, the founder of Pella. Also in Grand Rapids I encountered young women who preferred to speak English—young daughters especially delight in doing this. (I referred to this previously in my comments on Nieland's *Yankee-Dutch.*) In the colleges the greatest interest in the Dutch language was among young men, in part because it may come in handy if later on they become preachers in the West. Some of these observations do not agree with Dauzat's viewpoint. However, they do corroborate the opinion of Friedrich Schönemann, who points out "the dual nature of the modern American woman who on the one hand is staunchly conservative and on the other hand is boldly progressive."*[121] This is, after all, true of all women although perhaps not to this same degree.

I have previously emphasized the attachment of the men to our language. However, it is our leading preachers who are strongly urging the replacement of Dutch with English in the churches. But again this is not out of pure love or "*Sprachimperialismus*" [linguistic imperialism] but to make sure the young people will adhere to the faith of their fathers. Others who in the line of business have more contacts with Americans and those who have political ambitions endeavor, simply for this practical reason, to become more proficient in English. This is not the case for many women of Dutch descent whose main duty is the care of the family.

There are many who feel it their duty as American citizens first of all to speak the language of the country in which they live. This is an obligation also stressed by our fellow countryman, [Theodore] Roosevelt, in these words: "One country, one flag, one language." Dr. Beets shares and expresses a similar conviction, although we are aware of his deep affection for his native land. In an earlier era, Dr. A. Kuyper had likewise impressed upon our countrymen in America their duty in this respect.

Though there are many Dutch people here [in the U.S.A.] who for various reasons prefer to behave as Americans, nevertheless quite often the inflections of their grammatically correct English inevitably betray their origin. [W.] Wundt points out in his *Völkerpsychologie* [*Ethnic Psychology*] that in language mixing the greatest resistance and most numerous difficulties will be in the area of pronunciation or sound changes.[122] The changes are most radical in the target language, and the less educated a group of people is in adapting to a new language, the greater will be the sound

---

*"*die Doppelnatur der modernen Amerikanerin, die einerseits zäh konservativ und andererseits verwegen fortschrittlich ist.*"

changes. Our colonists have confirmed this in a striking manner. When Mrs. H. Laman Trip-de Beaufort visited the Michigan colony she chanced to get into conversation with the sexton of one of the many churches. She surmised at once by the accent of his English that he was of Gelders ancestry. When she spoke to him in "*Geldersch*" dialect he responded immediately.[123] I have had similar experiences myself. Recently an American woman approached me here [in Amsterdam] at the Centraal Station [the main railroad station] and asked for some information. From her inflections and also from her outer appearance I surmised at once that she was of Groningen ancestry. In my reply I let this be known and she confirmed it with amazement.

When a national language is lost many typically national characteristics disappear with it. Several competent and well-known writers have observed and expressed this. For example, Steinmetz analyzes and records his conclusions concerning the significance of the language in these words: "When language differences are wiped out, soon differences in national culture and lifestyle are obliterated with them."[124] I would like to remind the reader of an earlier remark made by Dr. J. H. Halbertsma concerning the relationship between language particularity and regional character. (See the third chapter of the first volume where I cited his quotation.) Many of our colonists agree. Dominie L. J. Hulst was opposed to the introduction of the English language in the Christian Reformed Chruch and to the organization of an "English" congregation. He suspected that the chief attraction was not primarily the language but the more informal style of the American worship service. He feared that secularization and externalization would be the result; in short, that they would succumb to typical American religious superficiality.[125]

While we are on the subject, it may be interesting to consider again the convictions of old Mister J. Ellerbroek, previously referred to. He had grandsons who spoke either "American" or Dutch and was therefore in a position to make comparisons. He was opposed to B. K. Kuiper's recommendation that for the sake of their religious faith and as their duty to their adopted country they should make every possible effort to learn English as quickly as possible, even if it meant that in so doing they would sacrifice their Dutch.[126] Ellerbroek wanted his children to learn both Dutch and English equally well and urged others to follow his example and teach their children Dutch at home. "Then the children will not absorb so much of that American frivolity. You understand, of course, that it is not primarily the language itself that counts, but I have so often noticed in my lifetime that when the Dutch language is lost, one no longer finds that typical staid Dutch spirit either."[127]

It appears inevitable, therefore, that over the years the distinguishable Dutch character traits will disappear. Indeed, I have already seen symptoms of it. One of the most obvious of these is certainly the restlessness, the instability that has apparently taken possession also of our fellow countrymen, not primarily due to the "spirit of the times" but certainly as being typically American or, shall I say more broadly as typically colonial. "Jack of all trades and master of none" appears to be no exception in America but rather it is the rule, due to the constraints of circumstances but also due to the broad range of opportunities available.

This unrest, if not already a natural inborn trait, begins with the uprooting, with the departure from their native village and increases in the new country to the same degree that one finds it harder to put down new roots. These rerooting problems result in part from the previously mentioned inborn restlessness and in part from the slow progress in being successful. Even among the staid and sober older men this phenomenon was manifested by their continually changing jobs. A case in point was the one of Worp Van Peyma at Lancaster, New York. It was also true of those in the West. "The iron monger of two years ago is now a banker, the farmer of last year is now a shopkeeper or hotel manager, the printer of the local paper defected from his trade for the sake of a more visual form of education and owns and operates a movie theater, the druggist suddenly became more interested in the automobile business and bought a garage, etc., etc.," so writes "a Frisian" recently from northwest Iowa.[128]

Among the Dutch farmers constant change has become the rule, not the exception, especially among those who rent land instead of buying it. They already look upon land in a completely different way, like a piece of merchandise that one buys and sells according to market fluctuations and that thus can be rented for no longer than one year. Longer rent contracts stand in the way of "marketability." A farm that was occupied by eight successive tenants in ten years was "not unusual." As a result some of our pioneer farmers in America, by going from one state to the next, traversed during their lifetime a territory greater than Europe. One of these, [?] Byker, in ten successive years, worked on farms at Center Lake, Michigan; Orange City, Iowa; three locations in Montana, viz., Shepherd, Columbus, and Manhattan; two years on the same farm in Crookston, Minnesota—and this was mentioned as something exceptional—and thereafter one year each in Hancock and Pease, Minnesota. This is not the only example of its kind.[129]

The new rental period begins on the first of March every year and this then becomes the all-important moving day, although the preparations are under way already the last week of February. In many settlements it is a veritable exodus, as one finds out when reading *De Volksvriend* and other newspapers. One could imagine oneself to be living among nomads. Long caravans of every kind of vehicle are moving on those days in many different directions. This restlessness among the Netherlanders, especially on the prairies but also in the cities, is undeniable proof of a character change deeper than the Americanizing of the language.

Though it is clear from the foregoing that the Americanization process continues, it would be going too far to conclude that in an area like Grand Rapids the homes, both inside and outside, could no longer be identified as Dutch; they are "not even non-American." If someone should still doubt this, he should take a careful look at the thoroughly Dutch faces of so many "Americans," even of those who were born and raised in America and their many children and grandchildren down to the third, fourth and fifth generation. Examine the accompanying photographs. We see that it is not unusual to be able to discern a patently Dutch physique even among the descendants of the seventeenth-century immigrants.

A different climate, a different diet, even a different lifestyle can cause physical as well as psychological changes in human beings. [Jedediah Hyde] Baxter and [Benjamin A.] Gould have shown that children born in America are taller than children born of the same parents in Europe. [Franz] Boas believed he had observed visible variations in cranial width and length and explains it thus: "The influence of the American environment is felt immediately and increases slowly in the period of time that elapses between the migration of the parents and the birth of the child."[130]* Although Boas has since re-evaluated some of his earlier conclusions, he is nevertheless convinced that the "Umwelt" [environment] has a "powerful influence" upon the body forms and its physiological functions.[131]

Not everyone agrees. Many regard Boas with suspicion and distrust, and doubt the rigor of his scientific methods. Others ascribe the variations to a certain natural selection process. [Otto] Ammon and others think that only the most energetic individuals choose to migrate and they have supposedly more elongated skulls or craniums; but I would be reluctant to confirm this statement as applying to Dutch immigrants. Steinmetz interprets this phenomenon as being due to the phasing out of the poverty class and defends the regeneration hypothesis.[132] Also [F.] Von Luschan in his studies on the population of Asia Minor notes the importance of "Auslese" [selection].[133] However that may be, with the recognition of Auslese, we must also admit that more credence is given to Boas' convictions. [Jacob] Bolk published related studies in the Netherlands. Whatever our judgment may be, the very conservative Eugen Fischer believes that "Umwelt-einflüsse" [enviromental influences], even on the shape of cranial structure, "however, can certainly not be denied" [indes gewisz nicht zu leugnen].[134]

These environmental influences cannot be denied in the case of the Dutch immigrants even though the changes in them were not great, as we saw previously, since the climate and the soil did not vary too much from those in the Old Country. Consequently, they did not have to change their life style too much, although their existence was greatly broadened. Their tall size is striking. I observed this repeatedly. The much better living standard appears to have been of great influence; the same can be observed in the Netherlands too.

I have not been able to discern on the whole any great alteration in the facial features, although I studied them carefully. I did see more lean and

---

*"der Einflusz der amerikanischen Umwelt macht sich sofort fühlbar und wächst langsam mit Zunahme des Zeitraumes der zwischen der Einwanderung der Eltern und der Geburt des Kindes liegt."

A prolific immigrant family. B. Mouw, originally from Elspeet, migrated to America in 1869, married a Dutch wife there and settled in Sioux Center, Sioux County, Iowa. From this marriage eleven children were born, all of whom married. Mouw now has fifty-eight grandchildren and one great-grandchild. Observe the thoroughly Dutch faces. (Original photo.)

slender figures among the immigrants (although not all by any means), which can be accounted for by their more restless lifestyle and also by climate extremes, in particular the great summer heat. [Karl] Lamprecht did research among the Germans in Wisconsin and he observed variations in physique such as sharper features and leanness, in short, "*Abwandlung genau in der Richtung, in der sich der englische Typ abgewandelt hat*" [modification quite in the direction in which the English type has developed].[135] Dr. H. Bouwman studied the facial features and skin colorings of many young Americans and thinks he can trace points of similarity with the Indians, including their melancholy expressions.[136] I have looked in vain for such similarities among the Dutch colonists. Indeed, many deny the tendency (formulated by some observers) that the American race-in-development is inclining towards that of the Indians. This is understandable because according to [Clark] Wissler there is no such thing as a homogeneous Indian population, hence there is no distinctly Indian genetic type.[137] In this connection, Steinmetz pointed out years ago the great contrasts in cranial width between the various Indian tribes—Hurons, Algonquins, Iroquois, and Omahas. He does not believe in a generally newly-formed basic "Yankee" type, at least he sees in this no new race but at best only a racial ideal.[138]

On the contrary I was struck (I repeat it) by the authentic Dutch faces. Following this lead and addressing the person in our language, without fail I received a reply in Dutch, although at times in a regional dialect. As concerns the first matter—facial features—we see that marriages tend to be of the same nationality, even among the highly educated or those who think themselves most Americanized. Therefore, these Dutch features may continue for centuries. This is quite understandable in the light of Mendel's laws of heredity. According to these laws the distinctly Dutch characteristics will also continue for centuries, based on the close connections between the physical and psychological predisposition. Strangers are more aware of this than those of the same nationality.

It can therefore be understood that whereas our people took for granted that all traces of our ancestry had practically disappeared in the nineteenth-century settlements, an American writer like Bercovici has ascertained that they still exist in "an unalloyed way." Another fact that has escaped the attention of our people but has been observed by others is that the Dutch national vitality of the nineteenth and twentieth centuries was of such power that it set its stamp upon the foreign immigrants who lived around and among our fellow countrymen. "Instead of adopting the customs and habits of others they impress their own upon other people, and later, when their children or grandchildren grow up, they take them back and accept them as if they were American customs and not of Dutch origin," says Bercovici in his *On New Shores* in 1925.[139] It is a judgment whose authority is mainly derived from the fact that the writer had a wide experience, having lived among many differing nationalities in the United States, not as a scholarly scientist but as an even more keenly perceptive artist.

Bercovici, reacting sensitively to the slightest nuance, must have seen what many others, including Americans, failed to see, namely that even the world metropolis of New York City still contains much that is "Dutch."[140] "And today, with all the hundreds of sky-scrapers, the tone of the city is still that of Dutch architecture. New York is still largely a Dutch city." Indeed this artist sees the entire Hudson River territory as "so strongly Dutch that one expects at any moment from the corners of the streets the wide hoops and wooden shoes and the clatter of them going down the terraced roads from the Palisades or from Spuyten Duyvil." A large part of New Jersey "is still strongly impregnated with the Dutch feeling and sense of things."

How much greater, then, must be the Dutch character of the much younger nineteenth-century settlements even when taking into account the totally different circumstances under which they took root and the fact that in the first half of that century our national vitality was at such a low ebb.

I find that I have recorded much of this in my 1921 diary and it was confirmed in 1926 by some articles in the *Algemeen Handelsblad*. The articles were written by a traveling reporter who had the good fortune to meet Dr. H. Beets. His conversations with Beets must have greatly deepened his insights. One of his colleagues, a reporter from Rotterdam, was not so fortunate and thus their reviews do not exactly coincide. The *Handelsblad* reporter visited Michigan some eight months earlier during the summer. He writes: "Over the whole of this Dutch-American region from Grand Rapids to Lake Michigan floats an atmosphere of Dutch rural friendliness and relaxation. Here and there, the country roads are even bordered on both sides by willows after the manner of the Netherlands, which is a graceful way of reinforcing the road. We do not know of any other area in America where this is found. The Dutch element has not been lost even in the fourth generation. In the language and daily customs many distinctly Dutch characteristics continue to survive."[141]

During the [First] World War Americans felt this very strongly, hypernervous as they were then, and they did not let any occasion go by to signal this to the Dutch. Certainly the Dutch colonists feel themselves to be true and loyal Americans. Indeed, they fully consider themselves as such. This is, after all, their firm resolve and on the basis of this resolve we must consider them as such and respect them. In another context Steinmetz makes statements concerning the formation of new national loyalties as follows: "It depends in particular upon this will to organize themselves and to separate themselves into a separate state."[142] Thus we must accept the fact that the majority of our countrymen in America have become a real part of the American nation. According to [W.] McDougall, the American nation " . . . is the creation of men who have desired that it should exist." Steinmetz and McDougall agree on the basics: " . . . that the being of a nation is not merely a physical or biological fact, but rather a psychological fact."[143]

This does not alter the circumstance that the colonists are of Dutch descent and that they remain attached to us with bonds that are hard to sever, even though they do not recognize this state of affairs either consciously or unconsciously. They think of themselves as 100 percent Americans, whether this be out of a sense of duty or because they have a youthful longing for the American way.

Previously I referred to the fact that during the [First] World War the "real" Americans have cruelly reminded our countrymen of this [duality]. However, once America was at war, our people did their patriotic duty as in the Civil War. Many a memorial monument for fallen soldiers, as in Grand Rapids, records the great sacrifices that also the Dutch element then made. How valiantly they conducted themselves! Merely judging by the number of awards and medals, one of the most valiant soldiers in the American army must have been a Young-Dutch American, Sergeant [?] Van Iersel of Passaic, New Jersey. However, during the [First] World War many Netherlanders in the United States were grossly insulted, even mistreated. I was told many tales of injuries inflicted upon them, and they often were no less than the outrageous behavior toward the German-American population. The burning of barns and schools in the Iowa area, as mentioned before, are examples.

It is evident that there was still a wide gap between even those Netherlanders most committed to the American way and the "ideal" upcoming American breed. The deepest cause was the nature of the fundamental conflicts. Even now with the war so many years behind us, the work of Edward Bok, who was apparently thoroughly American, is viewed with suspicion. To the "100% American" he is still seen as a "Dutchman" whose efforts to induce materialistic America to dedicate more time to spiritual pursuits are condemned as "not strictly American, for it is more prevalent in old and decadent countries"! This latter comment originated with the Harvard scholar T. N. Carver.[144] Also the attention of others, particularly [Friedrich] Schönemann, had been struck by the un-American character of Bok's famous *Ladies' Home Journal*, in particular its well-balanced editorial policy—["*ein gewisser anständiger Durchschnitt*"—a truly respectable middle-of-the-road (policy)]—also during the war years, although it was anti-German then.[145] Even the most moderate do not consider Bok a genuine American but along with [Horace] Kallen see him and others as being somewhat artificially American: "There 'Americanization' appears too much like an achievement, a tour de force, too little like a growth."[146]

In more than one conversation in an "American" home, or on the way to my hotel after the day's work was done and a certain quietness had come over "our" people, it happened that some educated Dutch-Americans revealed their deepest feelings to me and confessed that they actually did not feel at home in America even though they had lived here since their childhood and admitted that they "had it very good here." They felt it was impossible for them to become wrapped up in Yankee life, but they could not return to the Netherlands and to its spiritual atmosphere that they felt they needed. They felt therefore unbalanced, without a real identity, for they were no longer Netherlanders and actually they were not Americans either.

Only a steady job, constant work, could dispel this unrest for a time, this uncomfortable feeling of being an alien. So they continued to work ceaselessly. The result of this work and the "isolation" already noted previously engendered the progress I have described and that brought them prosperity and fame, but no deep, inner happiness.

Taking everything into account, it is this sense of being an alien that makes so many long for the old homeland and the mother tongue. This is a phenomenon one can detect in the colonies as well as among those scattered more widely among Americans. Even the most thoroughly Americanized among our fellow countrymen, who thought they had forgotten their mother tongue, revived it in their later years. Bok and others, whose finances enabled them to do so, often returned to the Old Country to restore the contacts they thought had already been lost. Others who can not afford such a trip are longing to hear some real Dutch spoken again. In 1921, when I was about to leave Pella, I was urgently asked to make a passing call on an elderly couple, Mr. and Mrs. C. They wanted so much to hear something about the Netherlands from the mouth of someone who actually lived there. The old lady told me of her deep disappointment in 1874 when she attended a lecture by Dr. M. Cohen Stuart (whom I have so often quoted). Instead of using her beloved Dutch, he spoke only in English! Let this be a hint to future speakers.

I am reminded of similar instances. The scholarly G. Vos, who had lived for more than thirty years among Americans in Princeton, proceeded in 1922 to write and publish his most cherished memoirs in the Dutch language. And there is F. H. Kuipers (Cooper), in his lifetime a world-renowned American. Often in his later years he revisited Akkrum, the village where he had been born. Even more extraordinary is the fact that although he died at New Rochelle, near New York City, after his death his last wish was fulfilled. He was buried at Akkrum in Frisian soil beside his first wife, A. De Graaf, a native of the province of Zeeland who had died in 1878; a mausoleum was erected over both graves.

In actuality then, the "Americanizing process" has gone forward very slowly, despite all sorts of exterior displays of being American. Our tribal instincts are too strong for that. Bercovici is not the only one who perceived this primeval force. Also others, even foreigners, notice this imprint of the Dutch archteype. The geographer [Albrecht] Penck, who spent several months in New York as an exchange professor, wrote in 1917: "The old New York families of Dutch origin remain closely knit together.... They constitute a very exclusive, fundamental aristocracy, which keeps its distance from the plutocrats of plebian descent."[147]*

The same tenacity can be observed at any time among the Young-Dutch Americans, all the more since the same orthodox religious faith binds them

*"Eng halten die alten New Yorker Familien holländischen Ursprungs zusammen.... Sie bilden eine sehr exklusive Grundaristokratie, die sich fern hält von den Plutokraten plebejischer Abkunft"

together even more strongly. The Americanization process assures this, although we concede that eventually, in a far future, the Dutch language will be lost.

Though the language may expire, the clan consciousness remains. How strong this is was demonstrated during the Boer War in South Africa. Wherever Netherlanders were living, local committees were formed and united into a Transvaal Bond for a cooperative effort. J. W. Warnshuis was one of the most ardent defenders of the Boer cause in Michigan.[148] However, nowhere was there any greater sympathy for their cause than in Iowa. Here M. P. Van Oosterhout was the soul of the Transvaal movement. Not only did people organize heavily attended meetings, but they also raised money—more than $10,000 in Iowa alone—for the benefit of the widows and orphans of the Transvaalers killed in the war. They tried to persuade their government to intervene and take action against the British outrages. Every defeat of the British murderers was hailed with the greatest enthusiasm. The post offices were kept open until late at night to get the very latest news and *Pella's Weekblad* printed and distributed bulletins. Several merchants organized "Transvaal Days" during which they donated a percentage of their proceeds to the Transvaal cause. In those days many wore insignia of "Oom Paul" |Paul Kruger, leader of the Boers|, and they even named their newborn children after the Transvaal heroes.

Official bodies, such as the city governments of Pella and Orange City, sent resolutions to the government. Representatives brought the matter of the Boer cause to the floor of their legislatures. American newspapers finally announced that hundreds of Netherlanders from Sioux County were preparing to go to South Africa, since it was reported that volunteer brigades had been formed.[149] Indeed, many young men suddenly disappeared in those days and sometime later turned up in Transvaal. Names like Klein, Dekker, and Te Veltrup were mentioned, who, like many volunteers from our country, fought shoulder to shoulder with our threatened countrymen in Africa. It was one of the most beautiful moments in the whole history of the Greater-Netherlands people.

The Dutch Americans sympathize with events in our own European Netherlands. The flood and ensuing calamity at Borculo* made a deep impression on them. Generous gifts for the relief of the needy flowed out of America also. Our "Republicans" even demonstrated great interest in our royal family. Recently Her Majesty the Queen and her husband celebrated their twenty-fifth wedding anniversary. Many Dutch-Americans joined in compiling a memorial book of annals as a gift to Her Majesty. Their delegates faithfully attend the Synods of our Reformed churches |in the Netherlands|.

The number of Dutch-American students who come to our country to

---

*Borculo, a town in Gelderland Province, was heavily damaged by a tornado on August 10, 1925.

study at the Free University [at Amsterdam] continues to increase. At the present time there are seven enrolled. Most of them are already preachers. They are accompanied by their wives and form a small Dutch-American colony in Amsterdam, holding weekly gatherings in the hospitable residence of Professor [Valentine] Hepp.* They cannot endure to hear false and ugly accusations made against our country, as, for example, when someone tries to justify the Belgian claims regarding the land bordering the Scheldt River, and mentions the "French" population of the Dutch Flanders area. [Zeeuwsch-Vlaanderen, north of Belgium]. Then John H. Van den Berge, "born near the Scheldt," joins the fray and "scores Belgian claims," to quote the headline above his warm and well-formulated plea for Dutch rights. Not only does he pick holes in the Belgian complaints but he points out that their claims have no legal basis. "Will some senator ever get it into his head to demand the banks of the St. Lawrence River simply to perfect our waterways?" he asks and quite to the point. He is firmly convinced that if Belgium ever tried to lay hands on Netherlands territory "you can bank on it that the Netherlanders are going to put up a fight and if left alone there is no doubt that Belgium is going to meet the same fate as in 1830."†

There are others who agree. G. Van den Berge registered protests against the Belgian demands. A. Van den Bosch, the Christian Reformed professor of history at the University of Kentucky, recently wrote *The Neutrality of the Netherlands During the World War*, published by Eerdmans at Grand Rapids, Michigan, in which he tried to make clear to the Americans once and for all what course of action the Netherlands was following and what difficulties also the Netherlands endured during the war. Our former ambassador at Washington, Jonkheer [A. C. D.] De Graeff, was deeply moved by the sympathy shown to the Netherlands by the Dutch colonists. Several times he visited the colony in Michigan and personally experienced it. He was struck by the warm concerns of the Young Dutch Americans, in contrast to the great indifference of the Old Dutch Americans.[151]

In return, Dutch Americans appreciate the interest our people demonstrate when delegates from the Netherlands attend their church conferences. And when they go through difficult times their thoughts go back to their Motherland as shown in this very moving telegram sent to us when America was involved in the [First] World War: "Holland, Michigan, and the entire Dutch colony in western Michigan, the largest Dutch-American community in America, ask the people of Holland in Europe, on this our American Independence Day, for their sympathy with the United States in this struggle, insofar as this is compatible with the policy of neutrality of your country."[152]

There are some other indications that in the United States the Nether-

---

*Valentine Hepp (1879–1950) was a professor in the Theology Department of the Free University who lectured in the United States on more than one occasion.

†The Netherlands took up arms in 1830 to prevent the Belgian secession, but ultimately failed.[150]

landers, despite themselves, will remain "Dutch" for centuries, no matter how loyal as Americans they will be, and even if our language has become a luxury or an object of academic study. Bercovici wrote recently: "I doubt whether the country has any better citizens than the Dutch."[153] In many towns in Reformed and Christian Reformed circles homes are being built exclusively for old people of Dutch descent: Holland Homes. There are such homes in Grand Rapids, Kalamazoo, and Muskegon in the state of Michigan; at Paterson in New Jersey; at Chicago in Illinois; and at Pella in Iowa. This year one is being built at Sheldon, Iowa and one is being planned at Orange City, also in Iowa.

Equally Dutch but somewhat more religious in character are various sanitariums. They are built and maintained chiefly for members of "Dutch" churches: a Christian hospital for the mentally retarded at Cutlerville, Michigan, a Christian sanatorium, "Bethesda," at Denver, Colorado, and a Christian sanatorium at Goffle Hill in New Jersey. There is a home in Hoboken, New Jersey, for the temporary use of incoming immigrants and seamen. (I have mentioned this in an earlier connection.) All of these are evidence of a still-existing "group spirit" among the Netherlanders in the United States.

That this "group spirit" is not limited to the "church-oriented" is shown by the celebrations held to commemorate Dutch holidays. There was one in Chicago in 1893, and at the present time one is occasionally held in the East. Various types of all-Dutch organizations take part. Dutch songs are sung and Dutch games are played that keep alive the memories of the Old Country.

"Racially and nationally we do not desire to remain Dutch," said Calvin College Professor, C[larence] Bouma recently.[154] But nature appears stronger than theory. Many are the examples I have cited such as the Dutch neighborhoods in the various cities. But the most patriotic Dutch American becomes most aware of his Dutchness when he considers marriage. The Netherlanders who settled in America in the mid-nineteenth century, even the educated ones, thought American girls were much too fond of pomp and splendor. "They all rustle with silk," said one young man somewhat contemptuously and added: "But if the girl who comes out of a log cabin is dressed in finery I feel three times as much aversion." "If you invite four or five dozen *Machteljes* and *Dieuwertjes* [Dutch female names] to come to one of our meetings or parties, *elles n'auront que l'embarras du choix* [they will find that there are too many young men to choose from]."[155]

Still more deprecating was the judgment of S. A. Sipma a few years previously: "The American women are terribly lazy. They do nothing but prepare food and drink. They neither sew nor mend. They wear their clothes until they fall from their bodies in rags and then buy new ones.... They are not willing to walk anywhere. To visit a neighbor they want a horse."[156] This view of the American woman is still prevalent today. For this reason a marriage between a Netherlander and an American woman is still more or less an exception although some of the differences between Dutch and American women are diminishing.

It is surprising to note that the Frisians, who were the first of the immigrants to adjust to American culture, and who more than many others felt like Americans, yet today disapprove of American women. Their opinion is as withering as it was seventy years ago. Indeed, they go beyond it. A Frisian who had lived among the Hollanders in Iowa for many years recently remarked that Frisians and Hollanders neither dared nor wished to marry a "thorough-bred" American girl. There were too many differences in their natures and the way they were reared. Such a marriage would be a total failure. Many go back to the Netherlands to find their life's companion. Those who are born in America visit the other Dutch settlements for such a purpose. We have seen that the Geldersman Bloemendaal did precisely that. The Frisian I have referred to, a well-educated man, still criticizes the slovenliness of many American women: "At home they appear untidy, but when they go out they are decked out like cockatoos." They have no natural aptitude for making the home a pleasant and congenial place. Then this same Frisian, ultra modern in running his business and a very refined person, raises the baffling question: "Should the American woman remain under consideration to be a suitable partner with whom to establish a household?"[157]

One could, of course, point out that this Frisian was born in the Netherlands, but many of those born in America are of the same opinion. It may be incidental, yet it speaks volumes, that recently one of the most Americanized, born-in-America Netherlanders—a Frisian again—the former member of Congress, G. J. Diekema, remarried a Dutch woman.[158]

It is true that at many levels of the Dutch-American communities a marriage between persons of the same origin is considered most desirable. You may recall that Dr. H. Beets and his followers openly acknowledged this in their plea for Christian schools. The charge that in free America we act therefore in a very clannish way was implicitly accepted as a virtue. "Now, clannishness may be overdone, we admit, but it is something of a virtue, even though it may degenerate into a vice sometimes."[159]

Since in subtle affairs of this kind the ethnic differences still assert themselves so strongly and since for undetermined lengths of time our families will have both a Dutch father and a Dutch mother, we can predict that even though the language may gradually be forgotten and even though many Dutch habits and customs may disappear, yet the Dutch nature will continue to assert itself for centuries to come and will be clearly recognized by the Bercovicis of the future.

We conclude, therefore, that the Dutch Americans, although scattered over the entire United States and seemingly absorbed in the great mass of people, are nevertheless still a rather highly visible ethnic unit. We see this most strongly of all in the old migrant settlements, the cores, so to speak, of all the Dutch stock in America whose influence has spread throughout the Union.

Young intellectuals enroute to and in America. 1. The departure from Rotterdam to New York. 2. Out of the harbor. 3. As cook's mate on a ship from New York to San Francisco. 4. After a busy workday at Martinez. 5. A vacation day in California. (Original photos.) [These five photos were owned by Van Hinte's brother, J. E. Van Hinte (second from left in photo 3), and depict his voyage in 1922-1923 from Hoboken to San Francisco on the ship W. A. *Luckenbach*, on which he worked as a messboy. After a brief vacation in California, Van Hinte took a job at Shell Oil refinery at Martinez, California. Letter of J. E. Van Hinte to Robert P. Swierenga, September 10, 1983.]

Should we mourn the loss of over 200,000 of our countrymen and all their potentialities? I do not think so. For many of them, the Netherlands was too small and at times also too narrow-minded. This was especially true with regard to our farmers, who were restricted by an increasing land shortage and exorbitant land taxes. For them in particular America has become an El Dorado in the highest sense of the word. They were able to continue to satisfy their love of countryside living, thanks to the Homestead Act and many other government ordinances. Finally, in these great open spaces they were able to develop all their abilities and to regain their self-confidence that was threatened with extinction in the Netherlands. Seen in this light, materialistic America, the land of multi-millionaires and of bloodily suppressed workers' strikes, acquires even for a communist like Henriëtte Roland Holst, a higher, consecrated significance. She wrote:

> Our eyes, full of dawning hope,
> turn to your beautiful distant countenance, O youthful Mater,
> that radiantly shines between sea mists like a baptismal
> child between veils.[160]*

Not only the farm workers but also others, especially among the *kleine luyden*, will give their assent.

For America the majority of the migrant Netherlanders were certainly not without value; indeed, in many respects they became a blessing. Our people occupy an increasingly more important place in American society. More and more our people rise to the opportunities that America offers, having been conditioned for this by their more or less typical Dutch characteristics. They could often develop these only as a result of the broad vision of their leaders, in particular Van Raalte, as I want to note here for the last time. His creation, Hope College, is an institution whose worth is more and more recognized and appreciated.

In conclusion, this migration was and still is of benefit to both the Netherlands and America, and the choicest individuals of the Dutch people, transplanted into American soil, already exercise an influence that extends beyond the borders of both countries. The contributions of men like Zwemer and Warnshuis, Bok, Kool (Cole), and Diekema illustrate this and promise still more for the future. Has not the Old-Dutch trunk given the United States two presidents, [Martin] Van Buren and [Theodore] Roosevelt, the only American heads of state not of English origin?†

Therefore we must hope for a number of reasons that America will again open wide its borders to our people. We must hope this primarily for the benefit of the Netherlands. The pressures of a too-dense population

*Onzeoogen gaan vol dagende hoop
naar uw schoon ver gelaat, o jonge Mater
dat tusschen zeedamp schittert als een doop-
kind tusschen sluiers.

†After this book was written (1928), Franklin Delano Roosevelt became the third president of Dutch descent.

threaten again to undermine seriously the typical, Old-Dutch qualities of independence, self-sufficiency, and relative honesty and loyalty at all levels of society. At the same time this population pressure engenders unhealthy practices in securing positions, which are often accompanied by unworthy flattery. This also causes an unprecedented corruption to spread through all layers of society. Therefore, we support Roland Holst in this regard, and wholeheartedly join in her plea:

Again, like once before, take up the lead and make us free, America.*

---

* *Neem weer, als eens, de leiding en maak ons vrij, Amerika.*

Notes

Volume One

Chapter 1. *The First Emigrants and Settlers: How America Became a Land of Promise.*

1. S. Muller Fz., *De Reis van Jan Cornelisz. May Naar de IJszee en de Amerikaansche kust, 1611–1612* (1909), xlv ff.

2. S. P. L'Honoré Naber, *Henry Hudson's Reize* (1921), xlv ff.

3. F. C. Wieder, "Onderzoek naar de oudste kaarten van de omgeving van New York," *Tijdschrift van het Koninklijk Nederlandsch Aardrijkskundig Genootschap* (1918), 236ff.

4. Naber, *Hudson's Reize*, lxx, lxxi.

5. Muller, *Reis*, xxiv.

6. Ibid., 35.

7. Ibid., xlix.

8. Joannes De Laet, *Nieuwe Wereldt ofte Beschrijvinghe van West-Indien* (1625), 88. My last reference does not concern Naber, who very accurately states: "He [De Laet] gives no data, only generalizations" liii.

9. J. Franklin Jameson, *Narratives of New Netherland* (1909), 67, n.2. On the same page see the animosity exhibited by the populace, according to Wassenaer. The connection with the ending of the privilege is my own interpretation.

10. F. C. Wieder, *De Stichting van New York in Juli 1625* (1925), 3–16.

11. Ibid., 11.

12. A. Eekhof, *Jonas Michaëlius* (1926), Doc. 9, 96–97. The significance of this was found by Wieder in the *Nieuwe Rotterdamsche Courant*, 1926.

13. Wieder, *Stichting*, 14.

14. Jameson, *Narratives*, 75. See also Wieder, *Stichting*, 12–13.

15. Wieder, *Stichting*, 26, 27ff.

16. Ibid., 24.

17. Eekhof, *Michaëlius*, letter of August 7, 1628, 103.

18. At any rate, according to G. Chinard, *Les Réfugiés Huguenots en Amérique* (1925), 43. I could not find this in [Wilhelmus] Baudartius's work, which is in the University of Amsterdam Library.

19. Jameson, *Narratives*, 76, 80, 82.

20. De Laet, *Nieuwe Wereldt*, 88–89.

21. Naber, *Hudson's Reize*, liii. The fact that colonization thoughts were also awakened among Hudson's men appears not only from Hudson's words, but also from [Robert] Juet's *Journal*, 70, 73. Here one can find a strengthening of the conviction that De Laet had seen one of Hudson's accounts; I had anticipated this.

22. De Laet, *Nieuwe Wereldt*, 89.

23. J. S. Catella Jessurun, *Kiliaen van Rensselaer van 1623 tot 1636* (1917), 26.

24. Naber, *Hudson's Reize* (Juet's *Journal*), 58–59, 70.

25. Jessurun, *Kiliaen van Rensselaer*, App. 4, VI; A. Eekhof, "De 'Memorie' van Isaack de Rasière voor Samuel Blommaert," *Nederlandsch Archief voor Kerkgeschiedenis* N.S. 15, No. 4 (1919).

26. Eekhof, *Michaëlius*, 101–102. Also Eekhof, *De Hervormde Kerk in Noord-Amerika* (1624–1664) (2 vols., 1913), II, App. I.

27. Eekhof, *Michaëlius*, 125.

28. Jessurun, *Kiliaen van Rensselaer*, 33.

29. Wieder, *Stichting*, 126.

30. David Pietersz. De Vries, *Korte histori-ael ende journaels aenteyckeninge van verscheyden voyagiens in de vier deelen des Wereldts-ronde* (H. T. Colenbrander, ed., 1911), 25–26. See also Jessurun, *Killiaen van Rensselaer.*

31. De Vries, *Voyagiens*, xxvii, 147.

32. Ibid., 247–248.

33. O. Van Rees, *Geschiedenis der Neder-landsche Volkplantingen in Noord-Amerika* (1855), 36, 41.

34. De Vries, *Voyagiens*, 233.

35. H. T. Colenbrander, *Koloniale Geschiede-nis* (2 vols., 1925), I, 55.

36. Van Rees, *Nederlandsche Volkplantingen,* 41.

37. De Vries, *Voyagiens*, 235, 248, 252; Jameson, *Narratives*, 215, n.1.

38. De Vries, *Voyagiens*, 250ff.; Van Rees, *Nederlandsche Volkplantingen*, 72.

39. Van Rees, *Nederlandsche Volkplantingen*, 101; Jameson, *Narratives.*

40. Jameson, *Narratives*, 288ff.

41. De Vries, *Voyagiens*, 237. Also see xxxvi and xxxvii.

42. Ibid., 238, 247, 256.

43. Ibid., 155, 249, 264, 241, 267.

44. Jameson, *Narratives*, 288. Van Rees, *Nederlandsche Volkplantingen*, using partly the same sources, came to the same conclusion.

45. Jameson, *Narratives*, 291. For an excel-lent translation of [Adriaen Van der Donck's] *Vertoogh*, 293–354.

46. An American translation, which con-tains a fervid account of Kieft's shipwreck, may be found in H. C. Murphy, *Representation from New-Nether-Lands and Broad-Advice* (1854), 127ff.

47. In order to let the people speak for themselves, I borrowed the following cita-tions from Van Rees, *Nederlandsche Volk-plantingen*, n. 14. Neither of these letters is available in Dutch in the University of Amsterdam Library. Sufficient for my pur-poses is Eekhof's *Hervormde Kerk*, I, 1, n.1, and I, 254, n.1; in addition see Jameson's transla-tion of *Vertoogh*, and Van Rees' detailed citation in *Nederlandsche Volkplantingen.*

48. Eekhof, *Hervormde Kerk*, II, 93–94.

49. G. M. Asher, *Bibliographic and Historical Essay on the Dutch Books and Pamphlets Related to New Netherland* (1868).

50. Eekhof, *Hervormde Kerk*, I, 252–63.

51. Asher, *Bibliographic and Historical Essay.*

52. Eekhof, *Hervormde Kerk*, II, 60ff.

53. H. P. G. Quack, *De Socialisten, Personen en Stelsels* (6 vols., 1911–1912), I, 155–73.

54. Eekhof, *Hervormde Kerk*, II, 65–67. It is notable that Eekhof does not mention Quack's much older account of 1892.

55. H. C. Murphy, *Jacob Steendam, Noch Vaster* (1861).

56. T. De Vries, *Dutch History, Art and Lit-erature* (1912), Ch. VII, "Jacob Steendam."

57. J. Prinsen J. L.zn., *Handboek tot de Ne-derlandsche Letterkundige Geschiedenis* (1916), 383–84.

58. Quack, *Socialisten*, I, 168–72.

59. Eekhof, *Hervormde Kerk*, I, 225, 217.

60. Jameson, *Narratives*, 260.

61. D. Buddingh, *De Kerk, School en Weten-schap in de Vereenigde Staten van Noord-Amerika* (1853), II, 5.

62. Jameson, *Narratives*, 259.

63. Eekhof, *Hervormde Kerk*, II, 176.

64. William Penn, *Een Kort Bericht (uyt het Engels overgeset) van de Provintie ofte Landschap Penn-Sylvania genaemt, leggende in Amerika* (1681), 4–5, 7–8, 17–18.

65. William Penn, *Missive van William Penn, Eygenaar en Gouverneur van Pennsylvania, in America* (2nd ed., 1684), 4–5, 26, 28.

66. C. Henry Smith, *The Mennonites of America* (1909), 91. Here he cites Broadhead with pleasure.

67. Chinard, *Réfugiés Huguenots*, 66.

68. A. B. Faust, *Das Deutschtum in den Ver-einigten Staaten in seiner geschichtlichen Entwicke-lung* (1912), 25ff., 31.

69. Ibid., 9.

70. Chinard, *Réfugiés Huguenots*, 44–45.

71. S. W. Pennypacker, "Abraham and Dirk op den Graeff," *The Penn Monthly*, Sept. 1875.

72. Pennypacker, "The Settlement of Ger-mantown and the Causes Which Led to It," *Pennsylvania Magazine*, 1880. From this account, as well as that of [A. C.] Myers, the names of the Dutch settlers have been taken.

73. A. C. Myers, *Narratives of Early Pennsyl-vania, West New Jersey, and Delaware, 1630–1707* (1912), 395.

74. J. G. De Hoop Scheffer, *Vriendschapsbe-trekkingen tusschen de Doopsgezinden hier te lande en die in Pennsylvania* (1869).

75. Faust, *Das Deutschtum* (Entwickelung), 31.

76. R. Cronau, *Drei Jahrhunderte deutschen Lebens in Amerika* (1924), 143–44.

77. Pennypacker, "Settlement of Ger-mantown," 35; Quack, *Socialisten*, I, 173.

78. Pennypacker, "Abraham and Dirck Op den Graeff;" see also *Yearbook of the Ne-therland Society of Philadelphia*, 1896 and 1897.

79. Ph. E. Gibbons, *Pennsylvania Dutch and Other Essays* (1882), "Mennonites from Holland were also among the early settlers of Germantown," 70. See also Smith, *Mennonites.*

80. De Hoop Scheffer, *Vriendschapsbetrekkingen.*

81. R. Bijlsma, "Rotterdams Amerikavaart in de eerste helft der seventiende eeuw," *Bijdragen voor Vaderlandsche Geschiedenis en Oudheidkunde,* V. Pt. 5, 127ff. Also see C. Te Lintum, "Emigratie over Rotterdam," *De Gids,* IV (1908).

82. Chinard, *Réfugiés Huguenots,* Ch. IV.

83. Faust, *Das Deutschtum (Entwickelung),* 135; Jameson, *Narratives,* 289ff.

84. Pennypacker, "Settlement of Germantown," 36.

85. Smith, *Mennonites,* Ch. VI.

86. Chinard, *Réfugiés Huguenots,* esp. Ch. V, 86.

87. P. J. Van Winter, *Het Aandeel van den Amsterdamschen handel aan den opbouw van het Amerikaansche Gemeenebest* (2 vols., 1927–1933), I, 14.

Chapter 2. Why the Number of America-Goers Remained Small in the Seventeenth and Eighteenth Centuries

1. For immigration statistics see Ch. VI and esp. n.78 and n.79.

2. Jan Huygen Van Linschoten, *Itinerario voyage ofte schipvaert van . . .* (Kern) (2 vols., 1910), I, xvii.

3. Hildebrand (Nicholaas Beets), *Camera Obscura* (23rd printing, 1904), 261.

4. Van Linschoten, *Itinerario,* I, 1.

5. David Pietersz. De Vries, *Korte historiael ende journaels aenteyckeninge van verscheyden voyagiens in de vier deelen des Wereldts-ronde* (J. H. Colenbrander, ed., 1911), xxvii, 147–148, 187ff., 231ff., 235ff.

6. J. S. C. Jessurun, *Kiliaen van Rensselaer* (1917).

7. Fr. Ratzel, *Politische Geographie* (1903), 104.

8. R. Gonnard, *L'Emigration européenne au XIXe siècle* (1906), 210ff.

9. Wilhelm Georg Friedrich Roscher, "Onderzoekingen omtrent het Koloniewe-zen," *Tijdschrift voor Staathuishoudkunde en Statistiek,* VI (1851), 280ff.

10. For the concept of "emigrant" see Ch. VI, n.78 and n.79.

11. A. Eekhof, *De Hervormde Kerk in Noord Amerika* (1624–1664), I, 72, E. T. Corwin, A *Manual of the Reformed Church in America* (1902), 30. Hereafter cited as *Corwin's Manual.* West India ships usually had a crew of about twenty-five men. No doubt there were others on board such as merchants. In addition there were some prisoners, in this case "political" prisoners, such as |Cornelis| Melyn and |Jochem Pietersz.| Kuyter. All in all, I would consider the total number at about fifty. This large number of remigrants may be ascribed to the Indian wars. These came to an end in 1645, and had reduced the Dutch population of three thousand in 1643 to one thousand in 1646. The restoration of order and the more lenient trade privileges, which the West India Company inaugurated for the colonists in 1645, doubtless resulted in a growth of emigration.

12. H. Blink, *Geschiedenis van den Boerenstand en den Landbouw in Nederland* (2 vols., 1904), II, 41. Also Emile Verviers, *De Nederlandsche Handelspolitiek tot aan de toepassing der vrijhandelsbeginselen* (n.d.), 9.

13. H. T. Colenbrander, *Koloniale Geschiedenis,* I, 55. The manner in which Rensselaer obtained his colonists may be found in Jesserun, where there is an entire version of Rensselaer's "Letterbook."

14. Eekhof, *Hervormde Kerk,* I, 248.

15. Gerhard Wilhelm Kernkamp, *Zweedsche Archivalia* |*Verslag van een onderzoek in Zweden, Noorwegen en Denemarken naar archivalia belangrijk voor de geschiedenis van Nederland* (1903)|, quoted in Eekhof, *Hervormde Kerk,* I, 248.

16. There is a considerable literature dealing with each of these "settlements," but I shall spare my readers.

17. F. C. Wieder, *De Stichting van New York in Juli 1625* (1925), 22.

18. De Vries, *Voyagiens,* XXXIV.

19. Ibid., 183.

20. O. Van Rees, *Geschiedenis der Nederlandsche Volkplantingen in Noord-Amerika* (1855), 99.

21. J. King Van Rensselaer, *The Social Ladder* (1925), 18–19.

22. William Penn, *Een kort Bericht* (1681), 5–6.

23. De Vries, *Voyagiens,* 277; Adriaen Van der Donck, *Vertoogh,* 13; see J. Franklin Jameson, *Narratives of New Netherland* (1909), 306.

Chapter 3 *What Happened to the Old Dutch Branch*

1. Rudolf Häpke, *Der deutsche Kaufman in den Niederlanden* (1912).

2. A. Eekhof, *Jonas Michaëlius* (1926), 118. Letter of Aug. 11, 1628.

3. C. H. Pierce, *New Harlem, Past and Present* (1903), 14, 25, 30, and 44.

4. Ibid., 72, 127–128.

5. *Corwin's Manual* (1922), 675.

6. G. Chinard, *Les Réfugiés Huguenots en Amérique* (1925), 178ff., 182. Especially see 180, n.3.

7. According to *Corwin's Manual*, 670.

8. G. Beernink, *De Geschiedschrijver en Rechtsgeleerde Dr. Arend van Slichtenhorst en zijn Vader Brant van Slichtenhorst* (1916), 179ff.

9. *Corwin's Manual*, 45–47, reprints Miller's account.

10. David Pietersz. De Vries, *Kort historiael ende journaels aenteyckeninge van verscheyden voyagiens in de vier deelen des Wereldts-ronde* (1911), 225.

11. De Vries, *Voyagiens*, xxxvi.

12. King Van Rensselaer, *The Social Ladder* (1925), 7.

13. Ibid., 8.

14. Eekhof, *Michaëlius*, 118. Letter of Aug. 11, 1628.

15. This account, among others, is in A. Eekhof, *De Hervormde Kerk in Noord-Amerika (1624–1664)* (2 vols., 1913), I, 84.

16. Eekhof, *Hervormde Kerk*, I, 115ff.

17. Beernink, *Geschiedschrijver*, 210.

18. Eekhof, *Hervormde Kerk*, I, 73.

19. Beernink, *Geschiedschrijver*, 157; 141, n.1; 152; 156; 159.

20. Ellen Semple, *American History and its Geographical Conditions* (1903), 126. The value of this citation lies in the general recognition of this fact; this is of importance because in a large part of American publications concerning Dutch colonization this is ignored, as for example, by F. J. Turner in *The Frontier in American History* (1921).

21. G. Myers, *Geschichte der grossen amerikanischen Vermögen* (2 vols., 1923), I, 26ff.

22. According to Myers, *Geschichte*, and also Turner, *Frontier in American History*, 80.

23. R. P. J. Tutein Nolthenius, "Westersch en Oostersch Nederland," *De Gids* (1909), 117ff.

24. It is worth the effort, with regard to the Leisler troubles, to pursue the emigrant literature. Corwin gives the "Netherlands Calvinist" view, 34ff.; for the "German" view see A. B. Faust, *Das Deutschtum in den Vereinigten Staaten in seiner geschichtlichen Entwickelung* (1912), 12ff.; for the "French" view see Chinard, *Réfugiés Huguenots*, 150ff. From all this it is clear that "science" is a rather vague idea!

25. Turner, *Frontier in American History*, 70.

26. A. Eekhof, *Bastiaen Janszoon Krol, Krankenbezoeker, Kommies en Kommandeur van Nieuw-Nederland, 1595–1645* (1910), 31. Also see Eekhof, *Michaëlius*, Ch. 1.

27. Eekhof, *Michaëlius*, has the most recent information about him.

28. With regard to this development, see Eekhof, *Hervormde Kerk*; especially the second volume gives a good account of colonial society and contains interesting material for the social geographer.

29. F. C. Wieder, "Onderzoek naar de oudste kaarten van de omgeving van New York" *Tijdschrift van het Koninklijk Nederlandsch Aardrijkskundig Genootschap* (1918), 242.

30. J. Franklin Jameson, *Narratives of New Netherland* (Van Wassenaer) (1909), 79.

31. Ibid. (Van der Donck), 296.

32. *Corwin's Manual*, 29.

33. Turner, *Frontier in American History*, 67ff.

34. *Corwin's Manual*, 57, 60, 64.

35. John Adams Todd, *Centennial Discourses* (2nd ed., 1877), 109–38.

36. Peter Kalm, *Reis door Noord Amerika* (2 vols., 1772), II, 56.

37. Turner, *Frontier in American History*, 80. The terms "Dutch" or "Netherlander" are scarcely mentioned, but the "Pennsylvania Dutch" (largely Germans) are cited.

38. Faust, *Das Deutschtum* (*Entwickelung*), 79. Faust speaks of "class prejudices."

39. *Corwin's Manual*, 528, 704.

40. Faust, *Das Deutschtum* (*Entwickelung*), 79.

41. Semi-Centennial Association, "Ridgewood," 2ff.

42. Rayner Wickersham Kelsey, *Cazenove Journal, 1974* (1922), 5ff.

43. *Corwin's Manual*, 627.

44. Ibid., 702.

45. Ben Lucien Burman, in Ernest Gruening, *These United States, A Symposium* (2 vols., 1923–1924), II, 218ff.

46. *Corwin's Manual*, 637, 690.

47. Meredith Nicholson, *The Valley of Democracy* (1919), 207, 209.

48. H. Quick, *Vandemark's Folly* (1922), "Introduction," 15, 32, 50ff.

49. Turner, *Frontier in American History*,

227, 233. Cf. A. C. Van Raalte's letter of Jan. 30, 1847, *Holland in Amerika of de Hollandsche Kolonisatie in den Staat Michigan*, A. Brummelkamp, comp. (Arnhem, 1847).

50. K. Jansz. Beukma, *Brieven van K. Jansz. Beukma*, Sept. 14, 1836.

51. Ibid.

52. Ibid., Jan. 20, 1838.

53. *Corwin's Manual*, 93, 82.

54. Ibid., 590–591.

55. "General G. H. Sharpe," Historical Society of New York *Yearbook* (1886–87), 45.

56. E. B. Swalue, *Brieven uit en over de Vereenigde Staten van Noord-Amerika, door Jonathan* (pseud.) (1853), ix.

57. Thomas De Witt, *A Discourse, Delivered in the North Reformed Dutch Church in the City of New York*, Aug. 1856 (1857), 42.

58. *Corwin's Manual*, 80.

59. "Sharpe," Historical Society of New York *Yearbook* (1886–87).

60. De Witt, *Discourse*, 85.

61. "Sharpe," Historical Society of New York *Yearbook* (1886–87).

62. Helen Lincklaen Fairchild, *Francis Adrian van der Kemp, 1751–1829* (1903), 113–14.

63. H. Van Eijk, *Dagboek mijner lotgevallen en ontmoetingen beginnende met de reis naar de Vereenigde Staten van Noord-Amerika* (1847); see also J. Hzn. Gunning, *Leven en Arbeid van H. J. Budding* (1909), 214.

64. Items in the *New York Courier and Enquirer* (184?) in the Scrapbook of Dr. H. Beets. Concerning this Marselus see also *Corwin's Manual*, 414.

65. Stegink in Dingeman Versteeg, *De Pelgrim-Vaders van het Westen* (1886), 37.

66. M. D. Teenstra, *Mentor*, 168.

67. B. De Beij and A. Zwemer, *Stemmen uit de Hollandsch-Gereformeerde Kerk in de Ver. Staten van Amerika* (1871), 23.

68. H. C. Dosker in N. H. Dosker, *De Hollandsche Gereformeerde Kerk in Amerika* (1888), 257.

69. D. Buddingh, *De Kerk, School en Wetenschap in the Vereenigde Staten van Noord-Amerika* (1853), I, 75, 155.

70. Ibid., I, 75.

71. J. Van Ginneken, S. J., *Handboek der Nederlandsche Taal* (1913), I, 289ff. See also Van Ginneken, *De Regenboogkleuren van Nederlands Taal* (1917), III, 219, 221.

72. M. Cohen Stuart, *Zes Maanden in Amerika* (2 vols., 1875), I, 97, 151.

73. J. Van 't Lindenhout, *Zes Weken tusschen de wielen of De Hollanders in Amerika* (1886), 100.

74. Netherlands Society of Philadelphia, *Fifth and Sixth Annual Banquets, 1896–1897*, 12.

75. H. P. Scholte, *Eene Stem uit Pella* (1847), 10.

76. Gunning, *Leven en Arbeid*, 214, 216.

77. Van Raalte's letter of Nov. 27, 1846, in Brummelkamp, *Stemmen*.

78. "Sheldon T. Viele," Historical Society of New York *Yearbook* (1888–89), 87.

79. Van Ginneken, *Handboek*, I, 287.

80. J. H. Halbertsma, "Rinse Posthumus," *De Vrije Fries* (1862), 223.

81. H. Beets, "The True Reformed Dutch Church, U.S.A.," a series of articles in *Religion and Culture*, May-Oct. 1921; see Corwin.

82. Beets, *Chr. Geref. Kerk*, 259.

83. Buddingh, *Kerk, School en Wetenschap*, 117, 119.

84. Ibid., 120ff., 166.

85. Cohen Stuart, *Zes Maanden*, II, 69, 73.

86. Dosker, *Hollandsche Gereformeerde Kerk*, 16. The original view is that of Dr. P. Schaff (1854) and was used by Dosker in the *Nederlandsch Hervormd Dagblad* in 1883.

87. Kalm, *Reis*, II, 55.

88. Gunning, *Leven en Arbeid* II, 215. Letter dated N.Y., Oct. 20, 1848.

89. Harriet Langdon Pruyn Rice, *Harmanus Bleecker, an Albany Dutchman 1779–1849* (New York, 1924), 180, 155.

90. St. Nicholas Society of New York; Record of the dinner given in honor of the officers of H. N. M. Frigate *Van Speijk*, May 8, 1893.

91. Rice, *Harmanus Bleecker*, 70ff.

92. Ibid., 2.

93. Ibid., 109–110; also 151.

94. G. Myers, *Great American Fortunes*, I, 156, 98.

95. Ibid., I, 261ff.

96. Paul Sabel, "Het echec der Van Sweringens," *De Groene Amsterdammer*, Mar. 13, 1926.

97. Ruth Putnam, "The Dutch Element in the United States," *Bijdragen voor Vaderlandsche Geschiedenis en Oudheidkunde*, (1910), 170ff.

98. Buddingh, *Kerk, School en Wetenschap*. There is much material on Verplanck in Buddingh, II, 126, 169, 226.

99. Ibid., II, 117ff.

100. Van Rensselaer, *Social Ladder*, 60ff, 173, 183.

101. Myers, *Great American Fortunes*, I, 310; "Sharpe" H.S.N.Y. *Yearbook* (1886–87); *Daily American Tribune*, Apr. 24, 1926.

102. Van Rensselaer, *Social Ladder*, 211–212.

103. See note 97.

104. Van Rensselaer, Social Ladder, 33.

105. Gruening, These United States, II, 187, 204.

106. A. B. Faust, Das Deutschtum in den Vereinigten Staaten in seiner Bedeutung für die amerikanische Kultur (1912), 16. Faust calculated the total number of Dutch descent in 1790 at 240,000 and assumed that the number doubled every twenty-three years. He gives the number of Old-Dutch in 1900 as 10.5 times this number, or an estimated 2,520,000. The U.S. Census Bureau estimated the Dutch number in 1790 to be scarcely 79,000, not including those who lived outside New York and New Jersey! Therefore, it also stated that by 1900, they had reached only 875,000. Lothrop Stoddard, in his Re-forging America (1927), III, reckons the "Dutch colonial element" at 1,500,000. Including the various "anglicized" Dutch and adding those in South Carolina, Kentucky, etc., a figure of 2,000,000 would not be too high.

107. Rev. J. H. Suydam, D.D., "Account of the Second Part of this Journey," Historical Society of New York Yearbook (1888–89), 141.

108. Ibid., 220ff.

109. Netherland Society of Philadelphia, Fifth and Sixth Annual Banquets, 1896 and 1897.

110. Suydam, "Account," 184.

111. Ibid., 193ff.

112. A. F. Pollard, Factors in American History (1925), 9, n.4.

113. Letter from a correspondent in New York dated May 3, 1926, appearing in the evening edition of Handelsblad, May 1926.

114. Interview of July 15, 1926.

115. Rice, Harmanus Bleecker, 175.

116. De Volksvriend, Feb. 15, 1923.

Chapter 4   The Causes of Emigration in the First Half of the Nineteenth Century

1. Clive Day, A History of Commerce in the United States (1917), Ch. XLVII and passim.

2. F. A. R. de Chateaubriand, Voyages en Amérique, en France et en Italie (1834), I, 100.

3. M. Jules Duval, Histoire de l'Emigration européene (1862), 49.

4. Commissioner General of Immigration, Annual Report to the Secretary of Labor,

Washington, 1920, app. All further immigration numbers, which are not identified, are taken from this appendix.

5. J. Van Hinte, "De Naam van Koning Willem I misbruikt," Tijdschrift van Geschiedenis, Land- en Volkenkunde, 33 (1918), 183–88.

6. H. Blink, Geschiedenis van den Boerenstand en den Landbouw in Nederland (1904), II, 285ff.; H. Blink and S. Koenen, "Inleiding" in De Nederlandsche Landbouw in het tijdvak, 1813–1913 ('s-Gravenhage, 1913).

7. J. H. Beucker Andreae, "Rapport," Tijdschrift voor Staathuishoudkunde en Statistiek (Sloet's Tijdschrift), VI (1851), 158ff.

8. J. Zeehuisen, "Statistieke Bijdrage," ibid., 380ff.

9. N. W. Posthumus, "Nota over den toestand van de Amsterdamsche handelshuizen in het jaar 1854," Economisch Historisch Jaarboek (1921), 196ff.

10. J. C. Ramaer, "Middelpunten der bewoning in Nederland voorheen en thans," Tijdschrift van het Koninklijk Nederlandsch Aardrijkskundig Genootschap (1921), 200ff.

11. H. E. Greve, "Hollandsche Spotprenten in de 19e Eeuw," Elsevier's Geïllustreerd Maandschrift (1909).

12. J. H. de Bosch Kemper, Geschiedkundig Onderzoek naar de Armoede in ons Vaderland (1851), 249ff.

13. B. P. Van Diggelen, Nederlandsche Belangen in betrekking tot Landverhuizing en Kolonisatie (1857), 30.

14. R. A. Gorter and C. W. De Vries, "Gegevens omtrent den Kinderarbeid in Nederland," Economisch Historisch Jaarboek (1922), 29.

15. Van Diggelen, Nederlandsche Belangen, 19.

16. De Bosch Kemper, Geschiedkundig Onderzoek, 11, 205ff.

17. Brummelkamp and Van Raalte, Landverhuizing, 1ff.

18. Van Diggelen, Nederlandsche Belangen, 12ff.

19. E. J. Potgieter, "Landverhuizing naar de Vereenigde Staten," De Gids (1855).

20. M. D. Teenstra, Mentor, 260ff.

21. W. Van Peyma, "Brieven van W. Van Peyma aan W. Eekhoff te Leeuwarden," No. 97, Apr. 8, 1845.

22. J. H. Halbertsma, "Rinse Posthumus," De Vrije Fries (1862), 244.

23. Beucker Andreae, "Rapport," 160ff.

24. De Bosch Kemper, Geschiedkundig Onderzoek, 215ff.

25. Anonymous, "Over de oorzaken van de Landverhuizing der Nederlanders naar

de Vereenigde Staten," *Tijdschrift voor Staathuishoudkunde en Statistiek* (Sloet's Tijdschrift) (1866). According to G. M. W. Jellinghaus, "De Staat tegenover de Landverhuizing," 54; this article was written by Prof. Van Rees.

26. De Bosch Kemper, *Geschiedkundig Onderzoek*, 174ff.

27. Beucker Andreae, "Rapport," 166–67.

28. Gorter and De Vries, *Gegevens omtrent den Kinderarbeid*, 20.

29. Beucker Andreae, "Rapport," 170ff.

30. De Bosch Kemper, *Geschiedkundig Onderzoek*, 262ff.

31. L. Knappert, *Geschiedenis der Ned. Herv. Kerk gedurende de 18e en 19e Eeuw* (1912), 265.

32. Beucker Andreae, "Rapport," 182.

33. Knappert, *Ned. Herv. Kerk*, 275ff.

34. H. P. G. Quack, "De Zwijndrechtsche Broederschap," *De Gids* (Aug. 1892), 230.

35. Knappert, *Ned. Herv. Kerk*, 272ff.

36. Mr. Sluis at Weesp, a son of a "Mazereeuwsche" [mother], told me this.

37. Knappert, *Ned. Herv. Kerk*, 280ff. Compare J. C. Rullmann, *De Afscheiding* (1916).

38. Rullmann, *Afscheiding*, 62.

39. Gorter and De Vries, *Gegevens omtrent den Kinderarbeid*, 9, n.

40. F., "Een Enkel Woord aan degenen die naar Noord-Amerika wenschen te verhuizen," *De Vereeniging: Christelijke Stemmen*, Pt. I (1847), 356.

41. Guillaume Groen van Prinsterer, *Brieven van J. A. Wormser* (Vol. I, 1874), 93.

42. Knappert, *Ned. Herv. Kerk*, 303. Rullmann, *Afscheiding*, 79ff., "De tragiek van het Reveil."

43. Knappert, *Ned. Herv. Kerk*, 255.

44. Rullmann, *Afscheiding*, 65ff.

45. R. H. Saltet, "De Gezondheidstoestand," *Eene Halve Eeuw*, I, 356.

46. J. A. Wormser, *Het Leven van Albertus Christiaan van Raalte* (1915), 13.

47. Jacob Van der Meulen, *Ter nagedachtenis van Rev. Cornelius van der Meulen* (1876), 12.

48. Knappert, *Ned. Herv. Kerk*, 301. Rullmann, *Afscheiding*.

49. J. A. Wormser, *Het Leven van Hendrik Peter Scholte* (1915), 9.

50. Jan Nollen, *De Afscheiding. Een gedenkschrift* (1898), 30ff.

51. Compare the struggle over the expression concerning the stadtholder "presently being waged" in the Union of Utrecht.

52. Knappert, *Ned. Herv. Kerk*, 307; J. A. Wormser, *De Vurige Oven* (1911), is a simple story that paints a good picture of the persecution of the Seceders.

53. Wormser and Rullmann have taken these and many other occurrences from Scholte's magazine, *De Reformatie* (1837–1847). The writer refers to the sympathetic remarks of Dr. H. Beets, *Chr. Geref. Kerk*, 37. Especially to A. J. Pieters, author of A *Dutch Settlement in Michigan*, is this recommended.

54. G. A. Wumkes, "Worp van Peyma en zijn Vrienden," *De Vrije Fries*, 22 (1914), 170ff.

55. H. Bouwman, *De Crisis der Jeugd* (1914); Beets, *Chr. Geref. Kerk*, 38.

56. Wormser, *Van Raalte*, n.100. The name comes from the brothers themselves!

57. Wormser, *Scholte*, 198–99, 129.

58. A. Goslinga, *Koning Willem I als verlicht Despoot* (1918), 43ff.

59. Halbertsma, "Rinse Posthumus," 215.

60. Van Peyma, "Brieven"; Wumkes, *Worp van Peyma*.

61. K. Jansz. Beukma, *Brieven van den Landbouwer* (Amsterdam, 1849), 45.

62. Anonymous, *Verzint Eer Gij Begint!*

63. Knappert, *Ned. Herv. Kerk*, 276.

64. Ibid., 294.

65. Compare, for instance, the salutation of his letters to Wormser.

66. Letter from J. A. Buekenhorst, in J. A. Brummelkamp and A. C. Van Raalte, *Landverhuizing of waarom bevorderen wij de Volksverhuizing en wel naar Noord-Amerika en niet naar Java?* (1846).

67. Letter of S. Bolks in *De toestand der Hollandsche Kolonisatie in den Staat Michigan* (1849).

68. Anonymous, "Over de oorzaken," 100.

69. Zeehuisen, "Statistieke Bijdrage," 380ff.

70. Anonymous, "Overzicht," *De Economist* (1869), Pt. 2, 975ff.

71. Warne, *Tide of Immigration*, 37–38.

72. Anonymous, "Overzicht," 949.

73. See n.25.

74. Letters from Arnoud, Sleyster, and Hartgerink in Brummelkamp and Van Raalte, *Landverhuizing*, and in Brummelkamp, *Stemmen uit Noord-Amerika* (1847).

75. Anonymous, *De Vereenigde Staten van Noord-Amerika en de Landerhuizing derwaarts* (1846), 20.

76. See n.25. Compare H. W. Heuvel, "Achterhoeksche menschen in Amerika," *Vragen van den Dag*, 38 (Apr.–May 1923), 275ff.

77. Anonymous, *Over Volksverhuizingen in het algemeen en over die naar Noord-Amerika in het bijzonder* (1846). The writer is probably a Dutch Reformed preacher—a Réveil man?

78. F., "Een Enkel Woord."

79. Nollen, *Afscheiding*, 41.

80. Van der Meulen, *Nagedachtenis*, 50, 71.

81. Lammert J. Hulst, *Drie en Zestig Jaren Prediker* (1913), 105ff.

82. Anonymous, *Verzint Eer Gij Begint!*

83. R. Gonnard, *L'émigration européenne au XIXe siècle* (1906), 101.

84. G. A. Wumkes, "Tjibbe Geerts Van der Meulen," *Nieuw Nederlandsch Bibliographisch Woordenboek*.

85. As his son, Mr. W. A. Van der Meulen, assured me in a letter of Feb. 3, 1922.

86. Unpublished letter of K. Koelewijn, Oct. 15, 1848.

87. J. Berkhout, *Brief uit Noord-Amerika* (1849), 25ff.

88. Letter of Koelewijn.

89. This letter can be found in Brummelkamp, *Stemmen*.

90. F. Vulpius, *Zevenjarige Ondervinding in Noord-Amerika* (1847).

91. M. P. Lindo, *Wenken voor Landverhuizers* (Reprinted from the *Volksbode*, Vol. 8).

92. Ibid., 4; Anonymous, *Over Volksverhuizingen*, 26.

93. Vulpius, *Ondervinding*. See introduction of H. Püttman.

94. Edith Abbot, *Immigration, Selected Documents and Case Records* (1924), 13ff. Compare Van Hinte, "Naam van Koning Willem I misbruikt."

95. M. D. Teenstra, *Mentor* (1855).

96. S. Osinga et al., *Tiental Brieven betrekkelijk de reis* (1848); S. Osinga, *Dagboek mijner reize naar Noord-Amerika's Vereenigde Staten in den jare 1847 gedaan* (1848).

97. Teenstra, *Mentor*.

98. Abbot, *Immigration*, 29, 30ff.

99. B. B. Haagsma, *Lotgevallen van den Heer O. H. Bonnema en zijne Togtgenooten* (1853).

100. J. F. Diederichs, "Letters and Diary," *Wisconsin Magazine of History*, VII (Mar. 1924), 352.

101. W. O. Van Eyck, "The Story of the Propellor Phoenix," ibid., 281ff.

102. Abbot, *Immigration*, 30.

103. Compare for instance, Osinga, *Tiental Brieven* and *Dagboek*.

104. Printed in Brummelkamp, *Stemmen*.

105. *Historical Souvenir of the Celebration of the Sixtieth Anniversary of the Colonization of the Hollanders in Western Michigan, held in Zeeland, Michigan, August 21, 1907* (1908), 101.

106. From the questionnaire prepared by Dr. H. Beets and filled out by the farmer, A. Meyles, at Eenigenburg. This questionnaire deals with colonists from Noord Holland who settled near Chicago. This questionnaire was shown to me by Dr. H. Beets.

107. J. Hzn. Gunning, *Leven en Arbeid van J. J. Budding* (1909), 210, n.1, where reference is made to "Pages from the Life of Miss J. Visser."

Chapter 5   *The Emigration*

1. P. J. Blok, *Geschiedenis van het Nederlandsche Volk* (2nd ed., 4 vols., 1918–1915), III, 630.

2. Ruth Putnam, "The Dutch Element in the United States," *Bijdragen voor Vaderlandsche Geschiedenis en Oudheidkunde* (1910), 180.

3. Helen Lincklaen Fairchild, *Francis Adrian Van der Kemp, 1751–1829* (1903), 83.

4. Pieter Stadnitski, *Voorafgaand Bericht Pieter Stadnitski wegens eene Negotiatie op landen in Amerika* (1792).

5. P. D. Evans, *The Holland Land Company* (1926), 21–30. Compare [?] Beaumez, "900,000 Acres of Land Offered for Sale" (n.d., n.p.).

6. Graaf G. Schimmelpenninck, *Rutger Jan Schimmelpenninck en eenige Gebeurtenissen van zijnen Tijd* (1845), 25.

7. Rayner Wickersham Kelsey, *Cazenove Journal, 1794* (1922), Intro.

8. Letter to the author from P. D. Evans, New Haven, Conn., Oct. 27, 1924. In the same year the interesting work of this gentleman about the Holland Land Company appeared. In 1927 the first volume of P. J. Van Winter appeared, who did not seem to know the work of Evans. I refer to both works. In my study, I am only interested in how far the Holland Land Company influenced emigration from our country.

9. Beaumez, "900,000 Acres," 40.

10. Stadnitski, *Voorafgaand Bericht*.

11. Fairchild, *Van der Kemp*, 194, n.

12. Letter of Evans, Oct. 27, 1924.

13. Evans, *Holland Land Company*, 170.

14. Fairchild, *Van der Kemp*, 88ff., 103.

15. Ibid., 123.

16. Evans, *Holland Land Company*, 15.

17. Ibid., ch. 3.

18. Fairchild, *Van der Kemp*, 185.

19. Ibid., 82.

20. Putnam, "Dutch Element," 182. N. M. and F. Tiffany have written his biography.

21. T. Greidanus, *The Dutch in New Netherland and the United States* (1909), 59.

22. Kelsey, *Cazenove Journal*, preface.

23. Blok, *History*, IV, 156.

24. All the names of these places are found in the Rand McNally Indexed Pocket Map of New York State.

25. K. Jansz. Beukma, Brieven van K. Jansz. Beukma (1835), 23.

26. Putnam, "Dutch Element," 180–81. Compare also Nieuwe Rotterdamsche Courant, Sept. 12, 1825, Evening ed. B, and Sept. 24, 1825, Morning ed. B.

27. Letter of Evans, Oct. 27, 1924.

28. Stadnitski, Voorafgaand Bericht, 16.

29. Beukma, Brieven, 2nd part, 86, etc., 39; 3rd part, 27.

30. Ibid., 2nd part, 17. The work of the duke appeared at Weimar in 1828; the Dutch translation, at Dordrecht in 1829.

31. Beukma, Brieven, 24.

32. Ibid., Rev. ed., 3rd part, 46.

33. S. Osinga, et al., Tiental Brieven betrekkelijk de reis (1848), 25–28.

34. Beukma, Brieven, Rev. ed., 2nd part, 77; 3rd part, 22–23, 40–41. Compare H. Quick, Vandemark's Folly (1922), 97.

35. Beukma, Brieven, 86ff.

36. Osinga, et. al., Tiental Brieven.

37. Yearbook, 1927; Report of the Reformed Synod, 1925. The Reformed statistics enumerate the number who made a confession of faith but not the number of souls.

38. Beukma, Brieven, 2nd part.

39. De Volksvriend Mar. 7, 1907.

40. S. F. Rederus, "The Dutch Settlements of Sheboygan County," Wisconsin Magazine of History, I (Mar. 1918), 256–65.

41. De Volksvriend, Mar. 7, 1907.

42. A. Copijn, Schets, van de Lotgevallen der Kolonisten (1855).

43. De Vestiging, 7.

44. W. Van Peyma, Letter of August 13, 1845, in "Brieven van W. Van Peyma aan W. Eekhof te Leeuwarden," 1845–1877, in the Provincial Archives at Leeuwarden.

45. A. Brummelkamp, Jr., Levensbeschrijving van wijlen Prof. A. Brummelkamp (1910), 201.

46. Fridrich Arends, Het Mississippi-dal (1839), 280.

47. Brummelkamp, Levensbeschrijving, 202; A. Brummelkamp and A. C. van Raalte, Landverhuizing of waarom bevorderen wij de Volksverhuizing en wel naar Noord-Amerika en niet naar Java? (1846), 14.

48. Beukma, Brieven, 2nd part.

49. From my correspondence with Mr. Heuvel at Borculo.

50. M. D. Teenstra, Mentor; de getrouwe Leidsman en Raadgever voor Landverhuizers, die naar Noord-Amerika willen vertrekken (1855), 272ff.

51. Jan Nollen, De Afscheiding: Een gedenkschrift (1898), 40. Also Brummelkamp, Levensbeschrijving, 202. Nollen, however, quotes Brummelkamp, Sr.'s own words.

52. Brummelkamp, Levensbeschrijving, 205. At the same time one finds here the complete Constitution.

53. H. P. Scholte in his periodical De Reformatie of 1846. Especially compare Nollen's Afscheiding, 41.

54. Brummelkamp, Levensbeschrijving, 211, which contains the letter of Rev. O. H. Heldring.

55. J. A. Wormser, Het Leven van Hendrik Peter Scholte (1915), 189–90.

56. Scholte objected to South Africa for the following reasons: one would have to deal with the English, the heathen Kaffirs might attack the whites, and the Boers favored slavery.

57. Letter of T. Hollerdijk in Brummelkamp and Van Raalte, Landverhuizing.

58. Scholte, De Reformatie, 3rd Series, 2nd part.

59. A. Brummelkamp, Stemmen uit Noord-Amerika met Begeleidend Woord aan A. Brummelkamp (1847), 17.

60. H. A. Dijkstra, "Geestelijk ontwaken in Drente," cited by Dr. H. Beets, De Chr. Geref. Kerk in N.A. (1918), 47.

61. J. C. Rullmann, De Afscheiding (1916), 269.

62. Jakob Noordewier, Een Tachtig-Jarige (1920), 8. Also compare Albert T. Huizinga in Historical Souvenir of the Celebration of the Sixtieth Anniversary of the Colonization of the Hollanders in Western Michigan held in Zeeland, Michigan, August 21, 1907 (1908), 104.

63. Cornelis Van Loo in ibid., 101.

64. M. P. Lindo, Wenken voor Landverhuizers (n.d.).

65. Jacob Van der Meulen, Ter nagedachtenis van Rev. Cornelius van der Meulen (1876), 50.

66. F., "Een Enkel Woord aan degenen die naar Noord-Amerika wenschen te verhuizen," De Vereeniging: Christelijke Stemmen, 1st part, 1847.

67. Lammert J. Hulst, Drie en Zestig Jaren Prediker (1913), 105.

68. F., "Een Enkel Woord."

69. Wormser, Een Schat in aarden Vaten, I. Het Leven van Albertus Christiaan Van Raalte (1915), 124.

70. See notes 65 and 72.

71. W. O. Van Eyck, "The Story of the Propeller Phoenix," Wisconsin Magazine of History, VII (Mar. 1924), 296.

72. Scholte, *De Reformatie*, 3rd Series, Pt. 3, 119. Also mentioned by Wormser, *Scholte*, 193.

73. Van Loo in *Historical Souvenir*, 66, 71.

74. In possession of the De Kruif family at Zeeland, Michigan. Extensively reported by Van Loo in *Historical Souvenir*, 67.

75. Cyrenus Cole, "A Bit of Holland in America," *The Midland Monthly*, 3 (Feb. 1895).

76. Brummelkamp, *Levensbeschrijving*, 264.

77. This letter is published in Brummelkamp and Van Raalte, *Landverhuizing*. Also in this letter the material and mystical factors come to expression. Brummelkamp, *Levensbeschrijving*, 214, casually mentions this letter. Wormser, *Van Raalte*, 119ff., gives more details. However, none of these letters illuminates my quoted passages.

78. See Brummelkamp and Van Raalte, *Landverhuizing*, Intro. Additionally, in 1841 John Romeyn Brodhead studied our archives. In 1846 Dr. Thomas De Witt visited our country in order to get possession of archival material. A. Eekhof, *De Hervormde Kerk in Noord-Amerika* (1624–1664) (2 vols., 1913), I, 13–14.

79. The word *especially* is used for a reason. In a letter of Wyckoff to Van Raalte, cited in Brummelkamp's *Stemmen*, it was emphatically noted: "No Roman Catholics to be promoted even if they are Dutch." Van Raalte himself had already departed and never received this letter.

80. Van Raalte in a letter from Buffalo, dated Nov. 27, 1846, included in Brummelkamp's *Stemmen*.

81. A. Brummelkamp, (ed.), A. C. Van Raalte, *Holland in America* (1847), Letter of Van Raalte from "Detroit in Michigan, Jan. 30, 1847." Also see Van Eyck, "Story of the Propellor Phoenix," and A. B. Faust, *Das Deutschtum in den Vereinigten Staaten in seiner geschichtlichen Entwickelung* (1912), 387ff.

82. E. Deckert, *Nordamerika* (3rd ed., 1913), 198ff, *Das Lorenzseenbecken*. See also Van Eyck, "Story of the Propellor Phoenix."

83. All these particulars, if not stated otherwise, are derived from Van Raalte's letters, edited and published by Brummelkamp, in *Holland in Amerika of de Hollandsche Kolonisatie in den Staat Michigan* (1847).

84. C. Van der Meulen, "Eerste Worstelingen," Address given at the 50th Anniversary in Holland, Michigan, published in G. Van Schelven, "Historische Schetsen uit het Koloniale Leven", *De Grondwet*, Dec. 1910.

85. G. Van den Elsen, *Twintig Brieven uit Amerika* (1907), 124ff.

86. G. Van Schelven, "Wat bracht U hier?" A series of articles in *De Grondwet*, beginning Mar. 24, 1908.

87. Van Schelven, *De Grondwet*, May 18, 1915.

88. A. J. Pieters, *A Dutch Settlement in Michigan* (1923), 56. The deed of purchase is dated Jan. 26, 1847.

89. D. Versteeg, *De Pelgrim-Vaders van het Westen* (1886), 27; Pieters, *Dutch Settlement*, 56, 62.

90. Wormser, *Scholte*, 194–95, 200.

91. Moritz Beyer, *Het boek der Landverhuizers* (1846). See Scholte's postscript.

92. K. Van Stigt, *Geschiedenis van Pella, Iowa en Omgeving* (3 vols., 1897), I, 75.

93. Ibid., I, 76 and passim. The interesting letter of H. Barendregt from St. Louis, Dec. 14, 1846, to H. P. Scholte is published here. An English translation of this letter is in Van der Zee, *Hollanders of Iowa*, App. A, and it was even translated from English into German in George Schnücker, *Die Ostfriesen in Amerika* (1917), 15–19.

94. Van Stigt, *Geschiedenis van Pella*, I, 87–124. The names of immigrants are also reported.

95. H. P. Scholte, *Eene Stem uit Pella* (1848), 6.

96. Van Stigt, *Geschiedenis van Pella*, I, 122ff. For the overland trip, however, see also Van der Zee, *Hollanders of Iowa*, 51 and 384, n.48. Also see Sipma's letter of Mar. 16, 1848, in S. A. Sipma, *Brief van Sjoerd Aukes Sipma aan de Ingezetenen van Bornwerd in Westdongeradeel* (1848), which speaks of "Columbe, not to be confused with Columbus in Ohio."

97. Scholte, *Eene Stem*, 11.

98. Ibid., 8.

99. Ibid., 3,5.

100. Van Stigt, *Geschiedenis van Pella*, I, 32.

101. Scholte, *Eene Stem*, 4–5.

102. Ibid., 14ff.

103. See Scholte's letter in *De toestand der Hollandsche Kolonisatie in den Staat Michigan* (1849), 18.

104. Ibid., 9.

105. Ibid., 17. Van Schelven emphatically points out this rivalry in his series of articles in *De Grondwet*, "Wat bracht U hier?" In *Historical and Business Compendium of Ottawa County*, Vol. I (1892–1893), an article of Van Schelven appears about the "Early Settlement of Holland" in which he reports a conversation with a man who spoke about "a sharp rivalry in recruiting."

106. *Historical Souvenir*, 65.

107. Van der Meulen, *Nagedachtenis*, 72. One part did not depart from Amsterdam, according to A. J. Pieters, *Dutch Settlement*, 58.

108. Van der Meulen, *Nagedachtenis*, 15.

109. S. Osinga, *Dagboek mijner reize naar Noord-Amerika's Vereenigde Staten in den jare 1847 gedaan* (1848), 19.

110. Van der Meulen, *Nagedachtenis*, 168.

111. See Van Schelven, "Wat bracht U hier?"

112. *Historical Souvenir*, 66.

113. Van der Meulen, *Nagedachtenis*, 56.

114. Ibid., 62.

115. Ibid., 76.

116. Ibid., 167.

117. The one-third figure is taken from the very reliable account of Nollen, *Afscheiding*, 43.

118. Versteeg, *Pelgrim-Vaders*, 46ff.

119. Letter from Rev. S. Bolks in *De toestand der Hollandsche Kolonisatie*, 24ff. See also Versteeg, *Pelgrim-Vaders*, 53ff. Friesland was nearly always written as "Vriesland," Overijssel as "Overisel."

120. Versteeg, *Pelgrim-Vaders*, 55.

121. Van Stigt, *Geschiedenis van Pella*, II, 57ff.

122. This was the impression I received during my visit in Pella in Aug. 1921.

123. Van Schelven, "Wat bracht U hier?", 81. Found in the collection of Henry Beets.

124. Letter of A. Hollerdijk in Brummelkamp and Van Raalte's *Landverhuizing*.

125. Letter of R. Sleyster printed in Brummelkamp's *Stemmen*.

126. Wormser, *Van Raalte*, 147.

127. Writings of P. Zonne in the *Groninger Courant*, July 26, 1853, No. 59, partially reprinted in Teenstra, *Mentor*, 285.

128. Rederus, "Dutch Settlements of Sheboygan County."

129. Letter of G. Baay Alto, Jan. 4, 1849 in *De toestand*.

130. Indeed there were many Catholics and Germans in Wisconsin, but as far as Roman Catholics were concerned, not in Waupun and environs. One should not forget also that Wisconsin is nearly six times the size of the Netherlands.

131. B. De Beij and A. Zwemer, *Stemmen uit de Hollandsch-Gereformeerde Kerk in de Ver. Staten van Amerika* (1871), 58.

132. *Corwin's Manual* (1902), 933.

133. R. A. Gouwens, "The Settlement and Growth of South Holland," in E. P. Beaudette-Niel, *Thornton Township, Cook County, Illinois* (1921), 97ff. The late P. De Jong, justice of the peace in South Holland, corrected for me the inaccuracies found here.

134. This date is found in De Beij and Zwemer, *Stemmen*, 58.

135. Particulars about these persons *in* the Netherlands are derived from information given by Mr. Meyles to Henry Beets. Information about the voyage and settlement in America is from an article of G. A. Brennan in *The Calumet Index*, Mar. 16, 1915, and the *60th Anniversary*, July 5, 1909.

136. C. Ton speaks of 160 acres, which is not in agreement with the figures of what each personally bought. The figure of 200 is according to the report of Brennan (1915), which is also later than Ton's sketch (1909).

137. This question about the town's name has been called to my attention by |Cornelius Lawrance| Clausing in Roseland on Aug. 13, 1921.

138. Letter from K. Koelewijn, Oct. 15, 1848. The total Scandinavian immigration (Norwegians, Swedes, and Danes) was not large, yet from 1846 to 1848 their numbers were 2,030, 1,320, and 1,113, respectively. But they preferred to go to the northern states and work particularly in lumbering, just as in earlier centuries.

139. *Provinciale Groninger Courant*, Oct. 14, 1854, No. 123; Teenstra, *Mentor*, 305ff.

140. H. Beets, *The Christian Reformed Church in North America* (1928), 28.

141. In the series "Der Auswanderer am Niederrhein," No. 3.

Chapter 6   *The Emigration (Continued)*

1. G. Keizer in one of his articles "Uit de Buitenlandsche kerken" in *De Reformatie, Weekblad tot ontwikkeling van het Gereformeerde leven*, Oct. 22, 1920, No. 4.

2. H. P. Scholte's Journal, *De Reformatie*, 3rd Series, Pt. 3, 119. See J. A. Wormser, *Een Schat in aarden Vaten, II. Het Leven Van Hendrik Peter Scholte* (1915), 191—193.

3. E. J. Tuuk, "Some Ideals of Dr. A. C. van Raalte," *Religion and Culture*, IV (Aug. 1924.)

4. *Historical Souvenir of the Celebration of the Sixtieth Anniversary of the Colonization of the Hollanders in Western Michigan, held in Zeeland, Michigan, August 21, 1907*, (1908), 70ff. Cf. H. E. Dosker, *Levensschets van Rev. A. C. van Raalte* (1893), 114, 184.

5. H. P. Scholte, *Eene Stem uit Pella* (1848), 35ff.; *Onze Tijd*, II (1849), 173.

6. A. Brummelkamp Jr., *Levensbeschrijving van wijlen Prof. A. Brummelkamp* (1910), 222.

7. K. Iz. Beukma, *Brieven van den Landbouwer*. Letter dated New York, Aug. 5, 1835.

8. Letter of A. C. Van Raalte, Buffalo, Nov. 27, 1846, published in A. Brummelkamp, *Stemmen uit Noord-Amerika* (1847); Jacob Van der Meulen, *Ter Nagedachtenis van Rev. Cornelius van der Meulen* (1876), 118–19.

9. G. A. Wumkes, "Worp Van Peyma en zijn Vrienden," *De Vrije Fries* (1914), 169ff.; H. Halbertsma, "Rinse Posthumus," *De Vrije Fries* (1862), 215ff.

10. Worp Van Peyma, "Brieven van Worp Van Peyma aan W. Eekhoff te Leeuwarden," Letter from Lancaster, Erie, County, New York, Nov. 19, 1877.

11. "A farewell extended to my brother and friend W. Van Peyma upon his departure with children and grandchildren and other good friends to America, "from R. Posthumus, Ljeauwert [Leeuwarden] 1849.

12. C. Borgman, *Bezoek in de Vereenigde Staten van Noord-Amerika in het jaar 1850* (1854), 52, 67, 118.

13. Ibid., 150.

14. So he himself wrote. Borgman spoke of sixteen ares [1,914 square yards].

15. Ibid., 163ff.

16. Van Peyma, "Brieven," Lancaster, Apr. 1865 (no. 103). It was necessary to indicate in detail Van Peyma's relationship to the Dutch language because Dr. Wumkes' above-mentioned account can lead to the wrong conclusions in this matter, especially his correct observation, as such, that Van Peyma always spoke Frisian or English, never Dutch, with his neighbours. Wumkes sees in Van Peyma only the Frisian and not the Dutchman. In my view, this is totally incorrect.

17. Van Peyma, "Brieven," Lancaster, Nov. 19, 1877.

18. Ibid., Apr. 5, 1877.

19. Ibid.

20. Ibid., Nov. 19, 1877.

21. Wumkes, *Worp van Peyma*, 176.

22. Van Peyma, "Brieven," Lancaster, Nov. 19, 1877. Why did Dr. Wumkes relate in Frisian this saying that was written in Dutch? Wumkes' article concerning Van Peyma gives the wrong impression concerning Van Peyma's relationship to the Dutch language.

23. Borgman, *Bezoek in de Vereenigde Staten*.

24. M. D. Teenstra, *Mentor; de getrouwe Leidsman en Raadgever voor Landverhuizers* (1855), 273. T. G. Van der Meulen visited the Van Houtens at Pella in 1880, where Van Houten made the remark, "He who murders his father and mother is still too good to be here." *Weekblad voor het Kanton Bergum*, No. 14 (Apr. 9, 1882). See here also Van der Meulen's remarks concerning "the Van Peymas who rose in the North and set in the West." See finally Borgman, *Bezoek in de Vereenigde Staten*, 188: "The moneyless working class shall finally see realized the great bait of America, that is, cheap land, bacon and bread, and good wages."

25. B. B. Haagsma, *Lotgevallen van den Heer O. H. Bonnema en zijne Togtgenooten* (1853); Haagsma, *Frisia of Schets der Friesche Volkplanting in Noord-Amerika* (1855).

26. Letter of E. Bonnema, Jelsum, Feb. 9, 1927.

27. S. Blaupot ten Cate, *Geschiedenis der Doopsgezinden in Friesland* (1839), 221–34.

28. Blaupot ten Cate, *Geschiedenis der Doopsgezinden in Holland, Zeeland, Utrecht en Gelderland*, (2 vols. in 1, 1847), II, 196.

29. Blaupot ten Cate, *Geschiedenis der Doopsgezinden in Friesland*, 223.

30. Ibid., App. XVIII, 370, 371.

31. Rev. J. M. Leendertz of Koog a/d Zaan, with whom I had an interview in Aug. 1924, concerning his visit to the Mennonites in the United States, showed me at that time this unpublished writing.

32. D. S. Gorter, *De Christelijke Lijdzaamheid* (1853), 23.

33. Blaupot ten Cate, *Geschiedenis der Doopsgezinden in Friesland*, 221.

34. Gorter, *Christelijke Lijdzaamheid*, 21.

35. Ibid., 4.

36. Rev. J. M. Leendertz was so kind as to inquire for me concerning this matter from one of his Balk co-religionists. Letter, Koog a/d Zaan, Sept. 16, 1924.

37. Gorter, *Christelijke Lijdzaamheid*, 5.

38. Letter of R. J. Symensma, Liverpool, Apr. 17, 1853, included in the "Vijf Brieven uit Amerika" in D. S. Gorter, *Godsdienstige Lectuur voor Doopsgezinden* (Sneek, 1854).

39. Letter of R. J. Symensma, Philadelphia, May 8, 1853.

40. Letter of R. J. Smit, June 15, 1853.

41. C. Henry Smith, *The Mennonites of America* (1909), 209ff.

42. Letter of R. J. Smit, June 15, 1853.

43. Letter of R. J. Smit and R. J. Symensma, "Aan de gemeente van Balk."

44. Smith, *Mennonites*, 283.

45. Leendertz, *Doopsgezind Pioniersleven in*

Amerika (n.d.), 6. Further, letter to me, Feb. 11, 1925.

46. Clipping from the Gospel Herald.

47. Letter of Rev. J. M. Leendertz to me, Feb. 11, 1925.

48. Anonymous, Over Volksverhuizingen in het algemeen en over die naar Noord-Amerika (1846), 23.

49. H. Blink, "Immigratie in Amerika en Emigratie uit Europa," Vragen van den Dag, 25 (1910).

50. H. Blink, "De Landverhuizing uit Nederland," Vragen van den Dag, 40 (Mar. 1925).

51. Letter, 's-Hertogenbosch, Nov. 4, 1919.

52. E. J. Potgieter, "Landverhuizing naar de Vereenigde Staten," De Gids (1855).

53. "Immigration from Holland and its Causes," an article in the English newspaper, London Patriot, reprinted in the Christian Intelligencer of June 3, 1847; also reprinted in De Grondwet Feb. 4, 1913.

54. A very brief overview of these Roman Catholic newspapers by P. J. Blok, Geschiedenis van het Nederlandsche Volk (4 vols., 1914–1915), IV, 365.

55. Anonymous, Verzint Eer Gij begint!, 19; Onze Tijd, II (1849), 169.

56. Catholijke Nederlandsche Stemmen, 12 (1846), (Grave, Publ. J. Witz), 367. Mr. L. Emond O.S.C. was so kind as to write me this and provide some additional information from some old, almost unobtainable newspapers that he copied for me.

57. The figures for Noord Holland Province are taken from the list "Staat der Landverhuizingen naar Noord-Amerika of andere Overzeesche gewesten," Noord Holland Province, 1846 and 1847, Rijksarchief in Noord Holland at Haarlem.

58. Catholijke Nederlandsche Stemmen, 13 (1847), 15ff.

59. B. G. Krijnen, Reisverhaal van den Wel Eerwaarden Heer B. G. Krijnen (1837), 7, 23, and 86ff. More interesting is Pater P. J. De Smet, S. J., Missiën van den Oregon en Reizen naar de Rotsbergen (1849).

60. I am indebted to Mr. Emond for a copy of this letter. In the English language one finds it in a small American work by M. A., The Story of Father Van den Broek, O. P. A Study of Holland and the Story of the Early Settlement of Wisconsin (1907), 40ff. This booklet also contains additional details, some of which are not always accurate, however.

61. Ibid., 74.

62. J. W. De Vries, O.P., "Een Hollandsche Kolonisatie in Wisconsin," a series of articles in the Katholieke Illustratie of Mar. 6, 1909. This essay is more reliable than "The Story." It is from this article that the data have been obtained.

63. Ibid., Mar. 20, 1909. "The Story," p. 75, reports that Gothard departed for Boston on the America.

64. De Godsdienstvriend, 64 (1850), 47.

65. Ibid., 65 (1850), 245.

66. L. Emond "De voormalige Missie der E. E. Kruisheeren in Wisconsin, I," Het Centrum, Mar. 20, 1915. Here the figure 200 is given and also the following data about the Crozier Fathers.

67. Potgieter, "Landverhuizing," 181.

68. Thus declared Mr. Emond to me in a letter dated St. Agatha (Cuyk), Aug. 12, 1921.

69. De Vries, "Hollandsche Kolonisatie," Mar. 6, 1909.

70. See Chapter 5, notes.

71. F. Von Raumer, De Vereenigde Staten van Noord-Amerika (tr. from German, 2 vols., 1849). Chapters "Revolts and Party Factions," II, 4, and "Religion and Church," 108.

72. Frank Julian Warne, The Tide of Immigration (1916), 237ff. Concerning Catholicism in the United States, see, among others, Firmin Roz, L'énergie américaine. Evolution des Etats-Unis (1820), chapter entitled "La Religion." Roz indicates there the part played by Roman Catholics in the War of Independence and denies the Protestant "nature" of it.

73. R. Mayo Smith, Emigration and Immigration: A Study in Social Science (1912), 81.

74. Warne, Tide of Immigration, 238.

75. Jeremiah W. Jenks and W. Jett Lauck, The Immigration Problem (4th ed., 1917), 43.

76. Mayo Smith, Emigration, 86.

77. Onze Tijd, II (1849), 173. Bijdragen tot bevordering van de kennis en den bloei der Mij. tot Nut van het Algemeen, 1848 and 1849, 7th annual. Even the archives of the Nut Society no longer possess these reports. Therefore, I must content myself with what Potgieter writes about them in his Gids article in 1855.

78. J. Van Hinte, "Werkloosheid en Emigratie," Tijdschrift voor Economische Geographie (Dec., 1922).

79. Warne, Tide of Immigration, Ch. 18.

80. Van Hinte, "Werkloosheid."

81. See Chapter "Emigratie" in the Sociaal Jaarboek voor Nederland, II (1918).

82. See note 77.

83. Potgieter, "Landverhuizing," 181ff.

84. Teenstra, Mentor, 145.

85. "Overzicht van de Hedendaagsche Landverhuizing," De Economist (no. 2, 1869), 631ff.

86. *Over Volksverhuizing in het algemeen*, 22ff. See also *De Grondwet*, Jan. 18, 1913.
87. Wilhelm G. F. Roscher, "Onderzoekingen omtrent het koloniewezen," *Tijdschrift voor Staathuishoudkunde en Statistiek*, VI (1851), 203.
88. J. C. Rullmann, *De Afscheiding* (1916), 266. See also Wormser's small works "Tegen beter weten in," because A. Brummelkamp pointed out Potgieter's attitude in Brummelkamp's *Levensbeschrijving*, 258.
89. Jacob Van der Meulen, *Ter nagedachtenis van Rev. Cornelius van der Meulen* (1876), 55.
90. Rullmann, *Afscheiding*, 266.
91. The famed antiquarian [?] De Vries of Amsterdam brought to my attention a copy which he had owned for a while.
92. Potgieter, "Landverhuizing," 165.
93. *Ontboezeming bij gelegenheid der Nederlandsche Landverhuizing naar Noord-Amerika* (1847).
94. C. Van Loo in *De Volksvriend*, Mar. 27, 1924, 6.
95. J. P. G. Moorrees, *Landverhuizing uit een volkshuishoudkundig oogpunt beschouwd. Eene voorlezing enz.* (1847), 5.
96. *Over Volksverhuizingen in het algemeen* (1846), 35ff.
97. Guillaume Groen van Prinsterer, *Brieven van J. A. Wormser*, I (1874), 391.
98. *Provinciaal Blad van Noord-Holland*, No. 82, which contains the Circular of Dec. 30, 1847, No. 219/10262, located in the Rijksarchief in Noord Holland at Haarlem.
99. Located in the Rijksarchief in Noord Holland at Haarlem. Scholte talks in *Eene Stem uit Pella*, 39, of "Geheime aanschrijvingen aan plaatselijke besturen" [Secret summonses to local administrations].
100. Halbertsma, *Rinse Posthumus*, for instance, 215ff.

Chapter 7 *The New Environment: Soil, Climate, and People*

1. L. A. Chase, *Rural Michigan* (1922), 42ff.
2. See the map of Iowa in Ch. 5.
3. K. Lamprecht, *Americana* (1906), 25; Kurt Hassert, *Australien und Neuseeland geographisch und wirtschaftlich* (1924), 101.
4. Letter, Detroit, Jan. 30, 1847, in A. C. van Raalte, *Holland in Amerika of de Hollandsche Kolonisatie in den Staat Michigan*, compiled by A. Brummelkamp (1847).
5. M. Cohen Stuart, *Zes Maanden in Ameri-

ka* (2 vols., 1875), I, 306. The description of Holland's harbor in the autobiography of the late Professor A. Brummelkamp is based on an error (p. 243). Cohen Stuart's sketch, which was used, was not of the Holland harbor but that of Grand Haven, located further north. See ibid., I, 321.
6. I. Bowman, *Forest Physiography* (1912), App. D. The geologic time table (with map). The classifications of Ch. Schuchert are here followed, in which the lower-carboniferous is called Mississippian and the productive upper-carboniferous is designated as Pennsylvanian. Compare also the geological chart in E. Deckert's *Nordamerika* (1916), opposite 53, where the Cambrium and the Ordovician layers are given the same coloration.
7. Scholte, *Eene Stem uit Pella* (1848), 21.
8. E. J. G. Bloemendaal, *Naar Amerika* (1911), 158.
9. Cohen Stuart, *Zes Maanden*, I, 316.
10. Chase, *Rural Michigan*, 99–100.
11. Bowman, *Forest Physiography*, 462ff.
12. Th. C. Chamberlin and R. D. Salisbury, *Geology* (2nd ed., 1909), III, 388.
13. Deckert, *Nordamerika*, 198; Bowman, *Forest Physiography*, 483.
14. Chamberlin and Salisbury, *Geology*, III, 392; Bowman, *Forest Physiography*, 468.
15. Chamberlin and Salisbury, *Geology*, III, 420. In this section we also find the definitions for drumlins (360) and kames (368).
16. Chase, *Rural Michigan*, 9ff.
17. Ibid., 14.
18. Bowman, *Forest Physiography*, 473; Chase, *Rural Michigan*, 7.
19. Cohen Stuart, *Zes Maanden*, I, 321. Cf. also I, 300ff.
20. R. P. J. Tutein Nolthenius; *Nieuwe Wereld* (1902), 224.
21. Emm. de Martonne, *Traité de Géographie Physique* (2nd ed., 1913), 769. Le loess est moins un sol en lui-même qu'une alluvion éolienne." [Loess is in itself not so much a soil as an aeolian alluvial deposit.]
22. Chamberlin and Salisbury, *Geology*, III, 405. Bowman's description of loess (p. 488) is based on this same passage, in spite of the notes. Compare also the "eluvial" concept of A. Supan, *Grundzüge der physischen Erdkunde* (1911).
23. De Martonne, *Traité*, 673.
24. Een Gelderschman, *De Hollanders in Iowa, Brieven uit Pella* (1858), twelve.
25. Iowa-Commissie, *Iowa, Het Land der Emigranten* (1870), 32. The term *loess* has been more universally used since F. Von

Richthofen's research, as is well known, *Vorlesungen über Allgemeine Siedlungs- und Verkehrgeographie* (1908).

26. E. C. Jul. Mohr, *De Grond van Java and Sumatra* (1922), Ch. III, presents an excellent survey of humus formation and the resulting variations in soil coloration.

27. Scholte, *Eene Stem*, 22.

28. See note 24.

29. Bloemendaal, *Naar Amerika*, 37, 77–78.

30. Bowman, *Forest Physiography*, 486.

31. Bloemendaal, *Naar Amerika*, 36.

32. Letter of K. Koelewijn, Oct. 15, 1848. See also Bolk's letter in *De toestand der Hollandsche Kolonisatie in den Staat Michigan, Noord-Amerika, in het begin van het jaar 1849.*

33. The data on the American climate are mostly quoted from Deckert, *Nordamerika*, in which the figures given on Chicago are obviously not all correct. See, for instance, notes 64 and 174.

34. Wladimir Peter Köppen, *Klimakunde* (1906). Deckert and some other writers call the snowstorms "blizzards." In the literature of the colony our Hollanders speak of "snow-blizzards." See the 25th Anniversary Jubilee issue of *De Volksvriend*, 2.

35. G. Draayom, "Schetsen uit het Verleden," *De Volksvriend*, May 1, 1924. "Een sneeuwstorm."

36. Deckert, *Nordamerika*, 73, 175.

37. K. Van Stigt, *Geschiedenis van Pella, Iowa en Omgeving* (3 vols., 1897), II, 46.

38. Ibid., III, 71.

39. Bloemendaal, *Naar Amerika*, 202ff.

40. Chase, *Rural Michigan*, 16ff. Climate of Michigan.

41. This account is an example of the Americanized Dutch language spoken by the many immigrants especially from Groningen living in the vicinity of Muskegon.

42. Supan, *Grundzüge*, maps 18 and 19.

43. Deckert, *Nordamerika*, 75ff.

44. Bowman, *Forest Physiography*, 3.

45. Ibid., 1.

46. Chase, *Rural Michigan*, 38, 63.

47. *De toestand der Hollandsche Kolonisatie*, 10.

48. J. P. Lotsy, *Van den Atlantischen Oceaan naar de Stille Zuidzee in 1922* (1923), 106, 109. Incidentally, types of cactus are found as far north as Saskatchewan. Compare with Deckert, *Nordamerika*, 79.

49. D. Versteeg, *De Pelgrim-Vaders van het Westen* (1886), 81.

50. Een Gelderschman, *Hollanders in Iowa*, 46.

51. Bowman, *Forest Physiography*, 428.

52. Lotsy, *Atlantischen Oceaan*, 97.

53. Unpublished letter.

54. J. W. De Vries, O.P., "Een Hollandsche Kolonisatie in Wisconsin, IV," *Katholieke Illustratie*, (1909), 272.

55. Corn. John Ton, *60th Anniversary of the Dutch Settlement at Roseland, Chicago, July 5th* 1909.

56. De Martonne, *Traité*, 800, where the quotation "*prairie nues*" must be understood as referring to "grass-steppes." Compare Bowman, *Forest Physiography*, 489, and Supan, *Grundzüge*, 844–45.

57. Deckert, *Nordamerika*, 83.

58. Versteeg, *Pelgrim-Vaders*, 118.

59. Letter from S. A. Sipma, Mar. 16, 1848.

60. Een Gelderschman, *Hollanders in Iowa*, 47ff.

61. For example, see Versteeg, *Pelgrim-Vaders*, 135.

62. Ibid., 133.

63. Edith Abbott, *Immigration, Select Documents and Case Records* (1924), 532–39. Also the Bureau "Landverhuizing" in the Hague has stories to tell about this!

64. Otto Hötzsch, *Die Vereinigte Staaten von Nordamerika* (1904), 52.

65. Compare the colored map in Hötzsch, *Vereinigte Staaten*, opposite 180. The date for Wisconsin as given on the map is 1849, which is incorrect, as also the statements by Teenstra and Colenbrander, giving the dates respectively as 1847 and 1840.

66. Iowa-Commissie, *Iowa*. The first chapter gives a condensed but explicit survey of the various changes in the government of the state of Iowa.

67. Chase, *Rural Michigan*, 127.

68. Cyrenus Cole, *A History of the People of Iowa* (1921), 95. See also the interesting account of this fellow Dutchman (*Cole* is *Kool* in Dutch) on the subject of the two treaties in Chs. XVIII and XXX.

69. In many "guide books" for immigrants are found information and instructions on the division of land and the terms of its purchase. I am indebted to the *Standard Historical Atlas of Sioux County* for data on surveying and division of land, and for data on its sale to Chase, *Rural Michigan*, 128, 137–38, and others.

70. Cole, *People of Iowa*, 130, 151. Concerning these claim associations or "land clubs," see also J. Huizinga, *Mensch en Menigte in Amerika* (1918), 34.

71. R. A. Gouwens, "The Settlement and

Growth of South Holland," in E. P. Beaudette-Niel, *Thornton Township, Cook County, Illinois* (1921), 77.

72. B. De Beij and A. Zwemer, *Stemmen
uit de Hollandsch-Gereformeerde Kerk in de Ver.
Staten van Amerika* (1871), 147.

73. Fridrich Arends, *Het Mississippi-dal*
(1839), 237.

74. K. Jz. Beukma, *Brieven van den Landbouwer* (1849), 30.

75. Van Raalte in A. Brummelkamp,
Stemmen uit Noord-Amerika (1847), 78ff.

76. S. A. Sipma, *Belangrijke Berigten uit
Pella* (1849), 8–9. Mrs. G. Van Horsen, "Oude
Herinneringen," in *Pella's Weekblad* of May 26,
1922, evidently gave an account of the same
chance meeting.

77. J. A. Wormser, *Een Schat in aarden
Vaten. II. Het Leven van Hendrik Peter Scholte*
(1915), 192–93, n.2.

Chapter 8 *The Rooting of the Young Dutch Branch in Michigan*

1. E. Frederiks, in "Anteekeningen," *De Grondwet*, Mar. 5, 1912.

2. D. Versteeg, *De Pelgrim-Vaders van het
Westen* (1886), 89.

3. G. Van Schelven "Historical Sketch of
Holland City and Colony, 1876." Reprinted
in *De Grondwet*, June 1, 1915.

4. Ibid.; Versteeg, *Pelgrim-Vaders*, 29.

5. Ibid., 55ff.

6. Engbertus Van der Veen, *Life History
and Reminiscenses* (1917), 5. Written shortly
before his death in 1917.

7. Van der Veen, *Life History*, 17.

8. Versteeg, *Pelgrim-Vaders*, 92.

9. Ibid., 55ff.; Van der Veen, *Life History*, 5.

10. Versteeg, *Pelgrim-Vaders*, 68ff.

11. Van Schelven, "Historical Sketch," *De
Grondwet*, June 15, 1915.

12. Jacob Van der Meulen, in *Ter nagedachtenis van Rev. C. van der Meulen* (1876), 65.
This eyewitness speaks of five sheds. So
also Versteeg, *Pelgrim-Vaders*, 40. A. J. Pieters,
A Dutch Settlement in Michigan (1923), 69,
mentions, in my opinion erroneously, the
number 3. Very likely this can be ascribed
to J. Van der Meulen's speech at the semi-
centennial twenty years after his "Herinneringen!"—where he speaks of three sheds.

13. J. D. Werkman, "Herinnering reis Nederland naar Noord-Amerika," *De Grondwet*,
Jan. 21, 1913.

14. C. M. Van Malsen, in "Achttal Brieven mijner Kinderen uit de Kolonie Holland
in Amerika, by A. Van Malsen." The letters
were written in 1847; cf. *De Grondwet*, Jan. 21,
1913.

15. H. Van Eijk, *Dagboek mijner lotgevallen
en ontmoetingen met de reis naar de Vereenigde
Staten van Noord-Amerika* (1847), Aug. 28,
1848.

16. Van der Veen, *Life History*, 4; also Versteeg, *Pelgrim-Vaders*, 38.

17. Versteeg, *Pelgrim-Vaders*, 69.

18. Van Schelven, "Historical Sketch," *De
Grondwet*, June 8, 1915.

19. Versteeg, *Pelgrim-Vaders*, 73.

20. L. A. Chase, *Rural Michigan* (1922), 9.

21. Rev. J. Van der Meulen, "Eerste Worstelingen," Speech at the Semi-Centennial,
De Grondwet, Feb. 7, 1913.

22. K. Jz. Beukma, *Brieven van K. Jz.
Beukma*, 3rd part, 2, Letter of July 8, 1837.

23. Versteeg, *Pelgrim-Vaders*, 73, 76.

24. Van der Veen, *Life History*, 8.

25. Ibid., 9.

26. J. A. Wormser, *Een Schat in aarden
Vaten I. Het Leven van Albertus Christiaan van
Raalte* (1915), 155.

27. Versteeg, *Pelgrim-Vaders*, 75.

28. H. Van Eijk, *Dagboek*, 51.

29. Versteeg, *Pelgrim-Vaders*, 74.

30. C. Van Loo, "Herinneringen" *Historical
Souvenir*, 100.

31. Van Schelven, "Historical Sketch," *De
Grondwet*, June 8, 1915. Further information
about the store in the colony, the ship, etc.,
are borrowed from Van der Veen, *Life History*,
19ff., and Versteeg, *Pelgrim-Vaders*, 143ff.

32. J. Van de Luyster, Jr., Letter Dec. 15,
1847 in the series *Achttal Brieven*.

33. Van Schelven, "Historical Sketch," *De
Grondwet*, June 8, 1915.

34. Pieters, *Dutch Settlement*, 109.

35. Van der Veen, *Life History*, 20.

36. Versteeg, *Pelgrim-Vaders*, 179.

37. Van Schelven, "Historical Sketch," *De
Grondwet*, June 8, 1915. Versteeg, *Pelgrim-
Vaders*, 153.

38. Versteeg, *Pelgrim-Vaders*, 144.

39. Ibid., 96ff., 82.

40. Van der Veen, *Life History*, 18. "It is a
historical road."

41. Pieters, *Dutch Settlement*, 154; cf. also
Van Schelven, "Historical Sketch," *De Grondwet*, June 15, 1915.

42. Versteeg, *Pelgrim-Vaders*, 45.

43. Van Raalte, "Letter," Feb. 11, 1849, in
De toestand der Hollandsche Kolonisatie, 11–12.

44. Pieters, *Dutch Settlement*, 86ff.

45. Van der Veen, *Life History*, 26–27.
46. Versteeg, *Pelgrim-Vaders*, 140ff.
47. Pieters, *Dutch Settlement*, 64.
48. Versteeg, *Pelgrim-Vaders*, 132.
49. Ibid., 136ff.
50. Van Raalte, Letter, Jan. 30, 1847, in Van Raalte, *Holland in Amerika*, 25ff. Thus it is incorrect to speak of a "discovery," as does Versteeg, *Pelgrim-Vaders*, 139.
51. Van Raalte, Letter, Feb. 11, 1849, in *De toestand*, 9.
52. Van der Meulen, Letter, Jan. 20, 1849, in *De toestand*.
53. Dr. Th. De Witt, Letter in the *Christian Intelligencer*, Oct. 28, 1847, quoted by Pieters, *Dutch Settlement*, 83.
54. Van der Veen, *Life History*, 11.
55. Versteeg, *Pelgrim-Vaders*, 155.
56. H. Van Eijk, "Reisverhaal en Waarnemingen," *De Grondwet*, Oct. 23, 1913.
57. Van der Veen, *Life History*, 18. About the success of this "steam," there are differences of opinion; cf. Versteeg, *Pelgrim-Vaders*, 154; Pieters, *Dutch Settlement*, 84.
58. Versteeg, *Pelgrim-Vaders*, 152.
59. Van der Veen, *Life History*, 11.
60. Van Raalte, Letter, Feb. 11, 1849; cf. Pieters, *Dutch Settlement*, 83.
61. About the stage drivers, Van Schelven, "Historical Sketch of the Post Office and Postal Services at Holland, Mich.," *The Holland Daily Sentinel*, Dec. 12, 1914; Van der Veen, *Life History*, 8.
62. Koelewijn, Letter, Oct. 15, 1848.
63. Van der Veen, *Life History*, 8.
64. G. E. Hohm, "Recollections of Holland in 1852," *De Grondwet*, Feb. 21, 1910, quoted in Pieters, *Dutch Settlement*, 82.
65. Clive Day, *A History of Commerce in the United States* (1917), 474.
66. G., *De Landverhuizing naar de Vereenigde Staten*, 58. A harsh statement, which is generally confirmed in Clive Day, *History of Commerce*, 475.
67. Van der Veen, *Life History*, 10. The ten mentioned were the merchants.
68. Ibid., 6; Versteeg, *Pelgrim-Vaders*, 142.
69. Versteeg, *Pelgrim-Vaders*, 145, 150.
70. Van Schelven, "Historical Sketch of the Post Office and Postal Services at Holland, Mich.," *The Holland Daily Sentinel*, Dec. 12, 1914.
71. Day, *History of Commerce*, 474.
72. Van der Veen, *Life History*, 12.
73. Versteeg, *Pelgrim-Vaders*, 162.
74. May F. Robinson, "Rix Robinson, Fur Trader," *Michigan History Magazine*, VI, no. 2–3 (1922).

75. Scholte, *Eene Stem uit Pella* (1848), App. 51.
76. Versteeg, *Pelgrim-Vaders*, 178.
77. Van Raalte, Letter, Feb. 11, 1849.
78. Van der Veen, *Life History*, 10.
79. Versteeg, *Pelgrim-Vaders*, 98.
80. Pieters, *Dutch Settlement*, 153.
81. Versteeg, *Pelgrim-Vaders*, 203.
82. Ibid., 179; cf. Van der Veen, *Life History*, 22; Pieters, *Dutch Settlement*, 155.
83. Cole, "People of Iowa," 133–134.
84. Van der Veen, *Life History*, 10. Pieters, *Dutch Settlement*, 151.
85. Van Schelven, "Historical Sketches," *De Grondwet*, June 15, 1915.
86. Pieters, *Dutch Settlement*, 118–119.
87. Van der Veen, *Life History*, 14.
88. Pieters, *Dutch Settlement*, 105, 117.
89. Van der Veen, *Life History*, 21.
90. Henry E. Dosker, *Levensschets van Rev. A. C. Van Raalte* (1893), 178.
91. Pieters, *Dutch Settlement*, 157.
92. Henry Griffin, "Herinneringen," in *Historical Souvenir*, 103.
93. Van der Veen, *Life History*, 21. Van Raalte was also present "on top of the pews."
94. Dosker, *Levensschets*, 99ff. Cf. also the typical statement of Van Schelven in *De Grondwet* of July 14, 1914, in which he speaks of "de stad" of Holland and "het dorp" of Zeeland. He then continues: "May we be forgiven for these two designations, they are still so typically colonial, and were heard for many years in daily conversation."
95. Pieters, *Dutch Settlement*, 108.
96. Versteeg, *Pelgrim-Vaders*, 173.
97. Van der Veen, *Life History*, 19.
98. Stegink in Versteeg, *Pelgrim-Vaders*, 174.
99. Isaak N. Wyckoff, *Report of a Visit to the Holland Colonies in Michigan and Wisconsin, made by order of the General Synod, and under Direction of the Domestic Missionary Society of the Reformed Dutch Church in May and June, 1849*. This report has been translated a few times into Dutch, among others by N. H. Dosker in *De Hollandsche Gereformeerde Kerk in Amerika* (1888), 139–155; and also by Wormser in his *Van Raalte*, 158ff. My citation is borrowed from the less expurgated Dutch but more typical Holland-American translation of Rev. G. K. Hemkes in *Het Rechtsbestaan der Holl. Chr. Ger. Kerk in Amerika* (Grand Rapids, n.d., however, presumably published in 1893; see p. 260, where *De Wachter* of June 14, 1893, is still referred to). Hemkes had moved to America in 1877, which is of some interest

to us in the evaluation of the "Americanization" of his Dutch language.

100. Van der Meulen, Letter, Holland, Oct. 8, 1847, mostly printed in *Nagedachtenis*, 59.

101. Versteeg, *Pelgrim-Vaders*, 182.

102. Van der Veen, *Life History*, 12; Versteeg, *Pelgrim-Vaders*, 181.

103. Van der Meulen, *Nagedachtenis*, 67.

104. Versteeg, *Pelgrim-Vaders*, 182.

105. Pieters, *Dutch Settlement*, 107. The marriage of Hendrik Grijpmoet Michmershuizen and Hendrika Johanna Rozendom, performed on Aug. 8, 1847, which is mentioned by Versteeg, *Pelgrim-Vaders*, 181, is thus incorrectly reported as the "first" marriage in the colony, by Wormser in *Van Raalte*, 180, and his source Dosker, in his *Levensschets*, 155.

106. Van der Veen, *Life History*, 13.

107. Pieters, *Dutch Settlement*, 91.

108. Van der Veen, *Life History*, 15.

109. Ibid., 16.

110. Cornelia M. Van de Luyster, nee Van Malsen, Letter, Nov. 16, 1847, included in Osinga et al., *Achttal Brieven*.

111. Wyckoff, *Report*, 6. Wyckoff exaggerates the most regarding the harbor.

112. Versteeg, *Pelgrim-Vaders*, 184.

113. Pieters, *Dutch Settlement*, 113–14.

114. Dosker, *Levensschets*, 162ff.

115. Wormser, *Van Raalte*, 183.

116. Van der Veen, *Life History*, 12.

117. Ibid., 14.

118. Pieters, *Dutch Settlement*, 115.

119. Van der Veen, *Life History*, 13.

120. Van Eijk, "Reisverhaal," *De Grondwet*, Dec. 23, 1913.

121. Versteeg, *Pelgrim-Vaders*, 183.

122. Van Eijk, "Reisverhaal," *De Grondwet*, Dec. 23, 1913.

123. Van der Veen, *Life History*, 12; Versteeg, *Pelgrim-Vaders*, 173ff.

124. T. Ulberg, in *Jaarboekje voor de Chr. Geref. Kerk in Amerika*, 1883. Quoted by Hemkes in *Het Rechtsbestaan*, 22.

125. Pieters, *Dutch Settlement*, 104.

126. "According to Versteeg," because one gets the impression that there is no certainty about this matter. The church historian Dr. H. Beets cites Versteeg, *Pelgrim-Vaders*, 189, in his well-known essay in the *Gedenkboek van het Vijftigjarig Jubileum der Christelijk Gereformeerde Kerk*, 13, but for safety's sake omits the place of the meeting. In his *De Chr. Geref. Kerk in N.A.* (1918), 65, Beets mentions the village of Zeeland but again omits this in *The Christian Reformed Church in*

North America (1923), 37. Pieters mentions Zeeland. No one, however, contradicts Versteeg's claim.

127. Versteeg, *Pelgrim-Vaders*, 189, mentions Allegan. Dr. Beets frequently mentions Graafschap, while Pieters, *Dutch Settlement*, 117, speaks of "the congregation of Allegan County (later Overisel)." Graafschap and Overisel are both in Allegan County. Graafschap organized a congregation first. Overisel, however, had a minister. That probably caused the confusion.

128. "Actually"; much has been written about the legality of this classis. Dosker, *Hollandsche Gereformeerde Kerk*, 132, speaks of "a kind of classical meeting." Beets especially denies in his frequently cited works "the legality," a concept, which in my opinion is very elastic. If one accepts the point of view of Beets, scores of regulations established in early "colonial" times could be called "illegal." Theoretically Beets and others might possibly be right; speaking practically, their claims seem to be "farfetched," an opinion seemingly shared by Rev. G. Keizer in *De Reformatie*, Nov. 19 and 26, 1920. See also Versteeg, *Pelgrim-Vaders*, 189 and Dosker, *Hollandsche Gereformeerde Kerk*, 269 n.82, about this first meeting.

129. Of importance seems to be the fact that Rev. G. Keizer in his series of articles in *De Reformatie* has reconsidered his former ideas influenced by Dosker's version in *Hollandsche Gereformeerde Kerk*. Beets, on the other hand, maintains his former opinions; cf. Beets, *Christian Reformed Church*, 44.

130. Dosker, *Hollandsche Gereformeerde Kerk*, 133.

131. Versteeg, *Pelgrim-Vaders*, 191.

132. See notes 99 and 111.

133. In the report itself, the date given is Thursday, June 1. Cf. Beets, *Chr. Geref. Kerk*, 68, n.12.

134. Report of Wyckoff, translated in Dosker, *Hollandsche Gereformeerde Kerk*, 142.

135. Ibid., 158.

136. Beets, in *Gedenkboek*, 19; *Chr. Geref. Kerk*, 72.

137. G. Keizer, in *De Reformatie*, Nov. 26, 1920.

138. Wormser, *Van Raalte*, 173.

139. Report in *The Christian Intelligencer*, May 9, 1850. Quoted in Dosker, *Hollandsche Gereformeerde Kerk*, 163.

140. Report in *The Christian Intelligencer*, June 13, 1850. Dutch translation in Dosker, *Hollandsche Gereformeerde Kerk*, 164ff.

141. Wormser, *Van Raalte*, 177.

142. Dosker, *Hollandsche Gereformeerde Kerk*, 136, 137.

143. Beets, *Chr. Geref. Kerk*, 72.

144. Hemkes, "Het Rechtsbestaan," 38ff. On p. 45 Rev. Hulst is quoted; cf. also n.136.

145. Dosker, *Hollandsche Gereformeerde Kerk*, 271, n.89.

146. G. Keizer, in *De Reformatie*, Mar. 4, 1921.

147. H. O. Bouwman, *Amerika, Schetsen en Herinneringen* (1912), 137. This wavering was probably stronger because of the fact that Dr. Bouwman on the same page a few lines above says: "The legality of this society is thus subject to legal objection!" Cf. also p. 136 of this work.

148. Keizer, in *De Reformatie*, Nov. 19, 1920.

149. Ibid., Nov. 26, 1920.

150. Cf. for example the last sentences of the article of Rev. G. Keizer in ibid., Mar. 4 and 25, 1921.

151. Versteeg, *Pelgrim-Vaders*, 186; Van Eijk, *Dagboek*.

152. Van der Veen, *Life History*, 11; Pieters, *Dutch Settlement*, 131.

153. Dosker, *Levensschets*, 194ff.

154. Prof. H. Boers, "Hope College at Holland, Michigan." Ch. XIV in *Corwin's Manual* (1902), 191.

155. Rev. H. E. Dosker, "The Western Seminary since 1884," in *Corwin's Manual* (1902), 207.

156. Boers in *Corwin's Manual* (1902), 193. Cf. Dosker, *Levensschets*, 198. "The real pillar of Hope College lies in the classical meeting of April 30, 1851."

157. Versteeg, *Pelgrim-Vaders*, 193.

158. Brummelkamp, *Levensbeschrijving*, 221.

159. Kleinheksels, "Historical Setting or the Semi-Centennial of Hope College" in *Fiftieth Anniversary Catalog of Hope College* (1916), 13.

160. Versteeg, *Pelgrim-Vaders*, 194, 195.

161. Dosker, *Levensschets*, 203.

162. G. J. Diekema, "Holland Emigration to Michigan: Its Causes and Results," *Michigan History Magazine*, I (Oct. 1917), reprint, p. 10.

163. E. J. Tuuk, "Some Ideals of Dr. A. C. van Raalte," *Religion and Culture*, May 1924.

164. Diekema, "Fruits of the Colonization for the Present Generation," in *Historical Souvenir*. Diekema repeated these words in his "Holland Emigration to Michigan," 7.

165. Van Raalte, Letter, Feb. 11, 1849, in *De toestand der Hollandsche Kolonisatie*.

166. Van Eijk, *Dagboek*, June 8, 1851, and especially what Van Eijk says on page 79: "In my loneliness on July 3, 1851." As far as I know this has never been referred to!

167. This report, among others, is reprinted in Dutch in Dosker, *Hollandsche Gereformeerde Kerk*, 133.

168. Diekema, "Holland Emigration," 7.

169. Van der Veen, *Life History*, 21.

170. Pieters, *Dutch Settlement*, 150.

171. Van der Veen, *Life History*, 22; cf. Pieters, *Dutch Settlement*, 155.

172. Georg Friederici, *Das puritanische New-England* (1924), 13–14. It is of interest to note here that this study was written before the World War, but is now reprinted. Documented elaborately, it amounts to an antidote against the extreme glorification of the Pilgrim Fathers. Its one-sidedness, however, will be recognized by even the most unsuspecting reader.

173. Versteeg, *Pelgrim-Vaders*, 205.

174. Pieters, *Dutch Settlement*, 95. She quotes Van der Veen in this connection, 20. He, however, does not speak of "new-comers" but of "settlers."

175. Van der Veen, *Life History*, 20.

176. Friederici, *Puritanische Neu-England*, 13, esp. n.4.

177. Versteeg, *Pelgrim-Vaders*, 207.

178. Ibid., 176.

179. Friederici, *Puritanische Neu-England*, 46.

180. Van der Meulen, Letter, Holland, Oct. 8, 1847, in *Nagedachtenis*, 59.

181. Van Raalte, Letter, Feb. 11, 1849.

182. De Beij and Zwemer, *Stemmen*, 146, 151.

183. Van der Veen, *Life History*, 10.

184. Ibid., 11.

185. See the report of this anniversary festival in *De Grondwet*, Nov. 21, 1922.

186. *De Hope*, Mar. 18, 1886, quoted in Versteeg, *Pelgrim-Vaders*, 169.

Chapter 9   *The Rooting of the Young Dutch Branch in Iowa*

1. Sjoerd Aukes Sipma, *Brief*, Pella, Mar. 16, 1848.

2. K. Van Stigt, *Geschiedenis van Pella, Iowa en Omgeving* (3 vols., 1897), II, 19.

3. Ibid., II, 18. This quotation shows at the same time how perfectly well he still

wrote his Dutch language in 1897, after having come to America in 1847.

4. Ibid., III, 20; D. Versteeg, *De Pelgrim-Vaders van het Westen* (1886), 19, did not understand the name "Straw town," "since no straw was to be seen," but he himself says on p. 20: "Still others stacked their straw in such a manner . . . "! Not only K. Van Stigt but also Mrs. G. Van Horsen, "Oude Herinneringen" in *Pella's Weekblad*, May 26, 1922, speaks of the dwellings covered with straw.

5. Van Stigt, *Geschiedenis van Pella*, II, 21. That Van Stigt overrates the "colonial" solidarity in this case will become apparent later on.

6. H. P. Scholte, *Eene Stem uit Pella* (1848), Supplement, 58–59. The street names can be found, among others, on the plan of Pella in Scholte's *Tweede Stem uit Pella* (1848).

7. J. Nollen, *De Afscheiding* (1898), 51; Van Stigt, *Geschiedenis van Pella*, II, 15 and 22.

8. Sipma, *Brief*, Pella, Sept. 26, 1848.

9. Nollen, *Afscheiding*, 52.

10. Scholte, *Eene Stem*, 29. It is important to note here that, according to L. Van Bergeyk in an unpublished work, "Geschiedenis van de eerste jaren in Pella," (1855), *Eene Stem* was read aloud to the colonists and approved by all before being sent to the Netherlands.

11. Van Stigt, *Geschiedenis van Pella*, II, 23.

12. Sipma, *Brief*, Pella, Sept. 26, 1848.

13. Scholte, *Tweede Stem*, 6.

14. Ibid., 7–8.

15. De Salmagundist, "Een Brief uit Pella, Oct. and Nov. 1854," *De Gids*, 1855, 202.

16. Van Stigt, *Geschiedenis van Pella*, II, 21 and 41.

17. Ibid., II, 36.

18. Scholte, *Eene Stem*, 30–31.

19. Scholte, *Tweede Stem*, 6.

20. Van Stigt, *Geschiedenis van Pella*, II, 41, 48.

21. Scholte, *Tweede Stem*, 8.

22. Van Stigt, *Geschiedenis van Pella*, II, 36.

23. Scholte, *Eene Stem*, 24. Scholte speaks here even of a "highway," but obviously means a state road. Van Stigt even speaks only of the state road. Further on, Scholte himself does so too. See, for instance, *Tweede Stem*. In the oldest pictures of Pella (see *Een Gelderschman*, *De Hollanders in Iowa. Brieven uit Pella* [1858]), there is nothing to be seen about a highway.

24. Scholte, *Eene Stem*, 34.

25. Scholte, *Tweede Stem*, 10.

26. Nollen, *Afscheiding*, 53.

27. Van Stigt, *Geschiedenis van Pella*, II, 52, 55, 74.

28. Jacob Van der Zee, *The Hollanders of Iowa* (1912), 39, n.97; Van Stigt, *Geschiedenis van Pella*, II, 57ff.

29. See *Pella's Weekblad*, Mar. 16, 1923. The paper probably was *The Whig* and the city was Keokuk. To use "Whig" to indicate a geographical place must again be an "American" inaccuracy.

30. De Salmagundist, "Een Brief uit Pella."

31. Van Stigt, *Geschiedenis van Pella*, II, 66ff.

32. Nollen, *Afscheiding*, 53–54. Both citations show again how the Dutch language maintained itself. Jan Nollen came to Pella in 1854. The booklet appeared in 1898. Van Stigt and Nollen list the year 1850. However, it is known that 1849 was the year of the "Rush." Van der Zee, *Hollanders of Iowa*, 84, therefore gives the year 1849.

33. Van Stigt, *Geschiedenis van Pella*, II, 73.

34. Ibid. Van Stigt does not speak of the "passing through of the Mormons," as Nollen does in *Afscheiding*, 54. This is important since Van Stigt had arrived in Pella a few years before Nollen. Van der Zee, *Hollanders of Iowa*, 84, does mention the Mormons, probably based on Nollen's report. Although very likely "Saints" may have gone through Pella, the main route of the Mormons, "the trail of the Mormons," passed south of the Des Moines River. See Cyrenus Cole, *A History of the People of Iowa* (1921), 227, and Sipma, *Brief*, Pella, Sept. 26, 1848.

35. Cole, *People of Iowa*, 240ff.

36. De Salmagundist, "Een Brief uit Pella."

37. *The Scottish Historical Review*, IX, 217. Mentioned by Van der Zee, *Hollanders of Iowa*, 383, n.45.

38. Sipma, *Brief*, Pella, Sept. 26, 1848.

39. Cole, *People of Iowa*, 212ff.; Van der Zee, *Hollanders of Iowa*, 388, n.69.

40. Scholte, *Eene Stem*, 25, 27.

41. Scholte, *Tweede Stem*, 9.

42. Ibid., 33. See also the map.

43. J. A. Wormser, *Een Schat in aarden Vaten. II. Het Leven van Hendrik Peter Scholte* (1915), 200.

44. Sipma, *Brief*, Pella, Sept. 26, 1848.

45. Scholte, *Tweede Stem*, 33; Van Stigt, *Geschiedenis van Pella*, II, 74.

46. Scholte, *Eene Stem*, 21.

47. Scholte, *Tweede Stem*, 32.

48. Cole, *People of Pella*, 214. Cole speaks of a "company" organized by the Hol-

landers "to build a New Amsterdam." The town was not called New Amsterdam—one could deduce this from Cole's version—but Amsterdam.

49. Van der Zee, *Hollanders of Iowa*, 390, n.88.

50. E. Deckert, *Nordamerika* (1916), 192.

51. Cole, *People of Pella*, 214.

52. Gratefully, I mention here the graciousness of Mr. Edward Cook of Pella for showing me the historic places of Pella and environs during my visit in August 1921.

53. Van Stigt, *Geschiedenis van Pella*, II, 68–70, 74; see also Van der Zee, *Hollanders of Iowa*, 91, among others, the citation from the *Annals of Iowa*. Van der Zee calls the flatboat attempts "partially and accidentally successful," but does not give any sources. Van Stigt speaks of "a total failure."

54. Cole, *People of Pella*, 216. It is curious that Cole does mention the Burlington-Mt. Pleasant road but does not mention the attempts of his fellow countryman A. E. Dudok Bousquet. It seems that, contrary to Van Stigt's opinion, Scholte had no part in the plank road project. See Van der Zee, *Hollanders of Iowa*, 390, n.89.

55. Scholte, *Eene Stem*, 25–26.

56. Van der Zee, *Hollanders of Iowa*, 92.

57. Ibid., 93: "led to no little speculation among them."

58. Scholte, *Eene Stem*, 37.

59. Van Stigt, *Geschiedenis van Pella*, II, 69; Van der Zee, *Hollanders of Iowa*, 91.

60. Sipma, *Brieven*, Pella, Mar. 16, Sept. 26, 1848. From Van Stigt's *Geschiedenis van Pella*, II, 67, one would conclude incorrectly that this neighborhood—called "Vrieze" at one time and "Vriesche" at another time—was formed no earlier than 1849. However, the Frisians already occur on the name lists of the first colonists.

61. Information of Mr. Gaass, Sr., of Pella, in whose home in Pella I spent a real Dutch evening.

62. Een Gelderschman, *De Hollanders in Iowa*. One gets the strong impression this "Gelderschman" (perhaps Nollen in cooperation with Hospers?) was not foreign to the speculation. See, for instance, on p. 72 his strongly colored, futuristic picture of the Des Moines River Valley; this was despite all the previous experiences.

63. Van Bergeyk, "Geschiedenis," 42.

64. Sipma, *Brief*, Pella, Sept. 26, 1848. From Bergeyk's "Geschiedenis" it appeared to me that Sipma's expression did not refer only to the Vereeniging, because in the con-

sistory the people could express their grievances against the "Vereeniging"! Thus in the consistory one could hear enough being said about this Vereeniging. Van der Zee, in his work, did not use Sipma's *Brieven* and did not even know by name Bergeyk's "Geschiedenis," which existed only in a few handwritten copies. I am giving the page number according to my own copy.

65. Scholte, *Eene Stem*, 32, App., 54ff.

66. Scholte, *Tweede Stem*, 10–12.

67. This difference in attitude toward the immigrants by "Northerners" and "Southerners," as was the case during the Dutch immigration in Michigan and Iowa (think, for instance, of Littlejohn in Michigan!), has been felt and is still felt elsewhere also. Read, for instance, Willa Cather, "Nebraska," in Ernest Gruening, *These United States*, A *Symposium* (2 vols., 1923–1924), II.

68. Anonymous, *Over Volksverhuizingen in het algemeen* (1846), 26ff.

69. Wyckoff, *Report*. See also Dosker, *De Hollandsche Gereformeerde Kerk*, 154, (Vertrouwelijk Rapport), and 271, n.92.

70. Scholte, *Eene Stem*, 34ff.

71. Van Stigt, *Geschiedenis van Pella*, II, 30ff. In March, 1848, the church building was "almost" ready and was put into use (p. 31). Later (p. 116), Van Stigt says that it was ready "around the month of April."

72. Sipma, *Brief*, Pella, Sept. 26, 1848. Also Van Stigt, *Geschiedenis van Pella*, II, 116; Nollen, *Afscheiding*, 59.

73. Van Stigt, *Geschiedenis van Pella*, II, 123, 124.

74. Ibid., II, 122.

75. Nollen, *Afscheiding*, 58. See also Wormser, *Scholte*, 221, among others.

76. Scholte, *Eene Stem*, 37.

77. Nollen, *Afscheiding*, 59. Also Van Stigt, *Geschiedenis van Pella*, II, 114.

78. Scholte, *Eene Stem*, 35.

79. Van Bergeyk, "Geschiedenis," 47.

80. Van Stigt, *Geschiedenis van Pella*, II, 110–114, lists the complete regulations, translated from the English language. Nollen, *Afscheiding*, p. 59, gives only a few excerpts. It is remarkable that Van Stigt continually speaks of "*Gemeente*" [Congregation], just as Scholte does, while Nollen speaks of "*Kerk*" [Church]. The members themselves spoke of "*gemeente*." See, for instance, Nollen, *Afscheiding*, 62. Since "The Christian Church of Pella" consisted for the time being of one single congregation, the use of both words could be justified. However, in 1851, a distantiation ("*verwijdering*") took place and a new division ("*afdeeling*") was formed

along the lines of the "Christelijke Kerk." Nollen does not mention this, however.

81. Van Bergeyk, "Geschiedenis," 48.

82. L. Knappert, *Geschiedenis der Neder-landsche Hervormde Kerk gedurende de 18e en 19e Eeuw* (1912), 309–310.

83. Scholte, *Eene Stem*, 37.

84. Van Stigt, *Geschiedenis van Pella*, II, 121.

85. Scholte, *Tweede Stem*, 13, 14, 15.

86. Van Stigt, *Geschiedenis van Pella*, II, 123.

87. Scholte, *Eene Stem*, 35.

88. De Salmagundist, "Een Brief uit Pella,"

89. Van Stigt, *Geschiedenis van Pella*, II, 87. "Viewed from a materialistic standpoint, this was a great acquisition for the town."

90. See for example, Nollen, *Afscheiding*, 59. "Therein the Vereeniging formulated its standpoint as follows." It was not the Vereeniging but the Church that formulated its standpoint in this case. Wormser, just as Nollen, commits this same error. See his *Een Schat in aarden Vaten*. II. *Het Leven van Hendrik Peter Scholte* (1915), 212.

91. Sipma, *Brief*, Pella, Sept. 26, 1848. From this letter have come also the following accusations. Sipma has shown himself to be a reliable person, and is described to us as "a serious and industrious young man." His letter form an important means of verification in relation to what Scholte writes, especially also in material affairs. See also the letters in Wormser, *Scholte*, 224–227, in particular, the writings of Hospers, 225–226.

92. Nollen, *Afscheiding*, 52. See Van Stigt, *Geschiedenis van Pella*, II, 165, "since 1848–1849 some tension arose."

93. Van Bergeyk, "Geschiedenis," 45. A heavy accusation. But would such a religious man as Van Bergeyk have dared to voice it, if he had but doubted ever so slightly? Could a Seceder have been so depraved?

94. Sipma, *Brief*, Pella, Sept. 26, 1848. Letter of Hospers in Wormser, *Scholte*, 226.

95. Wormser, *Scholte*, 215, and the listed letters. Nollen, Van Stigt, and Van der Zee say nothing about this censorship. But all the more, so does Van Bergeyk.

96. See the letters included in Wormser, *Scholte*.

97. Nollen, *Afscheiding*, 161. See the letters included in Wormser, *Scholte*.

98. Van Stigt, *Geschiedenis van Pella*, II, 124. See also Van Bergeyk, "Geschiedenis"!

99. See the letters in Wormser. Wormser says nothing about the "distantiation." He does not know the work of Van Stigt, neither Sipma's *Brieven*, nor Van Bergeyk's "Geschiedenis."

100. Van Bergeyk, "Geschiedenis," 2, 44.

101. Van Stigt, *Geschiedenis van Pella*, II, 127–128; Nollen, *Afscheiding*, 64.

102. Van Stigt, *Geschiedenis van Pella*, II, 82ff., 31.

103. Scholte, *Tweede Stem*, 11.

104. Cole, *People of Pella*, 256. See also Van Stigt, *Geschiedenis van Pella*, II, 187 and 190, about the "material" advantages.

105. Van Stigt, *Geschiedenis van Pella*, II, 122.

106. Ibid., II, 53–54. As we know, the expression "uit buurten gaan" |to go around the neighborhood| has still another meaning in the Netherlands: to announce a death. We are accustomed to speak of "*wanten breien*" |knitting mittens|, and therefore we speak of a "*breipen*" |knitting needle|, but we use other material. Thus we need not immediately think of a "*vervagen*" |blurring| of Van Stigt's written Dutch language.

107. A. J. Pieters, *A Dutch Settlement in Michigan* (1923), 103.

Chapter 10 *The Rooting of the Young Dutch Branch in Wisconsin and Illinois*

1. Letter of P. Zonne, Nov. 26, 1852. See M. D. Teenstra, *Mentor, de getrouwe Leidsman en Raadgever voor Landverhuizers* (1855), 285.

2. Letter of K. F. Wiersum, Sheboygan County, Kolonie Holland, Aug. 15, 1848; Teenstra, *Mentor*, 283.

3. See n.2.

4. Rev. G. Baay, Letter, Town Alto, Jan. 4, 1849, in *De toestand der Hollandsche Kolonisatie in den Staat Michigan, Noord-Amerika* (1849).

5. Letter of K. F. Wiersum, as above n.2.

6. Letter of Baay, Town Alto, Jan. 4, 1849.

7. The total of 2,000 I derive from a report in the *Sheboygan Nieuwsbode* of Apr. 11, 1851. The other data I took from the letter of Zonne (see n.1).

8. See note 1.

9. *Sheboygan Nieuwsbode*, July 4, 1850.

10. S. F. Rederus, "The Dutch Settlements of Sheboygan County," *Wisconsin Magazine of History*, I (Mar. 1918), reprint, p. 7.

11. Ibid.

12. *Sheboygan Nieuwsbode*, Mar. 19, 1850.

13. Ibid., Mar. 12, 1850.

14. Rederus, "Dutch Settlements," 7–8. The year 1853 has to be accepted with reservations unless the first elder, P. Daan, refers to the father and not to the son.

15. *Sheboygan Nieuwsbode*, Apr. 11, 1851.

16. Van Raalte, Letter, June 19, 1850. See D. Buddingh, *De Kerk*, 160; Isaac N. Wyckoff, *Report*, 7; Cf. H. N. Dosker, *De Hollandsche Gereformeerde Kerk in Amerika* (1888), 153, 271, n.271.

17. H. Beets, *De Chr. Geref. Kerk in N.A.* (1918), 56n.

18. Beets confirms this fact (see note 17). He ascribes the small influence, however, to the membership of the Presbyterian Church.

19. R. A. Gouwens, "The Settlement and Growth of South Holland," in E. P. Beaudette-Neil, *Thornton Township, Cook County, Illinois* (1921), 99.

20. Corn. John Ton, "A History of the First Dutch Settlement of Roseland," in *60th Anniversary of the Dutch Settlement at Roseland, Chicago, July 5th*, 1909.

21. Gouwens, "South Holland," 99. The article contains a few errors, which Peter De Jong (Zwarte Piet) of South Holland, Illinois, kindly pointed out to me. Such errors are characteristic of the work of many Holland Americans.

22. Ton, "Dutch Settlement of Roseland."

23. George A. Brennan, "Hollanders first to make Roseland Home," *Calumet Index, The Home Newspaper for the Calumet Towns*, Chicago, Ill., Mar. 26, 1925.

24. Ton, "Dutch Settlement of Roseland."

25. Brennan, "Hollanders first to make Roseland Home."

26. *Corwin's Manual* (1902), 920. From the article by Gouwens, "South Holland," one would get the impression that he already returned to the Netherlands in 1854.

27. Th. Van den Broek, Open Letter, Jan. 17, 1848, reprint in the *Katholieke Illustratie*, Mar. 6, 1909.

28. J. W. De Vries, O.P., "Een Hollandsche Kolonisatie in Wisconsin, IV, Holland," *Katholieke Illustratie*, Mar. 20, 1909.

29. Jan H. Wigman, "Oud dagboek," reprinted in the series by De Vries in the *Katholieke Illustratie*, Mar. 6, 1909.

30. G. Van den Elsen, *Twintig Brieven uit Amerika* (1907), 72.

31. Ibid., 68.

32. Ibid., 72. Erroneously, Van den Elsen thinks that Van den Broek had been in the Netherlands still another time. Also, his data are not entirely correct. Cf. M. A., *The Story of Father Van den Broek, O.P.: A Study of Holland and the Story of the Early Settlement of Wisconsin* (1907), 75. Van den Elsen further speaks of Father Goedhart, *Twintig Brieven uit Amerika*, 78; M. A. speaks of Godhart, *Story of Father Van den Broek*, 75; and De Vries speaks of Gothard, "Een Hollandsche Kolonisatie."

33. M. A., *The Story of Father Van den Broek*, 80–84; De Vries, "Een Hollandsche Kolonisatie," *Katholieke Illustratie*, Mar. 6, 1904. Both writers use the same sources.

34. Concerning the Ravenna settlement one finds a few disconnected news items in various *Grondwet* issues. Here also the data concerning Hodenpijl are vague; Van Raalte was far clearer about Hodenpijl's behavior! Compare *De Grondwet*, Nov. 11, May 20, 1913, (in which Pleune gives an account) and July 27, 1911, in which appears "Sketch of the Early Settlement of Ravenna, Michigan," by Professor L. d'Ooge. Further, Van Raalte letter, Holland, Ottawa, Michigan, Feb. 11, 1849, published in *De toestand der Hollandsche Kolonisatie*.

35. *De Grondwet*, Jan. 21, 1913. Concerning this Society, A. J. Pieters is rather elaborate in *A Dutch Settlement in Michigan* (1923), 43–44; she does not mention the name Hodenpijl, however, and she takes her data exclusively from *The Christian Intelligencer* of Jan. 7, Feb. 4, Mar. 18, 1847.

36. Baay, Letter, Town Alto, Jan. 4, 1849, in *De toestand der Hollandsche Kolonisatie*. Baay complains that the Society made him pay too much for the trip to the West. For example, for the trip Buffalo-Chicago, they asked twice the amount that this trip usually costs! One is rather surprised to see men like Van Raalte, Baay, and others, giving such a poor opinion of the Society, which after all had been founded by members of the Reformed Church. The whole affair, however, becomes incomprehensible when an educated immigrant, S. Osinga, notes in his *Dagboek mijner reize naar Noord-Amerika's Vereenigde Staten in den jare 1847 gedaan* (1848), 53–54, and also in one of his letters published in *Tiental Brieven betrekkelijk de reis* (1848), that he not only "strongly advises everybody against getting involved with the Nederlandsche Maatschappij established in New York," but in another letter he calls the agent of the Hollandsche Maatschappij "an impostor" and speaks of "frauds." Someone like J. Van de Luyster, Jr.,

even wrote in one of his letters published in Van Malsen's "Achttal": "Do not consult Reverend De Witt in New York; but if you go to Albany, go immediately to see the old godly and humanitarian Reverend Wyckoff. To him you can reveal all your affairs and plans; he will treat you well." I think I am able to solve the riddle. In the same building where the Netherlands Society had its office, 114 Greenwich Street, New York, there was also located, according to a printed circular that I received, the Nederlandsch Agentschap which was founded "to help the arriving Hollander with his departure for other locations in North America, as well as to assist him in the establishment of a business or to obtain a permanent job." The circular was signed by [?] Dooge, [?] Spaan, and [?] Hoffmann. This Spaan was unmasked by B[astiaan] Broere (see note 53) as "a wolf in sheep's clothing," with a tongue "more slippery than butter." It is very likely that a man such as Spaan, who had tried to sell Broere to an English sea captain, tried to make a handy use of the joint location with the Netherlands Society and that Dr. De Witt and others, having been less fortunate in the choice of their representatives, have been duped by this combination. The immigrants likewise were duped! Other conclusions may be drawn from this.

37. Teenstra, *Mentor*, 168.

38. J. Hzn. Gunning, *Leven en Arbeid van H. J. Budding* (1909), 209, 217. H. P. Scholte still remembered Budding's "many oddities" twenty years after his stay in the United States. See Scholte's letter, Pella, Iowa, May 16, 1866, in Gunning, *Leven*, 598–599.

39. D. Versteeg, *De Pelgrim-Vaders van het Westen* (1886), 185. Also Drenthe, Buffalo, and Albany called him in vain. See Gunning, *Leven*, 225, n.1. Gunning does not say anything about Ravenna, however. Something rotten?

40. Gunning, *Leven*, 225–26. This marriage request was the cause of his departure. The reason was his desire for the fatherland where the believing brothers wanted him back. He also longed for his father.

41. R., *Amerikaansche Levenservaring* (1892), 24. Most of the other details concerning this colonization have also been borrowed from this small work. The writer does not list his name; however, the drawings carry the name of J. H. Redelaar, Jr. The assumption is that the writer who in his younger

years had followed courses at the Academie van Beeldende Kunsten (Plastic Arts) in Amsterdam is the drawer. Therefore, I called him R. Some facts, whose correctness is specifically expressed in the introduction, corroborate data in letters of Beukma that have been mentioned earlier. Of great importance is that it appears from this that the Holland Land Company was still selling land in western New York State in 1855, contrary to the opinion of Paul Evans, *The Holland Land Company*.

42. Beukma, Letter, Tippecannoe County, State of Indiana, Sept. 14, 1836. R. found on the island a "monument" of Noah with his name and a Hebrew inscription. See R., *Amerikaansche Levenservaring*, 66.

43. Ibid., 43, 66, 69–71, 82.

44. D. Buddingh, *De Kerk, School en Wetenschap in de Vereenigde Staten van Noord-Amerika* (1853), 8, 75; O. Van Rees, *Geschiedenis der Nederlandsche Volksplantingen in Noord-Amerika* (1855), 2.

45. R., *Amerikaansche Levenservaring*, 84, 85, 95.

46. Ibid., 169.

47. Compare, for instance, Bercovici, *On New Shores* (1925), 172. However, one should be very careful with this writer.

48. G. Van Schelven, "Michigan and the Holland Immigration of 1847," *Michigan History Magazine*, I (Oct. 1917), reprint, p. 25. The italics are mine.

49. Bercovici, *On New Shores*, 172.

50. Van den Elsen, *Twintig Brieven*, 125. Van den Elsen visited Essexville, Oct. 5–7, 1906. The data concerning the Saginaw colonists have been taken mostly from these letters, and from Bercovici.

51. G. Van Schelven, *Wat bracht U hier?* (1908).

52. B. De Beij and A. Zwemer, *Stemmen uit de Hollandsch-Gereformeerde Kerk in de Ver. Staten van Amerika* (1871), 60.

53. H. De Vries, *Korte Beschrijving van het Leven van en de wonderbare Leidingen Gods met Bastiaan Broere*, 16ff. A letter of Budding was published in 1849 at Zierikzee.

54. Van den Elsen, *Twintig Brieven* 25.

55. Van Schelven, *Wat Bracht U hier?*

56. *New York Tribune*, Sat., Oct. 8, 1853.

57. *Grand Rapids Herald*, Oct. 26, 1913. Both news items were found by me among the newspaper clippings of Dr. Beets at Grand Rapids.

58. De Beij and Zwemer, *Stemmen*, 60; Wyckoff, *Report*. Note: Seceder Veenhuizen had joined the Presbyterians in America

just as so many of his coreligionists had done.

59. Wyckoff, *Report*; Buddingh, *De Kerk*, 160.

60. Albert Baxter, *History of Grand Rapids and Its Industries* (2 vols., 1906). This standard work (?) contains remarkably little concerning the Dutch. This is all the more remarkable since a large number of our fellow Dutch are living here. However, it can be explained to some extent in relation to my observations about the selection process.

61. J. W. Warnshuis and J. H. Karsten in "In Memoriam, Francis Van Drielé" (1900), 14 and 29.

62. F. Van Driele, cited by Rev. Pieter De Pree in *Ter nagedachtenis*, 120. See also "In Memoriam F. Van Driele."

63. Melis Stoke, Jr., Amerikaansche Brieven, II," *Neerlandia, Orgaan van het A.N.V.*, Nov. 1915. My suspicion that Melis Stoke, Jr. was Dr. Beets himself was confirmed to me personally by Beets during my visit in Grand Rapids in August, 1921! Part of the above-mentioned article appeared somewhat altered, under the title of "Dutch Journalism in Michigan," *Michigan History Magazine*, VI (1922), 435–41. Erroneously, in both articles Beets speaks of *De Hollander*. The newspaper was originally named *The Hollander*. See article and photograph in Theo De Veer, "Hollandsche Journalistiek in Amerika," *Elsevier's Geïllustreerd Maandschrift*. I have not been able to verify if *The Hollander* appeared somewhat earlier or somewhat later in 1850 than *De Nederlander*. *The Hollander* was published only partly in Dutch and thus I have listed it in the third place. Buddingh, *De Kerk*, 6, 159.

64. Prof. Albert Raap, who as a collector of funds for Hope College for many years had traveled through the various settlements, during an interview informed me of this and many other interesting details, during my stay in Holland, Michigan, in 1921.

65. De Beij and Zwemer, *Stemmen*, 60.

66. H. De Vries, *Korte Beschrijving*, 20ff. 31.

67. Letter, Ierseke, Mar. 25, 1920.

68. R., *Amerikaansche Levenservaring*, 43.

69. Jb. Van der Meulen, "Eerste Worstelingen" Speech, 50th Anniversary held at Holland, Mich., Aug. 25, 1897.

70. Wormser, *Scholte*, gives various examples, 52, esp. n.1. Cf. also the remark of Prof. L. Knappert in *Geschiedenis der Nederlandsch Hervormde Kerk gedurende de 18e en 19e Eeuw* (1912), 295.

71. Jacob Van der Zee, *The Hollanders of Iowa* (1912), 251, lists a number of towns where this paper had its agents.

72. Scholte, *Tweede Stem uit Pella* (1848), 4.

73. Van Driele, quoted in *Ter nagedachtenis*, 120.

74. Ton, "Dutch Settlement of Roseland."

75. Versteeg, *Pelgrim-Vaders*, 188ff., ch. "de Classis."

76. De Vries, *Korte Beschrijving*, 31–32.

Chapter 11 *The Material Growth of the Settlements*

1. Baron A. Van der Straten Ponthoz, *Onderzoek naar den toestand der Landverhuizers, in de Ver. Staten van Noord-Amerika* (1847), 1.

2. Cyrenus Cole, "A Bit of Holland in America," *The Midland Monthly*, 3 (Feb. 1845), 118. See n.5 of Ch. 5 above.

3. Cyrenus Cole, *A History of the People of Iowa* (1921), 230ff.

4. R. Gonnard, *L'émigration européenne au XIXe siècle* (1906), 131. Opinion of A. Dumont. See further nn. 7 and 97 below.

5. So, for example, the Hungarians, like the Netherlanders, have been very successful in sugarbeet cultivation in America. It is one of the heaviest forms of farming. See L. A. Chase, *Rural Michigan* (1922), 294.

6. S. R. Steinmetz, *Wat is Sociologie?* (1900), 37–39.

7. Van der Straten Ponthoz, *Onderzoek*, 97.

8. A. C. Van Raalte, Letter, Holland, Ottawa County, Michigan, Feb. 11, 1849, in *De toestand der Hollandsche Kolonisatie in den Staat Michigan* (1849).

9. Ellen Semple, *American History and its Geographic Conditions* (1903), 277.

10. H. P. Scholte, *Tweede Stem uit Pella* (1848), 4.

11. Van Raalte, Letter, Holland, Ottawa County, Michigan, Feb. 11, 1849, in *De toestand*.

12. D. Versteeg, *Pelgrim-Vaders van het Westen* (1886), 166–169.

13. Henry E. Dosker, *Levensschets van Rev. A. C. Van Raalte* (1893), 296ff.

14. S. F. Rederus, "The Dutch Settlements of Sheboygan County," *Wisconsin Magazine of History*, I (Mar. 1918), repr., p. 6.

15. Een Gelderschman, *De Hollanders in Iowa. Brieven uit Pella* (1858), 104.

16. Cole, *People of Iowa*, 216.

17. K. Van Stigt, *Geschiedenis van Pella, Iowa en Omgeving* (3 vols., 1897), II, 75.

18. Jacob Van der Zee, *The Hollanders of Iowa* (1912), 390 n.88.

19. Ibid., 112. Cf. Cole, *People of Iowa*, 279.

20. Numerous stories about this were told to me during my visit to Pella in August, 1921.

21. Van Stigt, *Geschiedenis van Pella*, III, 56. Cf. also Van der Zee, *Hollanders of Iowa*, 393, n.105.

22. G. Myers, *Geschichte der grossen amerikanischen Vermögen* (2 vols., 1923). See I, Chs. 3–4.

23. Cole, *People of Iowa*, 281–282.

24. Van Stigt, *Geschiedenis van Pella*, III, 56.

25. Van der Zee, *Hollanders of Iowa*, 114.

26. Chase, *Rural Michigan*, 242ff., 253.

27. Based on a report in the *New York Tribune* of Oct. 8, 1853, which I found in the scrap book of Dr. H. Beets.

28. A. E. Croockewit, "Amerikaansche Schetsen," *De Gids*, April 1870, 69.

29. E. J. G. Bloemendaal, *Naar Amerika* (1911), 25.

30. G. Van Schelven, "Historical Sketch of the Post Office and Postal Service at Holland, Mich.," *Holland Daily Sentinel*, Dec. 12, 1914.

31. Van Raalte speech, *De Grondwet*, Nov. 10, 1914.

32. J. W. De Vries, "Een Hollandsche Kolonisatie in Wisconsin, IV, Holland," *Katholieke Illustratie*, Mar. 20, 1909.

33. G. Baay, Letter, Town Alto, Jan. 4, 1849.

34. Rederus, "Dutch Settlements," 6.

35. Chase, *Rural Michigan*, 244.

36. Corn. John Ton, *60th Anniversary of the Dutch Settlement at Roseland*, Chicago, July 5th 1909. Ton speaks of the "Michigan and Illinois Central," a name no longer extant.

37. R. A. Gouwens, "The Settlement and Growth of South Holland" in E. P. Beaudette-Neil, *Thornton Township, Cook County, Illinois* (1921).

38. Van Stigt, *Geschiedenis van Iowa*, III, 33.

39. Van Schelven, "De Tweede Revival," *De Grondwet*, Dec. 23, 1913. A casual but very important remark concerning the "epochs" in the history of Holland, Mich., which strengthens my point of view.

40. Frederick Morley, *Michigan en zijne Hulpbronnen* (1882), 16–17.

41. Croockewit, "Amerikaansche Schetsen," 73ff., 95.

42. Bloemendaal, *Naar Amerika*, 35.

43. C. De Smit, *Naar Amerika? Schetsen uit de Portefeuille op reis naar en door de Nieuwe Wereld* (1882), 53.

44. J. P., *Naar Amerika! Indrukken van een Ooggetuige door* J.P. (1882), 51, 56.

45. Van Stigt, *Geschiedenis van Pella*, III, 10.

46. Clive Day, *A History of Commerce in the United States* (1917), 525, 556.

47. Bloemendaal, *Naar Amerika*, 135, 151.

48. In addition to the literature mentioned, see also Rederus, "Dutch Settlements," 9.

49. Bloemendaal, *Naar Amerika*, 134.

50. De Smit, *Naar Amerika?* 30, 43, 50.

51. Ibid., 53.

52. Van Stigt, *Geschiedenis van Pella*, III, 3. See also De Salmagundist, "Een brief uit Pella, Oct. and Nov. 1854," *De Gids*, 1855.

53. J. P., *Naar Amerika!* 56.

54. *Weekblad voor het Kanton Bergum*, April 1, 1882.

55. Croockewit, "Amerikaansche Schetsen," 89. Cf. Bloemendaal, *Naar Amerika*, 150.

56. De Smit, *Naar Amerika?* 47.

57. J. P., *Naar Amerika!* 32. Cf. G. J. Bieleman and H. B. Hijlkema, "Zuivelbereiding," in *De Nederlandsche Landbouw in het tijdvak 1813–1913*, 444.

58. Bloemendaal, *Naar Amerika*, 151, 35.

59. S. A. Sipma, *Belangrijke Berigten uit Pella* (1849).

60. J. P., *Naar Amerika!*, 57.

61. Day, *History of Commerce*, 525.

62. H. Van Maren in an interview, *Pella's Weekblad*, June 2, 1922.

63. Van Stigt, *Geschiedenis van Pella*, II, 70; III, 36–37.

64. Day, *History of Commerce*, 557.

65. Van Stigt, *Geschiedenis van Pella*, III, 77.

66. *Weekblad voor het Kanton Bergum*, April 1, 1882.

67. Van Stigt, *Geschiedenis van Pella*, II, 69.

68. *Weekblad voor het Kanton Bergum*, May 16, 1882.

69. Bloemendaal, *Naar Amerika*, 42.

70. De Smit, *Naar Amerika?*, 46.

71. H. N. Ter Veen, *De Haarlemmermeer als Kolonisatiegebied* (1925), 119.

72. See a similar comment in *Nederlandsche Landbouw*, 21.

73. Bloemendaal, *Naar Amerika*, 42.

74. De Smit, *Naar Amerika?*, 54.

75. Een Gelderschman, *Hollanders in Iowa*, 149.

76. Bloemendaal, *Naar Amerika*, 40.

77. C. Van Loo, "Zeeland township and village," in *Historical and Business Compendium of Ottawa County* (Vol. I, 1892–1893), 86.

78. M. Cohen Stuart, *Zes Maanden in Amerika* (2 vols., 1875), I, 314–15.

79. J. P., *Naar Amerika!*, 30, makes the remark about the woods. This is of importance because it becomes evident from this that many a Hollander was already at that time doing the same thing as the Finns are still doing now. See Chase, *Rural Michigan*, 9, 165ff. Here also it is again the similar circumstances, which . . . etc., etc.

80. De Smit, *Naar Amerika?*, 42, 43, 46.

81. J. P., *Naar Amerika!*, 30, 56.

82. Bloemendaal, *Naar Amerika*, 41, 151.

83. De Vries, *Katholieke Illustratie*, Mar. 6, 20, 1909.

84. Een Gelderschman, *Hollanders in Iowa*, 120; De Salmagundist, "Een Brief uit Pella."

85. Bloemendaal, *Naar Amerika*, 69; J. P., *Naar Amerika!*, 56.

86. De Salmagundist, "Een Brief uit Pella."

87. Croockewit, "Amerikaansche Schetsen," 94.

88. J. P., *Naar Amerika!*, 56.

89. Van Stigt, *Geschiedenis van Pella*, III, 3.

90. Ibid., III, 9.

91. Een Gelderschman, *Hollanders in Iowa*, 132ff.

92. Interview of Aug. 15, 1921, with A. Van Stigt, who as a child came with his parents to the United States and who belonged to the pioneers.

93. Van Stigt, *Geschiedenis van Pella*, III, 74. Most of the data concerning industry have been taken from both of these works.

94. J. Versteeg, "Een oude Geschiedenis nog eens oververteld," *Pella's Weekblad*, Oct. 6, 1922.

95. Van Stigt, *Geschiedenis van Pella*, III, 14.

96. Een Gelderschman, *Hollanders in Iowa*, IX.

97. Croockewit, "Amerikaansche Schetsen," 94.

98. Cohen Stuart, *Zes Maanden*, II, 7ff.

99. Van Raalte, Letter, Holland, Michigan, in *De toestand*. See also n.105 below and also *De Grondwet*, Nov. 10, 1914, etc.

100. Van Schelven, *Historische Schetsen uit het Koloniale Leven*; "The Burning of Holland, October 9, 1871," *De Grondwet*, Oct. 20, 1914.

101. These and the following figures are taken from the above-mentioned "Schetsen" in *De Grondwet*, Nov. 10, 17, 1914.

102. A. J. Pieters, *A Dutch Settlement in Michigan* (1923), 40, 89, taken from *De Grondwet* of Mar. 14, 1911, and of Aug. 13, 1912.

103. De Smit, *Naar Amerika?*, 40.

104. The Holland Board of Trade, *Holland: The Gateway of Western Michigan for Chicago and the Great West* (n.d.). Cf. G. F. Huizinga, *What the Dutch have Done in the West of the United States* (1909), 39.

105. Cohen Stuart, *Zes Maanden*, I, 317.

106. Ibid., I, 308, 316.

107. De Smit, *Naar Amerika?* 41.

108. R. T. Kuiper, *Eene Stem uit Amerika over Amerika* (1881), 68.

109. De Smit, *Naar Amerika?* 42.

110. Rederus, "Dutch Settlements," 6.

111. P. De Young in Beaudette-Neil, *Thornton Township*, 97.

112. George A. Brennan, "Hollanders first to make Roseland home," *Calumet Index*, Chicago, Ill., Mar. 26, 1915.

113. I had an interview, particularly pertaining to the arrival of Pullman, with this Dutch American who came from Alkmaar in Noord Holland. Many Roselanders came from Noord Holland. The interview took place on Aug. 13, 1921, at his home in Roseland, Ill.

114. See also the article of Brennan, "Hollanders first to make Roseland home."

115. G. Myers, *Geschichte der grossen Amerikanischen Vermögen* (2 vols., 1923), I, 163ff., 175.

116. This total of five hundred is from ibid., I, 175. This, however, does not say that all this land was bought exclusively from Netherlanders.

117. Ibid., I, 176ff. Cf. also G. Van den Elsen, *Twinting Brieven uit Amerika* (1907), 88.

118. Brennan, "Hollanders first to make Roseland home."

119. Charles Boissevain, *Van 't Noorden naar 't Zuiden, Schetsen en Indrukken van de Vereenigde Staten van Noord-Amerika* (2 vols., 1882), II, 54ff.

120. Brennan, "Hollanders first to make Roseland home."

121. Ton, *60th Anniversary*.

122. Cohen Stuart, *Zes Maanden*, I, 300.

123. J. P., *Naar Amerika!*, 9.

124. A. T. Chadwick, "In the days of early Paterson," *The Paterson School News*, Mar. 10, 24; Apr. 14, 28; May 12, 1921.

125. H. Van Eijk, *Dagboek mijner lotgevallen en ontmoetingen beginnende met de reis naar de Vereenigde Staten van Noord-Amerika* (1847). See the diary of Aug. 1, Sept. 9, and Nov. 24, 1847. For the relationships existing between the Old Dutch and Young Dutch, these "experiences" are very important. Nothing has ever been published from the first part of the diary.

126. Van Eijk, *Dagboek*, see Schenectady, May 6, (1847).

127. E. A. Ross, *The Foundations of Sociology* (Fifth ed., 1919), Ch. 5 "Mob Mind," 100ff.

128. J. P., *Naar Amerika!* 11. Here he warns against the low wages paid in Grand Rapids, although they were also low at that time in New York and New Jersey. See n.8.

129. *Herdenking van het Vijftigjarig Bestaan van de Chr. Geref. Gemeente,* 14th Street, Chicago, 1867–1917, 1.

130. Van Stigt, *Geschiedenis van Pella,* II, 91–92; III, 10–12.

131. Van Schelven, *Historische Schetsen,* "The Burning of Holland, Oct. 1871," *De Grondwet* of Oct. 20, 27; Nov. 3, 10, 17, 1914. The series contains, among others, the story of Van Schelven, a report in the *Allegan Gazette,* an address of Van Raalte, and a survey of the disaster published in the first issue of *De Grondwet* that appeared after the fire, on Oct. 10, 1871. My survey has been drawn from this material.

Chapter 12 *Cultural Change: Religious Life*

1. Van Raalte, Letter, Nov. 27, 1846, in A. Brummelkamp, *Stemmen uit Noord-Amerika met Begeleidend Woord van A. Brummelkamp* (1847).

2. M. Van de Luyster, Letter, Dec. 16, 1847, in *Achttal Brieven.* Reprinted in *De Grondwet,* July 14, 1914.

3. C. Van der Meulen, Letter, Holland, Oct. 8, 1947, in *Ter nagedachtenis van C. Van der Meulen* (1876), 58–59.

4. D. Versteeg, *De Pelgrim-Vaders van het Westen* (1886), 163.

5. E. J. G. Bloemendaal, *Naar Amerika* (1911), 41, 135; K. Van Stigt, *Geschiedenis van Pella, Iowa en Omgeving* (3 vols., 1897), also complains about this.

6. B. De Beij and A. Zwemer, *Stemmen uit de Hollandsch-Gereformeerde Kerk in de Ver. Staten van Amerika* (1871), 136–137.

7. Ibid., 150–52.

8. Ibid., 137, 152.

9. Ibid., 136, 146–47, 149, 153.

10. Ibid., 150, 155.

11. Van Stigt, *Geschiedenis van Pella,* III, 104.

12. H. Beets, *De Chr. Geref. Kerk in N. A.* (1918), 85.

13. De Beij and Zwemer, *Stemmen,* 143.

14. Beets, "De Chr. Geref. Kerk in haren oorsprong- en worstel-periode," in *Gedenk-boek van het Vijftigjarig Jubileum der Chr. Ger. Kerk,* A.D. 1857–1907 (1907), 3–4.

15. Henry E. Dosker, *Levensschets van Rev. A. C. Van Raalte* (1893), 224, 159. See also the critique in J. A. Wormser, *Een Schat in aarden Vaten* I. *Het Leven van Albertus Christiaan Van Raalte* (1915), 188.

16. Dosker, *Levensschets,* 278.

17. Van Schelven, *Historische Schetsen uit het Koloniale Leven* (1910), "De Tweede Revival," *De Grondwet,* Dec. 23, 1913.

18. Dosker, *Levensschets,* 281, 282.

19. L. Van Bergeyk, "Een Geschiedenis van de eerste jaren in Pella" (1855), 95.

20. Jan Nollen, *De Afscheiding. Een gedenk-schrift* (1898), 61ff.

21. Van Stigt, *Geschiedenis van Pella,* III, 134. Also the subsequent church affairs concerning Pella have mostly been taken from these two small works and from Van Bergeyk's remembrances.

22. Van Bergeyk, "Geschiedenis van de eerste jaren in Pella," 95.

23. Ibid., 99.

24. Ibid., 109.

25. E. A. Ross, *The Foundations of Sociology* (Fifth ed., 1919), Ch. V, "Mob Mind," 110.

26. Dosker, *Levensschets,* 240–41.

27. De Beij and Zwemer, *Stemmen,* 150.

28. Ibid., 142.

29. Dosker, *Levensschets,* 257.

30. Ibid.

31. A few American Frisians, among whom were some very educated ones, gave me this assurance during my trip through America in 1921.

32. These kinds of church switching ["over-loopen"], which was already observed in the case of Schepers in 1852, still occurs frequently today. Other factors also play a role in this.

33. Beets, *Chr. Geref. Kerk,* 86–87.

34. G. K. Hemkes, *Het Rechtsbestaan der Holl. Chr. Ger. Kerk in Amerika* (1893), 52.

35. Dosker, *Levensschets,* 242.

36. De Beij and Zwemer, *Stemmen,* 138.

37. I found these data in the Archives at the Prinsenhof, at Amsterdam. They are listed in a "Staat der Landverhuizingen naar Noord-Amerika," for the year 1847.

38. Beets, *Chr. Geref. Kerk,* 88–89. Budding thought the East to be orthodox. Cf. J. Hzn. Gunning, *Leven en Arbeid van H. J. Budding* (1909), 215–216.

39. De Beij and Zwemer, *Stemmen,* 148; Dosker, *Levensschets,* 246, 268.

40. Beets, *Chr. Geref. Kerk,* 90, 95.

41. De Beij and Zwemer, *Stemmen,* 148.

42. Beets, *Chr. Geref. Kerk*, 95.

43. De Beij and Zwemer, *Stemmen*, 144.

44. Beets, *Chr. Geref. Kerk*, 98.

45. Hemkes, *Het Rechtsbestaan*, 68, 66.

46. Very recently Dr. Beets pointed out, although in another context, the influence of the social advance also on the Reformed Churches in America. Editorial in *The Banner*, Oct. 9, 1925.

47. Beets, *Chr. Geref. Kerk*, 89.

48. Hemkes, *Het Rechtsbestaan*, 67.

49. Beets, *Chr. Geref. Kerk*, 122, 172, 256.

50. Dosker, *Levensschets*, 273.

51. Beets, *Chr. Geref. Kerk*, 124, 130.

52. De Beij and Zwemer, *Stemmen*, 153.

53. Beets, *Chr. Geref. Kerk*, 125.

54. Van Stigt, *Geschiedenis van Pella*, III, 131.

55. Beets, *Chr. Geref. Kerk*, 133.

56. De Salmagundist, "Een Brief uit Pella, Oct. and Nov. 1854," *De Gids*, 1855; Beets, *Chr. Geref. Kerk*, 132.

57. Dosker, *Levensschets*, 55.

58. Lammert J. Hulst, *Drie en Zestig Jaren Prediker* (1913), 15–17.

59. Dosker, *Levensschets*, 270.

60. N. H. Dosker, *De Hollandsche Gereformeerde Kerk in Amerika* (1888), 202.

61. Van Schelven, "Tweede Revival," *De Grondwet*, Dec. 30, 1913.

62. De Beij and Zwemer, *Stemmen*, 119.

63. Van Schelven, "Tweede Revival," *De Grondwet*, Dec. 23, 30, 1913. In order to give a description that is as correct and lively as possible, I have followed the writer literally at times.

64. Dosker, *Hollandsche Gereformeerde Kerk*, 206, especially 274, n.109.

65. H. J. Moerman, "Oostfriesland," *Tijdschrift van het Koninklijk Nederlandsch Aardrijkskundig Genootschap*, (1921), 665.

66. Dosker, *Levensschets*, 275.

67. Beets, *Chr. Geref. Kerk*, 136ff.

68. Ibid., 139. The Gelderlanders are not mentioned, probably for good reasons, because more than others they shared Van Raalte's views.

69. Jakob Noordewier, *Een Tachtig-Jarige* (1920), 23ff.

70. Dosker, *Hollandsche Gereformeerde Kerk*, 200.

71. W. P. De Jonge, *Eene Stem uit de Gereformeerde Kerk in Amerika* (1882), 76.

72. *Hollandsche Gereformeerde Kerk*, 201; De Jonge, *Eene Stem*, 6.

73. Beets, *Chr. Geref. Kerk*, 141–142.

74. Dosker, *Levensschets*, Appendix, 330. I have not used the other numbers given because the exclusively Dutch churches in the East (Paterson, Rochester, etc.), were not included.

75. De Beij and Zwemer, *Stemmen*, 77. The numbers given include Dutch churches in the East. Therefore I have used the year 1870.

76. Beets, *Chr. Geref. Kerk*, 173.

77. The Christian Reformed Church in America, *Yearbook* (1925), 132, 133. In the year 1875 only the total "souls" are mentioned in the statistics. If we figure five persons in the usually large immigrant families, then we have 1,613 families, if six persons then 1,344 families. Thus 1,500 families as an average.

78. De Beij and Zwemer, *Stemmen*, 77.

79. Christian Reformed Church in America, *Yearbook* (1925), 131–133.

80. Beets, *Chr. Geref. Kerk*, 173.

81. *Corwin's Manual* (1902), 140.

82. De Beij and Zwemer, *Stemmen*, 161.

83. Dosker, *Hollandsche Gereformeerde Kerk*, 205.

84. Hulst, *Drie en Zestig Jaren*, 120–122. See also "In Memoriam F. Van Driele."

85. Whitelaw Reid, "The Small Town" in Harold E. Stearns (ed.), *Civilization in the U.S., An enquiry by thirty Americans* (New York, 1922), 289.

86. Beets, *Chr. Geref. Kerk*, 174ff.

87. Hulst, *Drie en Zestig Jaren*, 123.

88. Ibid.; Dosker, *Hollandsche Gereformeerde Kerk*, 205ff.

89. *Corwin's Manual*, 656.

90. Dosker, *Levensschets*, Appendix, 331.

91. Beets, *Chr. Geref. Kerk*, 176ff., 178.

92. Hulst, *Drie en Zestig Jaren*, 121.

93. Beets, *Chr. Geref. Kerk*, 180.

94. Dosker, *Hollandsche Gereformeerde Kerk*, 217.

95. *Corwin's Manual*, 141; Beets, *Chr. Geref. Kerk*, 181, thinks this number is too low, without however indicating why it is wrong.

96. Engbertus Van der Veen, *Life History and Reminiscences* (1917), 15. Secessions occur chronically among the brothers. The question of to whom the church property belongs is still very current today.

97. Hulst, *Drie en Zestig Jaren*, 129; Cf. Beets, *Chr. Geref. Kerk*, 184.

98. Beets, *Chr. Geref. Kerk*, 187ff. Also see G. Keizer in *De Reformatie*, Mar. 25, 1921.

99. Beets, *Chr. Geref. Kerk*, 189.

100. Hulst, *Drie en Zestig Jaren*, 126.

101. Ibid., 119.

102. Beets, *Chr. Geref. Kerk*, 173–174, 266.

103. Dosker, *Levensschets*, Appendix, 329–330.

104. Van Schelven, A listing in "The Burning of Holland," *De Grondwet*, Nov. 10, 17, 1914.

105. Van Stigt, *Geschiedenis van Pella*, III, 94ff.

106. Noordewier, *Een Tachtig-Jarige*, 40.

107. Dosker, *Hollandsche Gereformeerde Kerk*, 274, n.107.

108. J. W. De Vries, "Een Hollandsche Kolonisatie in Wisconsin," *Katholieke Illustratie*, Feb. 20, 1909.

109. G. Van den Elsen, *Twintig Brieven uit Amerika* (1907), 28ff.

Chapter 13 *Cultural Change: Education and Missions*

1. Versteeg, *De Pelgrim-Vaders van het Westen* (1888), 194ff.

2. Engbertus Van der Veen, *Life History and Reminiscences* (1917), 21.

3. Versteeg, *Pelgrim-Vaders*, 200–01.

4. Henry E. Dosker, *Levensschets van Rev. A. C. van Raalte* (1893), 206.

5. Ibid., App., 329–30.

6. Ibid., 186–94. A. J. Pieters, *A Dutch Settlement in Michigan* (1923), 135, does not speak about the closing of this school, but inadvertently he suggests that it flourished.

7. C. Van Loo, "Zeeland township and village," 89.

8. See Chs. 4 and 5.

9. H. Beets, *De Chr. Gereformeerde Kerk in N. A.* (1918), 418ff.; K. Van Stigt, *Geschiedenis van Pella, Iowa en Omgeving* (3 vols., 1897), III, 110.

10. George Schnücker, *Die Ostfriesen in Amerika* (1917), 176–177.

11. Beets, *Chr. Geref. Kerk*, 418.

12. Versteeg, *Pelgrim-Vaders*, 196.

13. The fact that Van Raalte ceded these five acres at this meeting of Classis of Apr. 27, 1853, becomes clear from Dosker, *Levensschets*, 204; Versteeg, *Pelgrim-Vaders*, 196; Kleinheksel in *Fiftieth Anniversary Catalog of Hope College*, 12, etc. Nevertheless, in the "Chronological Memoranda" in this same Catalog and in many others, it is stated of Van Raalte in 1850: "Five acres donated . . . as a site for an Academy." Garretson had required a promise of five acres of land as a condition for support by the East. See *Corwin's Manual* (1902), 193. Seemingly, Van Raalte already gave this promise at that time. From there stems the confusion concerning 1850 and 1853.

14. Dosker, *Levensschets*, 204.

15. Versteeg, *Pelgrim-Vaders*, 196.

16. Pieters, *Dutch Settlement*, 138. An example of one of the many inaccuracies is found in the dismissal of Taylor. Was it in Oct. 1853 or in 1854? According to Pieters, *Dutch Settlement*, 138; Kleinheksel, 25, etc., it was in 1854. In the Hope College *Fiftieth Anniversary Catalog* of 1916 and the Hope College *Bulletin* of 1922, Oct. 1853 is listed among one of the "year reviews." Very likely the resignation came in Oct. 1853, when the balance was made, and the termination of the school task occurred in 1854.

17. Dosker, *Levensschets*, 205; Pieters, *Dutch Settlement*, 139, says sixteen students.

18. Pieters, *Dutch Settlement*, 141. Pages 136–37 are among the most interesting in this book.

19. Dosker, *Levensschets*, 206.

20. E. J. Tuuk, "Some Ideals of Dr. A. C. Van Raalte," *Religion and Culture*, (Grand Rapids), May 1924. In this essay the mentioned document is printed in its entirety. Van Raalte here gives in a very striking way his point of view concerning education .

21. Here again is one of those small American inaccuracies. One can read on the title page of the *Fiftieth Anniversary Catalog*: Pioneer School 1851 "reorganized as Holland Academy 1857." Kleinheksel in the same *Catalog* (p. 13) already speaks of the "Academy" in 1852, and on page 15 he mentions 1853, while under the "year review" (p. 189), the year 1855 is mentioned! This is typically American: all this in the same little book! How can this be explained? In popular parlance people already at an early date talked about the "acadamie" in addition to the "instituut." The name Academy first become official in 1855 at the appointment of Van Vleck as "Principal of the Holland Academy." See *Corwin's Manual* (1902), 194. But the title became really official when they had their own building in 1857.

22. Dosker, *Levensschets*, 213.

23. H. Boers, "Hope College at Holland, Michigan," *Corwin's Manual* (1902), 195. In the carelessly worded *Hope College Catalog*, 1916, J. N. Ferris is wrongly listed. Compare *Corwin's Manual* (1902), 461.

24. Corn. E. Crispell, "The Theological Seminary at Hope College," *Corwin's Manual* (1902).

25. Pieters, *Dutch Settlement*, 146.

26. Crispell, "Theological Seminary at Hope College," *Corwin's Manual* (1902), 199.

27. N. H. Dosker, De Hollandsche Gereformeerde Kerk in Amerika (1888), 83ff.

28. Western Theological Seminary, Semi-Centennial Catalog, Holland, Mich., 1919, "The Story of our Finances," 22.

29. H. E. Dosker, "The Western Seminary since 1884," Corwin's Manual (1902), 204.

30. Fiftieth Anniversary Catalog of Hope College, 52–53.

31. Schnücker, Ostfriesen, 128.

32. Western Theological Seminary, Semi-Centennial Catalog, Holland, Mich., 1919, 30. See also n.29.

33. The Milestone, 1866–1916 (Holland, Mich., 1916), 59 and 65.

34. Concerning student life one finds an amusing article, "60 jaren geleden," in De Volksvriend, Sept. 9, 1920.

35. Boers, "Hope College," Corwin's Manual (1902), 195.

36. De Volksvriend, Sept. 9, 1920.

37. L. A. Chase, Rural Michigan (1922), 165.

38. Pieters, Dutch Settlements, 143–44.

39. These figures have been taken from the alumni survey in the Fiftieth Anniversary Catalog of Hope College, 56–59.

40. E. J. G. Bloemendaal, Naar Amerika (1911), 71.

41. Van Stigt, Geschiedenis van Pella, II, 86.

42. Ibid., II, 85ff. With some reservations, I accept the statement that many gave support by "donating land." The present grounds of Central College still comprise the eight acres of Scholte. Thus, if more land was given, then the proceeds of it must have been used for the "University"; however, I have seen this mentioned nowhere.

43. Jan Nollen, De Afscheiding. Een gedenkschrift (1898), 60.

44. J. A. Wormser, Een Schat in aarden Vaten II. Het Leven van Hendrik Peter Scholte (1915), 213.

45. Van Stigt, Geschiedenis van Pella, II, 90. Jacob Van der Zee, The Hollanders of Iowa (1912), 278; "not a few Hollanders from Pella have attended Hope College."

46. Van Stigt, Geschiedenis van Pella, II, 87, 89.

47. Van der Zee Hollanders of Iowa, 279.

48. Van Stigt, Geschiedenis van Pella, III, 107 and 111.

49. G. K. Hemkes, Het Rechtsbestaan der Holl. Chr. Ger. Kerk in Amerika (1893), 86; De Theologische School.

50. Beets, Chr. Geref. Kerk, 147ff., 206ff.; G. D. De Jong, "Onze Theologische School" in

Gedenkboek van het vijftigjarig Jubileum der Chr. Ger. Kerk (1923), 93ff.

51. Dosker, Hollandsche Gereformeerde Kerk, 274, n.106.

52. De Grondwet, June 7, 1921. Cf. Fiftieth Anniversary Catalog of Hope College, 56–57, 64, 67.

53. Corwin's Manual (1902), 933–934.

54. De Volksvriend, Oct. 4, 1923.

55. Lammert J. Hulst, Drie en Zestig Jaren Prediker (1913), 134ff.

56. In an interesting interview at Grand Rapids, Aug. 6, 1921. Lack of time prevented me from availing myself of the friendly invitation by Dr. Hulst to spend some time at his home. I would have liked very much to meet the gifted Mrs. Hulst.

57. Hulst, Drie en Zestig Jaren, 135.

58. Words like "felle propaganda" [fierce propaganda] and "scherpe concurrentie" [sharp competition] would be more appropriate to commerce than to church affairs. Nevertheless, they fully apply in this case. When reading a book like Beets' De Chr. Geref. Kerk in Amerika, and even more so when one reads G. Schnücker's very frank book about the Ost Frisians, these types of expressions impose themselves on us as if by themselves. For instance, Beets speaks of the practice of "persuading" [overreden] when a congregation is pulled away from another church. See p. 126.

59. Van der Zee, Hollanders of Iowa, 103.

60. Schnücker, Die Ostfriesen, 301ff., 229

61. H. E. Dosker in Corwin's Manual, 206; Western Theological Seminary, Semi-Centennial Catalog, 19.

62. Schnücker, Ostfriesen, 230–231, 128. Van der Las worked for years among the Ost Frisians at Ackley, Iowa (1870–1886).

63. Many examples are mentioned by Beets' and Schnücker's works cited previously. One gets a strong impression that faith usually played a minor role in this.

64. Beets, Chr. Geref. Kerk, 246ff.

65. Schnücker, Ostfriesen, 302.

66. In places that were totally Roman Catholic, education was sometimes given in the District schools with the authorities looking the other way.

67. Firmin Roz, L'Energie américaine; Evolution des Etats-Unis (1920), 117ff.

68. J. W. De Vries, "Een Hollandsche Kolonisatie in Wisconsin," Katholieke Illustratie, Feb.–Mar., 1909.

69. See note 68.

70. A. Brummelkamp and A. C. Van Raalte, Landverhuizing of waarom bevorderen wij

de Volksverhuizing en wel naar Noord-Amerika en niet naar Iowa? (1846), 21ff.

71. This influence was recognized by the famous Dutch-American missionary S. M. Zwemer in his address, "The Influence of the Dutch Emigration of 1847 on Foreign Missions," in *Historical Souvenir*, 40ff.

72. Pieters, *Dutch Settlement*, 126.

73. Versteeg, *Pelgrim-Vaders*, 195.

74. The masses in the Netherlands did not think about missions.

75. *Corwin's Manual* (1902), 141, 241ff. See further the biographies in the chapter "The Ministry." See also the beautiful head of the Dutch-American Van Dijck. Further general data have also been taken from *Corwin's Manual*.

76. *De Hope*, Sept. 14, 1920, which includes an article from *De Volksvriend* entitled "Onze Zendingsfeesten."

77. The word *apparently* was used in relation with the request sent to the Reformed Church in 1858. See *Corwin's Manual* (1902), 245.

78. Zwemer, "The Influence," 40ff. Additional data were also taken from this source.

79. Pieters, *Dutch Settlement*, 127, reprints the complete "program." She gives the impression that the idea of a mission ship originated among the Hollanders. S. M. Zwemer (see n.78 above) however declares that the proposal was made by Dr. Phelps. This clears up many things.

80. Taken from Zwemer, "The Influence."

81. In the *Fiftieth Anniversary Catalog*, 56, Emme is listed erroneously; in *The Leader*, June 1, 1921, 3, mention is made erroneously of "Herren". In *Corwin's Manual* (1902), 520, there are two errors. The village of Uttun should be Uttum; Enne did not leave for America with his parents but with his father, a widower, and his brothers and sisters. See Schnücker, *Ostfriesen*, 90, 115.

82. Ibid., and especially *Corwin's Manual* (1902), 520.

83. *Corwin's Manual* (1902), 521–22. Survey of missionaries (Hope College alumni) in *The Leader*, June 1, 1921.

84. *Corwin's Manual* (1902), 459.

85. Ibid., 648, 254.

86. Ibid., 875ff. Notice the interesting portrait. Upon closer examination, it doesn't look American. Not everyone in the Netherlands seems to know that Verbeek lived only a relatively short time in America and was classified as a Young-Dutch American. See, for instance, the observation in Rich. P.

A. Van Rees, *Japan-Holland voor vijftig jaar* (1914), 137.

87. *Corwin's Manual*, 645, 273.

88. Ibid., 277.

89. Ibid., 934.

90. Beets, *Chr. Geref. Kerk*, 143ff., 189ff.

91. Ibid., 145.

92. Ibid., 198.

93. Ibid., 203.

Chapter 14 *Cultural Change: Political Life*

1. I had an interview with Mr. [C.] Van Loo at his residence in Zeeland, Mich., in August 1921. I had several discussions with [H.] Van Eyck, Democratic postmaster at Holland, Mich., concerning Dutch participation in politics.

2. Some of this is supported by my conversations in America. These ideas can be found in the literature, although they are expressed with great circumspection. See Jacob Van der Zee, *The Hollanders of Iowa* (1912), 224.

3. K. Van Stigt, *Geschiedenis van Pella, Iowa en Omgeving* (3 vols., 1897), III, 7–8.

4. Van Der Zee, *Hollanders of Iowa*, 223–224.

5. G. Van Schelven, in *Historical and Business Compendium of Ottawa County*, Vol. I (1892–1893), 34.

6. Van Stigt, *Geschiedenis van Pella*, III, 37, 78. It is evident from ibid., III, 4, that Fisher was an American.

7. R. A. Gouwens, "South-Holland. Incorporation of the Village," in E. P. Beaudette-Neil, *Thornton Township, Cook County, Illinois* (1921), 97.

8. Een Gelderschman, *De Hollanders in Iowa, Brieven uit Pella* (1858), 130.

9. E. J. G. Bloemendaal, *Naar Amerika* (1911), 55.

10. Van Stigt, *Geschiedenis van Pella*, II, 81.

11. G. Van Schelven, "Michigan and the Holland Immigration of 1847," *Michigan History Magazine*, I (Oct. 1917). The short biographies at the end of this work gave me some interesting data for my thesis (pp. 30, 32).

12. "Apparently" because [N. A.] Balch was postmaster under the Democratic President Buchanan, which in America in this context says it all.

13. Cyrenus Cole, A *History of the People of Iowa* (1921), 206.

14. *Sheboygan Nieuwsbode*, Nov. 14, 1851.

15. Otto Hötzsch, *Die Vereinigten Staaten von Nordamerika* (1904), 96.

16. Van der Zee, *Hollanders of Iowa*, 220, 222, 227–28.

17. Van der Zee, *Hollanders of Iowa*, 219–20; 406, n.192. Van Stigt, *Geschiedenis van Pella*, II, 82, gives the mistaken impression that the Dutch in Pella in the fall of 1852 "almost as one voted the Democratic ticket."

18. Van der Zee, *Hollanders of Iowa*, 220, 225. I cannot agree with Van der Zee's opinion that the Dutch voted against prohibition because it was a Republican law. Moreover, I cannot find it shown anywhere in Van der Zee's book. I agree with him that it was contrary to their concept of moderation. One should not idealize the Hollanders at the cost of the Germans, as Van der Zee does, in imitation of Scholte. It is possible that it was difficult "to find in the United States ten beer-shops kept by Dutchmen; they are commonly Germans." I had already indicated earlier that the Dutch liked to down a drink. Besides, a prominent Dutch American informed me how in the early days the Dutch immigrants used to elbow each other in the taverns in Paterson! Specifically, these were the extremely orthodox immigrants from Overflakkee!

19. Bloemendaal, *Naar Amerika*, 70.

20. A beautiful example of how Abraham Lincoln, a common man, made laughing stock of a Democratic Whig candidate is cited by H. Beets in his *Abraham Lincoln, Zijn tijd en zijn leven* (1909), 64.

21. Van Stigt, *Geschiedenis van Pella*, II, 81.

22. A. J. Pieters, *A Dutch Settlement in Michigan* (1923), 158, "the ideals of democracy as opposed to the so-called aristocracy as represented by the 'Whigs.'"

23. Van Schelven, "Michigan and the Holland Immigration," 34–35.

24. *Sheboygan Nieuwsbode*, Nov. 14, 1851.

25. Frank Julian Warne, *The Tide of Immigration* (1916), 235ff. Warne considers especially the Germans as part of the resistance, even though it was directed primarily at the Irish Catholics. Warne's book, however, which appeared in 1916, already betrays an anti-German sentiment. Warne still does not make plausible why they joined with the Republicans, who were their own enemies, when he considers the resistance as being strongly directed against the Germans also. See p. 240.

26. R. Mayo Smith, *Emigration and Immigration, A Study in Social Science* (1912), 81.

Smith's opinion is quite interesting. According to him, there has never been any defined movement against immigrants. Compare this with Warne, who is supported by the historians [James Bach] MacMaster and [James Ford] Rhodes. About the Nativism of 1850, Warne declares that "The magnitude is hardly conceivable to this generation!" See p. 240.

27. Jeremiah W. Jenks and W. Jett Lauck; *The Immigration Problem* (4th ed., 1917), 43. Here only actions against Catholics and the poor are mentioned. J. Huizinga, *Mensch en Menigte in Amerika* (1918), 39ff.; depicts the "type" of the Know-Nothing movement.

28. This should not be taken to mean, however, that Maryland is largely Democratic. The city of Baltimore, Md., has nearly half of the state's total population. Because of this, the state was sharply divided between Democrats and Republicans as early as the Civil War. For information about Maryland, see Henry L. Mencken, "Apex of Normalcy," in Ernest Gruening, *These United States, A Symposium* (2 vols., 1923–1924), I, 13.

29. Van der Zee, *Hollanders of Iowa*, 221; 225; 407, n.200. On the last two of these cited pages, Van der Zee cites sections of Scholte's editorials in the *Pella Gazette* of 1855, 1856, 1858. It appears from this that the Know Nothings, and certainly the Know-Nothing spirit, did not disappear as soon as, for example, Huizinga, *Mensch en Menigte*, p. 39, would indicate.

30. Pieters, *Dutch Settlement*, 158.

31. Van der Zee, *Hollanders of Iowa*, 229.

32. For discussions of this line and the relationships in Maryland, see Mencken, "Apex of Normalcy," I, 14ff.

33. Letters, 3rd Part, p. 27. Letter of July 8, 1837.

34. Ellen Semple, *American History and its Geographical Conditions* (1903), 284.

35. Quoted in ibid., 285.

36. H. T. Colenbrander, in his *Koloniale Geschiedenis* (1925), I, 87, incorrectly implies that the Wilmot Proviso was initiated by the Whigs. For background on political conditions in Iowa see Cole, *History of the People of Iowa*, 263ff.

37. Theo De Veer, "Hollandsche Journalistiek in Amerika," *Elsevier's Geïllustreerd Maandschrift* (Feb. 1909) 107, makes this completely erroneous statement. On the same page, and just as erroneous, is De Veer's remark that the Dutch during the Civil War were supposedly on the side of the Democrats.

38. J. A. Wormser, *Een Schat in aarden Vaten*. II. *Het Leven van Hendrik Peter Scholte* (1915), 192, esp. n.2.

39. Ibid., 192–93.

40. Versteeg, *Pelgrim-Vaders*, 177. Pieters, *Dutch Settlement*, 47–48.

41. H. De Vries and Bastiaan Broere, *Korte Beschrijving van het Leven van en de wonderbare Leidingen Gods met Bastiaan Broere in Nederland en in Amerika* (1887), 60–61.

42. George A. Brennan, "Hollanders first to make Roseland home," *Calumet Index* (Chicago), Mar. 26, 1915. See also "Roseland" in *Onze Toekomst* of Oct. 1, 1924.

43. De Veer, "Hollandsche Journalistiek," 107.

44. Beets, *Abraham Lincoln*, 150. This little book, which makes no pretensions whatsoever about being scholarly and thus can only be used with great reservations, has special significance for us since it was written by a prominent American of Dutch birth.

45. The Republican and Democratic sentiments in "*de Kolonie*" are a direct result of my discussions with Democrat [H.] Van Eyck and the Republicans G. J. Diekema, former member of Congress, Van Schelven, Van Loo, etc. Some sentiments were verified in the very small amount of literature available.

46. Van Schelven, "Michigan and the Holland Immigration of 1847," 30. Van Eyck confirmed to me that Van Raalte became a Republican especially after he came to Detroit; Van Eyck's father met Van Raalte several times. For additional information, see W. O. Van Eyck, *Landmarks of the Reformed Fathers* (Grand Rapids, Mich., 1922), 317.

47. Van der Zee, *Hollanders of Iowa*, 226; 228ff.; 408, n.201.

48. Ibid., 228; 407; 408, n.203.

49. Van Stigt, *Geschiedenis van Pella*, I, 37.

50. Ibid., III, 44.

51. Semple, *American History*, 284.

52. Van Stigt, *Geschiedens van Pella*, III, 44–45.

53. R. Cronau, *Drei Jahrhunderte deutschen Lebens in Amerika* (1924), 334. Cf. also the essay about Karl Schurz, 339ff.

54. Cole, *People of Pella*, 327.

55. Ibid., 334.

56. Colenbrander, *Koloniale Geschiedenis*, I, 89.

57. E. E. Miller, "Tennessee," in Gruening, *These United States*, I, 144.

58. Semple, *American History*, 285.

59. Cole, *People of Iowa*, 334.

60. De Vries, *Korte Beschrijving*, 50ff.

61. Henry E. Dosker, *Levensschets van Rev. A. C. Van Raalte* (1893), 227.

62. Beets, *Abraham Lincoln*, Appendix, "Hollanders in the armies of the Union." This title, however, is too broad. Beets (Van Schelven supplied this information to him) only cites the participation of the Michigan Hollanders, and is very incomplete concerning the Iowa colonists; those in Illinois, Wisconsin, New York State, etc., are completely ignored. The listing of the regimental titles tell us more than is usually the case. After all, they were formed during this time and not all at once, but gradually as they were needed. To a greater or lesser degree, they pinpoint the moment at which the enthusiasm or the sense of duty of the Hollanders awoke. I do this with reservation.

63. Dosker, *Levensschets*, 229.

64. S. F. Rederus, "The Dutch Settlements of Sheboygan County," *Wisconsin Magazine of History*, I (Mar. 1918), 5–6.

65. Brennan, "Hollanders first to make Roseland home."

66. Van der Zee, *Hollanders of Iowa*, 230; Van Stigt, *Geschiedenis van Pella*, II, 46.

67. Beets, *Abraham Lincoln*, App., 222. Beets only lists the above-mentioned G. Company, which numbered "ten officers," plus "soldiers" and "recruits." It is probable that also the non-commissioned officers (and the corporals?) were counted with the officers. The fact that the Michigan Dutch rose to the rank of sergeant, while the Iowa men rose to the rank of lieutenant, is once more an expression of the greater culture of the Pellians, in my view. It is also a result of the fact that the people in Michigan lived among Yankees, while those in Iowa lived among Southerners.

68. Van Stigt, *Geschiedenis van Pella*, III, 52–53; Dosker, *Levensschets*, 229.

69. Dosker, *Levensschets*, 228; Van Stigt, *Geschiedenis van Pella*, III, 47.

70. Dosker, *Levensschets*, 229.

71. Cole, *People of Iowa*, 336ff.

72. Ibid., 343 and 336, n.2.

73. Ibid., 361–62.

74. Van der Zee, *Hollanders of Iowa*, 230, ". . . there were no Hollanders implicated in such treasonable practices."

75. Beets, *Chr. Geref. Kerk*, 168.

76. Dosker, *Levensschets*, 228.

77. This was told to me in Holland, Michigan by very competent and completely reliable sources. See also G. Van Schelven *Wat Bracht U Hier?* p. 82.

78. Jan Nollen, *De Afscheiding. Een gedenk-schrift* (1898), 61.

79. Ibid., 66.

80. Ibid., 61.

81. Van Stigt, *Geschiedenis van Pella*, I, 36.

82. Cole, *People of Iowa*, 326. Cf. also 323, n.2, where Scholte is included in a group of men "famous in Iowa affairs."

83. Cronau, *Drei Jahrhunderte Deutschen Lebens in Amerika*, 340.

84. It was already during my visit to Holland, Mich., that I learned of Scholte's ambitions; however, they were only known there from rumors. These ambitions were later confirmed at Pella by Scholte's grandson (H. P. Scholte).

85. Van Stigt, *Geschiedenis van Pella*, I, 36, according to whom Scholte, in spite of everything, remained a "truly great man."

86. Beets, *Chr. Geref. Kerk*, 168.

87. Van der Zee, *Hollanders of Iowa*, 408, n.208; Cole, *History of the People of Iowa*, 343. One can read between the lines that this Copperhead convention was probably held at Pella. However, neither Van der Zee nor Cole actually say so. The latter only talks about Marion County.

88. Van Stigt, *Geschiedenis van Pella*, III, 47–48.

89. J. Versteeg, "Een oude geschiedenis nog eens oververteld," *Pella's Weekblad*, Oct. 6, 1922; Van Stigt, *Geschiedenis van Pella*, III, 48.

90. R., *Amerikaansche Levenservaring; Schetsen en Lotgevallen uit het leven van een Hollandsche emigrant met eene Gids voor den Landverhuizer naar Amerika* (1892), 144.

91. Wormser, *Scholte*, 192; 193, n.2.

92. *Weekblad voor het Kanton Bergum*, Apr. 1, 1882.

93. Dosker, *Levensschets*, 230.

94. This confession of love for America came from elderly C. Van Loo in *De Volksvriend*, Mar. 27, 1924, 5.

95. Beets, *Chr. Geref. Kerk*, 163–64.

96. Van Schelven, in "Revival," *De Grondwet*, Dec. 23, 1913.

97. Van der Zee, *Hollanders of Iowa*, 233.

98. Ibid., 232.

99. This was told to me by Mr. Van Eyck during my visit to Holland.

100. Taken from Van Loo, "Zeeland township and villages," in *Historical and Business Compendium of Ottawa County*, I (1892–1893), 92.

101. Van Loo, "Zeeland township," 92ff.

102. N. M. Butler, *Die Amerikaner* (1910), 6–7. Butler makes an unwarranted exception in the case of Great Britain.

103. Van der Zee, *Hollanders of Iowa*, 232.

104. Van Schelven, "Historical Sketch of the Post Office and Postal Service," at Holland, Michigan, *Holland Daily Sentinel*, Dec. 12, 1914. I want to remind the readers that Johnson wanted to restore "State rights" to the southern states before many Republicans considered it desirable to do so. He thus met the Democrats part-way. And of course it was also the local Holland Democrats who worked toward the resignation of Roest.

105. Van Stigt, *Geschiedenis van Pella*, II, 25; III, 13, 78.

106. R. A. Gouwens, "Story of South Holland Post Office," in E. P. Beaudette-Neil, *Thornton Township, Cook County, Illinois* (1921), 101.

107. Ernst Troeltsch, *Die Bedeutung des Protestantismus für die Entstehung der Modernen Welt* (1924), 43.

108. Ibid., 37.

109. Hans Baron, *Calvins Staatsanschauung und das Konfessionelle Zeitalter* (1924), 75.

110. The resistance of this "paus" [pope] that developed because of the aristocratic character of Van Raalte, which reminds us of the "paus" at Geneva [John Calvin], already came to our attention during the rooting time. This may also be the reason why Van Schelven, in his series of articles entitled "Wat Bracht U Hier?" considered Van Raalte as "a Whig from the outset" (p. 82), since Whigs and the aristocrats were considered one and the same. He was certainly so in his character and attitude. We know how little Scholte often concerned himself with his people and how haughty he was towards them at times. The Calvinist Netherlanders could be just as secretive as the Calvinist Yankees. Yet we should not consider character and religious beliefs as the same, even though they certainly are closely related.

Chapter 15 Cultural Change: The Dutch Press

1. The issues of the *Sheboygan Nieuwsbode*, 1849–1854, and *De Nieuwsbode*, 1855–1858, eight volumes altogether, are in the collection of the Grand Rapids Public Library. Unfortunately there was not enough time during my stay in Grand Rapids to go through these issues thoroughly. Later [Henry] Beets sent me some information from the *Sheboygan Nieuwsbode*.

2. Theo de Veer, "Hollandsche Journalistiek in Amerika," Elsevier's Geïllustreerd Maandschrift, Feb. 1909, 108. It is not right to cite H. Doesburg as the founder. Beets is also incorrect in his oft-mentioned essays in Neerlandia, Nov., 1915, and in the Michigan History Magazine, IV, No. 2–3 (1922), when he says that De Hollander was not brought to Holland, Mich., until 1852. See Henry E. Dosker, Levensschets van Rev. A. C. Van Raalte (1893), 175ff.

3. Dosker, Levensschets, 175. Clarification is needed regarding the statement made by Van Raalte on Oct. 30, 1850: "A certain Englishman is planning to publish a weekly paper." Yet the eighth issue, as depicted in Theo De Veer's essay, was dated Nov. 23, 1850. Since it was a weekly, the first issue must have come out as early as late Sept. or early Oct. 1850. In the issue Van Raalte cited, Holland—not Allegan—was mentioned at least twice as the place of publication. Therefore, 1852 must be the incorrect year for publication in Holland especially in view of what Dosker has indicated.

4. Engbertus Van der Veen, Life History and Reminiscences (1917), 14. "One of the elders saw Mr. H. D. come and sit down . . . took Mr. H. D. by the shoulders and requested that he withdraw." See also p. 21, where Van der Veen mentions "the Netherlander . . . published only for a short time by bad men, who gloried if they could publish some dirty articles." Van der Veen was apparently referring to The Hollander. Or did he perhaps have the De Nederlander of Kalamazoo in mind, a publication which lasted such a short time? After all, The Hollander existed for quite some time as De Hollander, also under Doesburg.

5. D. Versteeg, De Pelgrim-Vaders van het Westen (1886), 162.

6. Versteeg, Pelgrim-Vaders, 163; De Veer, "Hollandsche Journalistiek," 112. I acquired most of the information about De Grondwet, however, from an article about Leendert Mulder that precedes an advertisement premium in De Grondwet on Jan Malaban, Holland, Mich., 1897.

7. G. Haan, "De Grondleggers van onze Kerkengroep" in the Gedenkboek van het Vijftigjarig Jubileum der Christelijke Gereformeerde Kerk, AD 1857–1907 (1907), 248.

8. H. Beets, De Chr. Geref. Kerk in N. A. (1918), 157. It is surprising that Beets, normally such a precise Holland American, should twice cite Vorst as the publisher of this paper, both times in the publications I cited in

n.2 of this chapter. Haan (see my n.7) does not mention this; yet the article appeared in the Michigan History Magazine four years after publication of De Chr. Geref. Kerk.

9. G. Keizer, Onze Pers. Gedenboek, 165ff.; Cf. W. P. De Jonge, Eene Stem uit de Gereformeerde Kerk in Amerika (1882), 7.

10. Beets, Chr. Geref. Kerk, 218.

11. Versteeg, Pelgrim-Vaders, 162.

12. Beets, Neerlandia, Nov. 1915, and the article in the Michigan History Magazine, IV, No. 2–3 (1922).

13. Een Gelderschman, De Hollanders in Iowa. Brieven uit Pella (1858), 131.

14. Jacob Van der Zee, The Hollanders of Iowa (1912), 247–48.

15. Ibid., 245, where the "editorial" under consideration was printed.

16. K. Van Stigt, Geschiedenis van Pella, Iowa en Omgeving (3 vols., 1897), II, 92–93.

17. Ibid., III, 44; Van der Zee, Hollanders of Iowa, 248–49.

18. Van Stigt, Geschiedenis van Pella, III, 38, 69.

19. Ibid.; Van der Zee, Hollanders of Iowa, 250–51.

20. Van Stigt, Geschiedenis van Pella, III, 39ff.

21. Ibid., I, 41ff.

22. Ibid., III, 70. I have the issue dated June 21, 1882, in my possession.

23. Beets, Neerlandia, Nov. 1915; Michigan History Magazine, IV, Nos. 2, 3 (1922).

24. Some years of Stemmen uit de Vrije Hollandsche Gemeenten in Amerika are in the library of the Vrije Gemeente of Amsterdam, specifically for 1889 and 1890.

25. The "remigrant" Plugge, residing in Middelburg, told me this in a conversation. However, he no longer owned even a single copy of his newspaper, which was later changed to De Standaard. I have not been able to verify information concerning Plugge's publication at all.

26. Information concerning this paper is taken from the articles by Beets and De Veer.

27. E. Van Son in the Gedenkboek van het A.N.V. [Algemeen Nederlandsch Verbond].

28. "Landverhuizing naar de V. St. van N.-A.," Economist, II, 1869. The newspaper cited in this article was not mentioned by any of the emigrants.

29. G. Van der Meulen, "New-Yorksche Brieven" in the Weekblad voor het Kanton Bergum, No. 10, 1883, letter of Feb. 11, 1883.

30. Van Stigt, Geschiedenis van Pella, III, 31ff.

31. The Milestone, 1866–1916, Holland, Michigan, 73. Additional information was taken from copies in my possession.

32. Beets, *Chr. Geref. Kerk*, 219 and esp. 239.

33. *Stemmen uit de Vrije Hollandsche Gemeenten in Amerika*, V, 1890, No. 10.

34. Beets, *Chr. Geref. Kerk*, 106. Beets in this work also gives a list of Christian Reformed pamphlets, etc.

35. Beets, *Chr. Geref. Kerk*. I took further information from ads such as D. J. Doornink's at Grand Rapids, printed in 1877 at the back of "De Constitutie der Geref. Kerk in Amerika," from *Stemmen* in 1890, etc.

36. *Weekblad voor het Kanton Bergum*, Apr. 1, 1882.

Volume Two

Chapter 1   Sioux County, A Daughter Colony in the "Farther West"

1. E. A. Ross, *Changing America* (1912), 146.

2. Ibid., 148ff.

3. Een Gelderschman, *De Hollanders in Iowa, Brieven uit Pella* (1858), 167. "In the first place"; in my opinion this is not exclusive.

4. H. Hospers, "De Verhuizing," Jubileumnummer of *De Volksvriend*, Sept. 19, 1895.

5. K. Van Stigt, *Geschiedenis van Pella, Iowa en Omgeving* (3 vols., 1897), III, 65.

6. *De Volksvriend*, Sept. 9, 1920.

7. Ibid., Jan. 31, 1924. Oak Creek flows through Smith County. According to the Rand-McNally map of Kansas the town of Dispatch is located in Smith County. This is near a Netherlands settlement. However, *Corwin's Manual* (1902), 1026, gives the location in the bordering Jewell County. Either statement may be correct, due to the extensiveness of the rural congregations.

8. G. F. Huizinga, *What the Dutch Have Done in the West of the United States* (1909), 33.

9. Een Gelderschman, *Hollanders in Iowa*, 116.

10. X., "Herinneringen," Jubileumnummer, *De Volksvriend*. According to [Jacob] Van der Zee in *The Hollanders of Iowa* (1912), 394, n.111; X is the pseudonym of Scholte's son-in-law, Jan Nollen.

11. Albrecht Penck, *Die Natürlichen Grenzen Russlands* (1917), 5.

12. X., "Herinneringen."

13. M. R. Stone, "Idaho," in Ernest Gruening, *These United States, A Symposium* (2 vols., 1923–1924), II, 179.

14. E. A. Ross, *The Foundations of Sociology*, (5th ed., 1919), 359.

15. A. E. Croockewit, "Amerikaansche Schetsen," *De Gids*, Apr. 1870, 95ff.

16. Van Stigt, *Geschiedenis van Pella*, III, 2.

17. See n.15 above.

18. Hospers, "De Verhuizing;" Van Stigt, *Geschiedenis van Pella*, III, 62.

19. Ellen Semple, *American History and its Geographic Conditions* (1903), 240ff., 95ff.

20. Fr. Ratzel, *Politische Geographie* (3rd ed., 1903), 264.

21. H. J. Van der Waa, "The Beginning of the Colony," *Atlas of Sioux County, Iowa*. One gets the incorrect impression that it was Van der Waa who started the plans rolling for the colonization. However, Hospers gives that honor to J. Pelmulder. The account of the expedition that follows is adapted from this article.

22. E. J. G. Bloemendaal, *Naar Amerika* (1911), 75.

23. Van der Zee, *Hollanders of Iowa*, 123; 394, n.113.

24. A. E. Brunsting, "Herinneringen," *De Volksvriend*, Oct. 7, 1920.

25. Hospers, "De Verhuizing." Further statements are quoted from the above-mentioned article by Van der Waa, "Beginning of the Colony," and from Van der Zee, *Hollanders of Iowa*, 133ff.

26. Van der Waa, "Beginning of the Colony."

27. Hospers, "De Verhuizing."

28. Van Stigt, *Geschiedenis van Pella*, III, 64.

29. A. Van der Meide, "Reminiscence of early days in Sioux County," *Atlas of Sioux County, Iowa*.

30. Van der Waa, "Beginning of the Colony," see n.21 above. Cf. *De Volksvriend*, Jan. 17, 1924 (Correspondent, Okaton, S.D.).

31. "Biographical Sketch" in *Atlas of Sioux County*.

32. Bloemendaal, *Naar Amerika*, 77ff., 120ff.

33. G. Draayom, "Schetsen uit het Verleden. Herinneringen aan vroeger Dagen in Sioux County," *De Volksvriend*, May 22, 1924.

34. T. Wayenberg, "Sioux Center, Iowa," Jubileumnummer, De Volksvriend, Sept. 19, 1895.

35. Pella's Weekblad, Apr. 27, 1923. De Sprinkhanenplaag [The Grasshopper Plague].

36. Rev. J. De Pree, "Some Reminiscences of the early Settlement of Sioux Center," Atlas of Sioux County.

37. Bloemendaal, Naar Amerika, 124.

38. De Pree, "Reminiscences."

39. Draayom, "Schetsen uit het Verleden," De Volksvriend, Sept. 20, 1923.

40. E. O. Plumbe, "The History of Rock Township," Atlas of Sioux County.

41. Van der Meide, "Reminiscences."

42. Van Stigt, Geschiedenis van Pella, III, 66.

43. Van der Zee, Hollanders of Iowa, 145ff.; Van Hinte, "Nederland in Amerika, Orange City, 1870–1920," De Amsterdammer, Sept. 25, 1920.

44. A. J. Betten, Jr., "Geschiedenis," Jubileumnummer, De Volksvriend.

45. Van der Meide, "Orange City, Iowa," Jubileumnummer, De Volksvriend; Van der Zee, Hollanders of Iowa, 179, says that in 1871 Orange City had fifty inhabitants, in 1873 it had ninety-six. Not much for a county seat!

46. Van Stigt, Geschiedenis van Pella, III, 66.

47. Bloemendaal, Naar Amerika, 125ff. Also the reminiscences in the Sioux County Atlas are full of similar incidents, including the tale related by Van der Meide about "Mother Mouw."

48. Betten, "Geschiedenis." Van der Zee, Hollanders of Iowa, 180, reckons the number of inhabitants at 1,500 in 1873, but he is probably mistaken. On page 179 he gives the number for all of Sioux County for that same year as 2,872. See also p. 180.

49. De Pree, De Volksvriend, Oct. 7, 1920.

50. W. A. Bonger, Geloof en Misdaad (1913).

51. Betten, "Geschiedenis."

52. De Volksvriend, Jan. 17, 1924, includes this important data from the correspondent from Okaton, South Dakota, whose wife was one of the first in Sioux County.

53. Draayom, De Volksvriend, Nov. 8, 1923. N.52 indicates that the first worship service was not held in a sod hut as the Dr. thinks.

54. Van Stigt, Geschiedenis van Pella, III, 66.

55. John Engelsman, Historische Schets van de Eerste Gereformeerde Kerk van Orange City, Iowa, 1871–1921 (1921). The date of the organization in Betten's "Geschiedenis" is apparently incorrect, as is the number of families as given here and in the parallel account in the Atlas of Sioux County.

56. H. E. Dosker, "De Leiders der Colonizatie," an extremely interesting article in Historical Souvenir, 19.

57. Gleysteen, "Reminiscence," Atlas of Sioux County.

58. Betten, "Geschiedenis."

59. De Pree, "Reminiscences."

60. Engelsman, Historische Schets.

61. Van der Meide, "Orange City, Iowa." Data furnished by Dominie Breen.

62. Van der Meide, "Orange City, Iowa."

63. M. Cohen Stuart, Zes Maanden in Amerika (2 vols., 1875), II, 25ff.

64. Ross, Changing America, 146.,

65. Draayom in his "Schetsen uit het Verleden" uses both expressions readily, and refers especially to the "heroines." See De Volksvriend, July 12, 1923 and Mar. 20, 1924.

66. Van der Zee, Hollanders of Iowa, 136–138.

67. Betten, "Geschiedenis."

68. Van der Meide, "Reminiscence." Also see Betten, "Geschiedenis."

69. Betten, "Geschiedenis."

70. Van der Zee, Hollanders of Iowa, 180; 402, n.153.

71. Betten, "Geschiedenis."

72. Van der Zee, Hollanders of Iowa, 237, especially also the article, "Eeen en twintig jaren" in Jubileumnummer, De Volksvriend.

73. Van der Zee, Hollanders of Iowa, 239ff.

74. Ibid., 160ff.

75. [N.75 is missing in the original due to a typographical error].

76. Van der Meide, "Reminiscences"; Draayom, De Volksvriend, Sept. 20, 1923.

77. Van der Zee, Hollanders of Iowa, 164, 171.

78. Bloemendaal, Naar Amerika, 144. See especially also the "Reminiscences" of Van der Meide and Gleysteen in the Atlas of Sioux County.

79. Betten, "Geschiedenis."

80. Bloemendaal, Naar Amerika, 145, 140, and Betten, "Geschiedenis."

81. Bloemendaal, Naar Amerika, 142.

82. Draayom, De Volksvriend, Dec. 6, 1923.

83. Gleysteen, "Reminiscence."

84. Van der Zee, Hollanders of Iowa. 171.

85. Ibid., 172–173.

86. Draayom, De Volksvriend, Dec. 6, 1923.

87. Van Stigt, Geschiedenis van Pella, I, 96; III, 61ff.

88. X., "Herinneringen"; Van der Zee, Hollanders of Iowa, 150ff.

89. Ibid.

90. Ibid., 178. A walking stick with an inscription was then given to Hospers.

91. Ibid., 164–169. Information and data on help and support from other areas are quoted from this writing.

92. This is abundantly clear from the many personal names given in the *Sioux County Atlas*, where everyone's property is recorded on the ground plat.

93. Dr. H. Hospers, article published in *De Volksvriend* (Oct. 7, 1920) at the time of the fifty-year celebration.

94. D. Versteeg, *De Pelgrim-Vaders van het Westen* (1886), 184.

95. *Corwin's Manual* (1902), 335.

96. Bloemendaal, *Naar Amerika*, 142.

97. Van der Zee, *Hollanders of Iowa*, 169.

98. Bloemendaal, *Naar Amerika*, 146.

99. De Pree, "Reminiscences"; Cf. Draayom, *De Volksvriend*, May 1, 1924.

100. Draayom, *De Volksvriend*, Dec. 6, 1923. The figure, ⅓, I found in the very accurate writing by George Schnücker, *Die Ostfriesen in Amerika* (1917), 256.

101. Bloemendaal, *Naar Amerika*, 145, 142.

102. Draayom, *De Volksvriend*, Mar. 20, 1924.

103. Draayom, *De Volksvriend*, Apr. 24, 1924.

104. F. J. Turner, *The Frontier in American History* (1921), 319.

105. P. L. Haworth, *The United States in our Own Times 1865–1920* (1920), 118.

106. G. Myers, *Geschichte der groszen amerikanischen Vermögen* (Vol. 2, 1923), 450–452ff.

107. Haworth, *United States*, 159ff.

108. Ibid., 160.

109. Draayom, *De Volksvriend*, Apr. 24, May 8, 1924. The latter issue contains an account of the "kip-lerzen" meeting.

110. Draayom, *De Volksvriend*, Apr. 24, 1924.

111. J. Van 't Lindenhout, *Zes weken tusschen de Wielen of De Hollanders in Amerika* (1886), 187.

Chapter 2   The Growth of the Sioux County Colony To About 1895

1. E. J. G. Bloemendaal, *Naar Amerika* (1911), 139ff.

2. J. P., *Naar Amerika!* (1882), 45.

3. Gleysteen, "Reminiscence," *Standard Historical Atlas of Sioux County, Iowa*.

4. Betten, "Geschiedenis," Jubileumnummer, *De Volksvriend*, Sept. 19. 1895.

5. Jacob Van der Zee, *The Hollanders of Iowa* (1912); 398, n.134; 156.

6. Ibid., 157ff.

7. Ibid., 185. Compare with great caution the various articles concerning these townships in the *Atlas of Sioux County* and *De Volksvriend*, Feb. 21, 1924.

8. Van der Zee, *Hollanders of Iowa*, 186, 189. The total number of Netherlanders can not be determined with exactitude because the American statistics record all those born here as Americans. Only those born in a foreign country are listed separately with the country of origin.

9. Draayom, "Schetsen uit het Verleden," *De Volksvriend*, Feb. 21, 1924.

10. Articles on "Capel Township" and "Welcome Township" in the *Atlas of Sioux County*. There appear to be some very strange inconsistencies between the accounts in the *Atlas* and the things we were told in our national history. See the article on "Capel Township."

11. G. Van Peursem, "Maurice," Jubileumnummer, *De Volksvriend*.

12. James De Pree, "West Branch Township and the Town of Sioux Center" in the *Atlas of Sioux County*. North Sioux was the original name of the railroad village.

13. J. P., *Naar Amerika!*, 46.

14. Draayom, "Schetsen," *De Volksvriend*, Feb. 21, 1924.

15. Kl. J. Tiemersma, *Drie Jaren in Amerika* (1894), 53ff.

16. J. Dykstra, "Middleburgh," Jubileumnummer, *De Volksvriend*.

17. Betten, "Geschiedenis"; Van der Zee, *Hollanders of Iowa*, 182.

18. Tiemersma, *Drie Jaren*, 28.

19. Bloemendaal, *Naar Amerika*, 146.

20. J. P., *Naar Amerika!* 47.

21. J. Van 't Lindenhout, *Zes weken tusschen de Wielen of De Hollanders in Amerika* (1886), 176.

22. Ibid., 206, 203.

23. A. Van der Meide, "Orange City," Jubileumnummer, *De Volksvriend*.

24. Tiemersma, *Drie Jaren*, 67, 47.

25. Gleysteen, "Alton," Jubileumnummer, *De Volksvriend*.

26. Van 't Lindenhout, *Zes weken*, 184.

27. S. J. Menning, "Hospers," Jubileumnummer, *De Volksvriend*.

28. Gleysteen, "Reminiscence."

29. Gleysteen, "Alton;" Tiemersma, *Drie Jaren*, 67.

30. D. Haarsma, "Rock Valley," Jubileum-

nummer, *De Volksvriend*. Included in this is also an article about Hull.

31. F. Von Richthofen, *Vorlesungen über Allgemeine Siedlungs- und Verkehrsgeographie*, (1908), 259.

32. Kurt Hassert, *Die Städte geographisch betrachtet* (1907), 2. Hassert differentiates between three main types: the small hamlet, the village, and the city.

33. Van Stigt, *Geschiedenis van Pella*, III, 119.

34. De Pree, "West Branch Township."

35. John Engelsman, *Historische Schets*. The inaccurate data given in the Jubileumnummer is corrected here and also one error listed in *Corwin's Manual*, 188, (Maurice) an error which also appears in the 1922 ed., p. 664.

36. W. Van Rooyen, "Newkirk," Jubileumnummer, *De Volksvriend*.

37. Dijkstra, "Middleburgh."

38. De Pree, "West Branch Township."

39. J. P., *Naar Amerika!* 47.

40. Van 't Lindenhout, *Zes weken*, 205.

41. De Pree, "West Branch Township." T. Wayenberg, "Sioux Center," Jubileumnummer, *De Volksvriend*.

42. Van Peursem, "Maurice."

43. P. Vidal de la Blache, *Principes de Géographie Humaine* (1922), 172.

44. Van 't Lindenhout, *Zes weken*, 204.

45. Examine the various local accounts in Jubileumnummer, *De Volksvriend*.

46. Draayom, *De Volksvriend*, June 19, 26, 1924.

47. Tiemersma, *Drie Jaren*, 42ff., 47.

48. Van 't Lindenhout, *Zes weken*, 205.

49. Tiemersma, *Drie Jaren*, 10; Van der Meide, "Orange City."

50. Engelsman, *Historische Schets*.

51. F. J. Lohr, "Onze publieke School," Jubileumnummer, *De Volksvriend*; Van der Zee, *Hollanders of Iowa*, 280; Tiemersma, *Drie Jaren*, 106.

52. Betten, "Geschiedenis," J. A. De Spelder, "Wording der Akademie," Jubileumnummer, *De Volksvriend*.

53. Gleysteen, "Reminiscence."

54. J. F. Zwemer, "De Ontwikkeling," Jubileumnummer, *De Volksvriend*.

55. Van der Zee, *Hollanders of Iowa*, 280–81. Betten, "Geschiedenis."

56. "Een en twintig Jaren," Jubileumnummer, *De Volksvriend*.

57. Van der Zee, *Hollanders of Iowa*, 254.

58. Ibid., 243.

59. Wayenberg, "Sioux Center," and Van Peursem, "Maurice."

60. Tiemersma, *Drie Jaren*, 78.

61. Ibid., 16–17, 24.

62. Wm. E. West, "Buncombe Township and Hawarden," *Atlas of Sioux County*. The italics are mine.

Chapter 3   *A Colonization in Virginia that Failed*

1. Henry E. Dosker, *Levensschets van Rev. A. C. Van Raalte* (1893), 288ff., 291. There are errors in this chapter; events of 1868 are attributed to 1870 and vice versa. On p. 289 Dosker seems to indicate that Van Raalte had never been in Kansas, but on p. 305 he implies that he had. Nor is it clear who caused Van Raalte to be interested in the East.

2. Ibid., 290.

3. Ibid.

4. M. H. Jansen, *Stoomvaart op Amerika. Goedkooper brood en Meer werk* (1869).

5. M. H. Jansen, *Een Brug over den Oceaan* (1869), 47.

6. Dosker, *Levensschets*, 291–292.

7. Ibid., 291.

8. S. P. L'Honoré Naber, *Het Leven van een Vloothouder* (1925), 420.

9. Jansen, *Een Brug over den Oceaan*, 28–30.

10. Dosker, *Levensschets*, 292.

11. See n.8; Letter of the Secretary of the Netherlands Economic History Archives.

12. Jansen, *Stoomvaart op Amerika*.

13. *Corwin's Manual* (1902), 215–216, 956, 1027.

14. I found this very important data in a casual account in M. Cohen Stuart's *Zes Maanden in Amerika* (2 vols., 1875), II, 265. Here Cohen Stuart refers to Scheffelin as "our friend."

15. Dosker, *Levensschets*, 292.

16. Douglas Freeman, "Virginia," in Ernest Gruening, *These United States, A Symposium* (2 vols., 1923–1924), II, 2.

17. I. Bowman, *Forest Physiography* (1912), "Piedmont Plateau," 623ff.

18. Ibid., "Fall Line," 499.

19. J. Russell Smith, *Industrial and Commercial Geography* (1913), 377.

20. Bowman, *Forest Physiography*, "Fall Line," 499.

21. Dosker, *Levensschets*, 292.

22. Bowman, *Forest Physiography*, "Soils of the Piedmont Plateau," 633ff.

23. Cohen Stuart, *Zes Maanden*, II, 265ff.

24. Ibid., II, 268–269.

25. Ibid., II, 269.

26. Ibid., II.

27. Freeman, "Virginia," 11.

28. J. Russell Smith, North America (1925), 170.

29. Cohen Stuart, Zes Maanden, II, 269.

30. Russell Smith, North America, 186.

31. Ibid., 184.

32. Cohen Stuart, Zes Maanden, II, 270–273.

33. Dosker, Levensschets, 291.

34. Ibid., 292.

35. Beets, De Chr. Geref. Kerk in N.-A. (1918), 126.

36. Corwin's Manual (1902), 532.

37. Dosker, Levensschets, 293.

38. Cohen Stuart, Zes Maanden, II, 266.

39. Beets, Chr. Geref. Kerk, 126.

40. Dosker, Levensschets, 293.

41. Cohen Stuart, Zes Maanden, II, 267ff.

42. Ibid., II, 275–277.

43. Dosker, Levensschets, 294.

44. R. T. Kuiper, Eene Stem uit Amerika over Amerika (1881).

45. Cohen Stuart, Zes Maanden, I, 303.

46. Dosker, Levensschets, 310ff. and 316ff.

Chapter 4   *Daughter Colonies in Michigan, Nebraska, Kansas, Minnesota, Wisconsin, and Illinois*

1. Corwin's Manual (1902), 935–1044. Unless otherwise indicated, all data concerning the congregations are taken from this source. Data on further colonization is sporadic and not consistent. Various church sites cannot be found on the maps if they are not within an area served by a post office. This is the case, for example, with Harderwijk, which consists of scattered farms focused around a church.

2. Corwin's Manual, 402.

3. This material is from E. N. Van Halen. I found this clipping in the scrapbook of Dr. H. Beets in Grand Rapids.

4. Data concerning the Christian Reformed Church are taken from the Yearbook of the Christian Reformed Church in America (Grand Rapids, 1925).

5. Statistics concerning families in the Reformed churches, practically all composed of Dutch families, are taken from Michigan en zijn Hulpbronnen, 45.

6. R. T. Kuiper, Eene Stem uit Amerika over Amerika (1881), 116ff.

7. L. A. Chase, Rural Michigan (1922), 7, 45.

8. Ibid., 46.

9. Kuiper, Eene Stem, 116ff.

10. De Grondwet, Feb. 1, 1921.

11. Kuiper, Eene Stem, 141.

12. H. Lucas and J. H. Eppink, Nieuwe Hollandsche Nederzetting in Michigan gelegen, in Missaukee en Osceola Counties (1882), 1ff. Most of the following statistics are taken from this brochure.

13. It is suprising that Lucas and Eppink do not mention pine trees. This was due to their being agents and thus interested parties; so it is quite understandable. J. P. in Naar Amerika! (1882), 26, mentions the pine forests, which Chase describes as the chief reason.

14. J. P., Naar Amerika!, 27.

15. Chase, Rural Michigan, 46. Kalkaska County, north of Missaukee, had 8,097 residents in 1910 but only 5,577 in 1920!

16. Kuiper, Eene Stem, 116ff.

17. Corwin's Manual, 1038, 1024, etc. See headings under "Churches." Cf. 1922 ed., 714.

18. Lucas and Eppink, Nieuwe Hollandsche Nederzetting, 2.

19. S. R. Steinmetz, Die Philosophie des Krieges (1907), 256.

20. Ibid., 256.

21. Willa Cather, "Nebraska" in Ernest Gruening, These United States, A Symposium (2 vols., 1923–1924), II, 140.

22. Corwin's Manual, 791.

23. Jacob Van der Zee, The Hollanders of Iowa (1912), 199. Corwin's Manual, 1019, where Dragt is shown as the first preacher, 1894–96, whereas in the chapter "The Ministry" the year 1895–96 is given.

24. H. Beets, De Chr. Ger. Kerk in N.A. (1918), 191. The missionaries worked also among the Ost Frisians as well as among those from Bentheim.

25. William Allen White, "Kansas," in Gruening, These United States, I, 2.

26. Henry E. Dosker, Levensschets van Rev. A. C. Van Raalte (1893), 289, 305. Dosker is not clear on this and the same is true of J. A. Wormser, Een Schat in aarden Vaten I. Het Leven van Albertus Christiaan Van Raalte (1915), 227, 235, who follows Dosker closely and uncritically.

27. Corwin's Manual, 1032. See the Rand-McNally map of Kansas.

28. Corwin's Manual, 1026.

29. Van der Zee, *Hollanders of Iowa*, 199, 175. But by contrast compare G. F. Huizinga, *What the Dutch Have Done in the West of the United States* (1909), 33.

30. Van der Zee, *Hollanders of Iowa*, 174.

31. H. Beets, "The Editor in Sunflower State," *The Banner*, Sept. 5, 1924. Beets erroneously names these men as the first Dutch settlers in Phillips County, Kansas. They were preceded by others from Iowa and Michigan, however.

32. Beets mentions 1883 as the year of establishment (see n.31). In the Christian Reformed Church *Yearbooks* of 1919–21 as well as in the *Yearbook* of 1925, the date of 1885 is given. It is interesting to note this in relation to the "competing" Reformed Church community. Even dates can tell a tale!

33. Russell Smith, *North America*, 409ff.

34. Van der Zee, *Hollanders of Iowa*, 123.

35. Ibid., 199.

36. I. Bowman, *Forest Physiography* (1912), "Driftless Area," 494ff.

37. E. J. G. Bloemendaal, *Naar Amerika* (1911), 88.

38. According to an account in *De Volksvriend*, Sept. 9, 1920, and Oct. 25, 1923.

39. T. Tillema, "Korte Levensbeschrijving," *De Volksvriend*, June 9, 1921.

40. It is not clear from this account that Tillema was the founder of this Frisian colony, but Prof. |Albert| Raap of Hope College—being Frisian hismelf—informed me of this and also that he enjoyed the Frisian language there. In three days during Prof. Raap's stay, the hamlet of Friesland pledged $2,555 for Hope College. Also see *De Hope*, June 1, 1920.

41. See *Yearbooks*.

42. E. P. Beaudette-Neil, *Thornton Township, Cook County, Illinois* (1921), 113. Deals with the dispersion of the Dutch element and, among others, with the founding of Phoenix, Riverdale, Lansing, etc.

43. Ibid., 93.

44. Ibid. See the biographies of the onion growers in the Calumet area.

45. *Corwin's Manual*, 958. Here the name of Rev. L. J. Hulst seems to have been omitted on purpose. However, see p. 535.

46. Lammert J. Hulst, *Drie en Zestig Jaren Prediker* (1913), 109ff.

47. Albert Raap, "Good-Better-Best!" *De Hope*, Oct. 19, 1920, p. 8.

48. Our Consul-General in Chicago, J. Vennema, wrote me on Sept. 15, 1920, that in the largely Ost Frisian Baileyville there is a Dutch colony.

49. George Schnücker, *Die Ostfriesen in Amerika* (1917), 91ff. and especially 96, 114, 115, 117, 118, 119, 205, etc.

50. Schnücker, *Ostfriesen*, 194ff.

51. *De Grondwet*, Sept. 28, 1920. An advertisement asked for a person to head a colonization. Money would be contributed for the building of a church!

52. I am grateful for this information to Prof. Raap of Holland, Michigan, and Mr. J. Van Tijen, at that time residing in Port Arthur, Texas.

53. Beets, *Chr. Geref. Kerk*, 29.

54. G. Van den Elsen, *Twintig Brieven uit Amerika* (1907), 53.

55. Ibid., 54.

56. Ibid., 53, 59. Apparently the man from Winterswijk had been a Protestant.

57. Ibid., 88.

58. Ibid., 78.

59. Konrad Bercovici, *On New Shores* (1925), 176.

60. Van der Zee, *Hollanders of Iowa*, 195 and 404, n.168.

Chapter 5   *Granddaughters in the Dakotas and Minnesota*

1. P. L. Haworth, *The United States in our own Times, 1865–1920* (1920), 122.

2. G. Draayom, "Schetsen uit het Verleden," *De Volksvriend*, June 19, 1924.

3. N. J. Den Tex, *Amerikaansche Spoorwegen op de Amsterdamsche Beurs* (1873). On p. 43 there is a reference to this fierce rivalry. The Milwaukee and St. Paul is now the Chicago, Milwaukee and St. Paul.

4. J. Knuppe, *Land en dollars in Minnesota en Dakota* (1883), 4ff., 11.

5. E. J. G. Bloemendaal, *Naar Amerika* (1911), 147. This confirms Knuppe's comment: "One could obtain two 160-acre tracts of land for nothing."

6. E. A. Ross, *Changing America, Studies in Contemporary Society* (1912), 146–148.

7. Hayden Carruth, "South Dakota" in Ernest Gruening, *These United States, A Symposium* (2 vols., 1923–1924), I, 269ff.

8. Bloemendaal, *Naar Amerika*, 193.

9. Walt Whitman, *Leaves of Grass and Democratic Vistas* (1916), 194.

10. This trek can be deduced with reasonable certainty from the organization of mission stations and churches as related in "The Ministry" and "The Churches" in *Cor-*

win's *Manual* and in the yearbooks of the Christian Reformed Church. The definitive history of the Dakota colonists, as well as those in Nebraska and Kansas and other places, must still be written.

11. I am thankful for this to Dr. H. Beets, with whom I had an interview on Sept. 1, 1923, and also to a letter from him dated July 13, 1926. There is no reference to this "leadership" in the report of H. A. Kuipers (see following note).

12. H. A. Kuipers, "History of the Platte, S. D., Christian Reformed Church," *The Banner*, May 2, 1924.

13. I found a record of this family in "Staat der landverhuizingen" of 1847 in the Nieuw Archief in Amsterdam. See the facsimile. In 1847 the family consisted of the parents and six children. See K. Van Stigt, *Geschiedenis van Pella, Iowa en Omgeving* (3 vols., 1897), I, 103. I wish to thank Dr. H. Beets for the account of their arrival in the Harrison colony, given to me on Sept. 1, 1923.

14. Bloemendaal, *Naar Amerika*, 147–148, 169.

15. Ibid.

16. Carruth, "South Dakota," 266–267.

17. George Schnücker, *Die Ostfriesen in Amerika* (1917), 244.

18. *Corwin's Manual*, "The Ministry" and "The Churches."

19. H. Beets, *De Chr. Geref. Kerk in N.-A.* (1918), 191.

20. Ibid., 194.

21. Kuiper, "History of the Platte." See n.12 and cf. *Jaarboekje ten dienste der Christelijk Gereformeerde Kerk in Noord-Amerika* (1921).

22. J., "Korte Historische Schets van de Gemeente New Holland, So. Dak.," in *Jaarboekje ten dienste der Christelijk Gereformeerde Kerk*, 147.

23. Ibid.; Kuipers, "History of the Platte."

24. Kuipers, "History of the Platte."

25. Christian Reformed Church in America *Yearbook*, 1925.

26. From a very interesting conversation which I had with Professor [Albert] Raap at his home on Aug. 8, 1921, in Holland, Michigan. Professor Raap is a native of Wanswerd. He is no longer affiliated with Hope College and is thinking of moving to Florida—a typical American trait!

27. Schnücker, *Ostfriesen*, 260ff. "Die Kolonie bei Clara City. Chippewa County, Minnesota."

28. Ibid., 268. This parallels Van der Zee, *Hollanders of Iowa*, 204.

29. *Corwin's Manual*, 953. He gives 1897 as the year of founding; I am more inclined to follow Schnücker, who has always been very precise.

30. Bloemendaal, *Naar Amerika*, 173.

31. Van der Zee, *Hollanders of Iowa*, 204; G. F. Huizinga, *What the Dutch Have Done in the West of the United States* (1909), 34.

32. According to Bloemendaal, *Naar Amerika*, 182.

33. Den Tex, *Amerikaansche Spoorwegen*, 39, cf. 37. In this connection Den Tex (p. 22) refers to these "barons" as "great thieves."

34. Knuppe, *Land en dollars*, 29.

35. Bloemendaal, *Naar Amerika*, 170ff.

36. "Evidently," because Bloemendaal mentions a railroad running to the north and because some years later while enroute to South Dakota he traveled through this area and came through Leota and the more northerly situated Holland. The main point is, however, that the Bethel mission station was established in Leota already in 1891.

37. Bloemendaal, *Naar Amerika*, 191.

38. Ibid., 172ff, 179.

39. *De Volksvriend*, Feb. 3, 1921, gives an account of the death of Mrs. H. Daukenton.

40. These years denote the establishment of the Reformed and Christian Reformed churches. These usually followed so soon upon the founding of the colonies that we can consider them the years of settlement.

Chapter 6   *Emigration Since the Second Half of the Nineteenth Century*

1. Baron Johan d'Aulnis de Bourouill, "De Ontwikkeling der Volkswelvaart" in *Eene Halve Eeuw 1848–1898 Nederland*, (2 vols., 1898), I, 326.

2. R. P. A. Dozy, "Lectuur over Noord-Amerika, "*De Gids*, June, 1870.

3. H. Hartogh Heys van Zouteveen, *Californië Hulpbronnen en Toekomst, met het oog op een landverhuizing van Nederlanders derwaarts* (1871).

4. J. A. Obreen, *Opwekking tot Landverhuizing* (1871), 23.

5. H. Blink and S. Koenen, "A general review of economic history" in *De Nederlandsche Landbouw in het Tijdvak, 1813–1913* (1913), 17.

6. C. J. Sickesz van de Cloese and F. B. Löhnis, "Landbouw en Veeteelt" in *Eene*

Halve Eeuw 1848–1898 Nederland, I (1898), 251–252.

7. J. H. Rössing, *Verdwijnend Oud-Amsterdam* (1916), 29ff.

8. d'Aulnis de Bourouill, "Ontwikkeling," I, 351. Compare this with R. Schuiling. *Nederland; handboek der Aardrijkskunde* (Zwolle, 1915), 726ff.

9. Dr. R. A. Gorter and C. W. De Vries, "Gegevens omtrent den Kinderarbeid in Nederland," *Economisch Historisch Jaarboek,* VIII (1922), 30.

10. Ibid., 34.

11. Ibid., 200.

12. Ibid., 212. This report was prepared for the head of the Overijsel Bureau of Statistics. Note the figures on page 215.

13. Ibid., 233.

14. Professor |Albert| Raap, of Holland, Mich., related that Professor Boers, who had come from Overisel (Mich.), not only enjoyed Cremer's novels but was so interested in the "dialect" that he used it in writing letters.

15. Robert Cloutman Dexter, "Rhode Island" in Ernest Gruening, *These United States, A Symposium* (2 vols., 1923–1924), II, 280. In the past few years child labor here has increased by 6 percent. From 13 to 14 percent of all the children between ages ten and fifteen are being exploited in this state. In Woonsocket and Pawtucket the figures are 18.7 percent and 17.3 percent. Thousands of women work in the factories at night. Tuberculosis and asthma are common. Just as bad is the exploitation of children in home industries. See Dexter, in Gruening, II, 285.

16. Gorter and De Vries, "Kinderarbeid," 37.

17. J. J. Hasselman, *Eenige beschouwingen omtrent Kolonsatie* (1857).

18. Obreen, *Opwekking,* 21.

19. Hartogh Heys van Zouteveen, *Californië's Hulpbronnen,* VII.

20. I. J. Brugmans, *De Arbeidersklasse in Nederland in de 19ᵉ eeuw* (± 1813–1870), (1925). The figure " ± 1850," found on page 183 also includes laborers to about 1870 and that is why I cite it.

21. A. Caminetti, (*Bureau of Immigration*) *Annual Report of the Commissioner General of Immigration to the Secretary of Labor* (1920). These statistics have only limited value, although they come much closer to the reality; as noted before, some of our statistics also have but limited value.

22. Fr. Ratzel, *Politische Geographie* (3rd ed., 1903), 270.

23. George Schnüker, *Die Ostfriesen in Amerika* (1917), 5, 10.

24. G. Bonwetsch, *Geschichte der deutschen Kolonien an der Wolga* (1919), 117.

25. X., "Overzicht van de Hedendaagsche Landverhuizing," *De Economist,* II (1869), 630.

26. Bloemendaal, *Naar Amerika,* 32.

27. Ibid., 89–90, 104–105.

28. N.A.S.M., *Nederlandsch-Amerikaansche Gids en Tolk* (1887).

29. Jacob Van der Zee, *The Hollanders of Iowa* (1912), 150ff., includes large sections of Hospers' reports. Also see pages 397–398, notes 130 and 131.

30. Iowa Immigratie Commissie, *Iowa, Het Land Der Emigranten* (Pella, 1870), 115.

31. B., "Uit de grijze Oudheid," *Christian Reformed Church of America Yearbook* (1925), 133.

32. R. T. Kuiper, *Eene Stem uit Amerika over Amerika,* 11ff.

33. *Jaarboekje ten dienste der Chr. Geref. Kerk in Noord-Amerika* (1921), 135.

34. W. P. De Jonge, *Eene Stem uit de Gereformeerde Kerk in Amerika* (1882), 1–8. The years indicate their arrival in America. I have used these annual figures from this booklet as well as those from some biographies.

35. Jakob Noordewier, *Een Tachtig-Jarige* (1898), 23.

36. I found this total of seventy in *Neerlandia* (monthly Nederlandsch Verbond), Nov. 1917.

37. *Corwin's Manual,* 406.

38. M. Cohen Stuart, *Zes Maanden in Amerika* (2 vols., 1875), I, 11.

39. N. H. Dosker, *De Hollandsche Gereformeerde Kerk in Amerika* (1888), 201.

40. H. P. G. Quack, "De Zwijndrechtsche Broederschap," *De Gids,* Aug. 1892, p. 259ff.

41. Van Der Zee, *Hollanders of Iowa,* 159.

42. Frank I. Kooyman, "De Dageraad der Nederlandsche Zending," in *De Utah-Nederlander* (Salt Lake City), June 30, 1921. Also, see K., "Een heugelijk feit," *De Utah-Nederlander,* Mar. 31, 1921.

43. Kooyman, "De Dageraad," *De Utah-Nederlander,* June 30, 1921.

44. Lammer's short account in *De Utah-Nederlander,* Mar. 10, 1921.

45. *De Utah-Nederlander,* Mar. 7, 1921. Also see H. Bouwman's "Foreword" in I. Van Dellen, *Het Mormonisme* (Kampen, 1911).

46. *De Utah-Nederlander,* Mar. 8, 1923.

47. *De Utah-Nederlander,* Aug. 9, 1923. Some of their children were already living there.

48. Letter from E. Neuteboom to W. O. Van Eyck, Holland, Michigan, dated Feb. 12, 1920; it was written in Ogden, Utah, and is now in my possession.

49. *De Utah-Nederlander,* July 14, 1921.

50. W. F. Andriessen, "Is Emigratie naar de Ver. Staten van N.-A. nog langer aanbevelenswaardig?" *De Economist,* 1892, 1.

51. Sickesz van de Cloese and Löhnis, "Landbouw en Veeteelt," I, 252. Also see Blink and Koenen in *Nederlandsche Landbouw,* 18.

52. S. Koenen, *Inleiding tot de Landhuishoudkunde* (1924), Vol. 2, "De Landbouwcrisis van 1878–1895."

53. Blink and Koenen, "Algemeen Overzicht," in *Nederlandsche Landbouw.*

54. *Weekblad voor het Kanton Bergum,* Mar. 25, 1882.

55. Ibid., Aug. 19, 1882.

56. Van der Zee, *Hollanders of Iowa,* 189.

57. R. Van Zinderen Bakker, "F. Domela Nieuwenhuis, Zijn eerste optreden in de wouddorpen van Friesland," in *Gedenkboek, ter gelegenheid van den 70-sten verjaardag van F. Domela Nieuwenhuis 31 December 1916* (1916), 3.

58. W. Giezen, "Domela Nieuwenhuis en zijn werken voor de Arbeidersbeweging in Friesland," ibid., 62.

59. Among others, see the *Weekblad voor het Kanton Bergum,* Jan. 8, 1881; Mar. 4, 1882; Apr. 2, 1881; Apr. 8, 1882.

60. Ibid., May 6, 1882.

61. G. Van der Veen, Letter, dated Menodat, Oct. 1882, reprinted in *Weekblad voor het Kanton Bergum,* Nov. 18, 1882.

62. R. Mayo Smith, *Emigration and Immigration: A Study in Social Science* (1912), 47.

63. S. F. Van Oss, *Amerikaansche Spoorwegwaarden* (1903), 31. This corroborates Mayo Smith, *Emigration and Immigration,* 67.

64. Mayo Smith, 46.

65. G. M. W. Jellinghaus, *De Staat Tegenover de Landverhuizing* (1894), 56.

66. M. G. De Boer, *De Holland-Amerika Lijn 1873–1923* (1923), 19.

67. Cohen Stuart, *Zes Maanden in Amerika,* I, 10–11.

68. De Boer, *Holland-Amerika Lijn,* 32ff., 35.

69. *Algemeen Handelsblad,* May 9, 1882. "The Hartkamp papers" in the Amsterdam Archives.

70. *Algemeen Handelsblad,* May 9, 1882.

71. De Boer, *Holland-Amerika Lijn,* 36. One should not forget that De Boer was the "official historian." The lure of "dispensation

from military service" is therefore not mentioned in this official commemoration book; I received this information as an oral clarification. Note the repeated complaints about Prins and Zwanenburg in the *Weekblad voor het Kanton Bergum,* 1881–1884.

72. De Boer, *Holland-Amerika Lijn,* 40.

73. J. Van Lonkhuijzen, *Argentinië, Een belangrijk land ook voor Nederlanders* (1908), 155ff. Jellinghaus, *Landverhuizing,* 51.

74. Andriessen, "Een en ander over Landverhuizing, "Mij. tot Nut van het Algemeen (1892), 10.

75. Andriessen, "Emigratie naar de Ver. Staten," 115ff., 76.

76. Jellinghaus, *Landverhuizing,* 86.

77. E. Pelz, *Kompas voor Landverhuizers,* 13. Comments of the translator who mentions "the society for emigration to Minnesota" located in Amsterdam and "the society to sponsor emigration of the indigent to Minnesota."

78. Jellinghaus, *Landverhuizing,* 132. In 1893 the "Society for the Promotion of Emigration" decided to unite in 1894 with a similar group in Friesland.

79. *Algemeen Handelsblad,* May 9, 1882.

80. Andriessen, "Een en ander over Landverhuizing," 4.

81. Annual reports for 1890, 1891, 1893, and 1896 of the Dutch Consul-General in New York, in *Verzameling Verslagen en Berichten,* which is available at the Library of the University of Amsterdam.

82. W. F. Gevers Deynoot, *Aanteekeningen op eene Reis door de Ver. Staten van Noord-Amerika en Canada in 1859* (1860), 134.

83. H. Beets, *De Chr. Geref. Kerk in N.-A.* (1918), 277.

84. Gorter and De Vries, "Gegevens omtrent den Kinderarbeid," 197.

85. Kl. J. Tiemersma, *Drie Jaren in Amerika* (1894), 95.

86. N.A.S.M.,   *Nederlandsch-Amerikaansche Gids en Tolk* (1887). See the back page.

87. These and similar comments were made to me by W. A. Van der Meulen, a son of Van der Meulen in an interesting letter written from Bergum on Feb. 3, 1922, and confirmed in a letter from Leeuwarden of May 18, 1926.

88. "Wie veel geld wil verdienen." Article in the *Weekblad voor het Kanton Bergum,* Feb. 25, 1882.

89. Ibid., May 20, 1882.

90. Ibid., Feb. 3, 10, 1883.

91. See advertisements in ibid., Mar. 5, 12, 1881.

92. See n.87 above.

93. *Weekblad voor het Kanton Bergum*, Feb. 18, 1882.

94. Ibid., July 1, 1882.

95. Ibid., Oct. 22 and 29, 1881.

96. Ibid., July 2, 1881. As in the case of much of T. G.'s work, it is unfinished.

97. Jellinghaus, *Landverhuizing*, 126.

98. Beets, *Chr. Geref. Kerk*, 189.

99. Ibid., 91.

100. Ibid., 188.

101. B. B. Haagsma, "Annual Report of the Netherlands Consulate at St. Louis for 1892," in *Verzameling Verslagen en Berichten.* See n.81 above.

102. S. Koenen, *Inleiding tot de Landhuishoudkunde* (1924), Pt. 2, Ch. 3.

103. H. Blink, *Handboek voor de Kennis van Nederland en Koloniën* (1922), 38–39.

104. E. C. Van Dorp, *Officieel Gedenboek*, edited by Prof. H. Brugmans (1923), 211, 219.

105. C. Te Lintum, *Nederland en de Indiën, gedurende de laatste kwart-eeuw* (1923), 15.

106. Caminetti, *Annual Report.* I have previously commented about the validity of these statistics. One should be particularly careful with the last-cited figures because "Dutch and Flemish" were lumped together. On the other hand, as compensation for these figures, during the World War hundreds of Dutch sailors jumped ship in America, attracted by the high wages that were available. These "stowaways" were not officially recorded.

107. K. Reyne, *De Uittocht der Plattelandsbevolking* (1904), 535.

108. H. Brugmans, *Het Nieuwe Amsterdam, van 1795 tot den tegenwoordigen Tijd* (1925), 244.

109. J. C. C. Sandberg, "Prae-advies voor de Nationale Vereeniging tegen de Werkloosheid, "*Tijdschrift van den Nederlandschen Werkloosheids-Raad*, No. 4, 1922.

110. Van Lonkhuijzen, *Argentinë*, "Introduction," vi.

111. S. L. Veenstra, "Emigratie en de Nederlandsche Vereeniging 'Landverhuizing,'" reprint from *Vragen van den Dag*, 29 (Dec. 31, 1914).

112. Blink, "Landverhuizing," in ibid., 30 (Mar. 1915), 191. "Appeared" because the Netherlands statistics are incomplete. Others have come to an entirely different conclusion. J. Van Hinte, "Werkloosheid en Emigratie," *Tijdschrift voor Economisch Geografie* (Dec. 15, 1922).

113. J. Maurer, *De Nederlandsche Boer tegenover de Landverhuizing* (1912), 29.

114. Blink, "Immigratie in Amerika en Emigratie uit Europa," *Vragen van den Dag* (1910), 625.

115. Letter from C. J. Van der P., dated "Aan boord van de Nieuw Amsterdam, June 29, 1923."

116. Sandberg, "Landverhuizing," *Vragen van den Dag*, 36 (Feb. 1921), 96.

117. Ibid.

118. Nederlandsche Vereeniging "Landverhuizing," Annual Report for 1920.

119. I. Lippincott, *Economic Development of the United States* (1924), 512. This includes a review of American tariffs, based on Frank Taussig's book, *The Tariff History of the United States* (6th ed., New York, 1914).

120. J. and W. C. B. De Fremery, *Californië.* Excerpts from *Consular Reports*, Vol. II, 1876–1890 (1891), 59ff.

121. J. Jansen, "Een verblijf in Amerika," *Vragen van den Dag*, 36 (Aug. 1920), 628.

122. For a more complete account see Ch. 14.

123. Annual Report of J. R. Planten, Consul-General at New York, May 16, 1901, in *Verzameling Verslagen en Berichten.*

124. Ibid., 1906.

125. Ibid., 1906–1907.

126. Maurer, *Nederlandsche Boer.*

127. Sandberg, "Landverhuizing," 90.

128. Nederlandsche Vereeniging "Landverhuizing," Twelfth Annual Report for the Year 1925, 8, 9.

129. Ibid.

130. *Weekblad voor het Kanton Bergum*, June 11, 1881.

131. Extrapolated from one of the many accounts of Consul [F. E. H.] Groenman, then serving as Consul-at-large.

132. Mari Joseph Brusse, "Onder de Menschen. Canadeesche Brieven." Article series in the *Nieuwe Rotterdamsche Courant* for 1924 and 1925. In particular, note the evening edition, section D, for Feb. 4, and morning edition, section B, for Feb. 15, 1925.

133. *The Tide of Immigration*, Chs. 21–31.

134. A. Siegfried, *Les Etats-Unis d'Aujourd'hui* (1927), 117.

135. S. R. Steinmetz, "Het nieuwe menschenras in Amerika," *Nederlandsch Tijdschrift voor Geneeskunde* (1911, Part IIA), 342ff., 251.

136. C. E. Martin and W. H. George, *American Government and Citizenship* (1927), 730. Compare this to the unsympathetic twist which Lothrop Stoddard gives in his *Re forging America, The Problem of Immigration* (1927), 205ff.

137. Siegfried, Les Etats-Unis, 114–117.
138. Stoddard, Re-forging America, 206.
139. Ibid., 222, n.10.
140. Martin and George, American Government, 728.
141. Stoddard, Re-forging America, 211.

Chapter 7   New Attempts at Colonization in Minnesota, Directly from the Netherlands

1. J. Van Boven, De Eerste Hollandsche Nederzetting in Colorado (1893), 66.
2. "Landverhuizing," De Economist, II (1869), 647ff.
3. W. F. Gevers Deynoot, Aanteekeningen op eene Reis door de Ver. Staten van Noord-Amerika en Canada in 1859 (1860), 126.
4. E. Pelz, Kompas voor Landverhuizers naar Algiers (ca. 1872), 97.
5. S. R. J. Van Schevichaven, De Noord-Amerikaansche Staat Minnesota (1872), 60.
6. J. H. Kloos, Minnesota (V. St. van N.-Am) in zijne hulpbronnen . . . (1867), 60.
7. Kloos, "Introduction," Minnesota (2nd ed., 1867).
8. Ibid., 7.
9. J. J. Pas, Benton County in den Staat Minnesota als een geschikte plaats voor eene Kolonie van Nederlandsche landbouwers (1868).
10. See De Hope, Sept. 14, 1920. "In Memoriam, Mrs. H. Van den Hoek."
11. Pelz, Kompas voor Landverhuizers, 104.
12. E. J. G. Bloemendaal, Naar Amerika (1911), 174. Bloemendaal refers to "Klaas" but really means Kloos. He further speaks of a colony "in the vicinity of Benton County" where, as had been reported, the first group settled. Pas was probably one of them and later part of the group went northeastward to Benton County.
13. Gevers Deynoot, Aanteekeningen, 129.
14. Van Schevichaven, Noord-Amerikaansche Staat Minnesota, 65.
15. Kloos, Minnesota, 20ff.
16. Van Schevichaven, Noord-Amerikaansche Staat Minnesota, 69.
17. Bloemendaal, Naar Amerika, 182.
18. G. Hewitt, Minnesota: Zijn voordeelen voor landverhuizers en kolonisten, (2nd ed., 1868).
19. Pelz, Kompas voor Landverhuizers, 85, 89, 143, 91.
20. Hewitt, Minnesota, "Een woord van den (anonymen) vertaler."

21. Van Schevichaven, Noord-Amerikaansche Staat Minnesota, 73.
22. J. Knuppe, Land en dollars in Minnesota en Dakota (1883).
23. Ibid, 28.
24. F. G. Geerling, Gids voor Emigranten naar de Vereenigde Staten van Noord-Amerika (n.d.).
25. Ibid., 2.
26. Ibid., 11.
27. N. J. Den Tex, "Naar Amerika," De Gids, IV (1874), 419, 452ff.
28. Van der Meulen, Weekblad voor het Kanton Bergum, Feb. 25, Mar. 11, 1882.
29. Sinclair Lewis, "Minnesota, the Norse State, in Ernest Gruening, These States, A Symposium (2 vols., 1923–1924), II, 26.

Chapter 8   Colonization Attempts in California

1. C. L. Plasberg, Californië . . . Beschrijving van dat Land (1849).
2. Anon., Gids naar California, 30.
3. "De Goudmijnen van Californië," Onze Tijd, II (1849), 189; C. Te Lintum, De Geschiedenis van het Amerikaansche Volk (1917), 84; Te Lintum, Geschiedenis van Handel en Bedrijf vooral in Nederland, 2nd ed. (1925), 169. Interesting, since I know no other "adventures" of other Dutch gold-seekers of that time.
4. A. B. Faust, Das Deutschtum in den Vereinigten Staaten in seiner geschichtlichen Entwickelung (1912), 421.
5. James Wharton, In and Out of the Old Missions of California (1922), 24, 25, 156ff.; and J. Smeaton Chase, California Coast Trails (1913), 84, where Dana is cited.
6. J. Russell Smith, North America (1925), 572.
7. Onze Tijd, II (1849), 190. James and W. C. B. De Fremery, Californië, Excerpts from the consular Annual Reports, I, 1864–1874, 25.
8. De Fremery, Californië, Excerpts, II, 1876–90, 88.
9. Russell Smith, North America, 573.
10. De Fremery, Californië, II, 76ff.: I, 25ff.
11. De Fremery, Californië, II, 76ff., "Scheepvaart."
12. Anon., Gids naar Californië, 27.
13. Russell Smith, North America, 572.
14. Plasberg, Californië, 34ff. discusses the routes, just as the anonymous author of Gids naar Californië, 34.
15. De Fremery, Californië, I, under the title "Immigratie," 1864.

16. H. Hartogh Heys van Zouteveen, *Californië's Hulpbronnen en Toekomst* (1871), 79, gives the complete board. See also n.85.

17. De Fremery, *Californië*, I, "Immigratie," 1870, 1873, 1874.

18. Russell Smith, *North America*, 592.

19. Anon., *Gids naar California*, Preface.

20. R. P. A. Dozy, "Studiën over de Vereenigde Staten," *De Gids* (May 1871), 432ff.

21. J. A. Obreen, *Opwekking tot Landverhuizing naar de Republiek der Ver. Staten van Noord-Amerika* (1871), lists on pp. 23–24 this advertisement and gives at the same time the impression that that is how he learned about the plans for the colonization attempt in California.

22. Hartogh Heys van Zouteveen, *Californië's Hulpbronnen*, 77ff., which gives in the appendices the first and second plans.

23. Ibid., 79.

24. Ibid., pref., vii.

25. Dozy, "Studiën," 432. Compare with Hartogh Heys van Zouteveen, *Californië's Hulpbronnen*, 73.

26. Obreen, *Amerika. Land en Volk* (1872), 107; H. B. Van Daalen, "Californië (Reprint from *Onze Tijd* [1872], 74–76.)

27. Or would the previously mentioned investments by Dutch families in the San Francisco Savings Union refer to these would-be colonists? And was it also for them that the Dutch Nederlandsche Onderlinge Hulp Vereeniging was founded?

28. Hartogh Heys van Zouteveen, *Californië's Hulpbronnen*, 19ff., 45ff.

29. J. F. Niermeyer, "Indrukken van Amerika, VIII. Californisch Nederland," *Nieuws van den Dag*, Jan. 30, 1913.

30. Letter from Hotel National, Montreux, Switzerland, Dec. 11, 1923.

31. Niermeyer, "Indrukken," VIII.

32. De Fremery, *Californië*, II, "Varia 1887."

33. H. P. N. Muller, "Uit [In] het Verre Westen," reprint from *De Tijdspiegel*, May 1, 1905.

34. P. J. Van Löben Sels, *Uit Californië*. An interesting correspondence in *Hou en Trouw*, January, 1905.

35. A letter sent to me from Hotel National, Montreux, Switzerland, Dec. 11, 1923. From this letter it also becomes clear that the protest of P. J. Van Löben Sels in the Jan. 1905 issue of *Hou en Trouw* against a letter from Van Coenen Torchiana in the same periodical of Oct. 1904 had been somewhat premature!

36. Muller, *Uit [In] het Verre Westen*.

37. Letter from Montreux, Dec. 11, 1923. See n.35.

38. *Verzameling Verslagen en Berichten*, Annual Report for 1904 of the consulgeneral G. J. G. Marsily at San Francisco.

39. James G. Wharton, *In and Out of the Old Missions of California* (1922), 77.

40. Faust, *Das Deutschtum* (*Entwickelung*) (1912), 421, and *Das Deutschtum* (*Bedeutung*) (1912), 46.

41. Hartogh Heys van Zouteveen, *Californië's Hulpbronnen*, gives a description of Anaheim. Cf. also n.50 below.

42. I. Bowman, *Forest Physiography* (1912), 180.

43. A. Supan, *Grundzüge der Physischen Erdkunde* (5th ed., 1911), 542, 716.

44. Bowman, *Forest Physiography*, 181ff.

45. T. J. Van Outeren, et.al., *Een laatste woord in zake de Holland California Land Company en Raadgevingen aan hen die aan emigratie naar Californië denken* (1891), 13.

46. Bowman, *Forest Physiography*, 180; Russell Smith, *North America*, 576.

47. Hartogh Heys van Zouteveen, *Californië's Hulpbronnen*, 47–48.

48. W. A. Nijgh and J. H. De Veer, *Holland California Land Company* (1889), 10.

49. De Fremery, *Californië*, II, "Verslag Kolonisatie," 1890.

50. Orgaan der Holland California Land Company, *California* (hereafter H.C.L.C.), Vol. I (Oct. 1890).

51. Nijgh and De Veer, *Holland California Land Company*, 12ff.

52. Ibid., 35.

53. Ibid., 14.

54. Ibid., 16–18.

55. Ibid., 19, 20.

56. Van Outern, et.al., *Een laatste Woord*, 14.

57. H.C.L.C., *Californië*, No. 1, Oct. 1890.

58. W. F. Andriessen, *Californië met het oog op Nederlansche landverhuizers* (1892), 7.

59. H.C.L.C., *Californië*, No. 1, Oct. 7, 1890, and No. 12, Dec. 23, 1890.

60. Van Outeren, et.al., *Een laatste Woord*, 13.

61. H.C.L.C., *Californië*, Oct. 7, 1890.

62. Ibid., Oct. 14, 1890.

63. Van Outeren, et.al., *Een laatste Woord*, 5; H.C.L.C., *Californië*, No. 2.

64. De Fremery, *Californië*, II, "Kolonisatie," 188.

65. H.C.L.C., *Californië*, No. 2.

66. Van Outeren, et.al., *Een laatste Woord*, 6.

67. De Fremery, *Californië*, II, "Kolonisatie," 1889, 51.

68. Ibid., 1890, 54ff.

69. Van Löben Sels in his interesting letter in *Hou en Trouw*, Jan. 1905.

70. H.C.L.C., *Californië*, Nos. 3, 10, 12.

71. Van Outeren, et.al., *Een laatste Woord*, 9.

72. H.C.L.C., *Californië*, Nos. 15, 12. For this management see also Van Outeren et.al., *Een laatste Woord*, 8.

73. H.C.L.C., *Californië*, Nos. 17, 18.

74. Ibid., No. 12.

75. Ibid., No. 16.

76. Ibid., Nos. 1, 3, but especially also No. 38.

77. Ibid., Nos. 11, 12, and 41. See also Van Outeren, et.al., *Een laatste Woord*, 14.

78. Van Outeren, et.al., *Een laatste Woord*, 7; H.C.L.C., *Californië*, No. 2.

79. Ibid., No. 1.

80. Van Löben Sels, *Verzameling Verslagen en Berichten*, Jaarverslag, S. F. 1893.

81. H.C.L.C., *Californië*, No. 1.

82. Van Outeren, et.al., *Een laatste Woord*, 8.

83. H.C.L.C., *Californië*, Nos. 16, 33.

84. Ibid., 3, 8.

85. Ibid., 19, 1.

86. De Fremery, *Californië*, II, 54ff.

87. Ibid., No. 31.

88. Bowman, *Forest Physiography*, 190.

89. H.C.L.C., *Californië*, No. 37.

90. Jaarverslag, San Francisco, 1891. I must remind readers that De Fremery's separately bound reports concerning California do not go beyond the year 1890.

91. Ibid.

92. Van Outeren, et.al., *Een laatste Woord*, 9ff.

93. H.C.L.C., *Californië*, Nos. 40, 52.

94. Andriessen, *Californië*. From this booklet have been obtained most of the data concerning the Fresno Land Company. Even the most unsuspecting reader will notice that only pictures of Fresno illustrate this booklet, e.g., a picture of the Amsterdam Hotel. The reason why is evident.

95. H.C.L.C., *Californië*, No. 12. However also Van Outeren, et.al., *Een laatste Woord*, 8, 14, and 15.

96. Russell Smith, *North America*, 583.

97. H.C.L.C., *Californië*, No. 24.

98. Ibid., No. 13.

99. De Fremery, *Californië*, II, 52–53.

100. *Verzameling Verslagen en Berichten*, Jaarverslag, San Francisco, 1891.

101. See n.100 above.

102. Ibid., 1893; includes also the year 1892. It was given by consul J. P. Van Löben Sels.

103. This seems also to be the opinion of De Fremery in his latest report in which he observes that "with an adequate investigation" the presence of hardpan would have been found out much sooner. See n.100.

104. Ibid., 1891 (J. De Fremery) and 1893 (Van Löben Sels). Here is mentioned the largest number (104) of Netherlanders in the Rotterdam Colony. I will hold on to the number 135, which occurs repeatedly. The number of acres sold in the Rotterdam Colony is listed here as 1,265, and in another place as 1,400.

105 Ibid., 1898.

106. De Fremery, *Californië*, II, "Kolonisatie," 1890.

107. Jaarverslag, San Francisco, 1891, 18.

108. De Fremery, *Californië*, II, "Kolonisatie," 1890.

109. Russell Smith, *North America*, 550.

110. Jaarverslag, San Francisco, 1891 (J. De Fremery) and 1893 (P. J. Van Löben Sels).

111. Ibid., 1891.

112. J. H. De Veer, *Eene Vruchtencultuur-onderneming in Californië* (1891), 12–13, 5–6. De Veer collaborated with a German American, J. Schrader, whose advice was also highly esteemed by the H.C.L.C.—which makes one wonder.

113. Bowman, *Forest Physiography*, 183.

114. Van Outeren, et.al., *Een laatste Woord*, n.3 and n.8. Van Outeren and also Lens (see further on) and the consular reports only speak of Tulare County. It seems that later it was split into Tulare and King counties. That Lens also came from the Rotterdam colony can be deduced from this note, although not clearly.

115. L. C. Lens, *Geldbelegging in Californië en de Queen-Wilhelmina Kolonie* (1893).

116. Jaarverslag, San Francisco, 1898.

117. Ibid.

118. Census Bureau, Washington, D.C.

119. See note 117.

120. H.C.L.C., *Californië*, Nos. 8 and 52. See also No. 15.

121. H. A. Van Coenen Torchiana, "Uit Californië", a letter that appeared in *Hou en Trouw*—the publication of the organization Hou en Trouw—Oct. 1904. The letter appeared as a result of a request by the Hou en Trouw board to its members abroad to provide information for its Information Bu-

reau that had been set up for the purpose of "enlarging the Dutch element abroad."

122. This became apparent from a letter from Van Coenen Torchiana sent to me from San Francisco, Sept. 20, 1920, and in which he suggested that I query others concerning the Dutch established elsewhere in the USA; in view of an equitable "division of labor," this was also a reasonable point of view.

123. Van Löben Sels, "Protestbrief" in Hou en Trouw, Jan. 1905.

124. Van Coenen Torchiana, A letter from Watsonville, California, USA, Apr. 17, 1905, in Hou en Trouw, May 1905.

125. Van Coenen Torchiana, Uit Californië, see n.121 above. Van Coenen Torchiana was an attorney-solicitor and notary at Watsonville. The profession of notary is of a much lower standing in American than in the Netherlands and can be obtained there much more easily.

126. C. V. Gerritsen and H. Jacobs, Brieven uit en over Amerika (1806), 96, 98, 100–101. It is remarkable that Gerritsen mentions nowhere the attempts made at Merced and Fresno. Did he never hear from them or were these still too painful?

127. De Fremery, Californië, II, "Landbouw en Veeteelt," 1887.

128. Mr. Van Coenen Torchiana was kind enough to answer my questionnaire in an objective way in a very interesting letter from San Francisco, California, July 28, 1920. From this letter I took the Merced verdict, which I thought best to leave untranslated, so that no misgivings can possibly arise about the significance of Mr. Torchiana's words.

129. Rand McNally, Indexed Pocket Map, California.

130. Gerritsen and Jacobs, Brieven, 100.

131. State Commission of Immigration and Housing in California, Report on Fresno's Immigration Problem, 1918. It is possible that Belgians may have been included, that is, Flemish, who are not listed separately in these detailed statistics.

132. Russell Smith, North America, 582.

133. State Commission of Immigration, Report on Fresno's Immigration Problem.

134. Russell Smith, North America, 538–597.

135. Ibid., 552–553.

136. N.B. The names given here are the names of those who definitely were colonists around 1890. Van Löben Sels had named others but we are not sure they were colonists and therefore, in this instance, they are less important for our purpose.

Chapter 9 Settlements in Colorado and New Mexico

1. W. Blackmore, Colorado: Its Resources, Parks and Prospects as a new Field for Emigration (1869), 16.

2. I. Bowman, Forest Physiography (1912), 381–382.

3. N. J. Den Tex, Amerikaansche Spoorwegen op de Amsterdamsche Beurs (1873), 95.

4. R. P. A. Dozy, "Studiën over de Vereenigde Staten," De Gids, May, 1871. Dozy discusses Blackmore's Colorado, although it is only a publicity book.

5. Den Tex, Amerikaansche Spoorwegen, 93–94.

6. Concerning these practices, interesting data can be found in the "Eerste Verslag der Directie" published by Blikman and Sartorius (Amsterdam), 5ff.

7. I have not been able to obtain that brochure to verify its contents. Therefore, I relied on J. Obreen's version of it in Amerika, Land en Volk (1872).

8. Den Tex, Amerikaansche Spoorwegen, 95.

9. J. Van Boven, De Eerste Holandsche Nederzetting in Colorado (1893), 24. The word "Eerste" [First] does not tell us everything, but it does tell us something. After all, there are colonizations that people like to forget as soon as they can, and therefore an earlier attempt could have been completely forgotten!

10. A letter from H. A. Van Coenen Torchiana, San Francisoco, written to me Sept. 20, 1920.

11. A. J. G. W. Van Motz, Colorado uit een geographisch en huishoudkundig oogpunt beschouwd (1874).

12. W. J. Van Balen, Door Amerika (1913), 175.

13. Stemmen uit de Vrije Hollandsche Gemeenten in Amerika, V, 1890, Advertisement.

14. E. Bos, De Wachter, No. 46 and 48 1893. These important facts I found in a complete "Wachter series" by Dr. H. Beets. Bos speaks of Katon but it must be Raton.

15. Beets, De Chr. Geref. Kerk in N.-A. (1918), 274. Here he speaks of "ons volk" [our people] that is, the Christian Reformed fellow believers (see p. 284). A letter of Dr. Beets to me, dated Grand Rapids, Mich., July 13, 1926.

16. S. F. Van Oss, Effectenboek, 1906, 855; 1907, 984; 1926, II, 537. Information concerning this company can be found in these

annual reports. The founding dates, however, are given variously. Seemingly an older "Maxwell" Company was declared bankrupt in 1885 and a new one founded on June 16, 1888, also went bankrupt. And finally a third one was founded—our company—on May 3, 1890, at Amsterdam.

17. *Land- en Emigratie-Maatschappij der Vereenigde Staten van Noord-Amerika*, First Director's report, p. 17.

18. Van Boven, *Eerste Hollandsche Nederzetting*, 2. Most of the information is from this booklet, and also from Dutch-American newspapers, interviews, etc.

19. Ibid., 6.

20. Ibid., 6, 11. It is remarkable that I have not been able to obtain the brochure myself. Was it destroyed as much as possible?

21. Ibid., 33.

22. Ibid., 6, 80.

23. Ibid., 9.

24. Ibid., 10.

25. F. V. Hayden, *Report*, published in Blackmore, *Colorado*, 196ff.

26. Bowman, *Forest Physiography*, 381, 383ff. See the cross-section of the valley and the photograph; the latter corroborates the correctness of Van Boven's description.

27. Van Boven, *Eerste Hollandsche Nederzetting*, 10–11, 27.

28. Ibid., 12.

29. Ibid., 12–13.

30. Ibid., 13–14.

31. Ibid., 16ff. See also Ch. VI, "De Brochure eene bespotting der waarheid bevonden."

32. Ibid., 35–37.

33. Ibid., 51.

34. Ibid., 48–49.

35. Ibid., 52–54.

36. Ibid., 54–60.

37. Ch. A. Merriman, "Report." Reprinted as Suppl. 10 in Van Boven, ibid., 88ff.

38. Van Boven, 60–61. Especially Suppl. 11, Letter from the N. A. Land- en Emigratie-Mij.

39. Ibid., 61 and Supplements 1 and 9.

40. Ibid., 64–67.

41. Ibid., 62–63, 76, Suppl. 5.

42. *De Wachter*, No. 41, 1893, "Call for help for the Netherlanders in Rilland, Colo." See note 14 above.

43. Beets, *Chr. Geref. Kerk*, 274–275.

44. C. Bode in *De Wachter*, No. 43, 1893, "Nood uit Alamosa" [Need in Alamosa].

45. *De Wachter*, No. 44, 1893.

46. Beets, *Chr. Geref. Kerk*, 275.

47. Van Boven, *Eerste Hollandsche Nederzetting*, 26.

48. *De Wachter*, No. 45, 1893.

49. Ibid.

50. Van Boven, *Eerste Hollandsche Nederzetting*, 3. Van Boven declares that Zoutman's view of life was not Christian. Yet he continued to cooperate with him.

51. Annual report of consul B. B. Haagsma at St. Louis for 1892, in *Verzameling Verslagen en Berichten*.

52. *De Wachter*, No. 45, 1893.

53. Ibid.

54. Haagsma report in *Verzameling Verslagen en Berichten*, see n.51 above.

55. Dr. Beets told me this. See also *De Volksvriend*, Feb. 8, 1923.

56. A. Hof, "Uit Alamosa, Co.," *De Volksvriend*, Feb. 8, 1923. Also see Hof's correspondence in *De Volksvriend*, Mar. 1, 1923.

57. A. Hof, "Uit Alamosa, Co.," *De Volksvriend*, Jan. 11, 1923.

58. Christian Reformed Church in America *Yearbook*, 1925.

Chapter 10   *Settlements in the Northwest*

1. Wilhelm G. F. Roscher, "Onderzoekingen omtrent het Koloniewezen," *Tijdschrift voor Staathuishoudkunde en Statistiek*, 1851, VI, 222ff.

2. J. C. J. Kempees, "De Nederlandsche Hypotheekbanken in de Vereenigde Staten," article series in *De Economist* (Oct.–Dec. 1919), 905.

3. See the annual reports for 1922 and 1924 of the Northwestern and Pacific Hypotheekbank.

4. See n. 2 and 3 above.

5. See the annual reports of this company. I consulted the ones of 1903 and 1917–1920.

6. S. F. Van Oss, *Effectenboek*, 1907, 403ff. Mention is made incorrectly of Valkenberg. A number of interesting facts were provided to me by E. J. Everwijn Lange in his letter from Amsterdam, Dec. 24, 1919, and in an interview in Jan. 1920.

7. G. O. Van Wijk, *Brieven uit Amerika* (1895), 10.

8. Kempees, "Nederlandsche Hypotheekbanken." At the end of 1917 the invested capital of those banks was fl 14,421,100 in shares and fl 151,230,330 in bonds.

9. Annual report of the Holland-Texas

Hypotheekbank for 1923. This bank operates mainly in the city of Port Arthur.

10. *Nieuwe Rotterdamsche Courant*, June 24, 1925, morning ed., section B., in which an article appeared about the twelfth annual report. Since then the company went bankrupt, but appealed the bankruptcy.

11. Letter of Dec. 24, 1919; interview, Jan. 1920.

12. Letter, Gorinchem, Dec. 27, 1919 (Holland-Noord-Amerika Hypotheekbank). Furthermore, I received an answer from the Holland-Texas, the Northwestern and Pacific (the "Second" has the same board), de Nederlandsche-Amerikaansche and the Noord-Amerikaansche Hypotheekbanken.

13. Interview with Everwijn Lange, Jan. 1920; Annual report, Ned.-Am. Land Mij., 1903.

14. Van Wijk, *Brieven*, II, 12.

15. Ibid., 7–8.

16. From *Overzeesch Maandblad ter verspreiding van kennis over Noord-Amerika in Nederland* (Rotterdam 1919–1920).

17. I. Bowman, *Forest Physiography* (1912), 178ff.

18. Ibid., 192ff.

19. Pater P. J. De Smet, *Missiën van den Oregon en Reizen naar de Rotsbergen* (1849), 186.

20. Van Wijk, *Brieven*, 7.

21. Brief, postmarked Dec. 24, 1919.

22. Van Wijk, *Brieven*, 8.

23. Ibid., 5.

24. See the report of the Spokane Meelmolens for 1922. See also the report: Uitgifte Spokane Flour Mills, *Nieuwe Rotterdamsche Courant*, May, 1923.

25. Van Oss *Effectenboek*, 1917, 512ff.; 1926, II, 375ff. Further data from Everwijn Lange.

26. I received the most data from Everwijn Lange, and one or two I took from a letter of J. P. Guépin, director of the Northwestern and Pacific Hypotheekbank.

27. Information from J. C. J. Kempees, consul at Seattle, in an interview in July, 1920.

28. Van Oss *Effectenboek*, 1907, 350; 1927, I, 467. Further information from Everwijn Lange.

29. R. Insinger was president of this Chamber of Commerce at the time of Niermeyer's visit at Spokane (see his "Indrukken" in the *Nieuws van den Dag*, VII) and furthermore in July 1920 when I had an interview with Kempees.

30. J. Russell Smith, *North America* (1925), 534.

31. E. C. Leedy, *Nederlandsch-Belgische Colo-*

niën in de N. W. *Staten van Noord-Amerika* (n.d.), 43.

32. Russell Smith, *North America*, 531.

33. *Zillah's Quarter Centennial*, 1901–November–1926; *The Banner*, Dec. 24, 1926.

34. See the reprints of the *Handelsberichten*, Jan. 19, 1911, and the *Report* of Aug. 16, 1913, of the Netherlands ambassador at Washington, concerning "Emigratie naar de Vereenigde Staten."

35. Interview in July 1920.

36. Russell Smith, *North America*, Ch. XXXIII, "The Puget Sound—Willamette Valley."

37. R. Whitaker, "Washington," in Ernest Gruening, *These United States, A Symposium* (1923–1924), II, 233ff.

38. H. Beets, *De Chr. Geref. Kerk in N.-A.* (1918), 276–279.

39. *De Volksvriend*, May 27, June 10, 1920; Dec. 25, 1919.

40. J. J. Leys, *Nederlandsche Kolonisten in Canada; Rapport aan Zijne Exc. den Gouverneur van Suriname*, 31ff.

41. "Most Northwestern Church celebrates its Twenty-fifth Anniversary," *The Banner*, Aug. 28, 1928.

42. Annual report of the vice-consul at Seattle for 1913 in *Economische Verslagen*, see above.

43. *De Volksvriend*, Oct. 21, 1920.

44. Taken from Leys' report, *Nederlandsche Kolonisten*, see n.40 above.

45. *De Volksvriend*, Dec. 2, 1920.

46. To be prudent, I am speaking in the past tense, because these facts were given to me already in 1920 during an interview with Kempees.

47. C. Vriesman, "Everett, Wash.," in *The Banner*, Sept. 20, 1923, an article in which the restless and mixed character of the Dutch over there is also strongly evident.

48. Information fron consul Kempees.

49. Vriesman, "Everett, Wash."

50. R. H. Whitlock, "Irrigation in the United States," *The Geographical Journal* (Oct. 1919) 221ff.

51. F. E. H. Groenman, *Iets over Landverhuizing naar de Vereenigde Staten van Amerika* (1915), 12.

52. Whitlock, "Irrigation."

53. A. Fisher, "Montana," in Gruening, *These United States*, II, 43.

54. Bowman, *Forest Physiography*, 315ff.; E. Deckert, *Nordamerika* (1913); 349, 370, 395.

55. See report in *De Hope*, Dec. 9, 1919.

56. M. Borduin, "Conrad, Mont.," in *The Banner*, Feb. 12, 1926, and "Note of Editor"

(Dr. H. Beets) concerning an article of M. Borduin, "Home Mission Work in Montana," ibid., May 14, 1926.

57. Bowman, *Forest Physiography*, 100, 98.

58. C. S. Dent, "Northwestward Ho!" *World Traveler* (March 1924). Would it be mere chance that this article about the northwest appeared in the "Holland issue" of this magazine?

59. *Corwin's Manual*, 720, 646.

60. The figures concerning these Roman Catholic colonies are taken from the booklet of Leedy, *Nederlandsch-Belgische Coloniën*, which must be consulted very critically, and also from a very interesting report of the then vice-consul Groenman, "De Koloniale Maatschappij van pastoor Vermaat." Groenman advised me not to use full names. However, in the booklet of Leedy, the name Vermaat appears several times. Therefore, I consider it my *duty* to do the same.

61. Whitlock, "Irrigation."

62. J. Bs. Westerdijk, "Prae-advies van J. Bs. Westerdijk voor de Nationale Vereeniging tegen de Werkloosheid," *Tijdschrift van den Ned. Werkloosheids-Raad*, 5 (1922), Sec. 4, 154.

63. Henry L. Mencken, *Americana 1925* (1925), 293.

64. *De Grondwet*, June 15, 1920.

65. *De Volksvriend*, June 5, 1924.

66. Borduin, "Conrad, Mont."

67. Report, N.-Am. Hypotheekbank for the 12th Fiscal Year.

68. Fisher, "Montana," II, 44.

69. A. Woeikof, *Le Turkestan Russe* (1914), 115.

70. Russell Smith, *North America*, 414.

71. Letter of a hypotheekbank director in *De Financier*, reprinted in the *Nieuwe Rotterdamsche Courant*, morning ed., Apr. 15, 1926.

72. "Het tegengaan van irrationeele uitbreiding van het landbouwbedrijf in Amerika," ibid., Mar. 28, 1926.

73. *De Volksvriend*, June 9, 1921.

74. Ibid., Feb. 15, 1923. Probably this Apple Valley is the Payette Valley in which Germans also settled. See C. C. Eisse, *Früchte deutscher Arbeit* (1910).

75. *De Volksvriend*, ro/Feb. 8, 1923.

Chapter 11   *Colonization Attempts in the South*

1. C. G. Woodson, A *Century of Negro Migration* (1918), 121.

2. B. B. Haagsma, Annual report of 1893 in *Verzameling Verslagen en Berichten*

3. Ibid., 1895.

4. Ibid., 1894.

5. S. J. Menning, "Hospers, Iowa," in the Jubileumnummer, *De Volksvriend*, Sept. 19, 1895.

6. Charles Boissevain, *Van 't Noorden naar 't Zuiden, Schetsen en Indrukken van de Vereenigde Staten van Noord-Amerika* (2 vols., 1882), II, 283.

7. M. Cohen Stuart's work was published at Kruseman and Tjeenk Willink in 1875; Boissevain's work at the reorganized Tjeenk Willink, both at Haarlem.

8. Boissevain, *Van 't Noorden*, II, 292.

9. Correspondence, among others with A. A. H. Boissevain, datelined Lage Vuursche [Utrecht], Dec. 15, 1919, and with A. Boissevain, Ez., Amsterdam, Jan. 8. 1920. Conversation with J. De Bruyn (of Pierson and Co.), Dec. 23, 1919. Curiously, I received the information of Boissevain's part in connection with the Norfolk and Western from S. F. Van Oss, The Hague, Dec. 10, 1919.

10. Mr. J. P. André Mottu, Norfolk, Va. I asked for information years ago and after a renewed effort received the information on Apr. 18, 1927, which I've used.

11. Letter from J. P. André Mottu at Norfolk in the publication of the Association *Hou en Trouw*, Sept. 1906.

12. Letter of protest by J. P. André Mottu in the publication of the Association *Hou en Trouw*, Mar. 1905.

13. Beets, *De Chr. Geref. Kerk in N.-A.* (1918), 276, 284; J. P. André Mottu wrote to me (Norfolk, Va., Apr. 18, 1927) that "it never succeeded."

14. Robert Sloss, "Representative Hollanders in America Today" in *Van Norden, The World Mirror*, "Special Holland Number," Oct. 1909, 51. A "connection" between the Maryland colony and Van der Hoogt is all the more probable since he kept in contact with the Netherlanders in Michigan.

15. Boissevain, *Van 't Noorden*, II, 148, 204ff.

16. Haagsma, Annual Report of 1893 (St. Louis).

17. Ibid., 1894.

18. Boissevain, *Van 't Noorden*, II, 148.

19. The incorporated "data" I have gleaned especially from a letter of Jan. 17, 1920, from J. Van Tijen, who for a long time was the Dutch consul at Port Arthur. I received similar but less elaborate information from others.

20. Personal letter of J. De Goeijen from Arnhem, Apr. 24, 1920.

21. Most of these names are from a folder of the Kansas City Southern sent to me, together with other literature, by De Goeijen. Also Mr. Van Oss at The Hague gave information. Details about these towns, of which Mena and De Ridder became of some importance, are found in *The Ozark Region of Western Missouri and Arkansas*, n.d., Kansas City, Mo. (Immigration Dept.)

22. R. P. J. Tutein Nolthenius, *Nieuwe Wereld: Indrukken en aanteekleningen tijdens eene reis door de Vereenigde Staten van Noord-Amerika* (2nd. ed., 1902), 15ff., for his interesting trip on the Gulf Line Railroad.

23. I. Bowman, *Forest Physiography* (1912), 529–530, 541.

24. See the *Map . . . of the Port Arthur Land Co.*, Kansas City (n.d., but likely 1896, according to one of the pictures). Mr. Van Tijen kindly gave me a copy.

25. J. Russell Smith, *Industrial and Commercial Geography* (1913), 80. J. J. Parels, "Een en ander omtrent de Rijstcultuur in de Ver. Staten van Noord-Amerika," *Culture*, 31 (June 1909).

26. That the Netherlanders were expected to be successful in the growing of rice, was written to me by E. J. Everwijn Lange who reaffirmed this later. Van Tijen corroborated this.

27. F. E. H. Groenman, *Iets over Landverhuizing*, 10.

28. *Map . . . of Port Arthur Land Co.*

29. *Weekblad voor het Kanton Bergum*, Dec. 23, 1882. It raises questions!

30. This figure was given to me by a mortgage bank director. In the *Handelsberichten*, No. 201, Jan. 19, 1911, only the number of eighty-five persons is listed; however, neither the name "Nederland" nor the year of settlement, 1898, is given, which gives a vague impression.

31. I give credit for this to the correspondence and the interview with J. Van Tijen, Jan. 27, 1920, and July, 1920, respectively.

32. Letter, Port Arthur, Texas, dated Jan. 27, 1920.

33. Information credited to Dr. Beets in a conversation.

34. The interesting celebration program, which gives a tragic impression of the festive speech of Mr. J. E. Kroes, is in my possession, thanks to De Goeijen.

35. From a letter of H. Visscher, Kansas City, Mo., Oct. 8, 1920.

36. See in the above-named celebration program also the splendid fireworks probably dedicated to the "benefactor" of the colony. Hornbeck at that time was the general manager of the Land Co. The question remains whether the celebration was held at all and whether the program was used to encourage further immigration and settlement in the "jolly" colony, where one could get Oranje bier, which came directly from Haarlem.

37. Tutein Nolthenius, *Nieuwe Wereld*, 21, 22.

38. Information from J. Van Tijen in a conversation, July, 1920. Among the boardinghouse operators in the Ozark hill country at Lanagan, Mo., I saw a small guide of "Ozark Outings" in which occurred the name of F. M. Best, a name that often appears in Alkmaar's vicinity. Another possible example of the spreading of the Dutch element everywhere.

39. Russell Smith, *Industrial and Commercial Geography*, 80.

40. Immigration Bureau, Kansas City, Mo., *West Louisiana, East Texas, and the Gulf Coast* (n.d.), 28.

41. Letter from F. E. H. Groenman to me, 's Gravenhage, Dec. 1, 1919.

42. Letter from J. Van Tijen, Port Arthur, Texas, Jan. 27, 1920.

43. Letter from E. J. Everwijn Lange, Amsterdam, Dec. 29, 1919. Also see annual reports, among others, that of 1923.

44. Port Arthur Board of Trade, *Port Arthur, Texas, Pan-America Gateway* (1916).

45. See annual reports of this Syndicate. See also S. F. Van Oss, *Effectenboek*, 1907.

46. Immigration Bureau, *West Louisiana, East Texas, and Gulf Coast*, 41ff.

47. Information from conversations with E. J. Everwijn Lange and J. Van Tijen.

48. Kansas City Southern Railroad, "Ozark Outings," Kansas City, Mo. (n.d.).

49. "A City of ceaseless development." "A seaport storm-proof and safe," *Port Arthur, Texas Pan-America Gateway*.

50. *Weekblad voor het Kanton Bergum*, No. 51, Dec. 20, 1884.

51. Haagsma, Consular Report (St. Louis), Mar. 12, 1902, in *Verzameling Verslagen en Berichten*.

52. J. Van Tijen told me that Koch was a Netherlander. See also his information on Texas-Netherlanders in a report of the Dutch ambassador at Washington, Aug. 16, 1913, entitled "Emigratie naar de Vereenigde Staten."

53. E. J. G. Bloemendaal, *Naar Amerika* (1911), 231ff.

54. Information taken from a conversation with Van Tijen, July 1920.

55. See reports in *De Volksvriend*, Oct. 7, 21, 1920; *De Grondwet*. Nov. 23, 1920; *De Volksvriend*, Mar. 10, May 12, 1921.

56. Taken from a report of Groenman.

57. Information taken from a conversation with Van Tijen.

58. Kansas City Southern, *Current Events*, Apr. 1917, 56. See also the article here about the vicinity of the named towns, which are all in Benton Co., 39ff.

59. H. L. Mencken, *Americana 1925* (1925), 296.

60. Letter from S. F. Van Oss, The Hague, Dec. 10, 1919.

61. *Corwin's Manual*, 666.

62. *De Volksvriend*, July 19, 1923.

63. B. Rascoe, "Oklahoma," in Ernest Gruening, *These United States, A Symposium* (2 vols., 1923–1924), II, 155.

64. *Corwin's Manual*, 227.

65. Rascoe, "Oklahoma," II, 157.

66. J. B. Bogaerts, *Gids voor toekomstige kolonisten in Louisiana*, published by the Bureau for Colonization in the State of Louisiana, July 24, 1911, with approbation of J. H. Blenk, Archbishop of New Orleans and Cornelius Van de Ven, Bishop of Alexandria.

67. Letter of Hr. Ms. ambassador at Washington to the Minister of Foreign Affairs, July 28, 1912, No. 771/210. Reprinted in the *Oranjeboek* of 1912.

68. Letter of the Consulate at New Orleans to our ambassador at Washington, relayed by the latter, Aug. 16, 1913, in a report on "Emigration to the United States."

69. Catholic Colonization Society, U.S.A., *System in Catholic Colonization* (n.d.), 6ff.

70. A. J. Bruyn, "Nederlandsche Energie in het Buitenland," *Vragen van den Dag*, 1910.

71. Netherlands ambassador at Washington, "Emigratie naar de Vereenigde Staten," Report of Aug. 16, 1913.

72. Information of the Nederlandsche Vereeniging "Landverhuizing," No. 18, Alabama.

73. C. G. Stillman, "Florida," in Gruening, *These United States*, II, 51–52.

74. All this information taken from the report of Hr. Ms. ambassador at Washington, July 25, 1912 and reprinted in the *Oranjeboek* of that year.

75. Report of Groenman about his visit to this region, Nov. 16, 17, 1914.

76. Annual report of vice-consul Julsingha Blerick at Tampa in *Handelsberichten*, July 1, 1920. Other information taken from a very detailed and important letter of this gentleman to me, Tampa, Fla., Sept. 2, 1920.

77. *De Grondwet* (Holland, Mich.), May 25, 1920.

78. Compare with the information from the Ned. Vereen. "Landverhuizing."

79. Letter, Tampa, Fla., Sept. 2, 1920.

80. C. G. Stillman, "Florida," in Gruening, *These United States*, II.

81. B. H. Spalink, "Florida and our people there," *The Banner*, July 23, 1926.

82. J. Russell Smith, *North America* (1925), XIV, 277, for instance. However, Russell Smith borrowed much from the paper of C. G. Stillman.

83. Information from the Ned. Vereen. "Landverhuizing," *Landverhuizing naar de V. St. van Amerika* (n.d.).

84. N. V. Ned.-Am. Fruitteelt Mij. "Virginia," *De Hollandsche Fruitplantages in Virginia* (U.S.A).

85. The "misunderstanding" became apparent through an investigation on location by Groenman.

86. Boissevain, *Van 't Noorden*, II, 293.

87. Groenman, *Report*, 1915.

88. See *Handelsberichten*, No. 291, Jan. 19, 1911, and "Landverhuizing naar de V. St. van Amerika" in *Oranjeboek*, 1912.

89. "Landverhuizing naar de V. St. van Amerika," *Oranjeboek*, 1912.

90. Letter of H. Vogels to our ambassador at Washington, reprinted in "Emigratie naar de Vereenigde Staten, report, Aug. 16, 1913.

91. Ibid.

92. E. d'Oliveira, Jr., *De Mannen van '80 aan het Woord* (2nd ed., n.d.), 92.

93. J. Saks, *Socialistische Opstellen* (2nd vol., 1923), "De Pioniers van Bussum," 31.

94. A synopsis of Frederik van Eeden's America journey in G. Kalff, Jr., *Frederik Van Eeden, Psychologie van den Tachtiger* (1927), 290ff. Cf. also d'Oliveira, *Mannen*, 92.

95. See his report in the *Oranjeboek*, 1912.

96. Netherlands ambassador at Washington, "Emigratie naar de Vereenigde Staten," a report of Aug. 16, 1913, in which appeared a letter by H. Vogels.

97. Frederik Van Eeden, "Wenken en Waarschuwingen voor de werkers in Van Eeden Kolonie," in *Van Eeden Kolonie in N. Carolina, U.S.A.* (1912).

98. M. N. Beeking, *Emigratie naar de Vereenigde Staten en Kleine Boerderijen in Den Grooten Wintertuin* (n.d.).

99. Letter, Tampa, Fla., Sept. 2, 1920. In this writing J. B. names only "Castle

Haines" and in it he really puts all Hollanders in N.C. together.

100. Letter, Norfolk, Va., Apr. 18, 1927.
101. Ibid.
102. Neil Van Aken, *Broad Acre Farms in North Carolina,* U.S.A. (1926).
103. See note 100.
104. Groenman, *Report* (1915).
105. Netherlands ambassador at Washington, "Emigratie" (1913), which includes letter of J. Van Tijen.

Chapter 12   Roman Catholic and Miscellaneous Settlements

1. Catholic Colonization Society, U.S.A., (hereafter C.C.S.), *Common Sense in Colonization* (n.d.).
2. C.C.S., *System in Catholic Colonization* (n.d.).
3. C.C.S., *System,* 6ff.
4. J. A. Van Heertum, *Roman Catholics in the United States.* (A contribution in the *Gedenboek van het Algemeen Nederlandsche Verbond bij gelegenheid van zijn 25-jarige Bestaan, 1898-Mei-1923* (1923), presented by Holland Americans to the Queen on the twenty-fifth anniversary of her rule. Reprinted in *De Heidenwereld,* Holland, Mich., Dec., 1923, p. 19.
5. C.C.S., *System,* 20.
6. H. W. IJzermans, *Naar de Nieuwe Katholieke Kolonie te Butler in Minnesota,* Aug. 31, 1910.
7. C.C.S., *System,* 20.
8. IJzermans, *Nieuwe Katholieke Kolonie.*
9. C.C.S., *System.*
10. IJzermans, *Nieuwe Katholieke Kolonie.*
11. IJzermans, *Uit het Land der Yankees.* An interesting series of letters portraying the missionary activities of our Roman Catholic countrymen in the United States. The series is still running in *Het Centrum.* Letter dated at Verndale, Minn. on Sept. 9 and appearing in *Het Centurm,* Oct. 3, 1914.
12. IJzermans, *Land der Yankees.* Letter of Feb. 25, 1914, written in Verndale and printed in *Het Centrum,* Mar. 14, 1914.
13. Her Majesty's Ambassador at Washington, "Landverhuizing," in the *Oranjeboek* of 1912.
14. C.C.S., *System.*
15. F. E. H. Groenman, *Iets over landverhuizing naar de Vereenigde Staten van Amerika,* reprint from *Economische Verslagen,* 9, No. 5 and 4.
16. C.C.S., *Common Sense.*
17. C.C.S., *System.*

18. Letter from Rev. P. J. Cichozki, secretary of the C.C.S., Oct. 24, 1920.
19. Letter from H. Oyens and Sons, Amsterdam, Dec. 30, 1919.
20. Letter from A. Boissevain Ez., Amsterdam, Jan. 8, 1920.
21. Information for which I thank A. Colijn Jr., obtained in an interview on Jan. 5, 1920. Also see S. F. Van Oss, *Effectenboek,* 1927, I (Binnenland), 1564. My contacts with the Netherlandsche Handel Maatschappij were not particularly productive. The archivist, Peters, said that he could not recall any colonization. He concluded, "I can arrive at no other conclusion than that the company had no dealings with it." (Letter from Amsterdam, Mar. 19, 1927.)
22. See the *Annual Reports* of the Holland Dakota Landbouw Cie. for 1920, 1923, 1925.
23. Danaher Holton Co., "Hollanders Settle in Orchard Valley, Wisconsin," *Orchard Valley,* no date. Also see the report of F. E. H. Groenman who visited the colony on Aug. 13 and 14, 1914; among other things he mentions that he did not see the railroad to Duluth, although it was mentioned in the brochures.
24. J. Jansen, "Een verblijf in Amerika," *Vragen van den Dag,* 35 (Aug. 1920). H. Beets, "Our Frisian Settlement in Whitinsville, Mass.," *The Banner,* Oct. 1, 1926. Both accounts were used, mostly in a comparative fashion, to arrive at the facts.
25. Jansen, "Een verblijf," 634.
26. H. Beets, "The Reverend Frederick J. Drost, 1886, May 26, 1926," *The Banner,* June 4, 1926.
27. In various yearbooks of the Christian Reformed Church (1919, 1921, 1925), 1906 is given as the year in which the congregation was organized but this must be an error, in view of data from the listed articles.
28. Jansen, "Een verblijf," 631.
29. Beets, "Our Frisian Settlement."

Chapter 13   The Economic Development of the Settlements Since About 1895 and Their Present-Day Significance

1. Thomas Carlyle, *Zes lezingen over Helden, Heldenvereering en Heldengeest in de Geschiedenis* (n.d.), 9–10.

2. F. J. Turner, *The Frontier in American History* (1921), I, 297, 311–312.

3. *Die wissenschaftlichen Ergebnisse der Reise des Grafen Béla Széchenyi in Ost-Asien, 1877–1880*, Vol. I, Vienna (1893), 223. Cited by P. Vidal de la Blache, *Principes de Géographie Humaine* (1922), 44.

4. G. Chinard, *Les Réfugiés Huguenots en Amérique* (1925), 75, 100, 106, 204.

5. Max Weber, *Gesammelte Afusätze zur Religionssoziologie* (1922), I, 84ff.

6. Ibid., I, 167.

7. Emile Lauvrière, *La Tragédie d'un Peuple* (2 vols, new ed., 1924), II, 497ff.

8. Fridrich Arends, *Het Mississippi-dal* (1839), 246.

9. Anonymous, "Overzicht der Hedendaagsche Landverhuizing," *De Economist*, II (1869), 655.

10. Jean Brunhes and Camille Vallaux, *La Géographie de l'histoire* (1921), 212.

11. K. Lamprecht, *Americana* (1906), 55, 24.

12. A. B. Faust, *Das Deutschtum in den Vereinigten Staaten (Bedeutung)* (1912), 28, 29, n.1.

13. R. Gonnard, *L'Emigration européenne, au XIXe siècle* (1906), 148.

14. A. B. Faust, *Das Deutschtum (Bedeutung)* (1912), 30. Here is a list of real estate ownership; the Dutch are not treated separately.

15. Vidal de la Blache, *Principes*, 44.

16. George Schnücker, *Die Ostfriesen in America* (1917), 97; see also 91, 258, 293, 294.

17. Interview with G. Van Schelven, in Holland, Mich. Aug. 3, 1921; *De Grondwet*, Apr. 3, 1923.

18. Interviews with G. Van Schelven, Aug. 3, 1921, and G. J. Diekema, Aug. 9, 1921.

19. Van der Meulen, "Van Bergum naar Amerika," a series in the *Weekblad voor het Kanton Bergum*. No. 13, Apr. 1, 1882.

20. Interview with A. Oosterheerdt in Evergreen Park and visit to the town.

21. Jacob van der Zee, *The Hollanders of Iowa* (1912), 196ff.

22. Christian Reformed Church in America *Yearbook*, (1925), 18, "Classis Pella." Once again, I want to point out the value of these yearbooks.

23. *The Register and Leader*, July 28, 1909. Cited in Van der Zee, *Hollanders of Iowa*, 198.

24. I am using the year 1911 because the data were used in Van der Zee's work and were based on the tax records in Orange City and made available to him by H. Te Paske, a civil servant.

25. G. Draayom, "Schetsen uit het Verleden, Hospers," *De Volksvriend*, June 12, 1924.

26. Ibid., "Schetsen, Welcome Township," *De Volksvriend*, Mar. 6, 1924.

27. Van der Zee, *Hollanders of Iowa*, 202.

28. Draayom, "Schetsen, Hospers en Floyd Township," *De Volksvriend*, June 5, 1924.

29. Van der Zee, *Hollanders of Iowa*, 202.

30. Ibid., 203. Concerning Doon and its vicinity, see *The Banner*, Dec. 9, 1927.

31. Schnücker, *Ostfriesen*, 258ff.

32. Ibid., 259.

33. *De Volksvriend*, Dec. 25, 1919.

34. *Corwin's Manual* (1922), 342. Additional statistics concerning the Reformed Church may be found in the "Acts and Proceedings" of the General Synod of 1925.

35. During our most interesting automobile trip through Sioux and Lyon counties on Aug. 18, 1921, the mayor of Orange City, the Honorable G. Klay, acquainted me with the rivalry between the Gelderlanders and the Hollanders.

36. Van der Zee, *Hollanders of Iowa*, 243.

37. Draayom, "Schetsen, Onze noordelijke Buren," *De Volksvriend*, Jan. 31, 1924.

38. Ibid., "Grant en Lynn Townships," *De Volksvriend*, Feb. 14, 1924.

39. Ibid., "Hospers en Floyd Townships," *De Volksvriend*, June 5, 1924.

40. Ibid., "Een moeilijke Overtocht," *De Volksvriend*, June 19, 1924.

41. See various accounts in Ernest Gruening, *These United States, A Symposium* (2 vols., 1923–1924).

42. Chinard, *Réfugiés Huguenots*, 104ff., 110, 203, 204.

43. Faust, *Das Deutschtum (Bedeutung)*, 29.

44. An impression I got following a few discussions I had in Sioux County.

45. I am indebted to Rev. S. De Bruine for a letter dated Oskaloosa, Iowa, Jan. 28, 1920. At that time he was a minister in Oskaloosa—near the area that was threatened. The letter was addressed to the General Netherlands Association for Tourism in 's-Gravenhage. This information led to a very fruitful correspondence with Rev. De Bruine and provided me with extremely valuable information.

46. From an interesting letter written to me from Oskaloosa, Ia., Apr. 19, 1920.

47. S. R. Steinmetz, *Ethnologische Studien zur ersten Entwicklung der Strafe. Nebst einer psychologischen Abhandlung über Grausamkeit und Rachsucht*, (2 vols., 2nd ed., 1928), II, 3rd pt.

48. "Davis not guilty." From an account that probably appeared in *The Times* of Oska-

loosa under date of Apr. 19, 1920. See following note.

49. In this connection I received some valuable newspaper clippings. Of particular significance was a letter to the editor entitled "The Davis Trial," written by J. B. Mitchell in *The Times*, a local paper. I excerpted the "protest" from it. A clipping, "Davis not guilty" was probably from the same paper.

50. S. Berkenpas, "Veertigjarige Gedenkdag van Mr. and Mrs. Pl. de Zeeuw," *De Volksvriend*, Mar. 31, 1921.

51. E. J. G. Bloemendaal, *Naar Amerika* (1911), 146. Also, *De Volksvriend*, June 8, 1922.

52. *De Volksvriend*, Oct. 7, 1920.

53. Een Fries, "Uit het verre Westen," a series of letters appearing in the *Leeuwarder Courant* from which I obtained information about present-day farming. The writer cultivates 640 acres in northwestern Iowa. The *Leeuwarder Courant*, CXXV, Aug. 25, 1925.

54. Letter from Ben Mouw residing in Sioux Center, Sioux County. The letter had no date but reached me in 1924.

55. I am grateful for the hospitality I enjoyed while visiting Piet Mouw on his farm Aug. 17, 1921, and for my conversations with this recently deceased Gelderlander who still considered himself a real Dutchman in many respects.

56. See the account from Three Oaks, Michigan, in *De Volksvriend*, Dec. 2, 1920.

57. *De Grondwet*, June 15, 1920.

58. *De Volksvriend*, Oct. 21, 1920; Feb. 10, July 9, 1921, etc.

59. *De Volksvriend*, Sept. 9, 1920.

60. I learned much about it during my visit to Orange City, Aug. 16–18, 1921. Especially the elderly Mr. Oggel and the Honorable H. Klay, a lawyer, enlightened me about the guaranteed "homestead."

61. *De Volksvriend*, June 9, 1921.

62. Een Fries, "Uit het verre Westen," *Leeuwarder Courant*, LXXXIII, Jan. 30, 1924.

63. Johan J. Smertenko, "Iowa, A Mortgaged Eldorado," in Gruening, *These United States*, I, 222.

64. *De Volksvriend*, May 26, 1921.

65. *De Volksvriend*, Nov. 18, 1920.

66. *De Volksvriend*, Nov. 25, 1920.

67. *Het Oosten*, July 29, 1921.

68. *De Grondwet*, May 25, 1920.

69. *De Volksvriend*, Dec. 2, 1920.

70. *De Volksvriend*, Jan. 27, Feb. 3, 1921; Dec. 30, 1920, respectively.

71. *De Volksvriend*, June 5, 1924.

72. *De Grondwet*, Dec. 9, 1919.

73. *De Grondwet*, May 25, 1920; *Het Oosten*, May 21, 1920.

74. *De Volksvriend*, June 5, 1924.

75. *De Grondwet*, May 25, 1920.

76. *De Grondwet*, Nov. 16, 1920.

77. *De Grondwet*, July 6, 1920.

78. *De Grondwet*, Sept. 28, 1920.

79. L. A. Chase, *Rural Michigan* (1922), 199.

80. G. F. Huizinga, *What the Dutch Have Done in the West of the United States* (1909), 36.

81. Chase, *Rural Michigan*, 198.

82. J. Russell Smith, *North America* (1925), 284.

83. *De Grondwet*, May 10, 1921.

84. *De Grondwet*, Jan. 21, Feb. 8, 1921.

85. Een Fries, "Uit het verre Westen," *Leeuwarder Courant*, LVII, Feb. 9, 1923.

86. Chase, *Rural Michigan*, 455.

87. Huizinga, *What the Dutch Have Done*, 37.

88. Chase, *Rural Michigan*, 454.

89. *De Grondwet*, Dec. 9, 1919.

90. *De Grondwet*, Nov. 9, 1920.

91. Chase, *Rural Michigan*, 454. One should pay attention to the reservation "at least."

92. *De Grondwet*, June 1, Nov. 16, 1920.

93. Chase, *Rural Michigan*, 165.

94. I. Lippincott, *Economic Development of the United States* (1924), 416, 417ff.

95. Most of the information concerning modern industry in Holland was obtained—unless otherwise indicated—from a publication of the Holland Board of Trade, *Holland the Gateway of Western Michigan for Chicago and the Great West* (1914). This work was issued in 1914 and so gives a "normal" pre-war account. I obtained additional information from R. L. Polk and Company, *Polk's Holland City Directory* (1921). I was unable to obtain records for 1925 and 1926. The Board of Trade did not reply to my letters (although international answer coupons were included!) Dr. H. Beets, who was kind enough to inquire in turn for me had no result either. These are, it seems, indications of a greatly progressed Americanization!

96. Faust, *Das Deutschtum* (Bedeutung), 60.

97. Huizinga, *What the Dutch Have Done*, 36.

98. Chase, *Rural Michigan*, 293.

99. *De Grondwet*, Nov. 2, 1920; Dec. 9, 1919; Feb. 15, 1921.

100. *De Grondwet*, Feb. 20, 1923, has a report issued by the Census Bureau in Washington.

101. *De Grondwet*, Feb. 13, 1923.

102. *De Grondwet*, June 8, July 6, 1920.

103. Chase, *Rural Michigan*, 299.

104. Faust, *Das Deutschtum* (*Bedeutung*), 60. J. O. Schimmel of Jersey City, Bosman and Lohman in Norfolk—all Hollanders—are brazenly termed Germans by Faust and this was repeated in imitation by R. Cronau, *Drei Jahrhunderte deutschen Lebens in Amerika* (1924), 401.

105. *De Grondwet*, May 25, 1920.

106. |G. J.| Diekema and |J. B.| Nykerk gave me some interesting information in this regard.

107. *De Grondwet*, Dec. 9, 1919.

108. *De Grondwet*, Mar. 22, 1921.

109. Most of the information about Visscher was taken from "In Memoriam Mr. Arend Visscher," *Hope College Bulletin*, 59, No. 1, May, 1921.

110. I obtained information about Diekema from a conversation with the honorable gentleman in Holland, Aug. 9, 1921.

111. Polk's *Holland City Directory*; Yearbooks of the Reformed and Christian Reformed Churches.

112. *De Grondwet*, June 8, Sept. 14, 1920.

113. *De Volksvriend*, Dec. 25, 1919.

114. *De Grondwet*, May 25, 1920.

115. P. K. Dame in *De Hope*, Jan. 18, 1921.

116. *De Volksvriend*, Dec. 25, 1919.

117. *De Volksvriend*, Nov. 22, 1923. See "Berichten uit Sheboygan, Wisconsin."

118. *De Grondwet*, Sept. 14, Nov. 2, May 25, 1920.

119. *De Volksvriend*, Nov. 22, 1923.

120. Letter written by Rev. W. H. H. De Haan, New Franken, Wis. R.F.D., Apr. 1926.

121. J. W. De Vries, O.P., "Een Hollandsche Kolonisatie in Wisconsin, IV, Holland," *Katholieke Illustratie*, Mar. 20, 1909.

122. De Vries, "Een Hollandsche Kolonisatie in Wisconsin, I, Fox River Valley," *Katholieke Illustratie*, 1908.

123. De Vries, "Een Hollandsche Kolonisatie in Wisconsin, II, Green Bay," *Katholieke Illustratie*, Feb. 20, 1909.

124. From a letter written by Dr. G. Rijbroek on July 4, 1925, from Holy Family Convent, Alverno, Wisconsin.

125. E. P. Beaudette-Neil, *Thornton Township, Cook County, Illinois* (1921).

126. Ibid., 83–85.

127. Ibid., 113, 117, 119.

128. Conversation with P. De Jong in South Holland, Illinois, Aug. 12, 1921.

129. Beaudette-Neil, *Thornton Township*, 107. In 1910 a Hollander, M. Speyer, bought the store of A. Price.

130. "Schedule of Events" commemorating Pella's 75th anniversary. *Pella's Weekblad*, Sept. 8, 1922.

131. To the extent that I had not yet assembled these data during my visit to Pella in 1921, I obtained these from a letter written to me by G. G. Gaass, on behalf of Pella's Chamber of Commerce, Pella, Iowa, Aug. 21, 1926.

132. This last bank was not mentioned by G. G. Gaass. However, see *Pella's Weekblad*, Dec. 5, 1919. Has it since gone out of business?

133. *De Grondwet*, Feb. 1, 1921.

134. Letter from G. G. Gaass. See note 131.

135. *De Volksvriend*, June 19, 1924.

136. *De Volksvriend*, Sept. 9, 1920.

137. *Christian Journal*, Dec. 28, 1922, has an interesting article reprinted from *De Volksvriend*.

138. *De Volksvriend*, Oct. 20, 1920.

139. *De Volksvriend*, Dec. 25, 1919, June 8, 1922.

140. Huizinga, *What the Dutch Have Done*, 37.

141. *De Grondwet*, Apr. 26, 1921.

142. B. W. Lammers, "Correspontie uit Sodus," *De Volksvriend*, Jan. 18 and Mar. 1, 1923. I am also grateful to |Albert| Raap of Holland, Michigan, for some material.

143. In addition to the hundreds of advertisements and news items in the Dutch-American press, among others in *Neerlandia*, Dec. 1925, in which was published the letter of the *Algemeen Handelsblad*; see also Een Fries, "Uit het verre Westen," *Leeuwarder Courant*, Sept. 4, Oct. 12, 1923.

144. *De Volksvriend*, Oct. 7, 21, Nov. 18, 1920; Nov. 8, 1922; *De Grondwet*, Nov. 9, 1920, etc.

145. F. Schaap, in his "Magazine" *Holland-California*, Mar. 1, 1924, p. 12.

146. The Christian Reformed Church in America *Yearbook* (1927); *The Banner*, Dec. 30, 1927.

147. *The Banner*, June 24, 1927.

148. *The Banner*, May 8, 1925.

149. *De Volksvriend*, Apr. 7, 1921.

Chapter 14   Dutch Colonies in the Cities

1. H. Bass Hall in his foreword to T. N. Carver's *The Present Economic Revolution in the United States* (1926).

2. "De Boeren-staking in Noord-Amerika," *Algemeen Handelsblad*, evening ed., Mar. 25, 1927. From this it appears that in spite of the price rises I indicated the "flight" still continues. In 1925, 2,035,000 persons left the land as contrasted to 1,135,000 who settled on the land but did not compensate for the "flight."

3. These and other statistics have been abstracted from *Fourteenth Census of the United States* (1920).

4. Jeremiah W. Jenks and W. Jett Lauck, *The Immigration Problem* (4th ed., 1924), 516–517. Mr. Brons, secretary of Paterson's branch of the A. N. V. [Algemeen Nederlandsch Verbond] put me in touch with various individuals in Paterson and also supplied me with much interesting information himself. His comments on pre-war wages are largely substantiated in Jenks and Lauck, 521.

5. For this information I express my thanks to the convention and publicity committee of the Grand Rapids Chamber of Commerce with which I was in contact in August of 1921. The account in the *Algemeen Handelsblad*, evening ed., July 6, 1926, entitled "De Hollandsche Kolonie in Michigan" is most inaccurate. The account is obviously based on a brochure in my possession and issued in Grand Rapids, Michigan, by the Grand Rapids National Bank and titled "Het Hollandsche Element in Grand Rapids, Michigan" which has numerous errors. For example, the city of Holland is described as having 30,000 inhabitants when it has only 12,000! Both letters in the *Algemeen Handelsblad*, evening ed., July 5 and 6, 1926, swarm with inaccuracies.

6. Letter from J. Vennema, Chicago, Ill., Sept. 15, 1920.

7. Letter written from Grand Rapids on Mar. 29, 1925, by C. J. Van der Plasse to his parents in Ierseke [Zeeland Province].

8. Letter from Grand Rapids by C. J. Van der Plasse, Oct. 28, 1923.

9. Account of A. Couwenhoven in *The Banner*, Jan. 13, 1928. Conversation with Plugge in Middelburg, Aug. 1920. At that time Plugge was agent for the H.A.L. [Holland America Line]. Earlier he had lived as a factory hand in Grand Rapids and was a member of Hugenholtz' Independent Church. He knew about the orthodox element from personal experience!

10. L., "Leekenpraatjes," in *Stemmen uit de Vrije Hollandsche Gemeente*, IV, No. 9, 1889.

11. Max Weber, *Gesammelte Aufsätze zur Religionssoziologie* (Vol. I, 1922), I, 210, 211.

12. J. Jansen, "Een verblijf in Amerika," *Vragen van den Dag*, 36 (Aug. 1920), 633.

13. W. A. Bonger, *Geloof en Misdaad* (1913), 75.

14. Max Weber, *Gesammelte Aufsätze*, I, 209.

15. T. N. Carver, *Present Economic Revolution*, 90, 92.

16. *Pella's Weekblad*, Mar. 17, 1922.

17. Furniture Manufacturers Association of Grand Rapids, Michigan. *Grand Rapids, A Good Place to Work and a Good Place to Live.*

18. Grand Rapids National Bank, "Het Hollandsche Element in Grand Rapids," 13. Beets contributed to this publication.

19. Jenks and Lauck, *Immigration Problem*, 502–506. It is not indicated when this research took place; there is a reference (141) to a "recent study." It probably took place in 1912. See Pref., Third ed., 1913.

20. Carver, *Present Economic Revolution*, 89, 28.

21. See n.17 above.

22. S. J. Menning, "Uit Grand Rapids," *De Volksvriend*, June 5, 1924.

23. M. G. Levenbach, *Arbeid in Amerika, De sociale beweging in de Vereenigde Staten* (1926), 174.

24. See n.17 above.

25. R. P. J. Tutein Nolthenius, *Nieuwe Wereld* (1902), 227. That there had been a time when the general reliability of the Dutch came into question became evident to me from the manuscript of a lecture, "Holland Emigration to Michigan," by the Hon. G. Diekema and published in 1918 in Holland, Michigan. The printed copy omitted the following passage from the manuscript: "I am sorry to be obliged to chronicle here that some of their descendants have learned the ways of the land and do not entirely sustain the enviable reputation acquired by their fathers."

26. Tutein Nolthenius, *Nieuwe Wereld*, 225.

27. Article in *De Christelijke Heraut* (Pella, Iowa), June 21, 1882.

28. *Stemmen uit de Vrije Hollandsche Gemeenten in Amerika*, V. No. 6, 1890.

29. *Stemmen*, V, No. 5, 1890.

30. Jenks and Lauck, *Immigration Problem*, 548.

31. On my trip through the Dutch settlements I had many conversations and heard many curious things. Here I refer to some of these things.

32. Carver, *Present Economic Revolution*, 261–262.

33. *Onze Toekomst*, Apr. 14, 1926.

34. A. Feiler, *Amerika-Europa. Erfahrungen einer Reise* (1926), 223.

35. T. De Vries, "George Birkhoff, Sr. " [obituary], *Neerlandia*, Apr. 1911.

36. Een Fries, "Uit het verre Westen," *Leeuwarder Courant*, Mar. 10, 1925.

37. Jenks and Lauck, *Immigration Problem*, 496–497.

38. On Dec. 28 and 29, 1911, I stayed with Sjouke De Zee at Irnsum and learned much from my ship companion about many incidents during his stay among the Frisians. Also see *Sljucht en Rjucht*, 1912, No. 32ff. and esp. No. 35.

39. Letter from C. J. Van der Plasse, Grand Rapids, Oct. 28, 1923.

40. From a conversation on Aug. 4, 1921, with our consul in Grand Rapids, Jacob Steketee, grandson of the pioneer.

41. Grand Rapids National Bank, "Het Hollandsche Element in Grand Rapids," 3.

42. Extracted from the firm's publicity given to met at the time of my visit in Aug. 1921.

43. *Onze Toekomst*, Apr. 14, 1926.

44. From a conversation with Plugge in Aug. 1920, after he had remigrated to Middelburg.

45. Grand Rapids National Bank, "Het Hollandsche Element in Grand Rapids, Michigan."

46. For these data I express my thanks to Mr. De Zee whom I had visited in Rochester, July 31, 1921. I am also indebted to the valuable account of G. Elferink written from Rochester, N.Y., in Feb. 1922.

47. I visited Evergreen Park on Aug. 11, 1921. With respect to the other truck gardening areas, I obtained data from Mrs. R. Zoethout, Natoma Farm, Hinsdale, Ill., Jan. 25, 1922.

48. The consul-general, Steyny Parvé, gave me some very important introductions so that I could visit the notorious immigrant's island of Ellis Island. (See my article, "Ellis Island," *De Groene* [*Amsterdammer*], April 22, 1922.) On top of that, the list of official banquet guests—the only data—had been lost.

49. I visited these three gentlemen in July 1921, and they gave me some important information and some very interesting insights into immigrant life.

50. *Fourteenth Census of the United States*, 1920. I also express my thanks to the late Reverend [T.] Jongbloed of Hoboken.

51. On purpose, I remained in Hoboken several days so that I could get in touch with the most diverse Hollanders.

52. Membership roll as of March 1921, of the society "Eendracht maakt Macht," at New York.

53. Konrad Bercovici, *Around the World in New York* (1924), 414.

54. Jo Van Ammers-Küller, *Mijn Amerikaansche reis* (1926), 29ff.

55. Personal communication of Jhr. W. v. H., secretary of this group, whom I visited on July 22, 1921.

56. I traced this development through a careful comparison of accounts—not always in agreement with one other—which were made available to me in 1919 by Mr. Diamant, by the intercession of one of my former students, Miss C. Diamant in 1926, by my former student, Mr. M. Vigeveno, and by Mr. H. Polak in 1920. This account digresses slightly from the one given by Dr. F. Leviticus in his *Encyclopaedie der Diamantnijverheid*.

57. Leviticus, *Encyclopaedie*, 48.

58. Account of Mr. Diamant.

59. Leviticus, *Encyclopaedie*, 48, 49.

60. M. Barents, *De Diamantslijperij Maatschappij te Amsterdam, 1845–15 April–1920* (1920), 76.

61. Account of M. Vigeveno (Apr. 2, 1926).

62. Barents, *Diamantslijperij Maatschappij*, 80–81.

63. Figures given me by M. Vigeveno. According to H. Polak, the export in March, 1923 was *fl.* 23,000,000. See *De Telegraaf* of Aug. 23, 1924.

64. A letter sent me by H. Polak from Laren, Noord Holland, Jan. 10, 1920.

65. From a most interesting and extensive account by M. Vigeveno, Apr. 2, 1926.

66. Reprinted from the *Nieuwe Rotterdamsche Courant* in *Neerlandia*, Feb. 2, 1912, 38.

67. *Nieuwe Rotterdamsche Courant*, evening ed., Aug. 23, 1924, "Een belangrijk jubileum in de diamantnijverheid."

68. "De Diamantindustrie in Amerika," an article in the *Weekblad of the A.N.D.B.* [Algemeene Nederlandsche Diamantwerkers Bond], reprinted in *De Telegraaf*, July 7, 1923.

69. See nn. 65 and 67 above.

70. See n.64 above.

71. Various items from an elaborate correspondence with our consul-general in San Francisco and from a conversation with Miss S. Welters, secretary to the consul-general. Regarding orthodoxy see *The Banner*, May 8, 1925.

72. Letter from consul-general H. A. v. C. T. [H. A. Van Coenen Torchiana], July 28, 1920.

73. *Eleventh Yearbook* (1923) of the Holland American Chamber of Commerce, 43.

74. Letter from consul-general Van Coenen Torchiana, Sept. 20, 1920.

75. J. H. Van Hoboken, "Californië," in *Economische Verslagen van Nederlandsche diplomatieke en consulaire ambtenaren*, XVI, No. 7 (1922), 287. Supplement with the title "Handelsberichten," Jan. 25, 1923. Concerning land purchases at this time read, for instance, "Californië, het Goudland" in *Het Handelsblad*, morning ed., Dec. 22, 1917.

76. Letter from consul-general Van Coenen Torchiana, July 28, 1920; Van Hoboken, *Californië* (1923), 285.

Chapter 15   *Cultural Life in the Settlements*

1. J. Strong, *Ons Land: Deszelfs mogelijke toekomst en tegenwoordige crisis* (translated from English into Dutch by Rev. J. H. Karsten) (1889), 186.

2. W. McDougall, *The Group Mind* (2nd ed., 1927), 6, 197.

3. Ibid., "The Part of the Leaders in National Life," 137.

4. I heard this remark made by more than one side during my trip.

5. Cf also H. Beets, "Questionable Church Entertainments," Editorial in *The Banner*, Apr. 18, 1924.

6. *The Banner*, Nov. 11, 1920.

7. G. J. Stuart, "Our Group Psychology," *Religion and Culture*, Apr. 1924.

8. N. H. Dosker, *De Hollandsche Gereformeerde Kerk in Amerika* (1882), 263, n.53. These notes are really by Dosker's son, the very well known, recently deceased H. E. Dosker.

9. S. Van der Werf, "The Development of the Reformed Church in the West" in *Seventy-Fifth Anniversary Exercises, Celebrating the Admission of the Western Churches into the Reformed Church* (Oct. 13, 1925), 20.

10. Ibid., 25.

11. The Board of Publication and Bible School Work of the Reformed Church, *The Acts and Proceedings of the one hundred and nineteenth regular session of the General Synod of the Reformed Church in America* (1925), 1010.

12. The Christian Reformed Church in America Yearbook (1925), 22.

13. *Corwin's Manual* (1922), 89.

14. Van der Werf, "Development of the Reformed Church," 26.

15. Beets in *The Banner*, July 23, 1926.

16. Ibid., July 3, 1925.

17. *Corwin's Manual* (1922), 88.

18. Told to me by Rev. S. De Bruine in a letter from Oskaloosa, Iowa, Aug. 26, 1920.

19. Letter of S. De Bruine, Oskaloosa, Iowa, Apr. 19, 1920.

20. Franz Boas, *Kultur und Rasse* (1922), 128. Although Boas means here especially the "Landesnatur" [nature of the land], we may, after having studied McDougall's works, extend Boas's hypothesis to the social environment. See, for instance, Boas, *Kultur*, 131.

21. "Music in the Churches," *The Banner*, July 29, 1920. Also in many other issues of *The Banner* one can see that the hymns are in fact constantly defended. See *The Banner*, Oct. 28, Nov. 4, 1927.

22. *The Banner*, July 29, 1920. Cf. also P. H. Hugenholtz, Jr., *Licht en Schaduw. Indrukken van het godsdienstig leven in Amerika* (n.d.).

23. *De Wachter*, June 21, 1920.

24. *De Volksvriend*, Feb. 15, 1923.

25. *De Volksvriend*, Feb. 8, 1923.

26. N. J. Monsma, "Kerkelijk Besef," *Reformed Herald*, June, 1925.

27. *De Hollandsche Amerikaan*, Apr. 3, 1921. See also *De Grondwet*, Jan. 23, 1923.

28. I found examples in *De Volksvriend*, Jan. 27, 1921 (the Christian Reformed Church at Leota, Minn., called a Reformed minister) and in *De Volksvriend*, Feb. 10, 1921 (the Reformed Church at Bethel called a Christian Reformed Church minister). In *De Volksvriend*, Jan. 25, 1923, Oggel complained about the evil.

29. *Onze Toekomst*, Jan. 13, 1922.

30. Cf. also Dr. Beets in *The Banner*, Oct. 8, 1926.

31. *De Grondwet*, Nov. 16, 1920.

32. Ibid.

33. See Dr. A. C. Van Raalte, Editorial in *Religion and Culture*, Dec. 1921.

34. Address of Dr. H. Beets to the General Synod of the Reformed Church, *The Banner*, Oct. 8, 1926.

35. Ibid.

36. N. H. Dosker, *Hollandsche Gereformeerde Kerk*, n.106 (of H. E. Dosker). See also *The Leader*, July 3, 1918; H. Beets, *The Christian Reformed Church in North America* (1923), 122.

37. G. De Jonge, "The Union of the Classis in Holland with the Reformed Church in America" in *Seventy-Fifth Anniversary Exercises*, 16.

38. See details about these endeavors in H. Beets, *De Chr. Geref. Kerk in N.A.* (1918), 314ff.

39. *Corwin's Manual* (1922), 89.

40. Beets, *Chr. Geref. Kerk*, 314.

41. *The Banner*, Editorial, July 23, 1926.

42. Beets, *Chr. Geref. Kerk*, 316.

43. De Jonge, "Union of the Classis Holland," 17.

44. Van der Werf, "Development of the Reformed Church," 26, 24.

45. Ibid., 22. It is this Vanderwerf who has been working for years with Dr. H. Beets in *De Heidenwereld*.

46. *The Christian Journal*, Aug. 21, 1920, editorial by H. Van Andel. Instead of "historical growth," read "the power of the dead."

47. *The Banner*, Oct. 8, 1926, editorial by Dr. H. Beets.

48. *The Banner*, July 23, 1926, editorial by Dr. H. Beets.

49. That we should consider them as seceders is mentioned by Rev. G. De Jonge, "The Union of the Classis," 16. This is not entirely correct. Many must have belonged to the "Nederduitschen" while still in the Netherlands. The difference is also vague between "Nederduitsch" and "Oud-Gereformeerd." Even Dr. H. Beets (*The Banner*, Mar. 13, 1925) seems unable to make a clear cut differentiation. Some facts are taken from this article.

50. *De Volksvriend*, May 5, 1921; Dec. 2, 1920.

51. All one has to do is read the reports about "The Protesting Church of Hull and Sioux Center" in *The Banner*, Jan. 7, 1927.

52. *The Banner*, July 23, 1926, editorial by Dr. H. Beets.

53. Van der Werf, "Development of the Reformed Church," 24.

54. I want to point out emphatically that this citation of Dr. H. Beets is taken from his editorial in *The Banner*, Oct. 17, 1924, where it refers to a poem, which might be called "humility."

55. J. J. Hiemenga, "Address to the General Assembly of the United Presbyterian Church," *The Banner*, June 25, 1926.

56. M. E. Hepkema, *Eenige Weken in Amerika*, reprinted from *Nieuwsblad van Friesland* (n.d.), 229.

57. Some facts have been taken from previously mentioned sources, and others from a correspondence from Chicago in *De Maasbode*, June 19, 1926.

58. J. A. Van Heertum, "Roman Catholics in the United States," *De Heidenwereld* (Holland, Mich.), Dec. 1923. This essay appeared originally in the *Jubileum Album*, presented to Her Majesty, the Queen.

59. William McDougall, *An Introduction to Social Psychology* (1908), 116.

60. Beets, "Gebrek aan Leeraars," in the Christian Reformed Church in America Yearbook (1927), 142, 144.

61. *De Hope*, May 24, 1921.

62. B. K. Kuiper, *Ons Opmaken en Bouwen* (1918), 216, 230, 217.

63. Ibid., 217.

64. Ibid., 41, 39, 40.

65. Beets, editorial (extremely worthwhile reading!) in *The Banner*, July 29, 1920.

66. McDougall, *Introduction to Social Psychology*, 300.

67. F. J. Turner, *The Frontier in American History* (1921), 263.

68. S. C. Nettinga, "History of Hope College," Ch. XXI, in *Corwin's Manual* (1922).

69. *De Hope*, Feb. 1, 1921. Statistics of P. Hinkamp, communicated by A. Raap.

70. "Report of the Council of Hope College," Apr. 22, 1925, in *The Acts and Proceedings*, 821.

71. *Fiftieth Anniversary Catalog of Hope College* (May 1916), 17ff.

72. "Annual Report of the Board of Superintendents of the Western Theological Seminary," May, 1925, in *The Acts and Proceedings*, 807. See here also *Report*, New Brunswick Theological School, 793.

73. Western Theological Seminary, *Semi-Centennial Catalog*, 1869–1919, and *Catalog*, 1920–1921. See also Nettinga, "History of Western Theological Seminary," Ch. XXII, in *Corwin's Manual* (1922).

74. Nettinga, "History of Central College," Ch. XXIII, in *Corwin's Manual* (1922), 165.

75. *Central College Catalog*, 1922–1923.

76. "Ninth Annual Report" in *The Acts and Proceedings*. The total of 324 that is given by the Committee on Education is incorrect. See the *Acts*, 842. This is the gross total.

77. *Central College Catalog* 1922–1923.

78. "Ninth Annual Report" and "Committee on Education" in *The Acts and Proceedings*, 825, 842.

79. "Report of the Northwestern Classical Academy," April 1925 in *The Acts and Proceedings*, 837.

80. Northwestern Classical Academy, *Catalogue no. 37*, 1920–1921, 12.

81. Report of Pleasant Prairie Academy, 1925, in *The Acts and Proceedings*, 835.

82. "Twentieth Annual Report of the Board of Trustees of the Wisconsin Memorial Academy," March 22, 1921, in *The Acts*

and Proceedings, June, 1921, *The Acts* of 1925 contain no reports concerning this academy. S. C. Nettinga, "History of Academies," *Corwin's Manual* (1922), Ch. XXIV, gives an incorrect total of 56 (p. 167).

83. G. E. MacLean, "State Universities, School Systems, and Colleges, in the United States of America," in Gaillard Lapsley, *The America of Today* (1919), 188–189.

84. Kuiper, *Ons Opmaken,* 212.

85. J. J. Hiemenga, "Calvin's Past, Present and Future," *The Banner,* Mar. 26, 1926.

86. In addition to previously mentioned publications, see also the articles of Dominie J. Noordewier, "De Oorsprong van Onze Theologische School," and Rev. G. D. de Jong, "The History of the Development of the Theological School," in *Semi-Centennial Volume, Theological School and Calvin College, 1876–1926* (1926), 7–48.

87. B[eets], "Gebrek aan Leeraars," in Christian Reformed Church of America *Yearbook* (1927), 144.

88. B. K. Kuiper, *De Janssen Kwestie en Nog Iets* (Grand Rapids, 1922); R. Janssen, *Voortzetting van den Strijd* (Grand Rapids, 1922). For those who want to know what is understood by "science" in religious circles, this is interesting literature!

89. J. J. Hiemenga in *The Banner,* Mar. 26, 1926.

90. A. J. Rooks, "A History of Calvin College," in *Semi-Centennial Volume,* 49ff.

91. Christian Reformed Church *Yearbooks,* 1925, 1927.

92. *Yearbook of the Theological School and Calvin College at Grand Rapids, Mich.,* 1923–1924, 15ff.

93. J. J. Hiemenga in *The Banner,* Mar. 26, 1926.

94. B. K. Kuiper, *Ons Opmaken,* 265.

95. Beets, *Chr. Geref. Kerk,* 372 n.12. Cf. also *Onze Toekomst,* Sunday ed., Aug. 6, 1920, and *The Banner,* Oct. 2, 1925.

96. Beets, *Chr. Geref. Kerk,* 369ff. See also *De Wachter,* Dec. 24, 1919.

97. *De Wachter,* Dec. 24, 1919.

98. MacLean, "State Universities," 191.

99. M. C. Van Mourik Broekman, *De Yankee in Denken en Doen* (1914), 131ff.

100. Beets, "A Plea for Secondary Christian Schools," Editorial in *The Banner,* Nov. 19, 1926.

101. MacLean, "State Universities," 191.

102. J. L. Snethlage, *De Schoolopvoeding in Amerika en het Vraagstuk der Kennis* (n.d.), 22.

103. Most of these facts I take from more or less elaborate articles in *The Banner*

issue of Oct. 31, 1924 (H. H. Meeter), Dec. 3, 1926 (S. G. Ribbler), etc.

104. Snethlage, *De Schoolopvoeding,* 8.

105. Northwestern Classical Academy, *Catalogue no.* 37, 1920–1921, 11.

106. A real American-type article of a Christian Reformed person is in *The Banner,* Apr. 1, 1927 (C.E.R.W.).

107. Mark Fakkema, "The Growth of the Christian Schools," in *Onze Toekomst,* July 30, 1920.

108. Beets, *Chr. Geref. Kerk.* A clear overview of this education is given in Ch. 10, par. 10.

109. Beets, "To Which School our Sons and Daughters?" Editorial in *The Banner,* Sept. 3, 1926.

110. *Onze Toekomst,* Jan. 6, 1921.

111. Fakkema, "Growth of Christian Schools."

112. Beets, "Reply to Rev. J. Bovenkerk," Editorial in *The Banner,* Dec. 18, 1926.

113. J. G. Van den Bosch, "The Christian School and Christian Education," in *Semi-Centennial Volume,* 146.

114. "Rev. Bovenkerk's Reply," in *The Banner,* Nov. 5, 1926.

115. *The Banner,* Dec. 3, 1926.

116. Ibid., Dec. 10, 1926.

117. *De Wachter,* Dec. 24, 1919.

118. Beets in *The Banner,* Sept. 3, 1926.

119. Beets, "To Which Schools."

120. *The Banner,* Sept. 3, 1926.

121. Ate Dykstra, "Christian Education," *The Christian Journal,* Apr. 22, 1926.

122. *The Banner,* Sept. 24, 1926 ("Timely Topics" by Rev. E. J. Tanis); Ibid., Sept. 3, 1926, Editorial by Dr. H. Beets.

123. Ibid., Dec. 10, 1926.

124. Ibid., Sept. 3, 1926; ibid., Dec. 10, 1926.

125. *Onze Toekomst,* Jan. 6, 1921.

126. "The Plea for Secondary Christian Schools Continued," *The Banner,* Nov. 26, 1926.

127. See, for instance, a report in *De Grondwet,* May 3, 1921.

128. Ibid., Nov. 9, 1920. See the exhortation in *The Banner,* Aug. 15, 1924.

129. Hans Hansen, "Het Eucharistisch congres te Amsterdam, 20–27 Juli 1924," *Onze Toekomst,* Oct. 1, 1924.

130. *The Banner,* Oct. 31, 1924.

131. Ibid., Aug. 15, 1924.

132. Beets, "Chicago Eucharistic Congress," Editorial in *The Banner,* Feb. 12, 1926.

133. Rev. E. J. Tanis, "Timely Topics," *The Banner,* Oct. 1, 1926. See also ibid., Feb. 12, 1926.

134. Taken from Hans Hansen's outpouring, "Het Eucharistisch congres."

135. Dean A. J. Rooks, "A History of Calvin College, 1894–1926," *Semi-Centennial Volume*, 89.

136. "College Standards," *Religion and Culture*, Sept. 1921. During my stay in Grand Rapids and Holland, I had the opportunity to meet several teachers: A. J. Rooks, J. B. Nykerk, E. D. Dimnent, A. Raap, and Professor Blekkink.

137. *De Hope*, Feb. 9, 1926.

138. *Yearbook of the Theological School and Calvin College*, 1920–1921, "Alumni," 77ff.

139. *The Banner*, Dec. 31, 1926.

140. *Het Oosten*, Oct. 8, 1920.

141. S. Van der Werf, "Development of the Reformed Church," 24, 26.

142. "Ninety-third Annual Report of the Board of Foreign Missions," in *The Acts and Proceedings*, 94.

143. H. Ten Kate, *Psychologie en ethnologie in de koloniale politiek* (reprint from *De Indische Gids*, June, July, 1916), VI, "De Zending."

144. See note 142.

145. *De Hope*, May 17, 1921. Christiaan Snouck Hurgronje knew Zwemer personally and, in an interview with me on Dec. 29, 1927, called him a Muslim expert of renown who has a lot of optimism. This is so typical of Americans. In his beautiful lecture, given that day at Amsterdam, Snouck Hurgronje referred to several facts taken from Zwemer. See also *Achtste Koloniale Vacantiecursus voor Geografen* (1927), 23.

146. "De internationale zendingsraad en Dr. A. L. Warnshuis," *De Heidenwereld*, Dec. 1923.

147. "Ninety-fourth Annual Report of the Board of Domestic Missions" in *The Acts and Proceedings*, 28, 30, 33.

148. W. T. Demarest, "History of Domestic Missions" in *Corwin's Manual* (1922), 226.

149. Beets, *Chr. Geref. Kerk*, 287ff.

150. H. Ten Kate, *Reizen en Onderzoekingen in Noord-Amerika* (1885), esp. Chs. 7 and 8.

151. Beets, *The Christian Reformed Church in North America* (1923), 152ff.; *The Banner*, Nov. 19, 1926.

152. Beets, *Christian Reformed Church*, "Jewish Missions."

153. *De Volksvriend*, Dec. 16, 1920.

154. Beets, *Chr. Geref. Kerk*, 361ff.; *The Banner*, Nov. 11, 1920, etc.

155. *The Banner*, Nov. 11, 1920; Beets, "Eastern Problems," ibid., Feb. 11, 1927.

156. "Ninety-fourth Annual Report," "Meeting the Hollanders," 31.

157. Letter of P. Bleeker-Vos, dated Chicago, Oct. 25, 1926, to Mrs. Vis at Amsterdam.

158. This interesting remark I took from H. Beets, *Chr. Geref. Kerk*, 286.

159. Dr. L. S. Huizenga, "The China Mission," in Beets, *Chr. Geref. Kerk*, 164ff.

160. "Historisch bericht" in *The Banner*, Nov. 11, 1920.

161. L. S. Huizenga, "China Mission," 173.

162. Beets, "The Synod of 1926," Editorial in *The Banner*, June 18, 1926.

163. Ibid., Jan. 30, 1925.

164. Beets, *Chr. Geref. Kerk*, 177.

165. *The Banner*, Oct. 31, 1924.

166. *Onze Toekomst*, Jan. 13, 1922.

167. *De Volksvriend*, Dec. 9, 1920.

168. H. J. G. Van Andel, "Wij en de Wereld," *The Christian Journal*. W. Eerdmans obtained a bundle of these articles for me.

169. *De Volksvriend*, Sept. 20, 1923.

170. E. R. P. [E. R. Post], "The Calvin Club at the University of Michigan" in *Calvin Prism*, 1921.

171. *The Banner*, Oct. 29, 1926; Jan. 13, 1928.

172. G. F. Huizinga, *What the Dutch have done in the West of the United States* (1909), 272. Also *De Grondwet*, Apr. 5, May 10, 24, 1921.

173. Jacob Van der Zee, *The Hollanders of Iowa* (1912), 275.

174. Huizinga, *What the Dutch have done*.

175. *The Banner*, Oct. 29, 1926.

176. A. Oosterheerdt, "Critisch-Psychologische Beschouwingen over het Leven der Nederlanders in de V. St. v. N. Amerika," Unpublished work, 51ff.

177. Kuiper, *Ons Opmaken*, 24.

178. *De Grondwet*, May 3, 1921.

179. *De Volksvriend*, Nov. 11, 1920.

180. *De Volksvriend*, March 22, 1923.

181. *Het Oosten*, Dec. 5, 1919.

182. *De Telegraaf* (Paterson), Oct. 6, 13, 1920.

183. Information is borrowed from "City of Grand Rapids under Commission-Manager Government, 1924–1925 Review."

184. *Onze Toekomst*, Feb. 18, 1921.

185. Meredith Nicholson, *The Valley of Democracy* (1919), 194.

186. *De Volksvriend*, Jan. 27, 1920.

187. *De Hope*, Nov. 30, 1920.

188. *De Grondwet*, Feb. 8, 1921.

189. *De Grondwet*, Mar. 6, 1923.

190. *Pella's Weekblad*, Mar. 10, 1922.

191. *The Leader*, Feb. 17, 1926.

192. *The Banner*, Feb. 4, 18, 1927.

193. *De Hope*, Oct. 19, 1920.

194. *De Grondwet*, Oct. 19, 1920.

195. Upon my request, Mr. Hoekstra, an interesting figure among the Holland immigrants, wrote a short biography, from which I borrowed various facts.

196. G. Timmer in *De Volksvriend*, Aug. 30, 1923.

197. The Hon. J. G. Diekema gave me an interview from which much of the information is borrowed (Aug. 9, 1921, at Holland, Mich.).

198. C. C. Vaughan, *Michigan Official Directory and Legislative Manual for the Years 1917 and 1918*, 796.

199. Borrowed from a very short biography sent to me.

200. *The Banner*, Aug. 27, 1926.

201. Vaughan, *Michigan Official Directory*, 785–786, 126–229 provides a survey of all state politicians, from which I have derived the pure-blooded Young Dutch. Possibly there are more who have Americanized their names, however. My source goes no farther than 1916.

202. I visited his father in South Holland, Ill., Aug. 12, 1921.

203. The Legislative Voters League in its *Report on Outgoing Legislators*, 1916.

204. Borrowed from a few election documents which I was able to secure in 1921.

205. Van der Zee, *Hollanders of Iowa*, 234.

206. Ibid., 244.

207. The list of candidates in *De Volksvriend*, May 29, 1924.

208. M. G. Levenbach, *Arbeid in Amerika* (1926), 73.

209. This information I gathered at the time of my visit to Pella. Cf. also *Pella's Weekblad*, Mar. 31, 1922.

210. Jhr. De Graeff, for example, although an envoy at Washington for some years, heard the name for the first time from me.

211. Cyrenus Cole, *A History of the People of Iowa* (1921), 546. A "professional politician" would not have been able to write such a sensitive "Postscript Personal."

212. *The Pella Chronicle*, Oct. 27, 1921.

213. *Het Oosten*, Dec. 31, 1920.

214. M. R. Stone, "Idaho" in Gruening, *These United States, A Symposium* (2 vols., 1923–1924), II, 170ff.

215. C. C. Eisse, *Früchte deutscher Arbeit* (1910), 178.

216. Eisse, *Früchte*, 178ff.; "Die Ermordung des Gourverneurs Steunenberg." My efforts to secure more information about S.,

as in so many other cases, were in vain. Rev. Steunenberg of Orange City, for example, presumably a member of the family, has left my letters unanswered.

217. *The Banner*, Oct. 29, 1926.

218. Huizinga, *What the Dutch have done*, 41.

219. A. Brummelkamp, Jr., *Levensbeschrijving van wijlen Prof. A. Brummelkamp* (1910), 250; Van Bergeyk, *Een Geschiedenis van de eerste jaren in Pella* (1855), 8.

220. A Siegfried, *Les Etats-Unis d'Aujourd'hui* (1927), 275.

221. Van Mourik Broekman, *De Yankee in Denken en Doen*, (1914), 84.

222. *De Grondwet*, Nov. 9, 16, 1920; *De Volksvriend*, Nov. 4, 1920.

223. *Het Oosten*, Oct. 8, Nov. 12, 1920.

224. *Pella's Weekblad*, Nov. 10, 1922.

225. Cole, *History of the People of Iowa*, 528ff.

226. *Pella's Weekblad*, Nov. 10, 1922.

227. Van der Zee, *Hollanders of Iowa*, 241.

228. *De Grondwet*, Nov. 14, 1922. Most remarkably, the majority in Zeeland voted for the American Fortney. The old jealousy?

229. *The Banner*, Oct. 29, 1926.

230. R. A. Gouwens, "Story of South Holland Post Office" in E. P. Beaudette-Neil, *Thornton Township, Cook County, Illinois* (1921).

231. *De Volksvriend*, Oct. 21, 1920.

232. *De Volksvriend*, Oct. 7, Nov. 4, 1920.

233. *De Volksvriend*, Nov. 11, 1920.

234. *De Grondwet*, Nov. 9, 1920; *De Volksvriend*, Nov. 4, 1920.

235. *Het Oosten*, Sept. 17, 1920.

236. Siegfried, *Les Etats Unis*, 246.

237. Oosterheerdt, *Critisch-Psychologische Beschouwingen*, Ch. IV, "Politiek leven."

238. Van der Zee, *Hollanders of Iowa*, 241.

239. *De Grondwet*, June 15, 1920.

240. Oosterheerdt, *Critisch-Psychologische Beschouwingen*, Appendices.

241. *De Grondwet*, June 15, 1920.

242. Levenbach, *Arbeid in Amerika*, 108.

243. Kuiper, *Ons Opmaken*, 25.

244. *De Hope*, Oct. 19, 1920.

245. *De Grondwet*, Dec. 28, 1920.

246. H. J. G. Van Andel, "Social and Civic Activity," *Religion and Culture* (Jan. 1922).

247. Ibid.

248. Dykstra, "Civil Government," a column in *The Christian Journal*, a weekly in Grand Rapids. Dr. H. Beets refers to it in his "editorial": "A Christian Party—Why Not?" *The Banner*, June 26, 1925, from which also the following quotations are taken.

249. Levenbach, *Arbeid in Amerika*, 111ff.

250. *De Volksvriend*, Nov. 11, 1920.

251. Oosterheerdt, *Critisch-Psychologische Beschouwingen*, Appendices.

252. *Het Oosten*, Oct. 8, 1920. *De Grondwet*, Nov. 9, 1920.

253. Letter from Dirk Nieland, Grand Rapids, Mich., May 11, 1927.

254. Letter from C. J. Van der Plasse, Grand Rapids, Mich., Oct. 28, 1923.

255. Letter from P. Bleeker-Vos, Chicago, Ill., Oct. 25, 1926.

256. A. Feiler, *Amerika-Europa Erfahrungen einer Reise* (1926), 194.

257. From G. Elferink I received a very complete interesting communication, Rochester, N.Y., Feb. 1922.

258. Information about Velsing is borrowed from a letter from G. Elferink to S. de Zee at Irnsum (Rochester, Dec. 10, 1921).

259. G. Myers, *Geschichte der groszen Amerikanischen Vermögen* (2 vols., 1923), I, 177; *De Gereformeerde Amerikaan*, Vol. 3 (1899), 57.

260. I have this information also, thanks to Elferink in his letter of Feb. 1922. Cf. also *Neerlandia*, Nov., 1915.

261. Cf. note 258. Also N. A. De Vries *De Niewe Wereld, Amerika* (1923), 115.

262. Feiler, *Amerika-Europa*, 193.

263. E. J. Tanis, "Death of Debs. Death of Socialism?" *The Banner*, Oct. 29, 1926.

264. J. G. Van den Bosch, "Johannes Groen," *Religion and Culture* (April 1924). See also *Yearbook*, 1925, 176ff.

265. L. Berkhof, *The Church and Social Problems* (1913), 18–20.

266. Beets, *De Chr. Geref. Kerk*, 331–332.

267. R. B. Kuiper, *Christian Liberty*, 17ff.

268. *Acts of Synod*, 1926, of the Christian Reformed Church of North America, 60. Cf. also *The Banner*, Apr. 9, 16, 1927; Dec. 23, 1927.

269. Beets, *Chr. Geref. Kerk*, 332.

270. Kuiper, *Ons Opmaken*, 152; *Standard-Bulletin*, Dec. 6, 1919. Beets does not list any of these societies in his book about the Christian Reformed Church, which is dated 1923.

271. De Vries, *Nieuwe Wereld*, see the four maps adjoining p. 46.

272. Official program of the Holland National Day, Saturday, Aug. 27, 1910. Olympic Park, Newark, N.J.

273. Program of the Performance of the Roseland Division of the Algemeen Nederlandsch Verbond, on Thursday evening, Dec. 17, 1914.

274. Personal information from Sj. De Zee.

275. De Vries, *Nieuwe Wereld*, 64.

276. Van den Bosch, "Johannes Groen," 164; See *Yearbook* 1925, 179.

277. Letter to me from G. Elferink, Rochester, N.Y., Feb. 1922.

278. Information from Sj. De Zee.

279. *The Banner*, Nov. 12, 1926. Also J. Van Lonkhuyzen in *Onze Toekomst*, Apr. 21, 1926.

280. *The Banner*, Oct. 17, 1924. Also J. Huizinga, *Mensch en Menigte in Amerika* (1918), 42ff.

281. *The Banner*, Nov. 12, 1926.

282. A. F. Pollard, *Factors in American History* (1925), Ch. V, "Imperialism," 214, 125.

283. *De Grondwet*, March 22, 1921. The publisher of this paper is Mrs. Mulder. The Mulders from the same city of Holland are planters in Cuba When I asked about this on my visit to the editor in Holland, any connection was denied.

284. Pollard, *Factors*, 218.

285. Hans Hansen, "De Amerikanen in de Philippijnen," *Onze Toekomst*, Apr. 21, 1926.

286. Oosterheerdt, *Critisch-Psychologische Beschouwingen*, Ch. 4, "Political Life," Ch. 8, "Newspapers."

287. *Het Oosten*, Sept. 24, 1920.

288. "Civil Government" column in *The Christian Journal*, and *Standard-Bulletin*, two papers appearing in Grand Rapids, Mich., partly in Dutch and partly in English.

289. *Het Oosten*, Oct. 8, 1920.

290. The old content I borrowed from A. Kuyper, *Varia Americana*, 91.

291. *De Utah-Nederlander*, Dec. 8, 1921.

292. Dr. H. Beets, "Dutch Journalism in Michigan," *Michigan History Magazine*, VI (1922, Nos. 2–3), 439. Melis Stoke Jr. (Dr. H. Beets), "Amerikaansche Brieven, II" *Neerlandia* (Nov. 1915).

293. *De Gereformeerd Amerikaan*, Vols. 1–6, have been studied by me. Cf. also the *Gedenkboek*, 1907, 176, and Beets, *Chr. Geref. Kerk*, 308.

294. *Gedenkboek*, 1907, 177. The statistics cited are from the essay of De Veer in *Elsevier's Geïllustreerd Maandschrift* (Feb. 1909).

295. Personal information from W. Eerdmans. Some quotations were taken from the series of H. J. G. Van Andel, "Wij en de Wereld," *The Christian Journal*, as cultural expressions.

296. Several examples of both papers are in my possession.

297. Information from W. Eerdmans in a letter, Nijmegen, Jan. 16, 1921. I have a

Huisvriend of 1923. Theo De Veer speaks about *Het Huisgezin*, with a circulation of 8,000 copies, "which lies before him." It seems however that he means *De Huisvriend*. Neither of the two names, however, appears in his newspaper photo.

298. *Onze Toekomst*, Jan. 6. 1922. Theo De Veer in *Elsevier's Geïllustreerd Maandschrift* (Feb. 1909).

299. Letter from H. Beets, Aug. 26, 1927.

300. Melis Stoke Jr. (H. Beets) in *Neerlandia*, Nov. 1915. When I mention the year 1898, my information is taken from a list of A. Kuyper in his *Varia Americana*, 91–92. Cf. also Van der Zee, *Hollanders of Iowa*, 252.

301. Letter written to me by G. Elferink, Rochester, N.Y., Feb. 1922.

302. At the request of Poelstra I have personally endeavored, although in vain, to get the A.N.V. interested in this matter.

303. Thus W. Eerdmans wrote to me very emphatically from Nijmegen, Sept. 11, 1920.

304. Letter to me from Dr. G. Rijbroek, Holy Family Convent, Alverno, Route 1, Manitowoc, Wis., July 4, 1925.

305. Letter to me from W. H. H. De Haan, Roman Catholic priest, New Franken, Wis., Apr. 26, 1926.

306. Interview at Nijmegen, Aug. 1920.

307. Information from W. Eerdmans in a letter to me, Nijmegen, Sept. 11, 1920.

308. Van der Zee, *Hollanders of Iowa*, App. B, 349ff.

309. Dr. H. Beets gave me the statistics concerning the Grand Rapids papers in Aug. 1927; they are partly only "estimates." If it is not otherwise indicated, the figures and other information were obtained by me at the time of personal visits to the various editors in 1921. Advertising papers in the Dutch language like *De Huisvriend* recommending Dr. Zokoro's remedies and Holland-California of F. Schaap of San Francisco promoting land sales, I only mention here in passing.

310. *De Volksvriend*, Oct. 7, 1920.

311. *De Grondwet*, Nov. 21, 1922. Prohibition was in effect in Michigan before the federal prohibition law of 1920.

312. *De Volksvriend*, Sept. 9, 1920.

313. I have been a subscriber for a few years to this paper (1921 and 1922).

314. *De Volksvriend*, Feb. 4, 1924.

315. *De Heidenwereld*, Dec. 1923 even has a picture and article about this Netherlander born in Ost Friesland, who plays an important role in the spiritual life of the immigrants.

316. "Wij en de Wereld," series of articles in *The Christian Journal*.

317. *De Hollandsche Amerikaan*, Mar. 29, 1921.

318. *Neerlandia*, Nov. 1915 (Melis Stoke, Jr.).

319. *Het Oosten*, Jan. 7, 1921. *Het Oosten* will have nothing to do with the involvement of the church in social life. *Het Oosten*, June 1, 1920.

320. *Het Oosten*, May 21, 1920.

321. K. J. Van den Bussche, *Het Nederlandsch in Amerika, Noord en Zuid* (1881).

322. J. Te. Winkel, "Het Nederlandsch in Noord-Amerika en Zuid-Afrika," *Vragen van den Dag* (1896), 344.

323. S. J. Van Ginneken, *Handboek der Nederlandsche Taal* (Vol. 1, 1913), 292ff.

324. *De Grondwet*, Dec. 21, 28, 1920; Apr. 12; May 17; June 7, 1921.

325. J. Huizinga, *Amerika levend en denkend* (1926), 39.

326. *Pella's Weekblad*, Mar. 10, 17, 1921.

327. Read the description by G. Van der Veen from Menodat, Mo. in *Weekblad voor het Kanton Bergum*, Vol. 7 (1882), No. 46. Cf. *Het Oosten*, Jan. 7, 1921.

328. Beets, *Chr. Geref. Kerk*, 308.

329. *Corwin's Manual* (1922), 176–177.

330. *The Banner*, Oct. 1, 1926; *Yearbook*, 1927.

331. *The Calvin College Chimes*, Jan. 1920. See also *The Milestone* (1920 class), 75.

332. A few numbers are in my possession. Cf. also *The Banner*, Oct. 1926.

333. *De Volksvriend*, Oct. 25, 1923.

334. *Religion and Culture*, A Quarterly, Grand Rapids, Mich., I, No. 1.

335. *Religion and Culture*, I and II.

336. Ibid., IV (June 1922), "Our fourth Trip."

337. Ibid., VI, Dec. 1924, "Anatole France" (J. G. Van den Bosch).

338. See n.336 above.

339. Dr. J. Van Lonkhuyzen in the Sunday edition of *Onze Toekomst*, Oct. 1, 1924.

340. *The Witness*, I, No. 1.

341. *Reformed Herald*, Grand Rapids, Mich., I, No. 1, "Integration."

342. Much more carefully than I, Dr. H. Beets expresses his surprise about the dropping out of precisely the most talented of the editorial staff. Cf. *The Banner*, June 26, 1925. The brethren took offense because of this and for other reasons. Cf. *Reformed Herald*, I, No. 2.

343. *Reformed Herald*, May 1926, 185.

344. J. W. De Vries, O.P., "Een Hol-

landsche Kolonisatie in Wisconsin," *Katho-lieke Illustratie*, 1908; *De Volksvriend*, Oct. 25, 1923.

345. Van der Zee, *Hollanders of Iowa*, 255.

346. *De Volksvriend*, Sept. 27, 1923.

347. Letter of D. J. Van Löben Sels in *Hou en Trouw*, Jan. 1905.

348. Huizinga, *What the Dutch have done*, 40.

349. Van Norden, *The World Mirror*, Special Holland Number (Oct. 1909).

350. Mr. De Haan sent me a few copies of his paper which appears in Dubuque, Iowa.

351. See his "Publieke Verklaring," among others, in *Onze Toekomst*, Jan. 13, 1922.

352. *Het Oosten*, Mar. 25, 1921.

353. *De Hope*, Nov. 30, 1920; *Onze Toe-komst*, Sept. 3, 1920, "Weer Tehuis."

354. Borrowed from the issues of Dec. 29, 1920; Jan. 29, 1921; and Feb. 9, 1921, which are in my possession.

355. *The American Daily Standard*, Dec. 29, 1920. "To Our New Readers," which is an interesting bit of Dutch Americanism.

356. *De Hope*, June 7, 1921, has an extended excerpt from Monsma's book, "Why the American Daily Standard Failed." I have not been able to get a copy.

357. *Het Oosten*, Dec. 3, 1920.

358. *De Hope*, Nov. 30, 1920.

359. *De Volksvriend*, Mar. 24, 1921; *Het Oosten*, Mar. 25, 1921.

360. *De Hope*, June 14, 1921.

361. Cf. his apology "Publieke Verklaring" in *Onze Toekomst*, Jan. 13, 1922.

362. *Het Oosten*, Mar. 25, 1921.

363. *Onze Toekomst*, Sept. 3, 1920.

364. Van Andel, "Wij en de Wereld," *The Christian Journal*.

365. A. Oosterheerdt, *Opstellen mijner Jon-gelingsjaren* (1905). See the foreword by Prof. K. Schoolland.

366. Dr. H. Beets, "Prof. W. Heyns retiring," Editorial in *The Banner*, Nov. 5, 1926.

367. Cole, *People of Iowa*, 548.

368. D. M. Smeets, "Dr. Dosker, the Writer," in *Memorials Rev. H. E. Dosker, D.D.L.L.D., L.H.D. 1855–1926* (Louisville, 1926), 48.

369. For example, by Dr. A. Zijderveld in the article "Verwaarloosde Renaissance Literatuur" in the *Nieuw Theologisch Tijdschrift*, 16 (No. 2, 1927).

370. Peter Hoekstra is Christian Reformed and a professor at Calvin College.

371. *The Banner*, July 9, 1926.

372. Arnold Mulder, *The Outbound Road* (1919), 294.

373. That is the way the colonists feel about it, and not the least educated or most "narrow-minded" among them. See *The Christian Journal* in which J. G. Van den Bosch says something about *The Outbound Road*.

374. In *Gedenboek F. Domela Nieuwenhuis*, 9.

375. G. Andreae, "Leonard Charles Van Noppen, *Neerlandia*," Apr. 1916. Also Borel's "Zusje" is mentioned by Andreae among the translations.

376. J. Van Hinte, "Nederlandsche Nederzettingen in de Vereenigde Staten van Noord-Amerika," *Neerlandia*, April 1923.

377. Hepkema, *Eenige weken in Amerika*, 1265ff., reprint from *Het Nieuwsblad van Friesland*. See also "Het Jubileum van Coopersburg." *Leeuwarder Courant*, May 1, 1926, p. 4. An important article about Edward Bok in the *Nieuwe Rotterdamsche Courant*, Evening ed., Oct. 26, 1927.

378. Paul Sabel in *De Groene Amsterdammer*, Mar. 13, 1926.

379. A bragging survey, which can only be justified for being "truly American," concerning "Mr. Bok's Activities" in *Dollars Only*.

380. Horace Kallen, *Culture and Democracy in the United States* (1924), 86.

381. Carver, *The Present Economic Revolution*, 78–79.

382. Cf. *De Telegraaf*, Morning ed., Apr. 24, 1927. About Van Loon's famous work, see Huizinga, "Aanleeren of afleeren," *De Gids* II (1924), 130ff.; about Gompers, see Samuel Eliot Morison, *The Oxford History of the United States, 1783–1917* (2 vols., 1927), II, 372.

383. H. P. G. Quack, *De Socialisten, Personen en Stelsels* (6 vols., 1911–1912), II, 295.

384. Dr. A. J. Barnouw in the *Monthly Letter*, Sept. 1927; *Nieuwe Rotterdamsche Courant*, Evening ed., Oct. 10, 11, 15, 1927.

385. About J. O. Schimmel, etc., see A. B. Faust, *Das Deutschtum (Bedeutung)*, 60. Regarding the Netherlander A. Pincoff, see the *Rotterdamsch Jaarboekje*, 1927.

386. All these names, as far as not specifically mentioned, are taken from the letter of Van Löben Sels in *Hou en Trouw*, Jan. 1905. Letter of J. P. André Mottu, Norfolk, Va., Feb. 16, 1904; "De Hollanders in America" article in *Neerlandia*, Jan. 1908, and Van Noorden, *The World Mirror*, "Special Holland Number," Oct. 1909.

387. By Beets and others in different *Banner* articles; by the Algemeen Nederlandsch Verbond, for instance, in *Neerlandia*, Aug. 1927.

388. Letter, H. A. W. Van Coenen Torchiana in *Hou en Trouw*, Oct. 1904.

389. Interview with Mr. H. at Arnhem, July 1920.

390. Letter of H. Visscher, Kansas City, Mo., Oct. 8, 1920.

391. Letter of Prof. J. A. De Haas, Rotterdam, Aug. 28, 1920. Prof. De Haas lived in America for many years and is again living there now.

392. See the evening ed. of the *Algemeen Handelsblad* of May 19, 1919, in which the director of the Informatiebureau of the Nederlandsche Vereeniging "Landverhuizing" published judgments of government authorities.

393. I had the pleasure of meeting several times at Hoboken with Rev. J., since then deceased. In addition to providing interesting information, he also showed me this letter of Jan. 5, 1920, the answer to a new year's wish. Lothrop Stoddard, *Re-forging America*, p. 111. *Nieuwe Rotterdamsche Courant*, Feb. 26, 1928. *De Arbeidsmarkt, Orgaan voor de Praktijk*, Vol. 9, Issues 2 and 38.

394. R. Kjellen, *Schweden, Eine Politische Monographie* (1917), 88. About K. Velsing, see *Sljucht en Rjucht*, Nov. 12, 1927.

395. C. Borgman, *Bezoek in de Vereenigde Staten van Noord-Amerika in het jaar 1850* (1854), 147.

396. H. W. Heuvel, Letter, Borculo, June 23, 1924.

397. "Het Jubileum van Coopersburg," *Leeuwarder Courant*, May 1, 1926.

398. About H. Bierman, see *Nieuwe Rotterdamsche Courant*, Apr. 2, 1927; about Edward Bok, *ibid.*, Oct. 26, 1927 (Evening ed.).

399. *Weekblad voor het Kanton Bergum*, Sept. 23, 1882.

400. Taken from an interview with brother Symons at Amsterdam, Sept. 26, 1927.

401. Kjellen, *Schweden*, 87ff., 106, 113.

402. A. Van C. P. Huizinga, "De V. St. en de Landverhuizing," *Economische Statistische Berichten*, May 28, 1919.

403. J. C. C. Sandberg, "Behoud en Vermeerdering van Arbeidskrachten," *Economische Statistische Berichten*, July 31, 1918.

404. Maurer, *De Nederlandsche Boer tegenover de Landverhuizing* (1912), 27.

405. A. Van C. P. Huizinga, "The Dutch in America," *The Christian Journal*, Jan. 17, 1920.

406. Jeremiah W. Jenks and W. Jett Lauck, *The Immigration Problem*, (4th ed., 1917), 554. The official census cites 6,667 immigrants in 1912. Jenks and Lauck give

the total of 6,619. In percentages this does not cause much of a difference. It should not be forgotten that the years mentioned were considered to be a "flourishing period" for the Netherlands, although I have pointed out the elasticity of this concept.

407. R. T. Kuiper, *Eene Stem uit Amerika over Amerika* (1881), 20.

408. *De Grondwet*, June 1, 1920.

Chapter 16   From Netherlander to American

1. *Historical Souvenir of the Celebration of the Sixtieth Anniversary of the Colonization of Hollanders in Western Michigan, held in Zeeland, Michigan, August 21, 1907* (1908), 60.

2. G. J. Diekema, "Holland Emigration to Michigan: Its Causes and Results," *Michigan Historical Magazine* (Oct. 1917), 11.

3. *Nieuwe Rotterdamsche Courant*, Evening ed., May 3, 1927.

4. D. Versteeg, *De Pelgrim-Vaders van het Westen* (1886), 55, 50.

5. Letter in "Achttal Brieven mijner Kinderen," *De Grondwet*, July 14, 1914.

6. C. Te Lintum, "De oude Handelsstad Tiel en haar tegenwoordig voorkomen. *Tijdschrift van het Koninklijk Nederlandsch Agrarisch Genootschap* (1923), 107–117.

7. L. Mumford, "The City," in Harald E. Stearns, *Civilization in the United States* (1922), 8.

8. Jonkheer Gevers van Endegeest, *Over de Droogmaking van het Haarlemmermeer* (Vol. III, 1861), III, 219; H. N. Ter Veen, *De Haarlemmermeer als Kolonisatiegebied* (1925), 50.

9. J. H. Gallée, *Het Boerenhuis in Nederland en zijn Bewoners* (1908), 13.

10. B. B. Haagsma, *Frisia of Schets der Friesche Volkplanting in Noord-Amerika* (1855), 16.

11. C. Borgman, *Bezoek in de Vereenigde Staten van Noord-Amerika in het jaar 1850* (1854), 163.

12. T. G. Van der Meulen, "Van Bergum naar Amerika," *Weekblad voor het Kanton Bergum*, Apr. 1, 1882.

13. Gallée, *Boerenhuis*, 13.

14. *De Volksvriend*, Mar. 27, 1924.

15. Compare the "oude Kaapsche stijl" in Dorothea Fairbridge, *Historic Houses of South Africa* (London, 1922).

16. Conversations with Sjouke De Zee after his return from America, Dec. 28 and 29, 1921.

17. D. Nieland, Letter, Grand Rapids, May 11, 1927.

18. See, for example, *Pella's Weekblad*, Oct. 27, 1922; *De Grondwet*, Mar. 22, 1921.

19. *De Grondwet*, Feb. 8, 1921.

20. Ibid.

21. Christelijke Gereformeerde Kerk, *Acta der Synode* (1926), 308.

22. *De Grondwet*, Feb. 8, 1921.

23. *The Grand Rapids Spectator*, July 2, 1927.

24. Beets, "De Gereformeerde Nederlanders in Noord-Amerika," reprinted in *Nederlandsch Archief voor Kergeschiedenis*, XIX, 273.

25. *The Pella Chronicle*, Oct. 27, 1921.

26. *De Volksvriend*, Feb. 23, 1921.

27. Hamlin Garland, *A Son of the Middle Border* (1917), 236.

28. *De Volksvriend*, Mar. 27, 1924.

29. *De Volksvriend*, May 26, 1921.

30. L. R. Reid, "The Small Town" in Stearns, *Civilization*, 291.

31. *Het Oosten*, Sept. 17, 1920.

32. *De Grondwet*, Sept. 14, 1920.

33. J. Van Hinte, "Nederland in Amerika. Orange City, 1870–1920," *De Amsterdammer*, Sept. 25, 1920.

34. *Pella's Weekblad*, Sept. 1, 1922.

35. L. R. Reid, "Small Town."

36. Ph. E. Gibbons, *Pennsylvania Dutch and other Essays* (1882), 47, 406. Or are Oct. 31 and Sept. 29 (Michelsday) confused here?

37. Burns, *Poetical Works*, 18ff., 560. J. Schrijnen, *Nederlandsche Volkskunde* (2 vols., n.d.), I, 208; Gibbons, *Pennsylvania Dutch*, 406.

38. *De Volksvriend*, Nov. 4, 1920; *De Grondwet*, Nov. 16, 1920.

39. *De Volksvriend*, Nov. 4, 11, 1920.

40. *The Banner*, Apr. 18, 1924; Mar. 26, 1926; Jan. 7, 1927; etc. H. J. Kuiper, "In Our Circles, from 1915–1925," a series of articles in *The Reformed Herald*, 1925–1926.

41. B. K. Kuiper, *Ons Opmaken en Bouwen* (1918), 97, cf. 6, 126.

42. H. J. Kuiper, "In Our Circles, from 1915–1925," *The Reformed Herald*, Feb. 1926.

43. *De Volksvriend*, Feb. 3, 1921.

44. *De Volksvriend*, Aug. 9, 1923.

45. A. E. Crookewit, "Amerikaansche Schetsen," *De Gids*, Apr. 1870, 69.

46. *Nieuwe Rotterdamsche Courant*, Evening ed., May 3, 1927.

47. Peter Kalm, *Reis door Noord-Amerika* (2 vols., 1872), II, 57.

48. *De Volksvriend*, May 19, 1921.

49. L. R. Reid, "Small Town," 289. Cf. also the Pref. vii.

50. *De Volksvriend*, Jan. 26, 1922.

51. T. Greidanus, *The Dutch in New Netherlands and the United States* (1909), 62.

52. J. Van Hinte, "Nederlandsche Nederzettingen in de Vereenigde Staten van Noord-Amerika," *Neerlandia*, Apr., 1923; *Sljucht en Rjucht*, Mar. 26, 1927.

53. William McDougall, *An Introduction to Social Psychology* (1908), 338.

54. Information from Sjouke De Zee during my stay at Irnsum. Compare his travel accounts in *It Heitelân*, 1921, Nos. 26ff., and *Sljucht en Rjucht*, 1921, Nos. 32–52.

55. L. Knappert, *Verloving en Huwelijk in vroeger Dagen* (1914), 126, 164ff.

56. Gibbons, *Pennsylvania Dutch*, 406ff.

57. Schrijnen, *Nederlandsche Volkskunde*, I, 246.

58. F. Vulpius, *Zevenjarige Ondervinding in Noord-Amerika* (1847), 28.

59. *De Grondwet*, June 1, 1920.

60. *De Grondwet*, Mar. 22, 1921.

61. *De Volksvriend*, Dec. 4, 1919.

62. *De Volksvriend*, Mar. 3, 1921.

63. Interview, Aug. 10, 1921. Dimnent himself is partly of Dutch ancestry; however, he grew up among Irish, Germans and Yankees.

64. Diekema, "Holland Emigration," 11.

65. H. Schurtz, *Völkerkunde* (1903), 34.

66. G. G. Kloeke, *Reflexen van Hollandsche Expansie in de huidige Nederlandsche Dialecten* (1926), 8.

67. Letter in A. Brummelkamp, *Stemmen uit Noord-Amerika*.

68. Letter in "Achttal Brieven," published in *De Grondwet*, July 14, 1914.

69. Versteeg, *Pelgrim-Vaders*, Ch. XVI, "Onder de Amerikanen."

70. Engbertus Van der Veen, *Life History and Reminiscences* (1917), 7.

71. J. Schrijnen, *De Isoglossen van Ramisch in Nederland* (1920) I, 65.

72. Letter from B. Mouw, at Sioux Center.

73. Interview with Prof. |Albert| Raap, Aug. 8, 1921, at Holland, Mich., and with Cornelis Van Loo at Zeeland, Aug. 9, 1921.

74. G. Draayom, "Schetsen uit het Verleden. West Branch," *De Volksvriend*, May 22, 1924.

75. H. Bouwman, *Amerika, Schetsen en Herinneringen* (1912), 23.

76. Interview with C. Van Loo at Zeeland, Mich., Aug. 9, 1921.

77. Letter, Nijmegen, Sept. 24, 1920.

78. This unburdening |"*ontboezeming*"| is dated Sept. 22, 1921.

79. Letter, St. Anna Parochie, Dec. 20, 1917.

80. Jacob Van der Zee, *The Hollanders of Iowa* (1912), 203.

81. These data are taken from conversations with Eerdmans and Sj. De Zee, and from the latter's articles in *Sljucht and Rjucht*; from a letter from Irnsum, March, 1928; and from a news item in *Onze Toekomst*, Aug. 1, 1923.

82. W. Wundt, *Völkerpsychologie*, Vol. I, "Die Sprache," (1911), 405.

83. *De Grondwet*, May 31, 1921. The other quotations are from many other Holland-American newspapers in the years 1920 and 1921.

84. Henry E. Dosker, *Levensschets van Rev. A. C. van Raalte* (1893), 200.

85. W. Bode, "Onze Duitsche Germeenten" in the *Gedenkboek van het Vijftigjarig Jubileum der Christelijke Gereformeerde Kerk A.D. 1857–1907*, (1907), 73. Elaborated further in George Schnücker, *Die Ostfriesen in Amerika* (1917), 119.

86. Schnücker, *Ostfriesen*, 233.

87. M. J. Bosma, "Our American Churches" in *Gedenboek*, 81.

88. *The Banner*, May 6, 1920. Beets calls this a rapid increase. This depends on your point of view!

89. *The Banner*, May 2, 1924.

90. John Engelsman, *Historische Schets van de Eerste Gereformeerde Kerk van Orange City, Iowa, 1871–1921* (1921).

91. Letter, Grand Rapids, Mich., Nov. 28, 1927.

92. *The Banner*, Mar. 14, 1924.

93. For this information I am indebted to the two orthodox publishers, Bottenburg and Ten Have, who occasionally come in contact with Dutch Americans in the course of their business dealings (Dec. 15, 1917).

94. *The Banner*, July 16, 1926, "Editorial."

95. Letter from W. Eerdmans, Nijmegen, Sept. 11, 1920.

96. Interview, Dec. 15, 1917.

97. *De Grondwet*, June 15, 1920.

98. Interview, Aug. 1920.

99. *The Forty-ninth Annual Report of the Grand Rapids Public Library, April 1, 1919–March 31, 1920* (Grand Rapids, 1920), 55, App. E.

100. Personal research in the Rijksbibliotheek, Aug. 3, 1921.

101. *Bulletin of the Grand Rapids Public Library* (Jan.–Feb., 1921), 14.

102. Letter, Nijmegen, Sept. 11, 1920.

103. Letter, J. Kuiken, St. Anna Parochie, Dec. 20, 1917.

104. Letter, New York, Jan. 13, 1921.

105. A new Holland-America Line. Surprisingly, nothing is said about the Chicago accident and the Michigan attempts.

106. Very detailed is the article by Prof. Dr. A. Eekhof in the *Gedenkboek van het Algemeen Nederlandsch Verbond bij gelegenheid an zijn 25-jarig bestaan, 1898-Mei-1923* (1923).

107. *Neerlandia*, June, 1927. One need only scan the files of *Neerlandia* to confirm the anemic state.

108. "Editorial" in *The Banner*, July 16, 1926.

109. *Neerlandia*, Dec. 1926.

110. *Neerlandia*, Dec. 1917.

111. A. S. De Jong, "Observations on the Americanization of our People in the West," *Religion and Culture*, July, 1921.

112. Very stirring emotional outpouring about Americanization by J. Ellerbroek, *Pella's Weekblad*, Mar. 9, 1923.

113. *De Volksvriend*, April 3, 1924.

114. *Nieuwe Rotterdamsche Courant*, Evening ed., D., Mar. 5, 1927.

115. De Jong, "Observations on Americanization." W. Stuart, "Americanization in N. W. Iowa," *Religion and Culture*, Sept. 1921. The assertions Van der Zee (*Hollanders of Iowa*, 364), makes concerning the rapid phasing out of the Dutch language appear wholly unjustified.

116. I visited the Struyck family at Albany, July 30, 1921.

117. Konrad Bercovici, *On New Shores* (1925), 172, 177.

118. A. Eekhof, *De Hervormde Kerk in Noord-Amerika (1624–1664)* (2 vols., 1913), II, 203. The words were borrowed by Eekhof from Mrs. Schuyler (Mariana) Van Rensselaer, *History of the City of New York in the Seventeenth Century* (2 vols., 1909), II, 149–150.

119. T. Leviticus, *Encyclopaedie der Diamantnijverheid* (1908), 17–18.

120. A. Dauzat, *La géographie linguistique* (1922), 12.

121. F. Schönemann, *Die Kunst der Massenbeeinflüssung in den Vereinigten Staaten von Amerika* (1926), 89.

122. Wundt, *Völkerpsychologie*, I, "Die Sprache," 406.

123. Interview in July, 1920, at Oosterbeek.

124. S. R. Steinmetz, *De Nationaliteiten in Europa* (1920), 29.

125. Lammert J. Hulst, *Drie en Zestig Jaren Prediker* (1913), 154.

126. B. K. Kuiper, *Ons Opmaken en Bouwen* (1918), 250.

127. J. Ellerbroek, "Eenige gedachten

over Amerikanisatie," *Pella's Weekblad*, Mar. 23, 1923.

128. Een Fries, "Uit het verre Westen," *Leeuwarder Courant*, Mar. 25, 1924.

129. *De Volksvriend*, Feb. 23, 1922.

130. Franz Boas, *Kultur und Rasse* (1922), 63.

131. Ibid., 74.

132. S. R. Steinmetz, "Nieuw menschenras in Amerika," *Nederlandsch Tijdschrift voor Geneeskunde* (1911), II A., 351.

133. F. Von Luschan, *Völker, Rassen, Sprachen* (1922), 60, 69, 138.

134. E. Fischer, *Rasse und Rassenentstehung beim Menschen* (1927), 29.

135. K. Lamprecht, *Americana* (1906), 24.

136. H. Bouwman, *Amerika, Schetsen en Herinneringen* (1912), 177.

137. Clark Wissler, *The Relation of Nature to Man in Aboriginal America* (1926), 155ff.

138. Steinmetz, "Nieuw menschenras," 348, 344.

139. Bercovici, *On New Shores*, 172.

140. Ibid., 166.

141. *Algemeen Handelsblad*, Evening ed., July 5, 1926. "De Hollandsche Kolonie in Michigan."

142. Steinmetz, *Nationaliteiten*, 31.

143. W. McDougall, *The American Nation, Its Problems and Psychology* (1925), 5.

144. T. N. Carver, *The Present Economic Revolution in the United States* (1926), 79.

145. Schönemann, *Massenbeeinflüssung*, 97.

146. Horace M. Kallen, *Culture and Democracy in the United States* (1924), 86.

147. A. Penck, *U. S. Amerika* (1917), 30–31.

148. *Corwin's Manual*, 582.

149. Van der Zee, *The Hollanders of Iowa*, App. B, 349–362.

150. Clipping from *The Grand Rapids Press* in my possession.

151. Interview, July 1926.

152. *Algemeen Handelsblad*, July 11, 1918.

153. Bercovici, *On New Shores*, 172.

154. Bouma, "Our School and American Life" in *Semi-Centennial Volume, Theological School and Calvin College 1876–1926* (1926), 189.

155. "Brief uit Pella, Oct. en Nov. 1854," *De Gids*, 1855, 212ff.

156. Letter of S. A. Sipma, Sept. 26, 1848, in *Belangrijke Berigten uit Pella* (1849).

157. Een Fries, "Uit het verre Westen," *Leeuwarder Courant*, IX, IV, XXI. I know that this Frisian came directly from the Netherlands, but point out his very modern type of business and advanced education, which provide a defense for him against the charge of being "narrow-minded and bigoted."

158. *De Grondwet*, May 25, 1920.

159. Beets in *The Banner*, Nov. 26, 1926.

160. Henriëtte (Van der Schalk) Roland Holst, *Opwaartsche Wegen* (Rotterdam, 1914), 13–14.

Bibliography

Works Specifically Related to the Netherlanders in America.

Andreae, G. "Leonard Charles van Noppen," *Neerlandia*, Apr. 1916.

Andriessen, W. F. *Californië met het oog op Nederlandsche landverhuizers.* Amsterdam: 1892.

———. "Een en ander over Landverhui-zing," published by the *Nut van het Alge-meen*, 1892.

———. "Is Emigratie naar de Ver. Staten van Noord-Amerika nog langer aanbeve-lingswaardig?" *De Economist*, 1892.

Arends, Fridrich. *Het Mississippi-dal of het Westen der Vereenigde Staten van Noord-Amerika.* Translated from the High German. Groningen: 1839.

Asher, G. M. *Bibliographic and historical essay on the Dutch books and pamphlets related to New Netherland.* Amsterdam: 1868.

Baird, Robert. *Kerkelijke Geschiedenis. Kerkelijke Statistiek en Godsdienstig leven der Vereenigde Staten van Noord-Amerika.* First part of the German translation by Dr. R. Brandes. Translated into Dutch by A. W. v. d. Worm. Schoonhoven, 1846. Second part, directly translated into Dutch by E. B. Swalue from the revised American pub-lication and provided with an appendix. 1849.

Beaudette-Neil, E. P. *Thornton Township, Cook County, Illinois.* Hammond, Ind.: 1921.

Beeking, M. N. *Emigratie naar de Vereenigde Staten en Kleine Boerderijen in Den Grooten Wintertuin.* Hilversum: n.d.

Beernink, G. *De Geschiedschrijver en Rechts-geleerde Dr. Arend van Slichtenhorst en zijn Vader Brant van Slichtenhorst, Stichter van Albany, Hoofdstad van den Staat New-York.* Arnhem; 1916.

Beets, Henry. *Abraham Lincoln, zijn tijd en leven.* Grand Rapids: 1909.

———. "Amerikaansche Bibliotheken en hunne Ned. werken," reprint from *Tijd-schrift, Boek-en Bibliotheekwezen*, No. 5, 1915.

———. *De Chr. Geref. Kerk in N.-A.* Grand Rapids: 1918.

———. "De Gereformeerde Nederlanders in de Vereenigde Staten en in hoeverre zij hun vierderlei doel bereikt hebben na 75 jaren." As series of 3 articles in *De Reformatie*, June 9, 16, 23, 1922.

———. "De Gereformeerde Nederlanders in Noord-Amerika. Idealen verwerkelijkt binnen tachtig jaren?" *Nederlandsch Archief voor Kerkgeschiedenis*, 1927.

———. "Dutch Journalism in Michigan," *Michigan History Magazine*, VI (Sept. 1922), 435–41 (See also Melis Stoke).

———. "Het Psalmgezang in de Calv. Kerken van Noord-Amerika," *Nederlandsch Archief voor Kerkgeschiedenis*, Nieuwe Serie, Pt. X.

———. *The Christian Reformed Church in North America.* Grand Rapids: 1923.

———. "The True Reformed Dutch Church. U.S.A." A series of articles in *Religion and Culture*, 1921.

Behse, Karl Edward. *De Stephanische Landver-huizing. Eene waarschuwende proef van geestelijk belang.* (Dutch translator not named). Amsterdam: 1846.

Berkhof, L. *The Church and Social Problems*. Grand Rapids: 1913.

Berkhout, J. *Brief uit Noord-Amerika*. Amsterdam: 1849.

Beukma, K. Jz. *Brieven van den Landbouwer K. Jz. Beukma, verhuisd naar de Vereenigde Staten van Noord-Amerika. Opnieuw uitgegeven ten behoeve van allen, die naar Noord-Amerika willen en getrouwe berigten verlangen omtrent het land en den toestand aldaar*. Amsterdam: 1849.

_____. *Brieven van K. Jz. Beukma; Bevorens landbouwer op de boerderij Castor, in het kerspel Zuurdijk, Gemeente Leens, doch verhuisd naar de V. St. van N.-Am. in den jare 1835, aan deszelfs achtergelaten familie in de provincie Groningen*. Groningen: 1835.

Beyer, Moritz. *Het boek der Landverhuizers, of Gids en Raadsman bij de verhuizing naar Noord-Amerika*. Leipzig, 1846. Freely adapted from the 2nd edition in High German for the needs of the Dutch. Amsterdam: 1847.

Bijlsma, R. "Rotterdams Amerika-vaart in de eerste helft der zeventiende eeuw," *Bijdragen Voor Vaderlandsche Geschiedenis en Oudheidkunde*, V, 5th pt.

Blink, H. "De Landverhuizing uit Nederland." *Vragen van den Dag*, 30 (1915).

_____. *Handboek voor de Kennis van Nederland en Koloniën*. 's-Gravenhage: 1922.

Bloemendaal, E. J. G. *Naar Amerika*. Arnhem: 1911.

Bogaerts, J. B. *Gids voor toekomstige kolonisten in Louisiana. Uitgegeven door het Bureau van Kolonizatie in den Staat Louisiana*. (A printed letter, July 24, 1911.)

Bok, Edward. *The Americanization of Edward Bok. The Autobiography of a Dutch Boy Fifty Years After*. New York: 1920. (Also in the Dutch language.)

_____. *Dollars Only*. New York and London: 1926.

Borgman, C. *Bezoek in de Vereenigde Staten van Noord-Amerika in het jaar 1850*. Groningen: 1854.

Bouwman, H. *Amerika. Schetsen en Herinneringen*. Kampen: 1912.

_____. *De crisis der jeugd*. Kampen: 1914.

Brennan, George A. "Hollanders First to Make Roseland Home." *The Calumet Index* (Chicago), Mar. 26, 1915.

Broere, Bastiaan. *Korte Beschrijving van het Leven van en de wonderbare Leidingen Gods met Bastiaan Broere in Nederland en in Amerika*. (Compiled by H. De Vries). Amsterdam: n.d. [1887].

Brummelkamp, A. *Stemmen uit Noor-Amerika met Begeleidend Woord van A. Brummelkamp*. Amsterdam: 1847.

_____. Brummelkamp, A., and Van Raalte, A. C. *Bedienaren des Goddelijken Woords. Landverhuizing of waarom bevorderen wij de Volksverhuizing en wel naar Noord-Amerika en niet naar Java?* Amsterdam: 1846.

Brummelkamp, Jr., A. *Levensbeschrijving van wijlen Prof. A. Brummelkamp. Hoogleeraar aan de Theologische School te Kampen*. Kampen: 1910.

Brusse, Mari Joseph. "Onder de Menschen. Canadeesche Brieven." Articles in the *Nieuwe Rotterdamsche Courant*, 1924 and 1925.

Bruyn, A. J. "Nederlandsche Energie in het Buitenland," *Vragen van den Dag*, 25 (1910).

Casson, Herbert. "The Dutch in America." *Munsey's Magazine*, Nov. 1906.

Catella Jessurun, Jacob Spinoza. *Kiliaen van Rensselaer van 1623 tot 1636*. 's-Gravenhage: 1917.

Catholic Colonization Society, U.S.A. *System in Catholic Colonization*. n.p., n.d.

_____. *Common Sense in Colonization*. n.p., n.d.

Centennial Discourses. A Series of Sermons Delivered in the Year 1876, by the Order of the General Synod of the Reformed (Dutch) Church in America. 2nd ed. New York: 1877.

Chadwick, A. T. "In the Days of Early Paterson." A series of articles in *The Paterson School News*, Mar. 10, 24; Apr. 14, 28; May 12, 1921.

Christian Reformed Church In America, *Yearbooks*, 1919, 1921, 1925, 1927. Grand Rapids.

_____. *Acta der Synode 1926 van de Christelijke Gereformeerde Kerk. Gehouden van 9 Juni to 26 Juni, 1926 te Englewood, Chicago, Ill., U.S.A.*

Cohen, Stuart M. *Zes Maanden in Amerika*. 2 vols. Haarlem: 1875.

Cole, Cyrenus. "A Bit of Holland in America," *The Midland Monthly*, 3, No. 2 (Feb. 1895).

_____. *A History of the People of Iowa*. Cedar Rapids, Iowa: 1921.

Colenbrander, H. T. "The Dutch Element in

American History." *Annual Report of the American Historical Association.* 1909. pp. 191–201. Washington, D.C.: 1911.

Copijn, A. *Schets, van de Lotgevallen der Kolonisten, die aan de proeve van Europeesche Kolonisatie aan de Saramacea hebben deelgenomen.* Paramaribo: May, 1885.

Corwin, E. T. *A Manual of the Reformed Church in America.* (*Corwin's Manual*). 4th ed. New York: 1902; 5th ed. (more condensed), New York: 1922.

Croockewit, A. E. "Amerikaansche Schetsen," *De Gids,* Apr. 1870.

De Beij, B. and Zwemer, A. *Stemmen uit de Hollandsch-Gereformeerde Kerk in de Ver. Staten van Amerika.* Groningen: 1871.

De Fremery, J. and De Fremery, W. C. B. *Californië.* (Abstracted from consular Annual Reports. Vol. I, 1869–1874. Leiden: 1876; Vol. II, 1876–1890. Den Haag: 1891.)

De Hoop Scheffer, J. G. *Kerkelijk in huiselijk leven der Doopsgezinden in Pennsylvania.* Reprinted from *Doopsgezinden Bijdragen,* 1869.

————. *Vriendschapsbetrekkingen tusschen de Doopsgezinden hier te lande en die in Pennsylvania.* Reprinted from *Doopsgezinden Bijdragen,* 1869.

De Jong, A. S. "Observations on the Americanization of our People in the West," *Religion and Culture,* July 1921.

De Jonge, W. P. *Eene Stem uit de Gereformeerde Kerk in Amerika. Bijdrage tot de geschiedenis van den kerkelijken strijd, ter nadere en onpartijdige onderzoeking aanbevolen.* Winterswijk: n.d. |1882|.

De Laet, Joannes. *Nieuwe Wereldt ofte Beschrijvinghe van West-Indien, uit veelderhande Schriften ende Aen-teeckinghen van verscheyden Natien by een versamelt Door Joannes de Laet. Ende met Noodighe Kaerten ende Tafels voorsien, Tot Leyden. In de Druckerije van Isaack Elzevier, Anno 1625.*

De Landverhuizers in het Kanaal van Voorn in Mei 1847. Amsterdam: 1847.

De Peyster, J. Watts. *The Dutch at the North Pole and The Dutch in Maine.* New York: 1857.

De Salmagundist, "Een brief uit Pella, Oct. en Nov. 1854," *De Gids,* 1855. (See Potgieter).

De Smit, C. *Naar Amerika? Schetsen uit de Portefeuille, op reis naar en door de Nieuwe Wereld.* Winterswijk: n.d. |1882|.

————. *Stemmen uit Amerika.* Nijmegen: n.d. |1882|.

De toestand der Hollandsche Kolonisatie in den Staat Michigan, Noord-Amerika, in het begin van het jaar 1849, medegedeeld in drie brieven van de Wel Eerw. Heeren A. C. van Raalte, C. van der Meulen en S. Bolks, aan C. G. de Moen, Herder en leeraar der Chr. Afgescheiden Gemeente in den Ham. Benevens een Brief van G. Baay uit Alto. Wisconsin: 1849.

De Veer, J. H. *Eene Vruchtencultuur-onderneming in Californië.* Den Haag: 1891.

De Veer, Theo. "Hollandsche Journalistiek in Amerika," *Elsevier's Geïllustreerd Maandschrift,* Feb. 1909.

————. "Hope College," *Elsevier's Geïllustreerd Maandschrift,* Mar. 1909.

————. "Ons Hollanders in Michigan," *Eigen Haard,* 1907.

De Vereenigde Staten van Noord-Amerika en de Landverhuizing derwaarts. Tiel: 1846.

De Volksvriend Jubileumnummer, Orange City, Sioux County, Iowa: Sept. 19, 1895.

De Vries, David Pietersz. *Korte historiael ende journaels aenteyckeninge van verscheyden voyagiens in de vier deelen des Wereldts-ronde, als Europa, Africa, Asia ende America gedaen.* 's-Gravenhage: 1911.

De Vries, J. W. "Een Hollandsche Kolonisatie in Wisconsin." A series of articles in the *Katholieke Illustratie* of Feb. and Mar. 1909.

De Vries, T. *Dutch History, Art and Literature. Lectures given in the University of Chicago.* Grand Rapids: 1912.

De Witt, Th. A *Discourse Delivered in the North Reformed Dutch Church in the City of New York,* Aug. 1856. New York: 1857.

De Zee, Sjouke. "Brieven ùt Amerika, oan frjeonen en bikenden," *Sljucht en Rjucht,* Aug. 20, 1921—Jan. 7, 1922.

————. "Reisbrieven fen Sjouke De Zee," *It Heitelân,* Aug. 13, 1921—Dec. 17, 1921.

Den Tex, N. J. *Amerikaansche Spoorwegen op de Amsterdamsche Beurs door N. J. den Tex.* Amsterdam: 1873.

————. "Naar Amerika," *De Gids,* (1874), 4th pt., 417–57.

Diekema, G. J. "Holland Emigration to Michigan: Its Causes and Results," *Michigan History Magazine,* I (Oct. 1917), 78–108.

Dosker, Henry E. *Levensschets van Rev. A. C. v. Raalte.* Nijkerk: 1893.

Dosker, N. H. *De Hollandsche Gereformeerde Kerk in Amerika.* Nijmegen: 1888.

Draayom, G. "Schetsen uit het Verleden. Herinneringen aan vroeger Dagen in Sioux County." A series of articles in *De Volksvriend* of 1923 and 1924.

Eekhof, A. *Bastiaen Jansz. Krol. Krankenbezoeker, Kommies en Kommandeur van Nieuw-Nederland* (1595–1645). 's-Gravenhage: 1910.

―――. *De Hervormde Kerk in Noord-Amerika* (1624–1664). 2 vols. 's-Gravenhage: 1913.

―――. "De 'Memorie' van Isaack de Rasière voor Samuel Blommaert," *Nederlandsch Archief voor Kerkgeschiedenis*, Nieuwe Serie, 15, Pt. 4 (1919).

―――. *Jonas Michaëlius.* Leyden: 1926.

Een Amerikaan. *De Vereeniging van Kerk en Staat in Nieuw-Engeland, beschouwd in derzelver gevolgen voor de godsdienst in de V. St. door een Amerikaan.* Published by H. P. Scholte. V.D.M. Amsterdam: 1841.

Een Eigen Haard, voor Iedereen langs de baan der Chicago, Milwaukee and St. Paul Railway en daarmede verbonden Spoorwegen in het Noordwesten, het Verre Westen en de Zuidelijke Deelen der Vereenigde Staten van Amerika. Milwaukee: 1888.

Een Fries. "Uit het verre Westen." A series of articles that appeared since 1921 in *De Leeuwarder Courant.*

Een Gelderschman. *De Hollanders in Iowa. Brieven uit Pella.* Arnhem: 1858.

Eerdmans, W. B. "Momentopnamen in Europa." A few articles in *The Christian Journal,* 1920.

Emond, L. "De voormalige Missie der E. E. Kruisheeren in Wisconsin," *Het Centrum,* Mar. 20 and 27, 1915.

Engelsman, John. *Historische Schets van de Eerste Gereformeerde Kerk van Orange City, Iowa 1871–1921.* Orange City, Iowa: 1921.

Evans, P. D. *The Holland Land Company.* Buffalo: 1926.

F. "Een Enkel Woord aan degenen die naar Noord-Amerika wenschen te verhuizen," *De Vereeniging: Christelijke Stemmen.* 1st pt., 1847.

Fairchild, Helen Lincklaen. *Francis Adrian van der Kemp 1751–1829. An Autobiography with a Historical Sketch.* New York: 1903.

Gedenkboek Van Het Algemeen Nederlandsch Verbond bij gelegenheid van zijn 25-jarig bestaan, 1898–Mei–1923. Geschiedenis en invloed van den Nederlandschen stam. Amsterdam-Sloterdijk: 1923.

Gedenkboek van het Vijftigjarig Jubileum der Christelijke Gereformeerde Kerk. A.D. 1857–1907. Grand Rapids: 1907.

Geerling, F. G. *Gids voor Emigranten naar de Vereenigde Staten van Noord-Amerika.* Amsterdam: n.d.

Gerstacker, F. *Lotgevallen en Ontmoetingen van een Gezelschap Duitsche Landverhuizers naar en in Noord-Amerika.* Adapted from the High German. Amsterdam: 1847.

Gorter, D. S. *De Christelijke Lijdzaamheid, aangeprezen bij het vertrek der ouddoopsgezinden van Balk, die om vrijheid van krijgsdienst naar Noord-Amerika verhuisden,* Sneek: 1853.

―――. *Godsdienstige Lectuur voor Doopsgezinden.* Sneek: 1854.

Gorter, R. A. and De Vries, C. W, compilers. "Gegevens omtrent den Kinderarbeid in Nederland volgens de Enquêtes van 1841 en 1860," *Economisch Historisch Jaarboek,* 1922.

Grand Rapids Public Library. *The Forty-Ninth Annual Report.* Apr. 1, 1919—Mar. 31, 1920. Grand Rapids: 1920.

―――. *Bulletin,* Vol. 17, No. 1. Grand Rapids, Jan.–Feb. 1921.

Greidanus, T. *The Dutch in New Netherland and the United States.* New York: 1909.

Groenman, F. E. H. "Een reeks rapporten, als vice-consul in algemeenen dienst uitgebracht aan Ridder Van Rappard, Ned. gezant te Washington ter beantwoording van vragen gesteld door de Ned. Vereen. 'Landverhuizing,'" New York, Feb. 15, 1915. Unpublished.

―――. *Iets over Landverhuizing naar de Vereenigde Staten van Amerika.* Reprinted from *Economische Verslagen,* 9, No. 5, appendix of *Handelsberichten,* No. 427, May 20, 1915.

H. "Het verblijf van Hr. M. *Gelderland* te New York, 21 Juni—3 Juli 1907," *Eigen Haard,* 1907.

Haagsma, B. B. *Frisia of Schets der Friesche Volkplanting in Noord-Amerika, benevens raadgevingen en wenken voor landverhuizers, zijnde een vervolg op het werkje getiteld "O. Bonnema en zijne Togtgenooten."* Bolsward: n.d. |1855|.

―――. *Lotgevallen van den Heer O. H. Bonnema en zijne Togtgenooten, op reis uit Friesland naar de Vereenigde Staten van Noord-Amerika,* Harlingen: 1853.

Halbertsma, J. H. "Rinse Posthumus," *De Vrije Fries*, 1862.

Hansen, Hans (J. H. Hoekstra). *Een bundel korte schetsen*. Chicago: 1920.

Hartogh Heys van Zouteveen, H. *Californië's Hulpbronnen en Toekomst, met het oog op een landverhuizing van Naderlanders derwaarts*. 's-Gravenhage: 1871.

Hasselman, J. J. *Eenige beschouwingen omtrent Kolonisatie*. Amsterdam: 1857.

Hemkes, G. K. *Het Rechtsbestaan der Holl. Chr. Ger. Kerk in Amerika*. Grand Rapids: n.d. [1893].

Hepkema, M. E. *Eenige weken in Amerika*. Reprinted from the *Nieuwsblad van Friesland*. n.d.

Heuvel, H. W. "Achterhoeksche menschen in Amerika." *Vragen van den Dag*, 38, (Apr. and May 1923).

Hewitt, G. *Minnesota, zijn voordeelen voor landverhuizers en kolonisten*. 2nd ed. Heerenveen: 1868.

Historical And Business Compendium Of Ottawa County. Vol. I. *A Complete Historical, Statistical, Biographical and Geographical Compendium of Ottawa County's Public and Private Interests and Institutions*. Grand Haven, Mich.: 1892–1893.

Historical Souvenir of the Celebration of the Sixtieth Anniversary of the Colonization of the Hollanders in Western Michigan, held in Zeeland, Michigan, August 21, 1907. Zeeland, Mich.: 1908.

Hoeksema, H. *Dominee Kouwenaar of Zedelijk Dualisme*. Grand Rapids: 1919.

Holland aan de Vereenigde Staten van Noord-Amerika ten opzigte van de voldoening van derzelver schulden, ten voorbeeld voorgesteld. Amsterdam: 1842.

Holland-American Chamber of Commerce. *Eighth Yearbook, 1920: Eleventh Yearbook, 1923*. San Francisco.

Holland Board Of Trade. *Holland, the Gateway of Western Michigan for Chicago and the Great West*. Holland, Mich.: 1914.

Holland California Land Company, *Orgaan der Holland California Land Company*. Vol. I (1890).

Holland Land Company. "Verzameling van stukken (gebundeld) betreffende landverkoopen in de Vereenigde Staten aan het eind der 18e eeuw." Located in the University Library at Amsterdam.

Holland Society Of New York, *Yearbooks*, 1886–1889.

"Hollanders In De Vereenigde Staten." Private correspondence in the *Nieuwe Rotter-damsche Courant*, Apr. 15, 16, and 17, 1920, respectively in the Evening ed. C, Morning ed. C and B.

Hollandsch Genootschap van New York. *Eerste jaarl. maaltijd. 8ste van Louwmaand 1886 in het hotel Brunswick*. Published in the K. B.

Hope College. *Fiftieth Anniversary Catalog of Hope College*, Holland, Mich.: 1916.

Huizinga, A. Van C. P. "De V. St. en de Landverhuizing," *Economische Statistische Berichten*, May 28, 1919.

————. "Ned. Landverh. naar Amerika," *Neerlandia*, Oct. and Nov. 1918.

————. *Some Interesting Points of History to be Considered in Dutch-American Relations*. Publication division. "Nieuw Nederland," Algemeen Nederlandsch Verbond.

————. "The Dutch in America," *The Christian Journal*, Jan. 17, 1920.

Huizinga, G. F. *What the Dutch Have Done in the West of the United States*, Philadelphia: 1909.

Hulst, Lammert J. *Drie en Zestig Jaren Prediker*. Kampen: 1913.

IJzermans, H. W. "Naar de Nieuwe Katholieke Kolonie te Butler in Minnesota." Butler: Aug. 31, 1910.

————. "Uit het Land der Yankees." A series of letters in *Het Centrum*, 1924.

Iowa-Commissie. *Iowa, Het Land der Emigranten*. Pella: 1870.

J. P. *Naar Amerika! Indrukken van een Ooggetuige door J. P*. Zutphen: 1882.

Jameson, J. Franklin. *Narratives of New Netherland*. New York. 1909.

Jansen, J. "Een verblijf in Amerika." *Vragen van den Dag*, 35 (Aug. 1920).

Jonathan. *Brieven uit en over de Ver. Staten van Noord-Amerika, door Dr. E. B. Swalue*. Schoonhoven: 1853.

Kalff, G. *Een nieuwe Holland-Amerika Lijn*. n.d. (also available in English.)

Kalff, Jr., G. *Frederik Van Eeden, Psychologie van den Tachtiger*. Groningen and Den Haag: 1927.

Keizer, G. "Uit de Buitenlandsche Kerken." A series of articles in *De Reformatie*, 1920 and 1921.

Kelsey, Rayner Wickersham. *Cazenove Journal 1794*. Haverford, Pa.: 1922.

Kempees, J. C. J. "De Nederlandsche Hypotheekbanken in de Vereenigde Staten." A series of articles in *De Economist*, Oct. and Dec. 1919.

King Van Rensselaer, Mrs. J. *The Social Ladder*. London: 1925.

Kloos, J. H. *Minnesota (V. St. v. N.-Am.) in zijne hulpbronnen, vruchtbaarheid en ontwikkeling geschetst voor Landverhuizers en Kapitalisten*. Amsterdam: 1867.

Knuppe, J. *Land en dollars in Minnesota en Dakota*. Rotterdam: 1883.

Koelewijn, K. Unpublished letter of Oct. 15, 1848.

Kooyman, Frank I. "De Dageraad der Nederlandsche Zending." A series of articles in *De Utah-Nederlander* of 1921.

Krijnen, B. G. *Reisverhaal van den Wel Eerwaarden Heer B. G. Krijnen*. 's-Hertogenbosch: 1837.

Kuiper, B. K. *Ons Opmaken en Bouwen*, Grand Rapids: 1918.

Kuiper, G. *Nederland. Reisbeschrijving*. Translated from the English. Grand Rapids: n.d.

Kuiper, H. J. "In Our Circles, from 1915–1925." A series of articles in the *Reformed Herald*. 1925 and 1926.

Kuiper, R. T. *Eene Stem uit Amerika over Amerika*. Groningen: 1881.

Kuyper, A. *Varia Americana*. Amsterdam: n.d.

"Landverhuizing Naar Noord-Amerika," *Onze Tijd*, II, (1849).

Leedy, E. C. *Ned. Belg. Coloniën in de N. W. Staten van Noord-Amerika*. Publisher, Great Northern Railway, Antwerpen.

Leendertz, J. M. *Doopsgezind Pioniersleven in Amerika*. Amsterdam: n.d.

Lens, L. C. *Geldbelegging in Californië en de Queen-Wilhelmina Kolonie*. Rotterdam: 1893.

Leys, J. J. *Nederlandsche Kolonisten in Canada. Rapport aan Zijne Exc. den Gouverneur van Suriname*. n.p., n.d.

Lindo, M. P. *Wenken voor Landverhuizers*. Reprint from *De Volksbode*, Vol. 8.

Lucas, H. and Eppink, J. H. *Nieuwe Hollandsche Nederzetting in Michigan gelegen in Missaukee en Osceola Counties*. Holland, Mich.: 1882.

M. A. *The Story of Father Van den Broek, O.P., A Study of Holland and the Story of the Early Settlement of Wisconsin*. Chicago: 1907.

M. W. G. (?). *De Landverhuizing naar de Vereenigde Staten van Noord-Amerika*. Bergen op Zoom: 1853.

Maurer, J. *De Nederlandsche Boer tegenover de Landverhuizing. Een tweetal lezingen*. Haarlem: ca. 1912.

Memorials. *Henry Elias Dosker D.D., L.L.D., L.H.D. Professor of Church History, Louisville Presbyterian Theological Seminary. Died December 23, 1926.*

Meyere, J. L. F. *Jubileum Album van de Ned. Vereen. Eendracht maakt Macht. 1864–6 Maart—1914*. New York: 1914.

Moorrees, J. P. G. *Landverhuizing uit een volkshuishoudkundig Oogpunt beschouwd. Eene voorlezing enz*. Deventer: 1847.

Morley, Frederick. *Michigan en zijne Hulpbronnen*. Holland, Mich.: 1882.

Mulder, Arnold. *Bram of the Five Corners*. Chicago: 1915.

———. *The Dominie of Harlem*. Chicago: 1913.

———. *The Outbound Road*. Boston and New York: 1919.

———. *The Sand Doctor*. Boston and New York: 1921.

Muller Fz., S. *De Reis van Jan Cornelisz May naar de IJszee en de Amerikaansche kust, 1611–1612*. 's-Gravenhage: 1909.

Murphy, H. C. *Jacob Steendam. Noch Vaster. A memoir of the first poet in New Nederland*. The Hague: 1861.

———. *Representation From New-Nether-Lands and Broad-Advice*. New York: 1854.

Myers, A. C. *Narratives of Early Pennsylvania, West New Jersey and Delaware, 1630–1707*. New York: 1912.

N. A. S. M. *Nederlandsch-Amerikaansche Gids en Tolk*. Rotterdam: 1887.

Naber, S. P. L'Honoré. *Henry Hudson's Reize onder Nederlandsche Vlag van Amsterdam naar Nova Zembla, Amerika en terug naar Dartmouth in Engeland 1609, volgens het Journaal van Robert Juet*. 's-Gravenhage: 1921.

———. *Het Leven van een Vloothouder*. Utrecht: 1925.

Netherlands Ambassador at Washington. *Emigratie naar de Vereenigde Staten. Rapport 16 August 1913.*

Netherlands Society of Philadelphia. *Fifth and Sixth Annual Banquets*. Jan. 23, 1896 and 1897.

Nederlandsche Vereeniging "Landverhuizing." Various early Reports and Communications.

Nieland, D. *Yankee-Dutch. Humoristische Schetsen uit het Hollandsch-Amerikaansche Volksleven*. Grand Rapids: 1919.

Niermeyer, J. F. "Indrukken van Amerika." A series of articles in the *Nieuws van den Dag*, 1913.

Nijgh, A. Q. and De Veer, J. H. *Holland California Land Company*. Rotterdam: 1889.

Nollen, Jan. *De Afscheiding. Een gedenkschrift*. Orange City, Iowa: 1898.

Noordewier, Jakob. *Een Tachtig-Jarige*, Grand Rapids: 1920.

N.V. Ned.-Am. Fruitteelt Mij. "Virginia." *De Hollandsche Fruitteeltplantages in Virginia* (U.S.A.). Bussum: 1912.

Obreen, J.A. *Amerika, Land en Volk. Een gids voor hen, die tot landverhuizen genegen zijn*. Amsterdam, Grand Rapids, and New York: 1872.

——. *Opwekking tot Landverhuizing, naar de Republiek der Ver. Staten van Noord-Amerika*. Leiden: 1871.

Ontboezeming bij gelegenheid der Nederlandsche landverhuizing naar Noord-Amerika. Amsterdam: 1847.

Oosterheerdt, A. "Critisch-Psychologische Beschouwingen over het Leven van de Nederlanders in de V. St. v. N.-Amerika." Unpublished work.

——. *Opstellen mijner Jongelingsjaren*. Holland, Mich.: 1905.

Osinga, S. *Dagboek mijner reize naar Noord-Amerika's Vereenigde Staten in den jare 1847 gedaan; gevolgd door eenige aanteekeningen des lands. Eerste stukje*. Franeker: 1848.

——, and others. *Tiental Brieven betrekkelijk de reis, aankomst en vestiging naar en in Noord-Amerika, van eenige Landverhuizers vertrokken uit de Grietenijen Het Bildt en Barradeel in Vriesland*. Franeker: 1848.

"Over de oorzaken van de Landverhuizing der Nederlanders naar de Vereenigde Staten." *Tijdschrift voor Staathuishoudkunde en Statistiek*, 1866.

Over Volksverhuizingen in het algemeen en over die naar Noord-Amerika in het bijzonder. Een ernstig woord aan alle vrienden des vaderlands, bijzonder in betrekking tot het geschrift van de Heeren Brummelkamp en van Raalte.

"Overzicht van de Hedendaagsche Landverhuizing." *De Economist*, 1869, Pt. 2.

Pas, J. J. *Benton County in den Staat Minnesota als een geschikte plaats voor eene Kolonie van Nederlandsche landbouwers*. Amsterdam, 1868.

Pella Semi-Centennial 1847—1897. Compiled and published by the *Saturday Advertiser*. Pella, Iowa: 1897.

Pelz, E. *Kompas voor Landverhuizers naar Algiers, De Kaapkolonie, Australiën, De Zuid- en Mid-delamerikaansche Staten, De Vereenigde Staten van Noord-Amerika en Canada*. Adapted from the High German. Maassluis: n.d. [after 1872]

Penn, William. *Een kort bericht (uyt het Engels overgeset) van de Provintie ofte Landschap Penn-Sylvania genaemt, leggende in Ameri-ca; . . . Tot Rotterdam. Gedrukt bij Pieter van Wynbrugge, Anno 1681*.

——. *Missive van William Penn, Eygenaar en Gouverneur van Pennsylvania, in America . . .* 2nd ed. Jacob Claus, Boekverkooper in de Prince-straat. Amsterdam: 1684.

Pennypacker, S. W. "Abraham and Dirck Op den Graeff," *The Penn Monthly*, Sept. 1875. Reprinted in *Historical and Biographical Sketches*, 1883.

——. *Historical and Biographical Sketches*. Philadelphia: 1883.

——. *The Settlement of Germantown and the Causes Which Led to It*. Reprinted from *Pennsylvania Magazine*, (Philadelphia), 1880.

Pierce, C. H. *New Harlem Past and Present*. New York: 1903.

Pieters, A. J. *A Dutch Settlement in Michigan*. Grand Rapids: 1923.

Plasberg, C. L. *Californië. Beschrijving van dat Land*. Arnhem: 1849.

Polk and Co., R. L. *Polk's Holland City Directory*. Detroit: 1921.

Posthumus, N. W. "Gegevens over de Handelsrelaties van Nederland met de Vereenigde Staten van Noord-Amerika in de eerst jaren na het Herstel," *Bijdragen tot de Economische Geschiedenis van Nederland*. I. 's-Gravenhage: 1916.

Potgieter, E. J. "Landverhuizing naar de Vereenigde Staten. (Een brief uit Pella)." *De Gids*, 1855.

Pruyn Rice, H. L. *Harmanus Bleecker an Albany Dutchman 1779–1849*. Albany: 1924.

Putnam, Ruth. "The Dutch Element in the United States," *Bijdragen voor Vaderlandsche Geschiedenis en Oudheidkunde*, 1910.

Quick, H. *Vandemarks's Folly. A novel*. New York: 1922.

R., (?) *Amerikaansche Levenservaring. Schetsen en Lotgevallen uit het leven van een Hollandsche* emigrant met eene Gids voor den Landverhuizer naar Amerika. Amsterdam: 1892.

Rederus, S. F. "The Dutch Settlements of Sheboygan County." *Wisconsin Magazine of History*, I (Mar. 1918), 256–265.

Reformed Church, The Board of Publication and Bible School. Work of the. *The Acts and Proceedings of the one hundred and nineteenth regular session of the General Synod of the Reformed Church in America.* New York: 1925.

[Roseland] "The Growth of Roseland." A series of small articles in one of the local papers at Chicago, Ill., in July and Aug. 1922.

Sabel, Paul. "Het echec der Van Sweringens," *De (Groene) Amsterdammer*, Mar. 13, 1926.

Sandberg, J. C. C. "Behoud en Vermeerdering van Arbeidskrachten," *Economische Statistische Berichten*, July 31, 1918.

———. "Landverhuizing," *Vragen van den Dag*, 36 (Feb. 1921).

———. "Onaangename Toestanden in de Vereenigde Staten van Amerika. Vestiging van Ned. gezinnen in den Staat Iowa." *De Amsterdammer*, Oct. 9, 1920.

———. "Prae-advies voor de Nationale Vereeniging tegen de Werkloosheid," *Tijdschrift van den Nederlandschen Werkloosheids-Raad.* Ser. 4, 1922.

Scholte, H. P. *Eene Stem uit Pella.* Amsterdam: 1848.

———. *Tweede Stem uit Pella.* 's-Hertogenbosch: 1848.

Semi-Centennial Volume. Theological School and Calvin College, 1876–1926. Grand Rapids: 1926.

Seventy-Fifth Anniversary Exercises, Celebrating the Admission of the Western Churches into the Reformed Church. Holland, Mich.: Oct. 13, 1925.

Sipma, Sjoerd Aukes. *Belangrijke Berigten uit Pella, in de Vereenigde Staten van Noord-Amerika, of Tweede Brief van Sjoerd Aukes Sipma: van daar geschreven aan de ingezetenen van Bornwerd, waarin hij vele bijzonderheden, betreffende de Hollandsche Vereeniging in den Staat Iowa, de levenswijze en de gewoonten der Amerikanen, benevens vele nuttige wenken voor hen, die naar de Vereenigde Staten willen verhuizen, voorkomen. Voorzien met eenige aanmerkingen* door N. N. Dockum: 1849.

———. *Brief van Sjoerd Aukes Sipma aan de Ingezetenen van Bornwerd in Westdongeradeel, uit wier midden hij in het voorjaar van* 1847 *als landverhuizer is vertrokken naar Pella, in de V. St. van N.-Am., voorzien met ophelderende aanmerkingen door* N. N. Dockum: 1848.

St. Nicholas Society of the City of New York. *An Account of the Banquet Given by the St. Nicholas Society of the City of New York on the Occasion of the Visit of the Netherlands Frigate "Prins van Oranje" at New York, May* 1852.

———. *Record of the Dinner given in Honor of the officers of H. N. M. Frigate "van Speijk,"* 8 May 1893.

Stadnitski, Pieter. *Voorafgaand Bericht Pieter Stadnitski wegens eene Negotiatie op landen in Amerika.* Amsterdam: 1792.

Standard Historical Atlas of Sioux County, Iowa. (Issued as second part of *The Illustrated Historical Atlas of Sioux County, Iowa*). Chicago: 1908.

Stoke, Jr., Melis (H. Beets). "Amerikaansche Brieven," *Neerlandia. Orgaan van het A.N.V.* 1915.

Strong, J. *Ons Land: Deszelfs mogelijke toekomst en tegenwoordige crisis.* (Translated by Rev. J. H. Karsten.) Grand Rapids: 1889.

Stuart, W. "Americanization in N.W. Iowa," *Religion and Culture*, Sept. 1921.

Te Winkel, J. "Het Nederlandsch in Noord-Amerika en Zuid-Amerika," *Vragen van den Dag*, 11, 1896.

Teenstra, M. D. *Mentor; de getrouwe Leidsman en Raadgever voor Landverhuizers, die naar Noord-Amerika willen vertrekken.* Groningen: 1855.

Thomson, E. H. *Gids voor Landverhuizers naar den Staat Michigan in Noord-Amerika.* Translated according to the official edition. Amsterdam: 1850.

Tiemersma, Kl. J. *Drie Jaren in Amerika. Persoonlijke ervaringen in schrift gebracht door Kl. J. Tiemersma te Ee (Oost-Dongeradeel).* Leeuwarden: 1894.

Tillema, T. "Korte Levensbeschrijving," *De Volksvriend*, June 9, 1921.

Ton, Corn. John. *60th Anniversary of the Dutch Settlement at Roseland, Chicago.* July 5th 1909.

Tutein Noltthenius, R. P. J. *Nieuwe Wereld. Indrukken en aanteekeningen tijdens eene reis door de Vereenigde Staten van Noord-Amerika.* 2nd ed. Haarlem: 1902.

———. "Westersch en Oostersch Nederland," *De Gids*, 1909.

Tuuk, E. J."Some Ideals of Dr. A. C. van Raalte." A series of articles in *Religion and Culture*. 1924.

Van Aken, Neil. *Broad Acre Farms in North Carolina, U.S.A.* Terra Ceia, N.C.: 1926.

Van Andel, H. J. G. "Wij en de Wereld." A series of articles in *The Christian Journal*.

_____. "Social and Civic Activity." *Religion and Culture*. Jan. 1922.

Van Bergeijk, L. "Een Geschiedenis van de eerste jaren in Pella. Een Geschiedenis van vijf en twintig Jaren van den Wel Eerwaarde Leeraar H. P. Scholte. Bediener des Goddelijken Woords, opgesteld door Een Broeder van zijn Eerwaarde 'in Geloof Hoop en Liefde in onzen Heer en Hijland Jesus Christus Onzen Godt en Zaligmaker.' Die het leven en de onverdervelijkheid heeft aan het Ligt gebracht, Geboekt met zijn Goed en kwaad door L. van Bergeijk, Pella 22 July, 1855." (A copy of this unpublished manuscript is in my possession.)

Van Boven, J. *De Eerste Hollandsche Nederzetting in Colorado*. Utrecht: 1893.

Van Coenen Torchiana, H. A. *Holland, The Birthplace of American Political, Civic and Religious Liberty. An Historical Essay*. San Francisco: 1915.

_____. "Uit Californië." Letter appearing in *Hou en Trouw*, Oct. 1904.

Van Daalen, H. B. *Californië. Beschrijving van Land en Volk*. Reprint from *Onze Tijd*. 1873.

Van den Bosch, J. G. "Johannes Groen," *Religion and Culture*. April 1924.

Van den Bussche, K. J. *Het Nederlandsch in Amerika, Noord en Zuid* 1881.

Van den Elsen, G. *Twintig Brieven uit Amerika*. Helmond: n.d. [1907].

Van der Meulen, Jacob. *Ter nagedachtenis van Rev. Cornelius van der Meulen*. Grand Rapids: 1876.

Van der Meulen, T. G. "Van Bergum naar Amerika." A series of articles in the *Weekblad voor het Kanton Bergum*. (From July 2, 1881 to 1883).

Van der Straten Ponthoz, Baron A. *Onderzoek naar den toestand der Landverhuizers, in de Ver. Staten van Noord-Amerika*. Utrecht, 1847.

Van der Veen, Engbertus. *Life History and Reminiscences*, Holland, Mich.: 1917.

Van der Zee, Jacob. *The Hollanders of Iowa*. Iowa City: 1912.

Van Diggelen, B. P. G. *Nederlandsche Belangen in betrekking tot Landverhuizing en Kolonisatie*. Kampen; 1857.

Van Driele, Francis. *In Memoriam*. Grand Rapids; [1900].

Van Eeden, Frederik. *Van Eeden Kolonie in N. Carolina, U.S.A.* Amsterdam: 1912.

Van Eijk, H. "Dagboek mijner lotgevallen en ontmoetingen beginnende met de reis naar de Vereenigde Staten van Noord-Amerika" (1847). Unpublished.

Van Eyck, William O. *Landmarks of the Reformed Fathers*, Grand Rapids: 1922.

_____. "The Story of the Propellor Phoenix," *Wisconsin Magazine of History*, 7 (Mar. 1924), 281–300.

Van Ginneken, J. *Handboek der Nederlandsche Taal*. I. Nijmegen: 1913.

_____, and Endepols, J. *De Regenboogkleuren van Nederlands Taal*. III. Nijmegen: 1917.

Van Heertum, J. A. "Roman Catholics in the United States." *De Heidenwereld*, (Holland, Mich.), Dec. 1923.

Van Hinte, J. "De naam van Koning Willem I misbruikt. Een episode uit de Landverhuizersvervoer-misère," *Tijdschrift van Geschiedenis, Land- en Volkenkunde*, 33 (1918), 183–88.

_____. "Ellis Island," *De Amsterdammer*, April 22, 1922.

_____. "Les colonies néerlandaises aux Etats-Unis," *Revue anthropologique*, Apr.– June 1925.

_____. "Nederlandsche Nederzettingen in de Ver. Staten van Noord-Amerika," *Neerlandia*, Mar. and Apr. 1923.

_____. "Werkloosheid en Emigratie," *Tijdschrift voor Economische Geographie*. Dec. 1922.

Van Löben Sels, P. J. "Uit Californië," correspondence in *Hou en Trouw*. Jan. 1905.

Van Motz, A. J. G. W. *Colorado uit een geographisch en huishoudkundig oogpunt beschouwd*. Deventer: 1874.

Van Norden. *The World Mirror*. "Special Holland Number." Oct. 1909.

Van Outeren, T. J. and others. *Een laatste woord inzake de Holland Califorra Land Company en Raadgevingen aan hen die aan emigratie naar Californië denken*. Arnhem: 1891.

Van Peyma, W. Brieven van W. Van Peyma aan W. Eekhoff te Leeuwarden. (An unpublished packet of letters in the Provinciale Archief at Leeuwarden).

Van Raalte, A. C. *Holland in Amerika of de Hollandsche Kolonisatie in den Staat Michigan, medegedeeld door A. Brummelkamp.* Arnhem: 1847.

Van Rees, O. *Geschiedenis der Nederlandsche Volkplantingen in Noord-Amerika, beschouwd uit het Oogpunt der Koloniale Politiek.* Tiel: 1855.

Van Rees, Rich. P. A. *Japan-Holland voor vijftig jaar.* Amsterdam, n.d. [1914].

Van Schelven, G. "Historical Sketch of Holland City and Colony. 1876." *De Grondwet*, June 1, 1915.

———. "Historical Sketch of the Post Office and Postal Service, at Holland, Michigan." *The Holland Daily Sentinel*. Dec. 12, 1914.

———. "Historische Schetsen uit het Koloniale Leven. Onder Redactie van G. van Schelven." A collection of letters, reminiscences, addresses, etc. In *De Grondwet*, beginning Dec. 20, 1910.

———. "Michigan and the Holland Immigration of 1847," *Michigan History Magazine*, I (Oct. 1917), 72–96.

———. "Wat bracht U hier?" A series of articles in De *Grondwet*, beginning March 24, 1908.

Van Schevichaven, S. R. J. *De Noord-Amerikaansche Staat Minnesota.* Amsterdam: 1872.

Van Stigt, K. *Geschiedenis van Pella, Iowa en Omgeving.* 3 vols. Pella: 1897.

———. *Nekrologie. Sedert het jaar 1870, tot en met inbegrip van 1899 verzameld en gerangschikt door K. Van Stigt.* Pella, Iowa: 1900.

Van 't Lindenhout, J. *Eenige Gedachten over Amerikaansche Toestanden. Enkele Raadgevingen aan Landverhuizers.* Nijmegen: n.d.

———. *Zes weken tusschen de wielen of De Hollanders in Amerika.* Nijmegen: n.d. [1886].

Van Wijk, G. O. *Brieven uit Amerika.* Amsterdam, 1895. Reprinted from the *Nederlandsche Financier, Dagelijksche Beurscourant.* Jan. 15, 18, 24, 28, 31; Feb. 1, 1895.

Van Winter, P. J. *Het Aandeel van den Amsterdamschen handel aan den opbouw van het Amerikaansche Gemeenebest.* Vol. I. 's-Gravenhage: 1927.

Vaughan, C. C. *Michigan Offical Directory and Legislative Manual, 1917 and 1918.*

Veenstra, S. L. "Emigratie en de Nederlandsche Vereeniging 'Landverhuizing.'" Reprinted from *Vragen van den Dag*, 29 (Dec. 31, 1914).

Versteeg, D. *De Pelgrim-Vaders van het Westen.* Grand Rapids: 1886.

Versteeg, J. "Een oude geschiedenis nog eens oververteld," *Pella's Weekblad*, Oct. 6, 1922.

Verzameling Verslagen en Berichten. A collection of reports of our various consuls in America during the years 1890–1905.

Verzint Eer Gij Begint! Een hartelijk Woord aan mijne Landgenooten, over de, in ons Vaderland heerschende ziekte, genaamd: Landverhuizing. 's-Hertogenbosch; 1846.

Vulpius, F. *Zevenjarige Ondervinding in Noord-Amerika. Wenken en waarschuwingen voor Landverhuizers. Met een voorwoord van H. Püttmann.* Translated from the High German. Utrecht: 1847.

Weekblad voor het Kanton Bergum. Volume years 1881–1884.

Westerdijk, J. Bs. "Prae-advies van J. Bs. Westerdijk voor de Nationale Vereeniging tegen de Werkloosheid. ('In welke mate is de emigratie [tijdelijke en die met het doel zich blijvend buiten onze grenzen te vestigen] tijdens en na den oorlog, vergeleken met de jaren van vóór den oorlog, van invloed geweest op de tegenwoordige werkloosheid hier te lande en dienen er ook maatregelen getroffen te worden om de emigratie te bevorderen ten einde de werkloosheid te verminderen en zoo ja, welke?')" *Tijdschrift van den Nederlandschen Werkloosheids-Raad*. 5 (1922), Ser. 4.

Wieder, F. C. *De Stichting van New York in Juli 1625.* 's-Gravenhage, 1925.

———. "Onderzoek naar de oudste kaarten van de omgeving van New York." *Tijdschrift van het Koninklijk Nederlandsch Aardrijkskunding Genootschap*, 1918.

Wormser, J. A. *Een Schat in aarden Vaten, I. Het Leven van Albertus Christiaan van Raalte.* Nijverdal, 1915. II. *Het Leven van Hendrik Peter Scholte.* Nijverdal: 1915.

———. *De Vurige Oven.* Kampen: 1911.

Wumkes, G. A. "Tjibbe Geerts van der Meulen," *Nieuw Nederlandsch Bibliographisch Woordenboek.*

———. "Worp van Peyma en zijn Vrienden," *De Vrije Fries*, 22 (1914).

Wyckoff, Isaac N. *Report of a Visit to the Holland Colonies in Michigan and Wisconsin, made by order of the Great Synod, and under direction of the Domestic Missionary Society of the Reformed Dutch Church in May and June,* 1849.

General Works.

Abbot, Edith. *Immigration, Select Documents and Case Records.* Chicago: 1924.

Barents, M. *De Diamantslijperij Maatschappij te Amsterdam 1845, 15 April 1920.* Amsterdam: 1920.

Baron, Hans. *Calvins Staatsanschauung und das Konfessionelle Zeitalter.* Munich and Berlin: 1924.

Baxter, Albert. *History of Grand Rapids and Its Industries.* 2 vols. Chicago: 1906.

Bazin, Leon. "La Marine marchande et l'Emigration." Revue de la Marine marchande et des pêches maritimes. Jan. 1918.

Bercovici, Konrad. *Around the World in New York.* London: 1924.

————. *On New Shores.* New York and London: 1925.

Beucker Andreae, J. H. "Rapport, ingediend voor het 5e Landhuishoudkundig Congres te Leyden. 12 en 13 Juny, 1850." *Tijdschrift voor Staathuishoudkunde en Statistiek,* 1851.

Blackmore, W. *Colorado: its Resources, Parks and Prospects as a New Field for Emigration, with an Account of the Trenchara and Costilla Estates in the San Luis Park.* London: 1869.

Blaupot Ten Cate, S. *Geschiedenis der Doopsgezinden in Friesland.* Leeuwarden: 1839.

————. *Geschiedenis der Doopsgezinden in Holland, Zeeland, Utrecht, en Gelderland.* 2 vols. in 1. Amsterdam: 1847.

Blink, H. *Geschiedenis van den Boerenstand en den Landbouw in Nederland.* 2 vols. Groningen: 1904.

————. "Immigratie in Amerika en Emigratie uit Europa," *Vragen van den Dag,* 1910.

————. "Schetsen over de Economische Geografie der Vereen. Staten van Noord-Amerika," *Tijdschrift voor Economische Geographie,* 1915.

Blok, P. J. *Geschiedenis van het Nederlandsche Volk,* 4 vols. Leiden: 1914–1915.

Boas, Franz. *Kultur und Rasse.* Berlin and Leipzig: 1922.

Boissevain, Charles. *Van 't Noorden naar 't Zuiden. Schetsen en Indrukken van de Vereenigde Staten van Noord-Amerika.* 2 vols. Haarlem: 1882.

Bonger, W. A. *Geloof en Misdaad.* Leiden: 1913.

Bonwetsch, G. *Geschichte der deutschen Kolonien an der Wolga.* Stuttgart: 1919.

Bowman, I. *Forest Physiography.* New York: 1912.

Brugmans, H. *Het Nieuwe Amsterdam, van 1795 tot den tegenwoordigen Tijd.* Amsterdam: 1925.

Brugmans, I. J. *De Arbeidende Klasse in Nederland in de 19e eeuw, 1813–1870.* 's-Gravenhage: 1925.

Brunhes, Jean, and Vallaux, Camille. *La Géographie de l'histoire.* Paris: 1921.

Buddingh, D. *De Kerk, School en Wetenschap in de Vereenigde Staten van Noord-Amerika.* Utrecht: 1853.

Butler, N. M. *Die Amerikaner. Aus Natur und Geisteswelt.* Leipzig: 1910.

California State Commission of Immigration and Housing. *Report on Fresno's Immigration Problem.* 1918.

Caminetti, A. *Annual Report of the Commissioner General of Immigration to the Secretary of Labor. Fiscal Year ended June 30.* Washington, 1920.

Carlyle, Thomas. *Zes lezingen over Helden, Heldenvereering en Heldengeest in de Geschiedenis.* 3rd ed. Wereld Bibliotheek, Amsterdam: n.d.

Carver, Thomas N. *The Present Economic Revolution in the United States.* London: 1926.

Chamberlin, Thomas C. and Salisbury, Rollin D. *College Textbook of Geology.* III. 2nd ed. New York: 1909.

Chase, L. A. *Rural Michigan.* New York: 1922.

Chateaubriand, François René Auguste, Vicomte de. *Atala, René, Les Abencérages suivis du Voyage en Amérique.* Paris: n.d.

————. *Voyages en Amérique, en France et en Italie.* Paris: 1834.

Chinard, G. *Les Réfugiés Huguenots en Amérique.* Paris: 1925.

Colenbrander, H. T. *Koloniale Geschiedenis.* I. 's-Gravenhage: 1925.

Cronau, R. *Drei Jahrhunderte deutschen Lebens in Amerika.* 2nd., revised ed. Berlin: 1924.

Dauzat, A. La géographie linguistique. Paris: 1922.

Day, Clive. A History of Commerce in the United States. New York: 1917.

De Boer, M. G. De Holland Amerika Lijn, 1873–1923. Rotterdam: 1923.

_____. Geschiedenis der Amsterdamsche Stoomvaart. I. Amsterdam: 1923.

De Bosch Kemper, Jeronimo. H. Geschiedkundig Onderzoek naar de armoede in Ons Vaderland. 2nd ed. Haarlem: 1860.

"De Goudmijnen Van Californië," Onze Tijd, II, 1849.

De Martonne, Emm. Traité de Géographie Physique. 2nd ed. Paris: 1913.

De Smet, Pater P. J. Missiën van den Oregon en Reizen naar de Rotsbergen. Gent: 1849.

De Toekomst Der Maatschappij. Negen voordrachten. Amsterdam: 1907.

De Vries, Hugo. "Land en volk van Californië. Reisindrukken." Reprinted from De Aarde en haar Volken, Haarlem: n.d.

De Vries, N. A. De Nieuwe Wereld, Amerika, 1923. Groningen and Den Haag: 1924.

Deckert, E. Die Länder Nordamerikas in ihrer wirtschaftsgeographischen Ausrüstung. Frankfurt am Main: 1916.

_____. Nordamerika. 3rd rev. ed. Leipzig and Vienna: 1913.

Dent, C. S. "Northwestward Ho!" World Traveler, March 1924.

Diederichs, J. F. "Letters and Diary of John Fr. Diederichs," Wisconsin Magazine of History, 7 (March 1924), 350–368.

D'Oliveira Jr., E. De Mannen van '80 aan het Woord. 2nd ed. Amsterdam: n.d.

Dozy, R. P. A. "Lectuur over Noord-Amerika," De Gids. June 1870.

_____. "Studiën over de Vereenigde Staten," De Gids. May 1871.

Duval, M. Jules. Histoire de l'Emigration européenne, asiatique et africaine au XIXe siècle. Paris: 1862.

Eene Halve Eeuw 1848–1898, Nederland. Historisch Gedenkboek published by the Nieuws van den Dag. 2 vols. Amsterdam: 1898.

Eisse, C. C. Früchte deutscher Arbeit. Leipzig: 1910.

Fairbridge, Dorothea. Historic Houses of South Africa. London: 1922.

Faust, A. B. Das Deutschtum in den Vereinigten Staaten in seiner Bedeutung für die amerikanische Kultur. Leipzig: 1912.

_____. Das Deutschtum in den Vereinigten Staaten in seiner geschichtlichen Enwickelung. Leipzig: 1912.

Feiler, A. Amerika-Europa. Erfahrungen einer Reise. Frankfurt am Main: 1926.

Fischer, E. Rasse und Rassenentstehung beim Menschen, Berlin: 1927.

Friederici, Georg. Das puritanische Neu-England. Ein Beitrag zur Entwicklungsgeschichte der nordamerikanischen Union. Halle am Saale: 1924.

Gallee. J. H. Het Boerenhuis in Nederland en zijn Bewoners. Utrecht: 1908.

Gargas, S. Moderne Emigratie. Voordrachten gehouden aan de Ned. Handelshoogeschool te Rotterdam. Reprinted in De Economist, 1915.

Garland, Hamlin. A Son of the Middle Border. London: 1917.

Gedenkboek, ter gelegenheid van den 70sten verjaardag van F. Domela Nieuwenhuis 31 December 1916. Amsterdam: 1916.

Gerritsen, C. V. and Jacobs, Aletta H. Brieven uit en over Amerika. Amsterdam: 1906.

Gevers Deynoot, W. F. Aanteekeningen op eene reis door de Ver. Staten van Noord-Amerika en Canada in 1859. 's-Gravenhage: 1860.

Gevers van Endegeest, Jhr. Over de Droogmaking van het Haarlemmermeer. III. Amsterdam: 1861.

Gibbons, Ph. E. Pennsylvania Dutch and Other Essays. Philadelphia: 1882.

Goldberger, L. M. Das Land der unbegrenzten Möglichkeiten. Berlin and Leipzig: 1911.

Gonnard, R. L'émigration européenne au Xixe siècle. Paris: 1906.

Goslinga, A. Koning Willem I als verlicht Despoot. Baarn: 1918.

Greve, H. E. "Hollandsche Spotprenten in de 19e Eeuw." Elsevier's Geïllustreerd Maandschrift, 1909.

Groen van Prinsterer, Guillaume. Brieven van J. A. Wormser. I. Amsterdam: 1874.

Gruening, Ernest. These United States. A Symposium. 2 Series. New York: 1923–1924.

Gunning J. Hzn., J. H. Leven en Arbeid van H. J. Budding. Rhenen: 1909.

Handboek voor de Kennis van Nederland en Koloniën. 's-Gravenhage: 1922.

Häpke, Rudolf. Der deutsche Kaufman in den

Niederlanden. (In the series "Pfingstblätter des Hansischen Geschichtvereins"). Leipzig: 1912.

Hassert, Kurt. *Allgemeine Verkehrsgeographie.* Berlin and Leipzig: 1913.

———. *Australien und Neuseeland geographisch und wirtschaftlich.* Gotha-Stuttgart: 1924.

———. *Die Städte geographisch betrachtet.* Leipzig: 1907.

———. *Die Vereinigten Staaten von Amerika als politische und wirtschaftliche Weltmacht geographisch betrachtet.* Tübingen: 1922.

Haworth, P. L. *The United States in our own Times, 1865–1920.* London: 1920.

Heere, W. R. *Frédéric Le Play en zijne Volgelingen. De Methode der Monographieën.* Groningen: 1926.

Hildebrand, (Nicolaas Beets). *Camera Obscura,* 23rd ed. Haarlem: 1904.

Hötzsch, Otto. *Die Vereinigten Staaten von Nordamerika.* Bielefeld and Leipzig: 1904.

Hugenholtz, Jr., P. H. *Licht en Schaduw. Indrukken van het godsdienstig leven in Amerika.* Amsterdam: n.d.

Huizinga, J. *Amerika levend en denkend.* Haarlem: 1926.

———. *Mensch en Menigte in Amerika.* Haarlem; 1918.

Immigration Bureau, Kansas City, Mo. *West Louisiana, East Texas, and the Gulf Coast.* Kansas City, Mo.: n.d.

James, George Wharton. *In and Out of the Old Missions of California.* Boston: 1922.

Jansen, M. H. *Een Brug over den Oceaan. Stoomvaart op Amerika.* Delft: 1869.

———. *Stoomvaart op Amerika. Goedkooper brood en Meer werk.* Delft: 1869.

Jellinghaus, G. M. W. *De Staat tegenover de Landverhuizing.* Den Haag: 1894.

Jenks, Jeremiah W. and Lauck, W. Jett. *The Immigration Problem.* 4th ed. New York and London: 1917.

Kallen, Horace M. *Culture and Democracy in the United States. Studies in the Group Psychology of the American Peoples.* New York: 1924.

Kalm, Peter. *Reis door Noord Amerika.* 2 vols. Utrecht: 1872.

Kansas City Southern Railroad. "Ozark Outings," Kansas City, Mo.: n.d.

Kjellen, R. *Schweden. Eine Politische Monographie.* Munich and Berlin: 1917.

Kloeke, G. G. *Reflexen van Hollandsche Expansie in de huidige Nederlandsche Dialecten.* Amsterdam: 1926.

Knappert, L. *Geschiedenis der Ned. Herv. Kerk gedurende de 18e en 19e Eeuw.* Amsterdam: 1912.

———. *Verloving en Huwelijk in vroeger Dagen.* Amsterdam: 1914.

Koenen, S. *Inleiding tot de Landhuishoudkunde.* Haarlem: 1924.

Köppen, Wladimir Peter. *Klimakunde.* Leipzig: 1906.

Lamprecht, K. G. *Americana.* Freiburg im Breisgau: 1906.

Landbouw, Directie van den. *De Nederlandsche Landbouw in het tijdvak, 1813–1913.* 's-Gravenhage: n.d. [1913].

Lapsley, Gaillard. *The America of Today.* Cambridge: 1919.

Lauvrière, Emile. *La Tragédie d'un Peuple. Historie du Peuple acadien de ses origines à nos jours.* 2 vols. Paris: 1924.

Levenbach, M. G. *Arbeid in Amerika. De sociale beweging in de Vereenigde Staten.* Amsterdam: 1926.

Leviticus, T. *Encyclopaedie der Diamantnijverheid.* Haarlem: 1908.

Lippincott, I. *Economic Development of the United States.* New York: 1924.

Lotsy, J. P. *Van den Atlantischen Oceaan naar de Stille Zuidzee in 1922.* 's-Gravenhage: 1923.

Martin, C. E. and George, W. H. *American Government and Citizenship.* New York: 1927.

Mayo Smith, R. *Emigration and Immigration. A Study in Social Science.* New York: 1912.

McDougall, W. *An Introduction to Social Psychology.* London: 1908.

———. *The American Nation: Its Problems and Psychology.* London: 1925.

———. *The Group Mind.* 2nd ed. Cambridge: 1927.

Mencken, H. L. *Americana 1925.* London: 1925.

———. *The American Language,* 3rd. ed. New York: 1926.

Michigan, The Land Of Plenty. Publication of the Public Domain Commission and the Immigration Commission. 1914.

Moerman, H. J. "Oostfriesland," *Tijdschrift van het Koninklijk Nederlandsch Aardrijkskundig Genootschap.* 1921.

Mohr, E. C. Jul. *De Grond van Java en Sumatra.* Amsterdam: 1922.

Morison, S. E. *The Oxford History of the United States, 1783–1917.* 2 vols. London: 1927.

Muller, H. P. N. *In het Verre Westen.* Reprint from *De Tijdspiegel,* May 1, 1905.

Myers, G. *Geschichte der grossen amerikanischen Vermögen.* Translated from the English. 2 vols. Berlin: 1923.

Nicholson, Meredith. *The Valley of Democracy.* New York: 1919.

Officieel Gedenkboek, onder Redactie van Prof. Dr. H. Brugmans. Published in behalf of the Homage Commission, 1923 at Amsterdam. Amsterdam: 1923.

Oppenheim, A. *Vijf weken in Amerika.* Rotterdam: 1905.

Parels, J. J. "Een en ander omtrent de Rijstcultuur in de Ver. Staten van Noord-Amerika," *Cultura,* 31 (June 1909).

Penck, A. U. S. *Amerika. Gedanken und Erinnerungen eines Austauschprofessors.* Stuttgart:1917.

Pollard, A. F. *Factors in American History.* Cambridge: 1925.

Port Arthur Board of Trade. *Port Arthur Texas, Pan-American Gateway.* Port Arthur: 1916.

Posthumus, N. W. "Nota over den toestand van de Amsterdamsche handelshuizen in het jaar 1854," *Economisch Historisch Jaarboek,* 1921.

Prinsen J. L.zn., J. *Handboek tot de Nederlandsche letterkundige Geschiedenis.* 's-Gravenhage: 1916.

Quack, H. P. G. *De Socialisten. Personen en Stelsels.* 6 vols. Amsterdam: 1911–1912.

————. "De Zwijndrechtsche Broederschap," *De Gids,* Aug. 1892.

Ramaer, J. C. "Middelpunten der bewoning in Nederland voorheen en thans," *Tijdschrift van het Koninklijk Nederlandsch Aardrijkskundig Genootschap,* 1921.

Ratzel, Fr. *Politische Geographie,* 3rd ed. Munich and Berlin: 1903.

Reyne, K. *De Uittocht der Plattelandsbevolking. Studies in Volkskracht.* Haarlem: 1904.

Rijkens, R. H. *Licht en Schaduwbeelden uit het Amerikaansche Leven.* Den Haag: 1907.

Robinson, Mary F. "Rix Robinson, Fur Trader," *Michigan History Magazine,* VI (No. 2–3, 1922), 177–87.

Roland Holst, Henriëtte (Van der Schalk). *Opwaartsche Wegen.* Rotterdam: 1914.

Roscher, Wilhelm G. F. "Onderzoekingen omtrent het Koloniewezen," *Tijdschrift voor Staathuishoudkunde en Statistiek,* VI, 1851.

Ross, E. A. *Changing America. Studies in Contemporary Society.* London, 1912.

————. *The Foundations of Sociology.* 5th ed. New York: 1919.

————. *What is America?* New York, 1919.

Rössing, J. H. *Verdwijnend Oud-Amsterdam.* Amsterdam: 1916.

Roz, Firmin. *L'énergie américaine. Evolution des Etats-Unis.* Paris: 1920.

Rullmann, J. C. *De Afscheiding.* Amsterdam: 1916.

Russell Smith, J. *Industrial and Commercial Geography.* New York: 1913.

————. *North America.* London: 1925.

Saks, J. *Socialistische Opstellen.* 2nd vol. Rotterdam: 1923.

Schimmelpenninck, Graaf G. *Rutger Jan Schimmelpenninck en eenige Gebeurtenissen van zijnen Tijd.* 's-Gravenhage: 1845.

Schmuülling, E. *Ellis-eiland.* Reprinted in *Koloniaal Tijdschrift,* 7, No. 3.

Schnücker, George. *Die Ostfriesen in Amerika.* Cleveland: 1917.

Schönemann, F. *Die Kunst der Massenbeeinflüssung in den Vereinigten Staaten von Amerika.* Stuttgart, Berlin and Leipzig: 1926.

Schrijnen, J. *De Isoglossen van Ramisch in Nederland.* Bussum: 1920.

————. *Nederlandsche Volkskunde.* 2 vols. Zutphen: n.d.

Schuiling, Roelof. *Nederland, handboek der aardrijkskunde.* Zwolle; 1915.

Schurtz, H. *Völkerkunde,* Leipzig and Vienna: 1903.

Semple, Ellen. *American History and its Geographic Conditions.* Boston and New York: 1903.

————. *Influences of Geographic Environment.* New York and London: 1911.

Siegfried, A. *Les Etats-Unis d'Aujourd'hui.* Paris: 1927.

Smeaton Chase, J. *California Coast Trails.* Boston and New York: 1913.

Smith, C. Henry. *The Mennonites of America.* Goshen, Ind.: 1909.

Smithanders, Ernst. *Land und Leute in Nordamerika.* Berlin-Schöneberg: 1926.

Snethlage, J. L. *De Schoolopvoeding in Amerika en het Vraagstuk der Kennis.* Amsterdam: n.d.

Stearns, Harald E. *Civilization in the United States. An Enquiry by Thirty Americans.* London: 1922.

Steiner, Edw. A. *The Confession of a Hyphenated American.* New York, Chicago, etc.: 1916.

Steinmetz, S. R. *De Nationaliteiten in Europa.* Amsterdam: 1920.

———. "De Toekomst van ons Ras," *De Gids,* 1910. 4th part.

———. *Die Philosophie des Krieges.* Leipzig: 1907.

———. *Ethnologische Studien zur ersten Entwicklung der Strafe. Nebst einer psychologischen Abhandlung über Grausamkeit und Rachsucht.* II, Leiden, 1892; I. Leiden and Leipzig 1894; 2nd ed. Groningen: 1928.

———. "Nieuw Menschenras in Amerika," *Nederlandsch Tijdschrift voor Geneeskunde,* 1911. 2nd half A.

———. *Wat is Sociologie?* Leiden: 1900.

Stoddard, Lothrop. *Re-forging America, The Problem of Immigration.* London: 1927.

Supan, A. *Grundzüge der physischen Erdkunke.* Leipzig: 1911.

Te Lintum, C. *De Geschiedenis van het Amerikaansche Volk.* Zutphen: 1917.

———. "De oude Handelsstad Tiel en haar tegenwoordig voorkomen," *Tijdschrift van het Koninklijk Nederlandsch Aardrijkskundig Genootschap,* 1923.

———. "Emigratie over Rotterdam in de 18e eeuw." *De Gids,* 1908. Part IV.

———. *Geschiedenis van Handel en Bedrijf vooral in Nederland.* 2nd ed. Groningen and Den Haag: 1925.

———. *Nederland en de Indiën, gedurende de laatste kwart-eeuw.* Zutphen: 1923.

Ten Kate, H. "Psychologie en ethnologie in de koloniale politiek." Reprinted from *De Indische Gids,* June and July 1916.

———. *Reizen en Onderzoekingen in Noord-Amerika.* Leiden: 1885.

Ter Veen, H. N. *De Haarlemmermeer als Kolonisatiegebied.* Groningen: 1925.

Troeltsch, Ernst. *Die Bedeutung des Protestantismus für die Entstehung der Modernen Welt.* Munich and Berlin: 1924.

Turner, F. J. *The Frontier in American History.* New York: 1921.

U.S. Bureau of the Census, *Fourteenth Census of the United States, Taken in the Year 1920.* Vol. II, Population. Washington: 1923.

Van Ammers-Küller, Jo. *Mijn Amerikaansche reis.* Den Haag: 1926.

Van Balen, W. J. *Door Amerika.* Amsterdam: 1913.

Van Dellen, I. *Het Mormonisme* Kampen: 1911.

Van Linschoten, Jan Huygen. *Itinerario voyage ofte schipvaert van Jan Huygen van Linschoten.* 2 vols. 's-Gravenhage: 1910.

Van Lonkhuyzen, J. *Argentinië. Een belangrijk land, ook voor Nederlanders.* Washington: 1908.

Van Mourik Broekman, M. C. *De Yankee in Denken en Doen.* Haarlem: 1914.

Van Oss, S. F. *Amerikaansche Spoorwegwaarden.* Groningen: 1903.

Van Rensselaer, Mrs. Schuyler (Mariana). *History of the City of New-York in the Seventeenth Century.* 2 vols. New York: 1909.

Verviers, Emile. *De Nederlandsche Handelspolitiek tot aan de toepassing der vrijhandelsbeginselen.* Leiden: n.d.

Vidal de la Blache, P. *Principes de Géographie Humaine, publiés d'après les manuscrits de l'Auteur par Emmanuel de Martonne.* Paris: 1922.

Von Luschan, F. *Voelker, Rassen, Sprachen.* Berlin: 1922.

Von Raumer, F. *De Vereenigde Staten van Noord-Amerika.* 2 vols. Deventer: 1849.

Von Richthoven, F. *Vorlesungen über Allgemeine Siedlungs und Verkehrsgeographie.* Berlin: 1908.

Warne, Frank Julian. *The Tide of Immigration.* New York: 1916.

Weber, Max. *Gesammelte Aufsätze zur Religionssoziologie.* I. 3 vols. Tübingen: 1922–1923.

Whitlock, R. H. "Irrigation in the United States," *The Geographical Journal,* LIV (Oct. 1919), 721–31.

Whitman, Walt. *Leaves of Grass & Democratic Vistas.* London: 1916.

Wilde, Oscar. "L'Homme américain. Un inédit d'Oscar Wilde. (*Court and Society Review,* Apr. 13, 1887). Trans. Cecil George-Bazile. *La Grande Revue,* Nov. 1918.

Wissler, Clark. *The American Indian. An Introduction to the Anthropology of the New World.* New York: 1922.

———. *The Relation of Nature to Man in Aboriginal America.* New York: 1926.

Woeikof, A. *Le Turkestan Russe,* Paris: 1914.

Woodson, C. G. A *Century of Negro Migration.*
   Washington, D.C.: 1918.

Wundt, W. *Völkerpsychologie.* Vol. I. *Die Sprache,*
   1911.

Zeehuisen, J. "Statistieke Bijdrage tot de

kennis van den stoffelijken en zedelijken
toestand van de landbouwende klasse in
het kwartier Salland. Voorlezing." *Tijdschrift
voor Staathuishoudkunde en Statistiek,* VI,
1851.

Index

Groothof, P., 295
Group Mind, The, 843
Gruening, Ernest, 70
Grundy Center, Iowa, 867
Grundy College, 867
Guatemala, 98
Guepin, J. P., 686
Guild family, 310
Gunning, C. P., 959
Gunning, J. L., 959

Haagsma, B. B., 165, 167, 169, 703, 706, 714
Haan, G. G., 605, 606, 609, 690
Haan, G. T., 895
Haan, Gijsbert, 370–371, 372, 373, 374, 382
Haan, Ralph, xxxii
Haan, R. L., 918
Haarlemmer Courant, De, 588, 633
Haarlemmermeer polder, Neth., 334, 336, 623, 808
Haarlem, Mich., 772
Haarlem, N.Y., 40–41
Hackensack, N.J., 53, 64
Hagens, G. R., 897
Halbertsma, J. H., 62, 995, 1009
Haledon, N.J., 818
Hall, Claiborne, 267
Halloween, and young people's pranks, 981
Halma, A. T., 119
Halve Maan, 3, 72
Hamburg, Germany, 79, 160, 602
Hamilton, Alexander, 350
Hamilton, Mich., 535, 751, 780
Hamilton, Mrs., 59
Hamilton, Robert G., 417, 418–419
Hammond, S. M., 451
Hammond, Ind., 881
Hamsun, Knut, 949
Handboek der Nederlandsche Geshiedenis, 60
Handboek der Nederlandsche Taal, 60
Handelsblad, Het, 176, 603, 605, 630, 706, 808
Hanford, Cal., Dutch colony in, 655–656, 660, 808
Hanover, Pa., 54
Hansen, Hans ("du Fond"), 875, 876, 891, 900, 913, 914, 927, 954, 955
Häpke, Rudolf, 39
Hardenbergh, J. L. [R.], 51, 55

Harderwyk, Mich., 384, 535, 772
Harding, Warren G., 898 (sketch), 900, 914
Hardpan soils, in California, 649–650, 652–653, 656, 659
Hardy, Thomas, 950
Harkema family, 688
Harlem, Mont., 698
Harlingen, Neth., 104, 165, 710
Harmeling, S. J., 564, 565
"Harmonie, De," 1006
Harper's Magazine, 450
Harrington, E. J., 323
Harrington, George S., Sr., 215, 232
Harrison, S.D., 562, 565, 803
Hartgerink, A., 128
Hartogh, H. A., 667
Hartogh Heys van Zouteveen, H., 580, 633, 634–635, 644
Harvard University, 112
Harve, Le, France, 78, 154
Hasselaar [Hasselman, Adam P.], 794
Hasselman, J. J., 268, 584
Hassert, K., 194, 511
Hastings, Neb., 543
Havinga, Herman, 924
Hawarden, Iowa, 890
Hawks, Josiah L., 311, 446
Haworth, P. L., 498, 499
Hawthorne, N.J., 818
Hayden, F. V., 670
Hayes, Rutherford B., 439
Haynes, John, 11
Hazebroek family, 65
H. Bleecker, 63
Heald, 344, 354
Heemstede, N.Y., 21
Heemstra, Simon C., 891
Heemstra, Tjeerd, 475, 478, 479, 481, 484, 485, 523
Heeren, Enne J., 411
Heeris, F. J., 1001
Heersink, A., 672
Heersink, C. [Adolph], 677–678
Heersink family, 688
Heidenwereld, De, 851, 920, 936 (photo)
Heineken, 962
Heinz, H. J., 778
Hekhuis, Lambertus, 411

Hekman, 829, 867
Heldring, Otto G., 125, 408
Helene, Mont., 698
Hellendoorn, Mich., 150
Hellendoorn, Overijsel, 149
Hellevoetsluis, Neth., 103, 104, 146, 152
Helping Hand Mission (Chicago), 881
Hemert, H. J., 705
Hemkes, G. K., 402, 449, 589, 944
Hemmes, Jessie, 891
Henckler, G., 340
Hendricks, Gerhard, 27
Hengerveld, Hendrik, 130
Henry, Matthew, 1000
Henry, T. C., 672, 673, 674
Hepkema, Sietse, 1002
Hepner, E., 840
Hepp, Valentine, 1018
Heraut, De, 558, 916, 1001
Hereford cattle, 801
Heritage Hall Archives, Calvin College, xxxii
Herman, A., 28
Herman, I., 836
Heroes, Hero Worship, and the Heroic in History, 743
Herrick Public Library, xxxii
Herstelde Kerk van Christus, 89
Hertel, B. W., 933
Hervormde Kerk, 88, 124, 158, 845, 847
Herwijnen neighborhood (Pella), 280
Het Bilt, Friesland, 95, 103, 119, 600
Heukelum, Zuid Holland, 590–591
Heusdensche, De, 588
Heuvel, H. W., 965
Hewitt, G., 625
Heyns, G., 871, 944
Heyns, W., 866
Heyrman, 454
Heystek, W., 591, 592
Hibma, T., 575, 850
Hiemenga, J. J., 856, 865, 866, 867
Highland, Ind., 550, 551
High Prairie, Ill., 296–299, 314, 327, 346, 347, 496, 550, 551. See also Roseland, Ill.